Intermediate Accounting

ELEVENTH EDITION

INTERMEDIATE ACCOUNTING

Volume I

Donald E. Kieso Ph.D., C.P.A.
KPMG Peat Marwick Emeritus Professor of Accounting
Northern Illinois University
DeKalb, Illinois

Jerry J. Weygandt Ph.D., C.P.A.
Arthur Andersen Alumni Professor of Accounting
University of Wisconsin
Madison, Wisconsin

Terry D. Warfield Ph.D.
Associate Professor
University of Wisconsin
Madison, Wisconsin

WILEY

John Wiley & Sons, Inc.

Dedicated to our parents,
Lester and Mildred, Adolph and Sylvia, and Donald and Helen;
and to our fathers- and mothers-in-law,
William and Mathilda, Sigurd and Maxyne, and Mike and Flo,
for their love, support, and encouragement

PUBLISHER:	Susan Elbe
ACQUISITIONS EDITOR:	Mark Bonadeo
MARKETING MANAGER:	Keari Bedford
PROJECT EDITOR:	David B. Kear
MEDIA EDITOR:	Allison Keim
DEVELOPMENTAL EDITOR:	Ann Torbert
PRODUCTION SERVICES MANAGER:	Jeanine Furino
SENIOR DESIGNER:	Karin Kincheloe
ILLUSTRATION EDITOR:	Anna Melhorn
ASSOCIATE EDITOR:	Ed Brislin
TEXT DESIGNER:	Lee Goldstein
COVER DESIGNER:	David Levy
PROJECT MANAGEMENT:	Elm Street Publishing Services, Inc.
COVER PHOTOS:	© www.danheller.com

This book was set in Palatino by Techbooks and printed and bound by Von Hoffmann.
The cover was printed by Von Hoffmann.

This book is printed on acid-free paper. ∞

0-471-42639-3
Printed in the United States of America
10 9 8 7 6 5 4 3 2 1

About the Authors

Donald E. Kieso, Ph.D., C.P.A., received his bachelor's degree from Aurora University and his doctorate in accounting from the University of Illinois. He has served as chairman of the Department of Accountancy and is currently the KPMG Peat Marwick Emeritus Professor of Accounting at Northern Illinois University. He has public accounting experience with Price Waterhouse & Co. (San Francisco and Chicago) and Arthur Andersen & Co. (Chicago) and research experience with the Research Division of the American Institute of Certified Public Accountants (New York). He has done postdoctorate work as a Visiting Scholar at the University of California at Berkeley and is a recipient of NIU's Teaching Excellence Award and four Golden Apple Teaching Awards. Professor Kieso is the author of other accounting and business books and is a member of the American Accounting Association, the American Institute of Certified Public Accountants, and the Illinois CPA Society. He has served as a member of the Board of Directors of the Illinois CPA Society, the AACSB's Accounting Accreditation Committees, the State of Illinois Comptroller's Commission, as Secretary-Treasurer of the Federation of Schools of Accountancy, and as Secretary-Treasurer of the American Accounting Association. Professor Kieso served as a charter member of the national Accounting Education Change Commission. He is the recipient of the Outstanding Accounting Educator Award from the Illinois CPA Society, the FSA's Joseph A. Silvoso Award of Merit, and the NIU Foundation's Humanitarian Award for Service to Higher Education.

Jerry J. Weygandt, Ph.D., C.P.A., is Arthur Andersen Alumni Professor of Accounting at the University of Wisconsin—Madison. He holds a Ph.D. in accounting from the University of Illinois. Articles by Professor Weygandt have appeared in the *Accounting Review, Journal of Accounting Research, Accounting Horizons, Journal of Accountancy*, and other academic and professional journals. These articles have examined such financial reporting issues as accounting for price-level adjustments, pensions, convertible securities, stock option contracts, and interim reports. Professor Weygandt is author of other accounting and financial reporting books and is a member of the American Accounting Association, the American Institute of Certified Public Accountants, and the Wisconsin Society of Certified Public Accountants. He has served on numerous committees of the American Accounting Association and as a member of the editorial board of the *Accounting Review*; he also has served as President and Secretary-Treasurer of the American Accounting Association. In addition, he has been actively involved with the American Institute of Certified Public Accountants and has been a member of the Accounting Standards Executive Committee (AcSEC) of that organization. He has served on the FASB task force that examined the reporting issues related to accounting for income taxes and is presently a trustee of the Financial Accounting Foundation. Professor Weygandt has received the Chancellor's Award for Excellence in Teaching and the Beta Gamma Sigma Dean's Teaching Award. He is on the board of directors of M & I Bank of Southern Wisconsin and the Dean Foundation. He is the recipient of the Wisconsin Institute of CPA's Outstanding Educator's Award and the Lifetime Achievement Award. In 2001 he received the American Accounting Association's Outstanding Accounting Educator Award.

Terry D. Warfield, Ph.D., is associate professor of accounting at the University of Wisconsin—Madison. He received a B.S. and M.B.A. from Indiana University and a Ph.D. in accounting from the University of Iowa. Professor Warfield's area of expertise is financial reporting, and prior to his academic career, he worked for five years in the banking industry. He served as the Academic Accounting Fellow in the Office of the Chief Accountant at the U.S. Securities and Exchange Commission in Washington, D.C. from 1995–1996. Professor Warfield's primary research interests concern financial accounting standards and disclosure policies. He has published scholarly articles in *The Accounting Review, Journal of Accounting and Economics, Research in Accounting Regulation,* and *Accounting Horizons,* and he has served on the editorial boards of *The Accounting Review, Accounting Horizons,* and *Issues in Accounting Education.* He has served on the Financial Accounting Standards Committee of the American Accounting Association (Chair 1995–1996) and on the AAA-FASB Research Conference Committee. Professor Warfield has received teaching awards at both the University of Iowa and the University of Wisconsin, and he was named to the Teaching Academy at the University of Wisconsin in 1995. Professor Warfield has developed and published several case studies based on his research for use in accounting classes. These cases have been selected for the AICPA Professor-Practitioner Case Development Program and have been published in *Issues in Accounting Education.*

Preface

As we wrote this edition of *Intermediate Accounting*, the importance of financial accounting and reporting has never been more apparent. Recent failures of major corporations, such as **Enron**, **WorldCom**, and **Global Crossing**, have highlighted the need for relevant and reliable financial information to ensure that our capital market system functions efficiently. Although we are saddened by these failures and their negative consequences for companies, employees, investors, and creditors, we believe that much good can come from a renewed commitment to provide high-quality financial information to users of financial statements.

The Sarbanes-Oxley Act of 2002 will provide a framework that can be used to enhance the quality of financial information. For example, the Act mandates that managements and auditors meet higher standards in accounting and financial reporting in response to the recent business and accounting failures. Business executives must understand and certify to the accuracy of their company's financial statements. Consequently, it is imperative that every student of business understands the fundamentals of accounting and financial reporting.

In this edition of *Intermediate Accounting*, we continue a tradition begun nearly 30 years ago of helping students understand, prepare, and use financial information. As indicated above, the importance of students' understanding the role of financial information in capital markets has never been more important. For example, a recent *Wall Street Journal* ran the following headlines:

"The SEC Checks Whether Microsoft Was Too Conservative in Booking Revenues"

"Qwest Communications Acknowledges Some Off-Balance-Sheet Transactions"

"SEC Reviews Allegations That EMC Improperly Accounted for Some Sales"

"Krispy Kreme Makes Changes After an Accounting Technique Is Questioned"

"Marriott Is Set to Disclose Details of Write-Offs Related to Developer Franchising"

An important feature of *Intermediate Accounting*, therefore, is an enhanced effort to provide more perspective on the information available in financial reporting. As a result, special boxed insights titled "What Do the Numbers Mean?" illustrate how reporting methods affect the decisions of financial statement users. By means of these boxes, we hope to convey the excitement and ever-changing nature of accounting, illuminating its significance and highlighting its importance. During our years of teaching, we have found that many students, when introduced to the issues involved in financial reporting, genuinely enjoy the subject area.

A second key feature of this edition is the introduction of the *Take Action!* CD-ROM, which can be packaged with the text. The *Take-Action!* CD is an electronic gateway to a comprehensive set of materials that supplement the already comprehensive coverage of accounting topics in the textbook. Major elements of the *Take Action!* CD build on those contained in the *Gateway to the Profession Digital Tool* of the 10th Edition of *Intermediate Accounting*. In addition to updating the well-accepted material on the *Digital Tool*, the *Take Action!* CD has several new and enhanced features. These new features include self-assessment quizzes and interactive tutorials, which provide expanded discussion and explanation in a visual, audio, and narrative context. (Elements of the *Take Action!* CD are described in more detail later in the preface.)

The 11th Edition of *Intermediate Accounting* also introduces a new element to the "Using Your Judgment" section of the end-of-chapter material: A "Professional

Simulation" in each chapter provides students with a new and integrative context for applying the concepts introduced in the chapter. This new element is patterned after the new computerized CPA exam. It expands the focus of many of the elements of the *Take Action!* CD (writing, working in teams, using the analyst's toolkit) to help students learn how to use accounting facts and procedures in various business contexts.

We continue to strive for a balanced discussion of conceptual and procedural presentations so that these elements are mutually reinforcing. In addition, text discussions focus on explaining the rationale behind business transactions before addressing the accounting and reporting for those transactions. As in prior editions, we have thoroughly revised and updated the text to include all the latest developments in the accounting profession and practice. For example, the chapter on intangibles has been completely revised to reflect new accounting standards for intangible assets. Benefiting from the comments and recommendations of adopters of the 10th Edition, we have made significant revisions. Explanations have been expanded where necessary; complicated discussions and illustrations have been simplified; realism has been integrated to heighten interest and relevancy; and new topics and coverage have been added to maintain currency. We have deleted some 10th Edition coverage from the text. For example, the two chapters related to stockholders' equity have been combined and streamlined. Finally, to provide the instructor with flexibility of use and no loss in topic coverage, discussions of less commonly used methods and more complex or specialized topics have been moved to the *Take Action!* CD.

NEW FEATURES

Based on extensive reviews, focus groups, and interactions with other intermediate accounting instructors and students, we have developed a number of new pedagogical features and content changes designed both to help students learn more effectively and to answer the changing needs of the course.

New Chapters

As discussed, we have completely updated the chapter on intangibles, and we have streamlined the coverage of stockholders' equity by combining Chapters 15 and 16 of the 10th Edition.

New Pedagogy

With the introduction of the "What Do the Numbers Mean?" boxed insights and the Professional Simulations, we have enhanced the pedagogy in the book to better engage students in the material and to provide new opportunities for students to apply accounting concepts to various business contexts.

Take Action! CD

As described above, the *Take Action!* CD is a major resource of the 11th Edition, which can be packaged with the text or is available separately for purchase. Key elements of the *Take Action!* CD are described below.

Analyst's Toolkit

"Tools" in the Analyst's Toolkit consist of the following items.

Database of Real Companies. More than 20 annual reports of well-known companies, including three international companies, are provided on the *Take Action!* CD. These annual reports can be used in a variety of ways. For example, they can be used for illustrating different presentations of financial information or for comparing note disclosures across companies. In addition, these reports can be used to analyze a company's financial condition and compare its prospects with those of other companies in the same industry. Assignment material provides some examples of different types of analysis that can be performed.

Company Web Links. Each of the companies in the database of real companies is identified by a Web address to facilitate the gathering of additional information, if desired.

Additional Enrichment Material. A chapter on Financial Statement Analysis is provided on the CD, along with related assignment material. This chapter can also be used in conjunction with the database of annual reports of real companies.

Spreadsheet Tools. Present value templates are provided which can be used to solve time value of money problems.

Additional Internet Links. A number of useful links related to financial analysis are provided to expand expertise in this area.

Professional Toolkit

Consistent with expanding beyond technical accounting knowledge, the *Take Action!* CD emphasizes certain skills necessary to become a successful accountant and financial manager.

Writing Materials. A primer on professional communications gives students a framework for writing professional materials. This primer discusses issues such as the top ten writing problems, strategies for rewriting, how to do revisions, and tips on clarity. This primer has been class-tested and is effective in helping students enhance their writing skills.

Group Work Materials. Recent evaluations of accounting education have identified the need to develop more skills in group problem solving. The *Take Action!* CD provides a second primer dealing with the role that groups play in organizations. Information is included on what makes a successful group, how you can participate effectively in the group, and do's and don'ts of group formation.

Ethics. The Professional Toolkit contains expanded materials on the role of ethics in the profession, including references to:

- Speeches and articles on ethics in accounting.
- Codes of ethics for major professional bodies.
- Examples and additional case studies on ethics.

Career Professional Spotlights. Every student should have a good understanding of the profession he or she is entering. Career vignettes on the *Take Action!* CD indicate the types of work that accountants do. Other aspects of the spotlights on careers are included on the *Take Action!* CD to help students make successful career choices. These include professional Web links—important links to Web sites that can provide useful career information to facilitate the student's efforts in this area.

Student Toolkit

Also included on the *Take Action!* CD are features that help students process and understand the course materials. They are:

Interactive Tutorials. To help students better understand some of the more difficult topics in intermediate accounting, we have developed several interactive tutorials that provide expanded discussion and explanation in a visual and narrative context. Topics addressed include the accounting cycle; inventory methods, including dollar-value LIFO; depreciation and impairment of long-lived assets; and interest capitalization.

Note that these tutorials are for the benefit of the student and should require no use of class time on the part of instructors.

Expanded Discussions and Illustrations. The Expanded Discussion section provides additional topics not covered in depth in the textbook. The *Take Action!* CD gives the flexibility to enrich or expand the course by discussion of additional topics such as those listed below.

International Accounting. The *Take Action!* CD provides an expanded discussion of international accounting institutions, the evolution of international accounting standards, and a framework for understanding the differences in accounting practice. This discussion is designed to complement the International Reporting Cases in the "Using Your Judgment" sections.

Take Action! CD Topics. Topics included on the *Take Action!* CD are as follows (with appropriate chapter linkage identified).

Chapter 1

- Expanded discussion of international accounting.
- Expanded discussion of ethical issues in financial accounting.

Chapter 2

- Discussion of accounting for changing prices.

Chapter 3

- Presentation of work sheet using the periodic inventory method.
- Specialized journals and methods of processing accounting data.
- Tutorial on the accounting cycle.

Chapter 6

- Present-value-based measurements, including an expanded discussion of spreadsheet tools for solving present value problems.

Chapter 7

- Discussion of how a four-column bank reconciliation (the proof of cash) can be used for control purposes.
- Expanded example of transfers of receivables without recourse, with accounting entries.
- Tutorials on the accounting for bad debts and transfer of receivables.

Chapter 8

- Tutorial on inventory cost flow assumptions.
- Tutorial on LIFO issues, including dollar-value LIFO.

Chapter 10

- Tutorial on interest capitalization.

Chapter 11

- Discussion of lesser-used depreciation methods, such as the retirement and replacement methods.
- Tutorial on depreciation methods.
- Tutorial on impairments.

Chapter 12

- Expanded discussion on valuing goodwill.

Chapter 13

- Expanded discussion on property taxes.

Chapter 15

- Expanded discussion on the par value method for treasury stock.
- Expanded discussion on quasi-reorganizations.

Chapter 16

- Comprehensive earnings per share illustration.

Chapter 17

- Illustration of accounting entries for transfers of investment securities.
- Expanded discussion of special issues related to investments.

Chapter 19

- Discussion of the conceptual aspects of interperiod tax allocation, including the deferred and net of tax methods.
- Discussion of accounting for intraperiod tax allocation, with examples.

Chapter 21

- Discussion of real estate leases and leveraged leases.

Chapter 23

- Discussion of the T-account method for preparing a statement of cash flows. A detailed example is provided.

Chapter 24

- Discussion of accounting for changing prices both for general and specific price level changes.
- Financial analysis primer.

In addition to these materials, illustrative disclosures of financial reporting practices are provided.

Self-Study Tests and Additional Self-Tests. Each chapter on the *Take Action!* CD includes two sets of self-tests to allow students to check their understanding of key concepts from the chapter.

Glossary. A complete glossary of all the key terms used in the text is provided, in alphabetical order. Page numbers where these key terms appear in the text are also shown.

Learning Style Survey. Research on left brain/right brain differences and also on learning and personality differences suggests that each person has preferred ways to receive and communicate information. After taking this quiz, students will be able to pinpoint the study aids in the text that will help them learn the material based on their particular learning styles.

In summary, the *Take Action!* CD is a comprehensive complement to the 11th Edition of *Intermediate Accounting*, providing new materials as well as a new way to communicate that material.

ENHANCED FEATURES

We have continued and enhanced many of the features of the 10th Edition of *Intermediate Accounting*, including the following.

Chapter-Opening Vignettes

We have updated and introduced new chapter-opening vignettes to provide an even better real-world context that helps motivate student interest in the chapter topic.

"Using Your Judgment" Section

The "Using Your Judgment" section at the end of each chapter has been revised and updated. Elements in this section include a Financial Reporting Problem (featuring **3M Company**), Financial Statement Analysis Case, Comparative Analysis Case (featuring **The CocaCola Company** and **PepsiCo, Inc.**), Research Case(s), International Reporting Case, and the new Professional Simulation. Explicit writing and group assignments and ethics cases have been moved out of the Using Your Judgment sections and are instead integrated into the Exercises, Problems, and Conceptual Cases. Exercises, problems, and cases that are especially suited for group or writing assignments and those that specifically address ethics are identified with special icons, as shown here in the margin.

Real-World Emphasis

We believe that one of the goals of the intermediate accounting course is to orient students to the application of accounting principles and techniques in practice. Accordingly, we have continued our practice of using numerous examples from real corporations throughout the text. The names of these real companies are highlighted in red. Illustrations and exhibits marked by the icon shown here in the margin or by company logos are excerpts from actual financial statements of existing firms. In addition, the 2001 report of **3M Company** is included in Appendix 5B, and many real-company financial reports appear in the database on the *Take Action!* CD.

International Insights

INTERNATIONAL INSIGHT

International Insight paragraphs that describe or compare IASB standards and the accounting practices in other countries with U.S. GAAP are provided in the margin. We have continued this feature to help students understand that other countries sometimes use different recognition and measurement principles to report financial information. These insights are marked with the icon shown here in the margin.

Currency and Accuracy

Accounting continually changes as its environment changes; an up-to-date book is therefore a necessity. As in past editions, we have strived to make this edition the most up-to-date and accurate text available.

Streamlined Presentation

We have continued our efforts to keep the topical coverage of *Intermediate Accounting* in line with the way instructors are currently teaching the course. Accordingly, we have moved some optional topics into appendixes and have omitted altogether some topics that formerly were covered in appendixes, moving them to the *Take Action!* CD. Details are noted in the list of specific content changes below and in the earlier CD-content list.

CONTENT CHANGES

The following list outlines the revisions and improvements made in chapters of the 11th Edition.

Chapter 1 Financial Accounting and Accounting Standards

- New vignette.
- Discussion of Sarbanes-Oxley Act of 2002.
- Updated international discussion.

Chapter 2 Conceptual Framework Underlying Financial Accounting

- New vignette.
- Enhanced discussion of the new concepts statement on present values and cash flows.

Chapter 3 The Accounting Information System

- Updated vignette.
- Presentation of work sheet in spreadsheet format.
- The accounting equation analyses in the margin next to key journal entries now include indication of the cash flow effect.

Chapter 4 Income Statement and Related Information

- New vignette.
- Updated discussion of quality of earnings. Updated discussion of irregular items.
- Deleted appendix on discontinued operations, given changes in accounting standards.

Chapter 5 Balance Sheet and Statement of Cash Flows

- New vignette.
- New featured company.

Chapter 6 Accounting and the Time Value of Money

- Introduced new concepts statement on present values and expected cash flows.
- Moved appendix on spreadsheets to *Take Action!* CD.

Chapter 7 Cash and Receivables

- Updated vignette.
- Added new graphic on uncollectible accounts.

Chapter 8 Valuation of Inventories: A Cost Basis Approach

- New vignette on usefulness of inventory disclosures.
- Streamlined discussion of manufacturing costs and absorption costing.

Chapter 9 Inventories: Additional Valuation Issues

- Updated vignette.

Chapter 10 Acquisition and Disposition of Property, Plant, and Equipment

- New vignette on the significance of property, plant, and equipment.
- Updated discussion on capital additions and repairs.

Chapter 11 Depreciation, Impairments, and Depletion

- New vignette on impairments.
- Introduced component depreciation.

Chapter 12 Intangible Assets

- New chapter, given new standard on intangible assets.

Chapter 13 Current Liabilities and Contingencies

- Streamlined discussion of current liabilities.
- Moved property taxes payable to *Take Action!* CD.
- Introduced new standard on asset retirement obligations.
- Updated discussion on guarantees.

Chapter 14 Long-Term Liabilities

- New vignette on the impact of debt levels on equity markets.
- Streamlined discussion on types of bonds and bond ratings. Updated discussion on reporting of gains and losses on extinguishment of debt.
- Updated discussion of off-balance-sheet financing.

Chapter 15 Stockholders' Equity

- New combined chapter on stockholders' equity.

Chapter 16 Dilutive Securities and Earnings Per Share

- New vignette.
- Updated discussion of hybrid securities.
- New graphic on components of compensation.
- Updated discussion of stock options.

Chapter 17 Investments

- Updated vignette on equity method.
- Updated discussion on equity method and goodwill.
- Moved appendix on special issues related to investments to *Take Action!* CD.

Chapter 18 Revenue Recognition

- Updated discussion of regulatory environment related to revenue recognition.
- Introduced new International Insights.

Chapter 19 Accounting for Income Taxes

- Updated vignette.
- Streamlined discussion of alternative minimum tax.
- Streamlined discussion of multiple tax rates.

Chapter 20 Accounting for Pensions and Postretirement Benefits

- New vignette on pension funding.
- New graphic on magnitude of pension plans.
- Streamlined discussion of capitalization.

Chapter 21 Accounting for Leases

- Updated vignette and graphic on airline leases.
- Streamlined discussion of leasing advantages.
- Streamlined journal entries for lessor accounting.
- Moved summary lease illustrations to appendix.

Chapter 22 Accounting Changes and Error Analysis

- New vignette on restatements.
- Streamlined discussion on accounting change framework.
- Added spreadsheet presentation of accounting error work sheet.
- Updated appendix for equity method goodwill.

Chapter 23 Statement of Cash Flows

- Updated vignette on usefulness of cash flows.
- Introduced spreadsheet presentation of cash flow work sheet.

Chapter 24 Full Disclosure in Financial Reporting

- New vignette on quality financial reporting.
- New accounting policy illustration.
- Updated discussion of related party transactions.
- Updated discussion of fraudulent financial reporting.

END-OF-CHAPTER ASSIGNMENT MATERIAL

At the end of each chapter we have provided a comprehensive set of review and homework material consisting of Questions, Brief Exercises, Exercises, Problems, and short Conceptual Cases. For this edition, many of the exercises and problems have been revised or updated. In addition, the Using Your Judgment sections, which (as described earlier) include Financial Reporting Problems, Financial Statement Analysis Cases, Comparative Analysis Cases, Research Cases, International Reporting Cases, and Professional Simulations, have all been updated. All of the assignment materials have been class-tested and/or double-checked for accuracy and clarity.

The Questions are designed for review, self-testing, and classroom discussion purposes as well as for homework assignments. Typically, a Brief Exercise covers one topic, an Exercise one or two topics. Exercises require less time and effort to solve than do Problems. The Problems are designed to develop a professional level of achievement and are more challenging and time-consuming to solve than the Exercises. Those Exercises and Problems that are contained in the *Excel Problems* supplements are identified by the icon shown here in the margin.

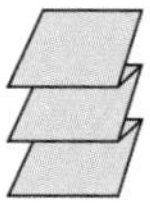

The Conceptual Cases generally require an essay as opposed to quantitative solutions. They are intended to confront the student with situations calling for conceptual analysis and the exercise of judgment in identifying problems and evaluating alternatives. The "Using Your Judgment" assignments, described earlier, are designed to develop students' critical thinking, analytical, research, and communication skills.

Probably no more than one-fourth of the total exercise, problem, and case material must be used to cover the subject matter adequately. Consequently, problem assignments may be varied from year to year without repetition.

SUPPLEMENTARY MATERIALS

Accompanying this textbook is an improved and expanded package of student learning aids and instructor teaching aids.

The *Intermediate Accounting,* 11th Edition, *Take Action!* CD, described in detail on pages viii–xi and available for packaging with the textbook, provides additional tools for students and instructors. Its three parts consist of the Analyst's Toolkit, the Professional Toolkit, and the Student Toolkit. Other teaching and learning aids are described below. In addition, other resources for students and instructors can be found at the book's companion Web site at www.wiley.com/college/kieso.

Instructor Teaching Aids

Instructor's Resource System on CD-ROM (IRCD)

- Resource manager with friendly interface for course development and presentation.
- Includes all instructor supplements, text art, and transparencies.

Instructor's Manual: Vol. 1: Chs. 1–14

Instructor's Manual: Vol. 2: Chs. 15–24

- Lecture outlines keyed to text learning objectives.
- Chapter reviews.
- Also available on the Kieso Web site and IRCD.

Solutions Manual, Vol. 1: Chs. 1–14

Solutions Manual, Vol. 2: Chs. 15–24

- Answers to all Brief Exercises, Exercises, Problems, and Case material provided.
- Classification Tables categorize the end-of-chapter material by topic to assist in assigning homework.
- Also available on the Kieso Web site and IRCD.
- Assignment Tables (of characteristics) describe the end-of-chapter material, its difficulty level, and estimated completion time.
- All solutions have been triple-checked to ensure accuracy.

Test Bank, Vol. 1: Chs. 1–14

Test Bank, Vol. 2: Chs. 15–24

- Essay questions with solutions for true-false, multiple choice, short answer, and essays help you test students' communication skills.
- Estimated completion times facilitate test planning.
- Computations for multiple-choice problems assist you in giving partial credit.
- Also available on the Kieso Web site and IRCD.

Computerized Test Bank IBM

- A large collection of objective questions and exercises with answers for each chapter in the text.
- Enables you to generate questions randomly or manually and modify/customize tests with your own material.
- Enables you to create versions of the same test by scrambling by type, character, number, or learning objective.
- Also available on the Kieso Web site and IRCD.

Test Preparation Service

- Simply call Wiley's Accounting Hotline (800-541-5602) with the questions you have selected for an exam. Wiley will provide a master within 24 hours.

Solutions Transparencies, Vol. 1: Chs. 1–14

Solutions Transparencies, Vol. 2: Chs. 15–24

- Provided in organizer box with chapter file folders.
- Large, bold type size for easier class presentation.
- Provided for all exercises, problems, and brief exercises.

PowerPoint Presentations

- Designed to enhance presentation of chapter topics and examples.
- Separate presentation for each chapter, available on the Kieso Web site and IRCD.

Teaching Transparencies

- More than 100 color figure illustrations and exhibits.

Checklist of Key Figures

- Available at the Kieso Web site to both students and instructors, and on the Instructor's Resource System CD (IRCD).

Solutions to Rockford Practice Set

- Available for download from the Kieso Web site, this supplement provides solutions to the *Rockford Practice Set.*

Solutions to Excel Templates

- Available for download from the Kieso Web site and IRCD, these are solutions to the *Solving Problems Using Excel Workbook* templates.

Course Management Resources

- Course content cartridges are available for both WebCT and Blackboard.

CPA Connection

The CPA Connection is a new resource developed for the 11th Edition. This booklet provides instructors with information about the computerized uniform Certified Public Accountant (CPA) examination scheduled to be administered for the first time in 2004. It provides knowledge about the changes in the exam and gives instructors ideas to assist their students in practicing the type of skills necessary to pass the Financial Accounting and Reporting section of the exam. Many of the ideas and tips included in the booklet are directly linked to *Intermediate Accounting*. Specifically, *The CPA Connection*: (1) develops awareness of the changed exam format, delivery, and content as it affects the financial accounting area, and (2) presents ideas and testing formats that instructors may choose to incorporate into their intermediate accounting classes. *The CPA Connection* should be viewed as a reference source, from which instructors can easily select and use the information that fits into their classroom situation. In addition, *The CPA Connection* booklet will be supplemented by an e-mail newsletter.

Student Learning Aids

Student Study Guide, Vol. 1: Chs. 1–14

Student Study Guide, Vol. 2: Chs. 15–24

- Chapter Learning Objectives
- Chapter Outline—a broad overview of general chapter content with space for note-taking in class.
- Chapter Review with summary of key concepts.
- Glossary of key terms.
- Review Questions and Exercises—self-test items with supporting computations.

Working Papers, Vol. 1: Chs. 1–14

Working Papers, Vol. 2: Chs. 15–24

- Solution forms and partially completed solutions forms for all end-of-chapter problems and exercises.
- Demonstrates how to correctly set up solution formats.

Excel Working Papers, Vol. 1: Chs. 1–14

Excel Working Papers, Vol. 2: Chs. 15–24

- Solution forms and partially completed solutions forms for all end-of-chapter problems and exercises; solution forms are available as Excel templates.
- Solutions can be typed directly into the templates, which are saved onto a hard drive or written manually after forms are printed.
- Students enter data electronically, enabling them to paste homework to a new file and e-mail the work sheet to their instructor.

Problem Solving Survival Guide, Vol. 1: Chs. 1–14

Problem Solving Survival Guide, Vol. 2: Chs. 15–24

- Provides additional questions and problems to develop students' problem-solving skills.
- Explanations assist in the approach, set-up, and completion of problems.
- Tips alert students to common pitfalls and misconceptions.

Solving Problems Using Excel Workbook

- Review of intermediate accounting and Excel concepts.
- Spreadsheet requirements range in difficulty (from data entry to developing spreadsheets).
- Each chapter consists of a basic tutorial, a more advanced tutorial, and two or three problems from the text.
- Each problem is followed by "what-if" questions to build students' analytical skills.

Rockford Corporation: An Accounting Practice Set

Rockford Corporation: A Computerized Accounting Practice Set

- Practice set that has been designed as a students' review and update of the accounting cycle and the preparation of financial statements.
- Available in a print version and in an updated computerized version.

Business Extra Web Site at www.wiley.com/college/businessextra

- Gives you instant access to a wealth of current articles dealing with all aspects of accounting.
- Articles are organized to correspond with the chapters of this text.
- To access Business Extra, you will need to purchase the "Doing Business in Turbulent Times" booklet.

ACKNOWLEDGMENTS

We thank the many users of our 10th Edition who contributed to the revision through their comments and instructive criticism. Special thanks are extended to the focus group participants and the primary reviewers of and contributors to our 11th Edition manuscript.

Janice Bell
California State University at Northridge

Larry Bergin
Winona State University

Robert Bloom
John Carroll University

Phillip Buchanan
George Mason University

Tom Buchman
University of Colorado, Boulder

Tom Carment
Northeastern State University

Joanne Duke
San Francisco State University

William Foster
New Mexico State University

Clyde Galbraith
West Chester University

Harold Goedde
SUNY Oneonta

Julia Higgs
Florida Atlantic University

Judy Hora
University of San Diego

Kathy Hsu
University of Louisiana, Lafayette

Daniel Ivancevich
University of North Carolina at Wilmington

Susan Ivancevich
University of North Carolina at Wilmington

James Johnston
Louisiana Tech University

Lisa Koonce
University of Texas at Austin

Steve Lafave
Augsburg College

Patsy Lee
University of Texas—Arlington

Gary Luoma
University of South Carolina

Joan Monnin-Callahan
University of Cincinnati

Patricia Parker
Columbus State Community College

Richard Parker
Olivet College

Marlene Plumlee
University of Utah

Debbie Rankin
Lincoln University

Paul Robertson
New Mexico State University

Larry Roman
Cuyahoga Community College

John Rossi
Moravian College

George Sanders
Western Washington University

Jerry Siebel
University of South Florida

Pamela Stuerke
Case Western Reserve University

Ron Stunda
Birmingham Southern College

Gary Taylor
University of Alabama

Gary Testa
Brooklyn College

Lynn Thomas
Kansas State University

Lynn Turner
Colorado State University

Elizabeth Venuti
Hofstra University

Jeannie Welsh
La Salle University

We would also like to thank other colleagues who provided helpful criticism and made valuable suggestions as members of focus groups or as adopters and reviewers of previous editions.

Charlene Abendroth
California State University—Hayward

Diana Adcox
University of North Florida

Noel Addy
Mississippi State University

Roberta Allen
Texas Tech University

James Bannister
University of Hartford

Kathleen Bauer
Midwestern State University

Jon A. Booker
Tennessee Technological University

John C. Borke
University of Wisconsin—Platteville

Suzanne M. Busch
California State University—Hayward

Eric Carlsen
Kean College of New Jersey

Robert Cluskey
Tennessee State University

Edwin Cohen
DePaul University

W. Terry Dancer
Arkansas State University

Lee Dexter
Moorhead State University

Judith Doing
University of Arizona

Dean S. Eiteman
Indiana University—Pennsylvania

Larry R. Falcetto
Emporia State University

Richard Fern
Eastern Kentucky University

Richard Fleischman
John Carroll University

Stephen L. Fogg
Temple University

Clyde Galbraith
West Chester University

Susan Gill
Washington State University

Lynford E. Graham
Rutgers University

Donald J. Griffin
Cayuga Community College

Marcia I. Halvorsen
University of Cincinnati

Garry Heesacker
Central Washington University

Wayne M. Higley
Buena Vista University

Geoffrey R. Horlick
St. Francis College

M. Zafar Iqbal
California Polytechnic State University—San Luis Obispo

Cynthia Jeffrey
Iowa State University

Jeff Jones
Auburn University

Celina Jozsi
University of South Florida

Douglas W. Kieso
University of California—Irvine

Paul D. Kimmel
University of Wisconsin—Milwaukee

Martha King
Emporia State University

Florence Kirk
State University of New York at Oswego

Mark Kohlbeck
University of Wisconsin—Madison

Lisa Koonce
University of Texas—Austin

David B. Law
Youngstown State University

Henry LeClerc
Suffolk Community College—Selden Campus

Barbara Leonard
Loyola University—Chicago

Brian Leventhal
University of Illinois—Chicago

Timothy Lindquist
University of Northern Iowa

Tom Linsmeier
Michigan State University

Daphne Main
University of New Orleans

Mostafa Maksy
Northeastern Illinois University

Danny Matthews
Midwestern State University

Robert J. Matthews
New Jersey City University

Robert Milbrath
University of Houston

John Mills
University of Nevada—Reno

Mohamed E. Moustafa
California State University—Long Beach

Siva Nathan
Georgia State University

Kermit Natho
Georgia State University

Obeau S. Persons
Rider University

Ray Pfeiffer
University of Massachusetts—Amherst

Tom Porter
Georgia State University

Robert Rambo
University of New Orleans

Vernon Richardson
University of Kansas

Richard Riley
West Virginia University

Jeffrey D. Ritter
St. Norbert College

Paul Robertson
New Mexico State University

Steven Rock
University of Colorado

Victoria Rymer
University of Maryland

James Sander
Butler University

John Sander
University of Southern Maine

Douglas Sharp
Wichita State University

John R. Simon
Northern Illinois University

Keith Smith
George Washington University

Pam Smith
Northern Illinois University

Billy S. Soo
Boston College

Carlton D. Stolle
Texas A & M University

William Stout
University of Louisville

Iris Stuart
California State University—Fullerton

Eric Sussman
University of California, Los Angeles

Diane L. Tanner
University of North Florida

Paula B. Thomas
Middle Tennessee State University

James D. Waddington, Jr.
Hawaii Pacific University

Dick Wasson
Southwestern College

Frank F. Weinberg
Golden Gate University

Shari H. Wescott
Houston Baptist University

Michael Willenborg
University of Connecticut

William H. Wilson
Oregon Health University

Kenneth Wooling
Hampton University

Joni Young
University of New Mexico

Paul Zarowin
New York University

Stephen A. Zeff
Rice University

We would also like to thank the following colleagues who contributed to several of the unique features of this edition.

Take Action! CD:

Andrew Prewitt, *KPMG, Chicago*
Jeff Seymour, *KPMG, Minneapolis*
Matt Sullivan, *Deloitte and Touche, Milwaukee*
Erin Viel, *PricewaterhouseCoopers, Milwaukee*

"Working in Teams" Materials:

Edward Wertheim, *Northeastern University*

The Writing Handbook:

Michelle Ephraim, *Worcester Polytechnic Institute*

Self-Test Materials:

Dick Wasson, *Southwestern College*

Perspectives and "From Classroom to Career" Interviews:

Stuart Weiss, *Stuart Weiss Business Writing, Inc.*

Ancillary Authors, Contributors, and Accuracy Checkers:

Shiela Ammons
Austin Community College

Maryann Benson
John C. Borke
University of Wisconsin—Platteville

Larry Falcetto
Emporia State University

Clyde Galbraith
West Chester University

Marc Giullian
Montana State University

Edwin Hackleman and Don Newell
Delta Software

Debra R. Hopkins
Northern Illinois University

Marilyn F. Hunt
University of Central Florida

Heather Johnson
Elm Street Publishing Services

Douglas W. Kieso
University of California—Irvine

Jennifer Laudermilch
Gary Lubin
Rex A. Schildhouse
University of Phoenix—San Diego

Barbara Muller
Arizona State University

Paul Jep Robertson
New Mexico State University

Alice Sineath
Forsyth Technical Community College

Dick D. Wasson
Southwestern College

Practicing Accountants and Business Executives

From the fields of corporate and public accounting, we owe thanks to the following practitioners for their technical advice and for consenting to interviews.

Tracy Barber
Deloitte & Touche

Ron Bernard
NFL Enterprises

Penelope Flugger
J.P. Morgan & Co.

John Gribble
PricewaterhouseCoopers

Darien Griffin
S.C. Johnson & Son Wax

Michael Lehman
Sun Microsystems, Inc.

Michele Lippert
Evoke.com

Sue McGrath
Vision Capital Management

David Miniken
Sweeney Conrad

Robert Sack
University of Virgina

Claire Schulte
Deloitte & Touche

Willie Sutton
Mutual Community Savings Bank, Durham, NC

Gary Valenzuela
Yahoo!

Rachel Woods
PricewaterhouseCoopers

Arthur Wyatt
Arthur Andersen & Co., and the University of Illinois—Urbana

In addition, we appreciate the exemplary support and professional commitment given us by the development, marketing, production, and editorial staffs of John Wiley & Sons, including Susan Elbe, Jay O'Callaghan, Mark Bonadeo, Keari Bedford, David Kear, Brian Kamins, Ed Brislin, Allie Keim, Jeanine Furino, Karen Kincheloe, Anna Melhorn, Lenore Belton, and Cynthia Taylor and to the management and staff at TechBooks. A special note of thanks also to Ann Torbert (editorial and content assistance) and Elm Street Publishing Services (Martha Beyerlein and Heather Johnson) for facilitating the production of the manuscript and the book. We also wish to thank Dick Wasson of Southwestern College for coordinating the efforts of the supplements authors and checkers. Finally, thanks to Maris Technologies for developing the format of the *Take Action!* CD. We appreciate the cooperation of the American Institute of Certified Public Accountants and the Financial Accounting Standards Board in permitting us to quote from their pronouncements. We thank 3M Company for permitting us to use its 2001 Annual Report for our specimen financial statements. We also acknowledge permission from the American Institute of Certified Public Accountants, the Institute of Management Accountants, and the Institute of Internal Auditors to adapt and use material from the Uniform CPA Examinations, the CMA Examinations, and the CIA Examination, respectively.

If this book helps teachers instill in their students an appreciation for the challenges, worth, and limitations of accounting, if it encourages students to evaluate critically and understand financial accounting theory and practice, and if it prepares students for advanced study, professional examinations, and the successful and ethical pursuit of their careers in accounting or business, then we will have attained our objective.

Suggestions and comments from users of this book will be appreciated.

Donald E. Kieso
Somonauk, Illinois

Jerry J. Weygandt
Madison, Wisconsin

Terry D. Warfield
Madison, Wisconsin

Brief Contents

Contents

CHAPTER 1

Financial Accounting and Accounting Standards

The Size of the New York City Phone Book . . .

Enron, **Global Crossing**, **Kmart**, **WorldCom**, **Williams Co.**, and **Xerox** are examples of companies that have come under the scrutiny of the Securities and Exchange Commission recently because of accounting issues. Share prices of all these companies have declined substantially, as investors punish any company whose quality of earnings is in doubt.

The unfortunate part of accounting scandals is that we all pay. Enron, for example, at one time had a market capitalization of $80 billion before disclosure of its accounting irregularities. Today it is bankrupt. Employees have lost their pension money, investors have lost their savings, and the entire stock market has become caught up in "Enronitis," which has led to substantial declines in the overall stock market. At one point, there were at least 10 congressional committees involved in inquiries regarding corporate governance issues, and over 30 Enron-related bills have addressed matters such as regulation of derivative securities, auditor-client conflicts, and development of an oversight body to regulate the accounting profession.

As a result of the many concerns expressed by investors about the completeness and the reliability of the accounting numbers, many companies have expanded their financial disclosures in their annual reports. For example, **General Electric**'s CEO Jeffery Immelt stated, "I want people to think about GE as we think of GE—as a transparent company." He noted that GE's annual report will be "the size of New York City's phone book, if necessary" to provide the information necessary to help investors and creditors make the proper investing decisions.

It is our hope that meaningful reform will come out of these recent investigations into sloppy or fraudulent accounting. Although the U.S. is still considered to have the finest reporting system in the world, we must do better. As former chair of the FASB Ed Jenkins recently remarked, "If anything positive results . . . it may be that [these accounting issues] serve as an indelible reminder to all that transparent financial reporting does matter and that lack of transparency imposes significant costs on all who participate [in our markets]."

LEARNING OBJECTIVES

After studying this chapter, you should be able to:

1. **Identify the major financial statements and other means of financial reporting.**
2. **Explain how accounting assists in the efficient use of scarce resources.**
3. **Identify some of the challenges facing accounting.**
4. **Identify the objectives of financial reporting.**
5. **Explain the need for accounting standards.**
6. **Identify the major policy-setting bodies and their role in the standards-setting process.**
7. **Explain the meaning of generally accepted accounting principles.**
8. **Describe the impact of user groups on the standards-setting process.**
9. **Understand issues related to ethics and financial accounting.**

PREVIEW OF CHAPTER 1

As the opening story indicates, relevant and reliable financial information must be provided so that our capital markets work efficiently. This chapter explains the environment of financial reporting and the many factors affecting it. The content and organization of this chapter are as follows.

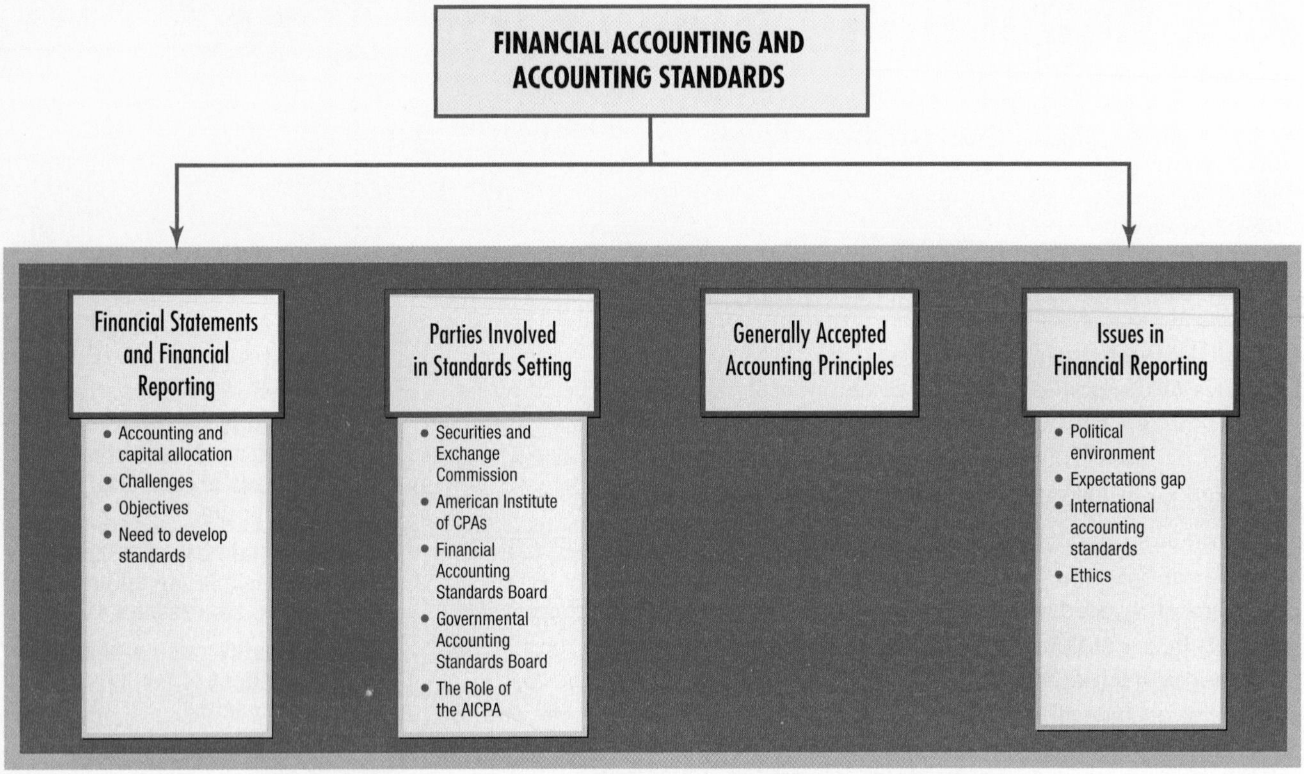

FINANCIAL STATEMENTS AND FINANCIAL REPORTING

The essential characteristics of accounting are: (1) identification, measurement, and communication of financial information about (2) economic entities to (3) interested parties. **Financial accounting** is the process that culminates in the preparation of financial reports on the enterprise as a whole for use by both internal and external parties. Users of these financial reports include investors, creditors, managers, unions, and government agencies. In contrast, **managerial accounting** is the process of identifying, measuring, analyzing, and communicating financial information needed by management to plan, evaluate, and control an organization's operations.

OBJECTIVE 1
Identify the major financial statements and other means of financial reporting.

Financial statements are the principal means through which financial information is communicated to those outside an enterprise. These statements provide the company's history quantified in money terms. The **financial statements** most frequently provided are (1) the balance sheet, (2) the income statement, (3) the statement of cash flows, and (4) the statement of owners' or stockholders' equity. In addition, note disclosures are an integral part of each financial statement.

Some financial information is better provided, or can be provided only, by means of **financial reporting** other than formal financial statements. Examples include the president's letter or supplementary schedules in the corporate annual report, prospectuses, reports filed with government agencies, news releases, management's forecasts, and certifications regarding internal controls and fraud. Such information may be required by authoritative pronouncement, regulatory rule, or custom. Or it may be supplied because management wishes to disclose it voluntarily.

The primary focus of this textbook concerns the development of two types of financial information: (1) the basic financial statements and (2) related disclosures.

Accounting and Capital Allocation

OBJECTIVE 2
Explain how accounting assists in the efficient use of scarce resources.

Because resources are limited, people try to conserve them, to use them effectively, and to identify and encourage those who can make efficient use of them. Through an efficient use of resources, our standard of living increases.

Markets, free enterprise, and competition determine whether a business is to be successful and thrive. This fact places a substantial burden on the accounting profession to measure performance accurately and fairly on a timely basis, so that the right managers and companies are able to attract investment capital. For example, relevant and reliable financial information enables investors and creditors to compare the income and assets employed by such companies as **IBM**, **McDonald's**, **Microsoft**, and **Ford**. As a result, they can assess the relative return and risks associated with investment opportunities and so channel resources more effectively. This process of capital allocation works as follows.

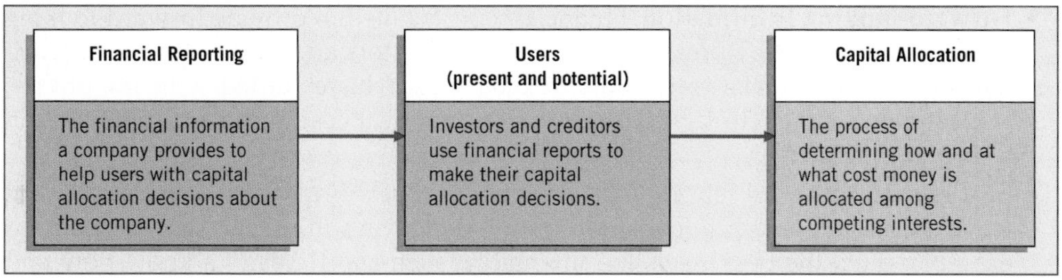

Financial Reporting
The financial information a company provides to help users with capital allocation decisions about the company.
Users (present and potential)
Investors and creditors use financial reports to make their capital allocation decisions.
Capital Allocation
The process of determining how and at what cost money is allocated among competing interests.

ILLUSTRATION 1-1
Capital Allocation Process

An effective process of capital allocation is critical to a healthy economy. It promotes productivity, encourages innovation, and provides an efficient and liquid market for buying and selling securities and obtaining and granting credit.[1] As indicated in our opening story, unreliable and irrelevant information leads to poor capital allocation, which adversely affects the securities markets.

IT'S NOT THE ECONOMY, ANYMORE, STUPID

WHAT DO THE NUMBERS MEAN?

It's not the economy anymore. It's the accounting. That's what many investors seem to be saying these days. As indicated in our opening story, even the slightest hint of any type of accounting irregularity at a company leads to a subsequent pounding of the company's stock. For example, a recent *Wall Street Journal* had the following headlines related to accounting and its effects on the economy.

Stocks take a beating as accounting worries spread beyond **Enron**

Williams Cos. delays earnings release to review a unit's obligations

Global Crossing's accounting method now being called aggressive

Bank stocks fall as investors take issue with **PNC**'s accounting

Investors, skeptical of **Tyco**'s breakup plan, send shares down 20%

It now has become clear that there must be trust in the numbers or investors will abandon the market and put their resources elsewhere. That is why overseas investors are pulling their money out of the U.S. market and why the dollar is dropping relative to other currencies. With investor uncertainty, the cost of capital increases for companies who need additional resources. In short, relevant and reliable financial information is necessary for markets to be efficient.

[1] AICPA Special Committee on Financial Reporting, "Improving Business Reporting — A Customer Focus," *Journal of Accountancy*, Supplement (October 1994).

The Challenges Facing Financial Accounting

OBJECTIVE 3
Identify some of the challenges facing accounting.

Although there is a crisis of confidence regarding corporate governance issues, of which one is proper accounting, much is right about financial reporting in the United States. The U.S. markets are still the most liquid, deep, secure, and efficient public capital markets of any country. One reason for this success is that our financial statements and related disclosures have captured and organized financial information in a useful and reliable fashion. However, much still needs to be done. For example, suppose you could move to the year 2020 and look back at financial reporting today. Here is what you might read:

- **Non-financial Measurements.** Financial reports failed to provide some key performance measures widely used by management. For example, nonfinancial measures such as customer satisfaction indexes, backlog information, and reject rates on goods purchased, all now used to evaluate the long-term stability of the company, were provided on an ad hoc basis, if at all.
- **Forward-looking Information.** Financial reports failed to provide forward-looking information needed by present and potential investors and creditors. One individual noted that financial statements in 2000 should have started with the phrase, "Once upon a time," to signify their use of historical cost and their accumulation of past events.
- **Soft Assets.** Financial reports focused on hard assets (inventory, plant assets) but failed to provide much information on a company's soft assets (intangibles). For example, often the best assets are intangible, such as **Microsoft**'s know-how and market dominance, **Dell**'s unique marketing setup and well-trained employees, and **J.Crew**'s brand image.
- **Timeliness.** Financial statements were prepared only quarterly, and audited financials were provided annually. Little to no real-time financial statement information was available.

INTERNATIONAL INSIGHT

The objectives of financial reporting differ across nations. Traditionally, the primary objective of accounting in many continental European nations and in Japan was conformity with the law. In contrast, Canada, the U.K., the Netherlands, and many other nations have shared the U.S. view that the primary objective is to provide information for investors. Insights into international standards and practices will be presented throughout the text.

We believe each of these challenges must be met for the accounting profession to continue to provide the type of information needed for an efficient capital allocation process. We are confident that changes will occur. Here are some positive signs:

- Already some companies are making voluntary disclosures on information deemed relevant to investors. Often such information is of a non-financial nature. Regional banking companies, like **BankOne Corp.**, **Fifth Third Bancorp**, **Sun Trust Banks**, and others, for example, now include, in addition to traditional financial information, data on loan growth, credit quality, fee income, operating efficiency, capital management, and management strategy.
- The World Wide Web was first used to provide limited financial data. Now most companies offer their annual reports in several formats on the Web. The most innovative companies are now offering sections of their annual reports in a format that can be readily manipulated by the user, such as in an Excel spreadsheet format.
- More accounting standards are now requiring the recording or disclosing of fair value information. For example, either investments in stocks and bonds, debt obligations, and derivatives are recorded at fair value, or information related to fair values is shown in the notes to the financial statements.

Changes in these directions will enhance the relevance of financial reporting and provide useful information to users of the financial statements.

Objectives of Financial Reporting

OBJECTIVE 4
Identify the objectives of financial reporting.

In an attempt to establish a foundation for financial accounting and reporting, a set of **objectives of financial reporting by business enterprises** has been identified. Financial reporting should provide information that:

❶ Is useful to present and potential investors and creditors and other users **in making rational investment, credit, and similar decisions**. The information should be comprehensible to those who have a **reasonable understanding** of business and economic activities and are willing to study the information with reasonable diligence.

❷ Helps present and potential investors, creditors, and other users **assess the amounts, timing, and uncertainty of prospective cash receipts** from dividends or interest and the proceeds from the sale, redemption, or maturity of securities or loans. Since investors' and creditors' cash flows are related to enterprise cash flows, financial reporting should provide information to help investors, creditors, and others assess the amounts, timing, and uncertainty of prospective net cash inflows to the related enterprise.

❸ **Clearly portrays the economic resources of an enterprise, the claims to those resources** (obligations of the enterprise to transfer resources to other entities and owners' equity), and the effects of transactions, events, and circumstances that change its resources and claims to those resources.[2]

In brief, the objectives of financial reporting are to provide (1) information that is useful in investment and credit decisions, (2) information that is useful in assessing cash flow prospects, and (3) information about enterprise resources, claims to those resources, and changes in them.

The emphasis on "assessing cash flow prospects" might lead one to suppose that the cash basis is preferred over the accrual basis of accounting. That is not the case. Information based on **accrual accounting generally provides a better indication of an enterprise's present and continuing ability to generate favorable cash flows** than does information limited to the financial effects of cash receipts and payments.[3]

Recall from your first accounting course that the objective of **accrual basis accounting** is to ensure that events that change an entity's financial statements are recorded in the periods in which the events occur, rather than only in the periods in which the entity receives or pays cash. Using the accrual basis to determine net income means recognizing revenues when earned rather than when cash is received, and recognizing expenses when incurred rather than when paid. Under accrual accounting, revenues, for the most part, are recognized when sales are made so they can be related to the economic environment of the period in which they occurred. Over the long run, trends in revenues are generally more meaningful than trends in cash receipts.

The Need to Develop Standards

OBJECTIVE ❺
Explain the need for accounting standards.

The main controversy in setting accounting standards is, "Whose rules should we play by, and what should they be?" The answer is not immediately clear because the users of financial accounting statements have both coinciding and conflicting needs for information of various types. To meet these needs, and to satisfy the fiduciary[4] reporting responsibility of management, a single set of **general-purpose financial statements** is prepared. These statements are expected to present fairly, clearly, and completely the financial operations of the enterprise.

As a result, the accounting profession has attempted to develop a set of standards that are generally accepted and universally practiced. Without these standards, each

[2]"Objectives of Financial Reporting by Business Enterprises," *Statement of Financial Accounting Concepts No. 1* (Stamford, Conn.: FASB, November 1978), pars. 5–8.

[3]*SFAC No. 1,* p. iv. As used here, cash flow means "cash generated and used in operations." The term **cash flows** is frequently used also to include cash obtained by borrowing and used to repay borrowing, cash used for investments in resources and obtained from the disposal of investments, and cash contributed by or distributed to owners.

[4]Management's responsibility to manage assets with care and trust is its **fiduciary** responsibility.

enterprise would have to develop its own standards, and readers of financial statements would have to familiarize themselves with every company's peculiar accounting and reporting practices. It would be almost impossible to prepare statements that could be compared.

This common set of standards and procedures is called **generally accepted accounting principles (GAAP)**. The term "generally accepted" means either that an authoritative accounting rule-making body has established a principle of reporting in a given area or that over time a given practice has been accepted as appropriate because of its universal application.[5] Although principles and practices have provoked both debate and criticism, most members of the financial community recognize them as the standards that over time have proven to be most useful. A more extensive discussion of what constitutes GAAP is presented later in this chapter.

PARTIES INVOLVED IN STANDARDS SETTING

OBJECTIVE 6
Identify the major policy-setting bodies and their role in the standards-setting process.

A number of organizations are instrumental in the development of financial accounting standards (GAAP) in the United States. Four major organizations are as follows.

1. Securities and Exchange Commission (SEC)
2. American Institute of Certified Public Accountants (AICPA)
3. Financial Accounting Standards Board (FASB)
4. Governmental Accounting Standards Board (GASB)

Securities and Exchange Commission (SEC)

INTERNATIONAL INSIGHT

The International Organization of Securities Commissions (IOSCO) is a group of more than 100 securities regulatory agencies or securities exchanges from all over the world. IOSCO was established in 1987. Collectively, its members represent a substantial proportion of the world's capital markets. The SEC is a member of IOSCO.

External financial reporting and auditing developed and evolved in tandem with the growth of America's industrial economy and its capital markets. However, when the stock market crashed in 1929 and the nation's economy plunged into the Great Depression, there were calls for increased government regulation and supervision of business generally and especially financial institutions and the stock market.

As a result, the federal government established the **Securities and Exchange Commission (SEC)** to help develop and standardize financial information presented to stockholders. The SEC is a federal agency. It administers the Securities Exchange Act of 1934 and several other acts. Most companies that issue securities to the public or are listed on a stock exchange are required to file audited financial statements with the SEC. In addition, the SEC has broad powers to prescribe, in whatever detail it desires, the accounting practices and standards to be employed by companies that fall within its jurisdiction. As a result, the SEC exercises oversight over 12,000 companies that are listed on the major exchanges (such as the New York Stock Exchange and Nasdaq).

Public/Private Partnership

At the time the SEC was created, no group—public or private—was issuing accounting standards. The SEC encouraged the creation of a private standards-setting body because it believed that the private sector had the resources and talent to develop appropriate accounting standards. As a result, accounting standards have generally developed in the private sector either through the American Institute of Certified Public Accountants (AICPA) or the Financial Accounting Standards Board (FASB).

The SEC has affirmed its support for the FASB by indicating that financial statements conforming to standards set by the FASB will be presumed to have substantial authoritative support. In short, the **SEC requires registrants to adhere to GAAP**. In addition, it has indicated in its reports to Congress that "it continues to believe that the

[5]The terms **principles** and **standards** are used interchangeably in practice and throughout this textbook.

initiative for establishing and improving accounting standards should remain in the private sector, subject to Commission oversight."

SEC Oversight

The SEC's partnership with the private sector has worked well. The SEC has acted with remarkable restraint in the area of developing accounting standards. Generally, **the SEC has relied on the AICPA and FASB to regulate the accounting profession and develop and enforce accounting standards**.

Over its history, however, the SEC's involvement in the development of accounting standards has varied. In some cases the private sector has attempted to establish a standard, but the SEC has refused to accept it. In other cases the SEC has prodded the private sector into taking quicker action on certain reporting problems, such as accounting for investments in debt and equity securities and the reporting of derivative instruments. In still other situations the SEC communicates problems to the FASB, responds to FASB exposure drafts, and provides the FASB with counsel and advice upon request.

The SEC has the mandate to establish accounting principles. The private sector, therefore, must listen carefully to the views of the SEC. In some sense the private sector is the formulator and the implementor of the standards.[6] While the partnership between the SEC and the private sector has worked well, it can be strained when accounting problems are not addressed as quickly as the SEC would like. This was apparent in the recent deliberations on the accounting for business combinations and intangible assets and concerns over the accounting for special-purpose entities, highlighted in the failure of **Enron**.

Enforcement

As indicated earlier, companies listed on a stock exchange are required to submit their financial statements to the SEC. If the SEC believes that an accounting or disclosure irregularity exists regarding the form or content of the financial statements, it sends a deficiency letter to the company. Usually these deficiency letters are resolved quickly. However, if disagreement continues, the SEC has the power to issue a "stop order," which prevents the registrant from issuing securities or trading securities on the exchanges. Criminal charges may also be brought by the Department of Justice for violations of certain laws. The SEC program, private sector initiatives, and civil and criminal litigation help to ensure the integrity of financial reporting for public companies.

American Institute of Certified Public Accountants (AICPA)

As indicated earlier, the **American Institute of Certified Public Accountants (AICPA)**, which is the national professional organization of practicing Certified Public Accountants (CPAs), has been vital to the development of GAAP. Various committees and boards established since the founding of the AICPA have contributed to this effort.

Committee on Accounting Procedure

At the urging of the SEC, the AICPA appointed the Committee on Accounting Procedure in 1939. The **Committee on Accounting Procedure (CAP)**, composed of practicing CPAs, issued 51 **Accounting Research Bulletins** during the years 1939 to 1959. (See

INTERNATIONAL INSIGHT

Nations also differ in the degree to which they have developed national standards and consistent accounting practices. One indicator of the level of a nation's accounting is the nature of the accounting profession within the country. Professional accounting bodies were established in the Netherlands, the U.K., Canada, and the U.S. in the nineteenth century. In contrast, public accountancy bodies were established in Hong Kong and Korea only in the last half century.

[6]One writer has described the relationship of the FASB and SEC and the development of financial reporting standards using the analogy of a pearl. The pearl (financial reporting standard) "is formed by the reaction of certain oysters (FASB) to an irritant (the SEC)—usually a grain of sand—that becomes embedded inside the shell. The oyster coats this grain with layers of nacre, and ultimately a pearl is formed. The pearl is a joint result of the irritant (SEC) and oyster (FASB); without both, it cannot be created." John C. Burton, "Government Regulation of Accounting and Information," *Journal of Accountancy* (June 1982).

list at the back of the book.) These bulletins deal with a variety of accounting problems. But this problem-by-problem approach failed to provide the structured body of accounting principles that was both needed and desired. In response, in 1959 the AICPA created the Accounting Principles Board.

Accounting Principles Board

The major purposes of the **Accounting Principles Board (APB)** were (1) to advance the written expression of accounting principles, (2) to determine appropriate practices, and (3) to narrow the areas of difference and inconsistency in practice. To achieve these objectives, the APB's mission was to develop an overall conceptual framework to assist in the resolution of problems as they become evident and to do substantive research on individual issues before pronouncements were issued.

The Board's 18 to 21 members, selected primarily from public accounting, also included representatives from industry and the academic community. The Board's official pronouncements, called **APB Opinions**, were intended to be based mainly on research studies and be supported by reasons and analysis. Between its inception in 1959 and its dissolution in 1973, the APB issued 31 opinions. (See complete list at the back of the book.)

Unfortunately, the APB came under fire early, charged with lack of productivity and failing to act promptly to correct alleged accounting abuses. Later the APB tackled numerous thorny accounting issues, only to meet a buzz saw of opposition from industry and CPA firms and occasional governmental interference. In 1971 the accounting profession's leaders, anxious to avoid governmental rule-making, appointed a Study Group on Establishment of Accounting Principles. Commonly known as the **Wheat Committee** for its chair Francis Wheat, this group was to examine the organization and operation of the APB and determine what changes would be necessary to attain better results. The Study Group's recommendations were submitted to the AICPA Council in the spring of 1972, adopted in total, and implemented by early 1973.

Financial Accounting Standards Board (FASB)

The Wheat Committee's recommendations resulted in the demise of the APB and the creation of a new standards-setting structure composed of three organizations—the Financial Accounting Foundation (FAF), the Financial Accounting Standards Board (FASB), and the Financial Accounting Standards Advisory Council (FASAC). The **Financial Accounting Foundation** selects the members of the FASB and the Advisory Council, funds their activities, and generally oversees the FASB's activities.

The major operating organization in this three-part structure is the **Financial Accounting Standards Board (FASB)**. Its mission is to establish and improve standards of financial accounting and reporting for the guidance and education of the public, which includes issuers, auditors, and users of financial information. The expectations of success and support for the new FASB were based upon several significant differences between it and its predecessor, the APB:

INTERNATIONAL INSIGHT

The U.S. legal system is based on English common law, whereby the government generally allows professionals to make the rules. These rules (standards) are therefore developed in the private sector. Conversely, some countries follow codified law, which leads to government-run accounting systems.

1. **Smaller Membership.** The FASB is composed of seven members, replacing the relatively large 18-member APB.
2. **Full-time, Remunerated Membership.** FASB members are well-paid, full-time members appointed for renewable 5-year terms. The APB members were unpaid and part-time.
3. **Greater Autonomy.** The APB was a senior committee of the AICPA, whereas the FASB is not an organ of any single professional organization. It is appointed by and answerable only to the Financial Accounting Foundation.
4. **Increased Independence.** APB members retained their private positions with firms, companies, or institutions. FASB members must sever all such ties.
5. **Broader Representation.** All APB members were required to be CPAs and members of the AICPA. Currently, it is not necessary to be a CPA to be a member of the FASB.

In addition to research help from its own staff, the FASB relies on the expertise of various task force groups formed for various projects and on the **Financial Accounting Standards Advisory Council (FASAC)**. FASAC consults with the FASB on major policy and technical issues and also helps select task force members.

Due Process

In establishing financial accounting standards, two basic premises of the FASB are: (1) The FASB should be responsive to the needs and viewpoints of the entire economic community, not just the public accounting profession. (2) It should operate in full view of the public through a "due process" system that gives interested persons ample opportunity to make their views known. To ensure the achievement of these goals, the steps shown in Illustration 1-2 are taken in the evolution of a typical FASB Statement of Financial Accounting Standards.

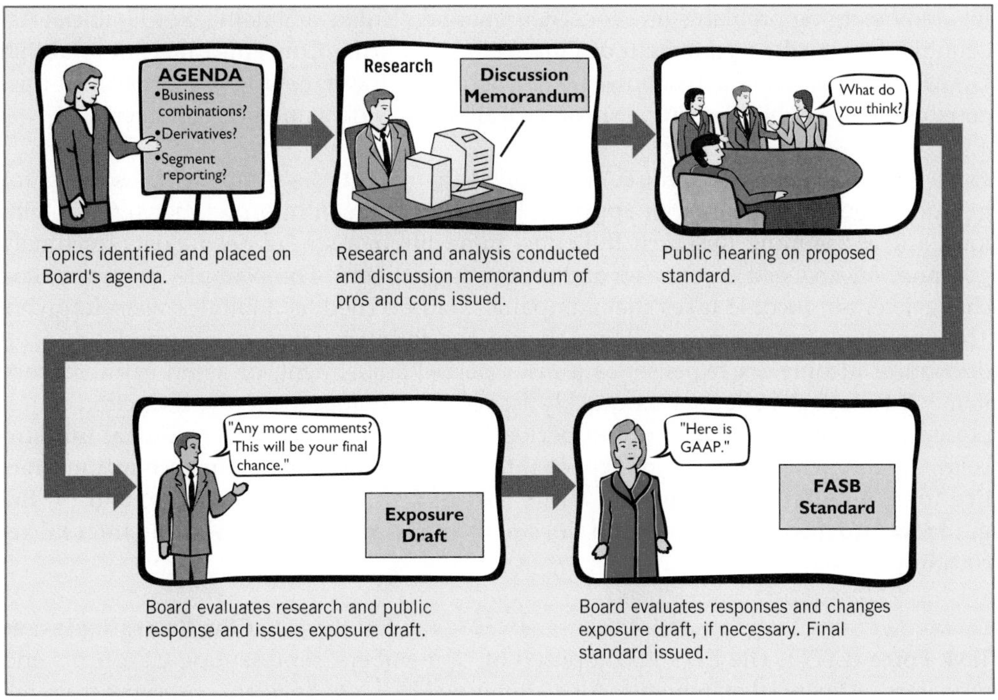

ILLUSTRATION 1-2
Due Process

The passage of a new FASB **Standards Statement** requires the support of four of the seven Board members. FASB Statements are considered GAAP and thereby binding in practice. All ARBs and APB Opinions that were in effect in 1973 when the FASB became effective continue to be effective until amended or superseded by FASB pronouncements. In recognition of possible misconceptions of the term "principles," the FASB uses the term **financial accounting standards** in its pronouncements.

Types of Pronouncements

The major types of pronouncements that the FASB issues are:

1. Standards and Interpretations.
2. Financial Accounting Concepts.
3. Technical Bulletins.
4. Emerging Issues Task Force Statements.

Standards and Interpretations. Financial accounting **standards** issued by the FASB are considered generally accepted accounting principles. In addition, the FASB also issues **interpretations** that represent modifications or extensions of existing standards. The

interpretations have the same authority as standards and require the same votes for passage as standards. However, interpretations do not require the FASB to operate in full view of the public through the due process system that is required for FASB Standards. The APB also issued interpretations of APB Opinions. Both types of interpretations are now considered authoritative support for purposes of determining GAAP. Since replacing the APB, the FASB has issued 147 standards and 44 interpretations. (See list at the back of the book.)

Financial Accounting Concepts. As part of a long-range effort to move away from the problem-by-problem approach, the FASB in November 1978 issued the first in a series of **Statements of Financial Accounting Concepts** as part of its conceptual framework project. (See list at the back of the book.) The purpose of the series is to set forth fundamental objectives and concepts that the Board will use in developing future standards of financial accounting and reporting. They are intended to form a cohesive set of interrelated concepts, a conceptual framework, that will serve as tools for solving existing and emerging problems in a consistent manner. Unlike a Statement of Financial Accounting Standards, **a Statement of Financial Accounting Concepts does not establish GAAP**. Concepts statements, however, pass through the same due process system (discussion memo, public hearing, exposure draft, etc.) as do standards statements.

FASB Technical Bulletins. The FASB receives many requests from various sources for guidelines on implementing or applying FASB Standards or Interpretations, APB Opinions, and Accounting Research Bulletins. In addition, a strong need exists for timely guidance on financial accounting and reporting problems. For example, in one tax law change, certain income taxes that companies had accrued as liabilities were forgiven. The immediate question was: How should the forgiven taxes be reported—as a reduction of income tax expense, as a prior period adjustment, or as an extraordinary item? A technical bulletin was quickly issued that required the tax reduction be reported as a reduction of the current period's income tax expense. A **technical bulletin** is issued only when (1) **it is not expected to cause a major change in accounting practice for a number of enterprises,** (2) **its cost of implementation is low, and** (3) **the guidance provided by the bulletin does not conflict with any broad fundamental accounting principle.**[7]

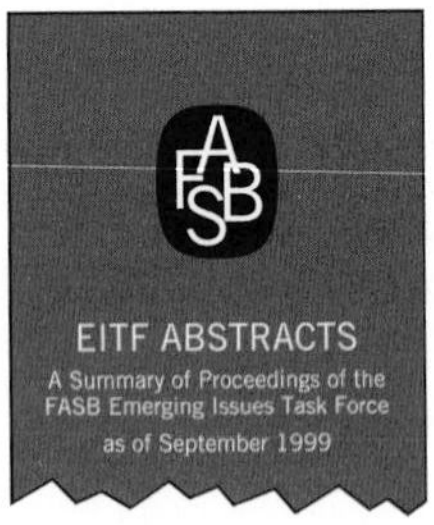

Emerging Issues Task Force Statements. In 1984 the FASB created the **Emerging Issues Task Force (EITF)**. The EITF is composed of 13 members, representing CPA firms and preparers of financial statements. Also attending EITF meetings are observers from the SEC and AICPA. The purpose of the task force is to reach a consensus on how to account for new and unusual financial transactions that have the potential for creating differing financial reporting practices. Examples include how to account for pension plan terminations; how to account for revenue from barter transactions by Internet companies; and how to account for excessive amounts paid to takeover specialists. The EITF also provided timely guidance for the reporting of the losses arising from the terrorist attacks on the World Trade Center on 9/11/01.

We cannot overestimate the importance of the EITF. In one year, for example, the task force examined 61 emerging financial reporting issues and arrived at a consensus on approximately 75 percent of them. The SEC has indicated that it will view consensus solutions as preferred accounting and will require persuasive justification for departing from them.

The EITF helps the FASB in many ways. For example, emerging issues often attract public attention. If they are not resolved quickly, they can lead to financial crises and scandal and can undercut public confidence in current reporting practices. The next step, possible governmental intervention, would threaten the continuance of standards setting in the private sector. In addition, the EITF identifies controversial accounting

[7]"Purpose and Scope of FASB Technical Bulletins and Procedures for Issuance," *FASB Technical Bulletin No. 79-1* (Revised) (Stamford, Conn.: FASB, June 1984).

problems as they arise and determines whether they can be quickly resolved, or whether the FASB should become involved in solving them. In essence, it becomes a "problem filter" for the FASB. Thus, it is hoped that the FASB will be able to work on more pervasive long-term problems, while the EITF deals with short-term emerging issues.

Governmental Accounting Standards Board (GASB)

Financial statements prepared by state and local governments are not comparable with financial reports prepared by private business organizations. This lack of comparability was highlighted in the 1970s when a number of large U.S. cities such as New York and Cleveland faced potential bankruptcy. As a result, the **Governmental Accounting Standards Board (GASB)**, under the oversight of the Financial Accounting Foundation, was created in 1984 to address state and local governmental reporting issues.

The operational structure of the GASB is similar to that of the FASB. That is, it has an advisory council called the **Governmental Accounting Standards Advisory Council (GASAC)**, and it is assisted by its own technical staff and task forces.

The creation of GASB was controversial. Many believe that there should be only one standards-setting body—the FASB. It was hoped that partitioning standards setting between the GASB, which deals only with state and local government reporting, and the FASB, which addresses reporting for all other entities, would not lead to conflict. Since we are primarily concerned with financial reports prepared by profit-seeking organizations, this textbook will focus on standards issued by the FASB only.

The formal organizational structure as it currently exists for the development of financial reporting standards is presented in Illustration 1-3.

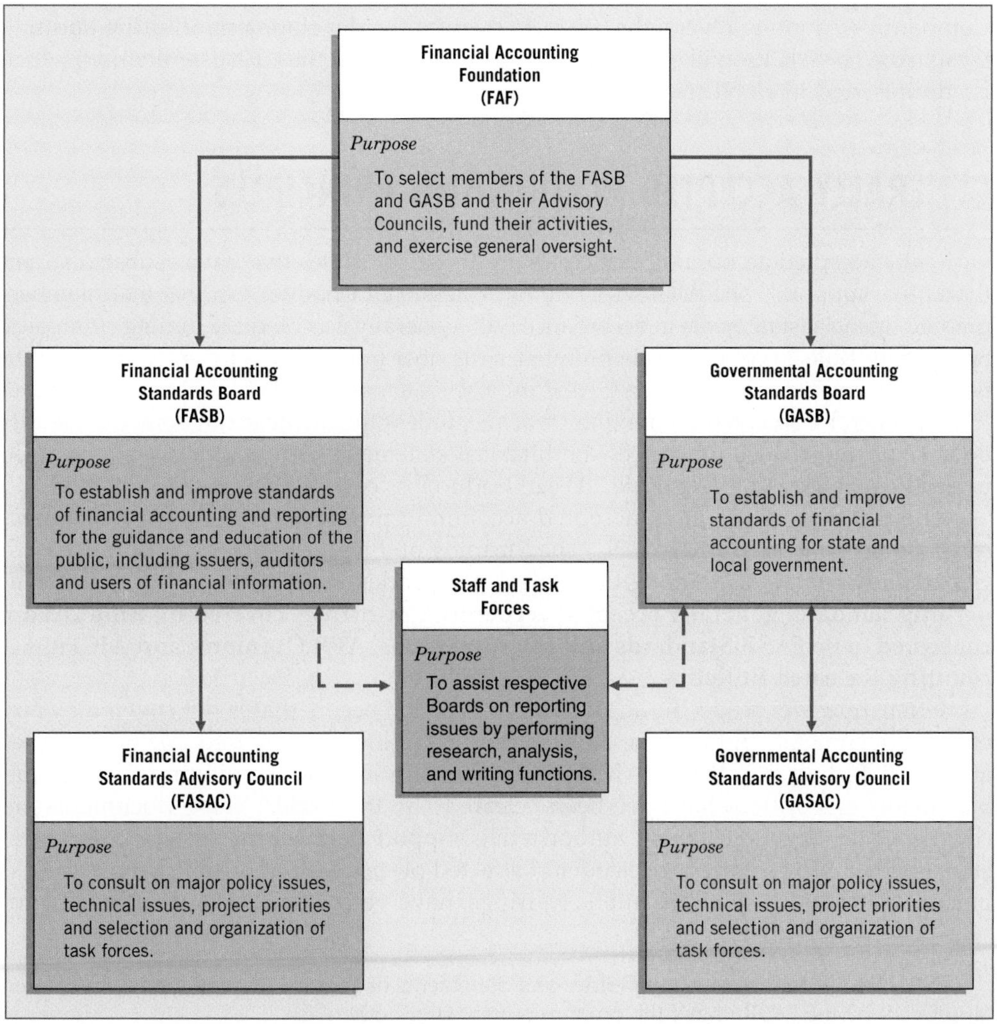

ILLUSTRATION 1-3
Organizational Structure for Setting Accounting Standards

The Role of the AICPA

For several decades the AICPA provided the leadership in the development of accounting principles and rules. It regulated the accounting profession and developed and enforced accounting practice more than did any other professional organization. When the Accounting Principles Board was dissolved and replaced with the FASB, the AICPA established the Accounting Standards Division to act as its official voice on accounting and reporting issues.

The **Accounting Standards Executive Committee (AcSEC)** was established within the Division and was designated as the senior technical committee authorized to speak for the AICPA in the area of financial accounting and reporting. It does so through various written communications:

Audit and Accounting Guidelines summarize the accounting practices of specific industries and provide specific guidance on matters not addressed by the FASB. Examples are accounting for casinos, airlines, colleges and universities, banks, insurance companies, and many others.

Statements of Position (SOP) provide guidance on financial reporting topics until the FASB sets standards on the issue in question. SOPs may update, revise, and clarify audit and accounting guides or provide free-standing guidance.

Practice Bulletins indicate AcSEC's views on narrow financial reporting issues not considered by the FASB.

The AICPA has been the leader in developing auditing standards through its **Auditing Standards Board**. However, the Sarbanes-Oxley Act of 2002 requires the Public Company Accounting Oversight Board to oversee the development of future auditing standards. The AICPA will continue to develop and grade the CPA examination, which is administered in all 50 states.

GENERALLY ACCEPTED ACCOUNTING PRINCIPLES

OBJECTIVE 7
Explain the meaning of generally accepted accounting principles.

Generally accepted accounting principles are those principles that have "substantial authoritative support." The AICPA's Code of Professional Conduct requires that members prepare financial statements in accordance with generally accepted accounting principles. Specifically, Rule 203 of this Code prohibits a member from expressing an opinion that financial statements conform with GAAP if those statements contain a material departure from a generally accepted accounting principle, unless the member can demonstrate that because of unusual circumstances the financial statements would otherwise have been misleading. Failure to follow Rule 203 can lead to loss of a CPA's license to practice.

The meaning of generally accepted accounting principles is defined by *Statement on Auditing Standards (SAS) No. 69*, "The Meaning of 'Present Fairly in Conformity With Generally Accepted Accounting Principles' in the Independent Auditor's Report." **Under this standard, generally accepted accounting principles covered by Rule 203 are construed to be FASB Standards and Interpretations, APB Opinions, and AICPA Accounting Research Bulletins.**

Often, however, a specific accounting transaction occurs that is not covered by any of these documents. In this case, other authoritative literature is used. Major examples are: FASB Technical Bulletins; AICPA Industry Auditing and Accounting Guides; and Statements of Position that have been "cleared" by the FASB.[8] These documents are considered to have substantial authoritative support because the recognized professional bodies, after giving interested and affected parties the opportunity to react to exposure drafts and respond at public hearings, have voted their issuance. If these pro-

[8] *SAS No. 69* states that Audit Guides and Statements of Position are assumed to be cleared (approved) by the FASB unless the pronouncement states otherwise.

nouncements are lacking in guidance, then other sources might be considered. The hierarchy of these sources is presented in Illustration 1-4.[9] If the accounting treatment of an event is not specified by a category (a) pronouncement, then categories (b) through (d) should be investigated. If there is a conflict between pronouncements in (b) through (d), the higher category is to be followed. For example, (b) is higher than (c).

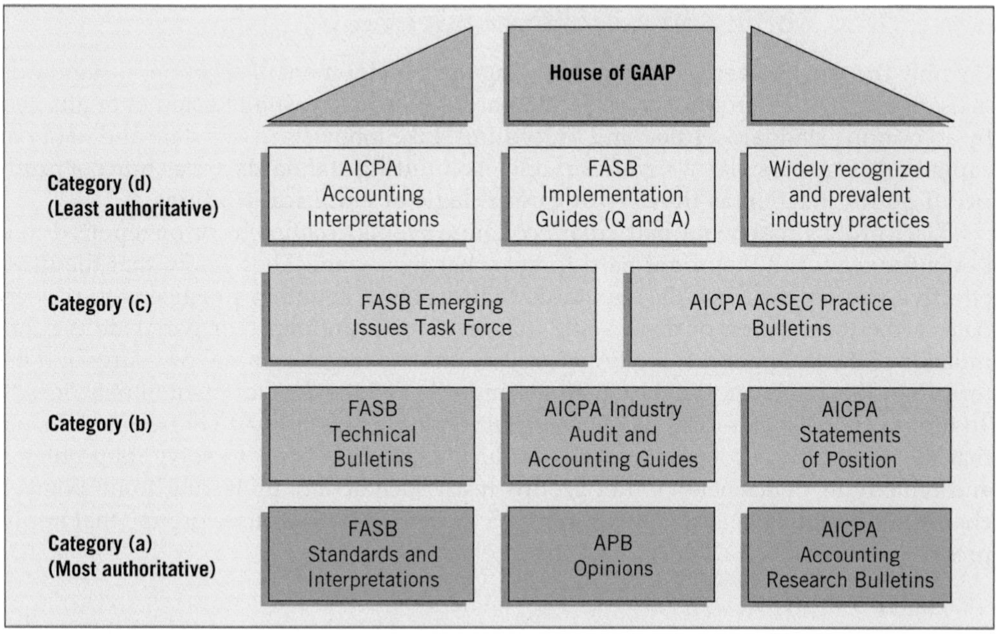

ILLUSTRATION 1-4
The House of GAAP

If none of these pronouncements addresses the event, the support is sought from other accounting literature. Examples of other accounting literature include FASB Concepts Statements, International Accounting Standards, and accounting articles.

YOU HAVE TO STEP BACK

WHAT DO THE NUMBERS MEAN?

Should the accounting profession have principle-based standards or rule-based standards? Critics of the profession today say that over the past three decades the standards-setters have moved away from establishing broad accounting principles aimed at ensuring that companies' financial statements are fairly presented.

Instead, these critics say, the standards-setters have moved toward drafting voluminous rules that may shield auditors and companies from legal liability if technically followed in check-box fashion. That can result in companies creating complex capital structures that technically comply with GAAP but hide billions of dollars of debt and other obligations. To add fuel to the fire, the chief accountant of the enforcement division of the SEC recently noted, "One can violate the SEC laws and still comply with GAAP."

In short, what he is saying is that it's not enough to check the boxes and do everything that GAAP requires. You have to then step back and determine whether the overall impression created by GAAP fairly portrays the underlying economics of the company. It is a tough standard and one that auditors and corporate management should work to achieve.

Source: Adapted from Steve Liesman, "SEC Accounting Cop's Warning: Playing by the Rules May Not Head Off Fraud Issues," *Wall Street Journal* (February 12, 2002), p. C7.

---

[9]See for example, "Remodeling the House of GAAP," by Douglas Sauter, *Journal of Accountancy* (July 1991), pp. 30–37.

ISSUES IN FINANCIAL REPORTING

Since many interests may be affected by the implementation of an accounting standard, it is not surprising that there is much discussion about who should develop these standards and to whom they should apply. Some of the major issues are discussed below.

Standards Setting in a Political Environment

OBJECTIVE 8
Describe the impact of user groups on the standards-setting process.

Possibly the most powerful force influencing the development of accounting standards is user groups. User groups consist of the parties who are most interested in or affected by accounting standards, rules, and procedures. Like lobbyists in our state and national capitals, user groups play a significant role. **Accounting standards are as much a product of political action as they are of careful logic or empirical findings.**

User groups may want particular economic events accounted for or reported in a particular way, and they fight hard to get what they want. They know that the most effective way to influence the standards that dictate accounting practice is to participate in the formulation of these standards or to try to influence or persuade the formulator of them. Therefore, the FASB has become the target of many pressures and efforts to influence changes in the existing standards and the development of new ones.[10] To top it off, these pressures have been multiplying. Some influential groups demand that the accounting profession act more quickly and decisively to solve its problems and remedy its deficiencies. Other groups resist such action, preferring to implement change more slowly, if at all. Illustration 1-5 shows the various user groups that apply pressure.

ILLUSTRATION 1-5
User Groups that Influence the Formulation of Accounting Standards

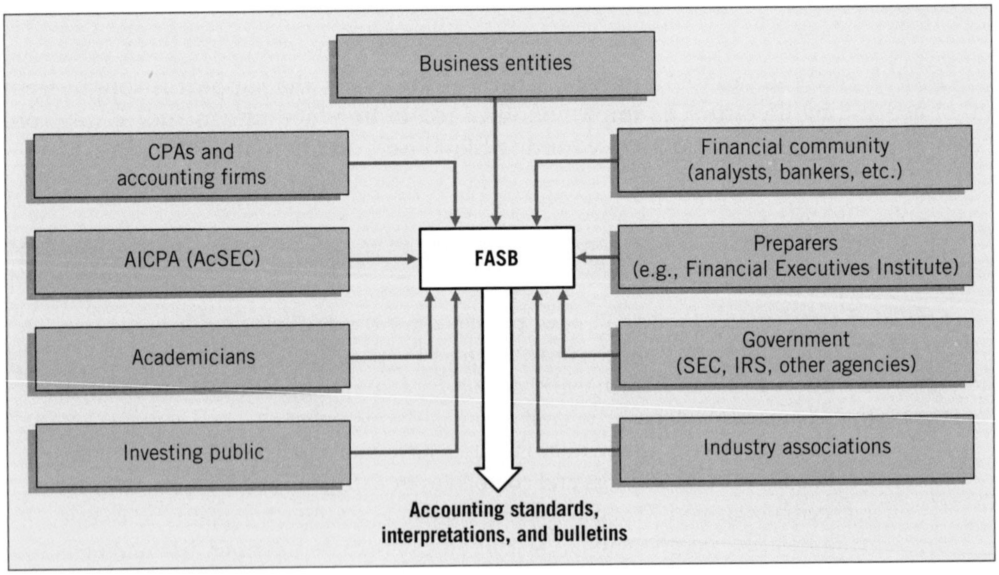

Should there be politics in setting standards for financial accounting and reporting? We have politics at home; at school; at the fraternity, sorority, and dormitory; at the office; at church, temple, and mosque—politics is everywhere. The FASB does not exist in a vacuum. Standards setting is part of the real world, and it cannot escape politics and political pressures.

[10]FASB board members have acknowledged that many of the Board's projects, such as "Accounting for Contingencies," "Accounting for Pensions," "Statement of Cash Flows," and "Accounting for Derivatives," were targets of political pressure.

That is not to say that politics in standards setting is evil. Considering the **economic consequences**[11] of many accounting standards, it is not surprising that special interest groups become vocal (some supporting, some opposing) when standards are being formulated. The Board must be attentive to the economic consequences of its actions. What the Board should *not* do is issue pronouncements that are primarily politically motivated. While paying attention to its constituencies, the Board should base its standards on sound research and a conceptual framework that has its foundation in economic reality. Even so, the FASB can continue to expect politics and special interest pressures, since as T. S. Eliot said, "Humankind cannot bear very much reality."

THE ECONOMIC CONSEQUENCES OF GOODWILL

WHAT DO THE NUMBERS MEAN?

Investors generally ignore an accounting change. But when it substantially affects net income, stockholders pay attention. One change that will affect many companies is the new goodwill rules. Before the change, companies that had goodwill were required to charge it against revenues over time. Under the new rules, companies no longer have to write off this cost on a systematic basis. The effect on the bottom line for some companies is substantial. For example, assuming no goodwill amortization, **International Paper** estimates an income increase of 21 percent, **Johnson Controls** 16 percent, and **Pepsi Bottling Group** 30 percent.

Some believe this change in the rules will make their stock more attractive. Others argue that it should have no effect because the write-off is a mere bookkeeping charge. Others argue that the change in the rules has no effect on cash flows, but that investors will perceive the company to be more profitable, and therefore a good buy in the marketplace. In short, the numbers have consequences. What do you think?

The Expectations Gap

All professions have come under increasing scrutiny by the government, whether it be the investment banking profession because of insider trading, the medical profession because of high costs and Medicare or Medicaid frauds, or engineers because of their failure to consider environmental consequences in their work.

Recently, it has been the accounting profession's turn. As indicated earlier, accounting scandals at companies like **Enron**, **Cendant**, **Sunbeam**, **Rite Aid**, **Xerox**, and **WorldCom** have attracted the attention of Congress. In 2002, legislation—the Sarbanes-Oxley Act—was enacted; the new law increases the resources for the SEC to combat fraud and curb poor reporting practices.[12] And the SEC has increased its policing efforts, approving new auditor independence rules and materiality guidelines for financial reporting. In addition, the Sarbanes-Oxley Act introduces sweeping changes to the institutional structure of the accounting profession. The following are some key provisions of the legislation:

- An accounting oversight board is being established. It will have oversight and enforcement authority and will establish auditing, quality control, and independence standards and rules.
- Stronger independence rules for auditors are now in place. Audit partners, for example, will be required to rotate every five years.

---

[11]"Economic consequences" in this context means the impact of accounting reports on the wealth positions of issuers and users of financial information and the decision-making behavior resulting from that impact. The resulting behavior of these individuals and groups could have detrimental financial effects on the providers of the financial information (enterprises). For a more detailed discussion of this phenomenon, see Stephen A. Zeff, "The Rise of 'Economic Consequences'," *Journal of Accountancy* (December 1978), pp. 56–63. Special appreciation is extended to Professor Zeff for his insights on this chapter.

[12]*Sarbanes-Oxley Act of 2002*, H. R. Rep. No. 107-610 (2002).

- CEOs and CFOs must forfeit bonuses and profits when there is an accounting restatement.
- CEOs and CFOs are required to certify that the financial statements and company disclosures are accurate and complete.
- Audit committees will need independent members and members with financial expertise.
- Codes of ethics must be in place for senior financial officers.

Will these changes be enough? The **expectations gap**—what the public thinks accountants should be doing and what accountants think they can do—is a difficult one to close. The instances of fraudulent reporting have caused some to question whether the profession is doing enough. Although the profession can argue rightfully that they cannot be responsible for every financial catastrophe, it must continue to strive to meet the needs of society. Efforts to meet these needs will become more costly to society because the development of a highly transparent, clear, and reliable system will require considerable resources.

International Accounting Standards

INTERNATIONAL INSIGHT

Foreign accounting firms that provide an audit report for a U.S.-listed company are subject to the authority of the accounting oversight board (mandated by the Sarbanes-Oxley Act).

Lawrence Summers, former Secretary of the Treasury, indicated that the single most important innovation shaping the capital market was the idea of generally accepted accounting principles. Summers went on to say that we need something similar internationally.

Most countries have recognized the need for more global standards. As a result, the **International Accounting Standards Committee (IASC)** was formed in 1973—the same year the FASB was born—to attempt to narrow the areas of divergence between standards of different countries.

The objective of the IASC in terms of standards setting was "to work generally for the improvement and harmonization of regulations, accounting standards and procedures relating to the presentation of financial statements." Eliminating differences is not easy. The objectives of financial reporting in the United States often differ from those in foreign countries, the institutional structures are often not comparable, and strong national tendencies are pervasive. Nevertheless, much headway has been made since IASC's inception.

Recently, the IASC has been restructured and renamed the **International Accounting Standards Board (IASB)**. This new body will work toward the development of a **single set of high-quality global standards**. The IASB has a structure similar to that of the FASB. It is hoped that the establishment of a fully independent international accounting standards setter will provide the essential convergence needed as we move to a global capital market system.

Expanded Discussion of International Accounting

It should be emphasized that the United States has a major voice in how international standards are being developed. As a result, there are many similarities between IASB- and U.S.-based standards. Throughout this textbook, international considerations are presented to help you understand the international reporting environment. In addition, as noted by the icon in the margin, there is an expanded discussion of international accounting on the Take Action! CD that accompanies this textbook. We strongly encourage you to access the material available on the CD.

Ethics in the Environment of Financial Accounting

OBJECTIVE 9
Understand issues related to ethics and financial accounting.

Robert Sack, a commentator on the subject of accounting ethics, noted that, "Based on my experience, new graduates tend to be idealistic . . . thank goodness for that! Still it is very dangerous to think that your armor is all in place and say to yourself 'I would have never given in to that.' The pressures don't explode on us; they build, and we often don't recognize them until they have us."

As indicated in this chapter, businesses' concentration on "maximizing the bottom line," "facing the challenges of competition," and "stressing short-term results" places accountants in an environment of conflict and pressure. Basic questions such as, "Is this way of communicating financial information good or bad?" "Is it right or wrong?" "What should I do in the circumstance?" cannot always be answered by simply adhering to GAAP or following the rules of the profession. Technical competence is not enough when ethical decisions are encountered.

Doing the right thing, making the right decision, is not always easy. Right is not always obvious. And the pressures "to bend the rules," "to play the game," "to just ignore it" can be considerable. For example, "Will my decision affect my job performance negatively?" "Will my superiors be upset?" "Will my colleagues be unhappy with me?" are often questions faced in making a tough ethical decision. The decision is more difficult because a public consensus has not emerged to formulate a comprehensive ethical system to provide guidelines. As discussed earlier, the issue has become of such importance that Congress has legislated that companies must develop a code of ethics for their senior financial officers.

Expanded Discussion of Ethical Issues in Financial Accounting

This whole process of ethical sensitivity and selection among alternatives can be complicated by pressures that may take the form of time pressures, job pressures, client pressures, personal pressures, and peer pressures. Throughout this textbook, **ethical considerations are presented for the purpose of sensitizing you** to the type of situations you may encounter in the performance of your professional responsibility.

HERE COME THE POLITICS

WHAT DO THE NUMBERS MEAN?

Given the current number of accounting scandals mentioned so far in the text, it is not surprising that both political parties are working hard to ensure that corporate management be ethical. President Bush, for example, has announced a set of proposals to crack down on unethical behavior by corporate officials, expanding the offenses subject to criminal and civil penalties. And both the SEC and the Justice Department are budgeted to get more funds to combat financial fraud. Bush has indicated "that the federal government will be vigilant in prosecuting wrongdoers" in American business. At the same time, the Democratic Party also is pushing for more corporate-reform initiatives. One thing is certain—recent events have undermined consumer confidence regarding corporate America and the capital markets. Because these issues are hurting the U.S. economy, politicians are now trying to find answers.

Conclusion

The FASB is in its thirtieth year as this textbook is written. Will the FASB survive in its present state, or will it be restructured or changed as its predecessors were? The next ten years will be interesting ones in the standards-setting arena. The possibility of global standards, the crisis of confidence in the capital markets caused by **Enron**, **Tyco**, **WorldCom**, and other accounting failures, and the issue of principle-based versus rule-based standards are major issues that will affect standards-setting in the United States.

At present, we believe that the accounting profession is reacting responsibly to remedy identified shortcomings. Because of its substantive resources and expertise, the private sector should be able to develop and maintain high standards. But it is a difficult process requiring time, logic, and diplomacy. By a judicious mix of these three ingredients, the profession should continue to develop its own reporting standards with SEC oversight.

SUMMARY OF LEARNING OBJECTIVES

KEY TERMS

Accounting Principles Board (APB), *8*
Accounting Research Bulletins, *7*
accrual basis accounting, *5*
American Institute of Certified Public Accountants (AICPA), *7*
APB Opinions, *8*
Auditing Standards Board, *12*
Committee on Accounting Procedure (CAP), *7*
economic consequences, *15*
Emerging Issues Task Force (EITF), *10*
expectations gap, *16*
financial accounting, *2*
Financial Accounting Standards Board (FASB), *8*
financial reporting, *2*
financial statements, *2*
generally accepted accounting principles (GAAP), *6*
Governmental Accounting Standards Board (GASB), *11*
International Accounting Standards Board (IASB), *16*
interpretations, *9*
objectives of financial reporting, *4*
Securities and Exchange Commission (SEC), *6*
standards, *9*
Standards Statement, *9*
Statement of Financial Accounting Concepts, *10*
technical bulletin, *10*
Wheat Committee, *8*

1 Identify the major financial statements and other means of financial reporting. The financial statements most frequently provided are (1) the balance sheet, (2) the income statement, (3) the statement of cash flows, and (4) the statement of owners' or stockholders' equity. Financial reporting other than financial statements may take various forms. Examples include the president's letter and supplementary schedules in the corporate annual report, prospectuses, reports filed with government agencies, news releases, management's forecasts, and certifications regarding internal controls and fraud.

2 Explain how accounting assists in the efficient use of scarce resources. Accounting provides reliable, relevant, and timely information to managers, investors, and creditors so that resources are allocated to the most efficient enterprises. Accounting also provides measurements of efficiency (profitability) and financial soundness.

3 Identify some of the challenges facing accounting. Financial reports fail to provide (1) some key performance measures widely used by management, (2) forward-looking information needed by investors and creditors, (3) sufficient information on a company's soft assets (intangibles), and (4) real-time financial information.

4 Identify the objectives of financial reporting. The objectives of financial reporting are to provide (1) information that is useful in investment and credit decisions, (2) information that is useful in assessing cash flow prospects, and (3) information about enterprise resources, claims to those resources, and changes in them.

5 Explain the need for accounting standards. The accounting profession has attempted to develop a set of standards that is generally accepted and universally practiced. Without this set of standards, each enterprise would have to develop its own standards, and readers of financial statements would have to familiarize themselves with every company's peculiar accounting and reporting practices. As a result, it would be almost impossible to prepare statements that could be compared.

6 Identify the major policy-setting bodies and their role in the standards-setting process. The *Securities and Exchange Commission (SEC)* is an agency of the federal government that has the broad powers to prescribe, in whatever detail it desires, the accounting standards to be employed by companies that fall within its jurisdiction. The *American Institute of Certified Public Accountants (AICPA)* issued standards through its Committee on Accounting Procedure and Accounting Principles Board. The *Financial Accounting Standards Board (FASB)* establishes and improves standards of financial accounting and reporting for the guidance and education of the public. The *Governmental Accounting Standards Board (GASB)* establishes and improves standards of financial accounting for state and local governments.

7 Explain the meaning of generally accepted accounting principles. Generally accepted accounting principles are those principles that have substantial authoritative support, such as FASB Standards and Interpretations, APB Opinions and Interpretations, AICPA Accounting Research Bulletins, and other authoritative pronouncements.

8 Describe the impact of user groups on the standards-setting process. User groups may want particular economic events accounted for or reported in a particular way, and they fight hard to get what they want. The FASB has become the target of many pressures and efforts to influence changes in the existing standards and the development of new ones. Because of the accelerated rate of change and the increased complexity of our economy, these pressures have been multiplying. Accounting standards are as much a product of political action as they are of careful logic or empirical findings.

9 Understand issues related to ethics and financial accounting. Financial accountants are called on for moral discernment and ethical decision making. The decision is more difficult because a public consensus has not emerged to formulate a comprehensive ethical system that provides guidelines in making ethical judgments.

QUESTIONS

1. Differentiate broadly between financial accounting and managerial accounting.
2. Differentiate between "financial statements" and "financial reporting."
3. How does accounting help the capital allocation process?
4. What are some of the major challenges facing the accounting profession?
5. What are the major objectives of financial reporting?
6. Of what value is a common set of standards in financial accounting and reporting?
7. What is the likely limitation of "general-purpose financial statements"?
8. What are some of the developments or events that occurred between 1900 and 1930 that helped bring about changes in accounting theory or practice?
9. In what way is the Securities and Exchange Commission concerned about and supportive of accounting principles and standards?
10. What was the Committee on Accounting Procedure, and what were its accomplishments and failings?
11. For what purposes did the AICPA in 1959 create the Accounting Principles Board?
12. Distinguish among Accounting Research Bulletins, Opinions of the Accounting Principles Board, and Statements of the Financial Accounting Standards Board.
13. If you had to explain or define "generally accepted accounting principles or standards," what essential characteristics would you include in your explanation?
14. In what ways was it felt that the statements issued by the Financial Accounting Standards Board would carry greater weight than the opinions issued by the Accounting Principles Board?
15. How are FASB discussion memoranda and FASB exposure drafts related to FASB "statements"?
16. Distinguish between FASB "statements of financial accounting standards" and FASB "statements of financial accounting concepts."
17. What is Rule 203 of the Code of Professional Conduct?
18. Rank from the most authoritative to the least authoritative, the following three items: FASB Technical Bulletins, AICPA Practice Bulletins, and FASB Standards.
19. The chairman of the FASB at one time noted that "the flow of standards can only be slowed if (1) producers focus less on quarterly earnings per share and tax benefits and more on quality products, and (2) accountants and lawyers rely less on rules and law and more on professional judgment and conduct." Explain his comment.
20. What is the purpose of FASB Technical Bulletins? How do FASB Technical Bulletins differ from FASB Interpretations?
21. Explain the role of the Emerging Issues Task Force in establishing generally accepted accounting principles.
22. What is the purpose of the Governmental Accounting Standards Board?
23. What are some possible reasons why another organization, such as the Governmental Accounting Standards Board, should not issue financial reporting standards?
24. What is AcSEC and what is its relationship to the FASB?
25. What are the sources of pressure that change and influence the development of accounting principles and standards?
26. Some individuals have indicated that the FASB must be cognizant of the economic consequences of its pronouncements. What is meant by "economic consequences"? What dangers exist if politics play too much of a role in the development of financial reporting standards?
27. If you were given complete authority in the matter, how would you propose that accounting principles or standards should be developed and enforced?
28. One writer recently noted that 99.4 percent of all companies prepare statements that are in accordance with GAAP. Why then is there such concern about fraudulent financial reporting?
29. What is the "expectations gap"? What is the profession doing to try to close this gap?
30. A number of foreign countries have reporting standards that differ from those in the United States. What are some of the main reasons why reporting standards are often different among countries?
31. How are financial accountants challenged in their work to make ethical decisions? Is technical mastery of GAAP not sufficient to the practice of financial accounting?

CONCEPTUAL CASES

C1-1 (Financial Accounting) Alan Rodriquez has recently completed his first year of studying accounting. His instructor for next semester has indicated that the primary focus will be the area of financial accounting.

Instructions

(a) Differentiate between financial accounting and managerial accounting.
(b) One part of financial accounting involves the preparation of financial statements. What are the financial statements most frequently provided?
(c) What is the difference between financial statements and financial reporting?

C1-2 (Objectives of Financial Reporting) Celia Cruz, a recent graduate of the local state university, is presently employed by a large manufacturing company. She has been asked by Angeles Ochoa, controller, to prepare the company's response to a current Discussion Memorandum published by the Financial Accounting Standards Board (FASB). Cruz knows that the FASB has issued seven *Statements of Financial Accounting Concepts,* and she believes that these concept statements could be used to support the company's response to the Discussion Memorandum. She has prepared a rough draft of the response citing *Statement of Financial Accounting Concepts No. 1,* "Objectives of Financial Reporting by Business Enterprises."

Instructions

(a) Identify the three objectives of financial reporting as presented in *Statement of Financial Accounting Concepts No. 1 (SFAC No. 1).*
(b) Describe the level of sophistication expected of the users of financial information by *SFAC No. 1.*

(CMA adapted)

C1-3 (Accounting Numbers and the Environment) Hardly a day goes by without an article appearing on the crises affecting many of our financial institutions in the United States. It is estimated that the savings and loan (S&L) debacle of the 1980s, for example, ended up costing $500 billion ($2,000 for every man, woman, and child in the United States). Some argue that if the S&Ls had been required to report their investments at market value instead of cost, large losses would have been reported earlier, which would have signaled regulators to close those S&Ls and, therefore, minimize the losses to U.S. taxpayers.

Instructions

Explain how reported accounting numbers might affect an individual's perceptions and actions. Cite two examples.

C1-4 (Need for Accounting Standards) Some argue that having various organizations establish accounting principles is wasteful and inefficient. Rather than mandating accounting standards, each company could voluntarily disclose the type of information it considered important. In addition, if an investor wants additional information, the investor could contact the company and pay to receive the additional information desired.

Instructions

Comment on the appropriateness of this viewpoint.

C1-5 (AICPA's Role in Standards Setting) One of the major groups involved in the standards-setting process is the American Institute of Certified Public Accountants. Initially it was the primary organization that established accounting principles in the United States. Subsequently it relinquished most of its power to the FASB.

Instructions

(a) Identify the two committees of the AICPA that established accounting principles prior to the establishment of the FASB.
(b) Speculate as to why these two organizations failed. In your answer, identify steps the FASB has taken to avoid failure.
(c) What is the present role of the AICPA in the standards-setting environment?

C1-6 (FASB Role in Standards Setting) A press release announcing the appointment of the trustees of the new Financial Accounting Foundation stated that the Financial Accounting Standards Board (to be appointed by the trustees) ". . . will become the established authority for setting accounting principles under which corporations report to the shareholders and others" (AICPA news release July 20, 1972).

Instructions

(a) Identify the sponsoring organization of the FASB and the process by which the FASB arrives at a decision and issues an accounting standard.

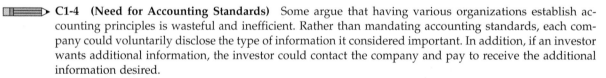

(b) Indicate the major types of pronouncements issued by the FASB and the purposes of each of these pronouncements.

C1-7 (Government Role in Standards Setting) Recently an article stated "the setting of accounting standards in the United States is now about 60 years old. It is a unique process in our society, one that has undergone numerous changes over the years. The standards are established by a private sector entity that has no dominant sponsor and is not part of any professional organization or trade association. The governmental entity that provides oversight, on the other hand, is far more a friend than a competitor or an antagonist."

Instructions

Identify the governmental entity that provides oversight and indicate its role in the standards-setting process.

C1-8 (Politicization of Standards Setting) Some accountants have said that politicization in the development and acceptance of generally accepted accounting principles (i.e., standards setting) is taking place. Some use the term "politicization" in a narrow sense to mean the influence by governmental agencies, particularly the Securities and Exchange Commission, on the development of generally accepted accounting principles. Others use it more broadly to mean the compromise that results when the bodies responsible for developing generally accepted accounting principles are pressured by interest groups (SEC, American Accounting Association, businesses through their various organizations, Institute of Management Accountants, financial analysts, bankers, lawyers, and so on).

Instructions

(a) The Committee on Accounting Procedures of the AICPA was established in the mid- to late 1930s and functioned until 1959, at which time the Accounting Principles Board came into existence. In 1973, the Financial Accounting Standards Board was formed and the APB went out of existence. Do the reasons these groups were formed, their methods of operation while in existence, and the reasons for the demise of the first two indicate an increasing politicization (as the term is used in the broad sense) of accounting standards setting? Explain your answer by indicating how the CAP, the APB, and the FASB operated or operate. Cite specific developments that tend to support your answer.

(b) What arguments can be raised to support the "politicization" of accounting standards setting?

(c) What arguments can be raised against the "politicization" of accounting standards setting?

(CMA adapted)

C1-9 (Models for Setting Accounting Standards) Presented below are three models for setting accounting standards.

1. The purely political approach, where national legislative action decrees accounting standards.
2. The private, professional approach, where financial accounting standards are set and enforced by private professional actions only.
3. The public/private mixed approach, where standards are basically set by private-sector bodies that behave as though they were public agencies and whose standards to a great extent are enforced through governmental agencies.

Instructions

(a) Which of these three models best describes standards setting in the United States? Comment on your answer.

(b) Why do companies, financial analysts, labor unions, industry trade associations, and others take such an active interest in standards setting?

(c) Cite an example of a group other than the FASB that attempts to establish accounting standards. Speculate as to why another group might wish to set its own standards.

C1-10 (Standards-Setting Terminology) Andrew Wyeth, an administrator at a major university, recently said, "I've got some CDs in my IRA, which I set up to beat the IRS." As elsewhere, in the world of accounting and finance, it often helps to be fluent in abbreviations and acronyms.

Instructions

Presented below is a list of common accounting acronyms. Identify the term for which each acronym stands, and provide a brief definition of each term.

(a) AICPA	**(e)** FAF	**(i)** CPA	**(m)** GASB
(b) CAP	**(f)** FASAC	**(j)** FASB	
(c) ARB	**(g)** SOP	**(k)** SEC	
(d) APB	**(h)** GAAP	**(l)** IASB	

C1-11 (Accounting Organizations and Documents Issued) Presented below are a number of accounting organizations and type of documents they have issued.

Instructions

Match the appropriate document to the organization involved. Note that more than one document may be issued by the same organization. If no document is provided for an organization, write in "0."

Organization	Document
	(a) Opinions
1. _____ Securities and Exchange Commission	**(b)** Practice Bulletins
2. _____ Accounting Standards Executive Committee	**(c)** Accounting Research Bulletins
3. _____ Accounting Principles Board	**(d)** Financial Reporting Releases
4. _____ Committee on Accounting Procedure	**(e)** Financial Accounting Standards
5. _____ Financial Accounting Standards Board	**(f)** Statements of Position
	(g) Technical Bulletins

C1-12 (Accounting Pronouncements) A number of authoritative pronouncements have been issued by standards-setting bodies in the last 50 years. A list is provided on the left, below, with a description of these pronouncements on the right.

Instructions

Match the description to the pronouncements.

1. _____ Technical Bulletin
2. _____ Interpretations (of the Financial Accounting Standards Board)
3. _____ Statement of Financial Accounting Standards
4. _____ EITF Statements
5. _____ Opinions
6. _____ Statement of Financial Accounting Concepts

(a) Official pronouncements of the APB.
(b) Sets forth fundamental objectives and concepts that will be used in developing future standards.
(c) Primary document of the FASB that establishes GAAP.
(d) Provides additional guidance on implementing or applying FASB Standards or Interpretations.
(e) Provides guidance on how to account for new and unusual financial transactions that have the potential for creating diversity in financial reporting practices.
(f) Represent extensions or modifications of existing standards.

C1-13 (Issues Involving Standards Setting) When the FASB issues new standards, the implementation date is usually 12 months from date of issuance, with early implementation encouraged. Paula Popovich, controller, discusses with her financial vice president the need for early implementation of a standard that would result in a fairer presentation of the company's financial condition and earnings. When the financial vice president determines that early implementation of the standard will adversely affect the reported net income for the year, he discourages Popovich from implementing the standard until it is required.

Instructions

Answer the following questions.

(a) What, if any, is the ethical issue involved in this case?
(b) Is the financial vice president acting improperly or immorally?
(c) What does Popovich have to gain by advocacy of early implementation?
(d) Which stakeholders might be affected by the decision against early implementation?

(CMA adapted)

C1-14 (Securities and Exchange Commission) The U.S. Securities and Exchange Commission (SEC) was created in 1934 and consists of five commissioners and a large professional staff. The SEC professional staff is organized into five divisions and several principal offices. The primary objective of the SEC is to support fair securities markets. The SEC also strives to foster enlightened stockholder participation in corporate decisions of publicly traded companies. The SEC has a significant presence in financial markets, the development of accounting practices, and corporation-shareholder relations, and has the power to exert influence on entities whose actions lie within the scope of its authority.

Instructions

(a) Explain from where the Securities and Exchange Commission receives its authority.

(b) Describe the official role of the Securities and Exchange Commission in the development of financial accounting theory and practices.

(c) Discuss the interrelationship between the Securities and Exchange Commission and the Financial Accounting Standards Board with respect to the development and establishment of financial accounting theory and practices.

(CMA adapted)

C1-15 (Standards-Setting Process) In 1973, the responsibility for developing and issuing rules on accounting practices was given to the Financial Accounting Foundation and, in particular, to an arm of the foundation called the Financial Accounting Standards Board (FASB). The generally accepted accounting principles established by the FASB are enunciated through a publication series entitled *Statements of Financial Accounting Standards.* These statements are issued periodically, and over 140 are currently in force. The statements have a significant influence on the way in which financial statements are prepared by U.S. corporations.

Instructions

(a) Describe the process by which a topic is selected or identified as appropriate for study by the Financial Accounting Standards Board (FASB).

(b) Once a topic is considered appropriate for consideration by the FASB, a series of steps is followed before a *Statement of Financial Accounting Standards* is issued. Describe the major steps in the process leading to the issuance of a standard.

(c) Identify at least three other organizations that influence the setting of generally accepted accounting principles (GAAP).

(CMA adapted)

C1-16 (History of Standards-Setting Organizations) Beta Alpha Psi, your university's accounting society, has decided to publish a brief pamphlet for seniors in high school, detailing the various facets of the accountancy profession. As a junior accounting major, you have been asked to contribute an article for this publication. Your topic is the evolution of accounting standards-setting organizations in the United States.

Instructions

Write a 1–2 page article on the historical development of the organizations responsible for giving us GAAP. (The most appropriate introduction would explain the increasing need for a more standardized approach to accounting for a company's assets.)

C1-17 (Economic Consequences) Presented below are comments made in the financial press.

Instructions

Prepare responses to the requirements in each item.

(a) Rep. John Dingell, the ranking Democrat on the House Commerce Committee, threw his support behind the FASB's controversial derivatives accounting standard and encouraged the FASB to adopt the rule promptly. Indicate why a member of Congress might feel obligated to comment on this proposed FASB standard.

(b) In a strongly worded letter to Senator Lauch Faircloth (R-NC) and House Banking Committee Chairman Jim Leach (R-IA), the American Institute of Certified Public Accountants (AICPA) cautioned against government intervention in the accounting standards-setting process, warning that it had the potential of jeopardizing U.S. capital markets. Explain how government intervention could possibly affect capital markets adversely.

C1-18 (Standards-Setting Process, Economic Consequences) The following letter was sent to the SEC and the FASB by leaders of the business community.

> Dear Sirs:
>
> The FASB has been struggling with accounting for derivatives and hedging for many years. The FASB has now developed, over the last few weeks, a new approach that it proposes to adopt as a final standard. We understand that the Board intends to adopt this new approach as a final standard without exposing it for public comment and debate, despite the evident complexity of the new approach, the speed with which it has been developed and the significant changes to the exposure draft since it was released more than one year ago. Instead, the Board plans to allow only a brief review by

selected parties, limited to issues of operationality and clarity, and would exclude questions as to the merits of the proposed approach.

As the FASB itself has said throughout this process, its mission does not permit it to consider matters that go beyond accounting and reporting considerations. Accordingly, the FASB may not have adequately considered the wide range of concerns that have been expressed about the derivatives and hedging proposal, including concerns related to the potential impact on the capital markets, the weakening of companies' ability to manage risk, and the adverse control implications of implementing costly and complex new rules imposed at the same time as other major initiatives, including the Year 2000 issues and a single European currency. We believe that these crucial issues must be considered, if not by the FASB, then by the Securities and Exchange Commission, other regulatory agencies, or Congress.

We believe it is essential that the FASB solicit all comments in order to identify and address all material issues that may exist before issuing a final standard. We understand the desire to bring this process to a prompt conclusion, but the underlying issues are so important to this nation's businesses, the customers they serve and the economy as a whole that expediency cannot be the dominant consideration. As a result, we urge the FASB to expose its new proposal for public comment, following the established due process procedures that are essential to acceptance of its standards, and providing sufficient time to affected parties to understand and assess the new approach.

We also urge the SEC to study the comments received in order to assess the impact that these proposed rules may have on the capital markets, on companies' risk management practices, and on management and financial controls. These vital public policy matters deserve consideration as part of the Commission's oversight responsibilities.

We believe that these steps are essential if the FASB is to produce the best possible accounting standard while minimizing adverse economic effects and maintaining the competitiveness of U.S. businesses in the international marketplace.

Very truly yours,

(This letter was signed by the chairs of 22 of the largest U.S. companies.)

Instructions

Answer the following questions.

(a) Explain the "due process" procedures followed by the FASB in developing a financial reporting standard.

(b) What is meant by the term "economic consequences" in accounting standards setting?

(c) What economic consequences arguments are used in this letter?

(d) What do you believe is the main point of the letter?

(e) Why do you believe a copy of this letter was sent by the business community to influential members of the United States Congress?

USING YOUR JUDGMENT

FINANCIAL REPORTING PROBLEM

Kate Jackson, a new staff accountant, is confused because of the complexities involving accounting standards setting. Specifically, she is confused by the number of bodies issuing financial reporting standards of one kind or another and the level of authoritative support that can be attached to these reporting standards. Kate decides that she must review the environment in which accounting standards are set, if she is to increase her understanding of the accounting profession.

Kate recalls that during her accounting education there was a chapter or two regarding the environment of financial accounting and the development of accounting standards. However, she remembers that little emphasis was placed on these chapters by her instructor.

Instructions

(a) Help Kate by identifying key organizations involved in accounting standards setting.

(b) Kate asks for guidance regarding authoritative support. Please assist her by explaining what is meant by authoritative support.

(c) Give Kate a historical overview of how standards setting has evolved so that she will not feel that she is the only one to be confused.

(d) What authority for compliance with GAAP has existed throughout the period of standards setting?

INTERNATIONAL REPORTING CASE

Michael Sharpe, former Deputy Chairman of the International Accounting Standards Committee (IASC), made the following comments before the 63rd Annual Conference of the Financial Executives Institute (FEI).

> There is an irreversible movement towards the harmonization of financial reporting throughout the world. The international capital markets require an end to:
>
> 1 The confusion caused by international companies announcing different results depending on the set of accounting standards applied. Recent announcements by Daimler-Benz [now **DaimlerChrysler**] highlight the confusion that this causes.
>
> 2 Companies in some countries obtaining unfair commercial advantages from the use of particular national accounting standards.
>
> 3 The complications in negotiating commercial arrangements for international joint ventures caused by different accounting requirements.
>
> 4 The inefficiency of international companies having to understand and use a myriad of different accounting standards depending on the countries in which they operate and the countries in which they raise capital and debt. Executive talent is wasted on keeping up to date with numerous sets of accounting standards and the never-ending changes to them.
>
> 5 The inefficiency of investment managers, bankers, and financial analysts as they seek to compare financial reporting drawn up in accordance with different sets of accounting standards.
>
> 6 Failure of many stock exchanges and regulators to require companies subject to their jurisdiction to provide comparable, comprehensive, and transparent financial reporting frameworks giving international comparability.
>
> 7 Difficulty for developing countries and countries entering the free market economy such as China and Russia in accessing foreign capital markets because of the complexity of and differences between national standards.
>
> 8 The restriction on the mobility of financial service providers across the world as a result of different accounting standards.
>
> Clearly the elimination of these inefficiencies by having comparable high-quality financial reporting used across the world would benefit international businesses.

Instructions

(a) What is the International Accounting Standards Board, and what is its relation to the International Accounting Standards Committee?

(b) What stakeholders might benefit from the use of International Accounting Standards?

(c) What do you believe are some of the major obstacles to harmonization?

PROFESSIONAL SIMULATION

Accounting — Generally Accepted Accounting Principles

Directions | Situation | Explanation | Research | Resources

Directions

In this simulation, you will be asked various questions regarding accounting principles. Prepare responses to all parts.

Situation

At the completion of Bloom Company's audit, the president, Judy Bloom, asks about the meaning of the phrase "in conformity with generally accepted accounting principles" that appears in your audit report on the management's financial statements. Judy observes that the meaning of the phrase must include something more and different than what she thinks of as "principles."

Explanation

(a) Explain the meaning of the term "accounting principles" as used in the audit report. (Do not discuss in this part the significance of "generally accepted.")

(b) President Bloom wants to know how you determine whether or not an accounting principle is generally accepted. Discuss the sources of evidence for determining whether an accounting principle has substantial authoritative support. Do not merely list the titles of publications.

www.wiley.com/college/kieso

Remember to check the ***Take Action! CD*** *and the book's* ***companion Web site*** *to find additional resources for this chapter.*

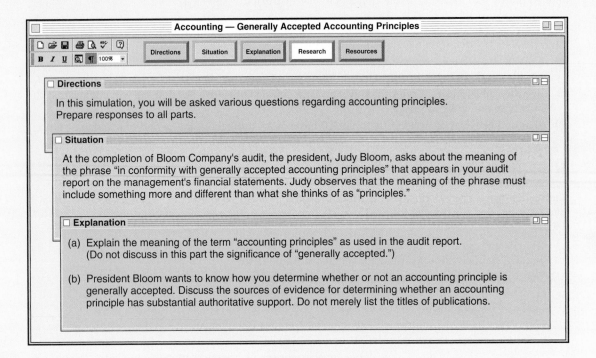

CHAPTER 2

Conceptual Framework Underlying Financial Accounting

Show Me the Earnings!

The growth of new-economy business on the Internet has led to the development of new measures of performance. When **Priceline.com** splashed on the dot-com scene, it touted steady growth in a measure called "unique offers by users" to explain its heady stock price. And **Drugstore.com** focused on "unique customers" at its Web site to draw investors to its stock. After all, new businesses call for new performance measures, right?

Not necessarily. The problem with such indicators is that they do not exhibit any consistent relationship with the ability of these companies to earn profits from the customers visiting their Web sites. Eventually, as the graphs below show, the profits never materialized, and stock price fell.

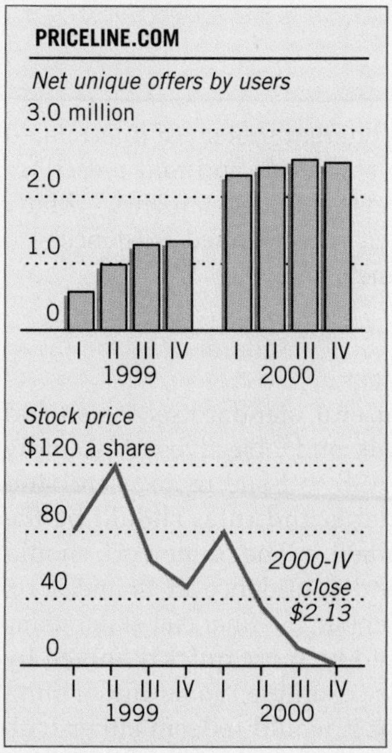

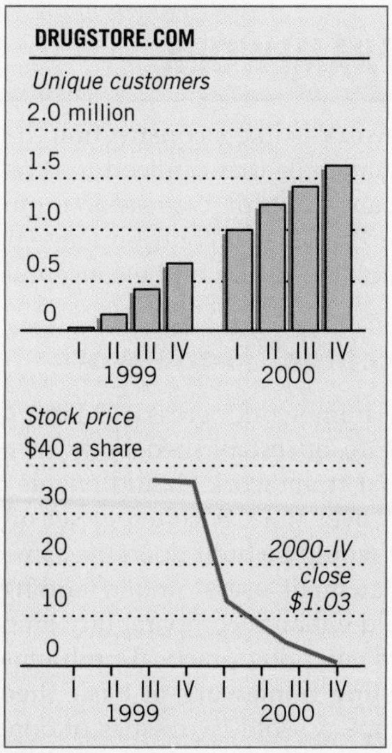

According to one accounting expert, investors' use of nonfinancial measures is not detrimental when combined with financial analysis, which is based on measures such as earnings and cash flows. The problem is that during the recent Internet craze, investors placed too much emphasis on nonfinancial data. Thus, the new economy may require some new measures but investors need to be careful not to forget the relevant and reliable traditional ones.[1]

[1]Story and graphs adapted from Gretchen Morgenson, "How Did They Value Stocks? Count the Absurd Ways," *New York Times* (March 18, 2001), section 3, p. 1.

LEARNING OBJECTIVES

After studying this chapter, you should be able to:

1. **Describe the usefulness of a conceptual framework.**
2. **Describe the FASB's efforts to construct a conceptual framework.**
3. **Understand the objectives of financial reporting.**
4. **Identify the qualitative characteristics of accounting information.**
5. **Define the basic elements of financial statements.**
6. **Describe the basic assumptions of accounting.**
7. **Explain the application of the basic principles of accounting.**
8. **Describe the impact that constraints have on reporting accounting information.**

PREVIEW OF CHAPTER 2

As indicated in the opening story about dot-com reporting, users of financial statements need relevant and reliable information. To help develop this type of financial information, a conceptual framework that guides financial accounting and reporting is used. This chapter discusses the basic concepts underlying this conceptual framework. The content and organization of this chapter are as follows.

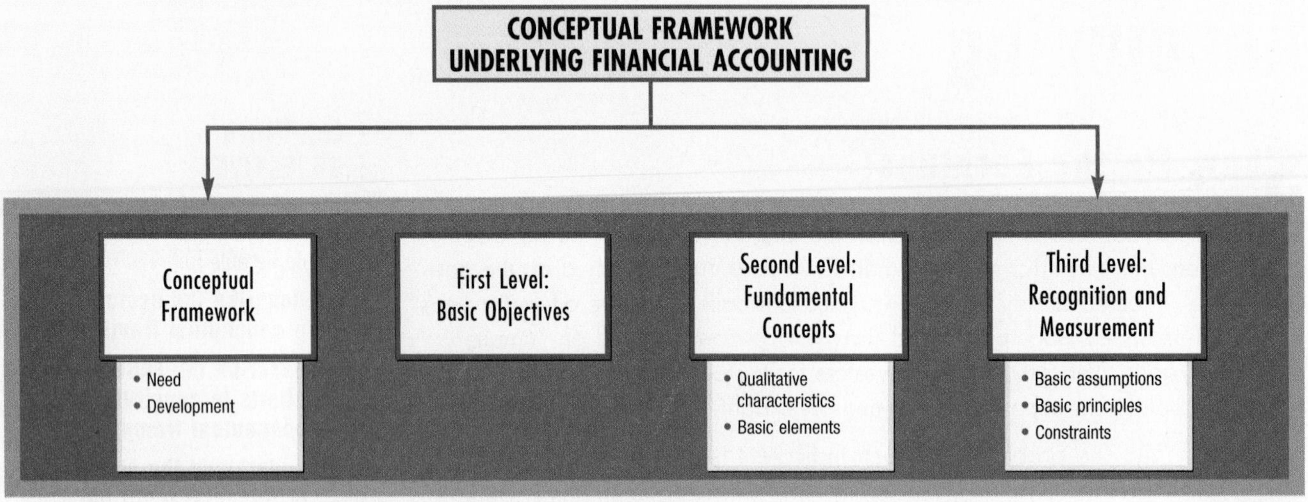

CONCEPTUAL FRAMEWORK

A **conceptual framework** is like a **constitution**: It is "a coherent system of interrelated objectives and fundamentals that can lead to consistent standards and that prescribes the nature, function, and limits of financial accounting and financial statements."[2] Many have considered the FASB's real contribution—and even its continued existence—to depend on the quality and utility of the conceptual framework.

Need for Conceptual Framework

OBJECTIVE 1
Describe the usefulness of a conceptual framework.

Why is a conceptual framework necessary? First, to be useful, standard setting should build on and relate to an established body of concepts and objectives. A soundly developed conceptual framework should enable the FASB to issue more useful and consistent standards over time. **A coherent set of standards and rules should be the result**, because they would be built upon the same foundation. The framework should increase financial statement users' understanding of and confidence in financial reporting, and it should enhance comparability among companies' financial statements.

Second, new and emerging **practical problems should be more quickly solved by reference to an existing framework of basic theory**. For example, Sunshine Mining (a silver mining company) sold two issues of bonds that it would redeem either with $1,000 in cash or with 50 ounces of silver, whichever was worth more at maturity. Both

[2]"Conceptual Framework for Financial Accounting and Reporting: Elements of Financial Statements and Their Measurement," *FASB Discussion Memorandum* (Stamford, Conn.: FASB, 1976), page 1 of the "Scope and Implications of the Conceptual Framework Project" section. For an excellent discussion of the functions of the conceptual framework, see Reed K. Storey and Sylvia Storey, Special Report, "The Framework of Financial Accounting and Concepts" (Norwalk, Conn.: FASB, 1998), pp. 85–88.

bond issues had a stated interest rate of 8.5 percent. At what amounts should the bonds have been recorded by Sunshine or the buyers of the bonds? What is the amount of the premium or discount on the bonds and how should it be amortized, if the bond redemption payments are to be made in silver (the future value of which was unknown at the date of issuance)?

It is difficult, if not impossible, for the FASB to prescribe the proper accounting treatment quickly for situations like this. Practicing accountants, however, must resolve such problems on a day-to-day basis. Through the exercise of good judgment and with the help of a universally accepted conceptual framework, practitioners can dismiss certain alternatives quickly and then focus on an acceptable treatment.

Development of Conceptual Framework

OBJECTIVE 2
Describe the FASB's efforts to construct a conceptual framework.

Over the years numerous organizations, committees, and interested individuals developed and published their own conceptual frameworks. But no single framework was universally accepted and relied on in practice. Recognizing the need for a generally accepted framework, the FASB in 1976 began work to develop a conceptual framework that would be a basis for setting accounting standards and for resolving financial reporting controversies. The FASB has issued six Statements of Financial Accounting Concepts that relate to financial reporting for business enterprises.[3] They are:

1. *SFAC No. 1*, "Objectives of Financial Reporting by Business Enterprises," presents the goals and purposes of accounting.
2. *SFAC No. 2*, "Qualitative Characteristics of Accounting Information," examines the characteristics that make accounting information useful.
3. *SFAC No. 3*, "Elements of Financial Statements of Business Enterprises," provides definitions of items in financial statements, such as assets, liabilities, revenues, and expenses.
4. *SFAC No. 5*, "Recognition and Measurement in Financial Statements of Business Enterprises," sets forth fundamental recognition and measurement criteria and guidance on what information should be formally incorporated into financial statements and when.
5. *SFAC No. 6*, "Elements of Financial Statements," replaces *SFAC No. 3* and expands its scope to include not-for-profit organizations.
6. *SFAC No. 7*, "Using Cash Flow Information and Present Value in Accounting Measurements," provides a framework for using expected future cash flows and present values as a basis for measurement.

INTERNATIONAL INSIGHT

The IASB has issued a conceptual framework that is broadly consistent with that of the United States.

Illustration 2-1 (on page 30) provides an overview of the conceptual framework.[4] At the first level, the **objectives** identify the goals and purposes of accounting. Ideally, accounting standards developed according to a conceptual framework will result in accounting reports that are more useful. At the second level are the **qualitative characteristics** that make accounting information useful and the **elements** of financial statements (assets, liabilities, and so on). At the third level are the **measurement and recognition concepts** used in establishing and applying accounting standards. These concepts include assumptions, principles, and constraints that describe the present reporting environment. The remainder of the chapter examines these three levels of the conceptual framework.

---

[3] The FASB has also issued a Statement of Financial Accounting Concepts that relates to nonbusiness organizations: *Statement of Financial Accounting Concepts No. 4*, "Objectives of Financial Reporting by Nonbusiness Organizations" (December 1980).

[4] Adapted from William C. Norby, *The Financial Analysts Journal* (March–April 1982), p. 22.

ILLUSTRATION 2-1
Conceptual Framework for Financial Reporting

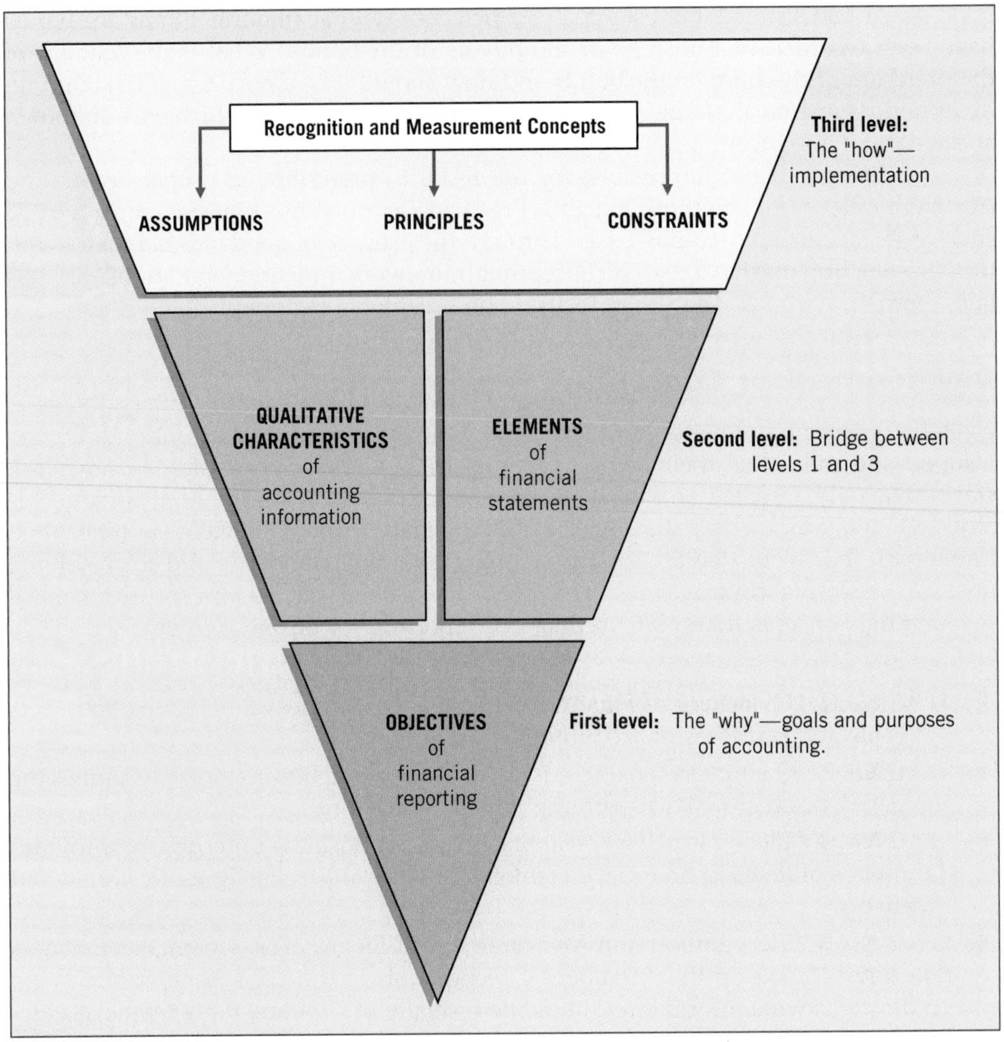

FIRST LEVEL: BASIC OBJECTIVES

OBJECTIVE 3
Understand the objectives of financial reporting.

As we discussed in Chapter 1, the **objectives of financial reporting** are to provide information that is: (1) useful to those making investment and credit decisions who have a reasonable understanding of business and economic activities; (2) helpful to present and potential investors, creditors, and other users in assessing the amounts, timing, and uncertainty of future cash flows; and (3) about economic resources, the claims to those resources, and the changes in them.

The objectives, therefore, begin with a broad concern about information that is useful to investor and creditor decisions. That concern narrows to the investors' and creditors' interest in the prospect of receiving cash from their investments in or loans to business enterprises. Finally, the objectives focus on the financial statements that provide information useful in the assessment of prospective cash flows to the business enterprise. This approach is referred to as **decision usefulness**. It has been said that the golden rule is the central message in many religions and the rest is elaboration. Similarly, decision usefulness is the message of the conceptual framework and the rest is elaboration.

In providing information to users of financial statements, general-purpose financial statements are prepared. These statements provide the most useful information possible at minimal cost to various user groups. Underlying these objectives is the notion that users need reasonable knowledge of business and financial accounting matters to understand the information contained in financial statements. This point is important. It means that in the preparation of financial statements a level of reasonable competence on the part of users can be assumed. This has an impact on the way and the extent to which information is reported.

INTERNATIONAL INSIGHT

In Switzerland, Germany, Korea, and other nations, capital is provided to business primarily by large banks. Creditors have very close ties to firms and can obtain information directly from them. Creditors do not need to rely on publicly available information, and financial information is focused on creditor protection. This process of capital allocation, however, is changing.

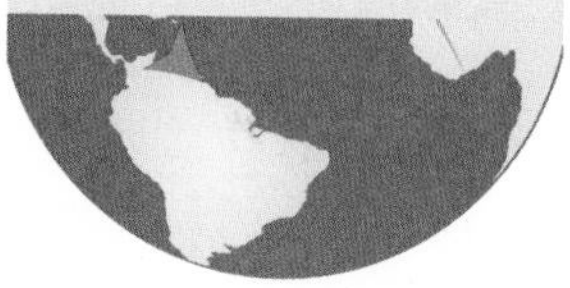

SECOND LEVEL: FUNDAMENTAL CONCEPTS

The objectives (first level) are concerned with the goals and purposes of accounting. Later, we will discuss the ways these goals and purposes are implemented (third level). Between these two levels it is necessary to provide certain conceptual building blocks that explain the qualitative characteristics of accounting information and define the elements of financial statements. These conceptual building blocks form a bridge between the **why** of accounting (the objectives) and the **how** of accounting (recognition and measurement).

Qualitative Characteristics of Accounting Information

How does one decide whether financial reports should provide information on how much a firm's assets cost to acquire (historical cost basis) or how much they are currently worth (current value basis)? Or how does one decide whether the three main segments that constitute **PepsiCo**—PepsiCola, Frito Lay, and Tropicana—should be combined and shown as one company, or disaggregated and reported as three separate segments for financial reporting purposes?

Choosing an acceptable accounting method, the amount and types of information to be disclosed, and the format in which information should be presented involves determining **which alternative provides the most useful information for decision making purposes (decision usefulness).** The FASB has identified the **qualitative characteristics** of accounting information that distinguish better (more useful) information from inferior (less useful) information for decision making purposes.[5] In addition, the FASB has identified certain constraints (cost-benefit and materiality) as part of the conceptual framework; these are discussed later in the chapter. The characteristics may be viewed as a hierarchy, as shown in Illustration 2-2 on the next page.

OBJECTIVE 4
Identify the qualitative characteristics of accounting information.

Decision Makers (Users) and Understandability

Decision makers vary widely in the types of decisions they make, how they make decisions, the information they already possess or can obtain from other sources, and their ability to process the information. For information to be useful, there must be a connection (linkage) between these users and the decisions they make. This link, **understandability**, is the quality of information that permits reasonably informed users to perceive its significance. To illustrate the importance of this linkage, assume that **IBM Corp.** issues a three-months' earnings report (interim report) that shows interim earnings way down. This report provides relevant and reliable information for decision making purposes. Some users, upon reading the report, decide to sell their stock. Other users do not understand the report's content and significance. They are surprised when IBM declares a smaller year-end dividend and the value of the stock declines. Thus, although the information presented was highly relevant and reliable, it was useless to those who did not understand it.

Primary Qualities: Relevance and Reliability

Relevance and reliability are the two primary qualities that make accounting information useful for decision making. As stated in FASB *Concepts Statement No. 2*, "the qualities that distinguish 'better' (more useful) information from 'inferior' (less useful)

[5] "Qualitative Characteristics of Accounting Information," *Statement of Financial Accounting Concepts No. 2* (Stamford, Conn.: FASB, May 1980).

ILLUSTRATION 2-2
Hierarchy of Accounting Qualities

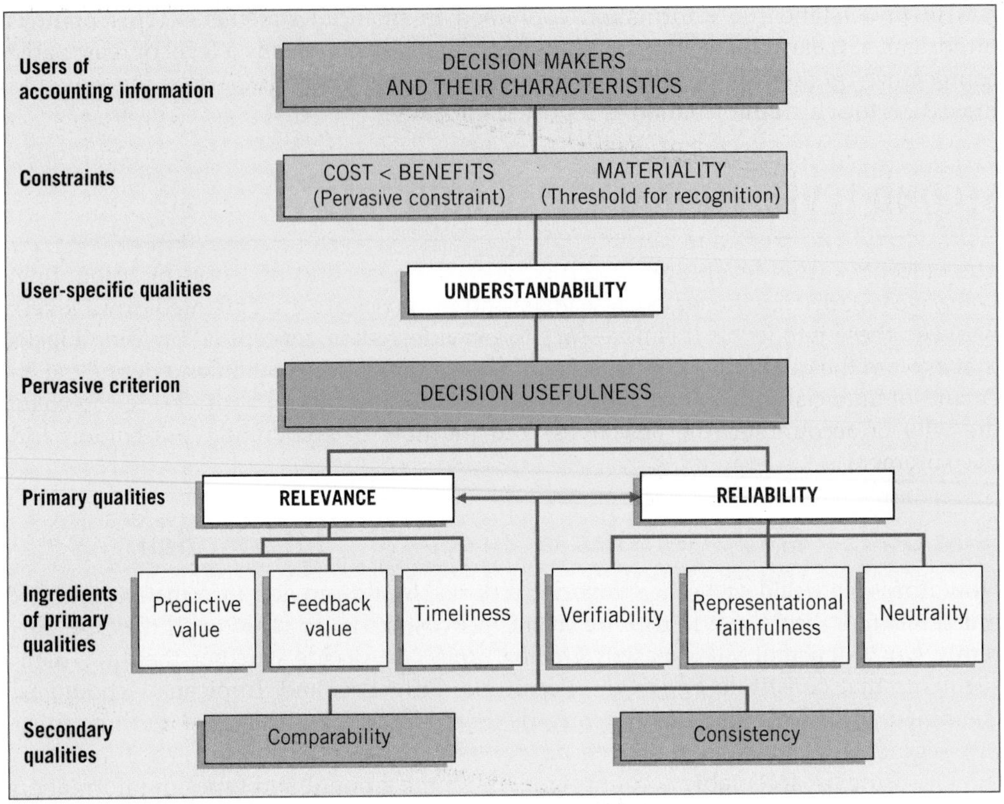

information are primarily the qualities of relevance and reliability, with some other characteristics that those qualities imply."[6]

Relevance. To be relevant, accounting information must be capable of making a difference in a decision.[7] If certain information has no bearing on a decision, it is irrelevant to that decision. Relevant information helps users make predictions about the ultimate outcome of past, present, and future events; that is, it has **predictive value**. Relevant information also helps users confirm or correct prior expectations; it has **feedback value**. For example, when **UPS (United Parcel Service)** issues an interim report, this information is considered relevant because it provides a basis for forecasting annual earnings and provides feedback on past performance. For information to be relevant, it must also be available to decision makers before it loses its capacity to influence their decisions. Thus **timeliness** is a primary ingredient. If UPS did not report its interim results until six months after the end of the period, the information would be much less useful for decision making purposes. **For information to be relevant, it should have predictive or feedback value, and it must be presented on a timely basis.**

Reliability. Accounting information is reliable to the extent that **it is verifiable, is a faithful representation, and is reasonably free of error and bias**. Reliability is a necessity for individuals who have neither the time nor the expertise to evaluate the factual content of the information.

Verifiability is demonstrated when independent measurers, using the same measurement methods, obtain similar results. For example, would several independent auditors come to the same conclusion about a set of financial statements? If outside parties using the same measurement methods arrive at different conclusions, then the statements are not verifiable. Auditors could not render an opinion on such statements.

---

[6]Ibid., par. 15.

[7]Ibid., par. 47.

Representational faithfulness means that the numbers and descriptions represent what really existed or happened. The accounting numbers and descriptions agree with the resources or events that these numbers and descriptions purport to represent. If **General Motors'** income statement reports sales of $150 billion when it had sales of $138.2 billion, then the statement is not a faithful representation.

Neutrality means that information cannot be selected to favor one set of interested parties over another. Factual, truthful, unbiased information must be the overriding consideration. For example, **R. J. Reynolds** should not be permitted to suppress information in the notes to its financial statements about the numerous lawsuits that have been filed against it because of tobacco-related health concerns—even though such disclosure is damaging to the company.

Neutrality in standard setting has come under increasing attack. Some argue that standards should not be issued if they cause undesirable economic effects on an industry or company. We disagree. Standards must be free from bias or we will no longer have credible financial statements. Without credible financial statements, individuals will no longer use this information. An analogy demonstrates the point: In the United States, we have both boxing and wrestling matches. Many individuals bet on boxing matches because such contests are assumed not to be fixed. But nobody bets on wrestling matches. Why? Because the public assumes that wrestling matches are rigged. If financial information is biased (rigged), the public will lose confidence and no longer use this information.

Secondary Qualities: Comparability and Consistency

Information about an enterprise is more useful if it can be compared with similar information about another enterprise (**comparability**) and with similar information about the same enterprise at other points in time (**consistency**).

Comparability. Information that has been measured and reported in a similar manner for different enterprises is considered comparable. Comparability enables users to identify the real similarities and differences in economic phenomena because these differences and similarities have not been obscured by the use of noncomparable accounting methods. For example, the accounting for pensions is different in the United States and Japan. In the U.S., pension cost is recorded as it is incurred, whereas in Japan there is little or no charge to income for these costs. As a result, it is difficult to compare and evaluate the financial results of **General Motors** or **Ford** to **Nissan** or **Honda**. Also, resource allocation decisions involve evaluations of alternatives; a valid evaluation can be made only if comparable information is available.

Consistency. When an entity applies the same accounting treatment to similar events, from period to period, the entity is considered to be consistent in its use of accounting standards. It does not mean that companies cannot switch from one method of accounting to another. Companies can change methods, but the changes are restricted to situations in which it can be demonstrated that the newly adopted method is preferable to the old. Then the nature and effect of the accounting change, as well as the justification for it, must be disclosed in the financial statements for the period in which the change is made.[8]

When there has been a change in accounting principles, the auditor refers to it in an explanatory paragraph of the audit report. This paragraph identifies the nature of the change and refers the reader to the note in the financial statements that discusses the change in detail.[9]

---

[8]Surveys of users indicate that users highly value consistency. They note that a change tends to destroy the comparability of data before and after the change. Some companies take the time to assist users to understand the pre- and post-change data. Generally, however, users say they lose the ability to analyze over time.

[9]"Reports on Audited Financial Statements," *Statement on Auditing Standards No. 58* (New York: AICPA, April 1988), par. 34.

In summary, accounting reports for any given year are more useful if they can be compared with reports from other companies and with prior reports of the same entity.

WHAT DO THE NUMBERS MEAN?

CAN YOU COMPARE PRO FORMAS?

Beyond touting nonfinancial measures to investors (see opening story), many companies are increasingly promoting the performance of their companies through the reporting of various "pro forma" earnings measures. A recent survey of newswire reports found 36 instances of the reporting of pro forma measures in just a 3-day period.

Pro forma measures are standard measures, such as earnings, that are adjusted, usually for one-time or nonrecurring items. For example, it is standard practice to adjust earnings for the effects of an extraordinary item. Such adjustments make the numbers more comparable to numbers reported in periods without the unusual item.

However, rather than increasing comparability, it appears that recent pro forma reporting is designed to accentuate the positive in company results. Examples of such reporting include **Yahoo!** and **Cisco**, which define pro forma income after adding back payroll tax expense. And **Level 8 Systems** transformed an operating loss into a pro forma profit by adding back expenses for depreciation and amortization of intangible assets.

Lynn Turner, former Chief Accountant at the SEC, calls such earnings measures EBS—"everything but bad stuff." He admonishes investors to view such reporting with caution and appropriate skepticism.

Source: Adapted from Gretchen Morgenson, "How Did They Value Stocks? Count the Absurd Ways," *New York Times* (March 18, 2001), section 3, p. 1; and Gretchen Morgenson, "Expert Advice: Focus on Profit," *New York Times* (March 18, 2001), section 3, p. 14.

Basic Elements

OBJECTIVE 5
Define the basic elements of financial statements.

An important aspect of developing any theoretical structure is the body of **basic elements** or definitions to be included in the structure. At present, accounting uses many terms that have distinctive and specific meanings. These terms constitute the language of business or the jargon of accounting.

One such term is **asset**. Is it something we own? If the answer is yes, can we assume that any leased asset would not be shown on the balance sheet? Is an asset something we have the right to use, or is it anything of value used by the enterprise to generate revenues? If the answer is yes, then why should the managers of the enterprise not be considered an asset? It seems necessary, therefore, to develop basic definitions for the elements of financial statements. *Concepts Statement No. 6* defines the ten interrelated elements that are most directly related to measuring the performance and financial status of an enterprise. We list them here for review and information purposes; you need not memorize these definitions at this point. Each of these elements will be explained and examined in more detail in subsequent chapters.

ELEMENTS OF FINANCIAL STATEMENTS

ASSETS. Probable future economic benefits obtained or controlled by a particular entity as a result of past transactions or events.

LIABILITIES. Probable future sacrifices of economic benefits arising from present obligations of a particular entity to transfer assets or provide services to other entities in the future as a result of past transactions or events.

EQUITY. Residual interest in the assets of an entity that remains after deducting its liabilities. In a business enterprise, the equity is the ownership interest.

INVESTMENTS BY OWNERS. Increases in net assets of a particular enterprise resulting from transfers to it from other entities of something of value to obtain or increase ownership interests (or equity) in it. Assets are most commonly received as investments by owners, but that which is received may also include services or satisfaction or conversion of liabilities of the enterprise.

DISTRIBUTIONS TO OWNERS. Decreases in net assets of a particular enterprise resulting from transferring assets, rendering services, or incurring liabilities by the enterprise to owners. Distributions to owners decrease ownership interests (or equity) in an enterprise.

COMPREHENSIVE INCOME. Change in equity (net assets) of an entity during a period from transactions and other events and circumstances from nonowner sources. It includes all changes in equity during a period except those resulting from investments by owners and distributions to owners.

REVENUES. Inflows or other enhancements of assets of an entity or settlement of its liabilities (or a combination of both) during a period from delivering or producing goods, rendering services, or other activities that constitute the entity's ongoing major or central operations.

EXPENSES. Outflows or other using up of assets or incurrences of liabilities (or a combination of both) during a period from delivering or producing goods, rendering services, or carrying out other activities that constitute the entity's ongoing major or central operations.

GAINS. Increases in equity (net assets) from peripheral or incidental transactions of an entity and from all other transactions and other events and circumstances affecting the entity during a period except those that result from revenues or investments by owners.

LOSSES. Decreases in equity (net assets) from peripheral or incidental transactions of an entity and from all other transactions and other events and circumstances affecting the entity during a period except those that result from expenses or distributions to owners.[10]

The FASB classifies the elements into two distinct groups. The first group of three elements (assets, liabilities, and equity) describes amounts of resources and claims to resources at a **moment in time**. The other seven elements (comprehensive income and its components—revenues, expenses, gains, and losses—as well as investments by owners and distributions to owners) describe transactions, events, and circumstances that affect an enterprise during a **period of time**. The first class is changed by elements of the second class and at any time is the cumulative result of all changes. This interaction is referred to as "articulation." That is, key figures in one statement correspond to balances in another.

THIRD LEVEL: RECOGNITION AND MEASUREMENT CONCEPTS

The third level of the framework consists of concepts that implement the basic objectives of level one. These concepts explain which, when, and how financial elements and events should be recognized, measured, and reported by the accounting system. Most of them are set forth in FASB *Statement of Financial Accounting Concepts No. 5,*

[10]"Elements of Financial Statements," *Statement of Financial Accounting Concepts No. 6* (Stamford, Conn.: FASB, December 1985), pp. ix and x.

"Recognition and Measurement in Financial Statements of Business Enterprises." According to *SFAC No. 5,* to be recognized, an item (event or transaction) must meet the definition of an "element of financial statements" as defined in *SFAC No. 6* and must be measurable. Most aspects of current practice are consistent with this recognition and measurement concept.

The accounting profession continues to use the concepts in *SFAC No. 5* as operational guidelines. For discussion purposes, we have chosen to identify the concepts as basic assumptions, principles, and constraints. Not everyone uses this classification system, so it is best to focus your attention more on **understanding the concepts** than on how they are classified and organized. These concepts serve as guidelines in developing rational responses to controversial financial reporting issues.

Basic Assumptions

OBJECTIVE 6
Describe the basic assumptions of accounting.

Four basic **assumptions** underlie the financial accounting structure: (1) **economic entity**, (2) **going concern**, (3) **monetary unit**, and (4) **periodicity**.

Economic Entity Assumption

The **economic entity assumption means that economic activity can be identified with a particular unit of accountability**. In other words, the activity of a business enterprise can be kept separate and distinct from its owners and any other business unit. For example, if the activities and elements of **General Motors** could not be distinguished from those of **Ford** or **DaimlerChrysler**, then it would be impossible to know which company financially outperformed the other two in recent years. If there were no meaningful way to separate all of the economic events that occur, no basis for accounting would exist.

The entity concept does not apply solely to the segregation of activities among given business enterprises. An individual, a department or division, or an entire industry could be considered a separate entity if we chose to define the unit in such a manner. Thus, **the entity concept does not necessarily refer to a legal entity**. A parent and its subsidiaries are separate **legal** entities, but merging their activities for accounting and reporting purposes does not violate the **economic entity** assumption.[11]

WHAT DO THE NUMBERS MEAN?

WHOSE COMPANY IS IT?

The importance of the entity assumption is illustrated by scandals involving **W.R. Grace**, and more recently, **Adelphia Communications Corp.** In both cases, top employees of these companies entered into transactions that blurred the line between the employee's financial interests and that of the company. At Adelphia, in one of many self-dealings, the company guaranteed over $2 billion of loans to the founding family. At W.R. Grace, company funds were used to pay for an apartment and chef for the company chairman. These insiders not only benefited at the expense of shareholders but also failed to disclose details of the transactions, which would allow shareholders to sort out the impact of the employee transactions on company results.

[11]The concept of the entity is changing. For example, it is now harder to define the outer edges of companies. There are public companies, such as **Enron**, with multiple public subsidiaries, each with joint ventures, licensing arrangements, and other affiliations. Increasingly, loose affiliations of enterprises in joint ventures or customer-supplier relationships are formed and dissolved in a matter of months or weeks. These "virtual companies" raise accounting issues about how to account for the entity. See Steven H. Wallman, "The Future of Accounting and Disclosure in an Evolving World: The Need for Dramatic Change," *Accounting Horizons* (September 1995).

Going Concern Assumption

Most accounting methods are based on the **going concern assumption—that the business enterprise will have a long life**. Experience indicates that, in spite of numerous business failures, companies have a fairly high continuance rate. Although accountants do not believe that business firms will last indefinitely, they do expect them to last long enough to fulfill their objectives and commitments.

The implications of this assumption are profound. The historical cost principle would be of limited usefulness if eventual liquidation were assumed. Under a liquidation approach, for example, asset values are better stated at net realizable value (sales price less costs of disposal) than at acquisition cost. **Depreciation and amortization policies are justifiable and appropriate only if we assume some permanence to the enterprise.** If a liquidation approach were adopted, the current-noncurrent classification of assets and liabilities would lose much of its significance. Labeling anything a fixed or long-term asset would be difficult to justify. Indeed, listing liabilities on the basis of priority in liquidation would be more reasonable.

The going concern assumption applies in most business situations. **Only where liquidation appears imminent is the assumption inapplicable.** In these cases a total revaluation of assets and liabilities can provide information that closely approximates the entity's net realizable value. Accounting problems related to an enterprise in liquidation are presented in advanced accounting courses.

Monetary Unit Assumption

The **monetary unit assumption** means that money is the common denominator of economic activity and provides an appropriate basis for accounting measurement and analysis. This assumption implies that the monetary unit is the most effective means of expressing to interested parties changes in capital and exchanges of goods and services. **The monetary unit is relevant, simple, universally available, understandable, and useful.** Application of this assumption depends on the even more basic assumption that quantitative data are useful in communicating economic information and in making rational economic decisions.

In the United States, price-level changes (inflation and deflation) are ignored in accounting, and the unit of measure—the dollar—is assumed to remain reasonably stable. This assumption about the monetary unit has been used to justify adding 1970 dollars to 2004 dollars without any adjustment. The FASB in *SFAC No. 5* indicated that it expects the dollar, unadjusted for inflation or deflation, to continue to be used to measure items recognized in financial statements. Only if circumstances change dramatically (such as if the United States were to experience high inflation similar to that in many South American countries) will the FASB again consider "inflation accounting."

INTERNATIONAL INSIGHT

Due to their experiences with persistent inflation, several South American countries produce "constant currency" financial reports. Typically, a general price-level index is used to adjust for the effects of inflation.

Accounting for Changing Prices

Periodicity Assumption

The most accurate way to measure the results of enterprise activity would be to measure them at the time of the enterprise's eventual liquidation. Business, government, investors, and various other user groups, however, cannot wait that long for such information. Users need to be apprised of performance and economic status on a timely basis so that they can evaluate and compare firms, and take appropriate actions. Therefore, information must be reported periodically.

The **periodicity** (or **time period**) **assumption** implies that **the economic activities of an enterprise can be divided into artificial time periods**. These time periods vary, but the most common are monthly, quarterly, and yearly.

The shorter the time period, the more difficult it becomes to determine the proper net income for the period. A month's results are usually less reliable than a quarter's results, and a quarter's results are likely to be less reliable than a year's results. Investors desire and demand that information be quickly processed and disseminated; yet the quicker the information is released, the more it is subject to error. **This**

phenomenon provides an interesting example of the trade-off between relevance and reliability in preparing financial data.

The problem of defining the time period is becoming more serious because product cycles are shorter and products become obsolete more quickly. Many believe that, given technology advances, more online, real-time financial information needs to be provided to ensure that relevant information is available.

Basic Principles of Accounting

OBJECTIVE 7
Explain the application of the basic principles of accounting.

Four basic **principles of accounting** are used to record transactions: (1) **historical cost**, (2) **revenue recognition**, (3) **matching**, and (4) **full disclosure**.

Historical Cost Principle

GAAP requires that most assets and liabilities be accounted for and reported on the basis of acquisition price. This is often referred to as the **historical cost principle**.

Cost has an important advantage over other valuations: **it is reliable**. To illustrate the importance of this advantage, consider the problems that would arise if we adopted some other basis for keeping records. If we were to select current selling price, for instance, we might have a difficult time in attempting to establish a sales value for a given item until it was sold. Every member of the accounting department might have a different opinion regarding an asset's value, and management might desire still another figure. And how often would it be necessary to establish sales value? All companies close their accounts at least annually, and some compute their net income every month. These companies would find it necessary to place a sales value on every asset each time they wished to determine income—a laborious task and one that would result in a figure of net income materially affected by opinion. Similar objections have been leveled against current cost (replacement cost, present value of future cash flows) and any other basis of valuation **except cost**.

What about liabilities? Are they accounted for on a cost basis? Yes, they are. **If we convert the term "cost" to "exchange price," we find that it applies to liabilities as well.** Liabilities, such as bonds, notes, and accounts payable, are issued by a business enterprise in exchange for assets, or perhaps services, upon which an agreed price has usually been placed. This price, established by the exchange transaction, is the "cost" of the liability and provides the figure at which it should be recorded in the accounts and reported in financial statements.

In general, users have indicated a preference for historical cost because it provides them a stable and consistent benchmark that can be relied upon to measure historical trends. However, fair value information is thought to be more useful for certain types of assets and liabilities and in certain industries. For example, many financial instruments, including derivatives, are reported at fair value, and inventories are reported at lower of cost or market. Certain industries, such as brokerage houses and mutual funds, prepare their basic financial statements on a fair value basis.

At initial acquisition, historical cost and fair value are the same. In subsequent periods, as market and economic conditions change, historical cost and fair value often diverge. Some believe that fair value measures or estimates are needed to provide relevant information about the expected future cash flows related to the asset or liability. For example, when long-lived assets decline in value, a fair value measure is needed to determine any impairment loss.

Statement of Financial Accounting Concepts No. 7 (SFAC No. 7), "Using Cash Flow Information and Present Value in Accounting Measurements," provides a framework for using expected cash flows and present value techniques to develop fair value estimates. These concepts are applied when reliable fair value information is not available for certain assets and liabilities. In the case of an impairment, reliable market values of long-lived assets often are not readily available. In this situation, the principles in *SFAC No. 7* can be applied to derive a fair value estimate for the asset.

As indicated, we presently have a "mixed attribute" system that permits the use of historical cost, fair value, and other valuation bases. Although the historical cost principle continues to be the primary basis for valuation, recording and reporting of fair value information is increasing.[12]

Revenue Recognition Principle

A crucial question for many enterprises is **when** revenue should be recognized. Revenue is generally recognized (1) when **realized** or **realizable** and (2) when **earned**. This approach has often been referred to as the **revenue recognition principle**. Revenues are **realized** when products (goods or services), merchandise, or other assets are exchanged for cash or claims to cash. Revenues are **realizable** when assets received or held are readily convertible into cash or claims to cash. Assets are readily convertible when they are salable or interchangeable in an active market at readily determinable prices without significant additional cost.

In addition to the first test (realized or realizable), revenues are not recognized until earned. Revenues are considered **earned** when the entity has substantially accomplished what it must do to be entitled to the benefits represented by the revenues.[13]

Generally, an objective test—confirmation by a sale to independent interests—is used to indicate the point at which revenue is recognized. Usually, only at the date of sale is there an objective and verifiable measure of revenue—the sales price. Any basis for revenue recognition short of actual sale opens the door to wide variations in practice. To give accounting reports uniform meaning, a rule of revenue recognition comparable to the cost rule for asset valuation is essential. **Recognition at the time of sale provides a uniform and reasonable test.**

There are, however, exceptions to the rule, as shown in Illustration 2-3.

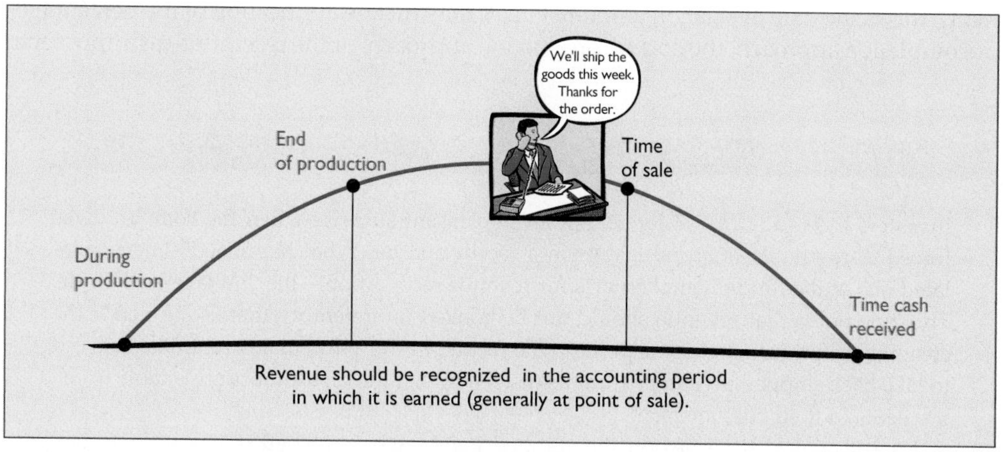

ILLUSTRATION 2-3
Timing of Revenue Recognition

During Production. **Recognition of revenue is allowed before the contract is completed in certain long-term construction contracts.** In this method revenue is recognized periodically based on the percentage of the job that has been completed, instead of waiting until the entire job has been finished. Although technically a transfer of ownership has not occurred, the earning process is considered substantially completed at

---

[12]The FASB and IASB currently are working on a project that will result in reporting all financial instruments, both assets and liabilities, at fair value. See for example, FASB, *Financial Accounting Series,* "Preliminary Views on Major Issues Related to Reporting Financial Instruments and Related Assets and Liabilities at Fair Value," No. 204B (December 14, 1999).

[13]"Recognition and Measurement in Financial Statements of Business Enterprises," *Statement of Financial Accounting Concepts No. 5* (Stamford, Conn.: FASB, December 1984), par. 83(a) and (b). The FASB and the IASB have recently added projects on revenue recognition to their agendas. The projects will develop a comprehensive statement that is conceptually based and can be applied to the wide range of revenue transactions that have emerged recently.

various stages as construction progresses. If it is not possible to obtain dependable estimates of cost and progress, then revenue recognition is delayed until the job is completed.

At End of Production. At times, **revenue might be recognized after the production cycle has ended but before the sale takes place**. This is the case when the selling price and the amount are certain. For instance, if products or other assets are salable in an active market at readily determinable prices without significant additional cost, then revenue can be recognized at the completion of production. An example would be the mining of certain minerals for which, once the mineral is mined, a ready market at a standard price exists. The same holds true for some artificial price supports set by the government in establishing agricultural prices.

Upon Receipt of Cash. **Receipt of cash is another basis for revenue recognition.** The cash basis approach is used only when it is impossible to establish the revenue figure at the time of sale because of the uncertainty of collection. One form of the cash basis is the installment sales method, in which payment is required in periodic installments over a long period of time. Its most common use is in the retail field. Farm and home equipment and furnishings are typically sold on an installment basis. The installment method is frequently justified on the basis that the risk of not collecting an account receivable is so great that the sale is not sufficient evidence for recognition to take place. In some instances, this reasoning may be valid. Generally, though, if a sale has been completed, it should be recognized; if bad debts are expected, they should be recorded as separate estimates.

Revenue, then, is recorded in the period when realized or realizable and earned. Normally, this is the date of sale. But circumstances may dictate application of the percentage-of-completion approach, the end-of-production approach, or the receipt-of-cash approach.

WHAT DO THE NUMBERS MEAN?

NO TAKE BACKS!

Investors in **Lucent Technologies** got an unpleasant surprise when the company was forced to restate its financial results in a recent quarter. What happened? Lucent violated one of the fundamental criteria for revenue recognition—the "no take-back" rule. This rule holds that revenue should not be booked on inventory that is shipped if the customer can return it at some point in the future. In this particular case, Lucent agreed to take back shipped inventory from its distributors, if the distributors are unable to sell the items to their customers.

Lucent booked the sales on the shipped goods, which helped it report continued sales growth. However, Lucent investors got a nasty surprise when those goods were returned by the distributors. The restatement erased $679 million in revenues, turning an operating profit into a loss. In response to this bad news, Lucent's stock price declined $1.31 per share or 8.5 percent.

Lucent has since changed its policy so that it will now record inventory as sold only if the final customer has bought the equipment, not when the inventory is shipped to the distributor. The lesson for investors is to review a company's revenue recognition policy for indications that revenues are being overstated due to generous return provisions for inventory. And remember, no take-backs!

Source: Adapted from S. Young, "Lucent Slashes First Quarter Outlook, Erases Revenue from Latest Quarter," *Wall Street Journal Online* (December 22, 2000).

Matching Principle

In recognizing expenses, the approach followed is, "Let the expense follow the revenues." Expenses are recognized not when wages are paid, or when the work is performed, or when a product is produced, but when the work (service) or the product actually makes its contribution to revenue. Thus, expense recognition is tied to revenue recognition. This practice is referred to as the **matching principle** because it dictates that **efforts (expenses) be matched with accomplishment (revenues) whenever it is reasonable and practicable to do so.**

For those costs for which it is difficult to adopt some type of rational association with revenue, some other approach must be developed. Often, a "rational and systematic" allocation policy is used that will approximate the matching principle. This type of expense recognition pattern involves assumptions about the benefits that are being received as well as the cost associated with those benefits. The cost of a long-lived asset, for example, must be allocated over all of the accounting periods during which the asset is used because the asset contributes to the generation of revenue throughout its useful life.

Some costs are charged to the current period as expenses (or losses) simply because no connection with revenue can be determined. Examples of these types of costs are officers' salaries and other administrative expenses.

Costs are generally classified into two groups: **product costs** and **period costs**. **Product costs** such as material, labor, and overhead attach to the product. They are carried into future periods if the revenue from the product is recognized in subsequent periods. **Period costs** such as officers' salaries and other administrative expenses are charged off immediately, even though benefits associated with these costs occur in the future, because no direct relationship between cost and revenue can be determined. These expense recognition procedures are summarized in Illustration 2-4.

ILLUSTRATION 2-4
Expense Recognition

Type of Cost	Relationship	Recognition
Product costs: • Material • Labor • Overhead	Direct relationship between cost and revenue.	Recognize in period of revenue (matching).
Period costs: • Salaries • Administrative costs	No direct relationship between cost and revenue.	Expense as incurred.

Hollywood Accounting

What do the numbers mean?

The problem of expense recognition is as complex as that of revenue recognition, as illustrated by Hollywood accounting. Major motion picture studios have been allowed to capitalize advertising and marketing costs and to amortize these costs against revenues over the life of the film. As a result, many investors have suggested that the studios' profit numbers were overstated. Under a new GAAP standard, these costs now must be amortized over no more than 3 months; in many cases, they must be expensed immediately. Similarly, the costs related to abandoned projects often were allocated to overhead and spread out over the lives of the successful projects. Not anymore. These costs now must be expensed as they are incurred. Here is a rough estimate of the amounts of capitalized advertising costs some major studios will have to write off.

Studio (Parent Company)	Capitalized Advertising (in millions)
Columbia Tri-Star (Sony)	$200
Paramount (Viacom)	200
20th Century Fox (News Corp)	150

Why the more conservative approach? A lot has to do with a stricter application of the definitions of assets and expenses. While many argue that advertising and marketing costs have future service potential, difficulty in reliably measuring these benefits suggests they are not assets. Therefore, a very short amortization period or immediate write-off is justified. Under these new guidelines, investors will have more reliable measures for assessing the performance of companies in this industry.

The conceptual validity of the matching principle has been a subject of debate. **A major concern is that matching permits certain costs to be deferred and treated as assets on the balance sheet when in fact these costs may not have future benefits.** If abused, this principle permits the balance sheet to become a "dumping ground" for unmatched costs. In addition, there appears to be no objective definition of "systematic and rational."

Full Disclosure Principle

In deciding what information to report, the general practice of providing information that is of sufficient importance to influence the judgment and decisions of an informed user is followed. Often referred to as the **full disclosure principle**, it recognizes that the nature and amount of information included in financial reports reflects a series of judgmental trade-offs. These trade-offs strive for (1) sufficient detail to disclose matters that **make a difference** to users, yet (2) sufficient condensation to make the **information understandable**, keeping in mind costs of preparing and using it.

Information about financial position, income, cash flows, and investments can be found in one of three places: (1) within the main body of financial statements, (2) in the notes to those statements, or (3) as supplementary information.

The **financial statements** are a formalized, structured means of communicating financial information. To be recognized in the main body of financial statements, **an item should meet the definition of a basic element, be measurable with sufficient certainty, and be relevant and reliable.**[14]

Disclosure is not a substitute for proper accounting. As a former chief accountant of the SEC recently noted: Good disclosure does not cure bad accounting any more than an adjective or adverb can be used without, or in place of, a noun or verb. Thus, for example, cash basis accounting for cost of goods sold is misleading, even if accrual basis amounts were disclosed in the notes to the financial statements.

The **notes to financial statements** generally amplify or explain the items presented in the main body of the statements. If the information in the main body of the financial statements gives an incomplete picture of the performance and position of the enterprise, additional information that is needed to complete the picture should be included in the notes. Information in the notes does not have to be quantifiable, nor does it need to qualify as an element. Notes can be partially or totally narrative. Examples of notes are: descriptions of the accounting policies and methods used in measuring the elements reported in the statements; explanations of uncertainties and contingencies; and statistics and details too voluminous for inclusion in the statements. The notes are not only helpful but also essential to understanding the enterprise's performance and position.

Supplementary information may include details or amounts that present a different perspective from that adopted in the financial statements. It may be quantifiable information that is high in relevance but low in reliability. Or it may be information that is helpful but not essential. One example of supplementary information is the data and schedules provided by oil and gas companies: Typically they provide information on proven reserves as well as the related discounted cash flows.

Supplementary information may also include management's explanation of the financial information and its discussion of the significance of that information. For example, many business combinations have produced innumerable conglomerate-type business organizations and financing arrangements that demand new and peculiar accounting and reporting practices and principles. In each of these situations, the same problem must be faced: making sure that enough information is presented to ensure that the **reasonably prudent investor** will not be misled.

The content, arrangement, and display of financial statements, along with other facets of full disclosure, are discussed in Chapters 4, 5, 23, and 24.

[14]*SFAC No. 5*, par. 63.

HOW'S YOUR LEVERAGE?

A classic illustration of the problem of determining adequate disclosure guidelines is the question of what banks should disclose about loans made for highly leveraged transactions such as leveraged buyouts. Investors want to know what percentage of a bank's loans are of this risky type. The problem is what do we mean by "leveraged"? As one regulator noted, "If it looks leveraged, it probably is leveraged, but most of us would be hard-pressed to come up with a definition." Is a loan to a company with a debt to equity ratio of 4 to 1 highly leveraged? Or is high leverage 8 to 1, or 10 to 1? The problem is complicated because some highly leveraged companies have cash flows that cover interest payments. Therefore, they are not as risky as they might appear. In short, providing the appropriate disclosure to help investors and regulators differentiate risky from safe is difficult.

WHAT DO THE NUMBERS MEAN?

Constraints

OBJECTIVE 8
Describe the impact that constraints have on reporting accounting information.

In providing information with the qualitative characteristics that make it useful, two overriding **constraints** must be considered: (1) the **cost-benefit relationship** and (2) **materiality**. Two other less dominant yet important constraints that are part of the reporting environment are **industry practices** and **conservatism**.

Cost-Benefit Relationship

Too often, users assume that information is a cost-free commodity. But preparers and providers of accounting information know that it is not. Therefore, the **cost-benefit relationship** must be considered: The costs of providing the information must be weighed against the benefits that can be derived from using the information. Standards-setting bodies and governmental agencies use cost-benefit analysis before making their informational requirements final. In order to justify requiring a particular measurement or disclosure, the benefits perceived to be derived from it must exceed the costs perceived to be associated with it.

The following remark, made by a corporate executive about a proposed standard, was addressed to the FASB: "In all my years in the financial arena, I have never seen such an absolutely ridiculous proposal. . . . To dignify these 'actuarial' estimates by recording them as assets and liabilities would be virtually unthinkable except for the fact that the FASB has done equally stupid things in the past. . . . For God's sake, use common sense just this once."[15] Although this remark is extreme, it does indicate the frustration expressed by members of the business community about standards setting and whether the benefits of a given standard exceed the costs.

The difficulty in cost-benefit analysis is that the costs and especially the benefits are not always evident or measurable. The costs are of several kinds, including costs of collecting and processing, costs of disseminating, costs of auditing, costs of potential litigation, costs of disclosure to competitors, and costs of analysis and interpretation. Benefits accrue to preparers (in terms of greater management control and access to capital) and to users (in terms of better information for allocation of resources, tax assessment, and rate regulation). But benefits are generally more difficult to quantify than are costs.

Most recently, the AICPA Special Committee on Financial Reporting submitted the following **constraints to limit the costs of reporting**.

1. Business reporting should exclude information outside of management's expertise or for which management is not the best source, such as information about competitors.
2. Management should not be required to report information that would significantly harm the company's competitive position.

---

[15]"Decision-Usefulness: The Overriding Objective," *FASB Viewpoints* (October 19, 1983), p. 4.

3. Management should not be required to provide forecasted financial statements. Rather, management should provide information that helps users forecast for themselves the company's financial future.
4. Other than for financial statements, management need only report the information it knows. That is, management should be under no obligation to gather information it does not have, or need, to manage the business.
5. Certain elements of business reporting should be presented only if users and management agree they should be reported—a concept of flexible reporting.
6. Companies should not have to report forward-looking information unless there are effective deterrents to unwarranted litigation that discourages companies from doing so.

Materiality

The constraint of **materiality** relates to an item's impact on a firm's overall financial operations. An item is material if its inclusion or omission would influence or change the judgment of a reasonable person.[16] It is immaterial and, therefore, irrelevant if it would have no impact on a decision maker. In short, **it must make a difference** or it need not be disclosed. The point involved here is one of **relative size and importance**. If the amount involved is significant when compared with the other revenues and expenses, assets and liabilities, or net income of the entity, sound and acceptable standards should be followed. If the amount is so small that it is unimportant when compared with other items, application of a particular standard may be considered of less importance.

It is difficult to provide firm guides in judging when a given item is or is not material because materiality varies both with relative amount and with relative importance. For example, the two sets of numbers presented below illustrate relative size.

ILLUSTRATION 2-5
Materiality Comparison

	Company A	Company B
Sales	$10,000,000	$100,000
Costs and expenses	9,000,000	90,000
Income from operations	$ 1,000,000	$ 10,000
Unusual gain	$ 20,000	$ 5,000

During the period in question, the revenues and expenses, and therefore the net incomes of Company A and Company B, have been proportional. Each has had an unusual gain. In looking at the abbreviated income figures for Company A, it does not appear significant whether the amount of the unusual gain is set out separately or merged with the regular operating income. It is only 2 percent of the net income and, if merged, would not seriously distort the net income figure. Company B has had an unusual gain of only $5,000, but it is relatively much more significant than the larger gain realized by A. For Company B, an item of $5,000 amounts to 50 percent of its net income. Obviously, the inclusion of such an item in ordinary operating income would affect the amount of that income materially. Thus we see the importance of the **relative size** of an item in determining its materiality.

Companies and their auditors for the most part have adopted the general rule of thumb that anything under 5 percent of net income is considered not material. Recently

[16]*SFAC No. 2* (par. 132) sets forth the essence of materiality: "The omission or misstatement of an item in a financial report is material if, in the light of surrounding circumstances, the magnitude of the item is such that it is probable that the judgment of a reasonable person relying upon the report would have been changed or influenced by the inclusion or correction of the item." This same concept of materiality has been adopted by the auditing profession. See "Audit Risk and Materiality in Conducting an Audit," *Statement on Auditing Standards No. 47* (New York: AICPA, 1983), par. 6.

the SEC has indicated that it is acceptable to use this percentage for an initial assessment of materiality, but that other factors must also be considered.[17] For example, companies can no longer fail to record items in order to meet consensus analysts' earnings numbers, preserve a positive earnings trend, convert a loss to a profit or vice versa, increase management compensation, or hide an illegal transaction like a bribe. In other words, **both quantitative and qualitative factors must be considered in determining whether an item is material.**

The SEC has also indicated that in determining materiality companies must consider each misstatement separately and the aggregate effect of all misstatements. For example, at one time, **General Dynamics** disclosed that its Resources Group had improved its earnings by $5.8 million at the same time that one of its other subsidiaries had taken write-offs of $6.7 million. Although both numbers were far larger than the $2.5 million that General Dynamics as a whole earned for the year, neither was disclosed as unusual because the net effect on earnings was considered immaterial. This practice is now prohibited because each item must be considered separately. In addition, even though an individual item may be immaterial, it may be considered material when added to other immaterial items. Such items must be disclosed.

Materiality is a factor in a great many internal accounting decisions, too. The amount of classification required in a subsidiary expense ledger, the degree of accuracy required in prorating expenses among the departments of a business, and the extent to which adjustments should be made for accrued and deferred items, are examples of judgments that should finally be determined on a basis of reasonableness and practicability, which is the materiality constraint sensibly applied. Only by **the exercise of good judgment and professional expertise** can reasonable and appropriate answers be found.

LIVING IN A MATERIAL WORLD

WHAT DO THE NUMBERS MEAN?

Arguing that a questionable accounting item is immaterial has been the first line of defense for many companies caught "cooking the books." That defense is not working so well lately, in the wake of recent accounting meltdowns at **Enron** and **Global Crossing** and the tougher rules on materiality issued by the SEC (*SAB 99*). For example, in its case against **Sunbeam**, the SEC alleged that the consumer-products maker racked up so many immaterial adjustments under CEO Al "Chainsaw" Dunlap that they added up to a material misstatement that misled investors about the company's financial position.

Responding to new concerns about materiality, blue-chip companies, such as **IBM** and **General Electric** are providing expanded disclosures of transactions that used to fall below the materiality radar. Thus, some good may yet come out of these recent accounting failures.

Source: Adapted from K. Brown and J. Weil, "A Lot More Information Is 'Material' After Enron," *Wall Street Journal Online* (February 22, 2002).

Industry Practices

Another practical consideration is **industry practices. The peculiar nature of some industries and business concerns** sometimes requires departure from basic theory. In the public utility industry, noncurrent assets are reported first on the balance sheet to highlight the industry's capital-intensive nature. Agricultural crops are often reported at market value because it is costly to develop accurate cost figures on individual crops. Such variations from basic theory are not many, yet they do exist. Whenever we find what appears to be a violation of basic accounting theory, we should determine whether

[17]"Materiality," *SEC Staff Accounting Bulletin No. 99* (Washington, D.C.: SEC, 1999).

it is explained by some peculiar feature of the type of business involved before we criticize the procedures followed.

INTERNATIONAL INSIGHT

In Japan, assets are often undervalued and liabilities overvalued by companies. These practices reduce the demand for dividends and protect creditors in event of a default.

Conservatism

Few conventions in accounting are as misunderstood as the constraint of conservatism. **Conservatism** means **when in doubt choose the solution that will be least likely to overstate assets and income**. Note that there is nothing in the conservatism convention urging that net assets or net income be *understated*. Unfortunately it has been interpreted by some to mean just that. All that conservatism does, properly applied, is provide a very reasonable guide in difficult situations: refrain from overstatement of net income and net assets. Examples of conservatism in accounting are the use of the lower of cost or market approach in valuing inventories and the rule that accrued net losses should be recognized on firm purchase commitments for goods for inventory. If the issue is in doubt, it is better to understate than overstate net income and net assets. Of course, if there is no doubt, there is no need to apply this constraint.

Summary of the Structure

Illustration 2-6 presents the conceptual framework discussed in this chapter. It is similar to Illustration 2-1, except that it provides additional information for each level. We cannot overemphasize the usefulness of this conceptual framework in helping to understand many of the problem areas that are examined in subsequent chapters.

ILLUSTRATION 2-6
Conceptual Framework for Financial Reporting

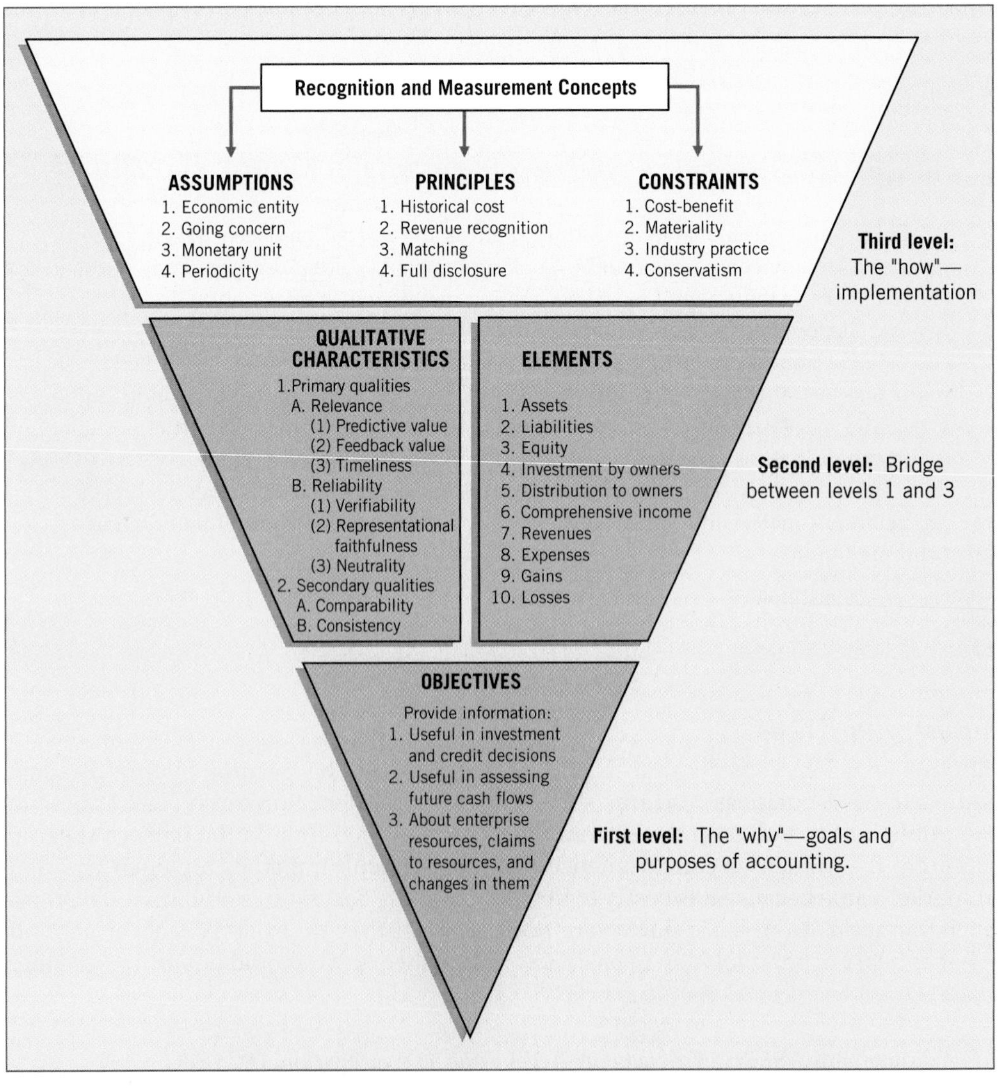

SUMMARY OF LEARNING OBJECTIVES

1 Describe the usefulness of a conceptual framework. A conceptual framework is needed to (1) build on and relate to an established body of concepts and objectives, (2) provide a framework for solving new and emerging practical problems, (3) increase financial statement users' understanding of and confidence in financial reporting, and (4) enhance comparability among companies' financial statements.

2 Describe the FASB's efforts to construct a conceptual framework. The FASB has issued six Statements of Financial Accounting Concepts that relate to financial reporting for business enterprises. These concept statements provide the framework for the conceptual framework. They include objectives, qualitative characteristics, and elements. In addition, measurement and recognition concepts are developed.

3 Understand the objectives of financial reporting. The objectives of financial reporting are to provide information that is (1) useful to those making investment and credit decisions who have a reasonable understanding of business activities; (2) helpful to present and potential investors, creditors, and others in assessing future cash flows; and (3) about economic resources and the claims to and changes in them.

4 Identify the qualitative characteristics of accounting information. The overriding criterion by which accounting choices can be judged is decision usefulness—that is, providing information that is most useful for decision making. Relevance and reliability are the two primary qualities, and comparability and consistency are the secondary qualities, that make accounting information useful for decision making.

5 Define the basic elements of financial statements. The basic elements of financial statements are: (1) assets, (2) liabilities, (3) equity, (4) investments by owners, (5) distributions to owners, (6) comprehensive income, (7) revenues, (8) expenses, (9) gains, and (10) losses. These ten elements are defined on pages 34 and 35.

6 Describe the basic assumptions of accounting. Four basic assumptions underlying the financial accounting structure are: (1) *Economic entity:* the assumption that the activity of a business enterprise can be kept separate and distinct from its owners and any other business unit. (2) *Going concern:* the assumption that the business enterprise will have a long life. (3) *Monetary unit:* the assumption that money is the common denominator by which economic activity is conducted, and that the monetary unit provides an appropriate basis for measurement and analysis. (4) *Periodicity:* the assumption that the economic activities of an enterprise can be divided into artificial time periods.

7 Explain the application of the basic principles of accounting. (1) *Historical cost principle:* Existing GAAP requires that most assets and liabilities be accounted for and reported on the basis of acquisition price. (2) *Revenue recognition:* Revenue is generally recognized when (a) realized or realizable and (b) earned. (3) *Matching principle:* Expenses are recognized when the work (service) or the product actually makes its contribution to revenue. (4) *Full disclosure principle:* Accountants follow the general practice of providing information that is of sufficient importance to influence the judgment and decisions of an informed user.

8 Describe the impact that constraints have on reporting accounting information. The constraints and their impact are: (1) *Cost-benefit relationship:* The costs of providing the information must be weighed against the benefits that can be derived from using the information. (2) *Materiality:* Sound and acceptable standards should be followed if the amount involved is significant when compared with the other revenues and expenses, assets and liabilities, or net income of the entity. (3) *Industry practices:* Follow the general practices in the firm's industry, which sometimes requires departure from basic theory. (4) *Conservatism:* When in doubt, choose the solution that will be least likely to overstate net assets and net income.

KEY TERMS

QUESTIONS

1. What is a conceptual framework? Why is a conceptual framework necessary in financial accounting?
2. What are the primary objectives of financial reporting as indicated in *Statement of Financial Accounting Concepts No. 1?*
3. What is meant by the term "qualitative characteristics of accounting information"?
4. Briefly describe the two primary qualities of useful accounting information.
5. According to the FASB conceptual framework, the objectives of financial reporting for business enterprises are based on the needs of the users of financial statements. Explain the level of sophistication that the Board assumes about the users of financial statements.
6. What is the distinction between comparability and consistency?
7. Why is it necessary to develop a definitional framework for the basic elements of accounting?
8. Expenses, losses, and distributions to owners are all decreases in net assets. What are the distinctions among them?
9. Revenues, gains, and investments by owners are all increases in net assets. What are the distinctions among them?
10. What are the four basic assumptions that underlie the financial accounting structure?
11. The life of a business is divided into specific time periods, usually a year, to measure results of operations for each such time period and to portray financial conditions at the end of each period.
    (a) This practice is based on the accounting assumption that the life of the business consists of a series of time periods and that it is possible to measure accurately the results of operations for each period. Comment on the validity and necessity of this assumption.
    (b) What has been the effect of this practice on accounting? What is its relation to the accrual system? What influence has it had on accounting entries and methodology?
12. What is the basic accounting problem created by the monetary unit assumption when there is significant inflation? What appears to be the FASB position on a stable monetary unit?
13. The chairman of the board of directors of the company for which you are chief accountant has told you that he has little use for accounting figures based on cost. He believes that replacement values are of far more significance to the board of directors than "out-of-date costs." Present some arguments to convince him that accounting data should still be based on cost.
14. When is revenue generally recognized? Why has that date been chosen as the point at which to recognize the revenue resulting from the entire producing and selling process?
15. Magnus Eatery operates a catering service specializing in business luncheons for large corporations. Magnus requires customers to place their orders 2 weeks in advance of the scheduled events. Magnus bills its customers on the tenth day of the month following the date of service and requires that payment be made within 30 days of the billing date. Conceptually, when should Magnus recognize revenue related to its catering service?
16. What is the difference between realized and realizable? Give an example of where the concept of realizable is used to recognize revenue.
17. What is the justification for the following deviations from recognizing revenue at the time of sale?
    (a) Installment sales method of recognizing revenue.
    (b) Recognition of revenue at completion of production for certain agricultural products.
    (c) The percentage-of-completion basis in long-term construction contracts.
18. Jane Hull Company paid $135,000 for a machine in 2005. The Accumulated Depreciation account has a balance of $46,500 at the present time. The company could sell the machine today for $150,000. The company president believes that the company has a "right to this gain." What does the president mean by this statement? Do you agree?
19. Three expense recognition methods (associating cause and effect, systematic and rational allocation, and immediate recognition) were discussed in the text under the matching principle. Indicate the basic nature of each of these types of expenses and give two examples of each.
20. *Statement of Financial Accounting Concepts No. 5* identifies four characteristics that an item must have before it is recognized in the financial statements. What are these four characteristics?
21. Briefly describe the types of information concerning financial position, income, and cash flows that might be provided: (a) within the main body of the financial statements, (b) in the notes to the financial statements, or (c) as supplementary information.
22. In January 2005, Alan Jackson Inc. doubled the amount of its outstanding stock by selling on the market an additional 10,000 shares to finance an expansion of the business. You propose that this information be shown by a footnote on the balance sheet as of December 31, 2004. The president objects, claiming that this sale took place after December 31, 2004, and, therefore, should not be shown. Explain your position.

23. Describe the two major constraints inherent in the presentation of accounting information.

24. What are some of the costs of providing accounting information? What are some of the benefits of accounting information? Describe the cost-benefit factors that should be considered when new accounting standards are being proposed.

25. How are materiality (and immateriality) related to the proper presentation of financial statements? What factors and measures should be considered in assessing the materiality of a misstatement in the presentation of a financial statement?

26. The treasurer of Joan Osborne Co. has heard that conservatism is a doctrine that is followed in accounting and, therefore, proposes that several policies be followed that are conservative in nature. State your opinion with respect to each of the policies listed below.

(a) The company gives a 2-year warranty to its customers on all products sold. The estimated warranty costs incurred from this year's sales should be entered as an expense this year instead of an expense in the period in the future when the warranty is made good.

(b) When sales are made on account, there is always uncertainty about whether the accounts are collectible. Therefore, the treasurer recommends recording the sale when the cash is received from the customers.

(c) A personal liability lawsuit is pending against the company. The treasurer believes there is an even chance that the company will lose the suit and have to pay damages of $200,000 to $300,000. The treasurer recommends that a loss be recorded and a liability created in the amount of $300,000.

(d) The inventory should be valued at "cost or market, whichever is lower" because the losses from price declines should be recognized in the accounts in the period in which the price decline takes place.

BRIEF EXERCISES

BE2-1 Discuss whether the changes described in each of the cases below require recognition in the CPA's report as to consistency. (Assume that the amounts are material.)

(a) After 3 years of computing depreciation under an accelerated method for income tax purposes and under the straight-line method for reporting purposes, the company adopted an accelerated method for reporting purposes.
(b) The company disposed of one of the two subsidiaries that had been included in its consolidated statements for prior years.
(c) The estimated remaining useful life of plant property was reduced because of obsolescence.
(d) The company is using an inventory valuation method that is different from those used by all other companies in its industry.

BE2-2 Identify which qualitative characteristic of accounting information is best described in each item below. (Do not use relevance and reliability.)

(a) The annual reports of **Best Buy Co.** are audited by certified public accountants.
(b) **Black & Decker** and **Cannondale Corporation** both use the FIFO cost flow assumption.
(c) **Starbucks Corporation** has used straight-line depreciation since it began operations.
(d) **Motorola** issues its quarterly reports immediately after each quarter ends.

BE2-3 For each item below, indicate to which category of elements of financial statements it belongs.

(a) Retained earnings
(b) Sales
(c) Additional paid-in capital
(d) Inventory
(e) Depreciation
(f) Loss on sale of equipment
(g) Interest payable
(h) Dividends
(i) Gain on sale of investment
(j) Issuance of common stock

BE2-4 Identify which basic assumption of accounting is best described in each item below.

(a) The economic activities of **FedEx Corporation** are divided into 12-month periods for the purpose of issuing annual reports.
(b) **Solectron Corporation, Inc.** does not adjust amounts in its financial statements for the effects of inflation.
(c) **Walgreen Co.** reports current and noncurrent classifications in its balance sheet.
(d) The economic activities of **General Electric** and its subsidiaries are merged for accounting and reporting purposes.

BE2-5 Identify which basic principle of accounting is best described in each item below.

(a) **Norfolk Southern Corporation** reports revenue in its income statement when it is earned instead of when the cash is collected.
(b) **Yahoo, Inc.** recognizes depreciation expense for a machine over the 2-year period during which that machine helps the company earn revenue.
(c) **Oracle Corporation** reports information about pending lawsuits in the notes to its financial statements.
(d) **Eastman Kodak Company** reports land on its balance sheet at the amount paid to acquire it, even though the estimated fair market value is greater.

BE2-6 Which constraints on accounting information are illustrated by the items below?

(a) Zip's Farms, Inc. reports agricultural crops on its balance sheet at market value.
(b) Crimson Tide Corporation does not accrue a contingent lawsuit gain of $650,000.
(c) Wildcat Company does not disclose any information in the notes to the financial statements unless the value of the information to financial statement users exceeds the expense of gathering it.
(d) Sun Devil Corporation expenses the cost of wastebaskets in the year they are acquired.

BE2-7 Presented below are three different transactions related to materiality. Explain whether you would classify these transactions as material.

(a) Marcus Co. has reported a positive trend in earnings over the last 3 years. In the current year, it reduces its bad debt allowance to ensure another positive earnings year. The impact of this adjustment is equal to 3% of net income.
(b) Sosa Co. has an extraordinary gain of $3.1 million on the sale of plant assets and a $3.3 million loss on the sale of investments. It decides to net the gain and loss because the net effect is considered immaterial. Sosa Co.'s income for the current year was $10 million.
(c) Seliz Co. expenses all capital equipment under $25,000 on the basis that it is immaterial. The company has followed this practice for a number of years.

BE2-8 If the going concern assumption is not made in accounting, what difference does it make in the amounts shown in the financial statements for the following items?

(a) Land.
(b) Unamortized bond premium.
(c) Depreciation expense on equipment.
(d) Merchandise inventory.
(e) Prepaid insurance.

BE2-9 What accounting assumption, principle, or modifying convention does **Target Corporation** use in each of the situations below?

(a) Target uses the lower of cost or market basis to value inventories.
(b) Target was involved in litigation over the last year. This litigation is disclosed in the financial statements.
(c) Target allocates the cost of its depreciable assets over the life it expects to receive revenue from these assets.
(d) Target records the purchase of a new IBM PC at its cash equivalent price.

BE2-10 Explain how you would decide whether to record each of the following expenditures as an asset or an expense. Assume all items are material.

(a) Legal fees paid in connection with the purchase of land are $1,500.
(b) Benjamin Bratt, Inc. paves the driveway leading to the office building at a cost of $21,000.
(c) A meat market purchases a meat-grinding machine at a cost of $3,500.
(d) On June 30, Alan and Alda, medical doctors, pay 6 months' office rent to cover the month of July and the next 5 months.
(e) Tim Taylor's Hardware Company pays $9,000 in wages to laborers for construction on a building to be used in the business.
(f) Nancy Kwan's Florists pays wages of $2,100 for November to an employee who serves as driver of their delivery truck.

EXERCISES

E2-1 (Qualitative Characteristics) *SFAC No. 2* identifies the qualitative characteristics that make accounting information useful. Presented below are a number of questions related to these qualitative characteristics and underlying constraints.

(a) What is the quality of information that enables users to confirm or correct prior expectations?
(b) Identify the two overall or pervasive constraints developed in *SFAC No. 2.*
(c) The chairman of the SEC at one time noted, "If it becomes accepted or expected that accounting principles are determined or modified in order to secure purposes other than economic measurement, we assume a grave risk that confidence in the credibility of our financial information system will be undermined." Which qualitative characteristic of accounting information should ensure that such a situation will not occur? (Do not use reliability.)
(d) Billy Owens Corp. switches from FIFO to average cost to FIFO over a 2-year period. Which qualitative characteristic of accounting information is not followed?
(e) Assume that the profession permits the savings and loan industry to defer losses on investments it sells, because immediate recognition of the loss may have adverse economic consequences on the industry. Which qualitative characteristic of accounting information is not followed? (Do not use relevance or reliability.)
(f) What are the two primary qualities that make accounting information useful for decision making?
(g) Rex Chapman, Inc. does not issue its first-quarter report until after the second quarter's results are reported. Which qualitative characteristic of accounting is not followed? (Do not use relevance.)
(h) Predictive value is an ingredient of which of the two primary qualities that make accounting information useful for decision-making purposes?
(i) Ronald Coles, Inc. is the only company in its industry to depreciate its plant assets on a straight-line basis. Which qualitative characteristic of accounting information may not be followed? (Do not use industry practices.)
(j) Jeff Malone Company has attempted to determine the replacement cost of its inventory. Three different appraisers arrive at substantially different amounts for this value. The president, nevertheless, decides to report the middle value for external reporting purposes. Which qualitative characteristic of information is lacking in these data? (Do not use reliability or representational faithfulness.)

E2-2 (Qualitative Characteristics) The qualitative characteristics that make accounting information useful for decision-making purposes are as follows.

Relevance	Timeliness	Representational faithfulness
Reliability	Verifiability	Comparability
Predictive value	Neutrality	Consistency
Feedback value		

Instructions

Identify the appropriate qualitative characteristic(s) to be used given the information provided below.

(a) Qualitative characteristic being employed when companies in the same industry are using the same accounting principles.
(b) Quality of information that confirms users' earlier expectations.
(c) Imperative for providing comparisons of a firm from period to period.
(d) Ignores the economic consequences of a standard or rule.
(e) Requires a high degree of consensus among individuals on a given measurement.
(f) Predictive value is an ingredient of this primary quality of information.
(g) Two qualitative characteristics that are related to both relevance and reliability.
(h) Neutrality is an ingredient of this primary quality of accounting information.
(i) Two primary qualities that make accounting information useful for decision-making purposes.
(j) Issuance of interim reports is an example of what primary ingredient of relevance?

E2-3 (Elements of Financial Statements) Ten interrelated elements that are most directly related to measuring the performance and financial status of an enterprise are provided below.

Assets	Distributions to owners	Expenses
Liabilities	Comprehensive income	Gains
Equity	Revenues	Losses
Investments by owners		

Instructions

Identify the element or elements associated with the 12 items below.

(a) Arises from peripheral or incidental transactions.
(b) Obligation to transfer resources arising from a past transaction.
(c) Increases ownership interest.
(d) Declares and pays cash dividends to owners.
(e) Increases in net assets in a period from nonowner sources.
(f) Items characterized by service potential or future economic benefit.
(g) Equals increase in assets less liabilities during the year, after adding distributions to owners and subtracting investments by owners.
(h) Arises from income statement activities that constitute the entity's ongoing major or central operations.
(i) Residual interest in the assets of the enterprise after deducting its liabilities.
(j) Increases assets during a period through sale of product.
(k) Decreases assets during the period by purchasing the company's own stock.
(l) Includes all changes in equity during the period, except those resulting from investments by owners and distributions to owners.

E2-4 (Assumptions, Principles, and Constraints) Presented below are the assumptions, principles, and constraints used in this chapter.

1. Economic entity assumption	**5.** Historical cost principle	**9.** Materiality
2. Going concern assumption	**6.** Matching principle	**10.** Industry practices
3. Monetary unit assumption	**7.** Full disclosure principle	**11.** Conservatism
4. Periodicity assumption	**8.** Cost-benefit relationship	

Instructions

Identify by number the accounting assumption, principle, or constraint that describes each situation below. Do not use a letter more than once.

(a) Allocates expenses to revenues in the proper period.
(b) Indicates that market value changes subsequent to purchase are not recorded in the accounts. (Do not use revenue recognition principle.)
(c) Ensures that all relevant financial information is reported.
(d) Rationale why plant assets are not reported at liquidation value. (Do not use historical cost principle.)
(e) Anticipates all losses, but reports no gains.
(f) Indicates that personal and business record keeping should be separately maintained.
(g) Separates financial information into time periods for reporting purposes.
(h) Permits the use of market value valuation in certain specific situations.
(i) Requires that information significant enough to affect the decision of reasonably informed users should be disclosed. (Do not use full disclosure principle.)
(j) Assumes that the dollar is the "measuring stick" used to report on financial performance.

E2-5 (Assumptions, Principles, and Constraints) Presented below are a number of operational guidelines and practices that have developed over time.

Instructions

Select the assumption, principle, or constraint that most appropriately justifies these procedures and practices. (Do not use qualitative characteristics.)

(a) Price-level changes are not recognized in the accounting records.
(b) Lower of cost or market is used to value inventories.
(c) Financial information is presented so that reasonably prudent investors will not be misled.
(d) Intangibles are capitalized and amortized over periods benefited.
(e) Repair tools are expensed when purchased.
(f) Brokerage firms use market value for purposes of valuation of all marketable securities.
(g) Each enterprise is kept as a unit distinct from its owner or owners.
(h) All significant postbalance sheet events are reported.
(i) Revenue is recorded at point of sale.
(j) All important aspects of bond indentures are presented in financial statements.
(k) Rationale for accrual accounting is stated.
(l) The use of consolidated statements is justified.

(m) Reporting must be done at defined time intervals.
(n) An allowance for doubtful accounts is established.
(o) All payments out of petty cash are charged to Miscellaneous Expense. (Do not use conservatism.)
(p) Goodwill is recorded only at time of purchase.
(q) No profits are anticipated and all possible losses are recognized.
(r) A company charges its sales commission costs to expense.

E2-6 (Full Disclosure Principle) Presented below are a number of facts related to R. Kelly, Inc. Assume that no mention of these facts was made in the financial statements and the related notes.

Instructions

Assume that you are the auditor of R. Kelly, Inc. and that you have been asked to explain the appropriate accounting and related disclosure necessary for each of these items.

(a) The company decided that, for the sake of conciseness, only net income should be reported on the income statement. Details as to revenues, cost of goods sold, and expenses were omitted.

(b) Equipment purchases of $170,000 were partly financed during the year through the issuance of a $110,000 notes payable. The company offset the equipment against the notes payable and reported plant assets at $60,000.

(c) During the year, an assistant controller for the company embezzled $15,000. R. Kelly's net income for the year was $2,300,000. Neither the assistant controller nor the money have been found.

(d) R. Kelly has reported its ending inventory at $2,100,000 in the financial statements. No other information related to inventories is presented in the financial statements and related notes.

(e) The company changed its method of depreciating equipment from the double-declining balance to the straight-line method. No mention of this change was made in the financial statements.

E2-7 (Accounting Principles—Comprehensive) Presented below are a number of business transactions that occurred during the current year for Fresh Horses, Inc.

Instructions

In each of the situations, discuss the appropriateness of the journal entries in terms of generally accepted accounting principles.

(a) The president of Fresh Horses, Inc. used his expense account to purchase a new Suburban solely for personal use. The following journal entry was made.

Miscellaneous Expense	29,000	
Cash		29,000

(b) Merchandise inventory that cost $620,000 is reported on the balance sheet at $690,000, the expected selling price less estimated selling costs. The following entry was made to record this increase in value.

Merchandise Inventory	70,000	
Revenue		70,000

(c) The company is being sued for $500,000 by a customer who claims damages for personal injury apparently caused by a defective product. Company attorneys feel extremely confident that the company will have no liability for damages resulting from the situation. Nevertheless, the company decides to make the following entry.

Loss from Lawsuit	500,000	
Liability for Lawsuit		500,000

(d) Because the general level of prices increased during the current year, Fresh Horses, Inc. determined that there was a $16,000 understatement of depreciation expense on its equipment and decided to record it in its accounts. The following entry was made.

Depreciation Expense	16,000	
Accumulated Depreciation		16,000

(e) Fresh Horses, Inc. has been concerned about whether intangible assets could generate cash in case of liquidation. As a consequence, goodwill arising from a purchase transaction during the current year and recorded at $800,000 was written off as follows.

Retained Earnings	800,000	
Goodwill		800,000

(f) Because of a "fire sale," equipment obviously worth $200,000 was acquired at a cost of $155,000. The following entry was made.

Equipment	200,000	
Cash		155,000
Revenue		45,000

E2-8 (Accounting Principles—Comprehensive) Presented below is information related to Garth Brooks, Inc.

Instructions

Comment on the appropriateness of the accounting procedures followed by Garth Brooks, Inc.

(a) Depreciation expense on the building for the year was $60,000. Because the building was increasing in value during the year, the controller decided to charge the depreciation expense to retained earnings instead of to net income. The following entry is recorded.

Retained Earnings	60,000	
Accumulated Depreciation — Buildings		60,000

(b) Materials were purchased on January 1, 2003, for $120,000 and this amount was entered in the Materials account. On December 31, 2003, the materials would have cost $141,000, so the following entry is made.

Inventory	21,000	
Gain on Inventories		21,000

(c) During the year, the company purchased equipment through the issuance of common stock. The stock had a par value of $135,000 and a fair market value of $450,000. The fair market value of the equipment was not easily determinable. The company recorded this transaction as follows.

Equipment	135,000	
Common Stock		135,000

(d) During the year, the company sold certain equipment for $285,000, recognizing a gain of $69,000. Because the controller believed that new equipment would be needed in the near future, she decided to defer the gain and amortize it over the life of any new equipment purchased.

(e) An order for $61,500 has been received from a customer for products on hand. This order was shipped on January 9, 2004. The company made the following entry in 2003.

Accounts Receivable	61,500	
Sales		61,500

CONCEPTUAL CASES

C2-1 (Conceptual Framework—General) Roger Morgan has some questions regarding the theoretical framework in which standards are set. He knows that the FASB and other predecessor organizations have attempted to develop a conceptual framework for accounting theory formulation. Yet, Roger's supervisors have indicated that these theoretical frameworks have little value in the practical sense (i.e., in the real world). Roger did notice that accounting standards seem to be established after the fact rather than before. He thought this indicated a lack of theory structure but never really questioned the process at school because he was too busy doing the homework.

Roger feels that some of his anxiety about accounting theory and accounting semantics could be alleviated by identifying the basic concepts and definitions accepted by the profession and considering them in light of his current work. By doing this, he hopes to develop an appropriate connection between theory and practice.

Instructions

(a) Help Roger recognize the purpose of and benefit of a conceptual framework.

(b) Identify any *Statements of Financial Accounting Concepts* issued by FASB that may be helpful to Roger in developing his theoretical background.

C2-2 (Conceptual Framework—General) The Financial Accounting Standards Board (FASB) has developed a conceptual framework for financial accounting and reporting. The FASB has issued seven

Statements of Financial Accounting Concepts. These statements are intended to set forth objectives and fundamentals that will be the basis for developing financial accounting and reporting standards. The objectives identify the goals and purposes of financial reporting. The fundamentals are the underlying concepts of financial accounting—concepts that guide the selection of transactions, events, and circumstances to be accounted for; their recognition and measurement; and the means of summarizing and communicating them to interested parties.

The purpose of *Statement of Financial Accounting Concepts No. 2,* "Qualitative Characteristics of Accounting Information," is to examine the characteristics that make accounting information useful. The characteristics or qualities of information discussed in *SFAC No. 2* are the ingredients that make information useful and the qualities to be sought when accounting choices are made.

Instructions

(a) Identify and discuss the benefits that can be expected to be derived from the FASB's conceptual framework study.

(b) What is the most important quality for accounting information as identified in *Statement of Financial Accounting Concepts No. 2*? Explain why it is the most important.

(c) *Statement of Financial Accounting Concepts No. 2* describes a number of key characteristics or qualities for accounting information. Briefly discuss the importance of any three of these qualities for financial reporting purposes.

(CMA adapted)

C2-3 (Objectives of Financial Reporting) Regis Gordon and Kathy Medford are discussing various aspects of the FASB's pronouncement *Statement of Financial Accounting Concepts No. 1,* "Objectives of Financial Reporting by Business Enterprises." Regis indicates that this pronouncement provides little, if any, guidance to the practicing professional in resolving accounting controversies. He believes that the statement provides such broad guidelines that it would be impossible to apply the objectives to present-day reporting problems. Kathy concedes this point but indicates that objectives are still needed to provide a starting point for the FASB in helping to improve financial reporting.

Instructions

(a) Indicate the basic objectives established in *Statement of Financial Accounting Concepts No. 1.*

(b) What do you think is the meaning of Kathy's statement that the FASB needs a starting point to resolve accounting controversies?

C2-4 (Qualitative Characteristics) Accounting information provides useful information about business transactions and events. Those who provide and use financial reports must often select and evaluate accounting alternatives. *FASB Statement of Financial Accounting Concepts No. 2,* "Qualitative Characteristics of Accounting Information," examines the characteristics of accounting information that make it useful for decision making. It also points out that various limitations inherent in the measurement and reporting process may necessitate trade-offs or sacrifices among the characteristics of useful information.

Instructions

(a) Describe briefly the following characteristics of useful accounting information.

(1) Relevance
(2) Reliability
(3) Understandability
(4) Comparability
(5) Consistency

(b) For each of the following pairs of information characteristics, give an example of a situation in which one of the characteristics may be sacrificed in return for a gain in the other.

(1) Relevance and reliability.
(2) Relevance and consistency.
(3) Comparability and consistency.
(4) Relevance and understandability.

(c) What criterion should be used to evaluate trade-offs between information characteristics?

C2-5 (Revenue Recognition and Matching Principle) After the presentation of your report on the examination of the financial statements to the board of directors of Bones Publishing Company, one of the new directors expresses surprise that the income statement assumes that an equal proportion of the revenue is earned with the publication of every issue of the company's magazine. She feels that the "crucial event" in the process of earning revenue in the magazine business is the cash sale of the subscription. She says that she does not understand why most of the revenue cannot be "recognized" in the period of the sale.

Instructions

(a) List the various accepted times for recognizing revenue in the accounts and explain when the methods are appropriate.

(b) Discuss the propriety of timing the recognition of revenue in Bones Publishing Company's accounts with:
  (1) The cash sale of the magazine subscription.
  (2) The publication of the magazine every month.
  (3) Both events, by recognizing a portion of the revenue with cash sale of the magazine subscription and a portion of the revenue with the publication of the magazine every month.

C2-6 (Revenue Recognition and Matching Principle) On June 5, 2003, McCoy Corporation signed a contract with Sulu Associates under which Sulu agreed (1) to construct an office building on land owned by McCoy, (2) to accept responsibility for procuring financing for the project and finding tenants, and (3) to manage the property for 35 years. The annual net income from the project, after debt service, was to be divided equally between McCoy Corporation and Sulu Associates. Sulu was to accept its share of future net income as full payment for its services in construction, obtaining finances and tenants, and management of the project.

By May 31, 2004, the project was nearly completed, and tenants had signed leases to occupy 90% of the available space at annual rentals totaling $4,000,000. It is estimated that, after operating expenses and debt service, the annual net income will amount to $1,500,000.

The management of Sulu Associates believed that (a) the economic benefit derived from the contract with McCoy should be reflected on its financial statements for the fiscal year ended May 31, 2004, and directed that revenue be accrued in an amount equal to the commercial value of the services Sulu had rendered during the year, (b) this amount should be carried in contracts receivable, and (c) all related expenditures should be charged against the revenue.

Instructions

(a) Explain the main difference between the economic concept of business income as reflected by Sulu's management and the measurement of income under generally accepted accounting principles.
(b) Discuss the factors to be considered in determining when revenue should be recognized for the purpose of accounting measurement of periodic income.
(c) Is the belief of Sulu's management in accordance with generally accepted accounting principles for the measurement of revenue and expense for the year ended May 31, 2004? Support your opinion by discussing the application to this case of the factors to be considered for asset measurement and revenue and expense recognition.

(AICPA adapted)

C2-7 (Matching Principle) An accountant must be familiar with the concepts involved in determining earnings of a business entity. The amount of earnings reported for a business entity is dependent on the proper recognition, in general, of revenue and expense for a given time period. In some situations, costs are recognized as expenses at the time of product sale. In other situations, guidelines have been developed for recognizing costs as expenses or losses by other criteria.

Instructions

(a) Explain the rationale for recognizing costs as expenses at the time of product sale.
(b) What is the rationale underlying the appropriateness of treating costs as expenses of a period instead of assigning the costs to an asset? Explain.
(c) In what general circumstances would it be appropriate to treat a cost as an asset instead of as an expense? Explain.
(d) Some expenses are assigned to specific accounting periods on the basis of systematic and rational allocation of asset cost. Explain the underlying rationale for recognizing expenses on the basis of systematic and rational allocation of asset cost.
(e) Identify the conditions under which it would be appropriate to treat a cost as a loss.

(AICPA adapted)

C2-8 (Matching Principle) Accountants try to prepare income statements that are as accurate as possible. A basic requirement in preparing accurate income statements is to match costs against revenues properly. Proper matching of costs against revenues requires that costs resulting from typical business operations be recognized in the period in which they expired.

Instructions

(a) List three criteria that can be used to determine whether such costs should appear as charges in the income statement for the current period.

(b) As generally presented in financial statements, the following items or procedures have been criticized as improperly matching costs with revenues. Briefly discuss each item from the viewpoint of matching costs with revenues and suggest corrective or alternative means of presenting the financial information.

(1) Receiving and handling costs.
(2) Valuation of inventories at the lower of cost or market.
(3) Cash discounts on purchases.

C2-9 (Matching Principle) Carlos Rodriguez sells and erects shell houses, that is, frame structures that are completely finished on the outside but are unfinished on the inside except for flooring, partition studding, and ceiling joists. Shell houses are sold chiefly to customers who are handy with tools and who have time to do the interior wiring, plumbing, wall completion and finishing, and other work necessary to make the shell houses livable dwellings.

Rodriguez buys shell houses from a manufacturer in unassembled packages consisting of all lumber, roofing, doors, windows, and similar materials necessary to complete a shell house. Upon commencing operations in a new area, Rodriguez buys or leases land as a site for its local warehouse, field office, and display houses. Sample display houses are erected at a total cost of $30,000 to $44,000 including the cost of the unassembled packages. The chief element of cost of the display houses is the unassembled packages, inasmuch as erection is a short, low-cost operation. Old sample models are torn down or altered into new models every 3 to 7 years. Sample display houses have little salvage value because dismantling and moving costs amount to nearly as much as the cost of an unassembled package.

Instructions

(a) A choice must be made between (1) expensing the costs of sample display houses in the periods in which the expenditure is made and (2) spreading the costs over more than one period. Discuss the advantages of each method.

(b) Would it be preferable to amortize the cost of display houses on the basis of (1) the passage of time or (2) the number of shell houses sold? Explain.

(AICPA adapted)

C2-10 (Qualitative Characteristics) Recently, your Uncle Waldo Ralph, who knows that you always have your eye out for a profitable investment, has discussed the possibility of your purchasing some corporate bonds. He suggests that you may wish to get in on the "ground floor" of this deal. The bonds being issued by Cricket Corp. are 10-year debentures which promise a 40% rate of return. Cricket manufactures novelty/party items.

You have told Waldo that, unless you can take a look at Cricket's financial statements, you would not feel comfortable about such an investment. Believing that this is the chance of a lifetime, Uncle Waldo has procured a copy of Cricket's most recent, unaudited financial statements which are a year old. These statements were prepared by Mrs. John Cricket. You peruse these statements, and they are quite impressive. The balance sheet showed a debt-to-equity ratio of 0.10 and, for the year shown, the company reported net income of $2,424,240.

The financial statements are not shown in comparison with amounts from other years. In addition, no significant note disclosures about inventory valuation, depreciation methods, loan agreements, etc. are available.

Instructions

Write a letter to Uncle Waldo explaining why it would be unwise to base an investment decision on the financial statements that he has provided to you. Be sure to explain why these financial statements are neither relevant nor reliable.

C2-11 (Matching) Hinckley Nuclear Power Plant will be "mothballed" at the end of its useful life (approximately 20 years) at great expense. The matching principle requires that expenses be matched to revenue. Accountants Jana Kingston and Pete Henning argue whether it is better to allocate the expense of mothballing over the next 20 years or ignore it until mothballing occurs.

Instructions

Answer the following questions.

(a) What stakeholders should be considered?
(b) What ethical issue, if any, underlies the dispute?
(c) What alternatives should be considered?
(d) Assess the consequences of the alternatives.
(e) What decision would you recommend?

USING YOUR JUDGMENT

FINANCIAL REPORTING PROBLEM

3M Company

The financial statements of **3M** are presented in Appendix 5B or can be accessed on the Take Action! CD.

Instructions

Refer to 3M's financial statements and the accompanying notes to answer the following questions.

(a) Using the notes to the consolidated financial statements, determine 3M's revenue recognition policies. Comment on the impact of SEC *SAB No. 101* on 3M's financial statements.

(b) Give two examples of where historical cost information is reported in 3M's financial statements and related notes. Give two examples of the use of fair value information reported in either the financial statements or related notes.

(c) How can we determine that the accounting principles used by 3M are prepared on a basis consistent with those of last year?

(d) What is 3M's accounting policy related to advertising? What accounting principle does 3M follow regarding accounting for advertising?

FINANCIAL STATEMENT ANALYSIS CASE

Weyerhaeuser Company

Presented below is a statement that appeared about **Weyerhaeuser Company** in a financial magazine.

> The land and timber holdings are now carried on the company's books at a mere $422 million. The value of the timber alone is variously estimated at $3 billion to $7 billion and is rising all the time. "The understatement of the company is pretty severe," conceded Charles W. Bingham, a senior vice-president. Adds Robert L. Schuyler, another senior vice-president: "We have a whole stream of profit nobody sees and there is no way to show it on our books."

Instructions

(a) What does Schuyler mean when he says, "We have a whole stream of profit nobody sees and there is no way to show it on our books"?

(b) If the understatement of the company's assets is severe, why does accounting not report this information?

COMPARATIVE ANALYSIS CASE

The Coca-Cola Company and PepsiCo, Inc.

Instructions

Go to the Take Action! CD, and use information found there to answer the following questions related to **The Coca-Cola Company** and **PepsiCo, Inc.**

(a) What are the primary lines of business of these two companies as shown in their notes to the financial statements?

(b) Which company has the dominant position in beverage sales?

(c) How are inventories for these two companies valued? What cost allocation method is used to report inventory? How does their accounting for inventories affect comparability between the two companies?

(d) Which company changed its accounting policies during 2001 which affected the consistency of the financial results from the previous year? What were these changes?

RESEARCH CASES

Case 1 Retrieval of Information on Public Company

There are several commonly available indexes that enable individuals to locate articles previously included in numerous business publications and periodicals. Articles can generally be searched by company or by subject matter. Four common indexes are the *Wall Street Journal Index, Business Abstracts* (formerly the *Business Periodical Index*), *Predicasts F&S Index,* and *ABI/Inform.*

Instructions

Use one of these resources to find an article about a company in which you are interested. Read the article and answer the following questions. (*Note:* Your library may have hard copy or CD-ROM versions of these indexes.)

(a) What is the article about?

(b) What company-specific information is included in the article?

(c) Identify any accounting-related issues discussed in the article.

Case 2

The February 11, 2002, *Wall Street Journal* includes an article by Susan Warren entitled "Dow Chemical Is Tight Lipped About Asbestos." (Subscribers to **Business Extra** can access the article at that site.)

Instructions

Read the article and answer the following questions.

(a) What ways of defining materiality are suggested in the article? Do you think these are better approaches than those of the Supreme Court or GAAP? Why or why not?

(b) Dow Chemical (Dow) says that its $230 million estimated asbestos liability is "not material." How has the Supreme Court defined materiality? How is materiality defined by FASB?

(c) Compare the asbestos-related information provided in the footnotes of Dow, Halliburton, and 3M. (You can see these footnotes at http://edgarscan.tc.pw.com/ or www. FreeEdgar.com.) Based on this comparison, which firm is doing the best job of providing the information that investors need? Justify your answer.

(d) Based on this comparison, what grade (A–F) would you give Dow's disclosures? Why?

INTERNATIONAL REPORTING CASE

As discussed in Chapter 1, the International Accounting Standards Board (IASB) develops accounting standards for many international companies. The IASB also has developed a conceptual framework to help guide the setting of accounting standards. Following is an Overview of the IASB Framework.

<u>Objective of Financial Statements:</u>
- To provide information about the financial position, performance, and changes in financial position of an enterprise that is useful to a wide range of users in making economic decisions.

<u>Underlying Assumptions</u>
- Accrual basis
- Going concern

<u>Qualitative Characteristics of Financial Statements</u>
- Understandability
- Relevance
  - Materiality
- Reliability
  - Faithful representation
  - Substance over form
  - Neutrality
  - Prudence
  - Completeness
- Comparability

<u>Constraints on Relevant and Reliable Information</u>
- Timeliness
- Balance between benefit and cost
- Balance between qualitative characteristics

<u>True and Fair Presentation</u>

Elements of Financial Statements

Asset: A resource controlled by the enterprise as a result of past events and from which future economic benefits are expected to flow to the enterprise.

Liability: A present obligation of the enterprise arising from past events, the settlement of which is expected to result in an outflow from the enterprise of resources embodying economic benefits.

Equity: The residual interest in the assets of the enterprise after deducting all its liabilities.

Income: Increases in economic benefits during the accounting period in the form of inflows or enhancements of assets or decreases of liabilities that result in increases in equity, other than those relating to contributions from equity participants.

Expenses: Decreases in economic benefits during the accounting period in the form of outflows or depletions of assets or incurrences of liabilities that result in decreases in equity, other than those relating to distributions to equity participants.

Instructions

Identify at least three similarities and at least three differences between the FASB and IASB conceptual frameworks as revealed in the above Overview.

PROFESSIONAL SIMULATION

Accounting — Conceptual Framework

Directions | Situation | Explanation | Research | Resources

Directions

In this simulation, you will be asked various questions regarding the FASB's Conceptual Framework. Prepare responses to all parts.

Situation

You are engaged to review the accounting records of Jeremy Roenick Corporation prior to the closing of the revenue and expense accounts as of December 31, the end of the current fiscal year. The following information comes to your attention.

1. During the current year, Jeremy Roenick Corporation changed its policy in regard to expensing purchases of small tools. In the past, these purchases had been expensed because they amounted to less than 2% of net income. Now, the president has decided that capitalization and subsequent depreciation be followed. It is expected that purchases of small tools will not fluctuate greatly from year to year.

2. On July 15 of the current year, Jeremy Roenick Corporation purchased an undeveloped tract of land at a cost of $320,000. The company spent $80,000 in subdividing the land and getting it ready for sale. An appraisal of the property at the end of the year indicated that the land was now worth $500,000. Although none of the lots were sold, the company recognized revenue of $180,000, less related expenses of $80,000, for a net income on the project of $100,000.

3. For a number of years the company used the FIFO method for inventory valuation purposes. During the current year, the president noted that all the other companies in their industry had switched to the LIFO method. The company decided not to switch to LIFO because net income would decrease $830,000.

Explanation

For each of the situations, prepare a brief explanation, stating whether or not you agree with the decisions made by Jeremy Roenick Corporation. Support your answers with reference, whenever possible, to the generally accepted principles, assumptions, and constraints in the circumstances.

www.wiley.com/college/kieso

Remember to check the **Take Action! CD**
and the book's **companion Web site**
to find additional resources for this chapter.

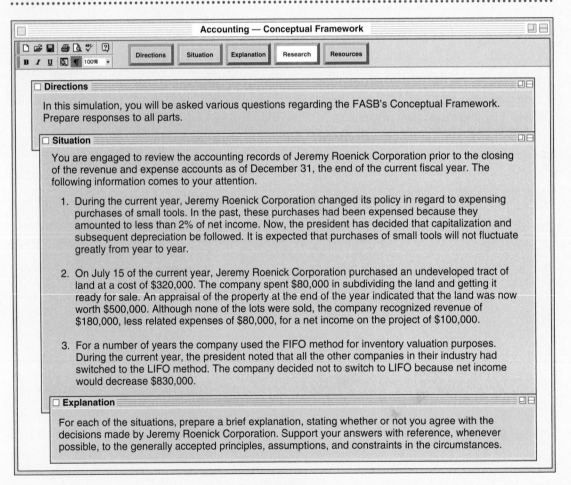

CHAPTER 3

The Accounting Information System

LEARNING OBJECTIVES

After studying this chapter, you should be able to:

1. **Understand basic accounting terminology.**
2. **Explain double-entry rules.**
3. **Identify steps in the accounting cycle.**
4. **Record transactions in journals, post to ledger accounts, and prepare a trial balance.**
5. **Explain the reasons for preparing adjusting entries.**
6. **Prepare closing entries.**
7. **Explain how inventory accounts are adjusted at year-end.**
8. **Prepare a 10-column work sheet.**

Needed: A Reliable Information System

Maintaining a set of accounting records is not optional. The Internal Revenue Service requires that businesses prepare and retain a set of records and documents that can be audited. The Foreign Corrupt Practices Act (federal legislation) requires public companies to ". . . make and keep books, records, and accounts, which, in reasonable detail, accurately and fairly reflect the transactions and dispositions of the assets. . . ." But beyond these two reasons, a company that does not keep an accurate record of its business transactions may lose revenue and is more likely to operate inefficiently.

Some companies are inefficient partly because of poor accounting systems. Consider, for example, the **Long Island Railroad**, once one of the nation's busiest commuter lines. The LIRR lost money because its cash position was unknown: Large amounts of money owed the railroad had not been billed; some payables were erroneously paid twice; and redemptions of bonds were not recorded. Also, consider **FFP Marketing**, which operates convenience stores in eleven states. It was forced to restate earnings in 1999 and 2000 when faulty bookkeeping was discovered for its credit card accounts and fuel payables.

Poor accounting and record keeping were also costly for the City of Cleveland, Ohio. A recent audit discovered over 313 examples of dysfunctional accounting, costing taxpayers over $1.3 million in 2001. Due to its poor accounting system, the Cleveland treasurer did not have a good record of the cash available for investment and missed out on returns that could have been earned if these funds were invested. And delayed recording of pension payments in the city ledgers created the false impression of $13 million in the city coffers, funds that actually were committed to the pensions.

Even the use of computers is no assurance of accuracy and efficiency. "The conversion to a new system called MasterNet fouled up data processing records to the extent that **Bank of America** was frequently unable to produce or deliver customer statements on a timely basis," said an executive at one of the country's largest banks.

Although these situations are not common in large organizations, they illustrate the point: Accounts and detailed records must be properly maintained; the cost of not doing so can be severe. At FFP Marketing, trading in its stock was suspended until it could sort out the errors and issue correct financial statements for 2001, and the City of Cleveland's municipal bond rating took a hit because of its poor accounting practices.

PREVIEW OF CHAPTER 3

As the opening story indicates, a reliable information system is a necessity for all companies. The purpose of this chapter is to explain and illustrate the features of an accounting information system. The content and organization of this chapter are as follows.

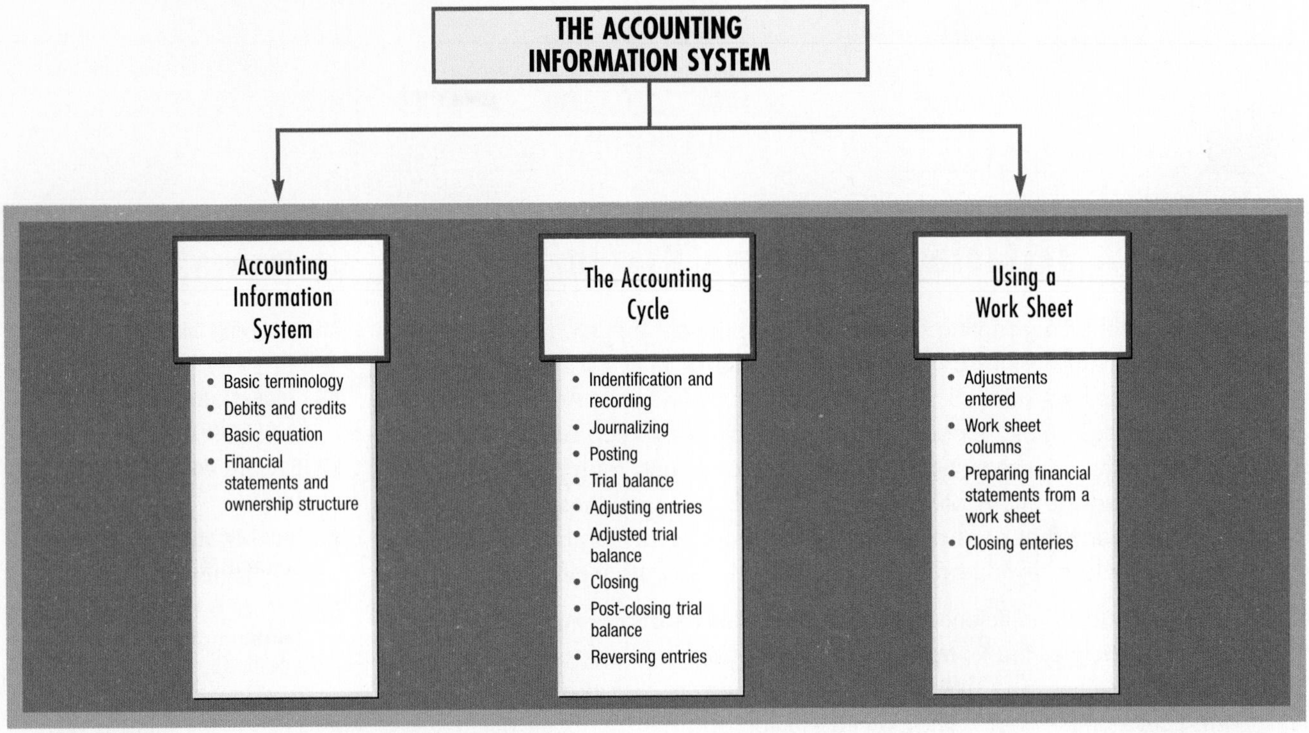

THE ACCOUNTING INFORMATION SYSTEM
Accounting Information System
• Basic terminology
• Debits and credits
• Basic equation
• Financial statements and ownership structure
The Accounting Cycle
• Indentification and recording
• Journalizing
• Posting
• Trial balance
• Adjusting entries
• Adjusted trial balance
• Closing
• Post-closing trial balance
• Reversing entries
Using a Work Sheet
• Adjustments entered
• Work sheet columns
• Preparing financial statements from a work sheet
• Closing enteries

ACCOUNTING INFORMATION SYSTEM

The system of collecting and processing transaction data and disseminating financial information to interested parties is known as the **accounting information system**. Accounting information systems vary widely from one business to another. Factors that shape these systems are the **nature of the business** and the transactions in which it engages, the **size of the firm**, the **volume of data** to be handled, and the **informational demands** that management and others place on the system. A good accounting information system helps management answer such questions as:

How much and what kind of debt is outstanding?
Were our sales higher this period than last?
What assets do we have?
What were our cash inflows and outflows?
Did we make a profit last period?
Are any of our product lines or divisions operating at a loss?
Can we safely increase our dividends to stockholders?
Is our rate of return on net assets increasing?

Many other questions can be answered when there is an efficient accounting system to provide the data. A well-devised accounting information system is beneficial for every business enterprise.

Basic Terminology

Financial accounting rests on a set of concepts (discussed in Chapters 1 and 2) for identifying, recording, classifying, and interpreting transactions and other events relating to enterprises. It is important to understand the **basic terminology employed in collecting accounting data**.

OBJECTIVE 1
Understand basic accounting terminology.

BASIC TERMINOLOGY

EVENT. A happening of consequence. An event generally is the source or cause of changes in assets, liabilities, and equity. Events may be external or internal.

TRANSACTION. An **external event** involving a transfer or exchange between two or more entities.

ACCOUNT. A systematic arrangement that shows the effect of transactions and other events on a specific asset or equity. A separate account is kept for each asset, liability, revenue, expense, and for capital (owners' equity).

REAL AND NOMINAL ACCOUNTS. Real (permanent) **accounts** are asset, liability, and equity accounts; they appear on the balance sheet. **Nominal** (temporary) **accounts** are revenue, expense, and dividend accounts; except for dividends, they appear on the income statement. Nominal accounts are periodically closed; real accounts are not.

LEDGER. The book (or computer printouts) containing the accounts. Each account usually has a separate page. A **general ledger** is a collection of all the asset, liability, owners' equity, revenue, and expense accounts. A **subsidiary ledger** contains the details related to a given general ledger account.

JOURNAL. The book of original entry where transactions and selected other events are initially recorded. Various amounts are transferred to the ledger from the book of original entry, the journal.

POSTING. The process of transferring the essential facts and figures from the book of original entry to the ledger accounts.

TRIAL BALANCE. A list of all open accounts in the ledger and their balances. A trial balance taken immediately after all adjustments have been posted is called an **adjusted trial balance.** A trial balance taken immediately after closing entries have been posted is designated as a **post-closing** or **after-closing trial balance**. A trial balance may be prepared at any time.

ADJUSTING ENTRIES. Entries made at the end of an accounting period to bring all accounts up to date on an accrual accounting basis so that correct financial statements can be prepared.

FINANCIAL STATEMENTS. Statements that reflect the collection, tabulation, and final summarization of the accounting data. Four statements are involved: (1) The **balance sheet** shows the financial condition of the enterprise at the end of a period. (2) The **income statement** measures the results of operations during the period. (3) The **statement of cash flows** reports the cash provided and used by operating, investing, and financing activities during the period. (4) The **statement of retained earnings** reconciles the balance of the retained earnings account from the beginning to the end of the period.

CLOSING ENTRIES. The formal process by which all nominal accounts are reduced to zero and the net income or net loss is determined and transferred to an owners' equity account; also known as "closing the ledger," "closing the books," or merely "closing."

Debits and Credits

OBJECTIVE 2
Explain double-entry rules.

The terms **debit** and **credit** mean left and right, respectively. They are commonly abbreviated as Dr. for debit and Cr. for credit. These terms do not mean increase or decrease. The terms debit and credit are used repeatedly in the recording process to describe where entries are made. For example, the act of entering an amount on the left side of an account is called **debiting** the account, and making an entry on the right side is **crediting** the account. When the totals of the two sides are compared, an account will have a **debit balance** if the total of the debit amounts exceeds the credits. An account will have a **credit balance** if the credit amounts exceed the debits.

The procedure of having debits on the left and credits on the right is an accounting custom or rule. We could function just as well if debits and credits were reversed. However, the custom of having debits on the left side of an account and credits on the right side (like the custom of driving on the right-hand side of the road) has been adopted in the United States. **This rule applies to all accounts.**

The equality of debits and credits provides the basis for the double-entry system of recording transactions (sometimes referred to as double-entry bookkeeping). Under the universally used **double-entry accounting system**, the dual (two-sided) effect of each transaction is recorded in appropriate accounts. This system provides a logical method for recording transactions. It also offers a means of proving the accuracy of the recorded amounts. If every transaction is recorded with equal debits and credits, then the sum of all the debits to the accounts must equal the sum of all the credits.

All asset and expense accounts are increased on the left (or debit side) and decreased on the right (or credit side). Conversely, all liability and revenue accounts are increased on the right (or credit side) and decreased on the left (or debit side). Stockholders' equity accounts, such as Common Stock and Retained Earnings, are increased on the credit side, whereas Dividends is increased on the debit side. The basic guidelines for an accounting system are presented in Illustration 3-1.

ILLUSTRATION 3-1
Double-entry (Debit and Credit) Accounting System

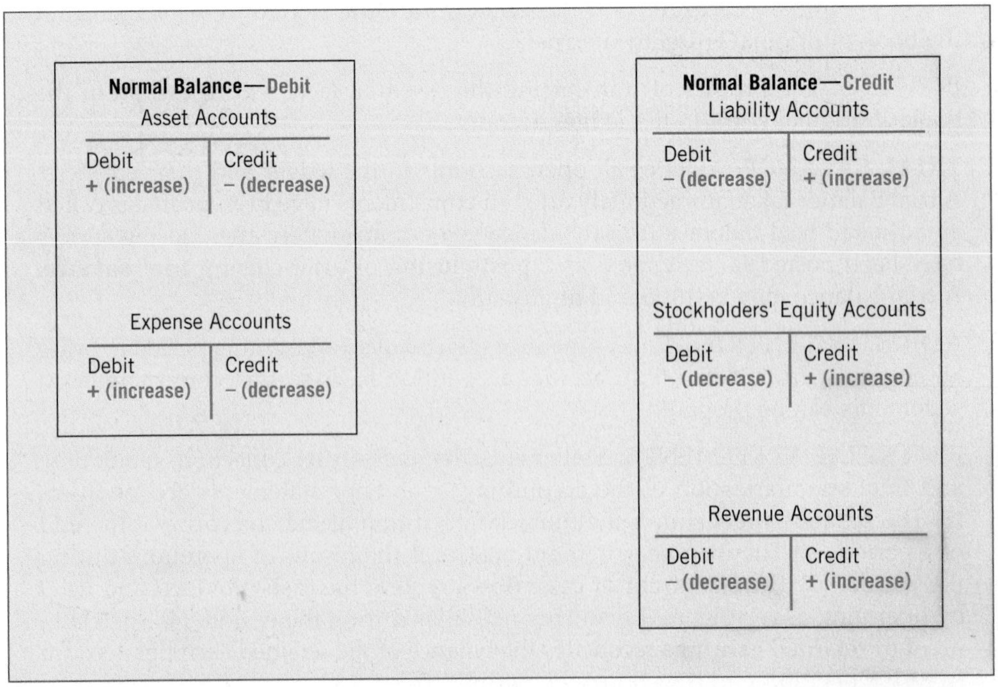

Basic Equation

In a double-entry system, for every debit there must be a credit, and vice versa. This leads us, then, to the basic equation in accounting (Illustration 3-2).

ILLUSTRATION 3-2
The Basic Accounting Equation

Assets	=	Liabilities	+	Stockholders' Equity

Illustration 3-3 expands this equation to show the accounts that comprise stockholders' equity. In addition, the debit/credit rules and effects on each type of account are illustrated. Study this diagram carefully. It will help you understand the fundamentals of the double-entry system. Like the basic equation, the expanded basic equation must be in balance (total debits equal total credits).

ILLUSTRATION 3-3
Expanded Basic Equation and Debit/Credit Rules and Effects

Basic Equation	Assets	=	Liabilities	+	Stockholders' Equity									
Expanded Basic Equation	Assets	=	Liabilities	+	Common Stock	+	Retained Earnings	−	Dividends	+	Revenues	−	Expenses	
Debit/Credit Rules	Dr. + | Cr. −		Dr. − | Cr. +		Dr. − | Cr. +		Dr. − | Cr. +		Dr. + | Cr. −		Dr. − | Cr. +		Dr. + | Cr. −	

Every time a transaction occurs, the elements of the equation change, but the basic equality remains. To illustrate, here are eight different transactions for Perez Inc.

1. Owners invest $40,000 in exchange for common stock.

Assets + 40,000	=	Liabilities	+	Stockholders' Equity + 40,000

2. Disburse $600 cash for secretarial wages.

Assets − 600	=	Liabilities	+	Stockholders' Equity − 600 (expense)

3. Purchase office equipment priced at $5,200, giving a 10 percent promissory note in exchange.

Assets + 5,200	=	Liabilities +5,200	+	Stockholders' Equity

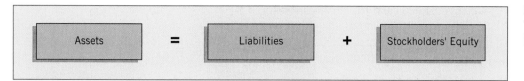

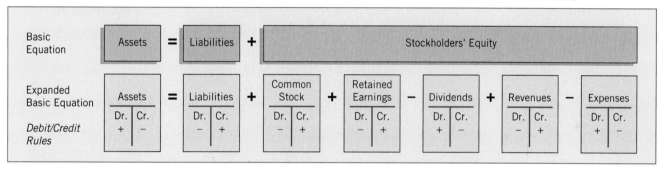

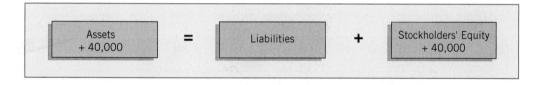

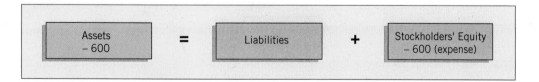

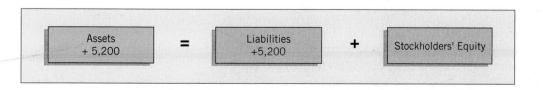

4 Receive $4,000 cash for services rendered.

Assets + 4,000	=	Liabilities	+	Stockholders' Equity + 4,000 (revenue)

5 Pay off a short-term liability of $7,000.

Assets – 7,000	=	Liabilities – 7,000	+	Stockholders' Equity

6 Declare a cash dividend of $5,000.

Assets	=	Liabilities + 5,000	+	Stockholders' Equity – 5,000

7 Convert a long-term liability of $80,000 into common stock.

Assets	=	Liabilities – 80,000	+	Stockholders' Equity + 80,000

8 Pay cash of $16,000 for a delivery van.

Assets –16,000 +16,000	=	Liabilities	+	Stockholders' Equity

Financial Statements and Ownership Structure

Common stock and retained earnings are reported in the stockholders' equity section of the balance sheet. Dividends are reported on the statement of retained earnings. Revenues and expenses are reported on the income statement. Dividends, revenues, and expenses are eventually transferred to retained earnings at the end of the period. As a result, a change in any one of these three items affects stockholders' equity. The relationships related to stockholders' equity are shown in Illustration 3-4.

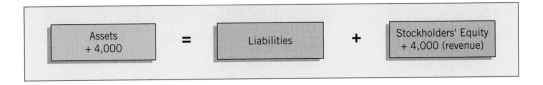

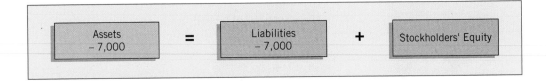

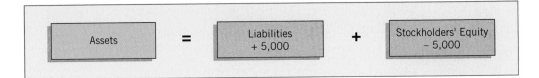

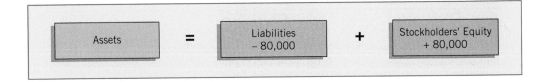

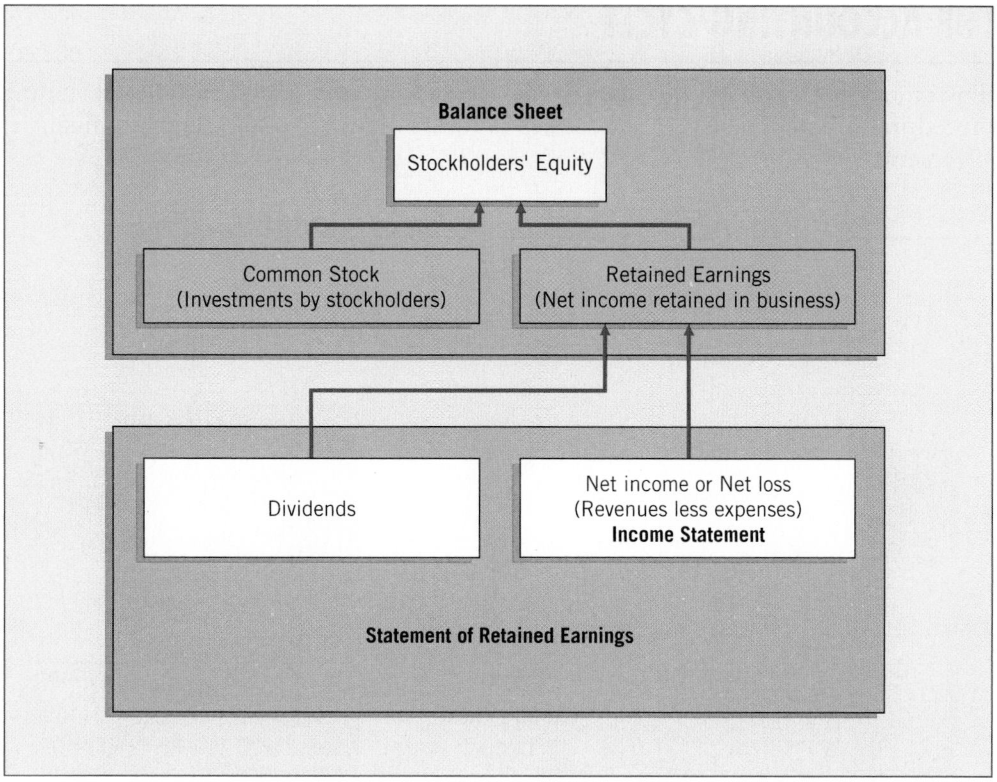

ILLUSTRATION 3-4
Financial Statements and Ownership Structure

The type of ownership structure employed by a business enterprise dictates the types of accounts that are part of or affect the equity section. In a corporation, **Common Stock**, **Additional Paid-in Capital**, **Dividends**, and **Retained Earnings** are accounts commonly used. In a proprietorship or partnership, a Capital account is used to indicate the owner's or owners' investment in the company. A Drawing account is used to indicate withdrawals by the owner(s).

Illustration 3-5 summarizes and relates the transactions affecting owners' equity to the nominal (temporary) and real (permanent) classifications and to the types of business ownership.

ILLUSTRATION 3-5
Effects of Transactions on Owners' Equity Accounts

		Ownership Structure			
		Proprietorships and Partnerships		Corporations	
Transactions Affecting Owners' Equity	Impact on Owners' Equity	Nominal (Temporary) Accounts	Real (Permanent) Accounts	Nominal (Temporary) Accounts	Real (Permanent) Accounts
Investment by owner(s)	Increase		Capital		Common Stock and related accounts
Revenues earned	Increase	Revenue	Capital	Revenue	Retained Earnings
Expenses incurred	Decrease	Expense	Capital	Expense	Retained Earnings
Withdrawal by owner(s)	Decrease	Drawing	Capital	Dividends	Retained Earnings

THE ACCOUNTING CYCLE

Illustration 3-6 flowcharts the steps in the **accounting cycle**. These are the accounting procedures normally used by enterprises to record transactions and prepare financial statements.

ILLUSTRATION 3-6
The Accounting Cycle

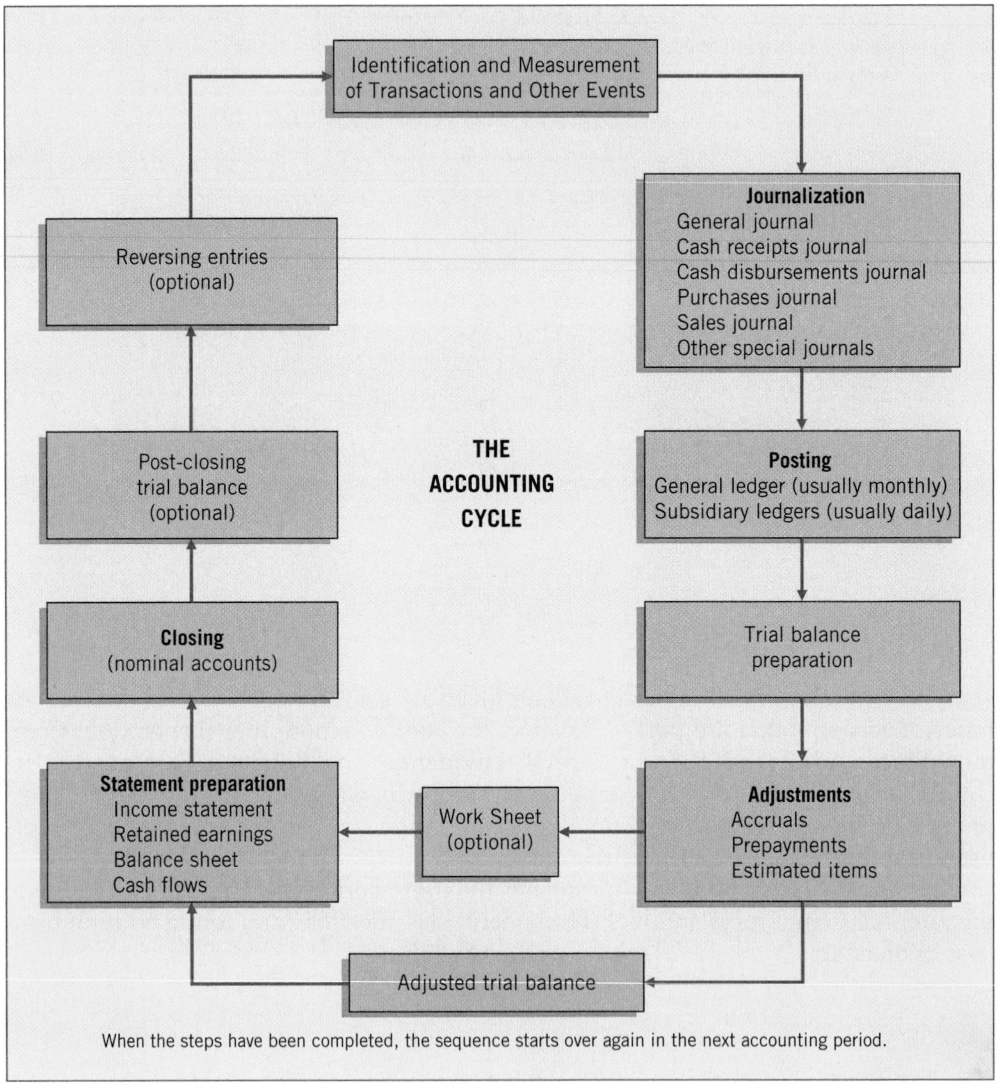

OBJECTIVE 3
Identify steps in the accounting cycle.

Accounting Cycle Tutorial

Identifying and Recording Transactions and Other Events

The first step in the accounting cycle is analysis of transactions and selected other events. The problem is to determine **what to record**. No simple rules exist that state whether an event should be recorded. Most agree that changes in personnel, changes in managerial policies, and the value of human resources, though important, should not be recorded in the accounts. On the other hand, when the company makes a cash sale or purchase—no matter how small—it should be recorded.

The phrase "transactions and other events and circumstances that affect a business enterprise" is used to describe the sources or causes of changes in an entity's assets, liabilities, and equity.[1] **Events** are of two types: (1) **External events** involve interaction

UNDERLYING CONCEPTS

Assets are probable economic benefits controlled by a particular entity as a result of a past transaction or event. Do human resources of a company meet this definition?

[1]"Elements of Financial Statements of Business Enterprises," *Statement of Financial Accounting Concepts No. 6* (Stamford, Conn.: FASB, 1985), pp. 259–60.

between an entity and its environment, such as a transaction with another entity, a change in the price of a good or service that an entity buys or sells, a flood or earthquake, or an improvement in technology by a competitor. (2) **Internal events** occur within an entity, such as using buildings and machinery in operations or transferring or consuming raw materials in production processes.

Many events have both external and internal elements. For example, acquiring the services of employees or others involves exchange transactions, which are external events. Using those services (labor), often simultaneously with their acquisition, is part of production, which is internal. Events may be initiated and controlled by an entity, such as the purchase of merchandise or the use of a machine. Or they may be beyond its control, such as an interest rate change, a theft or vandalism, or the imposition of taxes.

Transactions, as particular kinds of external events, may be an exchange in which each entity both receives and sacrifices value, such as purchases and sales of goods or services. Or transactions may be transfers in one direction in which an entity incurs a liability or transfers an asset to another entity without directly receiving (or giving) value in exchange. Examples include investments by owners, distributions to owners, payment of taxes, gifts, charitable contributions, casualty losses, and thefts.

In short, as many events as possible that affect the financial position of the enterprise are recorded. Some events are omitted because of tradition and others because the problems of measuring them are too complex. The accounting profession in recent years has shown signs of breaking with age-old traditions and is more receptive than ever to accepting the challenge of measuring and reporting events and phenomena previously viewed as too complex and immeasurable.

SHOULD I BOOK THAT OR NOT?

WHAT DO THE NUMBERS MEAN?

Deciding what to recognize in the accounts is governed by the concepts presented in Chapter 2. **An item should be recognized in the financial statements if it is an element, is measurable, and is relevant and reliable.** Consider human resources. R.G. Barry & Co. at one time reported as supplemental data total assets of $14,055,926, including $986,094 for "Net investments in human resources." AT&T and ExxonMobil Company have also experimented with human resource accounting. Should we value employees for balance sheet and income statement purposes? Certainly skilled employees are an important asset (highly relevant), but the problems of **determining their value and measuring it reliably have not yet been solved**. Consequently, human resources are not recorded. Perhaps when measurement techniques become more sophisticated and accepted, such information will be presented, if only in supplemental form.

Journalizing

Differing effects on the basic business elements (assets, liabilities, and equities) are categorized and collected in **accounts**. The **general ledger** is a collection of all the asset, liability, stockholders' equity, revenue, and expense accounts. A **T-account** (as shown in Illustration 3-8, on page 71) is a convenient method of illustrating the effect of transactions on particular asset, liability, equity, revenue, and expense items.

In practice, transactions and selected other events are not recorded originally in the ledger because a transaction affects two or more accounts, each of which is on a different page in the ledger. To circumvent this deficiency and to have a complete record of each transaction or other event in one place, a **journal** (also called "the book of original entry") is employed. The simplest journal form is a chronological listing of transactions and other events expressed in terms of debits and credits to particular accounts. This is called a **general journal**. It is illustrated on the next page (Illustration 3-7) for the following transactions.

OBJECTIVE 4
Record transactions in journals, post to ledger accounts, and prepare a trial balance.

Nov. 1 Buys a new delivery truck on account from Auto Sales Co., $22,400.
3 Receives an invoice from the *Evening Graphic* for advertising, $280.
4 Returns merchandise to Yankee Supply for credit, $175.
16 Receives a $95 debit memo from Confederate Co., indicating that freight on a purchase from Confederate Co. was prepaid but is our obligation.

Each **general journal entry** consists of four parts: (1) the accounts and amounts to be debited (Dr.), (2) the accounts and amounts to be credited (Cr.), (3) a date, and (4) an explanation. Debits are entered first, followed by the credits, which are slightly indented. The explanation is begun below the name of the last account to be credited and may take one or more lines. The "Ref." column is completed at the time the accounts are posted.

Expanded Discussion of Special Journals

In some cases, businesses use **special journals** in addition to the general journal. Special journals summarize transactions possessing a common characteristic (e.g., cash receipts, sales, purchases, cash payments), thereby reducing the time necessary to accomplish the various bookkeeping tasks.

Posting

The items entered in a general journal must be transferred to the general ledger. This procedure, **posting**, is part of the summarizing and classifying process.

For example, the November 1 entry in the general journal in Illustration 3-7 shows a debit to Delivery Equipment of $22,400 and a credit to Accounts Payable of $22,400. The amount in the debit column is posted from the journal to the debit side of the ledger account (Delivery Equipment). The amount in the credit column is posted from the journal to the credit side of the ledger account (Accounts Payable).

ILLUSTRATION 3-7
General Journal with Sample Entries

GENERAL JOURNAL — PAGE 12

Date 2005	Account Title and Explanation	Ref.	Amount Debit	Amount Credit
Nov. 1	Delivery Equipment	8	22,400	
	Accounts Payable	34		22,400
	(Purchased delivery truck on account from Auto Sales Co.)			
3	Advertising Expenses	65	280	
	Accounts Payable	34		280
	(Received invoice for advertising from *Evening Graphic*)			
4	Accounts Payable	34	175	
	Purchase Returns	53		175
	(Returned merchandise for credit to Yankee Supply)			
16	Transportation-In	55	95	
	Accounts Payable	34		95
	(Received debit memo for freight on merchandise purchased from Confederate Co.)			

The numbers in the "Ref." column of the general journal refer to the accounts in the ledger to which the respective items are posted. For example, the "34" placed in the column to the right of "Accounts Payable" indicates that this $22,400 item was posted to Account No. 34 in the ledger.

The posting of the general journal is completed when all of the posting reference numbers have been recorded opposite the account titles in the journal. Thus the number in the posting reference column serves two purposes: (1) It indicates the ledger account number of the account involved. And (2) it indicates that the posting has been completed for the particular item. Each business enterprise selects its own numbering system for its ledger accounts. One practice is to begin numbering with asset accounts and to follow with liabilities, owners' equity, revenue, and expense accounts, in that order.

The various ledger accounts in Illustration 3-8 show the accounts after the posting process is completed. The source of the data transferred to the ledger account is indicated by the reference GJ 12 (General Journal, page 12).

ILLUSTRATION 3-8
Ledger Accounts, in T-Account Format

Delivery Equipment — No. 8

Nov. 1	GJ 12	22,400			

Accounts Payable — No. 34

Nov. 4	GJ 12	175	Nov. 1	GJ 12	22,400
			3	GJ 12	280
			16	GJ 12	95

Purchase Returns — No. 53

			Nov. 4	GJ 12	175

Transportation-In — No. 55

Nov. 16	GJ 12	95			

Advertising Expense — No. 65

Nov. 3	GJ 12	280			

Trial Balance

A **trial balance** is a list of accounts and their balances at a given time. Customarily, a trial balance is prepared at the end of an accounting period. The accounts are listed in the order in which they appear in the ledger, with debit balances listed in the left column and credit balances in the right column. The totals of the two columns must be in agreement.

The primary purpose of a trial balance is to prove the mathematical equality of debits and credits after posting. Under the double-entry system this equality will occur when the sum of the debit account balances equals the sum of the credit account balances. **A trial balance also uncovers errors in journalizing and posting. In addition, it is useful in the preparation of financial statements.** The procedures for preparing a trial balance consist of:

1. Listing the account titles and their balances.
2. Totaling the debit and credit columns.
3. Proving the equality of the two columns.

The trial balance prepared from the ledger of Pioneer Advertising Agency Inc. is presented in Illustration 3-9 (page 72). Note that the total debits $287,000 equal the total credits $287,000. Account numbers to the left of the account titles in the trial balance are also often shown.

A trial balance does not prove that all transactions have been recorded or that the ledger is correct. Numerous errors may exist even though the trial balance columns agree. For example, the trial balance may balance even when (1) a transaction is not

ILLUSTRATION 3-9
Trial Balance
(Unadjusted)

PIONEER ADVERTISING AGENCY INC.
TRIAL BALANCE
OCTOBER 31, 2005

	Debit	Credit
Cash	$ 80,000	
Accounts Receivable	72,000	
Advertising Supplies	25,000	
Prepaid Insurance	6,000	
Office Equipment	50,000	
Notes Payable		$ 50,000
Accounts Payable		25,000
Unearned Service Revenue		12,000
Common Stock		100,000
Dividends	5,000	
Service Revenue		100,000
Salaries Expense	40,000	
Rent Expense	9,000	
	$287,000	$287,000

journalized, (2) a correct journal entry is not posted, (3) a journal entry is posted twice, (4) incorrect accounts are used in journalizing or posting, or (5) offsetting errors are made in recording the amount of a transaction. In other words, as long as equal debits and credits are posted, even to the wrong account or in the wrong amount, the total debits will equal the total credits.

Adjusting Entries

OBJECTIVE 5
Explain the reasons for preparing adjusting entries.

In order for revenues to be recorded in the period in which they are earned, and for expenses to be recognized in the period in which they are incurred, **adjusting entries** are made at the end of the accounting period. In short, **adjustments are needed to ensure that the revenue recognition and matching principles are followed.**

The use of adjusting entries makes it possible to report on the balance sheet the appropriate assets, liabilities, and owners' equity at the statement date and to report on the income statement the proper net income (or loss) for the period. However, the trial balance—the first pulling together of the transaction data—may not contain up-to-date and complete data. This is true for the following reasons.

1. Some events are not journalized daily because it is not expedient. Examples are the consumption of supplies and the earning of wages by employees.
2. Some costs are not journalized during the accounting period because these costs expire with the passage of time rather than as a result of recurring daily transactions. Examples of such costs are building and equipment deterioration and rent and insurance.
3. Some items may be unrecorded. An example is a utility service bill that will not be received until the next accounting period.

Adjusting entries are required every time financial statements are prepared. An essential starting point is an analysis of each account in the trial balance to determine whether it is complete and up-to-date for financial statement purposes. The analysis requires a thorough understanding of the company's operations and the interrelationship of accounts. The preparation of adjusting entries is often an involved process that requires the services of a skilled professional. In accumulating the adjustment data, the company may need to make inventory counts of supplies and repair parts. Also it may be desirable to prepare supporting schedules of insurance policies, rental agreements, and other contractual commitments. Adjustments are often prepared after the balance sheet date. However, the entries are dated as of the balance sheet date.

Types of Adjusting Entries

Adjusting entries can be classified as either prepayments or accruals. Each of these classes has two subcategories as shown below.

Prepayments	Accruals
1. **Prepaid Expenses.** Expenses paid in cash and recorded as assets before they are used or consumed.	3. **Accrued Revenues.** Revenues earned but not yet received in cash or recorded.
2. **Unearned Revenues.** Revenues received in cash and recorded as liabilities before they are earned.	4. **Accrued Expenses.** Expenses incurred but not yet paid in cash or recorded.

Specific examples and explanations of each type of adjustment are given in subsequent sections. Each example is based on the October 31 trial balance of Pioneer Advertising Agency Inc. (Illustration 3-9). We assume that Pioneer Advertising uses an accounting period of one month. Thus, monthly adjusting entries will be made. The entries will be dated October 31.

Adjusting Entries for Prepayments

As indicated earlier, prepayments are either prepaid expenses or unearned revenues. Adjusting entries for prepayments are required at the statement date to record the portion of the prepayment that represents the **expense incurred or the revenue earned** in the current accounting period. Assuming an adjustment is needed for both types of prepayments, the asset and liability are overstated and the related expense and revenue are understated. For example, in the trial balance, the balance in the asset Supplies shows only supplies purchased. This balance is overstated; the related expense account, Supplies Expense, is understated because the cost of supplies used has not been recognized. Thus the adjusting entry for prepayments will decrease a balance sheet account and increase an income statement account. The effects of adjusting entries for prepayments are graphically depicted in Illustration 3-10 (page 74).

Prepaid Expenses. Expenses paid in cash and recorded as assets before they are used or consumed are identified as **prepaid expenses**. When a cost is incurred, an asset account is debited to show the service or benefit that will be received in the future. Prepayments often occur in regard to insurance, supplies, advertising, and rent. In addition, prepayments are made when buildings and equipment are purchased.

Prepaid expenses expire either with the passage of time (e.g., rent and insurance) or through use and consumption (e.g., supplies). The expiration of these costs does not require daily recurring entries, which would be unnecessary and impractical. Accordingly, it is customary to postpone the recognition of such cost expirations until financial statements are prepared. At each statement date, adjusting entries are made to record the expenses that apply to the current accounting period and to show the unexpired costs in the asset accounts.

Prior to adjustment, assets are overstated and expenses are understated. **Thus, the prepaid expense adjusting entry results in a debit to an expense account and a credit to an asset account.**

ILLUSTRATION 3-10
Adjusting Entries for Prepayments

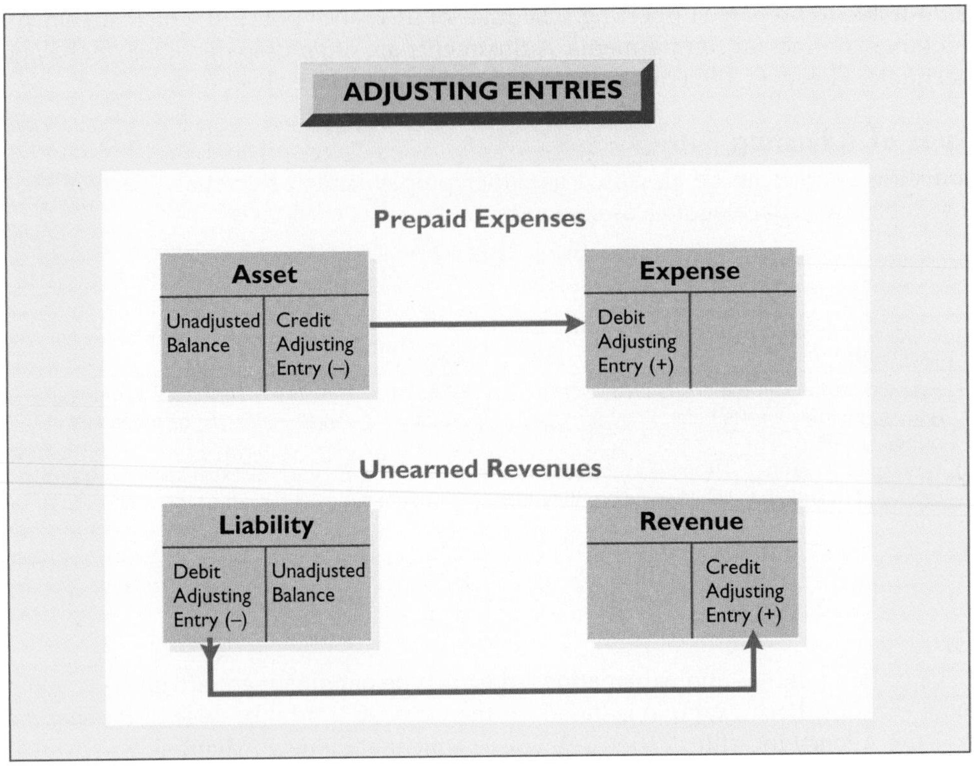

Supplies. Several different types of supplies are used in a business enterprise. For example, a CPA firm will have **office supplies** such as stationery, envelopes, and accounting paper. An advertising firm will have **advertising supplies** such as graph paper, video film, and poster paper. Supplies are generally debited to an asset account when they are acquired. During the course of operations, supplies are depleted or entirely consumed. However, recognition of supplies used is deferred until the adjustment process, when a physical inventory (count) of supplies is taken. The difference between the balance in the Supplies (asset) account and the cost of supplies on hand represents the supplies used (expense) for the period.

Pioneer Advertising Agency (see Illustration 3-9) purchased advertising supplies costing $25,000 on October 5. The debit was made to the asset Advertising Supplies. This account shows a balance of $25,000 in the October 31 trial balance. An inventory count at the close of business on October 31 reveals that $10,000 of supplies are still on hand. Thus, the cost of supplies used is $15,000 ($25,000 – $10,000), and the following adjusting entry is made.

A	= L +	SE
−15,000		−15,000

Cash Flows
no effect

Oct. 31		
Advertising Supplies Expense	15,000	
Advertising Supplies		15,000
(To record supplies used)		

After the adjusting entry is posted, the two supplies accounts in T-account form show the following.

ILLUSTRATION 3-11
Supplies Accounts after Adjustment

Advertising Supplies				Advertising Supplies Expense		
10/ 5	25,000	10/31	Adj. 15,000	10/31	Adj. 15,000	
10/31	Bal. 10,000					

The asset account Advertising Supplies now shows a balance of $10,000, which is equal to the cost of supplies on hand at the statement date. In addition, Advertising Supplies Expense shows a balance of $15,000, which equals the cost of supplies used in October. **If the adjusting entry is not made, October expenses will be understated and net income overstated by $15,000. Moreover, both assets and owners' equity will be overstated by $15,000 on the October 31 balance sheet.**

Insurance

Oct. 4

Insurance purchased; record asset

Insurance Policy			
Oct $500	Nov $500	Dec $500	Jan $500
Feb $500	March $500	April $500	May $500
June $500	July $500	Aug $500	Sept $500
I YEAR $6,000			

Oct. 31
Insurance expired; record insurance expense

Insurance. Most companies have fire and theft insurance on merchandise and equipment, personal liability insurance for accidents suffered by customers, and automobile insurance on company cars and trucks. The cost of insurance protection is determined by the payment of insurance premiums. The term and coverage are specified in the insurance policy. The minimum term is usually one year, but three- to five-year terms are available and offer lower annual premiums. Insurance premiums normally are charged to the asset account Prepaid Insurance when paid. At the financial statement date it is necessary to debit Insurance Expense and credit Prepaid Insurance for the cost that has expired during the period.

On October 4, Pioneer Advertising Agency Inc. paid $6,000 for a one-year fire insurance policy. The effective date of coverage was October 1. The premium was charged to Prepaid Insurance when it was paid, and this account shows a balance of $6,000 in the October 31 trial balance. An analysis of the policy reveals that $500 ($6,000 ÷ 12) of insurance expires each month. Thus, the following adjusting entry is made.

Oct. 31		
Insurance Expense	500	
Prepaid Insurance		500
(To record insurance expired)		

A	=	L	+	SE
−500				−500

Cash Flows
no effect

After the adjusting entry is posted, the accounts show:

Prepaid Insurance			
10/ 4	6,000	10/31	Adj. 500
10/31	Bal. 5,500		

Insurance Expense			
10/31	Adj. 500		

ILLUSTRATION 3-12
Insurance Accounts after Adjustment

The asset Prepaid Insurance shows a balance of $5,500, which represents the unexpired cost applicable to the remaining 11 months of coverage. At the same time, the balance in Insurance Expense is equal to the insurance cost that has expired in October. **If this adjustment is not made, October expenses will be understated by $500 and net income overstated by $500. Moreover, both assets and owners' equity also will be overstated by $500 on the October 31 balance sheet.**

Depreciation. A business enterprise typically owns a variety of productive facilities such as buildings, equipment, and motor vehicles. These assets provide a service for a number of years. The term of service is commonly referred to as the **useful life** of the asset. Because an asset such as a building is expected to provide service for many years, it is recorded as an asset, rather than an expense, in the year it is acquired. Such assets are recorded at cost, as required by the cost principle.

According to the matching principle, a portion of the cost of a long-lived asset should be reported as an expense during each period of the asset's useful life. **Depreciation** is the process of allocating the cost of an asset to expense over its useful life in a rational and systematic manner.

Depreciation

Oct. 1

Office equipment purchased; record asset ($50,000)

Office Equipment			
Oct $400	Nov $400	Dec $400	Jan $400
Feb $400	March $400	April $400	May $400
June $400	July $400	Aug $400	Sept $400
Depreciation = $4,800/year			

Oct. 31
Depreciation recognized; record depreciation expense

Need for depreciation adjustment. From an accounting standpoint, the acquisition of productive facilities is viewed essentially as a long-term prepayment for services. The need for making periodic adjusting entries for depreciation is, therefore, the same as described before for other prepaid expenses—that is, to recognize the cost that has expired (expense) during the period and to report the unexpired cost (asset) at the end of the period.

In determining the useful life of a productive facility, the primary causes of depreciation are actual use, deterioration due to the elements, and obsolescence. At the time an asset is acquired, the effects of these factors cannot be known with certainty, so they must be estimated. Thus, you should recognize that depreciation is an **estimate** rather than a factual measurement of the cost that has expired. A common procedure in computing depreciation expense is to divide the cost of the asset by its useful life. For example, if cost is $10,000 and useful life is expected to be 10 years, annual depreciation is $1,000.

For Pioneer Advertising, depreciation on the office equipment is estimated to be $4,800 a year (cost $50,000 less salvage value $2,000 divided by useful life of 10 years), or $400 per month. Accordingly, depreciation for October is recognized by the following adjusting entry.

A	=	L	+	SE
−400				−400

Cash Flows
no effect

Oct. 31		
Depreciation Expense	400	
Accumulated Depreciation—Office Equipment		400
(To record monthly depreciation)		

After the adjusting entry is posted, the accounts show the following.

ILLUSTRATION 3-13
Accounts after Adjustment for Depreciation

Office Equipment

Debit		Credit
10/1	50,000	

Accumulated Depreciation—Office Equipment

Debit	Credit		
	10/31	Adj.	400

Depreciation Expense

Debit			Credit
10/31	Adj.	400	

The balance in the accumulated depreciation account will increase $400 each month. Therefore, after journalizing and posting the adjusting entry at November 30, the balance will be $800.

Statement presentation. Accumulated Depreciation—Office Equipment is a contra asset account. A **contra asset account** is an account that is offset against an asset account on the balance sheet. This means that the accumulated depreciation account is offset against Office Equipment on the balance sheet and that its normal balance is a credit. This account is used instead of crediting Office Equipment in order to permit disclosure of **both the original cost** of the equipment **and the total cost that has expired to date**. In the balance sheet, Accumulated Depreciation—Office Equipment is deducted from the related asset account as follows.

ILLUSTRATION 3-14
Balance Sheet Presentation of Accumulated Depreciation

Office equipment	$50,000	
Less: Accumulated depreciation—office equipment	400	$49,600

The difference between the cost of any depreciable asset and its related accumulated depreciation is referred to as the **book value** of that asset. In Illustration 3-14, the book value of the equipment at the balance sheet date is $49,600. It is important to realize that the book value and the market value of the asset are generally two different amounts. The reason the two are different is that depreciation is not a matter of valuation but rather a means of cost allocation.

Note also that depreciation expense identifies that portion of the asset's cost that has expired in October. As in the case of other prepaid adjustments, the omission of this adjusting entry would cause total assets, total owners' equity, and net income to be overstated and depreciation expense to be understated.

If additional equipment is involved, such as delivery or store equipment, or if the company has buildings, depreciation expense is recorded on each of these items. Related accumulated depreciation accounts also are established. These accumulated depreciation accounts would be described in the ledger as follows: Accumulated Depreciation—Delivery Equipment; Accumulated Depreciation—Store Equipment; and Accumulated Depreciation—Buildings.

Unearned Revenues. Revenues received in cash and recorded as liabilities before they are earned are called **unearned revenues**. Such items as rent, magazine subscriptions, and customer deposits for further service may result in unearned revenues. Airlines such as **United**, **American**, and **Delta** treat receipts from the sale of tickets as unearned revenue until the flight service is provided. Similarly, tuition received prior to the start of a semester is considered to be unearned revenue. Unearned revenues are the opposite of prepaid expenses. Indeed, unearned revenue on the books of one company is likely to be a prepayment on the books of the company that has made the advance payment. For example, if identical accounting periods are assumed, a landlord will have unearned rent revenue when a tenant has prepaid rent.

Unearned Revenues

Oct. 2

Thank you in advance for your work
I will finish by Dec. 31
$12,000

Cash is received in advance; liability is recorded

Oct. 31

Service is provided; revenue is recorded

When the payment is received for services to be provided in a future accounting period, an unearned revenue (a liability) account should be credited to recognize the obligation that exists. Unearned revenues are subsequently earned through rendering service to a customer. During the accounting period it may not be practical to make daily recurring entries as the revenue is earned. In such cases, the recognition of earned revenue is delayed until the adjustment process. Then an adjusting entry is made to record the revenue that has been earned and to show the liability that remains. In the typical case, liabilities are overstated and revenues are understated prior to adjustment. Thus, **the adjusting entry for unearned revenues results in a debit (decrease) to a liability account and a credit (increase) to a revenue account**.

Pioneer Advertising Agency received $12,000 on October 2 from R. Knox for advertising services expected to be completed by December 31. The payment was credited to Unearned Service Revenue, and this account shows a balance of $12,000 in the October 31 trial balance. When analysis reveals that $4,000 of these services have been earned in October, the following adjusting entry is made.

Oct. 31		
Unearned Service Revenue	4,000	
Service Revenue		4,000
(To record revenue for services provided)		

A	=	L	+	SE
		−4,000		+4,000

Cash Flows
no effect

After the adjusting entry is posted, the accounts show the following.

ILLUSTRATION 3-15
Service Revenue Accounts after Prepayments Adjustment

Unearned Service Revenue						Service Revenue					
10/31	Adj.	4,000	10/ 2		12,000				10/31	Bal.	100,000
			10/31	Bal.	8,000				31	Adj.	4,000

The liability Unearned Service Revenue now shows a balance of $8,000, which represents the remaining advertising services expected to be performed in the future. At the same time, Service Revenue shows total revenue earned in October of $104,000. **If this adjustment is not made, revenues and net income will be understated by $4,000 in the income statement. Moreover, liabilities will be overstated and owners' equity will be understated by $4,000 on the October 31 balance sheet.**

Adjusting Entries for Accruals

The second category of adjusting entries is **accruals**. Adjusting entries for accruals are required to record revenues earned and expenses incurred in the current accounting period that have not been recognized through daily entries. If an accrual adjustment is needed, the revenue account (and the related asset account) and/or the expense account (and the related liability account) is understated. Thus, the adjusting entry for accruals will **increase both a balance sheet and an income statement account**. Adjusting entries for accruals are graphically depicted in Illustration 3-16.

ILLUSTRATION 3-16
Adjusting Entries for Accruals

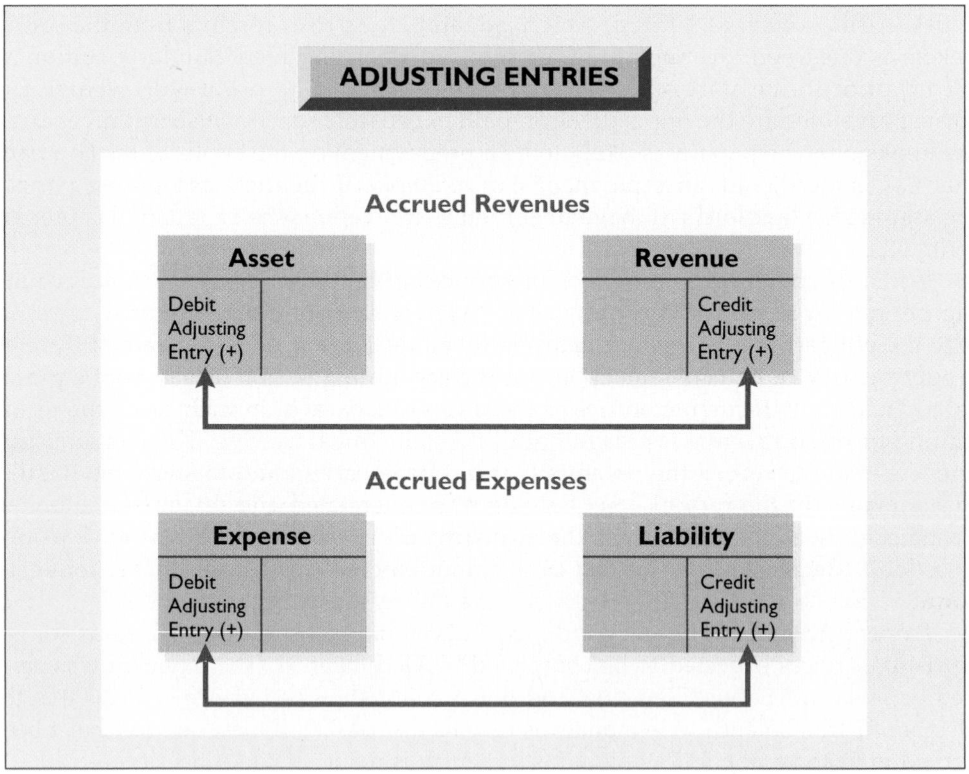

Accrued Revenues
Oct. 31
My fee is $2,000
Service is provided; revenue and receivable are recorded
Nov.
Cash is received; receivable is reduced

Accrued Revenues. Revenues earned but not yet received in cash or recorded at the statement date are **accrued revenues**. Accrued revenues may accumulate (accrue) with the passing of time, as in the case of interest revenue and rent revenue. Or they may result from services that have been performed but neither billed nor collected, as in the case of commissions and fees. The former are unrecorded because the earning of interest and rent does not involve daily transactions. The latter may be unrecorded because only a portion of the total service has been provided.

An adjusting entry is required to show the receivable that exists at the balance sheet date and to record the revenue that has been earned during the period. Prior to adjustment both assets and revenues are understated. Accordingly, **an adjusting entry for accrued revenues results in a debit (increase) to an asset account and a credit (increase) to a revenue account.**

In October Pioneer Advertising Agency earned $2,000 for advertising services that were not billed to clients before October 31. Because these services have not been billed, they have not been recorded. Thus, the following adjusting entry is made.

Oct. 31		
Accounts Receivable	2,000	
Service Revenue		2,000
(To record revenue for services provided)		

After the adjusting entry is posted, the accounts show the following.

ILLUSTRATION 3-17
Receivable and Revenue Accounts after Accrual Adjustment

Accounts Receivable			Service Revenue	
10/31	72,000		10/31	100,000
31 Adj.	2,000		31	4,000
			31 Adj.	2,000
			10/31	Bal. 106,000

The asset Accounts Receivable shows that $74,000 is owed by clients at the balance sheet date. The balance of $106,000 in Service Revenue represents the total revenue earned during the month ($100,000 + $4,000 + $2,000). **If the adjusting entry is not made, assets and owners' equity on the balance sheet, and revenues and net income on the income statement, will all be understated.**

Accrued Expenses. Expenses incurred but not yet paid or recorded at the statement date are called **accrued expenses**. Interest, rent, taxes, and salaries can be accrued expenses. Accrued expenses result from the same causes as accrued revenues. In fact, an accrued expense on the books of one company is an accrued revenue to another company. For example, the $2,000 accrual of service revenue by Pioneer is an accrued expense to the client that received the service.

Adjustments for accrued expenses are necessary to record the obligations that exist at the balance sheet date and to recognize the expenses that apply to the current accounting period. Prior to adjustment, both liabilities and expenses are understated. Therefore, **the adjusting entry for accrued expenses results in a debit (increase) to an expense account and a credit (increase) to a liability account.**

Accrued Interest. Pioneer Advertising Agency signed a three-month note payable in the amount of $50,000 on October 1. The note requires interest at an annual rate of 12 percent. The amount of the interest accumulation is determined by three factors: (1) the face value of the note, (2) the interest rate, which is always expressed as an annual rate, and (3) the length of time the note is outstanding. The total interest due on Pioneer's $50,000 note at its due date three months hence is $1,500 ($50,000 × 12% × 3/12), or $500 for one month. The formula for computing interest and its application to Pioneer Advertising Agency for October are shown in Illustration 3-18.

ILLUSTRATION 3-18
Formula for Computing Interest

Face Value of Note	×	Annual Interest Rate	×	Time in Terms of One Year	=	Interest
$50,000	×	12%	×	1/12	=	$500

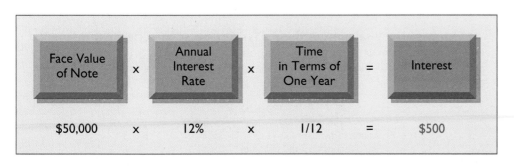

Note that the time period is expressed as a fraction of a year. The accrued expense adjusting entry at October 31 is as follows.

A	=	L	+	SE
		+500		−500

Cash Flows
no effect

Oct. 31		
Interest Expense	500	
Interest Payable		500
(To record interest on notes payable)		

After this adjusting entry is posted, the accounts show the following.

ILLUSTRATION 3-19
Interest Accounts after Adjustment

Interest Expense		Interest Payable	
10/31 500			10/31 500

Interest Expense shows the interest charges applicable to the month of October. The amount of interest owed at the statement date is shown in Interest Payable. It will not be paid until the note comes due at the end of three months. The Interest Payable account is used instead of crediting Notes Payable to disclose the two types of obligations (interest and principal) in the accounts and statements. **If this adjusting entry is not made, liabilities and interest expense will be understated, and net income and owners' equity will be overstated.**

Accrued Salaries. Some types of expenses, such as employee salaries and commissions, are paid for after the services have been performed. At Pioneer Advertising, salaries were last paid on October 26; the next payment of salaries will not occur until November 9. As shown in the calendar below, three working days remain in October (October 29–31).

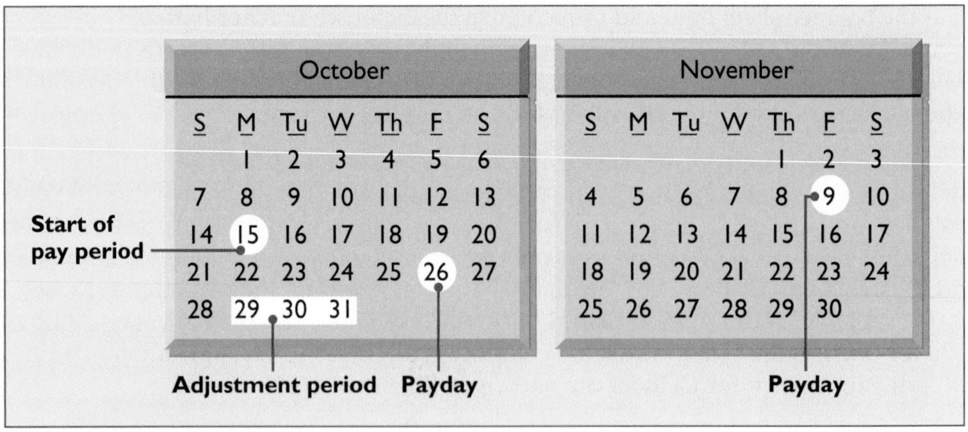

At October 31, the salaries for these days represent an accrued expense and a related liability to Pioneer Advertising. The employees receive total salaries of $10,000 for a five-day work week, or $2,000 per day. Thus, accrued salaries at October 31 are $6,000 ($2,000 × 3), and the adjusting entry is as follows.

A	=	L	+	SE
		+6,000		−6,000

Cash Flows
no effect

Oct. 31		
Salaries Expense	6,000	
Salaries Payable		6,000
(To record accrued salaries)		

After this adjusting entry is posted, the accounts show the following.

ILLUSTRATION 3-20
Salary Accounts after Adjustment

Salaries Expense			Salaries Payable		
10/26	40,000			10/31	Adj. 6,000
31	Adj. 6,000				
10/31	Bal. 46,000				

After this adjustment, the balance in Salaries Expense of \$46,000 (23 days × \$2,000) is the actual salary expense for October. The balance in Salaries Payable of \$6,000 is the amount of the liability for salaries owed as of October 31. **If the \$6,000 adjustment for salaries is not recorded, Pioneer's expenses will be understated \$6,000, and its liabilities will be understated \$6,000.**

At Pioneer Advertising, salaries are payable every two weeks. Consequently, the next payday is November 9, when total salaries of \$20,000 will again be paid. The payment consists of \$6,000 of salaries payable at October 31 plus \$14,000 of salaries expense for November (7 working days as shown in the November calendar × \$2,000). Therefore, the following entry is made on November 9.

Nov. 9		
Salaries Payable	6,000	
Salaries Expense	14,000	
Cash		20,000
(To record November 9 payroll)		

A	=	L	+	SE
−20,000		−6,000		−14,000

Cash Flows
−20,000

This entry eliminates the liability for Salaries Payable that was recorded in the October 31 adjusting entry and records the proper amount of Salaries Expense for the period between November 1 and November 9.

AM I COVERED?

WHAT DO THE NUMBERS MEAN?

Rather than purchasing insurance to cover casualty losses and other obligations, some companies "self-insure." Rather than paying premiums to an insurance company to cover unexpected obligations, a company decides to pay for any possible claims, as they arise, out of its own resources. An insurance policy may be purchased to cover only losses that exceed certain amounts. For example, **Almost Family, Inc.**, a health-care services company, has a self-insured employee health-benefit program. However, Almost Family ran into accounting problems when it failed to record an accrual of the liability for benefits not covered by its back-up insurance policy. This led to restatement of Almost Family's fiscal results for 2000 and 2001.

Bad Debts

Oct. 31
Uncollectible accounts; record bad debt expense

Bad Debts. Proper matching of revenues and expenses dictates recording bad debts as an expense of the period in which revenue is earned instead of the period in which the accounts or notes are written off. The proper valuation of the receivable balance also requires recognition of uncollectible, worthless receivables. Proper matching and valuation require an adjusting entry.

At the end of each period an estimate is made of the amount of current period revenue on account that will later prove to be uncollectible. The estimate is based on the amount of bad debts experienced in past years, general economic conditions, how long the receivables are past due, and other factors that indicate the element of uncollectibility. Usually it is expressed as a percentage of the revenue on account for the period. Or it may be computed by adjusting the Allowance for Doubtful Accounts to a certain percentage of the trade accounts receivable and trade notes receivable at the end of the period.

To illustrate, assume that experience indicates a reasonable estimate for bad debt expense for the month is $1,600. The adjusting entry for bad debts is:

Oct. 31		
Bad Debt Expense	1,600	
Allowance for Doubtful Accounts		1,600
(To record monthly bad debt expense)		

After the adjusting entry is posted, the accounts show the following.

ILLUSTRATION 3-21
Accounts after Adjustment for Bad Debt Expense

Accounts Receivable

Debit		Credit
10/ 1	72,000	
31	Adj. 2,000	

Allowance for Doubtful Accounts

Debit	Credit	
	10/31	Adj. 1,600

Bad Debt Expense

Debit		Credit
10/31	Adj. 1,600	

Adjusted Trial Balance

After all adjusting entries have been journalized and posted, another trial balance is prepared from the ledger accounts. This trial balance is called an **adjusted trial balance**. It shows the balance of all accounts, including those that have been adjusted, at the end of the accounting period. The purpose of an adjusted trial balance is to show the effects of all financial events that have occurred during the accounting period.

ILLUSTRATION 3-22
Adjusted Trial Balance

PIONEER ADVERTISING AGENCY, INC.
ADJUSTED TRIAL BALANCE
OCTOBER 31, 2005

	Debit	Credit
Cash	$ 80,000	
Accounts Receivable	74,000	
Allowance for Doubtful Accounts		$ 1,600
Advertising Supplies	10,000	
Prepaid Insurance	5,500	
Office Equipment	50,000	
Accumulated Depreciation—Office Equipment		400
Notes Payable		50,000
Accounts Payable		25,000
Interest Payable		500
Unearned Service Revenue		8,000
Salaries Payable		6,000
Common Stock		100,000
Dividends	5,000	
Service Revenue		106,000
Salaries Expense	46,000	
Advertising Supplies Expense	15,000	
Rent Expense	9,000	
Insurance Expense	500	
Interest Expense	500	
Depreciation Expense	400	
Bad Debt Expense	1,600	
	$297,500	$297,500

Closing

Basic Process

OBJECTIVE 6
Prepare closing entries.

The procedure generally followed to reduce the balance of nominal (temporary) accounts to zero in order to prepare the accounts for the next period's transactions is known as the **closing process**. In the closing process all of the revenue and expense account balances (income statement items) are transferred to a clearing or suspense account called Income Summary, which is used only at the end of each accounting period (yearly). Revenues and expenses are matched in the Income Summary account. The net result of this matching, which represents the net income or net loss for the period, is then transferred to an owners' equity account (retained earnings for a corporation, and capital accounts normally for proprietorships and partnerships). All such **closing entries** are posted to the appropriate general ledger accounts.

For example, assume that revenue accounts of Collegiate Apparel Shop have the following balances, after adjustments, at the end of the year.

Sales Revenue	$280,000
Rental Revenue	27,000
Interest Revenue	5,000

These **revenue accounts** would be closed and the balances transferred by the following closing journal entry.

Sales Revenue	280,000	
Rental Revenue	27,000	
Interest Revenue	5,000	
Income Summary		312,000
(To close revenue accounts to Income Summary)		

Assume that the expense accounts, including Cost of Goods Sold, have the following balances, after adjustments, at the end of the year.

Cost of Goods Sold	$206,000
Selling Expenses	25,000
General and Administrative Expenses	40,600
Interest Expense	4,400
Income Tax Expense	13,000

These **expense accounts** would be closed and the balances transferred through the following closing journal entry.

Income Summary	289,000	
Cost of Goods Sold		206,000
Selling Expenses		25,000
General and Administrative Expenses		40,600
Interest Expense		4,400
Income Tax Expense		13,000
(To close expense accounts to Income Summary)		

The Income Summary account now has a credit balance of $23,000, which is net income. The **net income is transferred to owners' equity** by closing the Income Summary account to Retained Earnings as follows.

A	=	L	+	SE
				−23,000
				+23,000

Cash Flows
no effect

Income Summary	23,000	
Retained Earnings		23,000
(To close Income Summary to Retained Earnings)		

Assuming that dividends of $7,000 were declared and distributed during the year, the Dividends account is closed directly to Retained Earnings as follows.

A	=	L	+	SE
				−7,000
				+7,000

Cash Flows
no effect

Retained Earnings	7,000	
Dividends		7,000
(To close Dividends to Retained Earnings)		

After the closing process is completed, each income statement (i.e., nominal) account is balanced out to zero and is ready for use in the next accounting period.

Illustration 3-23 shows the closing process in T-account form.

ILLUSTRATION 3-23
The Closing Process

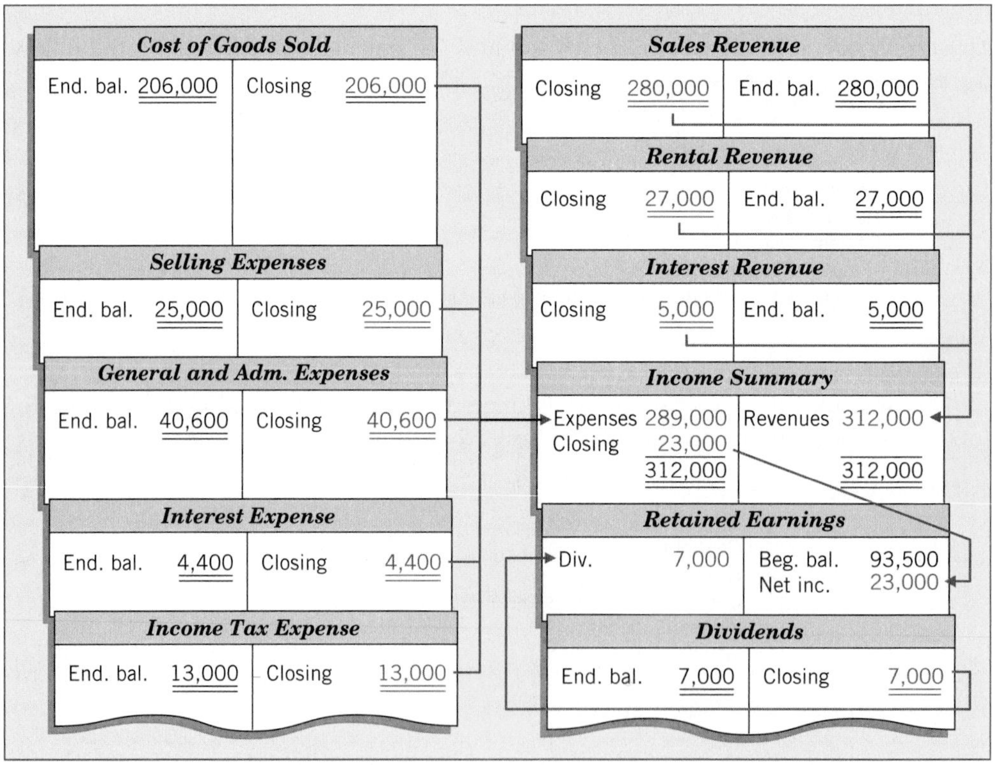

Inventory and Cost of Goods Sold

The closing procedures illustrated above assumed the use of the perpetual inventory system. With a **perpetual inventory system**, purchases and sales are recorded **directly in the Inventory account** as the purchases and sales occur. Therefore, the balance in the Inventory account should represent the ending inventory amount, and no adjusting entries are needed. To ensure this accuracy, a physical count of the items in the inventory is generally made annually. No Purchases account is used because the purchases are debited directly to the Inventory account. However, a Cost of Goods Sold account is used to accumulate the issuances from inventory. That is, when inventory items are sold, the cost of the sold goods is credited to Inventory and debited to Cost of Goods Sold.

With a **periodic inventory system**, a Purchases account is used, and the Inventory account is unchanged during the period. The Inventory account represents the beginning inventory amount throughout the period. At the end of the accounting period the Inventory account must be adjusted by **closing out the beginning inventory** amount and **recording the ending inventory** amount. The ending inventory is determined by physically counting the items on hand and valuing them at cost or at the lower of cost or market. Under the periodic inventory system, cost of goods sold is, therefore, determined by adding the beginning inventory together with net purchases and deducting the ending inventory.

OBJECTIVE 7
Explain how inventory accounts are adjusted at year-end.

To illustrate how cost of goods sold is computed with a periodic inventory system, assume that Collegiate Apparel Shop has a beginning inventory of $30,000; Purchases $200,000; Transportation-In $6,000; Purchase Returns and Allowances $1,000; Purchase Discounts $3,000; and the ending inventory is $26,000. The computation of cost of goods sold is as follows.

Beginning inventory			$ 30,000
Purchases		$200,000	
Less: Purchase returns and allowances	$1,000		
Purchase discounts	3,000	4,000	
Net purchases		196,000	
Plus: Transportation-in		6,000	
Cost of goods purchased			202,000
Cost of goods available for sale			232,000
Less: Ending inventory			26,000
Cost of goods sold			$206,000

ILLUSTRATION 3-24
Computation of Cost of Goods Sold Under Periodic Inventory System

Cost of goods sold will be the same whether the perpetual or periodic method is used.

Post-Closing Trial Balance

We already mentioned that a trial balance is taken after the regular transactions of the period have been entered and that a second trial balance (the adjusted trial balance) is taken after the adjusting entries have been posted. A third trial balance may be taken after posting the closing entries. The trial balance after closing, called the **post-closing trial balance**, shows that equal debits and credits have been posted to the Income Summary account. The post-closing trial balance consists only of asset, liability, and owners' equity (the real) accounts.

Reversing Entries

After the financial statements have been prepared and the books have been closed, it is often helpful to reverse some of the adjusting entries before recording the regular transactions of the next period. Such entries are called **reversing entries**. **A reversing entry is made at the beginning of the next accounting period and is the exact opposite of the related adjusting entry made in the previous period.** The recording of reversing entries is an **optional** step in the accounting cycle that may be performed at the beginning of the next accounting period. Appendix 3B discusses reversing entries in more detail.

The Accounting Cycle Summarized

A summary of the steps in the accounting cycle shows a logical sequence of the accounting procedures used during a fiscal period:

1. Enter the transactions of the period in appropriate journals.
2. Post from the journals to the ledger (or ledgers).
3. Take an unadjusted trial balance (trial balance).
4. Prepare adjusting journal entries and post to the ledger(s).
5. Take a trial balance after adjusting (adjusted trial balance).
6. Prepare the financial statements from the second trial balance.
7. Prepare closing journal entries and post to the ledger(s).
8. Take a trial balance after closing (post-closing trial balance).
9. Prepare reversing entries (optional) and post to the ledger(s).

This list of procedures constitutes a complete accounting cycle that is normally performed in every fiscal period.

WHAT DO THE NUMBERS MEAN?

24–7 ACCOUNTING

The ability to close the books quickly is a prerequisite to achieving the vision of "24–7 accounting." The concept of 24–7 accounting refers to a real-time financial reporting system in which companies update revenue, income, and balance sheet numbers every day within the quarter and publish them on the Internet. Such real-time reporting responds to the demand for **more timely financial information** made **available to all investors** (not just to analysts with access to management). Obstacles to achieving 24–7 reporting are the necessary accounting systems to close the books on a daily basis (only a few companies, such as Cisco Systems, have this capability) and reliability concerns associated with unaudited real-time data.

USING A WORK SHEET

OBJECTIVE 8
Prepare a 10-column work sheet.

To facilitate the end-of-period (monthly, quarterly, or annually) accounting and reporting process, a work sheet is often used. Such a work sheet can be prepared on columnar paper or within an electronic spreadsheet as shown in Illustration 3-25 on page 87. In either form, the **work sheet** is used to adjust account balances and to prepare financial statements. The **10-column work sheet** in Illustration 3-25 provides columns for the first trial balance, adjustments, adjusted trial balance, income statement, and balance sheet. Use of a work sheet helps the accountant prepare the financial statements on a more timely basis. It is not necessary to delay preparation of the financial statements until the adjusting and closing entries are journalized and posted.

The work sheet does not replace the financial statements. Instead, it is an informal device for accumulating and sorting information needed for the financial statements. Completing the work sheet provides considerable assurance that all of the details related to the end-of-period accounting and statement preparation have been properly brought together.

Adjustments Entered on the Work Sheet

Items (a) through (f) below and on page 87 serve as the basis for the adjusting entries made in the work sheet shown in Illustration 3-25.

(a) Furniture and equipment is depreciated at the rate of 10% per year based on original cost of $67,000.

(b) Estimated bad debts, one-quarter of 1 percent of sales ($400,000).

(c) Insurance expired during the year $360.

(d) Interest accrued on notes receivable as of December 31, $800.

(e) The Rent Expense account contains $500 rent paid in advance, which is applicable to next year.

(f) Property taxes accrued December 31, $2,000.

ILLUSTRATION 3-25
Use of a Work Sheet

UPTOWN CABINET CORP.
Ten-Column Work Sheet For The Year Ended December 31, 2005

	A	B	C	D	E	F	G	H	I	J	K
1	Accounts	Trial Balance Dr.	Trial Balance Cr.	Adjustments Dr.	Adjustments Cr.	Adjusted Trial Balance Dr.	Adjusted Trial Balance Cr.	Income Statement Dr.	Income Statement Cr.	Balance Sheet Dr.	Balance Sheet Cr.
2	Cash	1,200				1,200				1,200	
3	Notes receivable	16,000				16,000				16,000	
4	Accounts receivable	41,000				41,000				41,000	
5	Allowance for doubtful accounts		2,000		(b) 1,000		3,000				3,000
6	Merchandise inventory	40,000				40,000				40,000	
7	Prepaid insurance	900			(c) 360	540				540	
8	Furniture and equipment	67,000				67,000				67,000	
9	Accumulated depreciation–furniture and equipment		12,000		(a) 6,700		18,700				18,700
10	Notes payable		20,000				20,000				20,000
11	Accounts payable		13,500				13,500				13,500
12	Bonds payable		30,000				30,000				30,000
13	Common stock		50,000				50,000				50,000
14	Retained earnings, Jan. 1, 2005		14,200				14,200				14,200
15	Sales		400,000				400,000		400,000		
16	Cost of goods sold	316,000				316,000		316,000			
17	Sales salaries expense	20,000				20,000		20,000			
18	Advertising expense	2,200				2,200		2,200			
19	Traveling expense	8,000				8,000		8,000			
20	Salaries, office and general	19,000				19,000		19,000			
21	Telephone and Internet expense	600				600		600			
22	Rent expense	4,800			(e) 500	4,300		4,300			
23	Property tax expense	3,300		(f) 2,000		5,300		5,300			
24	Interest expense	1,700				1,700		1,700			
25	Totals	541,700	541,700								
26	Depreciation expense–furniture and equipment			(a) 6,700		6,700		6,700			
27	Bad debt expense			(b) 1,000		1,000		1,000			
28	Insurance expense			(c) 360		360		360			
29	Interest receivable			(d) 800		800				800	
30	Interest revenue				(d) 800		800		800		
31	Prepaid rent expense			(e) 500		500				500	
32	Property tax payable				(f) 2,000		2,000				2,000
33	Totals			11,360	11,360	552,200	552,200	385,160	400,800		
34	Income before income taxes							15,640			
35	Totals							400,800	400,800		
36	Income before income taxes								15,640		
37	Income tax expense			(g) 3,440				3,440			
38	Income tax payable				(g) 3,440						3,440
39	Net income							12,200			12,200
40	Totals							15,640	15,640	167,040	167,040
41											
42											

Sheet1 Sheet2 Sheet3

The adjusting entries shown on the December 31, 2005, work sheet are as follows.

(a)

Depreciation Expense—Furniture and Equipment	6,700	
Accumulated Depreciation—Furniture and Equipment		6,700

(b)

Bad Debt Expense	1,000	
Allowance for Doubtful Accounts		1,000

(c)

Insurance Expense	360	
Prepaid Insurance		360

	(d)		
Interest Receivable		800	
Interest Revenue			800
	(e)		
Prepaid Rent Expense		500	
Rent Expense			500
	(f)		
Property Tax Expense		2,000	
Property Tax Payable			2,000

These adjusting entries are transferred to the Adjustments columns of the work sheet, and each may be designated by letter. The accounts that are set up as a result of the adjusting entries and that are not already in the trial balance are listed below the totals of the trial balance, as illustrated on the work sheet. The Adjustments columns are then totaled and balanced.

Work Sheet Columns

Trial Balance Columns

Data for the trial balance are obtained from the ledger balances of Uptown Cabinet Corp. at December 31. The amount for Merchandise Inventory, $40,000, is the year-end inventory amount, which results from the application of a perpetual inventory system.

Adjustments Columns

After all adjustment data are entered on the work sheet, the equality of the adjustment columns is established. The balances in all accounts are then extended to the adjusted trial balance columns.

Adjusted Trial Balance

The adjusted trial balance shows the balance of all accounts after adjustment at the end of the accounting period. For example, the $2,000 shown opposite the Allowance for Doubtful Accounts in the Trial Balance Cr. column is added to the $1,000 in the Adjustments Cr. column. The $3,000 total is then extended to the Adjusted Trial Balance Cr. column. Similarly, the $900 debit opposite Prepaid Insurance is reduced by the $360 credit in the Adjustments column. The result, $540, is shown in the Adjusted Trial Balance Dr. column.

Income Statement and Balance Sheet Columns

All the debit items in the Adjusted Trial Balance columns are extended into the Income Statement or Balance Sheet columns to the right. All the credit items are similarly extended.

The next step is to total the Income Statement columns; the figure necessary to balance the debit and credit columns is the pretax income or loss for the period. The income before income taxes of $15,640 is shown in the Income Statement Dr. column because revenues exceeded expenses by that amount.

Income Taxes and Net Income

The federal and state income tax expense and related tax liability are computed next. The company applies an effective rate of 22 percent to arrive at $3,440. Because the Adjustments columns have been balanced, this adjustment is entered in the Income Statement Dr. column as Income Tax Expense and in the Balance Sheet Cr. column as Income Tax Payable. The following adjusting journal entry is recorded on December 31, 2005, and posted to the general ledger as well as entered on the work sheet.

A	=	L	+	SE
		+3,440		−3,440

Cash Flows
no effect

	(g)		
Income Tax Expense		3,440	
Income Tax Payable			3,440

Next, the Income Statement columns are balanced with the income taxes included. The $12,200 difference between the debit and credit columns in this illustration represents net income. The net income of $12,200 is entered in the Income Statement Dr. column to achieve equality and in the Balance Sheet Cr. column as the increase in retained earnings.

Preparing Financial Statements from a Work Sheet

The work sheet provides the information needed for preparation of the financial statements without reference to the ledger or other records. In addition, the data have been sorted into appropriate columns, which facilitates the preparation of the statements.

The financial statements prepared from the 10-column work sheet illustrated are as follows.

Using a Work Sheet—Periodic Inventory

1. Income Statement for the Year Ended December 31, 2005 (Illustration 3-26).
2. Statement of Retained Earnings for the Year Ended December 31, 2005 (Illustration 3-27).
3. Balance Sheet as of December 31, 2005 (Illustration 3-28).

These illustrations are shown below and on page 90.

Income Statement

The income statement presented is that of a trading or merchandising concern. If a manufacturing concern were illustrated, three inventory accounts would be involved: Raw Materials, Work in Process, and Finished Goods. When these accounts are used, a supplementary statement entitled Cost of Goods Manufactured must be prepared.

ILLUSTRATION 3-26
An Income Statement

UPTOWN CABINET CORP.
INCOME STATEMENT
FOR THE YEAR ENDED DECEMBER 31, 2005

Net sales			$400,000
Cost of goods sold			316,000
Gross profit on sales			84,000
Selling expenses			
Sales salaries expense		$20,000	
Advertising expense		2,200	
Traveling expense		8,000	
Total selling expenses		30,200	
Administrative expenses			
Salaries, office and general	$19,000		
Telephone and Internet expense	600		
Rent expense	4,300		
Property tax expense	5,300		
Depreciation expense—furniture and equipment	6,700		
Bad debt expense	1,000		
Insurance expense	360		
Total administrative expenses		37,260	
Total selling and administrative expenses			67,460
Income from operations			16,540
Other revenues and gains			
Interest revenue			800
			17,340
Other expenses and losses			
Interest expense			1,700
Income before income taxes			15,640
Income taxes			3,440
Net income			$ 12,200
Earnings per share			$1.22

Statement of Retained Earnings

The net income earned by a corporation may be retained in the business, or it may be distributed to stockholders by payment of dividends. In the illustration, the net income earned during the year was added to the balance of retained earnings on January 1, thereby increasing the balance of retained earnings to $26,400 on December 31. No dividends were declared during the year.

ILLUSTRATION 3-27
A Statement of Retained Earnings

UPTOWN CABINET CORP.
STATEMENT OF RETAINED EARNINGS
FOR THE YEAR ENDED DECEMBER 31, 2005

Retained earnings, Jan. 1, 2005	$14,200
Add: Net income for 2005	12,200
Retained earnings, Dec. 31, 2005	$26,400

ILLUSTRATION 3-28
A Balance Sheet

UPTOWN CABINET CORP.
BALANCE SHEET
AS OF DECEMBER 31, 2005

Assets			
Current assets			
Cash			$ 1,200
Notes receivable	$16,000		
Accounts receivable	41,000		
Interest receivable	800	$57,800	
Less: Allowance for doubtful accounts		3,000	54,800
Merchandise inventory			40,000
Prepaid insurance			540
Prepaid rent			500
Total current assets			97,040
Property, plant, and equipment			
Furniture and equipment		67,000	
Less: Accumulated depreciation		18,700	
Total property, plant, and equipment			48,300
Total assets			$145,340
Liabilities and Stockholders' Equity			
Current liabilities			
Notes payable			$ 20,000
Accounts payable			13,500
Property tax payable			2,000
Income tax payable			3,440
Total current liabilities			38,940
Long-term liabilities			
Bonds payable, due June 30, 2010			30,000
Total liabilities			68,940
Stockholders' equity			
Common stock, $5.00 par value, issued and outstanding, 10,000 shares		$50,000	
Retained earnings		26,400	
Total stockholders' equity			76,400
Total liabilities and stockholders' equity			$145,340

Balance Sheet

The balance sheet prepared from the 10-column work sheet contains new items resulting from year-end adjusting entries. Interest receivable, unexpired insurance, and prepaid rent expense are included as current assets. These assets are considered current because they will be converted into cash or consumed in the ordinary routine of the business within a relatively short period of time. The amount of Allowance for Doubtful Accounts is deducted from the total of accounts, notes, and interest receivable because it is estimated that only $54,800 of $57,800 will be collected in cash.

In the property, plant, and equipment section the accumulated depreciation is deducted from the cost of the furniture and equipment. The difference represents the book or carrying value of the furniture and equipment.

Property tax payable is shown as a current liability because it is an obligation that is payable within a year. Other short-term accrued liabilities would also be shown as current liabilities.

The bonds payable, due in 2010, are long-term liabilities and are shown in a separate section. (Interest on the bonds was paid on December 31.)

Because Uptown Cabinet Corp. is a corporation, the capital section of the balance sheet, called the stockholders' equity section in the illustration, is somewhat different from the capital section for a proprietorship. Total stockholders' equity consists of the common stock, which is the original investment by stockholders, and the earnings retained in the business.

Closing Entries

The entries for the closing process are as follows.

General Journal
December 31, 2005

Interest Revenue	800	
Sales	400,000	
Cost of Goods Sold		316,000
Sales Salaries Expense		20,000
Advertising Expense		2,200
Traveling Expense		8,000
Salaries, Office and General		19,000
Telephone and Internet Expense		600
Rent Expense		4,300
Property Tax Expense		5,300
Depreciation Expense—Furniture and Equipment		6,700
Bad Debt Expense		1,000
Insurance Expense		360
Interest Expense		1,700
Income Tax Expense		3,440
Income Summary		12,200
(To close revenues and expenses to Income Summary)		
Income Summary	12,200	
Retained Earnings		12,200
(To close Income Summary to Retained Earnings)		

Accounting Cycle Tutorial

STATEMENTS PLEASE

WHAT DO THE NUMBERS MEAN?

The use of a work sheet at the end of each month or quarter permits the preparation of interim financial statements even though the books are closed only at the end of each year. For example, assume that **Cisco Systems** closes its books on December 31 but that monthly financial statements are desired. At the end of January, a work sheet similar to the one illustrated in this chapter can be prepared to supply the information needed for statements for January. At the end of February, a work sheet can be used again. Note that because the accounts were not closed at the end of January, the income statement taken from the work sheet on February 28 will present the net income for two months. If an income statement for only the month of February is wanted, it can be obtained by subtracting the items in the January income statement from the corresponding items in the income statement for the two months of January and February. If such a process is executed on a daily basis, Cisco Systems can realize "24–7 accounting" (see box on page 86).

KEY TERMS

account, *63*
accounting cycle, *68*
accounting information system, *62*
accrued expenses, *79*
accrued revenues, *78*
adjusted trial balance, *63*
adjusting entry, *63, 72*
balance sheet, *63*
book value, *76*
closing entries, *63, 83*
closing process, *83*
contra asset account, *76*
credit, *64*
debit, *64*
depreciation, *75*
double-entry accounting, *64*
event, *63*
financial statements, *63*
general journal, *69*
general ledger, *69*
income statement, *63*
journal, *63*
ledger, *63*
nominal accounts, *63*
periodic inventory system, *85*
perpetual inventory system, *84*
post-closing trial balance, *63, 85*
posting, *63, 70*
prepaid expense, *73*
real accounts, *63*
reversing entries, *85*
special journals, *70*
statement of cash flows, *63*
statement of retained earnings, *63*
T-account, *69*
transaction, *63*
trial balance, *63, 71*
unearned revenues, *77*
useful life, *75*
work sheet, *86*

SUMMARY OF LEARNING OBJECTIVES

1 Understand basic accounting terminology. It is important to understand the following eleven terms: (1) Event. (2) Transaction. (3) Account. (4) Real and nominal accounts. (5) Ledger. (6) Journal. (7) Posting. (8) Trial balance. (9) Adjusting entries. (10) Financial statements. (11) Closing entries.

2 Explain double-entry rules. The left side of any account is the debit side; the right side is the credit side. All asset and expense accounts are increased on the left or debit side and decreased on the right or credit side. Conversely, all liability and revenue accounts are increased on the right or credit side and decreased on the left or debit side. Stockholders' equity accounts, Common Stock and Retained Earnings, are increased on the credit side. Dividends is increased on the debit side.

3 Identify steps in the accounting cycle. The basic steps in the accounting cycle are (1) identification and measurement of transactions and other events; (2) journalization; (3) posting; (4) unadjusted trial balance; (5) adjustments; (6) adjusted trial balance; (7) statement preparation; and (8) closing.

4 Record transactions in journals, post to ledger accounts, and prepare a trial balance. The simplest journal form is a chronological listing of transactions and events expressed in terms of debits and credits to particular accounts. The items entered in a general journal must be transferred (posted) to the general ledger. An unadjusted trial balance should be prepared at the end of a given period after the entries have been recorded in the journal and posted to the ledger.

5 Explain the reasons for preparing adjusting entries. Adjustments are necessary to achieve a proper matching of revenues and expenses, so as to determine net income for the current period and to achieve an accurate statement of end-of-the-period balances in assets, liabilities, and owners' equity accounts.

6 Prepare closing entries. In the closing process all of the revenue and expense account balances (income statement items) are transferred to a clearing account called Income Summary, which is used only at the end of the fiscal year. Revenues and expenses are matched in the Income Summary account. The net result of this matching represents the net income or net loss for the period. It is then transferred to an owners' equity account (retained earnings for a corporation and capital accounts for proprietorships and partnerships).

7 Explain how inventory accounts are adjusted at year-end. Under a perpetual inventory system the balance in the Inventory account should represent the ending inventory amount. When the inventory records are maintained in a periodic inventory system, a Purchases account is used; the Inventory account is unchanged during the period. The Inventory account represents the beginning inventory amount throughout the period. At the end of the accounting period the inventory account must be adjusted by closing out the beginning inventory amount and recording the ending inventory amount.

8 Prepare a 10-column work sheet. The 10-column work sheet provides columns for the first trial balance, adjustments, adjusted trial balance, income statement, and balance sheet. The work sheet does not replace the financial statements. Instead, it is the accountant's informal device for accumulating and sorting information needed for the financial statements.

APPENDIX 3A

Cash-Basis Accounting versus Accrual-Basis Accounting

DIFFERENCES BETWEEN CASH AND ACCRUAL BASES

OBJECTIVE 9
Differentiate the cash basis of accounting from the accrual basis of accounting.

Most companies use the **accrual basis of accounting**: They recognize revenue when it is earned and recognize expenses in the period incurred, without regard to the time of receipt or payment of cash. Some small enterprises and the average individual taxpayer, however, use a strict or modified cash-basis approach. Under the **strict cash basis** of accounting, revenue is recorded only when the cash is received, and expenses are recorded only when the cash is paid. The determination of income on the cash basis rests upon the collection of revenue and the payment of expenses. Under the cash basis, the revenue recognition and the matching principles are ignored. Consequently, cash-basis financial statements are not in conformity with generally accepted accounting principles.

To illustrate and contrast accrual-basis accounting and cash-basis accounting, assume that Quality Contractor signs an agreement to construct a garage for $22,000. In January, Quality Contractor begins construction, incurs costs of $18,000 on credit, and by the end of January delivers a finished garage to the buyer. In February, Quality Contractor collects $22,000 cash from the customer. In March, Quality pays the $18,000 due the creditors. The net incomes for each month under cash-basis accounting and accrual-basis accounting are as follows.

ILLUSTRATION 3A-1
Income Statement—Cash Basis

QUALITY CONTRACTOR
INCOME STATEMENT—CASH BASIS
For the Month of

	January	February	March	Total
Cash receipts	$-0-	$22,000	$ -0-	$22,000
Cash payments	-0-	-0-	18,000	18,000
Net income (loss)	$-0-	$22,000	$(18,000)	$ 4,000

ILLUSTRATION 3A-2
Income Statement—Accrual Basis

QUALITY CONTRACTOR
INCOME STATEMENT—ACCRUAL BASIS
For the Month of

	January	February	March	Total
Revenues	$22,000	$-0-	$-0-	$22,000
Expenses	18,000	-0-	-0-	18,000
Net income (loss)	$ 4,000	$-0-	$-0-	$ 4,000

For the three months combined, total net income is the same under both cash-basis accounting and accrual-basis accounting. The difference is in the **timing** of net income.

The balance sheet is also affected by the basis of accounting. For instance, if cash-basis accounting were used, Quality Contractor's balance sheets at each month-end would appear as follows.

ILLUSTRATION 3A-3
Balance Sheets—Cash Basis

QUALITY CONTRACTOR
BALANCE SHEETS—CASH BASIS
As of

	January 31	February 28	March 31
Assets			
Cash	$-0-	$22,000	$4,000
Total assets	$-0-	$22,000	$4,000
Liabilities and Owners' Equity			
Owners' equity	$-0-	$22,000	$4,000
Total liabilities and owners' equity	$-0-	$22,000	$4,000

If accrual-basis accounting were used, Quality Contractor's balance sheets at each month-end would appear as follows.

ILLUSTRATION 3A-4
Balance Sheets—Accrual Basis

QUALITY CONTRACTOR
BALANCE SHEETS—ACCRUAL BASIS
As of

	January 31	February 28	March 31
Assets			
Cash	$ -0-	$22,000	$4,000
Accounts receivable	22,000	-0-	-0-
Total assets	$22,000	$22,000	$4,000
Liabilities and Owners' Equity			
Accounts payable	$18,000	$18,000	$-0-
Owners' equity	4,000	4,000	4,000
Total liabilities and owners' equity	$22,000	$22,000	$4,000

An analysis of the preceding income statements and balance sheets shows the ways in which cash-basis accounting is inconsistent with basic accounting theory:

1. The cash basis understates revenues and assets from the construction and delivery of the garage in January. It ignores the $22,000 accounts receivable, representing a near-term future cash inflow.
2. The cash basis understates expenses incurred with the construction of the garage and the liability outstanding at the end of January. It ignores the $18,000 accounts payable, representing a near-term future cash outflow.
3. The cash basis understates owners' equity in January by not recognizing the revenues and the asset until February, and it overstates owners' equity in February by not recognizing the expenses and the liability until March.

In short, cash-basis accounting violates the theory underlying the elements of financial statements.

The **modified cash basis**, a mixture of the cash basis and the accrual basis, is the method often followed by professional services firms (doctors, lawyers, accountants, consultants) and by retail, real estate, and agricultural operations. It is the pure cash basis of accounting with modifications that have substantial support, such as capitalizing and depreciating plant assets or recording inventory.[1]

CONVERSION FROM CASH BASIS TO ACCRUAL BASIS

Not infrequently a cash basis or a modified cash basis set of financial statements is converted to the accrual basis for presentation to investors and creditors. To illustrate this conversion, assume that Dr. Diane Windsor keeps her accounting records on a cash basis. In the year 2005, Dr. Windsor received $300,000 from her patients and paid $170,000 for operating expenses, resulting in an excess of cash receipts over disbursements of $130,000 ($300,000 – $170,000). At January 1 and December 31, 2005, she has accounts receivable, unearned service revenue, accrued liabilities, and prepaid expenses as follows.

	January 1, 2005	December 31, 2005
Accounts receivable	$12,000	$9,000
Unearned service revenue	–0–	4,000
Accrued liabilities	2,000	5,500
Prepaid expenses	1,800	2,700

ILLUSTRATION 3A-5
Financial Information Related to Dr. Diane Windsor

Service Revenue Computation

To convert the amount of cash received from patients to service revenue on an accrual basis, changes in accounts receivable and unearned service revenue during the year must be considered. Accounts receivable at the beginning of the year represents revenues earned last year that are collected this year. Ending accounts receivable indicates revenues earned this year that are not yet collected. Therefore, beginning accounts receivable is subtracted and ending accounts receivable is added to arrive at revenue on an accrual basis, as shown in Illustration 3A-6.

Cash receipts from customers	– Beginning accounts receivable + Ending accounts receivable	= Revenue on an accrual basis

ILLUSTRATION 3A-6
Conversion of Cash Receipts to Revenue—Accounts Receivable

Using similar analysis, beginning unearned service revenue represents cash received last year for revenues earned this year. Ending unearned service revenue results from collections this year that will be recognized as revenue next year. Therefore, beginning unearned service revenue is added and ending unearned service revenue is subtracted to arrive at revenue on an accrual basis, as shown in Illustration 3A-7.

Cash receipts from customers	+ Beginning unearned service revenue – Ending unearned service revenue	= Revenue on an accrual basis

ILLUSTRATION 3A-7
Conversion of Cash Receipts to Revenue—Unearned Service Revenue

[1]A cash or modified cash basis might be used in the following situations.

(1) A company that is primarily interested in cash flows (for example, a group of physicians that distributes cash-basis earnings for salaries and bonuses).

(2) A company that has a limited number of financial statement users (small, closely held company with little or no debt).

(3) A company that has operations that are relatively straightforward (small amounts of inventory, long-term assets, or long-term debt).

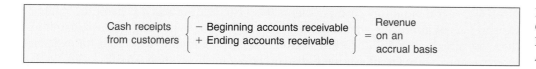

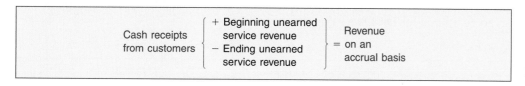

Cash collected from customers, therefore, is converted to service revenue on an accrual basis as follows.

ILLUSTRATION 3A-8
Conversion of Cash Receipts to Service Revenue

Cash receipts from customers		$300,000
− Beginning accounts receivable	$(12,000)	
+ Ending accounts receivable	9,000	
+ Beginning unearned service revenue	-0-	
− Ending unearned service revenue	(4,000)	(7,000)
Service revenue (accrual)		$293,000

Operating Expense Computation

To convert cash paid for operating expenses during the year to operating expenses on an accrual basis, you must consider changes in prepaid expenses and accrued liabilities during the year. Beginning prepaid expenses should be recognized as expenses this year. (The cash payment occurred last year.) Therefore, the beginning prepaid expenses balance is added to cash paid for operating expenses to arrive at operating expense on an accrual basis.

Conversely, ending prepaid expenses result from cash payments made this year for expenses to be reported next year. (The expense recognition is deferred to a future period.) As a result, ending prepaid expenses are deducted from cash paid for expenses, as shown in Illustration 3A-9.

ILLUSTRATION 3A-9
Conversion of Cash Payments to Expenses—Prepaid Expenses

Cash paid for operating expenses	+ Beginning prepaid expenses − Ending prepaid expenses	=	Expenses on an accrual basis

Using similar analysis, beginning accrued liabilities result from expenses recognized last year that require cash payments this year. Ending accrued liabilities relate to expenses recognized this year that have not been paid. Beginning accrued liabilities, therefore, are deducted and ending accrued liabilities added to cash paid for expenses to arrive at expense on an accrual basis, as shown in Illustration 3A-10.

ILLUSTRATION 3A-10
Conversion of Cash Payments to Expenses—Accrued Liabilities

Cash paid for operating expenses	− Beginning accrued liabilities + Ending accrued liabilities	=	Expenses on an accrual basis

Cash paid for operating expenses, therefore, is converted to operating expenses on an accrual basis for Dr. Diane Windsor as follows.

ILLUSTRATION 3A-11
Conversion of Cash Paid to Operating Expenses

Cash paid for operating expenses		$170,000
+ Beginning prepaid expense	$1,800	
− Ending prepaid expense	(2,700)	
− Beginning accrued liabilities	(2,000)	
+ Ending accrued liabilities	5,500	2,600
Operating expenses (accrual)		$172,600

This entire conversion can be completed in work sheet form as shown in Illustration 3A-12.

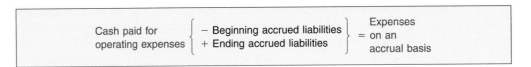

ILLUSTRATION 3A-12
Conversion of Statement of Cash Receipts and Disbursements to Income Statement

DIANE WINDSOR, D.D.S.
Conversion of Income Statement Data from Cash Basis to Accrual Basis
For the Year 2005

	Cash Basis	Adjustments Add	Adjustments Deduct	Accrual Basis
Collections from customers	$300,000			
− Accounts receivable, Jan. 1			$12,000	
+ Accounts receivable, Dec. 31		$9,000		
+ Unearned service revenue, Jan. 1		—	—	
− Unearned service revenue, Dec. 31			4,000	
Service revenue				$293,000
Disbursement for expenses	170,000			
+ Prepaid expenses, Jan. 1		1,800		
− Prepaid expenses, Dec. 31			2,700	
− Accrued liabilities, Jan. 1			2,000	
+ Accrued liabilities, Dec. 31		5,500		
Operating expenses				172,600
Excess of cash collections over disbursements—cash basis	$130,000			
Net income—accrual basis				$120,400

Using this approach, collections and disbursements on a cash basis are adjusted to revenue and expense on an accrual basis to arrive at accrual net income. In any conversion from the cash basis to the accrual basis, depreciation or amortization expense is an expense in arriving at net income on an accrual basis.

THEORETICAL WEAKNESSES OF THE CASH BASIS

The cash basis does report exactly when cash is received and when cash is disbursed. To many people that information represents something solid, something concrete. Isn't cash what it is all about? Does it make sense to invent something, design it, produce it, market and sell it, if you aren't going to get cash for it in the end? It is frequently said, "Cash is the real bottom line." It is also said, "Cash is the oil that lubricates the economy." If so, then what is the merit of accrual accounting?

Today's economy is considerably more lubricated by credit than by cash. And the accrual basis, not the cash basis, recognizes all aspects of the credit phenomenon. Investors, creditors, and other decision makers seek timely information about an enterprise's future cash flows. Accrual-basis accounting provides this information by reporting the cash inflows and outflows associated with earnings activities as soon as these cash flows can be estimated with an acceptable degree of certainty. Receivables and payables are forecasters of future cash inflows and outflows. In other words, accrual-basis accounting aids in predicting future cash flows by reporting transactions and other events with cash consequences at the time the transactions and events occur, rather than when the cash is received and paid.

SUMMARY OF LEARNING OBJECTIVE FOR APPENDIX 3A

9 **Differentiate the cash basis of accounting from the accrual basis of accounting.** Accrual-basis accounting provides information about cash inflows and outflows associated with earnings activities as soon as these cash flows can be estimated with an acceptable degree of certainty. That is, accrual-basis accounting aids in predicting future cash flows by reporting transactions and events with cash consequences at the time the transactions and events occur, rather than when the cash is received and paid.

KEY TERMS

accrual basis, *93*
modified cash basis, *94*
strict cash basis, *93*

APPENDIX 3B

Using Reversing Entries

OBJECTIVE 10
Identify adjusting entries that may be reversed.

The purpose of reversing entries is to simplify the recording of transactions in the next accounting period. The use of reversing entries does not change the amounts reported in the financial statements for the previous period.

ILLUSTRATION OF REVERSING ENTRIES—ACCRUALS

Reversing entries are most often used to reverse two types of adjusting entries: accrued revenues and accrued expenses. To illustrate the optional use of reversing entries for accrued expenses, we will use the following transaction and adjustment data.

1. October 24 (initial salary entry): $4,000 of salaries incurred between October 1 and October 24 are paid.
2. October 31 (adjusting entry): Salaries incurred between October 25 and October 31 are $1,200. These will be paid in the November 8 payroll.
3. November 8 (subsequent salary entry): Salaries paid are $2,500. Of this amount, $1,200 applied to accrued wages payable at October 31 and $1,300 was incurred between November 1 and November 8.

The comparative entries are shown in Illustration 3B-1.

ILLUSTRATION 3B-1
Comparison of Entries for Accruals, with and without Reversing Entries

REVERSING ENTRIES NOT USED				REVERSING ENTRIES USED			
Initial Salary Entry							
Oct. 24	Salaries Expense	4,000		Oct. 24	Salaries Expense	4,000	
	Cash		4,000		Cash		4,000
Adjusting Entry							
Oct. 31	Salaries Expense	1,200		Oct. 31	Salaries Expense	1,200	
	Salaries Payable		1,200		Salaries Payable		1,200
Closing Entry							
Oct. 31	Income Summary	5,200		Oct. 31	Income Summary	5,200	
	Salaries Expense		5,200		Salaries Expense		5,200
Reversing Entry							
Nov. 1	No entry is made.			Nov. 1	Salaries Payable	1,200	
					Salaries Expense		1,200
Subsequent Salary Entry							
Nov. 8	Salaries Payable	1,200		Nov. 8	Salaries Expense	2,500	
	Salaries Expense	1,300			Cash		2,500
	Cash		2,500				

The comparative entries show that the first three entries are the same whether or not reversing entries are used. The last two entries are different. The November 1 reversing entry eliminates the $1,200 balance in Salaries Payable that was created by the October 31 adjusting entry. The reversing entry also creates a $1,200 credit balance in the Salaries Expense account. As you know, it is unusual for an expense account to have a credit balance; however, the balance is correct in this instance. It is correct because the entire amount of the first salary payment in the new accounting period will be debited to Salaries Expense. This debit will eliminate the credit balance, and the resulting debit balance in the expense account will equal the salaries expense incurred in the new accounting period ($1,300 in this example).

When reversing entries are made, all cash payments of expenses can be debited to the expense account. This means that on November 8 (and every payday) Salaries Expense can be debited for the amount paid without regard to the existence of any accrued salaries payable. Being able to make the same entry each time simplifies the recording process in an accounting system.

ILLUSTRATION OF REVERSING ENTRIES—PREPAYMENTS

Up to this point, we have assumed that all prepayments are recorded as prepaid expense or unearned revenue. In some cases, prepayments are recorded directly in expense or revenue accounts. When this occurs, prepayments may also be reversed.

To illustrate the use of reversing entries for prepaid expenses, we will use the following transaction and adjustment data.

1. December 10 (initial entry): $20,000 of office supplies are purchased with cash.
2. December 31 (adjusting entry): $5,000 of office supplies on hand.

The comparative entries are shown in Illustration 3B-2.

ILLUSTRATION 3B-2
Comparison of Entries for Prepayments, with and without Reversing Entries

REVERSING ENTRIES NOT USED				REVERSING ENTRIES USED			
Initial Purchase of Supplies Entry							
Dec. 10	Office Supplies	20,000		Dec. 10	Office Supplies Expense	20,000	
	Cash		20,000		Cash		20,000
Adjusting Entry							
Dec. 31	Office Supplies Expense	15,000		Dec. 31	Office Supplies	5,000	
	Office Supplies		15,000		Office Supplies Expense		5,000
Closing Entry							
Dec. 31	Income Summary	15,000		Dec. 31	Income Summary	15,000	
	Office Supplies Expense		15,000		Office Supplies Expense		15,000
Reversing Entry							
Jan. 1	No entry			Jan. 1	Office Supplies Expense	5,000	
					Office Supplies		5,000

After the adjusting entry on December 31 (regardless of whether reversing entries are used), the asset account Office Supplies shows a balance of $5,000 and Office Supplies Expense a balance of $15,000. If Office Supplies Expense initially was debited when the supplies were purchased, a reversing entry is made to return to the expense account the cost of unconsumed supplies. The company then continues to debit Office Supplies Expense for additional purchases of office supplies during the next period.

With respect to prepaid items, why are all such items not entered originally into real accounts (assets and liabilities), thus making reversing entries unnecessary? Sometimes this practice is followed. It is particularly advantageous for items that need to be apportioned over several periods (e.g., supplies and parts inventories). However, items that do not follow this regular pattern and that may or may not involve two or more periods are ordinarily entered initially in revenue or expense accounts. The revenue and expense accounts may not require adjusting and are systematically closed to Income Summary. Using the nominal accounts adds consistency to the accounting system. It also makes the recording more efficient, particularly when a large number of such transactions occur during the year. For example, the bookkeeper knows that when an invoice is received for other than a capital asset acquisition, the amount is expensed. The bookkeeper need not worry at the time the invoice is received whether or not the item will result in a prepaid expense at the end of the period, because adjustments will be made at the end of the period.

SUMMARY OF REVERSING ENTRIES

A summary of guidelines for reversing entries is as follows.

1. All accrued items should be reversed.
2. All prepaid items for which the original cash transaction was debited or credited to an expense or revenue account should be reversed.
3. Adjusting entries for depreciation and bad debts are not reversed.

Recognize that reversing entries do not have to be used. Therefore, some accountants avoid them entirely.

SUMMARY OF LEARNING OBJECTIVE FOR APPENDIX 3B

10 **Identify adjusting entries that may be reversed.** Reversing entries are most often used to reverse two types of adjusting entries: accrued revenues and accrued expenses. Prepayments may also be reversed if the initial entry to record the transaction is made to an expense or revenue account.

Note: All **asterisked** Questions, Exercises, Problems, and Cases relate to material contained in the appendixes to the chapter.

QUESTIONS

1. Give an example of a transaction that results in:

(a) A decrease in an asset and a decrease in a liability.

(b) A decrease in one asset and an increase in another asset.

(c) A decrease in one liability and an increase in another liability.

2. Do the following events represent business transactions? Explain your answer in each case.

(a) A computer is purchased on account.

(b) A customer returns merchandise and is given credit on account.

(c) A prospective employee is interviewed.

(d) The owner of the business withdraws cash from the business for personal use.

(e) Merchandise is ordered for delivery next month.

3. Name the accounts debited and credited for each of the following transactions.

(a) Billing a customer for work done.

(b) Receipt of cash from customer on account.

(c) Purchase of office supplies on account.

(d) Purchase of 15 gallons of gasoline for the delivery truck.

4. Why are revenue and expense accounts called temporary or nominal accounts?

5. Omar Morena, a fellow student, contends that the double-entry system means that each transaction must be recorded twice. Is Omar correct? Explain.

6. Is it necessary that a trial balance be taken periodically? What purpose does it serve?

7. Indicate whether each of the items below is a real or nominal account and whether it appears in the balance sheet or the income statement.

(a) Prepaid Rent.

(b) Salaries and Wages Payable.

(c) Merchandise Inventory.

(d) Accumulated Depreciation.

(e) Office Equipment.

(f) Income from Services.

(g) Office Salaries Expense.

(h) Supplies on Hand.

8. Employees are paid every Saturday for the preceding work week. If a balance sheet is prepared on Wednesday, December 31, what does the amount of wages earned during the first three days of the week (12/29, 12/30, 12/31) represent? Explain.

9. (a) How do the components of revenues and expenses differ between a merchandising company and a service enterprise? (b) Explain the income measurement process of a merchandising company.

10. What is the purpose of the Cost of Goods Sold account? (Assume a periodic inventory system.)

11. Under a perpetual system, what is the purpose of the Cost of Goods Sold account?

12. If the $3,900 cost of a new microcomputer and printer purchased for office use were recorded as a debit to Purchases, what would be the effect of the error on the balance sheet and income statement in the period in which the error was made?

13. What differences are there between the trial balance before closing and the trial balance after closing with respect to the following accounts?

(a) Accounts Payable.

(b) Expense accounts.

(c) Revenue accounts.

(d) Retained Earnings account.

(e) Cash.

14. What are adjusting entries and why are they necessary?

15. What are closing entries and why are they necessary?

16. Paul Molitor, maintenance supervisor for Blue Jay Insurance Co., has purchased a riding lawnmower and accessories to be used in maintaining the grounds around corporate headquarters. He has sent the following information to the accounting department.

Cost of mower and accessories	$3,000	Date purchased	7/1/05
Estimated useful life	5 yrs	Monthly salary of groundskeeper	$1,100
		Estimated annual fuel cost	$150

Compute the amount of depreciation expense (related to the mower and accessories) that should be reported on Blue Jay's December 31, 2005, income statement. Assume straight-line depreciation.

17. Selanne Enterprises made the following entry on December 31, 2005.

Dec. 31, 2005	Interest Expense	10,000	
	Interest Payable		10,000
	(To record interest expense due on loan from Anaheim National Bank.)		

What entry would Anaheim National Bank make regarding its outstanding loan to Selanne Enterprises? Explain why this must be the case.

18. "A work sheet is a permanent accounting record, and its use is required in the accounting cycle." Do you agree? Explain.

***19.** Distinguish between cash-basis accounting and accrual-basis accounting. Why is accrual-basis accounting acceptable for most business enterprises and the cash-basis unacceptable in the preparation of an income statement and a balance sheet?

***20.** When wages expense for the year is computed, why are beginning accrued wages subtracted from, and ending accrued wages added to, wages paid during the year?

***21.** List two types of transactions that would receive different accounting treatment using (a) strict cash-basis accounting, and (b) a modified cash basis.

***22.** What are reversing entries, and why are they used?

BRIEF EXERCISES

BE3-1 Transactions for Argot Company for the month of May are presented below. Prepare journal entries for each of these transactions. (You may omit explanations.)

May	1	B.D. Argot invests $3,000 cash in exchange for common stock in a small welding corporation.
	3	Buys equipment on account for $1,100.
	13	Pays $400 to landlord for May rent.
	21	Bills Noble Corp. $500 for welding work done.

BE3-2 Brett Favre Repair Shop had the following transactions during the first month of business. Journalize the transactions.

Aug.	2	Invested $12,000 cash and $2,500 of equipment in the business.
	7	Purchased supplies on account for $400. (Debit asset account.)
	12	Performed services for clients, for which $1,300 was collected in cash and $670 was billed to the clients.
	15	Paid August rent $600.
	19	Counted supplies and determined that only $270 of the supplies purchased on August 7 are still on hand.

BE3-3 On July 1, 2005, Blair Co. pays $18,000 to Hindi Insurance Co. for a 3-year insurance contract. Both companies have fiscal years ending December 31. For Blair Co. journalize the entry on July 1 and the adjusting entry on December 31.

BE3-4 Using the data in BE3-3, journalize the entry on July 1 and the adjusting entry on December 31 for Hindi Insurance Co. Hindi uses the accounts Unearned Insurance Revenue and Insurance Revenue.

BE3-5 On August 1, George Bell Company paid $8,400 in advance for 2 years' insurance coverage. Prepare Bell's August 1 journal entry and the annual adjusting entry on December 31.

BE3-6 Mogilny Corporation owns a warehouse. On November 1, it rented storage space to a lessee (tenant) for 3 months for a total cash payment of $2,700 received in advance. Prepare Mogilny's November 1 journal entry and the December 31 annual adjusting entry.

BE3-7 Catherine Janeway Company's weekly payroll, paid on Fridays, totals $6,000. Employees work a 5-day week. Prepare Janeway's adjusting entry on Wednesday, December 31, and the journal entry to record the $6,000 cash payment on Friday, January 2.

BE3-8 Included in Martinez Company's December 31 trial balance is a note receivable of $10,000. The note is a 4-month, 12% note dated October 1. Prepare Martinez's December 31 adjusting entry to record $300 of accrued interest, and the February 1 journal entry to record receipt of $10,400 from the borrower.

BE3-9 Prepare the following adjusting entries at December 31 for DeGads Co.

(a) Interest on notes payable of $400 is accrued.
(b) Fees earned but unbilled total $1,400.
(c) Salaries earned by employees of $700 have not been recorded.
(d) Bad debt expense for year is $900.

Use the following account titles: Service Revenue, Accounts Receivable, Interest Expense, Interest Payable, Salaries Expense, Salaries Payable, Allowance for Doubtful Accounts, and Bad Debt Expense.

BE3-10 At the end of its first year of operations, the trial balance of Rafael Company shows Equipment $30,000 and zero balances in Accumulated Depreciation—Equipment and Depreciation Expense. Depreciation for the year is estimated to be $3,000. Prepare the adjusting entry for depreciation at December 31, and indicate the balance sheet presentation for the equipment at December 31.

BE3-11 Willis Corporation has beginning inventory $81,000; Purchases $540,000; Freight-in $16,200; Purchase Returns $5,800; Purchase Discounts $5,000; and ending inventory $70,200. Compute cost of goods sold.

BE3-12 Karen Sepaniak has year-end account balances of Sales $828,900; Interest Revenue $13,500; Cost of Goods Sold $556,200; Operating Expenses $189,000; Income Tax Expense $35,100; and Dividends $18,900. Prepare the year-end closing entries.

***BE3-13** Smith Company had cash receipts from customers in 2005 of $152,000. Cash payments for operating expenses were $97,000. Smith has determined that at January 1, accounts receivable was $13,000, and prepaid expenses were $17,500. At December 31, accounts receivable was $18,600, and prepaid expenses were $23,200. Compute (a) service revenue and (b) operating expenses.

***BE3-14** Pelican Company made a December 31 adjusting entry to debit Salaries Expense and credit Salaries Payable for $3,600. On January 2, Pelican paid the weekly payroll of $6,000. Prepare Pelican's (a) January 1 reversing entry; (b) January 2 entry (assuming the reversing entry was prepared); and (c) January 2 entry (assuming the reversing entry was not prepared).

EXERCISES

E3-1 (Transaction Analysis—Service Company) Beverly Crusher is a licensed CPA. During the first month of operations of her business (a sole proprietorship), the following events and transactions occurred.

April	2	Invested $32,000 cash and equipment valued at $14,000 in the business.
	2	Hired a secretary-receptionist at a salary of $290 per week payable monthly.
	3	Purchased supplies on account $700. (Debit an asset account.)
	7	Paid office rent of $600 for the month.
	11	Completed a tax assignment and billed client $1,100 for services rendered. (Use Service Revenue account.)
	12	Received $3,200 advance on a management consulting engagement.
	17	Received cash of $2,300 for services completed for Ferengi Co.
	21	Paid insurance expense $110.
	30	Paid secretary-receptionist $1,160 for the month.
	30	A count of supplies indicated that $120 of supplies had been used.
	30	Purchased a new computer for $6,100 with personal funds. (The computer will be used exclusively for business purposes.)

Instructions
Journalize the transactions in the general journal. (Omit explanations.)

E3-2 (Corrected Trial Balance) The trial balance of Wanda Landowska Company shown below does not balance. Your review of the ledger reveals the following: (a) Each account had a normal balance. (b) The debit footings in Prepaid Insurance, Accounts Payable, and Property Tax Expense were each understated $100. (c) A transposition error was made in Accounts Receivable; the correct balances for Accounts Receivable and Service Revenue are $2,750 and $6,690, respectively. (d) A debit posting to Advertising Expense of $300 was omitted. (e) A $1,500 cash drawing by the owner was debited to Wanda Landowska, Capital, and credited to Cash.

WANDA LANDOWSKA COMPANY
TRIAL BALANCE
APRIL 30, 2005

	Debit	Credit
Cash	$ 4,800	
Accounts Receivable	2,570	
Prepaid Insurance	700	
Equipment		$ 8,000
Accounts Payable		4,500
Property Tax Payable	560	
Wanda Landowska, Capital		11,200
Service Revenue	6,960	
Salaries Expense	4,200	
Advertising Expense	1,100	
Property Tax Expense		800
	$20,890	$24,500

Instructions
Prepare a correct trial balance.

E3-3 (Corrected Trial Balance) The trial balance of Blues Traveler Corporation (see next page) does not balance.

BLUES TRAVELER CORPORATION
TRIAL BALANCE
APRIL 30, 2005

	Debit	Credit
Cash	$ 5,912	
Accounts Receivable	5,240	
Supplies on Hand	2,967	
Furniture and Equipment	6,100	
Accounts Payable		$ 7,044
Common Stock		8,000
Retained Earnings		2,000
Service Revenue		5,200
Office Expense	4,320	
	$24,539	$22,244

An examination of the ledger shows these errors.

1. Cash received from a customer on account was recorded (both debit and credit) as $1,380 instead of $1,830.
2. The purchase on account of a computer costing $3,200 was recorded as a debit to Office Expense and a credit to Accounts Payable.
3. Services were performed on account for a client, $2,250, for which Accounts Receivable was debited $2,250 and Service Revenue was credited $225.
4. A payment of $95 for telephone charges was entered as a debit to Office Expenses and a debit to Cash.
5. The Service Revenue account was totaled at $5,200 instead of $5,280.

Instructions
From this information prepare a corrected trial balance.

E3-4 (Corrected Trial Balance) The trial balance of Antoine Watteau Co. shown below does not balance.

ANTOINE WATTEAU CO.
TRIAL BALANCE
JUNE 30, 2005

	Debit	Credit
Cash		$ 2,870
Accounts Receivable	$ 3,231	
Supplies	800	
Equipment	3,800	
Accounts Payable		2,666
Unearned Service Revenue	1,200	
Common Stock		6,000
Retained Earnings		3,000
Service Revenue		2,380
Wages Expense	3,400	
Office Expense	940	
	$13,371	$16,916

Each of the listed accounts has a normal balance per the general ledger. An examination of the ledger and journal reveals the following errors.

1. Cash received from a customer on account was debited for $570, and Accounts Receivable was credited for the same amount. The actual collection was for $750.

2. The purchase of a computer printer on account for $500 was recorded as a debit to Supplies for $500 and a credit to Accounts Payable for $500.
3. Services were performed on account for a client for $890. Accounts Receivable was debited for $890 and Service Revenue was credited for $89.
4. A payment of $65 for telephone charges was recorded as a debit to Office Expense for $65 and a debit to Cash for $65.
5. When the Unearned Service Revenue account was reviewed, it was found that $325 of the balance was earned prior to June 30.
6. A debit posting to Wages Expense of $670 was omitted.
7. A payment on account for $206 was credited to Cash for $206 and credited to Accounts Payable for $260.
8. A dividend of $575 was debited to Wages Expense for $575 and credited to Cash for $575.

Instructions
Prepare a correct trial balance. (*Note:* It may be necessary to add one or more accounts to the trial balance.)

E3-5 (Adjusting Entries) The ledger of Duggan Rental Agency on March 31 of the current year includes the following selected accounts before adjusting entries have been prepared.

	Debit	Credit
Prepaid Insurance	$ 3,600	
Supplies	2,800	
Equipment	25,000	
Accumulated Depreciation—Equipment		$ 8,400
Notes Payable		20,000
Unearned Rent Revenue		9,300
Rent Revenue		60,000
Interest Expense	–0–	
Wage Expense	14,000	

An analysis of the accounts shows the following.

1. The equipment depreciates $250 per month.
2. One-third of the unearned rent was earned during the quarter.
3. Interest of $500 is accrued on the notes payable.
4. Supplies on hand total $850.
5. Insurance expires at the rate of $300 per month.

Instructions
Prepare the adjusting entries at March 31, assuming that adjusting entries are made quarterly. Additional accounts are: Depreciation Expense; Insurance Expense; Interest Payable; and Supplies Expense.

E3-6 (Adjusting Entries) Karen Weller, D.D.S., opened a dental practice on January 1, 2005. During the first month of operations the following transactions occurred.

1. Performed services for patients who had dental plan insurance. At January 31, $750 of such services was earned but not yet billed to the insurance companies.
2. Utility expenses incurred but not paid prior to January 31 totaled $520.
3. Purchased dental equipment on January 1 for $80,000, paying $20,000 in cash and signing a $60,000, 3-year note payable. The equipment depreciates $400 per month. Interest is $500 per month.
4. Purchased a one-year malpractice insurance policy on January 1 for $12,000.
5. Purchased $1,600 of dental supplies. On January 31, determined that $500 of supplies were on hand.

Instructions
Prepare the adjusting entries on January 31. Account titles are: Accumulated Depreciation—Dental Equipment; Depreciation Expense; Service Revenue; Accounts Receivable; Insurance Expense; Interest Expense; Interest Payable; Prepaid Insurance; Supplies; Supplies Expense; Utilities Expense; and Utilities Payable.

E3-7 (Analyze Adjusted Data) A partial adjusted trial balance of Piper Company at January 31, 2005, shows the following.

PIPER COMPANY
ADJUSTED TRIAL BALANCE
JANUARY 31, 2005

	Debit	Credit
Supplies	$ 700	
Prepaid Insurance	2,400	
Salaries Payable		$ 800
Unearned Revenue		750
Supplies Expense	950	
Insurance Expense	400	
Salaries Expense	1,800	
Service Revenue		2,000

Instructions

Answer the following questions, assuming the year begins January 1.

(a) If the amount in Supplies Expense is the January 31 adjusting entry, and $850 of supplies was purchased in January, what was the balance in Supplies on January 1?
(b) If the amount in Insurance Expense is the January 31 adjusting entry, and the original insurance premium was for one year, what was the total premium and when was the policy purchased?
(c) If $2,500 of salaries was paid in January, what was the balance in Salaries Payable at December 31, 2004?
(d) If $1,600 was received in January for services performed in January, what was the balance in Unearned Revenue at December 31, 2004?

E3-8 (Adjusting Entries) Bjorn Borg is the new owner of Ace Computer Services. At the end of August 2005, his first month of ownership, Bjorn is trying to prepare monthly financial statements. Below is some information related to unrecorded expenses that the business incurred during August.

1. At August 31, Mr. Borg owed his employees $1,900 in wages that will be paid on September 1.
2. At the end of the month he had not yet received the month's utility bill. Based on past experience, he estimated the bill would be approximately $600.
3. On August 1, Mr. Borg borrowed $30,000 from a local bank on a 15-year mortgage. The annual interest rate is 8%.
4. A telephone bill in the amount of $117 covering August charges is unpaid at August 31.

Instructions

Prepare the adjusting journal entries as of August 31, 2005, suggested by the information above.

E3-9 (Adjusting Entries) Selected accounts of Urdu Company are shown below.

Supplies

Beg. Bal.	800	10/31	470

Accounts Receivable

10/15	2,400		
10/31	1,650		

Salaries Expense

10/15	800		
10/31	600		

Salaries Payable

		10/31	600

Unearned Service Revenue

10/31	400	10/20	650

Supplies Expense

10/31	470		

Service Revenue

		10/17	2,400
		10/31	1,650
		10/31	400

Instructions

From an analysis of the T-accounts, reconstruct (a) the October transaction entries, and (b) the adjusting journal entries that were made on October 31, 2005.

E3-10 (Adjusting Entries) Greco Resort opened for business on June 1 with eight air-conditioned units. Its trial balance on August 31 is as follows.

GRECO RESORT
TRIAL BALANCE
AUGUST 31, 2005

	Debit	Credit
Cash	$ 19,600	
Prepaid Insurance	4,500	
Supplies	2,600	
Land	20,000	
Cottages	120,000	
Furniture	16,000	
Accounts Payable		$ 4,500
Unearned Rent Revenue		4,600
Mortgage Payable		60,000
Common Stock		91,000
Retained Earnings		9,000
Dividends	5,000	
Rent Revenue		76,200
Salaries Expense	44,800	
Utilities Expense	9,200	
Repair Expense	3,600	
	$245,300	$245,300

Other data:

1. The balance in prepaid insurance is a one-year premium paid on June 1, 2005.
2. An inventory count on August 31 shows $450 of supplies on hand.
3. Annual depreciation rates are cottages (4%) and furniture (10%). Salvage value is estimated to be 10% of cost.
4. Unearned Rent Revenue of $3,800 was earned prior to August 31.
5. Salaries of $375 were unpaid at August 31.
6. Rentals of $800 were due from tenants at August 31.
7. The mortgage interest rate is 8% per year.

Instructions

(a) Journalize the adjusting entries on August 31 for the 3-month period June 1–August 31.
(b) Prepare an adjusted trial balance on August 31.

E3-11 (Closing Entries) The adjusted trial balance of Lopez Company shows the following data pertaining to sales at the end of its fiscal year, October 31, 2005: Sales $800,000, Freight-out $12,000, Sales Returns and Allowances $24,000, and Sales Discounts $15,000.

Instructions

(a) Prepare the sales revenue section of the income statement.
(b) Prepare separate closing entries for (1) sales and (2) the contra accounts to sales.

E3-12 (Closing Entries) Presented below is information related to Gonzales Corporation for the month of January 2005.

Cost of goods sold	$208,000	Salary expense	$ 61,000
Freight-out	7,000	Sales discounts	8,000
Insurance expense	12,000	Sales returns and allowances	13,000
Rent expense	20,000	Sales	350,000

Instructions

Prepare the necessary closing entries.

E3-13 (Work Sheet) Presented on the next page are selected accounts for Alvarez Company as reported in the work sheet at the end of May 2005.

Accounts	Adjusted Trial Balance		Income Statement		Balance Sheet	
	Dr.	Cr.	Dr.	Cr.	Dr.	Cr.
Cash	9,000					
Merchandise Inventory	80,000					
Sales		450,000				
Sales Returns and Allowances	10,000					
Sales Discounts	5,000					
Cost of Goods Sold	250,000					

Instructions

Complete the work sheet by extending amounts reported in the adjusted trial balance to the appropriate columns in the work sheet. Do not total individual columns.

E3-14 (Missing Amounts) Presented below is financial information for two different companies.

	Alatorre Company	Eduardo Company
Sales	$90,000	(d)
Sales returns	(a)	$ 5,000
Net sales	81,000	95,000
Cost of goods sold	56,000	(e)
Gross profit	(b)	38,000
Operating expenses	15,000	23,000
Net income	(c)	15,000

Instructions

Compute the missing amounts.

E3-15 (Find Missing Amounts—Periodic Inventory) Financial information is presented below for four different companies.

	Pamela's Cosmetics	Dean's Grocery	Anderson Wholesalers	Baywatch Supply Co.
Sales	$78,000	(c)	$144,000	$100,000
Sales returns	(a)	$ 5,000	12,000	9,000
Net sales	74,000	94,000	132,000	(g)
Beginning inventory	16,000	(d)	44,000	24,000
Purchases	88,000	100,000	(e)	85,000
Purchase returns	6,000	10,000	8,000	(h)
Ending inventory	(b)	48,000	30,000	28,000
Cost of goods sold	64,000	72,000	(f)	72,000
Gross profit	10,000	22,000	18,000	(i)

Instructions

Determine the missing amounts (a–i). Show all computations.

E3-16 (Cost of Goods Sold Section—Periodic Inventory) The trial balance of the Neville Mariner Company at the end of its fiscal year, August 31, 2005, includes the following accounts: Merchandise Inventory $17,500; Purchases $149,400; Sales $200,000; Freight-in $4,000; Sales Returns and Allowances $4,000; Freight-out $1,000; and Purchase Returns and Allowances $2,000. The ending merchandise inventory is $25,000.

Instructions

Prepare a cost of goods sold section for the year ending August 31.

E3-17 (Closing Entries for a Corporation) Presented below are selected account balances for Homer Winslow Co. as of December 31, 2005.

Merchandise Inventory 12/31/05	$ 60,000	Cost of Goods Sold	$225,700
Common Stock	75,000	Selling Expenses	16,000
Retained Earnings	45,000	Administrative Expenses	38,000
Dividends	18,000	Income Tax Expense	30,000
Sales Returns and Allowances	12,000		
Sales Discounts	15,000		
Sales	410,000		

Instructions
Prepare closing entries for Homer Winslow Co. on December 31, 2005.

E3-18 (Work Sheet Preparation) The trial balance of R. L. Stein Roofing at March 31, 2005, is as follows.

R. L. STEIN ROOFING
TRIAL BALANCE
MARCH 31, 2005

	Debit	Credit
Cash	$ 2,300	
Accounts Receivable	2,600	
Roofing Supplies	1,100	
Equipment	6,000	
Accumulated Depreciation—Equipment		$ 1,200
Accounts Payable		1,100
Unearned Service Revenue		300
Common Stock		6,400
Retained Earnings		600
Service Revenue		3,000
Salaries Expense	500	
Miscellaneous Expense	100	
	$12,600	$12,600

Other data:

1. A physical count reveals only $520 of roofing supplies on hand.
2. Equipment is depreciated at a rate of $120 per month.
3. Unearned service revenue amounted to $100 on March 31.
4. Accrued salaries are $850.

Instructions
Enter the trial balance on a work sheet and complete the work sheet, assuming that the adjustments relate only to the month of March. (Ignore income taxes.)

E3-19 (Work Sheet and Balance Sheet Presentation) The adjusted trial balance of Ed Bradley Co. work sheet for the month ended April 30, 2005, contains the following.

ED BRADLEY CO.
WORK SHEET (PARTIAL)
FOR THE MONTH ENDED APRIL 30, 2005

	Adjusted Trial Balance		Income Statement		Balance Sheet	
Account Titles	Dr.	Cr.	Dr.	Cr.	Dr.	Cr.
Cash	$19,472					
Accounts Receivable	6,920					
Prepaid Rent	2,280					
Equipment	18,050					
Accumulated Depreciation		$ 4,895				
Notes Payable		5,700				
Accounts Payable		5,472				
Bradley, Capital		34,960				
Bradley, Drawing	6,650					
Service Revenue		11,590				
Salaries Expense	6,840					
Rent Expense	2,260					
Depreciation Expense	145					
Interest Expense	83					
Interest Payable		83				

Instructions

Complete the work sheet and prepare a balance sheet as illustrated in this chapter.

E3-20 (Partial Work Sheet Preparation) Jurassic Park Co. prepares monthly financial statements from a work sheet. Selected portions of the January work sheet showed the following data.

JURASSIC PARK CO.
WORK SHEET (PARTIAL)
FOR MONTH ENDED JANUARY 31, 2005

	Trial Balance		Adjustments		Adjusted Trial Balance	
Account Title	Dr.	Cr.	Dr.	Cr.	Dr.	Cr.
Supplies	3,256			(a) 1,500	1,756	
Accumulated Depreciation		6,682		(b) 257		6,939
Interest Payable		100		(c) 50		150
Supplies Expense			(a) 1,500		1,500	
Depreciation Expense			(b) 257		257	
Interest Expense			(c) 50		50	

During February no events occurred that affected these accounts, but at the end of February the following information was available.

(a) Supplies on hand	$715
(b) Monthly depreciation	$257
(c) Accrued interest	$ 50

Instructions

Reproduce the data that would appear in the February work sheet, and indicate the amounts that would be shown in the February income statement.

E3-21 (Transactions of a Corporation, Including Investment and Dividend) Scratch Miniature Golf and Driving Range Inc. was opened on March 1 by Scott Verplank. The following selected events and transactions occurred during March.

Mar.	1	Invested $50,000 cash in the business in exchange for common stock.
	3	Purchased Lee Janzen's Golf Land for $38,000 cash. The price consists of land $10,000; building $22,000; and equipment $6,000. (Make one compound entry.)
	5	Advertised the opening of the driving range and miniature golf course, paying advertising expenses of $1,600.
	6	Paid cash $1,480 for a one-year insurance policy.
	10	Purchased golf equipment for $2,500 from Sluman Company, payable in 30 days.
	18	Received golf fees of $1,200 in cash.
	25	Declared and paid a $500 cash dividend.
	30	Paid wages of $900.
	30	Paid Sluman Company in full.
	31	Received $750 of fees in cash.

Scratch uses the following accounts: Cash; Prepaid Insurance; Land; Buildings; Equipment; Accounts Payable; Common Stock; Dividends; Service Revenue; Advertising Expense; and Wages Expense.

Instructions

Journalize the March transactions.

***E3-22 (Cash to Accrual Basis)** Jill Accardo, M.D., maintains the accounting records of Accardo Clinic on a cash basis. During 2005, Dr. Accardo collected $142,600 from her patients and paid $55,470 in expenses. At January 1, 2005, and December 31, 2005, she had accounts receivable, unearned service revenue, accrued expenses, and prepaid expenses as follows. (All long-lived assets are rented.)

	January 1, 2005	December 31, 2005
Accounts receivable	$9,250	$15,927
Unearned service revenue	2,840	4,111
Accrued expenses	3,435	2,108
Prepaid expenses	1,917	3,232

Instructions

Prepare a schedule that converts Dr. Accardo's "excess of cash collected over cash disbursed" for the year 2005 to net income on an accrual basis for the year 2005.

***E-23 (Cash and Accrual Basis)** Wayne Rogers Corp. maintains its financial records on the cash basis of accounting. Interested in securing a long-term loan from its regular bank, Wayne Rogers Corp. requests you as its independent CPA to convert its cash-basis income statement data to the accrual basis. You are provided with the following summarized data covering 2003, 2004, and 2005.

	2003	2004	2005
Cash receipts from sales:			
On 2003 sales	$295,000	$160,000	$30,000
On 2004 sales	–0–	355,000	90,000
On 2005 sales			408,000
Cash payments for expenses:			
On 2003 expenses	185,000	67,000	25,000
On 2004 expenses	40,000[a]	160,000	55,000
On 2005 expenses		45,000[b]	218,000

[a]Prepayments of 2004 expenses.
[b]Prepayments of 2005 expenses.

Instructions

(a) Using the data above, prepare abbreviated income statements for the years 2003 and 2004 on the cash basis.

(b) Using the data above, prepare abbreviated income statements for the years 2003 and 2004 on the accrual basis.

***E3-24 (Adjusting and Reversing Entries)** When the accounts of Daniel Barenboim Inc. are examined, the adjusting data listed below are uncovered on December 31, the end of an annual fiscal period.

1. The prepaid insurance account shows a debit of $5,280, representing the cost of a 2-year fire insurance policy dated August 1 of the current year.
2. On November 1, Rental Revenue was credited for $1,800, representing revenue from a subrental for a 3-month period beginning on that date.
3. Purchase of advertising materials for $800 during the year was recorded in the Advertising Expense account. On December 31, advertising materials of $290 are on hand.
4. Interest of $770 has accrued on notes payable.

Instructions

Prepare in general journal form: (a) the adjusting entry for each item and (b) the reversing entry for each item where appropriate.

PROBLEMS

P3-1 (Transactions, Financial Statements—Service Company) Listed below are the transactions of Isao Aoki, D.D.S., for the month of September.

Sept.	1	Isao Aoki begins practice as a dentist and invests $20,000 cash.
	2	Purchases furniture and dental equipment on account from Green Jacket Co. for $17,280.
	4	Pays rent for office space, $680 for the month.
	4	Employs a receptionist, Michael Bradley.
	5	Purchases dental supplies for cash, $942.
	8	Receives cash of $1,690 from patients for services performed.
	10	Pays miscellaneous office expenses, $430.
	14	Bills patients $5,120 for services performed.
	18	Pays Green Jacket Co. on account, $3,600.
	19	Withdraws $3,000 cash from the business for personal use.
	20	Receives $980 from patients on account.
	25	Bills patients $2,110 for services performed.
	30	Pays the following expenses in cash: office salaries $1,400; miscellaneous office expenses $85.
	30	Dental supplies used during September, $330.

Instructions

(a) Enter the transactions shown above in appropriate general ledger accounts. Use the following ledger accounts: Cash; Accounts Receivable; Supplies on Hand; Furniture and Equipment; Accumulated Depreciation; Accounts Payable; Isao Aoki, Capital; Service Revenue; Rent Expense; Miscellaneous Office Expense; Office Salaries Expense; Supplies Expense; Depreciation Expense; and Income Summary. Allow 10 lines for the Cash and Income Summary accounts, and 5 lines for each of the other accounts needed. Record depreciation using a 5-year life on the furniture and equipment, the straight-line method, and no salvage value. Do not use a drawing account.

(b) Prepare a trial balance.

(c) Prepare an income statement, a balance sheet, and a statement of owner's equity.

(d) Close the ledger.

(e) Prepare a post-closing trial balance.

P3-2 (Adjusting Entries and Financial Statements) Yount Advertising Agency was founded by Thomas Grant in January 2001. Presented below are both the adjusted and unadjusted trial balances as of December 31, 2005.

YOUNT ADVERTISING AGENCY
TRIAL BALANCE
DECEMBER 31, 2005

	Unadjusted		Adjusted	
	Dr.	Cr.	Dr.	Cr.
Cash	$ 11,000		$ 11,000	
Accounts Receivable	20,000		21,500	
Art Supplies	8,400		5,000	
Prepaid Insurance	3,350		2,500	
Printing Equipment	60,000		60,000	
Accumulated Depreciation		$ 28,000		$ 35,000
Accounts Payable		5,000		5,000
Interest Payable		–0–		150
Notes Payable		5,000		5,000
Unearned Advertising Revenue		7,000		5,600
Salaries Payable		–0–		1,300
Common Stock		10,000		10,000
Retained Earnings		3,500		3,500
Advertising Revenue		58,600		61,500
Salaries Expense	10,000		11,300	
Insurance Expense			850	
Interest Expense	350		500	
Depreciation Expense			7,000	
Art Supplies Expense			3,400	
Rent Expense	4,000		4,000	
	$117,100	$117,100	$127,050	$127,050

Instructions

(a) Journalize the annual adjusting entries that were made.

(b) Prepare an income statement and a statement of retained earnings for the year ending December 31, 2005, and a balance sheet at December 31.

(c) Answer the following questions.

(1) If the note has been outstanding 3 months, what is the annual interest rate on that note?

(2) If the company paid $13,500 in salaries in 2005, what was the balance in Salaries Payable on December 31, 2004?

P3-3 (Adjusting Entries) A review of the ledger of Oklahoma Company at December 31, 2005, produces the following data pertaining to the preparation of annual adjusting entries.

1. Salaries Payable $0. There are eight salaried employees. Salaries are paid every Friday for the current week. Five employees receive a salary of $700 each per week, and three employees earn $500 each per week. December 31 is a Tuesday. Employees do not work weekends. All employees worked the last 2 days of December.
2. Unearned Rent Revenue $369,000. The company began subleasing office space in its new building on November 1. Each tenant is required to make a $5,000 security deposit that is not refundable

until occupancy is terminated. At December 31, the company had the following rental contracts that are paid in full for the entire term of the lease.

Date	Term (in months)	Monthly Rent	Number of Leases
Nov. 1	6	$4,000	5
Dec. 1	6	$8,500	4

3. Prepaid Advertising $13,200. This balance consists of payments on two advertising contracts. The contracts provide for monthly advertising in two trade magazines. The terms of the contracts are as follows.

Contract	Date	Amount	Number of Magazine Issues
A650	May 1	$6,000	12
B974	Oct. 1	7,200	24

The first advertisement runs in the month in which the contract is signed.

4. Notes Payable $80,000. This balance consists of a note for one year at an annual interest rate of 12%, dated June 1.

Instructions

Prepare the adjusting entries at December 31, 2005. (Show all computations).

P3-4 (Work Sheet, Balance Sheet, Adjusting and Closing Entries) Noah's Ark has a fiscal year ending on September 30. Selected data from the September 30 work sheet are presented below.

NOAH'S ARK
WORK SHEET
FOR THE YEAR ENDED SEPTEMBER 30, 2005

	Trial Balance		Adjusted Trial Balance	
	Dr.	Cr.	Dr.	Cr.
Cash	37,400		37,400	
Supplies	18,600		1,200	
Prepaid Insurance	31,900		3,900	
Land	80,000		80,000	
Equipment	120,000		120,000	
Accumulated Depreciation		36,200		43,000
Accounts Payable		14,600		14,600
Unearned Admissions Revenue		2,700		1,700
Mortgage Payable		50,000		50,000
N. Y. Berge, Capital		109,700		109,700
N. Y. Berge, Drawing	14,000		14,000	
Admissions Revenue		278,500		279,500
Salaries Expense	109,000		109,000	
Repair Expense	30,500		30,500	
Advertising Expense	9,400		9,400	
Utilities Expense	16,900		16,900	
Property Taxes Expense	18,000		21,000	
Interest Expense	6,000		12,000	
Totals	491,700	491,700		
Insurance Expense			28,000	
Supplies Expense			17,400	
Interest Payable				6,000
Depreciation Expense			6,800	
Property Taxes Payable				3,000
Totals			507,500	507,500

Instructions

(a) Prepare a complete work sheet.

(b) Prepare a classified balance sheet. (*Note:* $10,000 of the mortgage payable is due for payment in the next fiscal year.)

(c) Journalize the adjusting entries using the work sheet as a basis.

(d) Journalize the closing entries using the work sheet as a basis.
(e) Prepare a post-closing trial balance.

P3-5 (Financial Statements, Adjusting and Closing Entries) The trial balance of Becky Bishop Fashion Center contained the following accounts at November 30, the end of the company's fiscal year.

BECKY BISHOP FASHION CENTER
TRIAL BALANCE
NOVEMBER 30, 2005

	Debit	Credit
Cash	$ 26,700	
Accounts Receivable	33,700	
Merchandise Inventory	45,000	
Store Supplies	5,500	
Store Equipment	85,000	
Accumulated Depreciation—Store Equipment		$ 18,000
Delivery Equipment	48,000	
Accumulated Depreciation—Delivery Equipment		6,000
Notes Payable		51,000
Accounts Payable		48,500
Common Stock		90,000
Retained Earnings		8,000
Sales		757,200
Sales Returns and Allowances	4,200	
Cost of Goods Sold	497,400	
Salaries Expense	140,000	
Advertising Expense	26,400	
Utilities Expense	14,000	
Repair Expense	12,100	
Delivery Expense	16,700	
Rent Expense	24,000	
	$978,700	$978,700

Adjustment data:

1. Store supplies on hand totaled $3,500.
2. Depreciation is $9,000 on the store equipment and $7,000 on the delivery equipment.
3. Interest of $11,000 is accrued on notes payable at November 30.

Other data:

1. Salaries expense is 70% selling and 30% administrative.
2. Rent expense and utilities expense are 80% selling and 20% administrative.
3. $30,000 of notes payable are due for payment next year.
4. Repair expense is 100% administrative.

Instructions

(a) Journalize the adjusting entries.
(b) Enter the trial balance on a work sheet and complete the work sheet.
(c) Prepare a multiple-step income statement and retained earnings statement for the year and a classified balance sheet as of November 30, 2005.
(d) Journalize the closing entries.
(e) Prepare a post-closing trial balance.

P3-6 (Adjusting Entries) The accounts listed below appeared in the December 31 trial balance of the Jane Alexander Theater.

	Debit	Credit
Equipment	$192,000	
Accumulated Depreciation—Equipment		$ 60,000
Notes Payable		90,000
Admissions Revenue		380,000
Advertising Expense	13,680	
Salaries Expense	57,600	
Interest Expense	1,400	

Instructions

(a) From the account balances listed above and the information given below, prepare the annual adjusting entries necessary on December 31.

(1) The equipment has an estimated life of 16 years and a salvage value of $40,000 at the end of that time. (Use straight-line method.)

(2) The note payable is a 90-day note given to the bank October 20 and bearing interest at 10%. (Use 360 days for denominator.)

(3) In December 2,000 coupon admission books were sold at $25 each. They could be used for admission any time after January 1.

(4) Advertising expense paid in advance and included in Advertising Expense $1,100.

(5) Salaries accrued but unpaid $4,700.

(b) What amounts should be shown for each of the following on the income statement for the year?

(1) Interest expense.

(2) Admissions revenue.

(3) Advertising expense.

(4) Salaries expense.

P3-7 (Adjusting Entries and Financial Statements) Presented below are the trial balance and the other information related to Muhammad Ali, a consulting engineer.

MUHAMMAD ALI, CONSULTING ENGINEER
TRIAL BALANCE
DECEMBER 31, 2005

	Debit	Credit
Cash	$ 31,500	
Accounts Receivable	49,600	
Allowance for Doubtful Accounts		$ 750
Engineering Supplies Inventory	1,960	
Unexpired Insurance	1,100	
Furniture and Equipment	25,000	
Accumulated Depreciation—Furniture and Equipment		6,250
Notes Payable		7,200
Muhammad Ali, Capital		35,010
Service Revenue		100,000
Rent Expense	9,750	
Office Salaries Expense	28,500	
Heat, Light, and Water Expense	1,080	
Miscellaneous Office Expense	720	
	$149,210	$149,210

1. Fees received in advance from clients $6,900.
2. Services performed for clients that were not recorded by December 31, $4,900.
3. Bad debt expense for the year is $1,430.
4. Insurance expired during the year $480.
5. Furniture and equipment is being depreciated at $12\frac{1}{2}$% per year.
6. Muhammad Ali gave the bank a 90-day, 10% note for $7,200 on December 1, 2005.
7. Rent of the building is $750 per month. The rent for 2005 has been paid, as has that for January 2006.
8. Office salaries earned but unpaid December 31, 2005, $2,510.

Instructions

(a) From the trial balance and other information given, prepare annual adjusting entries as of December 31, 2005.

(b) Prepare an income statement for 2005, a balance sheet, and a statement of owner's equity. Muhammad Ali withdrew $17,000 cash for personal use during the year.

P3-8 (Adjusting Entries and Financial Statements) Ana Alicia Advertising Corporation was founded by Ana Alicia in January 2001. Presented on the next page are both the adjusted and unadjusted trial balances as of December 31, 2005.

ANA ALICIA ADVERTISING CORPORATION
TRIAL BALANCE
DECEMBER 31, 2005

	Unadjusted		Adjusted	
	Dr.	Cr.	Dr.	Cr.
Cash	$ 7,000		$ 7,000	
Accounts Receivable	19,000		22,000	
Art Supplies	8,500		5,500	
Prepaid Insurance	3,250		2,500	
Printing Equipment	60,000		60,000	
Accumulated Depreciation		$ 27,000		$ 33,750
Accounts Payable		5,000		5,000
Interest Payable				150
Notes Payable		5,000		5,000
Unearned Service Revenue		7,000		5,600
Salaries Payable				1,500
Common Stock		10,000		10,000
Retained Earnings		4,500		4,500
Service Revenue		58,600		63,000
Salaries Expense	10,000		11,500	
Insurance Expense			750	
Interest Expense	350		500	
Depreciation Expense			6,750	
Art Supplies Expense	5,000		8,000	
Rent Expense	4,000		4,000	
	$117,100	$117,100	$128,500	$128,500

Instructions

(a) Journalize the annual adjusting entries that were made.

(b) Prepare an income statement and a statement of retained earnings for the year ending December 31, 2005, and a balance sheet at December 31.

(c) Answer the following questions.

(1) If the useful life of equipment is 8 years, what is the expected salvage value?

(2) If the note has been outstanding 3 months, what is the annual interest rate on that note?

(3) If the company paid $12,500 in salaries in 2005, what was the balance in Salaries Payable on December 31, 2004?

P3-9 (Adjusting and Closing) Following is the trial balance of the Platteville Golf Club, Inc. as of December 31. The books are closed annually on December 31.

PLATTEVILLE GOLF CLUB, INC.
TRIAL BALANCE
DECEMBER 31

	Debit	Credit
Cash	$ 15,000	
Accounts Receivable	13,000	
Allowance for Doubtful Accounts		$ 1,100
Unexpired Insurance	9,000	
Land	350,000	
Buildings	120,000	
Accumulated Depreciation of Buildings		38,400
Equipment	150,000	
Accumulated Depreciation of Equipment		70,000
Common Stock		400,000
Retained Earnings		82,000
Dues Revenue		200,000
Greens Fee Revenue		8,100
Rental Revenue		15,400
Utilities Expense	54,000	
Salaries Expense	80,000	
Maintenance Expense	24,000	
	$815,000	$815,000

Instructions

(a) Enter the balances in ledger accounts. Allow five lines for each account.

(b) From the trial balance and the information given, prepare annual adjusting entries and post to the ledger accounts.

(1) The buildings have an estimated life of 25 years with no salvage value (straight-line method).
(2) The equipment is depreciated at 10% per year.
(3) Insurance expired during the year $3,500.
(4) The rental revenue represents the amount received for 11 months for dining facilities. The December rent has not yet been received.
(5) It is estimated that 15% of the accounts receivable will be uncollectible.
(6) Salaries earned but not paid by December 31, $3,600.
(7) Dues paid in advance by members $8,900.

(c) Prepare an adjusted trial balance.

(d) Prepare closing entries and post.

P3-10 (Adjusting and Closing) Presented below is the December 31 trial balance of Nancy Drew Boutique.

NANCY DREW BOUTIQUE
TRIAL BALANCE
DECEMBER 31

	Debit	Credit
Cash	$ 18,500	
Accounts Receivable	42,000	
Allowance for Doubtful Accounts		$ 700
Inventory, December 31	80,000	
Prepaid Insurance	5,100	
Furniture and Equipment	84,000	
Accumulated Depreciation of Furniture and Equipment		35,000
Notes Payable		28,000
Common Stock		80,600
Retained Earnings		10,000
Sales		600,000
Cost of Goods Sold	398,000	
Sales Salaries Expense	50,000	
Advertising Expense	6,700	
Administrative Salaries Expense	65,000	
Office Expense	5,000	
	$754,300	$754,300

Instructions

(a) Construct T-accounts and enter the balances shown.

(b) Prepare adjusting journal entries for the following and post to the T-accounts. Open additional T-accounts as necessary. (The books are closed yearly on December 31.)

(1) Bad debts are estimated to be $1,400.
(2) Furniture and equipment is depreciated based on a 6-year life (no salvage).
(3) Insurance expired during the year $2,550.
(4) Interest accrued on notes payable $3,360.
(5) Sales salaries earned but not paid $2,400.
(6) Advertising paid in advance $700.
(7) Office supplies on hand $1,500, charged to Office Expense when purchased.

(c) Prepare closing entries and post to the accounts.

***P3-11 (Cash and Accrual Basis)** On January 1, 2005, Jill Monroe and Jenni Meno formed a computer sales and service enterprise in Soapsville, Arkansas, by investing $90,000 cash. The new company, Razorback Sales and Service, has the following transactions during January.

1. Pays $6,000 in advance for 3 months' rent of office, showroom, and repair space.
2. Purchases 40 personal computers at a cost of $1,500 each, 6 graphics computers at a cost of $3,000 each, and 25 printers at a cost of $450 each, paying cash upon delivery.
3. Sales, repair, and office employees earn $12,600 in salaries during January, of which $3,000 was still payable at the end of January.

4. Sells 30 personal computers at $2,550 each, 4 graphics computers for $4,500 each, and 15 printers for $750 each; $75,000 is received in cash in January, and $30,750 is sold on a deferred payment basis.
5. Other operating expenses of $8,400 are incurred and paid for during January; $2,000 of incurred expenses are payable at January 31.

Instructions

(a) Using the transaction data above, prepare (1) a cash-basis income statement, and (2) an accrual-basis income statement for the month of January.

(b) Using the transaction data above, prepare (1) a cash-basis balance sheet and (2) an accrual-basis balance sheet as of January 31, 2005.

(c) Identify the items in the cash basis financial statements that make cash-basis accounting inconsistent with the theory underlying the elements of financial statements.

USING YOUR JUDGMENT

FINANCIAL REPORTING PROBLEM

3M Company

The financial statements of 3M are presented in Appendix 5B or can be accessed on the Take Action! CD.

Instructions

Refer to these financial statements and the accompanying notes to answer the following questions.

(a) What were 3M's total assets at December 30, 2001? At December 31, 2000?

(b) How much cash (and cash equivalents) did 3M have on December 30, 2001?

(c) What were 3M's research and development costs in 1999? In 2001?

(d) What were 3M's revenues in 1999? In 2001?

(e) Using 3M's financial statements and related notes, identify items that may result in adjusting entries for prepayments and accruals.

(f) What were the amounts of 3M's depreciation expense in 1999, 2000, and 2001?

FINANCIAL STATEMENT ANALYSIS CASE

Kellogg Company

Kellogg Company has its headquarters in Battle Creek, Michigan. The company manufactures and sells ready-to-eat breakfast cereals and convenience foods including cookies, toaster pastries, and cereal bars.

Selected data from Kellogg Company's 2001 annual report follows (dollar amounts in millions).

	2001	2000	1999
Net sales	$8,853.3	$6,954.7	$6,984.2
Operating profit	1,167.9	989.8	828.8
Net cash flow provided by operations less capital expenditures	855.5	650.0	529.0
Net earnings	473.6	587.7	338.3

In its 2001 annual report, Kellogg Company discussed its strategies for "creating more value in the future." One of the principles designed to drive growth relates to the use of accounting measures:

> Set the Right Targets and Measures—Set targets that are both challenging and realistic and which do not risk long-term health for short-term gains.

Specifically, Kellogg has established performance incentives based on net sales, operating profit, and cash flow.

Instructions

(a) Compute the percentage change in sales, operating profit, net cash flow, and net earnings from year to year for the years presented.

(b) Evaluate Kellogg's performance. Which trend seems most favorable? Which trend seems least favorable? What are the implications of these trends for Kellogg's objective to "create more value in the future"? Explain.

COMPARATIVE ANALYSIS CASE

The Coca-Cola Company and PepsiCo, Inc.

Instructions

Go to the Take Action! CD and use information found there to answer the following questions related to The Coca-Cola Company and PepsiCo, Inc.

(a) Which company had the greater percentage increase in total assets from 2000 to 2001?

(b) Using the Selected Financial Data section of these two companies, determine their 5-year compound growth rates related to net sales and income from continuing operations.

(c) Which company had more depreciation and amortization expense for 2001? Provide a rationale as to why there is a difference in these amounts between the two companies.

RESEARCH CASE

The Enterprise Standard Industrial Classification (SIC) coding scheme, a published classification of firms into separate industries, is commonly used in practice. SIC codes permit identification of company activities on three levels of detail. Two-digit codes designate a "major group," three-digit codes designate an "industry group," and four-digit codes identify a specific "industry."

Instructions

Use the *Standard Industrial Classification Manual* (published by the U.S. Government's Office of Management and Budget in 1987) to answer the following questions.

(a) On what basis are SIC codes assigned to companies?

(b) Identify the major group/industry group/industry represented by the following codes.

12	3571	75
271	7033	872

(c) Identify the SIC code for the following industries.

(1) Golfing equipment—manufacturing.
(2) Worm farms.
(3) Felt tip markers—manufacturing.
(4) Household appliance stores, electric or gas—retail.
(5) Advertising agencies.

(d) You are interested in examining several companies in the passenger airline industry. Determine the appropriate two-, three-, and four-digit SIC codes. Use *Wards Business Directory of U.S. Private and Public Companies (Vol. 5)* to compile a list of the five largest parent companies (by total sales) in the industry. *Note:* If Wards is not available, alternative sources include *Standard & Poor's Register of Corporations, Directors, and Executives, Standard & Poor's Industry Surveys,* and the Dun & Bradstreet *Million Dollar Directory.*

PROFESSIONAL SIMULATIONS

Simulation 1

Accounting Information System

Directions | Situation | Journal Entries | Financial Statements | Explanation | Research | Resources

Directions

In this simulation, you will be asked various questions regarding the accounting information system. Prepare responses to all parts.

Situation

Nalezny Advertising Agency was founded by Casey Hayward in January 2002. Presented below are both the adjusted and unadjusted trial balances as of December 31, 2005.

Nalezny Advertising Agency
Trial Balance
December 31, 2005

	Unadjusted		Adjusted	
	Dr.	Cr.	Dr.	Cr.
Cash	$11,000		$11,000	
Accounts Receivable	20,000		21,500	
Art Supplies	8,400		5,000	
Printing Equipment	60,000		60,000	
Accumulated Depreciation		$28,000		$35,000
Accounts Payable		5,000		5,000
Unearned Advertising Revenue		7,000		5,600
Salaries Payable		–0–		1,300
Common Stock		10,000		10,000
Retained Earnings		4,800		4,800
Advertising Revenue		58,600		61,500
Salaries Expense	10,000		11,300	
Depreciation Expense			7,000	
Art Supplies Expense			3,400	
Rent Expense	4,000		4,000	
	$113,400	$113,400	$123,200	$123,200

Journal Entries

Journalize the annual adjusting entries that were made.

Financial Statements

Prepare an income statement for the year ending December 31, 2005, and a balance sheet at December 31.

Explanation

Describe the remaining steps in the accounting cycle to be completed by Nalezny for 2005.

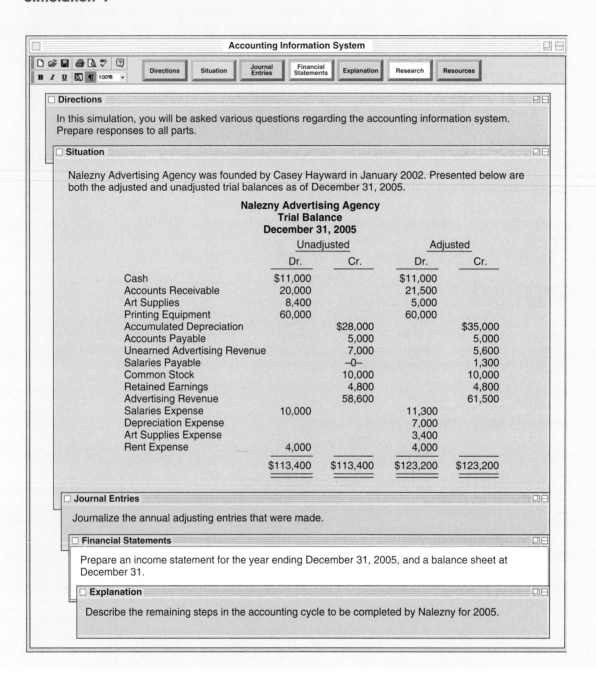

*Simulation 2

Cash Basis and Accrual Basis

Directions | Situation | Explanation | Research | Resources

Directions

In this simulation, you will be asked various questions regarding the cash and accrual bases of accounting. Prepare responses to all parts.

Situation

Dr. John Gleason, M.D., maintains the accounting records of Bones Clinic on a cash basis. During 2005, Dr. Gleason collected $146,000 from his patients and paid $55,470 in expenses.

At January 1, 2005, and December 31, 2005, he had accounts receivable, unearned service revenue, accrued expenses, and prepaid expenses as follows. (All long-lived assets are rented.)

	January 1, 2005	December 31, 2005
Accounts receivable	$9,250	$16,100
Unearned service revenue	2,840	1,620
Accrued expenses	3,435	2,200
Prepaid expenses	2,000	1,775

Resources

Using an electronic spreadsheet, prepare a schedule to calculate Dr. Gleason's income on the accrual basis.

Explanation

Draft a brief memorandum to Dr. Gleason explaining what you did to calculate net income on the accrual basis.

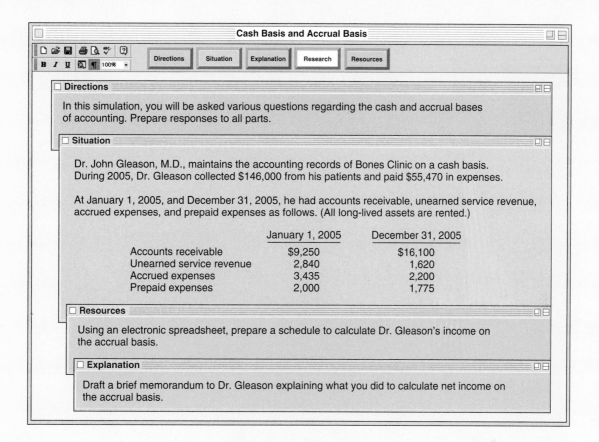

Remember to check the **Take Action! CD** and the book's **companion Web site** to find additional resources for this chapter.

CHAPTER 4

Income Statement and Related Information

Which Income Number?

Recently, companies have been providing investors a choice in reported income numbers. In addition to income measured according to generally accepted accounting principles (GAAP), companies also are reporting an income measure that has been adjusted for certain items. Companies make these adjustments because they believe the items are not representative of operating results. In some cases these adjustments are quite large. As shown in the following table, in a recent quarter the reporting of such "pro forma" income measures put a very different spin on operating results. In some cases (**JDS-Uniphase**, **PMC-Sierra**, and **Yahoo!**), a loss under GAAP measurement rules became an operating profit after pro forma adjustments.

Company	Earnings Per Share Pro Forma	Earnings Per Share GAAP
JDS-Uniphase	$0.14	−$1.13
Checkfree	0.04	−1.17
Amazon.com	−0.22	−0.66
PMC-Sierra	0.02	−0.38
Corning	0.29	0.14
Qualcomm	0.29	0.18
Yahoo!	0.01	−0.02

Characteristic of pro forma reporting practices is **Amazon.com**, which made adjustments for items such as stock-based compensation, amortization of goodwill and intangibles, impairment charges, and equity in losses of investees. All of these adjustments make pro forma earnings higher than GAAP income. In its earnings announcement, Amazon defended its pro forma reporting, saying that it gives better insight into the fundamental operations of the business.

So what's wrong with focusing investors on the fundamentals of the business? According to Ed Jenkins, former chair of the FASB, one problem is that there are no standards for the reporting of pro forma numbers. As a result, investors will have a hard time comparing Amazon's pro forma measure with that reported by another company, which has a different idea of what is fundamental to its business. Also, there is concern that many companies use pro forma reporting to deflect investor attention from bad news.

Rather than relying on management's choice of the number to focus on, GAAP income numbers are subject to the same rules for all companies, are audited, and give investors a more complete picture of company profitability, not the story preferred by management.[1]

LEARNING OBJECTIVES

After studying this chapter, you should be able to:

1. **Identify the uses and limitations of an income statement.**
2. **Prepare a single-step income statement.**
3. **Prepare a multiple-step income statement.**
4. **Explain how irregular items are reported.**
5. **Explain intraperiod tax allocation.**
6. **Explain where earnings per share information is reported.**
7. **Prepare a retained earnings statement.**
8. **Explain how other comprehensive income is reported.**

[1] Adapted from David Henry, "The Numbers Game," *Business Week* (May 14, 2001), pp. 100–110.

PREVIEW OF CHAPTER 4

As shown in the opening story, investors need complete and comparable information on income and its components to make valid assessments of company profitability. The purpose of this chapter is to examine the many different types of revenues, expenses, gains, and losses that affect the income statement and related information. The content and organization of this chapter are as follows.

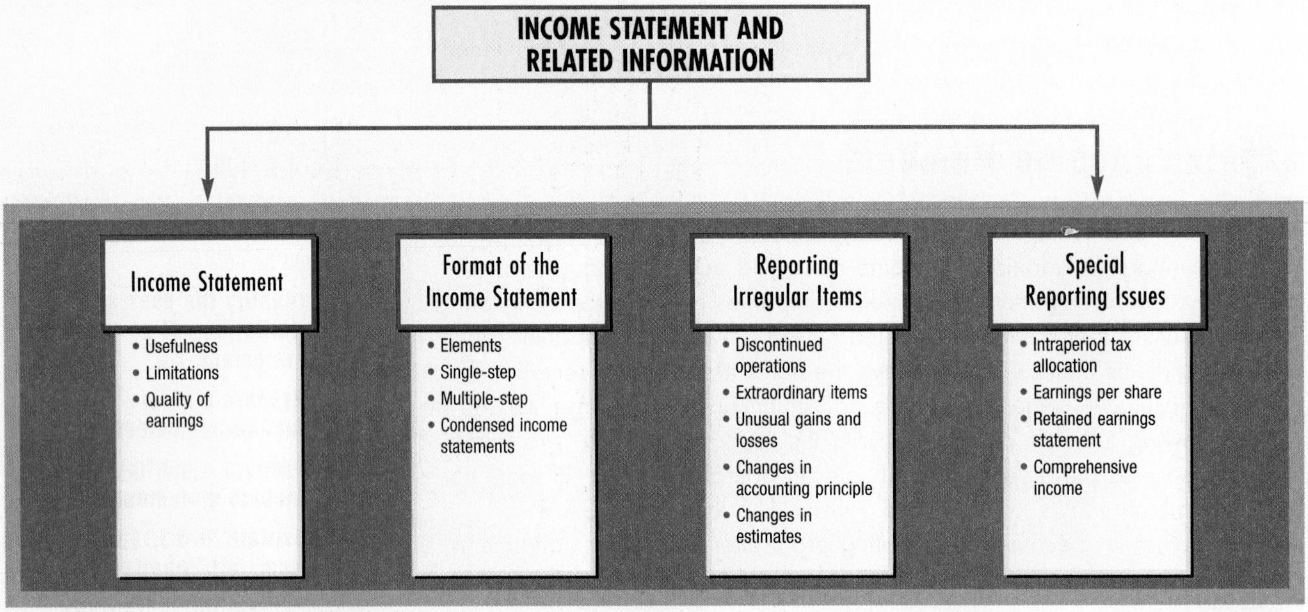

INCOME STATEMENT

OBJECTIVE 1
Identify the uses and limitations of an income statement.

The **income statement**, often called the statement of income or statement of earnings,[2] is the report that measures the success of enterprise operations for a given period of time. The business and investment community uses this report to determine profitability, investment value, and credit worthiness. It provides investors and creditors with information that helps them predict the **amounts, timing, and uncertainty of future cash flows**.

Usefulness of the Income Statement

The income statement helps users of financial statements predict future cash flows in a number of ways. For example, investors and creditors can use the information in the income statement to:

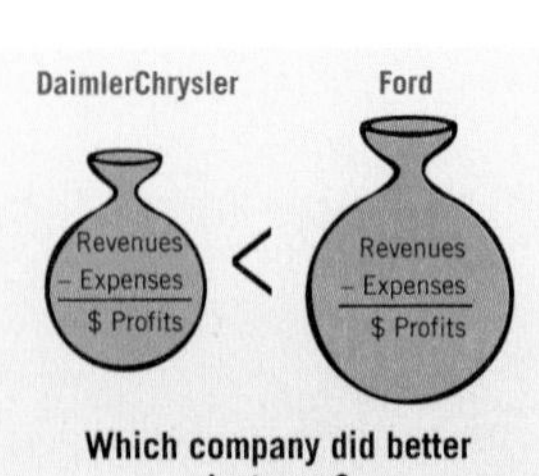

Which company did better last year?

1. **Evaluate the past performance of the enterprise.** By examining revenues and expenses, you can tell how the company performed and compare its performance to its competitors. For example, the income data provided by **DaimlerChrysler** can be used to compare its performance to that of **Ford**.
2. **Provide a basis for predicting future performance.** Information about past performance can be used to determine important trends that, if continued, provide

[2] *Accounting Trends and Techniques—2001* (New York: AICPA) indicates that for the 600 companies surveyed, the term *income* was employed in the title of 284 income statements. The term *operations* was second in acceptance with 198, and the term *earnings* was used by 108 companies.

information about future performance. For example, **General Electric** has reported consistent increases in revenues in recent years. Although success in the past does not necessarily mean the company will be successful in the future, predictions of future revenues, and hence earnings and cash flows, can be made with some confidence if a reasonable correlation exists between past and future performance.

Hmm....Where am I headed?

3. **Help assess the risk or uncertainty of achieving future cash flows.** Information on the various components of income—revenues, expenses, gains, and losses—highlights the relationships among them and can be used to assess the risk of not achieving a particular level of cash flows in the future. For example, segregating **IBM**'s operating performance from other nonrecurring sources of income is useful because operations are usually the primary means by which revenues and cash are generated. Thus, results from continuing operations usually have greater significance for predicting future performance than do results from nonrecurring activities and events.

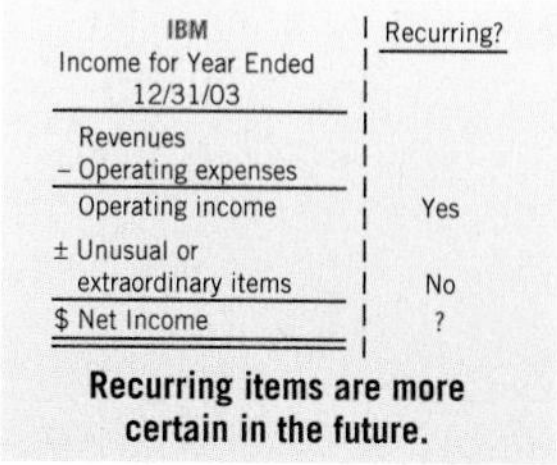

Recurring items are more certain in the future.

In summary, information in the income statement—revenues, expenses, gains, and losses—helps users evaluate past performance and provides insights into achieving a particular level of cash flows in the future.

Limitations of the Income Statement

Because net income is an estimate and reflects a number of assumptions, income statement users need to be aware of certain limitations associated with the information contained in the income statement. Some of these limitations include:

1. **Items that cannot be measured reliably are not reported in the income statement.** Current practice prohibits recognition of certain items from the determination of income even though the effects of these items arguably affect the performance of an entity from one point in time to another. For example, unrealized gains and losses on certain investment securities may not be recorded in income when there is uncertainty that the changes in value will ever be realized. In addition, more and more companies, like **Cisco Systems** and **Microsoft**, have experienced increases in value due to brand recognition, customer service, and product quality. Presently, a common framework for identifying and reporting these types of values has not been developed.

You left something out!

2. **Income numbers are affected by the accounting methods employed.** For example, one company may choose to depreciate its plant assets on an accelerated basis; another chooses straight-line depreciation. Assuming all other factors are equal, the income for the first company will be lower, even though the companies are essentially the same. In effect, we are comparing apples to oranges.

Hmm... Is the income the same?

3. **Income measurement involves judgment.** For example, one company in good faith may estimate the useful life of an asset to be 20 years while another company uses a 15-year estimate for the same type of asset. Similarly, some companies may make overly optimistic estimates of future warranty returns and bad debt write-offs, which results in lower expense and higher income.

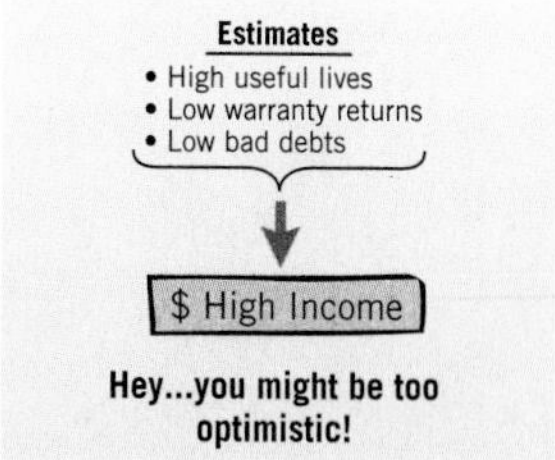

Hey...you might be too optimistic!

In summary, several limitations of the income statement reduce the usefulness of this statement for predicting the amounts, timing, and uncertainty of future cash flows.

Quality of Earnings

Our discussion to this point has highlighted the importance of information in the income statement for investment and credit decisions, including the evaluation of the company and its managers.[3] Companies try to meet or beat Wall Street expectations so that the market price of their stock and the value of management's stock options increase. As a result, companies have incentives to manage income to meet earnings targets or to make earnings look less risky.

The SEC has expressed concern that the motivations to meet earnings targets may be overriding good business practices. As a result, the quality of earnings and the quality of financial reporting are eroding. As indicated by a former SEC chairman, "Managing may be giving way to manipulation; integrity may be losing out to illusion."[4]

What is **earnings management**? It is often defined as the planned timing of revenues, expenses, gains, and losses to smooth out bumps in earnings. In most cases, earnings management is used to increase income in the current year at the expense of income in future years. For example, companies prematurely recognize sales before they are complete in order to boost earnings. As one commentator noted, " . . . it's like popping a cork in [opening] a bottle of wine before it is ready."

Earnings management can also be used to decrease current earnings in order to increase income in the future. The classic case is the use of "cookie jar" reserves. These are established by using unrealistic assumptions to estimate liabilities for such items as sales returns, loan losses, and warranty returns. These reserves can then be reduced in the future to increase income.

Such earnings management has a negative effect on the **quality of earnings** if it distorts the information in a way that is less useful for predicting future earnings and cash flows. As indicated in Chapter 1, markets are based on trust, and it is imperative

WHAT DO THE NUMBERS MEAN?

MANAGE UP, MANAGE DOWN

The quality of earnings is adversely affected whether earnings are managed up or down. For example, **W. R. Grace** managed earnings down by taking excess "cookie jar" reserves in good earnings years. During the early 1990s, Grace was growing fast, with profits increasing 30 percent annually. Analysts' targets had Grace growing 24 percent each year. Worried that they could not continue to meet these growth expectations, management began stashing away excess profits in an all-purpose reserve. In 1995, when profits were not meeting expectations, Grace wanted to reduce this reserve and so increase income. The SEC objected, noting that generally accepted accounting principles would be violated if Grace were to do so.

More recently, **MicroStrategy** managed earnings up by booking revenue for future software upgrades, even though it had not yet delivered on the upgrades. And **Rent-Way, Inc.** managed its earnings up by understating some $65 million in expenses relating to such items as automobile maintenance and insurance payments.

Does the market value accounting quality? Well, each of these companies took a beating in the marketplace when its earnings management practices were uncovered. For example, Rent-Way's stock price plummeted from above $25 per share to below $10 per share when it announced restatements for its improper expense accounting. So, whether earnings are managed up or down, companies had better be prepared to pay the price for poor accounting quality.

---

[3]In support of the usefulness of income information, accounting researchers have documented that the market prices of companies change when income is reported to the market. See W. H. Beaver, "The Information Content of Annual Earnings Announcements," *Empirical Research in Accounting: Selected Studies, Journal of Accounting Research* (Supplement 1968), pp. 67–92.

[4]A. Levitt, the "Numbers Game." Remarks to NYU Center for Law and Business, September 28, 1998 (Securities and Exchange Commission, 1998).

that the bond between shareholders and the company be strong. If investors or others lose faith in the numbers reported in the financial statements, U.S. capital markets will be damaged. As mentioned in the opening story, heightened scrutiny of income measurement and reporting is warranted to ensure the quality of earnings and investors' confidence in the income statement.

FORMAT OF THE INCOME STATEMENT

Elements of the Income Statement

Net income results from revenue, expense, gain, and loss transactions. These transactions are summarized in the income statement. This method of income measurement is called the **transaction approach** because it focuses on the income-related activities that have occurred during the period.[5] Income can be further classified by customer, product line, or function or by operating and nonoperating, continuing and discontinued, and regular and irregular categories.[6] More formal definitions of income-related items, referred to as the major **elements** of the income statement, are as follows.

ELEMENTS OF FINANCIAL STATEMENTS

REVENUES. Inflows or other enhancements of assets of an entity or settlements of its liabilities during a period from delivering or producing goods, rendering services, or other activities that constitute the entity's ongoing major or central operations.

EXPENSES. Outflows or other using-up of assets or incurrences of liabilities during a period from delivering or producing goods, rendering services, or carrying out other activities that constitute the entity's ongoing major or central operations.

GAINS. Increases in equity (net assets) from peripheral or incidental transactions of an entity except those that result from revenues or investments by owners.

LOSSES. Decreases in equity (net assets) from peripheral or incidental transactions of an entity except those that result from expenses or distributions to owners.[7]

Revenues take many forms, such as sales, fees, interest, dividends, and rents. Expenses also take many forms, such as cost of goods sold, depreciation, interest, rent, salaries and wages, and taxes. Gains and losses also are of many types, resulting from the sale of investments, sale of plant assets, settlement of liabilities, write-offs of assets due to obsolescence or casualty, and theft.

[5]The most common alternative to the transaction approach is the **capital maintenance approach** to income measurement. Under this approach, income for the period is determined based on the change in equity, after adjusting for capital contributions (e.g., investments by owners) or distributions (e.g., dividends). The main drawback associated with the capital maintenance approach is that the components of income are not evident in its measurement. The Internal Revenue Service uses the capital maintenance approach to identify unreported income and refers to this approach as the "net worth check."

[6]The term "irregular" encompasses transactions and other events that are derived from developments outside the normal operations of the business.

[7]"Elements of Financial Statements," *Statement of Financial Accounting Concepts No. 6* (Stamford, Conn.: FASB, 1985), pars. 78–89.

INTERNATIONAL INSIGHT

For some nations, financial reporting is prepared on the same basis as tax returns. In such cases, companies have incentives to minimize reported income.

The distinction between revenues and gains and the distinction between expenses and losses depend to a great extent on the typical activities of the enterprise. For example, when **McDonald's** sells a hamburger, the selling price is recorded as revenue. However, when McDonald's sells a french-fryer, any excess of the selling price over the book value would be recorded as a gain. This difference in treatment results because the sale of the hamburger is part of McDonald's regular operations while the sale of the french-fryer is not.

The importance of reporting these elements should not be underestimated. For most decision makers, the parts of a financial statement will often be more useful than the whole. As indicated earlier, investors and creditors are interested in predicting the amounts, timing, and uncertainty of future income and cash flows. Having income statement elements shown in some detail and in comparison form with prior years' data, decision makers are better able to assess future income and cash flows.

Single-Step Income Statements

In reporting revenues, gains, expenses, and losses, a format known as the **single-step income statement** is often used. In the single-step statement, just two groupings exist: revenues and expenses. Expenses are deducted from revenues to arrive at net income or loss. The expression "single-step" is derived from the single subtraction necessary to arrive at net income. Frequently income tax is reported separately as the last item before net income to indicate its relationship to income before income tax. Illustration 4-1 shows the single-step income statement of Dan Deines Company.

ILLUSTRATION 4-1
Single-step Income Statement

OBJECTIVE 2
Prepare a single-step income statement.

DAN DEINES COMPANY
INCOME STATEMENT
FOR THE YEAR ENDED DECEMBER 31, 2004

Revenues	
Net sales	$2,972,413
Dividend revenue	98,500
Rental revenue	72,910
Total revenues	3,143,823
Expenses	
Cost of goods sold	1,982,541
Selling expenses	453,028
Administrative expenses	350,771
Interest expense	126,060
Income tax expense	66,934
Total expenses	2,979,334
Net income	$ 164,489
Earnings per common share	$1.74

Because of its simplicity, the single-step income statement is widely used in financial reporting. In recent years, though, the multiple-step form has become more popular.[8]

The primary advantage of the single-step format lies in the simplicity of presentation and the absence of any implication that one type of revenue or expense item has priority over another. Potential classification problems are thus eliminated.

[8] *Accounting Trends and Techniques—2001.* Of the 600 companies surveyed by the AICPA, 466 employed the multiple-step form, and 134 employed the single-step income statement format. This is a reversal from 1983, when 314 used the single-step form and 286 used the multiple-step form.

Multiple-Step Income Statements

OBJECTIVE 3
Prepare a multiple-step income statement.

Some contend that including other important revenue and expense classifications makes the income statement more useful. These further classifications include:

1. A separation of operating and nonoperating activities of the company. For example, enterprises often present an income from operations figure and then sections entitled "Other revenues and gains" and "Other expenses and losses." These other categories include interest revenue and expense, gains or losses from sales of such items as investments and plant assets, and dividends received.
2. A classification of expenses by functions, such as merchandising (cost of goods sold), selling, and administration. This permits immediate comparison with costs of previous years and with other departments in the same year.

A **multiple-step income statement** is used to recognize these additional relationships. This statement recognizes a separation of operating transactions from nonoperating transactions and matches costs and expenses with related revenues. It highlights certain intermediate components of income that are used for the computation of ratios used to assess the performance of the enterprise.

Intermediate Components of the Income Statement

When a multiple-step income statement is used, some or all of the following sections or subsections may be prepared.

INCOME STATEMENT SECTIONS

1. **Operating Section.** A report of the revenues and expenses of the company's principal operations.
   (a) **Sales or Revenue Section.** A subsection presenting sales, discounts, allowances, returns, and other related information. Its purpose is to arrive at the net amount of sales revenue.
   (b) **Cost of Goods Sold Section.** A subsection that shows the cost of goods that were sold to produce the sales.
   (c) **Selling Expenses.** A subsection that lists expenses resulting from the company's efforts to make sales.
   (d) **Administrative or General Expenses.** A subsection reporting expenses of general administration.
2. **Nonoperating Section.** A report of revenues and expenses resulting from secondary or auxiliary activities of the company. In addition, special gains and losses that are infrequent or unusual, but not both, are normally reported in this section. Generally these items break down into two main subsections:
   (a) **Other Revenues and Gains.** A list of the revenues earned or gains incurred, generally net of related expenses, from nonoperating transactions.
   (b) **Other Expenses and Losses.** A list of the expenses or losses incurred, generally net of any related incomes, from nonoperating transactions.
3. **Income Tax.** A short section reporting federal and state taxes levied on income from continuing operations.
4. **Discontinued Operations.** Material gains or losses resulting from the disposition of a segment of the business.
5. **Extraordinary Items.** Unusual and infrequent material gains and losses.
6. **Cumulative Effect of a Change in Accounting Principle.**
7. **Earnings Per Share.**

Although the content of the operating section is always the same, the organization of the material need not be as described above. The breakdown above uses a **natural expense classification**. It is commonly used for manufacturing concerns and for merchandising companies in the wholesale trade. Another classification of operating expenses, recommended for retail stores, uses a **functional expense classification** of administrative, occupancy, publicity, buying, and selling expenses.

Usually, financial statements that are provided to external users have less detail than internal management reports. The latter tend to have more expense categories—usually grouped along lines of responsibility. This detail allows top management to judge staff performance. Furthermore, irregular transactions such as discontinued operations, extraordinary items, and cumulative effect of changes in accounting principles should be reported separately, following income from continuing operations.

To illustrate the multiple-step income statement, Dan Deines Company's statement of income is presented in Illustration 4-2. Items 1, 2, 3, and 7 from the list on page 129 are shown in the statement.[9] Note that in arriving at net income, three subtotals are presented:

1. Net sales revenue
2. Gross profit
3. Income from operations

The disclosure of net sales revenue is useful because regular revenues are reported as a separate item. Irregular or incidental revenues are disclosed elsewhere in the income statement. As a result, trends in revenue from continuing operations should be easier to understand and analyze.

Similarly, the reporting of gross profit provides a useful number for evaluating performance and assessing future earnings. A study of the trend in gross profits may show how successfully a company uses its resources; it may also be a basis for understanding how profit margins have changed as a result of competitive pressure.

Finally, disclosing income from operations highlights the difference between regular and irregular or incidental activities. This disclosure helps users recognize that incidental or irregular activities are unlikely to continue at the same level. Furthermore, disclosure of operating earnings may assist in comparing different companies and assessing operating efficiencies.

Condensed Income Statements

In some cases it is impossible to present in a single income statement of convenient size all the desired expense detail. This problem is solved by including only the totals of expense groups in the statement of income and preparing supplementary schedules to support the totals. With this format, the income statement itself may be reduced to a few lines on a single sheet. For this reason, readers who wish to study all the reported data on operations must give their attention to the supporting schedules. The income statement shown in Illustration 4-3 on page 132 for Dan Deines Company is a condensed version of the more detailed multiple-step statement presented earlier and is more representative of the type found in practice.

---

[9]Earnings per share or net loss per share is required to be included on the face of the income statement.

ILLUSTRATION 4-2
Multiple-step Income Statement

DAN DEINES COMPANY
INCOME STATEMENT
FOR THE YEAR ENDED DECEMBER 31, 2004

Sales Revenue			
Sales			$3,053,081
Less: Sales discounts		$ 24,241	
Sales returns and allowances		56,427	80,668
Net sales revenue			2,972,413
Cost of Goods Sold			
Merchandise inventory, Jan. 1, 2004		461,219	
Purchases	$1,989,693		
Less: Purchase discounts	19,270		
Net purchases	1,970,423		
Freight and transportation-in	40,612	2,011,035	
Total merchandise available for sale		2,472,254	
Less: Merchandise inventory, Dec. 31, 2004		489,713	
Cost of goods sold			1,982,541
Gross profit on sales			989,872
Operating Expenses			
Selling expenses			
Sales salaries and commissions	202,644		
Sales office salaries	59,200		
Travel and entertainment	48,940		
Advertising expense	38,315		
Freight and transportation-out	41,209		
Shipping supplies and expense	24,712		
Postage and stationery	16,788		
Depreciation of sales equipment	9,005		
Telephone and Internet expense	12,215	453,028	
Administrative expenses			
Officers' salaries	186,000		
Office salaries	61,200		
Legal and professional services	23,721		
Utilities expense	23,275		
Insurance expense	17,029		
Depreciation of building	18,059		
Depreciation of office equipment	16,000		
Stationery, supplies, and postage	2,875		
Miscellaneous office expenses	2,612	350,771	803,799
Income from operations			186,073
Other Revenues and Gains			
Dividend revenue		98,500	
Rental revenue		72,910	171,410
			357,483
Other Expenses and Losses			
Interest on bonds and notes			126,060
Income before income tax			231,423
Income tax			66,934
Net income for the year			$ 164,489
Earnings per common share			$1.74

Income Statements for Real Companies

ILLUSTRATION 4-3
Condensed Income Statement

DAN DEINES COMPANY
INCOME STATEMENT
FOR THE YEAR ENDED DECEMBER 31, 2004

Net sales		$2,972,413
Cost of goods sold		1,982,541
Gross profit		989,872
Selling expenses (see Note D)	$453,028	
Administrative expenses	350,771	803,799
Income from operations		186,073
Other revenues and gains		171,410
		357,483
Other expenses and losses		126,060
Income before income tax		231,423
Income tax		66,934
Net income for the year		$ 164,489
Earnings per share		$1.74

An example of a supporting schedule, cross-referenced as Note D and detailing the selling expenses, is shown in Illustration 4-4.

ILLUSTRATION 4-4
Sample Supporting Schedule

Note D: Selling expenses

Sales salaries and commissions	$202,644
Sales office salaries	59,200
Travel and entertainment	48,940
Advertising expense	38,315
Freight and transportation-out	41,209
Shipping supplies and expense	24,712
Postage and stationery	16,788
Depreciation of sales equipment	9,005
Telephone and Internet expense	12,215
Total selling expenses	$453,028

How much detail to include in the income statement is always a problem. On the one hand, we want to present a simple, summarized statement so that a reader can readily discover important factors. On the other hand, we want to disclose the results of all activities and to provide more than just a skeleton report. Certain basic elements are always included, but as we'll see, they can be presented in various formats.

REPORTING IRREGULAR ITEMS

OBJECTIVE 4
Explain how irregular items are reported.

As illustrated through the use of a multiple-step or condensed income statement, flexibility in the presentation of the components of income is permitted. In two important areas, however, specific guidelines have been developed. These two areas relate to what is included in income and how certain unusual or irregular items are reported.

What should be included in net income has been a controversy for many years. For example, should irregular gains and losses, and corrections of revenues and expenses of prior years be closed directly to Retained Earnings and therefore not be reported in the income statement? Or should they first be presented in the income statement and then carried to Retained Earnings along with the net income or loss for the period? In general, **income measurement follows an all-inclusive approach. This approach indicates that most items, even irregular ones, are recorded in income.**[10]

One exception is errors in prior years' income measurement. Because these items have affected earnings already reported in a prior period, errors from prior periods are not included in current income. Rather, these items are recorded as adjustments to retained earnings.[11]

Currently there is growing debate concerning **how** irregular items that are part of current income should be reported within the income statement. This issue is extremely important, because the reporting of irregular items on the income statement is substantial. For example, Illustration 4-5 identifies the most common types and number of irregular items reported in a survey of 600 large companies.

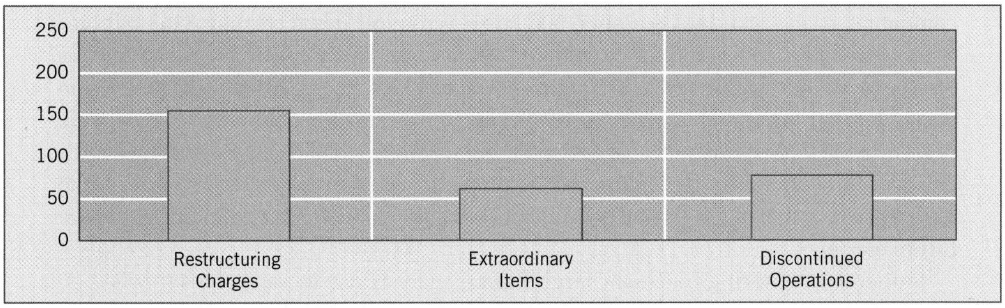

ILLUSTRATION 4-5
Number of Irregular Items Reported in a Recent Year by 600 Large Companies

As indicated, restructuring charges, which many times contain write-offs and other one-time items, were reported by more than one-fourth of the surveyed firms. About 20 percent of the surveyed firms reported either an extraordinary item or a discontinued operation charge.[12]

As discussed in the opening story, it is important to have consistent and comparable income reporting practices so that the information that companies disseminate is not too promotional. Developing a framework for reporting irregular items is important to ensure that financial statement users have reliable income information.[13]

Some users advocate a **current operating performance approach** to income reporting. These analysts argue that the most useful income measure will reflect only regular and recurring revenue and expense elements. Irregular items do not reflect an enterprise's future earning power. In contrast, others warn that a focus on operating income potentially misses important information about a firm's performance. Any gain or loss experienced by the firm, whether directly or indirectly related to operations, contributes to its long-run profitability. As one analyst notes, "write-offs matter. . . . They speak to the volatility of (past) earnings."[14] As a result, some nonoperating items

---

[10]As discussed later in this chapter, the FASB has issued a statement of concepts that offers some guidance on this topic—"Recognition and Measurement in Financial Statements of Business Enterprises," *Statement of Financial Accounting Concepts No. 5* (Stamford, Conn.: FASB, 1984).

[11]This is referred to as "prior period adjustments." Other examples that bypass the income statement are the gains or losses arising from certain investment securities and pension adjustments. Both examples are cases where there is uncertainty about the realization of the gains or losses. These gains and losses are recorded in owners' equity until they are realized.

[12]*Accounting Trends and Techniques—2001* (New York: AICPA).

[13]The FASB and other international accounting standard setters continue to study the best way to report income. See *Reporting Financial Performance: A Proposed Approach* (Norwalk, Conn.: FASB, September 1999).

[14]D. McDermott, "Latest Profit Data Stir Old Debate Between Net and Operating Income," *Wall Street Journal* (May 3, 1999).

can be used to assess the riskiness of future earnings. Furthermore, determining which items are operating and which items are irregular requires judgment and could lead to differences in the treatment of irregular items and to possible manipulation of income measures.

WHAT DO THE NUMBERS MEAN?

ARE ONE-TIME CHARGES BUGGING YOU?

Which number, net income or income from operations, should an analyst use in evaluating companies that have unusual items? Some argue that operating income is better because it is more representative of what will happen in the future. Others note that special items are often no longer special. For example, one study noted that in 2001, companies in the Standard & Poors' 500 index wrote off items totaling $165 billion—more than in the prior five years combined. And one study by **Multex.com** and the *Wall Street Journal* indicates that these charges should not be ignored. Based on data for companies taking unusual charges from 1996–2001, the study documented that companies reporting the largest unusual charges had more negative stock price performance in the period following the charge, compared to companies with smaller charges. Thus, rather than signaling that the bad times are behind, these unusual charges indicated poorer future earnings.

Rather than ignoring unusual charges, some analysts use these charges to weed out stocks that may be headed for a fall. Following the "cockroach theory," any charge indicating a problem raises the probability of more problems. Thus, investors should be wary of the increasing use of restructuring and other one-time charges, which may bury expenses that signal future performance declines.

Source: J. Weil and S. Liesman, "Stock Gurus Disregard Most Big Write-offs, But They Often Hold Vital Clues to Outlook," *Wall Street Journal Online* (December 31, 2001).

So, what to do? The accounting profession has **adopted a modified all-inclusive concept and requires application of this approach in practice. Irregular items** are required to be highlighted so that the reader of financial statements can better determine the long-run earning power of the enterprise. These items fall into five general categories:

1. Discontinued operations.
2. Extraordinary items.
3. Unusual gains and losses.
4. Changes in accounting principle.
5. Changes in estimates.

Discontinued Operations

As indicated in Illustration 4-5, one of the most common types of irregular items is discontinued operations. A **discontinued operation** occurs when (a) the results of operations and cash flows of a component of a company have been (or will be) eliminated from the ongoing operations, and (b) there is no significant continuing involvement in that component after the disposal transaction. To illustrate a **component**, **S. C. Johnson** manufactures and sells consumer products and has several product groups, each with different product lines and brands. For S. C. Johnson, a product group is the lowest level at which operations and cash flows can be clearly distinguished from the rest of the company's operations. Therefore each product group is a component of the company, and if disposed of, would be classified as a discontinued operation.

Here is another example. Assume that Softso Inc. has experienced losses with certain brands in its beauty-care products group. As a result, Softso decides to sell the beauty-care business. It will not have any continuing involvement in the product group after it is sold. In this case, the operations and the cash flows of the product group are eliminated from the ongoing operations of Softso and are reported as a discontinued operation. On the other hand, assume Softso decides to remain in the beauty-care business but will discontinue the brands that experienced losses. Because the cash flows from the brands cannot be differentiated from the cash flows of the product group as a whole, the brands are not considered a component. As a result, any gain or loss on the sale of the brands is not classified as a discontinued operation.

Discontinued operations are generally reported in a separate income statement category for the gain or loss from **disposal of a component of a business**. In addition, the **results of operations of a component that has been or will be disposed of** are also reported separately from continuing operations. The effects of discontinued operations are shown net of tax as a separate category, after continuing operations but before extraordinary items.[15]

To illustrate, Multiplex Products, Inc., a highly diversified company, decides to discontinue its electronics division. During the current year, the electronics division lost $300,000 (net of tax) and was sold at the end of the year at a loss of $500,000 (net of tax). The information is shown on the current year's income statement as follows.

Income from continuing operations		$20,000,000
Discontinued operations		
Loss from operation of discontinued electronics division (net of tax)	$300,000	
Loss from disposal of electronics division (net of tax)	500,000	800,000
Net income		$19,200,000

ILLUSTRATION 4-6
Income Statement Presentation of Discontinued Operations

Note that the phrase **"Income from continuing operations"** is used only when gains or losses on discontinued operations occur.

Extraordinary Items

Extraordinary items are defined as nonrecurring **material** items that differ significantly from the entity's typical business activities. The criteria for extraordinary items are as follows.

> Extraordinary items are events and transactions that are distinguished by their unusual nature **and** by the infrequency of their occurrence. **Both** of the following criteria must be met to classify an event or transaction as an extraordinary item:
>
> **(a) Unusual Nature.** The underlying event or transaction should possess a high degree of abnormality and be of a type clearly unrelated to, or only incidentally related to, the ordinary and typical activities of the entity, taking into account the environment in which the entity operates.
>
> **(b) Infrequency of Occurrence.** The underlying event or transaction should be of a type that would not reasonably be expected to recur in the foreseeable future, taking into account the environment in which the entity operates.[16]

[15]"Accounting for the Impairment or Disposal of Long-Lived Assets," *Statement of Financial Accounting Standards No. 144* (Norwalk, Conn.: FASB, 2001), par. 4.

[16]"Reporting the Results of Operations," *Opinions of the Accounting Principles Board No. 30* (New York: AICPA, 1973), par. 20.

Under current standards, the following gains and losses are **not extraordinary items**.

- **(a)** Write-down or write-off of receivables, inventories, equipment leased to others, deferred research and development costs, or other intangible assets.
- **(b)** Gains or losses from exchange or translation of foreign currencies, including those relating to major devaluations and revaluations.
- **(c)** Gains or losses on disposal of a component of an entity.
- **(d)** Other gains or losses from sale or abandonment of property, plant, or equipment used in the business.
- **(e)** Effects of a strike, including those against competitors and major suppliers.
- **(f)** Adjustment of accruals on long-term contracts.[17]

The items listed above are not considered extraordinary "because they are usual in nature and may be expected to recur as a consequence of customary and continuing business activities."

Only rarely does an event or transaction clearly meet the criteria for an extraordinary item.[18] For example, gains or losses such as (a) and (d) above would be classified as extraordinary if they are a **direct result of a major casualty** (such as an earthquake), **an expropriation**, or **a prohibition under a newly enacted law or regulation**. Such circumstances would clearly meet the criteria of unusual and infrequent. A good example of an extraordinary item is the approximately $36 million loss incurred by **Weyerhaeuser Company** (forest and lumber) as a result of volcanic activity at Mount St. Helens. Standing timber, logs, buildings, equipment, and transportation systems covering 68,000 acres were destroyed by the volcanic eruption.

INTERNATIONAL INSIGHT

Classification of items as extraordinary differs across nations. Even in countries in which the criteria for identifying extraordinary items are similar, they are not interpreted identically. Thus, what is extraordinary in the U.S. is not necessarily extraordinary elsewhere.

In determining whether an item is extraordinary, **the environment in which the entity operates is of primary importance**. The environment includes such factors as industry characteristics, geographic location, and the nature and extent of governmental regulations. Thus, extraordinary item treatment is accorded the loss from hail damages to a tobacco grower's crops because severe damage from hailstorms in its locality is rare. On the other hand, frost damage to a citrus grower's crop in Florida does not qualify as extraordinary because frost damage is normally experienced every three or four years. In this environment, the criterion of infrequency is not met.

Similarly, when a company sells the only significant security investment it has ever owned, the gain or loss meets the criteria of an extraordinary item. Another company, however, that has a portfolio of securities acquired for investment purposes would not have an extraordinary item. Sale of such securities would be considered part of its ordinary and typical activities.[19]

In addition, considerable judgment must be exercised in determining whether an item should be reported as extraordinary. For example, some paper companies have

[17]Ibid., par. 23, as amended by "Accounting for the Impairment or Disposal of Long-lived Assets," *Statement of Financial Accounting Standards No. 144* (Norwalk, Conn.: FASB, 2001).

[18]*Accounting Trends and Techniques—2001* (New York: AICPA) indicates that just 55 of the 600 companies surveyed reported an extraordinary item.

[19]Debt extinguishments had been the most common reason for companies reporting extraordinary items. In a recent four-year period, just 11 percent of surveyed companies reported an extraordinary item; over 90 percent of these were related to debt extinguishments (*Accounting Trends and Techniques—2001,* New York: AICPA). Recently the FASB eliminated extraordinary item treatment for these gains and losses in "Rescission of FASB Statements No. 4, 44, and 64 and Technical Corrections," *Statement of Financial Accounting Standards No. 145* (Norwalk, Conn.: FASB, 2002). Thus, reporting an extraordinary item is likely to become an even more rare event in the future.

had their forest lands condemned by the government for state or national parks or forests. Is such an event extraordinary, or is it part of normal operations? Such determination is not easy; much depends on the frequency of previous condemnations, the expectation of future condemnations, materiality, and the like.[20]

EXTRAORDINARY TIMES

WHAT DO THE NUMBERS MEAN?

No recent event better illustrates the difficulties of determining whether a transaction meets the definition of extraordinary than the financial impacts of the terrorist attacks on the World Trade Center on September 11, 2001. To many, this event, which resulted in the tragic loss of lives, jobs, and in some cases, entire businesses, clearly meets the criteria for unusual and infrequent. For example, in the wake of the terrorist attacks that destroyed the World Trade Center and turned much of lower Manhattan including Wall Street into a war zone, airlines, insurance companies, and other businesses recorded major losses due to property damage, business disruption, and suspension of airline travel and of securities trading. But, to the surprise of many, extraordinary item reporting was not permitted for losses arising from the terrorist attacks.

The reason? After much deliberation, the Emerging Issues Task Force (EITF) of the FASB decided that measurement of the possible loss was too difficult. Take the airline industry as an example: What portion of the airlines' losses after September 11 was related to the terrorist attack, and what portion was due to the ongoing recession? There also was concern that some companies would use the attacks as a reason for reporting as extraordinary some losses that had little direct relationship to the attacks. For example, shortly after the attacks, energy company **AES** and shoe retailer **Footstar**, who both were experiencing profit pressure before 9/11, put some of the blame for their poor performance on the attacks.

Source: J. Creswell, "Bad News Bearers Shift the Blame," *Fortune* (October 15, 2001), p. 44.

Extraordinary items are to be shown net of taxes in a separate section in the income statement, usually just before net income. After listing the usual revenues, costs and expenses, and income taxes, the remainder of the statement shows the following.

ILLUSTRATION 4-7
Income Statement Placement of Extraordinary Items

Income before extraordinary items
Extraordinary items (less applicable income tax of $________ . ________)
Net income

For example, the reporting of an extraordinary loss for **Keystone Consolidated Industries, Inc.** is shown in Illustration 4-8 on page 138.

Unusual Gains and Losses

Because of the restrictive criteria for extraordinary items, financial statement users must carefully examine the financial statements for items that are **unusual or infrequent but**

[20]It is often difficult to determine what is extraordinary, because assessing the materiality of individual items requires judgment. However, in making materiality judgments, extraordinary items should be considered individually, and not in the aggregate. "Reporting the Results of Operations," op. cit., par. 24.

ILLUSTRATION 4-8
Income Statement Presentation of Extraordinary Items

Keystone Consolidated Industries, Inc.

Income before extraordinary item	$11,638,000
Extraordinary item—flood loss (Note E)	1,216,000
Net income	$10,422,000

Note E: Extraordinary Item. The Keystone Steel and Wire Division's Steel Works experienced a flash flood on June 22. The extraordinary item represents the estimated cost, net of related income taxes of $1,279,000, to restore the steel works to full operation.

not both. As indicated earlier, items such as write-downs of inventories and transaction gains and losses from fluctuation of foreign exchange are not considered extraordinary items. Thus, these items are sometimes shown with the normal, recurring revenues, costs, and expenses. If they are not material in amount, they are combined with other items in the income statement. If they are material, they must be disclosed separately, but are shown **above** "Income (loss) before extraordinary items."

For example, **Pepsico, Inc.** presented an unusual charge in the following manner in its income statement.

ILLUSTRATION 4-9
Income Statement Presentation of Unusual Charges

PEPSICO

Pepsico, Inc.
(in millions)

Net sales	$20,917
Costs and expenses, net	
Cost of sales	8,525
Selling, general, and administrative expenses	9,241
Amortization of intangible assets	199
Unusual items (Note 2)	290
Operating income	$ 2,662

Note 2 (Restructuring Charge)

Dispose and write down assets	$183
Improve productivity	94
Strengthen the international bottler structure	13
Net loss	$290

The net charge to strengthen the international bottler structure includes proceeds of $87 million associated with a settlement related to a previous Venezuelan bottler agreement, which were partially offset by related costs.

Restructuring charges, like the one reported by Pepsico, have been common in recent years. A **restructuring charge** relates to a major reorganization of company affairs, such as costs associated with employee layoffs, plant closing costs, write-offs of assets, and so on. There has been a tendency to **report unusual items in a separate section just above "Income from operations before income taxes and Extraordinary items,"** especially when there are multiple unusual items. A restructuring charge should not be reported as an extraordinary item, because these write-offs are considered part of a company's ordinary and typical activities.

For example, when **General Electric Company** experienced multiple unusual items in one year, it reported them in a separate "Unusual items" section of the income statement below "Income before unusual items and income taxes." When a multiple-step income statement is being prepared for homework purposes, unusual gains and losses should be reported in the "Other revenues and gains" or "Other expenses and losses" section unless you are instructed to prepare a separate unusual items section.[21]

In dealing with events that are either unusual or nonrecurring but not both, the profession attempted to prevent a practice that many believed was misleading. Companies often reported such transactions on a net-of-tax basis and prominently displayed the earnings per share effect of these items. Although not captioned extraordinary items, they are presented in the same manner. Some had referred to these as "first cousins" to extraordinary items. As a consequence, the Board specifically **prohibited a net-of-tax treatment for such items**, to ensure that users of financial statements can easily differentiate extraordinary items—which are reported net of tax—from material items that are unusual or infrequent, but not both.

Changes in Accounting Principle

UNDERLYING CONCEPTS

Companies can change principles, but it must be demonstrated that the newly adopted principle is preferable to the old one. Such changes mean that consistency from period to period is lost.

Changes in accounting occur frequently in practice, because important events or conditions may be in dispute or uncertain at the statement date. One type of accounting change, therefore, comprises the normal recurring corrections and adjustments that are made by every business enterprise. Another accounting change results when an accounting principle is adopted that is different from the one previously used. Changes in accounting principle would include a change in the method of inventory pricing from FIFO to average cost or a change in depreciation from the double-declining to the straight-line method.[22]

Changes in accounting principle are recognized by including the cumulative effect as of the beginning of the year, net of tax in the current year's income statement. This amount is based on a retroactive computation of changing to a new accounting principle. **The effect on net income of adopting the new accounting principle should be disclosed as a separate item following extraordinary items in the income statement.**

To illustrate, Gaubert Inc. decided in March 2004 to change from an accelerated method of computing depreciation on its plant assets to the straight-line method. The assets originally cost $100,000 in 2002 and have a service life of four years. The data assumed for this illustration are as shown in Illustration 4-10.

ILLUSTRATION 4-10
Calculation of a Change in Accounting Principle

Year	Accelerated Depreciation	Straight-Line Depreciation	Excess of Accelerated over Straight-Line Method
2002	$40,000	$25,000	$15,000
2003	30,000	25,000	5,000
Total			$20,000

[21]Many companies are reporting "one-time items." However, some companies have taken restructuring charges practically every year. **Citicorp** (now **Citigroup**) took restructuring charges six years in a row, between 1988 and 1993; **Eastman Kodak Co.** did so five out of six years in 1989 to 1994. Recent research on the market reaction to income containing "one-time" items indicates that the market discounts the earnings of companies that report a series of "nonrecurring" items. Such evidence supports the contention that these elements reduce the quality of earnings. J. Elliott and D. Hanna, "Repeated Accounting Write-offs and the Information Content of Earnings," *Journal of Accounting Research* (Supplement, 1996).

[22]"Accounting Changes," *Opinions of the Accounting Principles Board No. 20* (New York: AICPA, 1971), par. 18. In Chapter 22, we examine in greater detail the problems related to accounting changes.

The information presented in the 2004 financial statements is shown in Illustration 4-11. (The tax rate was 30 percent.)

ILLUSTRATION 4-11
Income Statement Presentation of a Change in Accounting Principle

Income before extraordinary item and cumulative effect of a change in accounting principle	$120,000
Extraordinary item—casualty loss (net of $12,000 tax)	(28,000)
Cumulative effect on prior years of retroactive application of new depreciation method (net of $6,000 tax)	14,000
Net income	$106,000

Changes in Estimates

Estimates are inherent in the accounting process. Estimates are made, for example, of useful lives and salvage values of depreciable assets, of uncollectible receivables, of inventory obsolescence, and of the number of periods expected to benefit from a particular expenditure. Not infrequently, as time passes, as circumstances change, or as additional information is obtained, even estimates originally made in good faith must be changed. Such **changes in estimates** are accounted for in the period of change if they affect only that period, or in the period of change and future periods if the change affects both.

To illustrate a change in estimate that affects only the period of change, assume that DuPage Materials Corp. has consistently estimated its bad debt expense at 1 percent of credit sales. In 2003, however, DuPage's controller determines that the estimate of bad debts for the current year's credit sales must be revised upward to 2 percent, or double the prior years' percentage. Using 2 percent results in a bad debt charge of $240,000, or double the amount using the 1 percent estimate for prior years. The 2 percent rate is necessary to reduce accounts receivable to net realizable value. The provision is recorded at December 31, 2003, as follows.

Bad Debt Expense	240,000	
Allowance for Doubtful Accounts		240,000

The entire change in estimate is included in 2003 income because no future periods are affected by the change. **Changes in estimate are not handled retroactively.** That is, they are not carried back to adjust prior years. (Changes in estimate that affect both the current and future periods are examined in greater detail in Chapter 22.) **Changes in estimate are not considered errors (prior period adjustments) or extraordinary items.**

UNDERLYING CONCEPTS

The AICPA Special Committee on Financial Reporting indicates a company's core activities—usual and recurring events—provide the best historical data from which users determine trends and relationships and make their predictions about the future. Therefore, the effects of core and non-core activities should be separately displayed.

Summary of Irregular Items

The modified all-inclusive income concept is accepted in practice. Except for a couple of items (discussed later in this chapter) that are charged or credited directly to retained earnings, all other irregular gains or losses or nonrecurring items are closed to Income Summary and are included in the income statement. Of these, **discontinued operations of a component** of a business is classified as a separate item in the income statement after continuing operations. The **unusual, material, nonrecurring items** that are significantly different from the typical or customary business activities are shown in a separate section for "**Extraordinary items**" below discontinued operations. Other items of a material amount that are of an **unusual or nonrecurring** nature and are **not considered extraordinary** are separately disclosed. In addition, the cumulative adjustment that occurs when a change in accounting principles develops is disclosed as a separate item just before net income.

Because of the numerous intermediate income figures that are created by the reporting of these irregular items, careful evaluation of earnings information reported by the financial press is needed. Illustration 4-12 summarizes the basic concepts previously discussed. Although the chart is simplified, it provides a useful framework for determining the treatment of special items affecting the income statement.

ILLUSTRATION 4-12
Summary of Irregular Items in the Income Statement

Type of Situation[a]	Criteria	Examples	Placement on Financial Statements
Discontinued operations	Disposal of a component of a business for which the operations and cash flows can be clearly distinguished from the rest of the company's operations.	Sale by diversified company of major division that represents only activities in electronics industry. Food distributor that sells wholesale to supermarket chains and through fast-food restaurants decides to discontinue the division that sells to one of two classes of customers.	Shown in separate section of the income statement after continuing operations but before extraordinary items. (Shown net of tax.)
Extraordinary items	Material, and both unusual and infrequent (nonrecurring).	Gains or losses resulting from casualties, an expropriation, or a prohibition under a new law.	Separate section in the income statement entitled "Extraordinary items." (Shown net of tax.)
Unusual gains or losses, not considered extraordinary	Material; character typical of the customary business activities; unusual or infrequent but not both.	Write-downs of receivables, inventories; adjustments of accrued contract prices; gains or losses from fluctuations of foreign exchange; gains or losses from sales of assets used in business.	Separate section in income statement above income before extraordinary items. Often reported in "Other revenues and gains" or "Other expenses and losses" section. (Not shown net of tax.)
Changes in principle[b]	Change from one generally accepted principle to another.	Change in the basis of inventory pricing from FIFO to average cost; change in the method of depreciation from accelerated to straight-line.	Cumulative effect of the change is reflected in the income statement between the captions "Extraordinary items" and "Net income." (Shown net of tax.)
Changes in estimates	Normal, recurring corrections and adjustments.	Changes in the realizability of receivables and inventories; changes in estimated lives of equipment, intangible assets; changes in estimated liability for warranty costs, income taxes, and salary payments.	Change in income statement only in the account affected. (Not shown net of tax.)

[a]This summary provides only the general rules to be followed in accounting for the various situations described above. Exceptions do exist in some of these situations.

[b]The general rule per *APB Opinion No. 20* is to use the cumulative effect approach. However, recent FASB pronouncements require or permit the retroactive method whenever a new standard is adopted for the first time.

SPECIAL REPORTING ISSUES

Intraperiod Tax Allocation

OBJECTIVE 5
Explain intraperiod tax allocation.

We noted that certain irregular items are shown on the income statement net of tax. Many believe that the resulting income tax effect should be directly associated with that event or item. In other words, the tax expense for the year should be related, where possible, to **specific items** on the income statement to provide a more informative disclosure to statement users. This procedure is called **intraperiod tax allocation**, that is, allocation within a period. Its main purpose is to relate the income tax expense of the period to the items that affect the amount of the tax expense. Intraperiod tax allocation is used for the following items: (1) income from continuing operations, (2) discontinued operations, (3) extraordinary items, and (4) changes in accounting principle. The general concept is "**let the tax follow the income**."

The income tax expense attributable to "income from continuing operations" is computed by finding the income tax expense related to revenue and to expense transactions used in determining this income. In this tax computation, no effect is given to the tax consequences of the items excluded from the determination of "income from continuing operations." A separate tax effect is then associated with each irregular item.

Extraordinary Gains

In applying the concept of intraperiod tax allocation, assume that Schindler Co. has income before income tax and extraordinary item of $250,000 and an extraordinary gain from the sale of a single stock investment of $100,000. If the income tax rate is assumed to be 30 percent, the following information is presented on the income statement.

ILLUSTRATION 4-13
Intraperiod Tax Allocation, Extraordinary Gain

Income before income tax and extraordinary item		$250,000
Income tax		75,000
Income before extraordinary item		175,000
Extraordinary gain—sale of investment	$100,000	
Less: Applicable income tax	30,000	70,000
Net income		$245,000

The income tax of $75,000 ($250,000 × 30%) attributable to "Income before income tax and extraordinary item" is determined from revenue and expense transactions related to this income. In this income tax computation, the tax consequences of items excluded from the determination of "Income before income tax and extraordinary item" are not considered. The "Extraordinary gain—sale of investment" then shows a separate tax effect of $30,000.

Extraordinary Losses

To illustrate the reporting of an extraordinary loss, assume that Schindler Co. has income before income tax and extraordinary item of $250,000 and an extraordinary loss from a major casualty of $100,000. Assuming a 30 percent tax rate, the presentation of income tax on the income statement would be as shown in Illustration 4-14. In this case, the loss provides a positive tax benefit of $30,000 and, therefore, is subtracted from the $100,000 loss.

ILLUSTRATION 4-14
Intraperiod Tax Allocation, Extraordinary Loss

Income before income tax and extraordinary item		$250,000
Income tax		75,000
Income before extraordinary item		175,000
Extraordinary item—loss from casualty	$100,000	
Less: Applicable income tax reduction	30,000	70,000
Net income		$105,000

An extraordinary item may be reported "net of tax" with note disclosure, as shown in Illustration 4-15.

Income before income tax and extraordinary item	$250,000
Income tax	75,000
Income before extraordinary item	175,000
Extraordinary item, less applicable income tax reduction (Note 1)	70,000
Net income	$105,000

Note 1: During the year the Company suffered a major casualty loss of $70,000, net of applicable income tax reduction of $30,000.

ILLUSTRATION 4-15
Note Disclosure of Intraperiod Tax Allocation

Earnings per Share

OBJECTIVE 6
Explain where earnings per share information is reported.

The results of a company's operations are customarily summed up in one important figure: net income. As if this condensation were not enough of a simplification, the financial world has widely accepted an even more distilled and compact figure as its most significant business indicator—**earnings per share (EPS)**.

The computation of earnings per share is usually straightforward. **Net income minus preferred dividends (income available to common stockholders) is divided by the weighted average of common shares outstanding to arrive at earnings per share.**[23] To illustrate, assume that Lancer, Inc. reports net income of $350,000 and declares and pays preferred dividends of $50,000 for the year. The weighted average number of common shares outstanding during the year is 100,000 shares. Earnings per share is $3, as computed in Illustration 4-16.

$$\frac{\text{Net Income} - \text{Preferred Dividends}}{\text{Weighted Average of Common Shares Outstanding}} = \text{Earnings per Share}$$

$$\frac{\$350{,}000 - \$50{,}000}{100{,}000} = \$3$$

ILLUSTRATION 4-16
Equation Illustrating Computation of Earnings per Share

Note that the EPS figure measures the number of dollars earned by each share of common stock—not the dollar amount paid to stockholders in the form of dividends.

"Net income per share" or "earnings per share" is a ratio commonly used in prospectuses, proxy material, and annual reports to stockholders. It is also highlighted in the financial press, by statistical services like Standard & Poor's, and by Wall Street securities analysts. Because of its importance, **earnings per share is required to be disclosed on the face of the income statement**. A company that reports a discontinued operation, an extraordinary item, or the cumulative effect of a change in accounting principle must report per share amounts for these line items either on the face of the income statement or in the notes to the financial statements.[24]

To illustrate the income statement order of presentation and the earnings per share data, we present an income statement for Poquito Industries Inc. in Illustration 4-17 on page 144. Notice the order in which data are shown. In addition, per share information is shown at the bottom. Assume that the company had 100,000 shares outstanding for the entire year. The Poquito Industries Inc. income statement, in Illustration 4-17, is highly condensed. Items such as "Unusual charge," "Discontinued operations," "Extraordinary item," and the "Change in accounting principle" would have to be described fully and appropriately in the statement or related notes.

Many corporations have simple capital structures that include only common stock. For these companies, a presentation such as "earnings per common share" is

[23] In the calculation of earnings per share, preferred dividends are deducted from net income if declared or if cumulative though not declared.

[24] "Earnings Per Share," *Statement of Financial Accounting Standards No. 128* (Norwalk, Conn.: FASB, 1996).

ILLUSTRATION 4-17
Income Statement

POQUITO INDUSTRIES INC.
INCOME STATEMENT
FOR THE YEAR ENDED DECEMBER 31, 2004

Sales revenue		$1,480,000
Cost of goods sold		600,000
Gross profit		880,000
Selling and administrative expenses		320,000
Income from operations		560,000
Other revenues and gains		
Interest revenue		10,000
Other expenses and losses		
Loss on disposal of part of Textile Division	$ (5,000)	
Unusual charge—loss on sale of investments	(45,000)	(50,000)
Income from continuing operations before income tax		520,000
Income tax		208,000
Income from continuing operations		312,000
Discontinued operations		
Income from operations of Pizza Division, less applicable income tax of $24,800	54,000	
Loss on disposal of Pizza Division, less applicable income tax of $41,000	(90,000)	(36,000)
Income before extraordinary item and cumulative effect of accounting change		276,000
Extraordinary item—loss from earthquake, less applicable income tax of $23,000		(45,000)
Cumulative effect on prior years of retroactive application of new depreciation method, less applicable income tax of $30,900		(60,000)
Net income		$ 171,000
Per share of common stock		
Income from continuing operations		$3.12
Income from operations of discontinued division, net of tax		0.54
Loss on disposal of discontinued operation, net of tax		(0.90)
Income before extraordinary item and cumulative effect		2.76
Extraordinary loss, net of tax		(0.45)
Cumulative effect of change in accounting principle, net of tax		(0.60)
Net income		$1.71

appropriate on the income statement. In many instances, however, companies' earnings per share are subject to dilution (reduction) in the future because existing contingencies permit the issuance of additional common shares.[25]

In summary, the simplicity and availability of figures for per share earnings lead inevitably to their widespread use. Because of the undue importance that the public, even the well-informed public, attaches to earnings per share, the EPS figure must be made as meaningful as possible.

Retained Earnings Statement

OBJECTIVE 7
Prepare a retained earnings statement.

Net income increases retained earnings, and a net loss decreases retained earnings. Both cash and stock dividends decrease retained earnings. Prior period adjustments may either increase or decrease retained earnings. A **prior period adjustment** is a correction of an error in the financial statements of a prior period. Prior period adjustments (net of tax) are charged or credited to the opening balance of retained earnings, and thus excluded from the determination of net income for the current period.

[25]Ibid. The computational problems involved in accounting for these dilutive securities in earnings per share computations are discussed in Chapter 16.

Information related to retained earnings may be shown in different ways. For example, some companies prepare a separate retained earnings statement, as shown in Illustration 4-18.

ILLUSTRATION 4-18
Retained Earnings Statement

TIGER WOODS INC.
RETAINED EARNINGS STATEMENT
FOR THE YEAR ENDED DECEMBER 31, 2004

Balance, January 1, as reported		$1,050,000
Correction for understatement of net income in prior period (inventory error)		50,000
Balance, January 1, as adjusted		1,100,000
Add: Net income		360,000
		1,460,000
Less: Cash dividends	$100,000	
Stock dividends	200,000	300,000
Balance, December 31		$1,160,000

The reconciliation of the beginning to the ending balance in retained earnings provides information about why net assets increased or decreased during the year. The association of dividend distributions with net income for the period indicates what management is doing with earnings: It may be "plowing back" into the business part or all of the earnings, distributing all current income, or distributing current income plus the accumulated earnings of prior years.

Restrictions of Retained Earnings

Retained earnings is often restricted in accordance with contractual requirements, board of directors' policy, or the apparent necessity of the moment. The amounts of retained earnings restricted are generally disclosed in the notes to the financial statements. In some cases, the amount of retained earnings restricted is transferred to **Appropriated Retained Earnings**. The retained earnings section may therefore report two separate amounts—(1) retained earnings free (unrestricted) and (2) retained earnings appropriated (restricted). The total of these two amounts equals the total retained earnings.[26]

Comprehensive Income

As indicated earlier, the all-inclusive income concept is used in determining financial performance for a period of time. Under this concept, all revenues, expenses, and gains and losses recognized during the period are included in income. However, over time, specific exceptions to this general concept have developed. Certain items now bypass income and are reported directly in equity.

An example of one of these items is unrealized gains and losses on available-for-sale securities.[27] Why are these gains and losses on available-for-sale securities excluded from net income? Because disclosing them separately (1) reduces the volatility of net income due to fluctuations in fair value, yet (2) informs the financial statement user of the gain or loss that would be incurred if the securities were sold at fair value.

[26] *Accounting Trends and Techniques—2001* (New York: AICPA) indicates that most companies (577 of 600 surveyed) present changes in retained earnings either within the statement of stockholders' equity (534 firms) or in a separate statement of retained earnings. Only 10 of the 600 companies prepare a combined statement of income and retained earnings.

[27] Available-for-sale securities are further discussed in Chapter 17. Other examples of other comprehensive items are translation gains and losses on foreign currency, excess of additional pension liability over unrecognized prior service cost, and unrealized gains and losses on certain hedging transactions.

Items that bypass the income statement are included under the concept of comprehensive income. **Comprehensive income** includes all changes in equity during a period except those resulting from investments by owners and distributions to owners. Comprehensive income, therefore, includes all revenues and gains, expenses and losses reported in net income, and in addition it includes gains and losses that bypass net income but affect stockholders' equity. These items that bypass the income statement are referred to as **other comprehensive income**.

OBJECTIVE 8
Explain how other comprehensive income is reported.

The FASB decided that the components of other comprehensive income must be displayed in one of three ways: **(1) a second income statement; (2) a combined income statement of comprehensive income; or (3) as a part of the statement of stockholders' equity.**[28] Regardless of the format used, net income must be added to other comprehensive income to arrive at comprehensive income. Earnings per share information related to comprehensive income is not required.[29]

To illustrate these presentation formats, assume that V. Gill Inc. reports the following information for 2004: sales revenue $800,000, cost of goods sold $600,000, operating expenses $90,000, and an unrealized holding gain on available-for-sale securities of $30,000, net of tax.

Second Income Statement

The two-income statement format is shown in Illustration 4-19 below. Reporting comprehensive income in a separate statement indicates that the gains and losses identified as other comprehensive income have the same status as traditional gains and losses. In addition, the relationship of the traditional income statement to the comprehensive income statement is apparent because net income is the starting point in the comprehensive income statement.

ILLUSTRATION 4-19
Two-Statement Format: Comprehensive Income

V. GILL INC.
INCOME STATEMENT
FOR THE YEAR ENDED DECEMBER 31, 2004

Sales revenue	$800,000
Cost of goods sold	600,000
Gross profit	200,000
Operating expenses	90,000
Net income	$110,000

V. GILL INC.
COMPREHENSIVE INCOME STATEMENT
FOR THE YEAR ENDED DECEMBER 31, 2004

Net income	$110,000
Other comprehensive income	
Unrealized holding gain, net of tax	30,000
Comprehensive income	$140,000

[28]"Reporting Comprehensive Income," *Statement of Financial Accounting Standards No. 130* (Norwalk, Conn.: FASB, June 1997). *Accounting Trends and Techniques—2001* (New York: AICPA) indicates that for the 600 companies surveyed, 519 report comprehensive income. Most companies (422 of 497) include comprehensive income as part of the statement of stockholders' equity.

[29]A company is required to display the components of other comprehensive income either (1) net of related tax effects or (2) before related tax effects with one amount shown for the aggregate amount of tax related to the total amount of other comprehensive income. Under either alternative, each component of other comprehensive income must be shown, net of related taxes either in the face of the statement or in the notes.

Combined Income Statement

The second approach provides a combined statement of comprehensive income in which the traditional net income would be a subtotal, with total comprehensive income shown as a final total. The combined statement has the advantage of not requiring the creation of a new financial statement. However, burying net income in a subtotal on the statement is a disadvantage.

Statement of Stockholders' Equity

A third approach is to report other comprehensive income items in a **statement of stockholders' equity** (often referred to as statement of changes in stockholders' equity). This statement reports the changes in each stockholder's equity account and in total stockholders' equity during the year. The statement of stockholders' equity is often **prepared in columnar form** with columns for each account and for total stockholders' equity.

To illustrate its presentation, assume the same information related to V. Gill Inc. and that the company had the following stockholder equity account balances at the beginning of 2004: Common Stock $300,000; Retained Earnings $50,000; and Accumulated Other Comprehensive Income $60,000. No changes in the Common Stock account occurred during the year. A statement of stockholders' equity for V. Gill Inc. is shown in Illustration 4-20.

ILLUSTRATION 4-20
Presentation of Comprehensive Income Items in Stockholders' Equity Statement

V. GILL INC.
STATEMENT OF STOCKHOLDERS' EQUITY
FOR THE YEAR ENDED DECEMBER 31, 2004

	Total	Comprehensive Income	Retained Earnings	Accumulated Other Comprehensive Income	Common Stock
Beginning balance	$410,000		$ 50,000	$60,000	$300,000
Comprehensive income					
Net income	110,000	$110,000	110,000		
Other comprehensive income					
Unrealized holding gain, net of tax	30,000	30,000		30,000	
Comprehensive income		$140,000			
Ending balance	$550,000		$160,000	$90,000	$300,000

Examples of Comprehensive Income Reporting

Most companies use the statement of stockholders' equity approach to provide information related to the components of other comprehensive income. Because many companies already provide a statement of stockholders' equity, adding additional columns to display information related to comprehensive income is not costly.

Balance Sheet Presentation

Regardless of the display format used, the **accumulated other comprehensive income** of $90,000 is reported in the stockholders' equity section of the balance sheet of V. Gill Inc. as shown in Illustration 4-21.

ILLUSTRATION 4-21
Presentation of Accumulated Other Comprehensive Income in the Balance Sheet

V. GILL INC. BALANCE SHEET AS OF DECEMBER 31, 2004 (STOCKHOLDERS' EQUITY SECTION)	
Stockholders' equity	
Common stock	$300,000
Retained earnings	160,000
Accumulated other comprehensive income	90,000
Total stockholders' equity	$550,000

By providing information on the components of comprehensive income as well as total accumulated other comprehensive income, the company communicates information about all changes in net assets.[30] With this information, users will be better able to understand the quality of the company's earnings. This information should help users predict the amounts, timing, and uncertainty of future cash flows.

SUMMARY OF LEARNING OBJECTIVES

1 Identify the uses and limitations of an income statement. The income statement provides investors and creditors with information that helps them predict the amounts, timing, and uncertainty of future cash flows. Also, the income statement helps users determine the risk (level of uncertainty) of not achieving particular cash flows. The limitations of an income statement are: (1) The statement does not include many items that contribute to general growth and well-being of an enterprise. (2) Income numbers are often affected by the accounting methods used. (3) Income measures are subject to estimates.

The *transaction approach* focuses on the activities that have occurred during a given period. Instead of presenting only a net change, it discloses the components of the change. The transaction approach to income measurement requires the use of revenue, expense, loss, and gain accounts.

2 Prepare a single-step income statement. In a single-step income statement, just two groupings exist: revenues and expenses. Expenses are deducted from revenues to arrive at net income or loss—a single subtraction. Frequently, income tax is reported separately as the last item before net income to indicate its relationship to income before income tax.

3 Prepare a multiple-step income statement. A multiple-step income statement shows two further classifications: (1) a separation of operating results from those obtained through the subordinate or nonoperating activities of the company; and (2) a classification of expenses by functions, such as merchandising or manufacturing, selling, and administration.

4 Explain how irregular items are reported. Irregular gains or losses or nonrecurring items are generally closed to Income Summary and are included in the income statement. These are treated in the income statement as follows: (1) Discontinued operation of a component of a business is classified as a separate item, after continuing operations. (2) The unusual, material, nonrecurring items that are significantly different from the customary business activities are shown in a separate section for extraordinary items, below discontinued operations. (3) Other items of a material amount that

KEY TERMS

accumulated other comprehensive income, *147*
all-inclusive approach, *133*
appropriated retained earnings, *145*
capital maintenance approach, (n), *127*
changes in estimate, *140*
comprehensive income, *146*
current operating performance approach, *133*
discontinued operation, *134*
earnings management, *126*
earnings per share, *143*
extraordinary items, *135*
income statement, *124*
intraperiod tax allocation, *142*
irregular items, *134*
modified all-inclusive concept, *134*
multiple-step income statement, *129*
other comprehensive income, *146*
prior period adjustments, *144*

[30]Note that prior period adjustments and the cumulative effect of changes in accounting principle are not considered other comprehensive income items.

are of an unusual or nonrecurring nature and are not considered extraordinary are separately disclosed. (4) The cumulative adjustment that occurs when a change in accounting principles develops is disclosed as a separate item, just before net income.

5 Explain intraperiod tax allocation. The tax expense for the year should be related, where possible, to specific items on the income statement, to provide a more informative disclosure to statement users. This procedure is called intraperiod tax allocation, that is, allocation within a period. Its main purpose is to relate the income tax expense for the fiscal period to the following items that affect the amount of the tax provisions: (1) income from continuing operations, (2) discontinued operations, (3) extraordinary items, and (4) changes in accounting principle.

6 Explain where earnings per share information is reported. Because of the inherent dangers of focusing attention solely on earnings per share, earnings per share must be disclosed on the face of the income statement. A company that reports a discontinued operation, an extraordinary item, or the cumulative effect of a change in accounting principle must report per share amounts for these line items either on the face of the income statement or in the notes to the financial statements.

7 Prepare a retained earnings statement. The retained earnings statement should disclose net income (loss), dividends, prior period adjustments, and restrictions of retained earnings.

8 Explain how other comprehensive income is reported. The components of other comprehensive income are reported in a second statement, a combined income statement of comprehensive income, or in a statement of stockholders' equity.

quality of earnings, *126*
restructuring charge, *138*
single-step income statement, *128*
statement of stockholders' equity, *147*
transaction approach, *127*

QUESTIONS

1. What kinds of questions about future cash flows do investors and creditors attempt to answer with information in the income statement?

2. How can information based on past transactions be used to predict future cash flows?

3. Identify at least two situations in which important changes in value are not reported in the income statement.

4. Identify at least two situations in which application of different accounting methods or accounting estimates results in difficulties in comparing companies.

5. Explain the transaction approach to measuring income. Why is the transaction approach to income measurement preferable to other ways of measuring income?

6. What is earnings management?

7. How can earnings management affect the quality of earnings?

8. Why should caution be exercised in the use of the income figure derived in an income statement? What are the objectives of generally accepted accounting principles in their application to the income statement?

9. A *Wall Street Journal* article noted that **MicroStrategy** reported higher income than its competitors by using a more aggressive policy for recognizing revenue on future upgrades to its products. Some contend that MicroStrategy's quality of earnings is low. What does the term "quality of earnings" mean?

10. What is the major distinction (a) between revenues and gains and (b) between expenses and losses?

11. What are the advantages and disadvantages of the single-step income statement?

12. What is the basis for distinguishing between operating and nonoperating items?

13. Distinguish between the all-inclusive income statement and the current operating performance income statement. According to present generally accepted accounting principles, which is recommended? Explain.

14. How should prior period adjustments be reported in the financial statements? Give an example of a prior period adjustment.

15. Discuss the appropriate treatment in the financial statements of each of the following.

(a) An amount of $113,000 realized in excess of the cash surrender value of an insurance policy on the life of one of the founders of the company who died during the year.

(b) A profit-sharing bonus to employees computed as a percentage of net income.

(c) Additional depreciation on factory machinery because of an error in computing depreciation for the previous year.

(d) Rent received from subletting a portion of the office space.

(e) A patent infringement suit, brought 2 years ago against the company by another company, was settled this year by a cash payment of $725,000.

(f) A reduction in the Allowance for Doubtful Accounts balance, because the account appears to be considerably in excess of the probable loss from uncollectible receivables.

16. Indicate where the following items would ordinarily appear on the financial statements of Allepo, Inc. for the year 2004.

(a) The service life of certain equipment was changed from 8 to 5 years. If a 5-year life had been used previously, additional depreciation of $425,000 would have been charged.

(b) In 2004 a flood destroyed a warehouse that had a book value of $1,600,000. Floods are rare in this locality.

(c) In 2004 the company wrote off $1,000,000 of inventory that was considered obsolete.

(d) An income tax refund related to the 2001 tax year was received.

(e) In 2001, a supply warehouse with an expected useful life of 7 years was erroneously expensed.

(f) Allepo, Inc. changed its depreciation from double-declining to straight-line on machinery in 2004. The cumulative effect of the change was $925,000 (net of tax).

17. Give the section of a multiple-step income statement in which each of the following is shown.

(a) Loss on inventory write-down.

(b) Loss from strike.

(c) Bad debt expense.

(d) Loss on disposal of a component of the business.

(e) Gain on sale of machinery.

(f) Interest revenue.

(g) Depreciation expense.

(h) Material write-offs of notes receivable.

18. Barry Bonds Land Development, Inc. purchased land for $70,000 and spent $30,000 developing it. It then sold the land for $160,000. Tom Glavine Manufacturing purchased land for a future plant site for $100,000. Due to a change in plans, Glavine later sold the land for $160,000. Should these two companies report the land sales, both at gains of $60,000, in a similar manner?

19. You run into Rex Grossman at a party and begin discussing financial statements. Rex says, "I prefer the single-step income statement because the multiple-step format generally overstates income." How should you respond to Rex?

20. Federov Corporation has eight expense accounts in its general ledger which could be classified as selling expenses. Should Federov report these eight expenses separately in its income statement or simply report one total amount for selling expenses?

21. Jose DeLeon Investments reported an unusual gain from the sale of certain assets in its 2004 income statement. How does intraperiod tax allocation affect the reporting of this unusual gain?

22. What effect does intraperiod tax allocation have on reported net income?

23. Letterman Company computed earnings per share as follows.

$$\frac{\text{Net income}}{\text{Common shares outstanding at year-end}}$$

Letterman has a simple capital structure. What possible errors might the company have made in the computation? Explain.

24. Maria Shriver Corporation reported 2004 earnings per share of $7.21. In 2005, Maria Shriver reported earnings per share as follows.

On income before extraordinary item	$6.40
On extraordinary item	1.88
On net income	$8.28

Is the increase in earnings per share from $7.21 to $8.28 a favorable trend?

25. What is meant by "tax allocation within a period"? What is the justification for such practice?

26. When does tax allocation within a period become necessary? How should this allocation be handled?

27. During 2004, Natsume Sozeki Company earned income of $1,000,000 before income taxes and realized a gain of $450,000 on a government-forced condemnation sale of a division plant facility. The income is subject to income taxation at the rate of 34%. The gain on the sale of the plant is taxed at 30%. Proper accounting suggests that the unusual gain be reported as an extraordinary item. Illustrate an appropriate presentation of these items in the income statement.

28. On January 30, 2003, a suit was filed against Pierogi Corporation under the Environmental Protection Act. On August 6, 2004, Pierogi Corporation agreed to settle the action and pay $920,000 in damages to certain current and former employees. How should this settlement be reported in the 2004 financial statements? Discuss.

29. Tiger Paper Company decided to close two small pulp mills in Conway, New Hampshire, and Corvallis, Oregon. Would these closings be reported in a separate section entitled "Discontinued operations after income from continuing operations"? Discuss.

30. What major types of items are reported in the retained earnings statement?

31. Generally accepted accounting principles usually require the use of accrual accounting to "fairly present" income. If the cash receipts and disbursements method of accounting will "clearly reflect" taxable income, why does this method not usually also "fairly present" income?

32. State some of the more serious problems encountered in seeking to achieve the ideal measurement of periodic net income. Explain what accountants do as a practical alternative.

33. What is meant by the terms *components, elements,* and *items* as they relate to the income statement? Why might items have to be disclosed in the income statement?

34. What are the three ways that other comprehensive income may be displayed (reported)?

35. How should the disposal of a component of a business be disclosed in the income statement?

BRIEF EXERCISES

BE4-1 Tim Allen Co. had sales revenue of $540,000 in 2004. Other items recorded during the year were:

Cost of goods sold	$320,000
Wage expense	120,000
Income tax expense	25,000
Increase in value of company reputation	15,000
Other operating expenses	10,000
Unrealized gain on value of patents	20,000

Prepare a single-step income statement for Allen for 2004. Allen has 100,000 shares of stock outstanding.

BE4-2 Turner Corporation had net sales of $2,400,000 and interest revenue of $31,000 during 2004. Expenses for 2004 were: cost of goods sold $1,250,000; administrative expenses $212,000; selling expenses $280,000; interest expense $45,000. Turner's tax rate is 30%. The corporation had 100,000 shares of common stock authorized and 70,000 shares issued and outstanding during 2004. Prepare a single-step income statement for the year ended December 31, 2004.

BE4-3 Using the information provided in BE4-2, prepare a condensed multiple-step income statement for Turner Corporation.

BE4-4 Green Day Corporation had income from continuing operations of $12,600,000 in 2004. During 2004, it disposed of its restaurant division at an after-tax loss of $189,000. Prior to disposal, the division operated at a loss of $315,000 (net of tax) in 2004. Green Day had 10,000,000 shares of common stock outstanding during 2004. Prepare a partial income statement for Green Day beginning with income from continuing operations.

BE4-5 Boyz II Men Corporation had income before income taxes for 2004 of $7,300,000. In addition, it suffered an unusual and infrequent pretax loss of $770,000 from a volcano eruption. The corporation's tax rate is 30%. Prepare a partial income statement for Boyz II Men beginning with income before income taxes. The corporation had 5,000,000 shares of common stock outstanding during 2004.

BE4-6 Shawn Bradley Company changed from straight-line depreciation to double-declining balance depreciation at the beginning of 2004. The plant assets originally cost $1,500,000 in 2002. Using straight-line depreciation, depreciation expense is $60,000 per year. Under the double-declining balance method, depreciation expense would be $120,000, $110,400, and $101,568 for 2002, 2003, and 2004. If Bradley's tax rate is 30%, by what amount would the cumulative effect of a change in accounting principle increase or decrease 2004 net income?

BE4-7 Jana Kingston Company has recorded bad debt expense in the past at a rate of 1½% of net sales. In 2004, Kingston decides to increase its estimate to 2%. If the new rate had been used in prior years, cumulative bad debt expense would have been $380,000 instead of $285,000. In 2004, bad debt expense will be $120,000 instead of $90,000. If Kingston's tax rate is 30%, what amount should it report as the cumulative effect of changing the estimated bad debt rate?

BE4-8 In 2004, Kirby Puckett Corporation reported net income of $1,200,000. It declared and paid preferred stock dividends of $250,000. During 2004, Puckett had a weighted average of 190,000 common shares outstanding. Compute Puckett's 2004 earnings per share.

BE4-9 Lincoln Corporation has retained earnings of $675,000 at January 1, 2004. Net income during 2004 was $2,400,000, and cash dividends declared and paid during 2004 totaled $75,000. Prepare a retained earnings statement for the year ended December 31, 2004.

BE4-10 Using the information from BE4-9, prepare a retained earnings statement for the year ended December 31, 2004. Assume an error was discovered: land costing $80,000 (net of tax) was charged to repairs expense in 2001.

BE4-11 On January 1, 2004, Creative Works Inc. had cash and common stock of $60,000. At that date the company had no other asset, liability or equity balances. On January 2, 2004, it purchased for cash $20,000 of equity securities that it classified as available-for-sale. It received cash dividends of $3,000 during the year on these securities. In addition, it has an unrealized holding gain on these securities of $5,000 net of tax. Determine the following amounts for 2004: (a) net income; (b) comprehensive income; (c) other comprehensive income; and (d) accumulated other comprehensive income (end of 2004).

EXERCISES

E4-1 (Computation of Net Income) Presented below are changes in all the account balances of Fritz Reiner Furniture Co. during the current year, except for retained earnings.

	Increase (Decrease)		Increase (Decrease)
Cash	$ 79,000	Accounts Payable	$(51,000)
Accounts Receivable (net)	45,000	Bonds Payable	82,000
Inventory	127,000	Common Stock	125,000
Investments	(47,000)	Additional Paid-in Capital	13,000

Instructions

Compute the net income for the current year, assuming that there were no entries in the Retained Earnings account except for net income and a dividend declaration of $19,000 which was paid in the current year.

E4-2 (Income Statement Items) Presented below are certain account balances of Paczki Products Co.

Rental revenue	$ 6,500	Sales discounts	$ 7,800
Interest expense	12,700	Selling expenses	99,400
Beginning retained earnings	114,400	Sales	390,000
Ending retained earnings	134,000	Income tax	31,000
Dividend revenue	71,000	Cost of goods sold	184,400
Sales returns	12,400	Administrative expenses	82,500

Instructions

From the foregoing, compute the following: (a) total net revenue, (b) net income, (c) dividends declared during the current year.

E4-3 (Single-step Income Statement) The financial records of LeRoi Jones Inc. were destroyed by fire at the end of 2004. Fortunately the controller had kept certain statistical data related to the income statement as presented below.

1. The beginning merchandise inventory was $92,000 and decreased 20% during the current year.
2. Sales discounts amount to $17,000.
3. 20,000 shares of common stock were outstanding for the entire year.
4. Interest expense was $20,000.
5. The income tax rate is 30%.
6. Cost of goods sold amounts to $500,000.
7. Administrative expenses are 20% of cost of goods sold but only 8% of gross sales.
8. Four-fifths of the operating expenses relate to sales activities.

Instructions

From the foregoing information prepare an income statement for the year 2004 in single-step form.

E4-4 (Multiple-step and Single-step) Two accountants for the firm of Elwes and Wright are arguing about the merits of presenting an income statement in a multiple-step versus a single-step format. The discussion involves the following 2004 information related to P. Bride Company ($000 omitted).

Administrative expense	
Officers' salaries	$ 4,900
Depreciation of office furniture and equipment	3,960
Cost of goods sold	60,570
Rental revenue	17,230
Selling expense	
Transportation-out	2,690
Sales commissions	7,980
Depreciation of sales equipment	6,480
Sales	96,500
Income tax	9,070
Interest expense	1,860

Instructions

(a) Prepare an income statement for the year 2004 using the multiple-step form. Common shares outstanding for 2004 total 40,550 (000 omitted).
(b) Prepare an income statement for the year 2004 using the single-step form.
(c) Which one do you prefer? Discuss.

E4-5 (Multiple-step and Extraordinary Items) The following balances were taken from the books of Maria Conchita Alonzo Corp. on December 31, 2004.

Interest revenue	$ 86,000	Accumulated depreciation—equipment	$ 40,000
Cash	51,000	Accumulated depreciation—building	28,000
Sales	1,380,000	Notes receivable	155,000
Accounts receivable	150,000	Selling expenses	194,000
Prepaid insurance	20,000	Accounts payable	170,000
Sales returns and allowances	150,000	Bonds payable	100,000
Allowance for doubtful accounts	7,000	Administrative and general expenses	97,000
Sales discounts	45,000	Accrued liabilities	32,000
Land	100,000	Interest expense	60,000
Equipment	200,000	Notes payable	100,000
Building	140,000	Loss from earthquake damage (extraordinary item)	150,000
Cost of goods sold	621,000	Common stock	500,000
		Retained earnings	21,000

Assume the total effective tax rate on all items is 34%.

Instructions

Prepare a multiple-step income statement; 100,000 shares of common stock were outstanding during the year.

E4-6 (Multiple-step and Single-step) The accountant of Whitney Houston Shoe Co. has compiled the following information from the company's records as a basis for an income statement for the year ended December 31, 2004.

Rental revenue	$ 29,000
Interest on notes payable	18,000
Market appreciation on land above cost	31,000
Wages and salaries—sales	114,800
Materials and supplies—sales	17,600
Income tax	37,400
Wages and salaries—administrative	135,900
Other administrative expenses	51,700
Cost of goods sold	496,000
Net sales	980,000
Depreciation on plant assets (70% selling, 30% administrative)	65,000
Dividends declared	16,000

There were 20,000 shares of common stock outstanding during the year.

Instructions

(a) Prepare a multiple-step income statement.
(b) Prepare a single-step income statement.
(c) Which format do you prefer? Discuss.

E4-7 (Income Statement, EPS) Presented below are selected ledger accounts of Tucker Corporation as of December 31, 2004.

Cash	$ 50,000
Administrative expenses	100,000
Selling expenses	80,000
Net sales	540,000
Cost of goods sold	210,000
Cash dividends declared (2004)	20,000
Cash dividends paid (2004)	15,000
Discontinued operations (loss before income taxes)	40,000
Depreciation expense, not recorded in 2003	30,000
Retained earnings, December 31, 2003	90,000
Effective tax rate 30%	

Instructions

(a) Compute net income for 2004.

(b) Prepare a partial income statement beginning with income from continuing operations before income tax, and including appropriate earnings per share information. Assume 10,000 shares of common stock were outstanding during 2004.

E4-8 (Multiple-step Statement with Retained Earnings) Presented below is information related to Ivan Calderon Corp. for the year 2004.

Net sales	$1,300,000	Write-off of inventory due to obsolescence	$ 80,000
Cost of goods sold	780,000	Depreciation expense omitted by accident in 2003	55,000
Selling expenses	65,000	Casualty loss (extraordinary item) before taxes	50,000
Administrative expenses	48,000	Dividends declared	45,000
Dividend revenue	20,000	Retained earnings at December 31, 2003	980,000
Interest revenue	7,000	Effective tax rate of 34% on all items	

Instructions

(a) Prepare a multiple-step income statement for 2004. Assume that 60,000 shares of common stock are outstanding.

(b) Prepare a separate retained earnings statement for 2004.

E4-9 (Earnings Per Share) The stockholders' equity section of Tkachuk Corporation appears below as of December 31, 2004.

8% cumulative preferred stock, $50 par value, authorized 100,000 shares, outstanding 90,000 shares		$ 4,500,000
Common stock, $1.00 par, authorized and issued 10 million shares		10,000,000
Additional paid-in capital		20,500,000
Retained earnings	$134,000,000	
Net income	33,000,000	167,000,000
		$202,000,000

Net income for 2004 reflects a total effective tax rate of 34%. Included in the net income figure is a loss of $18,000,000 (before tax) as a result of a major casualty.

Instructions

Compute earnings per share data as it should appear on the income statement of Tkachuk Corporation.

E4-10 (Condensed Income Statement—Periodic Inventory Method) Presented below are selected ledger accounts of Spock Corporation at December 31, 2004.

Cash	$ 185,000	Travel and entertainment	$ 69,000
Merchandise inventory	535,000	Accounting and legal services	33,000
Sales	4,275,000	Insurance expense	24,000
Advances from customers	117,000	Advertising	54,000
Purchases	2,786,000	Transportation-out	93,000
Sales discounts	34,000	Depreciation of office equipment	48,000
Purchase discounts	27,000	Depreciation of sales equipment	36,000
Sales salaries	284,000	Telephone—sales	17,000
Office salaries	346,000	Utilities—office	32,000
Purchase returns	15,000	Miscellaneous office expenses	8,000
Sales returns	79,000	Rental revenue	240,000
Transportation-in	72,000	Extraordinary loss (before tax)	70,000
Accounts receivable	142,500	Interest expense	176,000
Sales commissions	83,000	Common stock ($10 par)	900,000

Spock's effective tax rate on all items is 34%. A physical inventory indicates that the ending inventory is $686,000.

Instructions

Prepare a condensed 2004 income statement for Spock Corporation.

E4-11 (Retained Earnings Statement) Eddie Zambrano Corporation began operations on January 1, 2001. During its first 3 years of operations, Zambrano reported net income and declared dividends as follows.

	Net income	Dividends declared
2001	$ 40,000	$ –0–
2002	125,000	50,000
2003	160,000	50,000

The following information relates to 2004.

Income before income tax	$240,000
Prior period adjustment: understatement of 2002 depreciation expense (before taxes)	$ 25,000
Cumulative decrease in income from change in inventory methods (before taxes)	$ 35,000
Dividends declared (of this amount, $25,000 will be paid on Jan. 15, 2005)	$100,000
Effective tax rate	40%

Instructions

(a) Prepare a 2004 retained earnings statement for Eddie Zambrano Corporation.

(b) Assume Eddie Zambrano Corp. restricted retained earnings in the amount of $70,000 on December 31, 2004. After this action, what would Zambrano report as total retained earnings in its December 31, 2004, balance sheet?

E4-12 (Earnings per Share) At December 31, 2003, Shiga Naoya Corporation had the following stock outstanding.

10% cumulative preferred stock, $100 par, 107,500 shares	$10,750,000
Common stock, $5 par, 4,000,000 shares	20,000,000

During 2004, Shiga Naoya's only stock transaction was the issuance of 400,000 shares of common on April 1. The following also occurred during 2004.

Income from continuing operations before taxes	$23,650,000
Discontinued operations (loss before taxes)	$ 3,225,000
Preferred dividends declared	$ 1,075,000
Common dividends declared	$ 2,200,000
Effective tax rate	35%

Instructions

Compute earnings per share data as it should appear in the 2004 income statement of Shiga Naoya Corporation.

E4-13 (Change in Accounting Principle) Tom Kothe Company placed an asset in service on January 2, 2002. Its cost was $450,000 with an estimated service life of 6 years. Salvage value was estimated to be $30,000. Using the double-declining-balance method of depreciation, the depreciation for 2002, 2003, and 2004 would be $150,000, $100,000, and $66,667 respectively. During 2004 the company's management decided to change to the straight-line method of depreciation. Assume a 35% tax rate.

Instructions

(a) How much depreciation expense will be reported in the income from continuing operations of the company's income statement for 2004? (*Hint:* Use the new depreciation in the current year.)

(b) What amount will be reported as the cumulative effect of the change in accounting principle for 2004?

E4-14 (Comprehensive Income) Roxanne Carter Corporation reported the following for 2004: net sales $1,200,000; cost of goods sold $750,000; selling and administrative expenses $320,000; and an unrealized holding gain on available-for-sale securities $18,000.

Instructions

Prepare a statement of comprehensive income, using the two-income statement format. Ignore income taxes and earnings per share.

E4-15 (Comprehensive Income) C. Reither Co. reports the following information for 2004: sales revenue $700,000; cost of goods sold $500,000; operating expenses $80,000; and an unrealized holding loss on available-for-sale securities for 2004 of $60,000. It declared and paid a cash dividend of $10,000 in 2004.

C. Reither Co. has January 1, 2004, balances in common stock $350,000; accumulated other comprehensive income $80,000; and retained earnings $90,000. It issued no stock during 2004.

Instructions

Prepare a statement of stockholders' equity.

E4-16 (Various Reporting Formats) The following information was taken from the records of Roland Carlson Inc. for the year 2004. Income tax applicable to income from continuing operations $187,000; income tax applicable to loss on discontinued operations $25,500; income tax applicable to extraordinary gain $32,300; income tax applicable to extraordinary loss $20,400; and unrealized holding gain on available-for-sale securities $15,000.

Extraordinary gain	$ 95,000	Cash dividends declared	$ 150,000
Loss on discontinued operations	75,000	Retained earnings January 1, 2004	600,000
Administrative expenses	240,000	Cost of goods sold	850,000
Rent revenue	40,000	Selling expenses	300,000
Extraordinary loss	60,000	Sales	1,900,000

Shares outstanding during 2004 were 100,000.

Instructions

(a) Prepare a single-step income statement for 2004.
(b) Prepare a retained earnings statement for 2004.
(c) Show how comprehensive income is reported using the second income statement format.

PROBLEMS

P4-1 (Multi-step Income, Retained Earnings) Presented below is information related to American Horse Company for 2004.

Retained earnings balance, January 1, 2004	$ 980,000
Sales for the year	25,000,000
Cost of goods sold	17,000,000
Interest revenue	70,000
Selling and administrative expenses	4,700,000
Write-off of goodwill (not tax deductible)	820,000
Income taxes for 2004	905,000
Gain on the sale of investments (normal recurring)	110,000
Loss due to flood damage—extraordinary item (net of tax)	390,000
Loss on the disposition of the wholesale division (net of tax)	440,000
Loss on operations of the wholesale division (net of tax)	90,000
Dividends declared on common stock	250,000
Dividends declared on preferred stock	70,000

Instructions

Prepare a multi-step income statement and a retained earnings statement. American Horse Company decided to discontinue its entire wholesale operations and to retain its manufacturing operations. On September 15, American Horse sold the wholesale operations to Rogers Company. During 2004, there were 300,000 shares of common stock outstanding all year.

P4-2 (Single-step Income, Retained Earnings, Periodic Inventory) Presented below is the trial balance of Mary J. Blige Corporation at December 31, 2004.

MARY J. BLIGE CORPORATION
TRIAL BALANCE
YEAR ENDED DECEMBER 31, 2004

	Debits	Credits
Purchase Discounts		$ 10,000
Cash	$ 205,100	
Accounts Receivable	105,000	
Rent Revenue		18,000
Retained Earnings		260,000
Salaries Payable		18,000
Sales		1,000,000

Notes Receivable	110,000	
Accounts Payable		49,000
Accumulated Depreciation—Equipment		28,000
Sales Discounts	14,500	
Sales Returns	17,500	
Notes Payable		70,000
Selling Expenses	232,000	
Administrative Expenses	99,000	
Common Stock		300,000
Income Tax Expense	38,500	
Cash Dividends	45,000	
Allowance for Doubtful Accounts		5,000
Supplies	14,000	
Freight-in	20,000	
Land	70,000	
Equipment	140,000	
Bonds Payable		100,000
Gain on Sale of Land		30,000
Accumulated Depreciation—Building		19,600
Merchandise Inventory	89,000	
Building	98,000	
Purchases	610,000	
Totals	$1,907,600	$1,907,600

A physical count of inventory on December 31 resulted in an inventory amount of $124,000.

Instructions

Prepare a single-step income statement and a retained earnings statement. Assume that the only changes in retained earnings during the current year were from net income and dividends. Thirty thousand shares of common stock were outstanding the entire year.

P4-3 (Irregular Items) Tony Rich Inc. reported income from continuing operations before taxes during 2004 of $790,000. Additional transactions occurring in 2004 but not considered in the $790,000 are as follows.

1. The corporation experienced an uninsured flood loss (extraordinary) in the amount of $80,000 during the year. The tax rate on this item is 46%.
2. At the beginning of 2002, the corporation purchased a machine for $54,000 (salvage value of $9,000) that had a useful life of 6 years. The bookkeeper used straight-line depreciation for 2002, 2003, and 2004 but failed to deduct the salvage value in computing the depreciation base.
3. Sale of securities held as a part of its portfolio resulted in a loss of $57,000 (pretax).
4. When its president died, the corporation realized $110,000 from an insurance policy. The cash surrender value of this policy had been carried on the books as an investment in the amount of $46,000 (the gain is nontaxable).
5. The corporation disposed of its recreational division at a loss of $115,000 before taxes. Assume that this transaction meets the criteria for discontinued operations.
6. The corporation decided to change its method of inventory pricing from average cost to the FIFO method. The effect of this change on prior years is to increase 2002 income by $60,000 and decrease 2003 income by $20,000 before taxes. The FIFO method has been used for 2004. The tax rate on these items is 40%.

Instructions

Prepare an income statement for the year 2004 starting with income from continuing operations before taxes. Compute earnings per share as it should be shown on the face of the income statement. Common shares outstanding for the year are 80,000 shares. (Assume a tax rate of 30% on all items, unless indicated otherwise.)

P4-4 (Multiple- and Single-step Income, Retained Earnings) The following account balances were included in the trial balance of J.R. Reid Corporation at June 30, 2004.

Sales	$1,678,500	Depreciation of office furniture and equipment	$ 7,250
Sales discounts	31,150		
Cost of goods sold	896,770	Real estate and other local taxes	7,320
Sales salaries	56,260	Bad debt expense—selling	4,850

Sales commissions	97,600	Building expense—prorated to administration	9,130
Travel expense—salespersons	28,930	Miscellaneous office expenses	6,000
Freight-out	21,400	Sales returns	62,300
Entertainment expense	14,820	Dividends received	38,000
Telephone and Internet expense—sales	9,030	Bond interest expense	18,000
Depreciation of sales equipment	4,980	Income taxes	133,000
Building expense—prorated to sales	6,200	Depreciation understatement due to error—2001 (net of tax)	17,700
Miscellaneous selling expenses	4,715	Dividends declared on preferred stock	9,000
Office supplies used	3,450	Dividends declared on common stock	32,000
Telephone and Internet expense—administration	2,820		

The Retained Earnings account had a balance of $337,000 at June 30, 2004, before closing. There are 80,000 shares of common stock outstanding.

Instructions

(a) Using the multiple-step form, prepare an income statement and a retained earnings statement for the year ended June 30, 2004.

(b) Using the single-step form, prepare an income statement and a retained earnings statement for the year ended June 30, 2004.

P4-5 (Irregular Items) Presented below is a combined single-step income and retained earnings statement for Sandy Freewalt Company for 2004.

		(000 omitted)
Net sales		$640,000
Costs and expenses		
Cost of goods sold		500,000
Selling, general, and administrative expenses		66,000
Other, net		17,000
		583,000
Income before income tax		57,000
Income tax		19,400
Net income		37,600
Retained earnings at beginning of period, as previously reported	$141,000	
Adjustment required for correction of error	(7,000)	
Retained earnings at beginning of period, as restated		134,000
Dividends on common stock		(12,200)
Retained earnings at end of period		$159,400

Additional facts are as follows.

1. "Selling, general, and administrative expenses" for 2004 included a usual but infrequently occurring charge of $10,500,000.
2. "Other, net" for 2004 included an extraordinary item (charge) of $9,000,000. If the extraordinary item (charge) had not occurred, income taxes for 2004 would have been $22,400,000 instead of $19,400,000.
3. "Adjustment required for correction of an error" was a result of a change in estimate (useful life of certain assets reduced to 8 years and a catch-up adjustment made).
4. Sandy Freewalt Company disclosed earnings per common share for net income in the notes to the financial statements.

Instructions

Determine from these additional facts whether the presentation of the facts in the Sandy Freewalt Company income and retained earnings statement is appropriate. If the presentation is not appropriate, describe the appropriate presentation and discuss its theoretical rationale. (Do not prepare a revised statement.)

P4-6 (Retained Earnings Statement, Prior Period Adjustment) Below is the retained earnings account for the year 2004 for LeClair Corp.

Retained earnings, January 1, 2004		$257,600
Add:		
Gain on sale of investments (net of tax)	$41,200	
Net income	84,500	

Refund on litigation with government, related to the year 2001 (net of tax)	21,600	
Recognition of income earned in 2003, but omitted from income statement in that year (net of tax)	25,400	172,700
		430,300
Deduct:		
Loss on discontinued operations (net of tax)	25,000	
Write-off of goodwill (net of tax)	60,000	
Cumulative effect on income in changing from straight-line depreciation to accelerated depreciation in 2004 (net of tax)	18,200	
Cash dividends declared	32,000	135,200
Retained earnings, December 31, 2004		$295,100

Instructions

(a) Prepare a corrected retained earnings statement. LeClair Corp. normally sells investments of the type mentioned above.

(b) State where the items that do not appear in the corrected retained earnings statement should be shown.

P4-7 (Income Statement, Irregular Items) Rap Corp. has 100,000 shares of common stock outstanding. In 2004, the company reports income from continuing operations before taxes of $1,210,000. Additional transactions not considered in the $1,210,000 are as follows.

1. In 2004, Rap Corp. sold equipment for $40,000. The machine had originally cost $80,000 and had accumulated depreciation of $36,000. The gain or loss is considered ordinary.
2. The company discontinued operations of one of its subsidiaries during the current year at a loss of $190,000 before taxes. Assume that this transaction meets the criteria for discontinued operations. The loss on operations of the discontinued subsidiary was $90,000 before taxes; the loss from disposal of the subsidiary was $100,000 before taxes.
3. In 2004, the company reviewed its accounts receivable and determined that $26,000 of accounts receivable that had been carried for years appeared unlikely to be collected.
4. An internal audit discovered that amortization of intangible assets was understated by $35,000 (net of tax) in a prior period. The amount was charged against retained earnings.
5. The company sold its only investment in common stock during the year at a gain of $145,000. The gain is taxed at a total effective rate of 40%. Assume that the transaction meets the requirements of an extraordinary item.

Instructions

Analyze the above information and prepare an income statement for the year 2004, starting with income from continuing operations before income taxes. Compute earnings per share as it should be shown on the face of the income statement. (Assume a total effective tax rate of 38% on all items, unless otherwise indicated.)

CONCEPTUAL CASES

C4-1 (Identification of Income Statement Deficiencies) John Amos Corporation was incorporated and began business on January 1, 2004. It has been successful and now requires a bank loan for additional working capital to finance expansion. The bank has requested an audited income statement for the year 2004. The accountant for John Amos Corporation provides you with the following income statement which John Amos plans to submit to the bank.

JOHN AMOS CORPORATION
INCOME STATEMENT

Sales		$850,000
Dividends		32,300
Gain on recovery of insurance proceeds from earthquake loss (extraordinary)		38,500
		920,800
Less:		
Selling expenses	$101,100	

Cost of goods sold	510,000	
Advertising expense	13,700	
Loss on obsolescence of inventories	34,000	
Loss on discontinued operations	48,600	
Administrative expense	73,400	780,800
Income before income tax		140,000
Income tax		56,000
Net income		$ 84,000

Instructions

Indicate the deficiencies in the income statement presented above. Assume that the corporation desires a single-step income statement.

C4-2 (Income Reporting Deficiencies) The following represents a recent income statement for **Boeing Company.**

	($ in millions)
Sales	$21,924
Costs and expenses	20,773
Income from operations	1,151
Other income	122
Interest and debt expense	(130)
Earnings before income taxes	1,143
Income taxes	(287)
Net income	$ 856

It includes only *five* separate numbers (two of which are in billions of dollars), *two* subtotals, and the net earnings figure.

Instructions

(a) Indicate the deficiencies in the income statement.
(b) What recommendations would you make to Boeing to improve the usefulness of its income statement?

C4-3 (All-inclusive vs. Current Operating) Information concerning the operations of a corporation is presented in an income statement. Some believe that income statements should be prepared on a "current operating performance" basis (earning power concept), whereas others prefer an "all-inclusive" basis (historical concept). Proponents of the two types of income statements do not agree upon the proper treatment of material nonrecurring charges and credits.

Instructions

(a) Define "current operating performance" and "all-inclusive" as used above.
(b) Explain the differences in content and organization of a "current operating performance" income statement and an "all-inclusive" income statement. Include a discussion of the proper treatment of material nonrecurring charges and credits.
(c) Give the principal arguments for the use of the "all-inclusive" income statement and the "current operating performance" income statement.

(AICPA adapted)

C4-4 (Extraordinary Items) Jeff Foxworthy, vice-president of finance for Red Neck Company, has recently been asked to discuss with the company's division controllers the proper accounting for extraordinary items. Jeff Foxworthy prepared the factual situations presented below as a basis for discussion.

1. An earthquake destroys one of the oil refineries owned by a large multinational oil company. Earthquakes are rare in this geographical location.
2. A publicly held company has incurred a substantial loss in the unsuccessful registration of a bond issue.
3. A large portion of a cigarette manufacturer's tobacco crops are destroyed by a hailstorm. Severe damage from hailstorms is rare in this locality.
4. A large diversified company sells a block of shares from its portfolio of securities acquired for investment purposes.
5. A company sells a block of common stock of a publicly traded company. The block of shares, which represents less than 10% of the publicly held company, is the only security investment the company has ever owned.

6. A company that operates a chain of warehouses sells the excess land surrounding one of its warehouses. When the company buys property to establish a new warehouse, it usually buys more land than it expects to use for the warehouse with the expectation that the land will appreciate in value. Twice during the past 5 years the company sold excess land.
7. A company experiences a material loss in the repurchase of a large bond issue that has been outstanding for 3 years. The company regularly repurchases bonds of this nature.
8. A railroad experiences an unusual flood loss to part of its track system. Flood losses normally occur every 3 or 4 years.
9. A machine tool company sells the only land it owns. The land was acquired 10 years ago for future expansion, but shortly thereafter the company abandoned all plans for expansion but decided to hold the land for appreciation.

Instructions

Determine whether the foregoing items should be classified as extraordinary items. Present a rationale for your position.

C4-5 (Earnings Management) Grace Inc. has recently reported steadily increasing income. The company reported income of $20,000 in 2001, $25,000 in 2002, and $30,000 in 2003. A number of market analysts have recommended that investors buy the stock because they expect the steady growth in income to continue. Grace is approaching the end of its fiscal year in 2004, and it again appears to be a good year. However, it has not yet recorded warranty expense.

Based on prior experience, this year's warranty expense should be around $5,000, but some managers have approached the controller to suggest a larger, more conservative warranty expense should be recorded this year. Income before warranty expense is $43,000. Specifically, by recording an $8,000 warranty accrual this year, Grace could report an increase in income for this year and still be in a position to cover its warranty costs in future years.

Instructions

(a) What is earnings management?
(b) What is the effect of the proposed accounting in 2004? In 2005? Assume income before warranty expense is $43,000 and that total warranty expense over the 2-year period is $10,000.
(c) What is the appropriate accounting in this situation?

C4-6 (Earnings Management) Arthur Miller, controller for the Salem Corporation, is preparing the company's income statement at year-end. He notes that the company lost a considerable sum on the sale of some equipment it had decided to replace. Since the company has sold equipment routinely in the past, Miller knows the losses cannot be reported as extraordinary. He also does not want to highlight it as a material loss since he feels that will reflect poorly on him and the company. He reasons that if the company had recorded more depreciation during the assets' lives, the losses would not be so great. Since depreciation is included among the company's operating expenses, he wants to report the losses along with the company's expenses, where he hopes it will not be noticed.

Instructions

(a) What are the ethical issues involved?
(b) What should Miller do?

C4-7 (Income Reporting Items) Woody Allen Corp. is an entertainment firm that derives approximately 30% of its income from the Casino Royale Division, which manages gambling facilities. As auditor for Woody Allen Corp., you have recently overheard the following discussion between the controller and financial vice-president.

VICE-PRESIDENT: If we sell the Casino Royale Division, it seems ridiculous to segregate the results of the sale in the income statement. Separate categories tend to be absurd and confusing to the stockholders. I believe that we should simply report the gain on the sale as other income or expense without detail.

CONTROLLER: Professional pronouncements would require that we disclose this information separately in the income statement. If a sale of this type is considered unusual and infrequent, it must be reported as an extraordinary item.

VICE-PRESIDENT: What about the walkout we had last month when employees were upset about their commission income? Would this situation not also be an extraordinary item?

CONTROLLER: I am not sure whether this item would be reported as extraordinary or not.

VICE-PRESIDENT: Oh well, it doesn't make any difference because the net effect of all these items is immaterial, so no disclosure is necessary.

Instructions

(a) On the basis of the foregoing discussion, answer the following questions: Who is correct about handling the sale? What would be the income statement presentation for the sale of the Casino Royale Division?

(b) How should the walkout by the employees be reported?

(c) What do you think about the vice-president's observation on materiality?

(d) What are the earnings per share implications of these topics?

C4-8 (Identification of Income Statement Weaknesses) The following financial statement was prepared by employees of Cynthia Taylor Corporation.

CYNTHIA TAYLOR CORPORATION
INCOME STATEMENT
YEAR ENDED DECEMBER 31, 2004

Revenues	
Gross sales, including sales taxes	$1,044,300
Less: Returns, allowances, and cash discounts	56,200
Net sales	988,100
Dividends, interest, and purchase discounts	30,250
Recoveries of accounts written off in prior years	13,850
Total revenues	1,032,200
Costs and expenses	
Cost of goods sold, including sales taxes	465,900
Salaries and related payroll expenses	60,500
Rent	19,100
Freight-in and freight-out	3,400
Bad debt expense	27,800
Total costs and expenses	576,700
Income before extraordinary items	455,500
Extraordinary items	
Loss on discontinued styles (Note 1)	71,500
Loss on sale of marketable securities (Note 2)	39,050
Loss on sale of warehouse (Note 3)	86,350
Total extraordinary items	196,900
Net income	$ 258,600
Net income per share of common stock	$2.30

Note 1: New styles and rapidly changing consumer preferences resulted in a $71,500 loss on the disposal of discontinued styles and related accessories.

Note 2: The corporation sold an investment in marketable securities at a loss of $39,050. The corporation normally sells securities of this nature.

Note 3: The corporation sold one of its warehouses at an $86,350 loss.

Instructions

Identify and discuss the weaknesses in classification and disclosure in the single-step income statement above. You should explain why these treatments are weaknesses and what the proper presentation of the items would be in accordance with recent professional pronouncements.

C4-9 (Classification of Income Statement Items) As audit partner for Noriyuki and Morita, you are in charge of reviewing the classification of unusual items that have occurred during the current year. The following material items have come to your attention.

1. A merchandising company incorrectly overstated its ending inventory 2 years ago. Inventory for all other periods is correctly computed.
2. An automobile dealer sells for $137,000 an extremely rare 1930 S type Invicta which it purchased for $21,000 10 years ago. The Invicta is the only such display item the dealer owns.
3. A drilling company during the current year extended the estimated useful life of certain drilling equipment from 9 to 15 years. As a result, depreciation for the current year was materially lowered.
4. A retail outlet changed its computation for bad debt expense from 1% to ½ of 1% of sales because of changes in its customer clientele.

5. A mining concern sells a foreign subsidiary engaged in uranium mining, although it (the seller) continues to engage in uranium mining in other countries.
6. A steel company changes from straight-line depreciation to accelerated depreciation in accounting for its plant assets.
7. A construction company, at great expense, prepared a major proposal for a government loan. The loan is not approved.
8. A water pump manufacturer has had large losses resulting from a strike by its employees early in the year.
9. Depreciation for a prior period was incorrectly understated by $950,000. The error was discovered in the current year.
10. A large sheep rancher suffered a major loss because the state required that all sheep in the state be killed to halt the spread of a rare disease. Such a situation has not occurred in the state for 20 years.
11. A food distributor that sells wholesale to supermarket chains and to fast-food restaurants (two distinguishable classes of customers) decides to discontinue the division that sells to one of the two classes of customers.

Instructions

From the foregoing information, indicate in what section of the income statement or retained earnings statement these items should be classified. Provide a brief rationale for your position.

C4-10 (Comprehensive Income) Ferguson Arthur, Jr., controller for Jenkins Corporation, is preparing the company's financial statements at year-end. Currently, he is focusing on the income statement and determining the format for reporting comprehensive income. During the year, the company earned net income of $400,000 and had unrealized gains on available-for-sale securities of $20,000. In the previous year net income was $410,000, and the company had no unrealized gains or losses.

Instructions

(a) Show how income and comprehensive income will be reported on a comparative basis for the current and prior years, using the separate income statement format.

(b) Show how income and comprehensive income will be reported on a comparative basis for the current and prior years, using the combined income statement format.

(c) Which format should Arthur recommend?

USING YOUR JUDGMENT

FINANCIAL REPORTING PROBLEM

3M Company

The financial statements of 3M are presented in Appendix 5B or can be accessed on the Take Action! CD.

Instructions

Refer to 3M's financial statements and the accompanying notes to answer the following questions.

(a) What type of income statement format does 3M use? Indicate why this format might be used to present income statement information.

(b) What are 3M's primary revenue sources?

(c) Compute 3M's gross profit for each of the years 1999–2001. Explain why gross profit declined in 2001.

(d) Why does 3M make a distinction between operating and nonoperating revenue?

(e) What financial ratios did 3M choose to report in its "Financial Summary" section covering the years 1991–2001?

FINANCIAL STATEMENT ANALYSIS CASES

Case 1: Bankruptcy Prediction

The Z-score bankruptcy prediction model uses balance sheet and income information to arrive at a Z-Score, which can be used to predict financial distress:

$$Z = \frac{\text{Working capital}}{\text{Total assets}} \times 1.2 + \frac{\text{Retained earnings}}{\text{Total assets}} \times 1.4 + \frac{\text{EBIT}}{\text{Total assets}} \times 3.3 + \frac{\text{Sales}}{\text{Total assets}} \times .99 + \frac{\text{MV equity}}{\text{Total liabilities}} \times 0.6$$

EBIT is earnings before interest and taxes. MV Equity is the market value of common equity, which can be determined by multiplying stock price by shares outstanding.

Following extensive testing, it has been shown that companies with Z-scores above 3.0 are unlikely to fail; those with Z-scores below 1.81 are very likely to fail. While the original model was developed for publicly held manufacturing companies, the model has been modified to apply to companies in various industries, emerging companies, and companies not traded in public markets.

Instructions

(a) Use information in the financial statements of a company like **PepsiCo** or **Coca-Cola** to compute the Z-score for the past 2 years.

(b) Interpret your result. Where does the company fall in the financial distress range?

(c) The Z-score uses EBIT as one of its elements. Why do you think this income measure is used?

Case 2: Dresser Industries

Dresser Industries provides products and services to oil and natural gas exploration, production, transmission and processing companies. A recent income statement is reproduced below. Dollar amounts are in millions.

Sales	$2,697.0
Service revenues	1,933.9
Share of earnings of unconsolidated affiliates	92.4
Total revenues	4,723.3
Cost of sales	1,722.7
Cost of services	1,799.9
Total costs of sales and services	3,522.6
Gross earnings	1,200.7
Selling, engineering, administrative and general expenses	(919.8)
Special charges	(70.0)
Other income (deductions)	
Interest expense	(47.4)
Interest earned	19.1
Other, net	4.8
Earnings before income taxes and other items below	187.4
Income taxes	(79.4)
Minority interest	(10.3)
Earnings from continuing operations	97.7
Discontinued operations	(35.3)
Earnings before extraordinary items and accounting changes	62.4
Extraordinary items	(6.3)
Cumulative effect of accounting changes	(393.8)
Net earnings (loss)	$(337.7)

Instructions

Assume that 177,636,000 shares of stock were issued and outstanding. Prepare the per-share portion of the income statement. Remember to begin with "Income from continuing operations."

COMPARATIVE ANALYSIS CASE

The Coca-Cola Company and PepsiCo, Inc.

Instructions

Go to the Take Action! CD and use information found there to answer the following questions related to **The Coca-Cola Company** and **PepsiCo, Inc.**

(a) What type of income format(s) is used by these two companies? Identify any differences in income statement format between these two companies.

(b) What are the gross profits, operating profit, and net income for these two companies over the 3-year period 1999–2001? Which company has had better financial results over this period of time?

(c) Identify the irregular items reported by these two companies in their income statements over the 3-year period 1999–2001. Do these irregular items appear to be significant?

(d) Refer to PepsiCo's Management Analysis section under "Items Affecting Comparability:" Briefly discuss how these items affect the comparability and consistency of PepsiCo's income over 1999–2001.

RESEARCH CASES

Case 1

Most libraries maintain the annual reports of large companies on file or on microfiche.

Instructions

Obtain the 2001 annual reports for **UAL Corp.** and **The Boeing Company**, and answer the following questions concerning their income statements. (*Note:* Larger libraries may have CD-ROM products such as *Laser Disclosure* or *Compact Disclosure*. UAL and Boeing are also on the Take Action! CD or can be found online in the SEC EDGAR database.)

(a) Describe the major differences between the income statement formats.

(b) Identify any irregular items on either of the income statements.

(c) UAL includes a separate line for depreciation expense, while Boeing does not. Why is this the case? Does Boeing's depreciation expense appear on another financial statement?

(d) UAL's income statement includes significantly more detail than Boeing's. Which presentation do you prefer? Why?

Case 2

The April 1996 issue of the *Journal of Accountancy* includes an article by Dennis R. Beresford, L. Todd Johnson, and Cheri L. Reither, entitled "Is a Second Income Statement Needed?"

Instructions

Read the article and answer the following questions.

(a) On what basis would the "second income statement" be prepared? Briefly describe this basis.

(b) Why is there a perceived need for a second income statement?

(c) Identify three alternatives for reporting the proposed measure of income.

INTERNATIONAL REPORTING CASE

Presented below is the income statement for a British company, **Avon Rubber PLC.**

Avon Rubber PLC

Consolidated Profit and Loss Account
for the year ended 30 September 2000

	2000		
	Before exceptional items £'000	Exceptional items (note 5) £'000	Total £'000
Turnover	277,997	—	277,997
Cost of sales	(231,842)	(1,984)	(233,826)
Gross profit	46,155	(1,984)	44,171
Net operating expenses (including £623,000 goodwill amortisation)	(30,891)	(4,688)	(35,579)
Share of profits/(losses) of joint ventures and associates	161	—	161
Operating profit	15,425	(6,672)	8,753
Profit on disposal of fixed assets	—	25	25
Profit on ordinary activities before interest	15,425	(6,647)	8,778
Interest receivable	2,871	—	2,871
Interest payable	(5,911)	—	(5,911)
Profit on ordinary activities before taxation	12,385	(6,647)	5,738
Taxation	(4,360)	1,400	(2,960)
Profit on ordinary activities after taxation	8,025	(5,247)	2,778
Minority interests	717	—	717
Profit for the year	8,742	(5,247)	3,495
Dividends	(6,735)	—	(6,735)
(Loss)/retained profit for the year	2,007	(5,247)	(3,240)
Basic earnings per ordinary share			12.4p

Instructions

(a) Review the Avon Rubber income statement and identify at least three differences between the British income statement and an income statement of a U.S. company as presented in the chapter.

(b) Identify any irregular items reported by Avon Rubber. Is the reporting of these irregular items in Avon's income statement similar to reporting of these items in U.S. companies' income statements? Explain.

PROFESSIONAL SIMULATION

Accounting — Income Statement

Directions | Situation | Explanation | Measurement | Research | Resources

Directions

In this simulation, you will be asked to compute various income amounts. Assume a tax rate of 30% and 100,000 shares of common stock outstanding during the year. Prepare responses to all parts.

Situation

Ritter Corporation provides you with the following pre-tax information for the period.

Sales	$3,200,000
Cost of goods sold	1,650,000
Interest revenue	10,000
Loss from abandonment of plant assets	40,000
Selling expenses	340,000
Administrative expenses	280,000
Effect of change from declining-balance to straight-line depreciation	50,000
Loss from earthquake (unusual and infrequent)	40,000
Gain on disposal of a component of Ritter's business	90,000

Explanation

Explain the proper accounting treatment for loss on abandonment of plant assets and gain on disposal of a component of a business.

Measurement

Compute the following five items.

(a) Gross profit.
(b) Income from operations.
(c) Income from continuing operations before income taxes.
(d) Net income.
(e) Earnings per share.

www.wiley.com/college/kieso

Remember to check the **Take Action! CD** and the book's **companion Web site** to find additional resources for this chapter.

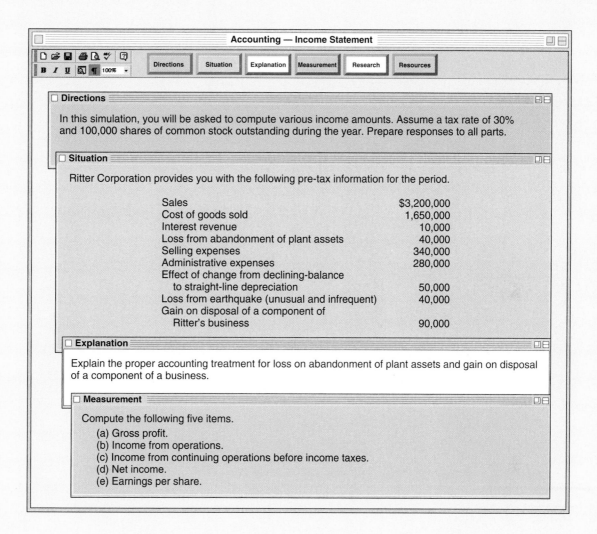

CHAPTER 5

Balance Sheet and Statement of Cash Flows

LEARNING OBJECTIVES

After studying this chapter, you should be able to:

1. **Identify the uses and limitations of a balance sheet.**
2. **Identify the major classifications of the balance sheet.**
3. **Prepare a classified balance sheet using the report and account formats.**
4. **Identify balance sheet information requiring supplemental disclosure.**
5. **Identify major disclosure techniques for the balance sheet.**
6. **Indicate the purpose of the statement of cash flows.**
7. **Identify the content of the statement of cash flows.**
8. **Prepare a statement of cash flows.**
9. **Understand the usefulness of the statement of cash flows.**

"There Ought to Be a Law"

When the Internet stock bubble burst during 2000, many investors learned the importance of analysis based on information in the balance sheet. As one money-manager noted, "There ought to be a law in this country that before you are allowed to buy a stock, you have to be able to read its balance sheet." Analysis based on balance sheet information was clearly missing during much of the bull market of late 1990s. Many investors in companies such as **Gateway 2000**, **Cisco Systems**, and **Alcatel** missed the information in the balance sheet indicating that inventories and receivables were growing. Increases in these assets indicate that sales are slowing and customers are facing more difficult economic times, both of which generally foretell declining future sales and profitability.[1]

Information on liabilities also is important for financial analysis, especially when the economy begins to slow. As shown in the graph below, in 2001 nonfinancial companies reported debt levels (as a percent of net worth) of nearly 60 percent. By comparison, debt levels during the prior recession in 1990–91 were only 51 percent.

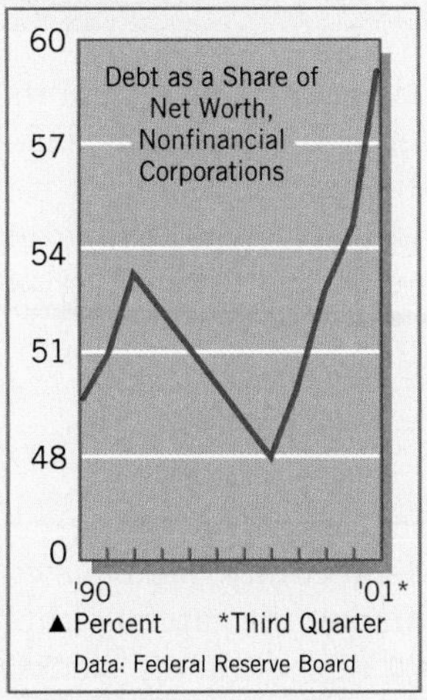

These high debt levels are troublesome because they indicate less of a financial cushion, making a company more vulnerable to unexpected shocks. For example, if inflation slows more than expected and companies cannot increase prices, the debt will be harder to pay. This situation further reduces a company's financial flexibility and reduces income as higher interest is paid on its risky debt. The statement of cash flows is very helpful in providing information on a company's liquidity and financial flexibility.

Thus, earnings declines (and falling stock prices) for many companies during the recent economic slowdown could have been predicted, based on the information in the balance sheet. And just as deteriorating balance sheets and statements of cash flow warned of trouble, improving balance sheet and cash flow information is a leading indicator for improved future earnings.

[1]Adapted from Gretchen Morgenson, "How Did They Value Stocks? Count the Absurd Ways," *New York Times on the Web* (March 18, 2001).

PREVIEW OF CHAPTER 5

Readers of the financial statements sometimes ignore important information in the balance sheet and statement of cash flows. As shown in the opening story involving **Cisco Systems** and **Gateway 2000**, surprises in earnings could have been anticipated if the balance sheet had not been overlooked. The purpose of this chapter is to examine the many different types of assets, liabilities, and stockholders' equity items that affect the balance sheet and the statement of cash flows. The content and organization of this chapter are as follows.

BALANCE SHEET AND STATEMENT OF CASH FLOWS

Balance Sheet

- Usefulness
- Limitations
- Classification
- Additional information reported
- Techniques of disclosure

Statement of Cash Flows

- Purpose
- Content and format
- Preparation
- Usefulness

SECTION 1 BALANCE SHEET

OBJECTIVE 1
Identify the uses and limitations of a balance sheet.

The **balance sheet**, sometimes referred to as the statement of financial position, reports the assets, liabilities, and stockholders' equity of a business enterprise at a specific date. This financial statement provides information about the nature and amounts of investments in enterprise resources, obligations to creditors, and the owners' equity in net resources.[2] It therefore helps in predicting the amounts, timing, and uncertainty of future cash flows.

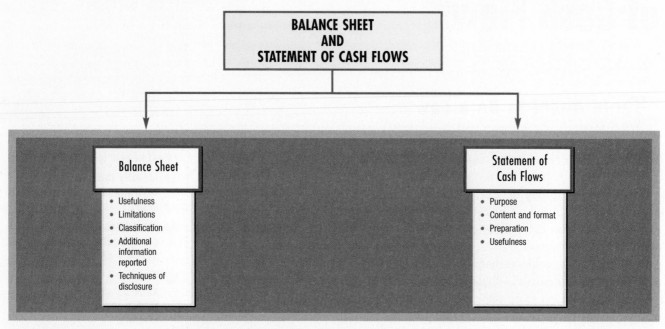

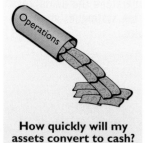

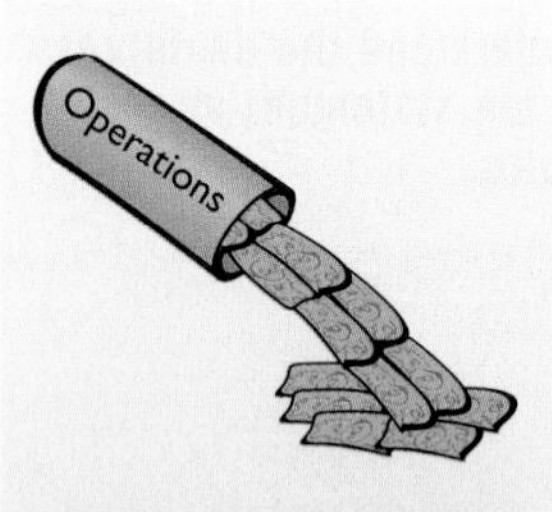

How quickly will my assets convert to cash?

USEFULNESS OF THE BALANCE SHEET

By providing information on assets, liabilities, and stockholders' equity, the balance sheet provides a basis for computing rates of return and evaluating the capital structure of the enterprise. As illustrated in the opening story about new-economy stocks, information in the balance sheet is also used to assess enterprise risk[3] and future cash

[2] *Accounting Trends and Techniques—2001* indicates that approximately 95 percent of the companies surveyed used the term "balance sheet." The term "statement of financial position" is used infrequently, although it is conceptually appealing.

[3] Risk is an expression of the unpredictability of future events, transactions, circumstances, and results of the enterprise.

flows. In this regard, the balance sheet is useful for analyzing a company's liquidity, solvency, and financial flexibility.

Liquidity describes "the amount of time that is expected to elapse until an asset is realized or otherwise converted into cash or until a liability has to be paid."[4] Creditors are interested in short-term liquidity ratios, such as the ratio of cash (or near cash) to short-term liabilities, because they indicate whether the enterprise will have the resources to pay its current and maturing obligations. Similarly, stockholders assess liquidity to evaluate the possibility of future cash dividends or the buyback of shares. In general, the greater the liquidity, the lower the risk of enterprise failure.

Obligation Ocean

We are drowning in a sea of debt!

Solvency refers to the ability of an enterprise to pay its debts as they mature. For example, when a company carries a high level of long-term debt relative to assets, it has lower solvency than a similar company with a low level of long-term debt. Companies with higher debt are relatively more risky because more of their assets will be required to meet these fixed obligations (such as interest and principal payments).

Liquidity and solvency affect an entity's **financial flexibility**, which measures the "ability of an enterprise to take effective actions to alter the amounts and timing of cash flows so it can respond to unexpected needs and opportunities."[5] For example, a company may become so loaded with debt—so financially inflexible—that its sources of cash to finance expansion or to pay off maturing debt are limited or nonexistent. An enterprise with a high degree of financial flexibility is better able to survive bad times, to recover from unexpected setbacks, and to take advantage of profitable and unexpected investment opportunities. Generally, the greater the financial flexibility, the lower the risk of enterprise failure.

GROUNDED

WHAT DO THE NUMBERS MEAN?

Lack of liquidity or solvency and inadequate financial flexibility seriously affected the U.S. airline industry over the last 25 years. For example, in the 1980s and again in the early 1990s, **American**, **Eastern**, **United**, and **TWA** all reported quarterly operating losses that stemmed primarily from high interest costs, increased fuel costs, and price cutting resulting from deregulation. In response to operating losses and lowered liquidity, some airlines asked their employees to sign labor contracts that provided no wage increases. Other airlines, already heavily in debt and lacking financial flexibility and liquidity, had to cancel orders for new, more efficient aircraft. TWA had to sell routes and planes to raise cash (and eventually was sold to American Airlines). Some of the major airlines (such as **Braniff**, **Continental**, **Eastern**, **Midway**, and **America West**) even declared bankruptcy. And the terrorist attacks of September 11, 2001, have shown how vulnerable the major airlines are to reduced demand for their services. This financial distress was not an insiders' secret. The airlines' balance sheets clearly revealed their financial inflexibility and low liquidity.

LIMITATIONS OF THE BALANCE SHEET

Some of the major limitations of the balance sheet are:

1. Most assets and liabilities are stated at **historical cost**. As a result, the information reported in the balance sheet has higher reliability but is subject to the criticism that a more relevant current fair value is not reported. For example, **Georgia**

[4]"Reporting Income, Cash Flows, and Financial Position of Business Enterprises," *Proposed Statement of Financial Accounting Concepts* (Stamford, Conn.: FASB, 1981), par. 29.

[5]"Reporting Income, Cash Flows, and Financial Position of Business Enterprises," *Proposed Statement of Financial Accounting Concepts* (Stamford, Conn.: FASB, 1981), par. 25.

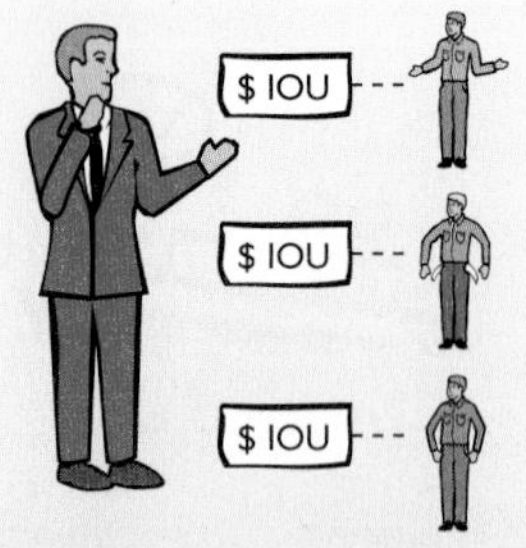

Hmm... I wonder if they will pay me back?

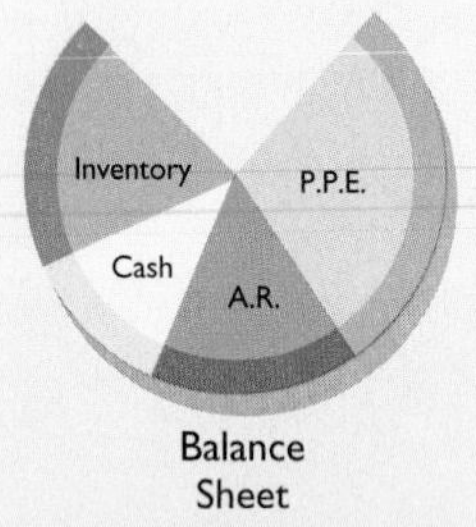

Hey....we left out the value of the employees!

OBJECTIVE 2
Identify the major classifications of the balance sheet.

Pacific owns timber and other assets that may appreciate in value after they are purchased; this increase is not reported unless the assets are sold.

2. **Judgments and estimates** are used in determining many of the items reported in the balance sheet. For example, **Gateway 2000** makes estimates of the amount of receivables that it will collect, the useful life of its warehouses, and the number of computers that will be returned under warranty in arriving at the amounts reported in its balance sheet.
3. The balance sheet necessarily **omits many items that are of financial value** to the business but cannot be recorded objectively. For example, the knowledge and skill of **Intel** employees in developing new computer chips are arguably the company's most significant asset. However, because it is difficult to reliably measure the value of employees and other intangible assets (such as customer base, research superiority, and reputation), these items are not recognized in the balance sheet. Similarly, many liabilities are also reported in an "off-balance-sheet" manner, if reported at all.[6]

The recent bankruptcy of the seventh largest U.S. company, **Enron**, highlights the fact that not all items of importance are reported in the balance sheet. In Enron's case, it had certain off-balance-sheet financing obligations which were not disclosed in the main financial statements.

CLASSIFICATION IN THE BALANCE SHEET

Balance sheet accounts are **classified** so that similar items are grouped together to arrive at significant subtotals. Furthermore, the material is arranged so that important relationships are shown.

The FASB has often noted that the parts and subsections of financial statements can be more informative than the whole. Therefore, as one would expect, the reporting of summary accounts alone (total assets, net assets, total liabilities, etc.) is discouraged. Individual items should be separately reported and classified in sufficient detail to permit users to assess the amounts, timing, and uncertainty of future cash flows, as well as the evaluation of liquidity and financial flexibility, profitability, and risk.

Classification in financial statements helps analysts by grouping items with similar characteristics and separating items with different characteristics:[7]

1. Assets that differ in their **type or expected function** in the central operations or other activities of the enterprise should be reported as separate items. For example, merchandise inventories should be reported separately from property, plant, and equipment.
2. Assets and liabilities with **different implications for the financial flexibility** of the enterprise should be reported as separate items. For example, assets used in operations should be reported separately from assets held for investment and assets subject to restrictions such as leased equipment.
3. Assets and liabilities with **different general liquidity characteristics** should be reported as separate items. For example, cash should be reported separately from inventories.

---

[6]Several of these omitted items (such as leases and other off-balance-sheet arrangements) are discussed in later chapters. See AICPA Special Committee on Financial Reporting, "Improving Business Reporting—A Customer Focus," *Journal of Accountancy*, Supplement (October 1994), for a discussion of issues surrounding off-balance-sheet items; and Wayne Upton, Jr., Special Report: *Business and Financial Reporting, Challenges from the New Economy* (Norwalk, Conn.: FASB, 2001).

[7]"Reporting Income, Cash Flows, and Financial Positions of Business Enterprises," *Proposed Statement of Financial Accounting Concepts* (Stamford, Conn.: FASB, 1981), par. 51.

The three general classes of items included in the balance sheet are assets, liabilities, and equity. We defined them in Chapter 2 as follows.

ELEMENTS OF THE BALANCE SHEET

1. *Assets.* Probable future economic benefits obtained or controlled by a particular entity as a result of past transactions or events.
2. *Liabilities.* Probable future sacrifices of economic benefits arising from present obligations of a particular entity to transfer assets or provide services to other entities in the future as a result of past transactions or events.
3. *Equity.* Residual interest in the assets of an entity that remains after deducting its liabilities. In a business enterprise, the equity is the ownership interest.[8]

These items are then divided into several subclassifications. Illustration 5-1 indicates the general format of balance sheet presentation.

ILLUSTRATION 5-1
Balance Sheet Classifications

Assets	Liabilities and Owners' Equity
Current assets	Current liabilities
Long-term investments	Long-term debt
Property, plant, and equipment	Owners' equity
Intangible assets	Capital stock
Other assets	Additional paid-in capital
	Retained earnings

The balance sheet may be classified in some other manner, but there is very little departure from these major subdivisions in practice. If a proprietorship or partnership is involved, the classifications within the owners' equity section are presented a little differently, as will be shown later in the chapter.

Current Assets

Current assets are cash and other assets expected to be converted into cash, sold, or consumed either in one year or in the operating cycle, whichever is longer. The operating cycle is the average time between the acquisition of materials and supplies and the realization of cash through sales of the product for which the materials and supplies were acquired. The cycle operates from cash through inventory, production, receivables, and back to cash. When there are several operating cycles within one year, the one-year period is used. If the operating cycle is more than one year, the longer period is used.

[8]"Elements of Financial Statements of Business Enterprises," *Statement of Financial Accounting Concepts No. 6* (Stamford, Conn.: FASB, 1985), paras. 25, 35, and 49.

Current assets are presented in the balance sheet in order of liquidity. The five major items found in the current assets section are cash, short-term investments, receivables, inventories, and prepayments. Valuation of these items is as follows: **Cash** is included at its stated value. **Short-term investments** are generally valued at fair value. **Accounts receivable** are stated at the estimated amount collectible. **Inventories** generally are included at cost or the lower of cost or market. **Prepaid items** are valued at cost.

These five items are not considered current assets if they are not expected to be realized in one year or in the operating cycle, whichever is longer. For example, cash restricted for purposes other than payment of current obligations or for use in current operations is excluded from the current assets section. **Generally, the rule is that if an asset is to be turned into cash or is to be used to pay a current liability within a year or the operating cycle, whichever is longer, it is classified as current.** This requirement is subject to exceptions. An investment in common stock is classified as either a current asset or a noncurrent asset depending on management's intent. When a company has small holdings of common stocks or bonds that are going to be held long-term, they should not be classified as current.

Although a current asset is well defined, certain theoretical problems develop. One problem is justifying the inclusion of prepaid expense in the current assets section. The normal justification is that if these items had not been paid in advance, they would require the use of current assets during the operating cycle. If we follow this logic to its ultimate conclusion, however, any asset purchased previously saves the use of current assets during the operating cycle and would be considered current.

Another problem occurs in the current asset definition when fixed assets are consumed during the operating cycle. A literal interpretation of the accounting profession's position on this matter would indicate that an amount equal to the current depreciation and amortization charges on the noncurrent assets should be placed in the current assets section at the beginning of the year, because they will be consumed in the next operating cycle. This conceptual problem is ignored, which illustrates that the formal distinction made between current and noncurrent assets is somewhat arbitrary.

Cash

Any restrictions on the general availability of cash or any commitments on its probable disposition must be disclosed. An example of such a presentation is excerpted from the Annual Report of **Alterra Healthcare Corp.** below.

ILLUSTRATION 5-2
Balance Sheet Presentation of Restricted Cash

Alterra Healthcare Corp.

Current assets	
Cash	$18,728,000
Restricted cash and investments (Note 7)	7,191,000

Note 7: Restricted Cash and Investments. Restricted cash and investments consist of certificates of deposit restricted as collateral for lease arrangements and debt service with interest rates ranging from 4.0% to 5.5%.

For Alterra Healthcare, cash was restricted to meet an obligation due currently and, therefore, was included under current assets. If cash is restricted for purposes other than current obligations, it is excluded from current assets. An example of current and noncurrent presentation is excerpted from the Annual Report of **Owens Corning, Inc.** in Illustration 5-3.

ILLUSTRATION 5-3
Balance Sheet Presentation of Current and Noncurrent Restricted Cash

Owens Corning, Inc.
(in millions)

Current assets	
Cash and cash equivalents	$ 70
Restricted securities—Fibreboard—current portion (Note 23)	900
Other assets	
Restricted securities—Fibreboard (Note 23)	938

Note 23 (in part). The Insurance Settlement funds are held in and invested by the Fibreboard Settlement Trust (the "Trust") and are available to satisfy Fibreboard's pending and future asbestos related liabilities. . . . The assets of the Trust are comprised of cash and marketable securities (collectively, the "Trust Assets") and are reflected on Owens Corning's consolidated balance sheet as restricted assets. These assets are reflected as current assets or other assets, with each category denoted "Restricted securities—Fibreboard."

Short-Term Investments

Investments in debt and equity securities are grouped into three separate portfolios for valuation and reporting purposes. These portfolios are categorized as follows.

Held-to-maturity: Debt securities that the enterprise has the positive intent and ability to hold to maturity.

Trading: Debt and equity securities bought and held primarily for sale in the near term to generate income on short-term price differences.

Available-for-sale: Debt and equity securities not classified as held-to-maturity or trading securities.

Trading securities (whether debt or equity) should be reported as current assets. Individual held-to-maturity and available-for-sale securities are classified as current or noncurrent depending upon the circumstances. All trading and available-for-sale securities are to be reported at fair value.[9] The example below is excerpted from the Annual Report of **Anchor Bancorp Wisconsin Inc.**

ILLUSTRATION 5-4
Balance Sheet Presentation of Investments in Securities

AnchorBank.

Anchor Bancorp Wisconsin Inc.
(in thousands)

Assets	
Cash and cash equivalents	$ 105,042
Investment securities available for sale	22,216
Investment securities held to maturity (fair value of $34,096)	33,913
Mortgage-related securities available for sale	173,968
Mortgage-related securities held to maturity (fair value of $207,669)	205,191
Loans receivable, net	
Held for sale	17,622
Held for investment	2,414,976
Foreclosed properties and repossessed assets, net	313

[9] "Accounting for Certain Investments in Debt and Equity Securities," *Statement of Financial Accounting Standards No. 115* (Norwalk, Conn.: FASB, 1993).

Receivables

Any anticipated loss due to uncollectibles, the amount and nature of any nontrade receivables, and any receivables designated or pledged as collateral should be clearly identified. **Mack Trucks, Inc.** reported its receivables as follows.

ILLUSTRATION 5-5
Balance Sheet Presentation of Receivables

Mack Trucks, Inc.

Current assets	
Trade receivables	
Accounts receivable	$102,212,000
Affiliated companies	1,157,000
Installment notes and contracts	625,000
Total	103,994,000
Less: Allowance for uncollectible accounts	8,194,000
Trade receivables—net	95,800,000
Receivables from unconsolidated financial subsidiaries	22,106,000

UNDERLYING CONCEPTS

The lower of cost or market valuation is an example of the use of conservatism in accounting.

Inventories

For a proper presentation of inventories, the basis of valuation (i.e., lower of cost or market) and the method of pricing (FIFO or LIFO) are disclosed. For a manufacturing concern (like **Abbott Laboratories**, shown below), the stage of completion of the inventories is also indicated.

ILLUSTRATION 5-6
Balance Sheet Presentation of Inventories, Showing Stage of Completion

Abbott Laboratories
(in thousands)

Current assets	
Inventories	
Finished products	$ 772,478
Work in process	338,818
Materials	384,148
Total inventories	1,495,444

Note 1 (in part): Inventories. Inventories are stated at the lower of cost (first-in, first-out basis) or market.

Weyerhaeuser Company, a forestry company and lumber manufacturer with several finished-goods product lines, reported its inventory as follows.

ILLUSTRATION 5-7
Balance Sheet Presentation of Inventories, Showing Product Lines

Weyerhaeuser Company

Current assets	
Inventories—at FIFO lower of cost or market	
Logs and chips	$ 68,471,000
Lumber, plywood and panels	86,741,000
Pulp, newsprint and paper	47,377,000
Containerboard, paperboard, containers and cartons	59,682,000
Other products	161,717,000
Total product inventories	423,988,000
Materials and supplies	175,540,000

Prepaid Expenses

Prepaid expenses included in current assets are expenditures already made for benefits (usually services) to be received within one year or the operating cycle, whichever is longer.[10] These items are current assets because if they had not already been paid, they would require the use of cash during the next year or the operating cycle. A common example is the payment in advance for an insurance policy. It is classified as a prepaid expense at the time of the expenditure because the payment precedes the receipt of the benefit of coverage. Other common prepaid expenses include prepaid rent, advertising, taxes, and office or operating supplies. Prepaid expenses are reported at the amount of the unexpired or unconsumed cost. **Knight Ridder, Inc.**, for example, listed its prepaid expenses in current assets as follows.

ILLUSTRATION 5-8
Balance Sheet Presentation of Prepaid Expenses

Knight Ridder, Inc.
(in thousands)

Current assets	
Cash, including short-term cash investments of $7,001	$ 41,661
Accounts receivable, net of allowances of $20,238	416,498
Inventories	52,786
Prepaids	30,767
Other current assets	34,382

Companies often include insurance and other prepayments for two or three years in current assets even though part of the advance payment applies to periods beyond one year or the current operating cycle.

Non-Current Assets

Non-current assets are those not meeting the definition of current assets. They include a variety of items, as discussed in the following sections.

Long-Term Investments

Long-term investments, often referred to simply as investments, normally consist of one of four types:

1. Investments in securities, such as bonds, common stock, or long-term notes.
2. Investments in tangible fixed assets not currently used in operations, such as land held for speculation.
3. Investments set aside in special funds such as a sinking fund, pension fund, or plant expansion fund. The cash surrender value of life insurance is included here.
4. Investments in nonconsolidated subsidiaries or affiliated companies.

Long-term investments are to be held for many years. They are not acquired with the intention of disposing of them in the near future. They are usually presented on the balance sheet just below "Current assets," in a separate section called Investments. Many securities that are properly shown among long-term investments are, in fact, readily marketable. But they are not included as current assets unless the intent is to convert them to cash in the short-term—within a year or in the operating cycle,

[10]*Accounting Trends and Techniques—2001* in its survey of 600 annual reports identified 343 companies that reported prepaid expenses.

whichever is longer. Securities classified as available-for-sale should be reported at fair value. Securities classified as held-to-maturity are reported at amortized cost.

Motorola, Inc. reported its investments section between "Property, plant, and equipment" and "Other assets" in the following manner.

ILLUSTRATION 5-9
Balance Sheet Presentation of Long-Term Investments

Motorola, Inc.
(in millions)

Investments	
Equity investments	$ 872
Other investments	2,567
Fair value adjustment to available-for-sale securities	2,487
Total	$5,926

Property, Plant, and Equipment

Property, plant, and equipment are properties of a durable nature used in the regular operations of the business. These assets consist of physical property such as land, buildings, machinery, furniture, tools, and wasting resources (timberland, minerals). With the exception of land, most assets are either depreciable (such as buildings) or depletable (such as timberlands or oil reserves).

Mattel, Inc., a manufacturer of toys and games, presented its property, plant, and equipment in its balance sheet as follows.

ILLUSTRATION 5-10
Balance Sheet Presentation of Property, Plant, and Equipment

Mattel, Inc.

Property, plant, and equipment	
Land	$ 32,793,000
Buildings	257,430,000
Machinery and equipment	564,244,000
Capitalized leases	23,271,000
Leasehold improvements	74,988,000
	952,726,000
Less: Accumulated depreciation	472,986,000
	479,740,000
Tools, dies and molds, net	168,092,000
Property, plant, and equipment, net	647,832,000

The basis of valuing the property, plant, and equipment, any liens against the properties, and accumulated depreciation should be disclosed—usually in notes to the statements.

Intangible Assets

Intangible assets lack physical substance and are not financial instruments (see definition on page 186). They include patents, copyrights, franchises, goodwill, trademarks, trade names, and secret processes. Limited-life intangible assets are written off (amortized) over their useful lives. Indefinite-life intangibles (such as goodwill) are not amortized but, instead, are assessed periodically for impairment. Intangibles can represent significant economic resources, yet financial analysts often ignore them, and accountants write them down or off arbitrarily because valuation is difficult.

PepsiCo, Inc. reported intangible assets in its balance sheet as follows.

PEPSICO
PepsiCo, Inc.
(in millions)

Intangible assets	
Goodwill	$3,374
Trademarks	1,320
Other identifiable intangibles	147
Total intangibles	$4,841

ILLUSTRATION 5-11
Balance Sheet Presentation of Intangible Assets

Other Assets

The items included in the section "Other assets" vary widely in practice. Some of the items commonly included are deferred charges (long-term prepaid expenses), non-current receivables, intangible assets, assets in special funds, deferred income taxes, property held for sale, and advances to subsidiaries. Such a section unfortunately is too general a classification. Instead, it should be restricted to unusual items sufficiently different from assets included in specific categories.

Liabilities

Similar to assets, liabilities are classified as current or long-term.

Current Liabilities

Current liabilities are the obligations that are reasonably expected to be liquidated either through the use of current assets or the creation of other current liabilities. This concept includes:

1. Payables resulting from the acquisition of goods and services: accounts payable, wages payable, taxes payable, and so on.
2. Collections received in advance for the delivery of goods or performance of services such as unearned rent revenue or unearned subscriptions revenue.
3. Other liabilities whose liquidation will take place within the operating cycle such as the portion of long-term bonds to be paid in the current period, or short-term obligations arising from purchase of equipment.

At times, a liability payable next year is not included in the current liabilities section. This occurs either when the debt is expected to be refinanced through another long-term issue,[11] or when the debt is retired out of non-current assets. This approach is used because liquidation does not result from the use of current assets or the creation of other current liabilities.

Current liabilities are not reported in any consistent order. The items most commonly listed first are notes payable, accounts payable, or short-term debt. Income taxes payable, current maturities of long-term debt, or other current liabilities are commonly

[11]"Classification of Short-term Obligations Expected to Be Refinanced," *Statement of Financial Accounting Standards No. 6* (Stamford, Conn.: FASB, 1975).

listed last. An example of **Halliburton Company**'s current liabilities section is shown below.

ILLUSTRATION 5-12
Balance Sheet Presentation of Current Liabilities

Halliburton Company
(in millions)

Current liabilities	
Short-term notes payable	$1,570
Accounts payable	782
Accrued employee compensation and benefits	267
Unearned revenues	386
Income taxes payable	113
Accrued special charges	6
Current maturities of long-term debt	8
Other current liabilities	694
Total current liabilities	3,826

Current liabilities include such items as trade and nontrade notes and accounts payable, advances received from customers, and current maturities of long-term debt. Income taxes and other accrued items are classified separately, if material. Any secured liability—for example, stock held as collateral on notes payable—is fully described in the notes so that the assets providing the security can be identified.

The excess of total current assets over total current liabilities is referred to as **working capital** (sometimes called **net working capital**). Working capital represents the net amount of a company's relatively liquid resources. That is, it is the liquid buffer available to meet the financial demands of the operating cycle. Working capital as an amount is seldom disclosed on the balance sheet, but it is computed by bankers and other creditors as an indicator of the short-run liquidity of a company. In order to determine the actual liquidity and availability of working capital to meet current obligations, however, one must analyze the composition of the current assets and their nearness to cash.

WHAT DO THE NUMBERS MEAN?

"SHOW ME THE ASSETS!"

Recently, concerns about liquidity and solvency of many dot-com companies have led creditors to demand more assurance that these companies can pay their bills when due. A key indicator for creditors is the amount of working capital. For example, when a report published early in 2001 predicted that **Amazon.com**'s working capital would turn negative, vendors who sell goods to Amazon on credit began to explore steps that could be taken to ensure that they will be paid.

Some vendors demanded that their Internet customers sign notes stating that the goods shipped to them serve as collateral for the transaction. Other vendors began shipping goods on consignment—an arrangement whereby the vendor retains ownership of the goods until they are bought and paid for by a third party. Such creditor protection measures for dot-coms arise from creditors' concerns about Internet companies' lack of tangible assets that can be converted to cash to meet short-term obligations. For example, the primary asset for many Internet companies is its customer list. However, these lists have little resale value because privacy agreements stipulate that the customer information is provided for the Internet company's use only.

Thus, with fewer hard assets that can be converted to cash, Internet companies can experience a more severe credit squeeze as vendors curtail shipments or take other measures to limit their financial risk to Internet customers. Such actions can further erode a company's liquidity and financial flexibility.

Long-Term Liabilities

Long-term liabilities are obligations that are not reasonably expected to be liquidated within the normal operating cycle but, instead, are payable at some date beyond that time. Bonds payable, notes payable, some deferred income tax amounts, lease obligations, and pension obligations are the most common examples. Generally, a great deal of supplementary disclosure is needed for this section, because most long-term debt is subject to various covenants and restrictions for the protection of lenders.[12] Long-term liabilities that mature within the current operating cycle are classified as current liabilities if their liquidation requires the use of current assets.

Generally, long-term liabilities are of three types:

1. Obligations arising from specific financing situations, such as the issuance of bonds, long-term lease obligations, and long-term notes payable.
2. Obligations arising from the ordinary operations of the enterprise, such as pension obligations and deferred income tax liabilities.
3. Obligations that are dependent upon the occurrence or nonoccurrence of one or more future events to confirm the amount payable, or the payee, or the date payable, such as service or product warranties and other contingencies.

It is desirable to report any premium or discount separately as an addition to or subtraction from the bonds payable. The terms of all long-term liability agreements (including maturity date or dates, rates of interest, nature of obligation, and any security pledged to support the debt) are frequently described in notes to the financial statements. An example of the financial statement and accompanying note presentation is shown in Illustration 5-13 in the excerpt from **The Great Atlantic & Pacific Tea Company**'s financials.

The Great Atlantic & Pacific Tea Company, Inc.

Total current liabilities	$978,109,000
Long-term debt (See note)	254,312,000
Obligations under capital leases	252,618,000
Deferred income taxes	57,167,000
Other non-current liabilities	127,321,000
Note: Indebtedness. Debt consists of:	
9.5% senior notes, due in annual installments of $10,000,000	$ 40,000,000
Mortgages and other notes due through 2011 (average interest rate of 9.9%)	107,604,000
Bank borrowings at 9.7%	67,225,000
Commercial paper at 9.4%	100,102,000
	314,931,000
Less: Current portion	(60,619,000)
Total long-term debt	$254,312,000

ILLUSTRATION 5-13
Balance Sheet Presentation of Long-Term Debt

[12]The pertinent rights and privileges of the various securities (both debt and equity) outstanding are usually explained in the notes to the financial statements. Examples of information that should be disclosed are dividend and liquidation preferences, participation rights, call prices and dates, conversion or exercise prices or rates and pertinent dates, sinking fund requirements, unusual voting rights, and significant terms of contracts to issue additional shares. "Disclosure of Information about Capital Structure," *Statement of Financial Accounting Standards No. 129* (Norwalk: FASB, 1997), par. 4.

Owners' Equity

The **owners' equity** (**stockholders' equity**) section is one of the most difficult sections to prepare and understand. This is due to the complexity of capital stock agreements and the various restrictions on residual equity imposed by state corporation laws, liability agreements, and boards of directors. The section is usually divided into three parts:

STOCKHOLDERS' EQUITY SECTION

1. *Capital Stock.* The par or stated value of the shares issued.
2. *Additional Paid-In Capital.* The excess of amounts paid in over the par or stated value.
3. *Retained Earnings.* The corporation's undistributed earnings.

The major disclosure requirements for capital stock are the authorized, issued, and outstanding par value amounts. The additional paid-in capital is usually presented in one amount, although subtotals are informative if the sources of additional capital are varied and material. The retained earnings section may be divided between the unappropriated (the amount that is usually available for dividend distribution) and restricted (e.g., by bond indentures or other loan agreements) amounts. In addition, any capital stock reacquired (treasury stock) is shown as a reduction of stockholders' equity.

The ownership or stockholders' equity accounts in a corporation are considerably different from those in a partnership or proprietorship. Partners' permanent capital accounts and the balance in their temporary accounts (drawing accounts) are shown separately. Proprietorships ordinarily use a single capital account that handles all of the owner's equity transactions.

Presented below is an example of the stockholders' equity section from **Quanex Corporation**.

ILLUSTRATION 5-14
Balance Sheet Presentation of Stockholders' Equity

Quanex Corporation
(in thousands)

Stockholders' equity (Note 12):	
Preferred stock, no par value, 1,000,000 shares authorized; 345,000 issued and outstanding	$ 86,250
Common stock, $0.50 par value, 25,000,000 shares authorized; 13,638,005 shares issued and outstanding	6,819
Additional paid-in capital	87,260
Retained earnings	57,263
	$237,592

Balance Sheet Format

OBJECTIVE 3
Prepare a classified balance sheet using the report and account formats.

One common arrangement followed in the presentation of a classified balance sheet is called the **account form**. It lists assets by sections on the left side, and liabilities and stockholders' equity by sections on the right side. The main disadvantage is the need for two facing pages.

To avoid the use of facing pages, the **report form**, shown in Illustration 5-15 (page 183), lists liabilities and stockholders' equity directly below assets on the same page.[13]

[13] *Accounting Trends and Techniques—2001* indicates that of the 600 companies surveyed, 502 use the "report form" and 98 use the "account form," sometimes collectively referred to as the "customary form."

SCIENTIFIC PRODUCTS, INC.
BALANCE SHEET
DECEMBER 31, 2003

Assets			
Current assets			
Cash		$ 42,485	
Available-for-sale securities—at fair value		28,250	
Accounts receivable	$165,824		
Less: Allowance for doubtful accounts	1,850	163,974	
Notes receivable		23,000	
Inventories—at average cost		489,713	
Supplies on hand		9,780	
Prepaid expenses		16,252	
Total current assets			$ 773,454
Long-term investments			
Investments in Warren Co.			87,500
Property, plant, and equipment			
Land—at cost		125,000	
Buildings—at cost	975,800		
Less: Accumulated depreciation	341,200	634,600	
Total property, plant, and equipment			759,600
Intangible assets			
Goodwill			100,000
Total assets			$1,720,554
Liabilities and Stockholders' Equity			
Current liabilities			
Notes payable to banks		$ 50,000	
Accounts payable		197,532	
Accrued interest on notes payable		500	
Income taxes payable		62,520	
Accrued salaries, wages, and other liabilities		9,500	
Deposits received from customers		420	
Total current liabilities			$ 320,472
Long-term debt			
Twenty-year 12% debentures, due January 1, 2013			500,000
Total liabilities			820,472
Stockholders' equity			
Paid in on capital stock			
Preferred, 7%, cumulative			
Authorized, issued, and outstanding, 30,000 shares of $10 par value	$300,000		
Common—			
Authorized, 500,000 shares of $1.00 par value; issued and outstanding, 400,000 shares	400,000		
Additional paid-in capital	37,500	737,500	
Earnings retained in the business		162,582	
Total stockholders' equity			900,082
Total liabilities and stockholders' equity			$1,720,554

ILLUSTRATION 5-15
Classified Report Form Balance Sheet

UNDERLYING CONCEPTS

The presentation of balance sheet information meets one of the objectives of financial reporting—to provide information about enterprise resources, claims to resources, and changes in them.

Other balance sheet formats are used infrequently. For example, current liabilities are sometimes deducted from current assets to arrive at working capital, or all liabilities are deducted from all assets.

WHAT DO THE NUMBERS MEAN?

WARNING SIGNALS

One of the uses of balance sheet information is in models used to predict financial distress. A bankruptcy-prediction model pioneered by Altman combines balance sheet and income measures in the following equation to derive a "Z-score."

$$Z = \frac{\text{Working capital}}{\text{Total assets}} \times 1.2 + \frac{\text{Retained earnings}}{\text{Total assets}} \times 1.4 + \frac{\text{EBIT}}{\text{Total assets}} \times 3.3 + \frac{\text{Sales}}{\text{Total assets}} \times 0.99 + \frac{\text{MV equity}}{\text{Total liabilities}} \times 0.6$$

Following extensive testing, Altman found that companies with Z-scores above 3.0 are unlikely to fail. Those with Z-scores below 1.81 are very likely to fail. While the original model was developed for publicly held manufacturing companies, the model has been modified to apply to companies in various industries, emerging companies, and companies not traded in public markets.

Until recently, the use of Z-scores was virtually unheard of among practicing accountants. Today this measure is used by auditors, management consultants, and courts of law, and as part of many database systems used for loan evaluation. While a low score does not guarantee bankruptcy, the model has been proven accurate in many situations in the past, and can be used to help evaluate the overall financial position and trends of a firm.

Source: Adapted from E. I. Altman, *Corporate Financial Distress and Bankruptcy*, 2nd edition (New York: John Wiley and Sons, 1993).

Presentation of Balance Sheet Formats for Various Real Companies

UNDERLYING CONCEPTS

The basis for inclusion of additional information should meet the full disclosure principle; that is, the information should be of sufficient importance to influence the judgment of an informed user.

ADDITIONAL INFORMATION REPORTED

The balance sheet is not complete simply because the assets, liabilities, and owners' equity accounts have been listed. Great importance is given to supplemental information. It may be information not presented elsewhere in the statement, or it may be an elaboration or qualification of items in the balance sheet. There are normally four types of information that are supplemental to the balance sheet.

OBJECTIVE 4
Identify balance sheet information requiring supplemental disclosure.

SUPPLEMENTAL BALANCE SHEET INFORMATION

1. *Contingencies.* Material events that have an uncertain outcome.
2. *Accounting Policies.* Explanations of the valuation methods used or the basic assumptions made concerning inventory valuations, depreciation methods, investments in subsidiaries, etc.
3. *Contractual Situations.* Explanations of certain restrictions or covenants attached to specific assets or, more likely, to liabilities.
4. *Fair Values.* Disclosures of fair values, particularly for financial instruments.

Contingencies

A **contingency** is defined as an existing situation involving uncertainty as to possible gain (gain contingency) or loss (loss contingency) that will ultimately be resolved when one or more future events occur or fail to occur. In short, they are material events that have an uncertain future. Examples of gain contingencies are tax operating loss carryforwards or company litigation against another party. Typical loss contingencies relate to litigation, environmental issues, possible tax assessments, or government investigation. The accounting and reporting requirements involving contingencies are examined fully in Chapter 13, and therefore additional discussion is not provided here.

Accounting Policies

APB Opinion No. 22 recommends disclosure for all significant accounting principles and methods that involve selection from among alternatives or those that are peculiar to a given industry.[14] For instance, inventories can be computed under several cost flow assumptions (such as LIFO and FIFO); plant and equipment can be depreciated under several accepted methods of cost allocation (such as double-declining balance and straight-line); and investments can be carried at different valuations (such as cost, equity, and fair value). Sophisticated users of financial statements know of these possibilities and examine the statements closely to determine the methods used.

Companies also are required to disclose information about the nature of their operations, the use of estimates in preparing financial statements, certain significant estimates, and vulnerabilities due to certain concentrations.[15] An example of such a disclosure is shown in Illustration 5-16.

Chesapeake Corporation

Risks and Uncertainties. Chesapeake operates in three business segments which offer a diversity of products over a broad geographic base. The Company is not dependent on any single customer, group of customers, market, geographic area or supplier of materials, labor or services. Financial statements include, where necessary, amounts based on the judgments and estimates of management. These estimates include allowances for bad debts, accruals for landfill closing costs, environmental remediation costs, loss contingencies for litigation, self-insured medical and workers' compensation insurance and income taxes and determinations of discount and other rate assumptions for pensions and postretirement benefit expenses.

ILLUSTRATION 5-16
Balance Sheet Disclosure of Significant Risks and Uncertainties

Disclosure of significant accounting principles and methods and of risks and uncertainties is particularly useful if given in a separate **Summary of Significant Accounting Policies** preceding the notes to the financial statements or as the initial note.

[14]"Disclosure of Accounting Policies," *Opinions of the Accounting Principles Board No. 22* (New York: AICPA, 1972).

[15]"Disclosure of Certain Significant Risks and Uncertainties," *Statement of Position 94–6* (New York: AICPA, 1994).

Contractual Situations

In addition to contingencies and different methods of valuation, contractual situations of significance should be disclosed in the notes to the financial statements. It is mandatory, for example, that the essential provisions of lease contracts, pension obligations, and stock option plans be clearly stated in the notes. The analyst who examines a set of financial statements wants to know not only the amount of the liabilities, but also how the different contractual provisions affect the company at present and in the future.

Commitments related to obligations to maintain working capital, to limit the payment of dividends, to restrict the use of assets, and to require the maintenance of certain financial ratios must all be disclosed if material. Considerable judgment is necessary to determine whether omission of such information is misleading. The axiom in this situation is, "When in doubt, disclose." It is better to disclose a little too much information than not enough.

Fair Values

As discussed in Chapter 2, historical cost is the primary valuation basis in financial statements. However, fair value information is thought to be more useful for certain types of assets and liabilities. This is particularly so in the case of financial instruments.

Financial instruments are defined as cash, an ownership interest, or a contractual right to receive or obligation to deliver cash or another financial instrument. Such contractual rights to receive cash or other financial instruments are assets. Contractual obligations to pay are liabilities. Cash, investments, accounts receivable, and payables are examples of financial instruments.

Financial instruments are increasing both in use and variety. As a consequence of the increasing use, companies are required to disclose both the carrying values and the estimated fair values of their financial instruments. For example, **Intel** provides extensive disclosures of the fair value of its financial instrument assets and liabilities, as shown in Illustration 5-17. More extensive discussion of financial instrument accounting and reporting is provided in Chapters 7, 13, 14, 15, and 17.

ILLUSTRATION 5-17
Disclosure of Financial Instrument Fair Values

Intel Corp.

Fair values of financial instruments. The estimated fair values of financial instruments outstanding at fiscal year-ends were as follows:

	2000	
(in millions)	Carrying amount	Estimated fair value
Cash and cash equivalents	$ 2,976	$ 2,976
Short-term investments	10,498	10,498
Trading assets	355	355
Marketable strategic equity securities	1,915	1,915
Other long-term investments	1,801	1,801
Non-marketable instruments	1,886	3,579
Swaps hedging investments in debt securities	12	12
Options hedging deferred compensation liabilities	(5)	(5)
Short-term debt	(378)	(378)
Long-term debt	(707)	(702)
Swaps hedging debt	—	(1)
Currency forward contracts	2	6

TECHNIQUES OF DISCLOSURE

The effect of various contingencies on financial condition, the methods of valuing assets, and the company's contracts and agreements should be disclosed as completely and as intelligently as possible. These methods of disclosing pertinent information are available: parenthetical explanations, notes, cross reference and contra items, and supporting schedules.

OBJECTIVE 5
Identify major disclosure techniques for the balance sheet.

Parenthetical Explanations

Additional information is often provided by parenthetical explanations following the item. For example, investments in available-for-sale securities are shown on the balance sheet under Investments as follows.

Investments in available-for-sale securities (cost, $330,586)—at fair value	$401,500

This device permits disclosure of additional pertinent balance sheet information that adds clarity and completeness. It has an advantage over a note because it brings the additional information into the body of the statement where it is less likely to be overlooked. Of course, lengthy parenthetical explanations that might distract the reader from the balance sheet information must be used with care.

UNDERLYING CONCEPTS

The user-specific quality of understandability requires accountants to be careful in describing transactions and events.

Notes

Notes are used if additional explanations cannot be shown conveniently as parenthetical explanations. For example, inventory costing methods are reported in **The Quaker Oats Company**'s accompanying notes as shown in Illustration 5-18.

ILLUSTRATION 5-18
Note Disclosure

The Quaker Oats Company

Inventories (Note 1)

Finished goods	$326,000,000
Grain and raw materials	114,100,000
Packaging materials and supplies	39,000,000
Total inventories	479,100,000

Note 1: Inventories. Inventories are valued at the lower of cost or market, using various cost methods, and include the cost of raw materials, labor, and overhead. The percentage of year-end inventories valued using each of the methods is as follows:

Average quarterly cost	21%
Last-in, first-out (LIFO)	65%
First-in, first-out (FIFO)	14%

If the LIFO method of valuing certain inventories was not used, total inventories would have been $60,100,000 higher than reported.

Notes are commonly used to disclose the following: the existence and amount of any preferred stock dividends in arrears, the terms of or obligations imposed by purchase commitments, special financial arrangements and instruments, depreciation policies, any changes in the application of accounting principles, and the existence of contingencies. The notes in Illustration 5-19 show a common method of presenting such information.

ILLUSTRATION 5-19
More Note Disclosures

Consolidated Papers, Inc.

Note 7: Commitments. The company had capital expenditure purchase commitments outstanding of approximately $17 million.

Alberto-Culver Company

Note 3: Long-Term Debt. Various borrowing arrangements impose restrictions on such items as total debt, working capital, dividend payments, treasury stock purchases and interest expense. The company was in compliance with these arrangements and $68 million of consolidated retained earnings was not restricted as to the payment of dividends and purchases of treasury stock.

Willamette Industries, Inc.

Note 4: Property, Plant, and Equipment (partial): The company changed its accounting estimates relating to depreciation. The estimated service lives for most machinery and equipment were extended five years. The change was based upon a study performed by the company's engineering department, comparisons to typical industry practices, and the effect of the company's extensive capital investments which have resulted in a mix of assets with longer productive lives due to technological advances. As a result of the change, net income was increased $51,900, or $0.46 per diluted share.

The notes must present all essential facts as completely and succinctly as possible. Careless wording may mislead rather than aid readers. Notes should add to the total information made available in the financial statements, not raise unanswered questions or contradict other portions of the statements.

Cross Reference and Contra Items

A direct relationship between an asset and a liability is "cross referenced" on the balance sheet. For example, on December 31, 2004, the following might be shown among the current assets.

Cash on deposit with sinking fund trustee for redemption of bonds payable—see Current liabilities	$800,000

Included among the current liabilities is the amount of bonds payable to be redeemed within one year:

Bonds payable to be redeemed in 2005—see Current assets	$2,300,000

This cross reference points out that $2,300,000 of bonds payable are to be redeemed currently, for which only $800,000 in cash has been set aside. Therefore, the additional cash needed must come from unrestricted cash, from sales of investments, from profits, or from some other source. The same information can be shown parenthetically, if this technique is preferred.

Another common procedure is to establish contra or adjunct accounts. A **contra account** on a balance sheet is an item that reduces either an asset, liability, or owners' equity account. Examples include Accumulated Depreciation and Discount on Bonds Payable. Contra accounts provide some flexibility in presenting the financial information. With the use of the Accumulated Depreciation account, for example, a reader of the statement can see the original cost of the asset as well as the depreciation to date.

An **adjunct account**, on the other hand, increases either an asset, liability, or owners' equity account. An example is Premium on Bonds Payable, which, when added to the Bonds Payable account, describes the total bond liability of the enterprise.

Supporting Schedules

Often a separate schedule is needed to present more detailed information about certain assets or liabilities, because the balance sheet provides just a single summary item.

ILLUSTRATION 5-20
Disclosure through Use of Supporting Schedules

Property, plant, and equipment	
Land, buildings, equipment, and other fixed assets—net (see Schedule 3)	$643,300

A separate schedule then might be presented as follows.

SCHEDULE 3
LAND, BUILDINGS, EQUIPMENT, AND OTHER FIXED ASSETS

	Total	Land	Buildings	Equip.	Other Fixed Assets
Balance January 1, 2004	$740,000	$46,000	$358,000	$260,000	$76,000
Additions in 2004	161,200		120,000	38,000	3,200
	901,200	46,000	478,000	298,000	79,200
Assets retired or sold in 2004	31,700			27,000	4,700
Balance December 31, 2004	869,500	46,000	478,000	271,000	74,500
Depreciation taken to January 1, 2004	196,000		102,000	78,000	16,000
Depreciation taken in 2004	56,000		28,000	24,000	4,000
	252,000		130,000	102,000	20,000
Depreciation on assets retired in 2004	25,800			22,000	3,800
Depreciation accumulated December 31, 2004	226,200		130,000	80,000	16,200
Book value of assets	$643,300	$46,000	$348,000	$191,000	$58,300

INTERNATIONAL INSIGHT

Internationally, accounting terminology is problematic. Confusing differences arise even between nations that share a language. For example, U.S. investors normally think of "stock" as "equity" or "ownership," but to the British "stocks" means inventory. In the U.S. "fixed assets" generally refers to "property, plant, and equipment," while in Britain the category includes more items.

Terminology

The account titles in the general ledger do not necessarily represent the best terminology for balance sheet purposes. Account titles are often brief and include technical terms that are understood only by accountants. But balance sheets are examined by many persons who are not acquainted with the technical vocabulary of accounting.

Thus, they should contain descriptions that will be generally understood and not be subject to misinterpretation.

For example, the profession has recommended that the word **reserve** be used only to describe an appropriation of retained earnings. This term had been used in several ways: to describe amounts deducted from assets (contra accounts such as accumulated depreciation and allowance for doubtful accounts), and as a part of the title of contingent or estimated liabilities. Because of the different meanings attached to this term, misinterpretation often resulted from its use. The use of "reserve" only to describe appropriated retained earnings has resulted in a better understanding of its significance when it appears in a balance sheet. However, the term "appropriated" appears more logical, and its use should be encouraged.

For years the profession has recommended that the use of the word **surplus** be discontinued in balance sheet presentations of owners' equity. The use of the terms capital surplus, paid-in surplus, and earned surplus is confusing. Although condemned by the profession, these terms appear all too frequently in current financial statements.

SECTION 2 STATEMENT OF CASH FLOWS

UNDERLYING CONCEPTS

The statement of cash flows meets one of the objectives of financial reporting—to help assess the amounts, timing, and uncertainty of future cash flows.

In Chapter 2, "assessing the amounts, timing, and uncertainty of cash flows" was presented as one of the three basic objectives of financial reporting. The balance sheet, the income statement, and the statement of stockholders' equity each present, to a limited extent, information about the cash flows of an enterprise during a period. For instance, comparative balance sheets might show what assets have been acquired or disposed of and what liabilities have been incurred or liquidated. The income statement provides information about resources provided by operations, but not exactly cash. The statement of stockholders' equity shows the amount of cash used to pay dividends or purchase treasury stock. But none of these statements presents a detailed summary of all the cash inflows and outflows, or the sources and uses of cash during the period. To fill this need, the FASB requires the **statement of cash flows** (also called the **cash flow statement**).[16]

PURPOSE OF THE STATEMENT OF CASH FLOWS

OBJECTIVE 6
Indicate the purpose of the statement of cash flows.

The primary purpose of a statement of cash flows is to provide relevant information about the cash receipts and cash payments of an enterprise during a period. To achieve this purpose, the statement of cash flows reports (1) the cash effects of operations during a period, (2) investing transactions, (3) financing transactions, and (4) the net increase or decrease in cash during the period.[17]

Reporting the sources, uses, and net increase or decrease in cash helps investors, creditors, and others know what is happening to a company's most liquid resource. Because most individuals maintain their checkbook and prepare their tax return on a cash basis, they can relate to the statement of cash flows and comprehend the causes and effects of cash inflows and outflows and the net increase or decrease in cash. The statement of cash flows provides answers to the following simple but important questions:

[16] "Statement of Cash Flows," *Statement of Financial Accounting Standards No. 95* (Stamford, Conn.: FASB, 1987).

[17] The basis recommended by the FASB is actually "cash and cash equivalents." **Cash equivalents** are short-term, highly liquid investments such as Treasury bills, commercial paper, and money market funds purchased with cash that is in excess of immediate needs.

1. Where did the cash come from during the period?
2. What was the cash used for during the period?
3. What was the change in the cash balance during the period?

WATCH THAT CASH FLOW

WHAT DO THE NUMBERS MEAN?

While investors usually focus on net income measured on an accrual basis, information on cash flows can be important for assessing a company's liquidity, financial flexibility, and overall financial performance. Presented below is a graph that shows W.T. Grant's financial performance over 7 years.

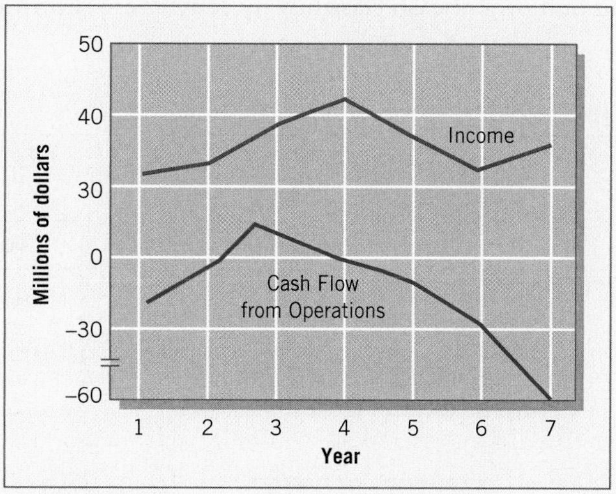

Although W.T. Grant showed consistent profits and even some periods of earnings growth, its cash flow began to "go south." W.T. Grant filed for bankruptcy shortly after year 7. Analysis of cash flows would have provided an early-warning signal of W.T. Grant's problems.

CONTENT AND FORMAT OF THE STATEMENT OF CASH FLOWS

OBJECTIVE 7
Identify the content of the statement of cash flows.

Cash receipts and cash payments during a period are classified in the statement of cash flows into three different activities—operating, investing, and financing activities. These classifications are defined as follows.

1. **Operating activities** involve the cash effects of transactions that enter into the determination of net income.
2. **Investing activities** include making and collecting loans and acquiring and disposing of investments (both debt and equity) and property, plant, and equipment.
3. **Financing activities** involve liability and owners' equity items. They include (a) obtaining resources from owners and providing them with a return on (and a return of) their investment and (b) borrowing money from creditors and repaying the amounts borrowed.

With cash flows classified into those three categories, the statement of cash flows has the following basic format.

ILLUSTRATION 5-21
Basic Format of Cash Flow Statement

Statement of Cash Flows

Cash flows from operating activities	$XXX
Cash flows from investing activities	XXX
Cash flows from financing activities	XXX
Net increase (decrease) in cash	XXX
Cash at beginning of year	XXX
Cash at end of year	$XXX

The inflows and outflows of cash classified by activity are shown in Illustration 5-22.

ILLUSTRATION 5-22 Cash Inflows and Outflows

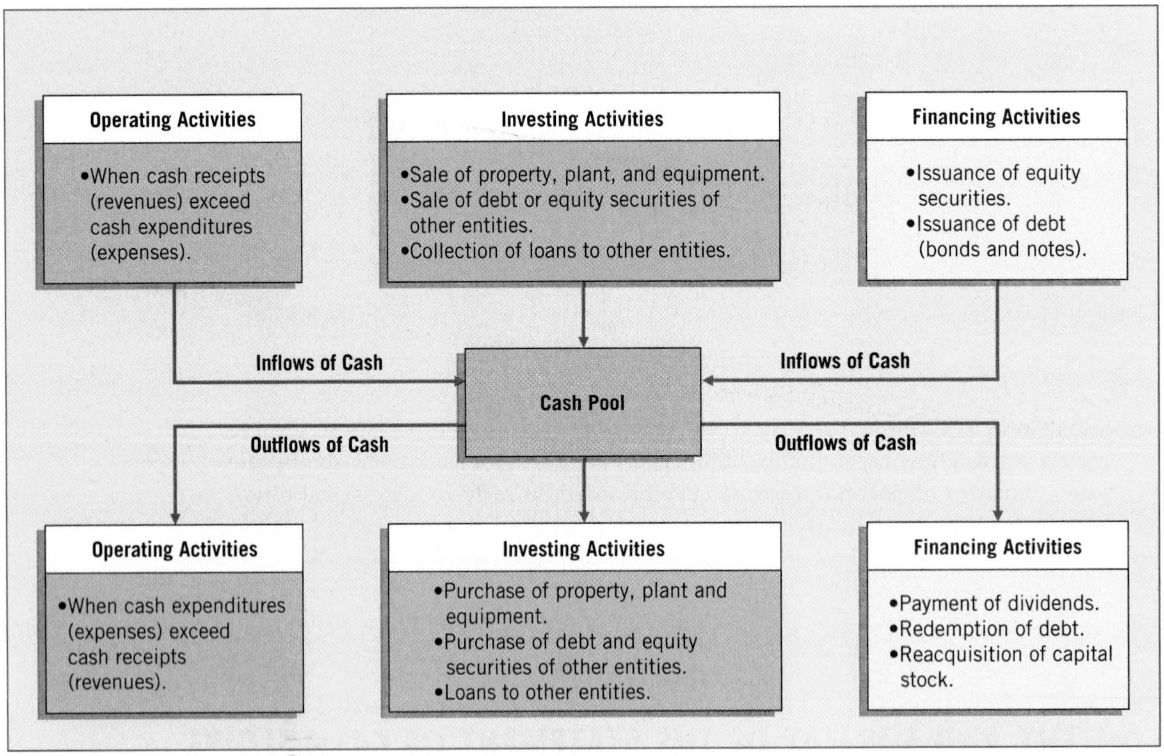

The statement's value is that it helps users evaluate liquidity, solvency, and financial flexibility. Liquidity refers to the "nearness to cash" of assets and liabilities. **Solvency** refers to the firm's ability to pay its debts as they mature. And **financial flexibility** refers to a firm's ability to respond and adapt to financial adversity and unexpected needs and opportunities.

We have devoted Chapter 23 entirely to the preparation and content of the statement of cash flows. Our comprehensive coverage of this topic has been deferred to that later chapter so that we can cover in the intervening chapters several elements and complex topics that make up the content of a typical statement of cash flows. The presentation in this chapter is introductory—a reminder of the existence of the statement of cash flows and its usefulness.

PREPARATION OF THE STATEMENT OF CASH FLOWS

OBJECTIVE 8
Prepare a statement of cash flows.

The information to prepare the statement of cash flows usually comes from (1) comparative balance sheets, (2) the current income statement, and (3) selected transaction data. Preparing the statement of cash flows from these sources involves four steps:

1. Determine the cash provided by operations.
2. Determine the cash provided by or used in investing and financing activities.
3. Determine the change (increase or decrease) in cash during the period.
4. Reconcile the change in cash with the beginning and the ending cash balances.

INTERNATIONAL INSIGHT

Statements of cash flows are not required in all countries. Some countries require a statement reporting sources and applications of "funds" (often defined as working capital). Others have no requirement for either cash or funds flow statements.

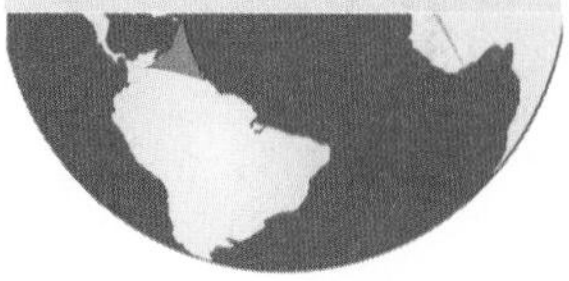

The following simple illustration demonstrates how these steps are applied in the preparation of a statement of cash flows.

On January 1, 2004, in its first year of operations, Telemarketing Inc. issued 50,000 shares of $1.00 par value common stock for $50,000 cash. The company rented its office space, furniture, and telecommunications equipment and performed surveys and marketing services throughout the first year. In June 2004 the company purchased land for $15,000. The comparative balance sheets at the beginning and end of the year 2004 are shown in Illustration 5-23.

ILLUSTRATION 5-23 Comparative Balance Sheets

TELEMARKETING INC.
BALANCE SHEETS

Assets	Dec. 31, 2004	Jan. 1, 2004	Increase/Decrease
Cash	$31,000	$–0–	$31,000 Increase
Accounts receivable	41,000	–0–	41,000 Increase
Land	15,000	–0–	15,000 Increase
Total	$87,000	$–0–	
Liabilities and Stockholders' Equity			
Accounts payable	$12,000	$–0–	12,000 Increase
Common stock	50,000	–0–	50,000 Increase
Retained earnings	25,000	–0–	25,000 Increase
Total	$87,000	$–0–	

The income statement and additional information for Telemarketing Inc. are as follows.

ILLUSTRATION 5-24
Income Statement Data

TELEMARKETING INC.
INCOME STATEMENT
FOR THE YEAR ENDED DECEMBER 31, 2004

Revenues	$172,000
Operating expenses	120,000
Income before income taxes	52,000
Income tax expense	13,000
Net income	$ 39,000

Additional information:
Dividends of $14,000 were paid during the year.

Cash provided by operations (the excess of cash receipts over cash payments) is determined by converting net income on an accrual basis to a cash basis. This is accomplished by adding to or deducting from net income those items in the income statement not affecting cash. This procedure requires an analysis not only of the current year's income statement but also of the comparative balance sheets and selected transaction data.

Analysis of Telemarketing's comparative balance sheets reveals two items that give rise to noncash credits or charges to the income statement: (1) The increase in accounts receivable reflects a noncash credit of $41,000 to revenues. (2) The increase in accounts payable reflects a noncash charge of $12,000 to expenses. **To arrive at cash provided by operations, the increase in accounts receivable must be deducted from net income, and the increase in accounts payable must be added back to net income.**

As a result of the accounts receivable and accounts payable adjustments, cash provided by operations is determined to be $10,000, computed as follows.

ILLUSTRATION 5-25
Computation of Net Cash Provided by Operations

Net income		$39,000
Adjustments to reconcile net income to net cash provided by operating activities:		
Increase in accounts receivable	$(41,000)	
Increase in accounts payable	12,000	(29,000)
Net cash provided by operating activities		$10,000

The increase of $50,000 in common stock resulting from the issuance of 50,000 shares for cash is classified as a financing activity. Likewise, the payment of $14,000 cash in dividends is a financing activity. Telemarketing Inc.'s only investing activity was the land purchase. The statement of cash flows for Telemarketing Inc. for 2004 is as follows.

ILLUSTRATION 5-26 Statement of Cash Flows

TELEMARKETING INC.
STATEMENT OF CASH FLOWS
FOR THE YEAR ENDED DECEMBER 31, 2004

Cash flows from operating activities		
Net income		$39,000
Adjustments to reconcile net income to net cash provided by operating activities:		
Increase in accounts receivable	$(41,000)	
Increase in accounts payable	12,000	(29,000)
Net cash provided by operating activities		10,000
Cash flows from investing activities		
Purchase of land	(15,000)	
Net cash used by investing activities		(15,000)
Cash flows from financing activities		
Issuance of common stock	50,000	
Payment of cash dividends	(14,000)	
Net cash provided by financing activities		36,000
Net increase in cash		31,000
Cash at beginning of year		–0–
Cash at end of year		$31,000

INTERNATIONAL INSIGHT

International Accounting Standard 7 requires a statement of cash flows. Both international standards and U.S. GAAP specify that the cash flows must be classified as operating, investing, or financing.

The increase in cash of $31,000 reported in the statement of cash flows agrees with the increase of $31,000 in the Cash account calculated from the comparative balance sheets.

An illustration of a more comprehensive statement of cash flows is presented in Illustration 5-27.

ILLUSTRATION 5-27
Comprehensive Statement of Cash Flows

NESTOR COMPANY
STATEMENT OF CASH FLOWS
FOR THE YEAR ENDED DECEMBER 31, 2004

Cash flows from operating activities		
Net income		$320,750
Adjustments to reconcile net income to net cash provided by operating activities:		
Depreciation expense	$88,400	
Amortization of intangibles	16,300	
Gain on sale of plant assets	(8,700)	
Increase in accounts receivable (net)	(11,000)	
Decrease in inventory	15,500	
Decrease in accounts payable	(9,500)	91,000
Net cash provided by operating activities		411,750
Cash flows from investing activities		
Sale of plant assets	90,500	
Purchase of equipment	(182,500)	
Purchase of land	(70,000)	
Net cash used by investing activities		(162,000)
Cash flows from financing activities		
Payment of cash dividend	(19,800)	
Issuance of common stock	100,000	
Redemption of bonds	(50,000)	
Net cash provided by financing activities		30,200
Net increase in cash		279,950
Cash at beginning of year		135,000
Cash at end of year		$414,950

Additional Disclosures of Cash Flow Reporting

USEFULNESS OF THE STATEMENT OF CASH FLOWS

OBJECTIVE 9
Understand the usefulness of the statement of cash flows.

"Happiness is a positive cash flow" is certainly true. Although net income provides a long-term measure of a company's success or failure, cash is the lifeblood of a company. Without cash, a company will not survive. For small and newly developing companies, cash flow is the single most important element for survival. Even medium and large companies indicate a major concern in controlling cash flow.

Creditors examine the cash flow statement carefully because they are concerned about being paid. A good starting point in their examination is to find net cash provided by operating activities. A high amount of net cash provided by operating activities indicates that a company is able to generate sufficient cash internally from operations to pay its bills without further borrowing. Conversely, a low or negative amount of net cash provided by operating activities indicates that a company cannot generate enough cash internally from its operations and, therefore, must borrow or issue equity securities to acquire additional cash. Consequently, creditors look for answers to the following questions in the company's cash flow statements.

1. How successful is the company in generating net cash provided by operating activities?
2. What are the trends in net cash flow provided by operating activities over time?
3. What are the major reasons for the positive or negative net cash provided by operating activities?

You should recognize that companies can fail even though they are profitable. The difference between net income and net cash provided by operating activities can be substantial. Companies such as **W.T. Grant Company** and **Prime Motor Inn**, for example, reported high net income numbers but negative net cash provided by operating activities. Eventually both these companies filed for bankruptcy.

As discussed in the opening story, the reasons for the difference between a positive net income and a negative net cash provided by operating activities are substantial increases in receivables and/or inventory. To illustrate more specifically, Ho Inc. in its first year of operations reported a net income of $80,000. Its net cash provided by operating activities, however, was a negative $95,000, as shown in Illustration 5-28.

ILLUSTRATION 5-28
Negative Net Cash Provided by Operating Activities

HO INC.
NET CASH FLOW FROM OPERATING ACTIVITIES

Cash flows from operating activities		
Net income		$ 80,000
Adjustments to reconcile net income to net cash provided by operating activities:		
Increase in receivables	$ (75,000)	
Increase in inventories	(100,000)	(175,000)
Net cash provided by operating activities		$(95,000)

Note that the negative net cash provided by operating activities occurred for Ho even though it reported a positive net income. Ho could easily experience a "cash crunch" because it has tied up its cash in receivables and inventory. If problems in collecting receivables occur, or if inventory is slow-moving or becomes obsolete, Ho's creditors may have difficulty collecting on their loans.

Financial Liquidity

One relationship (ratio) that is often used to assess liquidity is the **current cash debt coverage ratio**. It indicates whether the company can pay off its current liabilities in a given year from its operations. The formula for this ratio is:

ILLUSTRATION 5-29
Formula for Current Cash Debt Coverage Ratio

$$\frac{\text{Net Cash Provided by Operating Activities}}{\text{Average Current Liabilities}} = \text{Current Cash Debt Coverage Ratio}$$

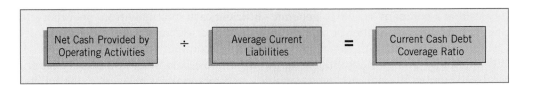

The higher this ratio, the less likely a company will have liquidity problems. For example, a ratio near 1:1 is good because it indicates that the company can meet all of its current obligations from internally generated cash flow.

Financial Flexibility

A more long-run measure which provides information on financial flexibility is the **cash debt coverage ratio**. This ratio indicates a company's ability to repay its liabilities from net cash provided by operating activities, without having to liquidate the assets employed in its operations. The formula for this ratio is:

Net Cash Provided by Operating Activities ÷ Average Total Liabilities = Cash Debt Coverage Ratio

ILLUSTRATION 5-30
Formula for Cash Debt Coverage Ratio

The higher this ratio, the less likely the company will experience difficulty in meeting its obligations as they come due. It signals whether the company can pay its debts and survive if external sources of funds become limited or too expensive.

Free Cash Flow

A more sophisticated way to examine a company's financial flexibility is to develop a free cash flow analysis. This analysis starts with net cash provided by operating activities and ends with **free cash flow**, which is calculated as net cash provided by operating activities less capital expenditures and dividends.[18] Free cash flow is the amount of discretionary cash flow a company has for purchasing additional investments, retiring its debt, purchasing treasury stock, or simply adding to its liquidity.

This measure indicates a company's level of financial flexibility. Questions that a free cash flow analysis answers are:

1. Is the company able to pay its dividends without resorting to external financing?
2. If business operations decline, will the company be able to maintain its needed capital investment?
3. What is the amount of discretionary cash flow that can be used for additional investment, retirement of debt, purchase of treasury stock, or addition to liquidity?

Presented on the top of the next page is a free cash flow analysis using the cash flow statement for Nestor Company that was shown in Illustration 5-27 (page 195).

[18]In determining free cash flows, some companies do not subtract dividends because they believe these expenditures to be discretionary.

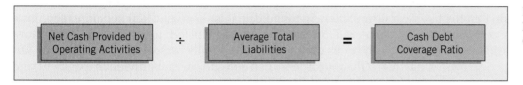

ILLUSTRATION 5-31
Free Cash Flow Computation

NESTOR COMPANY
FREE CASH FLOW ANALYSIS

Net cash provided by operating activities	$411,750
Less: Capital expenditures	(252,500)
Dividends	(19,800)
Free cash flow	$139,450

This analysis shows that Nestor has a positive, and substantial, net cash provided by operating activities of $411,750. Nestor reports on its statement of cash flows that it purchased equipment of $182,500 and land of $70,000 for total capital spending of $252,500. This amount is subtracted from net cash provided by operating activities because without continued efforts to maintain and expand facilities it is unlikely that Nestor can continue to maintain its competitive position. Capital spending is deducted first on the free cash flow statement to indicate it is the least discretionary expenditure a company generally makes. Dividends are then deducted, to arrive at free cash flow. Although a company can cut its dividend, it will usually do so only in a financial emergency. Nestor has more than sufficient cash flow to meet its dividend payment and therefore has satisfactory financial flexibility.

Nestor used its free cash flow to redeem bonds and add to its liquidity. If it finds additional investments that are profitable, it can increase its spending without putting its dividend or basic capital spending in jeopardy. Companies that have strong financial flexibility can take advantage of profitable investments, even in tough times. In addition, strong financial flexibility frees companies from worry about survival in poor economic times. In fact, those with strong financial flexibility often fare better in a poor economy because they can take advantage of opportunities that other companies cannot.

SUMMARY OF LEARNING OBJECTIVES

1 Identify the uses and limitations of a balance sheet. The balance sheet provides information about the nature and amounts of investments in enterprise resources, obligations to creditors, and the owners' equity in net resources. The balance sheet contributes to financial reporting by providing a basis for (1) computing rates of return, (2) evaluating the capital structure of the enterprise, and (3) assessing the liquidity, solvency, and financial flexibility of the enterprise.

The limitations of a balance sheet are: (1) The balance sheet does not reflect current value because accountants have adopted a historical cost basis in valuing and reporting assets and liabilities. (2) Judgments and estimates must be used in preparing a balance sheet. The collectibility of receivables, the salability of inventory, and the useful life of long-term tangible and intangible assets are difficult to determine. (3) The balance sheet omits many items that are of financial value to the business but cannot be recorded objectively, such as human resources, customer base, and reputation.

2 Identify the major classifications of the balance sheet. The general elements of the balance sheet are assets, liabilities, and equity. The major classifications within the balance sheet on the asset side are current assets; long-term investments; property, plant, and equipment; intangible assets; and other assets. The major classifications of liabilities are current and long-term liabilities. In a corporation, owners' equity is generally classified as capital stock, additional paid-in capital, and retained earnings.

KEY TERMS

account form, *182*
adjunct account, *189*
available-for-sale securities, *175*
balance sheet, *170*
cash debt coverage ratio, *197*
contingency, *185*
contra account, *189*
current assets, *173*
current cash debt coverage ratio, *196*
current liabilities, *179*
financial flexibility, *171*
financial instruments, *186*
financing activities, *191*
free cash flow, *197*
held-to-maturity securities, *175*

3 Prepare a classified balance sheet using the report and account formats. The report form lists liabilities and stockholders' equity directly below assets on the same page. The account form lists assets by sections on the left side and liabilities and stockholders' equity by sections on the right side.

4 Identify balance sheet information requiring supplemental disclosure. Four types of information normally are supplemental to account titles and amounts presented in the balance sheet: (1) *Contingencies:* Material events that have an uncertain outcome. (2) *Accounting policies:* Explanations of the valuation methods used or the basic assumptions made concerning inventory valuation, depreciation methods, investments in subsidiaries, etc. (3) *Contractual situations:* Explanations of certain restrictions or covenants attached to specific assets or, more likely, to liabilities. (4) *Fair values*: Disclosures related to fair values, particularly those related to financial instruments.

5 Identify major disclosure techniques for the balance sheet. There are four methods of disclosing pertinent information in the balance sheet: (1) *Parenthetical explanations:* Additional information or description is often provided by parenthetical explanations following the item. (2) *Notes:* Notes are used if additional explanations or descriptions cannot be shown conveniently as parenthetical explanations. (3) *Cross reference and contra items:* A direct relationship between an asset and a liability is "cross referenced" on the balance sheet. (4) *Supporting schedules:* Often a separate schedule is needed to present more detailed information about certain assets or liabilities, because the balance sheet provides just a single summary item.

6 Indicate the purpose of the statement of cash flows. The primary purpose of a statement of cash flows is to provide relevant information about the cash receipts and cash payments of an enterprise during a period. Reporting the sources, uses, and net increase or decrease in cash enables investors, creditors, and others to know what is happening to a company's most liquid resource.

7 Identify the content of the statement of cash flows. Cash receipts and cash payments during a period are classified in the statement of cash flows into three different activities: (1) *Operating activities:* Involve the cash effects of transactions that enter into the determination of net income. (2) *Investing activities:* Include making and collecting loans and acquiring and disposing of investments (both debt and equity) and property, plant, and equipment. (3) *Financing activities:* Involve liability and owners' equity items and include (a) obtaining capital from owners and providing them with a return on their investment and (b) borrowing money from creditors and repaying the amounts borrowed.

8 Prepare a statement of cash flows. The information to prepare the statement of cash flows usually comes from (1) comparative balance sheets, (2) the current income statement, and (3) selected transaction data. Preparing the statement of cash flows from these sources involves the following steps: (1) Determine the cash provided by operations. (2) Determine the cash provided by or used in investing and financing activities. (3) Determine the change (increase or decrease) in cash during the period. (4) Reconcile the change in cash with the beginning and the ending cash balances.

9 Understand the usefulness of the statement of cash flows. Creditors examine the cash flow statement carefully because they are concerned about being paid. The amount and trend of net cash flow provided by operating activities in relation to the company's liabilities is helpful in making this assessment. In addition, measures such as a free cash flow analysis provide creditors and stockholders with a better picture of the company's financial flexibility.

intangible assets, *178*
investing activities, *191*
liquidity, *171*
long-term investments, *177*
long-term liabilities, *181*
operating activities, *191*
owners' (stockholders') equity, *182*
property, plant, and equipment, *178*
report form, *182*
solvency, *171*
statement of cash flows, *190*
trading securities, *175*
working capital, *180*

APPENDIX 5A

Ratio Analysis—A Reference

USING RATIOS TO ANALYZE FINANCIAL PERFORMANCE

OBJECTIVE 10
Identify the major types of financial ratios and what they measure.

Qualitative information from financial statements can be gathered by examining relationships between items on the statements and identifying trends in these relationships. A useful starting point in developing this information is the application of ratio analysis.

A **ratio** expresses the mathematical relationship between one quantity and another. **Ratio analysis** expresses the relationship among selected financial statement data. The relationship is expressed in terms of either a percentage, a rate, or a simple proportion. To illustrate, recently **IBM Corporation** had current assets of $42,461 million and current liabilities of $35,119 million. The relationship is determined by dividing current assets by current liabilities. The alternative means of expression are:

Percentage: Current assets are 121% of current liabilities.
Rate: Current assets are 1.21 times as great as current liabilities.
Proportion: The relationship of current assets to liabilities is 1.21:1.

For analysis of financial statements, ratios can be classified into four types, as follows.

Expanded Discussion of Financial Statement Analysis

MAJOR TYPES OF RATIOS

Liquidity Ratios. Measures of the enterprise's short-run ability to pay its maturing obligations.

Activity Ratios. Measures of how effectively the enterprise is using the assets employed.

Profitability Ratios. Measures of the degree of success or failure of a given enterprise or division for a given period of time.

Coverage Ratios. Measures of the degree of protection for long-term creditors and investors.

In Chapter 5 two ratios related to the statement of cash flows were discussed. Throughout the remainder of the textbook, ratios are provided to help you understand and interpret the information presented. In an appendix to Chapter 24, a discussion of financial statement analysis, of which ratio analysis is one part, is presented. In Illustration 5A-1 are the ratios that will be used throughout the text. You should find this chart helpful as you examine these ratios in more detail in the following chapters.

ILLUSTRATION 5A-1 A Summary of Financial Ratios

Ratio	Formula	Purpose or Use
I. Liquidity		
1. Current ratio	Current assets / Current liabilities	Measures short-term debt-paying ability
2. Quick or acid-test ratio	Cash, marketable securities, and receivables (net) / Current liabilities	Measures immediate short-term liquidity
3. Current cash debt coverage ratio	Net cash provided by operating activities / Average current liabilities	Measures a company's ability to pay off its current liabilities in a given year from its operations
II. Activity		
4. Receivables turnover	Net sales / Average trade receivables (net)	Measures liquidity of receivables
5. Inventory turnover	Cost of goods sold / Average inventory	Measures liquidity of inventory
6. Asset turnover	Net sales / Average total assets	Measures how efficiently assets are used to generate sales
III. Profitability		
7. Profit margin on sales	Net income / Net sales	Measures net income generated by each dollar of sales
8. Rate of return on assets	Net income / Average total assets	Measures overall profitability of assets
9. Rate of return on common stock equity	Net income minus preferred dividends / Average common stockholders' equity	Measures profitability of owners' investment
10. Earnings per share	Net income minus preferred dividends / Weighted shares outstanding	Measures net income earned on each share of common stock
11. Price-earnings ratio	Market price of stock / Earnings per share	Measures the ratio of the market price per share to earnings per share
12. Payout ratio	Cash dividends / Net income	Measures percentage of earnings distributed in the form of cash dividends
IV. Coverage		
13. Debt to total assets	Total debt / Total assets or equities	Measures the percentage of total assets provided by creditors
14. Times interest earned	Income before interest charges and taxes / Interest charges	Measures ability to meet interest payments as they come due
15. Cash debt coverage ratio	Net cash provided by operating activities / Average total liabilities	Measures a company's ability to repay its total liabilities in a given year from its operations
16. Book value per share	Common stockholders' equity / Outstanding shares	Measures the amount each share would receive if the company were liquidated at the amounts reported on the balance sheet

SUMMARY OF LEARNING OBJECTIVE FOR APPENDIX 5A

(10) **Identify the major types of financial ratios and what they measure.** Ratios express the mathematical relationship between one quantity and another, in terms of either a percentage, a rate, or a proportion. Liquidity ratios measure the short-run ability to pay maturing obligations. Activity ratios measure the effectiveness of asset usage. Profitability ratios measure the success or failure of an enterprise. Coverage ratios measure the degree of protection for long-term creditors and investors.

KEY TERMS

activity ratios, *200*
coverage ratios, *200*
liquidity ratios, *200*
profitability ratios, *200*
ratio analysis, *200*

APPENDIX 5B

Specimen Financial Statements: 3M Company

To the Student:

The following pages contain the financial statements, accompanying notes, and other information from the 2001 Annual Report of **3M Company**.[1] 3M Company, formerly known as Minnesota Mining and Manufacturing Company, is an integrated enterprise characterized by substantial intercompany cooperation in research, manufacturing, and marketing of products. 3M's business has developed from its research and technology in coating and bonding for coated abrasives, the company's original product. Coating and bonding is the process of applying one material to another, such as abrasive granules to paper or cloth (coated abrasives), adhesives to a backing (pressure-sensitive tapes), ceramic coating to granular mineral (roofing granules), glass beads to plastic backing (reflective sheeting), and low-tack adhesives to paper (repositionable notes). The company conducts business through six operating segments: Industrial Markets; Transportation, Graphics and Safety Markets; Health Care Markets; Consumer and Office Markets; Electro and Communications Markets; and Specialty Material Markets.

We do not expect that you will comprehend 3M's financial statements and the accompanying notes in their entirety at your first reading. But we expect that by the time you complete the coverage of the material in this text, your level of understanding and interpretive ability will have grown enormously.

At this point we recommend that you take 20 to 30 minutes to scan the statements and notes, to familiarize yourself with the contents and accounting elements. Throughout the following 19 chapters, when you are asked to refer to specific parts of 3M's financials, do so! Then, when you have completed reading this book, we challenge you to reread 3M's financials to see how much greater and more sophisticated is your understanding of them.

3M

[1]The Annual Report of 3M Company can be found on the Take Action! CD. 3M's Management Discussion and Analysis is not shown in this appendix.

FINANCIAL HIGHLIGHTS

YEARS ENDED DECEMBER 31 (DOLLARS IN MILLIONS, EXCEPT PER-SHARE AMOUNTS)	2001	2000	% CHANGE IN U.S. DOLLARS	% CHANGE IN LOCAL CURRENCY
Net sales	**$ 16,079**	$ 16,724	(3.9)%	(.6)%
Operating income	**2,777**	3,081	(9.9)%	(4.2)%
% to sales	**17.3 %**	18.4 %		
Net income	**$ 1,742**	$ 1,872	(6.9)%	(1.9)%
% to sales	**10.8 %**	11.2 %		
Per share – diluted	**$ 4.36**	$ 4.68	(6.8)%	(1.7)%
Cash flows from operations	**3,078**	2,326	32.3 %	
Return on invested capital	**17.3 %**	19.3 %		
Cash dividends per share	**$ 2.40**	$ 2.32	3.4 %	

Operating income, net income and return on invested capital amounts presented above exclude non-recurring items and, therefore, are not in accordance with, or preferable to, amounts determined in conformity with generally accepted accounting principles. Reference should be made to the "Analysis of Financial Condition and Results of Operations" section and the Consolidated Financial Statements included in this report for additional information concerning non-recurring items excluded, and for information on amounts determined in accordance with generally accepted accounting principles. 2001 excludes non-recurring items that reduced net income by $312 million, or 78 cents per diluted share. 2000 excludes non-recurring items that reduced net income by $90 million, or 23 cents per diluted share.

NET SALES

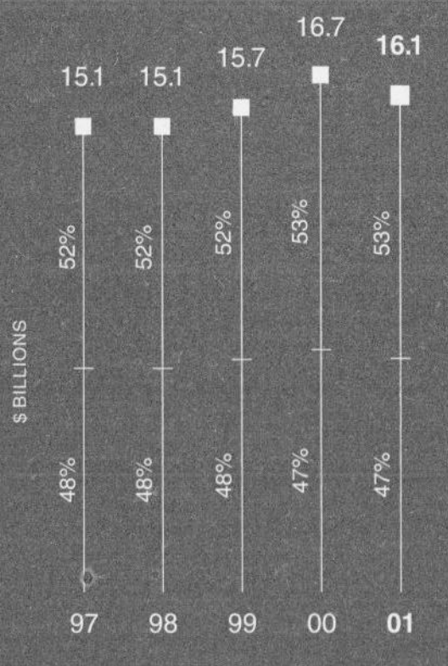

INTL.
U.S.

OPERATING INCOME*

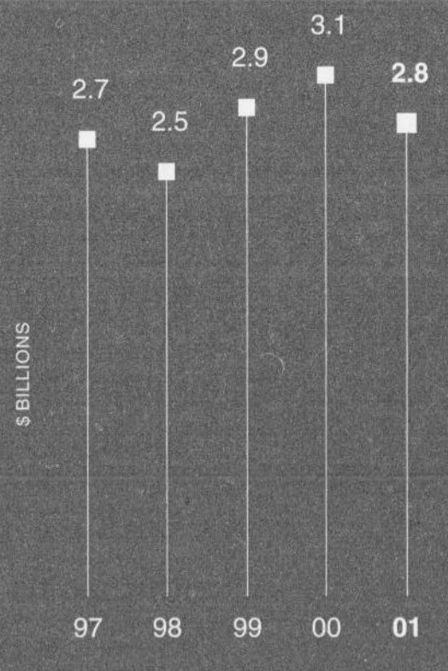

*excluding non-recurring items

DILUTED EARNINGS PER SHARE*

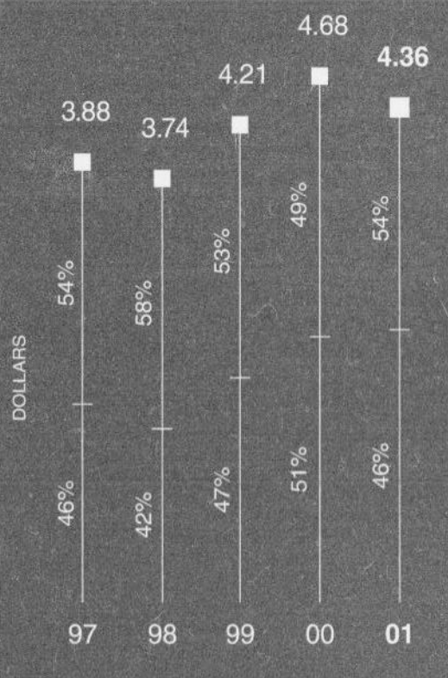

DIVIDENDS
RETAINED EARNINGS

*excluding non-recurring items

W. James McNerney, Jr.
Chairman of the Board and Chief Executive Officer

DEAR SHAREHOLDER:

From the synchronous slowdown in the world's major economies to the shock of September 11 and its profound and prolonged aftermath, 2001 was a year of continuous challenge. It was one of the most difficult years in memory, and the effects were felt in our markets and reflected in our results.

2001 RESULTS

More specifically, sales for the year decreased 3.9 percent, with currency translation accounting for most of that decline.

Earnings per share declined by about 7 percent, to $4.36 per share, excluding non-recurring items.

Despite the pressures on revenues and earnings last year, we reaffirmed both our ability and our commitment to fund our future. We generated an increase in cash flows from operations of more than 30 percent, and we continued to invest in research and development and related expenses at the $1 billion-plus level at a time when many companies reduced their R&D spending.

3M has always confronted periods of extraordinary challenge from a position of fundamental and enduring strength, and our diverse and innovative product base, our market leadership, and our powerful international position stood us in good stead again in 2001.

But 3M also confronts periods of challenge with action. In the first quarter, we addressed the sea change in global volumes by immediately imposing tighter control and discipline in our management of costs and assets. We quickly implemented a strategic global restructuring. And perhaps most importantly, we launched five initiatives to achieve both short-term cost benefits and longer-term increases in operational efficiency and growth. The initiatives were embraced by 3Mers everywhere, and the cost-oriented initiatives – *Sourcing Effectiveness* and *Indirect-Cost Control* – gained early traction and achieved impressive results. Together, the controls, restructuring and initiatives delivered an improvement of about $700 million to the 2001 cost base.

There's much more to 3M's story in 2001 than financial results, and our pride in fighting through a tough year should not be mistaken for satisfaction. While the market and economic outlook for 2002 remains very uncertain, we're confident in our long-term prospects. 3M has tremendous potential and a terrific future.

Today the initiatives are part of our everyday business processes and practices, and we will continue to drive improvement in productivity, efficiency and speed as they become increasingly operational throughout every corner of 3M.

3M PERFORMANCE INITIATIVES

SIX SIGMA

3M ACCELERATION

SOURCING EFFECTIVENESS

ePRODUCTIVITY

INDIRECT-COST CONTROL

CUSTOMER-FOCUSED GROWTH

In 2002, the initiatives will build on a strong employee engagement base to not only continue improvements on costs, but also to focus more strongly on customer service, customer solutions and growth. Examples include:

3M ACCELERATION – In 2001, we prioritized our investments and re-allocated about a third of our R&D investment into high-priority, high-potential projects like immune response modifiers (IRMs), fuel cells, and optical enhancement films for electronic displays. In fact, two of these examples really came to life last year: IRMs as a potential treatment for genital herpes (through a collaboration with Eli Lilly and Company) and new brightness enhancement films used in the fast-growing flat-panel desktop computer monitor and color cell phone display applications.

SIX SIGMA – Our primary and most fundamental initiative, Six Sigma, is improving costs, cash AND growth. In one of our service businesses, Health Information Systems, Six Sigma is advancing growth by increasing the efficiency of our sales force and improving the pricing and proposal process. Similarly, a Six Sigma team in 3M Unitek is working with our sales force and with our customers to successfully commercialize a new and sophisticated line of orthodontic products.

ePRODUCTIVITY – The Web is becoming a new platform for enhancing speed, customer service and customer relationships, while at the same time driving cost out of old processes. For example, by launching a suite of applications that provide online transactional and product support to customers, our Occupational Health and Environmental Safety business is improving speed and productivity for 3M and our customers alike.

In another example, end-users of electronic adhesive products can use our Web tools to specify and order product samples online, enabling them to quickly assess the feasibility of 3M products for their specific applications. Both of these applications drive productivity and growth.

To help bring these growth initiatives together at the customer level, I've established a Sales and Marketing Council to share best practices and promote boundaryless selling among 3M's diverse business units.

LEADERSHIP DEVELOPMENT

No matter how successful our initiatives may be, the future success of 3M is ultimately defined by the energy of our people and the quality of our leadership. In 2001, we fundamentally changed the dynamics of leadership development at 3M.

First, we established what we expect from our leaders and put programs in place to further their development. As part of that effort, the management team defined leadership attributes that will prepare our leaders to win in an increasingly competitive world. Leaders of 3M must chart the course, raise the bar, energize others, resourcefully innovate, live 3M values and deliver results.

Second, we formed the 3M Leadership Development Institute to foster the attainment of those attributes. The institute provides an intense, three-week accelerated development experience for some of our most promising leaders. During this program, participants work to develop real-world solutions to current business problems, all under the guidance of 3M executives.

Third, we're changing the focus of our employee assessment and compensation system to better motivate, reward and recognize our very best contributors.

Fourth, we're making the most of our "global brains"– facilitating the international transfer of knowledge, best practices and people to advance 3M's already powerful international capabilities.

And we're bolstering our very strong talent pool by selectively recruiting proven leaders from outside the company for key functional and business roles.

This renewed focus on leadership development motivates and encourages everyone to reach their full potential. When we raise the game of each individual and every team, we raise the game of the entire company.

3M LEADERSHIP ATTRIBUTES

CHART THE COURSE

RAISE THE BAR

ENERGIZE OTHERS

RESOURCEFULLY INNOVATE

LIVE 3M VALUES

DELIVER RESULTS

RESOLVE AND COMMITMENT

Since joining 3M in January of 2001, I continue to be impressed by the vast technological, market and geographic power of 3M. And I am more committed than ever to transforming those strengths into shareholder value.

We will continue to invest in successful technology platforms. While 3M's unique culture of innovation will always be the springboard for new products, we're infusing that culture with new energy – energy focused on speed, customer solutions and marketplace success. And we're aggressively pursuing multiple avenues for growth – for example, services, acquisitions and international – to complement and leverage 3M's historical organic growth engine.

3M's market leadership is being advanced by the power of our brands and a renewed commitment to communicate our brand promise to customers all around the world.

And by making the necessary capacity enhancements to our international organization, we are better positioned to increase penetration and to speed the delivery of technology, products and services to our customers around the world.

I want to recognize and thank 3M employees everywhere for their continued commitment and contributions to the company.

In particular, I would like to thank board member Ronald O. Baukol, executive vice president, International Operations, who retires from 3M and from the board this year. During his 35 years with 3M, Ron distinguished himself with strong leadership and operational contributions. We greatly appreciate his service.

I'm very proud of the performance of the 3M team in a very challenging 2001. You have my assurance that we will approach our 100th year in 2002 with the same resolve and commitment.

W. James McNerney, Jr.
Chairman of the Board and Chief Executive Officer
February 11, 2002

RESPONSIBILITY FOR FINANCIAL REPORTING

Management is responsible for the integrity and objectivity of the financial information included in this report. The financial statements have been prepared in accordance with accounting principles generally accepted in the United States of America. Where necessary, the financial statements reflect estimates based on management judgment.

Established accounting procedures and related systems of internal control provide reasonable assurance that assets are safeguarded, that the books and records properly reflect all transactions, and that policies and procedures are implemented by qualified personnel. Internal auditors continually review the accounting and control systems.

The Audit Committee, composed of four members of the Board of Directors who are not employees of the company, meets regularly with representatives of management, the independent auditors and the company's internal auditors to monitor the functioning of the accounting control systems and to review the results of the auditing activities. The Audit Committee recommends to the Board independent auditors for appointment, subject to shareholder ratification. The independent auditors have full and free access to the Audit Committee.

The independent auditors conduct an objective, independent audit of the financial statements. Their report appears at the right.

Patrick D. Campbell
Senior Vice President and Chief Financial Officer

REPORT OF INDEPENDENT AUDITORS

TO THE STOCKHOLDERS AND BOARD OF DIRECTORS
OF MINNESOTA MINING AND MANUFACTURING COMPANY:

In our opinion, the accompanying consolidated balance sheet and the related consolidated statements of income, of changes in stockholders' equity and comprehensive income, and of cash flows present fairly, in all material respects, the consolidated financial position of Minnesota Mining and Manufacturing Company and Subsidiaries at December 31, 2001 and 2000, and the consolidated results of their operations and their cash flows for each of the three years in the period ended December 31, 2001, in conformity with accounting principles generally accepted in the United States of America. These financial statements are the responsibility of the company's management; our responsibility is to express an opinion on these financial statements based on our audits. We conducted our audits of these statements in accordance with auditing standards generally accepted in the United States of America, which require that we plan and perform the audit to obtain reasonable assurance about whether the financial statements are free of material misstatement. An audit includes examining, on a test basis, evidence supporting the amounts and disclosures in the financial statements, assessing the accounting principles used and significant estimates made by management, and evaluating the overall financial statement presentation. We believe that our audits provide a reasonable basis for our opinion.

PricewaterhouseCoopers LLP
Minneapolis, Minnesota
February 11, 2002

CONSOLIDATED STATEMENT OF INCOME

MINNESOTA MINING AND MANUFACTURING COMPANY AND SUBSIDIARIES
YEARS ENDED DECEMBER 31

(Amounts in millions, except per-share amounts)	**2001**	2000	1999
Net sales	**$16,079**	$16,724	$15,748
Operating expenses			
Cost of sales	**8,749**	8,787	8,126
Selling, general and administrative expenses	**4,061**	3,963	3,712
Research, development and related expenses	**1,084**	1,101	1,056
Other expense (income)	**(88)**	(185)	(102)
Total	**13,806**	13,666	12,792
Operating income	**2,273**	3,058	2,956
Interest expense and income			
Interest expense	**124**	111	109
Interest income	**(37)**	(27)	(33)
Total	**87**	84	76
Income before income taxes, minority interest and cumulative effect of accounting change	**2,186**	2,974	2,880
Provision for income taxes	**702**	1,025	1,032
Minority interest	**54**	92	85
Income before cumulative effect of accounting change	**1,430**	1,857	1,763
Cumulative effect of accounting change	**—**	(75)	—
Net income	**$ 1,430**	$ 1,782	$ 1,763
Weighted average common shares outstanding – basic	**394.3**	395.7	402.0
Earnings per share – basic			
Income before cumulative effect of accounting change	**$ 3.63**	$ 4.69	$ 4.39
Cumulative effect of accounting change	**—**	(.19)	—
Net income	**$ 3.63**	$ 4.50	$ 4.39
Weighted average common shares outstanding – diluted	**399.9**	399.9	406.5
Earnings per share – diluted			
Income before cumulative effect of accounting change	**$ 3.58**	$ 4.64	$ 4.34
Cumulative effect of accounting change	**—**	(.19)	—
Net income	**$ 3.58**	$ 4.45	$ 4.34

The accompanying Notes to Consolidated Financial Statements are an integral part of this statement.

CONSOLIDATED BALANCE SHEET

MINNESOTA MINING AND MANUFACTURING COMPANY AND SUBSIDIARIES
AT DECEMBER 31

(Dollars in millions)	**2001**	2000
ASSETS		
Current assets		
Cash and cash equivalents	**$ 616**	$ 302
Accounts receivable – net	**2,482**	2,891
Inventories	**2,091**	2,312
Other current assets	**1,107**	874
Total current assets	**6,296**	6,379
Investments	**275**	310
Property, plant and equipment – net	**5,615**	5,823
Other assets	**2,420**	2,010
Total assets	**$14,606**	$14,522
LIABILITIES AND STOCKHOLDERS' EQUITY		
Current liabilities		
Short-term debt	**$ 1,373**	$ 1,866
Accounts payable	**753**	932
Payroll	**539**	382
Income taxes	**596**	462
Other current liabilities	**1,248**	1,112
Total current liabilities	**4,509**	4,754
Long-term debt	**1,520**	971
Other liabilities	**2,491**	2,266
Total liabilities	**8,520**	7,991
Stockholders' equity		
Common stock, par value $.01 per share	**5**	5
Shares outstanding – 2001: 391,303,636		
2000: 396,085,348		
Capital in excess of par value	**291**	291
Retained earnings	**11,914**	11,517
Treasury stock	**(4,633)**	(4,065)
Unearned compensation	**(286)**	(303)
Accumulated other comprehensive income (loss)	**(1,205)**	(914)
Stockholders' equity – net	**6,086**	6,531
Total liabilities and stockholders' equity	**$14,606**	$14,522

The accompanying Notes to Consolidated Financial Statements are an integral part of this statement.

CONSOLIDATED STATEMENT OF CHANGES IN STOCKHOLDERS' EQUITY AND COMPREHENSIVE INCOME

MINNESOTA MINING AND MANUFACTURING COMPANY AND SUBSIDIARIES

(Dollars in millions, except per-share amounts)	Total	Common Stock and Capital in Excess of Par	Retained Earnings	Treasury Stock	Unearned Compensation	Accumulated Other Comprehensive Income (Loss)
Balance at December 31, 1998	$ 5,936	$ 296	$ 9,980	$ (3,482)	$ (350)	$ (508)
Net income	1,763		1,763			
Cumulative translation adjustment – net of $2 million tax benefit	(176)					(176)
Minimum pension liability adjustment – net of $36 million tax benefit	(30)					(30)
Debt and equity securities, unrealized gain – net of $77 million tax provision	126					126
Total comprehensive income	1,683					
Dividends paid ($2.24 per share)	(901)		(901)			
Amortization of unearned compensation	23				23	
Reacquired stock (9.0 million shares)	(825)			(825)		
Issuances pursuant to stock option and benefit plans (5.7 million shares)	373		(101)	474		
Balance at December 31, 1999	$ 6,289	$ 296	$ 10,741	$ (3,833)	$ (327)	$ (588)
Net income	1,782		1,782			
Cumulative translation adjustment – net of $5 million tax provision	(191)					(191)
Minimum pension liability adjustment – net of $37 million tax benefit	(28)					(28)
Debt and equity securities, unrealized loss – net of $65 million tax benefit	(107)					(107)
Total comprehensive income	1,456					
Dividends paid ($2.32 per share)	(918)		(918)			
Amortization of unearned compensation	24				24	
Reacquired stock (9.1 million shares)	(814)			(814)		
Issuances pursuant to stock option and benefit plans (6.3 million shares)	483		(88)	571		
Issuances pursuant to acquisitions (129 thousand shares)	11			11		
Balance at December 31, 2000	$ 6,531	$ 296	$ 11,517	$ (4,065)	$ (303)	$ (914)
Net income	**1,430**		**1,430**			
Cumulative translation adjustment – net of $14 million tax provision	**(267)**					**(267)**
Minimum pension liability adjustment – net of $15 million tax benefit	**(16)**					**(16)**
Debt and equity securities, unrealized loss – net of $11 million tax benefit	**(17)**					**(17)**
Derivative financial instruments – unrealized gain – net of $5 million tax provision	**9**					**9**
Total comprehensive income	**1,139**					
Dividends paid ($2.40 per share)	**(948)**		**(948)**			
Amortization of unearned compensation	**17**				**17**	
Reacquired stock (12.0 million shares)	**(1,322)**			**(1,322)**		
Issuances pursuant to stock option and benefit plans (6.1 million shares)	**543**		**(85)**	**628**		
Issuances pursuant to acquisitions, net of returns of $1 million from escrow (net 1.1 million shares issued)	**126**			**126**		
Balance at December 31, 2001	**$ 6,086**	**$ 296**	**$ 11,914**	**$ (4,633)**	**$ (286)**	**$ (1,205)**

The accompanying Notes to Consolidated Financial Statements are an integral part of this statement.

CONSOLIDATED STATEMENT OF CASH FLOWS

MINNESOTA MINING AND MANUFACTURING COMPANY AND SUBSIDIARIES
YEARS ENDED DECEMBER 31

(Dollars in millions)	**2001**	2000	1999
CASH FLOWS FROM OPERATING ACTIVITIES			
Net income	**$ 1,430**	$ 1,782	$ 1,763
Adjustments to reconcile net income to net cash provided by operating activities			
Depreciation and amortization	**1,089**	1,025	900
Deferred income tax provision	**1**	89	95
Changes in assets and liabilities			
Accounts receivable	**345**	(171)	(186)
Inventories	**194**	(261)	96
Other current assets	**(97)**	(69)	(11)
Other assets – net of amortization	**(13)**	(145)	119
Income taxes payable	**148**	27	196
Accounts payable and other current liabilities	**(62)**	65	(63)
Other liabilities	**(27)**	(92)	173
Other – net	**70**	76	(1)
Net cash provided by operating activities	**3,078**	2,326	3,081
CASH FLOWS FROM INVESTING ACTIVITIES			
Purchases of property, plant and equipment	**(980)**	(1,115)	(1,050)
Proceeds from sale of property, plant and equipment	**102**	104	108
Acquisitions of businesses	**(218)**	(472)	(374)
Proceeds from sale of businesses	**11**	1	249
Purchases of investments	**(12)**	(12)	(56)
Proceeds from sale of investments	**47**	121	9
Net cash used in investing activities	**(1,050)**	(1,373)	(1,114)
CASH FLOWS FROM FINANCING ACTIVITIES			
Change in short-term debt – net	**(20)**	(236)	(164)
Repayment of debt (maturities greater than 90 days)	**(1,564)**	(23)	(179)
Proceeds from debt (maturities greater than 90 days)	**1,693**	495	2
Purchases of treasury stock	**(1,322)**	(814)	(825)
Reissuances of treasury stock	**462**	425	347
Dividends paid to stockholders	**(948)**	(918)	(901)
Distributions to minority interests	**(17)**	(60)	(51)
Net cash used in financing activities	**(1,716)**	(1,131)	(1,771)
Effect of exchange rate changes on cash	**2**	93	(20)
Net increase (decrease) in cash and cash equivalents	**314**	(85)	176
Cash and cash equivalents at beginning of year	**302**	387	211
Cash and cash equivalents at end of year	**$ 616**	$ 302	$ 387

The accompanying Notes to Consolidated Financial Statements are an integral part of this statement.

NOTES TO CONSOLIDATED FINANCIAL STATEMENTS

NOTE 1 SIGNIFICANT ACCOUNTING POLICIES

CONSOLIDATION: All significant subsidiaries are consolidated. All significant intercompany transactions are eliminated. As used herein, the term "3M" or "company" refers to Minnesota Mining and Manufacturing Company and subsidiaries unless the context indicates otherwise.

FOREIGN CURRENCY TRANSLATION: Local currencies generally are considered the functional currencies outside the United States, except in countries treated as highly inflationary. Assets and liabilities for operations in local-currency environments are translated at year-end exchange rates. Income and expense items are translated at average rates of exchange prevailing during the year. Cumulative translation adjustments are recorded as a component of accumulated other comprehensive income in stockholders' equity.

For operations in countries treated as highly inflationary, certain financial statement amounts are translated at historical exchange rates, with all other assets and liabilities translated at year-end exchange rates. These translation adjustments are reflected in income and are not material.

RECLASSIFICATIONS: Certain prior period balance sheet amounts have been reclassified to conform with the current-year presentation.

USE OF ESTIMATES: The preparation of financial statements in conformity with U.S. generally accepted accounting principles requires management to make estimates and assumptions that affect the reported amounts of assets and liabilities and the disclosure of contingent assets and liabilities at the date of the financial statements, and the reported amounts of revenues and expenses during the reporting period. Actual results could differ from these estimates.

CASH AND CASH EQUIVALENTS: Cash and cash equivalents consist of cash and temporary investments with maturities of three months or less when purchased.

INVESTMENTS: Investments primarily include the cash surrender value of life insurance policies and real estate and venture capital investments. Unrealized gains and losses relating to investments classified as available-for-sale are recorded as a component of accumulated other comprehensive income in stockholders' equity.

INVENTORIES: Inventories are stated at lower of cost or market, with cost generally determined on a first-in, first-out basis.

PROPERTY, PLANT AND EQUIPMENT: Property, plant and equipment are recorded at cost, including capitalized interest and internal engineering cost. Depreciation of property, plant and equipment generally is computed using the straight-line method based on estimated useful lives of the assets. Buildings and improvements estimated useful lives primarily range from 10 to 40 years, with the majority in the 20- to 40-year range. Machinery and equipment estimated useful lives primarily range from 3 to 15 years, with the majority in the 5- to 10-year range. Fully depreciated assets are retained in property and accumulated depreciation accounts until removed from service. Upon disposal, assets and related accumulated depreciation are removed from the accounts and the net amount, less proceeds from disposal, is charged or credited to operations.

OTHER ASSETS: Goodwill is amortized on a straight-line basis over the periods benefited, ranging from 5 to 40 years. Other intangible assets are amortized on a straight-line basis over their estimated economic lives. Refer to "New Accounting Pronouncements" that follows for information about the cessation of goodwill and other indefinite-lived intangible asset amortization effective January 1, 2002.

IMPAIRMENT OF LONG-LIVED ASSETS: Long-lived assets, including identifiable intangibles and goodwill, are reviewed for impairment whenever events or changes in circumstances indicate that the carrying amount of an asset may not be recoverable. An impairment loss would be recognized when the carrying amount of an asset exceeds the estimated undiscounted future cash flows expected to result from the use of the asset and its eventual disposition. The amount of the impairment loss to be recorded is calculated by the excess of the assets carrying value over its fair value. Fair value is determined using a discounted cash flow analysis.

REVENUE RECOGNITION: Revenue is recognized when the risks and rewards of ownership have substantively transferred to customers, regardless of whether legal title has transferred. This condition is normally met when the product has been delivered or upon performance of services. The company sells a wide range of products to a diversified base of customers around the world and, therefore, believes there is no material concentration of credit risk. Prior to 2000, the company recognized revenue upon shipment of goods to customers and upon performance of services (refer to Note 2 on page 40).

ADVERTISING AND MERCHANDISING: These costs are charged to operations in the year incurred.

INTERNAL-USE SOFTWARE: The company capitalizes direct costs of materials and services used in the development of internal-use software. Amounts capitalized are amortized on a straight-line basis over a period of 3 to 5 years and are reported as a component of machinery and equipment within property, plant and equipment.

ENVIRONMENTAL: Environmental expenditures relating to existing conditions caused by past operations that do not contribute to current or future revenues are expensed. Liabilities for remediation costs are recorded on an undiscounted basis when they are probable and reasonably estimable, generally no later than the completion of feasibility studies or the company's commitment to a plan of action.

ACCOUNTING FOR STOCK-BASED COMPENSATION: The company uses the intrinsic value method for its Management Stock Ownership Program (MSOP). The General Employees' Stock Purchase Plan is considered non-compensatory.

COMPREHENSIVE INCOME: Total comprehensive income and the components of accumulated other comprehensive income are presented in the Consolidated Statement of Changes in Stockholders' Equity and Comprehensive Income. Accumulated other comprehensive income is composed of foreign currency translation effects (including hedges of net investments in international companies), minimum pension liability adjustments, unrealized gains and losses on available-for-sale debt and equity securities, and unrealized gains and losses on cash flow hedging instruments.

EARNINGS PER SHARE: The difference in the weighted average shares outstanding for calculating basic and diluted earnings per share is attributable to the dilution associated with the company's stock-based compensation plans.

DERIVATIVES AND HEDGING ACTIVITIES: Effective January 1, 2001, the company adopted Statement of Financial Accounting Standards (SFAS) No. 133, "Accounting for Derivative Instruments and Hedging Activities," as amended by SFAS No. 138. This new accounting standard requires that all derivative instruments be recorded on the balance sheet at fair value and establishes criteria for designation and effectiveness of hedging relationships. The effect of adopting this standard was not material to the company's consolidated financial statements.

The company uses interest rate swaps, currency swaps, and forward and option contracts to manage risks generally associated with foreign exchange rate, interest rate and commodity market volatility. All hedging instruments are designated and effective as hedges, in accordance with U.S. generally accepted accounting principles. If the underlying hedged transaction ceases to exist, all changes in fair value of the related derivatives that have not been settled are recognized in current earnings. Instruments that do not qualify for hedge accounting are marked to market with changes recognized in current earnings. The company does not hold or issue derivative financial instruments for trading purposes and is not a party to leveraged derivatives.

NEW ACCOUNTING PRONOUNCEMENTS: In June 2001, the Financial Accounting Standards Board issued SFAS No. 141, "Business Combinations," and No. 142, "Goodwill and Other Intangible Assets." The most significant changes made by SFAS No. 141 are: 1) requiring that the purchase method of accounting be used for all business combinations initiated after June 30, 2001, and 2) establishing specific criteria for the recognition of intangible assets separately from goodwill.

SFAS No. 142 primarily addresses the accounting for acquired goodwill and intangible assets (i.e., the post-acquisition accounting). The provisions of SFAS No. 142 will be effective for fiscal years beginning after December 15, 2001. The most significant changes made by SFAS No. 142 are: 1) goodwill and indefinite-lived intangible assets will no longer be amortized; 2) goodwill and indefinite-lived intangible assets will be tested for impairment at least annually (a preliminary review indicated that no impairment existed at December 31, 2001); and 3) the amortization period of intangible assets with finite lives will no longer be limited to 40 years.

SFAS No. 141 applies to all business combinations with a closing date after June 30, 2001. SFAS No. 142 will be adopted effective January 1, 2002. Goodwill and intangible assets acquired after June 30, 2001, are subject immediately to the non-amortization and amortization provisions of this statement. These standards permit only prospective application of the new accounting; accordingly, adoption of these standards will not affect previously reported 3M financial information. The principal effect of SFAS No. 142 will be the elimination of goodwill amortization. Amortization of goodwill and indefinite-lived intangible assets in 2001 was $67 million (net income impact of $51 million, or 12 cents per diluted share).

In June 2001, the Financial Accounting Standards Board also issued Statement of Financial Accounting Standards (SFAS) No. 143, "Accounting for Asset Retirement Obligations," which must be adopted no later than January 1, 2003. This statement establishes accounting standards for recognition and measurement of a liability for an asset retirement obligation and the associated asset retirement cost. The company is reviewing the requirements of this standard. Although the company expects that this standard will not materially affect its financial position or results of operations, it has not yet finalized its determination of the impact of this standard on its consolidated financial statements.

In August 2001, the Financial Accounting Standards Board issued SFAS No. 144, "Accounting for the Impairment or Disposal of Long-Lived Assets," which will be adopted by the company on January 1, 2002. The company does not expect this standard to have a material impact on its consolidated financial statements. This standard broadens the presentation of discontinued operations to include more disposal transactions, thus the recognition of discontinued operations is expected to become more common under this new standard.

The company will adopt Emerging Issues Task Force Issue No. 00-25, "Vendor Income Statement Characterization of Consideration Paid to a Reseller of the Vendor's Products," effective January 1, 2002. This statement addresses whether certain consideration from a vendor to a reseller of the vendor's products is an adjustment to selling prices or a cost. It is estimated that this statement will result in Consumer and Office segment annual net sales and advertising cost (included in selling, general and administrative expenses) being reduced by approximately $25 million annually for years 1999 through 2001. This statement will have no effect on the company's net income or its financial position.

NOTE 2 CUMULATIVE EFFECT OF ACCOUNTING CHANGE

During the fourth quarter of 2000, the company changed its revenue recognition policies. Essentially, the new policies recognize that the risks and rewards of ownership in many transactions do not substantively transfer to customers until the product has been delivered, regardless of whether legal title has transferred. In addition to this change in accounting that affected a substantial portion of its product sales, the company has revised aspects of its accounting for services provided in several of its smaller businesses. These new policies are consistent with the guidance contained in SEC Staff Accounting Bulletin No. 101. The effect of these changes in revenue recognition policies, as of January 1, 2000, is reported as the cumulative effect of an accounting change in 2000. This change did not have a significant effect on previously reported 2000 quarters or on prior years.

NOTE 3 RESTRUCTURING CHARGES AND OTHER NON-RECURRING ITEMS

During the first half of 2001, the company developed and announced a restructuring plan that consolidates certain operations and streamlines the organization to increase speed and productivity. In June 2001, the company completed the identification of all significant actions to be taken and obtained final approvals from the appropriate level of management. In the fourth quarter of 2001, the company obtained approvals for certain additional actions. In 2001, the company recorded charges of $569 million ($353 million after tax and minority interest), principally related to the restructuring plan. These charges were classified as a component of cost of sales ($249 million); selling, general and administrative expenses ($300 million); and research, development and related expenses ($20 million). Of the total charges, $472 million related to employee severance and benefits, $80 million related to accelerated depreciation (incremental charges resulting from shortened depreciable lives, primarily related to downsizing or consolidating manufacturing operations), and $17 million related to other exit activities.

The accelerated depreciation (related to assets included in property, plant and equipment) primarily involved specialized 3M manufacturing machinery and equipment. Estimated salvage values were based on estimates of proceeds upon sale of certain affected assets. The charges related to other exit activities include incremental costs and contractual obligations for items such as lease termination payments and other facility exit costs incurred as a direct result of this plan.

In connection with its restructuring plan, the company expects to eliminate a total of about 6,000 positions, with most of these reductions occurring by June 30, 2002. Through December 31, 2001, the company had eliminated about 3,500 positions. These positions represent a wide range of functions throughout the company. Of the 6,000 employment reduction for the total plan, about 40 percent will occur in the United States, 35 percent in Europe, and the balance in other international areas. All business segments will be impacted directly and also indirectly through reduced allocations of corporate staff service costs. Employee severance and benefit charges totaling $472 million were taken during 2001. These charges were taken in the quarter when management approved the plans and after severance benefits had been communicated to the employees.

Of the company's remaining current liability at December 31, 2001, $185 million is classified in current liabilities (payroll) and $13 million is classified in other current liabilities on the Consolidated Balance Sheet. The company classified $124 million of the current year's charges as long-term liabilities. Special termination pension and medical benefits, aggregating $62 million, were offered to eligible employees. These benefits will generally be paid over their life expectancies. In addition, the company estimates that $62 million of deferred separation pay will be paid in 2003 and beyond. The company also recorded $8 million of non-cash stock option expense due to the reclassification of certain employees age 50 and older to retiree status, resulting in a modification of their original stock option awards for accounting purposes. The current liabilities and a portion of the non-current liabilities will be funded through cash provided by operations, with additional funding for non-current liabilities provided through established pension and postretirement trust funds.

The restructuring plan includes actions in 25 locations in the United States, 27 in Europe, eight in the Asia Pacific area, 13 in Latin America, and four in Canada. Substantially all actions required by the plan are expected to be completed by June 30, 2002. The company has not discontinued any major product lines as a result of the restructuring plan. The restructuring charges do not include any write-down of goodwill or other intangible assets.

Selected information related to these 2001 charges follows.

(Millions)	Employee Severance and Benefits	Accelerated Depreciation	Other	Total
2001 charges				
Second quarter	$ 386	$—	$ 11	$ 397
Third quarter	27	39	3	69
Fourth quarter	59	41	3	103
Total charges	$ 472	$ 80	$ 17	$ 569
Cash payments	(155)		(4)	(159)
Non-cash	(8)	(80)	—	(88)
Long-term portion of liability	(124)		—	(124)
Current liability at December 31, 2001	$ 185		$ 13	$ 198

Selected information related to the company's 1998 restructuring program follows.

(Millions)	Employee Severance and Benefits	Write-down of Property, Plant and Equipment	Other	Total
1998 charges	$ 271	$ 143	$ 79	$ 493
1999 changes in estimates	4	(31)	(1)	(28)
Total charges	$ 275	$ 112	$ 78	$ 465
December 31, 1998 liability	$ 232		$ 32	$ 264
1999 cash payments	(205)		(23)	(228)
1999 changes in estimates	4		(1)	3
December 31, 1999 liability	$ 31		$ 8	$ 39
2000 cash payments	(24)		(4)	(28)
December 31, 2000 liability	$ 7		$ 4	$ 11
2001 cash payments	(3)		(2)	(5)
December 31, 2001 liability	$ 4		$ 2	$ 6

NOTE 4 ACQUISITIONS AND DIVESTITURES

GENERAL: In 2001, 2000 and 1999, all business combinations completed by the company used the purchase method of accounting. Effective January 1, 2002, with the adoption of SFAS No. 142, goodwill and indefinite-lived intangibles will no longer be amortized.

YEAR 2001 ACQUISITIONS: In 2001, the company completed three notable business combinations, all in the first quarter of the year. 3M acquired MicroTouch Systems, Inc., a touch screen manufacturer, for $158 million in cash, net of cash acquired. 3M also acquired Robinson Nugent, Inc., a telecommunications supplier, in exchange for 1,124,135 shares of 3M common stock that had a fair market value of $127 million as of the acquisition date. 3M also combined its German dental business (3M Inter-Unitek GmbH, an existing 3M subsidiary) with ESPE Dental AG, a dental products manufacturer. 3M Inter-Unitek GmbH acquired 100 percent of the outstanding shares of ESPE Dental AG in exchange for 43 percent ownership in 3M Inter-Unitek and $25 million, net of cash acquired. Upon completion of this transaction, 3M holds a 57 percent controlling interest in 3M Inter-Unitek GmbH and consolidates it with a provision for the minority interest that does not have participating rights. 3M entered into put/call option agreements with former shareholders of ESPE Dental AG. Under the put agreements, 3M would be required to purchase the 43 percent minority interest in 3M Inter-Unitek GmbH from former shareholders of ESPE Dental AG for cash of approximately $266 million. These put options became exercisable on the acquisition date and expire on January 10, 2003. The call options, if exercised, would require the minority shareholders to sell their 3M Inter-Unitek GmbH shares to 3M, based upon a formula set forth in the agreement. These call options become exercisable on December 20, 2003, and expire on June 30, 2004.

The 2001 purchased intangible assets, including goodwill, through December 31, 2001, are being amortized on a straight-line basis over the periods benefited, ranging from 4 to 40 years. In-process research and development charges associated with these acquisitions were not material. Pro forma information related to these acquisitions is not provided because the impact of these acquisitions on the company's consolidated results of operations is not considered to be significant.

CONSOLIDATED BALANCE SHEET PURCHASE PRICE ALLOCATIONS: The purchase price allocations and the resulting impact on the Consolidated Balance Sheet relating to all 2001 business combinations, including five small acquisitions not discussed previously, are summarized in the following table. The impact on the Consolidated Balance Sheet for 2000 and 1999 acquisitions (discussed later) are also summarized in the table that follows.

ASSET (LIABILITY)

(Millions)	2001	2000	1999
Accounts receivable	**$ 67**	$ 86	$ 5
Inventories	**64**	112	8
Other current assets	**19**	13	6
Property, plant and equipment	**110**	179	14
Purchased intangible assets	**473**	326	254
Other assets	**23**	30	15
Accounts payable and other current liabilities	**(138)**	(93)	—
Interest-bearing debt	**(16)**	(123)	—
Minority interest liability	**(243)**	—	72
Other long-term liabilities	**(14)**	(47)	—
Net assets acquired	**$ 345**	$ 483	$ 374
Cash, net of cash acquired	**$ 218**	$ 472	$ 374
Non-cash (3M shares at fair value)	**127**	11	—
Net assets acquired	**$ 345**	$ 483	$ 374

YEAR 2000 ACQUISITIONS: During 2000, 3M acquired 91 percent (subsequently increased to 93 percent), of Quante AG (a telecommunications supplier), 100 percent of the multi-layer integrated circuit packaging line of W. L. Gore and Associates, and seven smaller businesses for a total purchase price of $472 million in cash (net of cash acquired) plus 128,994 shares of 3M common stock. The stock had a fair market value of $11 million at the acquisition date and was previously held as 3M treasury stock.

The 2000 purchased intangible assets, including goodwill, through December 31, 2001, are being amortized on a straight-line basis over the periods benefited, ranging from 3 to 20 years. In-process research and development charges associated with these acquisitions were not significant. Pro forma information related to these acquisitions is not included because the impact of these acquisitions on the company's consolidated results of operations is not considered to be significant.

YEAR 1999 ACQUISITIONS: During 1999, 3M had one notable acquisition and acquired seven smaller businesses. In December 1999, 3M finalized the acquisition of the outstanding 46 percent minority interest in Dyneon LLC from Celanese AG for approximately $340 million in cash, primarily financed by debt. The purchase price exceeded the fair value of the minority interest net assets by approximately $267 million, of which approximately $242 million represented goodwill and other intangible assets that are being amortized over 20 years or less. If these acquisitions had occurred at the beginning of 1999, the effect on consolidated results of operations would not have been significant.

YEAR 1999 DIVESTITURES: On June 30, 1999, the company closed the sale of Eastern Heights Bank, a subsidiary banking operation, and the sale of the assets of its cardiovascular systems business. These divestitures generated cash proceeds of $203 million and resulted in a pre-tax gain of $118 million ($69 million after tax) in the second quarter of 1999. 3M also recorded a pre-tax gain of $32 million ($20 million after tax) related to divestitures, mainly in the Health Care segment, in the third quarter of 1999. These pre-tax gains are recorded in the other expense (income) line within operating income. The primary impact of these divestitures on the 1999 Consolidated Balance Sheet was to reduce investments by about $350 million and decrease current and other liabilities by a similar amount.

NOTE 5 SUPPLEMENTAL STATEMENT OF INCOME INFORMATION

(Millions)	2001	2000	1999
Research, development and related expenses	**$1,084**	$1,101	$1,056
Advertising and merchandising costs	**432**	544	484

Research and development expenses, covering basic scientific research and the application of scientific advances to the development of new and improved products and their uses, totaled $745 million, $727 million and $688 million in 2001, 2000 and 1999, respectively. Related expenses primarily include technical support provided by the laboratories for existing products.

NOTE 6 SUPPLEMENTAL BALANCE SHEET INFORMATION

(Millions)	2001	2000
ACCOUNTS RECEIVABLE		
Accounts receivable	**$ 2,569**	$ 2,975
Less allowances	**87**	84
Accounts receivable – net	**$ 2,482**	$ 2,891
INVENTORIES		
Finished goods	**$ 1,103**	$ 1,231
Work in process	**611**	663
Raw materials	**377**	418
Total inventories	**$ 2,091**	$ 2,312
OTHER CURRENT ASSETS		
Product and other insurance receivables	**$ 304**	$ 267
Deferred income taxes	**290**	152
Other	**513**	455
Total other current assets	**$ 1,107**	$ 874
INVESTMENTS		
Available-for-sale (fair value)	**$ 37**	$ 72
Other (cost, which approximates fair value)	**238**	238
Total investments	**$ 275**	$ 310
PROPERTY, PLANT AND EQUIPMENT – AT COST		
Land	**$ 224**	$ 249
Buildings and leasehold improvements	**3,510**	3,477
Machinery and equipment	**10,208**	9,958
Construction in progress	**423**	486
	14,365	14,170
Less accumulated depreciation	**8,750**	8,347
Property, plant and equipment – net	**$ 5,615**	$ 5,823
OTHER ASSETS		
Goodwill	**$ 984**	$ 647
Patents	**141**	141
Tradenames	**52**	34
Other intangible assets	**36**	35
Prepaid pension benefits	**537**	412
Product and other insurance receivables	**481**	566
Deferred income taxes	**152**	143
Other	**37**	32
Total other assets	**$ 2,420**	$ 2,010

SUPPLEMENTAL BALANCE SHEET INFORMATION (continued)

(Millions)	2001	2000
OTHER CURRENT LIABILITIES		
Employee benefits and withholdings	**$ 295**	$ 237
Accrued trade payables	**267**	277
Deferred income	**188**	132
Property and other taxes	**153**	137
Product and other claims	**119**	107
Deferred income taxes	**16**	8
Other	**210**	214
Total other current liabilities	**$ 1,248**	$ 1,112
OTHER LIABILITIES		
Non-funded pension and postretirement benefits	**$ 633**	$ 754
Minority interest in subsidiaries	**527**	346
Deferred income taxes	**469**	362
Employee benefits	**355**	289
Product and other claims	**335**	339
Deferred income	**94**	12
Other	**78**	164
Total other liabilities	**$ 2,491**	$ 2,266

At December 31, 2001 and 2000, respectively, product and other insurance receivables (current and long-term) included $406 million and $519 million related to the breast implant matter, $223 million and $155 million related to respirator/mask/asbestos litigation, and $156 million and $159 million of other insurance receivables. Although at December 31, 2001, receivables for insurance recoveries related to the breast implant matter of $324 million continued to be contested by insurance carriers, management, based on the opinion of counsel, believes such amounts will ultimately be collected. Accounts payable included drafts payable on demand of $83 million at December 31, 2001, and $109 million at December 31, 2000.

NOTE 7 SUPPLEMENTAL STOCKHOLDERS' EQUITY AND COMPREHENSIVE INCOME INFORMATION

Common stock ($.01 par value per share; $.50 par value at December 31, 1999) of 1.5 billion shares is authorized (1 billion shares at December 31, 1999), with 472,016,528 shares issued in 2001, 2000 and 1999. Common stock and capital in excess of par includes $231 million transferred from common stock to capital in excess of par value during 2000 in connection with the change in par value of the company's common stock from $.50 to $.01 per share. Preferred stock, without par value, of 10 million shares is authorized but unissued.

The following table shows the ending balances of the components of accumulated other comprehensive income (loss).

ACCUMULATED OTHER COMPREHENSIVE INCOME (LOSS)

(Millions)	2001	2000	1999
Cumulative translation – net	**$ (1,152)**	$ (885)	$ (694)
Minimum pension liability adjustments – net	**(74)**	(58)	(30)
Debt and equity securities, unrealized gain – net	**12**	29	136
Cash flow hedging instruments, unrealized gain – net	**9**	—	—
Total accumulated other comprehensive income (loss)	**$ (1,205)**	$ (914)	$ (588)

Reclassification adjustments are made to avoid double counting in comprehensive income items that are also displayed as part of net income. A summary of these reclassification adjustments follows.

RECLASSIFICATION ADJUSTMENTS TO COMPREHENSIVE INCOME

(Millions)	2001	2000	1999
Gains on sale or donation of equity securities, net of tax provision of $9 million, $39 million and $16 million, respectively, for 2001, 2000 and 1999	**$ 14**	$ 62	$ 25
Write-down of equity securities, net of tax benefit of $3 million	**(5)**	—	—
Cash flow hedging instruments, gains, net of tax provision of $8 million	**$ 13**	—	—

In 1999, the equity security gains related to appreciated equity securities donated to the 3M Foundation. In 2001, 2000 and 1999, other reclassification adjustments were not material. No tax provision has been made for the translation of foreign currency financial statements into U.S. dollars.

NOTE 8 SUPPLEMENTAL CASH FLOW INFORMATION

(Millions)	2001	2000	1999
Cash income tax payments	**$ 520**	$ 852	$ 653
Cash interest payments	**137**	104	114
Capitalized interest	**26**	31	26
Depreciation	**916**	915	822
Amortization of software	**74**	45	39
Amortization of goodwill and indefinite-lived tradenames	**67**	44	24
Amortization of patents and other identifiable intangibles	**32**	21	15

Individual amounts on the Consolidated Statement of Cash Flows exclude the effects of acquisitions, divestitures and exchange rate impacts, which are presented separately. In 2000, the net impact of the cumulative effect of accounting changes is recorded in "Other – net" within operating activities.

Non-cash transactions occurring during 2001 included:

- 3M acquired Robinson Nugent, Inc. in exchange for shares of 3M common stock that had a fair market value of $127 million.
- The company exchanged 43 percent ownership in 3M Inter-Unitek GmbH, previously a wholly owned subsidiary, for 87 percent of ESPE Dental AG. The value of this transaction is estimated at approximately $245 million.
- Dividends declared, but not paid at December 31, 2001, of $40 million were payable to minority interests in consolidated subsidiaries.

In 1999, 3M exchanged assets used in the business, but not held for sale, with a fair market value of $61 million plus cash of $12 million, for similar assets having a fair market value of $73 million. No gain was recognized on this non-monetary exchange of productive assets. Also in 1999, 3M donated to the 3M Foundation appreciated equity securities with a market value of $66 million, resulting in $8 million of pre-tax expense, which represented the company's cost of the securities.

NOTE 9 DEBT

SHORT-TERM DEBT

(Millions)	Effective Interest Rate*	2001	2000
U.S. dollar commercial paper	2.60%	**$ 731**	$ 655
Non-U.S. dollar commercial paper	3.92%	**145**	—
5.6523% dealer remarketable securities	5.65%	**350**	352
Long-term debt – current portion	8.94%	**5**	616
Long-term debt – current portion – ESOP debt guarantee	5.62%	**32**	30
Other borrowings	7.25%	**110**	213
Total short-term debt		**$ 1,373**	$ 1,866

*Reflects the effects of interest rate and currency swaps at December 31.

LONG-TERM DEBT

(Millions)	Currency/ Fixed vs. Floating	Effective Interest Rate*	Maturity Date	2001	2000
U.S. dollar (USD)					
6.375% note	USD Fixed	6.38%	2028	**$ 330**	$330
ESOP debt guarantee	USD Fixed	5.62%	2003-2009	**271**	303
4.25% medium-term note	USD Floating	1.76%	2004	**200**	—
4.90% medium-term note	USD Floating	1.87%	2004	**150**	—
Japanese Yen (JPY)					
1% eurobond	JPY Fixed	1.00%	2003	**122**	139
4.57% medium-term note	USD Fixed	4.57%	2003	**100**	—
Dec. 2041 floating rate note	USD Floating	1.67%	2041	**100**	—
Sumitomo 3M Limited					
0.795% note	JPY Fixed	0.80%	2003	**76**	87
Other borrowings	Various	2.25%	2003-2040	**171**	112
Total long-term debt				**$1,520**	$971

WEIGHTED-AVERAGE EFFECTIVE INTEREST RATE*

At December 31	Total 2001	Total 2000	Excluding ESOP debt 2001	Excluding ESOP debt 2000
Short-term	**3.98%**	6.29%	**3.94%**	6.30%
Long-term	**3.60%**	4.84%	**3.15%**	4.48%

*Reflects the effects of interest rate and currency swaps at December 31.

In December 2001, the company's dealer remarketable securities were remarketed for one year. They were reissued with a fixed coupon rate of 5.6523 percent. The remarketable securities can be remarketed annually, at the option of the dealer, for a year each time, with a final maturity date of December 2010.

In October 2000, the company filed a shelf registration with the Securities and Exchange Commission relating to the potential offering of debt securities of up to $1.5 billion. After the shelf registration became effective, the company in May 2001 established under the shelf a medium-term notes program through which up to $1.4 billion of medium-term notes may be offered. As of December 31, 2001, $550 million of medium-term notes had been issued under the medium-term notes program and another $56 million of debt securities had been issued directly from the shelf, aggregating $606 million of debt securities offered for 2001 under the shelf.

The ESOP debt is serviced by dividends on stock held by the ESOP and by company contributions. These contributions are not reported as interest expense, but are reported as an employee benefit expense in the Consolidated Statement of Income. Other borrowings include debt held by 3M's international companies, and floating rate notes and industrial bond issues in the United States, with the long-term portion of this debt primarily comprised of U.S. dollar floating rate debt.

Maturities of long-term debt for the next five years are: 2002, $37 million; 2003, $331 million; 2004, $385 million; 2005, $37 million; and 2006, $39 million.

At year-end 2001, short-term lines of credit totaled about $658 million, of which $59 million was outstanding. An additional letter of credit of $266 million is dedicated to the reacquisition of 3M Inter-Unitek shares issued in connection with the ESPE Dental AG business combination, with the shares subject to put options exercisable by former shareholders of ESPE Dental AG from the date of acquisition until January 10, 2003. The company also has uncommitted lines of credit totaling $125 million. Debt covenants do not restrict the payment of dividends.

NOTE 10 OTHER FINANCIAL INSTRUMENTS

FOREIGN CURRENCY FORWARD AND OPTION CONTRACTS: The company enters into foreign exchange forward contracts, options and swaps to hedge against the effect of exchange rate fluctuations on cash flows denominated in foreign currencies and certain intercompany financing transactions. These transactions are designated as cash flow hedges. At December 31, 2001, the company had various open foreign exchange forward and option contracts, the majority of which had maturities of one year or less. The amounts at risk are not material because the company has the ability to generate offsetting foreign currency cash flows.

For foreign currency cash flow hedges, the net realized gain recorded in cost of sales for the year 2001 totaled $37 million, with the impact largely offset by underlying hedged items. The settlement or extension of these derivatives will result in reclassifications to earnings in the period during which the hedged transactions affect earnings (from other comprehensive income). If exchange rates are unchanged within the next 12 months, the company expects to reclassify to after-tax earnings a majority of the $17 million of unrealized net gains included in cash flow hedging instruments within other comprehensive income at December 31, 2001, with the impact largely offset by underlying hedged items. The maximum length of time over which 3M is hedging its exposure to the variability in future cash flows for a majority of the forecasted transactions, excluding those forecasted transactions related to the payment of variable interest on existing financial instruments, is 12 months. No foreign currency cash flow hedges were discontinued during 2001. Hedge ineffectiveness was not material for the year 2001.

INTEREST RATE AND CURRENCY SWAPS: The company manages interest expense using a mix of fixed and floating rate debt. To help manage borrowing costs, the company may enter into interest rate swaps. Under these arrangements, the company agrees to exchange, at specified intervals, the difference between fixed and floating interest amounts calculated by reference to an agreed-upon notional principal amount. The company uses interest rate and currency swaps to manage interest rate risk related to borrowings.

At December 31, 2001, the company had interest rate swaps with a fair value of $7 million designated as fair value hedges of underlying fixed rate obligations. The mark-to-market of these fair value hedges is recorded as gains or losses in interest expense and is offset by the gain or loss on the underlying debt instrument that is also recorded in interest expense. All existing fair value hedges are 100 percent effective and thus, there is no impact to earnings due to hedge ineffectiveness.

From time to time, the company also uses cross-currency interest rate swaps to hedge foreign currency and interest rates. There were no cross-currency interest rate swaps outstanding at December 31, 2001.

NET INVESTMENT HEDGING: From time to time, the company uses foreign currency debt and forwards to hedge portions of the company's net investments in foreign operations. For hedges that meet the effectiveness requirements, the net gains or losses are recorded in cumulative translation within other comprehensive income, with any ineffectiveness recorded in cost of sales. In 2001, an unrealized after-tax gain of $23 million was recorded in cumulative translation. Hedge ineffectiveness resulted in after-tax realized gains totaling $4 million in 2001.

COMMODITY PRICE MANAGEMENT: The company manages commodity price risks through negotiated supply contracts, price protection swaps and forward physical contracts. The company uses commodity price swaps as cash flow hedges of forecasted transactions to manage price volatility. The related mark-to-market gain or loss on qualifying hedges is included in other comprehensive income to the extent effective (typically 100 percent effective), and reclassified into cost of sales in the period during which the hedged transaction affects earnings. For total year 2001, an unrealized after-tax loss of $8 million was recorded in cash flow hedging instruments within other comprehensive income, with the majority expected to be reclassified to earnings beyond 12 months and expected to be largely offset by underlying hedged items. 3M has hedged its exposure to the variability of future cash flows for certain forecasted transactions through 2005. No commodity cash flow hedges were discontinued during the 12 months ended December 31, 2001.

CREDIT RISK: The company is exposed to credit loss in the event of non-performance by counterparties in interest rate swaps, currency swaps, and option and foreign exchange contracts. However, the company's risk is limited to the fair value of the instruments. The company actively monitors its exposure to credit risk through the use of credit approvals and credit limits, and by selecting major international banks and financial institutions as counterparties. The company does not anticipate non-performance by any of these counterparties.

FAIR VALUE OF FINANCIAL INSTRUMENTS: At December 31, 2001 and 2000, the company's financial instruments included cash and cash equivalents, accounts receivable, investments, accounts payable, borrowing, and derivative contracts. The fair values of cash and cash equivalents, accounts receivable, accounts payable, and short-term debt (except the $350 million dealer remarketable security) approximated carrying values because of the short-term nature of these instruments. Available-for-sale investments and year-end 2001 derivative contracts are reported at fair values. Fair values for investments held at cost are not readily available, but are believed to approximate fair value. The carrying amounts and estimated fair values of other financial instruments based on third-party quotes follow.

FINANCIAL INSTRUMENTS CARRYING AMOUNTS AND ESTIMATED FAIR VALUES

	December 31, 2001		December 31, 2000	
(Millions)	Carrying Amount	Fair Value	Carrying Amount	Fair Value
Short-term debt – dealer remarketable securities	**$ 350**	**$ 366**	$ 352	$ 362
Long-term debt	**1,520**	**1,494**	971	950

NOTE 11 INCOME TAXES

At December 31, 2001, about $3.3 billion of retained earnings attributable to international companies were considered to be indefinitely invested. No provision has been made for taxes that might be payable if these earnings were remitted to the United States. It is not practical to determine the amount of incremental taxes that might arise were these earnings to be remitted.

In 2000, the company recorded a cumulative effect of accounting change, reducing earnings by $75 million net of tax. The provision for income taxes excludes a $42 million tax benefit related to this cumulative effect.

INCOME BEFORE INCOME TAXES, MINORITY INTEREST AND CUMULATIVE EFFECT OF ACCOUNTING CHANGE

(Millions)	2001	2000	1999
United States	**$1,368**	$1,798	$2,020
International	**818**	1,176	860
Total	**$2,186**	$2,974	$2,880

PROVISION FOR INCOME TAXES

(Millions)	2001	2000	1999
Currently payable			
Federal	**$ 376**	$ 471	$ 543
State	**47**	64	72
International	**278**	401	322
Deferred			
Federal	**(7)**	92	100
State	**6**	7	9
International	**2**	(10)	(14)
Total	**$ 702**	$1,025	$1,032

COMPONENTS OF DEFERRED TAX ASSETS AND LIABILITIES

(Millions)	2001	2000
Accruals currently not deductible		
Employee benefit costs	**$ 225**	$ 278
Product and other claims	**173**	170
Severance and other restructuring costs	**73**	—
Product and other insurance receivables	**(286)**	(308)
Accelerated depreciation	**(464)**	(436)
Other	**236**	221
Net deferred tax asset (liability)	**$ (43)**	$ (75)

RECONCILIATION OF EFFECTIVE INCOME TAX RATE

	2001	2000	1999
Statutory U.S. tax rate	**35.0%**	35.0%	35.0%
State income taxes – net of federal benefit	**1.6**	1.6	1.8
International income taxes – net	**(.7)**	(.8)	.2
Tax benefit of foreign sales corporation	**(2.2)**	(.9)	(.9)
All other – net	**(1.6)**	(.4)	(.3)
Effective worldwide tax rate	**32.1%**	34.5%	35.8%

NOTE 12 BUSINESS SEGMENTS

3M's businesses are organized, managed and internally reported as six operating segments based on differences in products, technologies and services. These segments are Transportation, Graphics and Safety; Health Care; Industrial; Consumer and Office; Electro and Communications; and Specialty Material. These segments have worldwide responsibility for virtually all of the company's product lines. 3M is not dependent on any single product or market.

Transactions among reportable segments are recorded at cost. 3M is an integrated enterprise characterized by substantial intersegment cooperation, cost allocations and inventory transfers. Therefore, management does not represent that these segments, if operated independently, would report the operating income and other financial information shown. The allocations resulting from the shared utilization of assets are not necessarily indicative of the underlying activity for segment assets, depreciation and amortization, and capital expenditures.

Operating income in 2001 included non-recurring charges of $504 million. Non-recurring charges, principally related to the company's restructuring plan, totaled $569 million (recorded in Corporate and Unallocated). Acquisition-related costs totaled $23 million ($10 million recorded in Health Care; $7 million in Transportation, Graphics and Safety; and $6 million in Electro and Communications). Additional items recorded in Corporate and Unallocated included a reversal of a 1999 litigation accrual of $73 million, and a gain of $15 million related to the net impact of the sale and write-down of available-for-sale equity securities. Depreciation and amortization of $1.089 billion included accelerated depreciation (shortened lives) related to the restructuring of $80 million (recorded in Corporate and Unallocated).

Operating income in 2000 included a non-recurring net loss of $23 million. Non-recurring costs included $168 million in the Specialty Material segment related to the company's phase-out of perfluorooctanyl-based chemistry products. This $168 million included $56 million of accelerated depreciation (included in the Specialty Material segment depreciation and amortization), $48 million of impairment losses, and severance and other costs. Other non-recurring costs included a $20 million write-down of corporate and unallocated assets, and $20 million of other non-recurring expenses ($13 million related to acquisitions in the Electro and Communications segment). Non-recurring operating income gains in 2000 of $135 million were largely related to corporate and unallocated asset dispositions, principally the sale of available-for-sale equity securities. Operating income in 2000 also included a $50 million gain from the termination of a product distribution agreement in the Health Care segment.

Operating income in 1999 included a non-recurring net gain of $100 million. This related to divestitures of certain health care businesses

NOTES TO CONSOLIDATED FINANCIAL STATEMENTS

and Eastern Heights Bank, litigation expense, an investment valuation adjustment, and a change in estimate that reduced 1998 restructuring charges. Of this $100 million gain, $62 million was recorded in Health Care and $38 million in Corporate and Unallocated.

BUSINESS SEGMENT PRODUCTS

BUSINESS SEGMENT	MAJOR PRODUCTS
Transportation, Graphics and Safety	Reflective sheeting, commercial graphics systems, respirators, automotive components, safety and security products, and optical films
Health Care	Medical and surgical supplies, skin health and infection-prevention products, pharmaceuticals, drug delivery systems, dental and orthodontic products, health information systems, microbiology products, and closures for disposable diapers
Industrial	Tapes, coated and nonwoven abrasives, and specialty adhesives
Consumer and Office	Sponges, scouring pads, high performance cloths, consumer and office tapes, repositionable notes, carpet and fabric protectors, energy control products, home improvement products, floor matting and commercial cleaning products, and visual systems
Electro and Communications	Packaging and interconnection devices, insulating and splicing solutions for the electronics, telecommunications and electrical industries
Specialty Material	Specialty materials for automotive, electronics, telecommunications, textile and other industries, and roofing granules

BUSINESS SEGMENT INFORMATION

(Millions)		Net Sales	Operating Income	Assets**	Depr. and Amort.	Capital Expenditures
Transportation, Graphics and Safety	**2001**	**$ 3,526**	**$ 695**	**$ 2,621**	**$ 238**	**$ 208**
	2000	3,518	783	2,741	186	239
	1999	3,234	675	2,673	140	199
Health Care	**2001**	**3,419**	**760**	**2,264**	**193**	**179**
	2000	3,135	675	2,025	188	189
	1999	3,138	680	2,076	203	189
Industrial	**2001**	**3,199**	**518**	**2,134**	**185**	**191**
	2000	3,525	641	2,392	213	214
	1999	3,409	612	2,357	220	202

BUSINESS SEGMENT INFORMATION (continued)

(Millions)		Net Sales	Operating Income	Assets**	Depr. and Amort.	Capital Expenditures
Consumer and Office	**2001**	**2,724**	**447**	**1,514**	**121**	**106**
	2000	2,848	434	1,711	101	134
	1999	2,705	401	1,589	118	123
Electro and Communications	**2001**	**2,171**	**218**	**1,807**	**157**	**132**
	2000	2,467	404	1,961	158	208
	1999	2,017	402	1,359	130	194
Specialty Material	**2001**	**1,022**	**141**	**1,208**	**97**	**136**
	2000	1,197	57	1,230	144	131
	1999	1,194	185	1,323	79	143
Corporate and Unallocated*	**2001**	**18**	**(506)**	**3,058**	**98**	**28**
	2000	34	64	2,462	35	—
	1999	51	1	2,519	10	—
Total Company	**2001**	**$16,079**	**$2,273**	**$14,606**	**$1,089**	**$980**
	2000	16,724	3,058	14,522	1,025	1,115
	1999	15,748	2,956	13,896	900	1,050

*Corporate and Unallocated operating income principally includes corporate investment gains and losses, certain derivative gains and losses, insurance-related gains and losses, banking operating results (divested June 30, 1999), certain litigation expenses, restructuring charges and other miscellaneous items. Because this category includes a variety of miscellaneous items, it is subject to fluctuation on a quarterly and annual basis.

**Segment assets primarily include accounts receivable; inventory; property, plant and equipment – net; and other miscellaneous assets. Assets included in Corporate and Unallocated principally are cash and cash equivalents; insurance receivables; deferred income taxes; certain investments and other assets; and certain unallocated property, plant and equipment.

NOTE 13 GEOGRAPHIC AREAS

Information in the geographic area table is presented on the basis the company uses to manage its businesses. Export sales and certain income and expense items are reported within the geographic area where the final sales to customers are made. Prior-year amounts have been retroactively restated to conform to the current-year presentation.

In 2001, operating income for Eliminations and Other includes non-recurring net losses totaling $504 million, primarily related to the restructuring. Also included were a reversal of a 1999 litigation accrual, acquisition-related costs, and a net gain on the sale and write-down of available-for-sale equity securities. In 1999, operating income for Eliminations and Other includes a $100 million non-recurring net benefit related to gains on divestitures, litigation expense, an investment valuation adjustment, and a change in estimate that reduced 1998 restructuring charges.

GEOGRAPHIC AREA INFORMATION

(Millions)		United States	Europe and Middle East	Asia Pacific	Latin America, Africa and Canada	Elimina-tions and Other	Total Company
Net sales to customers	**2001**	**$ 7,546**	**$ 3,960**	**$ 3,043**	**$ 1,496**	**$ 34**	**$ 16,079**
	2000	7,858	3,946	3,329	1,564	27	16,724
	1999	7,559	3,808	2,887	1,467	27	15,748
Operating income	**2001**	**$ 1,028**	**$ 571**	**$ 807**	**$ 360**	**$ (493)**	**$ 2,273**
	2000	1,160	589	961	376	(28)	3,058
	1999	1,198	574	768	348	68	2,956
Property, plant and equipment – net	**2001**	**$ 3,675**	**$ 974**	**$ 634**	**$ 332**	**—**	**$5,615**
	2000	3,699	1,046	711	367	—	5,823
	1999	3,647	1,017	757	355	—	5,776

NOTE 14 PENSION AND POSTRETIREMENT BENEFIT PLANS

3M has various company-sponsored retirement plans covering substantially all U.S. employees and many employees outside the United States. Pension benefits are based principally on an employee's years of service and compensation near retirement. In addition to providing pension benefits, the company provides certain postretirement health care and life insurance benefits for substantially all of its U.S. employees who reach retirement age while employed by the company. Most international employees and retirees are covered by government health care programs. The cost of company-provided health care plans for these international employees is not material.

The company's pension funding policy is to deposit with independent trustees amounts at least equal to accrued liabilities, to the extent allowed by law. Trust funds and deposits with insurance companies are maintained to provide pension benefits to plan participants and their beneficiaries. In addition, the company has set aside funds for its U.S. postretirement plan with an independent trustee and makes periodic contributions to the plan.

During 2001, the company adopted a change in the measurement date of its U.S. employee benefit plans (qualified and non-qualified pension benefit plans and its U.S. postretirement benefit plan) from December 31 to September 30. Information presented in the tables for 2001 reflects a measurement date of September 30, 2001, and December 31 for prior periods. This change did not have a material impact on the determination of periodic pension cost or pension obligations. Management believes this change is preferable to the method previously employed, as it facilitates the benefit cost planning and forecasting process. The company's U.S. non-qualified pension plan had an unfunded accumulated benefit obligation of $196 million at September 30, 2001, and $187 million at December 31, 2000. There are no plan assets in the non-qualified plan due to its nature.

Certain international pension plans were underfunded as of year-end 2001 and 2000. The accumulated benefit obligations of these plans were $534 million in 2001 and $499 million in 2000. The assets of these plans were $287 million in 2001 and $300 million in 2000. The net underfunded amounts are included in current and other liabilities on the Consolidated Balance Sheet.

BENEFIT PLAN INFORMATION

(Millions)	Qualified and Non-qualified Pension Benefits: United States 2001	United States 2000	International 2001	International 2000	Postretirement Benefits 2001	Postretirement Benefits 2000
Reconciliation of benefit obligation						
Beginning balance	**$5,905**	$5,597	**$2,368**	$2,234	**$1,166**	$1,016
Service cost	**123**	125	**91**	83	**39**	39
Interest cost	**449**	416	**118**	98	**90**	82
Participant contributions	**—**	—	**8**	6	**10**	11
Foreign exchange rate changes	**—**	—	**23**	(199)	**—**	—
Plan amendments	**1**	1	**7**	—	**1**	—
Actuarial (gain) loss	**305**	117	**(90)**	199	**74**	109
Benefit payments	**(279)**	(351)	**(75)**	(53)	**(76)**	(91)
Settlements, curtailments, special termination benefits	**49**	—	**(5)**	—	**—**	—
Ending balance	**$6,553**	$5,905	**$2,445**	$2,368	**$1,304**	$1,166
Reconciliation of plan assets at fair value						
Beginning balance	**$6,954**	$6,813	**$2,011**	$2,155	**$ 601**	$ 537
Actual return on plan assets	**(726)**	384	**(99)**	5	**(117)**	4
Company contributions	**104**	90	**53**	60	**135**	139
Participant contributions	**—**	—	**8**	6	**10**	11
Foreign exchange rate changes	**—**	—	**60**	(157)	**—**	—
Benefit payments	**(279)**	(333)	**(73)**	(58)	**(75)**	(90)
Settlements, curtailments	**—**	—	**(5)**	—	**—**	—
Ending balance	**$6,053**	$6,954	**$1,955**	$2,011	**$ 554**	$ 601
Funded status of plans						
Plan assets at fair value less benefit obligation	**$ (500)**	$1,049	**$ (490)**	$ (357)	**$ (750)**	$ (565)
Unrecognized transition (asset) obligation	**—**	—	**—**	16	**—**	—
Unrecognized prior service cost	**117**	129	**32**	25	**(15)**	(26)
Unrecognized (gain) loss	**643**	(1,012)	**459**	311	**406**	160
Fourth-quarter contribution	**3**	—	**—**	—	**89**	—
Net amount recognized	**$ 263**	$ 166	**$ 1**	$ (5)	**$ (270)**	$ (431)
Amounts recognized in the Consolidated Balance Sheet consist of:						
Prepaid assets	**$ 424**	$ 319	**$ 102**	$ 80	**—**	—
Accrued liabilities	**(196)**	(187)	**(277)**	(229)	**$ (270)**	$ (431)
Intangible assets	**5**	5	**6**	8	**—**	—
Accumulated other comprehensive income – pre-tax	**30**	29	**170**	136	**—**	—
Net amount recognized	**$ 263**	$ 166	**$ 1**	$ (5)	**$ (270)**	$ (431)

BENEFIT PLAN INFORMATION

	Qualified and Non-qualified Pension Benefits						Postretirement Benefits		
	United States			International					
(Millions)	2001	2000	1999	2001	2000	1999	2001	2000	1999
Components of net periodic benefit cost									
Service cost	**$ 123**	$ 125	$ 150	**$ 91**	$ 83	$ 88	**$ 39**	$ 39	$ 42
Interest cost	**449**	416	387	**118**	98	98	**90**	82	69
Expected return on assets	**(615)**	(565)	(501)	**(142)**	(117)	(108)	**(53)**	(47)	(34)
Amortization of transition (asset) obligation	**—**	—	(37)	**1**	2	2	**—**	—	—
Amortization of prior service cost or benefit	**13**	13	45	**8**	8	8	**(11)**	(11)	(11)
Recognized net actuarial (gain) loss	**(9)**	(14)	14	**11**	7	2	**10**	3	—
Net periodic benefit cost	**$ (39)**	$ (25)	$ 58	**$ 87**	$ 81	$ 90	**$ 75**	$ 66	$ 66
Curtailments, settlements and special termination benefits	**49**	—	—	**1**	—	—	**12**	—	—
Net periodic benefit cost after curtailments and settlements	**$ 10**	$ (25)	$ 58	**$ 88**	$ 81	$ 90	**$ 87**	$ 66	$ 66
Weighted average assumptions									
Discount rate	**7.25%**	7.50%	7.50%	**5.23%**	5.40%	5.67%	**7.25%**	7.50%	7.50%
Expected return on assets	**9.00%**	9.00%	9.00%	**7.42%**	7.14%	6.69%	**9.50%**	8.19%	8.19%
Compensation rate increase	**4.60%**	4.65%	4.65%	**4.02%**	4.28%	4.12%	**4.60%**	4.65%	4.65%

The company expects its health care cost trend rate for postretirement benefits to slow from 8.5 percent in 2002 to 5.0 percent in 2006, after which the rate is expected to stabilize. A one percentage point change in the assumed health care cost trend rates would have the effects shown in the following table.

HEALTH CARE COST

(Millions)	One Percentage Point Increase	One Percentage Point Decrease
Effect on current year's service and interest cost	$ 16	$ (13)
Effect on benefit obligation	132	(113)

NOTE 15 LEASES

Rental expense under operating leases was $119 million in both 2001 and 2000, and $113 million in 1999. The table below shows minimum payments under operating leases with non-cancelable terms in excess of one year, as of December 31, 2001.

(Millions)	2002	2003	2004	2005	2006	After 2006	Total
Minimum lease payments	$79	$75	$40	$28	$20	$97	$339

NOTE 16 EMPLOYEE SAVINGS AND STOCK OWNERSHIP PLANS

The company sponsors employee savings plans under Section 401(k) of the Internal Revenue Code. These plans are offered to substantially all regular U.S. employees. Employee contributions of up to 6 percent of compensation are matched at rates ranging from 25 to 50 percent, with additional company contributions depending upon company performance. Only the company match is invested in 3M stock, with employee funds invested in a number of investment options. Vested employees may sell up to 50 percent of their 3M shares and diversify into other investment options.

The company maintains an Employee Stock Ownership Plan (ESOP). This plan was established in 1989 as a cost-effective way of funding the majority of the company's contributions under 401(k) employee savings plans. Total ESOP shares are considered to be shares outstanding for earnings per share calculations.

Dividends on shares held by the ESOP are paid to the ESOP trust and, together with company contributions, are used by the ESOP to repay principal and interest on the outstanding notes. Over the life of the notes, shares are released for allocation to participants based on the ratio of the current year's debt service to the remaining debt service prior to the current payment.

The ESOP has been the primary funding source for the company's employee savings plans. Expenses related to the ESOP include total debt service on the notes, less dividends. The company contributes treasury shares, accounted for at fair value, to employee savings plans to cover obligations not funded by the ESOP. These amounts are reported as an employee benefit expense. Unearned compensation, shown as a reduction of stockholders' equity, is reduced symmetrically as the ESOP makes principal payments on the debt.

EMPLOYEE SAVINGS AND STOCK OWNERSHIP PLANS

(Millions)	2001	2000	1999
Dividends on shares held by the ESOP	**$31**	$31	$31
Company contributions to the ESOP	**17**	15	7
Interest incurred on ESOP notes	**18**	19	21
Expenses related to ESOP debt service	**14**	12	14
Expenses related to treasury shares	**3**	35	50

ESOP DEBT SHARES

	2001	2000	1999
Allocated	**7,241,681**	6,898,666	6,596,898
Committed to be released	**49,135**	194,187	280,615
Unreleased	**5,549,275**	6,116,961	6,709,549
Total ESOP debt shares	**12,840,091**	13,209,814	13,587,062

NOTE 17 GENERAL EMPLOYEES' STOCK PURCHASE PLAN

In May 1997, shareholders approved 15 million shares for issuance under the company's General Employees' Stock Purchase Plan (GESPP). Substantially all employees are eligible to participate in the plan. Participants are granted options at 85 percent of market value at the date of grant. There are no GESPP shares under option at the beginning or end of each year because options are granted on the first business day and exercised on the last business day of the same month.

GENERAL EMPLOYEES' STOCK PURCHASE PLAN

	2001 Shares	2001 Exercise Price*	2000 Shares	2000 Exercise Price*	1999 Shares	1999 Exercise Price*
Options granted	**998,276**	**$93.85**	1,206,262	$77.40	1,210,189	$72.25
Options exercised	**(998,276)**	**$93.85**	(1,206,262)	$77.40	(1,210,189)	$72.25
Shares available for grant–						
Dec. 31	**9,565,450**		10,563,726		11,769,988	

*Weighted average

The weighted average fair value per option granted during 2001, 2000 and 1999 was $16.56, $13.65 and $12.75, respectively. The fair value of GESPP options was based on the 15 percent purchase discount.

NOTE 18 MANAGEMENT STOCK OWNERSHIP PROGRAM

In May 1997, shareholders approved 35 million shares for issuance under the Management Stock Ownership Program (MSOP). Management stock options are granted at market value at the date of grant. These options generally are exercisable one year after the date of grant and expire 10 years from the date of grant. Thus, outstanding shares under option include grants from previous plans. In May 2001, at the time of the last major grant, there were 11,784 participants in the plan.

MANAGEMENT STOCK OWNERSHIP PROGRAM

	2001 Shares	2001 Exercise Price*	2000 Shares	2000 Exercise Price*	1999 Shares	1999 Exercise Price*
Under option –						
Jan. 1	**32,347,256**	**$ 79.34**	30,702,415	$ 74.67	29,330,549	$ 67.72
Granted:						
Annual	**6,541,299**	**117.25**	6,040,196	88.33	5,194,766	95.00
Progressive (Reload)	**671,285**	**115.45**	572,511	98.33	502,567	87.33
Exercised	**(4,826,135)**	**71.41**	(4,684,779)	62.19	(4,201,886)	52.50
Canceled	**(183,517)**	**117.24**	(283,087)	86.77	(123,581)	93.35
Dec. 31	**34,550,188**	**$ 88.12**	32,347,256	$ 79.34	30,702,415	$ 74.67
Options exercisable –						
Dec. 31	**27,536,534**	**$ 80.98**	26,159,345	$ 77.02	25,213,683	$ 70.27
Shares available for grant –						
Dec. 31	**4,501,427**		11,738,624		18,088,285	

*Weighted average

MSOP OPTIONS OUTSTANDING AND EXERCISABLE AT DECEMBER 31, 2001

Range of Exercise Prices	Options Outstanding Shares	Options Outstanding Remaining Contractual Life (months)	Options Outstanding Exercise Price*	Options Exercisable Shares	Options Exercisable Exercise Price*
$46.01-63.10	8,397,652	42	$ 55.97	8,397,652	$ 55.97
80.24-96.87	18,638,304	87	91.59	18,638,304	91.59
103.05-122.90	7,514,232	117	115.79	500,578	110.78

*Weighted average

For annual and progressive (reload) options, the weighted average fair value at date of grant was calculated utilizing the Black-Scholes option-pricing model and the assumptions that follow.

MSOP ASSUMPTIONS

	Annual			Progressive (Reload)		
	2001	2000	1999	**2001**	2000	1999
Exercise price	**$117.25**	$88.33	$95.00	**$115.45**	$98.33	$87.33
Risk-free interest rate	**4.8%**	6.7%	5.4%	**3.8%**	6.3%	5.4%
Dividend growth rate	**4.6%**	4.3%	5.0%	**4.6%**	4.3%	5.0%
Volatility	**24.1%**	22.3%	22.3%	**23.7%**	25.4%	28.8%
Expected life (months)	**67**	68	66	**28**	28	26
Black-Scholes fair value	**$ 29.41**	$22.45	$22.86	**$ 17.62**	$17.18	$16.00

The MSOP options, if exercised, would have had the following dilutive effect on shares outstanding for the years ended 2001, 2000 and 1999, respectively: 5.6 million, 4.2 million and 4.5 million shares. Certain MSOP average options outstanding during the years 2001, 2000 and 1999 (4.2, 11.5 and 8.7 million shares, respectively) were not included in the computation of diluted earnings per share because they would not have had a dilutive effect.

NOTE 19 STOCK-BASED COMPENSATION

Generally no compensation cost is recognized for either the General Employees' Stock Purchase Plan (GESPP) or the Management Stock Ownership Program (MSOP). Pro forma amounts based on the options' estimated fair value, net of tax, at the grant dates for awards under the GESPP and MSOP are presented below.

PRO FORMA NET INCOME AND EARNINGS PER SHARE

(Millions)	**2001**	2000	1999
Net income			
As reported	**$ 1,430**	$ 1,782	$ 1,763
Pro forma	**1,278**	1,668	1,652
Earnings per share – basic			
As reported	**$ 3.63**	$ 4.50	$ 4.39
Pro forma	**3.24**	4.22	4.11
Earnings per share – diluted			
As reported	**$ 3.58**	$ 4.45	$ 4.34
Pro forma	**3.20**	4.17	4.06

NOTE 20 QUARTERLY DATA (Unaudited)

(Millions, except per-share amounts)	First	Second	Third	Fourth	Year
NET SALES					
2001	**$ 4,170**	**$ 4,079**	**$ 3,967**	**$ 3,863**	**$ 16,079**
2000	4,075	4,243	4,270	4,136	16,724
COST OF SALES*					
2001	**$ 2,196**	**$ 2,266**	**$ 2,156**	**$ 2,131**	**$ 8,749**
2000	2,091	2,181	2,295	2,220	8,787
INCOME BEFORE CUMULATIVE EFFECT OF ACCOUNTING CHANGE*					
2001	**$ 453**	**$ 202**	**$ 394**	**$ 381**	**$ 1,430**
2000	487	470	499	401	1,857
NET INCOME*					
2001	**$ 453**	**$ 202**	**$ 394**	**$ 381**	**$ 1,430**
2000	487	470	499	326	1,782
BASIC EARNINGS PER SHARE – INCOME BEFORE CUMULATIVE EFFECT*					
2001	**$ 1.14**	**$ .51**	**$ 1.00**	**$ .97**	**$3.63**
2000	1.22	1.19	1.26	1.02	4.69
BASIC EARNINGS PER SHARE – NET INCOME*					
2001	**$ 1.14**	**$ .51**	**$ 1.00**	**$ .97**	**$ 3.63**
2000	1.22	1.19	1.26	.83	4.50
DILUTED EARNINGS PER SHARE – INCOME BEFORE CUMULATIVE EFFECT*					
2001	**$ 1.13**	**$ .50**	**$ .99**	**$ .96**	**$ 3.58**
2000	1.21	1.18	1.25	1.00	4.64
DILUTED EARNINGS PER SHARE – NET INCOME*					
2001	**$ 1.13**	**$ .50**	**$ .99**	**$ .96**	**$ 3.58**
2000	1.21	1.18	1.25	.82	4.45
STOCK PRICE COMPARISONS (NYSE COMPOSITE TRANSACTIONS)					
2001 High	**$121.50**	**$127.00**	**$117.50**	**$121.90**	**$ 127.00**
2001 Low	**98.50**	**97.16**	**85.86**	**95.20**	**85.86**
2000 High	103.81	98.31	97.44	122.94	122.94
2000 Low	78.19	80.44	80.50	83.94	78.19

QUARTERLY DATA (Unaudited) (continued)

*The impact of non-recurring items in 2001 and 2000 by quarter are as follows:

NON-RECURRING ITEMS
(Millions, except per-share amounts)

2001	First	Second	Third	Fourth	Year
Cost of sales	$ 23	$ 141	$ 47	$ 61	$ 272
Selling, general and administrative expenses	—	242	16	42	300
Research, development and related expenses	—	14	6	—	20
Other expense (income)	—	—	—	(88)	(88)
Operating income (loss)	$ (23)	$(397)	$(69)	$ (15)	$ (504)
Net income (loss)	$ (14)	$(249)	$(43)	$ (6)	$ (312)
Diluted earnings (loss) per share	$(.03)	$ (.62)	$(.11)	$ (.02)	$ (.78)
Operating income (loss) detail:					
Acquisition-related	$ (23)	$ —	$ —	$ —	$ (23)
Restructuring-related	—	(397)	(69)	(103)	(569)
Reversal of a 1999 litigation accrual	—	—	—	73	73
Net gain on sale of equity securities, net of equity securities write-downs	—	—	—	15	15

NON-RECURRING ITEMS
(Millions, except per-share amounts)

2000	First	Second	Third	Fourth	Year
Cost of sales	$ —	$ —	$118	$ 90	$ 208
Other expense (income)	(50)		(119)	(16)	(185)
Operating income (loss)	$ 50	—	$1	$ (74)	$ (23)
Cumulative effect of accounting change (loss)	$ —	$ —	$ —	$ (75)	$ (75)
Net income (loss)	$ 31	$ —	$ —	$(121)	$ (90)
Diluted earnings (loss) per share	$ .08	$ —	$ —	$ (.30)	$ (.23)
Operating income (loss) detail:					
Gain from termination of distribution agreement	$ 50	$ —	$ —	$ —	$ 50
Phase-out of certain products	—	—	(106)	(62)	(168)
Gain on sale of equity securities and other	—	—	107	(12)	95

NOTE 21 LEGAL PROCEEDINGS

The company and some of its subsidiaries are named as defendants in a number of actions, governmental proceedings and claims, including environmental proceedings and products liability claims involving products now or formerly manufactured and sold by the company. In some actions, the claimants seek damages as well as other relief, which, if granted, would require substantial expenditures. The company has recorded liabilities, which represent reasonable estimates of its probable liabilities for these matters. The company also has recorded receivables for the probable amount of insurance recoverable with respect to these matters (refer to Note 6 on page 43).

Some of these matters raise difficult and complex factual and legal issues, and are subject to many uncertainties, including, but not limited to, the facts and circumstances of each particular action, the jurisdiction and forum in which each action is proceeding and differences in applicable law.

While the company believes that the ultimate outcome of all of its proceedings and claims, individually and in the aggregate, will not have a material adverse effect on its consolidated financial position, results of operations or cash flows, there can be no certainty that the company may not ultimately incur charges, whether for breast implant litigation, respirator/mask/asbestos litigation, environmental matters or other actions, in excess of presently recorded liabilities.

The company cannot always definitively determine possible liabilities that exceed recorded amounts related to its legal proceedings and claims. However, the company believes it is unlikely, based upon the nature of its legal proceedings and claims and its current knowledge of relevant facts and circumstances, that the possible liabilities exceeding recorded amounts would be material to its consolidated financial position, results of operations or cash flows. With respect to products liability claims, such a conclusion about possible liabilities considers insurance coverage available for such liabilities.

While the company believes that a material adverse impact on its consolidated financial position, results of operations or cash flows from any such future charges is unlikely, given the inherent uncertainty of litigation, a remote possibility exists that a future adverse ruling or unfavorable development could result in future charges that could have a material adverse impact on the company. The current estimates of the potential impact on the company's consolidated financial position, results of operations and cash flows for its legal proceedings and claims could change in the future.

FINANCIAL SUMMARY

(Dollars in millions, except per-share amounts)	**2001**	2000	1999	1998	1997	1996	1995	1994	1993	1992	1991
OPERATING RESULTS											
Net sales	**$16,079**	$16,724	$15,748	$15,094	$15,133	$14,295	$13,516	$12,199	$11,099	$10,862	$10,324
Operating income	**2,273**	3,058	2,956	2,039	2,675	2,491	2,221	2,095	1,796	1,811	1,683
Income from continuing operations	**1,430**	1,857	1,763	1,213	2,121	1,516	1,306	1,207	1,133	1,116	984
Per share – basic	**3.63**	4.69	4.39	3.01	5.14	3.63	3.11	2.85	2.61	2.55	2.24
Per share – diluted	**3.58**	4.64	4.34	2.97	5.06	3.59	3.09	2.84	2.59	2.54	2.23
Net income	**1,430**	1,782	1,763	1,175	2,121	1,526	976	1,322	1,263	1,233	1,154
Per share – basic	**3.63**	4.50	4.39	2.91	5.14	3.65	2.32	3.13	2.91	2.81	2.63
Per share – diluted	**3.58**	4.45	4.34	2.88	5.06	3.62	2.31	3.11	2.89	2.80	2.62
FINANCIAL RATIOS											
Percent of sales											
Cost of sales	**54.4%**	52.5%	51.6%	53.2%	52.0%	52.0%	52.6%	51.2%	51.9%	51.5%	52.1%
Selling, general and administrative expenses	**25.3**	23.7	23.6	23.5	23.7	24.0	23.9	24.8	24.7	25.2	24.7
Research, development and related expenses	**6.7**	6.6	6.7	6.8	6.6	6.6	6.5	6.8	7.2	7.4	6.9
Operating income	**14.1**	18.3	18.8	13.5	17.7	17.4	16.4	17.2	16.2	16.7	16.3
Income from continuing operations	**8.9**	11.1	11.2	8.0	14.0	10.6	9.7	9.9	10.2	10.3	9.5
Return on invested capital	**14.3**	19.2	19.1	13.0	18.0	17.3	16.3	17.4	16.0	16.8	16.1
Total debt to total capital	**32**	30	29	34	30	24	23	22	19	18	19
Current ratio	**1.4**	1.3	1.6	1.5	1.5	1.8	1.8	1.8	1.8	1.8	1.7
ADDITIONAL INFORMATION											
Cash dividends paid	**$ 948**	$ 918	$ 901	$ 887	$ 876	$ 803	$ 790	$ 744	$ 721	$ 701	$ 685
Per share	**2.40**	2.32	2.24	2.20	2.12	1.92	1.88	1.76	1.66	1.60	1.56
Stock price at year-end	**118.21**	120.50	97.88	71.13	82.06	83.00	66.38	53.38	54.38	50.31	47.63
Book value per share	**15.55**	16.49	15.77	14.77	14.64	15.08	16.44	16.04	15.16	15.06	14.36
Working capital	**1,787**	1,625	2,247	1,997	2,185	2,880	2,847	2,516	2,348	2,246	1,899
Total assets	**14,606**	14,522	13,896	14,153	13,238	13,364	14,183	13,068	11,795	11,528	10,886
Long-term debt (excluding current portion)	**1,520**	971	1,480	1,614	1,015	851	1,203	1,031	796	687	764
Capital expenditures	**980**	1,115	1,050	1,453	1,406	1,109	1,088	972	898	968	1,065
Depreciation	**916**	915	822	798	800	825	795	793	768	754	710
Research, development and related expenses	**1,084**	1,101	1,056	1,028	1,002	947	883	828	794	800	713
Number of employees at year-end*	**71,669**	75,026	70,549	73,564	75,639	74,289	85,313	85,296	85,940	86,793	88,370
Average shares outstanding basic (in millions)	**394.3**	395.7	402.0	403.3	412.7	418.2	419.8	423.0	434.3	438.2	439.1
Average shares outstanding diluted (in millions)	**399.9**	399.9	406.5	408.0	418.7	422.1	422.5	425.3	436.8	440.2	441.0

Cumulative effect of accounting changes and extraordinary items impact net income only, and are not included as part of income from continuing operations.

2001 results include a non-recurring net loss of $504 million ($312 million after tax and minority interest), or 78 cents per diluted share, principally related to charges in connection with 3M's restructuring plan, acquisition-related charges, a reversal of a 1999 litigation accrual, and a net gain related to the sale of available-for-sale equity securities, partially offset by the write-down of available-for-sale equity securities.

2000 results include a non-recurring net loss of $23 million ($15 million after tax), or 4 cents per diluted share, and a cumulative effect of accounting change related to revenue recognition that reduced net income by $75 million, or 19 cents per diluted share.

1999 results include non-recurring items of $100 million ($52 million after tax), or 13 cents per diluted share. Non-recurring items consist of a $73 million charge related to litigation; gains on divestitures of $147 million (net of an investment valuation adjustment); and a $26 million gain related to a change in estimate of the restructuring liability.

1998 results include restructuring charges of $493 million ($313 million after tax), or 77 cents per diluted share, and an extraordinary loss on early extinguishment of debt that reduced net income by $38 million, or 9 cents per diluted share.

1997 results include a gain of $803 million ($495 million after tax), or $1.18 per diluted share, on the sale of National Advertising Company.

* Includes both continuing and discontinued operations; decrease in 1996 primarily reflects Imation Corp. spin-off.

QUESTIONS

1. How does information from the balance sheet help users of the financial statements?

2. What is meant by solvency? What information in the balance sheet can be used to assess a company's solvency?

3. A recent financial magazine indicated that a drug company had good financial flexibility. What is meant by financial flexibility, and why is it important?

4. Discuss at least two situations in which estimates could affect the usefulness of information in the balance sheet.

5. Jones Company reported an increase in inventories in the past year. Discuss the effect of this change on the current ratio (current assets ÷ current liabilities). What does this tell a statement user about Jones Company's liquidity?

6. What is meant by liquidity? Rank the following assets from one to five in order of liquidity.

   (a) Goodwill.

   (b) Inventories.

   (c) Buildings.

   (d) Short-term investments.

   (e) Accounts receivable.

7. What are the major limitations of the balance sheet as a source of information?

8. Discuss at least two items that are important to the value of companies like **Intel** or **IBM** but that are not recorded in their balance sheets. What are some reasons why these items are not recorded in the balance sheet?

9. How does separating current assets from property, plant, and equipment in the balance sheet help analysts?

10. In its December 31, 2004, balance sheet Oakley Corporation reported as an asset, "Net notes and accounts receivable, $7,100,000." What other disclosures are necessary?

11. Should available-for-sale securities always be reported as a current asset? Explain.

12. What is the relationship between current assets and current liabilities?

13. The New York Knicks, Inc. sold 10,000 season tickets at $1,000 each. By December 31, 2004, 18 of the 40 home games had been played. What amount should be reported as a current liability at December 31, 2004?

14. What is working capital? How does working capital relate to the operating cycle?

15. In what section of the balance sheet should the following items appear, and what balance sheet terminology would you use?

    (a) Treasury stock (recorded at cost).

    (b) Checking account at bank.

    (c) Land (held as an investment).

    (d) Sinking fund.

    (e) Unamortized premium on bonds payable.

    (f) Copyrights.

    (g) Pension fund assets.

    (h) Premium on capital stock.

    (i) Long-term investments (pledged against bank loans payable).

16. Where should the following items be shown on the balance sheet, if shown at all?

    (a) Allowance for doubtful accounts receivable.

    (b) Merchandise held on consignment.

    (c) Advances received on sales contract.

    (d) Cash surrender value of life insurance.

    (e) Land.

    (f) Merchandise out on consignment.

    (g) Pension fund on deposit with a trustee (under a trust revocable at depositor's option).

    (h) Franchises.

    (i) Accumulated depreciation of plant and equipment.

    (j) Materials in transit—purchased f.o.b. destination.

17. State the generally accepted accounting principle (standard) applicable to the balance sheet valuation of each of the following assets.

    (a) Trade accounts receivable.

    (b) Land.

    (c) Inventories.

    (d) Trading securities (common stock of other companies).

    (e) Prepaid expenses.

18. Refer to the definition of assets on page 173. Discuss how a leased building might qualify as an asset of the lessee under this definition.

19. Christine Agazzi says, "Retained earnings should be reported as an asset, since it is earnings which are reinvested in the business." How would you respond to Agazzi?

20. The creditors of Nick Anderson Company agree to accept promissory notes for the amount of its indebtedness with a proviso that two-thirds of the annual profits must be applied to their liquidation. How should these notes be reported on the balance sheet of the issuing company? Give a reason for your answer.

21. What are some of the techniques of disclosure for the balance sheet?

22. What is a "Summary of Significant Accounting Policies"?

23. What types of contractual obligations must be disclosed in great detail in the notes to the balance sheet? Why do you think these detailed provisions should be disclosed?

24. What is the profession's recommendation in regard to the use of the term "surplus"? Explain.

25. What is the purpose of a statement of cash flows? How does it differ from a balance sheet and an income statement?

26. The net income for the year for Won Long, Inc. is $750,000, but the statement of cash flows reports that the cash provided by operating activities is $640,000. What might account for the difference?

27. Net income for the year for Jenkins, Inc. was $750,000, but the statement of cash flows reports that cash provided by operating activities was $860,000. What might account for the difference?

28. Differentiate between operating activities, investing activities, and financing activities.

29. Each of the following items must be considered in preparing a statement of cash flows. Indicate where each item is to be reported in the statement, if at all. Assume that net income is reported as $90,000.

(a) Accounts receivable increased from $32,000 to $39,000 from the beginning to the end of the year.

(b) During the year, 10,000 shares of preferred stock with a par value of $100 a share were issued at $115 per share.

(c) Depreciation expense amounted to $14,000, and bond premium amortization amounted to $5,000.

(d) Land increased from $10,000 to $30,000.

30. Marker Co. has net cash provided by operating activities of $900,000. Its average current liabilities for the period are $1,000,000, and its average total liabilities are $1,500,000. Comment on the company's liquidity and financial flexibility, given this information.

31. Net income for the year for Hatfield, Inc. was $750,000, but the statement of cash flows reports that cash provided by operating activities was $860,000. Hatfield also reported capital expenditures of $75,000 and paid dividends in the amount of $20,000. Compute Hatfield's free cash flow.

32. What is the purpose of a free cash flow analysis?

BRIEF EXERCISES

BE5-1 La Bouche Corporation has the following accounts included in its December 31, 2004, trial balance: Accounts Receivable $110,000; Inventories $290,000; Allowance for Doubtful Accounts $8,000; Patents $72,000; Prepaid Insurance $9,500; Accounts Payable $77,000; Cash $27,000. Prepare the current assets section of the balance sheet listing the accounts in proper sequence.

BE5-2 Jodi Corporation's adjusted trial balance contained the following asset accounts at December 31, 2004: Cash $7,000; Land $40,000; Patents $12,500; Accounts Receivable $90,000; Prepaid Insurance $5,200; Inventory $34,000; Allowance for Doubtful Accounts $4,000; Trading Securities $11,000. Prepare the current assets section of the balance sheet, listing the accounts in proper sequence.

BE5-3 Included in Goo Goo Dolls Company's December 31, 2004, trial balance are the following accounts: Prepaid Rent $5,200; Held-to-Maturity Securities $61,000; Unearned Fees $17,000; Land Held for Investment $39,000; Long-term Receivables $42,000. Prepare the long-term investments section of the balance sheet.

BE5-4 Adam Ant Company's December 31, 2004, trial balance includes the following accounts: Inventories $120,000; Buildings $207,000; Accumulated Depreciation–Equipment $19,000; Equipment $190,000; Land Held for Investment $46,000; Accumulated Depreciation–Buildings $45,000; Land $61,000; Capital Leases $70,000. Prepare the property, plant, and equipment section of the balance sheet.

BE5-5 Mason Corporation has the following accounts included in its December 31, 2004, trial balance: Trading Securities $21,000; Goodwill $150,000; Prepaid Insurance $12,000; Patents $220,000; Franchises $110,000. Prepare the intangible assets section of the balance sheet.

BE5-6 Mickey Snyder Corporation's adjusted trial balance contained the following asset accounts at December 31, 2004: Prepaid Rent $12,000; Goodwill $40,000; Franchise Fees Receivable $2,000; Franchises $47,000; Patents $33,000; Trademarks $10,000. Prepare the intangible assets section of the balance sheet.

BE5-7 John Hawk Corporation's adjusted trial balance contained the following liability accounts at December 31, 2004: Bonds Payable (due in 3 years) $100,000; Accounts Payable $72,000; Notes Payable (due in 90 days) $12,500; Accrued Salaries $4,000; Income Taxes Payable $7,000. Prepare the current liabilities section of the balance sheet.

BE5-8 Included in Ewing Company's December 31, 2004, trial balance are the following accounts: Accounts Payable $240,000; Obligations under Capital Leases $375,000; Discount on Bonds Payable $24,000; Advances from Customers $41,000; Bonds Payable $400,000; Wages Payable $27,000; Interest Payable $12,000; Income Taxes Payable $29,000. Prepare the current liabilities section of the balance sheet.

BE5-9 Use the information presented in BE5–8 for Ewing Company to prepare the long-term liabilities section of the balance sheet.

BE5-10 Kevin Flynn Corporation's adjusted trial balance contained the following accounts at December 31, 2004: Retained Earnings $120,000; Common Stock $700,000; Bonds Payable $100,000; Additional Paid-in Capital $200,000; Goodwill $55,000; Accumulated Other Comprehensive Loss $150,000. Prepare the stockholders' equity section of the balance sheet.

BE5-11 Young Company's December 31, 2004, trial balance includes the following accounts: Investment in Common Stock $70,000; Retained Earnings $114,000; Trademarks $31,000; Preferred Stock $172,000; Common Stock $55,000; Deferred Income Taxes $88,000; Additional Paid-in Capital $174,000. Prepare the stockholders' equity section of the balance sheet.

BE5-12 Midwest Beverage Company reported the following items in the most recent year.

Net income	$40,000
Dividends paid	5,000
Increase in accounts receivable	10,000
Increase in accounts payable	5,000
Purchase of equipment (capital expenditure)	8,000
Depreciation expense	4,000
Issue of notes payable	20,000

Compute cash flow from operations, the net change in cash during the year, and free cash flow.

BE5-13 Kes Company reported 2004 net income of $151,000. During 2004, accounts receivable increased by $13,000 and accounts payable increased by $9,500. Depreciation expense was $39,000. Prepare the cash flows from operating activities section of the statement of cash flows.

BE5-14 Yorkis Perez Corporation engaged in the following cash transactions during 2004.

Sale of land and building	$181,000
Purchase of treasury stock	40,000
Purchase of land	37,000
Payment of cash dividend	85,000
Purchase of equipment	53,000
Issuance of common stock	147,000
Retirement of bonds	100,000

Compute the net cash provided (used) by investing activities.

BE5-15 Use the information presented in BE5-14 for Yorkis Perez Corporation to compute the net cash used (provided) by financing activities.

BE5-16 Using the information in BE5-14, determine Yorkis Perez's free cash flow, assuming that it reported net cash provided by operating activities of $400,000.

EXERCISES

E5-1 (Balance Sheet Classifications) Presented below are a number of balance sheet accounts of Deep Blue Something, Inc.

(a) Investment in Preferred Stock.
(b) Treasury Stock.
(c) Common Stock Distributable.
(d) Cash Dividends Payable.
(e) Accumulated Depreciation.
(f) Warehouse in Process of Construction.
(g) Petty Cash.
(h) Accrued Interest on Notes Payable.
(i) Deficit.
(j) Trading Securities.
(k) Income Taxes Payable.
(l) Unearned Subscription Revenue.
(m) Work in Process.
(n) Accrued Vacation Pay.

Instructions

For each of the accounts above, indicate the proper balance sheet classification. In the case of borderline items, indicate the additional information that would be required to determine the proper classification.

E5-2 (Classification of Balance Sheet Accounts) Presented on the next page are the captions of Faulk Company's balance sheet.

(a) Current assets.
(b) Investments.
(c) Property, plant, and equipment.
(d) Intangible assets.
(e) Other assets.
(f) Current liabilities.
(g) Non-current liabilities.
(h) Capital stock.
(i) Additional paid-in capital.
(j) Retained earnings.

Instructions

Indicate by letter where each of the following items would be classified.

1. Preferred stock.
2. Goodwill.
3. Wages payable.
4. Trade accounts payable.
5. Buildings.
6. Trading securities.
7. Current portion of long-term debt.
8. Premium on bonds payable.
9. Allowance for doubtful accounts.
10. Accounts receivable.
11. Cash surrender value of life insurance.
12. Notes payable (due next year).
13. Office supplies.
14. Common stock.
15. Land.
16. Bond sinking fund.
17. Merchandise inventory.
18. Prepaid insurance.
19. Bonds payable.
20. Taxes payable.

E5-3 (Classification of Balance Sheet Accounts) Assume that Fielder Enterprises uses the following headings on its balance sheet.

(a) Current assets.
(b) Investments.
(c) Property, plant, and equipment.
(d) Intangible assets.
(e) Other assets.
(f) Current liabilities.
(g) Long-term liabilities.
(h) Capital stock.
(i) Paid-in capital in excess of par.
(j) Retained earnings.

Instructions

Indicate by letter how each of the following usually should be classified. If an item should appear in a note to the financial statements, use the letter "N" to indicate this fact. If an item need not be reported at all on the balance sheet, use the letter "X."

1. Unexpired insurance.
2. Stock owned in affiliated companies.
3. Unearned subscriptions revenue.
4. Advances to suppliers.
5. Unearned rent revenue.
6. Treasury stock.
7. Premium on preferred stock.
8. Copyrights.
9. Petty cash fund.
10. Sales tax payable.
11. Accrued interest on notes receivable.
12. Twenty-year issue of bonds payable that will mature within the next year. (No sinking fund exists, and refunding is not planned.)
13. Machinery retired from use and held for sale.
14. Fully depreciated machine still in use.
15. Accrued interest on bonds payable.
16. Salaries that company budget shows will be paid to employees within the next year.
17. Discount on bonds payable. (Assume related to bonds payable in No. 12.)
18. Accumulated depreciation.

E5-4 (Preparation of a Classified Balance Sheet) Assume that Denis Savard Inc. has the following accounts at the end of the current year.

1. Common Stock.
2. Discount on Bonds Payable.
3. Treasury Stock (at cost).
4. Note Payable, short-term.
5. Raw Materials.
6. Preferred Stock Investments—Long-term.
7. Unearned Rent Revenue.
8. Work in Process.
9. Copyrights.
10. Buildings.
11. Notes Receivable (short-term).
12. Cash.
13. Accrued Salaries Payable.
14. Accumulated Depreciation—Buildings.
15. Cash Restricted for Plant Expansion.
16. Land Held for Future Plant Site.
17. Allowance for Doubtful Accounts—Accounts Receivable.
18. Retained Earnings.
19. Premium on Common Stock.
20. Unearned Subscriptions Revenue.
21. Receivables—Officers (due in one year).
22. Finished Goods.
23. Accounts Receivable.
24. Bonds Payable (due in 4 years).

Instructions

Prepare a classified balance sheet in good form. (No monetary amounts are necessary.)

E5-5 (Preparation of a Corrected Balance Sheet) Uhura Company has decided to expand its operations. The bookkeeper recently completed the balance sheet presented below in order to obtain additional funds for expansion.

UHURA COMPANY
BALANCE SHEET
FOR THE YEAR ENDED 2004

Current assets	
Cash (net of bank overdraft of $30,000)	$200,000
Accounts receivable (net)	340,000
Inventories at lower of average cost or market	401,000
Trading securities—at cost (fair value $120,000)	140,000
Property, plant, and equipment	
Building (net)	570,000
Office equipment (net)	160,000
Land held for future use	175,000
Intangible assets	
Goodwill	80,000
Cash surrender value of life insurance	90,000
Prepaid expenses	12,000
Current liabilities	
Accounts payable	105,000
Notes payable (due next year)	125,000
Pension obligation	82,000
Rent payable	49,000
Premium on bonds payable	53,000
Long-term liabilities	
Bonds payable	500,000
Stockholders' equity	
Common stock, $1.00 par, authorized 400,000 shares, issued 290,000	290,000
Additional paid-in capital	160,000
Retained earnings	?

Instructions

Prepare a revised balance sheet given the available information. Assume that the accumulated depreciation balance for the buildings is $160,000 and for the office equipment, $105,000. The allowance for doubtful accounts has a balance of $17,000. The pension obligation is considered a long-term liability.

E5-6 (Corrections of a Balance Sheet) The bookkeeper for Geronimo Company has prepared the following balance sheet as of July 31, 2004.

GERONIMO COMPANY
BALANCE SHEET
AS OF JULY 31, 2004

Cash	$ 69,000	Notes and accounts payable	$ 44,000
Accounts receivable (net)	40,500	Long-term liabilities	75,000
Inventories	60,000	Stockholders' equity	155,500
Equipment (net)	84,000		$274,500
Patents	21,000		
	$274,500		

The following additional information is provided.

1. Cash includes $1,200 in a petty cash fund and $15,000 in a bond sinking fund.
2. The net accounts receivable balance is comprised of the following three items: (a) accounts receivable—debit balances $52,000; (b) accounts receivable—credit balances $8,000; (c) allowance for doubtful accounts $3,500.
3. Merchandise inventory costing $5,300 was shipped out on consignment on July 31, 2004. The ending inventory balance does not include the consigned goods. Receivables in the amount of $5,300 were recognized on these consigned goods.

4. Equipment had a cost of $112,000 and an accumulated depreciation balance of $28,000.
5. Taxes payable of $6,000 were accrued on July 31. Geronimo Company, however, had set up a cash fund to meet this obligation. This cash fund was not included in the cash balance, but was offset against the taxes payable amount.

Instructions

Prepare a corrected classified balance sheet as of July 31, 2004, from the available information, adjusting the account balances using the additional information.

E5-7 (Current Assets Section of the Balance Sheet) Presented below are selected accounts of Yasunari Kawabata Company at December 31, 2004.

Finished Goods	$ 52,000	Cost of Goods Sold	$2,100,000
Revenue Received in Advance	90,000	Notes Receivable	40,000
Bank Overdraft	8,000	Accounts Receivable	161,000
Equipment	253,000	Raw Materials	207,000
Work-in-Process	34,000	Supplies Expense	60,000
Cash	37,000	Allowance for Doubtful Accounts	12,000
Short-term Investments in Stock	31,000	Licenses	18,000
Customer Advances	36,000	Additional Paid-in Capital	88,000
Cash Restricted for Plant Expansion	50,000	Treasury Stock	22,000

The following additional information is available.

1. Inventories are valued at lower of cost or market using LIFO.
2. Equipment is recorded at cost. Accumulated depreciation, computed on a straight-line basis, is $50,600.
3. The short-term investments have a fair value of $29,000. (Assume they are trading securities.)
4. The notes receivable are due April 30, 2006, with interest receivable every April 30. The notes bear interest at 12%. (*Hint:* Accrue interest due on December 31, 2004.)
5. The allowance for doubtful accounts applies to the accounts receivable. Accounts receivable of $50,000 are pledged as collateral on a bank loan.
6. Licenses are recorded net of accumulated amortization of $14,000.
7. Treasury stock is recorded at cost.

Instructions

Prepare the current assets section of Yasunari Kawabata Company's December 31, 2004, balance sheet, with appropriate disclosures.

E5-8 (Current vs. Long-term Liabilities) Frederic Chopin Corporation is preparing its December 31, 2004, balance sheet. The following items may be reported as either a current or long-term liability.

1. On December 15, 2004, Chopin declared a cash dividend of $2.50 per share to stockholders of record on December 31. The dividend is payable on January 15, 2005. Chopin has issued 1,000,000 shares of common stock, of which 50,000 shares are held in treasury.
2. Also on December 31, Chopin declared a 10% stock dividend to stockholders of record on January 15, 2005. The dividend will be distributed on January 31, 2005. Chopin's common stock has a par value of $10 per share and a market value of $38 per share.
3. At December 31, bonds payable of $100,000,000 are outstanding. The bonds pay 12% interest every September 30 and mature in installments of $25,000,000 every September 30, beginning September 30, 2005.
4. At December 31, 2003, customer advances were $12,000,000. During 2004, Chopin collected $30,000,000 of customer advances, and advances of $25,000,000 were earned.

Instructions

For each item above indicate the dollar amounts to be reported as a current liability and as a long-term liability, if any.

E5-9 (Current Assets and Current Liabilities) The current assets and liabilities sections of the balance sheet of Allessandro Scarlatti Company appear as follows.

ALLESSANDRO SCARLATTI COMPANY
BALANCE SHEET (PARTIAL)
DECEMBER 31, 2004

Cash		$ 40,000	Accounts payable	$ 61,000
Accounts receivable	$89,000		Notes payable	67,000
Less: Allowance for doubtful accounts	7,000	82,000		$128,000
Inventories		171,000		
Prepaid expenses		9,000		
		$302,000		

The following errors in the corporation's accounting have been discovered:

1. January 2005 cash disbursements entered as of December 2004 included payments of accounts payable in the amount of $39,000, on which a cash discount of 2% was taken.
2. The inventory included $27,000 of merchandise that had been received at December 31 but for which no purchase invoices had been received or entered. Of this amount, $12,000 had been received on consignment; the remainder was purchased f.o.b. destination, terms 2/10, n/30.
3. Sales for the first four days in January 2005 in the amount of $30,000 were entered in the sales book as of December 31, 2004. Of these, $21,500 were sales on account and the remainder were cash sales.
4. Cash, not including cash sales, collected in January 2005 and entered as of December 31, 2004, totaled $35,324. Of this amount, $23,324 was received on account after cash discounts of 2% had been deducted; the remainder represented the proceeds of a bank loan.

Instructions

(a) Restate the current assets and liabilities sections of the balance sheet in accordance with good accounting practice. (Assume that both accounts receivable and accounts payable are recorded gross.)

(b) State the net effect of your adjustments on Allesandro Scarlatti Company's retained earnings balance.

E5-10 (Current Liabilities) Norma Smith is the controller of Baylor Corporation and is responsible for the preparation of the year-end financial statements. The following transactions occurred during the year.

(a) On December 20, 2004, an employee filed a legal action against Baylor for $100,000 for wrongful dismissal. Management believes the action to be frivolous and without merit. The likelihood of payment to the employee is remote.

(b) Bonuses to key employees based on net income for 2004 are estimated to be $150,000.

(c) On December 1, 2004, the company borrowed $600,000 at 8% per year. Interest is paid quarterly.

(d) Credit sales for the year amounted to $10,000,000. Baylor's expense provision for doubtful accounts is estimated to be 3% of credit sales.

(e) On December 15, 2004, the company declared a $2.00 per share dividend on the 40,000 shares of common stock outstanding, to be paid on January 5, 2005.

(f) During the year, customer advances of $160,000 were received; $50,000 of this amount was earned by December 31, 2004.

Instructions

For each item above, indicate the dollar amount to be reported as a current liability. If a liability is not reported, explain why.

E5-11 (Balance Sheet Preparation) Presented below is the adjusted trial balance of Kelly Corporation at December 31, 2004.

	Debits	Credits
Cash	$?	
Office Supplies	1,200	
Prepaid Insurance	1,000	
Equipment	48,000	
Accumulated Depreciation—Equipment		$ 4,000
Trademarks	950	
Accounts Payable		10,000
Wages Payable		500

Unearned Service Revenue		2,000
Bonds Payable, due 2011		9,000
Common Stock		10,000
Retained Earnings		25,000
Service Revenue		10,000
Wages Expense	9,000	
Insurance Expense	1,400	
Rent Expense	1,200	
Interest Expense	900	
Total	$?	$?

Additional information:

1. Net loss for the year was $2,500.
2. No dividends were declared during 2004.

Instructions

Prepare a classified balance sheet as of December 31, 2004.

E5-12 (Preparation of a Balance Sheet) Presented below is the trial balance of John Nalezny Corporation at December 31, 2004.

	Debits	Credits
Cash	$ 197,000	
Sales		$ 8,100,000
Trading Securities (at cost, $145,000)	153,000	
Cost of Goods Sold	4,800,000	
Long-term Investments in Bonds	299,000	
Long-term Investments in Stocks	277,000	
Short-term Notes Payable		90,000
Accounts Payable		455,000
Selling Expenses	2,000,000	
Investment Revenue		63,000
Land	260,000	
Buildings	1,040,000	
Dividends Payable		136,000
Accrued Liabilities		96,000
Accounts Receivable	435,000	
Accumulated Depreciation—Buildings		152,000
Allowance for Doubtful Accounts		25,000
Administrative Expenses	900,000	
Interest Expense	211,000	
Inventories	597,000	
Extraordinary Gain		80,000
Prior Period Adjustment—Depr. Error	140,000	
Long-term Notes Payable		900,000
Equipment	600,000	
Bonds Payable		1,000,000
Accumulated Depreciation—Equipment		60,000
Franchise (net of $80,000 amortization)	160,000	
Common Stock ($5 par)		1,000,000
Treasury Stock	191,000	
Patent (net of $30,000 amortization)	195,000	
Retained Earnings		218,000
Additional Paid-in Capital		80,000
Totals	$12,455,000	$12,455,000

Instructions

Prepare a balance sheet at December 31, 2004, for John Nalezny Corporation. Ignore income taxes.

E5-13 (Statement of Cash Flows—Classifications) The major classifications of activities reported in the statement of cash flows are operating, investing, and financing. Classify each of the transactions listed below as:

1. Operating activity—add to net income.
2. Operating activity—deduct from net income.
3. Investing activity.

4. Financing activity.
5. Not reported as a cash flow.

The transactions are as follows.

(a) Issuance of capital stock.
(b) Purchase of land and building.
(c) Redemption of bonds.
(d) Sale of equipment.
(e) Depreciation of machinery.
(f) Amortization of patent.
(g) Issuance of bonds for plant assets.
(h) Payment of cash dividends.
(i) Exchange of furniture for office equipment.
(j) Purchase of treasury stock.
(k) Loss on sale of equipment.
(l) Increase in accounts receivable during the year.
(m) Decrease in accounts payable during the year.

E5-14 (Preparation of a Statement of Cash Flows) The comparative balance sheets of Constantine Cavamanlis Inc. at the beginning and the end of the year 2004 appear below.

CONSTANTINE CAVAMANLIS INC.
BALANCE SHEETS

Assets	Dec. 31, 2004	Jan. 1, 2004	Inc./Dec.
Cash	$ 45,000	$ 13,000	$32,000 Inc.
Accounts receivable	91,000	88,000	3,000 Inc.
Equipment	39,000	22,000	17,000 Inc.
Less: Accumulated depreciation	(17,000)	(11,000)	6,000 Inc.
Total	$158,000	$112,000	
Liabilities and Stockholders' Equity			
Accounts payable	$ 20,000	$ 15,000	5,000 Inc.
Common stock	100,000	80,000	20,000 Inc.
Retained earnings	38,000	17,000	21,000 Inc.
Total	$158,000	$112,000	

Net income of $44,000 was reported, and dividends of $23,000 were paid in 2004. New equipment was purchased and none was sold.

Instructions
Prepare a statement of cash flows for the year 2004.

E5-15 (Preparation of a Statement of Cash Flows) Presented below is a condensed version of the comparative balance sheets for Zubin Mehta Corporation for the last two years at December 31.

	2004	2003
Cash	$177,000	$ 78,000
Accounts receivable	180,000	185,000
Investments	52,000	74,000
Equipment	298,000	240,000
Less: Accumulated depreciation	(106,000)	(89,000)
Current liabilities	134,000	151,000
Capital stock	160,000	160,000
Retained earnings	307,000	177,000

Additional information:
Investments were sold at a loss (not extraordinary) of $10,000; no equipment was sold; cash dividends paid were $30,000; and net income was $160,000.

Instructions
(a) Prepare a statement of cash flows for 2004 for Zubin Mehta Corporation.
(b) Determine Zubin Mehta Corporation's free cash flow.

E5-16 (Preparation of a Statement of Cash Flows) A comparative balance sheet for Shabbona Corporation is presented below.

	December 31	
Assets	2004	2003
Cash	$ 73,000	$ 22,000
Accounts receivable	82,000	66,000
Inventories	180,000	189,000
Land	71,000	110,000
Equipment	260,000	200,000
Accumulated depreciation—equipment	(69,000)	(42,000)
Total	$597,000	$545,000
Liabilities and Stockholders' Equity		
Accounts payable	$ 34,000	$ 47,000
Bonds payable	150,000	200,000
Common stock ($1 par)	214,000	164,000
Retained earnings	199,000	134,000
Total	$597,000	$545,000

Additional information:

1. Net income for 2004 was $125,000.
2. Cash dividends of $60,000 were declared and paid.
3. Bonds payable amounting to $50,000 were retired through issuance of common stock.

Instructions

(a) Prepare a statement of cash flows for 2004 for Shabbona Corporation.

(b) Determine Shabbona Corporation's current cash debt coverage ratio, cash debt coverage ratio, and free cash flow. Comment on its liquidity and financial flexibility.

E5-17 (Preparation of a Statement of Cash Flows and a Balance Sheet) Grant Wood Corporation's balance sheet at the end of 2003 included the following items.

Current assets	$235,000	Current liabilities	$150,000
Land	30,000	Bonds payable	100,000
Building	120,000	Common stock	180,000
Equipment	90,000	Retained earnings	44,000
Accum. depr.—building	(30,000)	Total	$474,000
Accum. depr.—equipment	(11,000)		
Patents	40,000		
Total	$474,000		

The following information is available for 2004.

1. Net income was $55,000.
2. Equipment (cost $20,000 and accumulated depreciation $8,000) was sold for $10,000.
3. Depreciation expense was $4,000 on the building and $9,000 on equipment.
4. Patent amortization was $2,500.
5. Current assets other than cash increased by $29,000. Current liabilities increased by $13,000.
6. An addition to the building was completed at a cost of $27,000.
7. A long-term investment in stock was purchased for $16,000.
8. Bonds payable of $50,000 were issued.
9. Cash dividends of $30,000 were declared and paid.
10. Treasury stock was purchased at a cost of $11,000.

Instructions

(a) Prepare a statement of cash flows for 2004.

(b) Prepare a balance sheet at December 31, 2004.

E5-18 (Preparation of a Statement of Cash Flows, Analysis) The comparative balance sheets of Madrasah Corporation at the beginning and end of the year 2004 appear on the next page.

MADRASAH CORPORATION
BALANCE SHEETS

Assets	Dec. 31, 2004	Jan. 1, 2004	Inc./Dec.
Cash	$ 20,000	$ 13,000	$ 7,000 Inc.
Accounts receivable	106,000	88,000	18,000 Inc.
Equipment	39,000	22,000	17,000 Inc.
Less: Accumulated depreciation	(17,000)	(11,000)	6,000 Inc.
Total	$148,000	$112,000	
Liabilities and Stockholders' Equity			
Accounts payable	$ 20,000	$ 15,000	5,000 Inc.
Common stock	100,000	80,000	20,000 Inc.
Retained earnings	28,000	17,000	11,000 Inc.
Total	$148,000	$112,000	

Net income of $44,000 was reported, and dividends of $33,000 were paid in 2004. New equipment was purchased and none was sold.

Instructions

(a) Prepare a statement of cash flows for the year 2004.
(b) Compute the current ratio as of January 1, 2004, and December 31, 2004, and compute free cash flow for the year 2004.
(c) In light of the analysis in (b), comment on Madrasah's liquidity and financial flexibility.

PROBLEMS

P5-1 (Preparation of a Classified Balance Sheet, Periodic Inventory) Presented below is a list of accounts in alphabetical order.

Accounts Receivable
Accrued Wages
Accumulated Depreciation—Buildings
Accumulated Depreciation—Equipment
Advances to Employees
Advertising Expense
Allowance for Doubtful Accounts
Bond Sinking Fund
Bonds Payable
Building
Cash in Bank
Cash on Hand
Cash Surrender Value of Life Insurance
Commission Expense
Common Stock
Copyright (net of amortization)
Dividends Payable
Equipment
FICA Taxes Payable
Gain on Sale of Equipment
Interest Receivable
Inventory—Beginning
Inventory—Ending
Land
Land for Future Plant Site
Loss from Flood
Notes Payable
Patent (net of amortization)
Pension Obligations
Petty Cash
Preferred Stock
Premium on Bonds Payable
Premium on Preferred Stock
Prepaid Rent
Purchases
Purchase Returns and Allowances
Retained Earnings
Sales
Sales Discounts
Sales Salaries
Trading Securities
Transportation-in
Treasury Stock (at cost)
Unearned Subscriptions Revenue

Instructions

Prepare a classified balance sheet in good form. (No monetary amounts are to be shown.)

P5-2 (Balance Sheet Preparation) Presented below are a number of balance sheet items for Letterman, Inc., for the current year, 2004.

Goodwill	$ 125,000	Accumulated depreciation—equipment	$ 292,000
Payroll taxes payable	177,591	Inventories	239,800
Bonds payable	300,000		

Discount on bonds payable	15,000	Rent payable—short-term	45,000
Cash	360,000	Taxes payable	98,362
Land	480,000	Long-term rental obligations	480,000
Notes receivable	545,700	Common stock, $1 par value	200,000
Notes payable to banks	265,000	Preferred stock, $10 par value	150,000
Accounts payable	590,000	Prepaid expenses	87,920
Retained earnings	?	Equipment	1,470,000
Refundable federal and state income taxes	97,630	Trading securities	121,000
Unsecured notes payable (long-term)	1,600,000	Accumulated depreciation—building	170,200
		Building	1,640,000

Instructions
Prepare a classified balance sheet in good form. Common stock authorized was 400,000 shares, and preferred stock authorized was 20,000 shares. Assume that notes receivable and notes payable are short-term, unless stated otherwise. Cost and fair value of marketable securities are the same.

P5-3 (Balance Sheet Adjustment and Preparation) The adjusted trial balance of Side Kicks Company and other related information for the year 2004 is presented below.

SIDE KICKS COMPANY
ADJUSTED TRIAL BALANCE
DECEMBER 31, 2004

	Debits	Credits
Cash	$ 41,000	
Accounts Receivable	163,500	
Allowance for Doubtful Accounts		$ 8,700
Prepaid Insurance	5,900	
Inventory	308,500	
Long-term Investments	339,000	
Land	85,000	
Construction Work in Progress	124,000	
Patents	36,000	
Equipment	400,000	
Accumulated Depreciation of Equipment		140,000
Unamortized Discount on Bonds Payable	20,000	
Accounts Payable		148,000
Accrued Expenses		49,200
Notes Payable		94,000
Bonds Payable		400,000
Capital Stock		500,000
Premium on Capital Stock		45,000
Retained Earnings		138,000
	$1,522,900	$1,522,900

Additional information:

1. The inventory has a replacement market value of $353,000. The LIFO method of inventory value is used.
2. The cost and fair value of the long-term investments that consist of stocks and bonds is the same.
3. The amount of the Construction Work in Progress account represents the costs expended to date on a building in the process of construction. (The company rents factory space at the present time.) The land on which the building is being constructed cost $85,000, as shown in the trial balance.
4. The patents were purchased by the company at a cost of $40,000 and are being amortized on a straight-line basis.
5. Of the unamortized discount on bonds payable, $2,000 will be amortized in 2005.
6. The notes payable represent bank loans that are secured by long-term investments carried at $120,000. These bank loans are due in 2005.
7. The bonds payable bear interest at 11% payable every December 31, and are due January 1, 2015.
8. 600,000 shares of common stock of a par value of $1 were authorized, of which 500,000 shares were issued and outstanding.

Instructions
Prepare a balance sheet as of December 31, 2004, so that all important information is fully disclosed.

P5-4 (Preparation of a Corrected Balance Sheet) Presented below is the balance sheet of Russell Crowe Corporation as of December 31, 2004.

RUSSELL CROWE CORPORATION
BALANCE SHEET
DECEMBER 31, 2004

Assets	
Goodwill (Note 2)	$ 120,000
Building (Note 1)	1,640,000
Inventories	312,100
Land	750,000
Accounts receivable	170,000
Treasury stock (50,000 shares, no par)	87,000
Cash on hand	175,900
Assets allocated to trustee for plant expansion	
Cash in bank	70,000
U.S. Treasury notes, at cost and fair value	138,000
	$3,463,000
Equities	
Notes payable (Note 3)	$ 600,000
Common stock, authorized and issued, 1,000,000 shares, no par	1,150,000
Retained earnings	658,000
Appreciation capital (Note 1)	570,000
Federal income taxes payable	75,000
Reserve for depreciation of building	410,000
	$3,463,000

Note 1: Buildings are stated at cost, except for one building that was recorded at appraised value. The excess of appraisal value over cost was $570,000. Depreciation has been recorded based on cost.

Note 2: Goodwill in the amount of $120,000 was recognized because the company believed that book value was not an accurate representation of the fair market value of the company. The gain of $120,000 was credited to Retained Earnings.

Note 3: Notes payable are long-term except for the current installment due of $100,000.

Instructions

Prepare a corrected classified balance sheet in good form. The notes above are for information only.

P5-5 (Balance Sheet Adjustment and Preparation) Presented below is the balance sheet of Stephen King Corporation for the current year, 2004.

STEPHEN KING CORPORATION
BALANCE SHEET
DECEMBER 31, 2004

Current assets	$ 435,000	Current liabilities	$ 330,000
Investments	640,000	Long-term liabilities	1,000,000
Property, plant, and equipment	1,720,000	Stockholders' equity	1,770,000
Intangible assets	305,000		$3,100,000
	$3,100,000		

The following information is presented.

1. The current assets section includes: cash $100,000, accounts receivable $170,000 less $10,000 for allowance for doubtful accounts, inventories $180,000, and unearned revenue $5,000. The cash balance is composed of $114,000, less a bank overdraft of $14,000. Inventories are stated on the lower of FIFO cost or market.
2. The investments section includes: the cash surrender value of a life insurance contract $40,000; investments in common stock, short-term (trading) $80,000 and long-term (available-for-sale) $270,000, and bond sinking fund $250,000. The cost and fair value of investments in common stock are the same.
3. Property, plant, and equipment includes: buildings $1,040,000 less accumulated depreciation $360,000; equipment $450,000 less accumulated depreciation $180,000; land $500,000; and land held for future use $270,000.

4. Intangible assets include: a franchise $165,000; goodwill $100,000; and discount on bonds payable $40,000.
5. Current liabilities include: accounts payable $90,000; notes payable—short-term $80,000 and long-term $120,000; and taxes payable $40,000.
6. Long-term liabilities are composed solely of 10% bonds payable due 2012.
7. Stockholders' equity has: preferred stock, no par value, authorized 200,000 shares, issued 70,000 shares for $450,000; and common stock, $1.00 par value, authorized 400,000 shares, issued 100,000 shares at an average price of $10. In addition, the corporation has retained earnings of $320,000.

Instructions

Prepare a balance sheet in good form, adjusting the amounts in each balance sheet classification as affected by the information given above.

P5-6 (Preparation of a Statement of Cash Flows and a Balance Sheet) Alistair Cooke Inc. had the following balance sheet at the end of operations for 2003.

ALISTAIR COOKE INC.
BALANCE SHEET
DECEMBER 31, 2003

Cash	$ 20,000	Accounts payable	$ 30,000
Accounts receivable	21,200	Long-term notes payable	41,000
Investments	32,000	Capital stock	100,000
Plant assets (net)	81,000	Retained earnings	23,200
Land	40,000		$194,200
	$194,200		

During 2004 the following occurred.

1. Alistair Cooke Inc. sold part of its investment portfolio for $17,000. This transaction resulted in a gain of $3,400 for the firm. The company often sells and buys securities of this nature.
2. A tract of land was purchased for $18,000 cash.
3. Long-term notes payable in the amount of $16,000 were retired before maturity by paying $16,000 cash.
4. An additional $24,000 in capital stock was issued at par.
5. Dividends totalling $8,200 were declared and paid to stockholders.
6. Net income for 2004 was $32,000 after allowing for depreciation of $12,000.
7. Land was purchased through the issuance of $30,000 in bonds.
8. At December 31, 2004, Cash was $39,000, Accounts Receivable was $41,600, and Accounts Payable remained at $30,000.

Instructions

(a) Prepare a statement of cash flows for 2004.
(b) Prepare the balance sheet as it would appear at December 31, 2004.
(c) How might the statement of cash flows help the user of the financial statements? Compute two cash flow ratios.

P5-7 (Preparation of a Statement of Cash Flows and Balance Sheet) Roger Mudd Inc. had the following balance sheet at the end of operations for 2003.

ROGER MUDD INC.
BALANCE SHEET
DECEMBER 31, 2003

Cash	$ 20,000	Accounts payable	$ 30,000
Accounts receivable	21,200	Bonds payable	41,000
Trading securities	32,000	Capital stock	100,000
Plant assets (net)	81,000	Retained earnings	23,200
Land	40,000		$194,200
	$194,200		

During 2004 the following occurred.

1. Mudd liquidated its investment portfolio at a loss of $3,000.
2. A tract of land was purchased for $38,000.
3. An additional $26,000 in common stock was issued at par.
4. Dividends totaling $10,000 were declared and paid to stockholders.
5. Net income for 2004 was $35,000, including $12,000 in depreciation expense.
6. Land was purchased through the issuance of $30,000 in additional bonds.
7. At December 31, 2004, Cash was $66,200, Accounts Receivable was $42,000, and Accounts Payable was $40,000.

Instructions

(a) Prepare a statement of cash flows for the year 2004 for Mudd.
(b) Prepare the balance sheet as it would appear at December 31, 2004.
(c) Compute the current and acid-test ratios for 2003 and 2004.
(d) Compute Mudd's free cash flow and the current cash debt coverage ratio for 2004.
(e) Use the analysis of Mudd to illustrate how information in the balance sheet and statement of cash flows helps the user of the financial statements.

CONCEPTUAL CASES

C5-1 (Reporting the Financial Effects of Varied Transactions) In an examination of Juan Acevedo Corporation as of December 31, 2004, you have learned that the following situations exist. No entries have been made in the accounting records for these items.

1. The corporation erected its present factory building in 1989. Depreciation was calculated by the straight-line method, using an estimated life of 35 years. Early in 2004, the board of directors conducted a careful survey and estimated that the factory building had a remaining useful life of 25 years as of January 1, 2004.
2. An additional assessment of 2003 income taxes was levied and paid in 2004.
3. When calculating the accrual for officers' salaries at December 31, 2004, it was discovered that the accrual for officers' salaries for December 31, 2003, had been overstated.
4. On December 15, 2004, Acevedo Corporation declared a 1% common stock dividend on its common stock outstanding, payable February 1, 2005, to the common stockholders of record December 31, 2004.

Instructions

Describe fully how each of the items above should be reported in the financial statements of Acevedo Corporation for the year 2004.

C5-2 (Current Asset and Liability Classification) Below are the titles of a number of debit and credit accounts as they might appear on the balance sheet of Ethan Allen Corporation as of October 31, 2004.

Debits	Credits
Interest Accrued on U.S. Government Securities	Capital Stock—Preferred
Notes Receivable	11% First Mortgage Bonds, due in 2011
Petty Cash Fund	Preferred Cash Dividend, payable Nov. 1, 2004
U.S. Government Securities	Allowance for Doubtful Accounts Receivable
Treasury Stock	Federal Income Taxes Payable
Unamortized Bond Discount	Customers' Advances (on contracts to be completed next year)
Cash in Bank	Premium on Bonds Redeemable in 2004
Land	Officers' 2004 Bonus Accrued
Inventory of Operating Parts and Supplies	Accrued Payroll
Inventory of Raw Materials	Notes Payable
Patents	Accrued Interest on Bonds
Cash and U.S. Government Bonds Set Aside for Property Additions	Accumulated Depreciation
Investment in Subsidiary	Accounts Payable
Accounts Receivable:	Capital in Excess of Par
U.S. Government Contracts	Accrued Interest on Notes Payable
Regular	8% First Mortgage Bonds, to be redeemed in 2004 out of current assets

Debits	Credits
Accounts Receivable (cont'd):	
Installments—Due Next Year	
Installments—Due After Next year	
Goodwill	
Inventory of Finished Goods	
Inventory of Work in Process	
Deficit	

Instructions

Select the current asset and current liability items from among these debits and credits. If there appear to be certain borderline cases that you are unable to classify without further information, mention them and explain your difficulty, or give your reasons for making questionable classifications, if any.

(AICPA adapted)

C5-3 (Identifying Balance Sheet Deficiencies) The assets of LaShon Johnson Corporation are presented below (000s omitted).

LASHON JOHNSON CORPORATION
BALANCE SHEET (PARTIAL)
DECEMBER 31, 2004

Assets		
Current assets		
Cash		$ 100,000
Unclaimed payroll checks		27,500
Marketable securities (cost $30,000) at fair value		37,000
Accounts receivable (less bad debt reserve)		75,000
Inventories—at lower of cost (determined by the next-in, first-out method) or market		240,000
Total current assets		479,500
Tangible assets		
Land (less accumulated depreciation)		80,000
Buildings and equipment	$800,000	
Less: Accumulated depreciation	250,000	550,000
Net tangible assets		630,000
Long-term investments		
Stocks and bonds		100,000
Treasury stock		70,000
Total long-term investments		170,000
Other assets		
Discount on bonds payable		19,400
Sinking fund		975,000
Total other assets		994,400
Total assets		$2,273,900

Instructions

Indicate the deficiencies, if any, in the foregoing presentation of LaShon Johnson Corporation's assets. Marketable securities are considered trading securities.

C5-4 (Critique of Balance Sheet Format and Content) Presented below is the balance sheet of Bellemy Brothers Corporation (000s omitted).

BELLEMY BROTHERS CORPORATION
BALANCE SHEET
DECEMBER 31, 2004

Assets		
Current assets		
Cash	$26,000	
Marketable securities	18,000	

Accounts receivable	25,000	
Merchandise inventory	20,000	
Supplies inventory	4,000	
Stock investment in Subsidiary Company	20,000	$113,000
Investments		
Treasury stock		25,000
Property, plant, and equipment		
Buildings and land	91,000	
Less: Reserve for depreciation	31,000	60,000
Other assets		
Cash surrender value of life insurance		19,000
		$217,000
Liabilities and Capital		
Current liabilities		
Accounts payable	$22,000	
Reserve for income taxes	15,000	
Customers' accounts with credit balances	1	$ 37,001
Deferred credits		
Unamortized premium on bonds payable		2,000
Long-term liabilities		
Bonds payable		60,000
Total liabilities		99,001
Capital stock		
Capital stock, par $5	85,000	
Earned surplus	24,999	
Cash dividends declared	8,000	117,999
		$217,000

Instructions

Evaluate the balance sheet presented. State briefly the proper treatment of any item criticized.

C5-5 (Presentation of Property, Plant, and Equipment) Andrea Pafko, corporate comptroller for Nicholson Industries, is trying to decide how to present "Property, plant, and equipment" in the balance sheet. She realizes that the statement of cash flows will show that the company made a significant investment in purchasing new equipment this year, but overall she knows the company's plant assets are rather old. She feels that she can disclose one figure titled "Property, plant, and equipment, net of depreciation," and the result will be a low figure. However, it will not disclose the age of the assets. If she chooses to show the cost less accumulated depreciation, the age of the assets will be apparent. She proposes the following.

Property, plant, and equipment, net of depreciation	$10,000,000
rather than	
Property, plant, and equipment	$50,000,000
Less: Accumulated depreciation	(40,000,000)
Net book value	$10,000,000

Instructions

Answer the following questions.

(a) What are the ethical issues involved?
(b) What should Pafko do?

C5-6 (Cash Flow Analysis) The partner in charge of the James Spencer Corporation audit comes by your desk and leaves a letter he has started to the CEO and a copy of the cash flow statement for the year ended December 31, 2003. Because he must leave on an emergency, he asks you to finish the letter by explaining: (1) the disparity between net income and cash flow; (2) the importance of operating cash flow; (3) the renewable source(s) of cash flow; and (4) possible suggestions to improve the cash position.

JAMES SPENCER CORPORATION
STATEMENT OF CASH FLOWS
FOR THE YEAR ENDED DECEMBER 31, 2003

Cash flows from operating activities		
Net income		$100,000
Adjustments to reconcile net income to net cash provided by operating activities:		
Depreciation expense	$ 10,000	
Amortization expense	1,000	
Loss on sale of fixed assets	5,000	
Increase in accounts receivable (net)	(40,000)	
Increase in inventory	(35,000)	
Decrease in accounts payable	(41,000)	(100,000)
Net cash provided by operating activities		–0–
Cash flows from investing activities		
Sale of plant assets	25,000	
Purchase of equipment	(100,000)	
Purchase of land	(200,000)	
Net cash used by investing activities		(275,000)
Cash flows from financing activities		
Payment of dividends	(10,000)	
Redemption of bonds	(100,000)	
Net cash used by financing activities		(110,000)
Net decrease in cash		(385,000)
Cash balance, January 1, 2003		400,000
Cash balance, December 31, 2003		$ 15,000

Date

James Spencer, III, CEO
James Spencer Corporation
125 Wall Street
Middleton, Kansas 67458

Dear Mr. Spencer:

I have good news and bad news about the financial statements for the year ended December 31, 2003. The good news is that net income of $100,000 is close to what we predicted in the strategic plan last year, indicating strong performance this year. The bad news is that the cash balance is seriously low. Enclosed is the Statement of Cash Flows, which best illustrates how both of these situations occurred simultaneously . . .

Instructions
Complete the letter to the CEO, including the four components requested by your boss.

USING YOUR JUDGMENT

FINANCIAL REPORTING PROBLEM

3M

3M Company
The financial statements of 3M are presented in Appendix 5B or can be accessed on the Take Action! CD.

Instructions

Refer to 3M's financial statements and the accompanying notes to answer the following questions.

(a) What alternative formats could 3M have adopted for its balance sheet? Which format did it adopt?

(b) Identify the various techniques of disclosure 3M might have used to disclose additional pertinent financial information. Which technique does it use in its financials?

(c) In what classifications are 3M's investments reported? What valuation basis does 3M use to report its investments? How much working capital did 3M have on December 31, 2001? December 31, 2000?

(d) What were 3M's cash flows from its operating, investing, and financing activities for 2001? What were its trends in net cash provided by operating activities over the period 1999 to 2001? Explain why the change in accounts payable and other current liabilities is deducted from net income to arrive at net cash provided by operating activities.

(e) Compute 3M's (1) current cash debt coverage ratio, (2) cash debt coverage ratio, and (3) free cash flow for 2001. What do these ratios indicate about 3M's financial condition?

FINANCIAL STATEMENT ANALYSIS CASES

Case 1: Uniroyal Technology Corporation

Uniroyal Technology Corporation (UTC), with corporate offices in Sarasota, Florida, is organized into three operating segments. The high-performance plastics segment is responsible for research, development, and manufacture of a wide variety of products, including orthopedic braces, graffiti-resistant seats for buses and airplanes, and a static-resistant plastic used in the central processing units of microcomputers. The coated fabrics segment manufactures products such as automobile seating, door and instrument panels, and specialty items such as waterproof seats for personal watercraft and stain-resistant, easy-cleaning upholstery fabrics. The foams and adhesives segment develops and manufactures products used in commercial roofing applications.

The following items relate to operations in a recent year.

1. Serious pressure was placed on profitability by sharply increasing raw material prices. Some raw materials increased in price 50% during the past year. Cost containment programs were instituted and product prices were increased whenever possible, which resulted in profit margins actually improving over the course of the year.
2. The company entered into a revolving credit agreement, under which UTC may borrow the lesser of $15,000,000 or 80% of eligible accounts receivable. At the end of the year, approximately $4,000,000 was outstanding under this agreement. The company plans to use this line of credit in the upcoming year to finance operations and expansion.

Instructions

(a) Should investors be informed of raw materials price increases, such as described in item 1? Does the fact that the company successfully met the challenge of higher prices affect the answer? Explain.

(b) How should the information in item 2 be presented in the financial statements of UTC?

Case 2: Sherwin-Williams Company

Sherwin-Williams, based in Cleveland, Ohio, manufactures a wide variety of paint and other coatings, which are marketed through its specialty stores and in other retail outlets. The company also manufactures paint for automobiles. The Automotive Division has had financial difficulty. During a recent year, five branch locations of the Automotive Division were closed, and new management was put in place for the branches remaining. The following titles were shown on Sherwin-Williams's balance sheet for that year.

Accounts payable	Machinery and equipment
Accounts receivable, less allowance	Other accruals
Accrued taxes	Other capital
Buildings	Other current assets
Cash and cash equivalents	Other long-term liabilities
Common stock	Postretirement obligations other than pensions
Employee compensation payable	Retained earnings
Finished goods inventories	Short-term investments
Intangibles and other assets	Taxes payable
Land	Work in process and raw materials inventories
Long-term debt	

Instructions

(a) Organize the accounts in the general order in which they would have been presented in a classified balance sheet.

(b) When several of the branch locations of the Automotive Division were closed, what balance sheet accounts were most likely affected? Did the balance in those accounts decrease or increase?

COMPARATIVE ANALYSIS CASE

The Coca-Cola Company and PepsiCo, Inc.

Instructions

Go to the Take Action! CD and use information found there to answer the following questions related to **The Coca-Cola Company** and **PepsiCo, Inc.**

(a) What format(s) did these companies use to present their balance sheets?

(b) How much working capital did each of these companies have at the end of 2001? Speculate as to their rationale for the amount of working capital they maintain.

(c) What is the most significant difference in the asset structure of the two companies? What causes this difference?

(d) What are the companies' annual and 4-year (1997–2001) growth rates in total assets and long-term debt?

(e) What were these two companies' trends in net cash provided by operating activities over the period 1999 to 2001?

(f) Compute both companies' (1) current cash debt coverage ratio, (2) cash debt coverage ratio, and (3) free cash flow. What do these ratios indicate about the financial condition of the two companies?

(g) What ratios do each of these companies use in the Management's Discussion and Analysis section of the Annual Report to explain their financial condition related to debt financing?

RESEARCH CASE

Publicly-owned companies registered with the Securities and Exchange Commission electronically file required reports via the EDGAR (Electronic Data Gathering, Analysis, and Retrieval) system.

EDGAR can easily be accessed via the Internet (**www.sec.gov**) using the following steps.

1. Select "EDGAR Database of Corporate Information" from the home page.
2. Select "Search the EDGAR Database."
3. Select "CIK (Central Index Key) and Ticker Symbol Lookup" and enter the name(s) of the company(ies) you are investigating. Write down the CIK number(s) and return to the previous page.
4. To examine filings, click on "Search the EDGAR Archives" and enter the appropriate CIK number (including all zeroes). When the list of filings appears, click on the desired filing under the "Company name" column.

Instructions

(a) Determine the CIK numbers for the following companies: **Ford Motor Company**, **Wisconsin Electric Power Company**, and **Orion Pictures**.

(b) Examine the balance sheet formats included in the following filings.

(1) Ford Motor Co. Form 10-K filed March 28, 2002.

(2) Wisconsin Electric Power Co. annual report to shareholders (10-K) filed March 30, 2001.

(3) Orion Pictures Form 10-K filed April 14, 1995.

Do you notice anything "unusual" about the balance sheet formats? Why do you think the balance sheets are presented in this manner?

INTERNATIONAL REPORTING CASE

Presented below is the balance sheet for **Tomkins PLC**, a British company.

Instructions

(a) Identify at least three differences in balance sheet reporting between British and U.S. firms, as shown in Tomkins's balance sheet.

(b) Review Tomkins's balance sheet and identify how the format of this financial statement provides useful information, as illustrated in the chapter.

TOMKINS

TOMKINS PLC
Consolidated Balance Sheet
at 30 April 2001

	£ million
Capital employed	
Fixed assets	
Intangible assets	199.7
Tangible assets	903.0
Investments	12.2
	1,114.9
Current assets	
Stock	473.5
Debtors	741.1
Cash	400.4
	1,615.0
Current liabilities	
Creditors: amounts falling due within one year	(813.3)
Net current assets	801.7
Total assets less current liabilities	1,916.6
Creditors: amounts falling due after more than one year	(425.8)
Provisions for liabilities and charges	(405.4)
Net assets	1,085.4
Capital and reserves	
Called up share capital	
Ordinary shares	39.1
Convertible preference shares	337.2
Redeemable preference shares	426.7
	803.0
Share premium account	89.7
Capital redemption reserve	64.8
Profit and loss account	94.5
Shareholders' funds	1,052.0
Equity minority interest	33.4
Total capital and reserves	1,085.4

PROFESSIONAL SIMULATION

Accounting — Statement of Cash Flows with Analysis

Directions | Situation | Financial Statements | Analysis | Explanation | Research | Resources

Directions

In this simulation, you will be asked to prepare a statement of cash flows. You will also analyze the balance sheet and the statement of cash flows for purposes of assessing liquidity and financial flexibility. Prepare responses to all parts.

Situation

A comparative balance sheet for Nicholson Industries Inc. is presented below.

Nicholson Industries Inc.
Balance Sheets

	December 31	
Assets	2004	2003
Cash	$ 13,000	$ 22,000
Accounts receivable	112,000	66,000
Inventories	220,000	189,000
Land	71,000	110,000
Equipment	260,000	200,000
Accumulated depreciation–equipment	(69,000)	(42,000)
Total	$607,000	$545,000
Liabilities and Stockholders' Equity		
Accounts payable	$ 44,000	$ 47,000
Bonds payable	150,000	200,000
Common stock ($1 par)	214,000	164,000
Retained earnings	199,000	134,000
Total	$607,000	$545,000

Additional information:
1. Net income for 2004 was $125,000.
2. Cash dividends of $60,000 were declared and paid.
3. Bonds payable amounting to $50,000 were retired through issuance of common stock.

Financial Statements

Prepare a statement of cash flows for the year 2004 for Nicholson Industries Inc.

Analysis

(a) Compute the free cash flow and the current cash debt coverage ratio for 2004.

(b) Compute the current and acid-test ratios for 2003 and 2004.

Explanation

Based on the previous analysis, assess Nicholson's liquidity and financial flexibility.

www.wiley.com/college/kieso

Remember to check the **Take Action! CD** and the book's **companion Web site** to find additional resources for this chapter.

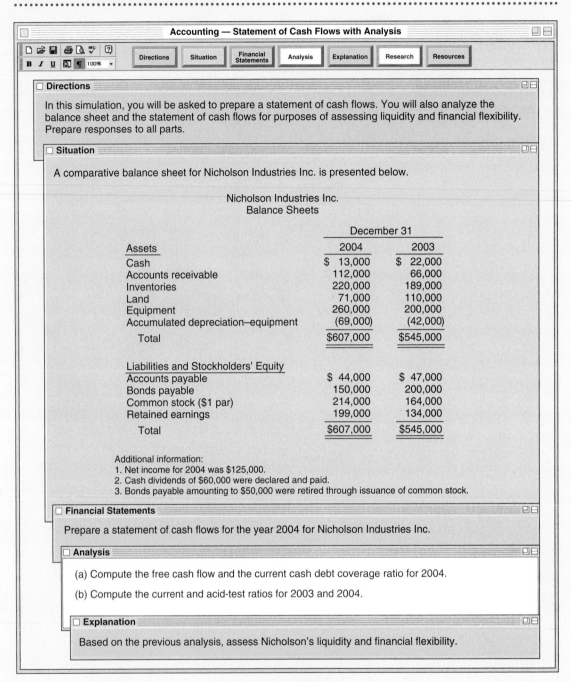

CHAPTER 6

Accounting and the Time Value of Money

The Magic of Interest

Sidney Homer, author of *A History of Interest Rates*, wrote, "$1,000 invested at a mere 8 percent for 400 years would grow to $23 quadrillion—$5 million for every human on earth. But the first 100 years are the hardest."

This startling quote highlights the power of time and compounding interest on money. Equally significant, although not mentioned in the quote, is the fact that a small difference in the interest rate makes a big difference in the amount of monies accumulated over time. Taking a more realistic example, assume that you had $20,000 in a tax-free retirement account. Half the money is in stocks returning 12 percent and the other half in bonds earning 8 percent. Assuming reinvested profits and quarterly compounding, your bonds would be worth $22,080 after ten years, a doubling of their value. But your stocks, returning 4 percent more, would be worth $32,620, or triple your initial value. The following chart shows this impact.

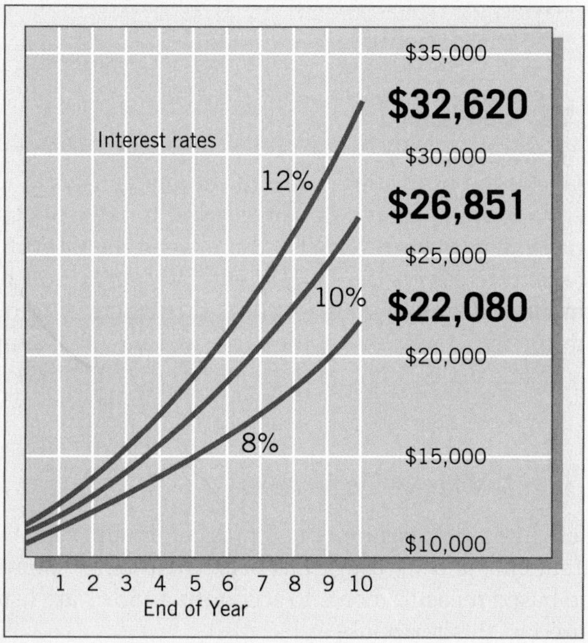

Money received tomorrow is not the same as money received today. Business people are acutely aware of this timing factor, and they invest and borrow only after carefully analyzing the relative present or future values of the cash flows.

LEARNING OBJECTIVES

After studying this chapter, you should be able to:

1. **Identify accounting topics where time value of money is relevant.**
2. **Distinguish between simple and compound interest.**
3. **Learn how to use appropriate compound interest tables.**
4. **Identify variables fundamental to solving interest problems.**
5. **Solve future and present value of 1 problems.**
6. **Solve future value of ordinary and annuity due problems.**
7. **Solve present value of ordinary and annuity due problems.**
8. **Solve present value problems related to deferred annuities and bonds.**
9. **Apply the expected cash flow approach to present value measurement.**

PREVIEW OF CHAPTER 6

As indicated in the opening story, the timing of the returns on investments has an important effect on the worth of the investment (asset), and the timing of debt repayments has a similarly important effect on the value of the debt commitment (liability). As a financial expert, you will be expected to make present and future value measurements and to understand their implications. The purpose of this chapter is to present the tools and techniques that will help you measure the present value of future cash inflows and outflows. The content and organization of the chapter are as follows.

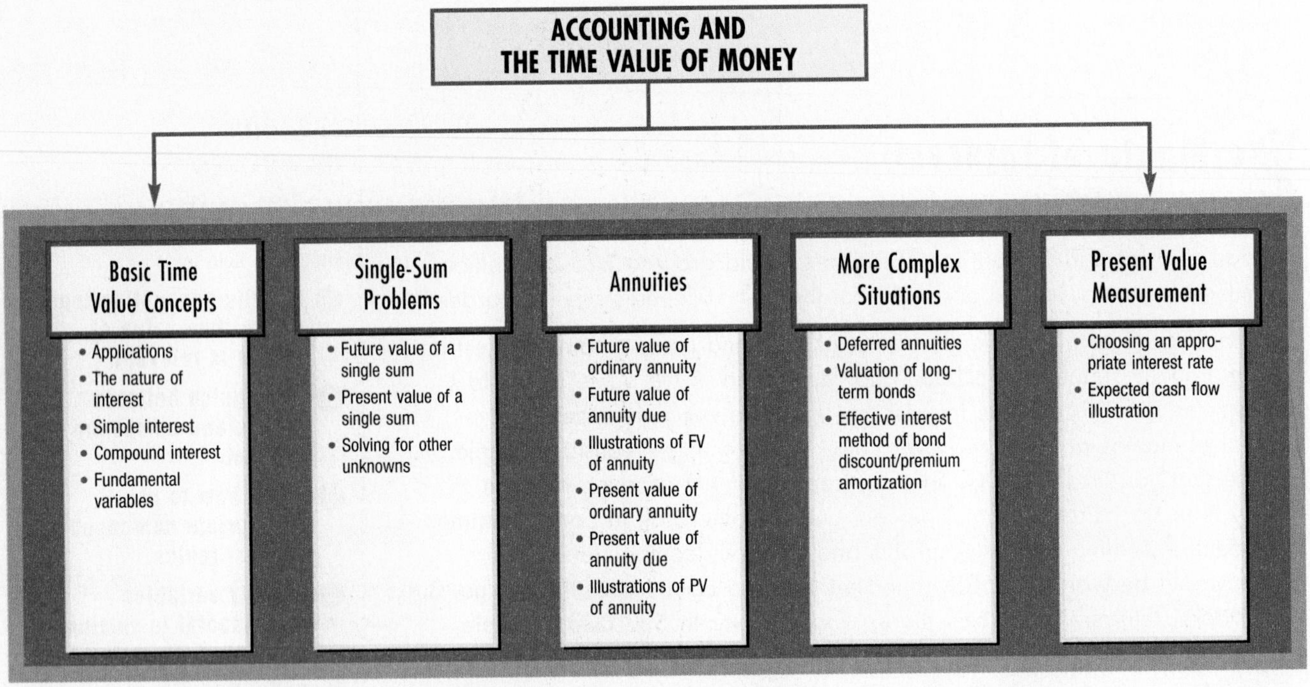

BASIC TIME VALUE CONCEPTS

OBJECTIVE 1
Identify accounting topics where the time value of money is relevant.

In accounting (and finance), the term **time value of money** is used to indicate a relationship between time and money—that a dollar received today is worth more than a dollar promised at some time in the future. Why? Because of the opportunity to invest today's dollar and receive interest on the investment. Yet, when you have to decide among various investment or borrowing alternatives, it is essential to be able to compare today's dollar and tomorrow's dollar on the same footing—to "compare apples to apples." We do that by using the concept of **present value**, which has many applications in accounting.

Applications of Time Value Concepts

Financial reporting uses different measurements in different situations. Present value is one of these measurements, and its usage has been increasing.[1] Some of the applications of present value-based measurements to accounting topics are listed below, several of which are required in this textbook.

[1] Many of the recent standards, such as *FASB Statements No. 106, 107, 109, 113, 114, 116, 141, 142,* and *144,* have addressed the issue of present value somewhere in the pronouncement or related basis for conclusions.

PRESENT VALUE-BASED ACCOUNTING MEASUREMENTS

1. *Notes.* Valuing noncurrent receivables and payables that carry no stated interest rate or a lower than market interest rate.
2. *Leases.* Valuing assets and obligations to be capitalized under long-term leases and measuring the amount of the lease payments and annual leasehold amortization.
3. *Pensions and Other Postretirement Benefits.* Measuring service cost components of employers' postretirement benefits expense and postretirement benefits obligation.
4. *Long-Term Assets.* Evaluating alternative long-term investments by discounting future cash flows. Determining the value of assets acquired under deferred payment contracts. Measuring impairments of assets.
5. *Sinking Funds.* Determining the contributions necessary to accumulate a fund for debt retirements.
6. *Business Combinations.* Determining the value of receivables, payables, liabilities, accruals, and commitments acquired or assumed in a "purchase."
7. *Disclosures.* Measuring the value of future cash flows from oil and gas reserves for disclosure in supplementary information.
8. *Installment Contracts.* Measuring periodic payments on long-term purchase contracts.

In addition to accounting and business applications, compound interest, annuity, and present value concepts apply to personal finance and investment decisions. In purchasing a home or car, planning for retirement, and evaluating alternative investments, you will need to understand time value of money concepts.

The Nature of Interest

Interest is payment for the use of money. It is the excess cash received or repaid over and above the amount lent or borrowed (**principal**). For example, if the Corner Bank lends you $1,000 with the understanding that you will repay $1,150, then the excess over $1,000, or $150, represents interest expense. Or if you lend your roommate $100 and then collect $110 in full payment, the $10 excess represents interest revenue.

The amount of interest to be paid is generally stated as a rate over a specific period of time. For example, if you used $1,000 for one year before repaying $1,150, the rate of interest is 15% per year ($150 ÷ $1,000). The custom of expressing interest as a percentage rate is an established business practice.[2] In fact, business managers make investing and borrowing decisions on the basis of the rate of interest involved rather than on the actual dollar amount of interest to be received or paid.

How is the interest rate determined? One of the most important factors is the level of credit risk (risk of nonpayment) involved. Other factors being equal, the higher the credit risk, the higher the interest rate. Low-risk borrowers like **Microsoft** or **Intel** can probably obtain a loan at or slightly below the going market rate of interest. You or the neighborhood delicatessen, on the other hand, would probably be charged several percentage points above the market rate—if you can get a loan at all.

[2]Federal law requires the disclosure of interest rates on an **annual basis** in all contracts. That is, instead of stating the rate as "1% per month," it must be stated as "12% per year" if it is simple interest or "12.68% per year" if it is compounded monthly.

The amount of interest involved in any financing transaction is a function of three variables:

VARIABLES IN INTEREST COMPUTATION

1. *Principal.* The amount borrowed or invested.
2. *Interest Rate.* A percentage of the outstanding principal.
3. *Time.* The number of years or fractional portion of a year that the principal is outstanding.

The larger the principal amount, or the higher the interest rate, or the longer the time period, the larger the dollar amount of interest.

Simple Interest

OBJECTIVE 2
Distinguish between simple and compound interest.

Simple interest is computed on the amount of the principal only. It is the return on (or growth of) the principal for one time period. Simple interest is commonly expressed as follows.[3]

$$\text{Interest} = p \times i \times n$$

where

$$p = \text{principal}$$
$$i = \text{rate of interest for a single period}$$
$$n = \text{number of periods}$$

To illustrate, if you borrow $1,000 for 3 years with a simple interest rate of 15% per year, the total interest you will pay is $450, computed as follows.

$$\begin{aligned}\text{Interest} &= p \times i \times n \\ &= \$1{,}000 \times .15 \times 3 \\ &= \$450\end{aligned}$$

If you borrow $1,000 for 3 months at 15%, the interest is $37.50, computed as follows.

$$\begin{aligned}\text{Interest} &= \$1{,}000 \times .15 \times .25 \\ &= \$37.50\end{aligned}$$

Compound Interest

John Maynard Keynes, the legendary English economist, supposedly called it magic. Mayer Rothschild, the founder of the famous European banking firm, is said to have proclaimed it the eighth wonder of the world. Today people continue to extol its wonder and its power. The object of their affection is compound interest.

Compound interest is computed on principal **and** on any interest earned that has not been paid or withdrawn. It is the return on (or growth of) the principal for two or more time periods. Compounding computes interest not only on the principal but also on the interest earned to date on that principal, assuming the interest is left on deposit.

To illustrate the difference between simple and compound interest, assume that you deposit $1,000 in the Last National Bank, where it will earn simple interest of 9%

[3]Simple interest is traditionally expressed in textbooks in business mathematics or business finance as: I(interest) = P(principal) × R(rate) × T(time).

per year, and you deposit another $1,000 in the First State Bank, where it will earn compound interest of 9% per year compounded annually. Also assume that in both cases you will not withdraw any interest until 3 years from the date of deposit. The computation of interest to be received and the accumulated year-end balance are indicated in Illustration 6-1.

ILLUSTRATION 6-1
Simple vs. Compound Interest

Last National Bank

Simple Interest Calculation	Simple Interest	Accumulated Year-end Balance
Year 1 $1,000.00 × 9%	$ 90.00	$1,090.00
Year 2 $1,000.00 × 9%	90.00	$1,180.00
Year 3 $1,000.00 × 9%	90.00	$1,270.00
	$270.00	

First State Bank

Compound Interest Calculation	Compound Interest	Accumulated Year-end Balance
Year 1 $1,000.00 × 9%	$ 90.00	$1,090.00
Year 2 $1,090.00 × 9%	98.10	$1,188.10
Year 3 $1,188.10 × 9%	106.93	$1,295.03
	$295.03	

$25.03 Difference

Note in the illustration above that simple interest uses the initial principal of $1,000 to compute the interest in all 3 years. **Compound interest uses the accumulated balance (principal plus interest to date) at each year-end to compute interest in the succeeding year—which explains why your compound interest account is larger.**

Obviously if you had a choice between investing your money at simple interest or at compound interest, you would choose compound interest, all other things—especially risk—being equal. In the example, compounding provides $25.03 of additional interest revenue. For practical purposes compounding assumes that unpaid interest earned becomes a part of the principal, and the accumulated balance at the end of each year becomes the new principal sum on which interest is earned during the next year.

Compound interest is the typical interest computation applied in business situations, particularly in our economy where large amounts of long-lived assets are used productively and financed over long periods of time. Financial managers view and evaluate their investment opportunities in terms of a series of periodic returns, each of which can be reinvested to yield additional returns. Simple interest is usually applicable only to short-term investments and debts that involve a time span of one year or less.

SPARE CHANGE

WHAT DO THE NUMBERS MEAN?

Here is an illustration of the power of *time* and *compounding* interest on money. In 1626, Peter Minuit bought Manhattan Island from the Manhattoe Indians for $24 worth of trinkets and beads. If the Indians had taken a boat to Holland, invested the $24 in Dutch securities returning just 6 percent per year, and kept the money and interest invested at 6 percent, by 1971 they would have had $13 billion, enough to buy back Manhattan and still have a couple of billion dollars left for doodads (*Forbes*, June 1, 1971). By 2002, 376 years after the trade, the $24 would have grown to approximately $79 billion.

OBJECTIVE 3
Learn how to use appropriate compound interest tables.

Compound Interest Tables (see pages 302—311)

Five different types of compound interest tables are presented at the end of this chapter. These tables should help you study this chapter as well as solve other problems involving interest. The titles of these five tables and their contents are:

INTEREST TABLES AND CONTENTS

1. ***Future Value of 1* table.** Contains the amounts to which 1 will accumulate if deposited now at a specified rate and left for a specified number of periods. (Table 6-1)
2. ***Present Value of 1* table.** Contains the amounts that must be deposited now at a specified rate of interest to equal 1 at the end of a specified number of periods. (Table 6-2)
3. ***Future Value of an Ordinary Annuity of 1* table.** Contains the amounts to which periodic rents of 1 will accumulate if the payments (rents) are invested at the **end** of each period at a specified rate of interest for a specified number of periods. (Table 6-3)
4. ***Present Value of an Ordinary Annuity of 1* table.** Contains the amounts that must be deposited now at a specified rate of interest to permit withdrawals of 1 at the **end** of regular periodic intervals for the specified number of periods. (Table 6-4)
5. ***Present Value of an Annuity Due of 1* table.** Contains the amounts that must be deposited now at a specified rate of interest to permit withdrawals of 1 at the beginning of regular periodic intervals for the specified number of periods. (Table 6-5)

Illustration 6-2 indicates the general format and content of these tables. It shows how much principal plus interest a dollar accumulates to at the end of each of five periods at three different rates of compound interest.

ILLUSTRATION 6-2
Excerpt from Table 6-1

FUTURE VALUE OF 1 AT COMPOUND INTEREST
(EXCERPT FROM TABLE 6-1, PAGE 303)

Period	9%	10%	11%
1	1.09000	1.10000	1.11000
2	1.18810	1.21000	1.23210
3	1.29503	1.33100	1.36763
4	1.41158	1.46410	1.51807
5	1.53862	1.61051	1.68506

The compound tables are computed using basic formulas. For example, the formula to determine the future value factor (*FVF*) for 1 is:

$$FVF_{n,i} = (1 + i)^n$$

where

$FVF_{n,i}$ = future value factor for n periods at i interest
n = number of periods
i = rate of interest for a single period

The $FVF_{n,i}$ and other time value of money formulas are programmed into financial calculators. The use of a financial calculator to solve time value of money problems is illustrated in Appendix 6A.

To illustrate the use of interest tables to calculate compound amounts, assuming an interest rate of 9%, the future value to which 1 accumulates (the future value factor) is shown below.

ILLUSTRATION 6-3
Accumulation of Compound Amounts

Period	Beginning-of-Period Amount	×	Multiplier $(1 + i)$	=	End-of-Period Amount*	Formula $(1 + i)^n$
1	1.00000		1.09		1.09000	$(1.09)^1$
2	1.09000		1.09		1.18810	$(1.09)^2$
3	1.18810		1.09		1.29503	$(1.09)^3$

*Note that these amounts appear in Table 6-1 in the 9% column.

Throughout the discussion of compound interest tables the use of the term **periods** instead of **years** is intentional. Interest is generally expressed in terms of an annual rate, but in many business circumstances the compounding period is less than one year. In such circumstances the annual interest rate must be converted to correspond to the length of the period. The process is to convert the "annual interest rate" into the "compounding period interest rate" by **dividing the annual rate by the number of compounding periods per year**.

In addition, the number of periods is determined by **multiplying the number of years involved by the number of compounding periods per year**. To illustrate, assume that $1.00 is invested for 6 years at 8% annual interest compounded **quarterly**. Using Table 6-1 from page 302, we can determine the amount to which this $1.00 will accumulate: Read the factor that appears in the 2% column on the 24th row—6 years × 4 compounding periods per year, namely 1.60844, or approximately $1.61. Thus, the term **periods**, not **years**, is used in all compound interest tables to express the quantity of n.

The following schedule shows how to determine (1) the interest rate per compounding period and (2) the number of compounding periods in four situations of differing compounding frequency.[4]

ILLUSTRATION 6-4
Frequency of Compounding

12% Annual Interest Rate over 5 Years Compounded	Interest Rate per Compounding Period	Number of Compounding Periods
Annually (1)	.12 ÷ 1 = .12	5 years × 1 compounding per year = 5 periods
Semiannually (2)	.12 ÷ 2 = .06	5 years × 2 compoundings per year = 10 periods
Quarterly (4)	.12 ÷ 4 = .03	5 years × 4 compoundings per year = 20 periods
Monthly (12)	.12 ÷ 12 = .01	5 years × 12 compoundings per year = 60 periods

[4]Because interest is theoretically earned (accruing) every second of every day, it is possible to calculate interest that is **compounded continuously**. Computations involving continuous compounding are facilitated through the use of the natural, or Napierian, system of logarithms. As a practical matter, however, most business transactions assume interest to be compounded no more frequently than daily.

How often interest is compounded can make a substantial difference in the rate of return. For example, a 9% annual interest compounded **daily** provides a 9.42% yield, or a difference of .42%. The 9.42% is referred to as the **effective yield.**[5] The annual interest rate (9%) is called the **stated, nominal,** or **face rate.** When the compounding frequency is greater than once a year, the effective interest rate will always be greater than the stated rate.

The schedule below shows how compounding for five different time periods affects the effective yield and the amount earned by an investment of $10,000 for one year.

ILLUSTRATION 6-5
Comparison of Different Compounding Periods

	Compounding Periods				
Interest Rate	Annually	Semiannually	Quarterly	Monthly	Daily
8%	8.00% $800	8.16% $816	8.24% $824	8.30% $830	8.33% $833
9%	9.00% $900	9.20% $920	9.31% $931	9.38% $938	9.42% $942
10%	10.00% $1,000	10.25% $1,025	10.38% $1,038	10.47% $1,047	10.52% $1,052

Fundamental Variables

OBJECTIVE 4
Identify variables fundamental to solving interest problems.

The following four variables are fundamental to all compound interest problems.

FUNDAMENTAL VARIABLES

1. ***Rate of Interest.*** This rate, unless otherwise stated, is an annual rate that must be adjusted to reflect the length of the compounding period if less than a year.
2. ***Number of Time Periods.*** This is the number of compounding periods. (A period may be equal to or less than a year.)
3. ***Future Value.*** The value at a future date of a given sum or sums invested assuming compound interest.
4. ***Present Value.*** The value now (present time) of a future sum or sums discounted assuming compound interest.

The relationship of these four fundamental variables is depicted in the **time diagram** on the following page.

---

[5]The formula for calculating the **effective rate** in situations where the compounding frequency (n) is greater than once a year is as follows.

$$\text{Effective rate} = (1 + i)^n - 1$$

To illustrate, if the stated annual rate is 8% compounded quarterly (or 2% per quarter), the effective annual rate is:

$$\begin{aligned}\text{Effective rate} &= (1 + .02)^4 - 1\\ &= (1.02)^4 - 1\\ &= 1.0824 - 1\\ &= .0824\\ &= 8.24\%\end{aligned}$$

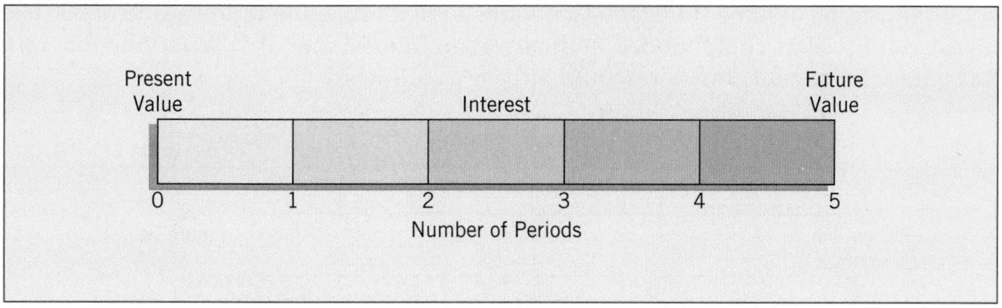

ILLUSTRATION 6-6
Basic Time Diagram

In some cases all four of these variables are known, but in many business situations at least one variable is unknown. As an aid to better understanding the problems and to finding solutions, we encourage you to sketch compound interest problems in the form of the preceding time diagram.

SINGLE-SUM PROBLEMS

Many business and investment decisions involve a single amount of money that either exists now or will in the future. Single-sum problems can generally be classified into one of the following two categories.

OBJECTIVE 5
Solve future and present value of 1 problems.

1. Computing the **unknown future value** of a known single sum of money that is invested now for a certain number of periods at a certain interest rate.
2. Computing the **unknown present value** of a known single sum of money in the future that is discounted for a certain number of periods at a certain interest rate.

When analyzing the information provided, you determine first whether it is a future value problem or a present value problem. **If you are solving for a future value**, all cash flows must be *accumulated* to a future point. In this instance, the effect of interest is to increase the amounts or values over time so that the future value is greater than the present value. However, **if you are solving for a present value**, all cash flows must be *discounted* from the future to the present. In this case, the **discounting** reduces the amounts or values so that the present value is less than the future amount.

Preparation of time diagrams aids in identifying the unknown as an item in the future or the present. Sometimes it is neither a future value nor a present value that is to be determined but, rather, the interest or discount rate or the number of compounding or discounting periods.

Future Value of a Single Sum

To determine the **future value** of a single sum, multiply the future value factor by its present value (principal), as follows.

$$FV = PV\ (FVF_{n,i})$$

where

FV = future value
PV = present value (principal or single sum)
$FVF_{n,i}$ = future value factor for n periods at i interest

To illustrate, assume Brueggen Co. wants to determine the future value of $50,000 invested for 5 years compounded annually at an interest rate of 11%. In time-diagram form, this investment situation would appear as follows.

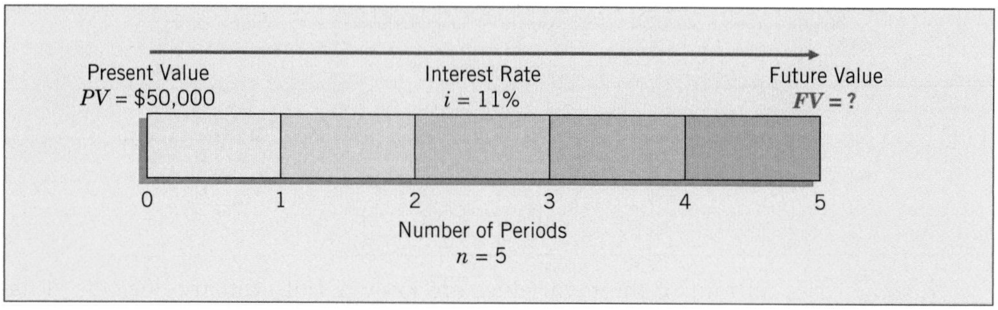

Using the formula, this investment problem is solved as follows.

$$\begin{aligned}\text{Future value} &= PV\ (FVF_{n,i}) \\ &= \$50{,}000\ (FVF_{5,11\%}) \\ &= \$50{,}000\ (1 + .11)^5 \\ &= \$50{,}000\ (1.68506) \\ &= \$84{,}253\end{aligned}$$

To determine the future value factor of 1.68506 in the formula above, use a financial calculator or read the appropriate table, in this case Table 6-1 (11% column and the 5-period row).

This time diagram and formula approach can be applied to a routine business situation. To illustrate, **Commonwealth Edison Company** deposited $250 million in an escrow account with the **Northern Trust Company** at the beginning of 2002 as a commitment toward a power plant to be completed December 31, 2005. How much will be on deposit at the end of 4 years if interest is 10%, compounded semi-annually?

With a known present value of $250 million, a total of 8 compounding periods (4 × 2), and an interest rate of 5% per compounding period (.10 ÷ 2), this problem can be time-diagrammed and the future value determined as follows.

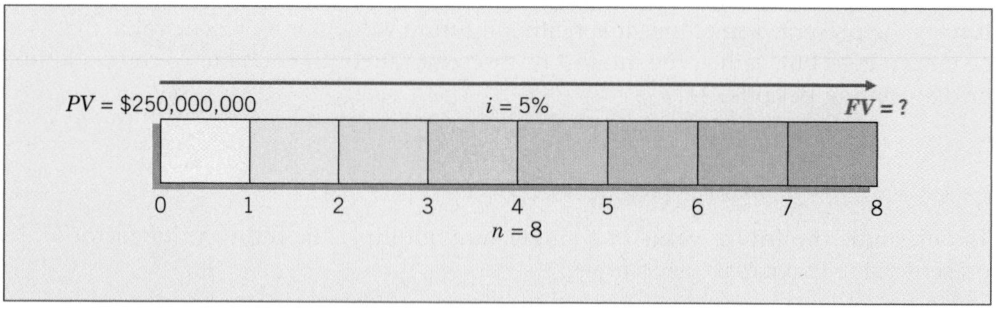

$$\begin{aligned}\text{Future value} &= \$250{,}000{,}000\ (FVF_{8,5\%}) \\ &= \$250{,}000{,}000\ (1 + .05)^8 \\ &= \$250{,}000{,}000\ (1.47746) \\ &= \$369{,}365{,}000\end{aligned}$$

Using a future value factor found in Table 6-1 (5% column, 8-period row), we find that the deposit of $250 million will accumulate to $369,365,000 by December 31, 2005.

Present Value of a Single Sum

The Brueggen Co. example on page 260 showed that $50,000 invested at an annually compounded interest rate of 11% will be worth $84,253 at the end of 5 years. It follows, then, that $84,253, 5 years in the future is worth $50,000 now. That is, $50,000 is the **present value** of $84,253. The **present value** is the amount that must be invested now to produce the known future value. **The present value is always a smaller amount than the known future value because interest will be earned and accumulated on the present value to the future date.** In determining the future value, we move forward in time using a process of **accumulation**. In determining present value, we move backward in time using a process of **discounting**.

As indicated earlier, a "present value of 1 table" appears at the end of this chapter as Table 6-2. Illustration 6-7 demonstrates the nature of such a table. It shows the present value of 1 for five different periods at three different rates of interest.

ILLUSTRATION 6-7
Excerpt from Table 6-2

PRESENT VALUE OF 1 AT COMPOUND INTEREST
(EXCERPT FROM TABLE 6-2, PAGE 305)

Period	9%	10%	11%
1	0.91743	0.90909	0.90090
2	0.84168	0.82645	0.81162
3	0.77218	0.75132	0.73119
4	0.70843	0.68301	0.65873
5	0.64993	0.62092	0.59345

The present value of 1 (present value factor) may be expressed as a formula:

$$PVF_{n,i} = \frac{1}{(1+i)^n}$$

where

$PVF_{n,i}$ = present value factor for n periods at i interest

To illustrate, assuming an interest rate of 9%, the present value of 1 discounted for three different periods is as follows.

ILLUSTRATION 6-8
Present Value of $1 Discounted at 9% for Three Periods

Discount Periods	1	÷ $(1+i)^n$	= Present Value*	Formula $1/(1+i)^n$
1	1.00000	1.09	.91743	$1/(1.09)^1$
2	1.00000	$(1.09)^2$	.84168	$1/(1.09)^2$
3	1.00000	$(1.09)^3$	.77218	$1/(1.09)^3$

*Note that these amounts appear in Table 6-2 in the 9% column.

The present value of any single sum (future value), then, is as follows.

$$PV = FV\,(PVF_{n,i})$$

where

PV = present value

FV = future value

$PVF_{n,i}$ = present value factor for n periods at i interest

To illustrate, what is the present value of $84,253 to be received or paid in 5 years discounted at 11% compounded annually? In time-diagram form, this problem is drawn as follows.

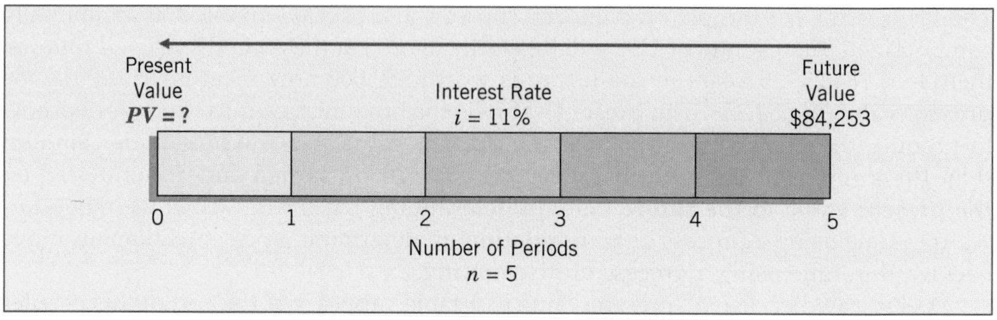

Using the formula, this problem is solved as follows.

$$\begin{aligned}\text{Present value} &= FV\,(PVF_{n,i})\\ &= \$84{,}253\,(PVF_{5,11\%})\\ &= \$84{,}253\left(\frac{1}{(1+.11)^5}\right)\\ &= \$84{,}253\,(.59345)\\ &= \$50{,}000\end{aligned}$$

To determine the present value factor of .59345, use a financial calculator or read the present value of a single sum in Table 6-2 (11% column, 5-period row).

The time diagram and formula approach can be applied in a variety of situations. For example, assume that your rich uncle proposes to give you $2,000 for a trip to Europe when you graduate from college 3 years from now. He proposes to finance the trip by investing a sum of money now at 8% compound interest that will provide you with $2,000 upon your graduation. The only conditions are that you graduate and that you tell him how much to invest now.

To impress your uncle, you might set up the following time diagram and solve this problem as follows.

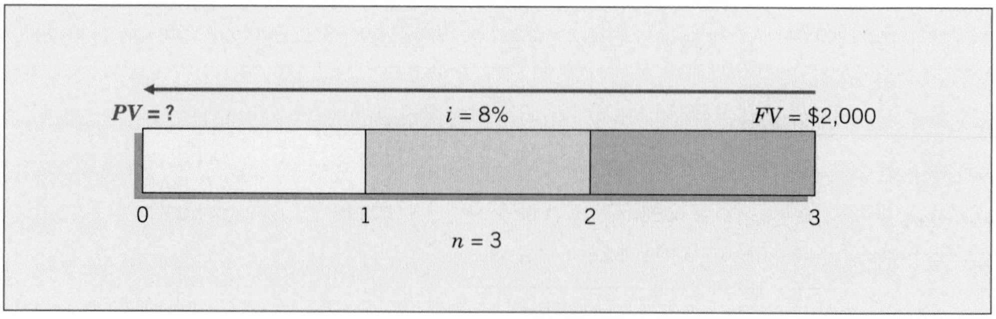

$$\begin{aligned}\text{Present value} &= \$2{,}000\,(PVF_{3,8\%})\\ &= \$2{,}000\left(\frac{1}{(1+.08)^3}\right)\\ &= \$2{,}000\,(.79383)\\ &= \$1{,}587.66\end{aligned}$$

Advise your uncle to invest \$1,587.66 now to provide you with \$2,000 upon graduation. To satisfy your uncle's other condition, you must pass this course, and many more.

Solving for Other Unknowns in Single-Sum Problems

In computing either the future value or the present value in the previous single-sum illustrations, both the number of periods and the interest rate were known. In many business situations, both the future value and the present value are known, but the number of periods or the interest rate is unknown. The following two illustrations are single-sum problems (future value and present value) with either an unknown number of periods (n) or an unknown interest rate (i). These illustrations and the accompanying solutions demonstrate that if any three of the four values (future value, FV; present value, PV; number of periods, n; interest rate, i) are known, the remaining unknown variable can be derived.

Illustration—Computation of the Number of Periods

The Village of Somonauk wants to accumulate \$70,000 for the construction of a veterans monument in the town square. If at the beginning of the current year the Village deposited \$47,811 in a memorial fund that earns 10% interest compounded annually, how many years will it take to accumulate \$70,000 in the memorial fund?

In this illustration, both the present value (\$47,811) and the future value (\$70,000) are known along with the interest rate of 10%. A time diagram of this investment problem is as follows.

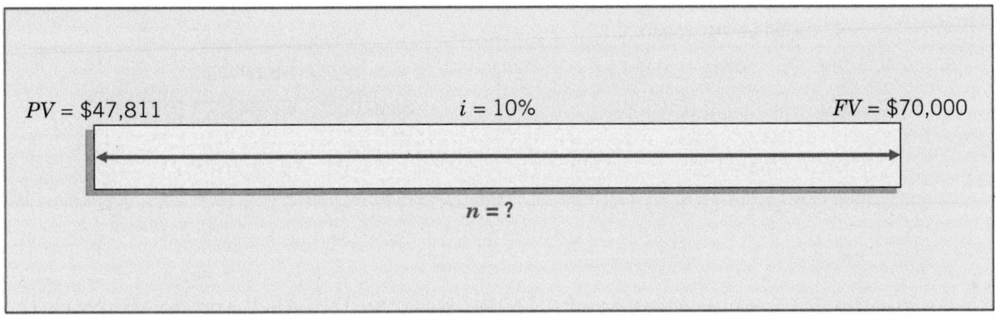

Because both the present value and the future value are known, we can solve for the unknown number of periods using either the future value or the present value formulas as shown below.

ILLUSTRATION 6-9
Solving for Unknown Number of Periods

Future Value Approach	Present Value Approach
$FV = PV\,(FVF_{n,10\%})$	$PV = FV\,(PVF_{n,10\%})$
$\$70{,}000 = \$47{,}811\,(FVF_{n,10\%})$	$\$47{,}811 = \$70{,}000\,(PVF_{n,10\%})$
$FVF_{n,10\%} = \dfrac{\$70{,}000}{\$47{,}811} = 1.46410$	$PVF_{n,10\%} = \dfrac{\$47{,}811}{\$70{,}000} = .68301$

Using the future value factor of 1.46410, refer to Table 6-1 and read down the 10% column to find that factor in the 4-period row. Thus, it will take 4 years for the \$47,811 to accumulate to \$70,000 if invested at 10% interest compounded annually. Using the present value factor of .68301, refer to Table 6-2 and read down the 10% column to find again that factor in the 4-period row.

Illustration—Computation of the Interest Rate

Advanced Design, Inc. wishes to have $1,409,870 for basic research 5 years from now. The firm currently has $800,000 to invest for that purpose. At what rate of interest must the $800,000 be invested to fund basic research projects of $1,409,870, 5 years from now?

A time diagram of this investment situation is as follows.

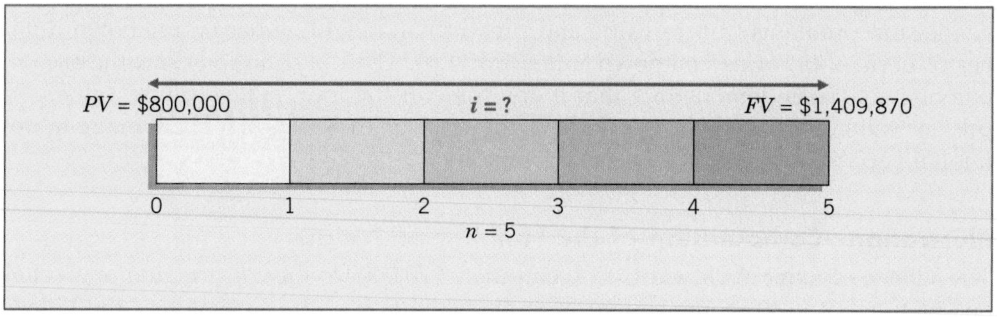

The unknown interest rate may be determined from either the future value approach or the present value approach as shown in Illustration 6-10.

ILLUSTRATION 6-10
Solving for Unknown Interest Rate

Future Value Approach	Present Value Approach
$FV = PV\,(FVF_{5,i})$	$PV = FV\,(PVF_{5,i})$
$\$1,409,870 = \$800,000\,(FVF_{5,i})$	$\$800,000 = \$1,409,870\,(PVF_{5,i})$
$FVF_{5,i} = \dfrac{\$1,409,870}{\$800,000} = 1.76234$	$PVF_{5,i} = \dfrac{\$800,000}{\$1,409,870} = .56743$

Using the future value factor of 1.76234, refer to Table 6-1 and read across the 5-period row to find that factor in the 12% column. Thus, the $800,000 must be invested at 12% to accumulate to $1,409,870 in 5 years. And, using the present value factor of .56743 and Table 6-2, again find that factor at the juncture of the 5-period row and the 12% column.

ANNUITIES

The preceding discussion involved only the accumulation or discounting of a single principal sum. Individuals frequently encounter situations in which a series of dollar amounts are to be paid or received periodically, such as loans or sales to be repaid in installments, invested funds that will be partially recovered at regular intervals, or cost savings that are realized repeatedly. A life insurance contract is probably the most common and most familiar type of transaction involving a series of equal payments made at equal intervals of time. Such a process of periodic saving represents the accumulation of a sum of money through an annuity. An **annuity**, by definition, requires that (1) the periodic payments or receipts (called **rents**) always be the same amount, (2) the **interval** between such rents always be the same, and (3) the **interest be compounded** once each interval. The **future value of an annuity** is the sum of all the rents plus the accumulated compound interest on them.

It should be noted that the rents may occur at either the beginning or the end of the periods. To distinguish annuities under these two alternatives, an annuity is classified as an **ordinary annuity** if the rents occur at the end of each period, and as an **annuity due** if the rents occur at the beginning of each period.

Future Value of an Ordinary Annuity

OBJECTIVE 6
Solve future value of ordinary and annuity due problems.

One approach to the problem of determining the future value to which an annuity will accumulate is to compute the value to which **each** of the rents in the series will accumulate and then total their individual future values. For example, assume that $1 is deposited at the **end** of each of 5 years (an ordinary annuity) and earns 12% interest compounded annually. The future value can be computed as follows using the "future value of 1" table (Table 6-1) for each of the five $1 rents.

ILLUSTRATION 6-11
Solving for the Future Value of an Ordinary Annuity

END OF PERIOD IN WHICH $1.00 IS TO BE INVESTED

Present	1	2	3	4	5	Value at End of Year 5
	$1.00					$1.57352
		$1.00				1.40493
			$1.00			1.25440
				$1.00		1.12000
					$1.00	1.00000
Total (future value of an ordinary annuity of $1.00 for 5 periods at 12%)						$6.35285

Because the rents that comprise an ordinary annuity are deposited at the end of the period, they can earn no interest during the period in which they are originally deposited. For example, the third rent earns interest for only two periods (periods four and five). Obviously the third rent earns no interest for the first two periods since it is not deposited until the third period. Furthermore, it can earn no interest for the third period since it is not deposited until the end of the third period. Any time the future value of an ordinary annuity is computed, the number of compounding periods will always be **one less than the number of rents.**

Although the foregoing procedure for computing the future value of an ordinary annuity will always produce the correct answer, it can become cumbersome if the number of rents is large. A more efficient way of expressing the future value of an ordinary annuity of 1 is in a formula that is a summation of the individual rents plus the compound interest:

$$FVF\text{-}OA_{n,i} = \frac{(1+i)^n - 1}{i}$$

where

$FVF\text{-}OA_{n,i}$ = future value factor of an ordinary annuity
i = rate of interest per period
n = number of compounding periods

For example, $FVF\text{-}OA_{5,12\%}$ refers to the value to which an ordinary annuity of 1 will accumulate in 5 periods at 12% interest.

Using the formula above, tables have been developed similar to those used for the "future value of 1" and the "present value of 1" for both an ordinary annuity and an annuity due. The table in Illustration 6-12 is an excerpt from the "future value of an ordinary annuity of 1" table.

ILLUSTRATION 6-12
Excerpt from Table 6-3

FUTURE VALUE OF AN ORDINARY ANNUITY OF 1
(EXCERPT FROM TABLE 6-3, PAGE 307)

Period	10%	11%	12%
1	1.00000	1.00000	1.00000
2	2.10000	2.11000	2.12000
3	3.31000	3.34210	3.37440
4	4.64100	4.70973	4.77933
5	6.10510	6.22780	6.35285*

*Note that this annuity table factor is the same as the sum of the future values of 1 factors shown in Illustration 6-11.

Interpreting the table, if $1 is invested at the end of each year for 4 years at 11% interest compounded annually, the value of the annuity at the end of the fourth year will be $4.71 (4.70973 × $1). Multiply the factor from the appropriate line and column of the table by the dollar amount of **one rent** involved in an ordinary annuity. The result: the accumulated sum of the rents and the compound interest to the date of the last rent.

The future value of an ordinary annuity is computed as follows.

$$\text{Future value of an ordinary annuity} = R\,(FVF\text{-}OA_{n,i})$$

where

$$R = \text{periodic rent}$$

$$FVF\text{-}OA_{n,i} = \text{future value of an ordinary annuity factor for } n \text{ periods at } i \text{ interest}$$

To illustrate, what is the future value of five $5,000 deposits made at the end of each of the next 5 years, earning interest of 12%? In time-diagram form, this problem is drawn as follows.

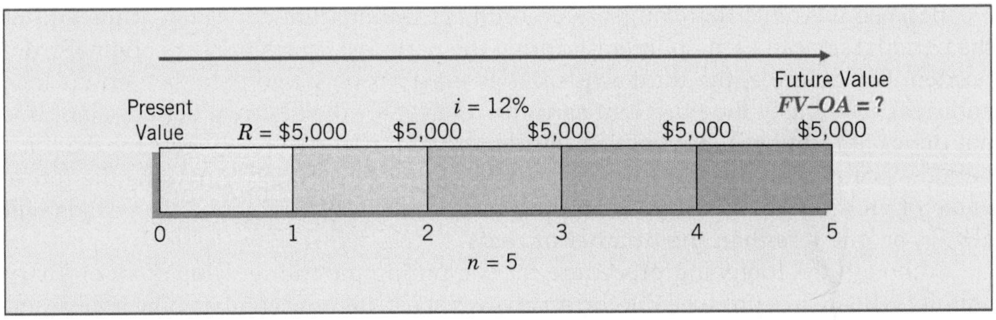

Using the formula, this investment problem is solved as follows.

$$\begin{aligned}\text{Future value of an ordinary annuity} &= R\,(FVF\text{-}OA_{n,i})\\ &= \$5{,}000\,(FVF\text{-}OA_{5,12\%})\\ &= \$5{,}000\left(\frac{(1+.12)^5-1}{.12}\right)\\ &= \$5{,}000\,(6.35285)\\ &= \$31{,}764.25\end{aligned}$$

We can determine the future value of an ordinary annuity factor of 6.35285 in the formula above using a financial calculator or by reading the appropriate table, in this case Table 6-3 (12% column and the 5-period row).

To illustrate these computations in a business situation, assume that Hightown Electronics decides to deposit $75,000 at the end of each 6-month period for the next 3 years for the purpose of accumulating enough money to meet debts that mature in 3 years. What is the future value that will be on deposit at the end of 3 years if the annual interest rate is 10%?

The time diagram and formula solution are as follows.

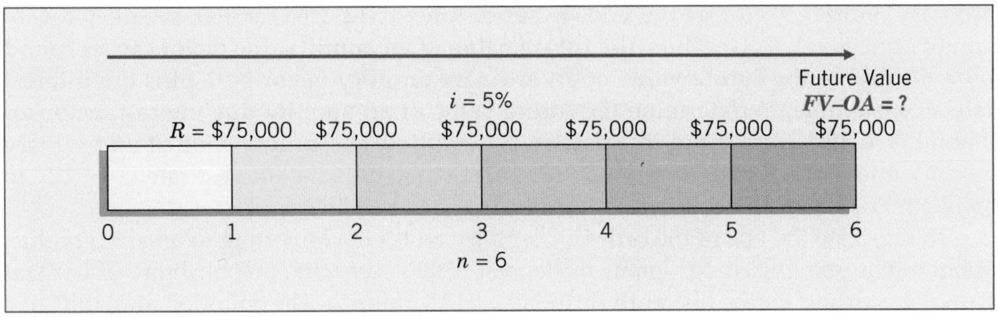

$$\text{Future value of an ordinary annuity} = R\,(FVF\text{-}OA_{n,i})$$
$$= \$75{,}000\,(FVF\text{-}OA_{6,5\%})$$
$$= \$75{,}000\left(\frac{(1+.05)^6-1}{.05}\right)$$
$$= \$75{,}000\,(6.80191)$$
$$= \$510{,}143.25$$

Thus, six 6-month deposits of $75,000 earning 5% per period will grow to $510,143.25.

Future Value of an Annuity Due

The preceding analysis of an ordinary annuity was based on the assumption that the periodic rents occur at the **end** of each period. An **annuity due** assumes periodic rents occur at the **beginning** of each period. This means an annuity due will accumulate interest during the first period, whereas an ordinary annuity rent will earn no interest during the first period because the rent is not received or paid until the end of the period. In other words, the significant difference between the two types of annuities is in the number of interest accumulation periods involved.

If rents occur at the end of a period (ordinary annuity), in determining the **future value of an annuity** there will be one less interest period than if the rents occur at the beginning of the period (annuity due). The distinction is shown in Illustration 6-13.

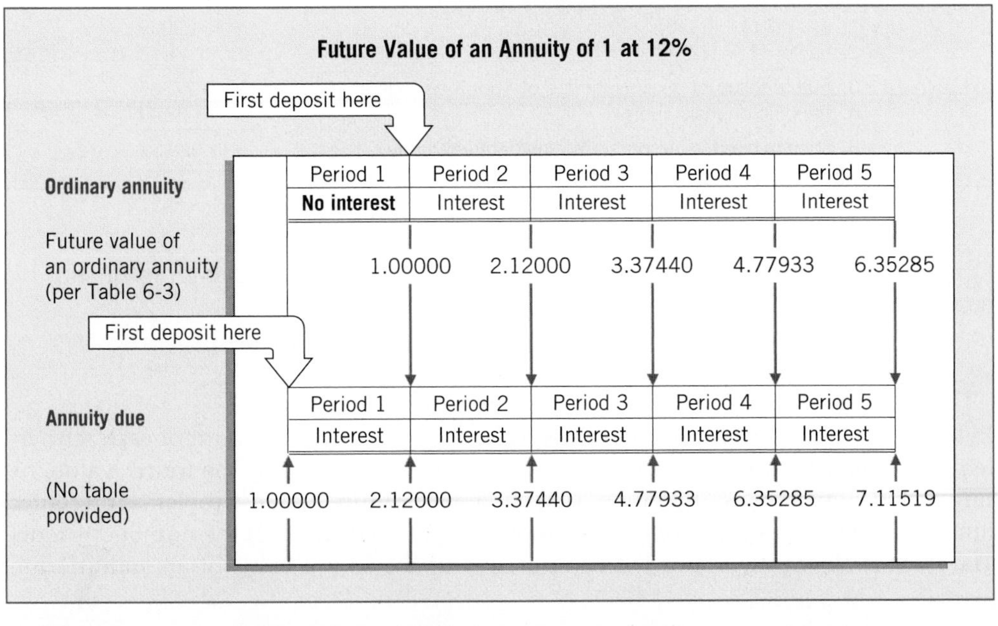

ILLUSTRATION 6-13
Comparison of the Future Value of an Ordinary Annuity with an Annuity Due

In this example, because the cash flows from the annuity due come exactly one period earlier than for an ordinary annuity, the future value of the annuity due factor is exactly 12% higher than the ordinary annuity factor. For example, the value of an ordinary annuity factor at the end of period one at 12% is 1.00000, whereas for an annuity due it is 1.12000. **Thus, the future value of an annuity due factor can be found by multiplying the future value of an ordinary annuity factor by 1 plus the interest rate.** For example, to determine the future value of an annuity due interest factor for 5 periods at 12% compound interest, simply multiply the future value of an ordinary annuity interest factor for 5 periods (6.35285) by one plus the interest rate (1 + .12), to arrive at 7.11519 (6.35285 × 1.12).

To illustrate the use of the ordinary annuity tables in converting to an annuity due, assume that Sue Lotadough plans to deposit $800 a year on each birthday of her son Howard, starting today, his tenth birthday, at 12% interest compounded annually. Sue wants to know the amount she will have accumulated for college expenses by her son's eighteenth birthday. If the first deposit is made on Howard's tenth birthday, Sue will make a total of 8 deposits over the life of the annuity (assume no deposit on the eighteenth birthday). Because all the deposits will be made at the beginning of the periods, they represent an annuity due.

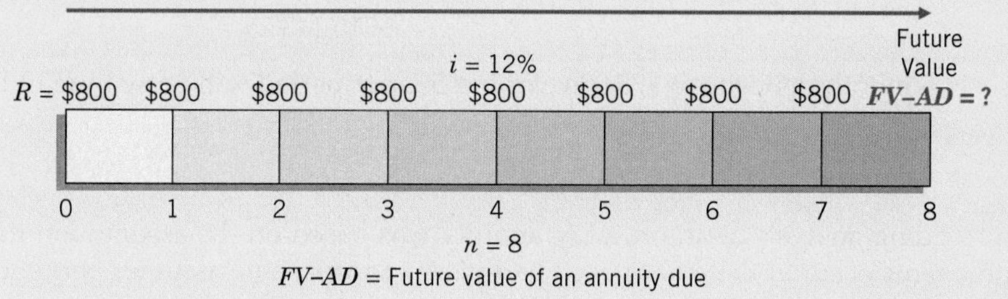

Referring to the "future value of an ordinary annuity of 1" table for 8 periods at 12%, we find a factor of 12.29969. This factor is then multiplied by (1 + .12) to arrive at the future value of an annuity due factor. As a result, the accumulated value on Howard's eighteenth birthday is $11,020.52 as shown in Illustration 6-14.

ILLUSTRATION 6-14
Computation of Accumulated Value of Annuity Due

1. Future value of an ordinary annuity of 1 for 8 periods at 12% (Table 6-3)		12.29969
2. Factor (1 + .12)	×	1.12
3. Future value of an annuity due of 1 for 8 periods at 12%		13.77565
4. Periodic deposit (rent)	×	$800
5. Accumulated value on son's eighteenth birthday		$11,020.52

Depending on the college he chooses, Howard may have only enough to finance his first year of school.

Illustrations of Future Value of Annuity Problems

In the foregoing annuity examples three values were known—amount of each rent, interest rate, and number of periods. They were used to determine the fourth value, future value, which was unknown. The first two future value problems presented illustrate the computations of (1) the amount of the rents and (2) the number of rents. The third problem illustrates the computation of the future value of an annuity due.

Computation of Rent

Assume that you wish to accumulate $14,000 for a down payment on a condominium apartment 5 years from now; for the next 5 years you can earn an annual return of 8% compounded semiannually. How much should you deposit at the end of each 6-month period?

The $14,000 is the future value of 10 (5 × 2) semiannual end-of-period payments of an unknown amount, at an interest rate of 4% (8% ÷ 2). This problem appears in the form of a time diagram as follows.

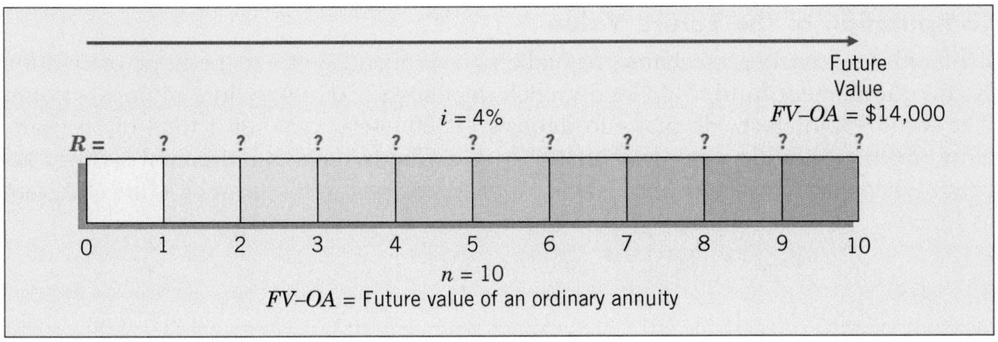

Using the formula for the future value of an ordinary annuity, the amount of each rent is determined as follows.

$$\text{Future value of an ordinary annuity} = R\,(FVF\text{-}OA_{n,i})$$

$$\$14{,}000 = R\,(FVF\text{-}OA_{10,4\%})$$

$$\$14{,}000 = R(12.00611)$$

$$\frac{\$14{,}000}{12.00611} = R$$

$$R = \$1{,}166.07$$

Thus, you must make 10 semiannual deposits of $1,166.07 each in order to accumulate $14,000 for your down payment.

Computation of the Number of Periodic Rents

Suppose that your company wishes to accumulate $117,332 by making periodic deposits of $20,000 at the end of each year that will earn 8% compounded annually while accumulating. How many deposits must be made?

The $117,332 represents the future value of n(?) $20,000 deposits, at an 8% annual rate of interest. This problem appears in the form of a time diagram as follows.

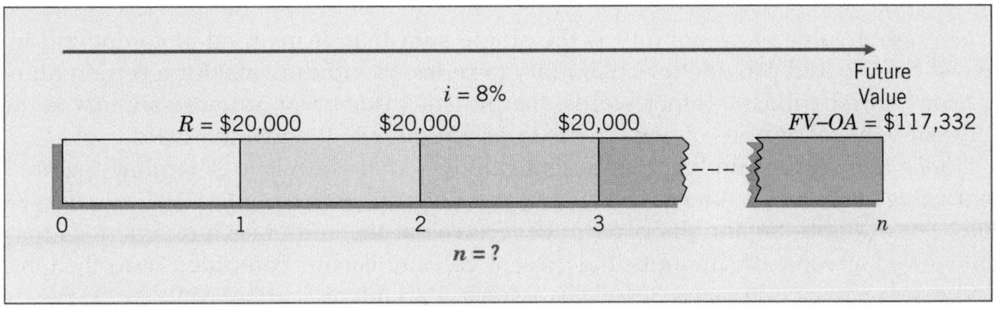

Using the future value of an ordinary annuity formula, we obtain the following factor.

$$\text{Future value of an ordinary annuity} = R\ (FVF\text{-}OA_{n,i})$$

$$\$117{,}332 = \$20{,}000\ (FVF\text{-}OA_{n,8\%})$$

$$FVF\text{-}OA_{n,8\%} = \frac{\$117{,}332}{\$20{,}000} = 5.86660$$

Using Table 6-3 and reading down the 8% column, we find 5.86660 in the 5-period row. Thus, five deposits of $20,000 each must be made.

Computation of the Future Value

Walter Goodwrench, a mechanic, has taken on weekend work in the hope of creating his own retirement fund. Mr. Goodwrench deposits $2,500 today in a savings account that earns 9% interest. He plans to deposit $2,500 every year for a total of 30 years. How much cash will have accumulated in Mr. Goodwrench's retirement savings account when he retires in 30 years? This problem appears in the form of a time diagram as follows.

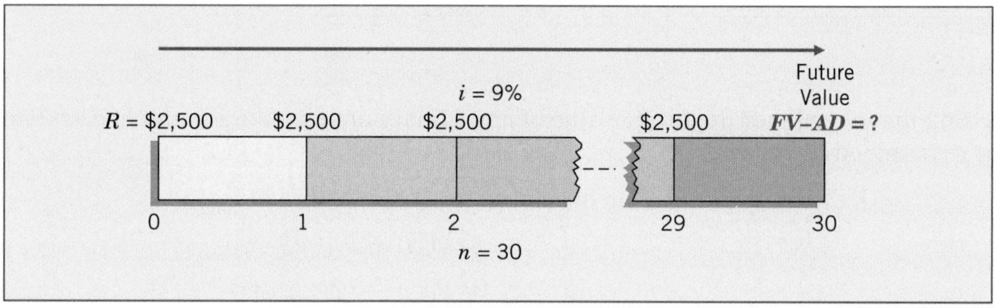

Using the "future value of an ordinary annuity of 1" table, the solution is computed as follows.

ILLUSTRATION 6-15
Computation of Accumulated Value of an Annuity Due

1. Future value of an ordinary annuity of 1 for 30 periods at 9%	136.30754
2. Factor (1 + .09)	× 1.09
3. Future value of an annuity due of 1 for 30 periods at 9%	148.57522
4. Periodic rent	× $2,500
5. Accumulated value at end of 30 years	$371,438

Present Value of an Ordinary Annuity

OBJECTIVE 7
Solve present value of ordinary and annuity due problems.

The present value of an annuity is **the single sum** that, if invested at compound interest now, would provide for an annuity (a series of withdrawals) for a certain number of future periods. In other words, the present value of an ordinary annuity is the present value of a series of equal rents to be withdrawn at equal intervals.

One approach to finding the present value of an annuity is to determine the present value of each of the rents in the series and then total their individual present values. For example, an annuity of $1 to be received at the **end** of each of 5 periods may be viewed as separate amounts; the present value of each is computed from the table of present values (see pages 304–305), assuming an interest rate of 12%.

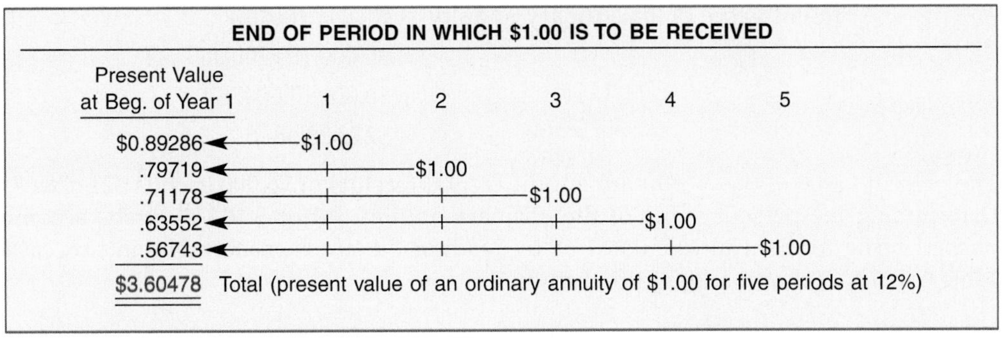
END OF PERIOD IN WHICH $1.00 IS TO BE RECEIVED
Present Value at Beg. of Year 1
1
2
3
4
5
$0.89286 ← $1.00
.79719 ← $1.00
.71178 ← $1.00
.63552 ← $1.00
.56743 ← $1.00
$3.60478 Total (present value of an ordinary annuity of $1.00 for five periods at 12%)

ILLUSTRATION 6-16
Solving for the Present Value of an Ordinary Annuity

This computation tells us that if we invest the single sum of \$3.60 today at 12% interest for 5 periods, we will be able to withdraw \$1 at the end of each period for 5 periods. This cumbersome procedure can be summarized by:

$$PVF\text{-}OA_{n,i} = \frac{1 - \dfrac{1}{(1+i)^n}}{i}$$

The expression $PVF\text{-}OA_{n,i}$ refers to the present value of an ordinary annuity of 1 factor for n periods at i interest. Using this formula, present value of ordinary annuity tables are prepared. An excerpt from such a table is shown below.

PRESENT VALUE OF AN ORDINARY ANNUITY OF 1
(EXCERPT FROM TABLE 6-4, PAGE 309)

Period	10%	11%	12%
1	0.90909	0.90090	0.89286
2	1.73554	1.71252	1.69005
3	2.48685	2.44371	2.40183
4	3.16986	3.10245	3.03735
5	3.79079	3.69590	3.60478*

*Note that this annuity table factor is equal to the sum of the present value of 1 factors shown in Illustration 6-16.

ILLUSTRATION 6-17
Excerpt from Table 6-4

The general formula for the present value of any ordinary annuity is as follows.

$$\text{Present value of an ordinary annuity} = R\,(PVF\text{-}OA_{n,i})$$

where

R = periodic rent (ordinary annuity)

$PVF\text{-}OA_{n,i}$ = present value of an ordinary annuity of 1 for n periods at i interest

To illustrate, what is the present value of rental receipts of \$6,000 each to be received at the end of each of the next 5 years when discounted at 12%? This problem may be time-diagrammed and solved as follows.

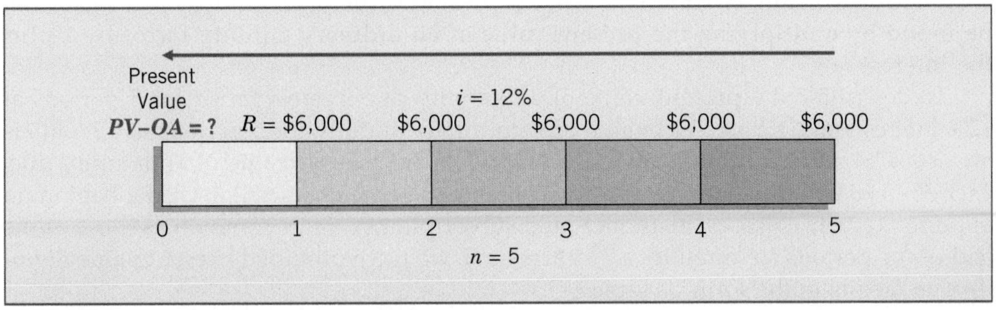

$$\begin{aligned}\text{Present value of an ordinary annuity} &= R\ (PVF\text{-}OA_{n,i}) \\ &= \$6{,}000\ (PVF\text{-}OA_{5,12\%}) \\ &= \$6{,}000\ (3.60478) \\ &= \$21{,}628.68\end{aligned}$$

The present value of the 5 ordinary annuity rental receipts of $6,000 each is $21,628.68. Determining the present value of the ordinary annuity factor 3.60478 can be accomplished using a financial calculator or by reading the appropriate table, in this case Table 6-4 (12% column and 5-period row).

WHAT DO THE NUMBERS MEAN?

UP IN SMOKE

Time value of money concepts also can be relevant to public policy debates. For example, several states are evaluating how to receive the payments from tobacco companies as settlement for a national lawsuit against the companies for the health-care costs of smoking.

The State of Wisconsin is due to collect 25 years of payments totaling $5.6 billion. The state could wait to collect the payments, or it can sell the payments to an investment bank (a process called *securitization*) and receive a lump-sum payment today of $1.26 billion. Assuming a discount rate of 8% and that the payments will be received in equal amounts, the present value of the tobacco payment annuity is:

$$\$5.6\text{ billion} \div 25 = \$224\text{ million} \times 10.67478^{*} = \$2.39\text{ billion}$$

$$^{*}PV\text{-}OA\ (i = 8\%, n = 25)$$

Why are some in the state willing to take just $1.26 billion today for an annuity, the present value of which is almost twice that value? One reason is that Wisconsin faces a hole in its budget today that can be plugged in part by the lump-sum payment. Also, some believe that the risk of getting paid by the tobacco companies in the future makes it prudent to get paid today.

If this latter reason has merit, then the present value computation above should have been based on a higher interest rate. Assuming a discount rate of 15%, the present value of the annuity is $1.448 billion ($5.6 billion ÷ 25 = $224 million; $224 million × 6.46415), which is much closer to the lump-sum payment offered to the State of Wisconsin.

Present Value of an Annuity Due

In the discussion of the present value of an ordinary annuity, the final rent was discounted back the same number of periods that there were rents. In determining the present value of an annuity due, there is always one fewer discount period. This distinction is shown graphically in Illustration 6-18.

Because each cash flow comes exactly one period sooner in the present value of the annuity due, the present value of the cash flows is exactly 12% higher than the present value of an ordinary annuity. Thus, **the present value of an annuity due factor can be found by multiplying the present value of an ordinary annuity factor by 1 plus the interest rate.**

To determine the present value of an annuity due interest factor for 5 periods at 12% interest, take the present value of an ordinary annuity for 5 periods at 12% interest (3.60478) and multiply it by 1.12 to arrive at the present value of an annuity due, 4.03735 (3.60478 × 1.12). Because the payment and receipt of rentals at the beginning of periods (such as leases, insurance, and subscriptions) are as common as those at the end of the periods (referred to as "in arrears"), we have provided present value annuity due factors in the form of Table 6-5.

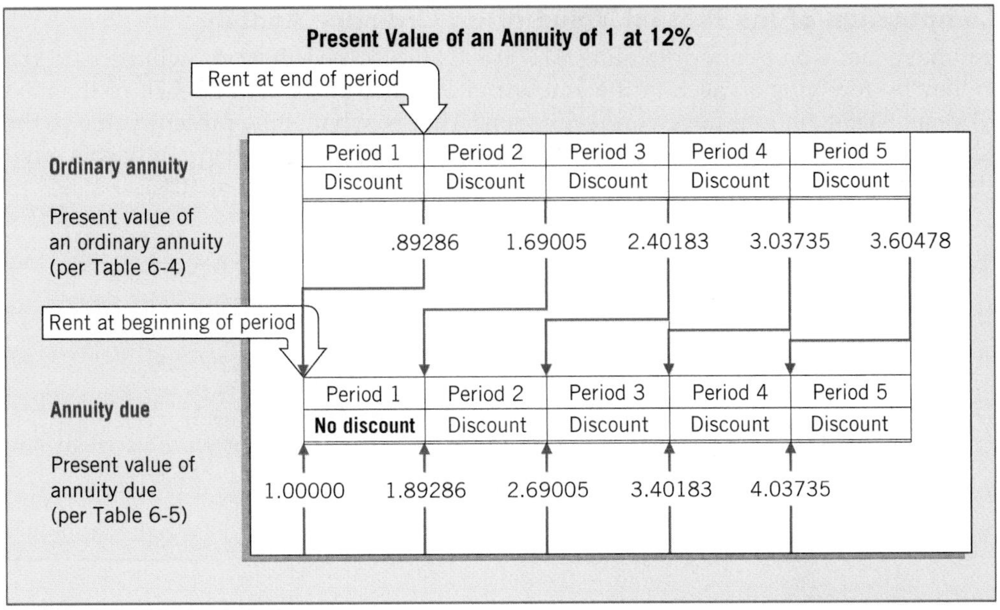

ILLUSTRATION 6-18
Comparison of Present Value of an Ordinary Annuity with an Annuity Due

Space Odyssey, Inc., rents a communications satellite for 4 years with annual rental payments of $4.8 million to be made at the beginning of each year. If the relevant annual interest rate is 11%, what is the present value of the rental obligations?

This problem is time-diagrammed as follows.

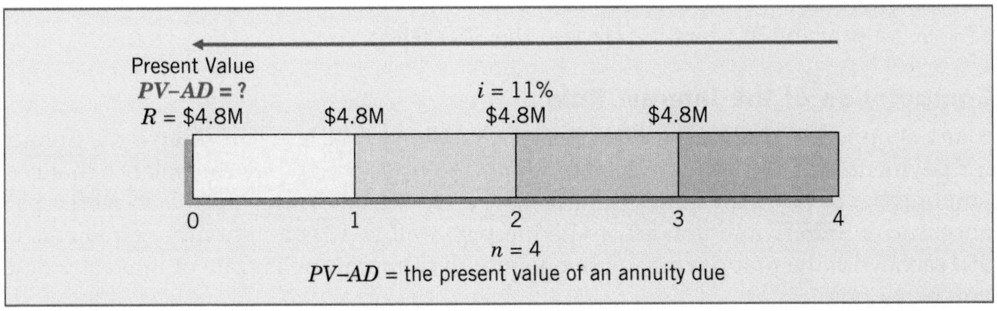

This problem is solved in the following manner.

ILLUSTRATION 6-19
Computation of Present Value of an Annuity Due

1. Present value of an ordinary annuity of 1 for 4 periods at 11% (Table 6-4)	3.10245
2. Factor (1 + .11)	× 1.11
3. Present value of an annuity due of 1 for 4 periods at 11%	3.44372
4. Periodic deposit (rent)	× $4,800,000
5. Present value of payments	$16,529,856

Since we have Table 6-5 for present value of an annuity due problems, we can also locate the desired factor 3.44372 and compute the present value of the lease payments to be $16,529,856.

Illustrations of Present Value of Annuity Problems

The following three illustrations demonstrate the computation of (1) the present value, (2) the interest rate, and (3) the amount of each rent.

Computation of the Present Value of an Ordinary Annuity

You have just won a lottery totaling $4,000,000 and learned that you will be paid the money by receiving a check in the amount of $200,000 at the end of each of the next 20 years. What amount have you really won? That is, what is the present value of the $200,000 checks you will receive over the next 20 years? A time diagram of this enviable situation is as follows (assuming an appropriate interest rate of 10%).

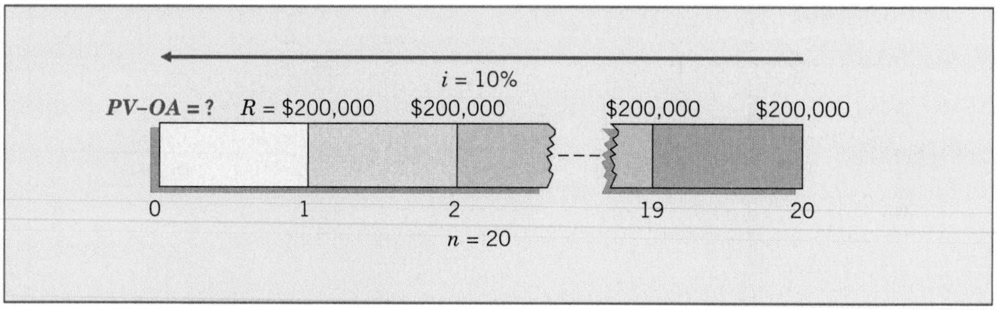

The present value is determined as follows:

$$
\begin{aligned}
\text{Present value of an ordinary annuity} &= R\,(PVF\text{-}OA_{n,i}) \\
&= \$200{,}000\,(PVF\text{-}OA_{20,10\%}) \\
&= \$200{,}000\,(8.51356) \\
&= \$1{,}702{,}712
\end{aligned}
$$

As a result, if the state deposits $1,702,712 now and earns 10% interest, it can withdraw $200,000 a year for 20 years to pay you the $4,000,000.

Computation of the Interest Rate

Many shoppers make purchases by using a credit card. When you receive the invoice for payment you may pay the total amount due or you may pay the balance in a certain number of payments. For example, if you receive an invoice from Visa with a balance due of $528.77 and you are invited to pay it off in 12 equal monthly payments of $50 each, with the first payment due one month from now, what rate of interest would you be paying?

The $528.77 represents the present value of the 12 payments of $50 each at an unknown rate of interest. This situation in the form of a time diagram appears as follows.

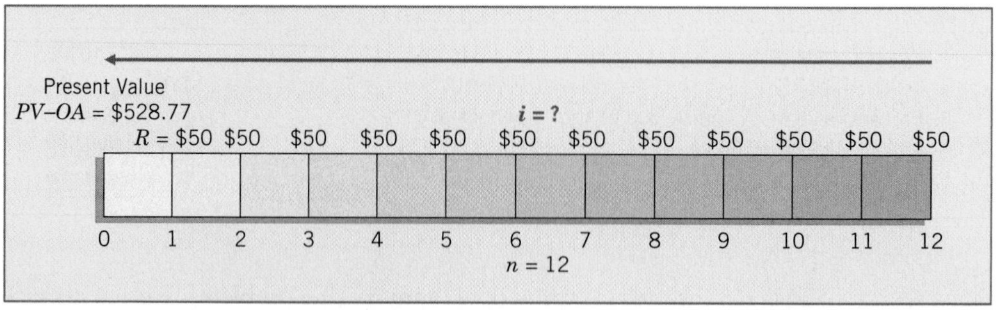

The rate is determined as follows.

$$
\begin{aligned}
\text{Present value of an ordinary annuity} &= R\,(PVF\text{-}OA_{n,i}) \\
\$528.77 &= \$50\,(PVF\text{-}OA_{12,i}) \\
(PVF\text{-}OA_{12,i}) &= \frac{\$528.77}{\$50} = 10.57540
\end{aligned}
$$

Referring to Table 6-4 and reading across the 12-period row, we find 10.57534 in the 2% column. Since 2% is a monthly rate, the nominal annual rate of interest is 24% (12 × 2%), and the effective annual rate is 26.82413% $[(1 + .02)^{12} - 1]$. Obviously, you're better off paying the entire bill now if you possibly can.

Computation of a Periodic Rent

Norm and Jackie Remmers have saved $18,000 to finance their daughter Dawna's college education. The money has been deposited in the Bloomington Savings and Loan Association and is earning 10% interest compounded semiannually. What equal amounts can their daughter withdraw at the end of every 6 months during the next 4 years while she attends college, without exhausting the fund? This situation is time-diagrammed as follows.

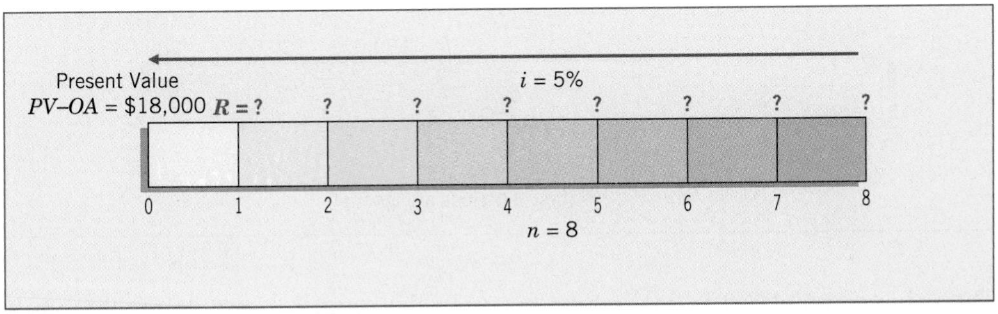

The answer is not determined simply by dividing $18,000 by 8 withdrawals because that would ignore the interest earned on the money remaining on deposit. Taking into consideration that interest is compounded semiannually at 5% (10% ÷ 2) for 8 periods (4 years × 2), and using the same present value of an ordinary annuity formula, we determine the amount of each withdrawal that she can make as follows.

$$\text{Present value of an ordinary annuity} = R\ (PVF\text{-}OA_{n,i})$$
$$\$18{,}000 = R\ (PVF\text{-}OA_{8,5\%})$$
$$\$18{,}000 = R\ (6.46321)$$
$$R = \$2{,}784.99$$

MORE COMPLEX SITUATIONS

Often it is necessary to use more than one table to solve time value problems. The business problem encountered may require that computations of both present value of a single sum and present value of an annuity be made. Two common situations are:

1. Deferred annuities.
2. Bond problems.

OBJECTIVE 8
Solve present value problems related to deferred annuities and bonds.

Deferred Annuities

A **deferred annuity** is an annuity in which the rents begin after a specified number of periods. A deferred annuity does not begin to produce rents until 2 or more periods have expired. For example, "an **ordinary annuity** of six annual rents deferred 4 years" means that no rents will occur during the first 4 years, and that the first of the six rents will occur at the end of the fifth year. "An **annuity due** of six annual rents deferred 4 years" means that no rents will occur during the first 4 years, and that the first of six rents will occur at the beginning of the fifth year.

Future Value of a Deferred Annuity

In the case of the future value of a deferred annuity the computations are relatively straightforward. Because there is no accumulation or investment on which interest may accrue, the future value of a deferred annuity is the same as the future value of an annuity not deferred. That is, the deferral period is ignored in computing the future value.

To illustrate, assume that Sutton Corporation plans to purchase a land site in 6 years for the construction of its new corporate headquarters. Because of cash flow problems, Sutton is able to budget deposits of $80,000 that are expected to earn 12% annually only at the end of the fourth, fifth, and sixth periods. What future value will Sutton have accumulated at the end of the sixth year?

A time diagram of this situation is as follows.

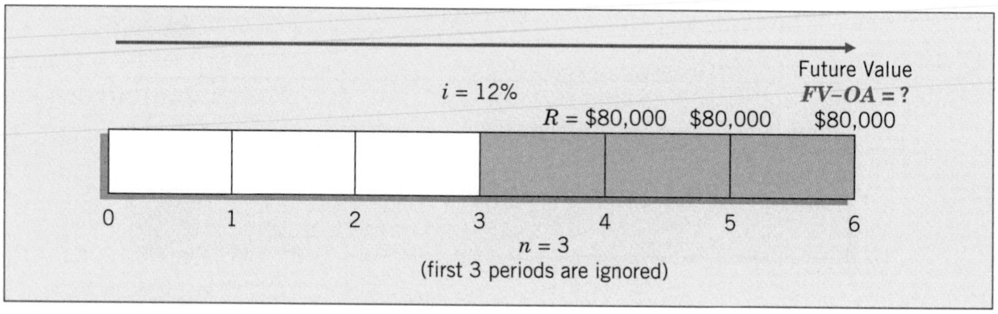

The value accumulated is determined by using the standard formula for the future value of an ordinary annuity:

$$\begin{aligned}\text{Future value of an ordinary annuity} &= R\ (FVF\text{-}OA_{n,i})\\ &= \$80{,}000\ (FVF\text{-}OA_{3,12\%})\\ &= \$80{,}000\ (3.37440)\\ &= \$269{,}952\end{aligned}$$

Present Value of a Deferred Annuity

In computing the present value of a deferred annuity, the interest that accrues on the original investment during the deferral period must be recognized.

To compute the present value of a deferred annuity, we compute the present value of an ordinary annuity of 1 as if the rents had occurred for the entire period, and then subtract the present value of rents which were not received during the deferral period. We are left with the present value of the rents actually received subsequent to the deferral period.

To illustrate, Tom Bytehead has developed and copyrighted a software computer program that is a tutorial for students in advanced accounting. He agrees to sell the copyright to Campus Micro Systems for six annual payments of $5,000 each. The payments are to begin 5 years from today. Given an annual interest rate of 8%, what is the present value of the six payments?

This situation is an ordinary annuity of 6 payments deferred 4 periods. The following time diagram helps to visualize this sales agreement.

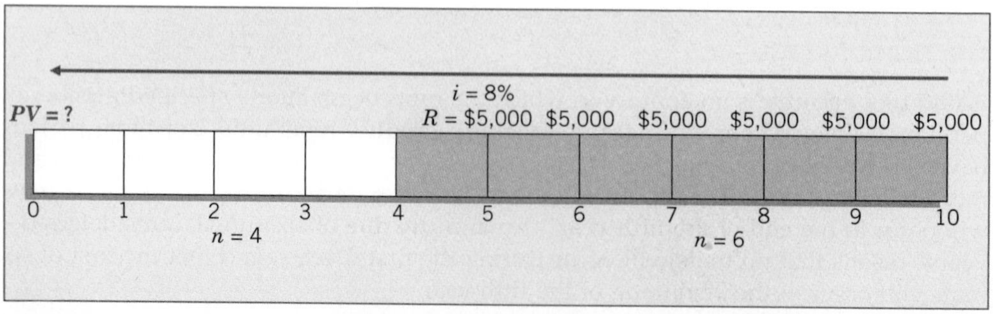

Two options are available to solve this problem. The first is to use only Table 6-4 as follows.

ILLUSTRATION 6-20
Computation of the Present Value of a Deferred Annuity

1. Each periodic rent		$5,000
2. Present value of an ordinary annuity of 1 for total periods (10) [number of rents (6) plus number of deferred periods (4)] at 8%	6.71008	
3. Less: Present value of an ordinary annuity of 1 for the number of deferred periods (4) at 8%	−3.31213	
4. Difference		× 3.39795
5. Present value of six rents of $5,000 deferred 4 periods		$16,989.75

The subtraction of the present value of an annuity of 1 for the deferred periods eliminates the nonexistent rents during the deferral period and converts the present value of an ordinary annuity of $1 for 10 periods to the present value of 6 rents of $1, deferred 4 periods.

Alternatively, the present value of the 6 rents could be computed using both Table 6-2 and Table 6-4. One can first discount the annuity 6 periods, but because the annuity is deferred 4 periods, the present value of the annuity must then be treated as a future amount to be discounted another 4 periods. A time diagram illustrates this two-step process as follows.

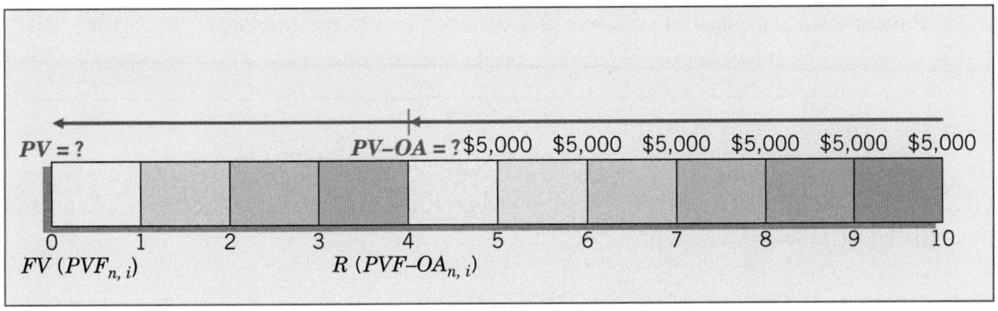

Step 1: Present value of an ordinary annuity $= R\ (PVF\text{-}OA_{n,i})$

$= \$5{,}000\ (PVF\text{-}OA_{6,8\%})$

$= \$5{,}000\ (4.62288)$
(Table 6-4 Present value of an ordinary annuity)

$= \$23{,}114.40$

Step 2: Present value $= FV\ (PVF_{n,i})$

$= \$23{,}114.40\ (PVF_{4,8\%})$

$= \$23{,}114.40\ (.73503)$
(Table 6-2 Present value of a single sum)

$= \$16{,}989.78$

The present value of $16,989.78 computed above is the same result although computed differently from the first illustration.

Valuation of Long-Term Bonds

A long-term bond produces two cash flows: (1) periodic interest payments during the life of the bond, and (2) the principal (face value) paid at maturity. At the date of issue, bond buyers determine the present value of these two cash flows using the market rate of interest.

The periodic interest payments represent an annuity, and the principal represents a single-sum problem. The current market value of the bonds is the combined present values of the interest annuity and the principal amount.

To illustrate, Alltech Corporation on January 1, 2003, issues $100,000 of 9% bonds due in 5 years with interest payable annually at year-end. The current market rate of interest for bonds of similar risk is 11%. What will the buyers pay for this bond issue?

The time diagram depicting both cash flows is shown below.

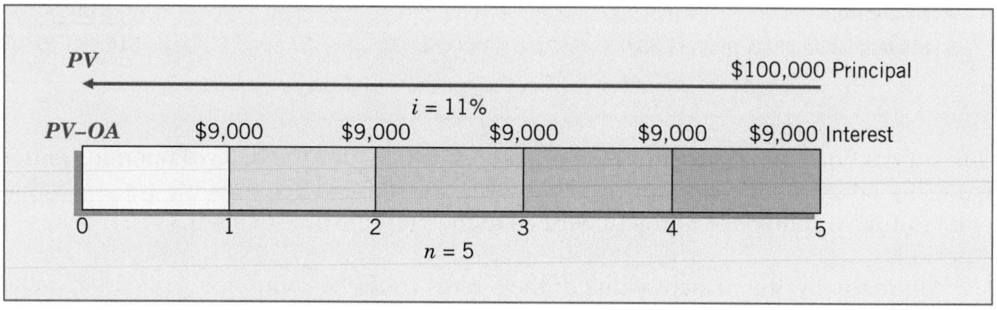

The present value of the two cash flows is computed by discounting at 11% as follows.

ILLUSTRATION 6-21
Computation of the Present Value of an Interest-Bearing Bond

1. Present value of the principal: $FV\ (PVF_{5,11\%})$ = $100,000 (.59345)	$59,345.00
2. Present value of the interest payments: $R\ (PVF\text{-}OA_{5,11\%})$ = $9,000 (3.69590)	33,263.10
3. Combined present value (market price)—carrying value of bonds	$92,608.10

By paying $92,608.10 at date of issue, the buyers of the bonds will realize an effective yield of 11% over the 5-year term of the bonds. This is true because the cash flows were discounted at 11%.

Effective Interest Method of Amortization of Bond Discount or Premium

In the Alltech Corporation bond issue, in Illustration 6-21, the bonds were issued at a discount computed as follows.

ILLUSTRATION 6-22
Computation of Bond Discount

Maturity value (face amount) of bonds		$100,000.00
Present value of the principal	$59,345.00	
Present value of the interest	33,263.10	
Proceeds (present value and cash received)		92,608.10
Discount on bonds issued		$ 7,391.90

This discount of $7,391.90 under acceptable accrual accounting is amortized (written off) over the life of the bond issue to interest expense.

Use of Spreadsheets to Calculate Bond Amortization

The profession's preferred procedure for amortization of a discount or premium is the **effective interest method** (also called **present value amortization**). Under the effective interest method:

1. Bond interest expense is computed first by multiplying the carrying value of the bonds at the beginning of the period by the effective interest rate.
2. The bond discount or premium amortization is then determined by comparing the bond interest expense with the interest to be paid.

The computation of the amortization is depicted graphically as follows.

Bond Interest Expense		Bond Interest Paid		
Carrying Value of Bonds at Beginning of Period × Effective Interest Rate	−	Face Amount of Bonds × Stated Interest Rate	=	Amortization Amount

ILLUSTRATION 6-23
Amortization Computation

The effective interest method produces a periodic interest expense equal to **a constant percentage of the carrying value of the bonds**. Since the percentage used is the effective rate of interest incurred by the borrower at the time of issuance, the effective interest method results in matching expenses with revenues.

The effective interest method of amortization can be illustrated using the data from the Alltech Corporation example, where \$100,000 face value of bonds were issued at a discount of \$7,391.90, resulting in a carrying value of \$92,608.10. The effective interest amortization schedule is shown in Illustration 6-24.

ILLUSTRATION 6-24
Effective Interest Amortization Schedule

SCHEDULE OF BOND DISCOUNT AMORTIZATION
5-YEAR, 9% BONDS SOLD TO YIELD 11%

Date	Cash Interest Paid	Interest Expense	Bond Discount Amortization	Carrying Value of Bonds
1/1/04				\$92,608.10
12/31/04	\$9,000[a]	\$10,186.89[b]	\$1,186.89[c]	93,794.99[d]
12/31/05	9,000	10,317.45	1,317.45	95,112.44
12/31/06	9,000	10,462.37	1,462.37	96,574.81
12/31/07	9,000	10,623.23	1,623.23	98,198.04
12/31/08	9,000	10,801.96	1,801.96	100,000.00
	\$45,000	\$52,391.90	\$7,391.90	

[a]\$100,000 × .09 = \$9,000
[b]\$92,608.10 × .11 = \$10,186.89
[c]\$10,186.89 − \$9,000 = \$1,186.89
[d]\$92,608.10 + \$1,186.89 = \$93,794.99

The amortization schedule illustrated above is used for note and bond transactions in Chapters 7 and 14.

PRESENT VALUE MEASUREMENT

OBJECTIVE 9
Apply the expected cash flow approach to present value measurement.

In the past, most accounting calculations of present value were based on the most likely cash flow amount. *Concepts Statement No.7*[6] introduces an **expected cash flow approach** that uses a range of cash flows and incorporates the probabilities of those cash flows to provide a more relevant measurement of present value.

To illustrate the expected cash flow model, assume that there is a 30% probability that future cash flows will be \$100, a 50% probability that they will be \$200, and a 20% probability that they will be \$300. In this case, the expected cash flow would be \$190 [(\$100 × 0.3) + (\$200 × 0.5) + (\$300 × 0.2)]. Under traditional present value approaches, the most likely estimate (\$200) would be used, but that estimate does not consider the different probabilities of the possible cash flows.

[6]"Using Cash Flow Information and Present Value in Accounting Measurements," *Statement of Financial Accounting Concepts No. 7* (Norwalk, Conn.: FASB, 2000).

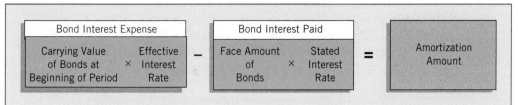

WHAT DO THE NUMBERS MEAN?

FED WATCHING

A popular pastime in today's financial markets is "Fed watching." Why is the practice of following the policy decisions of the Federal Reserve Bank and its chair, Alan Greenspan, of interest? Through a number of policy options, the Fed has the ability to move interest rates up or down—and these rate changes can affect the wealth of all market participants.

For example, if the Fed wants to raise rates (because the overall economy is getting overheated), it can raise the discount rate, which is the rate banks pay to borrow money from the Fed. This rate increase will factor into the rates used by banks and other creditors to lend money, and companies will think twice about borrowing money to expand their business. The result will be a slowing economy. A rate cut does just the opposite.

But not all companies are affected equally by rate changes. Following a recent Fed interest rate cut, the overall market experienced a positive 3-month return of 3.13 percent. Retailers, airlines, and investment banks benefited most, with a positive 3-month return of greater than 6 percent, while companies in the steel, aerospace, and auto-parts industries had negative returns of less than 5 percent. Although these latter companies did get some benefit from the rate cut, this effect was offset by the effects of general declining economic prospects, which prompted the Fed to cut rates to begin with.

Source: Adapted from David Franecki, "Thanks Alan: These Stock Groups Stand to Gain from Fed Rate Cuts," *Barrons Online* (January 22, 2001).

Choosing an Appropriate Interest Rate

After determining expected cash flows, the proper interest rate must then be used to discount the cash flows. The interest rate used for this purpose has three components:

THREE COMPONENTS OF INTEREST

1. ***Pure Rate of Interest (2%–4%).*** This would be the amount a lender would charge if there were no possibilities of default and no expectation of inflation.
2. ***Expected Inflation Rate of Interest (0%–?).*** Lenders recognize that in an inflationary economy, they are being paid back with less valuable dollars. As a result, they increase their interest rate to compensate for this loss in purchasing power. When inflationary expectations are high, interest rates are high.
3. ***Credit Risk Rate of Interest (0%–5%).*** The government has little or no credit risk (i.e., risk of nonpayment) when it issues bonds. A business enterprise, however, depending upon its financial stability, profitability, etc., can have a low or a high credit risk.

The FASB takes the position that after the expected cash flows are computed, they should be discounted by the **risk-free rate of return**, which is defined as **the pure rate of return plus the expected inflation rate**. The Board notes that the expected cash flow framework adjusts for credit risk because it incorporates the probability of receipt or payment into the computation of expected cash flows. Therefore the rate used to discount the expected cash flows should consider only the pure rate of interest and the inflation rate.

Expected Cash Flow Illustration

To illustrate application of these concepts, assume that Art's Appliance Outlet offers a 2-year warranty on all products sold. In 2003, Art sold $250,000 of a particular type of clothes dryer. Art's Appliance has entered into an agreement with Ralph's Repair to provide all warranty service on the dryers sold in 2003. Art's Appliance wishes to measure the fair value of the agreement to determine the warranty expense to record in 2003 and the amount of warranty liability to record on the December 31, 2003, balance sheet. Since there is not a ready market for these warranty contracts, Art's Appliance uses expected cash flow techniques to value the warranty obligation.

Based on prior warranty experience, Art's Appliance estimates the following expected cash outflows associated with the dryers sold in 2003.

ILLUSTRATION 6-25
Expected Cash Outflows—Warranties

	Cash Flow Estimate	×	Probability Assessment	=	Expected Cash Flow
2004	$3,800		20%		$ 760
	6,300		50%		3,150
	7,500		30%		2,250
			Total		$6,160
2005	$5,400		30%		$1,620
	7,200		50%		3,600
	8,400		20%		1,680
			Total		$6,900

Applying expected cash flow concepts to these data, Art's Appliance estimates warranty cash outflows of $6,160 in 2004 and $6,900 in 2005.

The present value of these cash flows, assuming a risk-free rate of 5 percent and cash flows occurring at the end of the year, is shown in the following schedule.

ILLUSTRATION 6-26
Present Value of Cash Flows

Year	Expected Cash Flow	×	PV Factor, $i = 5\%$	=	Present Value
2004	$6,160		0.95238		$ 5,870
2005	6,900		0.90703		6,260
			Total		$12,130

KEY TERMS

annuity, *264*
annuity due, *265*
compound interest, *254*
deferred annuity, *275*
discounting, *259*
effective interest method, *278*
effective yield, *258*
expected cash flow approach, *279*
face rate, *258*
future value, *259*
interest, *253*
nominal rate, *258*
ordinary annuity, *265*
present value, *261*
principal, *253*
risk-free rate of return, *280*
simple interest, *254*
stated rate, *258*
time value of money, *252*

SUMMARY OF LEARNING OBJECTIVES

1 Identify accounting topics where the time value of money is relevant. Some of the applications of present value–based measurements to accounting topics are: (1) notes, (2) leases, (3) pensions and other postretirement benefits, (4) long-term assets, (5) sinking funds, (6) business combinations, (7) disclosures, and (8) installment contracts.

2 Distinguish between simple and compound interest. See Fundamental Concepts following this Summary (on page 283).

3 Learn how to use appropriate compound interest tables. In order to identify the appropriate compound interest table to use, of the five given, you must identify whether you are solving for (1) the future value of a single sum, (2) the present value of a single sum, (3) the future value of a series of sums (an annuity), or (4) the present value of a series of sums (an annuity). In addition, when a series of sums (an annuity) is involved, you must identify whether these sums are received or paid (1) at the beginning of each period (annuity due) or (2) at the end of each period (ordinary annuity).

4 Identify variables fundamental to solving interest problems. The following four variables are fundamental to all compound interest problems: (1) *Rate of interest:* unless otherwise stated, an annual rate that must be adjusted to reflect the length of the compounding period if less than a year. (2) *Number of time periods:* the number of compounding periods (a period may be equal to or less than a year). (3) *Future value:* the value at a future date of a given sum or sums invested assuming compound interest. (4) *Present value:* the value now (present time) of a future sum or sums discounted assuming compound interest.

5 Solve future and present value of 1 problems. See Fundamental Concepts following this Summary, items 5(a) and 6(a).

6 Solve future value of ordinary and annuity due problems. See Fundamental Concepts following this Summary, item 5(b).

7 Solve present value of ordinary and annuity due problems. See Fundamental Concepts following this Summary, item 6(b).

8 Solve present value problems related to deferred annuities and bonds. Deferred annuities are annuities in which rents begin after a specified number of periods. The future value of a deferred annuity is computed the same as the future value of an annuity not deferred. The present value of a deferred annuity is found by computing the present value of an ordinary annuity of 1 as if the rents had occurred for the entire period, and then subtracting the present value of rents not received during the deferral period. The current market value of bonds is the combined present values of the interest annuity and the principal amount. The preferred procedure for amortization of bond discount or premium is the effective interest method, which first computes bond interest expense, next computes the cash interest to be paid, and then compares the two amounts to determine the amortization amount.

9 Apply the expected cash flow approach to present value measurement. The expected cash flow approach uses a range of cash flows and the probabilities of those cash flows to provide the most likely estimate of expected cash flows. The proper interest rate used to discount the cash flows is the risk-free rate of return.

FUNDAMENTAL CONCEPTS

1. *Simple Interest.* Interest on principal only, regardless of interest that may have accrued in the past.
2. *Compound Interest.* Interest accrues on the unpaid interest of past periods as well as on the principal.
3. *Rate of Interest.* Interest is usually expressed as an annual rate, but when the compounding period is shorter than one year, the interest rate for the shorter period must be determined.
4. *Annuity.* A series of payments or receipts (called rents) that occur at equal intervals of time. Types of annuities:
   - **(a)** *Ordinary Annuity.* Each rent is payable (receivable) at the end of the period.
   - **(b)** *Annuity Due.* Each rent is payable (receivable) at the beginning of the period.
5. *Future Value.* Value at a later date of a single sum that is invested at compound interest.
   - **(a)** *Future Value of 1* (or value of a single sum). The future value of $1 (or a single given sum), *FV*, at the end of *n* periods at *i* compound interest rate (Table 6-1).
   - **(b)** *Future Value of an Annuity.* The future value of a series of rents invested at compound interest. In other words, the accumulated total that results from a series of equal deposits at regular intervals invested at compound interest. Both deposits and interest increase the accumulation.
     - **(1)** *Future Value of an Ordinary Annuity.* The future value on the date of the last rent.
     - **(2)** *Future Value of an Annuity Due.* The future value one period after the date of the last rent. When an annuity due table is not available, use Table 6-3 with the following formula:

       Value of annuity due of 1 for *n* rents = (Value of ordinary annuity for *n* rents) × (1 + interest rate)
6. *Present Value.* The value at an earlier date (usually now) of a given future sum discounted at compound interest.
   - **(a)** *Present Value of 1* (or present value of a single sum). The present value (worth) of $1 (or a given sum), due *n* periods hence, discounted at *i* compound interest (Table 6-2).
   - **(b)** *Present Value of an Annuity.* The present value (worth) of a series of rents discounted at compound interest. In other words, it is the sum when invested at compound interest that will permit a series of equal withdrawals at regular intervals.
     - **(1)** *Present Value of an Ordinary Annuity.* The value now of $1 to be received or paid (rents) at the end of each period for *n* periods, discounted at *i* compound interest (Table 6-4).
     - **(2)** *Present Value of an Annuity Due.* The value now of $1 to be received or paid (rents) at the beginning of each period for *n* periods, discounted at *i* compound interest (Table 6-5). To use Table 6-4 for an annuity due, apply this formula:

       Present value of annuity due of 1 for *n* rents = (Present value of an ordinary annuity of *n* rents × (1 + interest rate)

APPENDIX 6A

Using Financial Calculators

OBJECTIVE 10
Use a financial calculator to solve time value of money problems.

Business professionals, once they have mastered the underlying concepts in Chapter 6, will often use a financial (business) calculator to solve time value of money problems. In many cases, calculators must be used if interest rates or time periods do not correspond with the information provided in the compound interest tables.

Financial calculators allow you to solve present and future value problems by entering the time value of money variables into the calculator. The five most common keys used to solve time value of money problems are pictured below.[1]

N	I	PV	PMT	FV

where

N = number of periods

I = interest rate per period (some calculators use I/YR or i)

PV = present value (occurs at the beginning of the first period)

PMT = payment (all payments are equal, and none are skipped)

FV = future value (occurs at the end of the last period)

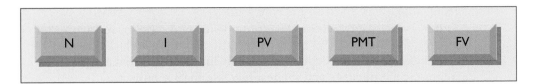

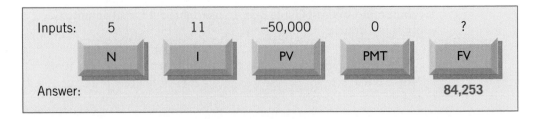

Use of Computer Spreadsheets to Solve Time Value of Money Problems

In solving time value of money problems in this appendix, you will generally be given three of four variables and will have to solve for the remaining variable. The fifth key (the key not used) is given a value of zero to ensure that this variable is not used in the computation.

FUTURE VALUE OF A SINGLE SUM

To illustrate the use of a financial calculator, let's assume that you want to know the future value of $50,000 invested to earn 11%, compounded annually for 5 years.

Inputs:	5	11	–50,000	0	?
	N	I	PV	PMT	FV
Answer:					84,253

[1]On many calculators, these keys are actual buttons on the face of the calculator; on others, they are shown on the display after accessing a present value menu.

The diagram shows you the information (inputs) to enter into the calculator: N = 5, I = 11, PV = −50,000, and PMT = 0. FV is then pressed to yield the answer: $84,253. This is the same answer as shown on page 260, when compound interest tables were used to compute the future value of a single sum. As indicated, the PMT key was given a value of zero because a series of payments did not occur in this problem.

Plus and Minus

The use of plus and minus signs in time value of money problems using a financial calculator can be confusing. Most financial calculators are programmed so that the positive and negative cash flows in any problem offset each other. In the future value problem above, we identified the 50,000 initial investment as a negative (outflow); the answer 84,253 was shown as a positive, reflecting a cash inflow. If the 50,000 were entered as a positive, then the final answer would have been reported as a negative (−84,253). Hopefully, the sign convention will not cause confusion. If you understand what is required in a problem, you should be able to interpret a positive or negative amount in determining the solution to a problem.

Compounding Periods

In the problem above, we assumed that compounding occurs once a year. Some financial calculators have a default setting, which assumes that compounding occurs 12 times a year. You must determine what default period has been programmed into your calculator and change it as necessary to arrive at the proper compounding period.

Rounding

Most financial calculators store and calculate using 12 decimal places. As a result, because compound interest tables generally have factors only up to 5 decimal places, a slight difference in the final answer can result. In most time value of money problems, the final answer will not include more than two decimal points.

PRESENT VALUE OF A SINGLE SUM

To illustrate how a present value problem is solved using a financial calculator, assume that you want to know the present value of $84,253 to be received in 5 years, discounted at 11% compounded annually.

Inputs:	5	11	?	0	84,253
	N	I	PV	PMT	FV
Answer:			**−50,000**		

In this case, you enter N = 5, I = 11, PMT = 0, FV = 84,253, and then press the PV key to find the present value of $50,000.

FUTURE VALUE OF AN ORDINARY ANNUITY

To illustrate the future value of an ordinary annuity, assume that you are asked to determine the future value of five $5,000 deposits made at the end of each of the next 5 years, each of which earns interest at 12%, compounded annually.

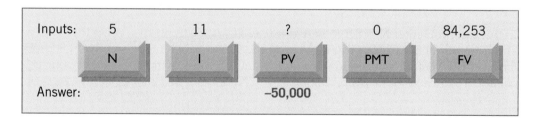

Inputs:	5	12	0	−5,000	?
	N	I	PV	PMT	FV
Answer:					31,764.24

In this case, you enter N = 5, I = 12, PV = 0, PMT = −5,000, and then press FV to arrive at the answer of $31,764.24.[2] The $5,000 payments are shown as negatives because the deposits represent cash outflows that will accumulate with interest to the amount to be received (cash inflow) at the end of 5 years.

FUTURE VALUE OF AN ANNUITY DUE

Recall from the discussion in Chapter 6 that in any annuity problem you must determine whether the periodic payments occur at the beginning or the end of the period. If the first payment occurs at the beginning of the period, most financial calculators have a key marked "Begin" (or "Due") that you press to switch from the end-of-period payment mode (for an ordinary annuity) to beginning-of-period payment mode (for an annuity due). For most calculators, the word BEGIN is displayed to indicate that the calculator is set for an annuity due problem. (Some calculators use DUE.)

To illustrate a future value of an annuity due problem, let's revisit a problem from Chapter 6: Sue Lotadough plans to deposit $800 per year in a fund on each of her son's birthdays, starting today (his tenth birthday). All amounts on deposit in the fund will earn 12% compounded annually. Sue wants to know the amount she will have accumulated for college expenses on her son's eighteenth birthday. She will make 8 deposits into the fund. (Assume no deposit will be made on the eighteenth birthday.)

Inputs:	8	12	0	−800	?
	N	I	PV	PMT	FV
Answer:					11,020.53

In this case, you enter N = 8, I = 12, PV = 0, PMT = −800, and then press FV to arrive at the answer of $11,020.53. You must be in the BEGIN or DUE mode to solve this problem correctly. Before starting to solve any annuity problem, make sure that your calculator is switched to the proper mode.

PRESENT VALUE OF AN ORDINARY ANNUITY

To illustrate how to solve a present value of an ordinary annuity problem using a financial calculator, assume that you are asked to determine the present value of rental receipts of $6,000 each to be received at the end of each of the next 5 years, when discounted at 12%.

[2]Note on page 266 that the answer using the compound interest tables is $31,764.25—a difference of 1 cent due to rounding.

Inputs:	5	12	?	6,000	0
	N	I	PV	PMT	FV
Answer:			**–21,628.66**		

In this case, you enter N = 5, I = 12, PMT = 6,000, FV = 0, and then press PV to arrive at the answer of $21,628.66.[3]

USEFUL FEATURES OF THE FINANCIAL CALCULATOR

With a financial calculator you can solve for any interest rate or for any number of periods in a time value of money problem. Here are some illustrations of these features.

Auto Loan

Assume you are financing a car with a 3-year loan. The loan has a 9.5% nominal annual interest rate, compounded monthly. The price of the car is $6,000, and you want to determine the monthly payments, assuming that the payments start one month after the purchase.

Inputs:	36	9.5	6,000	?	0
	N	I	PV	PMT	FV
Answer:				**–192.20**	

Thus, by entering N = 36 (12 × 3), I = 9.5, PV = 6,000, FV = 0, and then pressing PMT, you can determine that the monthly payments will be $192.20. Note that the payment key is usually programmed for 12 payments per year. Thus, you must change the default (compounding period) if the payments are different than monthly.

Mortgage Loan Amount

Let's say you are evaluating financing options for a loan on your house. You decide that the maximum mortgage payment you can afford is $700 per month. The annual interest rate is 8.4%. If you get a mortgage that requires you to make monthly payments over a 15-year period, what is the maximum purchase price you can afford?

Inputs:	180	8.4	?	–700	0
	N	I	PV	PMT	FV
Answer:			**71,509.81**		

[3]If the rental payments were received at the beginning of the year, then it would be necessary to switch to the BEGIN or DUE mode. In this case, the present value of the payments would be $24,224.10.

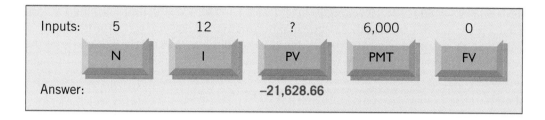

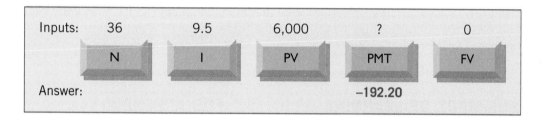

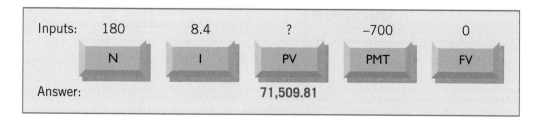

Entering N = 180 (12 × 15 years), I = 8.4, PMT = −700, FV = 0, and pressing PV, you find a present value of $71,509.81—the maximum house price you can afford, given that you want to keep your mortgage payments at $700. Note that by changing any of the variables, you can quickly conduct "what-if" analyses for different factual situations.

Individual Retirement Account (IRA)

Assume you opened an IRA on April 15, 1992, with a deposit of $2,000. Since then you have deposited $100 in the account every 2 weeks (26 deposits per year, with the first $100 deposit made on April 29, 1992). The account pays 7.6% annual interest compounded semi-monthly (with each deposit). How much will be in the account on April 15, 2002?

	N	I	PV	PMT	FV
Inputs:	260	7.6	-2,000	-100	?
Answer:					43,131.79

By entering N = 260 (26 × 10 years), I = 7.6, PV = −2,000, PMT = −100, and pressing FV, you determine the future value of $43,131.79. This is the amount that the IRA will grow to over the 10-year period. Note that in this problem we use four of the keys and solve for the fifth. Thus, we combine the future value of a single sum and of an annuity. Other problems similar to this are illustrated in Chapters 7 and 14.

SUMMARY OF LEARNING OBJECTIVE FOR APPENDIX 6A

10 **Use a financial calculator to solve time value of money problems.** A financial calculator can be used to solve time value of money problems. By entering into the calculator amounts for all but one of the unknown elements (periods, interest rate, payments, future or present value), a financial calculator can be used to solve the same and additional problems as those solved with the time value of money tables. Particularly useful situations involve interest rates and compounding periods not presented in the tables.

Note: All **asterisked** Exercises and Problems relate to material contained in the chapter appendix; a calculator is needed for these assignments.

QUESTIONS

1. What is the time value of money? Why should accountants have an understanding of compound interest, annuities, and present value concepts?

2. Identify three situations in which accounting measures are based on present values. Do these present value applications involve single sums or annuities, or both single sums and annuities? Explain.

3. What is the nature of interest? Distinguish between "simple interest" and "compound interest."

4. What are the components of an interest rate? Why is it important for accountants to understand these components?

5. Presented are a number of values taken from compound interest tables involving the same number of periods and the same rate of interest. Indicate what each of these four values represents.

(a) 6.71008 **(c)** .46319

(b) 2.15892 **(d)** 14.48656

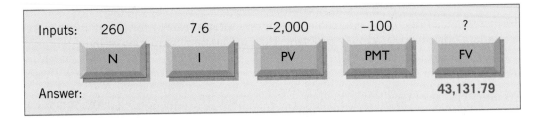

6. Bill Jones is considering two investment options for a $1,000 gift he received for graduation. Both investments have 8% annual interest rates. One offers quarterly compounding; the other compounds on a semiannual basis. Which investment should he choose? Why?

7. Brenda Starr deposited $18,000 in a money market certificate that provides interest of 10% compounded quarterly if the amount is maintained for 3 years. How much will Brenda Starr have at the end of 3 years?

8. Charlie Brown will receive $50,000 on December 31, 2009 (5 years from now) from a trust fund established by his father. Assuming the appropriate interest rate for discounting is 12% (compounded semiannually), what is the present value of this amount today?

9. What are the primary characteristics of an annuity? Differentiate between an "ordinary annuity" and an "annuity due."

10. Linus, Inc. owes $30,000 to Peanuts Company. How much would Linus have to pay each year if the debt is retired through four equal payments (made at the end of the year), given an interest rate on the debt of 12%? (Round to two decimal places.)

11. The Lockhorns are planning for a retirement home. They estimate they will need $160,000, 4 years from now to purchase this home. Assuming an interest rate of 10%, what amount must be deposited at the end of each of the 4 years to fund the home price? (Round to two decimal places.)

12. Assume the same situation as in Question 11, except that the four equal amounts are deposited at the beginning of the period rather than at the end. In this case, what amount must be deposited at the beginning of each period? (Round to two decimals.)

13. Explain how the future value of an ordinary annuity interest table is converted to the future value of an annuity due interest table.

14. Explain how the present value of an ordinary annuity interest table is converted to the present value of an annuity due interest table.

15. In a book named *Treasure,* the reader has to figure out where a 2.2 pound, 24 kt gold horse has been buried. If the horse is found, a prize of $25,000 a year for 20 years is provided. The actual cost of the publisher to purchase an annuity to pay for the prize is $210,000. What interest rate (to the nearest percent) was used to determine the amount of the annuity? (Assume end-of-year payments.)

16. Greg Norman Enterprises leases property to Tiger Woods, Inc. Because Tiger Woods, Inc. is experiencing financial difficulty, Norman agrees to receive five rents of $10,000 at the end of each year, with the rents deferred 3 years. What is the present value of the five rents discounted at 12%?

17. Answer the following questions.

   (a) On May 1, 2004, Liselotte Neumann Company sold some machinery to Tee-off Company on an installment contract basis. The contract required five equal annual payments, with the first payment due on May 1, 2004. What present value concept is appropriate for this situation?

   (b) On June 1, 2004, Mike Brisky Inc. purchased a new machine that it does not have to pay for until May 1, 2006. The total payment on May 1, 2006, will include both principal and interest. Assuming interest at a 12% rate, the cost of the machine would be the total payment multiplied by what time value of money concept?

   (c) Kelly Gibson Inc. wishes to know how much money it will have available in 5 years if five equal amounts of $35,000 are invested, with the first amount invested immediately. What interest table is appropriate for this situation?

   (d) Patty Sheehan invests in a "jumbo" $200,000, 3-year certificate of deposit at First Wisconsin Bank. What table would be used to determine the amount accumulated at the end of 3 years?

18. Recently Vickie Maher was interested in purchasing a Honda Acura. The salesperson indicated that the price of the car was either $27,000 cash or $6,900 at the end of each of 5 years. Compute the effective interest rate to the nearest percent that Vickie would pay if she chooses to make the five annual payments.

19. Recently, property/casualty insurance companies have been criticized because they reserve for the total loss as much as 5 years before it may happen. Recently the IRS has joined the debate because they say the full reserve is unfair from a taxation viewpoint. What do you believe is the IRS position?

BRIEF EXERCISES

BE6-1 Steve Allen invested $10,000 today in a fund that earns 8% compounded annually. To what amount will the investment grow in 3 years? To what amount would the investment grow in 3 years if the fund earns 8% annual interest compounded semiannually?

BE6-2 Itzak Perlman needs $20,000 in 4 years. What amount must he invest today if his investment earns 12% compounded annually? What amount must he invest if his investment earns 12% annual interest compounded quarterly?

BE6-3 Janet Jackson will invest $30,000 today. She needs $222,000 in 21 years. What annual interest rate must she earn?

BE6-4 Dan Webster will invest $10,000 today in a fund that earns 5% annual interest. How many years will it take for the fund to grow to $13,400?

BE6-5 Anne Boleyn will invest $5,000 a year for 20 years in a fund that will earn 12% annual interest. If the first payment into the fund occurs today, what amount will be in the fund in 20 years? If the first payment occurs at year-end, what amount will be in the fund in 20 years?

BE6-6 William Cullen Bryant needs $200,000 in 10 years. How much must he invest at the end of each year, at 11% interest, to meet his needs?

BE6-7 Jack Thompson's lifelong dream is to own his own fishing boat to use in his retirement. Jack has recently come into an inheritance of $400,000. He estimates that the boat he wants will cost $350,000 when he retires in 5 years. How much of his inheritance must he invest at an annual rate of 12% (compounded annually) to buy the boat at retirement?

BE6-8 Refer to the data in BE6-7. Assuming quarterly compounding of amounts invested at 12%, how much of Jack Thompson's inheritance must be invested to have enough at retirement to buy the boat?

BE6-9 Luther Vandross is investing $12,961 at the end of each year in a fund that earns 10% interest. In how many years will the fund be at $100,000?

BE6-10 Grupo Rana wants to withdraw $20,000 each year for 10 years from a fund that earns 8% interest. How much must he invest today if the first withdrawal is at year-end? How much must he invest today if the first withdrawal takes place immediately?

BE6-11 Mark Twain's VISA balance is $1,124.40. He may pay it off in 18 equal end-of-month payments of $75 each. What interest rate is Mark paying?

BE6-12 Corinne Dunbar is investing $200,000 in a fund that earns 8% interest compounded annually. What equal amounts can Corinne withdraw at the end of each of the next 20 years?

BE6-13 Bayou Inc. will deposit $20,000 in a 12% fund at the end of each year for 8 years beginning December 31, 2005. What amount will be in the fund immediately after the last deposit?

BE6-14 Hollis Stacy wants to create a fund today that will enable her to withdraw $20,000 per year for 8 years, with the first withdrawal to take place 5 years from today. If the fund earns 8% interest, how much must Hollis invest today?

BE6-15 Acadian Inc. issues $1,000,000 of 7% bonds due in 10 years with interest payable at year-end. The current market rate of interest for bonds of similar risk is 8%. What amount will Acadian receive when it issues the bonds?

BE6-16 Walt Frazier is settling a $20,000 loan due today by making 6 equal annual payments of $4,864.51. Determine the interest rate on this loan, if the payments begin one year after the loan is signed.

BE6-17 Consider the loan in BE6-16. What payments must Walt Frazier make to settle the loan at the same interest rate but with the 6 payments beginning on the day the loan is signed?

EXERCISES

(Interest rates are per annum unless otherwise indicated.)

E6-1 (Using Interest Tables) For each of the following cases, indicate (a) to what rate columns, and (b) to what number of periods you would refer in looking up the interest factor.

1. In a future value of 1 table

Annual Rate	Number of Years Invested	Compounded
a. 9%	9	Annually
b. 12%	5	Quarterly
c. 10%	15	Semiannually

2. In a present value of an annuity of 1 table

Annual Rate	Number of Years Involved	Number of Rents Involved	Frequency of Rents
a. 9%	25	25	Annually
b. 10%	15	30	Semiannually
c. 12%	7	28	Quarterly

E6-2 (Expected Cash Flows) For each of the following, determine the expected cash flows.

	Cash Flow Estimate	Probability Assessment
(a)	$ 3,800	20%
	6,300	50%
	7,500	30%
(b)	$ 5,400	30%
	7,200	50%
	8,400	20%
(c)	$(1,000)	10%
	2,000	80%
	5,000	10%

E6-3 (Expected Cash Flows and Present Value) Andrew Kelly is trying to determine the amount to set aside so that he will have enough money on hand in 2 years to overhaul the engine on his vintage used car. While there is some uncertainty about the cost of engine overhauls in 2 years, by conducting some research online, Andrew has developed the following estimates.

Engine Overhaul Estimated Cash Outflow	Probability Assessment
$200	10%
450	30%
550	50%
750	10%

Instructions

How much should Andrew Kelly deposit today in an account earning 6%, compounded annually, so that he will have enough money on hand in 2 years to pay for the overhaul?

E6-4 (Simple and Compound Interest Computations) Alan Jackson invests $20,000 at 8% annual interest, leaving the money invested without withdrawing any of the interest for 8 years. At the end of the 8 years, Alan withdrew the accumulated amount of money.

Instructions

(a) Compute the amount Alan would withdraw assuming the investment earns simple interest.
(b) Compute the amount Alan would withdraw assuming the investment earns interest compounded annually.
(c) Compute the amount Alan would withdraw assuming the investment earns interest compounded semiannually.

E6-5 (Computation of Future Values and Present Values) Using the appropriate interest table, answer each of the following questions. (Each case is independent of the others.)

(a) What is the future value of $7,000 at the end of 5 periods at 8% compounded interest?
(b) What is the present value of $7,000 due 8 periods hence, discounted at 11%?
(c) What is the future value of 15 periodic payments of $7,000 each made at the end of each period and compounded at 10%?
(d) What is the present value of $7,000 to be received at the end of each of 20 periods, discounted at 5% compound interest?

E6-6 (Computation of Future Values and Present Values) Using the appropriate interest table, answer the following questions. (Each case is independent of the others).

(a) What is the future value of 20 periodic payments of $4,000 each made at the beginning of each period and compounded at 8%?
(b) What is the present value of $2,500 to be received at the beginning of each of 30 periods, discounted at 10% compound interest?

(c) What is the future value of 15 deposits of $2,000 each made at the beginning of each period and compounded at 10%? (Future value as of the end of the fifteenth period.)
(d) What is the present value of six receipts of $1,000 each received at the beginning of each period, discounted at 9% compounded interest?

E6-7 (Computation of Present Value) Using the appropriate interest table, compute the present values of the following periodic amounts due at the end of the designated periods.

(a) $30,000 receivable at the end of each period for 8 periods compounded at 12%.
(b) $30,000 payments to be made at the end of each period for 16 periods at 9%.
(c) $30,000 payable at the end of the seventh, eighth, ninth, and tenth periods at 12%.

E6-8 (Future Value and Present Value Problems) Presented below are three unrelated situations.

(a) Kobe Bryant Company recently signed a lease for a new office building, for a lease period of 10 years. Under the lease agreement, a security deposit of $12,000 is made, with the deposit to be returned at the expiration of the lease, with interest compounded at 10% per year. What amount will the company receive at the time the lease expires?
(b) Serena Williams Corporation, having recently issued a $20 million, 15-year bond issue, is committed to make annual sinking fund deposits of $600,000. The deposits are made on the last day of each year and yield a return of 10%. Will the fund at the end of 15 years be sufficient to retire the bonds? If not, what will the deficiency be?
(c) Under the terms of his salary agreement, president Rex Walters has an option of receiving either an immediate bonus of $40,000, or a deferred bonus of $70,000 payable in 10 years. Ignoring tax considerations, and assuming a relevant interest rate of 8%, which form of settlement should Walters accept?

E6-9 (Computation of Bond Prices) What would you pay for a $50,000 debenture bond that matures in 15 years and pays $5,000 a year in interest if you wanted to earn a yield of:

(a) 8%? **(b)** 10%? **(c)** 12%?

E6-10 (Computations for a Retirement Fund) Clarence Weatherspoon, a super salesman contemplating retirement on his fifty-fifth birthday, decides to create a fund on an 8% basis that will enable him to withdraw $20,000 per year on June 30, beginning in 2011 and continuing through 2014. To develop this fund, Clarence intends to make equal contributions on June 30 of each of the years 2007–2010.

Instructions

(a) How much must the balance of the fund equal on June 30, 2010, in order for Clarence Weatherspoon to satisfy his objective?
(b) What are each of Clarence's contributions to the fund?

E6-11 (Unknown Rate) LEW Company purchased a machine at a price of $100,000 by signing a note payable, which requires a single payment of $123,210 in 2 years. Assuming annual compounding of interest, what rate of interest is being paid on the loan?

E6-12 (Unknown Periods and Unknown Interest Rate) Consider the following independent situations.

(a) Mike Finley wishes to become a millionaire. His money market fund has a balance of $92,296 and has a guaranteed interest rate of 10%. How many years must Mike leave that balance in the fund in order to get his desired $1,000,000?
(b) Assume that Venus Williams desires to accumulate $1 million in 15 years using her money market fund balance of $182,696. At what interest rate must Venus's investment compound annually?

E6-13 (Evaluation of Purchase Options) Sosa Excavating Inc. is purchasing a bulldozer. The equipment has a price of $100,000. The manufacturer has offered a payment plan that would allow Sosa to make 10 equal annual payments of $16,274.53, with the first payment due one year after the purchase.

Instructions

(a) How much total interest will Sosa pay on this payment plan?
(b) Sosa could borrow $100,000 from its bank to finance the purchase at an annual rate of 9%. Should Sosa borrow from the bank or use the manufacturer's payment plan to pay for the equipment?

E6-14 (Analysis of Alternatives) The Black Knights Inc., a manufacturer of high-sugar, low-sodium, low-cholesterol TV dinners, would like to increase its market share in the Sunbelt. In order to do so, Black Knights has decided to locate a new factory in the Panama City area. Black Knights will either buy or lease a site depending upon which is more advantageous. The site location committee has narrowed down the available sites to the following three buildings.

Building A: Purchase for a cash price of $600,000, useful life 25 years.

Building B: Lease for 25 years with annual lease payments of $69,000 being made at the beginning of the year.

Building C: Purchase for $650,000 cash. This building is larger than needed; however, the excess space can be sublet for 25 years at a net annual rental of $7,000. Rental payments will be received at the end of each year. The Black Knights Inc. has no aversion to being a landlord.

Instructions

In which building would you recommend that The Black Knights Inc. locate, assuming a 12% cost of funds?

E6-15 (Computation of Bond Liability) Lance Armstrong Inc. manufactures cycling equipment. Recently the vice president of operations of the company has requested construction of a new plant to meet the increasing demand for the company's bikes. After a careful evaluation of the request, the board of directors has decided to raise funds for the new plant by issuing $2,000,000 of 11% term corporate bonds on March 1, 2003, due on March 1, 2018, with interest payable each March 1 and September 1. At the time of issuance, the market interest rate for similar financial instruments is 10%.

Instructions

As the controller of the company, determine the selling price of the bonds.

E6-16 (Computation of Pension Liability) Nerwin, Inc. is a furniture manufacturing company with 50 employees. Recently, after a long negotiation with the local labor union, the company decided to initiate a pension plan as a part of its compensation plan. The plan will start on January 1, 2003. Each employee covered by the plan is entitled to a pension payment each year after retirement. As required by accounting standards, the controller of the company needs to report the pension obligation (liability). On the basis of a discussion with the supervisor of the Personnel Department and an actuary from an insurance company, the controller develops the following information related to the pension plan.

Average length of time to retirement	15 years
Expected life duration after retirement	10 years
Total pension payment expected each year after retirement for all employees. Payment made at the end of the year.	$700,000 per year

The interest rate to be used is 8%.

Instructions

On the basis of the information above, determine the present value of the pension obligation (liability).

E6-17 (Investment Decision) Jason Williams just received a signing bonus of $1,000,000. His plan is to invest this payment in a fund that will earn 8%, compounded annually.

Instructions

(a) If Williams plans to establish the JW Foundation once the fund grows to $1,999,000, how many years until he can establish the foundation?

(b) Instead of investing the entire $1,000,000, Williams invests $300,000 today and plans to make 9 equal annual investments into the fund beginning one year from today. What amount should the payments be if Williams plans to establish the $1,999,000 foundation at the end of 9 years?

E6-18 (Retirement of Debt) Jesper Parnevik borrowed $70,000 on March 1, 2002. This amount plus accrued interest at 12% compounded semiannually is to be repaid March 1, 2012. To retire this debt, Jesper plans to contribute to a debt retirement fund five equal amounts starting on March 1, 2007, and for the next 4 years. The fund is expected to earn 10% per annum.

Instructions

How much must be contributed each year by Jesper Parnevik to provide a fund sufficient to retire the debt on March 1, 2012?

E6-19 (Computation of Amount of Rentals) Your client, Ron Santo Leasing Company, is preparing a contract to lease a machine to Souvenirs Corporation for a period of 25 years. Santo has an investment cost of $365,755 in the machine, which has a useful life of 25 years and no salvage value at the end of that time. Your client is interested in earning an 11% return on its investment and has agreed to accept 25 equal rental payments at the end of each of the next 25 years.

Instructions

You are requested to provide Santo with the amount of each of the 25 rental payments that will yield an 11% return on investment.

E6-20 (Least Costly Payoff) Assume that **Sonic Foundry Corporation** has a contractual debt outstanding. Sonic has available two means of settlement: It can either make immediate payment of $2,600,000, or it can make annual payments of $300,000 for 15 years, each payment due on the last day of the year.

Instructions

Which method of payment do you recommend, assuming an expected effective interest rate of 8% during the future period?

E6-21 (Least Costly Payoff) Assuming the same facts as those in E6-20 except that the payments must begin now and be made on the first day of each of the 15 years, what payment method would you recommend?

***E6-22 (Determine Interest Rate)** Reba McEntire wishes to invest $19,000 on July 1, 2003, and have it accumulate to $49,000 by July 1, 2013.

Instructions

Use a financial calculator to determine at what exact annual rate of interest Reba must invest the $19,000.

***E6-23 (Determine Interest Rate)** On July 17, 2002, Tim McGraw borrowed $42,000 from his grandfather to open a clothing store. Starting July 17, 2003, Tim has to make ten equal annual payments of $6,500 each to repay the loan.

Instructions

Use a financial calculator to determine what interest rate Tim is paying.

***E6-24 (Determine Interest Rate)** As the purchaser of a new house, Patty Loveless has signed a mortgage note to pay the Memphis National Bank and Trust Co. $14,000 every 6 months for 20 years, at the end of which time she will own the house. At the date the mortgage is signed the purchase price was $198,000, and a down payment of $20,000 was made. The first payment will be made 6 months after the date the mortgage is signed.

Instructions

Using a financial calculator, compute the exact rate of interest earned on the mortgage by the bank.

PROBLEMS

(Interest rates are per annum unless otherwise indicated.)

P6-1 (Various Time Value Situations) Answer each of these unrelated questions.

(a) On January 1, 2003, Rather Corporation sold a building that cost $250,000 and that had accumulated depreciation of $100,000 on the date of sale. Rather received as consideration a $275,000 non-interest-bearing note due on January 1, 2006. There was no established exchange price for the building, and the note had no ready market. The prevailing rate of interest for a note of this type on January 1, 2003, was 9%. At what amount should the gain from the sale of the building be reported?

(b) On January 1, 2003, Rather Corporation purchased 200 of the $1,000 face value, 9%, 10-year bonds of Walters Inc. The bonds mature on January 1, 2013, and pay interest annually beginning January 1, 2004. Rather Corporation purchased the bonds to yield 11%. How much did Rather pay for the bonds?

(c) Rather Corporation bought a new machine and agreed to pay for it in equal annual installments of $4,000 at the end of each of the next 10 years. Assuming that a prevailing interest rate of 8% applies to this contract, how much should Rather record as the cost of the machine?

(d) Rather Corporation purchased a special tractor on December 31, 2003. The purchase agreement stipulated that Rather should pay $20,000 at the time of purchase and $5,000 at the end of each of the next 8 years. The tractor should be recorded on December 31, 2003, at what amount, assuming an appropriate interest rate of 12%?

(e) Rather Corporation wants to withdraw $100,000 (including principal) from an investment fund at the end of each year for 9 years. What should be the required initial investment at the beginning of the first year if the fund earns 11%?

P6-2 (Various Time Value Situations) Using the appropriate interest table, provide the solution to each of the following four questions by computing the unknowns.

(a) What is the amount of the payments that Tom Brokaw must make at the end of each of 8 years to accumulate a fund of $70,000 by the end of the eighth year, if the fund earns 8% interest, compounded annually?

(b) Peter Jennings is 40 years old today and he wishes to accumulate $500,000 by his sixty-fifth birthday so he can retire to his summer place on Lake Hopatcong. He wishes to accumulate this amount by making equal deposits on his fortieth through his sixty-fourth birthdays. What annual deposit must Peter make if the fund will earn 12% interest compounded annually?

(c) Jane Pauley has $20,000 to invest today at 9% to pay a debt of $56,253. How many years will it take her to accumulate enough to liquidate the debt?

(d) Maria Shriver has a $27,600 debt that she wishes to repay 4 years from today; she has $18,181 that she intends to invest for the 4 years. What rate of interest will she need to earn annually in order to accumulate enough to pay the debt?

P6-3 (Analysis of Alternatives) Assume that **Wal-Mart, Inc.** has decided to surface and maintain for 10 years a vacant lot next to one of its discount-retail outlets to serve as a parking lot for customers. Management is considering the following bids involving two different qualities of surfacing for a parking area of 12,000 square yards.

Bid A: A surface that costs $5.25 per square yard to install. This surface will have to be replaced at the end of 5 years. The annual maintenance cost on this surface is estimated at 20 cents per square yard for each year except the last year of its service. The replacement surface will be similar to the initial surface.

Bid B: A surface that costs $9.50 per square yard to install. This surface has a probable useful life of 10 years and will require annual maintenance in each year except the last year, at an estimated cost of 9 cents per square yard.

Instructions

Prepare computations showing which bid should be accepted by Wal-Mart Inc. You may assume that the cost of capital is 9%, that the annual maintenance expenditures are incurred at the end of each year, and that prices are not expected to change during the next 10 years.

P6-4 (Evaluating Payment Alternatives) Terry O'Malley has just learned he has won a $900,000 prize in the lottery. The lottery has given him two options for receiving the payments: (1) If Terry takes all the money today, the state and federal governments will deduct taxes at a rate of 46% immediately. (2) Alternatively, the lottery offers Terry a payout of 20 equal payments of $62,000 with the first payment occurring when Terry turns in the winning ticket. Terry will be taxed on each of these payments at a rate of 25%.

Instructions

Assuming Terry can earn an 8% rate of return (compounded annually) on any money invested during this period, which pay-out option should he choose?

P6-5 (Analysis of Alternatives) Sally Brown died, leaving to her husband Linus an insurance policy contract that provides that the beneficiary (Linus) can choose any one of the following four options.

(a) $55,000 immediate cash.

(b) $3,700 every 3 months payable at the end of each quarter for 5 years.

(c) $18,000 immediate cash and $1,600 every 3 months for 10 years, payable at the beginning of each 3-month period.

(d) $4,000 every 3 months for 3 years and $1,200 each quarter for the following 25 quarters, all payments payable at the end of each quarter.

Instructions

If money is worth 2½% per quarter, compounded quarterly, which option would you recommend that Linus exercise?

P6-6 (Expected Cash Flows and Present Value) Larry's Lawn Equipment sells high-quality lawn mowers and offers a 3-year warranty on all new lawn mowers sold. In 2003, Larry sold $300,000 of new specialty mowers for golf greens for which Larry's service department does not have the equipment to do the service. Larry has entered into an agreement with Mower Mavens to provide all warranty service on the special mowers sold in 2003. Larry wishes to measure the fair value of the agreement to determine the warranty liability for sales made in 2003. The controller for Larry's Lawn Equipment estimates the following expected warranty cash outflows associated with the mowers sold in 2003.

Year	Cash Flow Estimate	Probability Assessment
2004	$2,000	20%
	4,000	60%
	5,000	20%
2005	$2,500	30%
	5,000	50%
	6,000	20%
2006	$3,000	30%
	6,000	40%
	7,000	30%

Instructions

Using expected cash flow and present value techniques, determine the value of the warranty liability for the 2003 sales. Use an annual discount rate of 5%. Assume all cash flows occur at the end of the year.

P6-7 (Expected Cash Flows and Present Value) At the end of 2003, Richards Company is conducting an impairment test and needs to develop a fair value estimate for machinery used in its manufacturing operations. Given the nature of Richard's production process, the equipment is for special use. (No second-hand market values are available.) The equipment will be obsolete in 2 years, and Richard's accountants have developed the following cash flow information for the equipment.

Year	Net Cash Flow Estimate	Probability Assessment
2004	$6,000	40%
	8,000	60%
2005	$ (500)	20%
	2,000	60%
	3,000	20%
	Scrap value	
2005	$ 500	50%
	700	50%

Instructions

Using expected cash flow and present value techniques, determine the fair value of the machinery at the end of 2003. Use a 6% discount rate. Assume all cash flows occur at the end of the year.

P6-8 (Purchase Price of a Business) During the past year, Nicole Bobek planted a new vineyard on 150 acres of land that she leases for $27,000 a year. She has asked you as her accountant to assist her in determining the value of her vineyard operation.

The vineyard will bear no grapes for the first 5 years (1–5). In the next 5 years (6–10), Nicole estimates that the vines will bear grapes that can be sold for $60,000 each year. For the next 20 years (11–30) she expects the harvest will provide annual revenues of $100,000. But during the last 10 years (31–40) of the vineyard's life she estimates that revenues will decline to $80,000 per year.

During the first 5 years the annual cost of pruning, fertilizing, and caring for the vineyard is estimated at $9,000; during the years of production, 6–40, these costs will rise to $10,000 per year. The relevant market rate of interest for the entire period is 12%. Assume that all receipts and payments are made at the end of each year.

Instructions

Dick Button has offered to buy Nicole's vineyard business by assuming the 40-year lease. On the basis of the current value of the business, what is the minimum price Nicole should accept?

P6-9 (Time Value Concepts Applied to Solve Business Problems) Answer the following questions related to Mark Grace Inc.

(a) Mark Grace Inc. has $572,000 to invest. The company is trying to decide between two alternative uses of the funds. One alternative provides $80,000 at the end of each year for 12 years, and the other is to receive a single lump sum payment of $1,900,000 at the end of the 12 years. Which alternative should Grace select? Assume the interest rate is constant over the entire investment.

(b) Mark Grace Inc. has completed the purchase of new IBM computers. The fair market value of the equipment is $824,150. The purchase agreement specifies an immediate down payment of $200,000 and semiannual payments of $76,952 beginning at the end of 6 months for 5 years. What is the interest rate, to the nearest percent, used in discounting this purchase transaction?

(c) Mark Grace Inc. loans money to John Kruk Corporation in the amount of $600,000. Grace accepts an 8% note due in 7 years with interest payable semiannually. After 2 years (and receipt of interest for 2 years), Grace needs money and therefore sells the note to Chicago National Bank, which demands interest on the note of 10% compounded semiannually. What is the amount Grace will receive on the sale of the note?

(d) Mark Grace Inc. wishes to accumulate $1,300,000 by December 31, 2013, to retire bonds outstanding. The company deposits $300,000 on December 31, 2003, which will earn interest at 10% compounded quarterly, to help in the retirement of this debt. In addition, the company wants to know how much should be deposited at the end of each quarter for 10 years to ensure that $1,300,000 is available at the end of 2013. (The quarterly deposits will also earn at a rate of 10%, compounded quarterly.) Round to even dollars.

P6-10 (Analysis of Alternatives) Homer Simpson Inc., a manufacturer of steel school lockers, plans to purchase a new punch press for use in its manufacturing process. After contacting the appropriate vendors, the purchasing department received differing terms and options from each vendor. The Engineering Department has determined that each vendor's punch press is substantially identical and each has a useful life of 20 years. In addition, Engineering has estimated that required year-end maintenance costs will be $1,000 per year for the first 5 years, $2,000 per year for the next 10 years, and $3,000 per year for the last 5 years. Following is each vendor's sale package.

Vendor A: $45,000 cash at time of delivery and 10 year-end payments of $15,000 each. Vendor A offers all its customers the right to purchase at the time of sale a separate 20-year maintenance service contract, under which Vendor A will perform all year-end maintenance at a one-time initial cost of $10,000.

Vendor B: Forty seminannual payments of $8,000 each, with the first installment due upon delivery. Vendor B will perform all year-end maintenance for the next 20 years at no extra charge.

Vendor C: Full cash price of $125,000 will be due upon delivery.

Instructions

Assuming that both Vendor A and B will be able to perform the required year-end maintenance, that Simpson's cost of funds is 10%, and the machine will be purchased on January 1, from which vendor should the press be purchased?

P6-11 (Analysis of Business Problems) Jean-Luc is a financial executive with Starship Enterprises. Although Jean-Luc has not had any formal training in finance or accounting, he has a "good sense" for numbers and has helped the company grow from a very small company ($500,000 sales) to a large operation ($45 million in sales). With the business growing steadily, however, the company needs to make a number of difficult financial decisions in which Jean-Luc feels a little "over his head." He therefore has decided to hire a new employee with "numbers" expertise to help him. As a basis for determining whom to employ, he has decided to ask each prospective employee to prepare answers to questions relating to the following situations he has encountered recently. Here are the questions.

(a) In 2001, Starship Enterprises negotiated and closed a long-term lease contract for newly constructed truck terminals and freight storage facilities. The buildings were constructed on land owned by the company. On January 1, 2002, Starship took possession of the leased property. The 20-year lease is effective for the period January 1, 2002, through December 31, 2021. Advance rental payments of $800,000 are payable to the lessor (owner of facilities) on January 1 of each of the first 10 years of the lease term. Advance payments of $300,000 are due on January 1 for each of the last 10 years of the lease term. Starship has an option to purchase all the leased facilities for $1 on December 31, 2021. At the time the lease was negotiated, the fair market value of the truck terminals and freight storage facilities was approximately $7,200,000. If the company had borrowed the money to purchase the facilities, it would have had to pay 10% interest. Should the company have purchased rather than leased the facilities?

(b) Last year the company exchanged a piece of land for a non-interest-bearing note. The note is to be paid at the rate of $12,000 per year for 9 years, beginning one year from the date of disposal of the land. An appropriate rate of interest for the note was 11%. At the time the land was originally purchased, it cost $90,000. What is the fair value of the note?

(c) The company has always followed the policy to take any cash discounts on goods purchased. Recently the company purchased a large amount of raw materials at a price of $800,000 with terms 2/10, n/30 on which it took the discount. Starship has recently estimated its cost of funds at 10%. Should Starship continue this policy of always taking the cash discount?

P6-12 (Analysis of Lease vs. Purchase) Jose Rijo Inc. owns and operates a number of hardware stores in the New England region. Recently the company has decided to locate another store in a rapidly growing area of Maryland. The company is trying to decide whether to purchase or lease the building and related facilities.

Purchase: The company can purchase the site, construct the building, and purchase all store fixtures. The cost would be $1,650,000. An immediate down payment of $400,000 is required, and the remaining $1,250,000 would be paid off over 5 years at $300,000 per year (including interest). The property is expected to have a useful life of 12 years, and then it will be sold for $500,000. As the owner of the property, the company will have the following out-of-pocket expenses each period.

Property taxes (to be paid at the end of each year)	$40,000
Insurance (to be paid at the beginning of each year)	27,000
Other (primarily maintenance which occurs at the end of each year)	16,000
	$83,000

Lease: First National Bank has agreed to purchase the site, construct the building, and install the appropriate fixtures for Rijo Inc. if Rijo will lease the completed facility for 12 years. The annual costs for the lease would be $240,000. Rijo would have no responsibility related to the facility over the 12 years. The terms of the lease are that Rijo would be required to make 12 annual payments (the first payment to be made at the time the store opens and then each following year). In addition, a deposit of $100,000 is required when the store is opened. This deposit will be returned at the end of the twelfth year, assuming no unusual damage to the building structure or fixtures.

Currently the cost of funds for Rijo Inc. is 10%.

Instructions

Which of the two approaches should Rijo Inc. follow?

P6-13 (Pension Funding) You have been hired as a benefit consultant by Maugarite Alomar, the owner of Attic Angels. She wants to establish a retirement plan for herself and her three employees. Maugarite has provided the following information: The retirement plan is to be based upon annual salary for the last year before retirement and is to provide 50% of Maugarite's last-year annual salary and 40% of the last-year annual salary for each employee. The plan will make annual payments at the beginning of each year for 20 years from the date of retirement. Maugarite wishes to fund the plan by making 15 annual deposits beginning January 1, 2003. Invested funds will earn 12% compounded annually. Information about plan participants as of January 1, 2003, is as follows.

Maugarite Alomar, owner: Current annual salary of $40,000; estimated retirement date January 1, 2028.

Kenny Rogers, flower arranger: Current annual salary of $30,000; estimated retirement date January 1, 2033.

Anita Baker, sales clerk: Current annual salary of $15,000; estimated retirement date January 1, 2023.

Willie Nelson, part-time bookkeeper: Current annual salary of $15,000; estimated retirement date January 1, 2018.

In the past, Maugarite has given herself and each employee a year-end salary increase of 4%. Maugarite plans to continue this policy in the future.

Instructions

(a) Based upon the above information, what will be the annual retirement benefit for each plan participant? (Round to the nearest dollar.) (*Hint:* Maugarite will receive raises for 24 years.)

(b) What amount must be on deposit at the end of 15 years to ensure that all benefits will be paid? (Round to the nearest dollar.)

(c) What is the amount of each annual deposit Maugarite must make to the retirement plan?

P6-14 (Pension Funding) James Qualls, newly appointed controller of KBS, is considering ways to reduce his company's expenditures on annual pension costs. One way to do this is to switch KBS's pension fund assets from First Security to NET Life. KBS is a very well-respected computer manufacturer that recently has experienced a sharp decline in its financial performance for the first time in its 25-year history. Despite financial problems, KBS still is committed to providing its employees with good pension and postretirement health benefits.

Under its present plan with First Security, KBS is obligated to pay $43 million to meet the expected value of future pension benefits that are payable to employees as an annuity upon their retirement from the company. On the other hand, NET Life requires KBS to pay only $35 million for identical future pension benefits. First Security is one of the oldest and most reputable insurance companies in North America. NET Life has a much weaker reputation in the insurance industry. In pondering the significant difference in annual pension costs, Qualls asks himself, "Is this too good to be true?"

Instructions

Answer the following questions.

(a) Why might NET Life's pension cost requirement be $8 million less than First Security's requirement for the same future value?

(b) What ethical issues should James Qualls consider before switching KBS's pension fund assets?

(c) Who are the stakeholders that could be affected by Qualls's decision?

***P6-15 (Various Time Value of Money Situations)** Using a financial calculator, provide a solution to each of the following questions.

(a) What is the amount of the payments that Karla Zehms must make at the end of each of 8 years to accumulate a fund of $70,000 by the end of the eighth year, if the fund earns 7.25% interest, compounded annually?

(b) Bill Yawn is 40 years old today, and he wishes to accumulate $500,000 by his sixty-fifth birthday so he can retire to his summer place on Lake Winnebago. He wishes to accumulate this amount by making equal deposits on his fortieth through sixty-fourth birthdays. What annual deposit must Bill make if the fund will earn 9.65% interest compounded annually?

(c) Jane Mayer has a $26,000 debt that she wishes to repay 4 years from today. She has $17,000 that she intends to invest for the 4 years. What rate of interest will she need to earn annually in order to accumulate enough to pay the debt?

***P6-16 (Various Time Value of Money Situations)** Using a financial calculator, solve for the unknowns in each of the following situations.

(a) Wayne Eski wishes to invest $150,000 today to ensure payments of $20,000 to his son at the end of each year for the next 15 years. At what interest rate must the $150,000 be invested? (Round the answer to two decimal points.)

(b) On June 1, 2003, Shelley Long purchases lakefront property from her neighbor, Joey Brenner, and agrees to pay the purchase price in seven payments of $16,000 each, the first payment to be payable June 1, 2004. (Assume that interest compounded at an annual rate of 7.35% is implicit in the payments.) What is the purchase price of the property?

(c) On January 1, 2003, Cooke Corporation purchased 200 of the $1,000 face value, 8% coupon, 10-year bonds of Howe Inc. The bonds mature on January 1, 2013, and pay interest annually beginning January 1, 2004. Cooke purchased the bonds to yield 10.65%. How much did Cooke pay for the bonds?

***P6-17 (Various Time Value of Money Situations)** Using a financial calculator, provide a solution to each of the following situations.

(a) On March 12, 2004, William Scott invests in a $180,000 insurance policy that earns 5.25% compounded annually. The annuity policy allows William to receive annual payments, the first of which is payable to William on March 12, 2005. What will be the amount of each of the 20 equal annual receipts?

(b) Bill Schroeder owes a debt of $35,000 from the purchase of his new sport utility vehicle. The debt bears annual interest of 9.1% compounded monthly. Bill wishes to pay the debt and interest in equal monthly payments over 8 years, beginning one month hence. What equal monthly payments will pay off the debt and interest?

(c) On January 1, 2004, Sammy Sosa offers to buy Mark Grace's used snowmobile for $8,000, payable in five equal installments, which are to include 8.25% interest on the unpaid balance and a portion of the principal. If the first payment is to be made on January 1, 2004, how much will each payment be?

(d) Repeat the requirements in part (c), assuming Sosa makes the first payment on December 31, 2004.

USING YOUR JUDGMENT

FINANCIAL REPORTING PROBLEM

3M Company

The financial statements and accompanying notes of 3M are presented in Appendix 5B or can be accessed on the Take Action! CD.

Instructions

(a) Examining each item in 3M's balance sheet, identify those items that require present value, discounting, or interest computations in establishing the amount reported. (The accompanying notes are an additional source for this information.)

(b) (1) What interest rates are disclosed by 3M as being used to compute interest and present values? (2) Why are there so many different interest rates applied to 3M's financial statement elements (assets, liabilities, revenues, and expenses)?

FINANCIAL STATEMENT ANALYSIS CASE

Consolidated Natural Gas Company

Consolidated Natural Gas Company (CNG), with corporate headquarters in Pittsburgh, Pennsylvania, is one of the largest producers, transporters, distributors, and marketers of natural gas in North America.

Recently, the company experienced a decrease in the value of its gas and oil producing properties, and a special charge to income was recorded in order to reduce the carrying value of those assets. The company also wrote down oil and gas properties in the prior two years, and special charges were incurred for severance pay and early retirement incentives as CNG reduced its workforce.

Assume the following information: In 2002, CNG estimated the cash inflows from its oil and gas producing properties to be $350,000 per year. During 2003, the write-downs described above caused the estimate to be decreased to $275,000 per year. Production costs (cash outflows) associated with all these properties were estimated to be $125,000 per year in 2002, but this amount was revised to $175,000 per year in 2003.

Instructions

(Assume that all cash flows occur at the end of the year.)

(a) Calculate the present value of net cash flows for 2002–2004 (three years), using the 2002 estimates and a 10% discount factor.

(b) Calculate the present value of net cash flows for 2003–2005 (three years), using the 2003 estimates and a 10% discount factor.

(c) Compare the results using the two estimates. Is information on future cash flows from oil and gas producing properties useful, considering that the estimates must be revised each year? Explain.

RESEARCH CASES

Case 1

To access the Internet and EDGAR, follow the steps outlined in Research Case 1 on page 248.

Firms registered with the U.S. Securities and Exchange Commission (SEC) are required to file an annual report on Form 10-K within 90 days of their fiscal year end. The Form 10-K includes certain information not provided in a firm's annual report to shareholders.

Instructions

Examine the most recent Form 10-K of a company of your choice and answer the following questions.

(a) Each 10-K is required to include information regarding several aspects of a firm, referenced by item numbers. Identify the 14 items included in the 10-K.

(b) Each 10-K must include the firm's financial statements. Does the 10-K you examined include the firm's financial statements? If not, how did the firm comply with the financial statement requirement?

(c) What financial statement schedules are included with the 10-K you examined?

Case 2

In May 2001 the FASB published the first of a series of articles entitled *Understanding the Issues*, which are designed to enhance FASB constituents' understanding of various accounting issues. In the first installment, "Expected Cash Flows," Ed Trott and Wayne Upton explained issues related to *FASB Concepts Statement No. 7*.

Instructions

The article can be accessed at the FASB Web site (**www.fasb.org**). Read the article and answer the following questions.

(a) What are the three areas in which the FASB received objections to its exposure draft for *Concepts Statement No. 7*?

(b) What has been the traditional approach to estimating cash flows and present values? What were some of the problems with the "traditional approach to present value"?

(c) What are the principles the Board identified in application of present value to accounting measurements?

(d) How do present values computed using the model in *Concepts Statement No. 7* include the effects of inflation?

PROFESSIONAL SIMULATION

Accounting — Time Value of Money Applications

Directions | Situation | Research | Resources

Directions

In this simulation, you will be asked various questions concerning the application of time value of money concepts to accounting problems. Prepare responses to all parts.

Situation

Your company is considering the issuance of bonds in the amount of $100,000. The bonds mature in 5 years and have an annual coupon rate of interest of 10%. Market interest rates have been fluctuating in recent weeks, and the treasurer of your company would like to know the amount of proceeds that can be expected from issuance of the bonds.

Resources

*(a) Use a financial calculator to determine the amount of proceeds that will be received when the bonds are issued, assuming market interest rates for similar bonds are:
  1. 12%
  2. 8%

(b) Use a computer spreadsheet to prepare an amortization schedule for the bonds, assuming the bonds are issued when market interest rates are 12%.

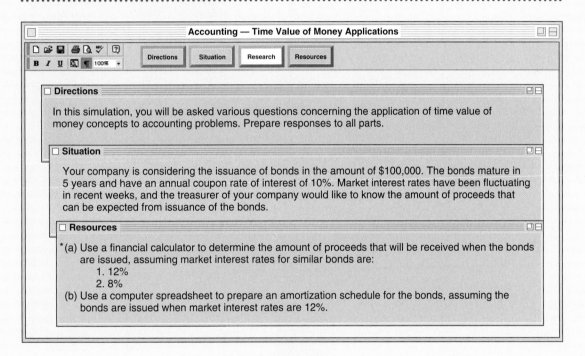

Remember to check the **Take Action! CD**
and the book's **companion Web site**
to find additional resources for this chapter.

TABLE 6-1 FUTURE VALUE OF 1 (FUTURE VALUE OF A SINGLE SUM)

$$FVF_{n,i} = (1 + i)^n$$

(n) Periods	2%	2½%	3%	4%	5%	6%
1	1.02000	1.02500	1.03000	1.04000	1.05000	1.06000
2	1.04040	1.05063	1.06090	1.08160	1.10250	1.12360
3	1.06121	1.07689	1.09273	1.12486	1.15763	1.19102
4	1.08243	1.10381	1.12551	1.16986	1.21551	1.26248
5	1.10408	1.13141	1.15927	1.21665	1.27628	1.33823
6	1.12616	1.15969	1.19405	1.26532	1.34010	1.41852
7	1.14869	1.18869	1.22987	1.31593	1.40710	1.50363
8	1.17166	1.21840	1.26677	1.36857	1.47746	1.59385
9	1.19509	1.24886	1.30477	1.42331	1.55133	1.68948
10	1.21899	1.28008	1.34392	1.48024	1.62889	1.79085
11	1.24337	1.31209	1.38423	1.53945	1.71034	1.89830
12	1.26824	1.34489	1.42576	1.60103	1.79586	2.01220
13	1.29361	1.37851	1.46853	1.66507	1.88565	2.13293
14	1.31948	1.41297	1.51259	1.73168	1.97993	2.26090
15	1.34587	1.44830	1.55797	1.80094	2.07893	2.39656
16	1.37279	1.48451	1.60471	1.87298	2.18287	2.54035
17	1.40024	1.52162	1.65285	1.94790	2.29202	2.69277
18	1.42825	1.55966	1.70243	2.02582	2.40662	2.85434
19	1.45681	1.59865	1.75351	2.10685	2.52695	3.02560
20	1.48595	1.63862	1.80611	2.19112	2.65330	3.20714
21	1.51567	1.67958	1.86029	2.27877	2.78596	3.39956
22	1.54598	1.72157	1.91610	2.36992	2.92526	3.60354
23	1.57690	1.76461	1.97359	2.46472	3.07152	3.81975
24	1.60844	1.80873	2.03279	2.56330	3.22510	4.04893
25	1.64061	1.85394	2.09378	2.66584	3.38635	4.29187
26	1.67342	1.90029	2.15659	2.77247	3.55567	4.54938
27	1.70689	1.94780	2.22129	2.88337	3.73346	4.82235
28	1.74102	1.99650	2.28793	2.99870	3.92013	5.11169
29	1.77584	2.04641	2.35657	3.11865	4.11614	5.41839
30	1.81136	2.09757	2.42726	3.24340	4.32194	5.74349
31	1.84759	2.15001	2.50008	3.37313	4.53804	6.08810
32	1.88454	2.20376	2.57508	3.50806	4.76494	6.45339
33	1.92223	2.25885	2.65234	3.64838	5.00319	6.84059
34	1.96068	2.31532	2.73191	3.79432	5.25335	7.25103
35	1.99989	2.37321	2.81386	3.94609	5.51602	7.68609
36	2.03989	2.43254	2.89828	4.10393	5.79182	8.14725
37	2.08069	2.49335	2.98523	4.26809	6.08141	8.63609
38	2.12230	2.55568	3.07478	4.43881	6.38548	9.15425
39	2.16474	2.61957	3.16703	4.61637	6.70475	9.70351
40	2.20804	2.68506	3.26204	4.80102	7.03999	10.28572

TABLE 6-1 FUTURE VALUE OF 1

8%	9%	10%	11%	12%	15%	(n) Periods
1.08000	1.09000	1.10000	1.11000	1.12000	1.15000	1
1.16640	1.18810	1.21000	1.23210	1.25440	1.32250	2
1.25971	1.29503	1.33100	1.36763	1.40493	1.52088	3
1.36049	1.41158	1.46410	1.51807	1.57352	1.74901	4
1.46933	1.53862	1.61051	1.68506	1.76234	2.01136	5
1.58687	1.67710	1.77156	1.87041	1.97382	2.31306	6
1.71382	1.82804	1.94872	2.07616	2.21068	2.66002	7
1.85093	1.99256	2.14359	2.30454	2.47596	3.05902	8
1.99900	2.17189	2.35795	2.55803	2.77308	3.51788	9
2.15892	2.36736	2.59374	2.83942	3.10585	4.04556	10
2.33164	2.58043	2.85312	3.15176	3.47855	4.65239	11
2.51817	2.81267	3.13843	3.49845	3.89598	5.35025	12
2.71962	3.06581	3.45227	3.88328	4.36349	6.15279	13
2.93719	3.34173	3.79750	4.31044	4.88711	7.07571	14
3.17217	3.64248	4.17725	4.78459	5.47357	8.13706	15
3.42594	3.97031	4.59497	5.31089	6.13039	9.35762	16
3.70002	4.32763	5.05447	5.89509	6.86604	10.76126	17
3.99602	4.71712	5.55992	6.54355	7.68997	12.37545	18
4.31570	5.14166	6.11591	7.26334	8.61276	14.23177	19
4.66096	5.60441	6.72750	8.06231	9.64629	16.36654	20
5.03383	6.10881	7.40025	8.94917	10.80385	18.82152	21
5.43654	6.65860	8.14028	9.93357	12.10031	21.64475	22
5.87146	7.25787	8.95430	11.02627	13.55235	24.89146	23
6.34118	7.91108	9.84973	12.23916	15.17863	28.62518	24
6.84847	8.62308	10.83471	13.58546	17.00000	32.91895	25
7.39635	9.39916	11.91818	15.07986	19.04007	37.85680	26
7.98806	10.24508	13.10999	16.73865	21.32488	43.53532	27
8.62711	11.16714	14.42099	18.57990	23.88387	50.06561	28
9.31727	12.17218	15.86309	20.62369	26.74993	57.57545	29
10.06266	13.26768	17.44940	22.89230	29.95992	66.21177	30
10.86767	14.46177	19.19434	25.41045	33.55511	76.14354	31
11.73708	15.76333	21.11378	28.20560	37.58173	87.56507	32
12.67605	17.18203	23.22515	31.30821	42.09153	100.69983	33
13.69013	18.72841	25.54767	34.75212	47.14252	115.80480	34
14.78534	20.41397	28.10244	38.57485	52.79962	133.17552	35
15.96817	22.25123	30.91268	42.81808	59.13557	153.15185	36
17.24563	24.25384	34.00395	47.52807	66.23184	176.12463	37
18.62528	26.43668	37.40434	52.75616	74.17966	202.54332	38
20.11530	28.81598	41.14479	58.55934	83.08122	232.92482	39
21.72452	31.40942	45.25926	65.00087	93.05097	267.86355	40

TABLE 6-2 PRESENT VALUE OF 1 (PRESENT VALUE OF A SINGLE SUM)

$$PVF_{n,i} = \frac{1}{(1 + i)^n} = (1 + i)^{-n}$$

(n) Periods	2%	2½%	3%	4%	5%	6%
1	.98039	.97561	.97087	.96154	.95238	.94340
2	.96117	.95181	.94260	.92456	.90703	.89000
3	.94232	.92860	.91514	.88900	.86384	.83962
4	.92385	.90595	.88849	.85480	.82270	.79209
5	.90573	.88385	.86261	.82193	.78353	.74726
6	.88797	.86230	.83748	.79031	.74622	.70496
7	.87056	.84127	.81309	.75992	.71068	.66506
8	.85349	.82075	.78941	.73069	.67684	.62741
9	.83676	.80073	.76642	.70259	.64461	.59190
10	.82035	.78120	.74409	.67556	.61391	.55839
11	.80426	.76214	.72242	.64958	.58468	.52679
12	.78849	.74356	.70138	.62460	.55684	.49697
13	.77303	.72542	.68095	.60057	.53032	.46884
14	.75788	.70773	.66112	.57748	.50507	.44230
15	.74301	.69047	.64186	.55526	.48102	.41727
16	.72845	.67362	.62317	.53391	.45811	.39365
17	.71416	.65720	.60502	.51337	.43630	.37136
18	.70016	.64117	.58739	.49363	.41552	.35034
19	.68643	.62553	.57029	.47464	.39573	.33051
20	.67297	.61027	.55368	.45639	.37689	.31180
21	.65978	.59539	.53755	.43883	.35894	.29416
22	.64684	.58086	.52189	.42196	.34185	.22751
23	.63416	.56670	.50669	.40573	.32557	.26180
24	.62172	.55288	.49193	.39012	.31007	.24698
25	.60953	.53939	.47761	.37512	.29530	.23300
26	.59758	.52623	.46369	.36069	.28124	.21981
27	.58586	.51340	.45019	.34682	.26785	.20737
28	.57437	.50088	.43708	.33348	.25509	.19563
29	.56311	.48866	.42435	.32065	.24295	.18456
30	.55207	.47674	.41199	.30832	.23138	.17411
31	.54125	.46511	.39999	.29646	.22036	.16425
32	.53063	.45377	.38834	.28506	.20987	.15496
33	.52023	.44270	.37703	.27409	.19987	.14619
34	.51003	.43191	.36604	.26355	.19035	.13791
35	.50003	.42137	.35538	.25342	.18129	.13011
36	.49022	.41109	.34503	.24367	.17266	.12274
37	.48061	.40107	.33498	.23430	.16444	.11579
38	.47119	.39128	.32523	.22529	.15661	.10924
39	.46195	.38174	.31575	.21662	.14915	.10306
40	.45289	.37243	.30656	.20829	.14205	.09722

TABLE 6-2 PRESENT VALUE OF 1

8%	9%	10%	11%	12%	15%	(n) Periods
.92593	.91743	.90909	.90090	.89286	.86957	1
.85734	.84168	.82645	.81162	.79719	.75614	2
.79383	.77218	.75132	.73119	.71178	.65752	3
.73503	.70843	.68301	.65873	.63552	.57175	4
.68058	.64993	.62092	.59345	.56743	.49718	5
.63017	.59627	.56447	.53464	.50663	.43233	6
.58349	.54703	.51316	.48166	.45235	.37594	7
.54027	.50187	.46651	.43393	.40388	.32690	8
.50025	.46043	.42410	.39092	.36061	.28426	9
.46319	.42241	.38554	.35218	.32197	.24719	10
.42888	.38753	.35049	.31728	.28748	.21494	11
.39711	.35554	.31863	.28584	.25668	.18691	12
.36770	.32618	.28966	.25751	.22917	.16253	13
.34046	.29925	.26333	.23199	.20462	.14133	14
.31524	.27454	.23939	.20900	.18270	.12289	15
.29189	.25187	.21763	.18829	.16312	.10687	16
.27027	.23107	.19785	.16963	.14564	.09293	17
.25025	.21199	.17986	.15282	.13004	.08081	18
.23171	.19449	.16351	.13768	.11611	.07027	19
.21455	.17843	.14864	.12403	.10367	.06110	20
.19866	.16370	.13513	.11174	.09256	.05313	21
.18394	.15018	.12285	.10067	.08264	.04620	22
.17032	.13778	.11168	.09069	.07379	.04017	23
.15770	.12641	.10153	.08170	.06588	.03493	24
.14602	.11597	.09230	.07361	.05882	.03038	25
.13520	.10639	.08391	.06631	.05252	.02642	26
.12519	.09761	.07628	.05974	.04689	.02297	27
.11591	.08955	.06934	.05382	.04187	.01997	28
.10733	.08216	.06304	.04849	.03738	.01737	29
.09938	.07537	.05731	.04368	.03338	.01510	30
.09202	.06915	.05210	.03935	.02980	.01313	31
.08520	.06344	.04736	.03545	.02661	.01142	32
.07889	.05820	.04306	.03194	.02376	.00993	33
.07305	.05340	.03914	.02878	.02121	.00864	34
.06763	.04899	.03558	.02592	.01894	.00751	35
.06262	.04494	.03235	.02335	.01691	.00653	36
.05799	.04123	.02941	.02104	.01510	.00568	37
.05369	.03783	.02674	.01896	.01348	.00494	38
.04971	.03470	.02430	.01708	.01204	.00429	39
.04603	.03184	.02210	.01538	.01075	.00373	40

TABLE 6-3 FUTURE VALUE OF AN ORDINARY ANNUITY OF 1

$$\text{FVF-OA}_{n,i} = \frac{(1 + i)^n - 1}{i}$$

(n) Periods	2%	2½%	3%	4%	5%	6%
1	1.00000	1.00000	1.00000	1.00000	1.00000	1.00000
2	2.02000	2.02500	2.03000	2.04000	2.05000	2.06000
3	3.06040	3.07563	3.09090	3.12160	3.15250	3.18360
4	4.12161	4.15252	4.18363	4.24646	4.31013	4.37462
5	5.20404	5.25633	5.30914	5.41632	5.52563	5.63709
6	6.30812	6.38774	6.46841	6.63298	6.80191	6.97532
7	7.43428	7.54743	7.66246	7.89829	8.14201	8.39384
8	8.58297	8.73612	8.89234	9.21423	9.54911	9.89747
9	9.75463	9.95452	10.15911	10.58280	11.02656	11.49132
10	10.94972	11.20338	11.46338	12.00611	12.57789	13.18079
11	12.16872	12.48347	12.80780	13.48635	14.20679	14.97164
12	13.41209	13.79555	14.19203	15.02581	15.91713	16.86994
13	14.68033	15.14044	15.61779	16.62684	17.71298	18.88214
14	15.97394	16.51895	17.08632	18.29191	19.59863	21.01507
15	17.29342	17.93193	18.59891	20.02359	21.57856	23.27597
16	18.63929	19.38022	20.15688	21.82453	23.65749	25.67253
17	20.01207	20.86473	21.76159	23.69751	25.84037	28.21288
18	21.41231	22.38635	23.41444	25.64541	28.13238	30.90565
19	22.84056	23.94601	25.11687	27.67123	30.53900	33.75999
20	24.29737	25.54466	26.87037	29.77808	33.06595	36.78559
21	25.78332	27.18327	28.67649	31.96920	35.71925	39.99273
22	27.29898	28.86286	30.53678	34.24797	38.50521	43.39229
23	28.84496	30.58443	32.45288	36.61789	41.43048	46.99583
24	30.42186	32.34904	34.42647	39.08260	44.50200	50.81558
25	32.03030	34.15776	36.45926	41.64591	47.72710	54.86451
26	33.67091	36.01171	38.55304	44.31174	51.11345	59.15638
27	35.34432	37.91200	40.70963	47.08421	54.66913	63.70577
28	37.05121	39.85980	42.93092	49.96758	58.40258	68.52811
29	38.79223	41.85630	45.21885	52.96629	62.32271	73.63980
30	40.56808	43.90270	47.57542	56.08494	66.43885	79.05819
31	42.37944	46.00027	50.00268	59.32834	70.76079	84.80168
32	44.22703	48.15028	52.50276	62.70147	75.29883	90.88978
33	46.11157	50.35403	55.07784	66.20953	80.06377	97.34316
34	48.03380	52.61289	57.73018	69.85791	85.06696	104.18376
35	49.99448	54.92821	60.46208	73.65222	90.32031	111.43478
36	51.99437	57.30141	63.27594	77.59831	95.83632	119.12087
37	54.03425	59.73395	66.17422	81.70225	101.62814	127.26812
38	56.11494	62.22730	69.15945	85.97034	107.70955	135.90421
39	58.23724	64.78298	72.23423	90.40915	114.09502	145.05846
40	60.40198	67.40255	75.40126	95.02552	120.79977	154.76197

TABLE 6-3 FUTURE VALUE OF AN ORDINARY ANNUITY OF 1

8%	9%	10%	11%	12%	15%	(n) Periods
1.00000	1.00000	1.00000	1.00000	1.00000	1.00000	1
2.08000	2.09000	2.10000	2.11000	2.12000	2.15000	2
3.24640	3.27810	3.31000	3.34210	3.37440	3.47250	3
4.50611	4.57313	4.64100	4.70973	4.77933	4.99338	4
5.86660	5.98471	6.10510	6.22780	6.35285	6.74238	5
7.33592	7.52334	7.71561	7.91286	8.11519	8.75374	6
8.92280	9.20044	9.48717	9.78327	10.08901	11.06680	7
10.63663	11.02847	11.43589	11.85943	12.29969	13.72682	8
12.48756	13.02104	13.57948	14.16397	14.77566	16.78584	9
14.48656	15.19293	15.93743	16.72201	17.54874	20.30372	10
16.64549	17.56029	18.53117	19.56143	20.65458	24.34928	11
18.97713	20.14072	21.38428	22.71319	24.13313	29.00167	12
21.49530	22.95339	24.52271	26.21164	28.02911	34.35192	13
24.21492	26.01919	27.97498	30.09492	32.39260	40.50471	14
27.15211	29.36092	31.77248	34.40536	37.27972	47.58041	15
30.32428	33.00340	35.94973	39.18995	42.75328	55.71747	16
33.75023	36.97371	40.54470	44.50084	48.88367	65.07509	17
37.45024	41.30134	45.59917	50.39593	55.74972	75.83636	18
41.44626	46.01846	51.15909	56.93949	63.43968	88.21181	19
45.76196	51.16012	57.27500	64.20283	72.05244	102.44358	20
50.42292	56.76453	64.00250	72.26514	81.69874	118.81012	21
55.45676	62.87334	71.40275	81.21431	92.50258	137.63164	22
60.89330	69.53194	79.54302	91.14788	104.60289	159.27638	23
66.76476	76.78981	88.49733	102.17415	118.15524	184.16784	24
73.10594	84.70090	98.34706	114.41331	133.33387	212.79302	25
79.95442	93.32398	109.18177	127.99877	150.33393	245.71197	26
87.35077	102.72314	121.09994	143.07864	169.37401	283.56877	27
95.33883	112.96822	134.20994	159.81729	190.69889	327.10408	28
103.96594	124.13536	148.63093	178.39719	214.58275	377.16969	29
113.28321	136.30754	164.49402	199.02088	241.33268	434.74515	30
123.34587	149.57522	181.94343	221.91317	271.29261	500.95692	31
134.21354	164.03699	201.13777	247.32362	304.84772	577.10046	32
145.95062	179.80032	222.25154	275.52922	342.42945	644.66553	33
158.62667	196.98234	245.47670	306.83744	384.52098	765.36535	34
172.31680	215.71076	271.02437	341.58955	431.66350	881.17016	35
187.10215	236.12472	299.12681	380.16441	484.46312	1014.34568	36
203.07032	258.37595	330.03949	422.98249	543.59869	1167.49753	37
220.31595	282.62978	364.04343	470.51056	609.83053	1343.62216	38
238.94122	309.06646	401.44778	523.26673	684.01020	1546.16549	39
259.05652	337.88245	442.59256	581.82607	767.09142	1779.09031	40

TABLE 6-4 PRESENT VALUE OF AN ORDINARY ANNUITY OF 1

$$\text{PVF-OA}_{n,i} = \frac{1 - \frac{1}{(1+i)^n}}{i}$$

(n) Periods	2%	2½%	3%	4%	5%	6%
1	.98039	.97561	.97087	.96154	.95238	.94340
2	1.94156	1.92742	1.91347	1.88609	1.85941	1.83339
3	2.88388	2.85602	2.82861	2.77509	2.72325	2.67301
4	3.80773	3.76197	3.71710	3.62990	3.54595	3.46511
5	4.71346	4.64583	4.57971	4.45182	4.32948	4.21236
6	5.60143	5.50813	5.41719	5.24214	5.07569	4.91732
7	6.47199	6.34939	6.23028	6.00205	5.78637	5.58238
8	7.32548	7.17014	7.01969	6.73274	6.46321	6.20979
9	8.16224	7.97087	7.78611	7.43533	7.10782	6.80169
10	8.98259	8.75206	8.53020	8.11090	7.72173	7.36009
11	9.78685	9.51421	9.25262	8.76048	8.30641	7.88687
12	10.57534	10.25776	9.95400	9.38507	8.86325	8.38384
13	11.34837	10.98319	10.63496	9.98565	9.39357	8.85268
14	12.10625	11.69091	11.29607	10.56312	9.89864	9.29498
15	12.84926	12.38138	11.93794	11.11839	10.37966	9.71225
16	13.57771	13.05500	12.56110	11.65230	10.83777	10.10590
17	14.29187	13.71220	13.16612	12.16567	11.27407	10.47726
18	14.99203	14.35336	13.75351	12.65930	11.68959	10.82760
19	15.67846	14.97889	14.32380	13.13394	12.08532	11.15812
20	16.35143	15.58916	14.87747	13.59033	12.46221	11.46992
21	17.01121	16.18455	15.41502	14.02916	12.82115	11.76408
22	17.65805	16.76541	15.93692	14.45112	13.16300	12.04158
23	18.29220	17.33211	16.44361	14.85684	13.48857	12.30338
24	18.91393	17.88499	16.93554	15.24696	13.79864	12.55036
25	19.52346	18.42438	17.41315	15.62208	14.09394	12.78336
26	20.12104	18.95061	17.87684	15.98277	14.37519	13.00317
27	20.70690	19.46401	18.32703	16.32959	14.64303	13.21053
28	21.28127	19.96489	18.76411	16.66306	14.89813	13.40616
29	21.84438	20.45355	19.18845	16.98371	15.14107	13.59072
30	22.39646	20.93029	19.60044	17.29203	15.37245	13.76483
31	22.93770	21.39541	20.00043	17.58849	15.59281	13.92909
32	23.46833	21.84918	20.38877	17.87355	15.80268	14.08404
33	23.98856	22.29188	20.76579	18.14765	16.00255	14.23023
34	24.49859	22.72379	21.13184	18.41120	16.19290	14.36814
35	24.99862	23.14516	21.48722	18.66461	16.37419	14.49825
36	25.48884	23.55625	21.83225	18.90828	16.54685	14.62099
37	25.96945	23.95732	22.16724	19.14258	16.71129	14.73678
38	26.44064	24.34860	22.49246	19.36786	16.86789	14.84602
39	26.90259	24.73034	22.80822	19.58448	17.01704	14.94907
40	27.35548	25.10278	23.11477	19.79277	17.15909	15.04630

TABLE 6-4 PRESENT VALUE OF AN ORDINARY ANNUITY OF 1

8%	9%	10%	11%	12%	15%	(n) Periods
.92593	.91743	.90909	.90090	.89286	.86957	1
1.78326	1.75911	1.73554	1.71252	1.69005	1.62571	2
2.57710	2.53130	2.48685	2.44371	2.40183	2.28323	3
3.31213	3.23972	3.16986	3.10245	3.03735	2.85498	4
3.99271	3.88965	3.79079	3.69590	3.60478	3.35216	5
4.62288	4.48592	4.35526	4.23054	4.11141	3.78448	6
5.20637	5.03295	4.86842	4.71220	4.56376	4.16042	7
5.74664	5.53482	5.33493	5.14612	4.96764	4.48732	8
6.24689	5.99525	5.75902	5.53705	5.32825	4.77158	9
6.71008	6.41766	6.14457	5.88923	5.65022	5.01877	10
7.13896	6.80519	6.49506	6.20652	5.93770	5.23371	11
7.53608	7.16073	6.81369	6.49236	6.19437	5.42062	12
7.90378	7.48690	7.10336	6.74987	6.42355	5.58315	13
8.24424	7.78615	7.36669	6.98187	6.62817	5.72448	14
8.55948	8.06069	7.60608	7.19087	6.81086	5.84737	15
8.85137	8.31256	7.82371	7.37916	6.97399	5.95424	16
9.12164	8.54363	8.02155	7.54879	7.11963	6.04716	17
9.37189	8.75563	8.20141	7.70162	7.24967	6.12797	18
9.60360	8.95012	8.36492	7.83929	7.36578	6.19823	19
9.81815	9.12855	8.51356	7.96333	7.46944	6.25933	20
10.01680	9.29224	8.64869	8.07507	7.56200	6.31246	21
10.20074	9.44243	8.77154	8.17574	7.64465	6.35866	22
10.37106	9.58021	8.88322	8.26643	7.71843	6.39884	23
10.52876	9.70661	8.98474	8.34814	7.78432	6.43377	24
10.67478	9.82258	9.07704	8.42174	7.84314	6.46415	25
10.80998	9.92897	9.16095	8.48806	7.89566	6.49056	26
10.93516	10.02658	9.23722	8.54780	7.94255	6.51353	27
11.05108	10.11613	9.30657	8.60162	7.98442	6.53351	28
11.15841	10.19828	9.36961	8.65011	8.02181	6.55088	29
11.25778	10.27365	9.42691	8.69379	8.05518	6.56598	30
11.34980	10.34280	9.47901	8.73315	8.08499	6.57911	31
11.43500	10.40624	9.52638	8.76860	8.11159	6.59053	32
11.51389	10.46444	9.56943	8.80054	8.13535	6.60046	33
11.58693	10.51784	9.60858	8.82932	8.15656	6.60910	34
11.65457	10.56682	9.64416	8.85524	8.17550	6.61661	35
11.71719	10.61176	9.67651	8.87859	8.19241	6.62314	36
11.77518	10.65299	9.70592	8.89963	8.20751	6.62882	37
11.82887	10.69082	9.73265	8.91859	8.22099	6.63375	38
11.87858	10.72552	9.75697	8.93567	8.23303	6.63805	39
11.92461	10.75736	9.77905	8.95105	8.24378	6.64178	40

TABLE 6-5 PRESENT VALUE OF AN ANNUITY DUE OF 1

$$\text{PVF-AD}_{n,i} = 1 + \frac{1 - \frac{1}{(1+i)^{n-1}}}{i}$$

(n) Periods	2%	2½%	3%	4%	5%	6%
1	1.00000	1.00000	1.00000	1.00000	1.00000	1.00000
2	1.98039	1.97561	1.97087	1.96154	1.95238	1.94340
3	2.94156	2.92742	2.91347	2.88609	2.85941	2.83339
4	3.88388	3.85602	3.82861	3.77509	3.72325	3.67301
5	4.80773	4.76197	4.71710	4.62990	4.54595	4.46511
6	5.71346	5.64583	5.57971	5.45182	5.32948	5.21236
7	6.60143	6.50813	6.41719	6.24214	6.07569	5.91732
8	7.47199	7.34939	7.23028	7.00205	6.78637	6.58238
9	8.32548	8.17014	8.01969	7.73274	7.46321	7.20979
10	9.16224	8.97087	8.78611	8.43533	8.10782	7.80169
11	9.98259	9.75206	9.53020	9.11090	8.72173	8.36009
12	10.78685	10.51421	10.25262	9.76048	9.30641	8.88687
13	11.57534	11.25776	10.95400	10.38507	9.86325	9.38384
14	12.34837	11.98319	11.63496	10.98565	10.39357	9.85268
15	13.10625	12.69091	12.29607	11.56312	10.89864	10.29498
16	13.84926	13.38138	12.93794	12.11839	11.37966	10.71225
17	14.57771	14.05500	13.56110	12.65230	11.83777	11.10590
18	15.29187	14.71220	14.16612	13.16567	12.27407	11.47726
19	15.99203	15.35336	14.75351	13.65930	12.68959	11.82760
20	16.67846	15.97889	15.32380	14.13394	13.08532	12.15812
21	17.35143	16.58916	15.87747	14.59033	13.46221	12.46992
22	18.01121	17.18455	16.41502	15.02916	13.82115	12.76408
23	18.65805	17.76541	16.93692	15.45112	14.16300	13.04158
24	19.29220	18.33211	17.44361	15.85684	14.48857	13.30338
25	19.91393	18.88499	17.93554	16.24696	14.79864	13.55036
26	20.52346	19.42438	18.41315	16.62208	15.09394	13.78336
27	21.12104	19.95061	18.87684	16.98277	15.37519	14.00317
28	21.70690	20.46401	19.32703	17.32959	15.64303	14.21053
29	22.28127	20.96489	19.76411	17.66306	15.89813	14.40616
30	22.84438	21.45355	20.18845	17.98371	16.14107	14.59072
31	23.39646	21.93029	20.60044	18.29203	16.37245	14.76483
32	23.93770	22.39541	21.00043	18.58849	16.59281	14.92909
33	24.46833	22.84918	21.38877	18.87355	16.80268	15.08404
34	24.98856	23.29188	21.76579	19.14765	17.00255	15.23023
35	25.49859	23.72379	22.13184	19.41120	17.19290	15.36814
36	25.99862	24.14516	22.48722	19.66461	17.37419	15.49825
37	26.48884	24.55625	22.83225	19.90828	17.54685	15.62099
38	26.96945	24.95732	23.16724	20.14258	17.71129	15.73678
39	27.44064	25.34860	23.49246	20.36786	17.86789	15.84602
40	27.90259	25.73034	23.80822	20.58448	18.01704	15.94907

TABLE 6-5 PRESENT VALUE OF AN ANNUITY DUE OF 1

8%	9%	10%	11%	12%	15%	(n) Periods
1.00000	1.00000	1.00000	1.00000	1.00000	1.00000	1
1.92593	1.91743	1.90909	1.90090	1.89286	1.86957	2
2.78326	2.75911	2.73554	2.71252	2.69005	2.62571	3
3.57710	3.53130	3.48685	3.44371	3.40183	3.28323	4
4.31213	4.23972	4.16986	4.10245	4.03735	3.85498	5
4.99271	4.88965	4.79079	4.69590	4.60478	4.35216	6
5.62288	5.48592	5.35526	5.23054	5.11141	4.78448	7
6.20637	6.03295	5.86842	5.71220	5.56376	5.16042	8
6.74664	6.53482	6.33493	6.14612	5.96764	5.48732	9
7.24689	6.99525	6.75902	6.53705	6.32825	5.77158	10
7.71008	7.41766	7.14457	6.88923	6.65022	6.01877	11
8.13896	7.80519	7.49506	7.20652	6.93770	6.23371	12
8.53608	8.16073	7.81369	7.49236	7.19437	6.42062	13
8.90378	8.48690	8.10336	7.74987	7.42355	6.58315	14
9.24424	8.78615	8.36669	7.98187	7.62817	6.72448	15
9.55948	9.06069	8.60608	8.19087	7.81086	6.84737	16
9.85137	9.31256	8.82371	8.37916	7.97399	6.95424	17
10.12164	9.54363	9.02155	8.54879	8.11963	7.04716	18
10.37189	9.75563	9.20141	8.70162	8.24967	7.12797	19
10.60360	9.95012	9.36492	8.83929	8.36578	7.19823	20
10.81815	10.12855	9.51356	8.96333	8.46944	7.25933	21
11.01680	10.29224	9.64869	9.07507	8.56200	7.31246	22
11.20074	10.44243	9.77154	9.17574	8.64465	7.35866	23
11.37106.	10.58021	9.88322	9.26643	8.71843	7.39884	24
11.52876	10.70661	9.98474	9.34814	8.78432	7.43377	25
11.67478	10.82258	10.07704	9.42174	8.84314	7.46415	26
11.80998	10.92897	10.16095	9.48806	8.89566	7.49056	27
11.93518	11.02658	10.23722	9.54780	8.94255	7.51353	28
12.05108	11.11613	10.30657	9.60162	8.98442	7.53351	29
12.15841	11.19828	10.36961	9.65011	9.02181	7.55088	30
12.25778	11.27365	10.42691	9.69379	9.05518	7.56598	31
12.34980	11.34280	10.47901	9.73315	9.08499	7.57911	32
12.43500	11.40624	10.52638	9.76860	9.11159	7.59053	33
12.51389	11.46444	10.56943	9.80054	9.13535	7.60046	34
12.58693	11.51784	10.60858	9.82932	9.15656	7.60910	35
12.65457	11.56682	10.64416	9.85524	9.17550	7.61661	36
12.71719	11.61176	10.67651	9.87859	9.19241	7.62314	37
12.77518	11.65299	10.70592	9.89963	9.20751	7.62882	38
12.82887	11.69082	10.73265	9.91859	9.22099	7.63375	39
12.87858	11.72552	10.75697	9.93567	9.23303	7.63805	40

CHAPTER 7

Cash and Receivables

Ugly Duckling or Swan?

Ugly Duckling Corporation is a used car dealer that has carved out a niche by selling cars to customers with questionable credit histories. Ugly Duckling and other "sub-prime lenders" attempt to make a profit by loaning money to riskier borrowers so they can purchase automobiles or homes. To compensate for the higher probability of default of these customers, sub-prime lenders charge higher rates of interest on these high-risk loans.

In theory, this strategy should work. Although some borrowers will not be able to repay their loans, Ugly Duckling plans to make up these losses based on the higher interest payments received from borrowers who do not default and who continue to pay on their loans. Furthermore, in many instances these companies are able to package their sub-prime loans and sell them as securities (a process called securitization). If they receive more for the securities than the amount at which the loans are recorded on the books, they record a gain on the sale of the asset. Recognition of these gains at the time of sale is appropriate if Ugly Duckling can arrive at a reasonable estimate of the proportion of the loans that will not be repaid.

However, estimating the proportion of these high-risk loans that are likely to default is difficult. If rates are not set high enough to cover unexpected higher rates of default, Ugly Duckling and other sub-prime lenders will be in a severe cash squeeze. In addition, if too many of the loans that were sold default, Ugly Duckling will have to take them back, thereby eliminating any gain they recorded on the original sale. Indeed, in 1999, **ContiFinancial** had to write off over $654 million in sub-prime loans. Similarly, **Superior Bank FSB**, which specialized in sub-prime loans, was taken over by bank regulators because it overestimated the value of its sub-prime loans.

Thus, the sub-prime lending business is a risky one. Depending on default and interest rate assumptions on these receivables, companies like Ugly Duckling may not survive to grow into lending swans.

LEARNING OBJECTIVES

After studying this chapter, you should be able to:

1. **Identify items considered cash.**
2. **Indicate how cash and related items are reported.**
3. **Define receivables and identify the different types of receivables.**
4. **Explain accounting issues related to recognition of accounts receivable.**
5. **Explain accounting issues related to valuation of accounts receivable.**
6. **Explain accounting issues related to recognition of notes receivable.**
7. **Explain accounting issues related to valuation of notes receivable.**
8. **Explain accounting issues related to disposition of accounts and notes receivable.**
9. **Explain how receivables are reported and analyzed.**

PREVIEW OF CHAPTER 7

As the opening story indicates, difficulties associated with estimating the collectibility of accounts receivable resulted in significant write-downs and restatements of earnings for businesses that rely on credit sales. The purpose of this chapter is to discuss two assets of importance to companies such as **Ugly Duckling**, **ContiFinancial**, and **Superior Bank FSB**—cash and receivables. The content and organization of the chapter are as follows.

CASH AND RECEIVABLES

Cash

- What is cash?
- Management and control of cash
- Reporting cash
- Summary of cash-related items

Receivables

- Recognition of accounts receivable
- Valuation of accounts receivable
- Recognition of notes receivable
- Valuation of notes receivable
- Disposition of accounts and notes receivable
- Presentation and analysis

SECTION 1 CASH

WHAT IS CASH?

OBJECTIVE 1
Identify items considered cash.

Cash, the most liquid of assets, is the standard medium of exchange and the basis for measuring and accounting for all other items. It is generally classified as a current asset. To be reported as **cash**, it must be readily available for the payment of current obligations, and it must be free from any contractual restriction that limits its use in satisfying debts.

Cash consists of coin, currency, and available funds on deposit at the bank. Negotiable instruments such as money orders, certified checks, cashier's checks, personal checks, and bank drafts are also viewed as cash. Savings accounts are usually classified as cash, although the bank has the legal right to demand notice before withdrawal. But, because prior notice is rarely demanded by banks, savings accounts are considered cash.

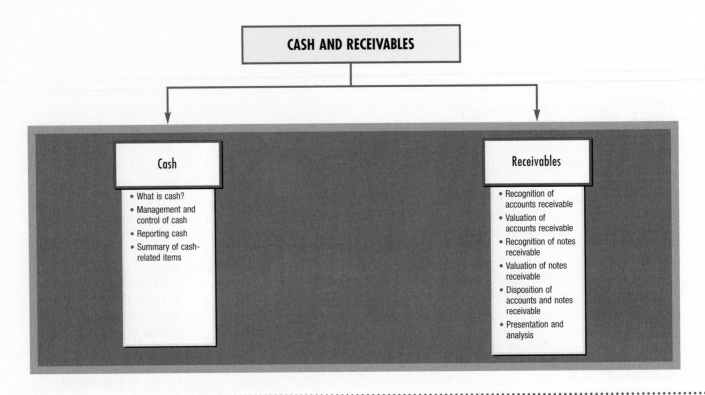

Money market funds, money market savings certificates, certificates of deposit (CDs), and similar types of deposits and "short-term paper"[1] that provide small investors with an opportunity to earn high rates of interest are more appropriately classified as temporary investments than as cash. The reason is that these securities usually contain restrictions or penalties on their conversion to cash. Money market funds that provide checking account privileges, however, are usually classified as cash.

Certain items present classification problems: **Postdated checks and I.O.U.s** are treated as receivables. **Travel advances** are properly treated as receivables if the advances are to be collected from the employees or deducted from their salaries. Otherwise, classification of the travel advance as a prepaid expense is more appropriate. **Postage stamps on hand** are classified as part of office supplies inventory or as a prepaid expense. **Petty cash funds and change funds** are included in current assets as cash because these funds are used to meet current operating expenses and to liquidate current liabilities.

MANAGEMENT AND CONTROL OF CASH

Cash is the asset most susceptible to improper diversion and use. Two problems of accounting for cash transactions face management: (1) Proper controls must be established to ensure that no unauthorized transactions are entered into by officers or employees. (2) Information necessary to the proper management of cash on hand and cash transactions must be provided. Yet even with sophisticated control devices errors can and do happen. The *Wall Street Journal* ran a story entitled "A $7.8 Million Error Has a Happy Ending for a Horrified Bank," which described how **Manufacturers Hanover Trust Co.** mailed about $7.8 million too much in cash dividends to its stockholders. As implied in the headline, most of the monies were subsequently returned.

To safeguard cash and to ensure the accuracy of the accounting records for cash, effective **internal control** over cash is imperative. There are new challenges to maintaining control over liquid assets as more and more transactions are conducted with the swipe of a debit or credit card. For example, over 25 percent of bill payments in the United States are now being made through the use of digital cash (credit cards, debit cards, and electronic transfers).[2] In addition, electronic commerce conducted over the Internet continues to grow. Estimated holiday sales over the Internet in 2001 were $9.6 billion, a 15 percent increase over the previous year. Each of these trends con-

---

[1]A variety of "short-term paper" is available for investment. For example, **certificates of deposit** (CDs) represent formal evidence of indebtedness, issued by a bank, subject to withdrawal under the specific terms of the instrument. Issued in $10,000 and $100,000 denominations, they mature in 30 to 360 days and generally pay interest at the short-term interest rate in effect at the date of issuance. **Money market savings certificates** are issued by banks and savings and loan associations in denominations of $10,000 or more for 6-month periods (6 to 48 months). The interest rate is tied to the 26-week Treasury bill rate. In **money market funds**, a variation of the mutual fund, the yield is determined by the mix of Treasury bills and commercial paper making up the fund's portfolio. Most money market funds require an initial minimum investment of $5,000; many allow withdrawal by check or wire transfer. **Treasury bills** are U.S. government obligations generally having 91- and 182-day maturities; they are sold in $10,000 denominations at weekly government auctions. **Commercial paper** is a short-term note (30 to 270 days) issued by corporations with good credit ratings. Issued in $5,000 and $10,000 denominations, these notes generally yield a higher rate than Treasury bills.

[2]Non-U.S. consumers are even bigger users of digital cash than U.S. consumers. For example, non-check payments in Japan and Europe comprise over 70 percent of all payment transactions. U.S. consumers' continued use of checks and cash for payment raises other fraud concerns, though, as duplication technology makes it easier for crooks to forge checks and currency.

tributes to the shift from cold cash to digital cash and poses new challenges for the control of cash. The appendix to this chapter discusses some of the basic control procedures used to ensure that cash is reported correctly.

WHAT DO THE NUMBERS MEAN?

LOSING CONTROL

The U.S. Federal Reserve (the Fed) also has an interest in controlling cash. The Fed relies on management of reserves on cash and checking account deposits held by banks as one of its tools for managing the money supply and interest rates. Thus, when Alan Greenspan wants to slow down the economy a bit, he can raise the required reserve ratio and keep more of the money in the bank, rather than allowing those dollars to circulate in the economy. However, as more transactions are executed through the use of stored-value cards or other forms of electronic cash, fewer funds are held by the banks. And as the cash disappears, the Fed is losing control of one of its monetary policy tools.

REPORTING CASH

OBJECTIVE 2
Indicate how cash and related items are reported.

Although the reporting of cash is relatively straightforward, there are a number of issues that merit special attention. These issues relate to the reporting of:

1. Restricted cash.
2. Bank overdrafts.
3. Cash equivalents.

Restricted Cash

Petty cash, payroll, and dividend funds are examples of cash set aside for a particular purpose. In most situations, these fund balances are not material and therefore are not segregated from cash when reported in the financial statements. When material in amount, restricted cash is segregated from "regular" cash for reporting purposes. The **restricted cash** is classified either in the current assets or in the long-term assets section, depending on the date of availability or disbursement. Classification in the current section is appropriate if the cash is to be used (within a year or the operating cycle, whichever is longer) for payment of existing or maturing obligations. On the other hand, if the cash is to be held for a longer period of time, the restricted cash is shown in the long-term section of the balance sheet.

Cash classified in the long-term section is frequently set aside for plant expansion, retirement of long-term debt or, in the case of **International Thoroughbred Breeders**, for entry fee deposits.

ILLUSTRATION 7-1
Disclosure of Restricted Cash

International Thoroughbred Breeders

Restricted cash and investments (See Note)	$3,730,000

Note: Restricted Cash. At year-end, the Company had approximately $3,730,000, which was classified as restricted cash and investments. These funds are primarily cash received from horsemen for nomination and entry fees to be applied to upcoming racing meets, purse winnings held in trust for horsemen, and amounts held for unclaimed ticketholder winnings.

Banks and other lending institutions often require customers to whom they lend money to maintain minimum cash balances in checking or savings accounts. These minimum balances, called **compensating balances**, are defined by the SEC as "that portion of any demand deposit (or any time deposit or certificate of deposit) maintained by a corporation which constitutes support for existing borrowing arrangements of the corporation with a lending institution. Such arrangements would include both outstanding borrowings and the assurance of future credit availability."[3]

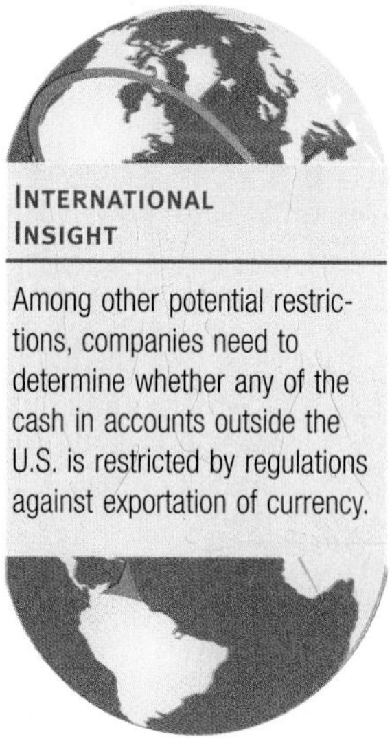

INTERNATIONAL INSIGHT

Among other potential restrictions, companies need to determine whether any of the cash in accounts outside the U.S. is restricted by regulations against exportation of currency.

To ensure that investors are not misled about the amount of cash available to meet recurring obligations, the SEC recommends that **legally restricted deposits** held as compensating balances against **short-term** borrowing arrangements be stated separately among the "Cash and cash equivalent items" in current assets. Restricted deposits held as compensating balances against **long-term** borrowing arrangements should be separately classified as noncurrent assets in either the investments or other assets sections, using a caption such as "Cash on deposit maintained as compensating balance." In cases where compensating balance arrangements exist without agreements that restrict the use of cash amounts shown on the balance sheet, the arrangements and the amounts involved should be described in the notes.

Bank Overdrafts

Bank overdrafts occur when a check is written for more than the amount in the cash account. They should be reported in the current liabilities section and are usually added to the amount reported as accounts payable. If material, these items should be separately disclosed either on the face of the balance sheet or in the related notes.[4]

Bank overdrafts are generally not offset against the cash account. A major exception is when available cash is present in another account in the same bank on which the overdraft occurred. Offsetting in this case is required.

Cash Equivalents

Additional Disclosures of Restricted Cash

A current classification that has become popular is "Cash and cash equivalents."[5] **Cash equivalents** are short-term, highly liquid investments that are both (a) readily convertible to known amounts of cash, and (b) so near their maturity that they present insignificant risk of changes in interest rates. Generally only investments with original maturities of three months or less qualify under these definitions. Examples of cash equivalents are Treasury bills, commercial paper, and money market funds. Some companies combine cash with temporary investments on the balance sheet. In these cases, the amount of the temporary investments is described either parenthetically or in the notes.

---

[3]*Accounting Series Release No. 148*, "Amendments to Regulations S-X and Related Interpretations and Guidelines Regarding the Disclosure of Compensating Balances and Short-Term Borrowing Arrangements," Securities and Exchange Commission (November 13, 1973). The SEC defines 15 percent of liquid assets (current cash balances, whether restricted or not, plus marketable securities) as being material.

[4]Bank overdrafts usually occur because of a simple oversight by the company writing the check. Banks often expect companies to have overdrafts from time to time and therefore negotiate a fee as payment for this possible occurrence. However, in the early 1980s, **E. F. Hutton** (a large brokerage firm) intentionally began overdrawing its accounts by astronomical amounts—on some days exceeding $1 billion—thus obtaining interest-free loans which it could invest. Because the amounts were so large and fees were not negotiated in advance, E. F. Hutton came under criminal investigation for its actions.

[5]*Accounting Trends and Techniques—2001* indicates that approximately 9 percent of the companies surveyed use the caption "Cash," 85 percent use "Cash and cash equivalents," and 5 percent use a caption such as "Cash and marketable securities" or similar terminology.

SUMMARY OF CASH-RELATED ITEMS

Cash and cash equivalents include the medium of exchange and most negotiable instruments. If the item cannot be converted to coin or currency on short notice, it is separately classified as an investment, as a receivable, or as a prepaid expense. Cash that is not available for payment of currently maturing liabilities is segregated and classified in the long-term assets section. Illustration 7-2 summarizes the classification of cash-related items.

ILLUSTRATION 7-2
Classification of Cash-Related Items

Classification of Cash, Cash Equivalents, and Noncash Items

Item	Classification	Comment
Cash	Cash	If unrestricted, report as cash. If restricted, identify and classify as current and noncurrent assets.
Petty cash and change funds	Cash	Report as cash.
Short-term paper	Cash equivalents	Investments with maturity of less than 3 months, often combined with cash.
Short-term paper	Temporary investments	Investments with maturity of 3 to 12 months.
Postdated checks and IOU's	Receivables	Assumed to be collectible.
Travel advances	Receivables	Assumed to be collected from employees or deducted from their salaries.
Postage on hand (as stamps or in postage meters)	Prepaid expenses	May also be classified as office supplies inventory.
Bank overdrafts	Current liability	If right of offset exists, reduce cash.
Compensating balances	Cash separately classified as a deposit maintained as compensating balance	Classify as current or noncurrent in the balance sheet. Disclose separately in notes details of the arrangement.

SECTION 2 RECEIVABLES

OBJECTIVE 3
Define receivables and identify the different types of receivables.

Receivables are claims held against customers and others for money, goods, or services. For financial statement purposes, receivables are classified as either **current** (short-term) or **noncurrent** (long-term). **Current receivables** are expected to be collected within a year or during the current operating cycle, whichever is longer. All other receivables are classified as **noncurrent**. Receivables are further classified in the balance sheet as either trade or nontrade receivables.

Trade receivables are amounts owed by customers for goods sold and services rendered as part of normal business operations. Trade receivables, usually the most significant an enterprise possesses, may be subclassified into accounts receivable and notes receivable. **Accounts receivable** are oral promises of the purchaser to pay for goods and services sold. They are normally collectible within 30 to 60 days and represent "open accounts" resulting from short-term extensions of credit. **Notes receivable** are written promises to pay a certain sum of money on a specified future date. They may arise from sales, financing, or other transactions. Notes may be short-term or long-term.

Nontrade receivables arise from a variety of transactions and can be written promises either to pay or to deliver. Some examples of nontrade receivables are:

1. Advances to officers and employees.
2. Advances to subsidiaries.
3. Deposits to cover potential damages or losses.
4. Deposits as a guarantee of performance or payment.
5. Dividends and interest receivable.
6. Claims against:
   - **(a)** Insurance companies for casualties sustained.
   - **(b)** Defendants under suit.
   - **(c)** Governmental bodies for tax refunds.
   - **(d)** Common carriers for damaged or lost goods.
   - **(e)** Creditors for returned, damaged, or lost goods.
   - **(f)** Customers for returnable items (crates, containers, etc.).

Because of the peculiar nature of nontrade receivables, they are generally classified and reported as separate items in the balance sheet. Illustration 7-3 shows the reporting of trade and non-trade receivables in the balance sheets of **Adolph Coors Company** and **Seaboard Corporation**.

ILLUSTRATION 7-3
Receivables Balance Sheet Presentations

Adolph Coors Company
(in thousands)

Current assets	
Cash and cash equivalents	$160,038
Short-term investments	96,190
Accounts and notes receivable	
Trade, less allowance for doubtful accounts of $299	106,962
Subsidiaries	11,896
Other, less allowance for certain claims of $584	7,751
Inventories	102,660
Other supplies, less allowance for obsolete supplies of $3,968	27,729
Prepaid expenses and other assets	12,848
Deferred tax asset	22,917
Total current assets	$548,991

Seaboard Corporation
(in thousands)

Current assets		
Cash and cash equivalents		$ 19,760
Short-term investments		91,375
Receivables		
Trade	$194,966	
Due from foreign affiliates	36,662	
Other	41,816	
		273,444
Allowance for doubtful receivables		(29,801)
Net receivables		243,643
Inventories		218,030
Deferred income taxes		14,132
Prepaid expenses and deposits		23,760
Current assets of discontinued operations		–
Total current assets		$610,700

The basic issues in accounting for accounts and notes receivable are the same: **recognition**, **valuation**, and **disposition**. We will discuss these basic issues of accounts and notes receivable in the following sequence.

1. Recognition and valuation of accounts receivable.
2. Recognition and valuation of notes receivable.
3. Disposition of accounts and notes receivable.

RECOGNITION OF ACCOUNTS RECEIVABLE

OBJECTIVE 4
Explain accounting issues related to recognition of accounts receivable.

In most receivables transactions, the amount to be recognized is the exchange price between the two parties. **The exchange price is the amount due from the debtor** (a customer or a borrower). It is generally evidenced by some type of business document, often an invoice. Two factors that may complicate the measurement of the exchange price are (1) the availability of discounts (trade and cash discounts), and (2) the length of time between the sale and the due date of payments (the interest element).

Trade Discounts

Customers are often quoted prices on the basis of list or catalog prices that may be subject to a trade or quantity discount. Such **trade discounts** are used to avoid frequent changes in catalogs, to quote different prices for different quantities purchased, or to hide the true invoice price from competitors.

Trade discounts are commonly quoted in percentages. For example, if your textbook has a list price of $90.00 and the publisher sells it to college bookstores for list less a 30 percent trade discount, the receivable recorded by the publisher is $63.00 per textbook. The normal practice is simply to deduct the trade discount from the list price and bill the customer net.

As another example, **Maxwell House** at one time sold a 10 oz. jar of its instant coffee listing at $4.65 to supermarkets for $3.90, a trade discount of approximately 16 percent. The supermarkets in turn sold the instant coffee for $3.99 per jar. Maxwell House records the receivable and related sales revenue at $3.90 per jar, not $4.65.

Cash Discounts (Sales Discounts)

Cash discounts (sales discounts) are offered as an inducement for prompt payment. They are communicated in terms that read, for example, 2/10, n/30 (2 percent if paid within 10 days, gross amount due in 30 days), or 2/10, E.O.M. (2 percent if paid within 10 days of the end of the month).

Companies that fail to take sales discounts are usually not using their money advantageously. An enterprise that receives a 1 percent reduction in the sales price for payment within 10 days, total payment due within 30 days, is effectively earning 18.25 percent (.01 ÷ [20/365]), or at least avoiding that rate of interest cost. For this reason, companies usually take the discount unless their cash is severely limited.

The easiest and most commonly used method of recording sales and related sales discount transactions is to enter the receivable and sale at the gross amount. Under this method, sales discounts are recognized in the accounts only when payment is received within the discount period. Sales discounts would then be shown in the income statement as a deduction from sales to arrive at net sales.

Some contend that sales discounts not taken reflect penalties added to an established price to encourage prompt payment. That is, the seller offers sales on account at a slightly higher price than if selling for cash, and the increase is offset by the cash discount offered. Thus, customers who pay within the discount period purchase at the cash price. Those who pay after expiration of the discount period are penalized because they must pay an amount in excess of the cash price. If this reasoning is used, sales and receivables are recorded net, and any discounts not taken are subsequently debited to Accounts Receivable and credited to Sales Discounts Forfeited. The entries in Illustration 7-4 on the next page show the difference between the gross and net methods.

If the gross method is employed, sales discounts are reported as a deduction from sales in the income statement. Proper matching would dictate that a reasonable estimate of material amounts of expected discounts to be taken also should be charged

Gross Method			Net Method		
Sales of $10,000, terms 2/10, n/30					
Accounts Receivable	10,000		Accounts Receivable	9,800	
Sales		10,000	Sales		9,800
Payment of $4,000 received within discount period					
Cash	3,920		Cash	3,920	
Sales Discounts	80		Accounts Receivable		3,920
Accounts Receivable		4,000			
Payment of $6,000 received after discount period					
Cash	6,000		Accounts Receivable	120	
Accounts Receivable		6,000	Sales Discounts Forfeited		120
			Cash	6,000	
			Accounts Receivable		6,000

ILLUSTRATION 7-4
Entries under Gross and Net Methods of Recording Cash (Sales) Discounts

against sales. If the net method is used, Sales Discounts Forfeited are considered as an "Other revenue" item.[6]

Theoretically, the recognition of Sales Discounts Forfeited is correct because the receivable is stated closer to its realizable value and the net sale figure measures the revenue earned from the sale. As a practical matter, however, the net method is seldom used because it requires additional analysis and bookkeeping. For one thing, the net method requires adjusting entries to record sales discounts forfeited on accounts receivable that have passed the discount period.

Nonrecognition of Interest Element

Ideally, receivables should be measured in terms of their present value, that is, the discounted value of the cash to be received in the future. When expected cash receipts require a waiting period, the receivable face amount is not worth the amount that is ultimately received.

To illustrate, assume that a company makes a sale on account for $1,000 with payment due in 4 months. The applicable annual rate of interest is 12 percent, and payment is made at the end of 4 months. The present value of that receivable is not $1,000 but $961.54 ($1,000 × .96154). In other words, $1,000 to be received 4 months from now is not the same as $1,000 received today.

Theoretically, any revenue after the period of sale is interest revenue. **In practice, interest revenue related to accounts receivable is ignored because the amount of the discount is not usually material in relation to the net income for the period.** Present value considerations are excluded for "receivables arising from transactions with customers in the normal course of business which are due in customary trade terms not exceeding approximately one year."[7]

UNDERLYING CONCEPTS

Materiality means it must make a difference to a decision maker. The FASB believes that present value concepts can be ignored for short-term receivables.

[6] To the extent that discounts not taken reflect a short-term financing, some argue that an interest revenue account could be used to record these amounts.

[7] "Interest on Receivables and Payables," *Opinions of the Accounting Principles Board No. 21* (New York: AICPA, 1971), par. 3(a).

VALUATION OF ACCOUNTS RECEIVABLE

OBJECTIVE 5
Explain accounting issues related to valuation of accounts receivable.

Reporting of receivables involves (1) classification and (2) valuation on the balance sheet. Classification involves determining the length of time each receivable will be outstanding. Receivables intended to be collected within a year or the operating cycle, whichever is longer, are classified as current; all other receivables are classified as long-term.

Short-term receivables are valued and reported at net realizable value—the net amount expected to be received in cash. Determining net realizable value requires an estimation of both uncollectible receivables and any returns or allowances to be granted.

Uncollectible Accounts Receivable

As one accountant so aptly noted, the credit manager's idea of heaven probably would be a place where everyone (eventually) paid his or her debts.[8] The recent experience of Sears, as shown in Illustration 7-5, indicates the importance of credit sales for many companies. Note that while credit cards represent the largest source of Sears's profits, its increased bad debt expense has led to a lower stock price.

ILLUSTRATION 7-5
Sears's Credit Card Growth and Stock Performance

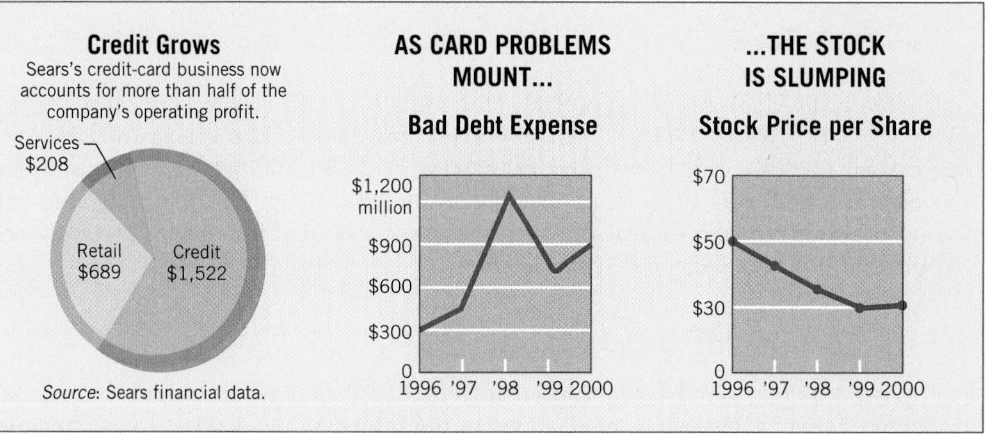

Sales on any basis other than cash make possible the subsequent failure to collect the account. An uncollectible account receivable is a loss of revenue that requires, through proper entry in the accounts, a decrease in the asset accounts receivable and a related decrease in income and stockholders' equity. The loss in revenue and the decrease in income are recognized by recording bad debt expense.

Two procedures are used to record uncollectible accounts:

METHODS FOR RECORDING UNCOLLECTIBLES

1. *Direct Write-Off Method.* No entry is made until a specific account has definitely been established as uncollectible. Then the loss is recorded by crediting Accounts Receivable and debiting Bad Debt Expense.
2. *Allowance Method.* An estimate is made of the expected uncollectible accounts from all sales made on account or from the total of outstanding receivables. This estimate is entered as an expense and an indirect reduction in accounts receivable (via an increase in the allowance account) in the period in which the sale is recorded.

[8]William J. Vatter, *Managerial Accounting* (Englewood Cliffs, N.J.: Prentice-Hall, 1950), p. 60.

The **direct write-off method** records the bad debt in the year in which it is determined that a specific receivable cannot be collected. In contrast, the **allowance method** enters the expense on an estimated basis in the accounting period in which the sales on account are made.

Supporters of the direct write-off method contend that facts, not estimates, are recorded. It assumes that a good account receivable resulted from each sale, and that later events proved certain accounts to be uncollectible and worthless. From a practical standpoint this method is simple and convenient to apply, although receivables do not generally become worthless at an identifiable moment of time. But the direct write-off method is theoretically deficient because it usually does not match costs with revenues of the period, nor does it result in receivables being stated at estimated realizable value on the balance sheet. **As a result, its use is not considered appropriate, except when the amount uncollectible is immaterial.**

Advocates of the allowance method believe that bad debt expense should be recorded in the same period as the sale, to obtain a proper matching of expenses and revenues and to achieve a proper carrying value for accounts receivable. They support the position that although estimates are involved, the percentage of receivables that will not be collected can be predicted from past experiences, present market conditions, and an analysis of the outstanding balances. Many companies set their credit policies to provide for a certain percentage of uncollectible accounts. (In fact, many feel that failure to reach that percentage means that sales are being lost by credit policies that are too restrictive.)

Because the collectibility of receivables is considered a loss contingency, the allowance method is appropriate in situations where it is probable that an asset has been impaired and that the amount of the loss can be reasonably estimated.[9]

A receivable is a prospective cash inflow, and the probability of its collection must be considered in valuing cash flows. These estimates normally are made either on (1) the basis of percentage of sales or (2) the basis of outstanding receivables.

GOING FOR BROKE

WHAT DO THE NUMBERS MEAN?

The start of the new millennium has been a tough one for companies and their investors, creditors, and employees. Recently **WorldCom**, **Enron**, and **Kmart** all declared bankruptcy. WorldCom, for example, is the largest company ever to declare bankruptcy, with Enron and Kmart not far behind. Industries like telecom, retail, and steel are in serious financial difficulty. And the trend seems to be continuing. In 2000, 176 publicly traded companies filed for bankruptcy. In 2001, 257 companies did so. And in 2001, companies defaulted on $64 billion, or 9.8 percent of outstanding debt.

It is not surprising that banks and other credit agencies are cracking down on companies, raising their lending standards. But even so, some question whether our financial institutions have set up reasonable bad debt allowances to ensure that their financial performance is reported accurately.

Source: Adapted from Julie Creswell, "First Going for Broke," *Fortune* (February 18, 2002), pp. 24–25.

UNDERLYING CONCEPTS

The percentage-of-sales method is a good illustration of the use of the matching principle which relates expenses to revenues earned.

Percentage-of-Sales (Income Statement) Approach

If there is a fairly stable relationship between previous years' credit sales and bad debts, then that relationship can be turned into a percentage and used to estimate this year's bad debt expense.

[9] "Accounting for Contingencies," *Statement of Financial Accounting Standards No. 5* (Stamford, Conn.: FASB, 1975), par. 8.

The **percentage-of-sales approach** matches costs with revenues because it relates the charge to the period in which the sale is recorded. To illustrate, assume that Chad Shumway Corp. estimates from past experience that about 2 percent of credit sales become uncollectible. If Shumway Corp. has credit sales of $400,000 in 2003, the entry to record bad debt expense using the percentage-of-sales method is as follows.

Bad Debt Expense	8,000	
Allowance for Doubtful Accounts		8,000

The Allowance for Doubtful Accounts is a valuation account (i.e., a contra asset) and is subtracted from trade receivables on the balance sheet.[10] The amount of bad debt expense and the related credit to the allowance account are unaffected by any balance currently existing in the allowance account. Because the bad debt expense estimate is related to a nominal account (Sales), and any balance in the allowance is ignored, this method is frequently referred to as the **income statement approach**. A proper matching of cost and revenues is therefore achieved.

Percentage-of-Receivables (Balance Sheet) Approach

Using past experience, a company can estimate the percentage of its outstanding receivables that will become uncollectible, without identifying specific accounts. This procedure provides a reasonably accurate estimate of the receivables' realizable value, but does not fit the concept of matching cost and revenues. Rather, its objective is to report receivables in the balance sheet at net realizable values. Hence it is referred to as the **percentage-of-receivables** (or **balance sheet**) **approach.**

The percentage of receivables may be applied using one **composite rate** that reflects an estimate of the uncollectible receivables. Another approach that is more sensitive to the actual status of the accounts receivable sets up an **aging schedule** and applies a different percentage based on past experience to the various age categories. An aging schedule is frequently used in practice. It indicates which accounts require special attention by providing the age of such accounts receivable. The following schedule of Wilson & Co. is an example.

ILLUSTRATION 7-6
Accounts Receivable Aging Schedule

WILSON & CO.
AGING SCHEDULE

Name of Customer	Balance Dec. 31	Under 60 days	61–90 days	91–120 days	Over 120 days
Western Stainless Steel Corp.	$ 98,000	$ 80,000	$18,000		
Brockway Steel Company	320,000	320,000			
Freeport Sheet & Tube Co.	55,000				$55,000
Allegheny Iron Works	74,000	60,000		$14,000	
	$547,000	$460,000	$18,000	$14,000	$55,000

Summary

Age	Amount	Percentage Estimated to be Uncollectible	Required Balance in Allowance
Under 60 days old	$460,000	4%	$18,400
61–90 days old	18,000	15%	2,700
91–120 days old	14,000	20%	2,800
Over 120 days	55,000	25%	13,750
Year-end balance of allowance for doubtful accounts			$37,650

[10]The account description employed for the allowance account is usually Allowance for Doubtful Accounts or simply Allowance. *Accounting Trends and Techniques—2001*, for example, indicates that approximately 78 percent of the companies surveyed used "allowance" in their description.

The amount $37,650 would be the bad debt expense to be reported for this year, assuming that no balance existed in the allowance account.

To change the illustration slightly, **assume that the allowance account had a credit balance of $800 before adjustment**. In this case, the amount to be added to the allowance account is $36,850 ($37,650 − $800), and the following entry is made.

Bad Debt Expense	36,850	
Allowance for Doubtful Accounts		36,850

The balance in the Allowance account is therefore stated at $37,650. **If the Allowance balance before adjustment had a debit balance of $200**, then the amount to be recorded for bad debt expense would be $37,850 ($37,650 desired balance + $200 debit balance). In the percentage-of-receivables method, the balance in the allowance account **cannot be ignored**, because the percentage is related to a real account (Accounts Receivable).

An aging schedule is usually not prepared to determine the bad debt expense. Rather, it is prepared as a control device to determine the composition of receivables and to identify delinquent accounts. The estimated loss percentage developed for each category is based on previous loss experience and the advice of credit department personnel. Regardless of whether a composite rate or an aging schedule is employed, the primary objective of the percentage of outstanding receivables method for financial statement purposes is to report receivables in the balance sheet at net realizable value. However, it is deficient in that it may not match the bad debt expense to the period in which the sale takes place.

Tutorial on Recording Uncollectible Accounts

The allowance for doubtful accounts as a percentage of receivables will vary, depending upon the industry and the economic climate. Companies such as **Eastman Kodak**, **General Electric**, and **Monsanto** have recorded allowances ranging from $3 to $6 per $100 of accounts receivable. Others such as **CPC International** ($1.48), **Texaco** ($1.23), and **United States Steel Corp.** ($0.78) are examples of large enterprises that have had bad debt allowances of less than $1.50 per $100. At the other extreme are hospitals that allow for $15 to $20 per $100 of accounts receivable.[11]

In summary, the percentage-of-receivables method results in a more accurate valuation of receivables on the balance sheet. From a matching viewpoint, the percentage-of-sales approach provides the better results. The following diagram relates these methods to the basic theory.

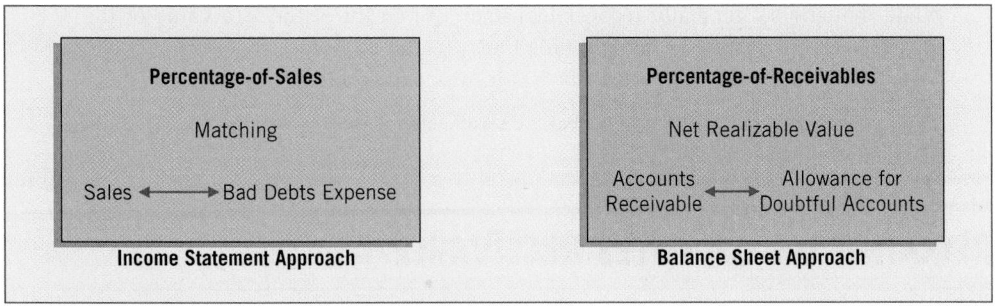

ILLUSTRATION 7-7
Comparison of Methods for Estimating Uncollectibles

[11]A U.S. Department of Commerce study indicated, as a general rule, the following relationships between the age of accounts receivable and their uncollectibility.

30 days or less	4% uncollectible
31–60 days	10% uncollectible
61–90 days	17% uncollectible
91–120 days	26% uncollectible

After 120 days, an approximate 3–4 percent increase in uncollectibles for every 30 days outstanding occurs for the remainder of the first year.

INTERNATIONAL INSIGHT

The U.S. has been critical of some countries' use of excess reserves to manage income. These same countries would argue that Suntrust Banks' accounting for loan losses is a similar practice.

The account title employed for the allowance account is usually Allowance for Doubtful Accounts or simply Allowance.

Regardless of the method chosen, determining the expense associated with uncollectible accounts is an area of accounting that is subject to a large degree of judgment. Recently there has been concern that some banks are using this judgment to manage earnings. By overestimating the amounts of uncollectible loans in a good earnings year, the bank can "save for a rainy day" in a future period. In future (less profitable) periods, the overly conservative allowance for loan loss account can be reduced to increase earnings. In this regard, the SEC brought action against **Suntrust Banks**, requiring a reversal of $100 million of bad debt expense. This reversal increased aftertax profit by $61 million.[12]

Collection of Accounts Receivable Written Off

When a particular account receivable is determined to be uncollectible, the balance is removed from the books by debiting Allowance for Doubtful Accounts and crediting Accounts Receivable. If a collection is eventually made on a receivable that was previously written off, the procedure is first to reestablish the receivable by debiting Accounts Receivable and crediting Allowance for Doubtful Accounts. An entry is then made to debit Cash and credit the customer's account for the amount received.

If the direct write-off approach is employed, the amount collected is debited to Cash and credited to a revenue account entitled Uncollectible Amounts Recovered, with proper notation in the customer's account.

WHAT DO THE NUMBERS MEAN?

COLLECTION IS A CLICK AWAY

What do lenders do when they determine that receivables are uncollectible? After they record bad debts on their books, the next step is to try to collect what they can from the deadbeat customers. Some lenders auction their bad loans in the market for distressed debt, usually paying a fee of 5–15 percent to a distressed debt broker, who arranges the sale. Recently, several Web sites have sprung up to provide a meeting place for lenders with bad loans and collectors who are willing to make a bid on the bad loans and then try to collect on them. These sites are sort of an "eBay of deadbeats." For example, **Bank One Corp.** listed $211 million of unpaid credit card receivables on **DebtforSale.com**. While the lendors generally recover less than 10 percent of the face value of the receivables in an auction, by going online they are able to reduce the costs of their bad debts. Online services charge just 0.5–1 percent for their auction services.

Source: Adapted from P. Gogoi, "An eBay of Deadbeats," *Business Week* (September 18, 2000), p. 124.

RECOGNITION OF NOTES RECEIVABLE

A note receivable is supported by a formal **promissory note**, a written promise to pay a certain sum of money at a specific future date. Such a note is a negotiable instrument that is signed by a **maker** in favor of a designated **payee** who may legally and readily sell or otherwise transfer the note to others. Although notes contain an interest element because of the time value of money, notes are classified as interest-bearing or non-interest-bearing. **Interest-bearing notes** have a stated rate of interest. **Zero-interest-bearing notes** (non-interest-bearing) include interest as part of their face amount instead of stating it explicitly. Notes receivable are considered fairly liquid, even if long-term, because they may be easily converted to cash.

[12]Recall from the earnings management discussion in Chapter 4 that increasing or decreasing income through management manipulation can reduce the quality of financial reports.

Notes receivable are frequently accepted from customers who need to extend the payment period of an outstanding receivable. Notes are also sometimes required of high-risk or new customers. In addition, notes are often used in loans to employees and subsidiaries and in the sales of property, plant, and equipment. In some industries (e.g., the pleasure and sport boat industry) all credit sales are supported by notes. The majority of notes, however, originate from lending transactions. The basic issues in accounting for notes receivable are the same as those for accounts receivable: recognition, valuation, and disposition.

Short-term notes are generally recorded at face value (less allowances) because the interest implicit in the maturity value is immaterial. A general rule is that notes treated as cash equivalents (maturities of 3 months or less) are not subject to premium or discount amortization.

OBJECTIVE 6
Explain accounting issues related to recognition of notes receivable.

Long-term notes receivable, however, should be recorded and reported at the **present value of the cash expected to be collected**. When the interest stated on an interest-bearing note is equal to the effective (market) rate of interest, the note sells at face value.[13] When the stated rate is different from the market rate, the cash exchanged (present value) is different from the face value of the note. The difference between the face value and the cash exchanged, either a discount or a premium, is then recorded and amortized over the life of a note to approximate the effective (market) interest rate. This illustrates one of the many situations in which time value of money concepts are applied to accounting measurement.

Note Issued at Face Value

To illustrate the discounting of a note issued at face value, assume that Bigelow Corp. lends Scandinavian Imports $10,000 in exchange for a $10,000, 3-year note bearing interest at 10 percent annually. The market rate of interest for a note of similar risk is also 10 percent. A time diagram depicting both cash flows is shown below.

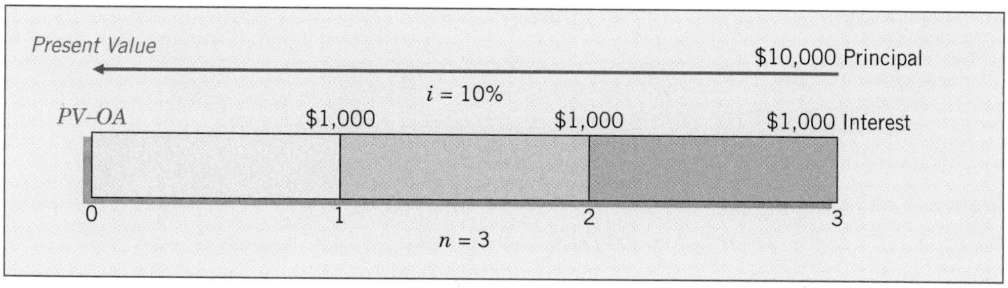

The present value or exchange price of the note is computed as follows.

ILLUSTRATION 7-8
Present Value of Note—Stated and Market Rates the Same

Face value of the note		$10,000
Present value of the principal:		
$10,000 ($PVF_{3,10\%}$) = $10,000 × .75132	$7,513	
Present value of the interest:		
$1,000 ($PVF\text{-}OA_{3,10\%}$) = $1,000 × 2.48685	2,487	
Present value of the note		10,000
Difference		$ –0–

[13]The **stated interest rate**, also referred to as the face rate or the coupon rate, is the rate contracted as part of the note. The **effective interest rate**, also referred to as the market rate or the effective yield, is the rate used in the market to determine the value of the note—that is, the discount rate used to determine present value.

As indicated in Appendix 6A, you can use a financial calculator to solve this problem.

Calculator Solution for Present Value of Note Receivable

	Inputs	Answer
N	3	
I	10	
PV	?	−10,000
PMT	1,000	
FV	10,000	

In this case, the present value of the note and its face value are the same, that is, $10,000, because the effective and stated rates of interest are also the same. The receipt of the note is recorded by Bigelow Corp. as follows.

Notes Receivable	10,000	
Cash		10,000

Bigelow Corp. would recognize the interest earned each year as follows.

Cash	1,000	
Interest Revenue		1,000

Note Not Issued at Face Value

Zero-Interest-Bearing Notes

If a zero-interest-bearing note is received solely for cash, its present value is the cash paid to the issuer. Because both the future amount and the present value of the note are known, the interest rate can be computed (i.e., it is implied). The **implicit interest rate** is the rate that equates the cash paid with the amounts receivable in the future. The difference between the future (face) amount and the present value (cash paid) is recorded as a discount and amortized to interest revenue over the life of the note.

To illustrate, Jeremiah Company receives a 3-year, $10,000 zero-interest-bearing note, the present value of which is $7,721.80. The implicit rate that equates the total cash to be received ($10,000 at maturity) to the present value of the future cash flows ($7,721.80) is 9 percent (the present value of 1 for 3 periods at 9 percent is .77218). The time diagram depicting the one cash flow is shown below.

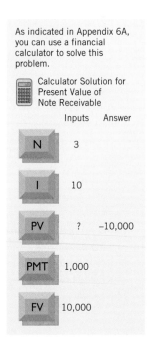

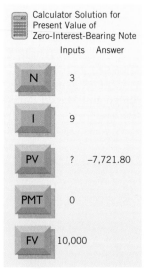

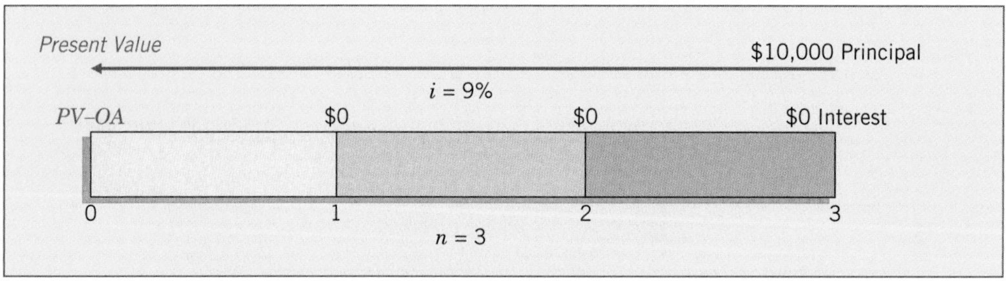

Calculator Solution for Present Value of Zero-Interest-Bearing Note

	Inputs	Answer
N	3	
I	9	
PV	?	−7,721.80
PMT	0	
FV	10,000	

The entry to record the transaction is as follows.

Notes Receivable	10,000.00	
Discount on Notes Receivable ($10,000 − $7,721.80)		2,278.20
Cash		7,721.80

The Discount on Notes Receivable is a valuation account. It is reported on the balance sheet as a contra-asset account to notes receivable. The discount is then amortized, and interest revenue is recognized annually using the **effective interest method**. The 3-year discount amortization and interest revenue schedule is shown in Illustration 7-9 on the next page.

Interest revenue at the end of the first year using the effective interest method is recorded as follows.

Discount on Notes Receivable	694.96	
Interest Revenue ($7,721.80 × 9%)		694.96

The amount of the discount, $2,278.20 in this case, represents the interest revenue to be received from the note over the 3 years.

ILLUSTRATION 7-9
Discount Amortization Schedule—Effective Interest Method

SCHEDULE OF NOTE DISCOUNT AMORTIZATION
EFFECTIVE INTEREST METHOD
0% NOTE DISCOUNTED AT 9%

	Cash Received	Interest Revenue	Discount Amortized	Carrying Amount of Note
Date of issue				$7,721.80
End of year 1	$ -0-	$ 694.96[a]	$ 694.96[b]	8,416.76[c]
End of year 2	-0-	757.51	757.51	9,174.27
End of year 3	-0-	825.73[d]	825.73	10,000.00
	$ -0-	$2,278.20	$2,278.20	

[a]$7,721.80 × .09 = $694.96
[b]$694.96 − 0 = $694.96
[c]$7,721.80 + $694.96 = $8,416.76
[d]5¢ adjustment to compensate for rounding

Interest-Bearing Notes

Often the stated rate and the effective rate are different. The zero-interest-bearing case above is one example of such a situation.

To illustrate a more common situation, assume that Morgan Corp. made a loan to Marie Co. and received in exchange a 3-year, $10,000 note bearing interest at 10 percent annually. The market rate of interest for a note of similar risk is 12 percent. The time diagram depicting both cash flows is shown below.

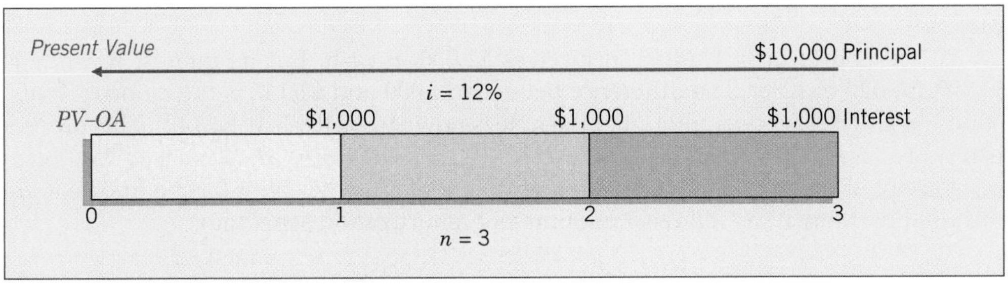

The present value of the two cash flows is computed as follows.

ILLUSTRATION 7-10
Computation of Present Value—Effective Rate Different from Stated Rate

Face value of the note		$10,000
Present value of the principal:		
$10,000 ($PVF_{3,12\%}$) = $10,000 × .71178	$7,118	
Present value of the interest:		
$1,000 ($PVF\text{-}OA_{3,12\%}$) = $1,000 × 2.40183	2,402	
Present value of the note		9,520
Difference (Discount)		$ 480

In this case, because the effective rate of interest (12 percent) is greater than the stated rate (10 percent), the present value of the note is less than the face value. That is, the note was exchanged **at a discount**. The receipt of the note at a discount is recorded by Morgan as follows.

Notes Receivable	10,000	
Discount on Notes Receivable		480
Cash		9,520

The discount is then amortized and interest revenue is recognized annually using the **effective interest method**. The 3-year discount amortization and interest revenue schedule is shown below.

ILLUSTRATION 7-11
Discount Amortization Schedule—Effective Interest Method

SCHEDULE OF NOTE DISCOUNT AMORTIZATION
EFFECTIVE INTEREST METHOD
10% NOTE DISCOUNTED AT 12%

	Cash Received	Interest Revenue	Discount Amortized	Carrying Amount of Note
Date of issue				$ 9,520
End of year 1	$1,000[a]	$1,142[b]	$142[c]	9,662[d]
End of year 2	1,000	1,159	159	9,821
End of year 3	1,000	1,179	179	10,000
	$3,000	$3,480	$480	

[a]$10,000 × 10% = $1,000
[b]$9,520 × 12% = $1,142
[c]$1,142 − $1,000 = $142
[d]$9,520 + $142 = $9,662

On the date of issue, the note has a present value of $9,520. Its unamortized discount—additional interest revenue to be spread over the 3-year life of the note—is $480.

At the end of year 1, Morgan receives $1,000 in cash. But its interest revenue is $1,142 ($9,520 × 12%). The difference between $1,000 and $1,142 is the amortized discount, $142. The carrying amount of the note is now $9,662 ($9,520 + $142). This process is repeated until the end of year 3.

Receipt of the annual interest and amortization of the discount for the first year are recorded by Morgan as follows (amounts per amortization schedule).

Cash	1,000	
Discount on Notes Receivable	142	
Interest Revenue		1,142

When the present value exceeds the face value, the note is exchanged at a premium. The premium on a note receivable is recorded as a debit and amortized using the effective interest method over the life of the note as annual reductions in the amount of interest revenue recognized.

Notes Received for Property, Goods, or Services

When a **note is received in exchange for property, goods, or services** in a bargained transaction entered into at arm's length, the stated interest rate is presumed to be fair unless:

1. No interest rate is stated, or
2. The stated interest rate is unreasonable, or
3. The face amount of the note is materially different from the current cash sales price for the same or similar items or from the current market value of the debt instrument.[14]

[14]"Interest on Receivables and Payables," *Opinions of the Accounting Principles Board No. 21* (New York: AICPA, 1971), par. 12.

In these circumstances, the present value of the note is measured by the fair value of the property, goods, or services or by an amount that reasonably approximates the market value of the note.

To illustrate, Oasis Development Co. sold a corner lot to Rusty Pelican as a restaurant site and accepted in exchange a 5-year note having a maturity value of $35,247 and no stated interest rate. The land originally cost Oasis $14,000 and at the date of sale had an appraised fair value of $20,000. Given the criterion above, it is acceptable to use the fair market value of the land, $20,000, as the present value of the note. The entry to record the sale therefore is:

Notes Receivable	35,247	
Discount on Notes Receivable ($35,247 – $20,000)		15,247
Land		14,000
Gain on Sale of Land ($20,000 – $14,000)		6,000

The discount is amortized to interest revenue over the 5-year life of the note using the effective interest method.

Calculator Solution for Effective Interest Rate on Note

	Inputs	Answer
N	5	
I	?	12
PV	20,000	
PMT	0	
FV	35,247	

Choice of Interest Rate

In note transactions, the effective or real interest rate is either evident or determinable by other factors involved in the exchange, such as the fair market value of what is given or received. But, if the fair value of the property, goods, services, or other rights is not determinable, and if the note has no ready market, the problem of determining the present value of the note is more difficult. To estimate the present value of a note under such circumstances, an applicable interest rate that may differ from the stated interest rate must be approximated. This process of interest-rate approximation is called **imputation**, and the resulting interest rate is called an **imputed interest rate**.

The choice of a rate is affected by the prevailing rates for similar instruments of issuers with similar credit ratings. It is also affected specifically by restrictive covenants, collateral, payment schedule, the existing prime interest rate, etc. Determination of the imputed interest rate is made when the note is received; any subsequent changes in prevailing interest rates are ignored.

VALUATION OF NOTES RECEIVABLE

OBJECTIVE 7
Explain accounting issues related to valuation of notes receivable.

Like accounts receivable, short-term notes receivable are recorded and reported at their net realizable value—that is, at their face amount less all necessary allowances. The primary notes receivable allowance account is Allowance for Doubtful Accounts. The computations and estimations involved in valuing short-term notes receivable and in recording bad debt expense and the related allowance are **exactly the same as for trade accounts receivable**. Either a percentage of sales revenue or an analysis of the receivables can be used to estimate the amount of uncollectibles.

Long-term notes receivable, however, pose additional estimation problems. For evidence, we need only look at the problems our financial institutions, most notably money-center banks, have had in collecting receivables from energy loans, real estate loans, and loans to less-developed countries.[15]

A note receivable is considered **impaired** when it is probable that the creditor will be unable to collect all amounts due (both principal and interest) according to the contractual terms of the loan. Impairments, as well as restructurings, of receivables and debts are discussed and illustrated in considerable detail in Appendix 14A.

---

[15]A wise person once said that a bank lending money to a Third World country is like lending money to one's children: You should never expect to get the interest, let alone the principal.

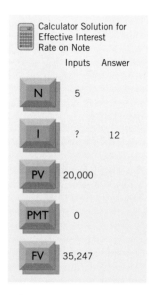

PUTTING THE SQUEEZE ON

WHAT DO THE NUMBERS MEAN?

When the economy slows, lenders, such as **J.P. Morgan** and **First Chicago**, get stingier in granting new loans or renewing loans to existing customers. This tightening of loans is referred to as a "credit squeeze." However, it is sometimes difficult for banks to cut back on lending when the economy goes from good times to bad. When times are good and banks are competing for lending business, lenders often grant business customers "lines of credit" as a sweetener in order to close a loan. In contrast to a term loan that is supported by a note, a line of credit allows borrowing on a day-to-day basis.

When times turn bad, the bank can cut back on loans via notes receivable, but it still must honor the lines of credit, even to weak customers. For example, **Xerox Inc.** got a $7 billion line of credit before it hit the skids during 2000. Although Xerox has not been able to access the traditional loan markets, it has been able to draw on its line of credit to make ends meet. Thus, what seemed like a good competitive tool in good times has put the squeeze on *lenders* when times have turned bad.

Source: Adapted from H. Timmons and D. Sparks, "Feeling a Credit Squeeze," *Business Week* (December 4, 2000), pp. 148–149.

DISPOSITION OF ACCOUNTS AND NOTES RECEIVABLE

OBJECTIVE 8
Explain accounting issues related to disposition of accounts and notes receivable.

In the normal course of events, accounts and notes receivable are collected when due and removed from the books. However, as credit sales and receivables have grown in size and significance, this "normal course of events" has evolved. **In order to accelerate the receipt of cash from receivables, the owner may transfer accounts or notes receivables to another company for cash.**

There are various reasons for this early transfer. First, for competitive reasons, providing sales financing for customers is virtually mandatory in many industries. In the sale of durable goods, such as automobiles, trucks, industrial and farm equipment, computers, and appliances, a large majority of sales are on an installment contract basis. Many major companies in these industries have created wholly-owned subsidiaries specializing in receivables financing. **General Motors Corp.** has **General Motors Acceptance Corp.** (GMAC), and **Sears** has **Sears Roebuck Acceptance Corp.** (SRAC).

Second, the **holder** may sell receivables because money is tight and access to normal credit is not available or is prohibitively expensive. Also, a firm may have to sell its receivables, instead of borrowing, to avoid violating existing lending agreements.

Finally, billing and collection of receivables are often time-consuming and costly. Credit card companies such as **MasterCard**, **VISA**, **American Express**, **Diners Club**, **Discover**, and others take over the collection process and provide merchants with immediate cash.

Conversely, some **purchasers** of receivables buy them to obtain the legal protection of ownership rights afforded a purchaser of assets versus the lesser rights afforded a secured creditor. In addition, banks and other lending institutions may be forced to purchase receivables because of legal lending limits. That is, they cannot make any additional loans but they can buy receivables and charge a fee for this service.

The transfer of receivables to a third party for cash is accomplished in one of two ways:

1. Secured borrowing.
2. Sales of receivables.

Secured Borrowing

Receivables are often used as collateral in a borrowing transaction. A creditor often requires that the debtor designate (assign) or pledge[16] receivables as security for the loan. If the loan is not paid when due, the creditor has the right to convert the collateral to cash—that is, to collect the receivables.

To illustrate, on March 1, 2003, Howat Mills, Inc. provides (assigns) $700,000 of its accounts receivable to Citizens Bank as collateral for a $500,000 note. Howat Mills will continue to collect the accounts receivable; the account debtors are not notified of the arrangement. Citizens Bank assesses a finance charge of 1 percent of the accounts receivable and interest on the note of 12 percent. Settlement by Howat Mills to the bank is made monthly for all cash collected on the receivables.

ILLUSTRATION 7-12
Entries for Transfer of Receivables—Secured Borrowing

Howat Mills, Inc.			Citizens Bank		
Transfer of accounts receivable and issuance of note on March 1, 2003					
Cash	493,000		Notes Receivable	500,000	
Finance Charge	7,000*		Finance Revenue		7,000*
Notes Payable		500,000	Cash		493,000
*(1% × $700,000)					
Collection in March of $440,000 of accounts less cash discounts of $6,000 plus receipt of $14,000 sales returns					
Cash	434,000				
Sales Discounts	6,000				
Sales Returns	14,000		(No entry)		
Accounts Receivable		454,000			
($440,000 + $14,000 = $454,000)					
Remitted March collections plus accrued interest to the bank on April 1					
Interest Expense	5,000*		Cash	439,000	
Notes Payable	434,000		Interest Revenue		5,000*
Cash		439,000	Notes Receivable		434,000
*($500,000 × .12 × 1/12)					
Collection in April of the balance of accounts less $2,000 written off as uncollectible					
Cash	244,000				
Allowance for Doubtful Accounts	2,000		(No entry)		
Accounts Receivable		246,000*			
*($700,000 − $454,000)					
Remitted the balance due of $66,000 ($500,000 − $434,000) on the note plus interest on May 1					
Interest Expense	660*		Cash	66,660	
Notes Payable	66,000		Interest Revenue		660*
Cash		66,660	Notes Receivable		66,000
*($66,000 × .12 × 1/12)					

In addition to recording the collection of receivables, all discounts, returns and allowances, and bad debts must be recognized. Each month the proceeds from the collection of the accounts receivable are used to retire the note obligation. In addition, interest on the note is paid.[17]

[16]If the receivables are transferred to the transferee for custodial purposes, the custodial arrangement is often referred to as a **pledge**.

[17]What happens if Citizens Bank collected the transferred accounts receivable rather than Howat Mills? Citizens Bank would simply remit the cash proceeds to Howat Mills, and Howat Mills would make the same entries shown in Illustration 7-12. As a result, the receivables used as collateral are reported as an asset on the transferor's balance sheet.

Sales of Receivables

Sales of receivables have increased substantially in recent years. A common type is a sale to a factor. **Factors** are finance companies or banks that buy receivables from businesses for a fee and then collect the remittances directly from the customers. **Factoring receivables** is traditionally associated with the textile, apparel, footwear, furniture, and home furnishing industries.[18] An illustration of a factoring arrangement is shown below.

ILLUSTRATION 7-13
Basic Procedures in Factoring

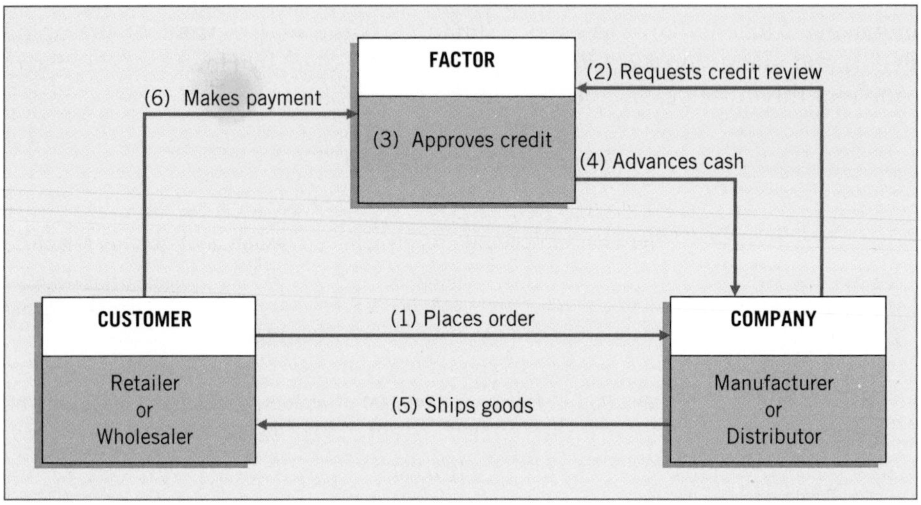

As indicated in the opening story, a recent phenomenon in the sale (transfer) of receivables is securitization. **Securitization** takes a pool of assets such as credit card receivables, mortgage receivables, or car loan receivables and sells shares in these pools of interest and principal payments (in effect, creating securities backed by these pools of assets). Virtually every asset with a payment stream and a long-term payment history is a candidate for securitization.

What are the differences between factoring and securitization? Factoring usually involves sale to only one company, fees are high, the quality of the receivables is low, and the seller afterward does not service the receivables. In a securitization, many investors are involved, margins are tight, the receivables are of higher quality, and the seller usually continues to service the receivables.

In either a factoring or a securitization transaction, receivables are sold on either a **without recourse** or a **with recourse** basis.[19]

Sale without Recourse

When receivables are sold **without recourse**, the purchaser assumes the risk of collectibility and absorbs any credit losses. The transfer of accounts receivable in a nonrecourse transaction is an outright sale of the receivables both in form (transfer of title) and substance (transfer of control). In nonrecourse transactions, as in any sale of assets, Cash is debited for the proceeds; Accounts Receivable is credited for the face

[18]Credit cards like **MasterCard** and **VISA** are a type of factoring arrangement. Typically the purchaser of the receivable charges a ¾–1½ percent commission of the receivables purchased (the commission is 4–5 percent for credit card factoring).

[19]**Recourse** is the right of a transferee of receivables to receive payment from the transferor of those receivables for (1) failure of the debtors to pay when due, (2) the effects of prepayments, or (3) adjustments resulting from defects in the eligibility of the transferred receivables. See "Accounting for Transfers and Servicing of Financial Assets and Extinguishments of Liabilities," *Statement of Financial Accounting Standards No. 140* (Stamford, Conn.: FASB, 2000), p. 155.

value of the receivables. The difference, reduced by any provision for probable adjustments (discounts, returns, allowances, etc.), is recognized as a Loss on the Sale of Receivables. The seller uses a Due from Factor account (reported as a receivable) to account for the proceeds retained by the factor to cover probable sales discounts, sales returns, and sales allowances.

Comprehensive Illustration of Sale Without Recourse

To illustrate, Crest Textiles, Inc. factors $500,000 of accounts receivable with Commercial Factors, Inc., on a **without recourse** basis. The receivable records are transferred to Commercial Factors, Inc., which will receive the collections. Commercial Factors assesses a finance charge of 3 percent of the amount of accounts receivable and retains an amount equal to 5 percent of the accounts receivable. The journal entries for both Crest Textiles and Commercial Factors for the receivables transferred without recourse are as follows.

ILLUSTRATION 7-14
Entries for Sale of Receivables Without Recourse

Crest Textiles, Inc.			Commercial Factors, Inc.		
Cash	460,000		Accounts (Notes) Receivable	500,000	
Due from Factor	25,000*		Due to Crest Textiles		25,000
Loss on Sale of Receivables	15,000**		Financing Revenue		15,000
Accounts (Notes) Receivable		500,000	Cash		460,000
*(5% × $500,000)					
**(3% × $500,000)					

In recognition of the sale of receivables, Crest Textiles records a loss of $15,000. The factor's net income will be the difference between the financing revenue of $15,000 and the amount of any uncollectible receivables.

Sale with Recourse

If receivables are sold **with recourse**, the seller guarantees payment to the purchaser in the event the debtor fails to pay. To record this type of transaction, a **financial components approach** is used, because the seller has a continuing involvement with the receivable.[20] In this approach, each party to the sale recognizes the assets and liabilities that it controls after the sale and no longer recognizes the assets and liabilities that were sold or extinguished.

To illustrate, assume the same information as in Illustration 7-14 for Crest Textiles and for Commercial Factors except that the receivables are sold on a with recourse basis. It is determined that this recourse obligation has a fair value of $6,000. To determine the loss on the sale of the receivables by Crest Textiles, the net proceeds from the sale are computed as follows.

ILLUSTRATION 7-15
Net Proceeds Computation

Cash received	$460,000	
Due from factor	25,000	$485,000
Less: Recourse obligation		6,000
Net proceeds		$479,000

[20]Previous accounting standards generally required that the transferor account for financial assets transferred as an inseparable unit that had been entirely sold or entirely retained. Those standards were difficult to apply and produced inconsistent and arbitrary results. Values are now assigned to such components as the recourse provision, servicing rights, and agreement to reacquire.

Net proceeds are cash or other assets received in a sale less any liabilities incurred. The loss is then computed as follows.

ILLUSTRATION 7-16
Loss on Sale Computation

Carrying (book) value	$500,000
Net proceeds	479,000
Loss on sale of receivables	$ 21,000

The journal entries for both Crest Textiles and Commercial Factors for the receivables sold with recourse are as follows.

ILLUSTRATION 7-17
Entries for Sale of Receivables with Recourse

Crest Textiles, Inc.			Commercial Factors, Inc.		
Cash	460,000		Accounts Receivable	500,000	
Due from Factor	25,000		Due to Crest Textiles		25,000
Loss on Sale of Receivables	21,000		Financing Revenue		15,000
Accounts (Notes) Receivable		500,000	Cash		460,000
Recourse Liability		6,000			

Tutorial on the Disposition of Receivables

In this case, Crest Textiles recognizes a loss of $21,000. In addition, a liability of $6,000 is recorded to indicate the probable payment to Commercial Factors for uncollectible receivables. If all the receivables are collected, Crest Textiles would eliminate its recourse liability and increase income. Commercial Factors' net income is the financing revenue of $15,000 because it will have no bad debts related to these receivables.

Secured Borrowing versus Sale

The FASB concluded that a sale occurs only if the seller surrenders control of the receivables to the buyer. The following three conditions must be met before a sale can be recorded:

1. The transferred asset has been isolated from the transferor (put beyond reach of the transferor and its creditors).
2. The transferees have obtained the right to pledge or exchange either the transferred assets or beneficial interests in the transferred assets.
3. The transferor does not maintain effective control over the transferred assets through an agreement to repurchase or redeem them before their maturity.

INTERNATIONAL INSIGHT

The IASB has a similar conceptual approach to the sale of receivables, although it provides more flexibility in implementation.

If the three conditions are met, a sale occurs. Otherwise, the transferor should record the transfer as a secured borrowing. If sale accounting is appropriate, it is still necessary to consider assets obtained and liabilities incurred in the transaction. The rules of accounting for transfers of receivables are shown in Illustration 7-18 on the next page. Illustration 7-18 shows that if there is continuing involvement in a sale transaction, the assets obtained and liabilities incurred must be recorded.

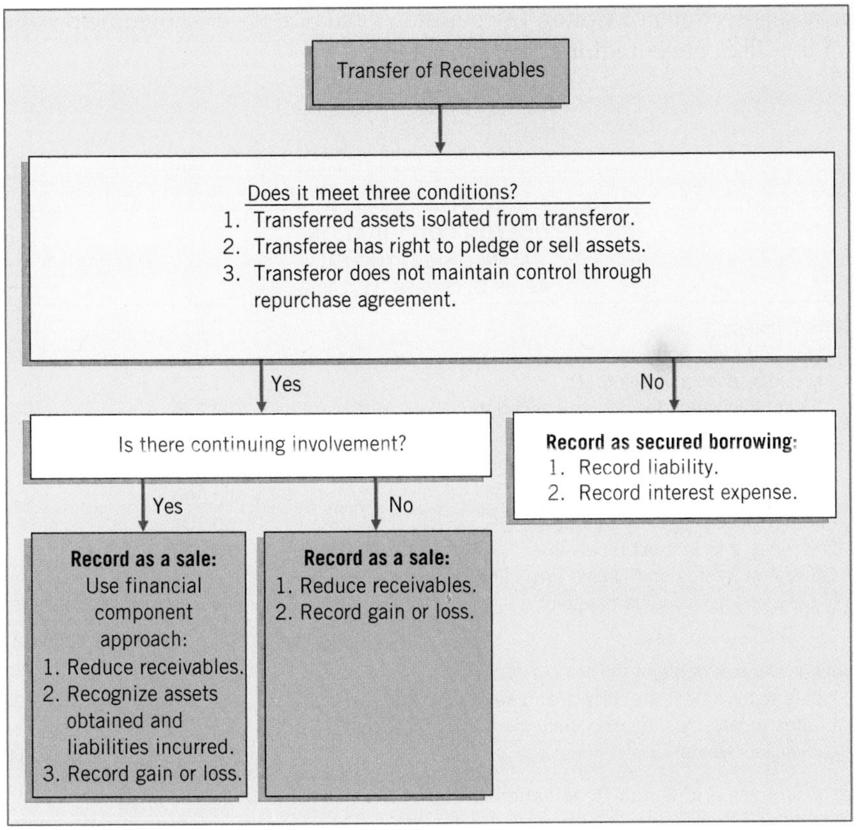

ILLUSTRATION 7-18
Accounting for Transfers of Receivables

PRESENTATION AND ANALYSIS

Presentation of Receivables

OBJECTIVE 9
Explain how receivables are reported and analyzed.

The general rules in classifying receivables are:

1. Segregate the different types of receivables that an enterprise possesses, if material.
2. Ensure that the valuation accounts are appropriately offset against the proper receivable accounts.
3. Determine that receivables classified in the current assets section will be converted into cash within the year or the operating cycle, whichever is longer.
4. Disclose any loss contingencies that exist on the receivables.
5. Disclose any receivables designated or pledged as collateral.
6. Disclose all significant concentrations of credit risk arising from receivables.[21]

[21]Concentrations of credit risk exist when receivables have common characteristics that may affect their collection. These common characteristics might be companies in the same industry or same region of the country. For example, users of financial statements want to know if a substantial amount of receivables are with defense contractors or with companies in the volatile parts of the world. No numerical guidelines are provided as to what is meant by a "concentration of credit risk." When a concentration is identified, three items should be disclosed: (1) information on the characteristic that determines the concentration, (2) the amount of loss that could occur upon nonperformance, and (3) information on any collateral related to the receivable. "Disclosures about Fair Value of Financial Instruments," *Statement of Financial Accounting Standards No. 107* (Norwalk, Conn.: FASB, 1991), par. 15.

The assets sections of Colton Corporation's balance sheet shown below illustrate many of the disclosures required for receivables.

ILLUSTRATION 7-19
Disclosure of Receivables

Additional Disclosures of Receivables

COLTON CORPORATION
BALANCE SHEET (PARTIAL)
AS OF DECEMBER 31, 2004

Current assets		
Cash and cash equivalents		$ 1,870,250
Accounts receivable (Note 2)	$8,977,673	
Less: Allowance for doubtful accounts	500,226	
	8,477,447	
Advances to subsidiaries due 9/30/05	2,090,000	
Notes receivable—trade (Note 2)	1,532,000	
Federal income taxes refundable	146,704	
Dividends and interest receivable	75,500	
Other receivables and claims (including debit balances in accounts payable)	174,620	12,496,271
Total current assets		14,366,521
Noncurrent receivables		
Notes receivable from officers and key employees		376,090
Claims receivable (litigation settlement to be collected over four years)		585,000

Note 2: Accounts and Notes Receivable. In November 2004, the Company arranged with a finance company to refinance a part of its indebtedness. The loan is evidenced by a 12% note payable. The note is payable on demand and is secured by substantially all the accounts receivable.

INTERNATIONAL INSIGHT

Holding receivables that will be paid in a foreign currency represents risk that the exchange rate may move against the company, causing a decrease in the amount collected in terms of U.S. dollars. Companies engaged in cross-border transactions often "hedge" these receivables by buying contracts to exchange currencies at specified amounts at future dates.

Analysis of Receivables

Financial ratios are frequently computed to evaluate the liquidity of a company's accounts receivable. The ratio used to assess the liquidity of the receivables is the **receivables turnover ratio**. This ratio measures the number of times, on average, receivables are collected during the period. The ratio is computed by dividing net sales by average (net) receivables outstanding during the year. Theoretically, the numerator should include only net credit sales. This information is frequently not available, however, and if the relative amounts of credit and cash sales remain fairly constant, the trend indicated by the ratio will still be valid. Unless seasonal factors are significant, average receivables outstanding can be computed from the beginning and ending balances of net trade receivables.

To illustrate, **Gateway** reported 2001 net sales of $6,080 million, and its beginning and ending accounts receivable balances were $545 million and $220 million, respectively. Its accounts receivables turnover ratio is computed in Illustration 7-20.

ILLUSTRATION 7-20
Computation of Accounts Receivable Turnover

$$\frac{\text{Net Sales}}{\text{Average Trade Receivables (net)}} = \text{Accounts Receivable Turnover}$$

$$\frac{\$6,080}{(\$545 + \$220)/2} = \text{15.9 times, or every 23 days } (365 \div 15.9)$$

This information provides some indication of the quality of the receivables, and also an idea of how successful the firm is in collecting its outstanding receivables. If possible, an aging schedule should also be prepared to determine how long receivables have been outstanding. It is possible that a satisfactory receivables turnover may have resulted because certain receivables were collected quickly though others have been outstanding for a relatively long period. An aging schedule would reveal such patterns.[22]

UNDERLYING CONCEPTS

Providing information that will help users assess an enterprises's current liquidity and prospective cash flows is a primary objective of accounting.

SUMMARY OF LEARNING OBJECTIVES

1 Identify items considered cash. To be reported as "cash," an asset must be readily available for the payment of current obligations and free from contractual restrictions that limit its use in satisfying debts. Cash consists of coin, currency, and available funds on deposit at the bank. Negotiable instruments such as money orders, certified checks, cashier's checks, personal checks, and bank drafts are also viewed as cash. Savings accounts are usually classified as cash.

2 Indicate how cash and related items are reported. Cash is reported as a current asset in the balance sheet. The reporting of other related items are: (1) *Restricted cash:* The SEC recommends that legally restricted deposits held as compensating balances against short-term borrowing be stated separately among the "Cash and cash equivalent items" in current assets. Restricted deposits held against long-term borrowing arrangements should be separately classified as noncurrent assets in either the investments or other assets sections. (2) *Bank overdrafts:* They should be reported in the current liabilities section and are usually added to the amount reported as accounts payable. If material, these items should be separately disclosed either on the face of the balance sheet or in the related notes. (3) *Cash equivalents:* This item is often reported together with cash as "Cash and cash equivalents."

3 Define receivables and identify the different types of receivables. Receivables are claims held against customers and others for money, goods, or services. The receivables are classified into three types: (1) current or noncurrent, (2) trade or nontrade, (3) accounts receivable or notes receivable.

4 Explain accounting issues related to recognition of accounts receivable. Two issues that may complicate the measurement of accounts receivable are: (1) The availability of discounts (trade and cash discounts), and (2) the length of time between the sale and the payment due dates (the interest element).

Ideally, receivables should be measured in terms of their present value—that is, the discounted value of the cash to be received in the future. The profession specifically excludes from the present-value considerations receivables arising from normal business transactions that are due in customary trade terms within approximately one year.

5 Explain accounting issues related to valuation of accounts receivable. Short-term receivables are valued and reported at net realizable value—the net amount expected to be received in cash, which is not necessarily the amount legally receivable. Determining net realizable value requires an estimation of uncollectible receivables.

6 Explain accounting issues related to recognition of notes receivable. Short-term notes are recorded at face value. Long-term notes receivable are recorded at the present value of the cash expected to be collected. When the interest stated on an interest-

KEY TERMS

accounts receivable, *318*
aging schedule, *324*
allowance method, *323*
bank overdrafts, *317*
cash, *314*
cash discounts, *320*
cash equivalents, *317*
compensating balances, *317*
direct write-off method, *323*
factoring receivables, *334*
financial components approach, *335*
imputed interest rate, *331*
net realizable value, *322*
nontrade receivables, *319*
notes receivable, *319*
percentage-of-receivables approach, *324*
percentage-of-sales approach, *324*
promissory note, *326*
receivables, *318*
receivables turnover ratio, *338*
restricted cash, *316*
sales discounts, *320*
securitization, *334*
trade discounts, *320*
trade receivables, *318*
with recourse, *335*
without recourse, *334*
zero-interest-bearing notes, *326*

[22]Often the receivables turnover is transformed to **days to collect accounts receivable** or days outstanding—an average collection period. In this case, 15.9 is divided into 365 days to obtain 23 days. Several figures other than 365 could be used here. A most common alternative is 360 days because it is divisible by 30 (days) and 12 (months). Use 365 days in any homework computations.

bearing note is equal to the effective (market) rate of interest, the note sells at face value. When the stated rate is different from the effective rate, either a discount or premium is recorded.

7 **Explain accounting issues related to valuation of notes receivable.** Like accounts receivable, short-term notes receivable are recorded and reported at their net realizable value. The same is also true of long-term receivables. Special issues relate to uncollectibles and impairments.

8 **Explain accounting issues related to disposition of accounts and notes receivable.** To accelerate the receipt of cash from receivables, the owner may transfer the receivables to another company for cash. The transfer of receivables to a third party for cash may be accomplished in one of two ways: (1) *Secured borrowing:* A creditor often requires that the debtor designate or pledge receivables as security for the loan. (2) *Sales (factoring) of receivables:* Factors are finance companies or banks that buy receivables from businesses and then collect the remittances directly from the customers. In many cases, transferors may have some continuing involvement with the receivable sold. A financial components approach is used to record this type of transaction.

9 **Explain how receivables are reported and analyzed.** Disclosure of receivables requires that valuation accounts be appropriately offset against receivables, receivables be appropriately classified as current or noncurrent, pledged or designated receivables be identified, and concentrations of risks arising from receivables be identified. Receivables may be analyzed based on turnover and the days outstanding.

APPENDIX 7A

Cash Controls

OBJECTIVE 10
Explain common techniques employed to control cash.

As indicated in Chapter 7, cash creates many management and control problems. The purpose of this appendix is to discuss some of the basic control issues related to cash.

USING BANK ACCOUNTS

A company can vary the number and location of banks and the types of bank accounts to obtain desired control objectives. For large companies operating in multiple locations, the location of bank accounts can be important. Establishing collection accounts in strategic locations can accelerate the flow of cash into the company by shortening the time between a customer's mailing of a payment and the company's use of the cash. Multiple collection centers generally are used to reduce the size of a company's **collection float**, which is the difference between the amount on deposit according to the company's records and the amount of collected cash according to the bank record.

The **general checking account** is the principal bank account in most companies and frequently the only bank account in small businesses. Cash is deposited in and disbursed from this account as all transactions are cycled through it. Deposits from and disbursements to all other bank accounts are made through the general checking account.

Imprest bank accounts are used to make a specific amount of cash available for a limited purpose. The account acts as a clearing account for a large volume of checks or for a specific type of check. The specific and intended amount to be cleared through the imprest account is deposited by transferring that amount from the general checking account or other source. Imprest bank accounts are often used for disbursing payroll checks, dividends, commissions, bonuses, confidential expenses (e.g., officers' salaries), and travel expenses.

Lockbox accounts are frequently used by large, multilocation companies to make collections in cities within areas of heaviest customer billing. The company rents a local post office box and authorizes a local bank to pick up the remittances mailed to that box number. The bank empties the box at least once a day and immediately credits the company's account for collections. The greatest advantage of a lockbox is that it accelerates the availability of collected cash. Generally, in a lockbox arrangement the bank microfilms the checks for record purposes and provides the company with a deposit slip, a list of collections, and any customer correspondence. If the control over cash is improved and if the income generated from accelerating the receipt of funds exceeds the cost of the lockbox system, then it is considered a worthwhile undertaking.

INTERNATIONAL INSIGHT

Multinational corporations often have cash accounts in more than one currency. For financial statement purposes, these currencies are typically translated into U.S. dollars using the exchange rate in effect at the balance sheet date.

THE IMPREST PETTY CASH SYSTEM

Almost every company finds it necessary to pay small amounts for a great many things such as taxi fares, minor office supplies, employees' lunches, and other miscellaneous expenses. It is frequently impractical to require that such disbursements be made by check, yet some control over them is important. A simple method of obtaining reasonable control, while adhering to the rule of disbursement by check, is the **imprest system for petty cash** disbursements. This is how the system works:

1. Someone is designated petty cash custodian and given a small amount of currency from which to make small payments. The transfer of funds to petty cash is recorded as:

Petty Cash	300	
Cash		300

2. As disbursements are made, the petty cash custodian obtains signed receipts from each individual to whom cash is paid. If possible, evidence of the disbursement should be attached to the petty cash receipt. Petty cash transactions are not recorded until the fund is reimbursed, and then such entries are recorded by someone other than the petty cash custodian.

3. When the supply of cash runs low, the custodian presents to the general cashier a request for reimbursement supported by the petty cash receipts and other disbursement evidence. The custodian receives a company check to replenish the fund. At this point, transactions are recorded based on petty cash receipts.

Office Supplies Expense	42	
Postage Expense	53	
Entertainment Expense	76	
Cash Over and Short	2	
Cash		173

4. If it is decided that the amount of cash in the petty cash fund is excessive, an adjustment may be made as follows (lowering the fund balance from \$300 to \$250).

Cash	50	
Petty Cash		50

Entries are made to the Petty Cash account only to increase or decrease the size of the fund.

A **Cash Over and Short** account is used when the petty cash fund fails to prove out. When this occurs, it is usually due to an error (failure to provide correct change, overpayment of expense, lost receipt, etc.). If cash proves out **short** (i.e., the sum of the receipts and cash in the fund is less than the imprest amount), the shortage is debited to the Cash Over and Short account. If cash proves out **over**, the overage is credited to Cash Over and Short. This account is left open until the end of the year, when it is closed. It is generally shown on the income statement as an "Other expense or revenue."

There are usually expense items in the fund except immediately after reimbursement. Therefore, if accurate financial statements are desired, the funds must be reimbursed at the end of each accounting period and also when nearly depleted.

Under the imprest system the petty cash custodian is responsible at all times for the amount of the fund on hand either as cash or in the form of signed receipts. These receipts provide the evidence required by the disbursing officer to issue a reimbursement check. Two additional procedures are followed to obtain more complete control over the petty cash fund:

1. Surprise counts of the fund are made from time to time by a superior of the petty cash custodian to determine that the fund is being accounted for satisfactorily.
2. Petty cash receipts are canceled or mutilated after they have been submitted for reimbursement, so that they cannot be used to secure a second reimbursement.

PHYSICAL PROTECTION OF CASH BALANCES

Not only must cash receipts and cash disbursements be safeguarded through internal control measures, but also the cash on hand and in banks must be protected. Because receipts become cash on hand and disbursements are made from cash in banks, adequate control of receipts and disbursements is a part of the protection of cash balances. Certain other procedures, however, should be given some consideration.

Physical protection of cash is so elementary a necessity that it requires little discussion. Every effort should be made to minimize the cash on hand in the office. A petty cash fund, the current day's receipts, and perhaps funds for making change should be all that is on hand at any one time. Insofar as possible, these funds should be kept in a vault, safe, or locked cash drawer. Each day's receipts should be transmitted intact to the bank as soon as practicable. Accurately stating the amount of available cash both in internal management reports and in external financial statements is also extremely important.

Every company has a record of cash received, disbursed, and the balance. Because of the many cash transactions, however, errors or omissions may be made in keeping this record. Therefore, it is necessary periodically to prove the balance shown in the general ledger. Cash actually present in the office—petty cash, change funds, and undeposited receipts—can be counted, for comparison with the company records. Cash on deposit is not available for count and is proved by preparing a bank reconciliation—a reconciliation of the company's record and the bank's record of the company's cash.

RECONCILIATION OF BANK BALANCES

At the end of each calendar month the bank supplies each customer with a **bank statement** (a copy of the bank's account with the customer) together with the customer's checks that have been paid by the bank during the month.[1] If no errors were made by

[1]As mentioned in Chapter 7, use of paper checks continues to be a popular means of payment. However, ready availability of desktop publishing software and hardware has created new opportunities for check fraud in the form of duplicate, altered, and forged checks. At the same time, new fraud-fighting technologies, such as ultraviolet imaging and high-capacity barcodes are being developed. These technologies convert paper documents into document files that are processed electronically, thereby reducing the risk of fraud.

the bank or the customer, if all deposits made and all checks drawn by the customer reached the bank within the same month, and if no unusual transactions occurred that affected either the company's or the bank's record of cash, the balance of cash reported by the bank to the customer would be the same as that shown in the customer's own records. This condition seldom occurs. Differences between the depositor's record of cash and the bank's record are usual and expected. Therefore, the two must be reconciled to determine the nature of the differences between the two amounts. Common reconciling items are shown below.

RECONCILING ITEMS

1. *Deposits in Transit.* End-of-month deposits of cash recorded on the depositor's books in one month are received and recorded by the bank in the following month.
2. *Outstanding Checks.* Checks written by the depositor are recorded when written but may not be recorded by (may not "clear") the bank until the next month.
3. *Bank Charges.* Charges recorded by the bank against the depositor's balance for such items as bank services, printing checks, **not-sufficient-funds (NSF) checks**, and safe-deposit box rentals. The depositor may not be aware of these charges until the receipt of the bank statement.
4. *Bank Credits.* Collections or deposits by the bank for the benefit of the depositor that may be unknown to the depositor until receipt of the bank statement. Examples are note collection for the depositor and interest earned on interest-bearing checking accounts.
5. *Bank or Depositor Errors.* Errors on either the part of the bank or the part of the depositor cause the bank balance to disagree with the depositor's book balance.

A **bank reconciliation** is a schedule explaining any differences between the bank's and the company's records of cash. If the difference results only from transactions not yet recorded by the bank, the company's record of cash is considered correct. But, if some part of the difference arises from other items, the bank's records or the company's records must be adjusted.

Two forms of bank reconciliation may be prepared. One form reconciles from the bank statement balance to the book balance or vice versa. The other form reconciles both the bank balance and the book balance to a correct cash balance. This latter form is more widely used. A sample of that form and its common reconciling items are shown in Illustration 7A-1.

ILLUSTRATION 7A-1
Bank Reconciliation Form and Content

Balance per bank statement (end of period)		$$$
Add: Deposits in transit	$$	
Undeposited receipts (cash on hand)	$$	
Bank errors that understate the bank statement balance	$$	$$
		$$$
Deduct: Outstanding checks	$$	
Bank errors that overstate the bank statement balance	$$	$$
Correct cash balance		$$$
Balance per depositor's books		$$$
Add: Bank credits and collections not yet recorded in the books	$$	
Book errors that understate the book balance	$$	$$
		$$$
Deduct: Bank charges not yet recorded in the books	$$	
Book errors that overstate the book balance	$$	$$
Correct cash balance		$$$

This form of reconciliation consists of two sections: (1) "Balance per bank statement" and (2) "Balance per depositor's books." Both sections end with the same "Correct cash balance." The correct cash balance is the amount to which the books must be adjusted and is the amount reported on the balance sheet. **Adjusting journal entries are prepared for all the addition and deduction items appearing in the "Balance per depositor's books" section.** Any errors attributable to the bank should be called to the bank's attention immediately.

To illustrate, Nugget Mining Company's books show a cash balance at the Denver National Bank on November 30, 2004, of $20,502. The bank statement covering the month of November shows an ending balance of $22,190. An examination of Nugget's accounting records and November bank statement identified the following reconciling items.

1. A deposit of $3,680 was mailed November 30 but does not appear on the bank statement.
2. Checks written in November but not charged to the November bank statement are:

Check #7327	$ 150
#7348	4,820
#7349	31

3. Nugget has not yet recorded the $600 of interest collected by the bank November 20 on Sequoia Co. bonds held by the bank for Nugget.
4. Bank service charges of $18 are not yet recorded on Nugget's books.
5. One of Nugget's customer's checks for $220 was returned with the bank statement and marked "NSF." The bank treated this bad check as a disbursement.
6. Nugget discovered that check #7322, written in November for $131 in payment of an account payable, had been incorrectly recorded in its books as $311.
7. A check for Nugent Oil Co. in the amount of $175 that had been incorrectly charged to Nugget Mining accompanied the bank statement.

The reconciliation of bank and book balances to the correct cash balance of $21,044 would appear as follows.

ILLUSTRATION 7A-2
Sample Bank Reconciliation

NUGGET MINING COMPANY
BANK RECONCILIATION
DENVER NATIONAL BANK, NOVEMBER 30, 2004

Balance per bank statement (end of period)			$22,190
Add: Deposit in transit	(1)	$3,680	
Bank error—incorrect check charged to account by bank	(7)	175	3,855
			26,045
Deduct: Outstanding checks	(2)		5,001
Correct cash balance			$21,044
Balance per books			$20,502
Add: Interest collected by the bank	(3)	$ 600	
Error in recording check #7322	(6)	180	780
			21,282
Deduct: Bank service charges	(4)	18	
NSF check returned	(5)	220	238
Correct cash balance			$21,044

The journal entries required to adjust and correct Nugget Mining's books in early December 2004 are taken from the items in the "Balance per books" section and are as follows.

Cash	600	
Interest Revenue		600
(To record interest on Sequoia Co. bonds, collected by bank)		
Cash	180	
Accounts Payable		180
(To correct error in recording amount of check #7322)		
Office Expense—Bank Charges	18	
Cash		18
(To record bank service charges for November)		
Accounts Receivable	220	
Cash		220
(To record customer's check returned NSF)		

Expanded Discussion of a Four-Column Bank Reconciliation

When the entries are posted, Nugget's cash account will have a balance of $21,044. Nugget should return the Nugent Oil Co. check to Denver National Bank, informing the bank of the error.

BOUNCE A CHECK, GET BANNED

WHAT DO THE NUMBERS MEAN?

Two years ago, Rebecca Cobos overdrew her checking account at a **Bank of America** branch in Los Angeles. When she couldn't immediately repay the bank, it not only closed her account, but also had her, in effect, banned for five years from opening a checking account at most other banks, too.

Bank of America did so by reporting the 23-year-old university secretary to **ChexSystems**, a national database to which 80 percent of bank branches in the country subscribe. Once lodged in ChexSystems, you automatically stay there for five years, whether your offense was bouncing a check or two or committing serious fraud. The large majority of banks using ChexSystems reject any checking-account applicant they find in the database.

ChexSystems, maintained by a unit of the check-printing company **Deluxe Corp.**, currently has about seven million names on file. Bank officials and executives of the unit, eFunds, defend the database as a valuable weapon in the battle against fraud and high-risk customers. And there is no denying that many of those who end up in the database have been financially careless, or worse.

Source: Paul Beckett, "It's Not in the Mail," *Wall Street Journal* (August 1, 2000), p. A1.

SUMMARY OF LEARNING OBJECTIVE FOR APPENDIX 7A

10 Explain common techniques employed to control cash. The common techniques employed to control cash are: (1) *Using bank accounts:* A company can vary the number and location of banks and the types of accounts to obtain desired control objectives. (2) *The imprest petty cash system:* It may be impractical to require small amounts of various expenses be paid by check, yet some control over them is important. (3) *Physical protection of cash balances:* Adequate control of receipts and disbursements is a part of the protection of cash balances. Every effort should be made to minimize the cash on hand in the office. (4) *Reconciliation of bank balances:* Cash on deposit is not available for count and is proved by preparing a bank reconciliation.

KEY TERMS

bank reconciliation, *343*

imprest system for petty cash, *341*

not-sufficient-funds (NSF) checks, *343*

Note: All **asterisked** Questions, Brief Exercises, Exercises, Problems, and Conceptual Cases relate to material covered in the appendix to the chapter.

QUESTIONS

1. What may be included under the heading of "cash"?

2. In what accounts should the following items be classified?

(a) Coins and currency.

(b) U.S. Treasury (government) bonds.

(c) Certificate of deposit.

(d) Cash in a bank that is in receivership.

(e) NSF check (returned with bank statement).

(f) Deposit in foreign bank (exchangeability limited).

(g) Postdated checks.

(h) Cash to be used for retirement of long-term bonds.

(i) Deposits in transit.

(j) 100 shares of stock (intention is to sell in one year or less).

(k) Savings and checking accounts.

(l) Petty cash.

(m) Stamps.

(n) Travel advances.

3. Define a "compensating balance." How should a compensating balance be reported?

4. Michael Tilsen Thomas Inc. reported in a recent annual report "Restricted cash for debt redemption." What section of the balance sheet would report this item?

5. What are the reasons that a company gives trade discounts? Why are trade discounts not recorded in the accounts like cash discounts?

6. What are two methods of recording accounts receivable transactions when a cash discount situation is involved? Which is more theoretically correct? Which is used in practice more of the time? Why?

7. What are the basic problems that occur in the valuation of accounts receivable?

8. What is the theoretical justification of the allowance method as contrasted with the direct write-off method of accounting for bad debts?

9. Indicate how well the percentage-of-sales method and the aging method accomplish the objectives of the allowance method of accounting for bad debts.

10. Of what merit is the contention that the allowance method lacks the objectivity of the direct write-off method? Discuss in terms of accounting's measurement function.

11. Explain how the accounting for bad debts can be used for earnings management.

12. Because of calamitous earthquake losses, Kishwaukee Company, one of your client's oldest and largest customers, suddenly and unexpectedly became bankrupt. Approximately 30% of your client's total sales have been made to Kishwaukee Company during each of the past several years. The amount due from Kishwaukee Company—none of which is collectible—equals 22% of total accounts receivable, an amount that is considerably in excess of what was determined to be an adequate provision for doubtful accounts at the close of the preceding year. How would your client record the write-off of the Kishwaukee Company receivable if it is using the allowance method of accounting for bad debts? Justify your suggested treatment.

13. What is the normal procedure for handling the collection of accounts receivable previously written off using the direct write-off method? The allowance method?

14. On January 1, 2004, John Singer Co. sells property for which it had paid $690,000 to Sargent Company, receiving in return Sargent's zero-interest-bearing note for $1,000,000 payable in 5 years. What entry would John Singer make to record the sale, assuming that John Singer frequently sells similar items of property for a cash sales price of $620,000?

15. What is "imputed interest"? In what situations is it necessary to impute an interest rate for notes receivable? What are the considerations in imputing an appropriate interest rate?

16. Indicate three reasons why a company might sell its receivables to another company.

17. When is the financial components approach to recording the transfers of receivables used? When should a transfer of receivables be recorded as a sale?

18. Hale Hardware is planning to factor some of its receivables. The cash received will be used to pay for inventory purchases. The factor has indicated that it will require "recourse" on the sold receivables. Explain to the controller of Hale Hardware what "recourse" is and how the recourse will be reflected in Hale's financial statements after the sale of the receivables.

19. Morley Safer Company includes in its trial balance for December 31 an item for Accounts Receivable $769,000. This balance consists of the following items:

Due from regular customers	$523,000
Refund receivable on prior year's income taxes (an established claim)	15,500
Travel advance to employees	22,000
Loan to wholly owned subsidiary	45,500
Advances to creditors for goods ordered	61,000
Accounts receivable assigned as security for loans payable	75,000

Notes receivable past due plus interest on these notes	27,000
Total	$769,000

Illustrate how these items should be shown in the balance sheet as of December 31.

20. What is the accounts receivable turnover ratio, and what type of information does it provide?

21. You are evaluating Hawthorn Downs Racetrack for a potential loan. An examination of the notes to the financial statements indicates restricted cash at year-end amounts to $100,000. Explain how you would use this information in evaluating Hawthorn's liquidity.

***22.** Distinguish among the following: (1) a general checking account, (2) an imprest bank account, and (3) a lockbox account.

BRIEF EXERCISES

BE7-1 Stowe Enterprises owns the following assets at December 31, 2004.

Cash in bank—savings account	63,000	Checking account balance	17,000
Cash on hand	9,300	Postdated checks	750
Cash refund due from IRS	31,400	Certificates of deposit (180-day)	90,000

What amount should be reported as cash?

BE7-2 Montoya Co. uses the gross method to record sales made on credit. On June 1, 2004, it made sales of $40,000 with terms 3/15, n/45. On June 12, 2004, Montoya received full payment for the June 1 sale. Prepare the required journal entries for Montoya Co.

BE7-3 Use the information from BE7-2, assuming Montoya Co. uses the net method to account for cash discounts. Prepare the required journal entries for Montoya Co.

BE7-4 Battle Tank, Inc. had net sales in 2004 of $1,200,000. At December 31, 2004, before adjusting entries, the balances in selected accounts were: Accounts Receivable $250,000 debit, and Allowance for Doubtful Accounts $2,100 credit. If Battle Tank estimates that 2% of its net sales will prove to be uncollectible, prepare the December 31, 2004, journal entry to record bad debt expense.

BE7-5 Use the information presented in BE7-4 for Battle Tank, Inc.

(a) Instead of estimating the uncollectibles at 2% of net sales, assume that 10% of accounts receivable will prove to be uncollectible. Prepare the entry to record bad debts expense.

(b) Instead of estimating uncollectibles at 2% of net sales, assume Battle Tank prepares an aging schedule that estimates total uncollectible accounts at $24,600. Prepare the entry to record bad debts expense.

BE7-6 Addams Family Importers sold goods to Acme Decorators for $20,000 on November 1, 2004, accepting Acme's $20,000, 6-month, 12% note. Prepare Addams's November 1 entry, December 31 annual adjusting entry, and May 1 entry for the collection of the note and interest.

BE7-7 Aero Acrobats lent $15,944 to Afterburner, Inc., accepting Afterburner's 2-year, $20,000, zero-interest-bearing note. The implied interest rate is 12%. Prepare Aero's journal entries for the initial transaction, recognition of interest each year, and the collection of $20,000 at maturity.

BE7-8 On October 1, 2004, Akira, Inc. assigns $1,000,000 of its accounts receivable to Alisia National Bank as collateral for a $700,000 note. The bank assesses a finance charge of 2% of the receivables assigned and interest on the note of 13%. Prepare the October 1 journal entries for both Akira and Alisia.

BE7-9 CRC Incorporated factored $100,000 of accounts receivable with Fredrick Factors Inc. on a without recourse basis. Fredrick assesses a 2% finance charge of the amount of accounts receivable and retains an amount equal to 6% of accounts receivable for possible adjustments. Prepare the journal entry for CRC Incorporated and Fredrick Factors to record the factoring of the accounts receivable to Fredrick.

BE7-10 Use the information in BE7-9 for CRC. Assume that the receivables are sold with recourse. Prepare the journal entry for CRC to record the sale, assuming that the recourse obligation has a fair value of $7,500.

BE7-11 Keyser Woodcrafters sells $200,000 of receivables to Commercial Factors, Inc. on a recourse basis. Commercial assesses a finance charge of 5% and retains an amount equal to 4% of accounts receivable. Keyser estimates the fair value of the recourse obligation to be $8,000. Prepare the journal entry for Keyser to record the sale.

BE7-12 Use the information presented in BE7-11 for Keyser Woodcrafters but assume that the recourse obligation has a fair value of $4,000, instead of $8,000. Discuss the effects of this change in the value of the recourse obligation on Keyser's balance sheet and income statement.

BE7-13 The financial statements of **General Mills, Inc.** report net sales of $5,416,000,000. Accounts receivable are $277,300,000 at the beginning of the year and $337,800,000 at the end of the year. Compute General Mills's accounts receivable turnover ratio. Compute General Mills's average collection period for accounts receivable in days.

***BE7-14** Genesis Company designated Alex Kidd as petty cash custodian and established a petty cash fund of $200. The fund is reimbursed when the cash in the fund is at $17. Petty cash receipts indicate funds were disbursed for office supplies $94 and miscellaneous expense $87. Prepare journal entries for the establishment of the fund and the reimbursement.

***BE7-15** Jaguar Corporation is preparing a bank reconciliation and has identified the following potential reconciling items. For each item, indicate if it is (1) added to balance per bank statement, (2) deducted from balance per bank statement, (3) added to balance per books, or (4) deducted from balance per books.

(a) Deposit in transit $5,500.
(b) Interest credited to Jaguar's account $31.
(c) Bank service charges $25.
(d) Outstanding checks $7,422.
(e) NSF check returned $377.

***BE7-16** Use the information presented in BE7-15 for Jaguar Corporation. Prepare any entries necessary to make Jaguar's accounting records correct and complete.

EXERCISES

E7-1 (Determining Cash Balance) The controller for Clint Eastwood Co. is attempting to determine the amount of cash to be reported on its December 31, 2003, balance sheet. The following information is provided.

1. Commercial savings account of $600,000 and a commercial checking account balance of $900,000 are held at First National Bank of Yojimbo.
2. Money market fund account held at Volonte Co. (a mutual fund organization) permits Eastwood to write checks on this balance, $5,000,000.
3. Travel advances of $180,000 for executive travel for the first quarter of next year (employee to reimburse through salary reduction).
4. A separate cash fund in the amount of $1,500,000 is restricted for the retirement of long-term debt.
5. Petty cash fund of $1,000.
6. An I.O.U. from Marianne Koch, a company customer, in the amount of $190,000.
7. A bank overdraft of $110,000 has occurred at one of the banks the company uses to deposit its cash receipts. At the present time, the company has no deposits at this bank.
8. The company has two certificates of deposit, each totaling $500,000. These CDs have a maturity of 120 days.
9. Eastwood has received a check that is dated January 12, 2004, in the amount of $125,000.
10. Eastwood has agreed to maintain a cash balance of $500,000 at all times at First National Bank of Yojimbo to ensure future credit availability.
11. Eastwood has purchased $2,100,000 of commercial paper of Sergio Leone Co. which is due in 60 days.
12. Currency and coin on hand amounted to $7,700.

Instructions

(a) Compute the amount of cash to be reported on Eastwood Co.'s balance sheet at December 31, 2003.
(b) Indicate the proper reporting for items that are not reported as cash on the December 31, 2003, balance sheet.

E7-2 (Determine Cash Balance) Presented below are a number of independent situations.

Instructions

For each individual situation, determine the amount that should be reported as cash. If the item(s) is not reported as cash, explain the rationale.

1. Checking account balance $925,000; certificate of deposit $1,400,000; cash advance to subsidiary of $980,000; utility deposit paid to gas company $180.
2. Checking account balance $600,000; an overdraft in special checking account at same bank as normal checking account of $17,000; cash held in a bond sinking fund $200,000; petty cash fund $300; coins and currency on hand $1,350.

3. Checking account balance $590,000; postdated check from customer $11,000; cash restricted due to maintaining compensating balance requirement of $100,000; certified check from customer $9,800; postage stamps on hand $620.
4. Checking account balance at bank $37,000; money market balance at mutual fund (has checking privileges) $48,000; NSF check received from customer $800.
5. Checking account balance $700,000; cash restricted for future plant expansion $500,000; short-term Treasury bills $180,000; cash advance received from customer $900 (not included in checking account balance); cash advance of $7,000 to company executive, payable on demand; refundable deposit of $26,000 paid to federal government to guarantee performance on construction contract.

E7-3 (Financial Statement Presentation of Receivables) Jack Gleason Company shows a balance of $181,140 in the Accounts Receivable account on December 31, 2003. The balance consists of the following.

Installment accounts due in 2004	$23,000
Installment accounts due after 2004	34,000
Overpayments to creditors	2,640
Due from regular customers, of which $40,000 represents accounts pledged as security for a bank loan	79,000
Advances to employees	1,500
Advance to subsidiary company (made in 1998)	81,000

Instructions

Illustrate how the information above should be shown on the balance sheet of Jack Gleason Company on December 31, 2003.

E7-4 (Determine Ending Accounts Receivable) Your accounts receivable clerk, Ms. Mitra Adams, to whom you pay a salary of $1,500 per month, has just purchased a new Cadillac. You decided to test the accuracy of the accounts receivable balance of $82,000 as shown in the ledger.

The following information is available for your *first year* in business.

(1) Collections from customers	$198,000
(2) Merchandise purchased	320,000
(3) Ending merchandise inventory	90,000
(4) Goods are marked to sell at 40% above cost	

Instructions

Compute an estimate of the ending balance of accounts receivable from customers that should appear in the ledger and any apparent shortages. Assume that all sales are made on account.

E7-5 (Record Sales Gross and Net) On June 3, Benedict Arnold Company sold to Chester Arthur merchandise having a sale price of $3,000 with terms of 2/10, n/60, f.o.b. shipping point. An invoice totaling $90, terms n/30, was received by Chester on June 8 from the John Booth Transport Service for the freight cost. On June 12, the company received a check for the balance due from Chester Arthur.

Instructions

(a) Prepare journal entries on the Benedict Arnold Company books to record all the events noted above under each of the following bases.

  (1) Sales and receivables are entered at gross selling price.

  (2) Sales and receivables are entered at net of cash discounts.

(b) Prepare the journal entry under basis 2, assuming that Chester Arthur did not remit payment until July 29.

E7-6 (Recording Sales Transactions) Presented below is information from Perez Computers Incorporated.

July	1	Sold $20,000 of computers to Robertson Company with terms 3/15, n/60. Perez uses the gross method to record cash discounts.
	10	Perez received payment from Robertson for the full amount owed from the July transactions.
	17	Sold $200,000 in computers and peripherals to The Clark Store with terms of 2/10, n/30.
	30	The Clark Store paid Perez for its purchase of July 17.

Instructions

Prepare the necessary journal entries for Perez Computers.

E7-7 (Recording Bad Debts) Shaquille Company reports the following financial information before adjustments.

	Dr.	Cr.
Accounts Receivable	$100,000	
Allowance for Doubtful Accounts		$ 2,000
Sales (all on credit)		900,000
Sales Returns and Allowances	50,000	

Instructions

Prepare the journal entry to record Bad Debt Expense assuming Shaquille Company estimates bad debts at (a) 1% of net sales and (b) 5% of accounts receivable.

E7-8 (Recording Bad Debts) At the end of 2004 Juarez Company has accounts receivable of $800,000 and an allowance for doubtful accounts of $40,000. On January 16, 2005, Juarez Company determined that its receivable from Maximillan Company of $6,000 will not be collected, and management authorized its write-off.

Instructions

(a) Prepare the journal entry for Juarez Company to write off the Maximillan receivable.

(b) What is the net realizable value of Juarez Company's accounts receivable before the write-off of the Maximillan receivable?

(c) What is the net realizable value of Juarez Company's accounts receivable after the write-off of the Maximillan receivable?

E7-9 (Computing Bad Debts and Preparing Journal Entries) The trial balance before adjustment of Patsy Cline Inc. shows the following balances.

	Dr.	Cr.
Accounts Receivable	$90,000	
Allowance for Doubtful Accounts	1,750	
Sales (all on credit)		$680,000

Instructions

Give the entry for estimated bad debts assuming that the allowance is to provide for doubtful accounts on the basis of (a) 4% of gross accounts receivable and (b) 1% of net sales.

E7-10 (Bad Debt Reporting) The chief accountant for Emily Dickinson Corporation provides you with the following list of accounts receivable written off in the current year.

Date	Customer	Amount
March 31	E. L. Masters Company	$7,800
June 30	Stephen Crane Associates	6,700
September 30	Amy Lowell's Dress Shop	7,000
December 31	R. Frost, Inc.	9,830

Emily Dickinson Corporation follows the policy of debiting Bad Debt Expense as accounts are written off. The chief accountant maintains that this procedure is appropriate for financial statement purposes because the Internal Revenue Service will not accept other methods for recognizing bad debts.

All of Emily Dickinson Corporation's sales are on a 30-day credit basis. Sales for the current year total $2,200,000, and research has determined that bad debt losses approximate 2% of sales.

Instructions

(a) Do you agree or disagree with Emily Dickinson Corporation policy concerning recognition of bad debt expense? Why or why not?

(b) By what amount would net income differ if bad debt expense was computed using the percentage-of-sales approach?

E7-11 (Bad Debts—Aging) Gerard Manley, Inc. includes the following account among its trade receivables.

Hopkins Co.

1/1	Balance forward	700	1/28	Cash (#1710)	1,100
1/20	Invoice #1710	1,100	4/2	Cash (#2116)	1,350
3/14	Invoice #2116	1,350	4/10	Cash (1/1 Balance)	155
4/12	Invoice #2412	1,710	4/30	Cash (#2412)	1,000
9/5	Invoice #3614	490	9/20	Cash (#3614 and part of #2412)	790
10/17	Invoice #4912	860	10/31	Cash (#4912)	860
11/18	Invoice #5681	2,000	12/1	Cash (#5681)	1,250
12/20	Invoice #6347	800	12/29	Cash (#6347)	800

Instructions
Age the balance and specify any items that apparently require particular attention at year-end.

E7-12 (Journalizing Various Receivable Transactions) Presented below is information related to James Garfield Corp.

July	1	James Garfield Corp. sold to Warren Harding Co. merchandise having a sales price of $8,000 with terms 2/10, net/60. Garfield records its sales and receivables net.
	5	Accounts receivable of $9,000 (gross) are factored with Andrew Jackson Credit Corp. without recourse at a financing charge of 9%. Cash is received for the proceeds; collections are handled by the finance company. (These accounts were all past the discount period.)
	9	Specific accounts receivable of $9,000 (gross) are pledged to Alf Landon Credit Corp. as security for a loan of $6,000 at a finance charge of 6% of the amount of the loan. The finance company will make the collections. (All the accounts receivable are past the discount period.)
Dec.	29	Warren Harding Co. notifies Garfield that it is bankrupt and will pay only 10% of its account. Give the entry to write off the uncollectible balance using the allowance method. (*Note*: First record the increase in the receivable on July 11 when the discount period passed.)

Instructions
Prepare all necessary entries in general journal form for Garfield Corp.

E7-13 (Assigning Accounts Receivable) On April 1, 2004, Rasheed Company assigns $400,000 of its accounts receivable to the Third National Bank as collateral for a $200,000 loan due July 1, 2004. The assignment agreement calls for Rasheed Company to continue to collect the receivables. Third National Bank assesses a finance charge of 2% of the accounts receivable, and interest on the loan is 10% (a realistic rate of interest for a note of this type).

Instructions
(a) Prepare the April 1, 2004, journal entry for Rasheed Company.
(b) Prepare the journal entry for Rasheed's collection of $350,000 of the accounts receivable during the period from April 1, 2004, through June 30, 2004.
(c) On July 1, 2004, Rasheed paid Third National all that was due from the loan it secured on April 1, 2004.

E7-14 (Journalizing Various Receivable Transactions) The trial balance before adjustment for Judy Collins Company shows the following balances.

	Dr.	Cr.
Accounts Receivable	$82,000	
Allowance for Doubtful Accounts	2,120	
Sales		$430,000

Instructions
Using the data above, give the journal entries required to record each of the following cases. (Each situation is independent.)

1. To obtain additional cash, Collins factors without recourse $25,000 of accounts receivable with Stills Finance. The finance charge is 10% of the amount factored.
2. To obtain a one-year loan of $55,000, Collins assigns $65,000 of specific receivable accounts to Crosby Financial. The finance charge is 8% of the loan; the cash is received and the accounts turned over to Crosby Financial.
3. The company wants to maintain the Allowance for Doubtful Accounts at 5% of gross accounts receivable.
4. The company wishes to increase the allowance by 1½% of net sales.

E7-15 (Transfer of Receivables with Recourse) Ames Quartet Inc. factors receivables with a carrying amount of $200,000 to Joffrey Company for $160,000 on a with recourse basis.

Instructions
The recourse provision has a fair value of $1,000. This transaction should be recorded as a sale. Prepare the appropriate journal entry to record this transaction on the books of Ames Quartet Inc.

E7-16 (Transfer of Receivables with Recourse) Whitney Houston Corporation factors $175,000 of accounts receivable with Kathleen Battle Financing, Inc. on a with recourse basis. Kathleen Battle Financing will collect the receivables. The receivables records are transferred to Kathleen Battle Financing on August 15, 2003. Kathleen Battle Financing assesses a finance charge of 2% of the amount of accounts receivable and also reserves an amount equal to 4% of accounts receivable to cover probable adjustments.

Instructions

(a) What conditions must be met for a transfer of receivables with recourse to be accounted for as a sale?

(b) Assume the conditions from part (a) are met. Prepare the journal entry on August 15, 2003, for Whitney Houston to record the sale of receivables, assuming the recourse obligation has a fair value of $2,000.

E7-17 (Transfer of Receivables without Recourse) JFK Corp. factors $300,000 of accounts receivable with LBJ Finance Corporation on a without recourse basis on July 1, 2003. The receivables records are transferred to LBJ Finance, which will receive the collections. LBJ Finance assesses a finance charge of 1½% of the amount of accounts receivable and retains an amount equal to 4% of accounts receivable to cover sales discounts, returns, and allowances. The transaction is to be recorded as a sale.

Instructions

(a) Prepare the journal entry on July 1, 2003, for JFK Corp. to record the sale of receivables without recourse.

(b) Prepare the journal entry on July 1, 2003, for LBJ Finance Corporation to record the purchase of receivables without recourse.

E7-18 (Note Transactions at Unrealistic Interest Rates) On July 1, 2004, Agincourt Inc. made two sales.

1. It sold land having a fair market value of $700,000 in exchange for a 4-year non-interest-bearing promissory note in the face amount of $1,101,460. The land is carried on Agincourt's books at a cost of $590,000.
2. It rendered services in exchange for a 3%, 8-year promissory note having a face value of $400,000 (interest payable annually).

Agincourt Inc. recently had to pay 8% interest for money that it borrowed from British National Bank. The customers in these two transactions have credit ratings that require them to borrow money at 12% interest.

Instructions

Record the two journal entries that should be recorded by Agincourt Inc. for the sales transactions above that took place on July 1, 2004.

E7-19 (Notes Receivable with Unrealistic Interest Rate) On December 31, 2002, Ed Abbey Co. performed environmental consulting services for Hayduke Co. Hayduke was short of cash, and Abbey Co. agreed to accept a $200,000 non-interest-bearing note due December 31, 2004, as payment in full. Hayduke is somewhat of a credit risk and typically borrows funds at a rate of 15%. Abbey is much more creditworthy and has various lines of credit at 6%.

Instructions

(a) Prepare the journal entry to record the transaction of December 31, 2002, for the Ed Abbey Co.

(b) Assuming Ed Abbey Co.'s fiscal year-end is December 31, prepare the journal entry for December 31, 2003.

(c) Assuming Ed Abbey Co.'s fiscal year-end is December 31, prepare the journal entry for December 31, 2004.

E7-20 (Analysis of Receivables) Presented below is information for Jones Company.

1. Beginning-of-the-year Accounts Receivable balance was $15,000.
2. Net sales for the year were $185,000. (Credit sales were $100,000 of the total sales.) Jones does not offer cash discounts.
3. Collections on accounts receivable during the year were $70,000.

Instructions

(a) Prepare (summary) journal entries to record the items noted above.

(b) Compute Jones' accounts receivable turnover ratio for the year.

(c) Use the turnover ratio computed in (b) to analyze Jones' liquidity. The turnover ratio last year was 13.65.

E7-21 (Transfer of Receivables) Use the information for Jones Company as presented in E7-20. Jones is planning to factor some accounts receivable at the end of the year. Accounts totaling $25,000 will be transferred to Credit Factors, Inc. with recourse. Credit Factors will retain 5% of the balances and assesses a finance charge of 4%. The fair value of the recourse obligation is $1,200.

Instructions

(a) Prepare the journal entry to record the sale of receivables.

(b) Compute Jones's accounts receivables turnover ratio for the year, assuming the receivables are sold, and discuss how factoring of receivables affects the turnover ratio.

***E7-22 (Petty Cash)** Carolyn Keene, Inc. decided to establish a petty cash fund to help ensure internal control over its small cash expenditures. The following information is available for the month of April.

1. On April 1, it established a petty cash fund in the amount of $200.
2. A summary of the petty cash expenditures made by the petty cash custodian as of April 10 is as follows.

Delivery charges paid on merchandise purchased	$60.00
Supplies purchased and used	25.00
Postage expense	33.00
I.O.U. from employees	17.00
Miscellaneous expense	36.00

The petty cash fund was replenished on April 10. The balance in the fund was $27.

3. The petty cash fund balance was increased $100 to $300 on April 20.

Instructions

Prepare the journal entries to record transactions related to petty cash for the month of April.

***E7-23 (Petty Cash)** The petty cash fund of Fonzarelli's Auto Repair Service, a sole proprietorship, contains the following.

1. Coins and currency		$ 15.20
2. Postage stamps		2.90
3. An I.O.U. from Richie Cunningham, an employee, for cash advance		40.00
4. Check payable to Fonzarelli's Auto Repair from Pottsie Weber, an employee, marked NSF		34.00
5. Vouchers for the following:		
Stamps	$ 20.00	
Two Rose Bowl tickets for Nick Fonzarelli	170.00	
Printer cartridge	14.35	204.35
		$296.45

The general ledger account Petty Cash has a balance of $300.

Instructions

Prepare the journal entry to record the reimbursement of the petty cash fund.

***E7-24 (Bank Reconciliation and Adjusting Entries)** Angela Lansbury Company deposits all receipts and makes all payments by check. The following information is available from the cash records.

June 30 Bank Reconciliation

Balance per bank	$ 7,000
Add: Deposits in transit	1,540
Deduct: Outstanding checks	(2,000)
Balance per books	$ 6,540

Month of July Results

	Per Bank	Per Books
Balance July 31	$8,650	$9,250
July deposits	5,000	5,810
July checks	4,000	3,100
July note collected (not included in July deposits)	1,000	—
July bank service charge	15	—
July NSF check from a customer, returned by the bank (recorded by bank as a charge)	335	—

Instructions

(a) Prepare a bank reconciliation going from balance per bank and balance per book to correct cash balance.

(b) Prepare the general journal entry or entries to correct the Cash account.

***E7-25 (Bank Reconciliation and Adjusting Entries)** Logan Bruno Company has just received the August 31, 2004, bank statement, which is summarized below.

County National Bank	Disbursements	Receipts	Balance
Balance, August 1			$ 9,369
Deposits during August		$32,200	41,569
Note collected for depositor, including $40 interest		1,040	42,609
Checks cleared during August	$34,500		8,109
Bank service charges	20		8,089
Balance, August 31			8,089

The general ledger Cash account contained the following entries for the month of August.

Cash			
Balance, August 1	10,050	Disbursements in August	34,903
Receipts during August	35,000		

Deposits in transit at August 31 are $3,800, and checks outstanding at August 31 total $1,050. Cash on hand at August 31 is $310. The bookkeeper improperly entered one check in the books at $146.50 which was written for $164.50 for supplies (expense); it cleared the bank during the month of August.

Instructions

(a) Prepare a bank reconciliation dated August 31, 2004, proceeding to a correct balance.
(b) Prepare any entries necessary to make the books correct and complete.
(c) What amount of cash should be reported in the August 31 balance sheet?

PROBLEMS

P7-1 (Determine Proper Cash Balance) Dumaine Equipment Co. closes its books regularly on December 31, but at the end of 2003 it held its cash book open so that a more favorable balance sheet could be prepared for credit purposes. Cash receipts and disbursements for the first 10 days of January were recorded as December transactions. The following information is given.

1. January cash receipts recorded in the December cash book totaled $39,640, of which $22,000 represents cash sales, and $17,640 represents collections on account for which cash discounts of $360 were given.
2. January cash disbursements recorded in the December check register liquidated accounts payable of $26,450 on which discounts of $250 were taken.
3. The ledger has not been closed for 2003.
4. The amount shown as inventory was determined by physical count on December 31, 2003.

Instructions

(a) Prepare any entries you consider necessary to correct Dumaine's accounts at December 31.
(b) To what extent was Dumaine Equipment Co. able to show a more favorable balance sheet at December 31 by holding its cash book open? (Use ratio analysis.) Assume that the balance sheet that was prepared by the company showed the following amounts:

	Dr.	Cr.
Cash	$39,000	
Receivables	42,000	
Inventories	67,000	
Accounts payable		$45,000
Other current liabilities		14,200

P7-2 (Bad Debt Reporting) Presented below are a series of unrelated situations.

1. Spock Company's unadjusted trial balance at December 31, 2003, included the following accounts.

	Debit	Credit
Allowance for doubtful accounts	$4,000	
Net sales		$1,500,000

Spock Company estimates its bad debt expense to be $1\frac{1}{2}$% of net sales. Determine its bad debt expense for 2003.

2. An analysis and aging of Scotty Corp. accounts receivable at December 31, 2003, disclosed the following.

Amounts estimated to be uncollectible	$ 180,000
Accounts receivable	1,750,000
Allowance for doubtful accounts (per books)	125,000

What is the net realizable value of Scotty's receivables at December 31, 2003?

3. Uhura Co. provides for doubtful accounts based on 3% of credit sales. The following data are available for 2003.

Credit sales during 2003	$2,100,000
Allowance for doubtful accounts 1/1/03	17,000
Collection of accounts written off in prior years (customer credit was reestablished)	8,000
Customer accounts written off as uncollectible during 2003	30,000

What is the balance in the Allowance for Doubtful Accounts at December 31, 2003?

4. At the end of its first year of operations, December 31, 2003, Chekov Inc. reported the following information.

Accounts receivable, net of allowance for doubtful accounts	$950,000
Customer accounts written off as uncollectible during 2003	24,000
Bad debt expense for 2003	84,000

What should be the balance in accounts receivable at December 31, 2003, before subtracting the allowance for doubtful accounts?

5. The following accounts were taken from Chappel Inc.'s balance sheet at December 31, 2003.

	Debit	Credit
Net credit sales		$750,000
Allowance for doubtful accounts	$ 14,000	
Accounts receivable	410,000	

If doubtful accounts are 3% of accounts receivable, determine the bad debt expense to be reported for 2003.

Instructions

Answer the questions relating to each of the five independent situations as requested.

P7-3 (Bad Debt Reporting—Aging) Ignace Paderewski Corporation operates in an industry that has a high rate of bad debts. Before any year-end adjustments, the balance in Paderewski's Accounts Receivable account was $555,000 and the Allowance for Doubtful Accounts had a credit balance of $35,000. The year-end balance reported in the balance sheet for the Allowance for Doubtful Accounts will be based on the aging schedule shown below.

Days Account Outstanding	Amount	Probability of Collection
Less than 16 days	$300,000	.98
Between 16 and 30 days	100,000	.90
Between 31 and 45 days	80,000	.85
Between 46 and 60 days	40,000	.75
Between 61 and 75 days	20,000	.40
Over 75 days	15,000	.00

Instructions

(a) What is the appropriate balance for the Allowance for Doubtful Accounts at year-end?
(b) Show how accounts receivable would be presented on the balance sheet.
(c) What is the dollar effect of the year-end bad debt adjustment on the before-tax income?

(CMA adapted)

P7-4 (Bad Debt Reporting) From inception of operations to December 31, 2004, Blaise Pascal Corporation provided for uncollectible accounts receivable under the allowance method: provisions were made monthly at 2% of credit sales; bad debts written off were charged to the allowance account; recoveries of bad debts previously written off were credited to the allowance account; and no year-end adjustments to the allowance account were made. Pascal's usual credit terms are net 30 days.

The balance in the Allowance for Doubtful Accounts was $154,000 at January 1, 2004. During 2004 credit sales totaled $9,000,000, interim provisions for doubtful accounts were made at 2% of credit sales, $95,000 of bad debts were written off, and recoveries of accounts previously written off amounted to $15,000. Pascal installed a computer facility in November 2004, and an aging of accounts receivable was prepared for the first time as of December 31, 2004. A summary of the aging is as follows.

Classification by Month of Sale	Balance in Each Category	Estimated % Uncollectible
November–December 2004	$1,080,000	2%
July–October	650,000	10%
January–June	420,000	25%
Prior to 1/1/04	150,000	70%
	$2,300,000	

Based on the review of collectibility of the account balances in the "prior to 1/1/04" aging category, additional receivables totaling $60,000 were written off as of December 31, 2004. The 70% uncollectible estimate applies to the remaining $90,000 in the category. Effective with the year ended December 31, 2004, Pascal adopted a new accounting method for estimating the allowance for doubtful accounts at the amount indicated by the year-end aging analysis of accounts receivable.

Instructions

(a) Prepare a schedule analyzing the changes in the Allowance for Doubtful Accounts for the year ended December 31, 2004. Show supporting computations in good form. (*Hint*: In computing the 12/31/04 allowance, subtract the $60,000 write-off).

(b) Prepare the journal entry for the year-end adjustment to the Allowance for Doubtful Accounts balance as of December 31, 2004.

(AICPA adapted)

P7-5 (Bad Debt Reporting) Presented below is information related to the Accounts Receivable accounts of Gulistan Inc. during the current year 2004.

1. An aging schedule of the accounts receivable as of December 31, 2004, is as follows.

Age	Net Debit Balance	% to Be Applied after Correction Is Made
Under 60 days	$172,342	1%
61–90 days	136,490	3%
91–120 days	39,924*	6%
Over 120 days	23,644	$4,200 definitely uncollectible; estimated remainder uncollectible is 25%
	$372,400	

*The $2,740 write-off of receivables is related to the 91-to-120 day category.

2. The Accounts Receivable control account has a debit balance of $372,400 on December 31, 2004.
3. Two entries were made in the Bad Debt Expense account during the year: (1) a debit on December 31 for the amount credited to Allowance for Doubtful Accounts, and (2) a credit for $2,740 on November 3, 2004, and a debit to Allowance for Doubtful Accounts because of a bankruptcy.
4. The Allowance for Doubtful Accounts is as follows for 2004.

Allowance for Doubtful Accounts

Nov. 3	Uncollectible accounts written off	2,740	Jan. 1	Beginning balance	8,750
			Dec. 31	5% of $372,400	18,620

5. A credit balance exists in the Accounts Receivable (61–90 days) of $4,840, which represents an advance on a sales contract.

Instructions

Assuming that the books have not been closed for 2004, make the necessary correcting entries.

P7-6 (Journalize Various Accounts Receivable Transactions) The balance sheet of Antonio Vivaldi Company at December 31, 2003, includes the following.

Notes receivable	$ 36,000	
Accounts receivable	182,100	
Less: Allowance for doubtful accounts	17,300	200,800

Transactions in 2004 include the following.

1. Accounts receivable of $138,000 were collected including accounts of $40,000 on which 2% sales discounts were allowed.
2. $6,300 was received in payment of an account which was written off the books as worthless in 2000. (*Hint:* Reestablish the receivable account.)
3. Customer accounts of $17,500 were written off during the year.
4. At year-end the Allowance for Doubtful Accounts was estimated to need a balance of $20,000. This estimate is based on an analysis of aged accounts receivable.

Instructions

Prepare all journal entries necessary to reflect the transactions above.

P7-7 (Assigned Accounts Receivable—Journal Entries) Nikos Company finances some of its current operations by assigning accounts receivable to a finance company. On July 1, 2004, it assigned, under guarantee, specific accounts amounting to $100,000. The finance company advanced to Nikos 80% of the accounts assigned (20% of the total to be withheld until the finance company has made its full recovery), less a finance charge of ½% of the total accounts assigned.

On July 31 Nikos Company received a statement that the finance company had collected $55,000 of these accounts and had made an additional charge of ½% of the total accounts outstanding as of July 31. This charge is to be deducted at the time of the first remittance due Nikos Company from the finance company. (*Hint*: Make entries at this time.) On August 31, 2004, Nikos Company received a second statement from the finance company, together with a check for the amount due. The statement indicated that the finance company had collected an additional $30,000 and had made a further charge of ½% of the balance outstanding as of August 31.

Instructions

Make all entries on the books of Nikos Company that are involved in the transactions above.

(AICPA adapted)

P7-8 (Notes Receivable with Realistic Interest Rate) On October 1, 2004, Jeppo Farm Equipment Company sold a pecan-harvesting machine to Lujan Brothers Farm, Inc. In lieu of a cash payment Lujan Brothers Farm gave Jeppo a 2-year, $100,000, 12% note (a realistic rate of interest for a note of this type). The note required interest to be paid annually on October 1. Jeppo's financial statements are prepared on a calendar-year basis.

Instructions

Assuming Lujan Brothers Farm fulfills all the terms of the note, prepare the necessary journal entries for Jeppo Farm Equipment Company for the entire term of the note.

P7-9 (Notes Receivable Journal Entries) On December 31, 2004, Menachem Inc. rendered services to Begin Corporation at an agreed price of $91,844.10, accepting $36,000 down and agreeing to accept the balance in four equal installments of $18,000 receivable each December 31. An assumed interest rate of 11% is imputed.

Instructions

Prepare the entries that would be recorded by Menachem Inc. for the sale and for the receipts and interest on the following dates. (Assume that the effective interest method is used for amortization purposes.)

(a) December 31, 2004. **(c)** December 31, 2006. **(e)** December 31, 2008.
(b) December 31, 2005. **(d)** December 31, 2007.

P7-10 (Comprehensive Receivables Problem) Connecticut Inc. had the following long-term receivable account balances at December 31, 2003.

Note receivable from sale of division	$1,800,000
Note receivable from officer	400,000

Transactions during 2004 and other information relating to Connecticut's long-term receivables were as follows.

1. The $1,800,000 note receivable is dated May 1, 2003, bears interest at 9%, and represents the balance of the consideration received from the sale of Connecticut's electronics division to New York Company. Principal payments of $600,000 plus appropriate interest are due on May 1, 2004, 2005, and 2006. The first principal and interest payment was made on May 1, 2004. Collection of the note installments is reasonably assured.
2. The $400,000 note receivable is dated December 31, 2003, bears interest at 8%, and is due on December 31, 2006. The note is due from Marcus Camby, president of Connecticut Inc. and is col-

lateralized by 10,000 shares of Connecticut's common stock. Interest is payable annually on December 31, and all interest payments were paid on their due dates through December 31, 2004. The quoted market price of Connecticut's common stock was $45 per share on December 31, 2004.

3. On April 1, 2004, Connecticut sold a patent to Pennsylvania Company in exchange for a $200,000 non-interest-bearing note due on April 1, 2006. There was no established exchange price for the patent, and the note had no ready market. The prevailing rate of interest for a note of this type at April 1, 2004, was 12%. The present value of $1 for two periods at 12% is 0.797 (use this factor). The patent had a carrying value of $40,000 at January 1, 2004, and the amortization for the year ended December 31, 2004, would have been $8,000. The collection of the note receivable from Pennsylvania is reasonably assured.
4. On July 1, 2004, Connecticut sold a parcel of land to Harrisburg Company for $200,000 under an installment sale contract. Harrisburg made a $60,000 cash down payment on July 1, 2004, and signed a 4-year 11% note for the $140,000 balance. The equal annual payments of principal and interest on the note will be $45,125 payable on July 1, 2005, through July 1, 2008. The land could have been sold at an established cash price of $200,000. The cost of the land to Connecticut was $150,000. Circumstances are such that the collection of the installments on the note is reasonably assured.

Instructions

(a) Prepare the long-term receivables section of Connecticut's balance sheet at December 31, 2004.
(b) Prepare a schedule showing the current portion of the long-term receivables and accrued interest receivable that would appear in Connecticut's balance sheet at December 31, 2004.
(c) Prepare a schedule showing interest revenue from the long-term receivables that would appear on Connecticut's income statement for the year ended December 31, 2004.

P7-11 (Income Effects of Receivables Transactions) Radisson Company requires additional cash for its business. Radisson has decided to use its accounts receivable to raise the additional cash and has asked you to determine the income statement effects of the following contemplated transactions.

1. On July 1, 2003, Radisson assigned $400,000 of accounts receivable to Stickum Finance Company. Radisson received an advance from Stickum of 85% of the assigned accounts receivable less a commission of 3% on the advance. Prior to December 31, 2003, Radisson collected $220,000 on the assigned accounts receivable, and remitted $232,720 to Stickum, $12,720 of which represented interest on the advance from Stickum.
2. On December 1, 2003, Radisson sold $300,000 of net accounts receivable to Wunsch Company for $250,000. The receivables were sold outright on a without recourse basis.
3. On December 31, 2003, an advance of $120,000 was received from First Bank by pledging $160,000 of Radisson's accounts receivable. Radisson's first payment to First Bank is due on January 30, 2004.

Instructions

Prepare a schedule showing the income statement effects for the year ended December 31, 2003, as a result of the above facts.

***P7-12 (Petty Cash, Bank Reconciliation)** Bill Howe is reviewing the cash accounting for Kappeler, Inc., a local mailing service. Howe's review will focus on the petty cash account and the bank reconciliation for the month ended May 31, 2003. He has collected the following information from Kappeler's bookkeeper for this task.

Petty Cash

1. The petty cash fund was established on May 10, 2003, in the amount of $250.
2. Expenditures from the fund by the custodian as of May 31, 2003, were evidenced by approved receipts for the following.

Postage expense	$33.00
Mailing labels and other supplies	75.00
I.O.U. from employees	30.00
Shipping charges	57.45
Newspaper advertising	22.80
Miscellaneous expense	15.35

On May 31, 2003, the petty cash fund was replenished and increased to $300; currency and coin in the fund at that time totaled $16.40.

Bank Reconciliation

THIRD NATIONAL BANK
BANK STATEMENT

	Disbursements	Receipts	Balance
Balance, May 1, 2003			$8,769
Deposits		$28,000	
Note payment direct from customer (interest of $30)		930	
Checks cleared during May	$31,150		
Bank service charges	27		
Balance, May 31, 2003			6,522

Kappeler's Cash Account

Balance, May 1, 2003	$ 9,150
Deposits during May 2003	31,000
Checks written during May 2003	(31,835)

Deposits in transit are determined to be $3,000, and checks outstanding at May 31 total $550. Cash on hand (besides petty cash) at May 31, 2003, is $246.

Instructions

(a) Prepare the journal entries to record the transactions related to the petty cash fund for May.
(b) Prepare a bank reconciliation dated May 31, 2003, proceeding to a correct cash balance, and prepare the journal entries necessary to make the books correct and complete.
(c) What amount of cash should be reported in the May 31, 2003, balance sheet?

***P7-13 (Bank Reconciliation and Adjusting Entries)** The cash account of Jose Orozco Co. showed a ledger balance of $3,969.85 on June 30, 2003. The bank statement as of that date showed a balance of $4,150. Upon comparing the statement with the cash records, the following facts were determined.

1. There were bank service charges for June of $25.
2. A bank memo stated that Bao Dai's note for $900 and interest of $36 had been collected on June 29, and the bank had made a charge of $5.50 on the collection. (No entry had been made on Orozco's books when Bao Dai's note was sent to the bank for collection.)
3. Receipts for June 30 for $2,890 were not deposited until July 2.
4. Checks outstanding on June 30 totaled $2,136.05.
5. The bank had charged the Orozco Co.'s account for a customer's uncollectible check amounting to $453.20 on June 29.
6. A customer's check for $90 had been entered as $60 in the cash receipts journal by Orozco on June 15.
7. Check no. 742 in the amount of $491 had been entered in the cashbook as $419, and check no. 747 in the amount of $58.20 had been entered as $582. Both checks had been issued to pay for purchases of equipment.

Instructions

(a) Prepare a bank reconciliation dated June 30, 2003, proceeding to a correct cash balance.
(b) Prepare any entries necessary to make the books correct and complete.

***P7-14 (Bank Reconciliation and Adjusting Entries)** Presented below is information related to Tanizaki Inc.

Balance per books at October 31, $41,847.85; receipts $173,523.91; disbursements $166,193.54. Balance per bank statement November 30, $56,274.20.

The following checks were outstanding at November 30.

1224	$1,635.29
1230	2,468.30
1232	3,625.15
1233	482.17

Included with the November bank statement and not recorded by the company were a bank debit memo for $27.40 covering bank charges for the month, a debit memo for $572.13 for a customer's check returned and marked NSF, and a credit memo for $1,400 representing bond interest collected by the bank in the name of Tanizaki Inc. Cash on hand at November 30 recorded and awaiting deposit amounted to $1,915.40.

Instructions

(a) Prepare a bank reconciliation (to the correct balance) at November 30, 2003, for Tanizaki Inc. from the information above.

(b) Prepare any journal entries required to adjust the cash account at November 30.

CONCEPTUAL CASES

C7-1 (Bad Debt Accounting) Ariel Company has significant amounts of trade accounts receivable. Ariel uses the allowance method to estimate bad debts instead of the direct write-off method. During the year, some specific accounts were written off as uncollectible, and some that were previously written off as uncollectible were collected.

Instructions

(a) What are the deficiencies of the direct write-off method?

(b) What are the two basic allowance methods used to estimate bad debts, and what is the theoretical justification for each?

(c) How should Ariel account for the collection of the specific accounts previously written off as uncollectible?

C7-2 (Various Receivable Accounting Issues) Anne Archer Company uses the net method of accounting for sales discounts. Anne Archer also offers trade discounts to various groups of buyers.

On August 1, 2003, Archer sold some accounts receivable on a without recourse basis. Archer incurred a finance charge.

Archer also has some notes receivable bearing an appropriate rate of interest. The principal and total interest are due at maturity. The notes were received on October 1, 2003, and mature on September 30, 2005. Archer's operating cycle is less than one year.

Instructions

(a) (1) Using the net method, how should Archer account for the sales discounts at the date of sale? What is the rationale for the amount recorded as sales under the net method?

(2) Using the net method, what is the effect on Archer's sales revenues and net income when customers do not take the sales discounts?

(b) What is the effect of trade discounts on sales revenues and accounts receivable? Why?

(c) How should Archer account for the accounts receivable factored on August 1, 2003? Why?

(d) How should Archer account for the note receivable and the related interest on December 31, 2003? Why?

C7-3 (Bad Debt Reporting Issues) Ben Gazarra conducts a wholesale merchandising business that sells approximately 5,000 items per month with a total monthly average sales value of $250,000. Its annual bad debt ratio has been approximately 1½% of sales. In recent discussions with his bookkeeper, Mr. Gazarra has become confused by all the alternatives apparently available in handling the Allowance for Doubtful Accounts balance. The following information has been shown.

1. An allowance can be set up (a) on the basis of a percentage of sales or (b) on the basis of a valuation of all past due or otherwise questionable accounts receivable. Those considered uncollectible can be charged to such allowance at the close of the accounting period, or specific items can be charged off directly against (1) Gross Sales or to (2) Bad Debt Expense in the year in which they are determined to be uncollectible.
2. Collection agency and legal fees, and so on, incurred in connection with the attempted recovery of bad debts can be charged to (a) Bad Debt Expense, (b) Allowance for Doubtful Accounts, (c) Legal Expense, or (d) General Expense.
3. Debts previously written off in whole or in part but currently recovered can be credited to (a) Other Revenue, (b) Bad Debt Expense, or (c) Allowance for Doubtful Accounts.

Instructions

Which of the foregoing methods would you recommend to Mr. Gazarra in regard to (1) allowances and charge-offs, (2) collection expenses, and (3) recoveries? State briefly and clearly the reasons supporting your recommendations.

C7-4 (Basic Note and Accounts Receivable Transactions)

Part 1

On July 1, 2004, Eve Arden Company, a calendar-year company, sold special-order merchandise on credit and received in return an interest-bearing note receivable from the customer. Eve Arden Company will receive interest at the prevailing rate for a note of this type. Both the principal and interest are due in one lump sum on June 30, 2005.

Instructions

When should Eve Arden Company report interest income from the note receivable? Discuss the rationale for your answer.

Part 2

On December 31, 2004, Eve Arden Company had significant amounts of accounts receivable as a result of credit sales to its customers. Eve Arden Company uses the allowance method based on credit sales to estimate bad debts. Past experience indicates that 2% of credit sales normally will not be collected. This pattern is expected to continue.

Instructions

(a) Discuss the rationale for using the allowance method based on credit sales to estimate bad debts. Contrast this method with the allowance method based on the balance in the trade receivables accounts.

(b) How should Eve Arden Company report the allowance for bad debts account on its balance sheet at December 31, 2004? Also, describe the alternatives, if any, for presentation of bad debt expense in Eve Arden Company's 2004 income statement.

(AICPA adapted)

C7-5 (Bad Debt Reporting Issues) Rosita Arenas Company sells office equipment and supplies to many organizations in the city and surrounding area on contract terms of 2/10, n/30. In the past, over 75% of the credit customers have taken advantage of the discount by paying within 10 days of the invoice date.

The number of customers taking the full 30 days to pay has increased within the last year. Current indications are that less than 60% of the customers are now taking the discount. Bad debts as a percentage of gross credit sales have risen from the 1.5% provided in past years to about 4% in the current year.

The controller has responded to a request for more information on the deterioration in collections of accounts receivable with the report reproduced below.

ROSITA ARENAS COMPANY
FINANCE COMMITTEE REPORT—ACCOUNTS RECEIVABLE COLLECTIONS
MAY 31, 2004

The fact that some credit accounts will prove uncollectible is normal. Annual bad debt write-offs have been 1.5% of gross credit sales over the past five years. During the last fiscal year, this percentage increased to slightly less than 4%. The current Accounts Receivable balance is $1,600,000. The condition of this balance in terms of age and probability of collection is as follows.

Proportion of Total	Age Categories	Probability of Collection
68%	not yet due	99%
15%	less than 30 days past due	96½%
8%	30 to 60 days past due	95%
5%	61 to 120 days past due	91%
2½%	121 to 180 days past due	70%
1½%	over 180 days past due	20%

The Allowance for Doubtful Accounts had a credit balance of $43,300 on June 1, 2003. Rosita Arenas Company has provided for a monthly bad debts expense accrual during the current fiscal year based on the assumption that 4% of gross credit sales will be uncollectible. Total gross credit sales for the 2003–04 fiscal year amounted to $4,000,000. Write-offs of bad accounts during the year totaled $145,000.

Instructions

(a) Prepare an accounts receivable aging schedule for Rosita Arenas Company using the age categories identified in the controller's report to the finance committee showing:

(1) The amount of accounts receivable outstanding for each age category and in total.

(2) The estimated amount that is uncollectible for each category and in total.

(b) Compute the amount of the year-end adjustment necessary to bring Allowance for Doubtful Accounts to the balance indicated by the age analysis. Then prepare the necessary journal entry to adjust the accounting records.

(c) In a recessionary environment with tight credit and high interest rates:
  (1) Identify steps Rosita Arenas Company might consider to improve the accounts receivable situation.
  (2) Then evaluate each step identified in terms of the risks and costs involved.

(CMA adapted)

C7-6 (Sale of Notes Receivable) Sergey Luzov Wholesalers Co. sells industrial equipment for a standard 3-year note receivable. Revenue is recognized at time of sale. Each note is secured by a lien on the equipment and has a face amount equal to the equipment's list price. Each note's stated interest rate is below the customer's market rate at date of sale. All notes are to be collected in three equal annual installments beginning one year after sale. Some of the notes are subsequently sold to a bank with recourse, some are subsequently sold without recourse, and some are retained by Luzov. At year end, Luzov evaluates all outstanding notes receivable and provides for estimated losses arising from defaults.

Instructions

(a) What is the appropriate valuation basis for Luzov's notes receivable at the date it sells equipment?
(b) How should Luzov account for the sale, without recourse, of a February 1, 2003, note receivable sold on May 1, 2003? Why is it appropriate to account for it in this way?
(c) At December 31, 2003, how should Luzov measure and account for the impact of estimated losses resulting from notes receivable that it
  (1) Retained and did **not** sell?
  (2) Sold to bank with recourse?

(AICPA adapted)

C7-7 (Non-interest-bearing Note Receivable) On September 30, 2003, Tiger Machinery Co. sold a machine and accepted the customer's non-interest-bearing note. Tiger normally makes sales on a cash basis. Since the machine was unique, its sales price was not determinable using Tiger's normal pricing practices.

After receiving the first of two equal annual installments on September 30, 2004, Tiger immediately sold the note with recourse. On October 9, 2005, Tiger received notice that the note was dishonored, and it paid all amounts due. At all times prior to default, the note was reasonably expected to be paid in full.

Instructions

(a) (1) How should Tiger determine the sales price of the machine?
  (2) How should Tiger report the effects of the non-interest-bearing note on its income statement for the year ended December 31, 2003? Why is this accounting presentation appropriate?
(b) What are the effects of the sale of the note receivable with recourse on Tiger's income statement for the year ended December 31, 2004, and its balance sheet at December 31, 2004?
(c) How should Tiger account for the effects of the note being dishonored?

C7-8 (Reporting of Notes Receivable, Interest, and Sale of Receivables) On July 1, 2004, Gale Sondergaard Company sold special-order merchandise on credit and received in return an interest-bearing note receivable from the customer. Sondergaard will receive interest at the prevailing rate for a note of this type. Both the principal and interest are due in one lump sum on June 30, 2005.

On September 1, 2004, Sondergaard sold special-order merchandise on credit and received in return a non-interest-bearing note receivable from the customer. The prevailing rate of interest for a note of this type is determinable. The note receivable is due in one lump sum on August 31, 2006.

Sondergaard also has significant amounts of trade accounts receivable as a result of credit sales to its customers. On October 1, 2004, some trade accounts receivable were assigned to Irene Dunne Finance Company on a non-notification (Sondergaard handles collections) basis for an advance of 75% of their amount at an interest charge of 12% on the balance outstanding.

On November 1, 2004, other trade accounts receivable were sold on a without recourse basis. The factor withheld 5% of the trade accounts receivable factored as protection against sales returns and allowances and charged a finance charge of 3%.

Instructions

(a) How should Sondergaard determine the interest income for 2004 on the:
  (1) Interest-bearing note receivable? Why?
  (2) Non-interest-bearing note receivable? Why?
(b) How should Sondergaard report the interest-bearing note receivable and the non-interest-bearing note receivable on its balance sheet at December 31, 2004?
(c) How should Sondergaard account for subsequent collections on the trade accounts receivable assigned on October 1, 2004, and the payments to Irene Dunne Finance? Why?

(d) How should Sondergaard account for the trade accounts receivable factored on November 1, 2004? Why?

(AICPA adapted)

C7-9 (Accounting for Non-interest-bearing Note) Soon after beginning the year-end audit work on March 10 at Engone Company, the auditor has the following conversation with the controller.

CONTROLLER: The year ended March 31st should be our most profitable in history and, as a consequence, the board of directors has just awarded the officers generous bonuses.

AUDITOR: I thought profits were down this year in the industry, according to your latest interim report.

CONTROLLER: Well, they were down, but 10 days ago we closed a deal that will give us a substantial increase for the year.

AUDITOR: Oh, what was it?

CONTROLLER: Well, you remember a few years ago our former president bought stock in Rocketeer Enterprises because he had those grandiose ideas about becoming a conglomerate. For 6 years we have not been able to sell this stock, which cost us $3,000,000 and has not paid a nickel in dividends. Thursday we sold this stock to Campbell Inc. for $4,000,000. So, we will have a gain of $700,000 ($1,000,000 pretax) which will increase our net income for the year to $4,000,000, compared with last year's $3,800,000. As far as I know, we'll be the only company in the industry to register an increase in net income this year. That should help the market value of the stock!

AUDITOR: Do you expect to receive the $4,000,000 in cash by March 31st, your fiscal year-end?

CONTROLLER: No. Although Campbell Inc. is an excellent company, they are a little tight for cash because of their rapid growth. Consequently, they are going to give us a $4,000,000 non-interest-bearing note with payments of $400,000 per year for the next 10 years. The first payment is due on March 31 of next year.

AUDITOR: Why is the note non-interest-bearing?

CONTROLLER: Because that's what everybody agreed to. Since we don't have any interest-bearing debt, the funds invested in the note do not cost us anything and besides, we were not getting any dividends on the Rocketeer Enterprises stock.

Instructions

Do you agree with the way the controller has accounted for the transaction? If not, how should the transaction be accounted for?

C7-10 (Receivables Management) As the manager of the accounts receivable department for Vicki Maher Leather Goods, Ltd., you recently noticed that Percy Shelley, your accounts receivable clerk who is paid $1,200 per month, has been wearing unusually tasteful and expensive clothing. (This is Vicki Maher's first year in business.) This morning, Shelley drove up to work in a brand new Lexus.

Naturally suspicious by nature, you decide to test the accuracy of the accounts receivable balance of $132,000 as shown in the ledger. The following information is available for your first year (precisely 9 months ended September 30, 2004) in business.

(1) Collections from customers	$198,000
(2) Merchandise purchased	360,000
(3) Ending merchandise inventory	90,000
(4) Goods are marked to sell at 40% above cost.	

Instructions

Assuming all sales were made on account, compute the ending accounts receivable balance that should appear in the ledger, noting any apparent shortage. Then, draft a memo dated October 3, 2004, to John Castle, the branch manager, explaining the facts in this situation. Remember that this problem is serious, and you do not want to make hasty accusations.

C7-11 (Bad Debt Reporting) Rudolph Company is a subsidiary of Hundley Corp. The controller believes that the yearly allowance for doubtful accounts for Rudolph should be 2% of net credit sales. The president, nervous that the parent company might expect the subsidiary to sustain its 10% growth rate, suggests that the controller increase the allowance for doubtful accounts to 3% yearly. The supervisor thinks that the lower net income, which reflects a 6% growth rate, will be a more sustainable rate for Rudolph Company.

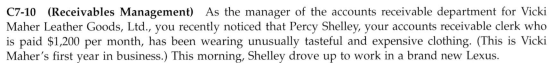

Instructions

(a) Should the controller be concerned with Rudolph Company's growth rate in estimating the allowance? Explain your answer.

(b) Does the president's request pose an ethical dilemma for the controller? Give your reasons.

USING YOUR JUDGMENT

FINANCIAL REPORTING PROBLEM

3M Company

The financial statements of 3M are presented in Appendix 5B or can be accessed on the Take Action! CD.

Instructions

Refer to 3M's financial statements and the accompanying notes to answer the following questions.

(a) What criteria does 3M use to classify "Cash and cash equivalents" as reported in its balance sheet?

(b) As of December 31, 2001, what balances did 3M have in cash and cash equivalents? What were the major uses of cash during the year?

(c) In recent years the accounting profession has encouraged companies to disclose any concentration of risk not apparent in their financial statements. What risks relative to accounts receivable does 3M disclose in its Notes to Consolidated Financial Statements?

FINANCIAL STATEMENT ANALYSIS CASE

Occidental Petroleum Corporation

Occidental Petroleum Corporation reported the following information in its 2000 Annual Report.

Occidental Petroleum Corporation
Consolidated Balance Sheets
(in millions)

Assets at December 31,	2000	1999
Current assets		
Cash and cash equivalents	$ 97	$ 214
Trade receivables, net of allowances	809	559
Receivables from joint ventures, partnerships, and other	517	215
Inventories	485	503
Prepaid expenses and other	159	197
Total current assets	2,067	1,688
Long-term receivables, net	2,119	168

Notes to Consolidated Financial Statements

Cash and Cash Equivalents. Cash equivalents consist of highly liquid money-market mutual funds and bank deposits with initial maturities of three months or less. Cash equivalents totaled approximately $46 million and $162 million at December 31, 2000 and 1999, respectively.

Trade Receivables. In 1992, Occidental entered into a new agreement to sell, under a revolving sale program, an undivided percentage ownership interest in a designated pool of trade receivables, with limited recourse. Under this program, Occidental serves as the collection agent with respect to the receivables sold. An interest in new receivables is sold as collections are made from customers. As of December 31, 2000, Occidental had received net cash proceeds totaling $360 million.

Instructions

(a) What items other than coin and currency may be included in "cash"?

(b) What items may be included in "cash equivalents"?

(c) What are compensating balance arrangements, and how should they be reported in financial statements?

(d) What are the possible differences between cash equivalents and short-term (temporary) investments?

(e) Occidental has sold some of its receivables. How much cash did it receive under this agreement in 2000?

(f) Assuming that the sale agreement meets the criteria for sale accounting, the carrying value of the receivables sold was $375 million, the finance charge was 4% of the balances sold, and the fair value of the limited recourse was $15 million, what was the effect on income from the sale of receivables?

(g) Briefly discuss the impact of the transaction in (f) on Occidental's liquidity.

COMPARATIVE ANALYSIS CASE

The Coca-Cola Company and PepsiCo, Inc.

Instructions

Go to the Take Action! CD and use the information found there to answer the following questions related to **The Coca-Cola Company** and **PepsiCo, Inc.**

(a) What were the cash and cash equivalents reported by Coca-Cola and PepsiCo at the end of 2001? What does each company classify as cash equivalents?

(b) What were the accounts receivable (net) for Coca-Cola and PepsiCo at the end of 2001? Which company reports the greater allowance for doubtful accounts receivable (amount and percentage of gross receivable) at the end of 2001?

(c) Assuming that all "net operating revenues" (Coca-Cola) and all "net sales" (PepsiCo) were net *credit* sales, compute the receivables turnover ratio for 2001 for Coca-Cola and PepsiCo; also compute the days outstanding for receivables. What is your evaluation of the difference?

RESEARCH CASES

Case 1

Accounting Trends and Techniques, published annually by the American Institute of Certified Public Accountants, is a survey of 600 annual reports to stockholders. The survey covers selected industrial, merchandising, and service companies.

Instructions

Examine the section regarding the use of receivables for financing and answer the following questions.

(a) For the most recent year, how many of the companies surveyed disclosed (1) receivables sold, and (2) receivables used as collateral?

(b) Examine the disclosure provided by a company that sold receivables and a company that used its receivables as collateral. Summarize the major terms of the transactions.

Case 2

The January 20, 1999, edition of the *Wall Street Journal* contained an article by Jonathan Weil entitled "**Americredit** Accounting Practices Are Criticized by Research Firm." (Subscribers to **Business Extra** can access the article at that site.)

Instructions

Read the article and answer the following questions.

(a) Why is Americredit's accounting for receivables criticized?

(b) How does the "cash-out" method of accounting for loan sales respond to the criticisms from part (a)?

(c) What are warning signs that investors can use to identify problems at sub-prime lenders?

PROFESSIONAL SIMULATION

Accounting for Receivables

Directions | Situation | Measurement | Financial Statements | Analysis | Explanation | Research | Resources

Directions

In this simulation, you will be asked to address various requirements regarding the accounting for receivables. Prepare responses to all parts.

Situation

Mike Horn Corporation manufactures sweatshirts for sale to athletic-wear retailers. The following information was available for Horn for the years ended December 31, 2003 and 2004.

	December 31, 2003	December 31, 2004
Cash	$ 20,000	$ 15,000
Trade accounts receivable	40,000	?
Allowance for doubtful accounts	5,500	?
Inventories	85,000	80,000
Current liabilities	80,000	86,000
Total credit sales	480,000	550,000
Collections on trade accounts receivable	440,000	500,000

During 2004, Horn had the following transactions.

1. On June 30, sales of $50,000 to a major customer were settled, with Horn accepting a 1-year $50,000 note bearing 11% interest, payable at maturity.

2. Horn factors some accounts receivable at the end of the year. Accounts totaling $40,000 are transferred to First Factors, Inc. with recourse. First Factors will receive the collections from Horn's customers and retain 6% of the balances. Horn is assessed a finance charge of 4% on this transfer. The fair value of the recourse obligation is $4,000.

3. On the basis of the latest available information, the 2004 provision for bad debts is estimated to be 0.8% of credit sales. Horn charged off as uncollectible, accounts with balances of $2,300.

Measurement

Based on the above transactions, determine the balance for Trade Accounts Receivable and the Allowance for Doubtful Accounts at December 31, 2004.

Financial Statements

Prepare the current assets section of Horn's balance sheet at December 31, 2004. The cash balance at December 31, 2004, reflects the following items: checking account $4,000; postage stamps $1,100; petty cash $300; currency $3,000; customers' checks (post-dated) $2,000.

Analysis

Compute the current ratio and the receivables turnover ratio for Horn at December 31, 2004. Use these measures to analyze Horn's liquidity. The receivables turnover ratio in 2003 was 10.37.

Explanation

Discuss how the Analysis above would be affected if Horn had transferred the receivables in a secured borrowing transaction.

www.wiley.com/college/kieso

Remember to check the **Take Action! CD** and the book's **companion Web site** to find additional resources for this chapter.

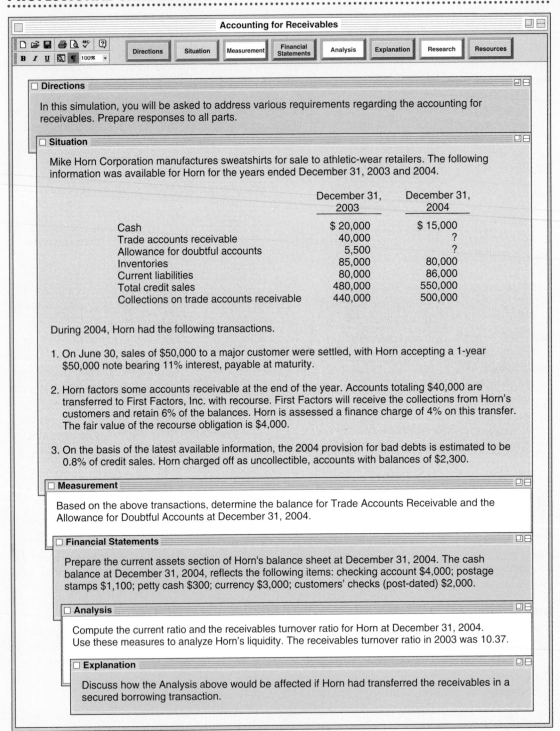

CHAPTER 8

Valuation of Inventories: A Cost Basis Approach

Inventories in the Crystal Ball

Policy makers, economists, and investors all want to know where the economy is headed. For example, if the economy is headed for a slow-down, it might be prudent on the part of the Federal Reserve to cut interest rates or for Congress to consider a tax cut to head off an economic downturn. Information on inventories is a key input into various decision makers' economic prediction models. For example, every month the U.S. Commerce Department reports data on inventory levels and sales. As shown in the table below, in a recent month these data indicated an increasing level of inventories.

November Inventory and Sales
(billions of dollars, seasonally adjusted)

	1999	2000	Percent Change
Total business inventories	$1,145	$1,221	+6.64%
Total business sales	$ 862	$ 896	+3.94%
Inventory/Sales ratio	1.33	1.36	

More importantly, not only were inventories rising, but they were rising at a faster rate than sales. These data raised some warnings about future economic growth, because rising inventory levels relative to sales indicate that consumers are trimming spending faster than companies can slow production.[1]

These data also raised warning flags for investors in individual companies. As one analyst remarked, "When inventory grows faster than sales, profits drop." That is, when companies face slowing sales and growing inventory, then markdowns in prices are usually not far behind. These markdowns, in turn, lead to lower sales revenue and income, as profit margins on sales are squeezed.[2]

Research supporting these observations has found that increases in retailers' inventory translate into lower prices and lower net income.[3] Interestingly, the same research found that for manufacturers, only increases in finished goods inventory lead to future profit declines. Increases in raw materials and work-in-process inventories provide a signal that the company is building its inventory to meet increased demand, and therefore future sales and income will be higher. These research results reinforce the usefulness of the GAAP requirement that a manufacturer's inventory components should be disclosed on the balance sheet or in related notes.

LEARNING OBJECTIVES

After studying this chapter, you should be able to:

1. **Identify major classifications of inventory.**
2. **Distinguish between perpetual and periodic inventory systems.**
3. **Identify the effects of inventory errors on the financial statements.**
4. **Identify the items that should be included as inventory cost.**
5. **Describe and compare the flow assumptions used in accounting for inventories.**
6. **Explain the significance and use of a LIFO reserve.**
7. **Explain the effect of LIFO liquidations.**
8. **Explain the dollar-value LIFO method.**
9. **Identify the major advantages and disadvantages of LIFO.**
10. **Identify the reasons why a given inventory method is selected.**

---

[1] N. Kulish, "Business Inventories Rose for November, Possibly Adding Evidence of Slowdown," *Wall Street Journal, Interactive Edition* (January 17, 2001).

[2] S. Pulliam, "Heard on the Street," *Wall Street Journal* (May 21, 1997), p. C1.

[3] Victor Bernard and J. Noel, "Do Inventory Disclosures Predict Sales and Earnings?" *Journal of Accounting, Auditing, and Finance* (March 1991), pp. 145–182.

PREVIEW OF CHAPTER 8

As indicated in the opening story, information on inventories can provide important signals to investors. As a result, proper accounting and reporting for this asset contributes to the usefulness of the financial statements. The purpose of this chapter is to discuss the basic issues related to accounting and reporting for the costs of inventory. The content and organization of the chapter are as follows.

VALUATION OF INVENTORIES: A COST BASIS APPROACH

- **Inventory Classification and Control**
  - Classification
  - Control
- **Physical Goods Included in Inventory**
  - Goods in transit
  - Consigned goods
  - Special sales agreements
  - Inventory errors
- **Costs Included in Inventory**
  - Product costs
  - Period costs
  - Purchase discounts
- **Cost Flow Assumptions**
  - Specific identification
  - Average cost
  - FIFO
  - LIFO
- **LIFO: Special Issues**
  - LIFO reserve
  - LIFO liquidation
  - Dollar-value LIFO
  - Comparison of LIFO approaches
  - Advantages of LIFO
  - Disadvantages of LIFO
- **Basis for Selection**
  - Summary of inventory valuation methods

INVENTORY CLASSIFICATION AND CONTROL

Classification

OBJECTIVE 1
Identify major classifications of inventory.

Inventories are asset items held for sale in the ordinary course of business or goods that will be used or consumed in the production of goods to be sold. The description and measurement of inventory require careful attention because the investment in inventories is frequently the largest current asset of merchandising (retail) and manufacturing businesses.

A **merchandising company**, such as **Wal-Mart**, ordinarily purchases its merchandise in a form ready for sale. It reports the cost assigned to unsold units left on hand as **merchandise inventory**. Only one inventory account, Merchandise Inventory, appears in the financial statements.

Manufacturing companies, on the other hand, produce goods which may be sold to merchandising companies. Many of the largest U.S. businesses are manufacturers—**Boeing, IBM, ExxonMobil, Procter & Gamble, Ford, Motorola**, to name only a few. Although the products they produce may be quite different, manufacturers normally have three inventory accounts—Raw Materials, Work in Process, and Finished Goods.

UNDERLYING CONCEPTS

Because inventory provides future economic benefits to the company (revenue from sales), it meets the definition of an asset. Inventory costs will be matched against revenue in the period that sales occur.

The cost assigned to goods and materials on hand but not yet placed into production is reported as **raw materials inventory**. Raw materials include the wood to make a baseball bat or the steel to make a car. These materials ultimately can be traced directly to the end product.

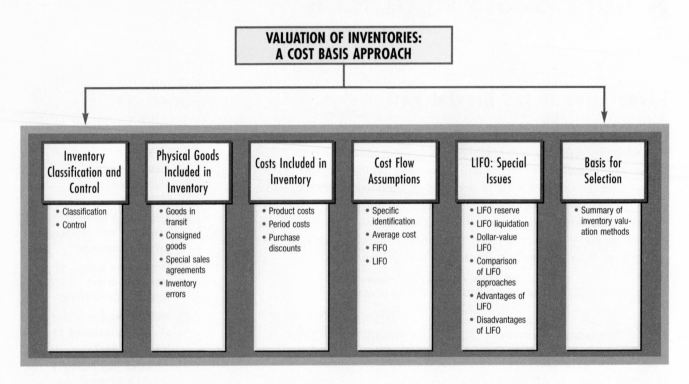

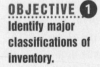

At any point in a continuous production process some units are not completely processed. The cost of the raw material on which production has been started but not completed, plus the direct labor cost applied specifically to this material and a ratable share of manufacturing overhead costs, constitute the **work in process inventory**.

The costs identified with the completed but unsold units on hand at the end of the fiscal period are reported as **finished goods inventory**. The current assets sections presented in Illustration 8-1 contrast the financial statement presentation of inventories of a merchandising company and those of a manufacturing company. The remainder of the balance sheet is essentially similar for the two types of companies.

ILLUSTRATION 8-1
Comparison of Current Assets Presentation for Merchandising and Manufacturing Companies

Merchandising Company
Wal-Mart
Balance Sheet
January 31, 2002

Current assets (in millions)	
Cash and cash equivalents	$ 2,161
Receivables	2,000
Inventories at LIFO cost	22,614
Prepaid expenses and other	1,471
Total current assets	$28,246

Manufacturing Company
Adolph Coors Company
Balance Sheet
December 30, 2001

Current assets (in millions)		
Cash and cash equivalents		$ 77
Short-term investments		233
Accounts and notes receivable (net)		109
Inventories		
Finished	$ 32	
In process	23	
Raw materials	42	
Packaging materials	18	
Total inventories		115
Prepaid expenses and other		73
Total current assets		$607

A manufacturing company also might include a **Manufacturing** or **Factory Supplies Inventory** account. In it would be items such as machine oils, nails, cleaning materials, and the like that are used in production but are not the primary materials being processed. The flow of costs through a merchandising company is different from that of a manufacturing company, as shown in Illustration 8-2.

Additional Inventory Disclosures

ILLUSTRATION 8-2
Flow of Costs through Manufacturing and Merchandising Companies

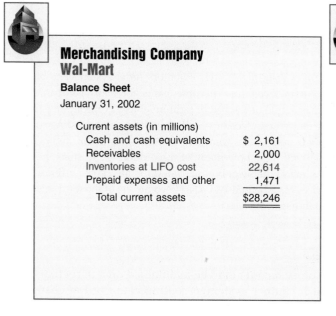

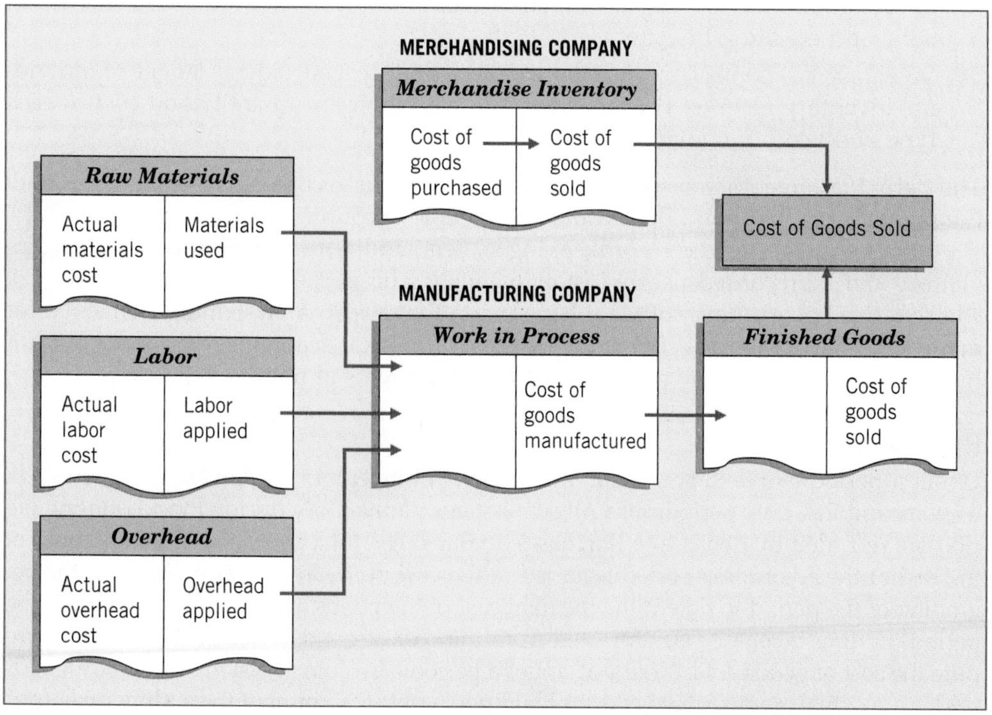

Control

For various reasons, management is vitally interested in inventory planning and control. An accurate accounting system with up-to-date records is essential. If unsalable items have accumulated in the inventory, a potential loss exists. Sales and customers may be lost if products ordered by customers are not available in the desired style, quality, and quantity. Also, businesses must monitor inventory levels carefully to limit the financing costs of carrying large inventories.

WHAT DO THE NUMBERS MEAN?

STAYING LEAN

With the introduction and use of "just-in-time"s (JIT) inventory order systems and better supplier relationships, inventory levels have become leaner for many companies.

Wal-Mart provides a classic example of the use of tight inventory controls. Department managers use a scanner that when placed over the bar code corresponding to a particular item, will tell them how many items were sold yesterday, last week, and over the same period last year. It will tell them how many of those items are in stock, how many are on the way, and how many the neighboring Wal-Marts are carrying (in case one store runs out). Such practices have helped Wal-Mart become one of the top-ranked companies on the Fortune 500 in terms of sales.

OBJECTIVE 2
Distinguish between perpetual and periodic inventory systems.

Perpetual System

As indicated in Chapter 3, inventory records may be maintained on a perpetual or periodic basis. Under a **perpetual inventory system**, a continuous record of changes in inventory is maintained in the Inventory account. That is, all purchases and sales (issues) of goods are recorded directly in the Inventory account **as they occur**. The accounting features of a perpetual inventory system are:

1. Purchases of merchandise for resale or raw materials for production are debited to Inventory rather than to Purchases.
2. Freight-in, purchase returns and allowances, and purchase discounts are recorded in Inventory rather than in separate accounts.
3. Cost of goods sold is recognized for each sale by debiting the account Cost of Goods Sold, and crediting Inventory.
4. Inventory is a control account that is supported by a subsidiary ledger of individual inventory records. The subsidiary records show the quantity and cost of each type of inventory on hand.

The perpetual inventory system provides a continuous record of the balances in both the Inventory account and the Cost of Goods Sold account.

Under a computerized recordkeeping system, additions to and issuances from inventory can be recorded nearly instantaneously. The popularity and affordability of computerized accounting software have made the perpetual system cost-effective for many kinds of businesses. Recording sales with optical scanners at the cash register has been incorporated into perpetual inventory systems at many retail stores.

Periodic System

Under a **periodic inventory system**, the quantity of inventory on hand is determined, as its name implies, only periodically. All acquisitions of inventory during the accounting period are recorded by debits to a Purchases account. The total in the Purchases account at the end of the accounting period is added to the cost of the inventory on hand at the beginning of the period to determine the total cost of the goods available for sale during the period. Ending inventory is subtracted from the cost of goods available for sale to compute the cost of goods sold. Note that under a periodic inventory system, the cost of goods sold is a residual amount that is dependent upon a physical count of the ending inventory.

The **physical inventory count** required by a periodic system is taken once a year at the end of the year.[4] However, most companies need more current information regarding their inventory levels to protect against stockouts or overpurchasing and to aid in the preparation of monthly or quarterly financial data. As a consequence, many companies use a **modified perpetual inventory system** in which increases and decreases in quantities only—not dollar amounts—are kept in a detailed inventory record. It is merely a memorandum device outside the double-entry system which helps in determining the level of inventory at any point in time.

Whether a company maintains a perpetual inventory in quantities and dollars, quantities only, or has no perpetual inventory record at all, it probably takes a physical inventory once a year. No matter what type of inventory records are in use or how well organized the procedures for recording purchases and requisitions, the danger of loss and error is always present. Waste, breakage, theft, improper entry, failure to prepare or record requisitions, and any number of similar possibilities may cause the inventory records to differ from the actual inventory on hand. This requires periodic verification of the inventory records by actual count, weight, or measurement. These counts are compared with the detailed inventory records. The records are corrected to agree with the quantities actually on hand.

Insofar as possible, the physical inventory should be taken near the end of a company's fiscal year so that correct inventory quantities are available for use in preparing annual accounting reports and statements. Because this is not always possible, however, physical inventories taken within two or three months of the year's end are satisfactory, if the detailed inventory records are maintained with a fair degree of accuracy.

To illustrate the difference between a perpetual and a periodic system, assume that Fesmire Company had the following transactions during the current year.

Beginning inventory	100 units at $ 6 = $ 600
Purchases	900 units at $ 6 = $5,400
Sales	600 units at $12 = $7,200
Ending inventory	400 units at $ 6 = $2,400

The entries to record these transactions during the current year are shown in Illustration 8-3.

ILLUSTRATION 8-3
Comparative Entries—Perpetual vs. Periodic

Perpetual Inventory System			Periodic Inventory System		
1. Beginning inventory, 100 units at $6:					
The inventory account shows the inventory on hand at $600.			The inventory account shows the inventory on hand at $600.		
2. Purchase 900 units at $6:					
Inventory	5,400		Purchases	5,400	
Accounts Payable		5,400	Accounts Payable		5,400
3. Sale of 600 units at $12:					
Accounts Receivable	7,200		Accounts Receivable	7,200	
Sales		7,200	Sales		7,200
Cost of Goods Sold (600 at $6)	3,600		(No entry)		
Inventory		3,600			
4. End-of-period entries for inventory accounts, 400 units at $6:					
No entry necessary.			Inventory (ending, by count)	2,400	
The account, Inventory, shows the ending balance of $2,400 ($600 + $5,400 − $3,600).			Cost of Goods Sold	3,600	
			Purchases		5,400
			Inventory (beginning)		600

[4]In recent years, some companies have developed methods of determining inventories, including statistical sampling, that are sufficiently reliable to make unnecessary an annual physical count of each item of inventory.

When a perpetual inventory system is used and a difference exists between the perpetual inventory balance and the physical inventory count, a separate entry is needed to adjust the perpetual inventory account. To illustrate, assume that at the end of the reporting period, the perpetual inventory account reported an inventory balance of $4,000, but a physical count indicated $3,800 was actually on hand. The entry to record the necessary writedown is as follows.

Inventory Over and Short	200	
Inventory		200

Perpetual inventory overages and shortages generally represent a misstatement of cost of goods sold. The difference is a result of normal and expected shrinkage, breakage, shoplifting, incorrect record keeping, and the like. Inventory Over and Short would therefore be an adjustment of cost of goods sold. In practice, the account Inventory Over and Short is sometimes reported in the "Other revenues and gains" or "Other expenses and losses" section of the income statement, depending on its balance.

Note that in a periodic inventory system the account Inventory Over and Short does not arise because there are no accounting records available against which to compare the physical count. Thus, inventory overages and shortages are buried in cost of goods sold.

BASIC ISSUES IN INVENTORY VALUATION

Because the goods sold or used during an accounting period seldom correspond exactly to the goods bought or produced during that period, the physical inventory either increases or decreases. The cost of all the goods available for sale or use should be allocated between the goods that were sold or used and those that are still on hand. The **cost of goods available for sale or use** is the sum of (1) the cost of the goods on hand at the beginning of the period and (2) the cost of the goods acquired or produced during the period. The **cost of goods sold** is the difference between the cost of goods available for sale during the period and the cost of goods on hand at the end of the period.

ILLUSTRATION 8-4
Computation of Cost of Goods Sold

Beginning inventory, Jan. 1	$100,000
Cost of goods acquired or produced during the year	800,000
Total cost of goods available for sale	900,000
Ending inventory, Dec. 31	200,000
Cost of goods sold during the year	$700,000

The valuation of inventories can be a complex process that requires determination of the following:

1. **The physical goods to be included in inventory** (who owns the goods?—goods in transit, consigned goods, special sales agreements).
2. **The costs to be included in inventory** (product vs. period costs, treatment of purchase discounts).
3. **The cost flow assumption to be adopted** (specific identification, average cost, FIFO, LIFO, retail, etc.).

We will explore these basic issues in the next three sections of the chapter.

PHYSICAL GOODS INCLUDED IN INVENTORY

Technically, purchases should be recorded when legal title to the goods passes to the buyer. General practice, however, is to record acquisitions when the goods are received, because it is difficult for the buyer to determine the exact time of legal passage of title for every purchase. In addition, no material error is likely to result from such a practice if it is consistently applied. Illustration 8-5 indicates the general guidelines used in evaluating whether the seller or the buyer reports an item as inventory.

ILLUSTRATION 8-5
Guidelines for Determining Ownership

Goods in Transit

Sometimes purchased merchandise is in transit—not yet received—at the end of a fiscal period. The accounting for these shipped goods depends on who owns them. That can be determined by application of the "passage of title" rule. If the goods are shipped **f.o.b. shipping point**, title passes to the buyer when the seller delivers the goods to the common carrier, who acts as an agent for the buyer. (The abbreviation f.o.b. stands for free on board.) If the goods are shipped **f.o.b. destination**, title does not pass until the buyer receives the goods from the common carrier. "Shipping point" and "destination" are often designated by a particular location, for example, f.o.b. Denver.

The accounting rule is that **goods to which legal title has passed should be recorded as purchases of the fiscal period**. Goods shipped f.o.b. shipping point that are in transit at the end of the period belong to the buyer and should be shown in the buyer's records. Legal title to these goods passed to the buyer when the goods were shipped. To disregard such purchases would result in an understatement of inventories and accounts payable in the balance sheet and an understatement of purchases and ending inventories in the income statement.

Consigned Goods

A specialized method of marketing certain products uses a device known as a **consignment** shipment. Under this arrangement, one party (the consignor) ships merchandise to another (the consignee), who acts as the consignor's agent in selling the **consigned goods**. The consignee agrees to accept the goods without any liability, except to exercise due care and reasonable protection from loss or damage, until the goods are sold to a third party. When the consignee sells the goods, the revenue, less a selling commission and expenses incurred in accomplishing the sale, is remitted to the consignor.

Goods out on consignment remain the property of the consignor and are included in the consignor's inventory at purchase price or production cost. Occasionally, the inventory out on consignment is shown as a separate item, but unless the amount is large there is little need for this. Sometimes the inventory on consignment is reported in the notes to the financial statements. For example, **Eagle Clothes, Inc.** reported the following related to consigned goods: "Inventories consist of finished goods shipped on consignment to customers of the Company's subsidiary **April-Marcus, Inc.**"

The consignee makes no entry to the inventory account for goods received because they are the property of the consignor. The consignee should be extremely careful *not* to include any of the goods consigned as a part of inventory.

Special Sales Agreements

As indicated earlier, transfer of legal title is the general guideline used to determine whether an item should be included in inventory. Unfortunately, transfer of legal title and the underlying substance of the transaction often do not match. For example, it is possible that legal title has passed to the purchaser, but the seller of the goods retains the risks of ownership. Conversely, transfer of legal title may not occur, but the economic substance of the transaction is such that the seller no longer retains the risks of ownership. Three special sales situations are illustrated here to indicate the types of problems encountered in practice. These are:

1. Sales with buyback agreement.
2. Sales with high rates of return.
3. Sales on installment.

Sales with Buyback Agreement

Sometimes an enterprise finances its inventory without reporting either the liability or the inventory on its balance sheet. Such an approach—often referred to as a **product financing arrangement**—usually involves a "sale" with either an implicit or explicit "buyback" agreement. To illustrate, Hill Enterprises transfers ("sells") inventory to Chase, Inc. and simultaneously agrees to repurchase this merchandise at a specified price over a specified period of time. Chase then uses the inventory as collateral and borrows against it. Chase uses the loan proceeds to pay Hill. Hill repurchases the inventory in the future, and Chase employs the proceeds from repayment to meet its loan obligation.

UNDERLYING CONCEPTS

Recognizing revenue at the time the inventory is "parked" violates the revenue recognition principle. This principle requires that the earning process be substantially completed; in this case, the economic benefits remain under the control of the seller.

The essence of this transaction is that Hill Enterprises is financing its inventory—and retaining risk of ownership—even though technical legal title to the merchandise was transferred to Chase. The advantage to Hill Enterprises in structuring a transaction in this manner is the avoidance of personal property taxes in certain states, the removal of the current liability from its balance sheet, and the ability to manipulate income. The advantages to Chase are that the purchase of the goods may solve a LIFO liquidation problem (discussed later), or that Chase may be interested in a reciprocal agreement at a later date.

These arrangements are often described in practice as "**parking transactions**," because the seller simply parks the inventory on another enterprise's balance sheet for a short period of time. When a repurchase agreement exists at a set price and this price covers all costs of the inventory plus related holding costs, the inventory and related liability should be reported on the seller's books.[5]

Sales with High Rates of Return

Formal or informal agreements often exist in industries such as publishing, music, toys, and sporting goods that permit inventory to be returned for a full or partial refund. To illustrate, Quality Publishing Company sells textbooks to Campus Bookstores with an agreement that any books not sold may be returned for full credit. In the past, approximately 25 percent of the textbooks sold to Campus Bookstores were returned. How should Quality Publishing report its sales transactions? One alternative is to record the sale at the full amount and establish an estimated sales returns and allowances account. A second possibility is to not record any sale until circumstances indicate the amount of inventory the buyer will return. The key question is: Under what circumstances should the inventory be considered sold and removed from Quality's inventory? The

[5]"Accounting for Product Financing Arrangements," *Statement of Financial Accounting Standards No. 49* (Stamford, Conn.: FASB, 1981).

answer is that **when the amount of returns can be reasonably estimated**, the goods should be considered sold. Conversely, if returns are unpredictable, removal of these goods from the inventory of the seller is inappropriate.[6]

Sales on Installment

"Goods sold on installment" describes any type of sale in which payment is required in periodic installments over an extended period of time. Because the risk of loss from uncollectibles is higher in installment sale situations than in other sales transactions, the seller often withholds legal title to the merchandise until all the payments have been made. The question is whether the inventory should be considered sold, even though legal title has not passed. The answer is that **the goods should be excluded from the seller's inventory if the percentage of bad debts can be reasonably estimated**. In some cases, the goods should be removed from inventory, although legal title may not have passed.

UNDERLYING CONCEPTS

Revenues should be recognized because they have been substantially earned and are reasonably estimable. Collection is not the most critical event because bad debts can be reasonably estimated.

NO PARKING!

WHAT DO THE NUMBERS MEAN?

At **Kurzweil Applied Intelligence Inc.** millions of dollars in phony inventory sales were booked during a two-year period that straddled two audits and an initial public stock offering. Employees dummied up phony shipping documents and logbooks to support bogus sales transactions. High-tech equipment was shipped all right, but not to customers. Instead, the goods were shipped to a public warehouse for "temporary" storage; Kurzweil still had ownership. Some "sold" equipment sat in storage for 17 months. To foil auditors' attempts to verify the existence of the "sold" inventory, Kurzweil employees moved the goods from warehouse to warehouse. To cover the fraudulently recorded sales transactions as auditors closed in, the still-hidden goods were brought back, under the pretense that they were returned by customers. When the fraud was finally exposed in mid-1994, the bottom dropped out of Kurzweil's stock.

Source: Adapted from "Anatomy of a Fraud," *Business Week* (September 16, 1996), pp. 90–94.

Effect of Inventory Errors

OBJECTIVE 3
Identify the effects of inventory errors on the financial statements.

Items incorrectly included or excluded in determining cost of goods sold by inventory misstatements will result in errors in the financial statements. Let's look at two cases.

Ending Inventory Misstated

What would happen if the beginning inventory and purchases are recorded correctly, but some items are not included in ending inventory? In this situation, we would have the following effects on the financial statements at the end of the period.

ILLUSTRATION 8-6
Financial Statement Effects of Misstated Ending Inventory

Balance Sheet		Income Statement	
Inventory	Understated	Cost of goods sold	Overstated
Retained earnings	Understated		
Working capital (current assets less current liabilities)	Understated	Net income	Understated
Current ratio (current assets divided by current liabilities)	Understated		

Working capital and the current ratio are understated because ending inventory is understated. Net income is understated because cost of goods sold is overstated.

[6]"Revenue Recognition When Right of Return Exists," *Statement of Financial Accounting Standards No. 48* (Stamford, Conn.: FASB, 1981).

UNDERLYING CONCEPTS

When inventory is misstated, its presentation lacks representational faithfulness.

To illustrate the effect on net income over a two-year period, assume that the ending inventory of Jay Weiseman Corp. is understated by $10,000 and that all other items are correctly stated. The effect of this error will be to decrease net income in the current year and to increase net income in the following year. The error will be counterbalanced (offset) in the next period because beginning inventory will be understated and net income will be overstated. Both net income figures are misstated, but the total for the two years is correct, as shown in Illustration 8-7.

ILLUSTRATION 8-7
Effect of Ending Inventory Error on Two Periods

JAY WEISEMAN CORP.
(All figures assumed)

	Incorrect Recording		Correct Recording	
	2003	2004	2003	2004
Revenues	$100,000	$100,000	$100,000	$100,000
Cost of goods sold				
Beginning inventory	25,000	20,000	25,000	30,000
Purchased or produced	45,000	60,000	45,000	60,000
Goods available for sale	70,000	80,000	70,000	90,000
Less: Ending inventory	20,000*	40,000	30,000	40,000
Cost of goods sold	50,000	40,000	40,000	50,000
Gross profit	50,000	60,000	60,000	50,000
Administrative and selling expenses	40,000	40,000	40,000	40,000
Net income	$ 10,000	$ 20,000	$ 20,000	$ 10,000
	Total income for two years = $30,000		Total income for two years = $30,000	

*Ending inventory understated by $10,000 in 2003.

If ending inventory is *overstated*, the reverse effect occurs. Inventory, working capital, current ratio, and net income are overstated, and cost of goods sold is understated. The effect of the error on net income will be counterbalanced in the next year, but both years' net income figures will be misstated.

Purchases and Inventory Misstated

Suppose that certain goods that the company owns are not recorded as a purchase and are not counted in ending inventory. The effect on the financial statements (assuming this is a purchase on account) is as follows.

ILLUSTRATION 8-8
Financial Statement Effects of Misstated Purchases and Inventory

Balance Sheet		Income Statement	
Inventory	Understated	Purchases	Understated
Retained earnings	No effect	Cost of goods sold	No effect
Accounts payable	Understated	Net income	No effect
Working capital	No effect	Inventory (ending)	Understated
Current ratio	Overstated		

Omission of goods from purchases and inventory results in an understatement of inventory and accounts payable in the balance sheet and an understatement of purchases and ending inventory in the income statement. Net income for the period is not affected by the omission of such goods. This is because purchases and ending inventory are both understated by the same amount—the error thereby offsetting itself in cost of goods sold. Total working capital is unchanged, but the current ratio is overstated because of the omission of equal amounts from inventory and accounts payable.

To illustrate the effect on the current ratio, assume that Larry Mall Company **understated** accounts payable and ending inventory by $40,000. The understated and correct data are shown below.

Purchases and Ending Inventory Understated		Purchases and Ending Inventory Correct	
Current assets	$120,000	Current assets	$160,000
Current liabilities	$ 40,000	Current liabilities	$ 80,000
Current ratio	3 to 1	Current ratio	2 to 1

ILLUSTRATION 8-9
Effects of Purchases and Ending Inventory Errors

The correct ratio is 2 to 1, rather than 3 to 1 as indicated by the understated data. Thus, understatement of accounts payable and ending inventory can lead to a "window dressing" of the current ratio. That is, they can make the current ratio appear better than it is.

If both purchases (on account) and ending inventory are **overstated**, then the effects on the balance sheet are exactly the reverse: Inventory and accounts payable are overstated, and the current ratio is understated. Working capital is not affected. Cost of goods sold and net income are not affected because the errors offset one another.

We cannot overemphasize the importance of a proper inventory measurement in presenting accurate financial statements. For example, **Leslie Fay**, a women's apparel maker, had accounting irregularities that wiped out one year's net income and caused a restatement of the prior year's earnings. One reason: it inflated inventory and deflated cost of goods sold. **Anixter Bros. Inc.** had to restate its income by $1.7 million because an accountant in the antenna manufacturing division overstated the ending inventory, thereby reducing its cost of sales. Similarly, **AM International** allegedly recorded as sold products that were only being rented. As a result, inaccurate inventory figures inappropriately added $7.9 million to pretax income.

COSTS INCLUDED IN INVENTORY

OBJECTIVE 4
Identify the items that should be included as inventory cost.

One of the most important problems in dealing with inventories concerns the amount at which the inventory should be carried in the accounts. **The acquisition of inventories, like other assets, is generally accounted for on a basis of cost.** (Other bases are discussed in Chapter 9.)

Product Costs

Product costs are those costs that "attach" to the inventory and are recorded in the inventory account. These costs are directly connected with the bringing of goods to the place of business of the buyer and converting such goods to a salable condition. Such charges would include freight charges on goods purchased, other direct costs of acquisition, and labor and other production costs incurred in processing the goods up to the time of sale.

It would seem proper also to allocate to inventories a share of any buying costs or expenses of a purchasing department, storage costs, and other costs incurred in storing or handling the goods before they are sold. Because of the practical difficulties involved in allocating such costs and expenses, however, these items are not ordinarily included in valuing inventories.

Period Costs

Selling expenses and, under ordinary circumstances, **general and administrative expenses** are not considered to be directly related to the acquisition or production of goods, and therefore they are not considered to be a part of inventories. Such costs are called **period costs**.

Conceptually, these expenses are as much a cost of the product as the initial purchase price and related freight charges attached to the product. Why then are these costs not considered inventoriable items? Selling expenses are generally considered as more directly related to the cost of goods sold than to the unsold inventory. In most cases, though, the costs, especially administrative expenses, are so unrelated or indirectly related to the immediate production process that any allocation is purely arbitrary.

Interest costs associated with getting inventories ready for sale usually are expensed as incurred. A major argument for this approach is that interest costs are really a cost of financing. Others have argued, however, that interest costs incurred to finance activities associated with bringing inventories to a condition and place ready for sale are as much a cost of the asset as materials, labor, and overhead and, therefore, should be capitalized.[7] **The FASB has ruled that interest costs related to assets constructed for internal use or assets produced as discrete projects (such as ships or real estate projects) for sale or lease should be capitalized.**[8] The FASB emphasized that these discrete projects should take considerable time, entail substantial expenditures, and be likely to involve significant amounts of interest cost. Interest costs should not be capitalized for inventories that are routinely manufactured or otherwise produced in large quantities on a repetitive basis, because the informational benefit does not justify the cost.

UNDERLYING CONCEPTS

In capitalizing interest, both constraints—materiality and cost/benefit—are applied.

Treatment of Purchase Discounts

The use of a **Purchase Discounts** account indicates that the company is reporting its purchases and accounts payable at the gross amount. Another approach is to record the purchases and accounts payable at an amount **net of the cash discounts**. This treatment is considered to be better for two reasons: (1) It provides a correct reporting of the cost of the asset and related liability. (2) It presents the opportunity to measure inefficiency of management if the discount is not taken. In the net approach, the failure to take a purchase discount within the discount period is recorded in a Purchase Discounts Lost account (for which management is responsible).

To illustrate the difference between the gross and net methods, assume the following transactions.

ILLUSTRATION 8-10
Entries under Gross and Net Methods

Gross Method			Net Method		
Purchase cost $10,000, terms 2/10, net 30:					
Purchases	10,000		Purchases	9,800	
Accounts Payable		10,000	Accounts Payable		9,800
Invoices of $4,000 are paid within discount period:					
Accounts Payable	4,000		Accounts Payable	3,920	
Purchase Discounts		80	Cash		3,920
Cash		3,920			
Invoices of $6,000 are paid after discount period:					
Accounts Payable	6,000		Accounts Payable	5,880	
Cash		6,000	Purchase Discounts Lost	120	
			Cash		6,000

UNDERLYING CONCEPTS

Not using the net method because of resultant difficulties is an example of the application of the cost-benefit constraint.

If the **gross method** is employed, purchase discounts should be reported as a deduction from purchases on the income statement. If the **net method** is used, purchase discounts lost should be considered a financial expense and reported in the "Other expenses and losses" section of the income statement.

[7]The reporting rules related to interest cost capitalization have their greatest impact in accounting for long-term assets and therefore are discussed in detail in Chapter 10.

[8]"Capitalization of Interest Cost," *Statement of Financial Accounting Standards No. 34* (Stamford, Conn.: FASB, 1979).

Many believe that the difficulty involved in using the somewhat more complicated net method is not justified considering the resulting benefits. This could account for the widespread use of the less logical but simpler gross method. In addition, some contend that management is reluctant to report in the financial statements the amount of purchase discounts lost.

YOU MAY NEED A MAP

WHAT DO THE NUMBERS MEAN?

Does it really matter where companies report certain costs in their income statements? As long as all the costs are included in expenses in the computation of income, why should the "geography" matter?

For e-tailers, such as **Amazon.com** or **Drugstore.com**, *where* certain selling costs are reported does appear to be important. Contrary to well-established retailer practices, these companies insist on reporting some selling costs—fulfillment costs related to inventory shipping and warehousing—as part of administrative expenses, instead of as cost of goods sold. While the practice doesn't affect the bottom line, it does make the e-tailers' gross margins look better. For example, in a recent quarter Amazon.com reported $265 million in these costs. Some experts thought those charges should be included in costs of goods sold, which would make Amazon's gross profit substantially lower than under usual retailer accounting practices, as shown below.

(in millions)

	E-tailer Reporting	Traditional Reporting
Sales	$2,795	$2,795
Cost of goods sold	2,132	2,397
Gross profit	$ 663	$ 398
Gross margin %	24%	14%

Similarly, if **Drugstore.com** and **eToys.com** were to make a similar adjustment, their gross margins would go from positive to negative.

Thus, if you want to be able to compare the operating results of e-tailers to other traditional retailers, it might be a good idea to have a good accounting map in order to navigate their income statements and how they report certain selling costs.

Source: Adapted from P. Elstrom, "The End of Fuzzy Math?" *Business Week*, e.Biz–Net Worth (December 11, 2000).

WHAT COST FLOW ASSUMPTION SHOULD BE ADOPTED?

OBJECTIVE 5
Describe and compare the flow assumptions used in accounting for inventories.

During any given fiscal period it is very likely that merchandise will be purchased at several different prices. If inventories are to be priced at cost and numerous purchases have been made at different unit costs, which of the various cost prices should be used? Conceptually, a specific identification of the given items sold and unsold seems optimal, but this measure is often not only expensive but impossible to achieve. Consequently, one of several systematic inventory **cost flow assumptions** is used. Indeed, the actual physical flow of goods and the cost flow assumption are often quite different. **There is no requirement that the cost flow assumption adopted be consistent with the physical movement of goods.** The major objective in selecting a method should be to choose the one that, under the circumstances, most clearly reflects periodic income.[9]

To illustrate, assume that Call-Mart Inc. had the following transactions in its first month of operations.

[9]"Restatement and Revision of Accounting Research Bulletins," *Accounting Research Bulletin No. 43* (New York: AICPA, 1953), Ch. 4, Statement 4.

Date	Purchases	Sold or Issued	Balance
March 2	2,000 @ $4.00		2,000 units
March 15	6,000 @ $4.40		8,000 units
March 19		4,000 units	4,000 units
March 30	2,000 @ $4.75		6,000 units

From this information, we can compute the ending inventory of 6,000 units and the cost of goods available for sale (beginning inventory + purchases) of $43,900 [(2,000 @ $4.00) + (6,000 @ $4.40) + (2,000 @ $4.75)]. The question is, which price or prices should be assigned to the 6,000 units of ending inventory? The answer depends on which cost flow assumption is employed.

Specific Identification

Specific identification calls for identifying each item sold and each item in inventory. The costs of the specific items sold are included in the cost of goods sold, and the costs of the specific items on hand are included in the inventory. This method may be used only in instances where it is practical to separate physically the different purchases made. It can be successfully applied in situations where a relatively small number of costly, easily distinguishable items are handled. In the retail trade this includes some types of jewelry, fur coats, automobiles, and some furniture. In manufacturing it includes special orders and many products manufactured under a job cost system.

To illustrate the specific identification method, assume that Call-Mart Inc.'s 6,000 units of inventory is composed of 1,000 units from the March 2 purchase, 3,000 from the March 15 purchase, and 2,000 from the March 30 purchase. The ending inventory and cost of goods sold would be computed as shown in Illustration 8-11.

ILLUSTRATION 8-11
Specific Identification Method

Date	No. of Units	Unit Cost	Total Cost
March 2	1,000	$4.00	$ 4,000
March 15	3,000	4.40	13,200
March 30	2,000	4.75	9,500
Ending inventory	6,000		$26,700

Cost of goods available for sale (computed in previous section)	$43,900
Deduct: Ending inventory	26,700
Cost of goods sold	$17,200

Conceptually, this method appears ideal because actual costs are matched against actual revenue, and ending inventory is reported at actual cost. In other words, under specific identification the cost flow matches the physical flow of the goods. On closer observation, however, this method has certain deficiencies.

One argument against specific identification is that it makes it possible to manipulate net income. For example, assume that a wholesaler purchases otherwise-identical plywood early in the year at three different prices. When the plywood is sold, the wholesaler can select either the lowest or the highest price to charge to expense simply by selecting the plywood from a specific lot for delivery to the customer. A business manager, therefore, can manipulate net income simply by delivering to the customer the higher- or lower-priced item, depending on whether higher or lower reported earnings is desired for the period.

Another problem relates to the arbitrary allocation of costs that sometimes occurs with specific inventory items. In certain circumstances, it is difficult to relate adequately, for example, shipping charges, storage costs, and discounts directly to a given inventory item. The alternative, then, is to allocate these costs somewhat arbitrarily, which leads to a "breakdown" in the precision of the specific identification method.[10]

Average Cost

As the name implies, the **average cost method** prices items in the inventory on the basis of the average cost of all similar goods available during the period. To illustrate, assuming that Call-Mart Inc. used the periodic inventory method, the ending inventory and cost of goods sold would be computed as follows using a **weighted-average method**.

ILLUSTRATION 8-12
Weighted-Average Method—Periodic Inventory

Date of Invoice	No. Units	Unit Cost	Total Cost
March 2	2,000	$4.00	$ 8,000
March 15	6,000	4.40	26,400
March 30	2,000	4.75	9,500
Total goods available	10,000		$43,900

Weighted-average cost per unit $\frac{\$43,900}{10,000} = \$4.39$

Inventory in units 6,000 units
Ending inventory 6,000 × $4.39 = $26,340

Cost of goods available for sale	$43,900
Deduct: Ending inventory	26,340
Cost of goods sold	$17,560

If the company has a beginning inventory, it is included both in the total units available and in the total cost of goods available in computing the average cost per unit.

Another average cost method is the **moving-average method**, which is used with perpetual inventory records. The application of the average cost method for perpetual records is shown in Illustration 8-13.

ILLUSTRATION 8-13
Moving-Average Method—Perpetual Inventory

Date	Purchased		Sold or Issued	Balance	
March 2	(2,000 @ $4.00)	$ 8,000		(2,000 @ $4.00)	$ 8,000
March 15	(6,000 @ 4.40)	26,400		(8,000 @ 4.30)	34,400
March 19			(4,000 @ $4.30) $17,200	(4,000 @ 4.30)	17,200
March 30	(2,000 @ 4.75)	9,500		(6,000 @ 4.45)	26,700

In this method, a **new average unit cost** is computed each time a purchase is made. On March 15, after 6,000 units are purchased for $26,400, 8,000 units costing $34,400 ($8,000 plus $26,400) are on hand. The average unit cost is $34,400 divided by 8,000, or $4.30. This unit cost is used in costing withdrawals until another purchase is made, at which time a new average unit cost is computed. Accordingly, the cost of the 4,000 units withdrawn on March 19 is shown at $4.30, a total cost of goods sold of $17,200. On March 30, following the purchase of 2,000 units for $9,500, a new unit cost of $4.45 is determined, resulting in an ending inventory of $26,700.

[10]A good illustration of the cost allocation problem arises in the motion picture industry. Often actors and actresses receive a percentage of net income for a given movie or television program. Some actors who had these arrangements have alleged that their programs have been extremely profitable to the motion picture studios but they have received little in the way of profit sharing. Actors contend that the studios allocate additional costs to successful projects to ensure that there will be no profits to share.

The use of the average cost methods is usually justified on the basis of practical rather than conceptual reasons. These methods are simple to apply, objective, and not as subject to income manipulation as some of the other inventory pricing methods. In addition, proponents of the average cost methods argue that it is often impossible to measure a specific physical flow of inventory, and therefore it is better to cost items on an average-price basis. This argument is particularly persuasive when the inventory involved is relatively homogeneous in nature.

First-In, First-Out (FIFO)

The **FIFO method** assumes that goods are used in the order in which they are purchased. In other words, it assumes that **the first goods purchased are the first used** (in a manufacturing concern) **or the first goods sold** (in a merchandising concern). The inventory remaining must therefore represent the most recent purchases.

To illustrate, assume that Call-Mart Inc. uses the periodic inventory system (amount of inventory computed only at the end of the month). The cost of the ending inventory is computed by taking the cost of the most recent purchase and working back until all units in the inventory are accounted for. The ending inventory and cost of goods sold are determined as shown in Illustration 8-14.

ILLUSTRATION 8-14
FIFO Method—Periodic Inventory

Date	No. Units	Unit Cost	Total Cost
March 30	2,000	$4.75	$ 9,500
March 15	4,000	4.40	17,600
Ending inventory	6,000		$27,100

Cost of goods available for sale	$43,900
Deduct: Ending inventory	27,100
Cost of goods sold	$16,800

If a perpetual inventory system in quantities and dollars is used, a cost figure is attached to each withdrawal. Then the cost of the 4,000 units removed on March 19 would be made up of the items purchased on March 2 and March 15. The inventory on a FIFO-basis perpetual system for Call-Mart Inc. is shown in Illustration 8-15.

ILLUSTRATION 8-15
FIFO Method—Perpetual Inventory

Date	Purchased		Sold or Issued	Balance	
March 2	(2,000 @ $4.00)	$ 8,000		2,000 @ $4.00	$ 8,000
March 15	(6,000 @ 4.40)	26,400		2,000 @ 4.00 6,000 @ 4.40	34,400
March 19			2,000 @ $4.00 2,000 @ 4.40 ($16,800)	4,000 @ 4.40	17,600
March 30	(2,000 @ 4.75)	9,500		4,000 @ 4.40 2,000 @ 4.75	27,100

The ending inventory in this situation is $27,100, and the cost of goods sold is $16,800 [(2,000 @ $4.00) + (2,000 @ $4.40)].

Notice that in these two FIFO examples, the cost of goods sold and ending inventory are the same. **In all cases where FIFO is used, the inventory and cost of goods sold would be the same at the end of the month whether a perpetual or periodic system is used.** This is true because the same costs will always be first in and, therefore, first out—whether cost of goods sold is computed as goods are sold throughout the accounting period (the perpetual system) or as a residual at the end of the accounting period (the periodic system).

One objective of FIFO is to approximate the physical flow of goods. When the physical flow of goods is actually first-in, first-out, the FIFO method closely approximates specific identification. At the same time, it does not permit manipulation of income because the enterprise is not free to pick a certain cost item to be charged to expense.

Another advantage of the FIFO method is that the ending inventory is close to current cost. Because the first goods in are the first goods out, the ending inventory amount will be composed of the most recent purchases. This is particularly true where the inventory turnover is rapid. This approach generally provides a reasonable approximation of replacement cost on the balance sheet when price changes have not occurred since the most recent purchases.

The basic disadvantage of the FIFO method is that current costs are not matched against current revenues on the income statement. The oldest costs are charged against the more current revenue, which can lead to distortions in gross profit and net income.

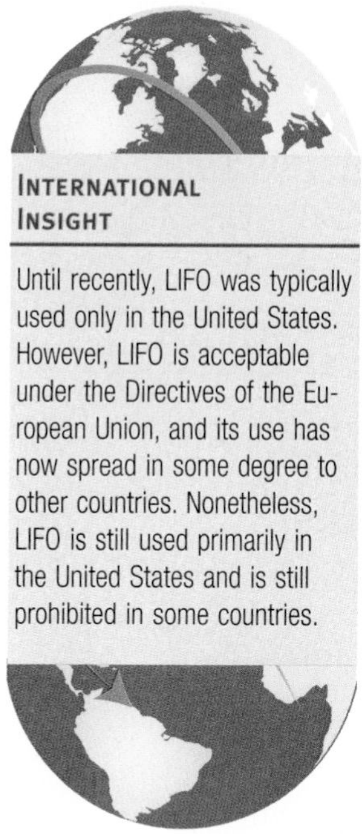

INTERNATIONAL INSIGHT

Until recently, LIFO was typically used only in the United States. However, LIFO is acceptable under the Directives of the European Union, and its use has now spread in some degree to other countries. Nonetheless, LIFO is still used primarily in the United States and is still prohibited in some countries.

Last-In, First-Out (LIFO)

The **LIFO method** first matches against revenue the cost of the last goods purchased. If a periodic inventory is used, then it would be assumed that **the cost of the total quantity sold or issued during the month would have come from the most recent purchases**. The ending inventory would be priced by using the total units as a basis of computation and disregarding the exact dates involved.

To illustrate, the example below assumes that the cost of the 4,000 units withdrawn absorbed the 2,000 units purchased on March 30 and 2,000 of the 6,000 units purchased on March 15. The inventory and related cost of goods sold would then be computed as shown in Illustration 8-16.

ILLUSTRATION 8-16
LIFO Method—Periodic Inventory

Date of Invoice	No. Units	Unit Cost	Total Cost
March 2	2,000	$4.00	$ 8,000
March 15	4,000	4.40	17,600
Ending inventory	6,000		$25,600

Goods available for sale	$43,900
Deduct: Ending inventory	25,600
Cost of goods sold	$18,300

If a perpetual inventory record is kept in quantities and dollars, application of the last-in, first-out method will result in **different ending inventory and cost of goods sold amounts**, as shown in Illustration 8-17.

ILLUSTRATION 8-17
LIFO Method—Perpetual Inventory

Date	Purchased		Sold or Issued	Balance	
March 2	(2,000 @ $4.00)	$ 8,000		2,000 @ $4.00	$ 8,000
March 15	(6,000 @ 4.40)	26,400		2,000 @ 4.00 6,000 @ 4.40	34,400
March 19			(4,000 @ $4.40) $17,600	2,000 @ 4.00 2,000 @ 4.40	16,800
March 30	(2,000 @ 4.75)	9,500		2,000 @ 4.00 2,000 @ 4.40 2,000 @ 4.75	26,300

The month-end periodic inventory computation presented in Illustration 8-16 (inventory $25,600 and cost of goods sold $18,300) shows a different amount from the perpetual inventory computation (inventory $26,300 and cost of goods sold $17,600). This is because the periodic system matches the total withdrawals for the month with the total purchases for the month in applying the last-in, first-out method. In contrast, the perpetual system matches each withdrawal with the immediately preceding purchases. In effect, the periodic computation assumed that the cost of the goods that were purchased on March 30 were included in the sale or issue on March 19.

Tutorial on Inventory Methods

SPECIAL ISSUES RELATED TO LIFO

LIFO Reserve

OBJECTIVE 6
Explain the significance and use of a LIFO reserve.

Many companies use LIFO for tax and external reporting purposes but maintain a FIFO, average cost, or standard cost system for internal reporting purposes. There are several reasons to do so: (1) Companies often base their pricing decisions on a FIFO, average, or standard cost assumption, rather than on a LIFO basis. (2) Record keeping on some other basis is easier because the LIFO assumption usually does not approximate the physical flow of the product. (3) Profit-sharing and other bonus arrangements are often not based on a LIFO inventory assumption. Finally, (4) the use of a pure LIFO system is troublesome for interim periods, for which estimates must be made of year-end quantities and prices.

The difference between the inventory method used for internal reporting purposes and LIFO is referred to as the Allowance to Reduce Inventory to LIFO or the **LIFO reserve**. The change in the allowance balance from one period to the next is called the **LIFO effect**. The LIFO effect is the adjustment that must be made to the accounting records in a given year. To illustrate, assume that Acme Boot Company uses the FIFO method for internal reporting purposes and LIFO for external reporting purposes. At January 1, 2004, the Allowance to Reduce Inventory to LIFO balance was $20,000, and the ending balance should be $50,000. The LIFO effect is therefore $30,000, and the following entry is made at year-end.

Cost of Goods Sold	30,000	
Allowance to Reduce Inventory to LIFO		30,000

The Allowance to Reduce Inventory to LIFO would be deducted from inventory to ensure that the inventory is stated on a LIFO basis at year-end.

The AICPA Task Force on LIFO Inventory Problems concluded that either the LIFO reserve or the replacement cost of the inventory should be disclosed.[11] Two types of this kind of disclosure are shown below.

ILLUSTRATION 8-18
Note Disclosures of LIFO Reserve

American Maize-Products Company

Inventories (Note 3)	$80,320,000

Note 3: Inventories. At December 31, $31,516,000 of inventories were valued using the LIFO method. This amount is less than the corresponding replacement value by $3,765,000.

BROWN SHOE

Brown Shoe Company, Inc.
(in thousands)

	1999	1998
Inventories, (Note 1)	$365,989	$362,274

Note 1 (partial): Inventories. Inventories are valued at the lower of cost or market determined principally by the last-in, first-out (LIFO) method. If the first-in, first-out (FIFO) cost method had been used, inventories would have been $11,709 higher in 1999 and $13,424 higher in 1998.

Additional LIFO Reserve Disclosures

[11]The AICPA Task Force on LIFO Inventory Problems defined **LIFO reserve** for its purposes as "the difference between (a) inventory at the lower of LIFO cost or market and (b) inventory at replacement cost or at the lower of cost determined by some acceptable inventory accounting method (such as FIFO or average cost) or market." *Issues Paper* (New York: AICPA, November 30, 1984), par. 2–24. The SEC has endorsed this issues paper, and therefore it has authoritative status for GAAP purposes.

COMPARING APPLES TO APPLES

WHAT DO THE NUMBERS MEAN?

A common ratio used by investors to evaluate a company's liquidity is the current ratio, which is computed as current assets divided by current liabilities. A higher current ratio indicates that a company is better able to meet its current obligations when they come due. However, it is not meaningful to compare the current ratio for a company using LIFO to one for a company using FIFO. It would be like comparing apples to oranges, since inventory (and cost of goods sold) would be measured differently for the two companies.

The LIFO reserve can be used to make the current ratio comparable on an apples-to-apples basis. To make the LIFO company comparable to the FIFO company, the following adjustments should do the trick:

Inventory Adjustment: LIFO inventory + LIFO reserve = FIFO inventory

(For cost of goods sold, the *change* in the LIFO reserve is deducted from LIFO cost of goods sold to yield the comparable FIFO amount.)

For **Brown Shoe Company, Inc.** (see Illustration 8-18), with current assets of \$487.8 million and current liabilities of \$217.8 million, the current ratio using LIFO is: \$487.8 ÷ \$217.8 = 2.2. After adjusting for the LIFO effect, Brown's current ratio under FIFO would be: (\$487.8 + \$11.7) ÷ \$217.8 = 2.3.

Thus, without the LIFO adjustment, the Brown Shoe current ratio is understated.

LIFO Liquidation

OBJECTIVE 7
Explain the effect of LIFO liquidations.

Up to this point, we have emphasized a **specific goods approach** to costing LIFO inventories (also called traditional LIFO or unit LIFO). This approach is often unrealistic for two reasons:

1. When a company has many different inventory items, the accounting cost of keeping track of each inventory item is expensive.
2. Erosion of the LIFO inventory can easily occur. Referred to as **LIFO liquidation**, this erosion often leads to distortions of net income and substantial tax payments.

To understand the LIFO liquidation problem, assume that Basler Co. has 30,000 pounds of steel in its inventory on December 31, 2004, costed on a specific goods LIFO approach.

Ending Inventory (2004)

	Pounds	Unit Cost	LIFO Cost
2001	8,000	\$ 4	\$ 32,000
2002	10,000	6	60,000
2003	7,000	9	63,000
2004	5,000	10	50,000
	30,000		\$205,000

As indicated, the ending 2004 inventory for Basler Co. comprises costs from past periods. These costs are called **layers** (increases from period to period).The first layer is identified as the base layer. The layers for Basler are shown in Illustration 8-19 on the next page.

The price of steel has increased over the 4-year period. In 2005, Basler Co. experienced metal shortages and had to liquidate much of its inventory (a LIFO liquidation). At the end of 2005, only 6,000 pounds of steel remained in inventory. Because the company is using LIFO, the most recent layer, 2004, is liquidated first, followed by the 2003

ILLUSTRATION 8-19
Layers of LIFO Inventory

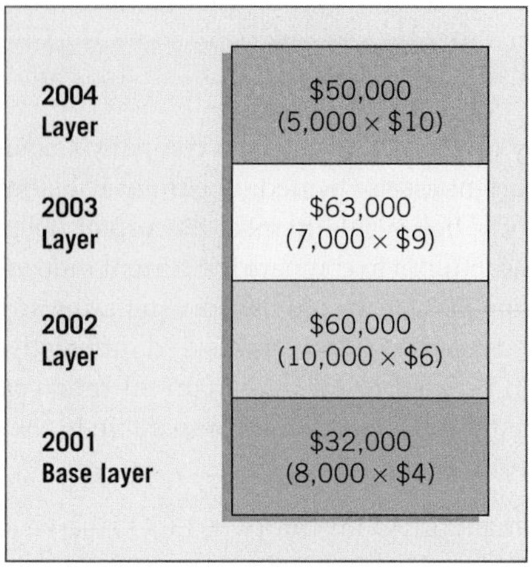

layer, and so on. The result: Costs from preceding periods are matched against sales revenues reported in current dollars. This leads to a distortion in net income and a substantial tax bill in the current period. These effects are shown in Illustration 8-20. Unfortunately, LIFO liquidations can occur frequently when a specific goods LIFO approach is employed.

ILLUSTRATION 8-20
LIFO Liquidation

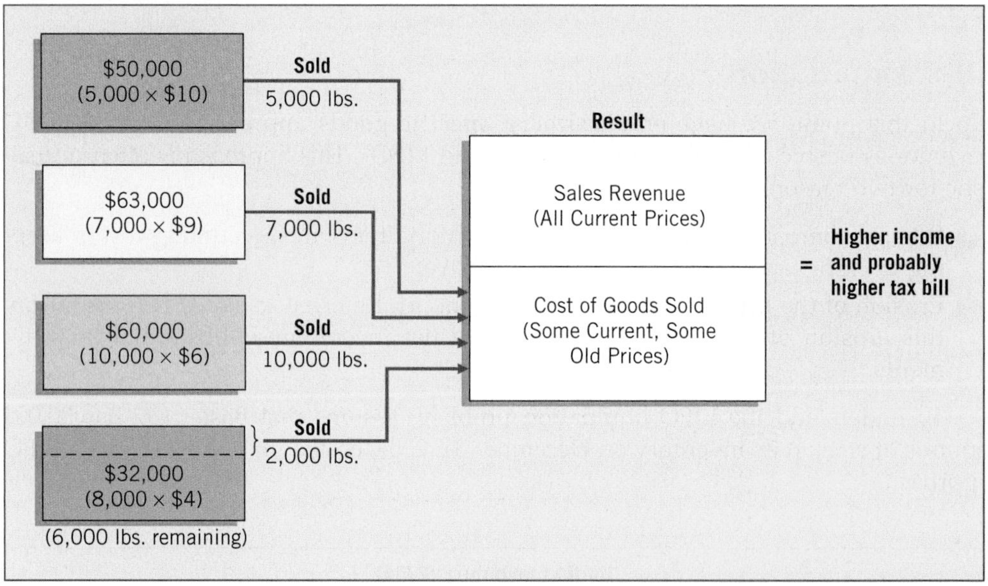

To alleviate the LIFO liquidation problems and to simplify the accounting, goods can be combined into pools. A **pool** is defined as a group of items of a similar nature. Thus, instead of only identical units, a number of similar units or products are combined and accounted for together. This method is referred to as the **specific goods pooled LIFO approach**. With the specific goods pooled LIFO approach, LIFO liquidations are less likely to happen because the reduction of one quantity in the pool may be offset by an increase in another.

The specific goods pooled LIFO approach eliminates some of the disadvantages of the specific goods (traditional) accounting for LIFO inventories. This pooled approach, using quantities as its measurement basis, however, creates other problems.

First, most companies are continually changing the mix of their products, materials, and production methods. A business once engaged in manufacturing train locomotives may now be involved in the automobile or aircraft business. A business that had used cotton fabric in its clothing now uses synthetic fabric (dacron, nylon, etc.). If a pooled approach using quantities is employed, such changes mean that the pools must be continually redefined; this can be time consuming and costly.

Second, even when such an approach is practical, an erosion (LIFO liquidation) of the layers often results, and much of the LIFO costing benefit is lost. An erosion of the layers results because a specific good or material in the pool may be replaced by another good or material either temporarily or permanently. This replacement may occur for competitive reasons or simply because a shortage of a certain material exists. Whatever the reason, the new item may not be similar enough to be treated as part of the old pool. Therefore any inflationary profit deferred on the old goods may have to be recognized as the old goods are replaced.

Dollar-Value LIFO

OBJECTIVE 8
Explain the dollar-value LIFO method.

To overcome the problems of redefining pools and eroding layers, the dollar-value LIFO method was developed. **An important feature of the dollar-value LIFO method is that increases and decreases in a pool are determined and measured in terms of total dollar value, not the physical quantity of the goods in the inventory pool.**

Such an approach has two important advantages over the specific goods pooled approach. First, a broader range of goods may be included in a dollar-value LIFO pool. Second, in a dollar-value LIFO pool, replacement is permitted if it is a similar material, or similar in use, or interchangeable. (In contrast, in a specific goods LIFO pool, an item may be replaced only with an item that is substantially identical.)

Thus, dollar-value LIFO techniques help protect LIFO layers from erosion. Because of this advantage, the dollar-value LIFO method is frequently used in practice.[12] Only in situations where few goods are employed and little change in product mix is predicted would the more traditional LIFO approaches be used.

Tutorial on Dollar-Value LIFO

Under the dollar-value LIFO method, it is possible to have the entire inventory in only one pool, although several pools are commonly employed.[13] In general, the more goods included in a pool, the more likely that decreases in the quantities of some goods will be offset by increases in the quantities of other goods in the same pool. Thus liquidation of the LIFO layers is avoided. It follows that having fewer pools means less cost and less chance of a reduction of a LIFO layer.[14]

Dollar-Value LIFO Illustration

To illustrate how the dollar-value LIFO method works, assume that dollar-value LIFO was first adopted (base period) on December 31, 2003, that the inventory at current prices on that date was $20,000, and that the inventory on December 31, 2004, at current prices is $26,400.

We should not conclude that the quantity has increased 32 percent during the year ($26,400 ÷ $20,000 = 132%). First, we need to ask: What is the value of the ending inventory in terms of beginning-of-the-year prices? Assuming that prices have increased 20 percent during the year, the ending inventory at beginning-of-the-year prices

[12]A study by James M. Reeve and Keith G. Stanga disclosed that the vast majority of respondent companies applying LIFO use the dollar-value method or the dollar-value retail method (explained in Chapter 9) to apply LIFO. Only a small minority of companies use the specific goods (unit LIFO) approach or the specific goods pooling approach. See "The LIFO Pooling Decision," *Accounting Horizons* (June 1987), p. 27.

[13]The Reeve and Stanga study (ibid.) reports that most companies have only a few pools (the median is six for retailers and three for nonretailers), but the distributions are highly skewed; some companies have 100 or more pools. Retailers that use LIFO have significantly more pools than nonretailers. About a third of the nonretailers (mostly manufacturers) use a single pool for their entire LIFO inventory.

[14]In a later study, William R. Coon and Randall B. Hayes point out that when quantities are increasing, multiple pools over a period of time may produce (under rather general conditions) significantly higher cost of goods sold deductions than a single-pool approach. When a stockout occurs, a single-pool approach may lessen the layer liquidation for that year, but it may not erase the cumulative cost of goods sold advantage accruing to the use of multiple pools built up over the preceding years. See "The Dollar Value LIFO Pooling Decision: The Conventional Wisdom Is Too General," *Accounting Horizons* (December 1989), pp. 57–70.

amounts to $22,000 ($26,400 ÷ 120%). Therefore, the inventory quantity has increased 10 percent, or from $20,000 to $22,000 in terms of beginning-of-the-year prices.

The next step is to price this real-dollar quantity increase. This real-dollar quantity increase of $2,000 valued at year-end prices is $2,400 (120% × $2,000). This increment (layer) of $2,400, when added to the beginning inventory of $20,000, gives a total of $22,400 for the December 31, 2004, inventory, as shown below.

First layer—(beginning inventory) in terms of 100	$20,000
Second layer—(2004 increase) in terms of 120	2,400
Dollar-value LIFO inventory, December 31, 2004	$22,400

It should be emphasized that **a layer is formed only when the ending inventory at base-year prices exceeds the beginning inventory at base-year prices**. And only when a new layer is formed must a new index be computed.

Comprehensive Dollar-Value LIFO Illustration

To illustrate the use of the dollar-value LIFO method in a more complex situation, assume that Bismark Company develops the following information.

December 31	Inventory at End-of-Year Prices	÷	Price Index (percentage)	=	End-of-Year Inventory at Base-Year Prices
(Base year) 2001	$200,000		100		$200,000
2002	299,000		115		260,000
2003	300,000		120		250,000
2004	351,000		130		270,000

At December 31, 2001, the ending inventory under dollar-value LIFO is simply the $200,000 computed as shown in Illustration 8-21.

ILLUSTRATION 8-21
Computation of 2001 Inventory at LIFO Cost

Ending Inventory at Base-Year Prices	Layer at Base-Year Prices		Price Index (percentage)		Ending Inventory at LIFO Cost
$200,000	$200,000	×	100	=	$200,000

At December 31, 2002, a comparison of the ending inventory at base-year prices ($260,000) with the beginning inventory at base-year prices ($200,000), indicates that the quantity of goods has increased $60,000 ($260,000 − $200,000). This increment (layer) is then priced at the 2002 index of 115 percent to arrive at a new layer of $69,000. Ending inventory for 2002 is $269,000, composed of the beginning inventory of $200,000 and the new layer of $69,000. These computations are shown in Illustration 8-22.

ILLUSTRATION 8-22
Computation of 2002 Inventory at LIFO Cost

Ending Inventory at Base-Year Prices	Layers at Base-Year Prices		Price Index (percentage)		Ending Inventory at LIFO Cost
$260,000	→2001 $200,000	×	100	=	$200,000
	→2002 60,000	×	115	=	69,000
	$260,000				$269,000

At December 31, 2003, a comparison of the ending inventory at base-year prices ($250,000) with the beginning inventory at base-year prices ($260,000) indicates that the quantity of goods has decreased $10,000 ($250,000 − $260,000). If the ending inventory at base-year prices is less than the beginning inventory at base-year prices, **the decrease must be subtracted from the most recently added layer. When a decrease occurs, previous layers must be "peeled off" at the prices in existence when the layers were**

added. In Bismark Company's situation, this means that $10,000 in base-year prices must be removed from the 2002 layer of $60,000 at base-year prices. The balance of $50,000 ($60,000 − $10,000) at base-year prices must be valued at the 2002 price index of 115%, so this 2002 layer now is valued at $57,500 ($50,000 × 115%). The ending inventory is therefore computed at $257,500, consisting of the beginning inventory of $200,000 and the second layer, $57,500. The computations for 2003 are shown in Illustration 8-23.

ILLUSTRATION 8-23
Computation of 2003 Inventory at LIFO Cost

Ending Inventory at Base-Year Prices	Layers at Base-Year Prices		Price Index (percentage)		Ending Inventory at LIFO Cost
$250,000	→2001 $200,000	×	100	=	$200,000
	→2002 50,000	×	115	=	57,500
	$250,000				$257,500

Note that if a layer or base (or portion thereof) has been eliminated, it cannot be rebuilt in future periods. That is, it is gone forever.

At December 31, 2004, a comparison of the ending inventory at base-year prices ($270,000) with the beginning inventory at base-year prices ($250,000) indicates that the dollar quantity of goods has increased $20,000 ($270,000 − $250,000) in terms of base-year prices. After converting the $20,000 increase to the 2004 price index, the ending inventory is $283,500, composed of the beginning layer of $200,000, a 2002 layer of $57,500, and a 2004 layer of $26,000 ($20,000 × 130%). This computation is shown in Illustration 8-24.

ILLUSTRATION 8-24
Computation of 2004 Inventory at LIFO Cost

Ending Inventory at Base-Year Prices	Layers at Base-Year Prices		Price Index (percentage)		Ending Inventory at LIFO Cost
	→2001 $200,000	×	100	=	$200,000
$270,000	→2002 50,000	×	115	=	57,500
	→2004 20,000	×	130	=	26,000
	$270,000				$283,500

The ending inventory at base-year prices must always equal the total of the layers at base-year prices. Checking that this situation exists will help to ensure that the dollar-value computation is made correctly.

Selecting a Price Index

Obviously, price changes are critical in dollar-value LIFO. How are the price indexes determined? Many companies use the general price-level index prepared and published monthly by the federal government. The most popular general external price-level index is the Consumer Price Index for Urban Consumers (CPI-U).[15] Specific external price indexes are also widely used. For instance, specific indexes are computed and published daily for most commodities (gold, silver, other metals, corn, wheat, and other farm products). Many trade associations prepare indexes for specific product lines or industries. Any of these indexes may be used for dollar-value LIFO purposes.

When a specific external price index is not readily available or relevant, a company may compute its own specific internal price index. The desired approach is to price ending inventory at the most current cost. Current cost is ordinarily determined by referring to the actual cost of those goods most recently purchased. The price index provides a measure of the change in price or cost levels between the base year and the

[15]Indexes may be **general** (composed of several commodities, goods, or services) or **specific** (for one commodity, good, or service). Additionally, they may be **external** (computed by an outside party, such as the government, commodity exchange, or trade association) or **internal** (computed by the enterprise for its own product or service).

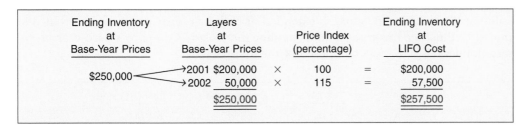

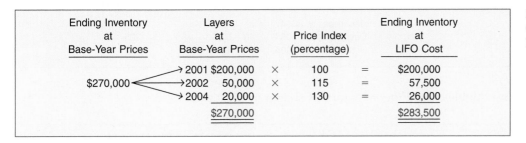

current year. An index is computed for each year after the base year. The general formula for computing the index is as follows.

ILLUSTRATION 8-25
Formula for Computing a Price Index

$$\frac{\text{Ending Inventory for the Period at Current Cost}}{\text{Ending Inventory for the Period at Base-Year Cost}} = \text{Price Index for Current Year}$$

This approach is generally referred to as the **double-extension method** because the value of the units in inventory is extended at both base-year prices and current-year prices. To illustrate this computation, assume that Toledo Company's base-year inventory (January 1, 2004) was composed of the following.

Items	Quantity	Cost per Unit	Total Cost
A	1,000	$ 6	$ 6,000
B	2,000	20	40,000
January 1, 2004, inventory at base-year costs			$46,000

Examination of the ending inventory indicates that 3,000 units of Item A and 6,000 units of Item B are held on December 31, 2004. The most recent actual purchases related to these items were as follows.

Items	Purchase Date	Quantity Purchased	Cost per Unit
A	December 1, 2004	4,000	$ 7
B	December 15, 2004	5,000	25
B	November 16, 2004	1,000	22

We double-extend the inventory as shown in Illustration 8-26.

ILLUSTRATION 8-26
Double-Extension Method of Determining a Price Index

	12/31/04 Inventory at Base-Year Costs			**12/31/04 Inventory at Current-Year Costs**		
Items	Units	Base-Year Cost per Unit	Total	Units	Current-Year Cost per Unit	Total
A	3,000	$ 6	$ 18,000	3,000	$ 7	$ 21,000
B	6,000	20	120,000	5,000	25	125,000
B				1,000	22	22,000
			$138,000			$168,000

After the inventories are double-extended, the formula in Illustration 8-25 is used to develop the index for the current year (2004), as follows.

ILLUSTRATION 8-27
Computation of 2004 Index

$$\frac{\text{Ending Inventory for the Period at Current Cost}}{\text{Ending Inventory for the Period at Base-Year Cost}} = \frac{\$168{,}000}{\$138{,}000} = 121.74\%$$

This index (121.74%) is then applied to the layer added in 2004. Note in this illustration that Toledo Company used the most recent actual purchases to determine current cost; other approaches such as FIFO and average cost may also be used. Whichever flow assumption is adopted, consistent use from one period to another is required.

Use of the double-extension method is time consuming and difficult where substantial technological change has occurred or where a large number of items is involved.

That is, as time passes, a new base-year cost must be determined for new products, and a base-year cost must be kept for each inventory item.[16]

Comparison of LIFO Approaches

Three different approaches to computing LIFO inventories are presented in this chapter—specific goods LIFO, specific goods pooled LIFO, and dollar-value LIFO. As indicated earlier, the use of the specific goods LIFO is unrealistic because most enterprises have numerous goods in inventory at the end of a period, and costing (pricing) them on a unit basis is extremely expensive and time consuming.

The specific goods pooled LIFO approach is better in that it reduces record keeping and clerical costs. In addition, it is more difficult to erode the layers because the reduction of one quantity in the pool may be offset by an increase in another. Nonetheless, the pooled approach using quantities as its measurement basis can lead to untimely LIFO liquidations.

As a result, **dollar-value LIFO is the method employed by most companies that currently use a LIFO system**. Although the approach appears complex, the logic and the computations are actually quite simple, once an appropriate index is determined.

This is not to suggest that problems do not exist with the dollar-value LIFO method. The selection of the items to be put in a pool can be subjective.[17] Such a determination, however, is extremely important because manipulation of the items in a pool without conceptual justification can affect reported net income. For example, the SEC noted that some companies have set up pools that are easy to liquidate. As a result, when the company wants to increase its income, it decreases inventory, thereby matching low-cost inventory items to current revenues.

To curb this practice, the SEC has taken a much harder line on the number of pools that companies may establish. In the well-publicized **Stauffer Chemical Company** case, Stauffer had increased the number of LIFO pools from 8 to 280, boosting its net income by $16,515,000 or approximately 13 percent.[18] Stauffer justified the change in its Annual Report on the basis of "achieving a better matching of cost and revenue." The SEC required Stauffer to reduce the number of its inventory pools, contending that some pools were inappropriate and alleging income manipulation.

Major Advantages of LIFO

OBJECTIVE 9
Identify the major advantages and disadvantages of LIFO.

One obvious advantage of LIFO approaches is that in certain situations the LIFO cost flow actually approximates the physical flow of the goods in and out of inventory. For instance, in the case of a coal pile, the last coal in is the first coal out because it is on the top of the pile. The coal remover is not going to take the coal from the bottom of the pile! The coal that is going to be taken first is the coal that was placed on the pile last.

However, the coal pile situation is one of only a few situations where the actual physical flow corresponds to LIFO. Therefore most adherents of LIFO use other arguments for its widespread employment, as follows.

---

[16]Another approach, which was initially sanctioned by the Internal Revenue Service for tax purposes, may be used to simplify the analysis. Under this method, an index is obtained by reference to an outside source or by double-extending only a sample portion of the inventory. For example, all companies are allowed to use 80 percent of the inflation rate reported by the appropriate consumer or producer price indexes prepared by the Bureau of Labor Statistics (BLS) as their inflation rate for a LIFO pool. Once the index is obtained, the ending inventory at current cost is divided by the index to find the base-year cost. Using generally available external indexes greatly simplifies LIFO computations, as internal indexes need not be computed.

[17]It is suggested that companies analyze how inventory purchases are affected by price changes, how goods are stocked, how goods are used, and if future liquidations are likely. See William R. Cron and Randall Hayes, "The Dollar Value LIFO Pooling Decision: The Conventional Wisdom Is Too General," *Accounting Horizons* (December 1989), p. 57.

[18]Commerce Clearing House, *SEC Accounting Rules* (Chicago: CCH, 1983), par. 4035.

Matching

In LIFO, the more recent costs are matched against current revenues to provide a better measure of current earnings. During periods of inflation, many challenge the quality of non-LIFO earnings, noting that by failing to match current costs against current revenues, **transitory or "paper" profits ("inventory profits") are created**. Inventory profits occur when the inventory costs matched against sales are less than the inventory replacement cost. The cost of goods sold therefore is understated and profit is overstated. Using LIFO (rather than a method such as FIFO), current costs are matched against revenues and inventory profits are thereby reduced.

Tax Benefits/Improved Cash Flow

Tax benefits are the major reason why LIFO has become popular. As long as the price level increases and inventory quantities do not decrease, a deferral of income tax occurs, because the items most recently purchased at the higher price level are matched against revenues. For example, when **Fuqua Industries** decided to switch to LIFO, it had a resultant tax savings of about $4 million. Even if the price level decreases later, the company has been given a temporary deferral of its income taxes. Thus, use of LIFO in such situations improves a company's cash flow.[19]

The tax law requires that if a company uses LIFO for tax purposes, it must also use LIFO for financial accounting purposes[20] (although neither tax law nor GAAP requires a company to pool its inventories in the same manner for book and tax purposes). This requirement is often referred to as the **LIFO conformity rule**. Other inventory valuation methods do not have this requirement.

Future Earnings Hedge

With LIFO, a company's future reported earnings will not be affected substantially by future price declines. LIFO eliminates or substantially minimizes write-downs to market as a result of price decreases. The reason: Since the most recent inventory is sold first, there isn't much ending inventory sitting around at high prices vulnerable to a price decline. In contrast, inventory costed under FIFO is more vulnerable to price declines, which can reduce net income substantially.

Major Disadvantages of LIFO Approaches

Despite its advantages, LIFO has the following drawbacks.

Reduced Earnings

Many corporate managers view the lower profits reported under the LIFO method in inflationary times as a distinct disadvantage. They would rather have higher reported profits than lower taxes. Some fear that an accounting change to LIFO may be misunderstood by investors and that, as a result of the lower profits, the price of the company's stock will fall. In fact, though, there is some evidence to refute this contention. Non-LIFO earnings are now highly suspect and may be severely punished by Wall Street.

[19]In periods of rising prices, the use of fewer pools will translate into greater income tax benefits through the use of LIFO. The use of fewer pools allows inventory reductions of some items to be offset by inventory increases in others. In contrast, the use of more pools increases the likelihood that old, low-cost inventory layers will be liquidated and tax consequences will be negative. See Reeve and Stanga, ibid., pp. 28–29.

[20]Management often selects an accounting procedure because a lower tax results from its use, instead of an accounting method that is conceptually more appealing. Throughout this textbook, an effort has been made to identify accounting procedures that provide income tax benefits to the user.

Inventory Understated

LIFO may have a distorting effect on a company's balance sheets: The inventory valuation is normally outdated because the oldest costs remain in inventory. This understatement makes the working capital position of the company appear worse than it really is.

The magnitude and direction of this variation between the carrying amount of inventory and its current price depend on the degree and direction of the price changes and the amount of inventory turnover. The combined effect of rising product prices and avoidance of inventory liquidations increases the difference between the inventory carrying value at LIFO and current prices of that inventory, thereby magnifying the balance sheet distortion attributed to the use of LIFO.

Physical Flow

LIFO does not approximate the physical flow of the items except in peculiar situations (such as the coal pile). Originally LIFO could be used only in certain circumstances. This situation has changed over the years to the point where physical flow characteristics no longer play an important role in determining whether LIFO may be employed.

Involuntary Liquidation/Poor Buying Habits

If the base or layers of old costs are eliminated, strange results can occur because old, irrelevant costs can be matched against current revenues. A distortion in reported income for a given period may result, as well as consequences that are detrimental from an income tax point of view.[21]

Because of the liquidation problem, LIFO may cause poor buying habits. A company may simply purchase more goods and match these goods against revenue to ensure that the old costs are not charged to expense. Furthermore, the possibility always exists with LIFO that a company will attempt to manipulate its net income at the end of the year simply by altering its pattern of purchases.[22]

One survey uncovered the following reasons why companies reject LIFO.[23]

ILLUSTRATION 8-28
Why Do Companies Reject LIFO? Summary of Responses

Reasons to Reject LIFO	Number	% of Total*
No expected tax benefits		
No required tax payment	34	16%
Declining prices	31	15
Rapid inventory turnover	30	14
Immaterial inventory	26	12
Miscellaneous tax related	38	17
	159	74%
Regulatory or other restrictions	26	12%
Excessive cost		
High administrative costs	29	14%
LIFO liquidation–related costs	12	6
	41	20%
Other adverse consequences		
Lower reported earnings	18	8%
Bad accounting	7	3
	25	11%

*Percentage totals more than 100% as some companies offered more than one explanation.

[21]The AICPA Task Force on LIFO Inventory Problems recommends that the effects on income of LIFO inventory liquidations be disclosed in the notes to the financial statements, but that the effects not receive special treatment in the income statement. *Issues Paper* (New York: AICPA, 1984), pp. 36–37.

[22]For example, one reason why **General Tire and Rubber** at one time accelerated raw material purchases at the end of the year was to minimize the book profit from a liquidation of LIFO inventories and to minimize income taxes for the year.

[23]Michael H. Granof and Daniel Short, "Why Do Companies Reject LIFO?" *Journal of Accounting, Auditing, and Finance* (Summer 1984), pp. 323–333, Table 1, p. 327.

BASIS FOR SELECTION OF INVENTORY METHOD

OBJECTIVE 10
Identify the reasons why a given inventory method is selected.

How does one choose among the various inventory methods? Although no absolute rules can be stated, preferability for LIFO can ordinarily be established in either of the following circumstances: (1) if selling prices and revenues have been increasing faster than costs, thereby distorting income, and (2) in situations where LIFO has been traditional, such as department stores and industries where a fairly constant "base stock" is present such as refining, chemicals, and glass.[24]

Conversely, LIFO would probably not be appropriate: (1) where prices tend to lag behind costs; (2) in situations where specific identification is traditional, such as in the sale of automobiles, farm equipment, art, and antique jewelry; or (3) where unit costs tend to decrease as production increases, thereby nullifying the tax benefit that LIFO might provide.[25]

Tax consequences are another consideration. Switching from FIFO to LIFO usually results in an immediate tax benefit. However, switching from LIFO to FIFO can result in a substantial tax burden. For example, when **Chrysler** (now **DaimlerChrysler**) changed from LIFO to FIFO, it became responsible for an additional $53 million in taxes that had been deferred over 14 years of LIFO inventory valuation. Why, then, would Chrysler, and other companies, change to FIFO? The major reason was the profit crunch of that era. Although Chrysler showed a loss of $7.6 million after the switch, the loss would have been $20 million *more* if the company had not changed its inventory valuation back to FIFO from LIFO.

It is questionable whether companies should switch from LIFO to FIFO for the sole purpose of increasing reported earnings.[26] Intuitively one would assume that companies with higher reported earnings would have a higher share valuation (common stock price). Some studies have indicated, however, that the users of financial data exhibit a much higher sophistication than might be expected. Share prices are the same and, in some cases, even higher under LIFO in spite of lower reported earnings.[27]

The concern about reduced income resulting from adoption of LIFO has even less substance now because the IRS has relaxed the LIFO conformity rule which required a company that employed LIFO for tax purposes to use it for book purposes as well. The IRS has relaxed restrictions against providing non-LIFO income numbers as supplementary information. As a result, the profession now permits supplemental non-LIFO disclosures but not on the face of the income statement. The supplemental disclosure, while not intended to override the basic LIFO method adopted for financial reporting, may be useful in comparing operating income and working capital with companies not on LIFO.

---

[24]*Accounting Trends and Techniques—2001* reports that of 887 inventory method disclosures, 283 used LIFO, 386 used FIFO, 180 used average cost, and 38 used other methods.

[25]See Barry E. Cushing and Marc J. LeClere, "Evidence on the Determinants of Inventory Accounting Policy Choice," *The Accounting Review* (April 1992), pp. 355–366, Table 4, p. 363, for a list of factors hypothesized to affect FIFO–LIFO choices.

[26]Because of steady or falling raw materials costs and costs savings from electronic data interchange and just-in-time technologies in recent years, many businesses using LIFO are no longer experiencing substantial tax benefits from LIFO. Even some companies for which LIFO is creating a benefit are finding that the administrative costs associated with LIFO are higher than the LIFO benefit obtained. As a result, some companies are deciding to move to FIFO or average cost.

[27]See, for example, Shyam Sunder, "Relationship Between Accounting Changes and Stock Prices: Problems of Measurement and Some Empirical Evidence," *Empirical Research in Accounting: Selected Studies, 1973* (Chicago: University of Chicago), pp. 1–40. But see Robert Moren Brown, "Short-Range Market Reaction to Changes to LIFO Accounting Using Preliminary Earnings Announcement Dates," *The Journal of Accounting Research* (Spring 1980), which found that companies that do change to LIFO suffer a short-run decline in the price of their stock. See also William E. Ricks, "Market's Response to the 1974 LIFO Adoptions," *The Journal of Accounting Research* (Autumn 1982), pp. 367–387.

For example, **JCPenney, Inc.** (a LIFO user) in its Annual Report presented the following information.

ILLUSTRATION 8-29
Supplemental Non-LIFO Disclosure

JCPenney, Inc.

Some companies in the retail industry use the FIFO method in valuing part or all of their inventories. Had JCPenney used the FIFO method and made no other assumptions with respect to changes in income resulting therefrom, income and income per share from continuing operations would have been:

Income from continuing operations (in millions)	$325
Income from continuing operations per share	$4.63

Relaxation of the LIFO conformity rule has led more companies to select LIFO as their inventory valuation method because they will be able to disclose FIFO income numbers in the financial reports if they so desire.[28]

Often the inventory methods are used in combination with other methods. For example, most companies never use LIFO totally, but rather use it in combination with other valuation approaches. One reason is that certain product lines can be highly susceptible to deflation instead of inflation. In addition, if the level of inventory is unstable, unwanted involuntary liquidations may result in certain product lines if LIFO is used. Finally, where inventory turnover in certain product lines is high, the additional recordkeeping and expense are not justified by LIFO. Average cost is often used in such cases because it is easy to compute.[29]

This variety of inventory methods has been devised to assist in accurate computation of net income rather than to permit manipulation of reported income. Hence, it is recommended that the pricing method most suitable to a company be selected and, once selected, be applied consistently thereafter. If conditions indicate that the inventory pricing method in use is unsuitable, serious consideration should be given to all other possibilities before selecting another method. Any change should be clearly explained and its effect disclosed in the financial statements.

Inventory Valuation Methods—Summary Analysis

A number of inventory valuation methods are described in the preceding sections of this chapter. A brief summary of the three major inventory methods, assuming periodic inventory procedures, is presented below to show the differing effects these valuation methods have on the financial statements. The first schedule provides selected data for the comparison as follows.

[28]Note that a company can use one variation of LIFO for financial reporting purposes and another for tax without violating the LIFO conformity rule. Such a relaxation has caused many problems because the general approach to accounting for LIFO has been "whatever is good for tax is good for financial reporting." The AICPA published a useful paper on this subject entitled "Identification and Discussion of Certain Financial Accounting and Reporting Issues Concerning LIFO Inventories" (New York: AICPA, November 30, 1984).

[29]For an interesting discussion of the reasons for and against the use of FIFO and average cost, see Michael H. Granof and Daniel G. Short "For Some Companies, FIFO Accounting Makes Sense," *Wall Street Journal* (August 30, 1982), and the subsequent rebuttal by Gary C. Biddle "Taking Stock of Inventory Accounting Choices," *Wall Street Journal* (September 15, 1982).

Selected Data

Given		
Beginning cash balance		$ 7,000
Beginning retained earnings		$10,000
Beginning inventory:	4,000 units @ $3	$12,000
Purchases:	6,000 units @ $4	$24,000
Sales:	5,000 units @ $12	$60,000
Operating expenses		$10,000
Income tax rate		40%

The comparative results of using average cost, FIFO, and LIFO on net income are computed as shown in Illustration 8-30.

ILLUSTRATION 8-30
Comparative Results of Average Cost, FIFO, and LIFO Methods

	Average Cost	FIFO	LIFO
Sales	$60,000	$60,000	$60,000
Cost of goods sold	18,000[a]	16,000[b]	20,000[c]
Gross profit	42,000	44,000	40,000
Operating expenses	10,000	10,000	10,000
Income before taxes	32,000	34,000	30,000
Income taxes (40%)	12,800	13,600	12,000
Net income	$19,200	$20,400	$18,000

[a]4,000 @ $3 = $12,000
6,000 @ $4 = 24,000
$36,000
$36,000 ÷ 10,000 = $3.60
$3.60 × 5,000 = $18,000

[b]4,000 @ $3 = $12,000
1,000 @ $4 = 4,000
$16,000

[c]5,000 @ $4 = $20,000

Notice that gross profit and net income are lowest under LIFO, highest under FIFO, and somewhere in the middle under average cost.

The table below then shows the final balances of selected items at the end of the period.

ILLUSTRATION 8-31
Balances of Selected Items Under Alternative Inventory Valuation Methods

	Inventory	Gross Profit	Taxes	Net Income	Retained Earnings	Cash
Average Cost	$18,000 (5,000 × $3.60)	$42,000	$12,800	$19,200	$29,200 ($10,000 + $19,200)	$20,200[a]
FIFO	$20,000 (5,000 × $4)	$44,000	$13,600	$20,400	$30,400 ($10,000 + $20,400)	$19,400[a]
LIFO	$16,000 (4,000 × $3) (1,000 × $4)	$40,000	$12,000	$18,000	$28,000 ($10,000 + $18,000)	$21,000[a]

[a]Cash at year-end	=	Beg. Balance	+	Sales	−	Purchases	−	Operating expenses	−	Taxes
Average cost—$20,200	=	$7,000	+	$60,000	−	$24,000	−	$10,000	−	$12,800
FIFO—$19,400	=	$7,000	+	$60,000	−	$24,000	−	$10,000	−	$13,600
LIFO—$21,000	=	$7,000	+	$60,000	−	$24,000	−	$10,000	−	$12,000

LIFO results in the highest cash balance at year-end because taxes are lower. This example assumes prices are rising. The opposite result occurs if prices are declining.

SUMMARY OF LEARNING OBJECTIVES

1 Identify major classifications of inventory. Only one inventory account, Merchandise Inventory, appears in the financial statements of a merchandising concern. A manufacturer normally has three inventory accounts: Raw Materials, Work in Process, and Finished Goods. The cost assigned to goods and materials on hand but not yet placed into production is reported as raw materials inventory. The cost of the raw materials on which production has been started but not completed, plus the direct labor cost applied specifically to this material and a ratable share of manufacturing overhead costs, constitute the work in process inventory. The costs identified with the completed but unsold units on hand at the end of the fiscal period are reported as finished goods inventory.

2 Distinguish between perpetual and periodic inventory systems. Under a perpetual inventory system, a continuous record of changes in inventory is maintained in the Inventory account. That is, all purchases and sales (issues) of goods are recorded directly in the Inventory account as they occur. Under a periodic inventory system, the quantity of inventory on hand is determined only periodically. The Inventory account remains the same, and a Purchases account is debited. Cost of goods sold is determined at the end of the period using a formula. Ending inventory is ascertained by physical count.

3 Identify the effects of inventory errors on the financial statements. *If the ending inventory is misstated,* (1) the inventory, retained earnings, working capital, and current ratio in the balance sheet will be misstated, and (2) the cost of goods sold and net income in the income statement will be misstated. *If purchases and inventory are misstated,* (1) the inventory, accounts payable, and current ratio will be misstated, and (2) purchases and ending inventory in the income statement will be misstated.

4 Identify the items that should be included as inventory cost. Product costs are directly connected with the bringing of goods to the place of business of the buyer and converting such goods to a salable condition. Such charges would include freight charges on goods purchased, other direct costs of acquisition, and labor and other production costs incurred in processing the goods up to the time of sale. Selling, administrative, and interest costs are generally not included as inventory costs.

5 Describe and compare the flow assumptions used in accounting for inventories. (1) *Average cost* prices items in the inventory on the basis of the average cost of all similar goods available during the period. (2) *First-in, first-out (FIFO)* assumes that goods are used in the order in which they are purchased. The inventory remaining must therefore represent the most recent purchases. (3) *Last-in, first-out (LIFO)* matches the cost of the last goods purchased against revenue.

6 Explain the significance and use of a LIFO reserve. The difference between the inventory method used for internal reporting purposes and LIFO is referred to as the Allowance to Reduce Inventory to LIFO. Either the LIFO reserve or the replacement cost of the inventory should be disclosed.

7 Explain the effect of LIFO liquidations. The effect of LIFO liquidations is that costs from preceding periods are matched against sales revenues reported in current dollars. This leads to a distortion in net income and a substantial tax bill in the current period. LIFO liquidations can occur frequently when a specific goods LIFO approach is employed.

8 Explain the dollar-value LIFO method. An important feature of the dollar-value LIFO method is that increases and decreases in a pool are determined and measured in terms of total dollar value, not the physical quantity of the goods in the inventory pool.

KEY TERMS

9 Identify the major advantages and disadvantages of LIFO. The major advantages of LIFO are as follows: (1) Recent costs are matched against current revenues to provide a better measure of current earnings. (2) As long as the price level increases and inventory quantities do not decrease, a deferral of income tax occurs in LIFO. (3) Because of the deferral of income tax, there is improvement of cash flow. (4) A company's future reported earnings will not be affected substantially by future price declines. Major disadvantages are: (1) reduced earnings, (2) understated inventory, (3) physical flow not approximated, except in peculiar situations, and (4) poor buying habits caused by involuntary liquidations.

10 Identify the reasons why a given inventory method is selected. Preferability of LIFO can ordinarily be established if: (1) selling prices and revenues have been increasing faster than costs, and (2) a company has a fairly constant "base stock." Conversely, LIFO would probably not be appropriate: (1) where prices tend to lag behind costs; (2) in situations where specific identification is traditional; and (3) where unit costs tend to decrease as production increases, thereby nullifying the tax benefit that LIFO might provide.

QUESTIONS

1. In what ways are the inventory accounts of a retailing company different from those of a manufacturing company?

2. Why should inventories be included in (a) a statement of financial position and (b) the computation of net income?

3. What is the difference between a perpetual inventory and a physical inventory? If a company maintains a perpetual inventory, should its physical inventory at any date be equal to the amount indicated by the perpetual inventory records? Why?

4. Mariah Carey, Inc. indicated in a recent annual report that approximately $19 million of merchandise was received on consignment. Should Mariah Carey, Inc. report this amount on its balance sheet? Explain.

5. What is a product financing arrangement? How should product financing arrangements be reported in the financial statements?

6. Where, if at all, should the following items be classified on a balance sheet?

(a) Goods out on approval to customers.

(b) Goods in transit that were recently purchased f.o.b. destination.

(c) Land held by a realty firm for sale.

(d) Raw materials.

(e) Goods received on consignment.

(f) Manufacturing supplies.

7. At the balance sheet date Paula Abdul Company held title to goods in transit amounting to $214,000. This amount was omitted from the purchases figure for the year and also from the ending inventory. What is the effect of this omission on the net income for the year as calculated when the books are closed? What is the effect on the company's financial position as shown in its balance sheet? Is materiality a factor in determining whether an adjustment for this item should be made?

8. Define "cost" as applied to the valuation of inventories.

9. Distinguish between product costs and period costs as they relate to inventory.

10. Ford Motor Co. is considering alternate methods of accounting for the cash discounts it takes when paying suppliers promptly. One method suggested was to report these discounts as financial income when payments are made. Comment on the propriety of this approach.

11. Harold Baines Inc. purchases 300 units of an item at an invoice cost of $30,000. What is the cost per unit? If the goods are shipped f.o.b. shipping point and the freight bill was $1,500, what is the cost per unit if Baines Inc. pays the freight charges? If these items were bought on 2/10, n/30 terms and the invoice and the freight bill were paid within the 10-day period, what would be the cost per unit?

12. Specific identification is sometimes said to be the ideal method of assigning cost to inventory and to cost of goods sold. Briefly indicate the arguments for and against this method of inventory valuation.

13. FIFO, weighted average, and LIFO methods are often used instead of specific identification for inventory valuation purposes. Compare these methods with the specific identification method, discussing the theoretical propriety of each method in the determination of income and asset valuation.

14. How might a company obtain a price index in order to apply dollar-value LIFO?

15. Describe the LIFO double-extension method. Using the following information, compute the index at December 31, 2004, applying the double-extension method to a

LIFO pool consisting of 25,500 units of product A and 10,350 units of product B. The base-year cost of product A is $10.20 and of product B is $37.00. The price at December 31, 2004, for product A is $19.00 and for product B is $45.60.

16. As compared with the FIFO method of costing inventories, does the LIFO method result in a larger or smaller net income in a period of rising prices? What is the comparative effect on net income in a period of falling prices?

17. What is the dollar-value method of LIFO inventory valuation? What advantage does the dollar-value method have over the specific goods approach of LIFO inventory valuation? Why will the traditional LIFO inventory costing method and the dollar-value LIFO inventory costing method produce different inventory valuations if the composition of the inventory base changes?

18. Explain the following terms.

(a) LIFO layer. (b) LIFO reserve. (c) LIFO effect.

19. On December 31, 2003, the inventory of Mario Lemieux Company amounts to $800,000. During 2004, the company decides to use the dollar-value LIFO method of costing inventories. On December 31, 2004, the inventory is $1,026,000 at December 31, 2004, prices. Using the December 31, 2003, price level of 100 and the December 31, 2004, price level of 108, compute the inventory value at December 31, 2004, under the dollar-value LIFO method.

20. In an article that appeared in the *Wall Street Journal*, the phrases "phantom (paper) profits" and "high LIFO profits" through involuntary liquidation were used. Explain these phrases.

BRIEF EXERCISES

BE8-1 Included in the December 31 trial balance of Billie Joel Company are the following assets.

Cash	$ 190,000	Work in process	$200,000
Equipment (net)	1,100,000	Receivables (net)	400,000
Prepaid insurance	41,000	Patents	110,000
Raw materials	335,000	Finished goods	150,000

Prepare the current assets section of the December 31 balance sheet.

BE8-2 Alanis Morrissette Company uses a perpetual inventory system. Its beginning inventory consists of 50 units that cost $30 each. During June, the company purchased 150 units at $30 each, returned 6 units for credit, and sold 125 units at $50 each. Journalize the June transactions.

BE8-3 Mayberry Company took a physical inventory on December 31 and determined that goods costing $200,000 were on hand. Not included in the physical count were $15,000 of goods purchased from Taylor Corporation, f.o.b. shipping point, and $22,000 of goods sold to Mount Pilot Company for $30,000, f.o.b. destination. Both the Taylor purchase and the Mount Pilot sale were in transit at year-end. What amount should Mayberry report as its December 31 inventory?

BE8-4 Gavin Bryars Enterprises reported cost of goods sold for 2004 of $1,400,000 and retained earnings of $5,200,000 at December 31, 2004. Gavin Bryars later discovered that its ending inventories at December 31, 2003 and 2004, were overstated by $110,000 and $45,000, respectively. Determine the corrected amounts for 2004 cost of goods sold and December 31, 2004, retained earnings.

BE8-5 Jose Zorilla Company uses a periodic inventory system. For April, when the company sold 700 units, the following information is available.

	Units	Unit Cost	Total Cost
April 1 inventory	250	$10	$ 2,500
April 15 purchase	400	12	4,800
April 23 purchase	350	13	4,550
	1,000		$11,850

Compute the April 30 inventory and the April cost of goods sold using the average cost method.

BE8-6 Data for Jose Zorilla Company are presented in BE8-5. Compute the April 30 inventory and the April cost of goods sold using the FIFO method.

BE8-7 Data for Jose Zorilla Company are presented in BE8-5. Compute the April 30 inventory and the April cost of goods sold using the LIFO method.

BE8-8 Easy-E Company had ending inventory at end-of-year prices of $100,000 at December 31, 2002; $123,200 at December 31, 2003; and $134,560 at December 31, 2004. The year-end price indexes were 100 at 12/31/02, 110 at 12/31/03, and 116 at 12/31/04. Compute the ending inventory for Easy-E Company for 2002 through 2004 using the dollar-value LIFO method.

BE8-9 Wingers uses the dollar-value LIFO method of computing its inventory. Data for the past 3 years follow.

Year Ended December 31	Inventory at Current-year Cost	Price Index
2002	$19,750	100
2003	21,708	108
2004	25,935	114

Instructions
Compute the value of the 2003 and 2004 inventories using the dollar-value LIFO method.

EXERCISES

E8-1 (Inventoriable Costs) Presented below is a list of items that may or may not be reported as inventory in a company's December 31 balance sheet.

1. Goods out on consignment at another company's store.
2. Goods sold on an installment basis (bad debts can be reasonably estimated).
3. Goods purchased f.o.b. shipping point that are in transit at December 31.
4. Goods purchased f.o.b. destination that are in transit at December 31.
5. Goods sold to another company, for which our company has signed an agreement to repurchase at a set price that covers all costs related to the inventory.
6. Goods sold where large returns are predictable.
7. Goods sold f.o.b. shipping point that are in transit at December 31.
8. Freight charges on goods purchased.
9. Interest costs incurred for inventories that are routinely manufactured.
10. Costs incurred to advertise goods held for resale.
11. Materials on hand not yet placed into production by a manufacturing firm.
12. Office supplies.
13. Raw materials on which a manufacturing firm has started production, but which are not completely processed.
14. Factory supplies.
15. Goods held on consignment from another company.
16. Costs identified with units completed by a manufacturing firm, but not yet sold.
17. Goods sold f.o.b. destination that are in transit at December 31.
18. Short-term investments in stocks and bonds that will be resold in the near future.

Instructions
Indicate which of these items would typically be reported as inventory in the financial statements. If an item should **not** be reported as inventory, indicate how it should be reported in the financial statements.

E8-2 (Inventoriable Costs) In your audit of Jose Oliva Company, you find that a physical inventory on December 31, 2004, showed merchandise with a cost of $441,000 was on hand at that date. You also discover the following items were all excluded from the $441,000.

1. Merchandise of $61,000 which is held by Oliva on consignment. The consignor is the Max Suzuki Company.
2. Merchandise costing $38,000 which was shipped by Oliva f.o.b. destination to a customer on December 31, 2004. The customer was expected to receive the merchandise on January 6, 2005.
3. Merchandise costing $46,000 which was shipped by Oliva f.o.b. shipping point to a customer on December 29, 2004. The customer was scheduled to receive the merchandise on January 2, 2005.
4. Merchandise costing $83,000 shipped by a vendor f.o.b. destination on December 30, 2004, and received by Oliva on January 4, 2005.
5. Merchandise costing $51,000 shipped by a vendor f.o.b. seller on December 31, 2004, and received by Oliva on January 5, 2005.

Instructions
Based on the above information, calculate the amount that should appear on Oliva's balance sheet at December 31, 2004, for inventory.

E8-3 (Inventoriable Costs) Assume that in an annual audit of **Brown Shoe Company, Inc.** at December 31, 2004, you find the following transactions near the closing date.

1. A special machine, fabricated to order for a customer, was finished and specifically segregated in the back part of the shipping room on December 31, 2004. The customer was billed on that date and the machine excluded from inventory although it was shipped on January 4, 2005.
2. Merchandise costing $2,800 was received on January 3, 2005, and the related purchase invoice recorded January 5. The invoice showed the shipment was made on December 29, 2004, f.o.b. destination.
3. A packing case containing a product costing $3,400 was standing in the shipping room when the physical inventory was taken. It was not included in the inventory because it was marked "Hold for shipping instructions." Your investigation revealed that the customer's order was dated December 18, 2004, but that the case was shipped and the customer billed on January 10, 2005. The product was a stock item of your client.
4. Merchandise received on January 6, 2005, costing $680 was entered in the purchase journal on January 7, 2005. The invoice showed shipment was made f.o.b. supplier's warehouse on December 31, 2004. Because it was not on hand at December 31, it was not included in inventory.
5. Merchandise costing $720 was received on December 28, 2004, and the invoice was not recorded. You located it in the hands of the purchasing agent; it was marked "on consignment."

Instructions
Assuming that each of the amounts is material, state whether the merchandise should be included in the client's inventory, and give your reason for your decision on each item.

E8-4 (Inventoriable Costs—Perpetual) Colin Davis Machine Company maintains a general ledger account for each class of inventory, debiting such accounts for increases during the period and crediting them for decreases. The transactions below relate to the Raw Materials inventory account, which is debited for materials purchased and credited for materials requisitioned for use.

1. An invoice for $8,100, terms f.o.b. destination, was received and entered January 2, 2004. The receiving report shows that the materials were received December 28, 2003.
2. Materials costing $28,000, shipped f.o.b. destination, were not entered by December 31, 2003, "because they were in a railroad car on the company's siding on that date and had not been unloaded."
3. Materials costing $7,300 were returned to the creditor on December 29, 2003, and were shipped f.o.b. shipping point. The return was entered on that date, even though the materials are not expected to reach the creditor's place of business until January 6, 2004.
4. An invoice for $7,500, terms f.o.b. shipping point, was received and entered December 30, 2003. The receiving report shows that the materials were received January 4, 2004, and the bill of lading shows that they were shipped January 2, 2004.
5. Materials costing $19,800 were received December 30, 2003, but no entry was made for them because "they were ordered with a specified delivery of no earlier than January 10, 2004."

Instructions
Prepare correcting general journal entries required at December 31, 2003, assuming that the books have not been closed.

E8-5 (Inventoriable Costs—Error Adjustments) Craig Company asks you to review its December 31, 2004, inventory values and prepare the necessary adjustments to the books. The following information is given to you.

1. Craig uses the periodic method of recording inventory. A physical count reveals $234,890 of inventory on hand at December 31, 2004.
2. Not included in the physical count of inventory is $13,420 of merchandise purchased on December 15 from Browser. This merchandise was shipped f.o.b. shipping point on December 29 and arrived in January. The invoice arrived and was recorded on December 31.
3. Included in inventory is merchandise sold to Champy on December 30, f.o.b. destination. This merchandise was shipped after it was counted. The invoice was prepared and recorded as a sale on account for $12,800 on December 31. The merchandise cost $7,350, and Champy received it on January 3.
4. Included in inventory was merchandise received from Dudley on December 31 with an invoice price of $15,630. The merchandise was shipped f.o.b. destination. The invoice, which has not yet arrived, has not been recorded.
5. Not included in inventory is $8,540 of merchandise purchased from Glowser Industries. This merchandise was received on December 31 after the inventory had been counted. The invoice was received and recorded on December 30.
6. Included in inventory was $10,438 of inventory held by Craig on consignment from Jackel Industries.
7. Included in inventory is merchandise sold to Kemp f.o.b. shipping point. This merchandise was shipped after it was counted. The invoice was prepared and recorded as a sale for $18,900 on December 31. The cost of this merchandise was $10,520, and Kemp received the merchandise on January 5.

8. Excluded from inventory was a carton labeled "Please accept for credit." This carton contains merchandise costing $1,500 which had been sold to a customer for $2,600. No entry had been made to the books to reflect the return, but none of the returned merchandise seemed damaged.

Instructions

(a) Determine the proper inventory balance for Craig Company at December 31, 2004.

(b) Prepare any correcting entries to adjust inventory to its proper amount at December 31, 2004. Assume the books have not been closed.

E8-6 (Determining Merchandise Amounts—Periodic) Two or more items are omitted in each of the following tabulations of income statement data. Fill in the amounts that are missing.

	2002	2003	2004
Sales	$290,000	$?	$410,000
Sales returns	11,000	13,000	?
Net sales	?	347,000	?
Beginning inventory	20,000	32,000	?
Ending inventory	?	?	?
Purchases	?	260,000	298,000
Purchase returns and allowances	5,000	8,000	10,000
Transportation-in	8,000	9,000	12,000
Cost of goods sold	233,000	?	293,000
Gross profit on sales	46,000	91,000	97,000

E8-7 (Purchases Recorded Net) Presented below are transactions related to Tom Brokaw, Inc.

May	10	Purchased goods billed at $15,000 subject to cash discount terms of 2/10, n/60.
	11	Purchased goods billed at $13,200 subject to terms of 1/15, n/30.
	19	Paid invoice of May 10.
	24	Purchased goods billed at $11,500 subject to cash discount terms of 2/10, n/30.

Instructions

(a) Prepare general journal entries for the transactions above under the assumption that purchases are to be recorded at net amounts after cash discounts and that discounts lost are to be treated as financial expense.

(b) Assuming no purchase or payment transactions other than those given above, prepare the adjusting entry required on May 31 if financial statements are to be prepared as of that date.

E8-8 (Purchases Recorded, Gross Method) Cruise Industries purchased $10,800 of merchandise on February 1, 2004, subject to a trade discount of 10% and with credit terms of 3/15, n/60. It returned $2,500 (gross price before trade or cash discount) on February 4. The invoice was paid on February 13.

Instructions

(a) Assuming that Cruise uses the perpetual method for recording merchandise transactions, record the purchase, return, and payment using the gross method.

(b) Assuming that Cruise uses the periodic method for recording merchandise transactions, record the purchase, return, and payment using the gross method.

(c) At what amount would the purchase on February 1 be recorded if the net method were used?

E8-9 (Periodic versus Perpetual Entries) The Fong Sai-Yuk Company sells one product. Presented below is information for January for the Fong Sai-Yuk Company.

Jan.	1	Inventory	100 units at $5 each
	4	Sale	80 units at $8 each
	11	Purchase	150 units at $6 each
	13	Sale	120 units at $8.75 each
	20	Purchase	160 units at $7 each
	27	Sale	100 units at $9 each

Fong Sai-Yuk uses the FIFO cost flow assumption. All purchases and sales are on account.

Instructions

(a) Assume Fong Sai-Yuk uses a periodic system. Prepare all necessary journal entries, including the end-of-month closing entry to record cost of goods sold. A physical count indicates that the ending inventory for January is 110 units.

(b) Compute gross profit using the periodic system.

(c) Assume Fong Sai-Yuk uses a perpetual system. Prepare all necessary journal entries.
(d) Compute gross profit using the perpetual system.

E8-10 (Inventory Errors—Periodic) Ann M. Martin Company makes the following errors during the current year.

1. Ending inventory is overstated, but purchases are recorded correctly.
2. Both ending inventory and purchases on account are understated. (Assume this purchase was recorded in the following year.)
3. Ending inventory is correct, but a purchase on account was not recorded. (Assume this purchase was recorded in the following year.)

Instructions
Indicate the effect of each of these errors on working capital, current ratio (assume that the current ratio is greater than 1), retained earnings, and net income for the current year and the subsequent year.

E8-11 (Inventory Errors) At December 31, 2003, Stacy McGill Corporation reported current assets of $370,000 and current liabilities of $200,000. The following items may have been recorded incorrectly.

1. Goods purchased costing $22,000 were shipped f.o.b. shipping point by a supplier on December 28. McGill received and recorded the invoice on December 29, but the goods were not included in McGill's physical count of inventory because they were not received until January 4.
2. Goods purchased costing $15,000 were shipped f.o.b. destination by a supplier on December 26. McGill received and recorded the invoice on December 31, but the goods were not included in McGill's physical count of inventory because they were not received until January 2.
3. Goods held on consignment from Claudia Kishi Company were included in McGill's physical count of inventory at $13,000.
4. Freight-in of $3,000 was debited to advertising expense on December 28.

Instructions
(a) Compute the current ratio based on McGill's balance sheet.
(b) Recompute the current ratio after corrections are made.
(c) By what amount will income (before taxes) be adjusted up or down as a result of the corrections?

E8-12 (Inventory Errors) The net income per books of Linda Patrick Company was determined without knowledge of the errors indicated.

Year	Net Income per Books	Error in Ending Inventory	
1999	$50,000	Overstated	$ 3,000
2000	52,000	Overstated	9,000
2001	54,000	Understated	11,000
2002	56,000	No error	
2003	58,000	Understated	2,000
2004	60,000	Overstated	8,000

Instructions
Prepare a work sheet to show the adjusted net income figure for each of the 6 years after taking into account the inventory errors.

E8-13 (FIFO and LIFO—Periodic and Perpetual) Inventory information for Part 311 of Monique Aaron Corp. discloses the following information for the month of June.

June 1	Balance	300 units @ $10	June 10	Sold	200 units @ $24
11	Purchased	800 units @ $12	15	Sold	500 units @ $25
20	Purchased	500 units @ $13	27	Sold	300 units @ $27

Instructions
(a) Assuming that the periodic inventory method is used, compute the cost of goods sold and ending inventory under (1) LIFO and (2) FIFO.
(b) Assuming that the perpetual inventory method is used and costs are computed at the time of each withdrawal, what is the value of the ending inventory at LIFO?
(c) Assuming that the perpetual inventory method is used and costs are computed at the time of each withdrawal, what is the gross profit if the inventory is valued at FIFO?
(d) Why is it stated that LIFO usually produces a lower gross profit than FIFO?

E8-14 (FIFO, LIFO and Average Cost Determination) John Adams Company's record of transactions for the month of April was as follows.

Purchases			Sales	
April	1 (balance on hand)	600 @ $6.00	April 3	500 @ $10.00
	4	1,500 @ 6.08	9	1,400 @ 10.00
	8	800 @ 6.40	11	600 @ 11.00
	13	1,200 @ 6.50	23	1,200 @ 11.00
	21	700 @ 6.60	27	900 @ 12.00
	29	500 @ 6.79		4,600
		5,300		

Instructions

(a) Assuming that perpetual inventory records are kept in units only, compute the inventory at April 30 using (1) LIFO and (2) average cost.

(b) Assuming that perpetual inventory records are kept in dollars, determine the inventory using (1) FIFO and (2) LIFO.

(c) Compute cost of goods sold assuming periodic inventory procedures and inventory priced at FIFO.

(d) In an inflationary period, which inventory method—FIFO, LIFO, average cost—will show the highest net income?

E8-15 (FIFO, LIFO, Average Cost Inventory) Shania Twain Company was formed on December 1, 2003. The following information is available from Twain's inventory records for Product BAP.

	Units	Unit Cost
January 1, 2004 (beginning inventory)	600	$ 8.00
Purchases:		
January 5, 2004	1,200	9.00
January 25, 2004	1,300	10.00
February 16, 2004	800	11.00
March 26, 2004	600	12.00

A physical inventory on March 31, 2004, shows 1,600 units on hand.

Instructions

Prepare schedules to compute the ending inventory at March 31, 2004, under each of the following inventory methods.

(a) FIFO. **(b)** LIFO. **(c)** Weighted average.

E8-16 (Compute FIFO, LIFO, Average Cost—Periodic) Presented below is information related to Blowfish radios for the Hootie Company for the month of July.

Date	Transaction	Units In	Unit Cost	Total	Units Sold	Selling Price	Total
July 1	Balance	100	$4.10	$ 410			
6	Purchase	800	4.20	3,360			
7	Sale				300	$7.00	$ 2,100
10	Sale				300	7.30	2,190
12	Purchase	400	4.50	1,800			
15	Sale				200	7.40	1,480
18	Purchase	300	4.60	1,380			
22	Sale				400	7.40	2,960
25	Purchase	500	4.58	2,290			
30	Sale				200	7.50	1,500
	Totals	2,100		$9,240	1,400		$10,230

Instructions

(a) Assuming that the periodic inventory method is used, compute the inventory cost at July 31 under each of the following cost flow assumptions.

  (1) FIFO.
  (2) LIFO.
  (3) Weighted-average.

(b) Answer the following questions.

  (1) Which of the methods used above will yield the lowest figure for gross profit for the income statement? Explain why.
  (2) Which of the methods used above will yield the lowest figure for ending inventory for the balance sheet? Explain why.

E8-17 (FIFO and LIFO—Periodic and Perpetual) The following is a record of Pervis Ellison Company's transactions for Boston Teapots for the month of May 2004.

May 1	Balance 400 units @ $20	May 10	Sale 300 units @ $38
12	Purchase 600 units @ $25	20	Sale 540 units @ $38
28	Purchase 400 units @ $30		

Instructions

(a) Assuming that perpetual inventories are **not** maintained and that a physical count at the end of the month shows 560 units on hand, what is the cost of the ending inventory using (1) FIFO and (2) LIFO?

(b) Assuming that perpetual records are maintained and they tie into the general ledger, calculate the ending inventory using (1) FIFO and (2) LIFO.

E8-18 (FIFO and LIFO; Income Statement Presentation) The board of directors of Ichiro Corporation is considering whether or not it should instruct the accounting department to shift from a first-in, first-out (FIFO) basis of pricing inventories to a last-in, first-out (LIFO) basis. The following information is available.

Sales	21,000 units @ $50
Inventory, January 1	6,000 units @ 20
Purchases	6,000 units @ 22
	10,000 units @ 25
	7,000 units @ 30
Inventory, December 31	8,000 units @ ?
Operating expenses	$200,000

Instructions

Prepare a condensed income statement for the year on both bases for comparative purposes.

E8-19 (FIFO and LIFO Effects) You are the vice-president of finance of Sandy Alomar Corporation, a retail company that prepared two different schedules of gross margin for the first quarter ended March 31, 2004. These schedules appear below.

	Sales ($5 per unit)	Cost of Goods Sold	Gross Margin
Schedule 1	$150,000	$124,900	$25,100
Schedule 2	150,000	129,400	20,600

The computation of cost of goods sold in each schedule is based on the following data.

	Units	Cost per Unit	Total Cost
Beginning inventory, January 1	10,000	$4.00	$40,000
Purchase, January 10	8,000	4.20	33,600
Purchase, January 30	6,000	4.25	25,500
Purchase, February 11	9,000	4.30	38,700
Purchase, March 17	11,000	4.40	48,400

Jane Torville, the president of the corporation, cannot understand how two different gross margins can be computed from the same set of data. As the vice-president of finance you have explained to Ms. Torville that the two schedules are based on different assumptions concerning the flow of inventory costs, i.e., FIFO and LIFO. Schedules 1 and 2 were not necessarily prepared in this sequence of cost flow assumptions.

Instructions

Prepare two separate schedules computing cost of goods sold and supporting schedules showing the composition of the ending inventory under both cost flow assumptions.

E8-20 (FIFO and LIFO—Periodic) Howie Long Shop began operations on January 2, 2004. The following stock record card for footballs was taken from the records at the end of the year.

Date	Voucher	Terms	Units Received	Unit Invoice Cost	Gross Invoice Amount
1/15	10624	Net 30	50	$20	$1,000
3/15	11437	1/5, net 30	65	16	1,040
6/20	21332	1/10, net 30	90	15	1,350
9/12	27644	1/10, net 30	84	12	1,008
11/24	31269	1/10, net 30	76	11	836
	Totals		365		$5,234

A physical inventory on December 31, 2004, reveals that 100 footballs were in stock. The bookkeeper informs you that all the discounts were taken. Assume that Howie Long Shop uses the invoice price less discount for recording purchases.

Instructions

(a) Compute the December 31, 2004, inventory using the FIFO method.
(b) Compute the 2004 cost of goods sold using the LIFO method.
(c) What method would you recommend to the owner to minimize income taxes in 2004, using the inventory information for footballs as a guide?

E8-21 (LIFO Effect) The following example was provided to encourage the use of the LIFO method.

In a nutshell, LIFO subtracts inflation from inventory costs, deducts it from taxable income, and records it in a LIFO reserve account on the books. The LIFO benefit grows as inflation widens the gap between current-year and past-year (minus inflation) inventory costs. This gap is:

	With LIFO	Without LIFO
Revenues	$3,200,000	$3,200,000
Cost of goods sold	2,800,000	2,800,000
Operating expenses	150,000	150,000
Operating income	250,000	250,000
LIFO adjustment	40,000	0
Taxable income	$210,000	$250,000
Income taxes @ 36%	$ 75,600	$ 90,000
Cash flow	$174,400	$160,000
Extra cash	$14,400	0
Increased cash flow	9%	0%

Instructions

(a) Explain what is meant by the LIFO reserve account.
(b) How does LIFO subtract inflation from inventory costs?
(c) Explain how the cash flow of $174,400 in this example was computed. Explain why this amount may not be correct.
(d) Why does a company that uses LIFO have extra cash? Explain whether this situation will always exist.

E8-22 (Alternative Inventory Methods—Comprehensive) Tori Amos Corporation began operations on December 1, 2003. The only inventory transaction in 2003 was the purchase of inventory on December 10, 2003, at a cost of $20 per unit. None of this inventory was sold in 2003. Relevant information is as follows.

Ending inventory units		
December 31, 2003		100
December 31, 2004, by purchase date		
December 2, 2004	100	
July 20, 2004	50	150

During the year the following purchases and sales were made.

Purchases		Sales	
March 15	300 units at $24	April 10	200
July 20	300 units at 25	August 20	300
September 4	200 units at 28	November 18	150
December 2	100 units at 30	December 12	200

The company uses the periodic inventory method.

Instructions

(a) Determine ending inventory under (1) specific identification, (2) FIFO, (3) LIFO and (4) average cost.
(b) Determine ending inventory using dollar-value LIFO. Assume that the December 2, 2004, purchase cost is the current cost of inventory. (*Hint:* The beginning inventory is the base layer priced at $20 per unit.)

E8-23 (Dollar-Value LIFO) Oasis Company has used the dollar-value LIFO method for inventory cost determination for many years. The following data were extracted from Oasis' records.

Date	Price Index	Ending Inventory at Base Prices	Ending Inventory at Dollar-Value LIFO
December 31, 2002	105	$92,000	$92,600
December 31, 2003	?	97,000	98,350

Instructions

Calculate the index used for 2003 that yielded the above results.

E8-24 (Dollar-Value LIFO) The dollar-value LIFO method was adopted by Enya Corp. on January 1, 2004. Its inventory on that date was $160,000. On December 31, 2004, the inventory at prices existing on that date amounted to $140,000. The price level at January 1, 2004, was 100, and the price level at December 31, 2004, was 112.

Instructions

(a) Compute the amount of the inventory at December 31, 2004, under the dollar-value LIFO method.

(b) On December 31, 2005, the inventory at prices existing on that date was $172,500, and the price level was 115. Compute the inventory on that date under the dollar-value LIFO method.

E8-25 (Dollar-Value LIFO) Presented below is information related to Dino Radja Company.

Date	Ending Inventory (End-of-Year Prices)	Price Index
December 31, 2001	$ 80,000	100
December 31, 2002	115,500	105
December 31, 2003	108,000	120
December 31, 2004	122,200	130
December 31, 2005	154,000	140
December 31, 2006	176,900	145

Instructions

Compute the ending inventory for Dino Radja Company for 2001 through 2006 using the dollar-value LIFO method.

E8-26 (Dollar-Value LIFO) The following information relates to the Jimmy Johnson Company.

Date	Ending Inventory (End-of-Year Prices)	Price Index
December 31, 2000	$ 70,000	100
December 31, 2001	90,300	105
December 31, 2002	95,120	116
December 31, 2003	105,600	120
December 31, 2004	100,000	125

Instructions

Use the dollar-value LIFO method to compute the ending inventory for Johnson Company for 2000 through 2004.

PROBLEMS

P8-1 (Various Inventory Issues) The following independent situations relate to inventory accounting.

1. Jag Co. purchased goods with a list price of $150,000, subject to trade discounts of 20% and 10%, with no cash discounts allowable. How much should Jag Co. record as the cost of these goods?
2. Francis Company's inventory of $1,100,000 at December 31, 2003, was based on a physical count of goods priced at cost and before any year-end adjustments relating to the following items.
   a. Goods shipped from a vendor f.o.b. shipping point on December 24, 2003, at an invoice cost of $69,000 to Francis Company were received on January 4, 2004.
   b. The physical count included $29,000 of goods billed to Sakic Corp. f.o.b. shipping point on December 31, 2003. The carrier picked up these goods on January 3, 2004.

   What amount should Francis report as inventory on its balance sheet?

3. Mark Messier Corp. had 1,500 units of part M.O. on hand May 1, 2003, costing $21 each. Purchases of part M.O. during May were as follows.

	Units	Unit Cost
May 9	2,000	$22.00
17	3,500	23.00
26	1,000	24.00

A physical count on May 31, 2003, shows 2,100 units of part M.O. on hand. Using the FIFO method, what is the cost of part M.O. inventory at May 31, 2003? Using the LIFO method, what is the inventory cost? Using the average cost method, what is the inventory cost?

4. Forsberg Company adopted the dollar-value LIFO method on January 1, 2003 (using internal price indexes and multiple pools). The following data are available for inventory pool A for the 2 years following adoption of LIFO.

Inventory	At Base-Year Cost	At Current-Year Cost
1/1/03	$200,000	$200,000
12/31/03	240,000	252,000
12/31/04	256,000	286,720

Computing an internal price index and using the dollar-value LIFO method, at what amount should the inventory be reported at December 31, 2004?

5. Eric Lindros Inc., a retail store chain, had the following information in its general ledger for the year 2004.

Merchandise purchased for resale	$909,400
Interest on notes payable to vendors	8,700
Purchase returns	16,500
Freight-in	22,000
Freight-out	17,100
Cash discounts on purchases	6,800

What is Lindros' inventoriable cost for 2004?

Instructions

Answer each of the preceding questions about inventories, and explain your answers.

P8-2 (Inventory Adjustments) James T. Kirk Company, a manufacturer of small tools, provided the following information from its accounting records for the year ended December 31, 2004.

Inventory at December 31, 2004 (based on physical count of goods in Kirk's plant, at cost, on December 31, 2004)	$1,520,000
Accounts payable at December 31, 2004	1,200,000
Net sales (sales less sales returns)	8,150,000

Additional information is as follows.

1. Included in the physical count were tools billed to a customer f.o.b. shipping point on December 31, 2004. These tools had a cost of $31,000 and were billed at $40,000. The shipment was on Kirk's loading dock waiting to be picked up by the common carrier.
2. Goods were in transit from a vendor to Kirk on December 31, 2004. The invoice cost was $71,000, and the goods were shipped f.o.b. shipping point on December 29, 2004.
3. Work in process inventory costing $30,000 was sent to an outside processor for plating on December 30, 2004.
4. Tools returned by customers and held pending inspection in the returned goods area on December 31, 2004, were not included in the physical count. On January 8, 2005, the tools costing $32,000 were inspected and returned to inventory. Credit memos totaling $47,000 were issued to the customers on the same date.
5. Tools shipped to a customer f.o.b. destination on December 26, 2004, were in transit at December 31, 2004, and had a cost of $21,000. Upon notification of receipt by the customer on January 2, 2005, Kirk issued a sales invoice for $42,000.
6. Goods, with an invoice cost of $27,000, received from a vendor at 5:00 p.m. on December 31, 2004, were recorded on a receiving report dated January 2, 2005. The goods were not included in the physical count, but the invoice was included in accounts payable at December 31, 2004.
7. Goods received from a vendor on December 26, 2004, were included in the physical count. However, the related $56,000 vendor invoice was not included in accounts payable at December 31, 2004, because the accounts payable copy of the receiving report was lost.

8. On January 3, 2005, a monthly freight bill in the amount of $6,000 was received. The bill specifically related to merchandise purchased in December 2004, one-half of which was still in the inventory at December 31, 2004. The freight charges were not included in either the inventory or in accounts payable at December 31, 2004.

Instructions

Using the format shown below, prepare a schedule of adjustments as of December 31, 2004, to the initial amounts per Kirk's accounting records. Show separately the effect, if any, of each of the eight transactions on the December 31, 2004, amounts. If the transactions would have no effect on the initial amount shown, enter NONE.

	Inventory	Accounts Payable	Net Sales
Initial amounts	$1,520,000	$1,200,000	$8,150,000
Adjustments—increase (decrease)			
1			
2			
3			
4			
5			
6			
7			
8			
Total adjustments			
Adjusted amounts	$	$	$

(AICPA adapted)

P8-3 (Purchases Recorded Gross and Net) Some of the transactions of William Dubois Company during August are listed below. Dubois uses the periodic inventory method.

August 10	Purchased merchandise on account, $9,000, terms 2/10, n/30.
13	Returned part of the purchase of August 10, $1,200, and received credit on account.
15	Purchased merchandise on account, $12,000, terms 1/10, n/60.
25	Purchased merchandise on account, $15,000, terms 2/10, n/30.
28	Paid invoice of August 15 in full.

Instructions

(a) Assuming that purchases are recorded at gross amounts and that discounts are to be recorded when taken:
  (1) Prepare general journal entries to record the transactions.
  (2) Describe how the various items would be shown in the financial statements.

(b) Assuming that purchases are recorded at net amounts and that discounts lost are treated as financial expenses:
  (1) Prepare general journal entries to enter the transactions.
  (2) Prepare the adjusting entry necessary on August 31 if financial statements are to be prepared at that time.
  (3) Describe how the various items would be shown in the financial statements.

(c) Which of the two methods do you prefer and why?

P8-4 (Compute FIFO, LIFO, and Average Cost—Periodic and Perpetual) Taos Company's record of transactions concerning part X for the month of April was as follows.

Purchases		Sales	
April 1 (balance on hand)	100 @ $5.00	April 5	300
4	400 @ 5.10	12	200
11	300 @ 5.30	27	800
18	200 @ 5.35	28	100
26	500 @ 5.60		
30	200 @ 5.80		

Instructions

(a) Compute the inventory at April 30 on each of the following bases. Assume that perpetual inventory records are kept in units only. Carry unit costs to the nearest cent.
  (1) First-in, first-out (FIFO).

(2) Last-in, first-out (LIFO).
(3) Average cost.

(b) If the perpetual inventory record is kept in dollars, and costs are computed at the time of each withdrawal, what amount would be shown as ending inventory in 1, 2, and 3 above? Carry average unit costs to four decimal places.

P8-5 (Compute FIFO, LIFO and Average Cost—Periodic and Perpetual) Some of the information found on a detail inventory card for David Letterman Inc. for the first month of operations is as follows.

	Received		Issued,	Balance,
Date	No. of Units	Unit Cost	No. of Units	No. of Units
January 2	1,200	$3.00		1,200
7			700	500
10	600	3.20		1,100
13			500	600
18	1,000	3.30	300	1,300
20			1,100	200
23	1,300	3.40		1,500
26			800	700
28	1,500	3.60		2,200
31			1,300	900

Instructions

(a) From these data compute the ending inventory on each of the following bases. Assume that perpetual inventory records are kept in units only. Carry unit costs to the nearest cent and ending inventory to the nearest dollar.
(1) First-in, first-out (FIFO).
(2) Last-in, first-out (LIFO).
(3) Average cost.

(b) If the perpetual inventory record is kept in dollars, and costs are computed at the time of each withdrawal, would the amounts shown as ending inventory in 1, 2, and 3 above be the same? Explain and compute.

P8-6 (Compute FIFO, LIFO, Average Cost—Periodic and Perpetual) Iowa Company is a multiproduct firm. Presented below is information concerning one of its products, the Hawkeye.

Date	Transaction	Quantity	Price/Cost
1/1	Beginning inventory	1,000	$12
2/4	Purchase	2,000	18
2/20	Sale	2,500	30
4/2	Purchase	3,000	23
11/4	Sale	2,000	33

Instructions

Compute cost of goods sold, assuming Iowa uses:

(a) Periodic system, FIFO cost flow.
(b) Perpetual system, FIFO cost flow.
(c) Periodic system, LIFO cost flow.
(d) Perpetual system, LIFO cost flow.
(e) Periodic system, weighted-average cost flow.
(f) Perpetual system, moving-average cost flow.

P8-7 (Financial Statement Effects of FIFO and LIFO) The management of Maine Company has asked its accounting department to describe the effect upon the company's financial position and its income statements of accounting for inventories on the LIFO rather than the FIFO basis during 2004 and 2005. The accounting department is to assume that the change to LIFO would have been effective on January 1, 2004, and that the initial LIFO base would have been the inventory value on December 31, 2003. Presented below are the company's financial statements and other data for the years 2004 and 2005 when the FIFO method was employed.

	Financial Position as of		
	12/31/03	12/31/04	12/31/05
Cash	$ 90,000	$130,000	$ 141,600
Accounts receivable	80,000	100,000	120,000
Inventory	120,000	140,000	180,000
Other assets	160,000	170,000	200,000
Total assets	$450,000	$540,000	$ 641,600

Accounts payable	$ 40,000	$ 60,000	$ 80,000
Other liabilities	70,000	80,000	110,000
Common stock	200,000	200,000	200,000
Retained earnings	140,000	200,000	251,600
Total equities	$450,000	$540,000	$ 641,600

	Income for Years Ended	
	12/31/04	12/31/05
Sales	$900,000	$1,350,000
Less: Cost of goods sold	505,000	770,000
Other expenses	205,000	304,000
	710,000	1,074,000
Income before income taxes	190,000	276,000
Income taxes (40%)	76,000	110,400
Net income	$114,000	$ 165,600

Other data:

1. Inventory on hand at December 31, 2003, consisted of 40,000 units valued at $3.00 each.
2. Sales (all units sold at the same price in a given year):

   2004—150,000 units @ $6.00 each   2005—180,000 units @ $7.50 each

3. Purchases (all units purchased at the same price in given year):

   2004—150,000 units @ $3.50 each   2005—180,000 units @ $4.50 each

4. Income taxes at the effective rate of 40% are paid on December 31 each year.

Instructions

Name the account(s) presented in the financial statements that would have different amounts for 2005 if LIFO rather than FIFO had been used, and state the new amount for each account that is named. Show computations.

(CMA adapted)

P8-8 (Dollar-Value LIFO) Falcon's Televisions produces television sets in three categories: portable, midsize, and console. On January 1, 2003, Falcon adopted dollar-value LIFO and decided to use a single inventory pool. The company's January 1 inventory consists of:

Category	Quantity	Cost per Unit	Total Cost
Portable	6,000	$100	$ 600,000
Midsize	8,000	250	2,000,000
Console	3,000	400	1,200,000
	17,000		$3,800,000

During 2003, the company had the following purchases and sales.

Category	Quantity Purchased	Cost per Unit	Quantity Sold	Selling Price per Unit
Portable	15,000	$120	14,000	$150
Midsize	20,000	300	24,000	405
Console	10,000	460	6,000	600
	45,000		44,000	

Instructions

(Round to four decimals.)

(a) Compute ending inventory, cost of goods sold, and gross profit.
(b) Assume the company uses three inventory pools instead of one. Repeat instruction (a).

P8-9 (Internal Indexes—Dollar-Value LIFO) On January 1, 2003, Adis Abeba Wholesalers Inc. adopted the dollar-value LIFO inventory method for income tax and external financial reporting purposes. However, Abeba continued to use the FIFO inventory method for internal accounting and management purposes. In applying the LIFO method, Abeba uses internal conversion price indexes and the multiple pools approach under which substantially identical inventory items are grouped into LIFO inventory pools. The following data were available for inventory pool no. 1, which comprises products A and B, for the 2 years following the adoption of LIFO.

	FIFO Basis per Records		
	Units	Unit Cost	Total Cost
Inventory, 1/1/03			
Product A	10,000	$30	$300,000
Product B	9,000	25	225,000
			$525,000
Inventory, 12/31/03			
Product A	17,000	35	$595,000
Product B	9,000	26	234,000
			$829,000
Inventory, 12/31/04			
Product A	13,000	40	$520,000
Product B	10,000	32	320,000
			$840,000

Instructions

(a) Prepare a schedule to compute the internal conversion price indexes for 2003 and 2004. Round indexes to two decimal places.

(b) Prepare a schedule to compute the inventory amounts at December 31, 2003 and 2004, using the dollar-value LIFO inventory method.

(AICPA adapted)

P8-10 (Internal Indexes—Dollar-Value LIFO) Presented below is information related to Mellon Collie Corporation for the last 3 years.

Item	Quantities in Ending Inventories	Base-Year Cost Unit Cost	Base-Year Cost Amount	Current-Year Cost Unit Cost	Current-Year Cost Amount
December 31, 2002					
A	9,000	$2.00	$18,000	$2.40	$21,600
B	6,000	3.00	18,000	3.55	21,300
C	4,000	5.00	20,000	5.40	21,600
		Totals	$56,000		$64,500
December 31, 2003					
A	9,000	$2.00	$18,000	$2.60	$23,400
B	6,800	3.00	20,400	3.75	25,500
C	6,000	5.00	30,000	6.40	38,400
		Totals	$68,400		$87,300
December 31, 2004					
A	8,000	$2.00	$16,000	$2.70	$21,600
B	8,000	3.00	24,000	4.00	32,000
C	6,000	5.00	30,000	6.20	37,200
		Totals	$70,000		$90,800

Instructions

Compute the ending inventories under the dollar-value LIFO method for 2002, 2003, and 2004. The base period is January 1, 2002, and the beginning inventory cost at that date was $45,000. Compute indexes to two decimal places.

P8-11 (Dollar-Value LIFO) Warren Dunn Company cans a variety of vegetable-type soups. Recently, the company decided to value its inventories using dollar-value LIFO pools. The clerk who accounts for inventories does not understand how to value the inventory pools using this new method, so, as a private consultant, you have been asked to teach him how this new method works.

He has provided you with the following information about purchases made over a 6-year period.

Date	Ending Inventory (End-of-Year Prices)	Price Index
Dec. 31, 2000	$ 80,000	100
Dec. 31, 2001	115,500	105
Dec. 31, 2002	108,000	120
Dec. 31, 2003	131,300	130
Dec. 31, 2004	154,000	140
Dec. 31, 2005	174,000	145

You have already explained to him how this inventory method is maintained, but he would feel better about it if you were to leave him detailed instructions explaining how these calculations are done and why he needs to put all inventories at a base-year value.

Instructions

(a) Compute the ending inventory for Warren Dunn Company for 2000 through 2005 using dollar-value LIFO.

(b) Using your computation schedules as your illustration, write a step-by-step set of instructions explaining how the calculations are done. Begin your explanation by briefly explaining the theory behind this inventory method, including the purpose of putting all amounts into base-year price levels.

CONCEPTUAL CASES

C8-1 (Inventoriable Costs) You are asked to travel to Milwaukee to observe and verify the inventory of the Milwaukee branch of one of your clients. You arrive on Thursday, December 30, and find that the inventory procedures have just been started. You spot a railway car on the sidetrack at the unloading door and ask the warehouse superintendent, Predrag Danilovic, how he plans to inventory the contents of the car. He responds, "We are not going to include the contents in the inventory."

Later in the day, you ask the bookkeeper for the invoice on the carload and the related freight bill. The invoice lists the various items, prices, and extensions of the goods in the car. You note that the carload was shipped December 24 from Albuquerque, f.o.b. Albuquerque, and that the total invoice price of the goods in the car was $35,300. The freight bill called for a payment of $1,500. Terms were net 30 days. The bookkeeper affirms the fact that this invoice is to be held for recording in January.

Instructions

(a) Does your client have a liability that should be recorded at December 31? Discuss.

(b) Prepare a journal entry(ies), if required, to reflect any accounting adjustment required. Assume a perpetual inventory system is used by your client.

(c) For what possible reason(s) might your client wish to postpone recording the transaction?

C8-2 (Inventoriable Costs) Alonzo Spellman, an inventory control specialist, is interested in better understanding the accounting for inventories. Although Alonzo understands the more sophisticated computer inventory control systems, he has little knowledge of how inventory cost is determined. In studying the records of Ditka Enterprises, which sells normal brand-name goods from its own store and on consignment through Wannstedt Inc., he asks you to answer the following questions.

Instructions

(a) Should Ditka Enterprises include in its inventory normal brand-name goods purchased from its suppliers but not yet received if the terms of purchase are f.o.b. shipping point (manufacturer's plant)? Why?

(b) Should Ditka Enterprises include freight-in expenditures as an inventory cost? Why?

(c) If Ditka Enterprises purchases its goods on terms 2/10, net 30, should the purchases be recorded gross or net? Why?

(d) What are products on consignment? How should they be reported in the financial statements?

(AICPA adapted)

C8-3 (Inventoriable Costs) Jack McDowell, the controller for McDowell Lumber Company, has recently hired you as assistant controller. He wishes to determine your expertise in the area of inventory accounting and therefore asks you to answer the following unrelated questions.

(a) A company is involved in the wholesaling and retailing of automobile tires for foreign cars. Most of the inventory is imported, and it is valued on the company's records at the actual inventory cost plus freight-in. At year-end, the warehousing costs are prorated over cost of goods sold and ending inventory. Are warehousing costs considered a product cost or a period cost?

(b) A certain portion of a company's "inventory" is composed of obsolete items. Should obsolete items that are not currently consumed in the production of "goods or services to be available for sale" be classified as part of inventory?

(c) A company purchases airplanes for sale to others. However, until they are sold, the company charters and services the planes. What is the proper way to report these airplanes in the company's financial statements?

(d) A company wants to buy coal deposits but does not want the financing for the purchase to be reported on its financial statements. The company therefore establishes a trust to acquire the coal deposits. The company agrees to buy the coal over a certain period of time at specified prices. The trust is able to finance the coal purchase and pay off the loan as it is paid by the company for the minerals. How should this transaction be reported?

C8-4 (Accounting Treatment of Purchase Discounts) Wayne Gretzky Corp., a household appliances dealer, purchases its inventories from various suppliers. Gretzky has consistently stated its inventories at the lower of cost (FIFO) or market.

Instructions

Gretzky is considering alternate methods of accounting for the cash discounts it takes when paying its suppliers promptly. From a theoretical standpoint, discuss the acceptability of each of the following methods.

(a) Financial income when payments are made.
(b) Reduction of cost of goods sold for the period when payments are made.
(c) Direct reduction of purchase cost.

(AICPA adapted)

C8-5 (General Inventory Issues) In January 2004, Wesley Crusher Inc. requested and secured permission from the commissioner of the Internal Revenue Service to compute inventories under the last-in, first-out (LIFO) method and elected to determine inventory cost under the dollar-value LIFO method. Crusher Inc. satisfied the commissioner that cost could be accurately determined by use of an index number computed from a representative sample selected from the company's single inventory pool.

Instructions

(a) Why should inventories be included in (1) a balance sheet and (2) the computation of net income?
(b) The Internal Revenue Code allows some accountable events to be considered differently for income tax reporting purposes and financial accounting purposes, while other accountable events must be reported the same for both purposes. Discuss why it might be desirable to report some accountable events differently for financial accounting purposes than for income tax reporting purposes.
(c) Discuss the ways and conditions under which the FIFO and LIFO inventory costing methods produce different inventory valuations. Do not discuss procedures for computing inventory cost.

(AICPA adapted)

C8-6 (LIFO Inventory Advantages) Jean Honore, president of Fragonard Co., recently read an article that claimed that at least 100 of the country's largest 500 companies were either adopting or considering adopting the last-in, first-out (LIFO) method for valuing inventories. The article stated that the firms were switching to LIFO to (1) neutralize the effect of inflation in their financial statements, (2) eliminate inventory profits, and (3) reduce income taxes. Ms. Honore wonders if the switch would benefit her company.

Fragonard currently uses the first-in, first-out (FIFO) method of inventory valuation in its periodic inventory system. The company has a high inventory turnover rate, and inventories represent a significant proportion of the assets.

Ms. Honore has been told that the LIFO system is more costly to operate and will provide little benefit to companies with high turnover. She intends to use the inventory method that is best for the company in the long run rather than selecting a method just because it is the current fad.

Instructions

(a) Explain to Ms. Honore what "inventory profits" are and how the LIFO method of inventory valuation could reduce them.
(b) Explain to Ms. Honore the conditions that must exist for Fragonard Co. to receive tax benefits from a switch to the LIFO method.

C8-7 (Average Cost, FIFO, and LIFO) Prepare a memorandum containing responses to the following items.

(a) Describe the cost flow assumptions used in average cost, FIFO, and LIFO methods of inventory valuation.
(b) Distinguish between weighted-average cost and moving-average cost for inventory costing purposes.
(c) Identify the effects on both the balance sheet and the income statement of using the LIFO method instead of the FIFO method for inventory costing purposes over a substantial time period when purchase prices of inventoriable items are rising. State why these effects take place.

C8-8 (LIFO Application and Advantages) Neshki Corporation is a medium-sized manufacturing company with two divisions and three subsidiaries, all located in the United States. The Metallic Division manufactures metal castings for the automotive industry, and the Plastic Division produces small plastic items for electrical products and other uses. The three subsidiaries manufacture various products for other industrial users.

Neshki Corporation plans to change from the lower of first-in, first-out (FIFO) cost or market method of inventory valuation to the last-in, first-out (LIFO) method of inventory valuation to obtain tax benefits. To make the method acceptable for tax purposes, the change also will be made for its annual financial statements.

Instructions

(a) Describe the establishment of and subsequent pricing procedures for each of the following LIFO inventory methods.
- **(1)** LIFO applied to units of product when the periodic inventory system is used.
- **(2)** Application of the dollar-value method to LIFO units of product.

(b) Discuss the specific advantages and disadvantages of using the dollar-value LIFO application as compared to specific goods LIFO (unit LIFO). Ignore income tax considerations.

(c) Discuss the general advantages and disadvantages claimed for LIFO methods.

C8-9 (Dollar-Value LIFO Issues) Maria Callas Co. is considering switching from the specific goods LIFO approach to the dollar-value LIFO approach. Because the financial personnel at Callas know very little about dollar-value LIFO, they ask you to answer the following questions.

(a) What is a LIFO pool?
(b) Is it possible to use a LIFO pool concept and not use dollar-value LIFO? Explain.
(c) What is a LIFO liquidation?
(d) How are price indexes used in the dollar-value LIFO method?
(e) What are the advantages of dollar-value LIFO over specific goods LIFO?

C8-10 (FIFO and LIFO) Günter Grass Company is considering changing its inventory valuation method from FIFO to LIFO because of the potential tax savings. However, the management wishes to consider all of the effects on the company, including its reported performance, before making the final decision.

The inventory account, currently valued on the FIFO basis, consists of 1,000,000 units at $7 per unit on January 1, 2004. There are 1,000,000 shares of common stock outstanding as of January 1, 2004, and the cash balance is $400,000.

The company has made the following forecasts for the period 2004–2006.

	2004	2005	2006
Unit sales (in millions of units)	1.1	1.0	1.3
Sales price per unit	$10	$10	$12
Unit purchases (in millions of units)	1.0	1.1	1.2
Purchase price per unit	$7	$8	$9
Annual depreciation (in thousands of dollars)	$300	$300	$300
Cash dividends per share	$0.15	$0.15	$0.15
Cash payments for additions to and replacement of plant and equipment (in thousands of dollars)	$350	$350	$350
Income tax rate	40%	40%	40%
Operating expenses (exclusive of depreciation) as a percent of sales	15%	15%	15%
Common shares outstanding (in millions)	1	1	1

Instructions

(a) Prepare a schedule that illustrates and compares the following data for Günter Grass Company under the FIFO and the LIFO inventory method for 2004–2006. Assume the company would begin LIFO at the beginning of 2004.
- **(1)** Year-end inventory balances.
- **(2)** Annual net income after taxes.
- **(3)** Earnings per share.
- **(4)** Cash balance.

Assume all sales are collected in the year of sale and all purchases, operating expenses, and taxes are paid during the year incurred.

(b) Using the data above, your answer to (a), and any additional issues you believe need to be considered, prepare a report that recommends whether or not Günter Grass Company should change to the LIFO inventory method. Support your conclusions with appropriate arguments.

(CMA adapted)

C8-11 (LIFO Choices) Gamble Company uses the LIFO method for inventory costing. In an effort to lower net income, company president Oscar Gamble tells the plant accountant to take the unusual step of recommending to the purchasing department a large purchase of inventory at year-end. The price of the item to be purchased has nearly doubled during the year, and the item represents a major portion of inventory value.

Instructions

Answer the following questions.

(a) Identify the major stakeholders. If the plant accountant recommends the purchase, what are the consequences?

(b) If Gamble Company were using the FIFO method of inventory costing, would Oscar Gamble give the same order? Why or why not?

USING YOUR JUDGMENT

FINANCIAL STATEMENT ANALYSIS CASES

Case 1: T J International

T J International was founded in 1969 as Trus Joist International. The firm, a manufacturer of specialty building products, has its headquarters in Boise, Idaho. The company, through its partnership in the Trus Joist MacMillan joint venture, develops and manufactures engineered lumber. This product is a high-quality substitute for structural lumber, and uses lower-grade wood and materials formerly considered waste. The company also is majority owner of the Outlook Window Partnership, which is a consortium of three wood and vinyl window manufacturers.

Following is T J International's adapted income statement and information concerning inventories from its annual report.

T J International

Sales	$618,876,000
Cost of goods sold	475,476,000
Gross profit	143,400,000
Selling and administrative expenses	102,112,000
Income from operations	41,288,000
Other expense	24,712,000
Income before income tax	16,576,000
Income taxes	7,728,000
Net income	$ 8,848,000

Inventories. Inventories are valued at the lower of cost or market and include material, labor, and production overhead costs. Inventories consisted of the following:

	Current Year	Prior Year
Finished goods	$27,512,000	$23,830,000
Raw materials and work-in-progress	34,363,000	33,244,000
	61,875,000	57,074,000
Reduction to LIFO cost	(5,263,000)	(3,993,000)
	$56,612,000	$53,081,000

The last-in, first-out (LIFO) method is used for determining the cost of lumber, veneer, Microllam lumber, TJI joists, and open web joists. Approximately 35 percent of total inventories at the end of the current year were valued using the LIFO method. The first-in, first-out (FIFO) method is used to determine the cost of all other inventories.

Instructions

(a) How much would income before taxes have been if FIFO costing had been used to value all inventories?

(b) If the income tax rate is 46.6%, what would income tax have been if FIFO costing had been used to value all inventories? In your opinion, is this difference in net income between the two methods material? Explain.

(c) Does the use of a different costing system for different types of inventory mean that there is a different physical flow of goods among the different types of inventory? Explain.

Case 2: Noven Pharmaceuticals, Inc.

Noven Pharmaceuticals, Inc., headquartered in Miami, Florida, describes itself in a recent annual report as follows.

> **Noven Pharmaceuticals, Inc.**
>
> Noven is a place of ideas—a company where scientific excellence and state-of-the-art manufacturing combine to create new answers to human needs. Our transdermal delivery systems speed drugs painlessly and effortlessly into the bloodstream by means of a simple skin patch. This technology has proven applications in estrogen replacement, but at Noven we are developing a variety of systems incorporating bestselling drugs that fight everything from asthma, anxiety and dental pain to cancer, heart disease and neurological illness. Our research portfolio also includes new technologies, such as iontophoresis, in which drugs are delivered through the skin by means of electrical currents, as well as products that could satisfy broad consumer needs, such as our anti-microbial mouthrinse.

Noven also reported in its annual report that its activities to date have consisted of product development efforts, some of which have been independent and some of which have been completed in conjunction with **Rhone-Poulenc Rorer (RPR)** and **Ciba-Geigy**. The revenues so far have consisted of money received from licensing fees, "milestone" payments (payments made under licensing agreements when certain stages of the development of a certain product have been completed), and interest on its investments. The company expects that it will have significant revenue in the upcoming fiscal year from the launch of its first product, a transdermal estrogen delivery system.

The current assets portion of Noven's balance sheet follows.

Cash and cash equivalents	$12,070,272
Securities held to maturity	23,445,070
Inventory of supplies	1,264,553
Prepaid and other current assets	825,159
Total current assets	$37,605,054

Inventory of supplies is recorded at the lower of cost (first-in, first-out) or net realizable value and consists mainly of supplies for research and development.

Instructions

(a) What would you expect the physical flow of goods for a pharmaceutical manufacturer to be most like: FIFO, LIFO, or random (flow of goods does not follow a set pattern)? Explain.

(b) What are some of the factors that Noven should consider as it selects an inventory measurement method?

(c) Suppose that Noven had $49,000 in an inventory of transdermal estrogen delivery patches. These patches are from an initial production run, and will be sold during the coming year. Why do you think that this amount is not shown in a separate inventory account? In which of the accounts shown is the inventory likely to be? At what point will the inventory be transferred to a separate inventory account?

RESEARCH CASES

Case 1

As indicated in the chapter, the FIFO and LIFO inventory methods can result in significantly different income statement and balance sheet figures. However, it is possible to convert income for a LIFO firm to its FIFO-based equivalent. To assist financial statement users in this task, firms using LIFO are required to disclose in their footnotes the "LIFO reserve" (LR)—i.e., the difference between the inventory balance shown on the balance sheet and the amount that would have been reported had the firm used current cost (or FIFO), as illustrated for **Brown Shoe Company** on page 384.

The following equation can be used to convert LIFO cost of goods sold (COGS) to FIFO COGS.

$$COGS_{FIFO} = COGS_{LIFO} - \text{LIFO effect}$$

where

$$\text{LIFO effect} = [LR_{ending} - LR_{beginning}]$$

The following equation can be used to convert LIFO net income (NI) to FIFO net income.

$$NI_{FIFO} = NI_{LIFO} + (\text{LIFO effect})\ (1 - \text{tax rate})$$

Instructions

Obtain the annual report of a firm that reports a LIFO reserve in its footnotes.

(a) Identify the LIFO reserve at the two most recent balance sheet dates.

(b) Determine the LIFO effect during the most recent year.

(c) By how much would cost of goods sold during the most recent year change if the firm used FIFO?

(d) By how much would net income during the most recent year change if the firm used FIFO? (*Hint:* To estimate the tax rate, divide income tax expense by income before taxes.)

Case 2

The "Fortune 500" issue of *Fortune* magazine can serve as a useful reference. This annual issue, generally appearing in late April or early May, contains a great deal of information regarding the largest U.S. industrial and service companies.

Instructions

Examine the most recent edition and answer the following questions.

(a) Identify the three largest U.S. corporations in terms of revenue, profit, assets, market value, and employees.

(b) Identify the largest corporation in your state (by total revenue).

PROFESSIONAL SIMULATION

Inventory Valuation

Directions | Situation | Analysis | Explanation | Research | Resources

Directions

In this simulation, you will be asked questions regarding inventory valuation and measurement. Prepare responses to all parts.

Situation

Norwel Company makes miniature circuit boards that are components of wireless phones and personal organizers. The company has experienced strong growth, and you are especially interested in how well Norwel is managing its inventory balances. You have collected the following information for the current year.

Inventory at the beginning of year	$125.5 million
Inventory at the end of year, before any adjustments	$116.7 million
Total cost of goods sold, before any adjustments	$1,776.4 million

The company values inventory at lower of cost (using LIFO cost flow assumption) or market.

Analysis

Compute Norwel's inventory turnover ratio for the current year.

Resources

Use a computer spreadsheet to prepare a schedule showing the impact of the following items on Norwel's inventory turnover ratio.

(a) During the year, Norwel recorded sales and costs of goods sold on $2 million of units shipped to various wholesalers on consignment. At year-end, none of these units have been sold by wholesalers.

(b) Shipping contracts changed 2 months ago from f.o.b. shipping point to f.o.b. destination. At the end of the year, $5 million of products are en route to China (and will not arrive until after financial statements are released). Current inventory balances do not reflect this change in policy.

(c) To be more consistent with industry inventory valuation practices, Norwel changed from LIFO to FIFO for its inventory of high-speed circuit boards. This inventory is currently carried at $724 million (cost of goods sold, $941 million). Data for this item of inventory for the year are as follows.

Month	Units purchased	Inventory sold	Price per unit	Units balance
January 1	100		$3.10	100
April 10	150		3.20	250
October 20		130		120
November 20	250		3.50	370
December 15		150		220

Explanation

Prepare a brief memorandum to Norwel's management discussing the advantages of adopting the LIFO cost flow assumption.

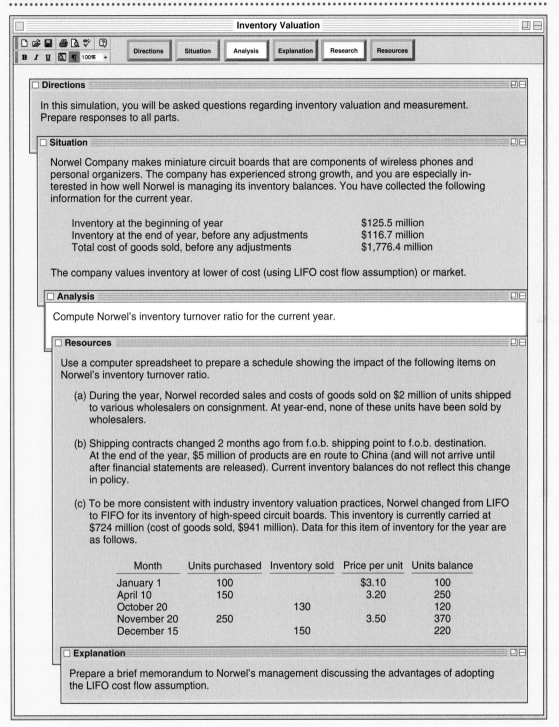

Remember to check the **Take Action! CD** and the book's **companion Web site** to find additional resources for this chapter.

CHAPTER 9

Inventories: Additional Valuation Issues

What Do Inventory Changes Tell Us?

Department stores face an ongoing challenge: They need to keep enough inventory on hand to meet customer demand, but at the same time not to accumulate too much inventory if demand for the product is less than expected. If demand falls short of expectations, the department store may be forced to reduce prices, thus losing sales revenue.

For example, the following table shows recent annual sales and inventory trends for major retailers, compared to the prior year.

Company	Sales	Inventory
Nordstrom	+ 7.36%	+18.53%
Sears	+ 3.49%	+10.83%
Federated Department Stores	+ 4.32%	+10.13%
Kmart	+ 6.68%	+ 8.64%
Target	+ 9.96%	+10.89%
May Department Stores	+ 5.93%	+ 6.10%
Wal-Mart	+19.91%	+14.94%
JCPenney	+ 6.66%	− 1.86%

Source: Company reports, fiscal years 1999 and 2000.

Note that for six of these eight retailers, inventories grew faster than sales from one year to the next. This trend should raise warning flags for investors in retail company stocks. Rising levels of inventories indicate that fewer shoppers are turning out to buy merchandise compared to activity in the prior period. Such a scenario will be reflected in lower inventory turnover ratios. As one analyst remarked, ". . . when inventory grows faster than sales, profits drop." That is, when retailers face slower sales and growing inventory, then markdowns in prices are usually not far behind. These markdowns, in turn, lead to lower sales revenue and income as profit margins on sales are squeezed.

The recent bankruptcies of retailers like **Ames Department Stores**, **Montgomery Ward**, and **Bradlees Stores** indicate the consequences of poor inventory management. And **Kmart**, which filed for bankruptcy in January 2002, was in an inventory "Catch-22." In order to work out of bankruptcy, Kmart needed to keep its shelves stocked so that customers would continue to shop in its remaining stores. However, vendors who were worried about Kmart's ability to manage its inventory were reluctant to ship goods without assurances that they would get paid. Thus, investors, creditors, and vendors keep an eye on information about inventories in the retail industry.

LEARNING OBJECTIVES

After studying this chapter, you should be able to:

1. **Explain and apply the lower of cost or market rule.**
2. **Identify when inventories are valued at net realizable value.**
3. **Explain when the relative sales value method is used to value inventories.**
4. **Explain accounting issues related to purchase commitments.**
5. **Determine ending inventory by applying the gross profit method.**
6. **Determine ending inventory by applying the retail inventory method.**
7. **Explain how inventory is reported and analyzed.**

PREVIEW OF CHAPTER 9

As indicated in the opening story, information on inventories and on changes in inventory is relevant to predicting profits. The purpose of this chapter is to discuss and illustrate some of the valuation and estimation concepts that are used to develop relevant inventory information.

The content and organization of the chapter are as follows.

INVENTORIES: ADDITIONAL VALUATION ISSUES

Lower of Cost or Market
- Ceiling and floor
- How LCM works
- Application of LCM
- "Market"
- Evaluation of rule

Valuation Bases
- Net realizable value
- Relative sales value
- Purchase commitments

Gross Profit Method
- Gross profit percentage
- Evaluation of method

Retail Inventory Method
- Terminology
- Conventional method
- Special items
- Evaluation of method

Presentation and Analysis
- Presentation
- Analysis

LOWER OF COST OR MARKET

OBJECTIVE 1
Explain and apply the lower of cost or market rule.

As noted in Chapter 8, inventories are recorded at their original cost. However, a major departure from the historical cost principle is made in the area of inventory valuation if inventory declines in value below its original cost. Whatever the reason for a decline—obsolescence, price-level changes, or damaged goods—the inventory should be written down to reflect this loss. **The general rule is that the historical cost principle is abandoned when the future utility (revenue-producing ability) of the asset is no longer as great as its original cost.**

Inventories that experience a decline in utility therefore are valued on the basis of the lower of cost or market (LCM), instead of on original cost. **Cost** is the acquisition price of inventory computed using one of the historical cost-based methods—specific identification, average cost, FIFO, or LIFO. The term **market** in the phrase "the lower of cost or market" generally means the cost to replace the item by purchase or reproduction. In a retailing business, the term "market" refers to the market in which goods were purchased, not the market in which they are sold. In manufacturing, the term "market" refers to the cost to reproduce the goods. Thus the rule really means that **goods are to be valued at cost or at cost to replace, whichever is lower**. For example, a Casio calculator wristwatch that costs a retailer $30 when purchased, that can be sold for $48.95, and that can be replaced for $25 should be valued at $25 for inventory purposes under the lower of cost or market rule. The lower of cost or market rule of valuation can be used after any of the cost flow methods discussed in Chapter 8 have been applied to determine the inventory cost.

UNDERLYING CONCEPTS

The use of the lower of cost or market method is an excellent example of the conservatism constraint.

A departure from cost is justified because **a loss of utility should be charged against revenues in the period in which the loss occurs**, not in the period in which it is sold. In addition, the lower of cost or market method is **a conservative approach to inventory valuation**. That is, when doubt exists about the value of an asset, it is preferable to undervalue rather than to overvalue it.

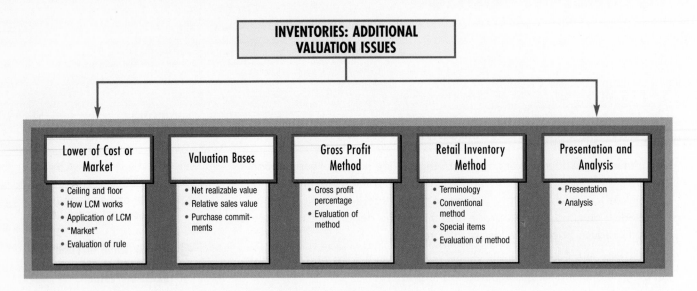

Lower of Cost or Market—Ceiling and Floor

Why use replacement cost to represent market value? The reason is that a decline in the replacement cost of an item usually reflects or predicts a decline in selling price. Using replacement cost allows a company to maintain a consistent rate of gross profit on sales (a normal profit margin).

Sometimes, however, a reduction in the replacement cost of an item does not indicate a corresponding reduction in its utility. Then, two additional valuation limitations are used to value ending inventory—net realizable value and net realizable value less a normal profit margin. **Net realizable value (NRV)** is defined as the estimated selling price in the ordinary course of business less reasonably predictable costs of completion and disposal. A normal profit margin is subtracted from that amount to arrive at **net realizable value less a normal profit margin**.

To illustrate, assume that Jerry Mander Corp. has unfinished inventory with a sales value of $1,000, estimated cost of completion of $300, and a normal profit margin of 10 percent of sales. The net realizable value can be determined as follows.

Inventory—sales value	$1,000
Less: Estimated cost of completion and disposal	300
Net realizable value	700
Less: Allowance for normal profit margin (10% of sales)	100
Net realizable value less a normal profit margin	$ 600

ILLUSTRATION 9-1
Computation of Net Realizable Value

The general rule of **lower of cost or market** is this: **Inventory is valued at the lower of cost or market, with market limited to an amount that is not more than net realizable value nor less than net realizable value less a normal profit margin.**[1]

What is the rationale for these two limitations? The **upper (ceiling)** and **lower (floor) limits** for the value of the inventory are intended to prevent the inventory from being reported at an amount in excess of the net selling price or at an amount less than the net selling price less a normal profit margin. The maximum limitation—**not to exceed the net realizable value (ceiling)**—covers obsolete, damaged, or shopworn material. It prevents overstatement of inventories and understatement of the loss in the current period.

That is, if the replacement cost of an item is greater than its net realizable value, inventory should not be reported at replacement cost because the company can receive only the selling price less cost of disposal. To report the inventory at replacement cost would result in an **overstatement of inventory** and an **understated loss** in the current period. To illustrate, assume that **Staples** paid $600 for a laser printer that can now be replaced for $500 and whose net realizable value is $350. At what amount should the laser printer be reported in the financial statements? To report the replacement cost of $500 overstates the ending inventory and understates the loss for the period. The printer should therefore be reported at $350.

UNDERLYING CONCEPTS

Setting a floor and a ceiling increases the relevancy of the inventory presentation. The inventory figure provides a better understanding of how much revenue the inventory will generate.

The minimum limitation—**not to be less than net realizable value reduced by an allowance for an approximately normal profit margin (floor)**—deters understatement of inventory and overstatement of the loss in the current period. It establishes a floor below which the inventory should not be priced, regardless of replacement cost. It makes no sense to price inventory below net realizable value less a normal margin because this minimum amount (floor) measures what the company can receive for the inventory and still earn a normal profit.

These ceiling and floor guidelines are illustrated graphically in Illustration 9-2.

[1]"Restatement and Revision of Accounting Research Bulletins," *Accounting Research Bulletin No. 43* (New York: AICPA, 1953), Ch. 4, par. 8.

ILLUSTRATION 9-2
Inventory Valuation—
Lower of Cost or Market

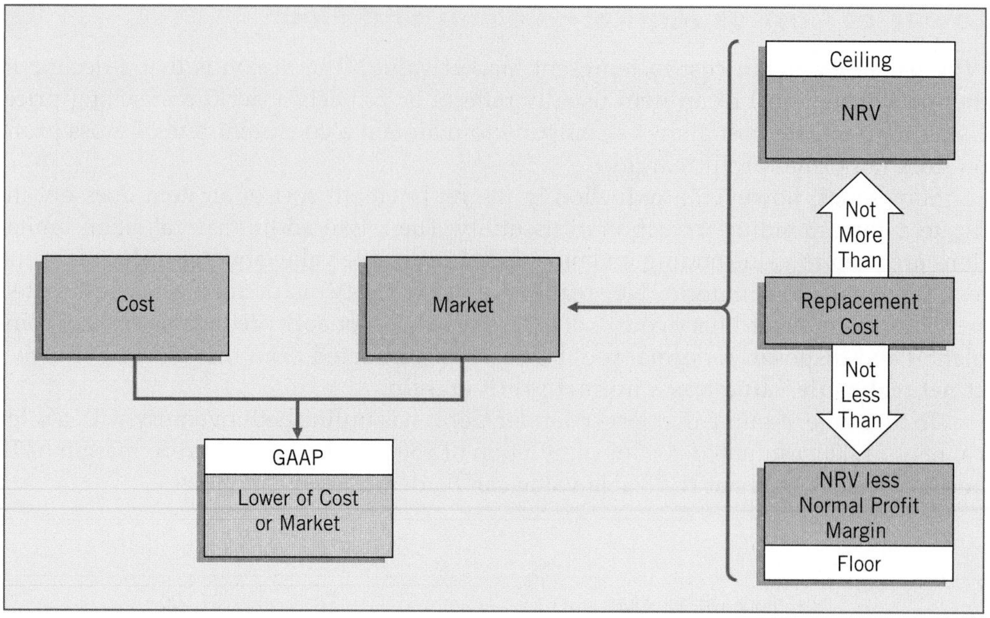

How Lower of Cost or Market Works

The amount that is compared to cost, often referred to as **designated market value**, is **always the middle value of three amounts**: replacement cost, net realizable value, and net realizable value less a normal profit margin. To illustrate how designated market value is computed, assume the following information relative to the inventory of Regner Foods, Inc.

ILLUSTRATION 9-3
Computation of
Designated Market Value

Food	Replacement Cost	Net Realizable Value (Ceiling)	Net Realizable Value Less a Normal Profit Margin (Floor)	Designated Market Value
Spinach	$ 88,000	$120,000	$104,000	$104,000
Carrots	90,000	100,000	70,000	90,000
Cut beans	45,000	40,000	27,500	40,000
Peas	36,000	72,000	48,000	48,000
Mixed vegetables	105,000	92,000	80,000	92,000

Designated Market Value Decision:

Spinach	Net realizable value less a normal profit margin is selected because it is the middle value.
Carrots	Replacement cost is selected because it is the middle value.
Cut beans	Net realizable value is selected because it is the middle value.
Peas	Net realizable value less a normal profit margin is selected because it is the middle value.
Mixed vegetables	Net realizable value is selected because it is the middle value.

Designated market value is then compared to cost to determine the lower of cost or market. To illustrate, the final inventory value for Regner Foods is determined as follows.

ILLUSTRATION 9-4
Determining Final Inventory Value

Food	Cost	Replacement Cost	Net Realizable Value (Ceiling)	Net Realizable Value Less a Normal Profit Margin (Floor)	Designated Market Value	Final Inventory Value
Spinach	$ 80,000	$ 88,000	$120,000	$104,000	$104,000	$ 80,000
Carrots	100,000	90,000	100,000	70,000	90,000	90,000
Cut beans	50,000	45,000	40,000	27,500	40,000	40,000
Peas	90,000	36,000	72,000	48,000	48,000	48,000
Mixed vegetables	95,000	105,000	92,000	80,000	92,000	92,000
						$350,000

Final Inventory Value:

Spinach	Cost ($80,000) is selected because it is lower than designated market value (net realizable value less a normal profit margin).
Carrots	Designated market value (replacement cost, $90,000) is selected because it is lower than cost.
Cut beans	Designated market value (net realizable value, $40,000) is selected because it is lower than cost.
Peas	Designated market value (net realizable value less a normal profit margin, $48,000) is selected because it is lower than cost.
Mixed vegetables	Designated market value (net realizable value, $92,000) is selected because it is lower than cost.

The application of the lower of cost or market rule incorporates only losses in value that occur in the normal course of business from such causes as style changes, shift in demand, or regular shop wear. Damaged or deteriorated goods are reduced to net realizable value. When material, such goods may be carried in separate inventory accounts.

Methods of Applying Lower of Cost or Market

In the previous illustration for Regner Foods, we assumed that the lower of cost or market rule was applied to each individual type of food. However, the lower of cost or market rule may be applied in different ways: either directly to each item, to each category, or to the total of the inventory. If a major category or total inventory approach is followed, increases in market prices tend to offset decreases in market prices. To illustrate, assume that Regner Foods separates its food products into frozen and canned for purposes of designating major categories.

ILLUSTRATION 9-5
Alternative Applications of Lower of Cost or Market

			Lower of Cost or Market By:		
	Cost	Designated Market	**Individual Items**	**Major Categories**	**Total Inventory**
Frozen					
Spinach	$ 80,000	$104,000	$ 80,000		
Carrots	100,000	90,000	90,000		
Cut beans	50,000	40,000	40,000		
Total frozen	230,000	234,000		$230,000	
Canned					
Peas	90,000	48,000	48,000		
Mixed vegetables	95,000	92,000	92,000		
Total canned	185,000	140,000		140,000	
Total	$415,000	$374,000	$350,000	$370,000	$374,000

As shown in Illustration 9-5, if the lower of cost or market rule is applied to individual items, the amount of inventory is $350,000. If LCM is applied to major categories, it is $370,000. If it is applied to the total inventory, it is $374,000. The reason for the difference is that when the major categories or total inventory approach is adopted, market values higher than cost are offset against market values lower than cost. For Regner Foods, the high market value for spinach is partially offset when the major categories approach is adopted, and it is totally offset when the total inventory approach is used.

The most common practice is to price the inventory on an item-by-item basis. For one thing, tax rules require that an individual-item basis be used unless it involves practical difficulties. In addition, the individual-item approach gives the most conservative valuation for balance sheet purposes.[2] Inventory is often priced on a total-inventory basis when there is only one end product (comprised of many different raw materials) because the main concern is the pricing of the final inventory. If several end products are produced, a category approach might be used. The method selected should be the one that most clearly reflects income. **Whichever method is selected, it should be applied consistently from one period to another.**[3]

Recording "Market" Instead of Cost

Two methods are used for recording inventory at market. One method, referred to as the **direct method**, substitutes the market value figure for cost when valuing the inventory. As a result, no loss is reported in the income statement because the loss is buried in cost of goods sold. The second method, referred to as the **indirect method** or **allowance method**, does not change the cost amount, but establishes a separate contra asset account and a loss account to record the writeoff.

To illustrate entries under both methods, we use the following inventory data.

Cost of goods sold (before adjustment to market)	$108,000
Ending inventory (cost)	82,000
Ending inventory (at market)	70,000

The following entries assume the use of a **perpetual** inventory system.

ILLUSTRATION 9-6
Accounting for the Reduction of Inventory to Market—Perpetual Inventory System

Direct Method			Indirect or Allowance Method		
To reduce inventory from cost to market:					
Cost of Goods Sold	12,000		Loss Due to Market Decline of Inventory	12,000	
Inventory		12,000	Allowance to Reduce Inventory to Market		12,000

[2]If a company uses dollar-value LIFO, determining the LIFO cost of an individual item may be more difficult. The company might decide that it is more appropriate to apply the lower of cost or market rule to the total amount of each pool. The AICPA Task Force on LIFO Inventory Problems concluded that the most reasonable approach to applying the lower of cost or market provisions to LIFO inventories is to base the determination on reasonable groupings of items and that a pool constitutes a reasonable grouping. Both the Task Force and AcSEC, however, support the use of the item-by-item approach for identifying product obsolescence and product discontinuance write-downs and write-offs.

[3]Inventory accounting for financial statement purposes can be different from the accounting for income tax purposes. For example, the lower of cost or market rule cannot be used with LIFO for tax purposes. There is nothing, however, to prevent the use of the lower of cost or market and LIFO for financial accounting purposes. In addition, for financial accounting purposes, companies often write down slow-moving inventory because experience indicates that some of it will not be sold for many years, if at all. However, to be deductible for tax purposes a write-down in inventory value resulting from the application of the lower of cost or market rule can be taken only in the year in which the actual decline in the sale price of the item occurs. Also, the write-down must be computed on an individual-item basis rather than on classes of inventory or on the inventory as a whole.

The advantage of identifying the loss due to market decline is that it is shown separately from cost of goods sold in the income statement (not as an extraordinary item). Therefore, the cost of goods sold for the year is not distorted. The data from the preceding illustration are used to contrast the differing amounts reported in the income statements below.

ILLUSTRATION 9-7
Income Statement Presentation—Direct and Indirect Methods of Reducing Inventory to Market

Direct Method

Revenue from sales	$200,000
Cost of goods sold (after adjustment to market*)	120,000
Gross profit on sales	$ 80,000

Indirect or Allowance Method

Revenue from sales	$200,000
Cost of goods sold	108,000
Gross profit on sales	92,000
Loss due to market decline of inventory	12,000
	$ 80,000

*Cost of goods sold (before adjustment to market)	$ 108,000
Difference between inventory at cost and market ($82,000–$70,000)	12,000
Cost of goods sold (after adjustment to market)	$ 120,000

The second presentation is preferable, because it clearly discloses the loss resulting from the market decline of inventory prices. The first presentation buries the loss in the cost of goods sold. The Allowance to Reduce Inventory to Market would be reported on the balance sheet as a $12,000 deduction from the inventory. This deduction permits both the income statement and the balance sheet to show the ending inventory of $82,000, although the balance sheet shows a net amount of $70,000. It also keeps subsidiary inventory ledgers and records in correspondence with the control account without changing unit prices.

UNDERLYING CONCEPTS

The income statement under the direct method presentation lacks *representational faithfulness.* The cost of goods sold does not represent what it purports to represent. However, allowing this presentation illustrates the concept of materiality. That is, the presentation does not affect net income and would not "change the judgment of a reasonable person."

Although use of an allowance account permits balance sheet disclosure of the inventory at cost and at the lower of cost or market, it raises the problem of how to dispose of the balance of the new account in the following period. If the merchandise in question is still on hand, the allowance account should be retained. Otherwise, beginning inventory and cost of goods are overstated. But if the goods have been sold, then the account should be closed. A "new allowance account" is then established for any decline in inventory value that has taken place in the current year.[4]

Some accountants leave this account on the books and merely adjust the balance at the next year-end to agree with the discrepancy between cost and the lower of cost or market at that balance sheet date. Thus, if prices are falling, a loss is recorded. If prices are rising, a loss recorded in prior years is recovered and a "gain" (which is not really a gain, but a recovery of a previously recognized loss) is recorded, as illustrated in the example below.

ILLUSTRATION 9-8
Effect on Net Income of Reducing Inventory to Market

Date	Inventory at Cost	Inventory at Market	Amount Required in Valuation Account	Adjustment of Valuation Account Balance	Effect on Net Income
Dec. 31, 2003	$188,000	$176,000	$12,000	$12,000 inc.	Loss
Dec. 31, 2004	194,000	187,000	7,000	5,000 dec.	Gain
Dec. 31, 2005	173,000	174,000	0	7,000 dec.	Gain
Dec. 31, 2006	182,000	180,000	2,000	2,000 inc.	Loss

[4]The AICPA Task Force on LIFO Inventory Problems concluded that for LIFO inventories the allowance from the prior year should be closed and that the allowance at the end of the year should be based on a new lower of cost or market computation. *Issues Paper* (New York: AICPA, November 30, 1984), pp. 50–55.

UNDERLYING CONCEPTS

The inconsistency in the presentation of inventory is an example of the trade-off between *relevancy and reliability.* Market is more relevant than cost, and cost is more reliable than market. Apparently, relevance takes precedence in a down market, and reliability is more important in an up market.

This net "gain" can be thought of as the excess of the credit effect of closing the beginning allowance balance over the debit effect of setting up the current year-end allowance account. Recognition of gain or loss has the same effect on net income as closing the allowance balance to beginning inventory or to cost of goods sold. Recovery of the loss up to the original cost is permitted, **but it may not exceed original cost.**

Evaluation of the Lower of Cost or Market Rule

The lower of cost or market rule suffers some conceptual deficiencies.

1. Decreases in the value of the asset and the charge to expense are recognized in the period in which the loss in utility occurs—not in the period of sale. On the other hand, increases in the value of the asset are recognized only at the point of sale. This treatment is inconsistent and can lead to distortions in income data.
2. Application of the LCM rule results in inconsistency because the inventory of a company may be valued at cost in one year and at market in the next year.
3. Lower of cost or market values the inventory in the balance sheet conservatively, but its effect on the income statement may or may not be conservative. Net income for the year in which the loss is taken is definitely lower. But net income of the subsequent period may be higher than normal if the expected reductions in sales price do not materialize.
4. Application of the lower of cost or market rule uses a "normal profit" in determining inventory values. Since "normal profit" is an estimated figure based upon past experience (and might not be attained in the future), it is subjective in nature and presents an opportunity for income manipulation.

Many financial statement users appreciate the lower of cost or market rule because they at least know that the inventory is not overstated. In addition, recognizing all losses but anticipating no gains generally results in lower income.

WHAT DO THE NUMBERS MEAN?

ALL ITS BERRIES IN ONE BASKET

The latest quarter has not been very good for **Northland Cranberries**. The Wisconsin cranberry producer reported lower sales compared to the same quarter in the prior year and an operating loss:

	Current Quarter	Same Quarter, Prior Year
Revenues	$61,206,000	$76,609,000
Net income	(79,846,000)	3,577,000

Things are so bad that Northland is in violation of several debt covenants and is looking to sell assets in order to generate cash for paying its debts.

What is behind these dismal numbers? Northland cites declining market prices for cranberries which have led the company to take an inventory write-down of $30.4 million in the current quarter. All companies in this industry are affected by declining market prices for cranberries, but Northland is particularly vulnerable because so much of its business is concentrated in the cranberry market. What's more, Northland is a small competitor in a cranberry and juice market dominated by major producers, such as **Ocean Spray**, **Tropicana** (owned by **PepsiCo**), and **Minute-Maid** (owned by **Coca-Cola**). These large producers are able to withstand market pressures in the cranberry market with sales in other juices and beverages. Northland must take its lumps in the cranberry market with inventory write-downs and operating losses.

VALUATION BASES

Valuation at Net Realizable Value

For the most part, inventory is recorded at cost or at the lower of cost or market.[5] However, many believe that market should always be defined as net realizable value (selling price less estimated costs to complete and sell), rather than replacement cost, for purposes of applying the lower of cost or market rule. This argument is based on the fact that net realizable value is the amount that will be collected from this inventory in the future.[6]

OBJECTIVE 2
Identify when inventories are valued at net realizable value.

Under limited circumstances, support exists for **recording inventory at net realizable value** even if that amount is above cost. This exception to the normal recognition rule is permitted under the following conditions: when (1) there is a controlled market with a quoted price applicable to all quantities and (2) no significant costs of disposal are involved. Inventories of certain minerals (rare metals especially) are ordinarily reported at selling prices because there is often a controlled market without significant costs of disposal. A similar treatment is given agricultural products that are immediately marketable at quoted prices.

INTERNATIONAL INSIGHT

In the Netherlands, Canada, and the United Kingdom, inventory is valued at "lower of cost or market," but in contrast to the U.S., *market* in these nations is defined as "net realizable value." The U.S. is the only country that defines *market* as something other than net realizable value.

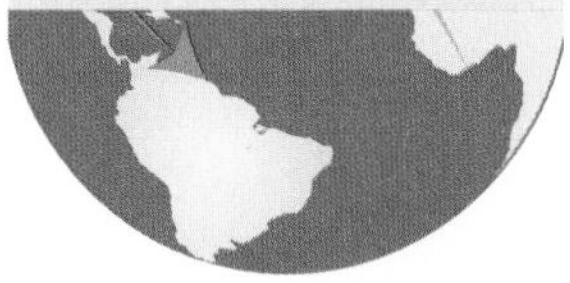

Another reason for allowing this method of valuation is that sometimes the cost figures are too difficult to obtain. In a manufacturing plant, various raw materials and purchased parts are put together to create a finished product. The various items in inventory, whether completely or partially finished, can be accounted for on a basis of cost because the cost of each individual component part is known. In a meat-packing plant, however, a different situation prevails. The "raw material" consists of cattle, hogs, or sheep, each unit of which is purchased as a whole and then divided into parts that are the products. Instead of one product out of many raw materials or parts, many products are made from one "unit" of raw material. To allocate the cost of the animal "on the hoof" into the cost of ribs, chucks, and shoulders, for instance, is a practical impossibility. It is much easier and more useful to determine the market price of the various products and value them in the inventory at selling price less the various costs necessary to get them to market (costs such as shipping and handling). Hence, because of a peculiarity of the meat-packing industry, **inventories are sometimes carried at sales price less distribution costs**.

Valuation Using Relative Sales Value

A special problem arises when a group of varying units is bought in a single **lump sum purchase**, a so-called **basket purchase**. Assume that Woodland Developers purchases land for $1 million that can be subdivided into 400 lots. These lots are of different sizes

OBJECTIVE 3
Explain when the relative sales value method is used to value inventories.

[5]Manufacturing companies frequently employ a **standardized cost system** that predetermines the unit costs for material, labor, and manufacturing overhead and values raw materials, work in process, and finished goods inventories at their standard costs. For financial reporting purposes, the pricing of inventories at standard costs is acceptable if there is no significant difference between the actual costs and standard costs. If there is a significant difference, the inventory amounts should be adjusted to actual cost. In *Accounting Research and Terminology Bulletin, Final Edition,* the profession notes that "**standard costs are acceptable if adjusted at reasonable intervals to reflect current conditions**." **Burlington Industries** and **Hewlett-Packard** are examples of companies that use standard costs for valuing at least a portion of their inventory.

[6]"The Accounting Basis of Inventories," *Accounting Research Study No. 13* (New York: AICPA, 1973) recommends that net realizable value be adopted. It also should be noted that a literal interpretation of the rules of lower of cost or market is frequently not applied in practice. For example, the lower limit—net realizable value less a normal markup—is rarely computed and applied because it is a fairly subjective computation. In addition, inventory is often not reduced to market unless its disposition is expected to result in a loss. Furthermore, if the net realizable value of finished goods exceeds cost, it is usually assumed that both work in process and raw materials do also. In practice, therefore, *ARB No. 43* is considered a guide, and professional judgment is often exercised in lieu of following this pronouncement literally.

and shapes but can be roughly sorted into three groups graded A, B, and C. As lots are sold, the purchase cost of $1 million is apportioned among the lots sold and the lots remaining on hand.

It is inappropriate to divide 400 lots into the total cost of $1 million to get a cost of $2,500 for each lot, because they vary in size, shape, and attractiveness. When such a situation is encountered—and it is not at all unusual—the common and most logical practice is to allocate the total cost among the various units on the basis of their relative sales value. For the example given, the allocation works out as follows.

ILLUSTRATION 9-9
Allocation of Costs, Using Relative Sales Value

Lots	Number of Lots	Sales Price Per Lot	Total Sales Price	Relative Sales Price	Total Cost	Cost Allocated to Lots	Cost Per Lot
A	100	$10,000	$1,000,000	100/250	$1,000,000	$ 400,000	$4,000
B	100	6,000	600,000	60/250	1,000,000	240,000	2,400
C	200	4,500	900,000	90/250	1,000,000	360,000	1,800
			$2,500,000			$1,000,000	

Using the amounts given in the "Cost Per Lot" column, the cost of lots sold and the gross profit can be determined as follows.

ILLUSTRATION 9-10
Determination of Gross Profit, Using Relative Sales Value

Lots	Number of Lots Sold	Cost Per Lot	Cost of Lots Sold	Sales	Gross Profit
A	77	$4,000	$308,000	$ 770,000	$ 462,000
B	80	2,400	192,000	480,000	288,000
C	100	1,800	180,000	450,000	270,000
			$680,000	$1,700,000	$1,020,000

The ending inventory is therefore $320,000 ($1,000,000 − $680,000).

This inventory amount can also be computed in another manner. The ratio of cost to selling price for all the lots is $1 million divided by $2,500,000, or 40 percent. Accordingly, if the total sales price of lots sold is, say $1,700,000, then the cost of these lots sold is 40 percent of $1,700,000, or $680,000. The inventory of lots on hand is then $1 million less $680,000, or $320,000.

The relative sales value method is used throughout the petroleum industry to value (at cost) the many products and by-products obtained from a barrel of crude oil.

Purchase Commitments—A Special Problem

OBJECTIVE 4
Explain accounting issues related to purchase commitments.

In many lines of business, the survival and continued profitability of a firm depends on its having a sufficient stock of merchandise to meet all customer demands. Consequently, it is quite common for a company to agree to buy inventory weeks, months, or even years in advance. Such arrangements may be made on the basis of estimated or firm sales commitments by the company's customers. Generally, title to the merchandise or materials described in these **purchase commitments** has not passed to the buyer. Indeed, the goods may exist only as natural resources, or in the case of commodities, as unplanted seed, or in the case of a product, as work in process.

Usually it is neither necessary nor proper for the buyer to make any entries to reflect commitments for purchases of goods that have not been shipped by the seller. Ordinary orders, for which the prices are determined at the time of shipment and **which are subject to cancellation** by the buyer or seller, do not represent either an asset or a liability to the buyer. Therefore they need not be recorded in the books or reported in the financial statements.

Even with formal, noncancelable purchase contracts, no asset or liability is recognized at the date of inception, **because the contract is "executory" in nature**: Neither party has fulfilled its part of the contract. However, if material, such contract details should be disclosed in the buyer's balance sheet in a note, an example of which is shown in Illustration 9-11.

Note 1: Contracts for the purchase of raw materials in 2002 have been executed in the amount of $600,000. The market price of such raw materials on December 31, 2001, is $640,000.

ILLUSTRATION 9-11
Disclosure of Purchase Commitment

In the foregoing illustration the contracted price was less than the market price at the balance sheet date. **If the contracted price is in excess of market and it is expected that losses will occur when the purchase is effected, losses should be recognized in the period during which such declines in market prices take place.**[7]

In the early 1980s, many Northwest forest product companies such as **Boise Cascade**, **Georgia-Pacific**, **Weyerhaeuser**, and **St. Regis Paper Co.** signed long-term timber-cutting contracts with the U.S. Forest Service. These contracts required that the companies pay $310 per thousand board feet for timber-cutting rights. Unfortunately, the market price for timber-cutting rights in late 1984 dropped to $80 per thousand board feet. As a result, a number of these companies had long-term contracts that, if fulfilled, projected substantial future losses.

To illustrate the accounting problem, assume that St. Regis Paper Co. signed timber-cutting contracts to be executed in 2005 at a firm price of $10,000,000 and that the market price of the timber cutting rights on December 31, 2004, dropped to $7,000,000. The following entry is made on December 31, 2004.

Unrealized Holding Gain or Loss—Income (Purchase Commitments)	3,000,000	
Estimated Liability on Purchase Commitments		3,000,000

UNDERLYING CONCEPTS

Reporting the loss is *conservative*. However, reporting the decline in market price is debatable because no asset is recorded. This area demonstrates the need for good definitions of assets and liabilities.

This unrealized holding loss would be reported in the income statement under "Other expenses and losses." The Estimated Liability on Purchase Commitments is reported in the current liabilities section of the balance sheet because the contract is to be executed within the next fiscal year. When St. Regis cuts the timber at a cost of $10 million, the following entry would be made.

Purchases (Inventory)	7,000,000	
Estimated Liability on Purchase Commitments	3,000,000	
Cash		10,000,000

The company paid $10 million for a contract worth only $7 million. The loss was recorded in the previous period—when the price actually declined.

If the price is partially or fully recovered before the timber is cut, the Estimated Liability on Purchase Commitments is reduced. A resulting gain is then reported in the period of the price increase for the amount of the partial or full recovery. For example, Congress permitted some of these companies to buy out of their contracts at reduced prices in order to avoid some potential bankruptcies. To illustrate, assume that St. Regis is permitted to reduce its contract price and therefore its commitment by $1,000,000. The entry to record this transaction is as follows.

Estimated Liability on Purchase Commitments	1,000,000	
Unrealized Holding Gain or Loss—Income (Purchase Commitments)		1,000,000

If the market price at the time the timber is cut is more than $2,000,000 below the contract price, St. Regis will have to recognize an additional loss in the period of cutting and record the purchase at the lower of cost or market.

[7] *Accounting Research Bulletin No. 43*, op. cit., par. 16.

The purchasers in purchase commitments can protect themselves against the possibility of market price declines of goods under contract by hedging. **Hedging** is accomplished through a futures contract in which the purchaser in the purchase commitment simultaneously contracts to a future **sale** of the same quantity of the same or similar goods at a fixed price. When a company holds a buy position in a purchase commitment and a sell position in a futures contract in the same commodity, it will be better off under one contract by approximately (maybe exactly) the same amount by which it is worse off under the other contract. That is, a loss on one will be offset by a gain on the other. For example, if St. Regis Paper Co. had hedged its purchase commitment contract by selling futures contracts for timber rights of the same amount, its loss of $3,000,000 on the purchase commitment would have been offset by a $3,000,000 gain on the futures contract.[8]

Accounting for purchase commitments (and, for that matter, all commitments) is unsettled and controversial. Some argue that these contracts should be reported as assets and liabilities at the time the contract is signed.[9] Others believe that the present recognition at the delivery date is more appropriate. *FASB Concepts Statement No. 6* states, "a purchase commitment involves both an item that might be recorded as an asset and an item that might be recorded as a liability. That is, it involves both a right to receive assets and an obligation to pay. . . . If both the right to receive assets and the obligation to pay were recorded at the time of the purchase commitment, the nature of the loss and the valuation account that records it when the price falls would be clearly seen." Although the discussion in *Concepts Statement No. 6* does not exclude the possibility of recording assets and liabilities for purchase commitments, it contains no conclusions or implications about whether they should be recorded.[10]

THE GROSS PROFIT METHOD OF ESTIMATING INVENTORY

OBJECTIVE 5
Determine ending inventory by applying the gross profit method.

Recall that the basic purpose of taking a physical inventory is to verify the accuracy of the perpetual inventory records or, if no records exist, to arrive at an inventory amount. Sometimes, taking a physical inventory is impractical. In such cases, substitute measures are used to approximate inventory on hand.

One substitute method of verifying or determining the inventory amount is called the **gross profit method** (often called the gross margin method). This method is widely used by auditors in situations (e.g., interim reports) where only an estimate of the company's inventory is needed. It is also used where either inventory or inventory records have been destroyed by fire or other catastrophe.

The **gross profit method** is based on three assumptions: (1) The beginning inventory plus purchases equal total goods to be accounted for. (2) Goods not sold must be on hand. (3) If the sales, reduced to cost, are deducted from the sum of the opening inventory plus purchases, the result is the ending inventory.

[8]A complete discussion regarding hedging and the use of derivatives such as futures is provided in Appendix 17A.

[9]See, for example, Yuji Ijiri, *Recognition of Contractual Rights and Obligations, Research Report* (Stamford, Conn.: FASB, 1980), who argues that firm purchase commitments should be capitalized. "Firm" means that it is unlikely that performance under the contract can be avoided without a severe penalty.

Also, see Mahendra R. Gujarathi and Stanley F. Biggs, "Accounting for Purchase Commitments: Some Issues and Recommendations," *Accounting Horizons* (September 1988), pp. 75–78, who conclude, "Recording an asset and liability on the date of inception for the noncancelable purchase commitments is suggested as the first significant step towards alleviating the accounting problems associated with the issue. At year-end, the potential gains and losses should be treated as contingencies under *FASB 5* which provides a coherent structure for the accounting and informative disclosure for such gains and losses."

[10]"Elements of Financial Statements," *Statement of Financial Accounting Concepts No. 6* (Stamford, Conn.: FASB, 1985), pars. 251–253.

To illustrate, assume that Cetus Corp. has a beginning inventory of $60,000 and purchases of $200,000, both at cost. Sales at selling price amount to $280,000. The gross profit on selling price is 30 percent. The gross margin method is applied as follows.

ILLUSTRATION 9-12
Application of Gross Profit Method

Beginning inventory (at cost)		$ 60,000
Purchases (at cost)		200,000
Goods available (at cost)		260,000
Sales (at selling price)	$280,000	
Less: Gross profit (30% of $280,000)	84,000	
Sales (at cost)		196,000
Approximate inventory (at cost)		$ 64,000

All the information needed to compute Cetus's inventory at cost, except for the gross profit percentage, is available in the current period's records. The gross profit percentage is determined by reviewing company policies or prior period records. In some cases, this percentage must be adjusted if prior periods are not considered representative of the current period.[11]

Computation of Gross Profit Percentage

In most situations, the **gross profit percentage** is given as a percentage of selling price. The previous illustration, for example, used a 30 percent gross profit on sales. Gross profit on selling price is the common method for quoting the profit for several reasons: (1) Most goods are stated on a retail basis, not a cost basis. (2) A profit quoted on selling price is lower than one based on cost, and this lower rate gives a favorable impression to the consumer. (3) The gross profit based on selling price can never exceed 100 percent.[12]

In the previous example, the gross profit was a given. But how was that figure derived? To see how a gross profit percentage is computed, assume that an article cost $15 and sells for $20, a gross profit of $5. This markup is ¼ or 25 percent of retail and ⅓ or 33⅓ percent of cost:

ILLUSTRATION 9-13
Computation of Gross Profit Percentage

$$\frac{\text{Markup}}{\text{Retail}} = \frac{\$5}{\$20} = 25\% \text{ at retail} \qquad \frac{\text{Markup}}{\text{Cost}} = \frac{\$5}{\$15} = 33\tfrac{1}{3}\% \text{ on cost}$$

[11]An alternative method of estimating inventory using the gross profit percentage, considered by some to be less complicated than the traditional method illustrated above, uses the standard income statement format as follows. (Assume the same data as in the Cetus Corp. illustration above.)

Sales		$280,000			$280,000
Cost of sales					
Beginning inventory	$ 60,000			$ 60,000	
Purchases	200,000			200,000	
Goods available for sale	260,000			260,000	
Ending inventory	(3) ?			(3) 64,000 Est.	
Cost of goods sold		(2) ?			(2)196,000 Est.
Gross profit on sales (30%)		(1) ?			(1) 84,000 Est.

Compute the unknowns as follows: first the gross profit amount, then cost of goods sold, and then the ending inventory.

(1) $280,000 × 30% = $84,000 (gross profit on sales).
(2) $280,000 − $84,000 = $196,000 (cost of goods sold).
(3) $260,000 − $196,000 = $64,000 (ending inventory).

[12]The terms "gross margin percentage," "rate of gross profit," and "percentage markup" are synonymous, although "markup" is more commonly used in reference to cost and "gross profit" in reference to sales.

Although it is normal to compute the gross profit on the basis of selling price, you should understand the basic relationship between markup on cost and markup on selling price.

For example, assume that you were told that the markup on cost for a given item is 25 percent. What, then, is the **gross profit on selling price**? To find the answer, assume that the selling price of the item is $1. In this case, the following formula applies.

$$\text{Cost} + \text{Gross profit} = \text{Selling price}$$
$$C + .25C = SP$$
$$(1 + .25)C = SP$$
$$1.25C = \$1.00$$
$$C = \$0.80$$

The gross profit equals $0.20 ($1.00 − $0.80), and the rate of gross profit on selling price is therefore 20 percent ($0.20/$1.00).

Conversely, assume that you were told that the gross profit on selling price is 20 percent. What is the **markup on cost**? To find the answer, again assume that the selling price is $1. Again, the same formula holds.

$$\text{Cost} + \text{Gross profit} = \text{Selling price}$$
$$C + .20SP = SP$$
$$C = (1 - .20)SP$$
$$C = .80SP$$
$$C = .80(\$1.00)$$
$$C = \$0.80$$

Here, as in the example above, the markup equals $0.20 ($1.00 − $0.80), and the markup on cost is 25 percent ($0.20/$0.80).

Retailers use the following formulas to express these relationships.

ILLUSTRATION 9-14
Formulas Relating to Gross Profit

$$1.\ \text{Gross profit on selling price} = \frac{\text{Percentage markup on cost}}{100\% + \text{Percentage markup on cost}}$$

$$2.\ \text{Percentage markup on cost} = \frac{\text{Gross profit on selling price}}{100\% - \text{Gross profit on selling price}}$$

To understand how these formulas are employed, consider the following calculations.

ILLUSTRATION 9-15
Application of Gross Profit Formulas

Gross Profit on Selling Price		Percentage Markup on Cost
Given: 20%	→	$\frac{.20}{1.00 - .20} = 25\%$
Given: 25%	→	$\frac{.25}{1.00 - .25} = 33\frac{1}{3}\%$
$\frac{.25}{1.00 + .25} = 20\%$	←	Given: 25%
$\frac{.50}{1.00 + .50} = 33\frac{1}{3}\%$	←	Given: 50%

Because selling price is greater than cost, and with the gross profit amount the same for both, **gross profit on selling price will always be less than the related percentage based on cost.** It should be emphasized that sales may not be multiplied by a cost-based markup percentage; the gross profit percentage must be converted to a percentage based on selling price.

THE SQUEEZE

WHAT DO THE NUMBERS MEAN?

Gross profits are closely followed by managements and analysts. A small change in the gross profit rate can have a significant effect on the bottom line. In the mid-1990s, **Apple Computer** suffered a textbook case of shrinking gross profits. In response to pricing wars in the personal computer market, Apple was forced to quickly reduce the price of its signature Macintosh computers—reducing prices more quickly than it could reduce its costs. As a result its gross profit rate fell 4 percent relative to the prior year. Although a drop of 4 percent may appear small, its impact on the bottom line caused Apple's stock price to drop from $57 per share to $27.50 over a 6-week period following release of the lower numbers.

More recently, **Debenham Plc**, the second largest department store in the United Kingdom, experienced a 14 percent share price decline in the summer of 2002. The cause? Markdowns on slow-moving inventory, which reduced its gross margin.

Source: Alison Smith, "Debenham's Shares Hit by Warning," *Financial Times* (July 24, 2002), p. 21.

Evaluation of Gross Profit Method

What are the major disadvantages of the gross profit method? One major disadvantage is that **it provides an estimate**. As a result, a physical inventory must be taken once a year to verify that the inventory is actually on hand. Second, the gross profit method **uses past percentages** in determining the markup. Although the past can often provide answers to the future, a current rate is more appropriate. It is important to emphasize that whenever significant fluctuations occur, the percentage should be adjusted as appropriate. Third, **care must be taken in applying a blanket gross profit rate**. Frequently, a store or department handles merchandise with widely varying rates of gross profit. In these situations, the gross profit method may have to be applied by subsections, lines of merchandise, or a similar basis that classifies merchandise items according to their respective rates of gross profit.

The gross profit method is **not normally acceptable for financial reporting purposes** because it provides only an estimate. A physical inventory is needed as additional verification that the inventory indicated in the records is actually on hand. Nevertheless, the gross profit method is permitted to determine ending inventory for **interim** (generally quarterly) **reporting purposes** provided the use of this method is disclosed. Note that the gross profit method will follow closely the inventory method used (FIFO, LIFO, average cost) because it is based on historical records.

RETAIL INVENTORY METHOD

OBJECTIVE 6
Determine ending inventory by applying the retail inventory method.

Accounting for inventory in a retail operation presents several challenges. Retailers with certain types of inventory may use the specific identification method to value their inventories. Such an approach makes sense when individual inventory units are significant, such as automobiles, pianos, or fur coats. However, imagine attempting to use such an approach at **Target**, **True-Value Hardware**, **Sears**, or **Bloomingdale's**—high-volume retailers that have many different types of merchandise. It would be extremely difficult to determine the cost of each sale, to enter cost codes on the tickets, to change the codes to reflect declines in value of the merchandise, to allocate costs such as transportation, and so on.

An alternative is to compile the inventories at retail prices. In most retail concerns, an observable pattern between cost and price exists. Retail prices can then be converted to cost through formula. This method, called the **retail inventory method, requires that a record be kept of (1) the total cost and retail value of goods purchased, (2) the total cost and retail value of the goods available for sale, and (3) the sales for the period.**

Here is how it works: The sales for the period are deducted from the retail value of the goods available for sale, to determine an estimated inventory (goods on hand) at retail. The ratio of cost to retail for all goods passing through a department or firm is then computed by dividing the total goods available for sale at cost by the total goods available at retail. The inventory valued at retail is converted to ending inventory at cost by applying the cost-to-retail ratio. Use of the retail inventory method is very common. For example, **Safeway** supermarkets uses the retail inventory method, as do the department stores of **Target Corp.** The retail inventory method is illustrated below for Jordan-Guess Inc.

ILLUSTRATION 9-16
Retail Inventory Method

JORDAN-GUESS INC.
(current period)

	Cost	Retail
Beginning inventory	$14,000	$ 20,000
Purchases	63,000	90,000
Goods available for sale	$77,000	110,000
Deduct: Sales		85,000
Ending inventory, at retail		$ 25,000

Ratio of cost to retail ($77,000 ÷ $110,000) = 70%
Ending inventory at cost (70% of $25,000) = $ 17,500

To avoid a potential overstatement of the inventory, periodic inventory counts are made, especially in retail operations where loss due to shoplifting or breakage is common.

There are different versions of the retail inventory method—the conventional (lower of average cost or market) method, the cost method, the LIFO retail method, and the dollar-value LIFO retail method. Regardless of which version is used, the retail inventory method is sanctioned by the IRS, various retail associations, and the accounting profession. One of its advantages is that the inventory balance **can be approximated without a physical count.**

The retail inventory method is particularly useful for any type of interim report, because a fairly quick and reliable measure of the inventory value is usually needed. Insurance adjusters often use this approach to estimate losses from fire, flood, or other type of casualty. This method also acts as a **control device** because any deviations from a physical count at the end of the year have to be explained. In addition, the retail method **expedites the physical inventory count** at the end of the year. The crew taking the physical inventory need record only the retail price of each item. The crew does not need to look up each item's invoice cost, thereby saving time and expense.

Retail Method Terminology

The amounts shown in the Retail column of Illustration 9-16 represent the original retail prices, assuming no price changes. Sales prices are frequently marked up or down. For retailers, the term **markup** means an additional markup of the original retail price. (In another context, such as the gross profit discussion on page 433, we often think of markup on the basis of cost.) **Markup cancellations** are decreases in prices of merchandise that had been marked up above the original retail price.

Markdowns below the original sales prices may be necessary because of a decrease in the general level of prices, special sales, soiled or damaged goods, overstocking, and competition. Markdowns are common in retailing these days. **Markdown cancellations** occur when the markdowns are later offset by increases in the prices of goods that had been marked down—such as after a one-day sale, for example. Neither a markup cancellation nor a markdown cancellation can exceed the original markup or markdown.

To illustrate these different concepts, assume that Designer Clothing Store recently purchased 100 dress shirts from Marroway, Inc. The cost for these shirts was $1,500, or

$15 a shirt. Designer Clothing established the selling price on these shirts at $30 a shirt. The manager noted that the shirts were selling quickly, so he added a markup of $5 per shirt. This markup made the price too high for customers and sales lagged. The manager then reduced the price to $32. At this point we would say that Designer Clothing has had a markup of $5 and a markup cancellation of $3. As soon as the major marketing season passed, the manager marked the remaining shirts down to a sale price of $23. At this point, an additional markup cancellation of $2 has taken place, and a $7 markdown has occurred. If the shirts are later written up to $24, a markdown cancellation of $1 would occur.

Retail Inventory Method with Markups and Markdowns—Conventional Method

Retailers use markup and markdown concepts in developing the proper inventory valuation at the end of the accounting period. To obtain the appropriate inventory figures, proper treatment must be given to markups, markup cancellations, markdowns, and markdown cancellations.

To illustrate the different possibilities, consider the data for In-Fashion Stores Inc., shown in Illustration 9-17. In-Fashion's ending inventory at cost can be calculated under two assumptions, A and B. (The reasons for the two will be explained later.)

Assumption A: Computes a cost ratio after markups (and markup cancellations) but before markdowns.

Assumption B: Computes a cost ratio after both markups and markdowns (and cancellations).

ILLUSTRATION 9-17
Retail Inventory Method with Markups and Markdowns

	Cost	Retail
Beginning inventory	$ 500	$ 1,000
Purchases (net)	20,000	35,000
Markups		3,000
Markup cancellations		1,000
Markdowns		2,500
Markdown cancellations		2,000
Sales (net)		25,000

IN-FASHION STORES INC.

	Cost		Retail
Beginning inventory	$ 500		$ 1,000
Purchases (net)	20,000		35,000
Merchandise available for sale	20,500		36,000
Add: Markups		$3,000	
Less: Markup cancellations		(1,000)	
Net markups			2,000
	20,500		38,000
(A) Cost-to-retail ratio	$\frac{\$20,500}{\$38,000}$	= 53.9%	
Deduct:			
Markdowns		2,500	
Less: Markdown cancellations		(2,000)	
Net markdowns			500
	$20,500		37,500
(B) Cost-to-retail ratio	$\frac{\$20,500}{\$37,500}$	= 54.7%	
Deduct: Sales (net)			25,000
Ending inventory at retail			$12,500

The computations for In-Fashion Stores are:

Ending inventory at retail × Cost ratio	= Value of ending inventory
Assumption A: $12,500 × 53.9%	= $6,737.50
Assumption B: $12,500 × 54.7%	= $6,837.50

The question becomes: Which assumption and which percentage should be employed to compute the ending inventory valuation?

The answer depends on the retail inventory method chosen. **The conventional retail inventory method uses assumption A only. It is designed to approximate the lower of average cost or market.** We will refer to this approach as the **lower of cost or market approach** or the **conventional retail inventory method**. To understand why the markups but not the markdowns are considered in the cost percentage, you must understand how a retail outlet operates. Markup normally indicates that the market value of the item has increased. On the other hand, a markdown means that a decline in the utility of that item has occurred. Therefore, if we attempt to approximate the lower of cost or market, markdowns are considered a current loss and are not involved in the calculation of the cost-to-retail ratio. Thus, the cost-to-retail ratio is lower, which leads to an approximate lower of cost or market.

An example will make this clear. Two items were purchased for $5 apiece, and the original sales price was established at $10 each. One item was subsequently written down to $2. Assuming no sales for the period, **if markdowns are considered** in the cost-to-retail ratio (assumption B, above), we compute the ending inventory in the following manner.

ILLUSTRATION 9-18
Retail Inventory Method Including Markdowns—Cost Method

Markdowns Included in Cost-to-Retail Ratio

	Cost	Retail
Purchases	$10	$20
Deduct: Markdowns		8
Ending inventory, at retail		$12

Cost-to-retail ratio $\frac{\$10}{\$12} = 83.3\%$

Ending inventory at cost ($12 × .833) = $10

This approach is the **cost method**. It reflects an **average cost** of the two items of the commodity without considering the loss on the one item.

If markdowns are not considered, the result is the lower of cost or market method (assumption A). The calculation is made as shown below.

ILLUSTRATION 9-19
Retail Inventory Method Excluding Markdowns—Conventional Method (LCM)

Markdowns Not Included in Cost-to-Retail Ratio

	Cost	Retail
Purchases	$10	$20

Cost-to-retail ratio $\frac{\$10}{\$20} = 50\%$

Deduct: Markdowns		8
Ending inventory, at retail		$12

Ending inventory, at cost ($12 × .50) = $6

Under the conventional retail inventory method (when markdowns are **not considered** in computing the cost-to-retail ratio), the ratio would be 50 percent ($10/$20), and ending inventory would be $6 ($12 × .50).

The inventory valuation of $6 reflects two inventory items, one inventoried at $5, the other at $1. Basically, the sales price was reduced from $10 to $2, and the cost reduced from $5 to $1.[13] To approximate the lower of cost or market, therefore, the **cost-to-retail ratio** must be established by dividing the cost of goods available by the sum of the original retail price of these goods plus the net markups. The markdowns and markdown cancellations are excluded. The basic format for the retail inventory method using the lower of cost or market approach is shown in Illustration 9-20 using the In-Fashion Stores information.

ILLUSTRATION 9-20
Comprehensive Conventional Retail Inventory Method Format

IN-FASHION STORES INC.

	Cost		Retail
Beginning inventory	$ 500.00		$ 1,000.00
Purchases (net)	20,000.00		35,000.00
Totals	20,500.00		36,000.00
Add: Net markups			
Markups		$3,000.00	
Markup cancellations		1,000.00	2,000.00
Totals	$20,500.00 ←		→ 38,000.00
Deduct: Net markdowns			
Markdowns		2,500.00	
Markdown cancellations		2,000.00	500.00
Sales price of goods available			37,500.00
Deduct: Sales (net)			25,000.00
Ending inventory, at retail			$12,500.00

$$\text{Cost-to-retail ratio} = \frac{\text{Cost of goods available}}{\text{Original retail price of goods available, plus net markups}}$$

$$= \frac{\$20{,}500}{\$38{,}000} = 53.9\%$$

Ending inventory at lower of cost or market (53.9% × $12,500.00) = $ 6,737.50

Because an averaging effect occurs, an exact lower of cost or market inventory valuation is ordinarily not obtained, but an adequate approximation can be achieved. In contrast, adding net markups **and** deducting net markdowns yields **approximate cost**.

Special Items Relating to Retail Method

The retail inventory method becomes more complicated when such items as freight-in, purchase returns and allowances, and purchase discounts are involved. **Freight costs** are treated as a part of the purchase cost. **Purchase returns** are ordinarily considered as a reduction of the price at both cost and retail. **Purchase discounts and allowances** usually are considered as a reduction of the cost of purchases. When the purchase allowance is not reflected by a reduction in the selling price, no adjustment is made to the retail column. In short, the treatment for the items affecting the cost column of the retail inventory approach follows the computation for cost of goods available for sale.

Note also that **sales returns and allowances** are considered as proper adjustments to gross sales. **Sales discounts,** however, are not recognized when sales are recorded gross. To adjust for the sales discount account in such a situation would provide an ending inventory figure at retail that would be overvalued.

In addition, a number of special items require careful analysis. **Transfers-in** from another department, for example, should be reported in the same way as purchases from an outside enterprise. **Normal shortages** (breakage, damage, theft, shrinkage) should reduce the retail column because these goods are no longer available for sale. Such costs

[13]This figure is not really market (replacement cost), but it is net realizable value less the normal margin that is allowed. In other words, the sale price of the goods written down is $2, but subtracting a normal margin of 50% ($5 cost, $10 price), the figure becomes $1.

are reflected in the selling price because a certain amount of shortage is considered normal in a retail enterprise. As a result, this amount is not considered in computing the cost to retail percentage. Rather, it is shown as a deduction similar to sales to arrive at ending inventory at retail. **Abnormal shortages** should be deducted from both the cost and retail columns and reported as a special inventory amount or as a loss. To do otherwise distorts the cost-to-retail ratio and overstates ending inventory. Finally, companies often provide their employees with special discounts to encourage loyalty, better performance, and so on. **Employee discounts** should be deducted from the retail column in the same way as sales. These discounts should not be considered in the cost-to-retail percentage because they do not reflect an overall change in the selling price.

Illustration 9-21 shows some of these concepts. The company, Feminine Executive Apparel, determines its inventory using the conventional retail inventory method.

ILLUSTRATION 9-21
Conventional Retail Inventory Method—Special Items Included

FEMININE EXECUTIVE APPAREL

	Cost		Retail
Beginning inventory	$ 1,000		$ 1,800
Purchases	30,000		60,000
Freight-in	600		—
Purchase returns	(1,500)		(3,000)
Totals	30,100		58,800
Net markups			9,000
Abnormal shortage	(1,200)		(2,000)
Totals	$28,900 ⟷		65,800
Deduct:			
Net markdowns			1,400
Sales		$36,000	
Sales returns		(900)	35,100
Employee discounts			800
Normal shortage			1,300
			$27,200

Cost-to-retail ratio = $\frac{\$28,900}{\$65,800}$ = 43.9%

Ending inventory at lower of cost or market (43.9% × $27,200) = $11,940.80

Evaluation of Retail Inventory Method

The retail inventory method of computing inventory is used widely for the following reasons: (1) to permit the computation of net income without a physical count of inventory, (2) as a control measure in determining inventory shortages, (3) in regulating quantities of merchandise on hand, and (4) for insurance information.

One characteristic of the retail inventory method is that it **has an averaging effect on varying rates of gross profit**. When applied to an entire business where rates of gross profit vary among departments, no allowance is made for possible distortion of results because of such differences. Some companies refine the retail method under such conditions by computing inventory separately by departments or by classes of merchandise with similar gross profits. In addition, the reliability of this method assumes that the distribution of items in inventory is similar to the "mix" in the total goods available for sale.

PRESENTATION AND ANALYSIS

Presentation of Inventories

OBJECTIVE 7
Explain how inventory is reported and analyzed.

Accounting standards require financial statement disclosure of the composition of the inventory, inventory financing arrangements, and the inventory costing methods employed. The standards also require the consistent application of costing methods from one period to another.

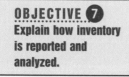

Manufacturers should report the inventory composition either in the balance sheet or in a separate schedule in the notes. As discussed in Chapter 8, the relative mix of raw materials, work in process, and finished goods is important in assessing liquidity and in computing the stage of inventory completion.

Additional Inventory Disclosures

Significant or unusual financing arrangements relating to inventories may require note disclosure. Examples are: transactions with related parties, product financing arrangements, firm purchase commitments, involuntary liquidation of LIFO inventories, and pledging of inventories as collateral. Inventories pledged as collateral for a loan should be presented in the current assets section rather than as an offset to the liability.

The basis upon which inventory amounts are stated (lower of cost or market) and the method used in determining cost (LIFO, FIFO, average cost, etc.) should also be reported. For example, the annual report of **Mumford of Wyoming** contains the following disclosures.

ILLUSTRATION 9-22
Disclosure of Inventory Methods

Mumford of Wyoming

Note A: Significant Accounting Policies

Live feeder cattle and feed—last-in, first-out (LIFO) cost, which is below approximate market	$854,800
Live range cattle—lower of principally identified cost or market	$1,240,500
Live sheep and supplies—lower of first-in, first-out (FIFO) cost or market	$674,000
Dressed meat and by-products—principally at market less allowances for distribution and selling expenses	$362,630

INTERNATIONAL INSIGHT

In Switzerland, inventory may be reported on the balance sheet at amounts substantially (one-third or more) below cost or market due to provisions of the tax code. Further, Swiss accounting principles do not require any specific disclosures related to inventories.

The preceding illustration shows that a company can use different pricing methods for different elements of its inventory. If Mumford changes the method of pricing any of its inventory elements, a change in accounting principle must be reported. For example, if Mumford changes its method of accounting for live sheep from FIFO to average cost, this change, along with the effect on income, should be separately reported in the financial statements. Changes in accounting principle require an explanatory paragraph in the auditor's report describing the change in method.

Fortune Brands, Inc. reported its inventories in its Annual Report as follows. Note the "trade practice" followed in classifying inventories among the current assets.

ILLUSTRATION 9-23
Disclosure of Trade Practice in Valuing Inventories

Fortune Brands, Inc.

Current assets	
Inventories (Note 2)	
Leaf tobacco	$ 563,424,000
Bulk whiskey	232,759,000
Other raw materials, supplies and work in process	238,906,000
Finished products	658,326,000
	$1,693,415,000

Note 2: Inventories

Inventories are priced at the lower of cost (average; first-in, first-out; and minor amounts at last-in, first-out) or market. In accordance with generally recognized trade practice, the leaf tobacco and bulk whiskey inventories are classified as current assets, although part of such inventories due to the duration of the aging process, ordinarily will not be sold within one year.

The following inventory disclosures by **Newmont Gold Company** reveal the application of different bases of valuation, including market value, for different classifications of inventory.

ILLUSTRATION 9-24
Disclosure of Different Bases of Valuation

Newmont Gold Company

Current assets		
Inventories (Note 2)		$44,303,000
Noncurrent assets		
Inventories—ore in stockpiles (Note 2)		$5,250,000

Note 2: Inventories

Inventories included in current assets at December 31 were:

Ore and in-process inventory	$11,303,000
Gold bullion and gold precipitates	24,209,000
Materials and supplies	8,791,000
	$44,303,000

Ore and in-process inventory and materials and supplies are stated at the lower of average cost or net realizable value. Gold bullion and gold precipitates are stated at market value, less a provision for estimated refining and delivery charges. Expenditures capitalized as ore and in-process inventory include labor, material and other production costs.

Noncurrent inventories are stated at the lower of average cost or net realizable value and represent ore in stockpiles anticipated to be processed in future years.

Analysis of Inventories

As illustrated in the opening story, the amount of inventory that a company carries can have significant economic consequences. As a result, inventories must be managed. Inventory management is a double-edged sword that requires constant attention. On the one hand, management wants to have a great variety and quantity on hand so customers have the greatest selection and always find what they want in stock. But, such an inventory policy may incur excessive carrying costs (e.g., investment, storage, insurance, taxes, obsolescence, and damage). On the other hand, low inventory levels lead to stockouts, lost sales, and disgruntled customers. Financial ratios can be used to help chart a middle course between these two dangers. Common ratios used in the management and evaluation of inventory levels are inventory turnover and a related measure, average days to sell the inventory.

The **inventory turnover ratio** measures the average number of times the inventory was sold during the period. Its purpose is to measure the liquidity of the inventory. A manager may extrapolate from past turnover experience how long the inventory now in stock will take to be sold. The inventory turnover is computed by dividing the cost of goods sold by the average inventory on hand during the period. Unless seasonal factors are significant, average inventory can be computed from the beginning and ending inventory balances. For example, in its 2001 annual report **Kellogg Company** reported a beginning inventory of $443.8 million, an ending inventory of $574.5 million, and cost of goods sold of $4,129 million for the year. The inventory turnover formula and Kellogg Company's 2001 ratio computation are shown below.

ILLUSTRATION 9-25
Inventory Turnover Ratio

$$\text{Inventory Turnover} = \frac{\text{Cost of Goods Sold}}{\text{Average Inventory}}$$

$$= \frac{\$4{,}129}{(\$574.5 + \$443.8)/2} = 8.1 \text{ times}$$

A variant of the inventory turnover ratio is the **average days to sell inventory**. This measure represents the average number of days' sales for which inventory is on hand. For example, the inventory turnover for **Kellogg Company** of 8.1 times divided into 365 is approximately 45.1 days.

There are typical levels of inventory in every industry. However, companies that are able to keep their inventory at lower levels with higher turnovers than those of their competitors, and still satisfy customer needs, are the most successful.

SUMMARY OF LEARNING OBJECTIVES

1 Explain and apply the lower of cost or market rule. If inventory declines in value below its original cost, for whatever reason, the inventory should be written down to reflect this loss. The general rule is that the historical cost principle is abandoned when the future utility (revenue-producing ability) of the asset is no longer as great as its original cost.

2 Identify when inventories are valued at net realizable value. Inventories are valued at net realizable value when (1) there is a controlled market with a quoted price applicable to all quantities, (2) no significant costs of disposal are involved, and (3) the cost figures are too difficult to obtain.

3 Explain when the relative sales value method is used to value inventories. When a group of varying units is purchased at a single lump sum price—a so-called basket purchase—the total purchase price may be allocated to the individual items on the basis of relative sales value.

4 Explain accounting issues related to purchase commitments. Accounting for purchase commitments is controversial. Some argue that these contracts should be reported as assets and liabilities at the time the contract is signed. Others believe that the present recognition at the delivery date is most appropriate. The FASB neither excludes nor recommends the recording of assets and liabilities for purchase commitments, but it notes that if they were recorded at the time of commitment, "the nature of the loss and the valuation account...when the price falls would be clearly seen."

5 Determine ending inventory by applying the gross profit method. The steps to determine ending inventory by applying the gross profit method are as follows: (1) Compute the gross profit percentage on selling price. (2) Compute gross profit by multiplying net sales by the gross profit percentage. (3) Compute cost of goods sold by subtracting gross profit from net sales. (4) Compute ending inventory by subtracting cost of goods sold from total goods available for sale.

6 Determine ending inventory by applying the retail inventory method. The steps to determine ending inventory by applying the conventional retail method are: (1) Deduct the sales for the period from the retail value of the goods available for sale to determine an estimated inventory at retail. (2) Find the ratio of cost to retail for all goods passing through a department or firm by dividing the total goods available for sale at cost by the total goods available at retail. (3) Convert the inventory valued at retail to approximate cost by applying the cost-to-retail ratio.

7 Explain how inventory is reported and analyzed. Accounting standards require financial statement disclosure of: (1) the composition of the inventory (in the balance sheet or a separate schedule in the notes); (2) significant or unusual inventory financing arrangements; and (3) inventory costing methods employed (which may differ for different elements of inventory). Accounting standards also require the consistent application of costing methods from one period to another. Common ratios used in the management and evaluation of inventory levels are inventory turnover and a related measure, average days to sell the inventory.

KEY TERMS

APPENDIX 9A

LIFO Retail Methods

Many argue that the conventional retail method follows a flow assumption that does not match current cost against current revenues. They suggest that a LIFO assumption be adopted to obtain a better matching of costs and revenues.

LIFO RETAIL METHODS

OBJECTIVE 8
Determine ending inventory by applying the LIFO retail methods.

Many retail establishments have changed from the more conventional treatment to a **LIFO retail method** for the tax advantages associated with valuing inventories on a LIFO basis.

The application of LIFO retail is made under two assumptions: (1) stable prices and (2) fluctuating prices.

Stable Prices—LIFO Retail Method

Computing the final inventory balance assuming a LIFO flow is much more complex than the calculation for the conventional retail method. Under the LIFO retail method, **both markups and markdowns are considered** in obtaining the proper cost-to-retail percentage. Furthermore, since the LIFO method is concerned only with the additional layer, or the amount that should be subtracted from the previous layer, the beginning inventory is excluded from the cost-to-retail percentage.

A major assumption of the LIFO retail method—one that is debatable—is that the markups and markdowns apply only to the goods purchased during the current period and not to the beginning inventory. In addition, to simplify the accounting, we have assumed that the price level has remained unchanged. The concepts are presented in Illustration 9A-1.

ILLUSTRATION 9A-1
LIFO Retail Method—Stable Prices

	Cost	Retail
Beginning inventory—2004	$ 27,000	$ 45,000
Net purchases during the period	346,500	480,000
Net markups		20,000
Net markdowns		(5,000)
Total (excluding beginning inventory)	346,500 ←→	495,000
Total (including beginning inventory)	$373,500	540,000
Net sales during the period		(484,000)
Ending inventory at retail		$ 56,000

Establishment of cost-to-retail percentage under assumptions of LIFO retail ($346,500 ÷ $495,000) = 70%

Illustration 9A-2 indicates that the inventory is composed of two layers: the beginning inventory and the additional increase that occurred in the inventory this period (2004). When we start the next period (2005), the beginning inventory will be composed of those two layers, and if an increase in inventory occurs again, an additional layer will be added.

ILLUSTRATION 9A-2
Ending Inventory at LIFO Cost, 2004—Stable Prices

Ending Inventory at Retail Prices—2004	Layers at Retail Prices			Cost-to-Retail (Percentage)		Ending Inventory at LIFO Cost
$56,000 →	2003	$45,000	×	60%*	=	$27,000
→	2004	11,000	×	70	=	7,700
		$56,000				$34,700

*$27,000 / $45,000 (prior year's cost-to-retail)

However, if the final inventory figure is below the beginning inventory, it is necessary to reduce the beginning inventory starting with the most recent layer. For example, assume that the ending inventory for 2005 at retail is $50,000. The computation of the ending inventory at cost is shown below.

ILLUSTRATION 9A-3
Ending Inventory at LIFO Cost, 2005—Stable Prices

Ending Inventory at Retail Prices—2005	Layers at Retail Prices			Cost-to-Retail (Percentage)		Ending Inventory at LIFO Cost
$50,000 →	2003	$45,000	×	60%	=	$27,000
→	2004	5,000	×	70	=	3,500
		$50,000				$30,500

Notice that the 2004 layer is reduced from $11,000 to $5,000.

Fluctuating Prices—Dollar-Value LIFO Retail Method

The computation of the LIFO retail method was simplified in the previous illustration because changes in the selling price of the inventory were ignored. Let us now assume that a change in the price level of the inventories occurs (as is usual). If the price level does change, **the price change must be eliminated** because we are measuring the real increase in inventory, not the dollar increase.

To illustrate, assume that the beginning inventory had a retail market value of $10,000 and the ending inventory a retail market value of $15,000. If the price level has risen from 100 to 125, it is inappropriate to suggest that a real increase in inventory of $5,000 has occurred. Instead, the ending inventory at retail should be deflated as indicated by the computation shown below.

ILLUSTRATION 9A-4
Ending Inventory at Retail—Deflated and Restated

Ending inventory at retail (deflated) $15,000 ÷ 1.25*	$12,000	
Beginning inventory at retail	10,000	
Real increase in inventory at retail	$ 2,000	
Ending inventory at retail on LIFO basis:		
First layer	$10,000	
Second layer ($2,000 × 1.25)	2,500	$12,500

*1.25 = 125 ÷ 100

This approach is essentially the dollar-value LIFO method previously discussed in Chapter 8. In computing the LIFO inventory under a dollar-value LIFO approach, the dollar increase in inventory is found and deflated to beginning-of-the-year prices. This indicates whether actual increases or decreases in quantity have occurred. If an increase in quantities occurs, this increase is priced at the new index to compute the value of the new layer. If a decrease in quantities happens, it is subtracted from the most recent layers to the extent necessary.

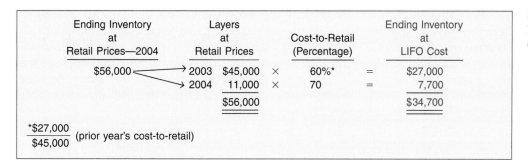

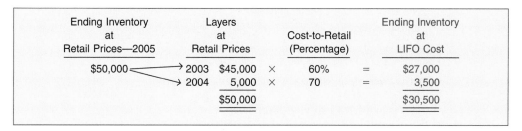

The following computations, taken from Illustration 9A-1, illustrate the differences between the **dollar-value LIFO retail method** and the regular LIFO retail approach. Assume that the current 2004 price index is 112 (prior year = 100) and that the inventory ($56,000) has remained unchanged. In comparing these two illustrations, note that the computations involved in finding the cost-to-retail percentage are exactly the same. However, the dollar-value method determines the increase that has occurred in the inventory in terms of base-year prices.

ILLUSTRATION 9A-5
Dollar-Value LIFO Retail Method—Fluctuating Prices

	Cost	Retail
Beginning inventory—2004	$ 27,000	$ 45,000
Net purchases during the period	346,500	480,000
Net markups		20,000
Net markdowns		(5,000)
Total (excluding beginning inventory)	346,500 ⟷	495,000
Total (including beginning inventory)	$373,500	540,000
Net sales during the period at retail		(484,000)
Ending inventory at retail		$ 56,000

Establishment of cost-to-retail percentage under assumptions of LIFO retail ($346,500 ÷ $495,000) =	70%
A. Ending inventory at retail prices deflated to base-year prices $56,000 ÷ 112 =	$50,000
B. Beginning inventory (retail) at base-year prices	45,000
C. Inventory increase (retail) from beginning of period	$ 5,000

From this information, we compute the inventory amount at cost:

ILLUSTRATION 9A-6
Ending Inventory at LIFO Cost, 2004—Fluctuating Prices

Ending Inventory at Base-Year Retail Prices—2004	Layers at Base-Year Retail Prices			Price Index (percentage)		Cost-to-Retail (percentage)		Ending Inventory at LIFO Cost
$50,000 →	2003	$45,000	×	100%	×	60%	=	$27,000
→	2004	5,000	×	112	×	70	=	3,920
		$50,000						$30,920

As illustrated above, before the conversion to cost takes place, layers of a particular year must be restated to the prices in effect in the year when the layer was added.

Note the difference between the LIFO approach (stable prices) and the dollar-value LIFO method as indicated below.

ILLUSTRATION 9A-7
Comparison of Effect of Price Assumptions

	LIFO (stable prices)	LIFO (fluctuating prices)
Beginning inventory	$27,000	$27,000
Increment	7,700	3,920
Ending inventory	$34,700	$30,920

The difference of $3,780 ($34,700 − $30,920) is a result of an increase in the **price** of goods, not of an increase in the **quantity** of goods.

Subsequent Adjustments Under Dollar-Value LIFO Retail

The dollar-value LIFO retail method follows the same procedures in subsequent periods as the traditional dollar-value method discussed in Chapter 8. That is, when a real increase in inventory occurs, a new layer is added. Using the data from the previous illustration, assume that the retail value of the 2005 ending inventory at current prices is $64,800, the 2005 price index is 120 percent of base-year, and the cost-to-retail percentage is 75 percent. In base-year dollars, the ending inventory is therefore $54,000 ($64,800/120%). The computation of the ending inventory at LIFO cost is as follows.

ILLUSTRATION 9A-8
Ending Inventory at LIFO Cost, 2005—Fluctuating Prices

Ending Inventory at Base-Year Retail Prices—2005	Layers at Base-Year Retail Prices			Price Index (percentage)		Cost-to-Retail (percentage)		Ending Inventory at LIFO Cost
$54,000 →	2003	$45,000	×	100%	×	60%	=	$27,000
	2004	5,000	×	112	×	70	=	3,920
	2005	4,000	×	120	×	75	=	3,600
		$54,000						$34,520

Conversely, when a real decrease in inventory develops, previous layers are "peeled off" at prices in existence when the layers were added. To illustrate, assume that in 2005 the ending inventory in base-year prices is $48,000. The computation of the LIFO inventory is as follows.

ILLUSTRATION 9A-9
Ending Inventory at LIFO Cost, 2005—Fluctuating Prices

Ending Inventory at Base-Year Retail Prices—2005	Layers at Base-Year Retail Prices			Price Index (percentage)		Cost-to-Retail (percentage)		Ending Inventory at LIFO Cost
$48,000 →	2003	$45,000	×	100%	×	60%	=	$27,000
	2004	3,000	×	112	×	70	=	2,352
		$48,000						$29,352

The advantages and disadvantages of the lower of cost or market method (conventional retail) versus LIFO retail are the same for retail operations as for nonretail operations. As a practical matter, the selection of the retail inventory method to be used often involves determining which method provides a lower taxable income. Although it might appear that retail LIFO will provide the lower taxable income in a period of rising prices, such is not always the case. LIFO will provide an approximate current cost matching, but the ending inventory is stated at cost. The conventional retail method may have a large write-off because of the use of the lower of cost or market approach which may offset the LIFO current cost matching.

CHANGING FROM CONVENTIONAL RETAIL TO LIFO

When changing from the conventional retail method to LIFO retail, neither a cumulative adjustment nor a retroactive adjustment can be made easily. Because conventional retail is a lower of cost or market approach, the beginning inventory must be restated to a cost basis. The usual approach is to compute the cost basis from the purchases of the prior year, adjusted for both markups and markdowns.[1] To illustrate, assume that Clark Clothing Store employs the conventional retail method but wishes to change to the LIFO retail method beginning in 2005. The amounts shown by the firm's books are as follows.

	At Cost	At Retail
Inventory, January 1, 2004	$ 5,210	$ 15,000
Net purchases in 2004	47,250	100,000
Net markups in 2004		7,000
Net markdowns in 2004		2,000
Sales in 2004		95,000

[1]A logical question to ask is, "Why are only the purchases from the prior period considered and not also the beginning inventory?" Apparently the IRS believes that "the purchases-only approach" provides a more reasonable cost basis. The IRS position is debatable. However, for our purposes, it seems appropriate to use the purchases-only approach.

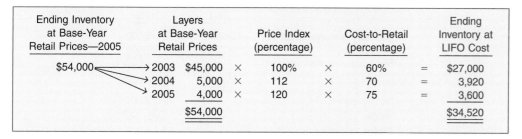

Ending inventory under the **conventional retail method** for 2004 is computed as shown in Illustration 9A-10.

ILLUSTRATION 9A-10
Conventional Retail Inventory Method

	Cost	Retail
Inventory January 1, 2004	$ 5,210	$ 15,000
Net purchases	47,250	100,000
Net additional markups		7,000
	$52,460	122,000
Net markdowns		(2,000)
Sales		(95,000)
Ending inventory at retail		$ 25,000
Establishment of cost-to-retail percentage ($52,460 ÷ $122,000) =		43%
December 31, 2003, inventory at cost		
Inventory at retail		$ 25,000
Cost-to-retail ratio		× 43%
Inventory at cost under conventional retail		$ 10,750

The ending inventory for 2004 under the **LIFO retail method** can then be quickly approximated in the following way.

ILLUSTRATION 9A-11
Conversion to LIFO Retail Inventory Method

December 31, 2004, Inventory at LIFO Cost

$$\text{Ending inventory} \quad \frac{\text{Retail}}{\$25{,}000} \times \frac{\text{Ratio}}{45\%^*} = \frac{\text{LIFO}}{\$11{,}250}$$

*The cost-to-retail ratio was computed as follows:

$$\frac{\text{Net purchases at cost}}{\text{Net purchases at retail plus markups less markdowns}} = \frac{\$47{,}250}{\$100{,}000 + \$7{,}000 - \$2{,}000} = 45\%$$

The difference of $500 ($11,250 − $10,750) between the LIFO retail method and the conventional retail method in the ending inventory for 2004 is the amount by which the beginning inventory for 2005 must be adjusted. The entry to adjust the inventory to a cost basis is as follows.

Inventory	500	
Adjustment to Record Inventory at Cost		500

SUMMARY OF LEARNING OBJECTIVE FOR APPENDIX 9A

KEY TERMS

dollar-value LIFO retail method, 446

LIFO retail method, 444

8 Determine ending inventory by applying the LIFO retail methods. The application of LIFO retail is made under two assumptions: stable prices and fluctuating prices.

Procedures under stable prices: (a) Because the LIFO method is a cost method, both the markups and the markdowns must be considered in obtaining the proper cost-to-retail percentage. (b) Since the LIFO method is concerned only with the additional layer, or the amount that should be subtracted from the previous layer, the beginning inventory is excluded from the cost-to-retail percentage. (c) The markups and markdowns apply only to the goods purchased during the current period and not to the beginning inventory.

Procedures under fluctuating prices: The steps are the same as for stable prices except that in computing the LIFO inventory under a dollar-value LIFO approach, the dollar increase in inventory is found and deflated to beginning-of-the-year prices to determine whether actual increases or decreases in quantity have occurred. If quantities increase, this increase is priced at the new index to compute the new layer. If quantities decrease, the decrease is subtracted from the most recent layers to the extent necessary.

Note: All **asterisked** Questions, Brief Exercises, Exercises, Problems, and Conceptual Cases relate to material contained in the appendix to the chapter.

QUESTIONS

1. Where there is evidence that the utility of inventory goods, as part of their disposal in the ordinary course of business, will be less than cost, what is the proper accounting treatment?

2. Explain the rationale for the ceiling and floor in the lower of cost or market method of valuing inventories.

3. Why are inventories valued at the lower of cost or market? What are the arguments against the use of the lower of cost or market method of valuing inventories?

4. What approaches may be employed in applying the lower of cost or market procedure? Which approach is normally used and why?

5. In some instances accounting principles require a departure from valuing inventories at cost alone. Determine the proper unit inventory price in the following cases.

	Cases				
	1	2	3	4	5
Cost	$15.90	$16.10	$15.90	$15.90	$15.90
Net realizable value	14.30	19.20	15.20	10.40	16.40
Net realizable value less normal profit	12.80	17.60	13.75	8.80	14.80
Market (replacement cost)	14.80	17.20	12.80	9.70	16.80

6. What method(s) might be used in the accounts to record a loss due to a price decline in the inventories? Discuss.

7. What factors might call for inventory valuation at sales prices (net realizable value or market price)?

8. Under what circumstances is relative sales value an appropriate basis for determining the price assigned to inventory?

9. At December 31, 2005, James Arness Co. has outstanding purchase commitments for purchase of 150,000 gallons, at $6.40 per gallon, of a raw material to be used in its manufacturing process. The company prices its raw material inventory at cost or market, whichever is lower. Assuming that the market price as of December 31, 2005, is $5.90, how would you treat this situation in the accounts?

10. What are the major uses of the gross profit method?

11. Distinguish between gross profit as a percentage of cost and gross profit as a percentage of sales price. Convert the following gross profit percentages based on cost to gross profit percentages based on sales price: 20% and 33⅓%. Convert the following gross profit percentages based on sales price to gross profit percentages based on cost: 33⅓% and 60%.

12. Carole Lombard Co. with annual net sales of $6 million maintains a markup of 25% based on cost. Lombard's expenses average 15% of net sales. What is Lombard's gross profit and net profit in dollars?

13. A fire destroys all of the merchandise of Rosanna Arquette Company on February 10, 2005. Presented below is information compiled up to the date of the fire.

Inventory, January 1, 2005	$ 400,000
Sales to February 10, 2005	1,750,000
Purchases to February 10, 2005	1,140,000
Freight-in to February 10, 2005	60,000
Rate of gross profit on selling price	40%

What is the approximate inventory on February 10, 2005?

14. What conditions must exist for the retail inventory method to provide valid results?

15. The conventional retail inventory method yields results that are essentially the same as those yielded by the lower of cost or market method. Explain. Prepare an illustration of how the retail inventory method reduces inventory to market.

16. **(a)** Determine the ending inventory under the conventional retail method for the furniture department of Gin Blossoms Department Stores from the following data.

	Cost	Retail
Inventory, Jan. 1	$ 149,000	$ 283,500
Purchases	1,400,000	2,160,000
Freight-in	70,000	
Markups, net		92,000
Markdowns, net		48,000
Sales		2,235,000

(b) If the results of a physical inventory indicated an inventory at retail of $240,000, what inferences would you draw?

17. Bodeans Company reported inventory in its balance sheet as follows:

Inventories	$115,756,800

What additional disclosures might be necessary to present the inventory fairly?

18. Of what significance is inventory turnover to a retail store?

***19.** What modifications to the conventional retail method are necessary to approximate a LIFO retail flow?

BRIEF EXERCISES

BE9-1 Presented below is information related to Alstott Inc.'s inventory.

(per unit)	Skis	Boots	Parkas
Historical cost	$190.00	$106.00	$53.00
Selling price	217.00	145.00	73.75
Cost to distribute	19.00	8.00	2.50
Current replacement cost	203.00	105.00	51.00
Normal profit margin	32.00	29.00	21.25

Determine the following: (a) the two limits to market value (i.e., the ceiling and the floor) that should be used in the lower of cost or market computation for skis; (b) the cost amount that should be used in the lower of cost or market comparison of boots; and (c) the market amount that should be used to value parkas on the basis of the lower of cost or market.

BE9-2 Robin Corporation has the following four items in its ending inventory.

Item	Cost	Replacement Cost	Net Realizable Value (NRV)	NRV Less Normal Profit Margin
Jokers	$2,000	$1,900	$2,100	$1,600
Penguins	5,000	5,100	4,950	4,100
Riddlers	4,400	4,550	4,625	3,700
Scarecrows	3,200	2,990	3,830	3,070

Determine the final lower of cost or market inventory value for each item.

BE9-3 Battletoads Inc. uses a perpetual inventory system. At January 1, 2005, inventory was $214,000 at both cost and market value. At December 31, 2005, the inventory was $286,000 at cost and $269,000 at market value. Prepare the necessary December 31 entry under (a) the direct method and (b) the indirect method.

BE9-4 PC Plus buys 1,000 computer game CDs from a distributor who is discontinuing those games. The purchase price for the lot is $6,000. PC Plus will group the CDs into three price categories for resale, as indicated below.

Group	No. of CDs	Price per CD
1	100	$ 5.00
2	800	10.00
3	100	15.00

Determine the cost per CD for each group, using the relative sales value method.

BE9-5 Beavis Company signed a long-term noncancelable purchase commitment with a major supplier to purchase raw materials in 2005 at a cost of $1,000,000. At December 31, 2004, the raw materials to be purchased have a market value of $930,000. Prepare any necessary December 31 entry.

BE9-6 Use the information for Beavis Company from BE9-5. In 2005, Beavis paid $1,000,000 to obtain the raw materials which were worth $930,000. Prepare the entry to record the purchase.

BE9-7 Big Hurt Corporation's April 30 inventory was destroyed by fire. January 1 inventory was $150,000, and purchases for January through April totaled $500,000. Sales for the same period were $700,000. Big Hurt's normal gross profit percentage is 31%. Using the gross profit method, estimate Big Hurt's April 30 inventory that was destroyed by fire.

BE9-8 Bimini Inc. had beginning inventory of $12,000 at cost and $20,000 at retail. Net purchases were $120,000 at cost and $170,000 at retail. Net markups were $10,000; net markdowns were $7,000; and sales were $157,000. Compute ending inventory at cost using the conventional retail method.

BE9-9 In its 2002 Annual Report, **Wal-Mart** reported inventory of $22,614 million on January 31, 2002, and $21,442 million on January 31, 2001, cost of sales of $171,562 million for fiscal year 2002, and net sales of $217,799 million. Compute Wal-Mart's inventory turnover and the average days to sell inventory for the fiscal year 2002.

***BE9-10** Use the information for Bimini Inc. from BE9-8. Compute ending inventory at cost using the LIFO retail method.

***BE9-11** Use the information for Bimini Inc. from BE9-8, and assume the price level increased from 100 at the beginning of the year to 120 at year-end. Compute ending inventory at cost using the dollar-value LIFO retail method.

EXERCISES

E9-1 (Lower of Cost or Market) The inventory of 3T Company on December 31, 2005, consists of the following items.

Part No.	Quantity	Cost per Unit	Cost to Replace per Unit
110	600	$90	$100
111	1,000	60	52
112	500	80	76
113	200	170	180
120	400	205	208
121[a]	1,600	16	14
122	300	240	235

[a]Part No. 121 is obsolete and has a realizable value of $0.20 each as scrap.

Instructions

(a) Determine the inventory as of December 31, 2005, by the lower of cost or market method, applying this method directly to each item.

(b) Determine the inventory by the lower of cost or market method, applying the method to the total of the inventory.

E9-2 (Lower of Cost or Market) Smashing Pumpkins Company uses the lower of cost or market method, on an individual-item basis, in pricing its inventory items. The inventory at December 31, 2005, consists of products D, E, F, G, H, and I. Relevant per-unit data for these products appear below.

	Item D	Item E	Item F	Item G	Item H	Item I
Estimated selling price	$120	$110	$95	$90	$110	$90
Cost	75	80	80	80	50	36
Replacement cost	120	72	70	30	70	30
Estimated selling expense	30	30	30	25	30	30
Normal profit	20	20	20	20	20	20

Instructions

Using the lower of cost or market rule, determine the proper unit value for balance sheet reporting purposes at December 31, 2005, for each of the inventory items above.

E9-3 (Lower of Cost or Market) Michael Bolton Company follows the practice of pricing its inventory at the lower of cost or market, on an individual-item basis.

Item No.	Quantity	Cost per Unit	Cost to Replace	Estimated Selling Price	Cost of Completion and Disposal	Normal Profit
1320	1,200	$3.20	$3.00	$4.50	$0.35	$1.25
1333	900	2.70	2.30	3.50	0.50	0.50
1426	800	4.50	3.70	5.00	0.40	1.00
1437	1,000	3.60	3.10	3.20	0.25	0.90
1510	700	2.25	2.00	3.25	0.80	0.60
1522	500	3.00	2.70	3.80	0.40	0.50
1573	3,000	1.80	1.60	2.50	0.75	0.50
1626	1,000	4.70	5.20	6.00	0.50	1.00

Instructions

From the information above, determine the amount of Bolton Company inventory.

E9-4 (Lower of Cost or Market—Journal Entries) Corrs Company began operations in 2004 and determined its ending inventory at cost and at lower of cost or market at December 31, 2004, and December 31, 2005. This information is presented below.

	Cost	Lower of Cost or Market
12/31/04	$346,000	$327,000
12/31/05	410,000	395,000

Instructions

(a) Prepare the journal entries required at December 31, 2004, and December 31, 2005, assuming that the inventory is recorded at market, and a perpetual inventory system (direct method) is used.

(b) Prepare journal entries required at December 31, 2004, and December 31, 2005, assuming that the inventory is recorded at cost and an allowance account is adjusted at each year-end under a perpetual system.

(c) Which of the two methods above provides the higher net income in each year?

E9-5 (Lower of Cost or Market—Valuation Account) Presented below is information related to Candlebox Enterprises.

	Jan. 31	Feb. 28	Mar. 31	Apr. 30
Inventory at cost	$15,000	$15,100	$17,000	$13,000
Inventory at the lower of cost or market	14,500	12,600	15,600	12,300
Purchases for the month		20,000	24,000	26,500
Sales for the month		29,000	35,000	40,000

Instructions

(a) From the information, prepare (as far as the data permit) monthly income statements in columnar form for February, March, and April. The inventory is to be shown in the statement at cost, the gain or loss due to market fluctuations is to be shown separately, and a valuation account is to be set up for the difference between cost and the lower of cost or market.

(b) Prepare the journal entry required to establish the valuation account at January 31 and entries to adjust it monthly thereafter.

E9-6 (Lower of Cost or Market—Error Effect) Winans Company uses the lower of cost or market method, on an individual-item basis, in pricing its inventory items. The inventory at December 31, 2004, included product X. Relevant per-unit data for product X appear below.

Estimated selling price	$45
Cost	40
Replacement cost	35
Estimated selling expense	14
Normal profit	9

There were 1,000 units of product X on hand at December 31, 2004. Product X was incorrectly valued at $35 per unit for reporting purposes. All 1,000 units were sold in 2005.

Instructions

Compute the effect of this error on net income for 2004 and the effect on net income for 2005, and indicate the direction of the misstatement for each year.

E9-7 (Relative Sales Value Method) Phil Collins Realty Corporation purchased a tract of unimproved land for $55,000. This land was improved and subdivided into building lots at an additional cost of $34,460. These building lots were all of the same size but owing to differences in location were offered for sale at different prices as follows.

Group	No. of Lots	Price per Lot
1	9	$3,000
2	15	4,000
3	17	2,400

Operating expenses for the year allocated to this project total $18,200. Lots unsold at the year-end were as follows.

Group 1	5 lots
Group 2	7 lots
Group 3	2 lots

Instructions

At the end of the fiscal year Phil Collins Realty Corporation instructs you to arrive at the net income realized on this operation to date.

E9-8 (Relative Sales Value Method) During 2005, Pretenders Furniture Company purchases a carload of wicker chairs. The manufacturer sells the chairs to Pretenders for a lump sum of $59,850, because it is discontinuing manufacturing operations and wishes to dispose of its entire stock. Three types of chairs are included in the carload. The three types and the estimated selling price for each are listed below.

Type	No. of Chairs	Estimated Selling Price Each
Lounge chairs	400	$90
Armchairs	300	80
Straight chairs	700	50

During 2005, Pretenders sells 200 lounge chairs, 100 armchairs, and 120 straight chairs.

Instructions
What is the amount of gross profit realized during 2005? What is the amount of inventory of unsold wicker chairs on December 31, 2005?

E9-9 (Purchase Commitments) Marvin Gaye Company has been having difficulty obtaining key raw materials for its manufacturing process. The company therefore signed a long-term noncancelable purchase commitment with its largest supplier of this raw material on November 30, 2005, at an agreed price of $400,000. At December 31, 2005, the raw material had declined in price to $365,000.

Instructions
What entry would you make on December 31, 2005, to recognize these facts?

E9-10 (Purchase Commitments) At December 31, 2005, Indigo Girls Company has outstanding noncancelable purchase commitments for 36,000 gallons, at $3.00 per gallon, of raw material to be used in its manufacturing process. The company prices its raw material inventory at cost or market, whichever is lower.

Instructions
(a) Assuming that the market price as of December 31, 2005, is $3.30, how would this matter be treated in the accounts and statements? Explain.
(b) Assuming that the market price as of December 31, 2005, is $2.70, instead of $3.30, how would you treat this situation in the accounts and statements?
(c) Give the entry in January 2006, when the 36,000-gallon shipment is received, assuming that the situation given in (b) above existed at December 31, 2005, and that the market price in January 2006 was $2.70 per gallon. Give an explanation of your treatment.

E9-11 (Gross Profit Method) Each of the following gross profit percentages is expressed in terms of cost.

1. 20%. **3.** 33⅓%.
2. 25%. **4.** 50%.

Instructions
Indicate the gross profit percentage in terms of sales for each of the above.

E9-12 (Gross Profit Method) Mark Price Company uses the gross profit method to estimate inventory for monthly reporting purposes. Presented below is information for the month of May.

Inventory, May 1	$ 160,000
Purchases (gross)	640,000
Freight-in	30,000
Sales	1,000,000
Sales returns	70,000
Purchase discounts	12,000

Instructions
(a) Compute the estimated inventory at May 31, assuming that the gross profit is 30% of sales.
(b) Compute the estimated inventory at May 31, assuming that the gross profit is 30% of cost.

E9-13 (Gross Profit Method) Tim Legler requires an estimate of the cost of goods lost by fire on March 9. Merchandise on hand on January 1 was $38,000. Purchases since January 1 were $72,000; freight-in, $3,400; purchase returns and allowances, $2,400. Sales are made at 33⅓% above cost and totaled $100,000 to March 9. Goods costing $10,900 were left undamaged by the fire; remaining goods were destroyed.

Instructions
(a) Compute the cost of goods destroyed.
(b) Compute the cost of goods destroyed, assuming that the gross profit is 33⅓% of sales.

E9-14 (Gross Profit Method) Rasheed Wallace Company lost most of its inventory in a fire in December just before the year-end physical inventory was taken. The corporation's books disclosed the following.

Beginning inventory	$170,000	Sales	$650,000
Purchases for the year	390,000	Sales returns	24,000
Purchase returns	30,000	Rate of gross margin on net sales	40%

Merchandise with a selling price of $21,000 remained undamaged after the fire. Damaged merchandise with an original selling price of $15,000 had a net realizable value of $5,300.

Instructions
Compute the amount of the loss as a result of the fire, assuming that the corporation had no insurance coverage.

E9-15 (Gross Profit Method) You are called by Jay Williams of Bulls Co. on July 16 and asked to prepare a claim for insurance as a result of a theft that took place the night before. You suggest that an inventory be taken immediately. The following data are available.

Inventory, July 1	$ 38,000
Purchases—goods placed in stock July 1–15	85,000
Sales—goods delivered to customers (gross)	116,000
Sales returns—goods returned to stock	4,000

Your client reports that the goods on hand on July 16 cost $30,500, but you determine that this figure includes goods of $6,000 received on a consignment basis. Your past records show that sales are made at approximately 40% over cost.

Instructions

Compute the claim against the insurance company.

E9-16 (Gross Profit Method) Gheorghe Moresan Lumber Company handles three principal lines of merchandise with these varying rates of gross profit on cost.

Lumber	25%
Millwork	30%
Hardware and fittings	40%

On August 18, a fire destroyed the office, lumber shed, and a considerable portion of the lumber stacked in the yard. To file a report of loss for insurance purposes, the company must know what the inventories were immediately preceding the fire. No detail or perpetual inventory records of any kind were maintained. The only pertinent information you are able to obtain are the following facts from the general ledger, which was kept in a fireproof vault and thus escaped destruction.

	Lumber	Millwork	Hardware
Inventory, Jan. 1, 2005	$ 250,000	$ 90,000	$ 45,000
Purchases to Aug. 18, 2005	1,500,000	375,000	160,000
Sales to Aug. 18, 2005	2,080,000	533,000	210,000

Instructions

Submit your estimate of the inventory amounts immediately preceding the fire.

E9-17 (Gross Profit Method) Presented below is information related to Warren Moon Corporation for the current year.

Beginning inventory	$ 600,000	
Purchases	1,500,000	
Total goods available for sale		$2,100,000
Sales		2,500,000

Instructions

Compute the ending inventory, assuming that **(a)** gross profit is 45% of sales; **(b)** gross profit is 60% of cost; **(c)** gross profit is 35% of sales; and **(d)** gross profit is 25% of cost.

E9-18 (Retail Inventory Method) Presented below is information related to Bobby Engram Company.

	Cost	Retail
Beginning inventory	$ 58,000	$100,000
Purchases (net)	122,000	200,000
Net markups		10,345
Net markdowns		26,135
Sales		186,000

Instructions

(a) Compute the ending inventory at retail.

(b) Compute a cost-to-retail percentage (round to two decimals) under the following conditions.

  (1) Excluding both markups and markdowns.
  (2) Excluding markups but including markdowns.
  (3) Excluding markdowns but including markups.
  (4) Including both markdowns and markups.

(c) Which of the methods in (b) above (1, 2, 3, or 4) does the following?

  (1) Provides the most conservative estimate of ending inventory.
  (2) Provides an approximation of lower of cost or market.
  (3) Is used in the conventional retail method.

(d) Compute ending inventory at lower of cost or market (round to nearest dollar).
(e) Compute cost of goods sold based on (d).
(f) Compute gross margin based on (d).

E9-19 (Retail Inventory Method) Presented below is information related to Ricky Henderson Company.

	Cost	Retail
Beginning inventory	$ 200,000	$ 280,000
Purchases	1,375,000	2,140,000
Markups		95,000
Markup cancellations		15,000
Markdowns		35,000
Markdown cancellations		5,000
Sales		2,200,000

Instructions
Compute the inventory by the conventional retail inventory method.

E9-20 (Retail Inventory Method) The records of Ellen's Boutique report the following data for the month of April.

Sales	$99,000	Purchases (at cost)	$48,000
Sales returns	2,000	Purchases (at sales price)	88,000
Additional markups	10,000	Purchase returns (at cost)	2,000
Markup cancellations	1,500	Purchase returns (at sales price)	3,000
Markdowns	9,300	Beginning inventory (at cost)	30,000
Markdown cancellations	2,800	Beginning inventory (at sales price)	46,500
Freight on purchases	2,400		

Instructions
Compute the ending inventory by the conventional retail inventory method.

E9-21 (Analysis of Inventories) The financial statements of **General Mills, Inc**'s. 2001 Annual Report disclose the following information.

(in millions)	May 27, 2001	May 28, 2000	May 26, 1999
Inventories	$518.9	$510.5	$ 426.7

	Fiscal Year	
	2001	2000
Sales	$7,077.7	$6,700.2
Cost of goods sold	2,841.2	2,697.6
Net income	665.1	614.4

Instructions
Compute General Mills's **(a)** inventory turnover and **(b)** the average days to sell inventory for 2001 and 2000.

***E9-22 (Retail Inventory Method—Conventional and LIFO)** Helen Keller Company began operations on January 1, 2003, adopting the conventional retail inventory system. None of its merchandise was marked down in 2003 and, because there was no beginning inventory, its ending inventory for 2003 of $38,100 would have been the same under either the conventional retail system or the LIFO retail system. On December 31, 2004, the store management considers adopting the LIFO retail system and desires to know how the December 31, 2004, inventory would appear under both systems. All pertinent data regarding purchases, sales, markups, and markdowns are shown below. There has been no change in the price level.

	Cost	Retail
Inventory, Jan. 1, 2004	$ 38,100	$ 60,000
Markdowns (net)		13,000
Markups (net)		22,000
Purchases (net)	130,900	178,000
Sales (net)		167,000

Instructions
Determine the cost of the 2004 ending inventory under both **(a)** the conventional retail method and **(b)** the LIFO retail method.

***E9-23 (Retail Inventory Method—Conventional and LIFO)** Leonard Bernstein Company began operations late in 2003 and adopted the conventional retail inventory method. Because there was no beginning inventory for 2003 and no markdowns during 2003, the ending inventory for 2003 was $14,000 under both the conventional retail method and the LIFO retail method. At the end of 2004, management wants to compare the results of applying the conventional and LIFO retail methods. There was no change in the price level during 2004. The following data are available for computations.

	Cost	Retail
Inventory, January 1, 2004	$14,000	$20,000
Sales		80,000
Net markups		9,000
Net markdowns		1,600
Purchases	58,800	81,000
Freight-in	7,500	
Estimated theft		2,000

Instructions

Compute the cost of the 2004 ending inventory under both **(a)** the conventional retail method and **(b)** the LIFO retail method.

***E9-24 (Dollar-Value LIFO Retail)** You assemble the following information for Seneca Department Store, which computes its inventory under the dollar-value LIFO method.

	Cost	Retail
Inventory on January 1, 2004	$216,000	$300,000
Purchases	364,800	480,000
Increase in price level for year		9%

Instructions

Compute the cost of the inventory on December 31, 2004, assuming that the inventory at retail is **(a)** $294,300 and **(b)** $365,150.

***E9-25 (Dollar-Value LIFO Retail)** Presented below is information related to Langston Hughes Corporation.

	Price Index	LIFO Cost	Retail
Inventory on December 31, 2005, when dollar-value LIFO is adopted	100	$36,000	$ 74,500
Inventory, December 31, 2006	110	?	100,100

Instructions

Compute the ending inventory under the dollar-value LIFO method at December 31, 2006. The cost-to-retail ratio for 2006 was 60%.

***E9-26 (Conventional Retail and Dollar-Value LIFO Retail)** Black Feet Corporation began operations on January 1, 2004, with a beginning inventory of $30,100 at cost and $50,000 at retail. The following information relates to 2004.

	Retail
Net purchases ($108,500 at cost)	$150,000
Net markups	10,000
Net markdowns	5,000
Sales	126,900

Instructions

(a) Assume Black Feet decided to adopt the conventional retail method. Compute the ending inventory to be reported in the balance sheet.

(b) Assume instead that Black Feet decides to adopt the dollar-value LIFO retail method. The appropriate price indexes are 100 at January 1 and 110 at December 31. Compute the ending inventory to be reported in the balance sheet.

(c) On the basis of the information in part (b), compute cost of goods sold.

***E9-27 (Dollar-Value LIFO Retail)** The Connie Chung Corporation adopted the dollar-value LIFO retail inventory method on January 1, 2003. At that time the inventory had a cost of $54,000 and a retail price of $100,000. The following information is available.

	Year-End Inventory at Retail	Current Year Cost—Retail %	Year-End Price Index
2003	$118,720	57%	106
2004	138,750	60%	111
2005	125,350	61%	115
2006	162,500	58%	125

The price index at January 1, 2003, is 100.

Instructions

Compute the ending inventory at December 31 of the years 2003–2006. Round to the nearest dollar.

***E9-28 (Change to LIFO Retail)** John Olerud Ltd., a local retailing concern in the Bronx, N.Y., has decided to change from the conventional retail inventory method to the LIFO retail method starting on January 1, 2005. The company recomputed its ending inventory for 2004 in accordance with the procedures necessary to switch to LIFO retail. The inventory computed was $212,600.

Instructions

Assuming that John Olerud Ltd.'s ending inventory for 2004 under the conventional retail inventory method was $205,000, prepare the appropriate journal entry on January 1, 2005.

PROBLEMS

P9-1 (Lower of Cost or Market) Grant Wood Company manufactures desks. Most of the company's desks are standard models and are sold on the basis of catalog prices. At December 31, 2005, the following finished desks appear in the company's inventory.

Finished Desks	A	B	C	D
2005 catalog selling price	$450	$480	$900	$1,050
FIFO cost per inventory list 12/31/05	470	450	830	960
Estimated current cost to manufacture (at December 31, 2005, and early 2006)	460	440	610	1,000
Sales commissions and estimated other costs of disposal	45	60	90	130
2006 catalog selling price	500	540	900	1,200

The 2005 catalog was in effect through November 2005 and the 2006 catalog is effective as of December 1, 2005. All catalog prices are net of the usual discounts. Generally, the company attempts to obtain a 20% gross margin on selling price and has usually been successful in doing so.

Instructions

At what amount should each of the four desks appear in the company's December 31, 2005, inventory, assuming that the company has adopted a lower of FIFO cost or market approach for valuation of inventories on an individual-item basis?

P9-2 (Lower of Cost or Market) T. Allen Home Improvement Company installs replacement siding, windows, and louvered glass doors for single family homes and condominium complexes in northern New Jersey and southern New York. The company is in the process of preparing its annual financial statements for the fiscal year ended May 31, 2004, and Tim Taylor, controller for T. Allen, has gathered the following data concerning inventory.

At May 31, 2004, the balance in T. Allen's Raw Material Inventory account was $408,000, and the Allowance to Reduce Inventory to Market had a credit balance of $29,500. Taylor summarized the relevant inventory cost and market data at May 31, 2004, in the schedule below.

Taylor assigned Patricia Richardson, an intern from a local college, the task of calculating the amount that should appear on T. Allen's May 31, 2004, financial statements for inventory under the lower of cost or market rule as applied to each item in inventory. Richardson expressed concern over departing from the cost principle.

	Cost	Replacement Cost	Sales Price	Net Realizable Value	Normal Profit
Aluminum siding	$ 70,000	$ 62,500	$ 64,000	$ 56,000	$ 5,100
Cedar shake siding	86,000	79,400	94,000	84,800	7,400
Louvered glass doors	112,000	124,000	186,400	168,300	18,500
Thermal windows	140,000	122,000	154,800	140,000	15,400
Total	$408,000	$387,900	$499,200	$449,100	$46,400

Instructions

(a) (1) Determine the proper balance in the Allowance to Reduce Inventory to Market at May 31, 2004.
(2) For the fiscal year ended May 31, 2004, determine the amount of the gain or loss that would be recorded due to the change in the Allowance to Reduce Inventory to Market.

(b) Explain the rationale for the use of the lower of cost or market rule as it applies to inventories.

(CMA adapted)

P9-3 (Entries for Lower of Cost or Market—Direct and Allowance) Mary Stuart Company determined its ending inventory at cost and at lower of cost or market at December 31, 2003, December 31, 2004, and December 31, 2005, as shown below.

	Cost	Lower of Cost or Market
12/31/03	$650,000	$650,000
12/31/04	780,000	722,000
12/31/05	900,000	830,000

Instructions

(a) Prepare the journal entries required at December 31, 2004, and at December 31, 2005, assuming that a perpetual inventory system and the direct method of adjusting to market is used.

(b) Prepare the journal entries required at December 31, 2004, and at December 31, 2005, assuming that a perpetual inventory is recorded at cost and reduced to market through the use of an allowance account (indirect method).

P9-4 (Gross Profit Method) David Hasselhoff Company lost most of its inventory in a fire in December just before the year-end physical inventory was taken. Corporate records disclose the following.

Inventory (beginning)	$ 80,000	Sales	$415,000
Purchases	280,000	Sales returns	21,000
Purchase returns	28,000	Gross profit % based on net selling price	34%

Merchandise with a selling price of $30,000 remained undamaged after the fire, and damaged merchandise has a salvage value of $7,150. The company does not carry fire insurance on its inventory.

Instructions

Prepare a formal labeled schedule computing the fire loss incurred. (Do not use the retail inventory method.)

P9-5 (Gross Profit Method) On April 15, 2005, fire damaged the office and warehouse of John Kimmel Corporation. The only accounting record saved was the general ledger, from which the trial balance below was prepared.

JOHN KIMMEL CORPORATION
Trial Balance
March 31, 2005

Cash	$ 20,000	
Accounts receivable	40,000	
Inventory, December 31, 2004	75,000	
Land	35,000	
Building and equipment	110,000	
Accumulated depreciation		$ 41,300
Other assets	3,600	
Accounts payable		23,700
Other expense accruals		10,200
Capital stock		100,000
Retained earnings		52,000
Sales		135,000
Purchases	52,000	
Other expenses	26,600	
	$362,200	$362,200

The following data and information have been gathered.

1. The fiscal year of the corporation ends on December 31.
2. An examination of the April bank statement and canceled checks revealed that checks written during the period April 1–15 totaled $13,000: $5,700 paid to accounts payable as of March 31, $3,400

for April merchandise shipments, and $3,900 paid for other expenses. Deposits during the same period amounted to $12,950, which consisted of receipts on account from customers with the exception of a $950 refund from a vendor for merchandise returned in April.

3. Correspondence with suppliers revealed unrecorded obligations at April 15 of $10,600 for April merchandise shipments, including $2,300 for shipments in transit (f.o.b. shipping point) on that date.
4. Customers acknowledged indebtedness of $36,000 at April 15, 2005. It was also estimated that customers owed another $8,000 that will never be acknowledged or recovered. Of the acknowledged indebtedness, $600 will probably be uncollectible.
5. The companies insuring the inventory agreed that the corporation's fire-loss claim should be based on the assumption that the overall gross profit ratio for the past 2 years was in effect during the current year. The corporation's audited financial statements disclosed this information:

	Year Ended December 31	
	2004	2003
Net sales	$530,000	$390,000
Net purchases	280,000	235,000
Beginning inventory	50,000	75,200
Ending inventory	75,000	50,000

6. Inventory with a cost of $7,000 was salvaged and sold for $3,500. The balance of the inventory was a total loss.

Instructions

Prepare a schedule computing the amount of inventory fire loss. The supporting schedule of the computation of the gross profit should be in good form.

(AICPA adapted)

P9-6 (Retail Inventory Method) The records for the Clothing Department of Magdalena Aguilar's Discount Store are summarized below for the month of January.

Inventory, January 1: at retail $25,000; at cost $17,000
Purchases in January: at retail $137,000; at cost $86,500
Freight-in: $7,000
Purchase returns: at retail $3,000; at cost $2,300
Purchase allowances: $2,200
Transfers in from suburban branch: at retail $13,000; at cost $9,200
Net markups: $8,000
Net markdowns: $4,000
Inventory losses due to normal breakage, etc.: at retail $400
Sales at retail: $85,000
Sales returns: $2,400

Instructions

Compute the inventory for this department as of January 31, at **(a)** retail and **(b)** lower of average cost or market.

P9-7 (Retail Inventory Method) Presented below is information related to Edward Braddock Inc.

	Cost	Retail
Inventory, 12/31/04	$250,000	$ 390,000
Purchases	914,500	1,460,000
Purchase returns	60,000	80,000
Purchase discounts	18,000	—
Gross sales (after employee discounts)	—	1,460,000
Sales returns	—	97,500
Markups	—	120,000
Markup cancellations	—	40,000
Markdowns	—	45,000
Markdown cancellations	—	20,000
Freight-in	79,000	—
Employee discounts granted	—	8,000
Loss from breakage (normal)	—	2,500

Instructions

Assuming that Edward Braddock Inc. uses the conventional retail inventory method, compute the cost of its ending inventory at December 31, 2005.

P9-8 (Retail Inventory Method) Jared Jones Inc. uses the retail inventory method to estimate ending inventory for its monthly financial statements. The following data pertain to a single department for the month of October 2005.

Inventory, October 1, 2005	
At cost	$ 52,000
At retail	78,000
Purchases (exclusive of freight and returns)	
At cost	262,000
At retail	423,000
Freight-in	16,600
Purchase returns	
At cost	5,600
At retail	8,000
Additional markups	9,000
Markup cancellations	2,000
Markdowns (net)	3,600
Normal spoilage and breakage	10,000
Sales	380,000

Instructions

(a) Using the conventional retail method, prepare a schedule computing estimated lower of cost or market inventory for October 31, 2005.

(b) A department store using the conventional retail inventory method estimates the cost of its ending inventory as $60,000. An accurate physical count reveals only $47,000 of inventory at lower of cost or market. List the factors that may have caused the difference between the computed inventory and the physical count.

P9-9 (Statement and Note Disclosure, LCM, and Purchase Commitment) Garth Brooks Specialty Company, a division of Fresh Horses Inc., manufactures three models of gear shift components for bicycles that are sold to bicycle manufacturers, retailers, and catalog outlets. Since beginning operations in 1972, Brooks has used normal absorption costing and has assumed a first-in, first-out cost flow in its perpetual inventory system. Except for overhead, manufacturing costs are accumulated using actual costs. Overhead is applied to production using predetermined overhead rates. The balances of the inventory accounts at the end of Brooks's fiscal year, November 30, 2004, are shown below. The inventories are stated at cost before any year-end adjustments.

Finished goods	$647,000
Work-in-process	112,500
Raw materials	240,000
Factory supplies	69,000

The following information relates to Brooks's inventory and operations.

1. The finished goods inventory consists of the items analyzed below.

	Cost	Market
Down tube shifter		
Standard model	$ 67,500	$ 67,000
Click adjustment model	94,500	87,000
Deluxe model	108,000	110,000
Total down tube shifters	270,000	264,000
Bar end shifter		
Standard model	83,000	90,050
Click adjustment model	99,000	97,550
Total bar end shifters	182,000	187,600
Head tube shifter		
Standard model	78,000	77,650
Click adjustment model	117,000	119,300
Total head tube shifters	195,000	196,950
Total finished goods	$647,000	$648,550

2. One-half of the head tube shifter finished goods inventory is held by catalog outlets on consignment.
3. Three-quarters of the bar end shifter finished goods inventory has been pledged as collateral for a bank loan.
4. One-half of the raw materials balance represents derailleurs acquired at a contracted price 20 percent above the current market price. The market value of the rest of the raw materials is $127,400.
5. The total market value of the work-in-process inventory is $108,700.
6. Included in the cost of factory supplies are obsolete items with an historical cost of $4,200. The market value of the remaining factory supplies is $65,900.
7. Brooks applies the lower of cost or market method to each of the three types of shifters in finished goods inventory. For each of the other three inventory accounts, Brooks applies the lower of cost or market method to the total of each inventory account.
8. Consider all amounts presented above to be material in relation to Brooks' financial statements taken as a whole.

Instructions

(a) Prepare the inventory section of Brooks's statement of financial position as of November 30, 2004, including any required note(s).

(b) Without prejudice to your answer to (a), assume that the market value of Brooks' inventories is less than cost. Explain how this decline would be presented in Brooks' income statement for the fiscal year ended November 30, 2004.

(c) Assume that Brooks has a firm purchase commitment for the same type of derailleur included in the raw materials inventory as of November 30, 2004, and that the purchase commitment is at a contracted price 15% greater than the current market price. These derailleurs are to be delivered to Brooks after November 30, 2004. Discuss the impact, if any, that this purchase commitment would have on Brooks's financial statements prepared for the fiscal year ended November 30, 2004.

(CMA adapted)

P9-10 (Lower of Cost or Market) Fortner Co. follows the practice of valuing its inventory at the lower of cost or market. The following information is available from the company's inventory records as of December 31, 2003.

Item	Quantity	Unit Cost	Replacement Cost/Unit	Estimated Selling Price/Unit	Completion & Disposal Cost/Unit	Normal Profit Margin/Unit
A	1,100	$7.50	$8.40	$10.50	$1.50	$1.80
B	800	8.20	8.00	9.40	0.90	1.20
C	1,000	5.60	5.40	7.20	1.10	0.60
D	1,000	3.80	4.20	6.30	0.80	1.50
E	1,400	6.40	6.30	6.80	0.70	1.00

Instructions

Finn Berge is an accounting clerk in the accounting department of Fortner Co., and he cannot understand why the market value keeps changing from replacement cost to net realizable value to something that he cannot even figure out. Finn is very confused, and he is the one who records inventory purchases and calculates ending inventory. You are the manager of the department and an accountant.

(a) Calculate the lower of cost or market using the "individual item" approach.

(b) Show the journal entry he will need to make in order to write down the ending inventory from cost to market.

(c) Then write a memo to Finn explaining what designated market value is as well as how it is computed. Use your calculations to aid in your explanation.

***P9-11 (Conventional and Dollar-Value LIFO Retail)** As of January 1, 2005, Carl Sandburg Inc. installed the retail method of accounting for its merchandise inventory.

To prepare the store's financial statements at June 30, 2005, you obtain the following data.

	Cost	Selling Price
Inventory, January 1	$ 30,000	$ 43,000
Markdowns		10,500
Markups		9,200
Markdown cancellations		6,500
Markup cancellations		3,200
Purchases	108,800	155,000
Sales		159,000
Purchase returns and allowances	2,800	4,000
Sales returns and allowances		8,000

Instructions

(a) Prepare a schedule to compute Sandburg's June 30, 2005, inventory under the conventional retail method of accounting for inventories.

(b) Without prejudice to your solution to part (a), assume that you computed the June 30, 2005, inventory to be $54,000 at retail and the ratio of cost to retail to be 70%. The general price level has increased from 100 at January 1, 2005, to 108 at June 30, 2005. Prepare a schedule to compute the June 30, 2005, inventory at the June 30 price level under the dollar-value LIFO retail method.

(AICPA adapted)

***P9-12 (Retail, LIFO Retail, and Inventory Shortage)** Late in 2001, Sara Teasdale and four other investors took the chain of Sprint Department Stores private, and the company has just completed its third year of operations under the ownership of the investment group. Elinor Wylie, controller of Sprint Department Stores, is in the process of preparing the year-end financial statements. Based on the preliminary financial statements, Teasdale has expressed concern over inventory shortages, and she has asked Wylie to determine whether an abnormal amount of theft and breakage has occurred. The accounting records of Sprint Department Stores contain the following amounts on November 30, 2004, the end of the fiscal year.

	Cost	Retail
Beginning inventory	$ 68,000	$100,000
Purchases	248,200	400,000
Net markups		50,000
Net markdowns		110,000
Sales		330,000

According to the November 30, 2004, physical inventory, the actual inventory at retail is $107,000.

Instructions

(a) Describe the circumstances under which the retail inventory method would be applied and the advantages of using the retail inventory method.

(b) Assuming that prices have been stable, calculate the value, at cost, of Sprint Department Stores' ending inventory using the last-in, first-out (LIFO) retail method. Be sure to furnish supporting calculations.

(c) Estimate the amount of shortage, at retail, that has occurred at Sprint Department Stores during the year ended November 30, 2004.

(d) Complications in the retail method can be caused by such items as (1) freight-in expense, (2) purchase returns and allowances, (3) sales returns and allowances, and (4) employee discounts. Explain how each of these four special items is handled in the retail inventory method.

(CMA adapted)

***P9-13 (Change to LIFO Retail)** Ulysses Grant Stores Inc., which uses the conventional retail inventory method, wishes to change to the LIFO retail method beginning with the accounting year ending December 31, 2004.

Amounts as shown below appear on the store's books before adjustment.

	At Cost	At Retail
Inventory, January 1, 2004	$ 13,600	$ 24,000
Purchases in 2004	116,200	184,000
Markups in 2004		12,000
Markdowns in 2004		5,500
Sales in 2004		170,000

You are to assume that all markups and markdowns apply to 2004 purchases, and that it is appropriate to treat the entire inventory as a single department.

Instructions

Compute the inventory at December 31, 2004, under the following methods.

(a) The conventional retail method.

(b) The last-in, first-out retail method, effecting the change in method as of January 1, 2004. Assume that the cost-to-retail percentage for 2003 was recomputed correctly in accordance with procedures necessary to change to LIFO. This ratio was 57%.

(AICPA adapted)

***P9-14 (Change to LIFO Retail; Dollar-Value LIFO Retail)** Rudyard Kipling Department Store converted from the conventional retail method to the LIFO retail method on January 1, 2003, and is now considering converting to the dollar-value LIFO inventory method. During your examination of the financial statements for the year ended December 31, 2004, management requested that you furnish a summary showing certain computations of inventory cost for the past 3 years.

Here is the available information.

1. The inventory at January 1, 2002, had a retail value of $56,000 and cost of $26,700 based on the conventional retail method.
2. Transactions during 2002 were as follows.

	Cost	Retail
Gross purchases	$311,000	$554,000
Purchase returns	5,200	10,000
Purchase discounts	6,000	
Gross sales (after employee discounts)		551,000
Sales returns		9,000
Employee discounts		3,000
Freight-in	17,600	
Net markups		20,000
Net markdowns		12,000

3. The retail value of the December 31, 2003, inventory was $73,500, the cost ratio for 2003 under the LIFO retail method was 61%, and the regional price index was 105% of the January 1, 2003, price level.
4. The retail value of the December 31, 2004, inventory was $65,880, the cost ratio for 2004 under the LIFO retail method was 60%, and the regional price index was 108% of the January 1, 2003, price level.

Instructions

(a) Prepare a schedule showing the computation of the cost of inventory on hand at December 31, 2002, based on the conventional retail method.

(b) Prepare a schedule showing the recomputation of the inventory to be reported on December 31, 2002, in accordance with procedures necessary to convert from the conventional retail method to the LIFO retail method beginning January 1, 2003. Assume that the retail value of the December 31, 2002, inventory was $63,000.

(c) Without prejudice to your solution to part (b), assume that you computed the December 31, 2002, inventory (retail value $63,000) under the LIFO retail method at a cost of $34,965. Prepare a schedule showing the computations of the cost of the store's 2003 and 2004 year-end inventories under the dollar-value LIFO method.

(AICPA adapted)

CONCEPTUAL CASES

C9-1 (Lower of Cost or Market) You have been asked by the financial vice-president to develop a short presentation on the lower of cost or market method for inventory purposes. The financial VP needs to explain this method to the president, because it appears that a portion of the company's inventory has declined in value.

Instructions

The financial VP asks you to answer the following questions.

(a) What is the purpose of the lower of cost or market method?

(b) What is meant by market? (*Hint*: Discuss the ceiling and floor constraints.)

(c) Do you apply the lower of cost or market method to each individual item, to a category, or to the total of the inventory? Explain.

(d) What are the potential disadvantages of the lower of cost or market method?

C9-2 (Lower of Cost or Market) The market value of Lake Corporation's inventory has declined below its cost. Vickie Maher, the controller, wants to use the allowance method to write down inventory because it more clearly discloses the decline in market value and does not distort the cost of goods sold. Her supervisor, financial vice-president Doug Brucki, prefers the direct method to write down inventory because it does not call attention to the decline in market value.

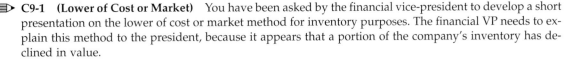

Instructions

Answer the following questions.

(a) What, if any, is the ethical issue involved?
(b) Is any stakeholder harmed if Brucki's preference is used?
(c) What should Vickie Maher do?

C9-3 (Lower of Cost or Market) Lena Horne Corporation purchased a significant amount of raw materials inventory for a new product that it is manufacturing.

Horne uses the lower of cost or market rule for these raw materials. The replacement cost of the raw materials is above the net realizable value, and both are below the original cost.

Horne uses the average cost inventory method for these raw materials. In the last 2 years, each purchase has been at a lower price than the previous purchase, and the ending inventory quantity for each period has been higher than the beginning inventory quantity for that period.

Instructions

(a) **(1)** At which amount should Horne's raw materials inventory be reported on the balance sheet? Why?
(2) In general, why is the lower of cost or market rule used to report inventory?
(b) What would have been the effect on ending inventory and cost of goods sold had Horne used the LIFO inventory method instead of the average cost inventory method for the raw materials? Why?

C9-4 (Retail Inventory Method) Aragon Company, your client, manufactures paint. The company's president, Ms. Catherine Aragon, has decided to open a retail store to sell Aragon paint as well as wallpaper and other supplies that would be purchased from other suppliers. She has asked you for information about the conventional retail method of pricing inventories at the retail store.

Instructions

Prepare a report to the president explaining the retail method of pricing inventories. Your report should include the following points.

(a) Description and accounting features of the method.
(b) The conditions that may distort the results under the method.
(c) A comparison of the advantages of using the retail method with those of using cost methods of inventory pricing.
(d) The accounting theory underlying the treatment of net markdowns and net markups under the method.

(AICPA adapted)

C9-5 (Cost Determination, LCM, Retail Method) E. A. Poe Corporation, a retailer and wholesaler of national brand-name household lighting fixtures, purchases its inventories from various suppliers.

Instructions

(a) **(1)** What criteria should be used to determine which of Poe's costs are inventoriable?
(2) Are Poe's administrative costs inventoriable? Defend your answer.
(b) **(1)** Poe uses the lower of cost or market rule for its wholesale inventories. What are the theoretical arguments for that rule?
(2) The replacement cost of the inventories is below the net realizable value less a normal profit margin, which, in turn, is below the original cost. What amount should be used to value the inventories? Why?
(c) Poe calculates the estimated cost of its ending inventories held for sale at retail using the conventional retail inventory method. How would Poe treat the beginning inventories and net markdowns in calculating the cost ratio used to determine its ending inventories? Why?

(AICPA adapted)

C9-6 (Purchase Commitments) Vineland Company signed a long-term purchase contract to buy timber from the U.S. Forest Service at $300 per thousand board feet. Under these terms, Vineland must cut and pay $6,000,000 for this timber during the next year. Currently the market value is $250 per thousand board feet. At this rate, the market price is $5,000,000. Ruben Walker, the controller, wants to recognize the loss in value on the year-end financial statements, but the financial vice-president, Billie Hands, argues that the loss is temporary and should be ignored. Walker notes that market value has remained near $250 for many months, and he sees no sign of significant change.

Instructions

Answer the following questions.

(a) What are the ethical issues, if any?
(b) Is any particular stakeholder harmed by the financial vice-president's decision?
(c) What should the controller do?

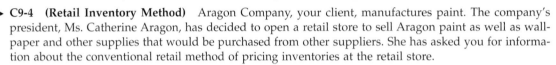

*C9-7 **(Retail Inventory Method and LIFO Retail)** Presented below are a number of items that may be encountered in computing the cost to retail percentage when using the conventional retail method or the LIFO retail method.

1. Markdowns.
2. Markdown cancellations.
3. Cost of items transferred in from other departments.
4. Retail value of items transferred in from other departments.
5. Sales discounts.
6. Purchases discounts (purchases recorded gross).
7. Estimated retail value of goods broken or stolen.
8. Cost of beginning inventory.
9. Retail value of beginning inventory.
10. Cost of purchases.
11. Retail value of purchases.
12. Markups.
13. Markup cancellations.
14. Employee discounts (sales recorded net).

Instructions

For each of the items listed above, indicate whether this item would be considered in the cost to retail percentage under **(a)** conventional retail and **(b)** LIFO retail.

USING YOUR JUDGMENT

FINANCIAL REPORTING PROBLEM

3M Company

The financial statements of 3M are presented in Appendix 5B or can be accessed on the Take Action! CD.

Instructions

Refer to 3M's financial statements and the accompanying notes to answer the following questions.

(a) How does 3M value its inventories? Which inventory costing method does 3M use as a basis for reporting its inventories?

(b) How does 3M report its inventories in the balance sheet? In the notes to its financial statements, what three descriptions are used to classify its inventories?

(c) What was 3M's inventory turnover ratio in 2001? What is its gross profit percentage? Evaluate 3M's inventory turnover ratio and its gross profit percentage.

FINANCIAL STATEMENT ANALYSIS CASES

Case 1 Sonic, Inc.

Sonic, Inc., reported the following information regarding 2002–2003 inventory.

SONIC, INC.

	2003	2002
Current assets		
Cash	$ 153,010	$ 538,489
Accounts receivable, net of allowance for doubtful accounts of $46,000 in 2003 and $160,000 in 2002	1,627,980	2,596,291
Inventories (Note 2)	1,340,494	1,734,873
Other current assets	123,388	90,592
Assets of discontinued operations	—	32,815
Total current assets	3,244,872	4,993,060

Notes to Consolidated Financial Statements

Note 1 (in part): Nature of Business and Significant Accounting Policies

Inventories—Inventories are stated at the lower of cost or market. Cost is determined by the last-in, first-out (LIFO) method by the parent company and by the first-in, first-out (FIFO) method by its subsidiaries.

Note 2: Inventories

Inventories consist of the following.

	2003	2002
Raw materials	$1,264,646	$2,321,178
Work in process	240,988	171,222
Finished goods and display units	129,406	711,252
Total inventories	1,635,040	3,203,652
Less: Amount classified as long-term	294,546	1,468,779
Current portion	$1,340,494	$1,734,873

Inventories are stated at the lower of cost determined by the LIFO method or market for Sonic, Inc. Inventories for the two wholly-owned subsidiaries, Sonic Command, Inc. (U.S.) and Sonic Limited (U.K.) are stated on the FIFO method which amounted to $566,000 at October 31, 2002. No inventory is stated on the FIFO method at October 31, 2003. Included in inventory stated at FIFO cost was $32,815 at October 31, 2002, of Sonic Command inventory classified as an asset from discontinued operations (see Note 14). If the FIFO method had been used for the entire consolidated group, inventories after an adjustment to the lower of cost or market, would have been approximately $2,000,000 and $3,800,000 at October 31, 2003 and 2002, respectively.

Inventory has been written down to estimated net realizable value, and results of operations for 2003, 2002, and 2001 include a corresponding charge of approximately $868,000, $960,000, and $273,000, respectively, which represents the excess of LIFO cost over market.

Inventory of $294,546 and $1,468,779 at October 31, 2003 and 2002, respectively, shown on the balance sheet as a noncurrent asset represents that portion of the inventory that is not expected to be sold currently.

Reduction in inventory quantities during the years ended October 31, 2003, 2002, and 2001 resulted in liquidation of LIFO inventory quantities carried at a lower cost prevailing in prior years as compared with the cost of fiscal 2000 purchases. The effect of these reductions was to decrease the net loss by approximately $24,000, $157,000 and $90,000 at October 31, 2003, 2002, and 2001, respectively.

Instructions

(a) Why might Sonic, Inc., use two different methods for valuing inventory?

(b) Comment on why Sonic, Inc. might disclose how its LIFO inventories would be valued under FIFO.

(c) Why does the LIFO liquidation reduce operating costs?

(d) Comment on whether Sonic would report more or less income if it had been on a FIFO basis for all its inventory.

Case 2 Barrick Gold Corporation

Barrick Gold Corporation, with headquarters in Toronto, Canada, is the world's most profitable and largest gold mining company outside South Africa. Part of the key to Barrick's success has been due to its ability to maintain cash flow while improving production and increasing its reserves of gold-containing property. During 2000, Barrick achieved record growth in cash flow, production, and reserves.

The company maintains an aggressive policy of developing previously identified target areas that have the possibility of a large amount of gold ore, and that have not been previously developed. Barrick limits the riskiness of this development by choosing only properties that are located in politically stable regions, and by the company's use of internally generated funds, rather than debt, to finance growth.

Barrick's inventories are as follows:

Inventories (in millions, US dollars)	
Current	
Gold in process	$85
Mine operating supplies	43
	$128
Non-current (included in property, plant, and equipment)	
Ore in stockpiles	$202

Instructions

(a) Why do you think that there are no finished goods inventories? Why do you think the raw material, ore in stockpiles, is considered to be a non-current asset?

(b) Consider that Barrick has no finished goods inventories. What journal entries are made to record a sale?

(c) Suppose that gold bullion that cost $1.8 million to produce was sold for $2.4 million. The journal entry was made to record the sale, but no entry was made to remove the gold from the gold in process inventory. How would this error affect the following?

Balance Sheet		Income Statement	
Inventory	?	Cost of goods sold	?
Retained earnings	?	Net income	?
Accounts payable	?		
Working capital	?		
Current ratio	?		

COMPARATIVE ANALYSIS CASE

The Coca-Cola Company and PepsiCo, Inc.

Instructions

Go to the Take Action! CD and use information found there to answer the following questions related to **The Coca-Cola Company** and **PepsiCo, Inc.**

(a) What is the amount of inventory reported by Coca-Cola at December 31, 2001, and by PepsiCo at December 31, 2001? What percent of total assets is invested in inventory by each company?

(b) What inventory costing methods are used by Coca-Cola and PepsiCo? How does each company value its inventories?

(c) In the notes, what classifications (description) are used by Coca-Cola and PepsiCo to categorize their inventories?

(d) Compute and compare the inventory turnover ratios and days to sell inventory for Coca-Cola and PepsiCo for 2001. Indicate why there might be a significant difference between the two companies.

RESEARCH CASES

Case 1

Numerous companies have established home pages on the Internet, for example, **Boston Beer Company** (www.samadams.com), **Ford Motor Company** (www.ford.com), and **Kodak** (www.kodak.com). You undoubtedly have noticed company Internet addresses in television commercials or magazine advertisements.

Instructions

Examine the home pages of any two companies and answer the following questions.

(a) What type of information is available?

(b) Is any accounting-related information presented?

(c) Would you describe the home page as informative, promotional, or both? Why?

Case 2

The September 23, 1994, edition of the *Wall Street Journal* includes an article entitled "**CompUSA** Auctions Notebook Computers Through Bulk Sale." (Subscribers to **Business Extra** can access the article at that site.)

Instructions

Read the article and answer the following questions.

(a) At what amount did CompUSA estimate the retail value of the computers? What was the estimate made by one of the bidders?

(b) What was wrong with the computers?

(c) What were the rules of the auction as specified by CompUSA?

(d) CompUSA had just recorded a $3 million inventory write-down in the preceding quarter. Based on the information in the article, does it appear that additional write-downs were called for?

PROFESSIONAL SIMULATION

Inventory Valuation

Directions | Situation | Journal Entries | Explanation | Research | Resources

Directions

In this simulation, you will be asked various questions related to inventory valuation. Prepare responses to all parts.

Situation

YoYoMa Inc. manufactures and sells four products, the inventories of which are priced at cost or market, whichever is lower. A normal profit margin rate of 30% is usually maintained on each of the four products.

The following information was compiled as of December 31, 2004.

Product	Original Cost	Cost to Replace	Estimated Cost to Dispose	Expected Selling Price*
A	$17.50	$14.00	$ 6.00	$ 30.00
B	48.00	78.00	26.00	100.00
C	35.00	42.00	15.00	80.00
D	47.50	45.00	20.50	95.00

*Normal margin is 30% of selling price.

Resources

Use a computer spreadsheet to prepare a schedule containing unit values (including "floor" and "ceiling") for determining the lower of cost or market on an individual-product basis. The last column of the schedule should contain, for each product, the unit value for the purpose of inventory valuation resulting from the application of the lower of cost or market rule.

Journal Entry

Prepare the journal entry to record the lower of cost or market for YoYoMa. Assume 1,000 units of each product and that YoYoMa uses a perpetual inventory system.

Explanation

Prepare a brief memorandum to explain why expected selling prices are important in the application of the lower of cost or market rule.

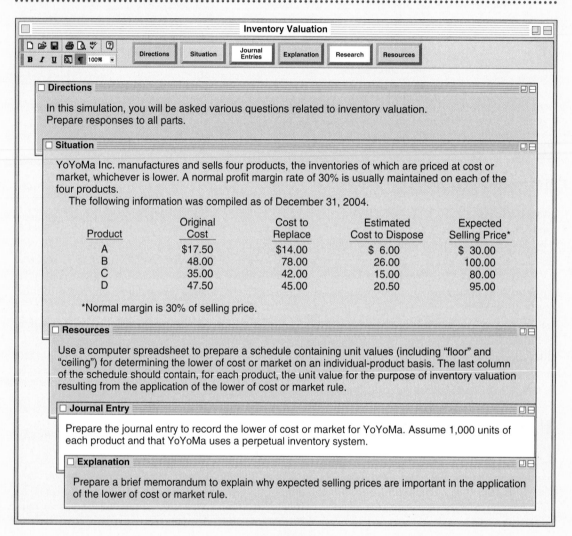

Remember to check the **Take Action! CD** and the book's **companion Web site** to find additional resources for this chapter.

CHAPTER 10

Acquisition and Disposition of Property, Plant, and Equipment

Where Have All the Assets Gone?

Investments in long-lived assets, such as property, plant, and equipment, are important elements in many companies' balance sheets. As indicated in the chart below, major companies, such as **Wal-Mart** and **Southwest Airlines** recently reported property, plant, and equipment (PP&E) as a percent of total assets ranging from 40 percent up to nearly 90 percent.

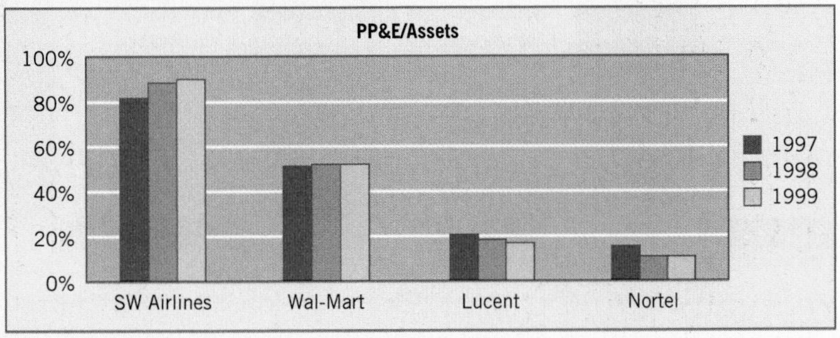

However, for various strategic reasons, a number of companies are now shedding property, plant, and equipment. They are using the proceeds to pay other companies to perform manufacturing and assembly functions—functions that were previously performed in company-owned facilities. As a result, some companies, such as **Lucent** and **Nortel**, do not need to invest as much in long-lived assets.

Nortel is a good example of the specifics of this strategy. The company is in the midst of a 36-month plan to sell and outsource certain facilities in order to reduce its direct manufacturing activities and costs. Nortel also sold its training and headset businesses and plans to more aggressively outsource other operations to reduce costs. Reductions in these areas will enable Nortel to concentrate on its core operations. The market seems to approve of this strategy. As measured by price-earnings (P-E) ratios early in 2000, Nortel's P-E ratio was above that of competitors not pursuing aggressive outsourcing strategies.[1]

LEARNING OBJECTIVES

After studying this chapter, you should be able to:

1. **Describe the major characteristics of property, plant, and equipment.**
2. **Identify the costs included in the initial valuation of land, buildings, and equipment.**
3. **Describe the accounting problems associated with self-constructed assets.**
4. **Describe the accounting problems associated with interest capitalization.**
5. **Understand accounting issues related to acquiring and valuing plant assets.**
6. **Describe the accounting treatment for costs subsequent to acquisition.**
7. **Describe the accounting treatment for the disposal of property, plant, and equipment.**

[1] Adapted from Chapter 1 in Grady Means and David Schneider, *MetaCapitalism: The e-Business Revolution and the Design of 21st-Century Companies and Markets* (New York: John Wiley and Sons, 2000).

PREVIEW OF CHAPTER 10

As indicated in the opening story, a company like **Southwest Airlines** has a substantial investment in property, plant, and equipment. Conversely, other companies such as **Nortel** have a minor investment in these types of assets.

The purpose of this chapter is to discuss (1) the proper accounting for costs related to property, plant, and equipment and (2) the accounting methods used to record the retirement or disposal of these costs. Depreciation—allocating costs of property, plant, and equipment to accounting periods—is presented in Chapter 11. The content and organization of this chapter are as follows.

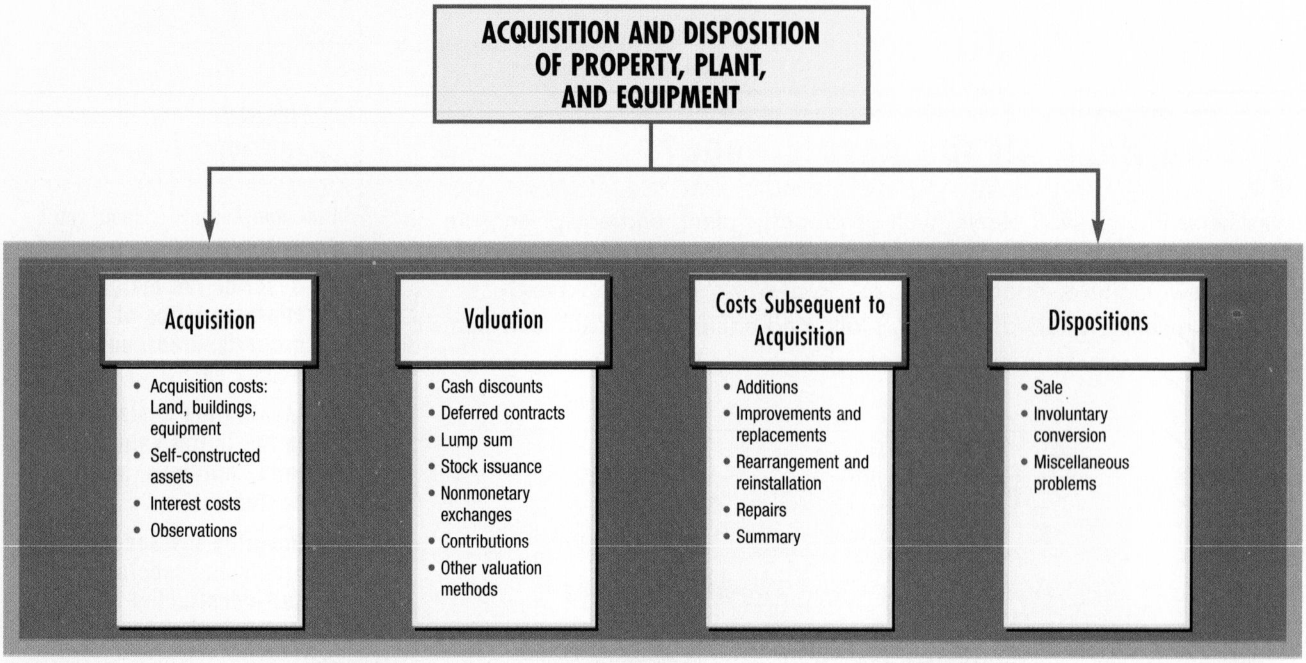

OBJECTIVE 1
Describe the major characteristics of property, plant, and equipment.

Almost every business enterprise of any size or activity uses assets of a durable nature. Such assets are commonly referred to as **property, plant, and equipment**; **plant assets**; or **fixed assets**. They include land, building structures (offices, factories, warehouses), and equipment (machinery, furniture, tools). These terms are used interchangeably throughout this textbook. The major characteristics of property, plant, and equipment are:

1. ***They are acquired for use in operations and not for resale.*** Only assets used in normal business operations should be classified as property, plant, and equipment. An idle building is more appropriately classified separately as an investment. Land held by land developers or subdividers is classified as inventory.
2. ***They are long-term in nature and usually subject to depreciation.*** Property, plant, and equipment yield services over a number of years. The investment in these assets is assigned to future periods through periodic depreciation charges. The exception is land. Land is not depreciated unless a material decrease in value occurs, such as a loss in fertility of agricultural land because of poor crop rotation, drought, or soil erosion.
3. ***They possess physical substance.*** Property, plant, and equipment are characterized by physical existence or substance and thus are differentiated from intangible assets, such as patents or goodwill. Unlike raw material, however, property, plant, and equipment do not physically become part of a product held for resale.

ACQUISITION OF PROPERTY, PLANT, AND EQUIPMENT

Historical cost is the usual basis for valuing property, plant, and equipment. **Historical cost is measured by the cash or cash equivalent price of obtaining the asset and bringing it to the location and condition necessary for its intended use.** The purchase price, freight costs, sales taxes, and installation costs of a productive asset are considered part of the asset's cost. These costs are allocated to future periods through depreciation. Any related costs incurred **after the asset's acquisition**, such as additions, improvements, or replacements, are **added to the asset's cost if they provide future service potential**. Otherwise they are expensed immediately.

OBJECTIVE 2
Identify the costs included in the initial valuation of land, buildings, and equipment.

Cost should be the basis used at the acquisition date. The reason is that the cash or cash equivalent price best measures the asset's value at that time. Disagreement does exist concerning differences between historical cost and other valuation methods (such as replacement cost or fair market value) arising after acquisition. *APB Opinion No. 6* states that "property, plant, and equipment should not be written up to reflect appraisal, market, or current values which are above cost." Although minor exceptions are noted, current standards indicate that departures from historical cost are rare.

The main reasons for this position are as follows: (1) At the date of acquisition, cost reflects fair value. (2) Historical cost involves actual, not hypothetical, transactions and as a result is the most reliable. (3) Gains and losses should not be anticipated but should be recognized when the asset is sold.

UNDERLYING CONCEPTS

Market value is relevant to inventory but less so for property, plant, and equipment which, consistent with the going concern assumption, are held for use in the business, not for sale like inventory.

Cost of Land

All expenditures made to acquire land and to ready it for use are considered part of the land cost. Land costs typically include the following: (1) the purchase price, (2) closing costs, such as title to the land, attorney's fees, and recording fees, (3) costs incurred in getting the land in condition for its intended use, such as grading, filling, draining, and clearing, (4) assumption of any liens, mortgages, or encumbrances on the property, and (5) any additional land improvements that have an indefinite life.

Expanded Discussion of Alternative Valuation Methods

When land has been purchased for the purpose of constructing a building, all costs incurred up to the excavation for the new building are considered land costs. **Removal of old buildings—clearing, grading, and filling—are considered land costs because these costs are necessary to get the land in condition for its intended purpose.** Any proceeds obtained in the process of getting the land ready for its intended use, such as salvage receipts on the demolition of an old building or the sale of cleared timber, are treated as **reductions in the price of the land**.

In some cases, the purchaser of land has to assume certain obligations on the land such as back taxes or liens. In such situations, the cost of the land is the cash paid for it, plus the encumbrances. In other words, if the purchase price of the land is $50,000 cash, and accrued property taxes of $5,000 and liens of $10,000 are assumed, the cost of the land is $65,000.

INTERNATIONAL INSIGHT

In many nations, such as Great Britain and Brazil, companies are allowed to revalue their fixed assets at amounts above historical cost. These revaluations may be at appraisal values or at amounts linked to a specified index. Other nations, such as Japan and Germany, do not allow such revaluations.

Special assessments for local improvements, such as pavements, street lights, sewers, and drainage systems, are usually charged to the Land account. They are relatively permanent in nature and after installation, are maintained and replaced by the local government body. In addition, permanent improvements made by the owner, such as landscaping, are properly chargeable to the Land account. **Improvements with limited lives**, such as private driveways, walks, fences, and parking lots, are recorded separately as Land Improvements so they can be depreciated over their estimated lives.

Generally, land is part of property, plant, and equipment. However, if the major purpose of acquiring and holding land is speculative, it is more appropriately classified as an investment. If the land is held by a real estate concern for resale, it should be classified as inventory.

In cases where land is held as an investment, what accounting treatment should be given taxes, insurance, and other direct costs incurred while holding the land? Many believe these costs should be capitalized because the revenue from the investment still has not been received. This approach is reasonable and seems justified except in cases where the asset is currently producing revenue (such as rental property).

Cost of Buildings

The cost of buildings should include all expenditures related directly to their acquisition or construction. These costs include (1) materials, labor, and overhead costs incurred during construction and (2) professional fees and building permits. Generally, companies contract to have their buildings constructed. All costs incurred, from excavation to completion, are considered part of the building costs.

INTERNATIONAL INSIGHT

Under international accounting standards, historical cost is the benchmark (preferred) treatment for property, plant, and equipment. However, it is also allowable to use revalued amounts. If revaluation is used, companies are required to revalue the class of assets regularly.

One accounting problem is deciding what to do about an old building that is on the site of a newly proposed building. Is the cost of removal of the old building a cost of the land or a cost of the new building? The answer is that if land is purchased with an old building on it, then the cost of demolition less its salvage value is a cost of getting the land ready for its intended use. Therefore the cost of removal relates to the land rather than to the new building. As indicated earlier, all costs of getting an asset ready for its intended use are costs of that asset.

Cost of Equipment

The term "equipment" in accounting includes delivery equipment, office equipment, machinery, furniture and fixtures, furnishings, factory equipment, and similar fixed assets. The cost of such assets includes the purchase price, freight and handling charges incurred, insurance on the equipment while in transit, cost of special foundations if required, assembling and installation costs, and costs of conducting trial runs. Costs thus include all expenditures incurred in acquiring the equipment and preparing it for use.

Self-Constructed Assets

OBJECTIVE 3
Describe the accounting problems associated with self-constructed assets.

Occasionally companies (particularly in the railroad and utility industries) construct their own assets. Determining the cost of such machinery and other fixed assets can be a problem. Without a purchase price or contract price, the company must allocate costs and expenses in order to arrive at the cost of the **self-constructed asset**. Materials and direct labor used in construction pose no problem; these costs can be traced directly to work and material orders related to the fixed assets constructed.

However, the assignment of **indirect costs** of manufacturing creates special problems. These indirect costs, called **overhead** or burden, include power, heat, light, insurance, property taxes on factory buildings and equipment, factory supervisory labor, depreciation of fixed assets, and supplies. These costs might be handled in one of two ways:

1. *Assign No Fixed Overhead to the Cost of the Constructed Asset.* The major argument for this treatment is that indirect overhead is generally fixed in nature and does not increase as a result of constructing one's own plant or equipment. This approach assumes that the company will have the same costs regardless of whether the company constructs the asset or not. Therefore, to charge a portion of the overhead costs to the equipment will normally relieve current expenses and consequently overstate income of the current period. In contrast, variable overhead costs that increase as a result of the construction are assigned to the cost of the asset.
2. *Assign a Portion of All Overhead to the Construction Process.* This approach, a **full costing** concept, is appropriate if one believes that costs attach to all products and assets manufactured or constructed. This procedure assigns overhead costs to construction as it would to normal production. Advocates say that failure to allo-

cate overhead costs understates the initial cost of the asset and results in an inaccurate future allocation.

A pro rata portion of the fixed overhead should be assigned to the asset to obtain its cost. This treatment is employed extensively because many believe a better matching of costs with revenues is obtained. If the allocated overhead results in recording construction costs in excess of the costs that would be charged by an outside independent producer, the excess overhead should be recorded as a period loss rather than be capitalized, to avoid capitalizing the asset at more than its probable market value.[2]

Interest Costs During Construction

OBJECTIVE 4
Describe the accounting problems associated with interest capitalization.

The proper accounting for interest costs has been a long-standing controversy. Three approaches have been suggested to account for the interest incurred in financing the construction or acquisition of property, plant, and equipment:

1. ***Capitalize No Interest Charges During Construction.*** Under this approach interest is considered a cost of financing and not a cost of construction. It is contended that if the company had used stock financing rather than debt financing, this expense would not have been incurred. The major argument against this approach is that an implicit interest cost is associated with the use of cash regardless of its source; if stock financing is employed, a real cost exists to the stockholders although a contractual claim does not take place.
2. ***Charge Construction with All Costs of Funds Employed, Whether Identifiable or Not.*** This method maintains that one part of the cost of construction is the cost of financing, whether by debt, cash, or stock financing. An asset should be charged with all costs necessary to get it ready for its intended use. Interest, whether actual or imputed, is a cost of building, just as labor, materials, and overhead are costs. A major criticism of this approach is that imputation of a cost of equity capital is subjective and outside the framework of an historical cost system.
3. ***Capitalize Only the Actual Interest Costs Incurred During Construction.*** This approach relies on the historical cost concept that only actual transactions are recorded. It is argued that interest incurred is as much a cost of acquiring the asset as the cost of the materials, labor, and other resources used. As a result, a company that uses debt financing will have an asset of higher cost than an enterprise that uses stock financing. The results achieved by this approach are considered unsatisfactory by some because the cost of an asset should be the same whether cash, debt financing, or stock financing is employed.

Illustration 10-1 on the next page shows the interest costs (if any) that would be added to the cost of an asset under the three capitalization approaches.

---

[2]Recently, the Accounting Standards Executive Committee (AcSEC) of the AICPA issued an exposure draft related to property, plant, and equipment. In this exposure draft, AcSEC argues against allocation of overhead. Instead, it basically supports capitalization of only direct costs (costs directly related to the specific activities involved in the construction process). AcSEC was concerned that the allocation of overhead costs may lead to overly aggressive allocations and therefore misstatements of income. In addition, not reporting these costs as period costs during the construction period may affect favorably the comparison of period costs and resulting net income from one period to the next. See Accounting Standards Executive Committee, "Accounting for Certain Costs and Activities Related to Property, Plant, and Equipment," *Exposure Draft* (New York: AICPA, June 29, 2001).

ILLUSTRATION 10-1
Capitalization of Interest Costs

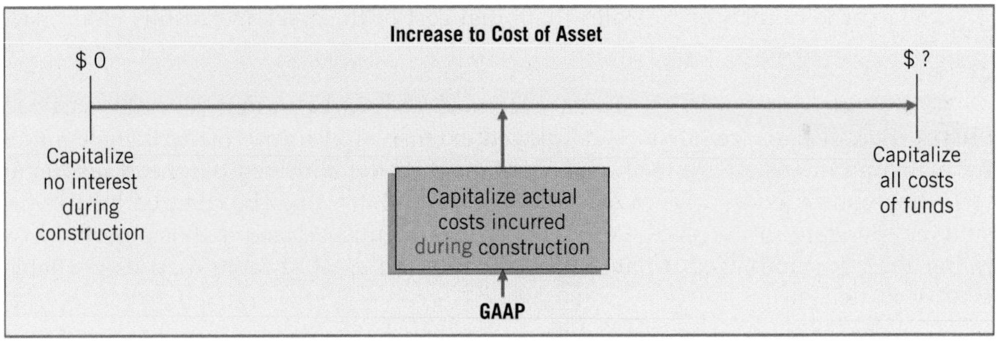

As indicated, in general, capitalizing actual interest (with modification) is the approach recommended under GAAP. This method is in accordance with the concept that the historical cost of acquiring an asset includes all costs (including interest) incurred to bring the asset to the condition and location necessary for its intended use. The rationale for this approach is that during construction the asset is not generating revenues, and therefore interest costs should be deferred (capitalized).[3] Once construction is completed, the asset is ready for its intended use and revenues can be earned. At this point interest should be reported as an expense and matched to these revenues. It follows that any interest cost incurred in purchasing an asset that is ready for its intended use should be expensed.

To implement this general approach, three items must be considered:

1. Qualifying assets.
2. Capitalization period.
3. Amount to capitalize.

Qualifying Assets

To qualify for interest capitalization, assets must require a period of time to get them ready for their intended use. Interest costs are capitalized starting with the first expenditure related to the asset. Capitalization continues until the asset is substantially completed and ready for its intended use.

Assets that qualify for interest cost capitalization include two types: (1) assets under construction for an enterprise's own use (including buildings, plants, and large machinery), and (2) assets intended for sale or lease that are constructed or otherwise produced as discrete projects (e.g., ships or real estate developments).

Examples of assets that do not qualify for interest capitalization are (1) assets that are in use or ready for their intended use, and (2) assets that are not being used in the earnings activities of the enterprise and that are not undergoing the activities necessary to get them ready for use. Examples would be land that is not being developed and assets not being used because of obsolescence, excess capacity, or need for repair.

INTERNATIONAL INSIGHT

Under international accounting standards, capitalization of interest is allowed, but it is not the preferred treatment. The benchmark treatment is to expense interest in the period incurred.

Capitalization Period

The **capitalization period** is the period of time during which interest must be capitalized. It begins when three conditions are present:

1. Expenditures for the asset have been made.
2. Activities that are necessary to get the asset ready for its intended use are in progress.
3. Interest cost is being incurred.

Interest capitalization **continues as long as these three conditions are present**. The capitalization period ends when the asset is substantially complete and ready for its intended use.

---

[3] "Capitalization of Interest Cost," *Statement of Financial Accounting Standards No. 34* (Stamford, Conn.: FASB, 1979).

Amount to Capitalize

The amount of interest to be capitalized is limited to the lower of actual interest cost incurred during the period or avoidable interest. **Avoidable interest** is the amount of interest cost during the period that theoretically could have been avoided if expenditures for the asset had not been made. If the actual interest cost for the period is $90,000 and the avoidable interest is $80,000, only $80,000 is capitalized. If the actual interest cost is $80,000 and the avoidable interest is $90,000, only $80,000 is capitalized. In no situation should interest cost include a cost of capital charge for stockholders' equity. And, interest capitalization is required for a qualifying asset only if its effect, compared with the effect of expensing interest, is material.[4]

To apply the avoidable interest concept, the potential amount of interest that may be capitalized during an accounting period is determined by multiplying the interest rate(s) by the **weighted-average accumulated expenditures** for qualifying assets during the period.

Weighted-Average Accumulated Expenditures. In computing the weighted-average accumulated expenditures, the construction expenditures are weighted by the amount of time (fraction of a year or accounting period) that interest cost could be incurred on the expenditure.

To illustrate, assume a 17-month bridge construction project with current-year payments to the contractor of $240,000 on March 1, $480,000 on July 1, and $360,000 on November 1. The weighted-average accumulated expenditures for the year ended December 31 are computed as follows.

ILLUSTRATION 10-2
Computation of Weighted-Average Accumulated Expenditures

Expenditures					
Date	Amount	×	Capitalization Period*	=	Weighted-Average Accumulated Expenditures
March 1	$ 240,000		10/12		$200,000
July 1	480,000		6/12		240,000
November 1	360,000		2/12		60,000
	$1,080,000				$500,000

*Months between date of expenditure and date interest capitalization stops or end of year, whichever comes first (in this case December 31).

To compute the weighted-average accumulated expenditures, we weight the expenditures by the amount of time that interest cost could be incurred on each one. For the March 1 expenditure, 10 months' interest costs can be associated with the expenditure. For the expenditure, on July 1, only 6 months' interest costs can be incurred. For the expenditure made on November 1, only 2 months of interest cost is incurred.

Interest Rates. The principles to be used in selecting the appropriate interest rates to be applied to the weighted-average accumulated expenditures are as follows.

1. For the portion of weighted-average accumulated expenditures that is less than or equal to any amounts borrowed specifically to finance construction of the assets, **use the interest rate incurred on the specific borrowings.**

[4]Ibid., summary paragraph.

❷ For the portion of weighted-average accumulated expenditures that is greater than any debt incurred specifically to finance construction of the assets, **use a weighted average of interest rates incurred on all other outstanding debt during the period.**[5]

An illustration of the computation of a weighted-average interest rate for debt greater than the amount incurred specifically to finance construction of the assets is shown in Illustration 10-3.

ILLUSTRATION 10-3
Computation of Weighted-Average Interest Rate

	Principal	Interest
12%, 2-year note	$ 600,000	$ 72,000
9%, 10-year bonds	2,000,000	180,000
7.5%, 20-year bonds	5,000,000	375,000
	$7,600,000	$627,000

$$\text{Weighted-average interest rate} = \frac{\text{Total interest}}{\text{Total principal}} = \frac{\$627,000}{\$7,600,000} = 8.25\%$$

Comprehensive Illustration of Interest Capitalization

To illustrate the issues related to interest capitalization, assume that on November 1, 2003, Shalla Company contracted with Pfeifer Construction Co. to have a building constructed for $1,400,000 on land costing $100,000 (purchased from the contractor and included in the first payment). Shalla made the following payments to the construction company during 2004.

January 1	March 1	May 1	December 31	Total
$210,000	$300,000	$540,000	$450,000	$1,500,000

Construction was completed and the building was ready for occupancy on December 31, 2004. Shalla Company had the following debt outstanding at December 31, 2004.

Specific Construction Debt	
1. 15%, 3-year note to finance purchase of land and construction of the building, dated December 31, 2003, with interest payable annually on December 31	$750,000
Other Debt	
2. 10%, 5-year note payable, dated December 31, 2000, with interest payable annually on December 31	$550,000
3. 12%, 10-year bonds issued December 31, 1999, with interest payable annually on December 31	$600,000

The weighted-average accumulated expenditures during 2004 are computed as follows.

ILLUSTRATION 10-4
Computation of Weighted-Average Accumulated Expenditures

Expenditures			Current Year		
Date	Amount	×	Capitalization Period	=	Weighted-Average Accumulated Expenditures
January 1	$ 210,000		12/12		$210,000
March 1	300,000		10/12		250,000
May 1	540,000		8/12		360,000
December 31	450,000		0		0
	$1,500,000				$820,000

[5]The interest rate to be used may be based exclusively on an average rate of all the borrowings, if desired. For our purposes, we will use the specific borrowing rate followed by the average interest rate because we believe it to be more conceptually consistent. Either method can be used; *FASB Statement No. 34* does not provide explicit guidance on this measurement. For a discussion of this issue and others related to interest capitalization, see Kathryn M. Means and Paul M. Kazenski, "SFAS 34: Recipe for Diversity," *Accounting Horizons* (September 1988); and Wendy A. Duffy, "A Graphical Analysis of Interest Capitalization," *Journal of Accounting Education* (Fall 1990).

Note that the expenditure made on December 31, the last day of the year, does not have any interest cost.

The avoidable interest is computed as follows.

ILLUSTRATION 10-5
Computation of Avoidable Interest

Weighted-Average Accumulated Expenditures	×	Interest Rate	=	Avoidable Interest
$750,000		.15 (construction note)		$112,500
70,000[a]		.1104 (weighted average of other debt)[b]		7,728
$820,000				$120,228

[a]The amount by which the weighted-average accumulated expenditures exceeds the specific construction loan.

[b]Weighted-average interest rate computation:

	Principal	Interest
10%, 5-year note	$ 550,000	$ 55,000
12%, 10-year bonds	600,000	72,000
	$1,150,000	$127,000

$$\text{Weighted-average interest rate} = \frac{\text{Total interest}}{\text{Total principal}} = \frac{\$127,000}{\$1,150,000} = 11.04\%$$

The actual interest cost, which represents the maximum amount of interest that may be capitalized during 2004, is computed as shown below.

ILLUSTRATION 10-6
Computation of Actual Interest Cost

Construction note	$750,000 × .15	=	$112,500
5-year note	$550,000 × .10	=	55,000
10-year bonds	$600,000 × .12	=	72,000
Actual interest			$239,500

The interest cost to be capitalized is the lesser of avoidable interest ($120,228) or actual interest ($239,500). In this case, the interest cost to be capitalized is $120,228.

The journal entries made by Shalla Company during 2004 would be as follows.

January 1		
Land	100,000	
Building (or Construction in Process)	110,000	
Cash		210,000
March 1		
Building	300,000	
Cash		300,000
May 1		
Building	540,000	
Cash		540,000
December 31		
Building	450,000	
Cash		450,000
Building (Capitalized Interest)	120,228	
Interest Expense ($239,500 − $120,228)	119,272	
Cash ($112,500 + $55,000 + $72,000)		239,500

Tutorial on Interest Capitalization

Capitalized interest cost should be written off as part of depreciation over the useful life of the assets involved—and not over the term of the debt. The total interest cost incurred during the period should be disclosed, with the portion charged to expense and the portion capitalized indicated.

At December 31, 2004, Shalla would disclose the amount of interest capitalized either as part of the nonoperating section of the income statement or in the notes accompanying the financial statements. Both forms of disclosure are shown in Illustrations 10-7 and 10-8.

ILLUSTRATION 10-7
Capitalized Interest Reported in the Income Statement

Income from operations		XXXX
Other expenses and losses:		
Interest expense	$239,500	
Less: Capitalized interest	120,228	119,272
Income before taxes on income		XXXX
Income taxes		XXX
Net income		XXXX

ILLUSTRATION 10-8
Capitalized Interest Disclosed in a Note

Note 1: Accounting Policies. *Capitalized Interest.* During 2004 total interest cost was $239,500, of which $120,228 was capitalized and $119,272 was charged to expense.

Special Issues Related to Interest Capitalization

Two issues related to interest capitalization merit special attention:

1. Expenditures for land.
2. Interest revenue.

Expenditures for Land. When land is purchased with the intent of developing it for a particular use, interest costs associated with those expenditures qualify for interest capitalization. If land is purchased as a site for a structure (such as a plant site), interest costs capitalized during the period of construction are part of the cost of the plant, not the land. In the Shalla illustration, where land was acquired for a structure, all interest costs capitalized (including those related to land expenditures) should be allocated to the cost of the building. Conversely, if land is being developed for lot sales, any capitalized interest cost should be part of the acquisition cost of the developed land.

Interest costs involved in purchasing land held **for speculation** should **not** be capitalized because the asset is ready for its intended use.

INTERNATIONAL INSIGHT

Under international accounting standards *(IAS No. 23)*, capitalization of interest is allowed, but it is not the preferred treatment. Thus, the financial statements of U.S. and IAS companies may not be comparable if capitalized interest costs are significant and the IAS company uses the preferred treatment. An analyst can use the information disclosed by the U.S. company to convert the U.S. GAAP numbers to be comparable to the IAS company.

Interest Revenue. Companies frequently borrow money to finance construction of assets and temporarily invest the excess borrowed funds in interest-bearing securities until the funds are needed to pay for construction. During the early stages of construction, interest revenue earned may exceed the interest cost incurred on the borrowed funds.

The question is whether it is appropriate to offset interest revenue against interest cost when determining the amount of interest to be capitalized as a part of the construction cost of assets. According to *FASB Statement No. 62* on capitalization of interest cost, **interest revenue should not be netted or offset against interest cost**, except in cases involving externally restricted tax-exempt borrowings. Temporary or short-term investment decisions are not related to the interest incurred as part of the acquisition cost of assets. Therefore, the interest incurred on qualifying assets should be capitalized whether or not excess funds are temporarily invested in short-term securities. Some are critical of this accounting because a company can defer the interest cost but report the interest revenue in the current period.

Observations

The interest capitalization requirement, while now universally adopted, is still debated. From a conceptual viewpoint, many believe that either **no** interest cost should be capitalized or **all** interest costs, actual or imputed, should be capitalized for the reasons mentioned earlier in this section.

WHAT'S IN YOUR INTEREST?

WHAT DO THE NUMBERS MEAN?

The requirement to capitalize interest can have a significant impact on financial statements. For example, when earnings of building manufacturer **Jim Walter's Corporation** dropped from $1.51 to $1.17 per share, the company was able to offset 11 cents per share of the decline by capitalizing the interest on coal mining projects and several plants under construction.

How can statement users determine the impact of interest capitalization on a company's bottom line? They can examine the notes to the financial statements. Companies with material interest capitalization are required to disclose the amounts of capitalized interest relative to total interest costs. For example, **Anadarko Petroleum Corporation** capitalized nearly 30 percent of its total interest costs in a recent year and provided the following footnote related to capitalized interest.

Financial Footnotes

Total interest costs incurred during the year were $82,415,000. Of this amount, the Company capitalized $24,716,000. Capitalized interest is included as part of the cost of oil and gas properties. The capitalization rates are based on the Company's weighted-average cost of borrowings used to finance the expenditures.

VALUATION

We have seen that **an asset should be recorded at the fair market value of what is given up or at the fair value of the asset received, whichever is more clearly evident.** Fair market value, however, is sometimes obscured by the process through which the asset is acquired. As an example, assume that land and buildings are bought together for one price. How are separate values for the land and buildings determined? A number of accounting problems of this nature are examined in the following sections.

Cash Discounts

When plant assets are purchased subject to cash discounts for prompt payment, how should the discount be reported? If the discount is taken, it should be considered a reduction in the purchase price of the asset. What is not clear, however, is whether a reduction in the asset cost should occur even if the discount is not taken.

OBJECTIVE 5
Understand accounting issues related to acquiring and valuing plant assets.

Two points of view exist on this matter. Under one approach, the discount—whether taken or not—is considered a reduction in the cost of the asset. The rationale for this approach is that the real cost of the asset is the cash or cash equivalent price of the asset. In addition, some argue that the terms of cash discounts are so attractive that failure to take them indicates management error or inefficiency. Proponents of the other approach argue that the discount should not always be considered a loss because the terms may be unfavorable or because it might not be prudent for the company to take the discount. At present, both methods are employed in practice. The former method is generally preferred.

Deferred Payment Contracts

Plant assets are purchased frequently on long-term credit contracts through the use of notes, mortgages, bonds, or equipment obligations. **To properly reflect cost, assets purchased on long-term credit contracts should be accounted for at the present value of the consideration exchanged between the contracting parties at the date of the transaction.** For example, an asset purchased today in exchange for a $10,000 zero-interest-bearing note payable 4 years from now should not be recorded at $10,000. The present value of the $10,000 note establishes the exchange price of the transaction (the purchase price of the asset). Assuming an appropriate interest rate of 12 percent at which to discount this single payment of $10,000 due 4 years from now, this asset should be recorded at $6,355.20 ($10,000 × .63552). [See Table 6-2 for the present value of a single sum, $PV = \$10,000\ (PVF_{4,12\%})$.]

When no interest rate is stated, or if the specified rate is unreasonable, an appropriate interest rate must be imputed. The objective is to approximate the interest rate that the buyer and seller would negotiate at arm's length in a similar borrowing transaction. Factors to be considered in imputing an interest rate are the borrower's credit rating, the amount and maturity date of the note, and prevailing interest rates. **If determinable, the cash exchange price of the asset acquired should be used as the basis for recording the asset and measuring the interest element.**

To illustrate, Sutter Company purchases a specially built robot spray painter for its production line. The company issues a $100,000, 5-year, zero-interest-bearing note to Wrigley Robotics, Inc. for the new equipment when the prevailing market rate of interest for obligations of this nature is 10 percent. Sutter is to pay off the note in five $20,000 installments made at the end of each year. The fair market value of this specially built robot is not readily determinable and must therefore be approximated by establishing the market value (present value) of the note. Computation of the present value of the note and the date of purchase and dates of payment entries are as follows.

Date of Purchase

Equipment	75,816*	
Discount on Notes Payable	24,184	
Notes Payable		100,000

*Present value of note = $20,000 ($PVF\text{-}OA_{5,10\%}$)
= $20,000 (3.79079); Table 6-4
= $75,816

End of First Year

Interest Expense	7,582	
Notes Payable	20,000	
Cash		20,000
Discount on Notes Payable		7,582

Interest expense in the first year under the effective-interest approach is $7,582 [($100,000 − $24,184) × 10%]. The entry at the end of the second year to record interest and principal payment is as follows.

End of Second Year

Interest Expense	6,340	
Notes Payable	20,000	
Cash		20,000
Discount on Notes Payable		6,340

Interest expense in the second year under the effective-interest approach is $6,340 [($100,000 − $24,184) − ($20,000 − $7,582)] × 10%.

If an interest rate were not imputed for such deferred payment contracts, the asset would be recorded at an amount greater than its fair value. In addition, interest expense reported in the income statement would be understated for all periods involved.

Lump-Sum Purchases

A special problem of pricing fixed assets arises when a group of plant assets is purchased at a single **lump-sum price**. Such a situation is not at all unusual. When it occurs, the practice is to allocate the total cost among the various assets on the basis of their relative fair market values. The assumption is that costs will vary in direct proportion to sales value. This is the same principle that is applied to allocate a lump-sum cost among different inventory items.

To determine fair market value, any of the following might be used: an appraisal for insurance purposes, the assessed valuation for property taxes, or simply an independent appraisal by an engineer or other appraiser.

To illustrate, Norduct Homes, Inc. decides to purchase several assets of a small heating concern, Comfort Heating, for $80,000. Comfort Heating is in the process of liquidation, and its assets sold are:

	Book Value	Fair Market Value
Inventory	$30,000	$ 25,000
Land	20,000	25,000
Building	35,000	50,000
	$85,000	$100,000

Assuming specific identification of costs is not practicable, the $80,000 purchase price would be allocated on the basis of the relative fair market values in the following manner.

ILLUSTRATION 10-9
Allocation of Purchase Price—Relative Fair Market Value Basis

Inventory	$\frac{\$25{,}000}{\$100{,}000} \times \$80{,}000 = \$20{,}000$
Land	$\frac{\$25{,}000}{\$100{,}000} \times \$80{,}000 = \$20{,}000$
Building	$\frac{\$50{,}000}{\$100{,}000} \times \$80{,}000 = \$40{,}000$

Issuance of Stock

When property is acquired by issuance of securities (such as common stock), the cost of the property is not properly measured by the par or stated value of such stock. If the stock is actively traded, **the market value of the stock issued is a fair indication of the cost of the property acquired because the stock is a good measure of the current cash equivalent price.**

For example, Upgrade Living Co. decides to purchase some adjacent land for expansion of its carpeting and cabinet operation. In lieu of paying cash for the land, the company issues to Deedland Company 5,000 shares of common stock (par value $10) that have a fair market value of $12 per share. Upgrade Living Co. would make the following entry.

Land (5,000 × $12)	60,000	
Common Stock		50,000
Additional Paid-In Capital		10,000

If the market value of the common stock exchanged is not determinable, the market value of the property should be established and used as the basis for recording the asset and issuance of the common stock.[6]

[6]When the fair market value of the stock is used as the basis of valuation, careful consideration must be given to the effect that the issuance of additional shares will have on the existing market price. Where the effect on market price appears significant, an independent appraisal of the asset received should be made. This valuation should be employed as the basis for valuation of the asset as well as for the stock issued. In the unusual case where the fair market value of the stock or the fair market value of the asset cannot be determined objectively, the board of directors of the corporation may set the value.

Exchanges of Nonmonetary Assets

The proper accounting for exchanges of nonmonetary assets (such as inventories and property, plant, and equipment) is controversial.[7] Some argue that the accounting for these types of exchanges should be based on the fair value of the asset given up or the fair value of the asset received, with a gain or loss recognized. Others believe that the accounting should be based on the recorded amount (book value) of the asset given up, with no gain or loss recognized. Still others favor an approach that would recognize losses in all cases, but defer gains in special situations.

Ordinarily accounting for the exchange of **nonmonetary assets** should be based on **the fair value of the asset given up or the fair value of the asset received, whichever is clearly more evident**.[8] Thus, any gains or losses on the exchange **should be recognized immediately**. The rationale for such immediate recognition is that the earnings process related to these assets is completed, and therefore a gain or loss should be recognized. This approach is always employed when the assets are **dissimilar** in nature, such as the exchange of computers for a truck or the exchange of equipment for inventory. If the fair value of either asset is not reasonably determinable, the book value of the asset given up is usually used as the basis for recording the nonmonetary exchange. The alternative exchange situations are summarized in Illustration 10-10.

ILLUSTRATION 10-10
Accounting for Exchanges

Type of Exchange	Accounting Guidance	Rationale
Dissimilar assets 	Recognize gains and losses immediately.	Earnings process is complete.
Similar assets — No cash received 	Defer gains; recognize losses immediately.	Earnings process is not complete.
Similar assets — Cash received 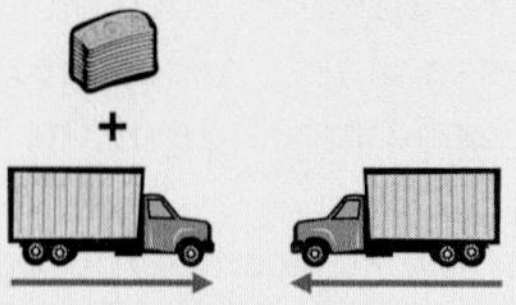	Recognize partial gain; recognize losses immediately.* *If cash is 25% or more of the fair value of the exchange, recognize entire gain because earnings process is complete.	Earnings process is partially complete.*

The general rule of immediate recognition is modified when exchanges of **similar** nonmonetary assets occur for gain situations. For example, when a company exchanges its inventory items with inventory of another company because of color, size, etc. to facilitate sale to an outside customer, the earnings process is not considered completed and a **gain should not be recognized**. Likewise, if a company trades **similar productive assets** such as land for land or equipment for equipment, the earnings process is not considered complete and **a gain should not be recognized**. However, if the exchange transaction involving **similar assets** would result in a loss, **the loss is recognized immediately**.

In certain situations, gains on exchange of similar nonmonetary assets may be recognized where **monetary consideration (boot)** is received. When monetary considera-

[7]Nonmonetary assets are items whose price in terms of the monetary unit may change over time. Monetary assets—cash and short- or long-term accounts and notes receivable—are fixed in terms of units of currency by contract or otherwise.

[8]"Accounting for Nonmonetary Transactions," *Opinions of the Accounting Principles Board No. 29* (New York: AICPA, 1973), par 18.

tion such as cash is received in addition to the nonmonetary asset, it is assumed that a portion of the earnings process is completed, and therefore a partial gain is recognized.[9]

To illustrate the accounting for these different types of transactions, we will look at the following three situations:

1. Accounting for dissimilar assets.
2. Accounting for similar assets—loss situation.
3. Accounting for similar assets—gain situation.

Dissimilar Assets

The cost of a nonmonetary asset acquired in exchange for a **dissimilar nonmonetary asset** is usually recorded at the **fair value of the asset given up**, and a gain or loss is recognized. The **fair value of the asset received** should be used only if it is more clearly evident than the fair value of the asset given up.

To illustrate, Interstate Transportation Company exchanged a number of used trucks plus cash for vacant land that might be used for a future plant site. The trucks have a combined book value of $42,000 (cost $64,000 less $22,000 accumulated depreciation). Interstate's purchasing agent, who has had previous dealings in the second-hand market, indicates that the trucks have a fair market value of $49,000. In addition to the trucks, Interstate must pay $17,000 cash for the land. The cost of the land to Interstate is $66,000 computed as follows.

ILLUSTRATION 10-11
Computation of Land Cost

Fair value of trucks exchanged	$49,000
Cash paid	17,000
Cost of land	$66,000

The journal entry to record the exchange transaction is:

Land	66,000	
Accumulated Depreciation—Trucks	22,000	
Trucks		64,000
Gain on Disposal of Trucks		7,000
Cash		17,000

The gain is the difference between the fair value of the trucks and their book value. It is verified as follows.

ILLUSTRATION 10-12
Computation of Gain on Disposal of Used Trucks

Fair value of trucks		$49,000
Cost of trucks	$64,000	
Less: Accumulated depreciation	22,000	
Book value of trucks		42,000
Gain on disposal of used trucks		$ 7,000

It follows that if the fair value of the trucks was $39,000 instead of $49,000, a loss on the exchange of $3,000 ($42,000 − $39,000) would be reported. In either case, as a result of the exchange of dissimilar assets, the earnings process on the used trucks has been completed and **a gain or loss should be recognized.**

---

[9]When the monetary consideration is significant, i.e., **25 percent or more** of the fair value of the exchange, the transaction is considered a **monetary exchange** by both parties. In such monetary exchanges the fair values are used to measure the gains or losses that are recognized in their entirety. *EITF Issue No. 86–29*, "Nonmonetary Transactions: Magnitude of Boot and the Exception to the Use of Fair Value," *Emerging Issues Task Force Abstracts* (October 1, 1987).

Similar Assets—Loss Situation

Similar nonmonetary assets are those that are of the same general type, or that perform the same function, or that are employed in the same line of business. When similar nonmonetary assets are exchanged and a loss results, the loss should be recognized immediately.

For example, Information Processing, Inc. trades its used machine for a new model. The machine given up has a book value of $8,000 (original cost $12,000 less $4,000 accumulated depreciation) and a fair value of $6,000. It is traded for a new model that has a list price of $16,000. In negotiations with the seller, a trade-in allowance of $9,000 is finally agreed on for the used machine. The cash payment that must be made for the new asset and the cost of the new machine are computed as follows.

ILLUSTRATION 10-13
Computation of Cost of New Machine

List price of new machine	$16,000
Less: Trade-in allowance for used machine	9,000
Cash payment due	7,000
Fair value of used machine	6,000
Cost of new machine	$13,000

The journal entry to record this transaction is:

Equipment	13,000	
Accumulated Depreciation—Equipment	4,000	
Loss on Disposal of Equipment	2,000	
Equipment		12,000
Cash		7,000

The loss on the disposal of the used machine can be verified as follows.

ILLUSTRATION 10-14
Computation of Loss on Disposal of Used Machine

Fair value of used machine	$6,000
Book value of used machine	8,000
Loss on disposal of used machine	$2,000

Why was the trade-in allowance or the book value of the old asset not used as a basis for the new equipment? The trade-in allowance is not used because it included a price concession (similar to a price discount) to the purchaser. For example, few individuals pay list price for a new car. Trade-in allowances on the used car are often inflated so that actual selling prices are below list prices. To record the car at list price would state it at an amount in excess of its cash equivalent price because the new car's list price is usually inflated. Similarly, use of book value in this situation would overstate the value of the new machine by $2,000. Because assets should not be valued at more than their cash equivalent price, the loss should be recognized immediately rather than added to the cost of the newly acquired asset.

Similar Assets—Gain Situation, No Cash Received

The accounting treatment for exchanges of **similar** nonmonetary assets when a gain develops is more complex. If the exchange does not complete the earnings process, then any **gain should be deferred**.

The real estate industry provides a good example of why the accounting profession decided not to recognize gains on exchanges of similar nonmonetary assets. In this industry, it is common practice for companies to "swap" real estate holdings. Assume that Landmark Company and Hillfarm, Inc. each had undeveloped land on which they intended to build shopping centers. Appraisals indicated that the land of both companies had increased significantly in value. The companies decided to exchange (swap) their undeveloped land, record a gain, and report their new parcels of land at current fair values. But should gains be recognized at this point? No—the earnings process is not completed because the companies remain in the same economic position after the swap as before. Therefore, the asset acquired should be recorded at book value with **no gain** recognized. In contrast, had book value exceeded fair value, a loss would be recognized immediately.

Davis Rent-A-Car has a rental fleet of automobiles consisting primarily of Ford Motor Company products. Davis's management is interested in increasing the variety of automobiles in its rental fleet by adding numerous General Motors models. Davis arranges with Nertz Rent-A-Car to exchange a group of Ford automobiles with a fair value of $160,000 and a book value of $135,000 (cost $150,000 less accumulated depreciation $15,000) for a number of GM models with a fair value of $170,000. Davis pays $10,000 in cash in addition to the Ford automobiles exchanged. The total gain to Davis Rent-A-Car is computed as shown in Illustration 10-15.

ILLUSTRATION 10-15
Computation of Gain (Unrecognized)

Fair value of Ford automobiles exchanged	$160,000
Book value of Ford automobiles exchanged	135,000
Total gain (unrecognized)	$ 25,000

But the earnings process is not considered completed in this transaction. The company still has a fleet of cars, although different models. Therefore, the total gain is deferred, and the basis of the General Motors automobiles is reduced via two different but acceptable computations as shown below.

ILLUSTRATION 10-16
Basis of New Automobiles—Fair Value vs. Book Value

Fair value of GM automobiles	$170,000		Book value of Ford automobiles	$135,000
Less: Gain deferred	(25,000)	OR	Cash paid	10,000
Basis of GM automobiles	$145,000		Basis of GM automobiles	$145,000

The entry by Davis to record this transaction is as follows.

Automobiles (GM)	145,000	
Accumulated Depreciation—Automobiles	15,000	
Automobiles (Ford)		150,000
Cash		10,000

The gain that reduced the basis of the new automobiles will be recognized when those automobiles are sold to an outside party. While these automobiles are held, depreciation charges will be lower and net income will be higher in subsequent periods because of the reduced basis.

Similar Assets—Gain Situation, Some Cash Received

The accounting issue of gain recognition becomes more difficult if monetary consideration such as cash is **received** in an exchange of similar nonmonetary assets. When cash is received, part of the nonmonetary asset is considered sold and part exchanged; therefore, only a portion of the gain is deferred. The general formula for gain recognition when some cash is received is as follows.

ILLUSTRATION 10-17
Formula for Gain Recognition, Some Cash Received

$$\frac{\text{Cash Received (Boot)}}{\text{Cash Received (Boot)} + \text{Fair Value of Other Assets Received}} \times \text{Total Gain} = \text{Recognized Gain}$$

If the book value of Nertz's GM automobiles exchanged in the foregoing example is $136,000 (cost $200,000 less accumulated depreciation $64,000), then the total gain on the exchange to Nertz would be computed as shown on the next page.

ILLUSTRATION 10-18
Computation of Total Gain

Fair value of GM automobiles exchanged	$170,000
Book value of GM automobiles exchanged	136,000
Total gain	$ 34,000

But because Nertz received $10,000 in cash, the recognized gain on this transaction is computed as follows.

ILLUSTRATION 10-19
Computation of Recognized Gain Based on Ratio of Cash Received

$$\frac{\$10{,}000}{\$10{,}000 + \$160{,}000} \times \$34{,}000 = \$2{,}000$$

The ratio of monetary assets ($10,000) to the total consideration received ($10,000 + $160,000) is the portion of the total gain ($34,000) to be recognized—that is, $2,000. Because only a gain of $2,000 is recognized on this transaction, the remaining $32,000 ($34,000 − $2,000) is deferred and reduces the basis (recorded cost) of the new automobiles. The computation of the basis is as follows.

ILLUSTRATION 10-20
Basis of New Automobiles—Fair Value vs. Book Value

Fair value of Ford automobiles	$160,000		Book value of GM automobiles	$136,000
Less: Gain deferred	(32,000)	OR	Portion of book value presumed sold	(8,000)*
Basis of Ford automobiles	$128,000		Basis of Ford automobiles	$128,000

$$^*\frac{\$10{,}000}{\$170{,}000} \times \$136{,}000 = \$8{,}000$$

The entry by Nertz to record this transaction is as follows.

Cash	10,000	
Automobiles (Ford)	128,000	
Accumulated Depreciation—Automobiles (GM)	64,000	
Automobiles (GM)		200,000
Gain on Disposal of GM Automobiles		2,000

The rationale for this treatment is as follows: Before the exchange, Nertz Rent-A-Car had an unrecognized gain of $34,000, as evidenced by the difference between the book value ($136,000) and the fair value ($170,000) of its GM automobiles. When the exchange occurred, a portion of the fair value ($10,000/$170,000 or 1/17) was converted to a more liquid asset. The ratio of this liquid asset ($10,000) to the total consideration received ($160,000 + $10,000) is the portion of the gain realized ($34,000). Thus, a gain of $2,000 (1/17 × $34,000) is recognized and recorded.

Presented below in summary form are the accounting requirements for recognizing gains and losses on exchanges of nonmonetary assets.[10]

ILLUSTRATION 10-21
Summary of Gain and Loss Recognition on Exchanges of Nonmonetary Assets

1. Compute the total gain or loss on the transaction. This amount is equal to the difference between the fair value of the asset given up and the book value of the asset given up.
2. If a loss is computed in 1, always recognize the entire loss.
3. If a gain is computed in 1,
   (a) and the earnings process is considered completed, the entire gain is recognized (dissimilar assets).
   (b) and the earnings process is not considered completed (similar assets),
      (1) and no cash is involved, no gain is recognized.
      (2) and some cash is given, no gain is recognized.
      (3) and some cash is received, the following portion of the gain is recognized:

$$\frac{\text{Cash Received (Boot)}}{\text{Cash Received (Boot)} + \text{Fair Value of Other Assets Received}} \times \text{Total Gain}^*$$

*If the amount of cash exchanged is 25% or more, recognize entire gain.

[10]Adapted from an article by Robert Capettini and Thomas E. King, "Exchanges of Nonmonetary Assets: Some Changes," *The Accounting Review* (January 1976).

An enterprise that engages in one or more nonmonetary exchanges during a period should disclose in financial statements for the period the nature of the transactions, the method of accounting for the assets transferred, and gains or losses recognized on transfers.[11]

About Those Swaps

What do the numbers mean?

In a press release, Roy Olofson, former vice president of finance for **Global Crossing**, accused company executives of improperly describing the company's revenue to the public. Olofson said Global Crossing had improperly recorded long-term sales immediately rather than over the term of the contract, that the company improperly booked swaps of capacity with other carriers as cash transactions, and that Global Crossing fired him when he blew the whistle.

The accounting for the swaps is of particular interest here. The accounting for swaps involves exchanges of similar network capacity. Companies engaged in such deals, they have said, because it was less costly and quicker than building segments that their own networks lacked, or because such pacts provided redundancies to make their own networks more reliable to customers. In one expert's view, an exchange of similar network capacity is the equivalent of trading a blue truck for a red truck—it shouldn't boost a company's revenue.

But Global Crossing and **Qwest**, among others, used the transactions to do just that, counting as revenue the money received from the company on the other end of the deal. (In general, in transactions involving leased capacity, the companies booked the revenue over the life of the contract.) Some of these companies then treated their own purchases as capital expenditures, which weren't run through the income statement. Instead, the spending led to the addition of assets on the balance sheet.

Both congressional and Securities and Exchange Commission investigators are seeking to determine whether some of these capacity exchanges may have been a device to pad revenue. Revenue growth was a key factor in the valuation of some of these companies, such as Global Crossing and Qwest, throughout the craze for tech stocks in the late 1990s and 2000.

Source: Adapted from Henny Sender, "Telecoms Draw Focus for Moves in Accounting," *Wall Street Journal* (March 26, 2002), p. C7.

Accounting for Contributions

Companies sometimes receive or make contributions (donations or gifts). Such contributions are referred to as **nonreciprocal transfers** because they are transfers of assets in one direction. A contribution is often some type of asset (such as cash, securities, land, buildings, or use of facilities), but it also could be the forgiveness of a debt.

When assets are acquired as a donation, a strict cost concept dictates that the valuation of the asset should be zero. A departure from the cost principle seems justified, however, because the only costs incurred (legal fees and other relatively minor expenditures) do not constitute a reasonable basis of accounting for the assets acquired. To record nothing is to ignore the economic realities of an increase in wealth and assets. Therefore, the **fair value of the asset** should be used to establish its value on the books.

Two general approaches have been used to record the credit for the asset received. Some believe the credit should be to Donated Capital (an additional paid-in capital account). The increase in assets as a result of a donation is viewed more as contributed capital than as earned revenue. Others argue that capital is contributed only by the owners of the business and that donations are benefits to the enterprise that should be reported as revenues from contributions. At issue is whether the revenue should be

[11]"Accounting for Nonmonetary Transactions," op. cit., par. 28.

reported immediately or over the period that the asset is employed. For example, to attract new industry a city may offer land, but the receiving enterprise may incur additional costs in the future (transportation, higher state income taxes, etc.) because the location is not the most desirable. As a consequence, some argue that the revenue should be deferred and recognized as the costs are incurred.

The FASB has taken the position that, **in general, contributions received should be recognized as revenues in the period received.**[12] Contributions would be measured at the fair value of the assets received.[13] To illustrate, Max Wayer Meat Packing, Inc. has recently accepted a donation of land with a fair value of $150,000 from the Memphis Industrial Development Corp. in return for a promise to build a packing plant in Memphis. Max Wayer's entry is:

Land	150,000	
Contribution Revenue		150,000

When a nonmonetary asset is contributed, the amount of the donation should be recorded as an expense at the fair value of the donated asset. If a difference exists between the fair value of the asset and its book value, a gain or loss should be recognized. To illustrate, Kline Industries donates land that cost $80,000 and has a fair market value of $110,000 to the city of Los Angeles for a city park. The entry to record this donation would be:

Contribution Expense	110,000	
Land		80,000
Gain on Disposal of Land		30,000

In some cases, companies will promise to give (pledge) some type of asset in the future. The question is whether this promise should be recorded immediately or at the time the assets are given. If the promise is **unconditional** (depends only on the passage of time or on demand by the recipient for performance), the contribution expense and related payable should be reported. If the promise is **conditional**, the expense is recognized in the period benefited by the contribution, which is generally when the asset is transferred.

Other Asset Valuation Methods

As indicated above, an exception to the historical cost principle arises in the acquisition of plant assets through donation, which is based on fair value. Another approach that is sometimes allowed and not considered a violation of historical cost is a concept often referred to as **prudent cost**. This concept states that if for some reason you were ignorant about a certain price and paid too much for the asset originally, it is theoretically preferable to charge a loss immediately.

As an example, assume that a company constructs an asset at a cost substantially in excess of its present economic usefulness. In this case, it would be appropriate to charge these excess costs as a loss to the current period, rather than capitalize them as part of the cost of the asset. This problem seldom develops because at the outset individuals either use good reasoning in paying a given price or fail to recognize any such errors.

On the other hand, a purchase that is obtained at a bargain, or a piece of equipment internally constructed at a cost savings, should not result in immediate recognition of a gain under any circumstances. Although immediate recognition of a gain is conceptually appealing, the implications of such a treatment would be to change completely the entire basis of accounting.

---

[12]"Accounting for Contributions Received and Contributions Made," *Statement of Financial Accounting Standards No. 116* (Norwalk, Conn.: FASB, 1993). Transfers of assets from governmental units to business enterprises are excluded from the scope of this standard. However, we believe that the basic requirements should hold also for these types of contributions, and therefore all assets should be recorded at fair value and all credits should be recorded as revenue.

[13]"Accounting for Nonmonetary Transactions," op. cit., par. 18. Also, *FASB No. 116* indicates that expenses on contributions made should be recorded at the fair value of the assets given up.

COSTS SUBSEQUENT TO ACQUISITION

OBJECTIVE 6
Describe the accounting treatment for costs subsequent to acquisition.

After plant assets are installed and ready for use, additional costs are incurred that range from ordinary repair to significant additions. The major problem is allocating these costs to the proper time periods. **In general, costs incurred to achieve greater future benefits should be capitalized, and expenditures that simply maintain a given level of services should be expensed.**

In order for costs to be capitalized, one of three conditions must be present:

1. The useful life of the asset must be increased.
2. The quantity of units produced from the asset must be increased.
3. The quality of the units produced must be enhanced.

Expenditures that do not increase an asset's future benefits should be expensed. Ordinary repairs are expenditures that maintain the existing condition of the asset or restore it to normal operating efficiency. Such repairs should be expensed immediately.

Most expenditures below an established arbitrary minimum amount are expensed rather than capitalized. Many enterprises have adopted the rule that expenditures below, say, $100 or $500, should always be expensed. Although conceptually this treatment may not be correct, expediency demands it. Otherwise, depreciation schedules would have to be set up for such items as wastepaper baskets and ash trays.

UNDERLYING CONCEPTS

Expensing long-lived ash trays and waste baskets is an application of the materiality constraint.

DISCONNECTED

WHAT DO THE NUMBERS MEAN?

It all started with a check of the books by an internal auditor for **WorldCom, Inc.** The telecom giant's newly installed chief executive had asked for a financial review, and the auditor's job was to spot-check records of capital expenditures. What she found was that the company was using an unorthodox technique to account for one of the long-distance company's biggest expenses: charges paid to local telephone networks to complete calls. Instead of recording them as operating expenses, a significant portion was moved to the category of capital expenditures. The maneuver was worth hundreds of millions of dollars to WorldCom's bottom line, effectively turning a loss for all of 2001 and the first quarter of 2002 into a profit. Presented below in graphical form is a comparison of WorldCom's accounting to that under GAAP.

WorldCom's accounting

1. Accounts for $3.1 billion in "line costs," including telecom access and transport charges, as capital expenditures.
2. Plans to amortize $3.1 billion over a period of time, possibly as much as 10 years.
3. Reports net income of $1.38 billion for 2001.

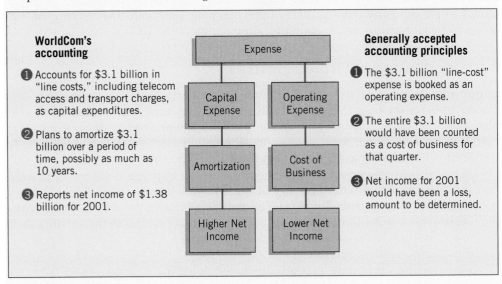

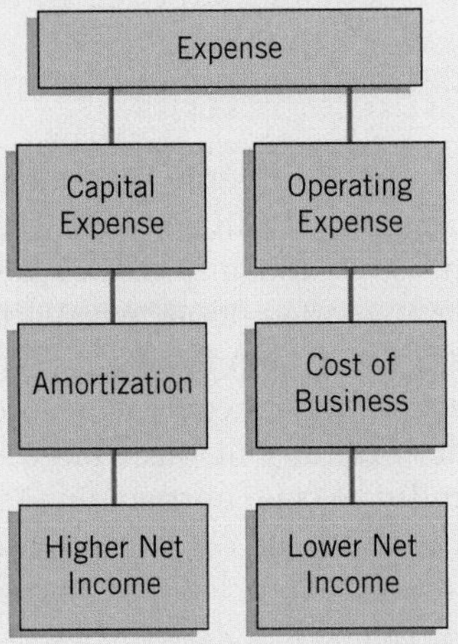

Generally accepted accounting principles

1. The $3.1 billion "line-cost" expense is booked as an operating expense.
2. The entire $3.1 billion would have been counted as a cost of business for that quarter.
3. Net income for 2001 would have been a loss, amount to be determined.

Soon after this discovery, WorldCom filed for bankruptcy.

Source: Adapted from Jared Sandberg, Deborah Solomon, and Rebecca Blumenstein, "Inside WorldCom's Unearthing of a Vast Accounting Scandal," *Wall Street Journal* (June 27, 2002), p. A1.

The distinction between a **capital (asset) expenditure** and a **revenue (expense) expenditure** is not always clear-cut. Determining the **property unit** with which costs should be associated is critical. If a fully equipped steamship is considered a property unit, then replacement of the engine might be considered an expense. On the other hand, if the ship's engine is considered a property unit, then its replacement would be capitalized.

Generally, four major types of expenditures are incurred relative to existing assets.

MAJOR TYPES OF EXPENDITURES

ADDITIONS. Increase or extension of existing assets.

IMPROVEMENTS AND REPLACEMENTS. Substitution of an improved asset for an existing one.

REARRANGEMENT AND REINSTALLATION. Movement of assets from one location to another.

REPAIRS. Expenditures that maintain assets in condition for operation.

Additions

Additions should present no major accounting problems. By definition, **any addition to plant assets is capitalized** because a new asset has been created. The addition of a wing to a hospital or the addition of an air conditioning system to an office, for example, increases the service potential of that facility. Such expenditures should be capitalized and matched against the revenues that will result in future periods.

The most difficult problem that develops in this area is accounting for any changes related to the existing structure as a result of the addition. Is the cost that is incurred to tear down an old wall to make room for the addition a cost of the addition or an expense or loss of the period? The answer is that it depends on the original intent. If the company had anticipated that an addition was going to be added later, then this cost of removal is a proper cost of the addition. But if the company had not anticipated this development, it should properly be reported as a loss in the current period on the basis that the company was inefficient in its planning. Normally, the carrying amount of the old wall remains in the accounts, although theoretically it should be removed.

Improvements and Replacements

Improvements (often referred to as **betterments**) and **replacements** are substitutions of one asset for another. What is the difference between an improvement and a replacement? An improvement is the substitution of a **better asset** for the one currently used (say, a concrete floor for a wooden floor). A replacement, on the other hand, is the substitution of a **similar asset** (a wooden floor for a wooden floor).

Many times improvements and replacements result from a general policy to modernize or rehabilitate an older building or piece of equipment. The problem is differentiating these types of expenditure from normal repairs. Does the expenditure increase the **future service potential** of the asset, or does it merely **maintain the existing level** of service? Frequently, the answer is not clear-cut, and good judgment must be used in order to classify these expenditures.

If it is determined that the expenditure increases the future service potential of the asset and, therefore, should be capitalized, the accounting is handled in one of three ways, depending on the circumstances:

1. ***Substitution Approach.*** Conceptually, the substitution approach is the correct procedure if the carrying amount of the old asset is available. If the carrying amount

of the old asset can be determined, it is a simple matter to remove the cost of the old asset and replace it with the cost of the new asset.

To illustrate, Instinct Enterprises decides to replace the pipes in its plumbing system. A plumber suggests that in place of the cast iron pipes and copper tubing, a newly developed plastic tubing be used. The old pipe and tubing have a book value of $15,000 (cost of $150,000 less accumulated depreciation of $135,000) and a scrap value of $1,000. The plastic tubing system has a cost of $125,000. Assuming that Instinct has to pay $124,000 for the new tubing after exchanging the old tubing, the entry is:

Plumbing System	125,000	
Accumulated Depreciation	135,000	
Loss on Disposal of Plant Assets	14,000	
Plumbing System		150,000
Cash ($125,000 − $1,000)		124,000

The problem is determining the book value of the old asset. Generally, the components of a given asset depreciate at different rates, but no separate accounting is made. As an example, the tires, motor, and body of a truck depreciate at different rates, but most companies use only one depreciation rate for the entire truck. Separate depreciation rates could be set for each component. If the carrying amount of the old asset cannot be determined, one of two other approaches is adopted.

❷ ***Capitalizing the New Cost.*** The justification for capitalizing the cost of the improvement or replacement is that even though the carrying amount of the old asset is not removed from the accounts, sufficient depreciation was taken on the item to reduce the carrying amount almost to zero. Although this assumption may not be true in every case, the differences are not often significant. Improvements are usually handled in this manner.

❸ ***Charging to Accumulated Depreciation.*** There are times when the quantity or quality of the asset itself has not been improved, but its useful life has been extended. Replacements, particularly, may extend the useful life of the asset, yet may not improve its quality or quantity. In these circumstances, the expenditure may be debited to Accumulated Depreciation rather than to an asset account. The theory behind this approach is that the replacement extends the useful life of the asset and thereby recaptures some or all of the past depreciation. The net carrying amount of the asset is the same whether the asset is debited or the accumulated depreciation is debited.

Rearrangement and Reinstallation

Rearrangement and reinstallation costs, which are expenditures intended to benefit future periods, are different from additions, replacements, and improvements. An example is the rearrangement and reinstallation of a group of machines to facilitate future production. If the original installation cost and the accumulated depreciation taken to date can be determined or estimated, the rearrangement and reinstallation cost is handled as a replacement. If not—and this is generally the case—the new costs (if material in amount) should be capitalized as an asset to be amortized over those future periods expected to benefit. If these costs are not material, if they cannot be separated from other operating expenses, or if their future benefit is questionable, they should be immediately expensed.

Repairs

Ordinary repairs are expenditures made to maintain plant assets in operating condition. They are charged to an expense account in the period in which they are incurred on the basis that **it is the primary period benefited**. Replacing minor parts, lubricating and adjusting equipment, repainting, and cleaning are examples of maintenance charges that occur regularly and are treated as ordinary operating expenses.

It is often difficult to distinguish a repair from an improvement or replacement. The major consideration is whether the expenditure benefits more than one year or one operating cycle, whichever is longer. If a **major repair** (such as an overhaul) occurs, several periods will benefit, and the cost should be handled as an addition, improvement, or replacement.[14]

If income statements are prepared for short periods of time, say, monthly or quarterly, the same principles apply. Ordinary repairs and other regular maintenance charges for an annual period may benefit several quarters, and allocation of the cost among the periods concerned might be required. A company will often find it advantageous to concentrate its repair program at a certain time of the year, perhaps during the period of least activity or when the plant is shut down for vacation. Short-term comparative statements might be misleading if such expenditures were shown as expenses of the quarter in which they were incurred. To give comparability to monthly or quarterly income statements, an account such as Allowance for Repairs might be used so that repair costs could be better assigned to periods benefited.

To illustrate, Cricket Tractor Company estimated that its total repair expense for the year would be $720,000. It decided to charge each quarter for a portion of the repair cost even though the total cost for the year would occur in only two quarters.

End of First Quarter (zero repair costs incurred)		
Repair Expense	180,000	
Allowance for Repairs (¼ × $720,000)		180,000
End of Second Quarter ($344,000 repair costs incurred)		
Allowance for Repairs	344,000	
Cash, Wages Payable, Inventory, etc.		344,000
Repair Expense	180,000	
Allowance for Repairs (¼ × $720,000)		180,000
End of Third Quarter (zero repair costs incurred)		
Repair Expense	180,000	
Allowance for Repairs (¼ × $720,000)		180,000
End of Fourth Quarter ($380,800 repair costs incurred)		
Allowance for Repairs	380,800	
Cash, Wages Payable, Inventory, etc.		380,800
Repair Expense	184,800	
Allowance for Repairs ($344,000 + $380,800 − $180,000 − $180,000 − $180,000)		184,800

No balance in the Allowance for Repairs account should be carried over to the following year. The fourth quarter would normally absorb the variation from estimates. If balance sheets are prepared during the year, the Allowance account should be added to or subtracted from the property, plant, and equipment section to determine a proper valuation.[15]

Summary of Costs Subsequent to Acquisition

Illustration 10-22 on the next page summarizes the accounting treatment for various costs incurred subsequent to the acquisition of capitalized assets.

---

[14]AcSEC in a recent exposure draft (see footnote 2) argues that costs involved for planned major expenditures should be expensed as incurred unless they represent an additional component or the replacement of an existing component. The "expense as incurred" approach is justified on the basis that these costs are relatively consistent from period to period, that they are not separately identifiable assets or property units in and of themselves, and that they serve only to restore other assets to their original operating condition.

[15]Some might argue that the Allowance for Repairs account should be reported as a liability, because it has a credit balance. However, reporting a liability is inappropriate because to whom do you owe the amount? Placement in the stockholders' equity section is also illogical because no addition to the stockholders' investment has taken place.

ILLUSTRATION 10-22
Summary of Costs Subsequent to Acquisition of Property, Plant, and Equipment

Type of Expenditure	Normal Accounting Treatment
Additions	Capitalize cost of addition to asset account.
Improvements and replacements	(a) **Carrying value known:** Remove cost of and accumulated depreciation on old asset, recognizing any gain or loss. Capitalize cost of improvement/replacement. (b) **Carrying value unknown:** 1. If the asset's useful life is extended, debit accumulated depreciation for cost of improvement/replacement. 2. If the quantity or quality of the asset's productivity is increased, capitalize cost of improvement/replacement to asset account.
Rearrangement and reinstallation	(a) If original installation cost is **known**, account for cost of rearrangement/reinstallation as a replacement (carrying value known). (b) If original installation cost is **unknown** and rearrangement/reinstallation cost is **material** in amount and benefits future periods, capitalize as an asset. (c) If original installation cost is **unknown** and rearrangement/reinstallation cost is **not material or future benefit is questionable**, expense the cost when incurred.
Repairs	(a) **Ordinary:** Expense cost of repairs when incurred. (b) **Major:** As appropriate, treat as an addition, improvement, or replacement.

DISPOSITIONS OF PLANT ASSETS

OBJECTIVE 7
Describe the accounting treatment for the disposal of property, plant, and equipment.

Plant assets may be retired voluntarily or disposed of by sale, exchange, involuntary conversion, or abandonment. Regardless of the time of disposal, depreciation must be taken up to the date of disposition, and then all accounts related to the retired asset should be removed. Ideally, the book value of the specific plant asset would be equal to its disposal value, but this is generally not the case. As a result, a gain or loss develops. The reason: Depreciation is an estimate of cost allocation and not a process of valuation. **The gain or loss is really a correction of net income** for the years during which the fixed asset was used. If it had been possible at the time of acquisition to forecast the exact date of disposal and the amount to be realized at disposition, then a more accurate estimate of depreciation could have been recorded and no gain or loss would be incurred.

Gains or losses on the retirement of plant assets should be shown in the income statement along with other items that arise from customary business activities. If, however, the "operations of a component of a business" are sold, abandoned, spun off, or otherwise disposed of, then the results of "continuing operations" should be reported separately from "discontinued operations." Any gain or loss from disposal of a component of a business should be reported with the related results of discontinued operations, and not as an extraordinary item.

Sale of Plant Assets

Depreciation must be recorded for the period of time between the date of the last depreciation entry and the date of sale. To illustrate, assume that depreciation on a machine costing $18,000 has been recorded for 9 years at the rate of $1,200 per year. If the machine is sold in the middle of the tenth year for $7,000, the entry to record depreciation to the date of sale is:

Depreciation Expense	600	
Accumulated Depreciation—Machinery		600

This separate entry ordinarily is not made because most companies enter all depreciation, including this amount, in one entry at the end of the year. In either case the entry for the sale of the asset is:

Cash	7,000	
Accumulated Depreciation—Machinery [($1,200 × 9)+ $600]	11,400	
Machinery		18,000
Gain on Disposal of Machinery		400

The book value of the machinery at the time of the sale is $6,600 ($18,000 − $11,400). Because it is sold for $7,000, the amount of the gain on the sale is $400.

Involuntary Conversion

Sometimes, an asset's service is terminated through some type of **involuntary conversion** such as fire, flood, theft, or condemnation. The gains or losses are treated no differently from those in any other type of disposition except that **they are often reported in the extraordinary items section of the income statement.**

To illustrate, Camel Transport Corp. was forced to sell a plant located on company property that stood directly in the path of an interstate highway. For a number of years the state had sought to purchase the land on which the plant stood, but the company resisted. The state ultimately exercised its right of eminent domain and was upheld by the courts. In settlement, Camel received $500,000, which was substantially in excess of the $200,000 book value of the plant and land (cost of $400,000 less accumulated depreciation of $200,000). The following entry was made.

Cash	500,000	
Accumulated Depreciation—Plant Assets	200,000	
Plant Assets		400,000
Gain on Disposal of Plant Assets		300,000

However, some object to the recognition of a gain or loss in certain involuntary conversions. For example, the federal government often condemns forests for national parks. As a result, the paper companies that owned these forests are required to report a gain or loss on the condemnation. However, companies such as **Georgia-Pacific** contend that because they must replace this condemned forest land immediately, they are in the same economic position as they were before and so no gain or loss should be reported. The issue is whether the condemnation and subsequent purchase should be viewed as one or two transactions. *FASB Interpretation No. 30* rules against the companies by requiring "that gain or loss be recognized when a nonmonetary asset is involuntarily converted to monetary assets even though an enterprise reinvests or is obligated to reinvest the monetary assets in replacement nonmonetary assets."[16]

The gain or loss that develops on these types of unusual, nonrecurring transactions should be shown as an extraordinary item. Similar treatment is given to other types of involuntary conversions such as those resulting from a major casualty (such as an earthquake) or an expropriation, assuming that it meets other conditions for extraordinary item treatment. The difference between the amount recovered (condemnation award or insurance recovery), if any, and the asset's book value is reported as a gain or loss.

Miscellaneous Problems

If an asset is scrapped or abandoned without any cash recovery, a loss should be recognized equal to the asset's book value. If scrap value exists, the gain or loss that occurs is the difference between the asset's scrap value and its book value. If an asset still can be used even though it is fully depreciated, it may be kept on the books at historical cost less depreciation.

Disclosure of the amount of fully depreciated assets in service should be made in notes to the financial statements. For example, **Petroleum Equipment Tools Inc.** in its Annual Report disclosed, "The amount of fully depreciated assets included in property, plant, and equipment at December 31 amounted to approximately $98,900,000."

[16]"Accounting for Involuntary Conversions of Nonmonetary Assets to Monetary Assets," *FASB Interpretation No. 30* (Stamford, Conn.: FASB, 1979), summary paragraph.

SUMMARY OF LEARNING OBJECTIVES

1 Describe the major characteristics of property, plant, and equipment. The major characteristics of property, plant, and equipment are: (1) They are acquired for use in operations and not for resale; (2) they are long-term in nature and usually subject to depreciation; and (3) they possess physical substance.

2 Identify the costs included in the initial valuation of land, buildings, and equipment. *Cost of land:* Includes all expenditures made to acquire land and to ready it for use. Land costs typically include (1) the purchase price; (2) closing costs, such as title to the land, attorney's fees, and recording fees; (3) costs incurred in getting the land in condition for its intended use, such as grading, filling, draining, and clearing; (4) assumption of any liens, mortgages, or encumbrances on the property; and (5) any additional land improvements that have an indefinite life.

Cost of buildings: Includes all expenditures related directly to their acquisition or construction. These costs include (1) materials, labor, and overhead costs incurred during construction and (2) professional fees and building permits.

Cost of equipment: Includes the purchase price, freight and handling charges incurred, insurance on the equipment while in transit, cost of special foundations if required, assembling and installation costs, and costs of conducting trial runs.

3 Describe the accounting problems associated with self-constructed assets. The assignment of indirect costs of manufacturing creates special problems because these costs cannot be traced directly to work and material orders related to the fixed assets constructed. These costs might be handled in one of two ways: (1) Assign no fixed overhead to the cost of the constructed asset or (2) assign a portion of all overhead to the construction process. The second method is used extensively in practice.

4 Describe the accounting problems associated with interest capitalization. Only actual interest (with modifications) should be capitalized. The rationale for this approach is that during construction the asset is not generating revenue and therefore interest cost should be deferred (capitalized). Once construction is completed, the asset is ready for its intended use and revenues can be earned. Any interest cost incurred in purchasing an asset that is ready for its intended use should be expensed.

5 Understand accounting issues related to acquiring and valuing plant assets. The following issues relate to acquiring and valuing plant assets: (1) *Cash discounts:* Whether taken or not, they are generally considered a reduction in the cost of the asset. The real cost of the asset is the cash or cash equivalent price of the asset. (2) *Assets purchased on long-term credit contracts:* Such assets are accounted for at the present value of the consideration exchanged between the contracting parties. (3) *Lump-sum purchase:* For such purchases, allocate the total cost among the various assets on the basis of their relative fair market values. (4) *Issuance of stock:* If the stock is actively traded, the market value of the stock issued is a fair indication of the cost of the property acquired. If the market value of the common stock exchanged cannot be determined, the value of the property should be established and used as the basis for recording the asset and issuance of the common stock. (5) *Exchanges of property, plant, and equipment.* See Illustrations 10-10 and 10-21 for summaries of how to account for exchanges. (6) *Contributions:* These should be recorded at the fair value of the asset received, and a related credit should be made to revenue for the same amount.

6 Describe the accounting treatment for costs subsequent to acquisition. See Illustration 10-22 for a summary of how to account for costs subsequent to acquisition.

7 Describe the accounting treatment for the disposal of property, plant, and equipment. Regardless of the time of disposal, depreciation must be taken up to the date of disposition, and then all accounts related to the retired asset should be removed. Gains

KEY TERMS

additions, *490*
avoidable interest, *475*
betterments, *490*
capital expenditure, *490*
capitalization period, *474*
dissimilar nonmonetary asset, *483*
fixed assets, *470*
historical cost, *471*
improvements (betterments), *490*
involuntary conversion, *494*
lump-sum price, *480*
major repairs, *492*
nonmonetary assets, *482*
nonreciprocal transfers, *487*
ordinary repairs, *491*
plant assets, *470*
property, plant, and equipment, *470*
prudent cost, *488*
rearrangement and reinstallation costs, *491*
replacements, *490*
revenue expenditure, *490*
self-constructed asset, *472*
similar nonmonetary assets, *484*
weighted-average accumulated expenditures, *475*

or losses on the retirement of plant assets should be shown in the income statement along with other items that arise from customary business activities. Gains or losses on involuntary conversions should be reported as extraordinary items. If an asset is scrapped or abandoned without any cash recovery, a loss should be recognized equal to the asset's book value. If scrap value exists, the gain or loss that occurs is the difference between the asset's scrap value and its book value.

QUESTIONS

1. What are the major characteristics of plant assets?

2. Esplanade Inc. owns land that it purchased on January 1, 1997, for $420,000. At December 31, 2004, its current value is $770,000 as determined by appraisal. At what amount should Esplanade report this asset on its December 31, 2004, balance sheet? Explain.

3. Name the items, in addition to the amount paid to the former owner or contractor, that may properly be included as part of the acquisition cost of the following plant assets.

(a) Land.

(b) Machinery and equipment.

(c) Buildings.

4. Indicate where the following items would be shown on a balance sheet.

(a) A lien that was attached to the land when purchased.

(b) Landscaping costs.

(c) Attorney's fees and recording fees related to purchasing land.

(d) Variable overhead related to construction of machinery.

(e) A parking lot servicing employees in the building.

(f) Cost of temporary building for workers during construction of building.

(g) Interest expense on bonds payable incurred during construction of a building.

(h) Assessments for sidewalks that are maintained by the city.

(i) The cost of demolishing an old building that was on the land when purchased.

5. Two positions have normally been taken with respect to the recording of fixed manufacturing overhead as an element of the cost of plant assets constructed by a company for its own use:

(a) It should be excluded completely.

(b) It should be included at the same rate as is charged to normal operations.

What are the circumstances or rationale that support or deny the application of these methods?

6. The Buildings account of Diego Rivera Inc. includes the following items that were used in determining the basis for depreciating the cost of a building.

(a) Organization and promotion expenses.

(b) Architect's fees.

(c) Interest and taxes during construction.

(d) Commission paid on the sale of capital stock.

(e) Bond discount.

Do you agree with these charges? If not, how would you deal with each of the items above in the corporation's books and in its annual financial statements?

7. Jones Company has purchased two tracts of land. One tract will be the site of its new manufacturing plant, while the other is being purchased with the hope that it will be sold in the next year at a profit. How should these two tracts of land be reported in the balance sheet?

8. One financial accounting issue encountered when a company constructs its own plant is whether the interest cost on funds borrowed to finance construction should be capitalized and then amortized over the life of the assets constructed. What is a common accounting justification for capitalizing such interest?

9. Provide examples of assets that do not qualify for interest capitalization.

10. What interest rates should be used in determining the amount of interest to be capitalized? How should the amount of interest to be capitalized be determined?

11. How should the amount of interest capitalized be disclosed in the notes to the financial statements? How should interest revenue from temporarily invested excess funds borrowed to finance the construction of assets be accounted for?

12. Discuss the basic accounting problem that arises in handling each of the following situations.

(a) Assets purchased by issuance of capital stock.

(b) Acquisition of plant assets by gift or donation.

(c) Purchase of a plant asset subject to a cash discount.

(d) Assets purchased on a long-term credit basis.

(e) A group of assets acquired for a lump sum.

(f) An asset traded in or exchanged for another asset.

13. Yukio Mishima Industries acquired equipment this year to be used in its operations. The equipment was delivered by the suppliers, installed by Mishima, and placed into operation. Some of it was purchased for cash with discounts available for prompt payment. Some of it was purchased under long-term payment plans for which the interest charges approximated prevailing rates. What costs should Mishima capitalize for the new equipment purchased this year? Explain.

14. Adam Mickiewicz Co. purchased for $2,200,000 property that included both land and a building to be used in operations. The seller's book value was $300,000 for the land and $900,000 for the building. By appraisal, the fair market value was estimated to be $500,000 for the land and $2,000,000 for the building. At what amount should Mickiewicz report the land and the building at the end of the year?

15. Richardson Co. acquires machinery by paying $10,000 cash and signing a $5,000, 2-year, zero-interest-bearing note payable. The note has a present value of $4,058, and Richardson purchased a similar machine last month for $13,500. At what cost should the new equipment be recorded?

16. Ron Dayne is evaluating two recent transactions involving exchanges of equipment. In one case, similar assets were exchanged. In the second situation, dissimilar assets were exchanged. Explain to Ron the differences in accounting for these two situations.

17. Saadi Company purchased a heavy-duty truck on July 1, 2001, for $30,000. It was estimated that it would have a useful life of 10 years and then would have a trade-in value of $6,000. It was traded on August 1, 2005, for a similar truck costing $39,000; $13,000 was allowed as trade-in value (also fair value) on the old truck and $26,000 was paid in cash. What is the entry to record the trade-in? The company uses the straight-line method.

18. Once equipment has been installed and placed in operation, subsequent expenditures relating to this equipment are frequently thought of as repairs or general maintenance and, hence, chargeable to operations in the period in which the expenditure is made. Actually, determination of whether such an expenditure should be charged to operations or capitalized involves a much more careful analysis of the character of the expenditure. What are the factors that should be considered in making such a decision? Discuss fully.

19. What accounting treatment is normally given to the following items in accounting for plant assets?

(a) Additions.

(b) Major repairs.

(c) Improvements and replacements.

20. New machinery, which replaced a number of employees, was installed and put in operation in the last month of the fiscal year. The employees had been dismissed after payment of an extra month's wages, and this amount was added to the cost of the machinery. Discuss the propriety of the charge. If it was improper, describe the proper treatment.

21. To what extent do you consider the following items to be proper costs of the fixed asset? Give reasons for your opinions.

(a) Overhead of a business that builds its own equipment.

(b) Cost of constructing new models of machinery.

(c) Cash discounts on purchases of equipment.

(d) Interest paid during construction of a building.

(e) Cost of a safety device installed on a machine.

(f) Freight on equipment returned before installation, for replacement by other equipment of greater capacity.

(g) Cost of moving machinery to a new location.

(h) Cost of plywood partitions erected as part of the remodeling of the office.

(i) Replastering of a section of the building.

(j) Cost of a new motor for one of the trucks.

22. Recently, Michelangelo Manufacturing Co. presented the account "Allowance for Repairs" in the long-term liabilities section. Evaluate this procedure.

23. Dimitri Enterprises has a number of fully depreciated assets that are still being used in the main operations of the business. Because the assets are fully depreciated, the president of the company decides not to show them on the balance sheet or disclose this information in the notes. Evaluate this procedure.

24. What are the general rules for how gains or losses on retirement of plant assets should be reported in income?

BRIEF EXERCISES

BE10-1 Bonanza Brothers Inc. purchased land at a price of $27,000. Closing costs were $1,400. An old building was removed at a cost of $12,200. What amount should be recorded as the cost of the land?

BE10-2 Brett Hull Company is constructing a building. Construction began on February 1 and was completed on December 31. Expenditures were $1,500,000 on March 1, $1,200,000 on June 1, and $3,000,000 on December 31. Compute Hull's weighted-average accumulated expenditures for interest capitalization purposes.

BE10-3 Brett Hull Company (see BE10-2) borrowed $1,000,000 on March 1 on a 5-year, 12% note to help finance construction of the building. In addition, the company had outstanding all year a 13%, 5-year, $2,000,000 note payable and a 15%, 4-year, $3,500,000 note payable. Compute the weighted-average interest rate used for interest capitalization purposes.

BE10-4 Use the information for Brett Hull Company from BE10-2 and BE10-3. Compute avoidable interest for Brett Hull Company.

BE10-5 Chavez Corporation purchased a truck by issuing an $80,000, 4-year, non-interest-bearing note to Equinox Inc. The market rate of interest for obligations of this nature is 12%. Prepare the journal entry to record the purchase of this truck.

BE10-6 Cool Spot Inc. purchased land, building, and equipment from Pinball Wizard Corporation for a cash payment of $306,000. The estimated fair values of the assets are land $60,000, building $220,000, and equipment $80,000. At what amounts should each of the three assets be recorded?

BE10-7 Dark Wizard Company obtained land by issuing 2,000 shares of its $10 par value common stock. The land was recently appraised at $85,000. The common stock is actively traded at $41 per share. Prepare the journal entry to record the acquisition of the land.

BE10-8 Strider Corporation traded a used truck (cost $20,000, accumulated depreciation $18,000) for a small computer worth $3,700. Strider also paid $1,000 in the transaction. Prepare the journal entry to record the exchange.

BE10-9 Sloan Company traded a used welding machine (cost $9,000, accumulated depreciation $3,000) for office equipment with an estimated fair value of $5,000. Sloan also paid $2,000 cash in the transaction. Prepare the journal entry to record the exchange.

BE10-10 Bubey Company traded a used truck for a new truck. The used truck cost $30,000 and has accumulated depreciation of $27,000. The new truck is worth $35,000. Bubey also made a cash payment of $33,000. Prepare Bubey's entry to record the exchange.

BE10-11 Buck Rogers Corporation traded a used truck for a new truck. The used truck cost $20,000 and has accumulated depreciation of $17,000. The new truck is worth $35,000. Rogers also made a cash payment of $33,000. Prepare Rogers' entry to record the exchange.

BE10-12 Indicate which of the following costs should be expensed when incurred.

- **(a)** $13,000 paid to rearrange and reinstall machinery.
- **(b)** $200 paid for tune-up and oil change on delivery truck.
- **(c)** $200,000 paid for addition to building.
- **(d)** $7,000 paid to replace a wooden floor with a concrete floor.
- **(e)** $2,000 paid for a major overhaul on a truck, which extends useful life.
- **(f)** $700,000 paid for relocation of company headquarters.

BE10-13 Sim City Corporation owns machinery that cost $20,000 when purchased on January 1, 2001. Depreciation has been recorded at a rate of $3,000 per year, resulting in a balance in accumulated depreciation of $9,000 at December 31, 2003. The machinery is sold on September 1, 2004, for $10,500. Prepare journal entries to (a) update depreciation for 2004 and (b) record the sale.

BE10-14 Use the information presented for Sim City Corporation in BE10-13, but assume the machinery is sold for $5,200 instead of $10,500. Prepare journal entries to (a) update depreciation for 2004 and (b) record the sale.

EXERCISES

E10-1 (Acquisition Costs of Realty) The following expenditures and receipts are related to land, land improvements, and buildings acquired for use in a business enterprise. The receipts are enclosed in parentheses.

(a)	Money borrowed to pay building contractor (signed a note)	$(275,000)
(b)	Payment for construction from note proceeds	275,000
(c)	Cost of land fill and clearing	8,000
(d)	Delinquent real estate taxes on property assumed by purchaser	7,000
(e)	Premium on 6-month insurance policy during construction	6,000
(f)	Refund of 1-month insurance premium because construction completed early	(1,000)
(g)	Architect's fee on building	22,000
(h)	Cost of real estate purchased as a plant site (land $200,000 and building $50,000)	250,000
(i)	Commission fee paid to real estate agency	9,000
(j)	Installation of fences around property	4,000
(k)	Cost of razing and removing building	11,000

(l)	Proceeds from salvage of demolished building	(5,000)
(m)	Interest paid during construction on money borrowed for construction	13,000
(n)	Cost of parking lots and driveways	19,000
(o)	Cost of trees and shrubbery planted (permanent in nature)	14,000
(p)	Excavation costs for new building	3,000

Instructions
Identify each item by letter and list the items in columnar form, using the headings shown below. All receipt amounts should be reported in parentheses. For any amounts entered in the Other Accounts column also indicate the account title.

Item	Land	Land Improvements	Building	Other Accounts

E10-2 (Acquisition Costs of Realty) Martin Buber Co. purchased land as a factory site for $400,000. The process of tearing down two old buildings on the site and constructing the factory required 6 months.

The company paid $42,000 to raze the old buildings and sold salvaged lumber and brick for $6,300. Legal fees of $1,850 were paid for title investigation and drawing the purchase contract. Martin Buber paid $2,200 to an engineering firm for a land survey, and $68,000 for drawing the factory plans. The land survey had to be made before definitive plans could be drawn. Title insurance on the property cost $1,500, and a liability insurance premium paid during construction was $900. The contractor's charge for construction was $2,740,000. The company paid the contractor in two installments: $1,200,000 at the end of 3 months and $1,540,000 upon completion. Interest costs of $170,000 were incurred to finance the construction.

Instructions
Determine the cost of the land and the cost of the building as they should be recorded on the books of Martin Buber Co. Assume that the land survey was for the building.

E10-3 (Acquisition Costs of Trucks) Alexei Urmanov Corporation operates a retail computer store. To improve delivery services to customers, the company purchases four new trucks on April 1, 2004. The terms of acquisition for each truck are described below.

1. Truck #1 has a list price of $15,000 and is acquired for a cash payment of $13,900.
2. Truck #2 has a list price of $16,000 and is acquired for a down payment of $2,000 cash and a non-interest-bearing note with a face amount of $14,000. The note is due April 1, 2005. Urmanov would normally have to pay interest at a rate of 10% for such a borrowing, and the dealership has an incremental borrowing rate of 8%.
3. Truck #3 has a list price of $16,000. It is acquired in exchange for a computer system that Urmanov carries in inventory. The computer system cost $12,000 and is normally sold by Urmanov for $15,200. Urmanov uses a perpetual inventory system.
4. Truck #4 has a list price of $14,000. It is acquired in exchange for 1,000 shares of common stock in Urmanov Corporation. The stock has a par value per share of $10 and a market value of $13 per share.

Instructions
Prepare the appropriate journal entries for the foregoing transactions for Urmanov Corporation.

E10-4 (Purchase and Self-Constructed Cost of Assets) Worf Co. both purchases and constructs various equipment it uses in its operations. The following items for two different types of equipment were recorded in random order during the calendar year 2005.

Purchase	
Cash paid for equipment, including sales tax of $5,000	$105,000
Freight and insurance cost while in transit	2,000
Cost of moving equipment into place at factory	3,100
Wage cost for technicians to test equipment	4,000
Insurance premium paid during first year of operation on this equipment	1,500
Special plumbing fixtures required for new equipment	8,000
Repair cost incurred in first year of operations related to this equipment	1,300
Construction	
Material and purchased parts (gross cost $200,000; failed to take 2% cash discount)	$200,000
Imputed interest on funds used during construction (stock financing)	14,000
Labor costs	190,000
Allocated overhead costs (fixed—$20,000; variable—$30,000)	50,000
Profit on self-construction	30,000
Cost of installing equipment	4,400

Instructions

Compute the total cost for each of these two pieces of equipment. If an item is not capitalized as a cost of the equipment, indicate how it should be reported.

E10-5 (Treatment of Various Costs) Ben Sisko Supply Company, a newly formed corporation, incurred the following expenditures related to Land, to Buildings, and to Machinery and Equipment.

Abstract company's fee for title search		$ 520
Architect's fees		2,800
Cash paid for land and dilapidated building thereon		87,000
Removal of old building	$20,000	
Less: Salvage	5,500	14,500
Surveying before construction		370
Interest on short-term loans during construction		7,400
Excavation before construction for basement		19,000
Machinery purchased (subject to 2% cash discount, which was not taken)		55,000
Freight on machinery purchased		1,340
Storage charges on machinery, necessitated by noncompletion of building when machinery was delivered		2,180
New building constructed (building construction took 6 months from date of purchase of land and old building)		485,000
Assessment by city for drainage project		1,600
Hauling charges for delivery of machinery from storage to new building		620
Installation of machinery		2,000
Trees, shrubs, and other landscaping after completion of building (permanent in nature)		5,400

Instructions

Determine the amounts that should be debited to Land, to Buildings, and to Machinery and Equipment. Assume the benefits of capitalizing interest during construction exceed the cost of implementation. Indicate how any costs not debited to these accounts should be recorded.

E10-6 (Correction of Improper Cost Entries) Plant acquisitions for selected companies are as follows.

1. Belanna Industries Inc. acquired land, buildings, and equipment from a bankrupt company, Torres Co., for a lump-sum price of $700,000. At the time of purchase, Torres's assets had the following book and appraisal values.

	Book Values	Appraisal Values
Land	$200,000	$150,000
Buildings	250,000	350,000
Equipment	300,000	300,000

To be conservative, the company decided to take the lower of the two values for each asset acquired. The following entry was made.

Land	150,000	
Buildings	250,000	
Equipment	300,000	
Cash		700,000

2. Harry Enterprises purchased store equipment by making a $2,000 cash down payment and signing a 1-year, $23,000, 10% note payable. The purchase was recorded as follows.

Store Equipment	27,300	
Cash		2,000
Note Payable		23,000
Interest Payable		2,300

3. Kim Company purchased office equipment for $20,000, terms 2/10, n/30. Because the company intended to take the discount, it made no entry until it paid for the acquisition. The entry was:

Office Equipment	20,000	
Cash		19,600
Purchase Discounts		400

4. Kaisson Inc. recently received at zero cost land from the Village of Cardassia as an inducement to locate its business in the Village. The appraised value of the land is $27,000. The company made no entry to record the land because it had no cost basis.
5. Zimmerman Company built a warehouse for $600,000. It could have purchased the building for $740,000. The controller made the following entry.

Warehouse	740,000	
Cash		600,000
Profit on Construction		140,000

Instructions

Prepare the entry that should have been made at the date of each acquisition.

E10-7 (Capitalization of Interest) Harrisburg Furniture Company started construction of a combination office and warehouse building for its own use at an estimated cost of $5,000,000 on January 1, 2004. Harrisburg expected to complete the building by December 31, 2004. Harrisburg has the following debt obligations outstanding during the construction period.

Construction loan—12% interest, payable semiannually, issued December 31, 2003	$2,000,000
Short-term loan—10% interest, payable monthly, and principal payable at maturity on May 30, 2005	1,400,000
Long-term loan—11% interest, payable on January 1 of each year. Principal payable on January 1, 2008	1,000,000

Instructions

(Carry all computations to two decimal places.)

(a) Assume that Harrisburg completed the office and warehouse building on December 31, 2004, as planned at a total cost of $5,200,000, and the weighted average of accumulated expenditures was $3,600,000. Compute the avoidable interest on this project.

(b) Compute the depreciation expense for the year ended December 31, 2005. Harrisburg elected to depreciate the building on a straight-line basis and determined that the asset has a useful life of 30 years and a salvage value of $300,000.

E10-8 (Capitalization of Interest) On December 31, 2003, Alma-Ata Inc. borrowed $3,000,000 at 12% payable annually to finance the construction of a new building. In 2004, the company made the following expenditures related to this building: March 1, $360,000; June 1, $600,000; July 1, $1,500,000; December 1, $1,500,000. Additional information is provided as follows.

1. Other debt outstanding

10-year, 13% bond, December 31, 1997, interest payable annually	$4,000,000
6-year, 10% note, dated December 31, 2001, interest payable annually	$1,600,000

2. March 1, 2004, expenditure included land costs of $150,000

3. Interest revenue earned in 2004 — $49,000

Instructions

(a) Determine the amount of interest to be capitalized in 2004 in relation to the construction of the building.

(b) Prepare the journal entry to record the capitalization of interest and the recognition of interest expense, if any, at December 31, 2004.

E10-9 (Capitalization of Interest) On July 31, 2004, Amsterdam Company engaged Minsk Tooling Company to construct a special-purpose piece of factory machinery. Construction was begun immediately and was completed on November 1, 2004. To help finance construction, on July 31 Amsterdam issued a $300,000, 3-year, 12% note payable at Netherlands National Bank, on which interest is payable each July 31. $200,000 of the proceeds of the note was paid to Minsk on July 31. The remainder of the proceeds was temporarily invested in short-term marketable securities at 10% until November 1. On November 1, Amsterdam made a final $100,000 payment to Minsk. Other than the note to Netherlands, Amsterdam's only outstanding liability at December 31, 2004, is a $30,000, 8%, 6-year note payable, dated January 1, 2001, on which interest is payable each December 31.

Instructions

(a) Calculate the interest revenue, weighted-average accumulated expenditures, avoidable interest, and total interest cost to be capitalized during 2004. Round all computations to the nearest dollar.

(b) Prepare the journal entries needed on the books of Amsterdam Company at each of the following dates.

(1) July 31, 2004.

(2) November 1, 2004.

(3) December 31, 2004.

E10-10 (Capitalization of Interest) The following three situations involve the capitalization of interest.

Situation I

On January 1, 2004, Oksana Baiul, Inc. signed a fixed-price contract to have Builder Associates construct a major plant facility at a cost of $4,000,000. It was estimated that it would take 3 years to complete the project. Also on January 1, 2004, to finance the construction cost, Oksana Baiul borrowed $4,000,000 payable in 10 annual installments of $400,000, plus interest at the rate of 10%. During 2004, Oksana Baiul made deposit and progress payments totaling $1,500,000 under the contract; the weighted-average amount of accumulated expenditures was $800,000 for the year. The excess borrowed funds were invested in short-term securities, from which Oksana Baiul realized investment income of $250,000.

Instructions

What amount should Oksana Baiul report as capitalized interest at December 31, 2004?

Situation II

During 2004, Midori Ito Corporation constructed and manufactured certain assets and incurred the following interest costs in connection with those activities.

	Interest Costs Incurred
Warehouse constructed for Ito's own use	$30,000
Special-order machine for sale to unrelated customer, produced according to customer's specifications	9,000
Inventories routinely manufactured, produced on a repetitive basis	8,000

All of these assets required an extended period of time for completion.

Instructions

Assuming the effect of interest capitalization is material, what is the total amount of interest costs to be capitalized?

Situation III

Peggy Fleming, Inc. has a fiscal year ending April 30. On May 1, 2004, Peggy Fleming borrowed $10,000,000 at 11% to finance construction of its own building. Repayments of the loan are to commence the month following completion of the building. During the year ended April 30, 2005, expenditures for the partially completed structure totaled $7,000,000. These expenditures were incurred evenly throughout the year. Interest earned on the unexpended portion of the loan amounted to $650,000 for the year.

Instructions

How much should be shown as capitalized interest on Peggy Fleming's financial statements at April 30, 2005?

(CPA adapted)

E10-11 (Entries for Equipment Acquisitions) Jane Geddes Engineering Corporation purchased conveyor equipment with a list price of $10,000. The vendor's credit terms were 2/10, n/30. Presented below are three independent cases related to the equipment. Assume that the purchases of equipment are recorded gross. (Round to nearest dollar.)

(a) Geddes paid cash for the equipment 8 days after the purchase.

(b) Geddes traded in equipment with a book value of $2,000 (initial cost $8,000), and paid $9,500 in cash one month after the purchase. The old equipment could have been sold for $400 at the date of trade (assume similar equipment).

(c) Geddes gave the vendor a $10,800 non-interest-bearing note for the equipment on the date of purchase. The note was due in one year and was paid on time. Assume that the effective interest rate in the market was 9%.

Instructions

Prepare the general journal entries required to record the acquisition and payment in each of the independent cases above. Round to the nearest dollar.

E10-12 (Entries for Asset Acquisition, Including Self-Construction) Below are transactions related to Fred Couples Company.

(a) The City of Pebble Beach gives the company 5 acres of land as a plant site. The market value of this land is determined to be $81,000.

(b) 13,000 shares of common stock with a par value of $50 per share are issued in exchange for land and buildings. The property has been appraised at a fair market value of $810,000, of which $180,000 has been allocated to land and $630,000 to buildings. The stock of Fred Couples Company is not listed on any exchange, but a block of 100 shares was sold by a stockholder 12 months ago at $65 per share, and a block of 200 shares was sold by another stockholder 18 months ago at $58 per share.

(c) No entry has been made to remove from the accounts for Materials, Direct Labor, and Overhead the amounts properly chargeable to plant asset accounts for machinery constructed during the year. The following information is given relative to costs of the machinery constructed.

Materials used	$12,500
Factory supplies used	900
Direct labor incurred	15,000
Additional overhead (over regular) caused by construction of machinery, excluding factory supplies used	2,700
Fixed overhead rate applied to regular manufacturing operations	60% of direct labor cost
Cost of similar machinery if it had been purchased from outside suppliers	44,000

Instructions

Prepare journal entries on the books of Fred Couples Company to record these transactions.

E10-13 (Entries for Acquisition of Assets) Presented below is information related to Zonker Company.

1. On July 6 Zonker Company acquired the plant assets of Doonesbury Company, which had discontinued operations. The appraised value of the property is:

Land	$ 400,000
Building	1,200,000
Machinery and equipment	800,000
Total	$2,400,000

Zonker Company gave 12,500 shares of its $100 par value common stock in exchange. The stock had a market value of $168 per share on the date of the purchase of the property.

2. Zonker Company expended the following amounts in cash between July 6 and December 15, the date when it first occupied the building.

Repairs to building	$105,000
Construction of bases for machinery to be installed later	135,000
Driveways and parking lots	122,000
Remodeling of office space in building, including new partitions and walls	161,000
Special assessment by city on land	18,000

3. On December 20, the company paid cash for machinery, $260,000, subject to a 2% cash discount, and freight on machinery of $10,500.

Instructions

Prepare entries on the books of Zonker Company for these transactions.

E10-14 (Purchase of Equipment with Non-Interest-Bearing Debt) Chippewas Inc. has decided to purchase equipment from Central Michigan Industries on January 2, 2004, to expand its production capacity to meet customers' demand for its product. Chippewas issues an $800,000, 5-year, non-interest-bearing note to Central Michigan for the new equipment when the prevailing market rate of interest for obligations of this nature is 12%. The company will pay off the note in five $160,000 installments due at the end of each year over the life of the note.

Instructions

(a) Prepare the journal entry(ies) at the date of purchase. (Round to nearest dollar in all computations.)

(b) Prepare the journal entry(ies) at the end of the first year to record the payment and interest, assuming that the company employs the effective-interest method.

(c) Prepare the journal entry(ies) at the end of the second year to record the payment and interest.

(d) Assuming that the equipment had a 10-year life and no salvage value, prepare the journal entry necessary to record depreciation in the first year. (Straight-line depreciation is employed.)

E10-15 (Purchase of Computer with Non-Interest-Bearing Debt) Cardinals Corporation purchased a computer on December 31, 2003, for $105,000, paying $30,000 down and agreeing to pay the balance in five equal installments of $15,000 payable each December 31 beginning in 2004. An assumed interest rate of 10% is implicit in the purchase price.

Instructions

(a) Prepare the journal entry(ies) at the date of purchase. (Round to two decimal places.)
(b) Prepare the journal entry(ies) at December 31, 2004, to record the payment and interest (effective-interest method employed).
(c) Prepare the journal entry(ies) at December 31, 2005, to record the payment and interest (effective-interest method employed).

E10-16 (Asset Acquisition) Hayes Industries purchased the following assets and constructed a building as well. All this was done during the current year.

Assets 1 and 2
These assets were purchased as a lump sum for $100,000 cash. The following information was gathered.

Description	Initial Cost on Seller's Books	Depreciation to Date on Seller's Books	Book Value on Seller's Books	Appraised Value
Machinery	$100,000	$50,000	$50,000	$85,000
Office equipment	60,000	10,000	50,000	45,000

Asset 3
This machine was acquired by making a $10,000 down payment and issuing a $30,000, 2-year, zero-interest-bearing note. The note is to be paid off in two $15,000 installments made at the end of the first and second years. It was estimated that the asset could have been purchased outright for $35,900.

Asset 4
This machinery was acquired by trading in similar used machinery. Facts concerning the trade-in are as follows.

Cost of machinery traded	$100,000
Accumulated depreciation to date of sale	40,000
Fair market value of machinery traded	80,000
Cash received	10,000
Fair market value of machinery acquired	70,000

Asset 5
Office equipment was acquired by issuing 100 shares of $8 par value common stock. The stock had a market value of $11 per share.

Construction of Building
A building was constructed on land purchased last year at a cost of $150,000. Construction began on February 1 and was completed on November 1. The payments to the contractor were as follows.

Date	Payment
2/1	$120,000
6/1	360,000
9/1	480,000
11/1	100,000

To finance construction of the building, a $600,000, 12% construction loan was taken out on June 1. The loan was repaid on November 1. The firm had $200,000 of other outstanding debt during the year at a borrowing rate of 8%.

Instructions
Record the acquisition of each of these assets.

E10-17 (Nonmonetary Exchange with Boot) Busytown Corporation, which manufactures shoes, hired a recent college graduate to work in its accounting department. On the first day of work, the accountant was assigned to total a batch of invoices with the use of an adding machine. Before long, the accountant, who had never before seen such a machine, managed to break the machine. Busytown Corporation gave the machine plus $340 to Dick Tracy Business Machine Company (dealer) in exchange for a new machine. Assume the following information about the machines.

	Busytown Corp. (Old Machine)	Dick Tracy Co. (New Machine)
Machine cost	$290	$270
Accumulated depreciation	140	–0–
Fair value	85	425

Instructions
For each company, prepare the necessary journal entry to record the exchange.

E10-18 (Nonmonetary Exchange with Boot) Cannondale Company purchased an electric wax melter on April 30, 2005, by trading in its old gas model and paying the balance in cash. The following data relate to the purchase.

List price of new melter	$15,800
Cash paid	10,000
Cost of old melter (5-year life, $700 residual value)	11,200
Accumulated depreciation—old melter (straight-line)	6,300
Second-hand market value of old melter	5,200

Instructions
Prepare the journal entry(ies) necessary to record this exchange, assuming that the melters exchanged are **(a)** similar in nature, and **(b)** dissimilar in nature. Cannondale's fiscal year ends on December 31, and depreciation has been recorded through December 31, 2004.

E10-19 (Nonmonetary Exchange with Boot) Carlos Arruza Company exchanged equipment used in its manufacturing operations plus $3,000 in cash for similar equipment used in the operations of Tony LoBianco Company. The following information pertains to the exchange.

	Carlos Arruza Co.	Tony LoBianco Co.
Equipment (cost)	$28,000	$28,000
Accumulated depreciation	19,000	10,000
Fair value of equipment	12,500	15,500
Cash given up	3,000	

Instructions
Prepare the journal entries to record the exchange on the books of both companies.

E10-20 (Nonmonetary Exchange with Boot) Dana Ashbrook Inc. has negotiated the purchase of a new piece of automatic equipment at a price of $8,000 plus trade-in, f.o.b. factory. Dana Ashbrook Inc. paid $8,000 cash and traded in used equipment. The used equipment had originally cost $62,000; it had a book value of $42,000 and a secondhand market value of $47,800, as indicated by recent transactions involving similar equipment. Freight and installation charges for the new equipment required a cash payment of $1,100.

Instructions
- **(a)** Prepare the general journal entry to record this transaction, assuming that the assets Dana Ashbrook Inc. exchanged are similar in nature.
- **(b)** Assuming the same facts as in (a) except that the assets exchanged are dissimilar in nature, prepare the general journal entry to record this transaction.

E10-21 (Analysis of Subsequent Expenditures) King Donovan Resources Group has been in its plant facility for 15 years. Although the plant is quite functional, numerous repair costs are incurred to maintain it in sound working order. The company's plant asset book value is currently $800,000, as indicated below.

Original cost	$1,200,000
Accumulated depreciation	400,000
	$ 800,000

During the current year, the following expenditures were made to the plant facility.

- **(a)** Because of increased demands for its product, the company increased its plant capacity by building a new addition at a cost of $270,000.
- **(b)** The entire plant was repainted at a cost of $23,000.
- **(c)** The roof was an asbestos cement slate. For safety purposes it was removed and replaced with a wood shingle roof at a cost of $61,000. Book value of the old roof was $41,000.
- **(d)** The electrical system was completely updated at a cost of $22,000. The cost of the old electrical system was not known. It is estimated that the useful life of the building will not change as a result of this updating.
- **(e)** A series of major repairs were made at a cost of $47,000, because parts of the wood structure were rotting. The cost of the old wood structure was not known. These extensive repairs are estimated to increase the useful life of the building.

Instructions

Indicate how each of these transactions would be recorded in the accounting records.

E10-22 (Analysis of Subsequent Expenditures) The following transactions occurred during 2005. Assume that depreciation of 10% per year is charged on all machinery and 5% per year on buildings, on a straight-line basis, with no estimated salvage value. Depreciation is charged for a full year on all fixed assets acquired during the year, and no depreciation is charged on fixed assets disposed of during the year.

Jan. 30	A building that cost \$132,000 in 1988 is torn down to make room for a new building. The wrecking contractor was paid \$5,100 and was permitted to keep all materials salvaged.
Mar. 10	Machinery that was purchased in 1998 for \$16,000 is sold for \$2,900 cash, f.o.b. purchaser's plant. Freight of \$300 is paid on this machinery.
Mar. 20	A gear breaks on a machine that cost \$9,000 in 2000. The gear is replaced at a cost of \$385. The replacement does not extend the useful life of the machine.
May 18	A special base installed for a machine in 1999 when the machine was purchased has to be replaced at a cost of \$5,500 because of defective workmanship on the original base. The cost of the machinery was \$14,200 in 1999. The cost of the base was \$3,500, and this amount was charged to the Machinery account in 1999.
June 23	One of the buildings is repainted at a cost of \$6,900. It had not been painted since it was constructed in 2001.

Instructions

Prepare general journal entries for the transactions. (Round to the nearest dollar.)

E10-23 (Analysis of Subsequent Expenditures) Plant assets often require expenditures subsequent to acquisition. It is important that they be accounted for properly. Any errors will affect both the balance sheets and income statements for a number of years.

Instructions

For each of the following items, indicate whether the expenditure should be capitalized (C) or expensed (E) in the period incurred.

(a) ________ Improvement.
(b) ________ Replacement of a minor broken part on a machine.
(c) ________ Expenditure that increases the useful life of an existing asset.
(d) ________ Expenditure that increases the efficiency and effectiveness of a productive asset but does not increase its salvage value.
(e) ________ Expenditure that increases the efficiency and effectiveness of a productive asset and increases the asset's salvage value.
(f) ________ Expenditure that increases the quality of the output of the productive asset.
(g) ________ Improvement to a machine that increased its fair market value and its production capacity by 30% without extending the machine's useful life.
(h) ________ Ordinary repairs.
(i) ________ Interest on borrowing necessary to finance a major overhaul of machinery. The overhaul extended the life of the machinery.

E10-24 (Entries for Disposition of Assets) On December 31, 2004, Travis Tritt Inc. has a machine with a book value of \$940,000. The original cost and related accumulated depreciation at this date are as follows.

Machine	\$1,300,000
Accumulated depreciation	360,000
	\$ 940,000

Depreciation is computed at \$60,000 per year on a straight-line basis.

Instructions

Presented below is a set of independent situations. For each independent situation, indicate the journal entry to be made to record the transaction. Make sure that depreciation entries are made to update the book value of the machine prior to its disposal.

(a) A fire completely destroys the machine on August 31, 2005. An insurance settlement of \$430,000 was received for this casualty. Assume the settlement was received immediately.
(b) On April 1, 2005, Tritt sold the machine for \$1,040,000 to Dwight Yoakam Company.
(c) On July 31, 2005, the company donated this machine to the Mountain King City Council. The fair market value of the machine at the time of the donation was estimated to be \$1,100,000.

E10-25 (Disposition of Assets) On April 1, 2004, Gloria Estefan Company received a condemnation award of $430,000 cash as compensation for the forced sale of the company's land and building, which stood in the path of a new state highway. The land and building cost $60,000 and $280,000, respectively, when they were acquired. At April 1, 2004, the accumulated depreciation relating to the building amounted to $160,000. On August 1, 2004, Estafan purchased a piece of replacement property for cash. The new land cost $90,000, and the new building cost $400,000.

Instructions

Prepare the journal entries to record the transactions on April 1 and August 1, 2004.

PROBLEMS

P10-1 (Classification of Acquisition and Other Asset Costs) At December 31, 2003, certain accounts included in the property, plant, and equipment section of Craig Ehlo Company's balance sheet had the following balances.

Land	$230,000
Buildings	890,000
Leasehold improvements	660,000
Machinery and equipment	875,000

During 2004 the following transactions occurred.

1. Land site number 621 was acquired for $850,000. In addition, to acquire the land Ehlo paid a $51,000 commission to a real estate agent. Costs of $35,000 were incurred to clear the land. During the course of clearing the land, timber and gravel were recovered and sold for $13,000.
2. A second tract of land (site number 622) with a building was acquired for $420,000. The closing statement indicated that the land value was $300,000 and the building value was $120,000. Shortly after acquisition, the building was demolished at a cost of $41,000. A new building was constructed for $330,000 plus the following costs.

Excavation fees	$38,000
Architectural design fees	11,000
Building permit fee	2,500
Imputed interest on funds used during construction (stock financing)	8,500

   The building was completed and occupied on September 30, 2004.
3. A third tract of land (site number 623) was acquired for $650,000 and was put on the market for resale.
4. During December 2004 costs of $89,000 were incurred to improve leased office space. The related lease will terminate on December 31, 2006, and is not expected to be renewed. (*Hint:* Leasehold improvements should be handled in the same manner as land improvements.)
5. A group of new machines was purchased under a royalty agreement that provides for payment of royalties based on units of production for the machines. The invoice price of the machines was $87,000, freight costs were $3,300, installation costs were $2,400, and royalty payments for 2004 were $17,500.

Instructions

(a) Prepare a detailed analysis of the changes in each of the following balance sheet accounts for 2004.

Land	Leasehold improvements
Buildings	Machinery and equipment

Disregard the related accumulated depreciation accounts.

(b) List the items in the situation that were not used to determine the answer to (a) above, and indicate where, or if, these items should be included in Ehlo's financial statements.

(AICPA adapted)

P10-2 (Classification of Acquisition Costs) Selected accounts included in the property, plant, and equipment section of Spud Webb Corporation's balance sheet at December 31, 2003, had the following balances.

Land	$ 300,000
Land improvements	140,000
Buildings	1,100,000
Machinery and equipment	960,000

During 2004 the following transactions occurred.

1. A tract of land was acquired for $150,000 as a potential future building site.
2. A plant facility consisting of land and building was acquired from Ken Norman Company in exchange for 20,000 shares of Webb's common stock. On the acquisition date, Webb's stock had a closing market price of $37 per share on a national stock exchange. The plant facility was carried on Norman's books at $110,000 for land and $320,000 for the building at the exchange date. Current appraised values for the land and building, respectively, are $230,000 and $690,000.
3. Items of machinery and equipment were purchased at a total cost of $400,000. Additional costs were incurred as follows.

Freight and unloading	$13,000
Sales taxes	20,000
Installation	26,000

4. Expenditures totaling $95,000 were made for new parking lots, streets, and sidewalks at the corporation's various plant locations. These expenditures had an estimated useful life of 15 years.
5. A machine costing $80,000 on January 1, 1996, was scrapped on June 30, 2004. Double-declining-balance depreciation has been recorded on the basis of a 10-year life.
6. A machine was sold for $20,000 on July 1, 2004. Original cost of the machine was $44,000 on January 1, 2001, and it was depreciated on the straight-line basis over an estimated useful life of 7 years and a salvage value of $2,000.

Instructions

(a) Prepare a detailed analysis of the changes in each of the following balance sheet accounts for 2004.

Land
Land improvements
Buildings
Machinery and equipment

(*Hint:* Disregard the related accumulated depreciation accounts.)

(b) List the items in the fact situation that were not used to determine the answer to (a), showing the pertinent amounts and supporting computations in good form for each item. In addition, indicate where, or if, these items should be included in Spud Webb's financial statements.

(AICPA adapted)

P10-3 (Classification of Land and Building Costs) Lenny Wilkins Company was incorporated on January 2, 2005, but was unable to begin manufacturing activities until July 1, 2005, because new factory facilities were not completed until that date.

The Land and Building account at December 31, 2005, was as follows.

January 31, 2005	Land and building	$160,000
February 28, 2005	Cost of removal of building	9,800
May 1, 2005	Partial payment of new construction	60,000
May 1, 2005	Legal fees paid	3,770
June 1, 2005	Second payment on new construction	40,000
June 1, 2005	Insurance premium	2,280
June 1, 2005	Special tax assessment	4,000
June 30, 2005	General expenses	36,300
July 1, 2005	Final payment on new construction	40,000
December 31, 2005	Asset write-up	43,800
		399,950
December 31, 2005	Depreciation—2005 at 1%	4,000
	Account balance	$395,950

The following additional information is to be considered.

1. To acquire land and building the company paid $80,000 cash and 800 shares of its 8% cumulative preferred stock, par value $100 per share. Fair market value of the stock is $107 per share.
2. Cost of removal of old buildings amounted to $9,800, and the demolition company retained all materials of the building.
3. Legal fees covered the following.

Cost of organization	$ 610
Examination of title covering purchase of land	1,300
Legal work in connection with construction contract	1,860
	$3,770

4. Insurance premium covered the building for a 2-year term beginning May 1, 2005.
5. The special tax assessment covered street improvements that are permanent in nature.
6. General expenses covered the following for the period from January 2, 2005, to June 30, 2005.

President's salary	$32,100
Plant superintendent covering supervision of new building	4,200
	$36,300

7. Because of a general increase in construction costs after entering into the building contract, the board of directors increased the value of the building $43,800, believing that such an increase was justified to reflect the current market at the time the building was completed. Retained earnings was credited for this amount.
8. Estimated life of building—50 years.
   Write-off for 2005—1% of asset value (1% of $400,000, or $4,000).

Instructions

(a) Prepare entries to reflect correct land, building, and depreciation allowance accounts at December 31, 2005.

(b) Show the proper presentation of land, building, and depreciation on the balance sheet at December 31, 2005.

(AICPA adapted)

P10-4 (Dispositions, Including Condemnation, Demolition, and Trade-in) Presented below is a schedule of property dispositions for Frank Thomas Co.

Schedule of Property Dispositions

	Cost	Accumulated Depreciation	Cash Proceeds	Fair Market Value	Nature of Disposition
Land	$40,000	—	$31,000	$31,000	Condemnation
Building	15,000	—	3,600	—	Demolition
Warehouse	70,000	$11,000	74,000	74,000	Destruction by fire
Machine	8,000	3,200	900	7,200	Trade-in
Furniture	10,000	7,850	—	3,100	Contribution
Automobile	8,000	3,460	2,960	2,960	Sale

The following additional information is available.

Land

On February 15, a condemnation award was received as consideration for unimproved land held primarily as an investment, and on March 31, another parcel of unimproved land to be held as an investment was purchased at a cost of $35,000.

Building

On April 2, land and building were purchased at a total cost of $75,000, of which 20% was allocated to the building on the corporate books. The real estate was acquired with the intention of demolishing the building, and this was accomplished during the month of November. Cash proceeds received in November represent the net proceeds from demolition of the building.

Warehouse

On June 30, the warehouse was destroyed by fire. The warehouse was purchased January 2, 2001, and had depreciated $11,000. On December 27, the insurance proceeds and other funds were used to purchase a replacement warehouse at a cost of $90,000.

Machine

On December 26, the machine was exchanged for another machine having a fair market value of $6,300 and cash of $900 was received.

Furniture

On August 15, furniture was contributed to a qualified charitable organization. No other contributions were made or pledged during the year.

Automobile

On November 3, the automobile was sold to Ozzie Guillen, a stockholder.

Instructions

Indicate how these items would be reported on the income statement of Frank Thomas Co.

(AICPA adapted)

P10-5 (Classification of Costs and Interest Capitalization) On January 1, 2004, George Solti Corporation purchased for $600,000 a tract of land (site number 101) with a building. Solti paid a real estate broker's commission of $36,000, legal fees of $6,000, and title guarantee insurance of $18,000. The closing statement indicated that the land value was $500,000 and the building value was $100,000. Shortly after acquisition, the building was razed at a cost of $54,000.

Solti entered into a $3,000,000 fixed-price contract with Slatkin Builders, Inc. on March 1, 2004, for the construction of an office building on land site number 101. The building was completed and occupied on September 30, 2005. Additional construction costs were incurred as follows.

Plans, specifications, and blueprints	$21,000
Architects' fees for design and supervision	82,000

The building is estimated to have a 40-year life from date of completion and will be depreciated using the 150% declining balance method.

To finance construction costs, Solti borrowed $3,000,000 on March 1, 2004. The loan is payable in 10 annual installments of $300,000 plus interest at the rate of 10%. Solti's weighted-average amounts of accumulated building construction expenditures were as follows.

For the period March 1 to December 31, 2004	$1,200,000
For the period January 1 to September 30, 2005	1,900,000

Instructions

(a) Prepare a schedule that discloses the individual costs making up the balance in the land account in respect of land site number 101 as of September 30, 2005.

(b) Prepare a schedule that discloses the individual costs that should be capitalized in the office building account as of September 30, 2005. Show supporting computations in good form.

(AICPA adapted)

P10-6 (Interest During Construction) Jerry Landscaping began construction of a new plant on December 1, 2002. On this date the company purchased a parcel of land for $142,000 in cash. In addition, it paid $2,000 in surveying costs and $4,000 for a title insurance policy. An old dwelling on the premises was demolished at a cost of $3,000, with $1,000 being received from the sale of materials.

Architectural plans were also formalized on December 1, 2002, when the architect was paid $30,000. The necessary building permits costing $3,000 were obtained from the city and paid for on December 1 as well. The excavation work began during the first week in December with payments made to the contractor as follows.

Date of Payment	Amount of Payment
March 1	$240,000
May 1	360,000
July 1	60,000

The building was completed on July 1, 2003.

To finance construction of this plant, Jerry borrowed $600,000 from the bank on December 1, 2002. Jerry had no other borrowings. The $600,000 was a 10-year loan bearing interest at 8%.

Instructions

Compute the balance in each of the following accounts at December 31, 2002, and December 31, 2003.

(a) Land.

(b) Buildings.

(c) Interest Expense.

P10-7 (Capitalization of Interest) Wordcrafters Inc. is a book distributor that had been operating in its original facility since 1979. The increase in certification programs and continuing education requirements in several professions has contributed to an annual growth rate of 15% for Wordcrafters since 1999. Wordcrafters' original facility became obsolete by early 2004 because of the increased sales volume and the fact that Wordcrafters now carries tapes and disks in addition to books.

On June 1, 2004, Wordcrafters contracted with Favre Construction to have a new building constructed for $5,000,000 on land owned by Wordcrafters. The payments made by Wordcrafters to Favre Construction are shown in the schedule below.

Date	Amount
July 30, 2004	$1,200,000
January 30, 2005	1,500,000
May 30, 2005	1,300,000
Total payments	$4,000,000

Construction was completed and the building was ready for occupancy on May 27, 2005. Wordcrafters had no new borrowings directly associated with the new building but had the following debt outstanding at May 31, 2005, the end of its fiscal year.

14½%, 5-year note payable of $2,000,000, dated April 1, 2001, with interest payable annually on April 1.

12%, 10-year bond issue of $3,000,000 sold at par on June 30, 1997, with interest payable annually on June 30.

The new building qualifies for interest capitalization. The effect of capitalizing the interest on the new building, compared with the effect of expensing the interest, is material.

Instructions

(a) Compute the weighted average accumulated expenditures on Wordcrafters' new building during the capitalization period.

(b) Compute the avoidable interest on Wordcrafters' new building.

(c) Some interest cost of Wordcrafters Inc. is capitalized for the year ended May 31, 2005.

  (1) Identify the items relating to interest costs that must be disclosed in Wordcrafters' financial statements.

  (2) Compute the amount of each of the items that must be disclosed.

(CMA adapted)

P10-8 (Nonmonetary Exchanges with Boot) Susquehanna Corporation wishes to exchange a machine used in its operations. Susquehanna has received the following offers from other companies in the industry.

1. Choctaw Company offered to exchange a similar machine plus $23,000.
2. Powhatan Company offered to exchange a similar machine.
3. Shawnee Company offered to exchange a similar machine, but wanted $8,000 in addition to Susquehanna's machine.

In addition, Susquehanna contacted Seminole Corporation, a dealer in machines. To obtain a new machine, Susquehanna must pay $93,000 in addition to trading in its old machine.

	Susquehanna	Choctaw	Powhatan	Shawnee	Seminole
Machine cost	$160,000	$120,000	$147,000	$160,000	$130,000
Accumulated depreciation	50,000	45,000	71,000	75,000	–0–
Fair value	92,000	69,000	92,000	100,000	185,000

Instructions

For each of the four independent situations, prepare the journal entries to record the exchange on the books of each company. (Round to nearest dollar.)

P10-9 (Nonmonetary Exchanges with Boot) On August 1, Arna, Inc. exchanged productive assets with Bontemps, Inc. Arna's asset is referred to below as "Asset A," and Bontemps' is referred to as "Asset B." The following facts pertain to these assets.

	Asset A	Asset B
Original cost	$96,000	$110,000
Accumulated depreciation (to date of exchange)	45,000	52,000
Fair market value at date of exchange	60,000	75,000
Cash paid by Arna, Inc.	15,000	
Cash received by Bontemps, Inc.		15,000

Instructions

(a) Assuming that Assets A and B are dissimilar, record the exchange for both Arna, Inc. and Bontemps, Inc. in accordance with generally accepted accounting principles.

(b) Assuming that Assets A and B are similar, record the exchange for both Arna, Inc. and Bontemps, Inc. in accordance with generally accepted accounting principles.

P10-10 (Nonmonetary Exchanges with Boot) During the current year, Garrison Construction trades an old crane that has a book value of $80,000 (original cost $140,000 less accumulated depreciation $60,000) for a new crane from Keillor Manufacturing Co. The new crane cost Keillor $165,000 to manufacture and is classified as inventory. The following information is also available.

	Garrison Const.	Keillor Mfg. Co.
Fair market value of old crane	$ 72,000	
Fair market value of new crane		$190,000
Cash paid	118,000	
Cash received		118,000

Instructions

(a) Assuming that this exchange is considered to involve dissimilar assets, prepare the journal entries on the books of (1) Garrison Construction and (2) Keillor Manufacturing.

(b) Assuming that this exchange is considered to involve similar assets, prepare the journal entries on the books of (1) Garrison Construction and (2) Keillor Manufacturing.

(c) Assuming the same facts as those in (a), except that the fair market value of the old crane is $98,000 and the cash paid is $92,000, prepare the journal entries on the books of (1) Garrison Construction and (2) Keillor Manufacturing.

(d) Assuming the same facts as those in (b), except that the fair market value of the old crane is $87,000 and the cash paid $103,000, prepare the journal entries on the books of (1) Garrison Construction and (2) Keillor Manufacturing.

P10-11 (Purchases by Deferred Payment, Lump-sum, and Nonmonetary Exchanges) Kent Adamson Company, a manufacturer of ballet shoes, is experiencing a period of sustained growth. In an effort to expand its production capacity to meet the increased demand for its product, the company recently made several acquisitions of plant and equipment. Tod Mullinger, newly hired in the position of fixed-asset accountant, requested that Watt Kaster, Adamson's controller, review the following transactions.

Transaction 1

On June 1, 2004, Adamson Company purchased equipment from Venghaus Corporation. Adamson issued a $20,000, 4-year, non-interest-bearing note to Venghaus for the new equipment. Adamson will pay off the note in four equal installments due at the end of each of the next 4 years. At the date of the transaction, the prevailing market rate of interest for obligations of this nature was 10%. Freight costs of $425 and installation costs of $500 were incurred in completing this transaction. The appropriate factors for the time value of money at a 10% rate of interest are given below.

Future value of $1 for 4 periods	1.46
Future value of an ordinary annuity for 4 periods	4.64
Present value of $1 for 4 periods	0.68
Present value of an ordinary annuity for 4 periods	3.17

Transaction 2

On December 1, 2004, Adamson Company purchased several assets of Haukap Shoes Inc., a small shoe manufacturer whose owner was retiring. The purchase amounted to $210,000 and included the assets listed below. Adamson Company engaged the services of Tennyson Appraisal Inc., an independent appraiser, to determine the fair market values of the assets which are also presented below.

	Haukap Book Value	Fair Market Value
Inventory	$ 60,000	$ 50,000
Land	40,000	80,000
Building	70,000	120,000
	$170,000	$250,000

During its fiscal year ended May 31, 2005, Adamson incurred $8,000 for interest expense in connection with the financing of these assets.

Transaction 3

On March 1, 2005, Adamson Company exchanged a number of used trucks plus cash for vacant land adjacent to its plant site. Adamson intends to use the land for a parking lot. The trucks had a combined book value of $35,000, as Adamson had recorded $20,000 of accumulated depreciation against these assets. Adamson's purchasing agent, who has had previous dealings in the second-hand market, indicated that the trucks had a fair market value of $46,000 at the time of the transaction. In addition to the trucks, Adamson Company paid $19,000 cash for the land.

Instructions

(a) Plant assets such as land, buildings, and equipment receive special accounting treatment. Describe the major characteristics of these assets that differentiate them from other types of assets.

(b) For each of the three transactions described above, determine the value at which Adamson Company should record the acquired assets. Support your calculations with an explanation of the underlying rationale.

(c) The books of Adamson Company show the following additional transactions for the fiscal year ended May 31, 2005.

(1) Acquisition of a building for speculative purposes.
(2) Purchase of a 2-year insurance policy covering plant equipment.
(3) Purchase of the rights for the exclusive use of a process used in the manufacture of ballet shoes.

For each of these transactions, indicate whether the asset should be classified as a plant asset. If it is a plant asset, explain why it is. If it is not a plant asset, explain why not, and identify the proper classification.

(CMA adapted)

CONCEPTUAL CASES

C10-1 (Acquisition, Improvements, and Sale of Realty) William Bradford Company purchased land for use as its corporate headquarters. A small factory that was on the land when it was purchased was torn down before construction of the office building began. Furthermore, a substantial amount of rock blasting and removal had to be done to the site before construction of the building foundation began. Because the office building was set back on the land far from the public road, Bradford Company had the contractor construct a paved road that led from the public road to the parking lot of the office building.

Three years after the office building was occupied, Bradford Company added four stories to the office building. The four stories had an estimated useful life of 5 years more than the remaining estimated useful life of the original office building.

Ten years later the land and building were sold at an amount more than their net book value, and Bradford Company had a new office building constructed in another state for use as its new corporate headquarters.

Instructions

(a) Which of the expenditures above should be capitalized? How should each be depreciated or amortized? Discuss the rationale for your answers.
(b) How would the sale of the land and building be accounted for? Include in your answer an explanation of how to determine the net book value at the date of sale. Discuss the rationale for your answer.

C10-2 (Accounting for Self-Constructed Assets) Shanette Medical Labs, Inc., began operations 5 years ago producing stetrics, a new type of instrument it hoped to sell to doctors, dentists, and hospitals. The demand for stetrics far exceeded initial expectations, and the company was unable to produce enough stetrics to meet demand.

The company was manufacturing its product on equipment that it built at the start of its operations. To meet demand, more efficient equipment was needed. The company decided to design and build the equipment, because the equipment currently available on the market was unsuitable for producing stetrics.

In 2004, a section of the plant was devoted to development of the new equipment and a special staff was hired. Within 6 months a machine developed at a cost of $714,000 increased production dramatically and reduced labor costs substantially. Elated by the success of the new machine, the company built three more machines of the same type at a cost of $441,000 each.

Instructions

(a) In general, what costs should be capitalized for self-constructed equipment?
(b) Discuss the propriety of including in the capitalized cost of self-constructed assets:
    (1) The increase in overhead caused by the self-construction of fixed assets.
    (2) A proportionate share of overhead on the same basis as that applied to goods manufactured for sale.
(c) Discuss the proper accounting treatment of the $273,000 ($714,000 − $441,000) by which the cost of the first machine exceeded the cost of the subsequent machines. This additional cost should not be considered research and development costs.

C10-3 (Capitalization of Interest) Zucker Airline is converting from piston-type planes to jets. Delivery time for the jets is 3 years, during which substantial progress payments must be made. The multimillion-dollar cost of the planes cannot be financed from working capital; Zucker must borrow funds for the payments.

Because of high interest rates and the large sum to be borrowed, management estimates that interest costs in the second year of the period will be equal to one-third of income before interest and taxes, and one-half of such income in the third year.

After conversion, Zucker's passenger-carrying capacity will be doubled with no increase in the number of planes, although the investment in planes would be substantially increased. The jet planes have a 7-year service life.

Instructions
Give your recommendation concerning the proper accounting for interest during the conversion period. Support your recommendation with reasons and suggested accounting treatment. (Disregard income tax implications.)

(AICPA adapted)

C10-4 (Capitalization of Interest) Petri Magazine Company started construction of a warehouse building for its own use at an estimated cost of $6,000,000 on January 1, 2002, and completed the building on December 31, 2002. During the construction period, Petri has the following debt obligations outstanding.

Construction loan—12% interest, payable semiannually, issued December 31, 2001	$2,000,000
Short-term loan—10% interest, payable monthly, and principal payable at maturity, on May 30, 2003	1,400,000
Long-term loan—11% interest, payable on January 1 of each year. Principal payable on January 1, 2005	2,000,000

Total cost amounted to $6,200,000, and the weighted average of accumulated expenditures was $4,000,000.

Dee Pettepiece, the president of the company, has been shown the costs associated with this construction project and capitalized on the balance sheet. She is bothered by the "avoidable interest" included in the cost. She argues that, first, all the interest is unavoidable—no one lends money without expecting to be compensated for it. Second, why can't the company use all the interest on all the loans when computing this avoidable interest? Finally, why can't her company capitalize all the annual interest that accrued over the period of construction?

Instructions
You are the manager of accounting for the company. In a memo, explain what avoidable interest is, how you computed it (being especially careful to explain why you used the interest rates that you did), and why the company cannot capitalize all its interest for the year. Attach a schedule supporting any computations that you use.

C10-5 (Nonmonetary Exchanges) You have two clients that are considering trading machinery with each other. Although the machines are different from each other, you believe that they are "similar" for the purposes of recording a nonmonetary exchange. Your clients would prefer that the machines be considered dissimilar, to allow them to record gains. Here are the facts:

	Client A	Client B
Original cost	$100,000	$150,000
Accumulated depreciation	40,000	80,000
Market value	95,000	125,000
Cash received (paid)	(30,000)	30,000

Instructions
- **(a)** Record the trade-in on Client A's books assuming the assets are dissimilar.
- **(b)** Record the trade-in on Client A's books assuming the assets are similar.
- **(c)** Write a memo to the controller of Company A indicating and explaining the dollar impact on current and future statements of treating the assets as "similar" versus "dissimilar."
- **(d)** Record the entry on Client B's books assuming the assets are dissimilar.
- **(e)** Record the entry on Client B's books assuming the assets are similar.
- **(f)** Write a memo to the controller of Company B indicating and explaining the dollar impact on current and future statements of treating the assets as "similar" versus "dissimilar."

C10-6 (Costs of Acquisition) The invoice price of a machine is $40,000. Various other costs relating to the acquisition and installation of the machine including transportation, electrical wiring, special base, and so on amount to $7,500. The machine has an estimated life of 10 years, with no residual value at the end of that period.

The owner of the business suggests that the incidental costs of $7,500 be charged to expense immediately for the following reasons.

1. If the machine should be sold, these costs cannot be recovered in the sales price.
2. The inclusion of the $7,500 in the machinery account on the books will not necessarily result in a closer approximation of the market price of this asset over the years, because of the possibility of changing demand and supply levels.
3. Charging the $7,500 to expense immediately will reduce federal income taxes.

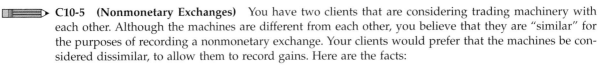

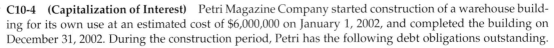

Instructions
Discuss each of the points raised by the owner of the business.

(AICPA adapted)

C10-7 (Cost of Land vs. Building) Field Company purchased a warehouse in a downtown district where land values are rapidly increasing. Adolph Phillips, controller, and Wilma Smith, financial vice-president, are trying to allocate the cost of the purchase between the land and the building. Noting that depreciation can be taken only on the building, Phillips favors placing a very high proportion of the cost on the warehouse itself, thus reducing taxable income and income taxes. Smith, his supervisor, argues that the allocation should recognize the increasing value of the land, regardless of the depreciation potential of the warehouse. Besides, she says, net income is negatively impacted by additional depreciation and will cause the company's stock price to go down.

Instructions
Answer the following questions.

(a) What stakeholder interests are in conflict?
(b) What ethical issues does Phillips face?
(c) How should these costs be allocated?

USING YOUR JUDGMENT

FINANCIAL STATEMENT ANALYSIS CASE

Johnson & Johnson

Johnson & Johnson, the world's leading and most diversified health-care corporation, serves its customers through specialized worldwide franchises. Each of its franchises consists of a number of companies throughout the world that focus on a particular health care market, such as surgical sutures, consumer pharmaceuticals, or contact lenses. Information related to its property, plant, and equipment in its 2001 annual report is shown in the notes to the financial statements as follows.

Note 1: Property, Plant, and Equipment and Depreciation
Property, plant, and equipment are stated at cost. The Company utilizes the straight-line method of depreciation on estimated useful lives of the assets:

Building and building equipment	20–40 years
Land and leasehold improvements	10–20 years
Machinery and equipment	2–13 years

Note 3: Property, Plant, and Equipment
At the end of 2001 and 2000, property, plant, and equipment at cost and accumulated depreciation were:

(dollars in millions)	2001	2000
Land and land improvements	$ 459	$ 427
Buildings and building equipment	3,911	3,659
Machinery and equipment	6,805	6,312
Construction in progress	1,283	1,468
	12,458	11,866
Less: Accumulated depreciation	4,739	4,457
	$ 7,719	$ 7,409

The Company capitalizes interest expense as part of the cost of construction of facilities and equipment. Interest expense capitalized in 2001, 2000, and 1999 was $95 million, $97 million, and $84 million, respectively.

Upon retirement or other disposal of fixed assets, the cost and related amount of accumulated depreciation or amortization are eliminated from the asset and accumulated depreciation accounts, respectively. The difference, if any, between the net asset value and the proceeds is adjusted to earnings.

In Johnson & Johnson's cash flow statement for 2001, the following selected information is provided.

Johnson & Johnson
2001 Annual Report
Consolidated Financial Statements (excerpts)

Net cash flows from operating activities	$ 8,864
Cash flows from investing activities	
Additions to property, plant and equipment	(1,731)
Proceeds from the disposal of assets	163
Acquisition of businesses, net of cash acquired (Note 17)	(225)
Purchases of investments	(8,188)
Sales of investments	5,967
Other	(79)
Net cash used by investing activities	(4,093)
Cash flows from financing activities	
Dividends to shareowners	(2,047)
Repurchase of common stock	(2,570)
Proceeds from short-term debt	338
Retirement of short-term debt	(1,109)
Proceeds from long-term debt	14
Retirement of long-term debt	(391)
Proceeds from the exercise of stock options	514
Net cash used by financing activities	(5,251)
Effect of exchange rate changes on cash and cash equivalents	(40)
(Decrease)/increase in cash and cash equivalents	(520)
Cash and cash equivalents, beginning of year (Note 1)	4,278
Cash and cash equivalents, end of year (Note 1)	$ 3,758
Supplemental cash flow data	
Cash paid during the year for:	
Interest	$ 185
Income taxes	2,090

Instructions

(a) What was the cost of buildings and building equipment at the end of 2001?

(b) Does Johnson & Johnson use a conservative or liberal method to depreciate its property, plant, and equipment?

(c) What was the actual interest expense incurred by the company in 2001?

(d) What is Johnson & Johnson's free cash flow? From the information provided, comment on Johnson & Johnson's financial flexibility.

RESEARCH CASE

BUSINESS EXTRA

The March 26, 2002, *Wall Street Journal* includes an article by Henny Sender entitled "Telecoms Draw Focus for Moves in Accounting." (Subscribers to **Business Extra** can access the article at that site.)

Instructions

Read the article and answer the following questions.

(a) What is the EITF referred to in this article?

(b) Explain the accounting issue related to the exchange of similar network capacity.

(c) Why did the EITF not address the issues related to swaps that occurred at companies such as **Global Crossing** and **Qwest Communications**?

PROFESSIONAL SIMULATION

Accounting–Property, Plant, and Equipment

Directions | Situation | Measurement | Journal Entries | Financial Statements | Analysis | Research | Resources

Directions

In this simulation, you will be asked various questions regarding accounting for property, plant, and equipment. Prepare responses to all parts.

Situation

Norwel Company manufactures miniature circuit boards used in wireless phones and personal organizers. On January 2, 2003, Norwel purchased a circuit board stamping machine at a retail price of $12,000. Norwel paid 5% sales tax on this purchase. Norwel paid a contractor $1,400 for a specially wired platform for the machine, to ensure non-interrupted power to the machine. Norwel estimates the machine will have a 4-year useful life, with a salvage value of $2,000 at the end of 4 years. Norwel uses straight-line depreciation and employs the "half-year" convention in accounting for partial-year depreciation (that is, it takes a half year of depreciation in the first year of an asset's useful life).
Norwel's fiscal year ends on December 31.

Measurement

At what amount should Norwel record the acquisition cost of the machine?

Journal Entry

What journal entry should Norwel record in 2003?

Financial Statements

At what amount will the machine be reported in Norwel's balance sheet at December 31, 2004?

Analysis

On July 1, 2005, Norwel decides to outsource its circuit board operations to Boards-R-Us Inc. As part of this plan, Norwel sells the machine (and the platform) to Boards-R-Us for $7,000. What is the impact of this disposal on Norwel's 2005 income before taxes?

www.wiley.com/college/kieso

Remember to check the **Take Action! CD**
and the book's **companion Web site**
to find additional resources for this chapter.

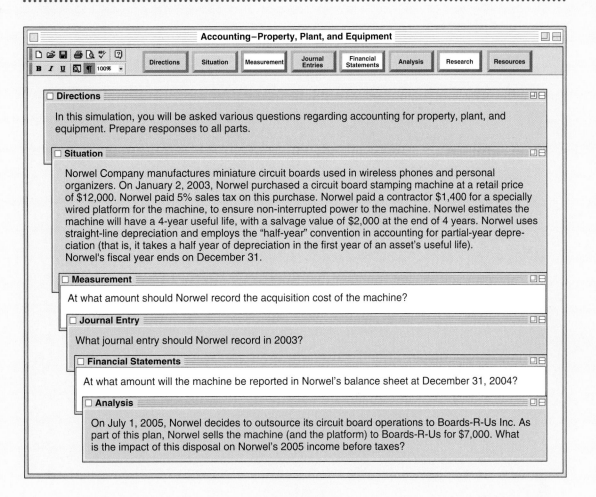

CHAPTER 11

Depreciation, Impairments, and Depletion

Do They Matter?

The axiom on Wall Street has always been that huge one-time charges don't really count; they are highly unusual events that don't truly reflect how a company is faring. Wall Street simply ignores them. Many companies must believe this axiom because in the last few years write-offs have approached the all-time highs of the early 1990s when the U.S. went through massive corporate restructurings.

However, some companies have been taking write-offs so regularly that they really are a reflection of ongoing business. When you adjust for the write-offs, earnings turn out to be far worse—and the companies' shares of stock turn out to be far more expensive. Presented below are data from three companies that have had charges every year for the last 5 years, showing their income before and after the write-offs, adjusted earnings after the write-offs, and related EPS data.

Company	Net Income Before Write-Offs ($mil)	Net Income After Write-Offs ($mil)	Percentage Difference	EPS 2002 Mean $	EPS 2002 Adjusted $	P/E 2002 Mean	P/E 2002 Adjusted
International Paper	$591	$ 95	84%	$2.82	$0.46	15	90
Waste Management	755	130	83	1.43	0.25	18	102
Fortune Brands	322	61	81	3.30	0.63	13	67

For example, this chart shows that International Paper's adjusted earnings will come in closer to $0.46 per share than $2.82. This means that its price to earnings ratio is closer to 90 than to 15! In short, these companies may be overpriced and are likely set for stock price declines.[1]

One reason for more write-offs may be the tougher guidelines established in the U.S. to determine when impairments of property, plant, and equipment occur. Thus, while impairments are on the rise in the United States and elsewhere, investors are now receiving better information about fixed asset values in financial statements.

LEARNING OBJECTIVES

After studying this chapter, you should be able to:

1. **Explain the concept of depreciation.**
2. **Identify the factors involved in the depreciation process.**
3. **Compare activity, straight-line, and decreasing-charge methods of depreciation.**
4. **Explain special depreciation methods.**
5. **Explain the accounting issues related to asset impairment.**
6. **Explain the accounting procedures for depletion of natural resources.**
7. **Explain how property, plant, equipment, and natural resources are reported and analyzed.**

[1]Adapted from "Were Profits Inflated?" *Business Week* (March 4, 2002), p. 14, and from Michael K. Ozanian, "The Serial Chargers," *Forbes* (March 4, 2002), p. 102.

PREVIEW OF CHAPTER 11

As noted in the opening story, accounting standards-setters have developed new rules on impairments. These rules recognize that when economic conditions change, some type of write-off of cost is needed to indicate that the usefulness of an asset has declined. The purpose of this chapter is to examine the depreciation process and the methods of writing off the cost of tangible assets and natural resources.

The content and organization of the chapter are as follows.

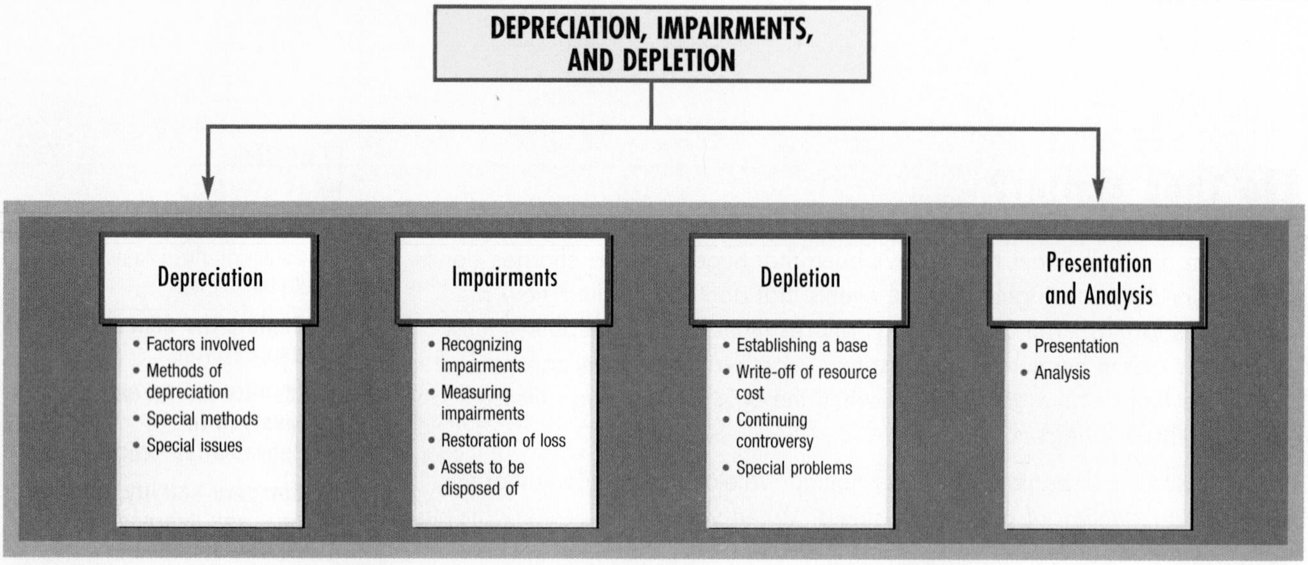

DEPRECIATION—A METHOD OF COST ALLOCATION

OBJECTIVE 1
Explain the concept of depreciation.

Most individuals at one time or another purchase and trade in an automobile. In discussions with the automobile dealer, depreciation is a consideration on two points. First, how much has the old car "depreciated"? That is, what is the trade-in value? Second, how fast will the new car depreciate? That is, what will its trade-in value be several years in the future? In both cases depreciation is thought of as a loss in value.

To accountants, however, **depreciation is not a matter of valuation but a means of cost allocation**. Assets are not depreciated on the basis of a decline in their fair market value, but on the basis of systematic charges to expense. **Depreciation is defined as the accounting process of allocating the cost of tangible assets to expense in a systematic and rational manner to those periods expected to benefit from the use of the asset.**

This approach is employed because the value of the asset may fluctuate between the time the asset is purchased and the time it is sold or junked. Attempts to measure these interim value changes have not been successful because values are difficult to measure objectively. Therefore, the asset's cost is charged to depreciation expense over its estimated life, making no attempts to value the asset at fair value between acquisition and disposition. The cost allocation approach is used because a matching of costs with revenues occurs and because fluctuations in fair value are tenuous and difficult to measure.

When long-lived assets are written off, the term **depreciation** is most often used to indicate that tangible plant assets have declined in value. Where natural resources, such as timber, gravel, oil, and coal, are involved, the term **depletion** is employed. The expiration of intangible assets, such as patents or goodwill, is called **amortization**.

Factors Involved in the Depreciation Process

OBJECTIVE 2
Identify the factors involved in the depreciation process.

Three basic questions must be answered before depreciation expense can be determined.

1. What depreciable base is to be used for the asset?
2. What is the asset's useful life?
3. What method of cost apportionment is best for this asset?

Answering these questions involves distilling several estimates into one single figure, which is itself an estimate. The calculations on which depreciation is based assume perfect knowledge of the future, which is never attainable.

Depreciable Base for the Asset

Tutorial on Depreciation Methods

The base established for depreciation is a function of two factors: the original cost and the salvage or disposal value. We discussed historical cost in Chapter 10. **Salvage value** is the estimated amount that will be received at the time the asset is sold or removed from service. It is the amount to which the asset must be written down or depreciated during its useful life. To illustrate, if an asset has a cost of $10,000 and a salvage value of $1,000, its depreciation base is $9,000.

ILLUSTRATION 11-1
Computation of Depreciation Base

Original cost	$10,000
Less: Salvage value	1,000
Depreciation base	$ 9,000

From a practical standpoint, salvage value is often considered to be zero because its valuation is small. Some long-lived assets, however, have substantial salvage values.

Estimation of Service Lives

The service life of an asset and its physical life are often not the same. A piece of machinery may be physically capable of producing a given product for many years beyond its service life. But the equipment may not be used for all of those years because the cost of producing the product in later years may be too high. For example, the old **Slater** cotton mill in Pawtucket, Rhode Island, is preserved in remarkable physical condition as an historic landmark in American industrial development, although its service life was terminated many years ago.[2]

Assets are retired for two reasons: **physical factors** (such as casualty or expiration of physical life) and **economic factors** (obsolescence). Physical factors are the wear and tear, decay, and casualties that make it difficult for the asset to perform indefinitely. These physical factors set the outside limit for the service life of an asset.

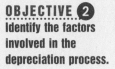

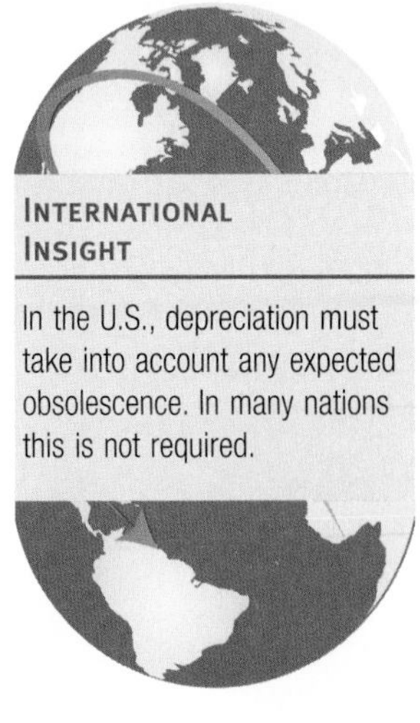

INTERNATIONAL INSIGHT

In the U.S., depreciation must take into account any expected obsolescence. In many nations this is not required.

The economic or functional factors can be classified into three categories: inadequacy, supersession, and obsolescence. **Inadequacy** results when an asset ceases to be useful to a given enterprise because the demands of the firm have increased. An example would be the need for a larger building to handle increased production. Although the old building may still be sound, it may have become inadequate for that enterprise's purposes. **Supersession** is the replacement of one asset with another more efficient and economical asset. Examples would be the replacement of the mainframe computer with a PC network, or the replacement of the Boeing 767 with the Boeing 777. **Obsolescence** is the catchall for situations not involving inadequacy and supersession. Because the distinction between these categories appears artificial, it is proba-

[2]Taken from J. D. Coughlan and W. K. Strand, *Depreciation Accounting, Taxes and Business Decisions* (New York: The Ronald Press, 1969), pp. 10–12.

bly best to consider economic factors totally instead of trying to make distinctions that are not clear-cut.

To illustrate the concepts of physical and economic factors, consider a new nuclear power plant. Which do you think would be more important in determining the useful life of a nuclear power plant—physical factors or economic factors? The limiting factors seem to be (1) ecological considerations, (2) competition from other power sources, and (3) safety concerns. Physical life does not appear to be the primary factor affecting useful life. Although the plant's physical life may be far from over, the plant may become obsolete in 10 years.

For a house, physical factors undoubtedly are more important than the economic or functional factors relative to useful life. Whenever the physical nature of the asset is the primary determinant of useful life, maintenance plays an extremely vital role. The better the maintenance, the longer the life of the asset.[3]

In some cases, arbitrary service lives are selected. In others, sophisticated statistical methods are employed to establish a useful life for accounting purposes. In many cases, the primary basis for estimating the useful life of an asset is the company's past experience with the same or similar assets. In a highly industrial economy such as that of the United States, where research and innovation are so prominent, technological factors have as much effect, if not more, on service lives of tangible plant assets as physical factors do.

WHAT DO THE NUMBERS MEAN?

ALPHABET DUPE

Some companies try to imply that depreciation is not a cost. For example, in their press releases they will often make a bigger deal over earnings before interest, taxes, depreciation and amortization (often referred to as Ebitda) than net income under GAAP. They like it because it "dresses up" their earnings numbers, and some on Wall Street buy it because they don't like the allocations that have to be made to determine net income. Some banks, without batting an eyelash, even let companies base their loan covenants on Ebitda.

For example, look at **Premier Parks**, which operates the Six Flags chain of amusement parks. Premier touts its Ebitda performance, but that masks a big part of how the company operates—and how it spends its money. Premier argues that depreciation for big-ticket items like roller coasters should be ignored because rides have a long life. Critics, however, say that the amusement industry has to spend as much as 50 percent of its Ebitda just to keep its rides and attractions current. Those expenses are not optional—let the rides get a little rusty, and ticket sales start to trail off. That means depreciation associated with the costs of maintaining rides (or buying new ones) should really be viewed as an everyday expense. It also means investors in those companies should have strong stomachs.

What's the risk of trusting a fad accounting trick? Just look at a recent year's bankruptcy numbers. Of the 147 companies tracked by Moody's that defaulted on their debt, most borrowed money based on Ebitda performance. The bankers in those deals probably wish they'd looked at a few other factors. Maybe it's time more investors did so too.

Source: Adapted from Herb Greenberg, "Alphabet Dupe: Why Ebitda Falls Short," *Fortune* (July 10, 2000), p. 240.

[3]The airline industry also illustrates the type of problem involved in estimation. In the past, aircraft were assumed not to wear out—they just became obsolete. However, some jets have been in service as long as 20 years, and maintenance of these aircraft has become increasingly expensive. Also, the public's concern about worn-out aircraft has been heightened by some recent air disasters. As a result, some airlines are finding it necessary to replace aircraft not because of obsolescence but because of physical deterioration.

Methods of Depreciation

The third factor involved in the depreciation process is the **method** of cost apportionment. The profession requires that the depreciation method employed be "systematic and rational." A number of depreciation methods are used. They may be classified as follows.

1. Activity method (units of use or production).
2. Straight-line method.
3. Decreasing-charge methods (accelerated):
   (a) Sum-of-the-years'-digits.
   (b) Declining-balance method.
4. Special depreciation methods:
   (a) Group and composite methods.
   (b) Hybrid or combination methods.[4]

UNDERLYING CONCEPTS

Depreciation is an attempt to match the cost of an asset to the periods that benefit from the use of that asset.

To illustrate some of these depreciation methods, assume that Stanley Coal Mines recently purchased an additional crane for digging purposes. Pertinent data concerning the purchase of the crane are:

Cost of crane	$500,000
Estimated useful life	5 years
Estimated salvage value	$ 50,000
Productive life in hours	30,000 hours

ILLUSTRATION 11-2
Data Used to Illustrate Depreciation Methods

Activity Method

OBJECTIVE 3
Compare activity, straight-line, and decreasing-charge methods of depreciation.

The **activity method** (also called the variable charge approach) assumes that depreciation is **a function of use or productivity instead of the passage of time**. The life of the asset is considered in terms of either the **output** it provides (units it produces), or an **input** measure such as the number of hours it works. Conceptually, the proper cost association is established in terms of output instead of hours used, but often the output is not easily measurable. In such cases, an input measure such as machine hours is a more appropriate method of measuring the dollar amount of depreciation charges for a given accounting period.

The crane poses no particular problem because the usage (hours) is relatively easy to measure. If the crane is used 4,000 hours the first year, the depreciation charge is:

$$\frac{\text{(Cost less salvage)} \times \text{Hours this year}}{\text{Total estimated hours}} = \text{Depreciation charge}$$

$$\frac{(\$500{,}000 - \$50{,}000) \times 4{,}000}{30{,}000} = \$60{,}000$$

ILLUSTRATION 11-3
Depreciation Calculation, Activity Method—Crane Example

The major limitation of this method is that it is not appropriate in situations in which depreciation is a function of time instead of activity. For example, a building is subject to a great deal of steady deterioration from the elements (time) regardless of its use. In addition, where an asset is subject to economic or functional factors, independent

[4] *Accounting Trends and Techniques—2001* reports that of its 600 surveyed companies various depreciation methods were used for financial reporting purposes: straight-line 576; declining-balance 22; sum-of-the-years'-digits 7; accelerated method (not specified) 53; units of production 34. No utility or transportation companies (the ones that use the "special depreciation methods") are included in the AICPA's survey.

of its use, the activity method loses much of its significance. For example, if a company is expanding rapidly, a particular building may soon become obsolete for its intended purposes. In both cases, activity is irrelevant. Another problem in using an activity method is that an estimate of units of output or service hours received is often difficult to determine.

Where loss of services is a result of activity or productivity, the activity method will best match costs and revenues. Companies that desire low depreciation during periods of low productivity and high depreciation during high productivity either adopt or switch to an activity method. In this way, a plant running at 40 percent of capacity generates 60 percent lower depreciation charges. **Inland Steel**, for example, switched to units-of-production depreciation at one time and reduced its losses by $43 million, or $1.20 per share.[5]

UNDERLYING CONCEPTS

If those benefits flow on a "straight-line" basis, then justification exists for matching the cost of the asset on a straight-line basis with these benefits.

Straight-Line Method

The **straight-line method** considers depreciation a **function of time rather than a function of usage**. This method is widely employed in practice because of its simplicity. The straight-line procedure is often the most conceptually appropriate, too. When creeping obsolescence is the primary reason for a limited service life, the decline in usefulness may be constant from period to period. The depreciation charge for the crane is computed as follows.

ILLUSTRATION 11-4
Depreciation Calculation, Straight-Line Method—Crane Example

$$\frac{\text{Cost less salvage}}{\text{Estimated service life}} = \text{Depreciation charge}$$

$$\frac{\$500{,}000 - \$50{,}000}{5} = \$90{,}000$$

The major objection to the straight-line method is that it rests on two unrealistic assumptions: (1) The asset's economic usefulness is the same each year, and (2) the repair and maintenance expense is essentially the same each period.

One additional problem that occurs in using straight-line is that distortions in the rate of return analysis (income/assets) develop. Illustration 11-5 indicates how the rate of return increases, given constant revenue flows, because the asset's book value decreases.

ILLUSTRATION 11-5
Depreciation and Rate of Return Analysis—Crane Example

Year	Depreciation Expense	Undepreciated Asset Balance (book value)	Income (after depreciation expense)	Rate of Return (Income ÷ Assets)
0		$500,000		
1	$90,000	410,000	$100,000	24.4%
2	90,000	320,000	100,000	31.2%
3	90,000	230,000	100,000	43.5%
4	90,000	140,000	100,000	71.4%
5	90,000	50,000	100,000	200.0%

UNDERLYING CONCEPTS

The matching concept does not justify a constant charge to income. If the benefits from the asset decline as the asset gets older, then a decreasing charge to income would better match cost to benefits.

Decreasing-Charge Methods

The **decreasing-charge methods**—often called **accelerated depreciation methods**—provide for a higher depreciation cost in the earlier years and lower charges in later periods. The main justification for this approach is that more depreciation should be charged in earlier years because the asset suffers its greatest loss of services in those years. Another argument presented is that the accelerated methods provide a constant cost because the depreciation charge is lower in the later periods, at the time when the repair and maintenance costs are often higher. Generally, one of two decreasing-charge methods is employed: the sum-of-the-years'-digits method or the declining-balance method.

[5]"Double Standard," *Forbes* (November 22, 1982), p. 178.

Sum-of-the-Years'-Digits. The **sum-of-the-years'-digits method** results in a decreasing depreciation charge based on a decreasing fraction of depreciable cost (original cost less salvage value). Each fraction uses the sum of the years as a denominator (5 + 4 + 3 + 2 + 1 = 15) and the number of years of estimated life remaining as of the beginning of the year as a numerator. In this method, the numerator decreases year by year and the denominator remains constant (5/15, 4/15, 3/15, 2/15, and 1/15). At the end of the asset's useful life, the balance remaining should be equal to the salvage value. This method of computation is shown in Illustration 11-6.[6]

ILLUSTRATION 11-6
Sum-of-the-Years'-Digits Depreciation Schedule—Crane Example

Year	Depreciation Base	Remaining Life in Years	Depreciation Fraction	Depreciation Expense	Book Value, End of Year
1	$450,000	5	5/15	$150,000	$350,000
2	450,000	4	4/15	120,000	230,000
3	450,000	3	3/15	90,000	140,000
4	450,000	2	2/15	60,000	80,000
5	450,000	1	1/15	30,000	50,000[a]
		15	15/15	$450,000	

[a]Salvage value.

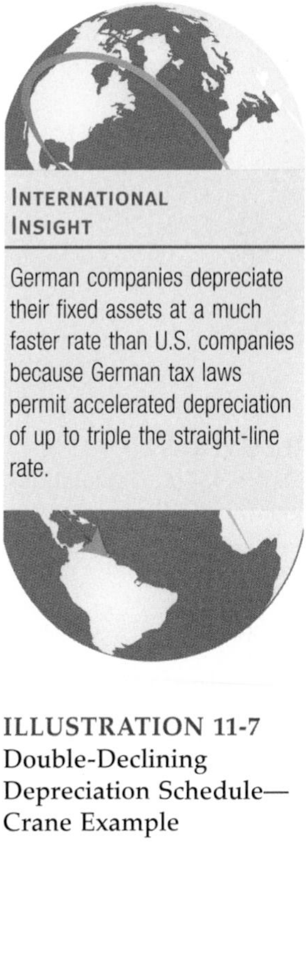

INTERNATIONAL INSIGHT

German companies depreciate their fixed assets at a much faster rate than U.S. companies because German tax laws permit accelerated depreciation of up to triple the straight-line rate.

Declining-Balance Method. Another decreasing-charge method is the **declining-balance method**, which utilizes a depreciation rate (expressed as a percentage) that is some multiple of the straight-line method. For example, the double-declining rate for a 10-year asset would be 20 percent (double the straight-line rate, which is 1/10 or 10 percent). The declining-balance rate remains constant and is applied to the reducing book value each year. Unlike other methods, in the declining-balance method the salvage value is not deducted in computing the depreciation base. The declining-balance rate is multiplied by the book value of the asset at the beginning of each period. Since the book value of the asset is reduced each period by the depreciation charge, the constant-declining-balance rate is applied to a successively lower book value, which results in lower depreciation charges each year. This process continues until the book value of the asset is reduced to its estimated salvage value, at which time depreciation is discontinued.

As indicated above, various multiples are used in practice, such as twice (200%) the straight-line rate (**double-declining-balance method**) and 150% of the straight-line rate. Using the double-declining approach in the crane example, Stanley Coal Mines would have the depreciation charges shown in Illustration 11-7.

ILLUSTRATION 11-7
Double-Declining Depreciation Schedule—Crane Example

Year	Book Value of Asset First of Year	Rate on Declining Balance[a]	Depreciation Expense	Balance Accumulated Depreciation	Book Value, End of Year
1	$500,000	40%	$200,000	$200,000	$300,000
2	300,000	40%	120,000	320,000	180,000
3	180,000	40%	72,000	392,000	108,000
4	108,000	40%	43,200	435,200	64,800
5	64,800	40%	14,800[b]	450,000	50,000

[a]Based on twice the straight-line rate of 20% ($90,000/$450,000 = 20%; 20% × 2 = 40%).
[b]Limited to $14,800 because book value should not be less than salvage value.

[6]What happens if the estimated service life of the asset is, let us say, 51 years? How would you calculate the sum-of-the-years'-digits? Fortunately mathematicians have developed a formula that permits easy computation. It is as follows:

$$\frac{n(n+1)}{2} = \frac{51(51+1)}{2} = 1{,}326$$

Near the end of the asset's useful life, enterprises often switch from the declining-balance method to the sum-of-the-years'-digits or straight-line method to ensure that the asset is depreciated only to its salvage value.[7]

Special Depreciation Methods

OBJECTIVE 4
Explain special depreciation methods.

Sometimes an enterprise does not select one of the more popular depreciation methods because the assets involved have unique characteristics, or the nature of the industry dictates that a special depreciation method be adopted. Two of these special methods are discussed below.

1. Group and composite methods.
2. Hybrid or combination methods.

Group and Composite Methods

Multiple-asset accounts are often depreciated using one rate. For example, an enterprise such as **AT&T** might depreciate telephone poles, microwave systems, or switchboards by groups.

Two methods of depreciating multiple-asset accounts are employed: the group method and the composite method. The term **"group" refers to a collection of assets that are similar in nature. "Composite" refers to a collection of assets that are dissimilar in nature**. The **group method** is frequently used when the assets are fairly homogeneous and have approximately the same useful lives. The **composite approach** is used when the assets are heterogeneous and have different lives. The group method more closely approximates a single-unit cost procedure because the dispersion from the average is not as great. The method of computation for group or composite is essentially the same: find an average and depreciate on that basis.

To illustrate, Mooney Motors depreciates its fleet of cars, trucks, and campers on a composite basis. The depreciation rate is established in the following manner.

ILLUSTRATION 11-8
Depreciation Calculation, Composite Basis

Asset	Original Cost	Residual Value	Depreciable Cost	Estimated Life (yrs.)	Depreciation per Year (straight-line)
Cars	$145,000	$25,000	$120,000	3	$40,000
Trucks	44,000	4,000	40,000	4	10,000
Campers	35,000	5,000	30,000	5	6,000
	$224,000	$34,000	$190,000		$56,000

$$\text{Composite depreciation rate} = \frac{\$56{,}000}{\$224{,}000} = 25\%$$

Composite life = 3.39 years ($190,000 ÷ $56,000)

The **composite depreciation rate** is determined by dividing the depreciation per year by the total cost of the assets. If there are no changes in the asset account, the

[7]A pure form of the declining-balance method (sometimes appropriately called the "fixed percentage of book value method") has also been suggested as a possibility. This approach finds a rate that depreciates the asset exactly to salvage value at the end of its expected useful life. The formula for determination of this rate is as follows.

$$\text{Depreciation rate} = 1 - \sqrt[n]{\frac{\text{Salvage value}}{\text{Acquisition cost}}}$$

The life in years is n. Once the depreciation rate is computed, it is applied on the declining book value of the asset from period to period, which means that depreciation expense will be successively lower. This method is not used extensively in practice because the computations are cumbersome, and it is not permitted for tax purposes.

group of assets will be depreciated to the residual or salvage value at the rate of $56,000 ($224,000 × 25%) a year. As a result, it will take Mooney 3.39 years (composite life as indicated in Illustration 11-8) to depreciate these assets.

The differences between the group or composite method and the single-unit depreciation method become accentuated when we look at asset retirements. If an asset is retired before, or after, the average service life of the group is reached, the resulting gain or loss is buried in the Accumulated Depreciation account. This practice is justified because some assets will be retired before the average service life and others after the average life. For this reason, the debit to Accumulated Depreciation is the difference between original cost and cash received. No gain or loss on disposition is recorded. To illustrate, suppose that one of the campers with a cost of $5,000 was sold for $2,600 at the end of the third year. The entry is:

Accumulated Depreciation	2,400	
Cash	2,600	
Cars, Trucks, and Campers		5,000

If a new type of asset is purchased (mopeds, for example), a new depreciation rate must be computed and applied in subsequent periods.

A typical financial statement disclosure of the group depreciation method is shown for **Ampco-Pittsburgh Corporation** as follows.

Ampco-Pittsburgh Corporation

Depreciation rates are based on estimated useful lives of the asset groups. Gains or losses on normal retirements or replacements of depreciable assets, subject to composite depreciation methods, are not recognized; the difference between the cost of the assets retired or replaced and the related salvage value is charged or credited to the accumulated depreciation.

ILLUSTRATION 11-9
Disclosure of Group Depreciation Method

The group or composite method simplifies the bookkeeping process and tends to average out errors caused by over- or underdepreciation. As a result, periodic income is not distorted by gains or losses on disposals of assets.

On the other hand, the unit method has several advantages over the group or composite methods: (1) It simplifies the computation mathematically. (2) It identifies gains and losses on disposal. (3) It isolates depreciation on idle equipment. (4) It represents the best estimate of the depreciation of each asset, not the result of averaging the cost over a longer period of time. As a consequence, the unit method is generally used in practice and is generally assumed to be used in homework problems unless stated otherwise.[8]

Hybrid or Combination Methods

In addition to the aforementioned depreciation methods, companies are free to develop their own special or tailor-made depreciation methods. GAAP requires only that the method result in the allocation of an asset's cost over the asset's life in a systematic and rational manner.

Discussion of Other Special Depreciation Methods

[8]Recently, AcSEC has indicated in an exposure draft that the unit approach should be used whenever feasible. In fact, it indicates that an even better way to depreciate property, plant, and equipment is to use component depreciation. Under component depreciation, any part or portion of property, plant, and equipment that can be separately identified as an asset should be depreciated over its expected useful life. For example, a building might be divided into various components such as roof, heating and cooling system, elevator, leasehold improvements, and so on. Each of these components would be depreciated over its useful life.

A hybrid depreciation method widely used in the steel industry is a combination straight-line/activity approach referred to as the **production variable method**. The following note from **WHX Corporation**'s Annual Report explains one variation of this method.

ILLUSTRATION 11-10
Disclosure of Hybrid Depreciation Method

WHX Corporation

The Company utilizes the modified units of production method of depreciation which recognizes that the depreciation of steelmaking machinery is related to the physical wear of the equipment as well as a time factor. The modified units of production method provides for straight-line depreciation charges modified (adjusted) by the level of raw steel production. In the prior year depreciation under the modified units of production method was $21.6 million or 40% less than straight-line depreciation, and in the current year it was $1.1 million or 2% more than straight-line depreciation.

WHAT DO THE NUMBERS MEAN?

DECELERATING DEPRECIATION

Which depreciation method should management select? Many believe that the method that best matches revenues with expenses should be used. For example, if revenues generated by the asset are constant over its useful life, straight-line depreciation should be selected. On the other hand, if revenues are higher (or lower) at the beginning of the asset's life, then a decreasing (or increasing) method should be used. Thus, if revenues from the asset can be reliably estimated, selecting a depreciation method that best matches costs with those revenues would seem to provide the most useful information to investors and creditors for assessing the future cash flows from the asset. Other factors that might also be considered are record-keeping costs and effects on income and asset book values.

Managers in the real estate industry face a different challenge when considering depreciation choices. Real estate managers are frustrated with depreciation accounting because in their view, real estate often does not decline in value. In addition, because real estate is highly debt-financed, most real estate concerns report losses in earlier years of operations when the sum of depreciation and interest exceeds the revenue from the real estate project. As a result, real estate companies, like **Kimco Realty**, argue for some form of **increasing-charge method** of depreciation (lower depreciation at the beginning and higher depreciation at the end). With such a method, higher total assets and net income would be reported in the earlier years of the project.[9]

Special Depreciation Issues

Several special issues related to depreciation remain to be discussed. The major issues are:

1. How should depreciation be computed for partial periods?
2. Does depreciation provide for the replacement of assets?
3. How are revisions in depreciation rates handled?

---

[9]In this regard, real estate investment trusts (REITs) often report (in addition to net income) an earnings measure, funds from operations (FFO), that adjusts income for depreciation expense and other noncash expenses. This method is not GAAP, and there is mixed empirical evidence about whether FFO or GAAP income is more useful to real estate investment trust investors. See, for example, Richard Gore and David Stott, "Toward a More Informative Measure of Operating Performance in the REIT Industry: Net Income vs. FFO," *Accounting Horizons* (December 1998), and Linda Vincent, "The Information Content of FFO for REITs," *Journal of Accounting and Economics* (January 1999).

Depreciation and Partial Periods

Plant assets are seldom purchased on the first day of a fiscal period or disposed of on the last day of a fiscal period. A practical question is: How much depreciation should be charged for the partial periods involved?

Assume, for example, that an automated drill machine with a 5-year life is purchased by Steeltex Company for $45,000 (no salvage value) on June 10, 2003. The company's fiscal year ends December 31, and depreciation is charged for 6⅔ months during that year. The total depreciation for a full year (assuming straight-line depreciation) is $9,000 ($45,000/5), and the depreciation for the first, partial year is:

$$\frac{6\tfrac{2}{3}}{12} \times \$9{,}000 = \$5{,}000$$

The partial-period calculation is relatively simple when straight-line depreciation is used. But how is partial-period depreciation handled when an accelerated method such as sum-of-the-years'-digits or double-declining balance is used? As an illustration, assume that an asset was purchased for $10,000 on July 1, 2003, with an estimated useful life of 5 years. The depreciation figures for 2003, 2004, and 2005 are shown in Illustration 11-11.

ILLUSTRATION 11-11
Calculation of Partial-Period Depreciation, Two Methods

	Sum-of-the-Years'-Digits		Double-Declining Balance	
1st full year	(5/15 × $10,000) =	$3,333.33	(40% × $10,000) =	$4,000
2nd full year	(4/15 × 10,000) =	2,666.67	(40% × 6,000) =	2,400
3rd full year	(3/15 × 10,000) =	2,000.00	(40% × 3,600) =	1,440
Depreciation from July 1, 2003, to December 31, 2003				
6/12 × $3,333.33 =		$1,666.67	6/12 × $4,000 =	$2,000
Depreciation for 2004				
6/12 × $3,333.33 =		$1,666.67	6/12 × $4,000 =	$2,000
6/12 × 2,666.67 =		1,333.33	6/12 × 2,400 =	1,200
		$3,000.00		$3,200
			or ($10,000 − $2,000) × 40% =	$3,200
Depreciation for 2005				
6/12 × $2,666.67 =		$1,333.33	6/12 × $2,400 =	$1,200
6/12 × 2,000.00 =		1,000.00	6/12 × 1,440 =	720
		$2,333.33		$1,920
			or ($10,000 − $5,200) × 40% =	$1,920

In computing depreciation expense for partial periods, it is necessary to determine the depreciation expense for the full year and then to prorate this depreciation expense between the two periods involved. This process should continue throughout the useful life of the asset.

Sometimes the process of allocating costs to a partial period is modified to handle acquisitions and disposals of plant assets more simply. Depreciation may be computed for the full period on the opening balance in the asset account, and no depreciation is charged on acquisitions during the year. Some other variations: Charge a full year's depreciation on assets used during the year. Or, charge one-half year's depreciation in the year of acquisition and in the year of disposal (referred to as the "half-year" convention). Or, charge a full year in the year of acquisition and none in the year of disposal.

A company is at liberty to adopt any one of these several fractional-year policies in allocating cost to the first and last years of an asset's life so long as the method is applied consistently. However, **unless otherwise stipulated, depreciation is normally computed on the basis of the nearest full month.** Illustration 11-12 shows depreciation allocated under five different fractional-year policies using the straight-line method on the $45,000 automated drill machine purchased on June 10, 2003, by Steeltex Company, discussed earlier.

ILLUSTRATION 11-12
Fractional-Year Depreciation Policies

Machine Cost = $45,000	Depreciation Allocated per Period Over 5-Year Life*					
Fractional-Year Policy	2003	2004	2005	2006	2007	2008
1. Nearest fraction of a year.	$5,000[a]	$9,000	$9,000	$9,000	$9,000	$4,000[b]
2. Nearest full month.	5,250[c]	9,000	9,000	9,000	9,000	3,750[d]
3. Half year in period of acquisition and disposal.	4,500	9,000	9,000	9,000	9,000	4,500
4. Full year in period of acquisition, none in period of disposal.	9,000	9,000	9,000	9,000	9,000	–0–
5. None in period of acquisition, full year in period of disposal.	–0–	9,000	9,000	9,000	9,000	9,000

[a]6.667/12 ($9,000) [b]5.333/12 ($9,000) [c]7/12 ($9,000) [d]5/12 ($9,000)
*Rounded to nearest dollar.

Depreciation and Replacement of Fixed Assets

A common misconception about depreciation is that it provides funds for the replacement of fixed assets. Depreciation is similar to any other expense in that it reduces net income. It differs in that **it does not involve a current cash outflow.**

To illustrate why depreciation does not provide funds for replacement of plant assets, assume that a business starts operating with plant assets of $500,000 that have a useful life of 5 years. The company's balance sheet at the beginning of the period is:

Plant assets	$500,000	Owners' equity	$500,000

Now if we assume that the enterprise earned no revenue over the 5 years, the income statements are:

	Year 1	Year 2	Year 3	Year 4	Year 5
Revenue	$ –0–	$ –0–	$ –0–	$ –0–	$ –0–
Depreciation	(100,000)	(100,000)	(100,000)	(100,000)	(100,000)
Loss	$(100,000)	$(100,000)	$(100,000)	$(100,000)	$(100,000)

The balance sheet at the end of the 5 years is:

Plant assets	–0–	Owners' equity	–0–

This extreme example illustrates that depreciation in no way provides funds for the replacement of assets. **The funds for the replacement of the assets come from the revenues** (generated through use of the asset). Without the revenues, no income materializes and no cash inflow results. A separate decision must be made by management to set aside cash to accumulate asset replacement funds.

Revision of Depreciation Rates

When a plant asset is purchased, depreciation rates are carefully determined based on past experience with similar assets and other pertinent information. The provisions for depreciation are only estimates, however, and it may be necessary to revise them during the life of the asset. Unexpected physical deterioration or unforeseen obsolescence may make the useful life of the asset less than originally estimated. Improved maintenance procedures, revision of operating procedures, or similar developments may prolong the life of the asset beyond the expected period.[10]

For example, assume that machinery originally costing $90,000 is estimated to have a 20-year life with no salvage value. However, during year 11 it is estimated that the machine will be used an additional 20 years. Its total life, therefore, will be 30 years instead of 20. Depreciation has been recorded at the rate of 1/20 of $90,000, or $4,500 per year by the straight-line method. On the basis of a 30-year life, depreciation should have been 1/30 of $90,000, or $3,000 per year. Depreciation, therefore, has been overestimated, and net income has been understated by $1,500 for each of the past 10 years, or a total amount of $15,000. The amount of the difference can be computed as shown below.

ILLUSTRATION 11-13
Computation of Accumulated Difference Due to Revisions

	Per Year	For 10 Years
Depreciation charged per books (1/20 × $90,000)	$4,500	$45,000
Depreciation based on a 30-year life (1/30 × $90,000)	3,000	30,000
Excess depreciation charged	$1,500	$15,000

Changes in estimate should be handled in the current and prospective periods. No changes should be made in previously reported results. Opening balances are not adjusted, and no attempt is made to "catch up" for prior periods. The reason is that changes in estimates are a continual and inherent part of any estimation process. Continual restatement of prior periods would occur for revisions of estimates unless they are handled prospectively. Therefore, no entry is made at the time the change in estimate occurs, and charges for depreciation in subsequent periods (assuming use of the straight-line method) are based on **dividing the remaining book value less any salvage value by the remaining estimated life**.

ILLUSTRATION 11-14
Computing Depreciation after Revision of Estimated Life

Machinery	$90,000
Less: Accumulated depreciation	45,000
Book value of machinery at end of 10th year	$45,000

Depreciation (future periods) = $45,000 book value ÷ 20 years remaining life = $2,250

[10]As an example of a change in operating procedures, **General Motors** (GM) used to write off its tools—such as dies and equipment used to manufacture car bodies—over the life of the body type. Through this procedure, it expensed tools twice as fast as **Ford** and three times as fast as **DaimlerChrysler**. However, it slowed the depreciation process on these tools and lengthened the lives on its plant and equipment. These revisions had the effect of reducing depreciation and amortization charges by approximately $1.23 billion, or $2.55 per share, in the year of the change.

The entry to record depreciation for each of the remaining 20 years is:

Depreciation Expense	2,250	
Accumulated Depreciation—Machinery		2,250

WHAT DO THE NUMBERS MEAN?

DEPRECIATION CHOICES

The amount of depreciation expense recorded depends on both the depreciation method used and estimates of service lives and salvage values of the assets. Differences in these choices and estimates can have a significant impact on a company's reported results and can make it difficult to compare the depreciation numbers of different companies. For example, when **DuPont** switched its depreciation method from accelerated to straight-line, it reported a $250 million decrease in depreciation expense (and an increase in income) in the year of the change. And when **Willamette Industries** extended by 5 years the estimated service lives of its machinery and equipment, the effect on income was an increase of nearly $54 million.

An analyst can determine the impact of these management choices and judgments on the amount of depreciation expense by examining the notes to financial statements. For example, Willamette Industries provided the following note to its financial statements to explain the rationale for the change in estimated useful lives and to provide information that can be used to compare the useful lives of its assets to those of other companies.

Note 4: Property, Plant, and Equipment (partial)

	Range of useful lives
Land	—
Buildings	15–35
Machinery & equipment	5–25
Furniture & fixtures	3–15

In 1999, the estimated service lives for most machinery and equipment were extended five years. The change was based upon a study performed by the company's engineering department, comparisons to typical industry practices, and the effect of the company's extensive capital investments which have resulted in a mix of assets with longer productive lives due to technological advances. As a result of the change, 1999 net income was increased by $54,000,000.

IMPAIRMENTS

OBJECTIVE 5
Explain the accounting issues related to asset impairment.

The general accounting standard of **lower of cost or market for inventories does not apply to property, plant, and equipment**. Even when property, plant, and equipment has suffered partial obsolescence, accountants have been reluctant to reduce the carrying amount of the asset. This reluctance occurs because, unlike inventories, it is difficult to arrive at a fair value for property, plant, and equipment that is not subjective and arbitrary. For example, **Falconbridge Ltd. Nickel Mines** had to decide whether all or a part of its property, plant, and equipment in a nickel-mining operation in the Dominican Republic should be written off. The project had been incurring losses because nickel prices were low and operating costs were high. Only if nickel prices increased by approximately 33 percent would the project be reasonably profitable. Whether a write-off was appropriate depended on the future price of nickel. Even if the decision were made to write off the asset, another important question would be: How much should be written off?

Recognizing Impairments

As discussed in the opening story, a new standard on impairments of long-lived assets was recently issued.[11] In this standard, an **impairment** occurs when the carrying amount of an asset is not recoverable, and therefore a write-off is needed. Various events and changes in circumstances might lead to an impairment. Examples are:

a. A significant decrease in the market value of an asset.

b. A significant change in the extent or manner in which an asset is used.

c. A significant adverse change in legal factors or in the business climate that affects the value of an asset.

d. An accumulation of costs significantly in excess of the amount originally expected to acquire or construct an asset.

e. A projection or forecast that demonstrates continuing losses associated with an asset.

UNDERLYING CONCEPTS

The *going concern* concept assumes that the firm can recover the cost of the investment in its assets. Under GAAP the fair value of long-lived assets is not reported because a *going* concern does not plan to sell such assets. However, if the assumption of being able to recover the cost of the investment is not valid, then a reduction in value should be reported.

If these events or changes in circumstances indicate that the carrying amount of the asset may not be recoverable, a **recoverability test** is used to determine whether an impairment has occurred. To apply the first step of the recoverability test, you estimate the future net cash flows expected from the **use of that asset and its eventual disposition**. If the sum of the expected future net cash flows (undiscounted) is **less than the carrying amount** of the asset, the asset is considered impaired. Conversely, if the sum of the expected future net cash flows (undiscounted) is **equal to or greater than the carrying amount** of the asset, no impairment has occurred.

The recoverability test is a screening device to determine whether an impairment has occurred. For example, if the expected future net cash flows from an asset are $400,000 and its carrying amount is $350,000, no impairment has occurred. However, if the expected future net cash flows are $300,000, an impairment has occurred. The rationale for the recoverability test is the basic presumption that a balance sheet should report long-lived assets at no more than the carrying amounts that are recoverable.

Measuring Impairments

If the recoverability test indicates that an impairment has occurred, a loss is computed. **The impairment loss is the amount by which the carrying amount of the asset exceeds its fair value.** The fair value of an asset is measured by its market value if an active market for it exists. If no active market exists, the **present value of expected future net cash flows** should be used. To summarize, the process of determining an impairment loss is as follows.

1. Review events or changes in circumstances for possible impairment.
2. If the review indicates impairment, apply the recoverability test. If the sum of the expected future net cash flows from the long-lived asset is less than the carrying amount of the asset, an impairment has occurred.
3. Assuming an impairment, the impairment loss is the amount by which the carrying amount of the asset is greater than the fair value of the asset. The fair value is the market value or the present value.

[11] "Accounting for the Impairment or Disposal of Long-lived Assets," *Statement of Financial Accounting Standards No. 144* (Norwalk, Conn.: 2001).

Illustration One

M. Alou Inc. has an asset that, due to changes in its use, is reviewed for possible impairment. The asset's carrying amount is $600,000 ($800,000 cost less $200,000 accumulated depreciation). The expected future net cash flows (undiscounted) from the use of the asset and its eventual disposition are determined to be $650,000.

The recoverability test indicates that the $650,000 of expected future net cash flows from the asset's use exceed its carrying amount of $600,000. As a result, no impairment is assumed to have occurred. The undiscounted future net cash flows must be less than the carrying amount for an asset to be deemed impaired and for the impairment loss to be measured. Therefore, M. Alou Inc. will not recognize an impairment loss in this case.

Illustration Two

Assume the same facts as Illustration One, except that the expected future net cash flows from Alou's equipment are $580,000 (instead of $650,000). The recoverability test indicates that the expected future net cash flows of $580,000 from the use of the asset are less than its carrying amount of $600,000. Therefore an impairment has occurred. The difference between the carrying amount of Alou's asset and its fair value is the impairment loss. This asset has a market value of $525,000. The computation of the loss is:

ILLUSTRATION 11-15
Computation of Impairment Loss

Carrying amount of the equipment	$600,000
Fair value of equipment (market value)	525,000
Loss on impairment	$ 75,000

The entry to record the impairment loss is as follows.

Loss on Impairment	75,000	
Accumulated Depreciation		75,000

The impairment loss is reported as part of income from continuing operations, generally in the "Other expenses and losses" section. This loss should **not be reported as an extraordinary item**. Costs associated with an impairment loss are the same costs that would flow through operations and be reported as part of continuing operations. These assets will continue to be used in operations, and therefore the loss should not be reported below income from continuing operations.

A company that recognizes an impairment loss should disclose the asset(s) impaired, the events leading to the impairment, the amount of the loss, and how fair value was determined (disclosing the interest rate used, if appropriate).

U.S. oil companies are particularly affected by this new impairment standard because they now have to assess each of their producing fields on a case-by-case basis. In the past, oil fields were evaluated on a total company basis. **Texaco** (now **ChevronTexaco**), for instance, took a $640 million fourth-quarter charge at one time that swung a quarterly profit into a loss. Other oil company impairment charges in the same year were reported by **Mobil** (now **ExxonMobil**), $487 million, **Amoco** (now **BP PLC**), $380 million, **Ashland Inc.**, $90 million, and **Phillips Petroleum**, $49 million.

Restoration of Impairment Loss

Once an impairment loss is recorded, the reduced carrying amount of an asset held for use becomes its new cost basis. As a result, the new cost basis is not changed except for depreciation in future periods or for additional impairments. To illustrate, assume that Ortiz Company at December 31, 2003, has equipment with a carrying amount of $500,000, which is impaired and is written down to its fair value of $400,000. At the end of 2004, assume that the fair value of this asset is $480,000. The carrying amount of the asset should not change in 2004 except for the depreciation taken in 2004. **The impairment loss may not be restored for an asset held for use.** The rationale for not writing the asset up in value is that the new cost basis puts the impaired asset on an equal basis with other assets that are not impaired.

IMPAIRMENT, IMPAIRMENT EVERYWHERE

WHAT DO THE NUMBERS MEAN?

As shown below, companies reported significant impairments on long-lived assets in the late 1990s.

Company	Nature of Impairment	Amount
Hanneford Brothers Co.	Stores	$40 million
Sodak Gaming Inc.	Riverboat	6 million
Au Bon Pain Co.	Fixed assets of business unit to be sold	17.7 million
Ross Technologies	Subsidiary and other assets	11.2 million
Damark International	Computer software and hardware, and furniture and fixtures	10.2 million

Each of these write-offs is recorded in accordance with the impairment standard. For example, **Sodak Gaming Inc.** reported that its write-down on the Miss Marquette Riverboat was recorded after the company decided that this asset would not be as profitable as originally thought. Similarly, both **Au Bon Pain Co.** and **Ross Technologies** recorded impairments on assets in businesses that they were planning to sell. Before the new standard, companies generally waited to record impairments or write-downs until it was certain that the impairment was permanent. As a result, investors and creditors often learned too late that long-lived assets had declined in value.

INTERNATIONAL INSIGHT

International accounting standards permit write-ups for subsequent recoveries of impairment, whereas U.S. GAAP prohibits those write-ups, except for assets to be disposed of.

Assets to Be Disposed Of

What happens if the impaired asset is intended to be disposed of instead of held for use? In this case, the impaired asset is reported at the lower of cost or fair value less cost to sell (net realizable value). Because the asset is intended to be disposed of in a short period of time, net realizable value is used in order to provide a better measure of the net cash flows that will be received from this asset.

Assets that are being held for disposal are not depreciated during the period they are held. The rationale is that depreciation is inconsistent with the notion of assets to be disposed of and with the use of the lower of cost or net realizable value. In other words, **assets held for disposal are like inventory and should be reported at the lower of cost or net realizable value**.

Because assets held for disposal will be recovered through sale rather than through operations, they are continually revalued. They are reported each period at the lower of cost or net realizable value. Thus **an asset held for disposal can be written up or down in future periods, as long as the write-up is never to an amount greater than the carrying amount of the asset before the impairment**. Losses or gains related to these impaired assets should be reported as part of **income from continuing operations**. The disclosure requirements for these assets are complex; we leave that issue for an advanced course.

A summary of the key concepts in accounting for impairments is presented in Illustration 11-16.

ILLUSTRATION 11-16
Graphic of Accounting for Impairments

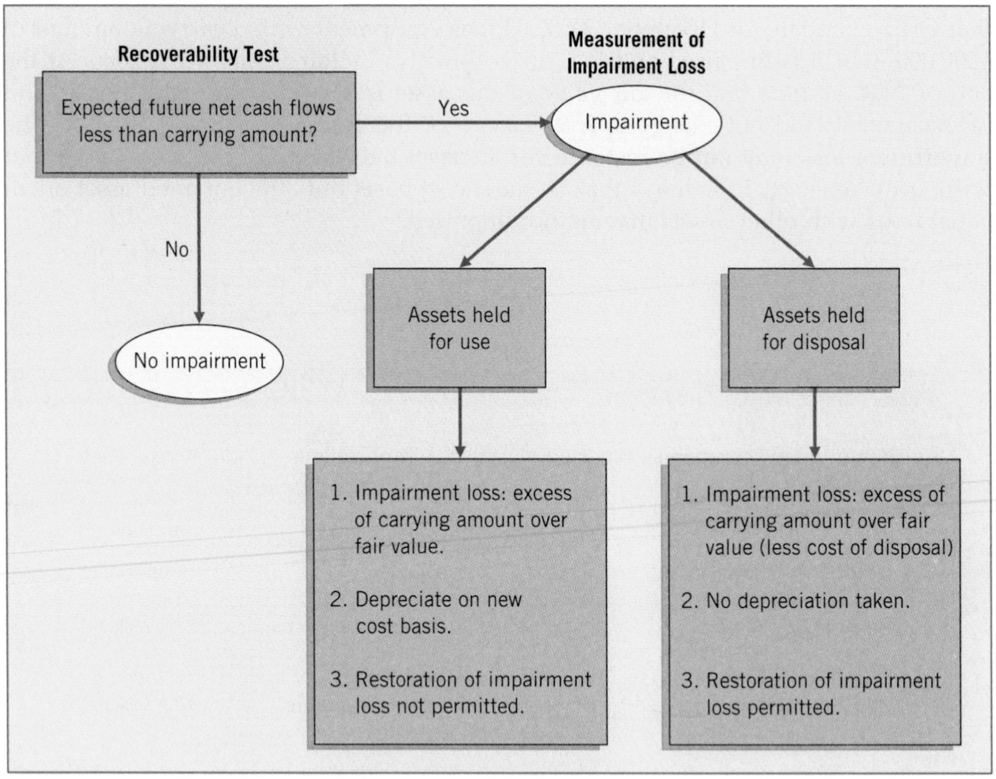

DEPLETION

OBJECTIVE 6
Explain the accounting procedures for depletion of natural resources.

Natural resources, often called wasting assets, include petroleum, minerals, and timber. They are characterized by two main features: (1) the complete removal (consumption) of the asset, and (2) replacement of the asset only by an act of nature. Unlike plant and equipment, natural resources are consumed physically over the period of use and do not maintain their physical characteristics. Still, the accounting problems associated with natural resources are similar to those encountered with fixed assets. The questions to be answered are:

1. How is the cost basis for write-off (depletion) established?
2. What pattern of allocation should be employed?

Establishing a Depletion Base

How do we determine the depletion base for natural resources? Sizable expenditures are needed to find these natural resources, and for every successful discovery there are many failures. Furthermore, long delays are encountered between the time the costs are incurred and the benefits are obtained from the extracted resources. As a result, a conservative policy frequently is adopted in accounting for the expenditures incurred in finding and extracting natural resources. The computation of the depletion base involves four factors: (1) acquisition cost of the deposit, (2) exploration costs, (3) development costs, and (4) restoration costs.

Acquisition Costs

Acquisition cost is the price paid to obtain the property right to search and find an undiscovered natural resource or the price paid for an already discovered resource. In some cases, property is leased and special royalty payments paid to the owner if a productive natural resource is found and is commercially profitable. Generally, the acquisition cost is placed in an account titled Undeveloped Property. That cost is assigned to the natural resource if exploration efforts are successful. If they are unsuccessful, the cost is written off as a loss.

Exploration Costs

As soon as a company has the right to use the property, **exploration costs** are often needed to find the resource. In most cases, these costs are expensed as incurred. When these costs are substantial and the risks of finding the resource uncertain (such as in the oil and gas industry), capitalization may occur. The unique issues related to the oil and gas industry are examined on page 538.

Development Costs

Development costs are divided into: (1) tangible equipment costs and (2) intangible development costs. Tangible equipment costs include all of the transportation and other heavy equipment necessary to extract the resource and get it ready for production or shipment. Because the asset can be moved from one drilling or mining site to another, **tangible equipment costs are normally not considered in the depletion base**. Instead, separate depreciation charges are employed. Tangible assets that cannot be moved should be depreciated over their useful life or the life of the resource, whichever is shorter.

Intangible development costs, on the other hand, are for such items as drilling costs, tunnels, shafts, and wells. These costs have no tangible characteristics but are needed for the production of the natural resource. **Intangible development costs are considered part of the depletion base.**

Restoration Costs

Companies sometimes incur substantial costs to restore property to its natural state after extraction has occurred. These **restoration costs** should be **added to the depletion base** for purposes of computing the depletion cost per unit. It follows that any salvage value received on the property should be deducted from the depletion base.

Write-Off of Resource Cost

As soon as the depletion base is established, the next problem is determining how the cost of the natural resource should be allocated to accounting periods. Normally, depletion is computed on the units of production method (activity approach). This means that depletion is a function of the number of units withdrawn during the period. In adopting this approach, the total cost of the natural resource less salvage value is divided by the number of units estimated to be in the resource deposit, to obtain a cost per unit of product. This cost per unit is multiplied by the number of units extracted to compute depletion.

For example, MaClede Co. has acquired the right to use 1,000 acres of land in Alaska to mine for gold. The lease cost is $50,000, and the related exploration costs on the property are $100,000. Intangible development costs incurred in opening the mine are $850,000. Total costs related to the mine before the first ounce of gold is extracted are, therefore, $1,000,000. MaClede estimates that the mine will provide approximately 100,000 ounces of gold. The depletion rate established is computed in the following manner.

ILLUSTRATION 11-17
Computation of Depletion Rate

$$\frac{\text{Total cost} - \text{Salvage value}}{\text{Total estimated units available}} = \text{Depletion cost per unit}$$

$$\frac{\$1{,}000{,}000}{100{,}000} = \$10 \text{ per ounce}$$

If 25,000 ounces are extracted in the first year, then the depletion for the year is $250,000 (25,000 ounces × $10). The entry to record the depletion is:

Inventory	250,000	
Accumulated Depletion		250,000

Inventory is first debited for the total depletion for the year, and then is credited for the cost of materials sold during the year. The amount not sold remains in inventory and is reported in the current assets section.

In some instances an Accumulated Depletion account is not used, and the credit goes directly to the natural resources asset account. The balance sheet presents the cost of the property and the amount of accumulated depletion entered to date as follows:

ILLUSTRATION 11-18
Balance Sheet Presentation of Natural Resource

Gold mine (at cost)	$1,000,000	
Less: Accumulated depletion	250,000	$750,000

In the income statement the depletion cost is part of the cost of goods sold.

The tangible equipment used in extracting the gold may also be depreciated on a units-of-production basis, especially if the estimated lives of the equipment can be directly assigned to one given resource deposit. If the equipment is used on more than one job, other cost allocation methods such as straight-line or accelerated depreciation methods would be more appropriate.

Continuing Controversy

A major controversy relates to the accounting for exploration costs in the oil and gas industry. Conceptually, the question is whether unsuccessful exploration costs are a cost of those that are successful. Some believe that unsuccessful ventures are a cost of those that are successful. This is called the **full cost concept**. Its rationale is that the cost of drilling a dry hole is a cost that is needed to find the commercially profitable wells. Others believe that only the costs of successful projects should be capitalized. This is the **successful efforts concept**. Its rationale is that an unsuccessful company will end up capitalizing many costs that will make it, over a short period of time, show no less income than does one that is successful.[12] In addition, in the view of successful efforts proponents, the only relevant measure for a single property unit is the cost directly related to that unit. The remainder of the costs should be reported as period charges.

The FASB has attempted to narrow the available alternatives but has met with little success. Here is a brief history of the debate.

1. **1977—The FASB issued *Statement No. 19*, which required oil and gas companies to follow successful efforts accounting.** However, after small oil and gas producers, voicing strong opposition, lobbied extensively in Congress, governmental agencies assessed the implications of this standard from a public interest perspective and reacted contrary to the FASB's position.[13]
2. **1978—In response to criticisms of the FASB's actions, the SEC reexamined the issue and found both the successful efforts and full cost approaches inadequate because neither reflects the economic substance of oil and gas exploration.** As a

[12]Large international oil companies such as **ExxonMobil** use the successful efforts approach. The full cost approach is used by most of the smaller, exploration-oriented companies. The differences in net income figures under the two methods can be staggering. It was estimated that the full cost approach used by **Texaco** (now **ChevronTexaco**) increased the company's reported profits by $500 million over a 10-year period.

[13]The Department of Energy indicated that companies using the full cost method at that time would reduce their exploration activities because of the unfavorable earnings impact associated with successful efforts accounting. The Justice Department asked the SEC to postpone adoption of one uniform method of accounting in the oil and gas industry until the SEC could determine whether the information reported to investors would be enhanced and competition constrained by adoption of the successful efforts method.

substitute, the SEC argued in favor of a yet-to-be developed method, **reserve recognition accounting (RRA)**, which it believed would provide more useful information. Under RRA, as soon as a company discovers oil, it reports the value of the oil on the balance sheet and in the income statement. Thus, RRA is a current value approach as opposed to full costing and successful efforts, which are historical cost approaches.[14]

3. **1979–1981—As a result of the SEC's actions, the FASB had no choice but to issue another standard that suspended the requirement that companies follow successful efforts accounting.** Therefore, full costing again became permissible. In attempting to implement RRA, however, the SEC encountered practical problems in estimating **(1) the amount of the reserves, (2) the future production costs, (3) the periods of expected disposal, (4) the discount rate, and (5) the selling price**. An estimate for each of these elements is necessary to arrive at an accurate valuation of existing oil or gas reserves. If the oil or gas reserves are not to be extracted and sold for several years, estimating the future selling price, the appropriate discount rate, and the future costs of extraction and delivery can each be a formidable task.
4. **1981—The SEC announced that it had abandoned RRA as a potential accounting recognition method in the primary financial statements of oil and gas producers.** Because of the inherent uncertainty of determining recoverable quantities of proved oil and gas reserves, the SEC indicated that RRA does not currently possess the required degree of reliability for use as a primary method of financial reporting. However, the SEC continued to stress that some form of value-based disclosure was needed for oil and gas reserves. As a result, the FASB issued *Statement No. 69*, "Disclosure about Oil and Gas Producing Activities," which requires current value disclosures.
5. **1986—One requirement of the full cost approach is that costs can be capitalized only up to a ceiling, the height of which is determined by the present value of company reserves.** Capitalized costs above that ceiling have to be expensed. In 1986 the price of oil plummeted, and a number of companies faced massive write-offs of their reserves as a result (because capitalized costs exceeded the present value of the companies' reserves). Companies lobbied for leniency, but the SEC decided that the write-offs had to be taken. **Mesa Limited Partnerships**' $31 million profit was restated to a $169 million loss, and **Pacific Lighting**'s $44.5 million profit was changed to a $70.5 million loss.

Currently, either the full cost approach or the successful efforts approach is acceptable. It does seem ironic that Congress directed the FASB to develop one method of accounting for the oil and gas industry, and when the FASB did so, the government chose not to accept it. Subsequently, the government (SEC) attempted to develop a new approach, failed, and then urged the FASB to develop the disclosure requirements in this area. After all these changes, alternatives still exist in the oil and gas industry.

This controversy in the oil and gas industry provides a number of lessons to the student in accounting. First, it demonstrates the strong influence that the federal government has in financial reporting matters. Second, the concern for economic consequences places considerable pressure on the FASB to weigh the economic effects of any required standard. Third, the experience with RRA highlights the problems that are encountered when a change from an historical cost to a current value approach is proposed. Fourth, this controversy illustrates the difficulty of establishing standards when affected groups have differing viewpoints. And finally, it reinforces the need for a conceptual framework with carefully developed guidelines for recognition, measurement, and reporting, so that issues of this nature hopefully may be more easily resolved in the future.

UNDERLYING CONCEPTS

Failure to consider the economic consequences of accounting principles is a frequent criticism of the profession. However, the neutrality concept requires that the statements be free from bias. Freedom from bias requires that the statements reflect economic reality, even if undesirable effects occur.

[14]The use of RRA would make a substantial difference in the balance sheets and income statements of oil companies. For example, **Atlantic Richfield Co.** at one time reported net producing property of $2.6 billion. If RRA were adopted, the same properties would be valued at $11.8 billion. Similarly, **Standard Oil of Ohio**, which reported net producing properties of $1.7 billion, would have reported approximately $10.7 billion under RRA.

Special Problems in Depletion Accounting

Accounting for natural resources has some interesting problems that are uncommon to most other types of assets. These problems are divided into four categories:

1. Difficulty of estimating recoverable reserves.
2. Problems of discovery value.
3. Tax aspects of natural resources.
4. Accounting for liquidating dividends.

Estimating Recoverable Reserves

Not infrequently the estimate of recoverable reserves has to be changed, either because new information has become available or because production processes have become more sophisticated. Natural resources such as oil and gas deposits and some rare metals have recently provided the greatest challenges. Estimates of these reserves are in large measure "knowledgeable guesses."

This problem is the **same as accounting for changes in estimates for the useful lives of plant and equipment**. The procedure is to revise the depletion rate on a **prospective basis** by dividing the remaining cost by the new estimate of the recoverable reserves. This approach has much merit because the required estimates are so tenuous.

Discovery Value

Discovery value accounting and reserve recognition accounting are similar. RRA is specifically related to the oil and gas industry, whereas **discovery value** is a broader term associated with the whole natural resources area. As indicated earlier, discovery values are presently not recognized. However, if discovery value were to be recorded, an asset account would be debited and an Unrealized Appreciation account would be credited. Unrealized Appreciation is part of stockholders' equity. Unrealized Appreciation would then be transferred to revenue as the natural resources are sold.

A similar issue arises with resources such as growing timber, aging liquor, and maturing livestock that increase in value over time. One method is to record the increase in value as the accretion occurs: Debit the asset account and credit revenue or an unrealized revenue account. These increases can be substantial. **Boise Cascade**'s timber resources were at one time valued at $1.7 billion, whereas its book value was approximately $289 million. Accountants have been hesitant to record these increases because of the uncertainty regarding the final sales price and the problem of estimating the costs involved in getting the resources ready for sale.

Tax Aspects of Natural Resources

The tax aspects of accounting for most natural resources have comprised some of the most controversial provisions of the Internal Revenue Code. The tax law has long provided a deduction for the greater of **cost** or **percentage depletion** against revenue from oil, gas, and most minerals. The percentage or statutory depletion allows a write-off ranging from 5 percent to 22 percent (depending on the natural resource) of gross revenue received. As a result, the amount of depletion may exceed the cost assigned to a given natural resource. An asset's carrying amount may be zero, but a depletion deduction may still be taken if the enterprise has gross revenue. The significance of the percentage depletion allowance is now greatly reduced because it has been repealed for most oil and gas companies and is of only limited use in most other situations.

Liquidating Dividends

A company often owns as its only major asset a certain property from which it intends to extract natural resources. If the company does not expect to purchase additional properties, it may distribute gradually to stockholders their capital investments by paying dividends greater than the amount of accumulated net income. The major accounting problem is to distinguish between dividends that are a return of capital and those that are not. The company issuing a **liquidating dividend** should debit Paid-in Capital in Excess of Par for that portion related to the original investment instead of Retained Earnings, because the dividend is a return of part of the investor's original contribution.

To illustrate, at year-end, Callahan Mining had a retained earnings balance of $1,650,000, accumulated depletion on mineral properties of $2,100,000, and paid-in capital in excess of par of $5,435,493. Callahan's board declared a dividend of $3 a share on the 1,000,000 shares outstanding. The entry to record the $3,000,000 cash dividend is as follows.

Retained Earnings	1,650,000	
Paid-in Capital in Excess of Par	1,350,000	
Cash		3,000,000

Stockholders must be informed that each $3 dividend per share represents a $1.65 ($1,650,000 ÷ 1,000,000 shares) per share return on investment and a $1.35 ($1,350,000 ÷ 1,000,000 shares) per share liquidating dividend.

PRESENTATION AND ANALYSIS

Presentation of Property, Plant, Equipment, and Natural Resources

OBJECTIVE 7
Explain how property, plant, equipment, and natural resources are reported and analyzed.

The basis of valuation—usually historical cost—for property, plant, equipment, and natural resources should be disclosed along with pledges, liens, and other commitments related to these assets. Any liability secured by property, plant, equipment, and natural resources should not be offset against these assets, but should be reported in the liabilities section. Property, plant, equipment, and natural resources not currently employed as producing assets in the business (such as idle facilities or land held as an investment) should be segregated from assets used in operations.

When assets are depreciated, a valuation account normally called Accumulated Depreciation is credited. The employment of an Accumulated Depreciation account permits the user of the financial statements to see the original cost of the asset and the amount of depreciation that has been charged to expense in past years. When assets are depleted, some companies use an Accumulated Depletion account. Many companies, however, simply credit the natural resource account directly. The rationale for this approach is that the natural resources are physically consumed and therefore direct reduction of the cost of the natural resources is appropriate.

Because of the significant impact on the financial statements of the depreciation method(s) used, the following disclosures should be made.

a. Depreciation expense for the period.
b. Balances of major classes of depreciable assets, by nature and function.
c. Accumulated depreciation, either by major classes of depreciable assets or in total.
d. A general description of the method or methods used in computing depreciation with respect to major classes of depreciable assets.[15]

For natural resources, special disclosure requirements relate to the oil and gas industry. Companies engaged in these activities must disclose the following in their financial statements: (1) the basic method of accounting for those costs incurred in oil and gas producing activities (e.g., full cost versus successful efforts), and (2) the man-

[15]"Omnibus Opinion—1967," *Opinions of the Accounting Principles Board No. 12* (New York: AICPA, 1967), par. 5. Some believe that the average useful life of the assets or the range of years for asset life is significant information that should be disclosed.

ner of disposing of costs relating to oil and gas producing activities (e.g., expensing immediately versus depreciation and depletion).[16]

The 2001 Annual Report of **Boise Cascade Corporation** in Illustration 11-19 represents an acceptable disclosure using condensed balance sheet data supplemented with details and policies in notes to the financial statements.

ILLUSTRATION 11-19
Disclosures for Property, Plant, Equipment, and Natural Resources

Boise Cascade Corporation

	2001	2000
	(expressed in thousands)	
Property		
Property and equipment		
Land and land improvements	$ 68,482	$ 70,551
Buildings and improvements	675,905	648,256
Machinery and equipment	4,606,102	4,447,628
	5,350,489	5,166,435
Accumulated depreciation	(2,742,650)	(2,584,784)
	2,607,839	2,581,651
Timber, timberlands, and timber deposits	322,132	291,132
	$2,929,971	$2,872,783

Notes to Financial Statements

Note 1 (in part): Summary of Significant Accounting Policies

Property. Property and equipment are recorded at cost. Cost includes expenditures for major improvements and replacements and the net amount of interest cost associated with significant capital additions. Capitalized interest was $1.9 million in 2001, $1.5 million in 2000, and $0.2 million in 1999. Gains and losses from sales and retirements are included in income as they occur. Most of our paper and wood products manufacturing facilities determine depreciation by the units-of-production method; other operations use the straight-line method.

Depreciation is computed over the following estimated useful lives:

Buildings and improvements	20 to 40 years
Furniture and fixtures	5 to 10 years
Machinery, equipment, and delivery trucks	4 to 20 years
Leasehold improvements	10 to 40 years

Timber and Timberlands. Timber and timberlands are stated at cost, less the accumulated cost of timber previously harvested. The vast majority of our timberlands are long-rotation, which have growing cycles averaging over 40 years. Capitalized costs for these timberlands include site preparation, seeding, and planting. Other costs, including thinning, fertilization, pest control, herbicide application, leases of timberland, property taxes, and interest costs, are expensed as incurred.

We acquire a portion of our wood requirements from outside sources. Except for deposits required pursuant to wood supply contracts, no amounts are recorded until we become obligated to purchase the timber. At December 31, 2001, based on average prices at the time, the unrecorded amount of those contracts was estimated to be approximately $29 million.

Additional Property, Plant, Equipment, and Natural Resources Disclosures

Analysis of Property, Plant, Equipment, and Natural Resources

Assets may be analyzed relative to activity (turnover) and profitability. How efficiently a company uses its assets to generate sales is measured by the **asset turnover ratio.** This ratio is determined by dividing net sales by average total assets for the period.

[16]Public companies, in addition to these two required disclosures, must include as supplementary information numerous schedules reporting reserve quantities; capitalized costs; acquisition, exploration, and development activities; and a standardized measure of discounted future net cash flows related to proved oil and gas reserve quantities. See "Disclosures about Oil and Gas Producing Activities," *Statement of Financial Accounting Standards Board No. 69* (Stamford, Conn.: FASB, 1982).

The resulting number is the dollars of sales produced by each dollar invested in assets. To illustrate, we will use the following data from the 2001 Annual Report of **Tootsie Roll Industries**.

Tootsie Roll Industries

	(in millions)
Net sales	$423.5
Total assets, 12/31/01	618.7
Total assets, 12/31/00	562.4
Net income	65.6

ILLUSTRATION 11-20
Asset Turnover Ratio

$$\text{Asset turnover} = \frac{\text{Net sales}}{\text{Average total assets}}$$
$$= \frac{\$423.5}{(\$618.7 + \$562.4)/2}$$
$$= 0.717$$

The asset turnover ratio shows that Tootsie Roll generated sales of $0.72 per dollar of assets in the year ended December 31, 2001.

Asset turnover ratios vary considerably among industries. For example, a large utility company like **Ameren U/E** has a ratio of 0.36 times, and a large grocery chain like **Atlantic and Pacific Tea** (A&P) has a ratio of 3.6 times.

Employment of the **profit margin on sales ratio** (rate of return on sales) in conjunction with the asset turnover ratio offers an interplay that leads to a **rate of return on total assets**. By using the Tootsie Roll Industries data shown above, the profit margin on sales ratio and the rate of return on total assets are computed as follows.

ILLUSTRATION 11-21
Profit Margin on Sales

$$\text{Profit margin on sales} = \frac{\text{Net income}}{\text{Net sales}}$$
$$= \frac{\$65.6}{\$423.5}$$
$$= 15.49\%$$
$$\text{Rate of return on total assets} = \text{Profit margin on sales} \times \text{Asset turnover}$$
$$= 15.49\% \times 0.717$$
$$= 11.11\%$$

The profit margin on sales ratio does not answer the question of how profitably a company uses its assets. But by relating the profit margin on sales to the asset turnover during a period of time, it is possible to ascertain how profitably the assets were used during that period of time.

The **rate of return on assets** (ROA) can be directly computed by dividing net income by average total assets. By using Tootsie Roll's data, the ratio is computed as follows.

ILLUSTRATION 11-22
Rate of Return on Assets

$$\text{Rate of return on assets} = \frac{\text{Net income}}{\text{Average total assets}}$$
$$= \frac{\$65.6}{(\$618.7 + \$562.4)/2}$$
$$= 11.11\%$$

The 11.11 percent rate of return computed in this manner is identical to the 11.11 percent rate computed by multiplying the profit margin on sales by the asset turnover. The rate of return on assets is a good measure of profitability because it combines the effects of profit margin and asset turnover.

SUMMARY OF LEARNING OBJECTIVES

KEY TERMS

accelerated depreciation methods, 524
activity method, 523
amortization, 520
asset turnover ratio, 542
composite approach, 526
composite depreciation rate, 526
declining-balance method, 525
decreasing-charge methods, 524
depletion, 520
depreciation, 520
development costs, 537
discovery value, 540
double-declining-balance method, 525
exploration costs, 537
full cost concept, 538
group method, 526
impairment, 533
inadequacy, 521
liquidating dividends, 541
natural resources, 536
obsolescence, 521
percentage depletion, 540
profit margin on sales ratio, 543
rate of return on assets (ROA), 543
recoverability test, 533
reserve recognition accounting (RRA), 539
restoration costs, 537
salvage value, 521
straight-line method, 524
successful efforts concept, 538
sum-of-the-years'-digits method, 525
supersession, 521

1 Explain the concept of depreciation. Depreciation is the accounting process of allocating the cost of tangible assets to expense in a systematic and rational manner to those periods expected to benefit from the use of the asset.

2 Identify the factors involved in the depreciation process. Three factors involved in the depreciation process are: (1) determining the depreciation base for the asset, (2) estimating service lives, and (3) selecting a method of cost apportionment (depreciation).

3 Compare activity, straight-line, and decreasing-charge methods of depreciation. (1) *Activity method*: Assumes that depreciation is a function of use or productivity instead of the passage of time. The life of the asset is considered in terms of either the output it provides or an input measure such as the number of hours it works. (2) *Straight-line method*: Considers depreciation a function of time instead of a function of usage. This method is widely employed in practice because of its simplicity. The straight-line procedure is often the most conceptually appropriate when the decline in usefulness is constant from period to period. (3) *Decreasing-charge methods*: Provide for a higher depreciation cost in the earlier years and lower charges in later periods. The main justification for this approach is that the asset suffers the greatest loss of services in those years.

4 Explain special depreciation methods. Two special depreciation methods are: (1) *Group and composite methods*: The term *group* refers to a collection of assets that are similar in nature; *composite* refers to a collection of assets that are dissimilar in nature. The group method is frequently used when the assets are fairly homogeneous and have approximately the same useful lives. The composite approach is used when the assets are heterogeneous and have different lives. (2) *Hybrid or combination methods*: A hybrid depreciation method widely used in the steel industry is a combination straight-line/activity approach referred to as the production variable method.

5 Explain the accounting issues related to asset impairment. The process to determine an impairment loss is as follows: (1) Review events and changes in circumstances for possible impairment. (2) If events or changes suggest impairment, determine if the sum of the expected future net cash flows from the long-lived asset is less than the carrying amount of the asset. If less, measure the impairment loss. (3) The impairment loss is the amount by which the carrying amount of the asset is greater than the fair value of the asset.

After an impairment loss is recorded, the reduced carrying amount of the long-lived asset is considered its new cost basis. Impairment losses may not be restored for assets held for use. If the asset is expected to be disposed of, the impaired asset should be reported at the lower of cost or net realizable value. It is not depreciated. It can be continuously revalued, as long as the write-up is never to an amount greater than the carrying amount before impairment.

6 Explain the accounting procedures for depletion of natural resources. The accounting procedures for depletion of natural resources are (1) establishing the depletion base, and (2) writing off resource cost. Four factors are involved in establishing the depletion base: (a) *acquisition costs*, (b) *exploration costs*, (c) *development costs*, and (d) *restoration costs*. To write off resource cost, depletion normally is computed on the units of production method. This means that depletion is a function of the number of units withdrawn during the period. In adopting this approach, the total cost of the natural resource less salvage value is divided by the number of units estimated to be in the resource deposit, to obtain a cost per unit of product. To compute depletion, this cost per unit is multiplied by the number of units withdrawn.

7 **Explain how property, plant, equipment, and natural resources are reported and analyzed.** The basis of valuation for property, plant, equipment and for natural resources should be disclosed along with pledges, liens, and other commitments related to these assets. Any liability secured by property, plant, equipment or by natural resources should not be offset against these assets, but should be reported in the liabilities section. When assets are depreciated, a valuation account normally called Accumulated Depreciation is credited. When assets are depleted, an accumulated depletion account may be used, or the depletion may be credited directly to the natural resource account. Companies engaged in significant oil and gas producing activities must provide special additional disclosures about these activities. Analysis may be performed to evaluate the asset turnover rate, the profit margin on sales, and the rate of return on assets.

APPENDIX 11A

Income Tax Depreciation

OBJECTIVE 8
Describe income tax methods of depreciation.

For the most part, issues related to the computation of income taxes are not discussed in a financial accounting course. However, because the concepts of tax depreciation are similar to those of book depreciation, and because tax depreciation methods are sometimes adopted for book purposes, an overview of this subject is presented.

Efforts to stimulate capital investment through faster write-offs and to bring more uniformity to the write-off period resulted in enactment of the Accelerated Cost Recovery System (ACRS) as part of the Economic Recovery Tax Act of 1981. For assets purchased in the years 1981 through 1986, ACRS and its preestablished "cost recovery periods" for various classes of assets are used.

A **Modified Accelerated Cost Recovery System**, known as **MACRS**, was enacted by Congress in the Tax Reform Act of 1986. It applies to depreciable assets placed in service in 1987 and later. The following discussion is based on these MACRS rules. Tax depreciation rules are subject to change annually.

MODIFIED ACCELERATED COST RECOVERY SYSTEM

The computation of depreciation under MACRS differs from the computation under GAAP in three respects: (1) a mandated tax life, which is generally shorter than the economic life; (2) cost recovery on an accelerated basis; and (3) an assigned salvage value of zero.

Tax Lives (Recovery Periods)

Each item of depreciable property is assigned to a property class. The recovery period (depreciable tax life) of an asset depends on the property class.[1] The MACRS property classes are presented in Illustration 11A-1.

[1]Tax depreciation changed numerous times in the 1980s and 1990s. For example, since 1980, six different depreciation requirements have been enacted. The tax life of certain real property has moved from 35 years in 1980 to 15 in 1981, 18 in 1982, 19 in 1984, 31.5 in 1986, and 39 in 1993. As one writer noted, "It appears that the useful life of a depreciation law is 2.2 years."

ILLUSTRATION 11A-1
MACRS Property Classes

3-year property—includes small tools, horses, and assets used in research and development activities
5-year property—includes automobiles, trucks, computers and peripheral equipment, and office machines
7-year property—includes office furniture and fixtures, agriculture equipment, oil exploration and development equipment, railroad track, manufacturing equipment, and any property not designated by law as being in any other class
10-year property—includes railroad tank cars, mobile homes, boilers, and certain public utility property
15-year property—includes roads, shrubbery, and certain low-income housing
20-year property—includes waste-water treatment plants and sewer systems
27.5-year property—includes residential rental property
39-year property—includes nonresidential real property

Tax Depreciation Methods

The depreciation expense is computed based on the tax basis—usually the cost—of the asset. The depreciation method depends on the life of the assets as mandated by the MACRS property class, as shown below.

ILLUSTRATION 11A-2
Depreciation Method for Various MACRS Property Classes

MACRS Property Class	Depreciation Method
3-, 5-, 7-, and 10-year property	Double-declining-balance
15- and 20-year property	150% declining-balance
27.5- and 39-year property	Straight-line

When one of the accelerated methods is used, a change is made to the straight-line method in the first year in which straight-line depreciation exceeds the accelerated depreciation. Depreciation computations for income tax purposes are based on the **half-year convention**. That is, a half year of depreciation is allowable in the year of acquisition and in the year of disposition.[2] An asset is depreciated to a zero value so that there is no salvage value at the end of its MACRS life.

The application of these depreciation methods is simplified by using IRS-published tables as shown in Illustration 11A-3 (page 547).

Illustration—MACRS System

To illustrate depreciation computations under both the MACRS system and GAAP straight-line accounting, assume the following facts for a computer and peripheral equipment purchased by Denise Rode Company on January 1, 2003.

Acquisition date	January 1, 2003
Cost	$100,000
Estimated useful life	7 years
Estimated salvage value	$16,000
MACRS class life	5 years
MACRS method	200% declining-balance
GAAP method	Straight-line
Disposal proceeds—January 2, 2010	$11,000

[2]Mid-quarter and mid-month conventions are required for MACRS purposes in certain circumstances.

ILLUSTRATION 11A-3
IRS Table of MACRS Depreciation Rates, by Property Class

MACRS Depreciation Rates by Class of Property						
Recovery Year	3-year (200% DB)	5-year (200% DB)	7-year (200% DB)	10-year (200% DB)	15-year (150% DB)	20-year (150% DB)
1	33.33	20.00	14.29	10.00	5.00	3.750
2	44.45	32.00	24.49	18.00	9.50	7.219
3	14.81*	19.20	17.49	14.40	8.55	6.677
4	7.41	11.52*	12.49	11.52	7.70	6.177
5		11.52	8.93*	9.22	6.93	5.713
6		5.76	8.92	7.37	6.23	5.285
7			8.93	6.55*	5.90*	4.888
8			4.46	6.55	5.90	4.522
9				6.56	5.91	4.462*
10				6.55	5.90	4.461
11				3.28	5.91	4.462
12					5.90	4.461
13					5.91	4.462
14					5.90	4.461
15					5.91	4.462
16					2.95	4.461
17						4.462
18						4.461
19						4.462
20						4.461
21						2.231

*Switchover to straight-line depreciation.

Using the rates from the MACRS depreciation rate schedule for a 5-year class of property, depreciation is computed as follows for tax purposes.

ILLUSTRATION 11A-4
Computation of MACRS Depreciation

MACRS Depreciation			
2003	$100,000 × .20	=	$ 20,000
2004	$100,000 × .32	=	32,000
2005	$100,000 × .192	=	19,200
2006	$100,000 × .1152	=	11,520
2007	$100,000 × .1152	=	11,520
2008	$100,000 × .0576	=	5,760
Total depreciation			$100,000

The depreciation under GAAP straight-line method with $16,000 of estimated salvage value and an estimated useful life of 7 years is computed as follows.

ILLUSTRATION 11A-5
Computation of GAAP Depreciation

GAAP Depreciation	
($100,000 − $16,000) ÷ 7 =	$12,000 annual depreciation
	× 7 years
1/1/03–1/2/10	$84,000 total depreciation

The MACRS depreciation recovers the total cost of the asset on an accelerated basis. But, a taxable gain of $11,000 results from the sale of the asset at January 2, 2010. Therefore, the net effect on taxable income for the years 2003 through 2010 is $89,000 ($100,000 depreciation − $11,000 gain).

Under GAAP, a loss on disposal of $5,000 ($16,000 book value − $11,000 disposal proceeds) is recognized. The net effect on income before income taxes for the years 2003 through 2010 is $89,000 ($84,000 depreciation + $5,000 loss), the same as the net effect of MACRS on taxable income.

Even though the net effects are equal in amount, the deferral of income tax payments under MACRS from early in the life of the asset to later in life is desirable when considering present value concepts. The different amounts of depreciation for income tax reporting and financial GAAP reporting in each year are a matter of timing and result in temporary differences, which require interperiod tax allocation. (See Chapter 19 for an extended treatment of this topic.)

Optional Straight-Line Method

An alternate MACRS method to determine depreciation deductions is based on the straight-line method. Often referred to as the **optional** (elective) **straight-line method**, it applies to the six classes of property described earlier. Under the alternate MACRS, the straight-line method is generally applied to the MACRS recovery periods. Salvage value is ignored. Under the optional straight-line method, in the first year the property is placed in service, half of the amount of depreciation that would be permitted for a full year is generally deducted (half-year convention). Use the half-year convention for homework problems.

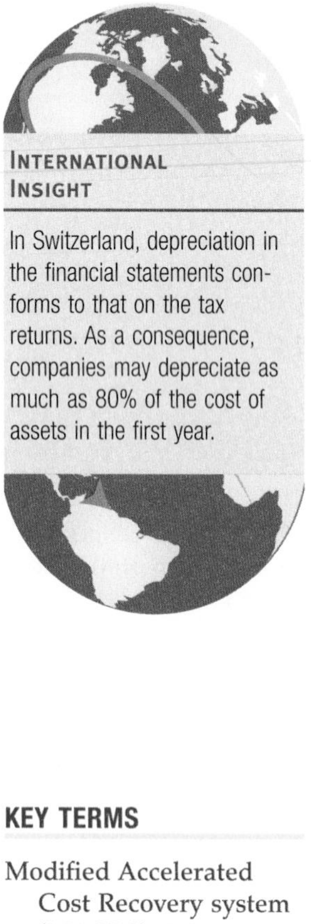

INTERNATIONAL INSIGHT

In Switzerland, depreciation in the financial statements conforms to that on the tax returns. As a consequence, companies may depreciate as much as 80% of the cost of assets in the first year.

Tax versus Book Depreciation

GAAP requires that the cost of depreciable assets be allocated to expense over the expected useful life of the asset in a systematic and rational manner. Some argue that from a cost-benefit perspective it would be better for companies to adopt the MACRS approach in order to eliminate the necessity of maintaining two different sets of records. However, the objectives of the tax laws and financial reporting are different. The purpose of taxation is to raise revenue from constituents in an equitable manner. The purpose of financial reporting is to reflect the economic substance of a transaction as closely as possible and to help predict the amounts, timing, and uncertainty of future cash flows. Because these objectives differ, the adoption of one method for both tax and book purposes in all cases would be unfortunate.

SUMMARY OF LEARNING OBJECTIVE FOR APPENDIX 11A

KEY TERMS

Modified Accelerated Cost Recovery system (MACRS), *545*

8 Describe income tax methods of depreciation. A Modified Accelerated Cost Recovery System (MACRS) was enacted by Congress in the Tax Reform Act of 1986. It applies to depreciable assets placed in service in 1987 and later. The computation of depreciation under MACRS differs from the computation under GAAP in three respects: (1) a mandated tax life, which is generally shorter than the economic life; (2) cost recovery on an accelerated basis; and (3) an assigned salvage value of zero.

Note: All **asterisked** Questions, Brief Exercises, Exercises, Problems, and Conceptual Cases relate to material contained in the appendix to the chapter.

QUESTIONS

1. Distinguish between depreciation, depletion, and amortization.
2. Identify the factors that are relevant in determining the annual depreciation charge, and explain whether these factors are determined objectively or whether they are based on judgment.
3. Some believe that accounting depreciation measures the decline in the value of fixed assets. Do you agree? Explain.
4. Explain how estimation of service lives can result in unrealistically high valuations of fixed assets.
5. The plant manager of a manufacturing firm suggested in a conference of the company's executives that accountants should speed up depreciation on the machinery in the finishing department because improvements were rapidly making those machines obsolete and a depreciation fund big enough to cover their replacement is needed. Discuss

the accounting concept of depreciation and the effect on a business concern of the depreciation recorded for plant assets, paying particular attention to the issues raised by the plant manager.

6. For what reasons are plant assets retired? Define inadequacy, supersession, and obsolescence.

7. What basic questions must be answered before the amount of the depreciation charge can be computed?

8. Elizabeth Ashley Company purchased a machine on January 2, 2003, for $600,000. The machine has an estimated useful life of 5 years and a salvage value of $100,000. Depreciation was computed by the 150% declining-balance method. What is the amount of accumulated depreciation at the end of December 31, 2004?

9. Linda Blair Company purchased machinery for $120,000 on January 1, 2004. It is estimated that the machinery will have a useful life of 20 years, scrap value of $15,000, production of 84,000 units, and working hours of 42,000. During 2004 the company uses the machinery for 14,300 hours, and the machinery produces 20,000 units. Compute depreciation under the straight-line, units-of-output, working-hours, sum-of-the-years'-digits, and declining-balance (use 10% as the annual rate) methods.

10. What are the major factors considered in determining what depreciation method to use?

11. Under what conditions is it appropriate for a business to use the composite method of depreciation for its plant assets? What are the advantages and disadvantages of this method?

12. If Ed Asner, Inc. uses the composite method and its composite rate is 7.5% per year, what entry should it make when plant assets that originally cost $50,000 and have been used for 10 years are sold for $16,000?

13. A building that was purchased December 31, 1979, for $2,400,000 was originally estimated to have a life of 50 years with no salvage value at the end of that time. Depreciation has been recorded through 2003. During 2004 an examination of the building by an engineering firm discloses that its estimated useful life is 15 years after 2003. What should be the amount of depreciation for 2004?

14. Armand Assante, president of Flatbush Company, has recently noted that depreciation increases cash provided by operations and therefore depreciation is a good source of funds. Do you agree? Discuss.

15. Melanie Mayron purchased a computer for $6,000 on July 1, 2004. She intends to depreciate it over 4 years using the double-declining balance method. Salvage value is $1,000. Compute depreciation for 2005.

16. Astaire Inc. is considering the write-down of its long-term plant because of a lack of profitability. Explain to the management of Astaire how to determine whether a write-off is permitted.

17. Last year Wilde Company recorded an impairment on an asset held for use. Recent appraisals indicate that the asset has increased in value. Should Wilde record this recovery in value?

18. Kuga Co. has equipment with a carrying amount of $700,000. The expected future net cash flows from the equipment are $705,000, and its fair value is $590,000. The equipment is expected to be used in operations in the future. What amount (if any) should Kuga report as an impairment to its equipment?

19. Explain how gains or losses on impaired assets should be reported in income.

20. It has been suggested that plant and equipment could be replaced more quickly if depreciation rates for income tax and accounting purposes were substantially increased. As a result, business operations would receive the benefit of more modern and more efficient plant facilities. Discuss the merits of this proposition.

21. Neither depreciation on replacement cost nor depreciation adjusted for changes in the purchasing power of the dollar has been recognized as generally accepted accounting principles for inclusion in the primary financial statements. Briefly present the accounting treatment that might be used to assist in the maintenance of the ability of a company to replace its productive capacity.

22. List (a) the similarities and (b) the differences in the accounting treatments of depreciation and cost depletion.

23. Describe cost depletion and percentage depletion. Why is the percentage depletion method permitted?

24. In what way may the use of percentage depletion violate sound accounting theory?

25. In the extractive industries, businesses may pay dividends in excess of net income. What is the maximum permissible? How can this practice be justified?

26. The following statement appeared in a financial magazine: "RRA—or Rah-Rah, as it's sometimes dubbed—has kicked up quite a storm. Oil companies, for example, are convinced that the approach is misleading. Major accounting firms agree." What is RRA? Why might oil companies believe that this approach is misleading?

27. Adriana Oil uses successful efforts accounting and also provides full-cost results as well. Under full-cost, Adriana Oil would have reported retained earnings of $42 million and net income of $4 million. Under successful efforts, retained earnings were $29 million, and net income was $3 million. Explain the difference between full costing and successful efforts accounting.

28. **Target Corporation** in 2001 reported net income of $1.4 billion, net sales of $39.2 billion, and average total assets of $21.8 billion. What is Target's asset turnover ratio? What is Target's rate of return on assets?

***29.** What is a modified accelerated cost recovery system (MACRS)? Speculate as to why this system is now required for tax purposes.

BRIEF EXERCISES

BE11-1 Castlevania Corporation purchased a truck at the beginning of 2004 for $42,000. The truck is estimated to have a salvage value of $2,000 and a useful life of 160,000 miles. It was driven 23,000 miles in 2004 and 31,000 miles in 2005. Compute depreciation expense for 2004 and 2005.

BE11-2 Cheetah Company purchased machinery on January 1, 2004, for $60,000. The machinery is estimated to have a salvage value of $6,000 after a useful life of 8 years. (a) Compute 2004 depreciation expense using the straight-line method. (b) Compute 2004 depreciation expense using the straight-line method assuming the machinery was purchased on September 1, 2004.

BE11-3 Use the information for Cheetah Company given in BE11-2. (a) Compute 2004 depreciation expense using the sum-of-the-years'-digits method. (b) Compute 2004 depreciation expense using the sum-of-the-years'-digits method assuming the machinery was purchased on April 1, 2004.

BE11-4 Use the information for Cheetah Company given in BE11-2. (a) Compute 2004 depreciation expense using the double-declining balance method. (b) Compute 2004 depreciation expense using the double-declining balance method assuming the machinery was purchased on October 1, 2004.

BE11-5 Garfield Company purchased a machine on July 1, 2005, for $25,000. Garfield paid $200 in title fees and county property tax of $125 on the machine. In addition, Garfield paid $500 shipping charges for delivery, and $475 was paid to a local contractor to build and wire a platform for the machine on the plant floor. The machine has an estimated useful life of 6 years with a scrap value of $3,000. Determine the depreciation base of Garfield's new machine. Garfield uses straight-line depreciation.

BE11-6 Battlesport Inc. owns the following assets.

Asset	Cost	Salvage	Estimated Useful Life
A	$70,000	$ 7,000	10 years
B	50,000	10,000	5 years
C	82,000	4,000	12 years

Compute the composite depreciation rate and the composite life of Battlesport's assets.

BE11-7 Myst Company purchased a computer for $7,000 on January 1, 2003. Straight-line depreciation is used, based on a 5-year life and a $1,000 salvage value. In 2005, the estimates are revised. Myst now feels the computer will be used until December 31, 2006, when it can be sold for $500. Compute the 2005 depreciation.

BE11-8 Dinoland Company owns machinery that cost $900,000 and has accumulated depreciation of $360,000. The expected future net cash flows from the use of the asset are expected to be $500,000. The fair value of the equipment is $400,000. Prepare the journal entry, if any, to record the impairment loss.

BE11-9 Genghis Khan Corporation acquires a coal mine at a cost of $400,000. Intangible development costs total $100,000. After extraction has occurred, $75,000 will be spent to restore the property, after which it can be sold for $160,000. Khan estimates that 4,000 tons of coal can be extracted. If 700 tons are extracted the first year, prepare the journal entry to record depletion.

BE11-10 In its 2001 Annual Report **Campbell Soup Company** reports beginning-of-the-year total assets of $5,196 million, end-of-the-year total assets of $5,927 million, total sales of $6,664 million, and net income of $649 million. (a) Compute Campbell's asset turnover ratio. (b) Compute Campbell's profit margin on sales. (c) Compute Campbell's rate of return on assets (1) using asset turnover and profit margin and (2) using net income.

***BE11-11** Timecap Corporation purchased an asset at a cost of $40,000 on March 1, 2005. The asset has a useful life of 8 years and a salvage value of $4,000. For tax purposes, the MACRS class life is 5 years. Compute tax depreciation for each year 2005–2010.

EXERCISES

E11-1 (Depreciation Computations—SL, SYD, DDB) Deluxe Ezra Company purchases equipment on January 1, Year 1, at a cost of $469,000. The asset is expected to have a service life of 12 years and a salvage value of $40,000.

Instructions

(a) Compute the amount of depreciation for each of Years 1 through 3 using the straight-line depreciation method.

(b) Compute the amount of depreciation for each of Years 1 through 3 using the sum-of-the-years'-digits method.

(c) Compute the amount of depreciation for each of Years 1 through 3 using the double-declining balance method. (In performing your calculations, round constant percentage to the nearest one-hundredth of a point and round answers to the nearest dollar.)

E11-2 (Depreciation—Conceptual Understanding) Rembrandt Company acquired a plant asset at the beginning of Year 1. The asset has an estimated service life of 5 years. An employee has prepared depreciation schedules for this asset using three different methods to compare the results of using one method with the results of using other methods. You are to assume that the following schedules have been correctly prepared for this asset using (1) the straight-line method, (2) the sum-of-the-years'-digits method, and (3) the double-declining balance method.

Year	Straight-Line	Sum-of-the-Years'-Digits	Double-Declining Balance
1	$ 9,000	$15,000	$20,000
2	9,000	12,000	12,000
3	9,000	9,000	7,200
4	9,000	6,000	4,320
5	9,000	3,000	1,480
Total	$45,000	$45,000	$45,000

Instructions

Answer the following questions.

(a) What is the cost of the asset being depreciated?

(b) What amount, if any, was used in the depreciation calculations for the salvage value for this asset?

(c) Which method will produce the highest charge to income in Year 1?

(d) Which method will produce the highest charge to income in Year 4?

(e) Which method will produce the highest book value for the asset at the end of Year 3?

(f) If the asset is sold at the end of Year 3, which method would yield the highest gain (or lowest loss) on disposal of the asset?

E11-3 (Depreciation Computations—SYD, DDB—Partial Periods) Judds Company purchased a new plant asset on April 1, 2004, at a cost of $711,000. It was estimated to have a service life of 20 years and a salvage value of $60,000. Judds' accounting period is the calendar year.

Instructions

(a) Compute the depreciation for this asset for 2004 and 2005 using the sum-of-the-years'-digits method.

(b) Compute the depreciation for this asset for 2004 and 2005 using the double-declining balance method.

E11-4 (Depreciation Computations—Five Methods) Jon Seceda Furnace Corp. purchased machinery for $315,000 on May 1, 2004. It is estimated that it will have a useful life of 10 years, scrap value of $15,000, production of 240,000 units, and working hours of 25,000. During 2005 Seceda Corp. uses the machinery for 2,650 hours, and the machinery produces 25,500 units.

Instructions

From the information given, compute the depreciation charge for 2005 under each of the following methods. (Round to three decimal places.)

(a) Straight-line.

(b) Units-of-output.

(c) Working hours.

(d) Sum-of-the-years'-digits.

(e) Declining-balance (use 20% as the annual rate).

E11-5 (Depreciation Computations—Four Methods) Robert Parish Corporation purchased a new machine for its assembly process on August 1, 2004. The cost of this machine was $117,900. The company estimated that the machine would have a trade-in value of $12,900 at the end of its service life. Its life is estimated at 5 years and its working hours are estimated at 21,000 hours. Year-end is December 31.

Instructions

Compute the depreciation expense under the following methods. Each of the following should be considered unrelated.

(a) Straight-line depreciation for 2004.
(b) Activity method for 2004, assuming that machine usage was 800 hours.
(c) Sum-of-the-years'-digits for 2005.
(d) Double-declining balance for 2005.

E11-6 (Depreciation Computations—Five Methods, Partial Periods) Muggsy Bogues Company purchased equipment for $212,000 on October 1, 2003. It is estimated that the equipment will have a useful life of 8 years and a salvage value of $12,000. Estimated production is 40,000 units and estimated working hours 20,000. During 2003, Bogues uses the equipment for 525 hours and the equipment produces 1,000 units.

Instructions

Compute depreciation expense under each of the following methods. Bogues is on a calendar-year basis ending December 31.

(a) Straight-line method for 2003.
(b) Activity method (units of output) for 2003.
(c) Activity method (working hours) for 2003.
(d) Sum-of-the-years'-digits method for 2005.
(e) Double-declining balance method for 2004.

E11-7 (Different Methods of Depreciation) Jackel Industries presents you with the following information.

Description	Date Purchased	Cost	Salvage Value	Life in Years	Depreciation Method	Accumulated Depreciation to 12/31/04	Depreciation for 2005
Machine A	2/12/03	$142,500	$16,000	10	**(a)**	$33,350	**(b)**
Machine B	8/15/02	**(c)**	21,000	5	SL	29,000	**(d)**
Machine C	7/21/01	75,400	23,500	8	DDB	**(e)**	**(f)**
Machine D	10/12/**(g)**	219,000	69,000	5	SYD	70,000	**(h)**

Instructions

Complete the table for the year ended December 31, 2005. The company depreciates all assets using the half-year convention.

E11-8 (Depreciation Computation—Replacement, Nonmonetary Exchange) George Zidek Corporation bought a machine on June 1, 2002, for $31,000, f.o.b. the place of manufacture. Freight to the point where it was set up was $200, and $500 was expended to install it. The machine's useful life was estimated at 10 years, with a scrap value of $2,500. On June 1, 2003, an essential part of the machine is replaced, at a cost of $1,980, with one designed to reduce the cost of operating the machine.

On June 1, 2006, the company buys a new machine of greater capacity for $35,000, delivered, trading in the old machine which has a fair market value and trade-in allowance of $20,000. To prepare the old machine for removal from the plant cost $75, and expenditures to install the new one were $1,500. It is estimated that the new machine has a useful life of 10 years, with a scrap value of $4,000 at the end of that time.

Instructions

Assuming that depreciation is to be computed on the straight-line basis, compute the annual depreciation on the new equipment that should be provided for the fiscal year beginning June 1, 2006. (Round to the nearest dollar.)

E11-9 (Composite Depreciation) Presented below is information related to Dell Curry Manufacturing Corporation.

Asset	Cost	Estimated Scrap	Estimated Life (in years)
A	$40,500	$5,500	10
B	33,600	4,800	9
C	36,000	3,600	9
D	19,000	1,500	7
E	23,500	2,500	6

Instructions

(a) Compute the rate of depreciation per year to be applied to the plant assets under the composite method.

(b) Prepare the adjusting entry necessary at the end of the year to record depreciation for the year.
(c) Prepare the entry to record the sale of fixed asset D for cash of $4,800. It was used for 6 years, and depreciation was entered under the composite method.

E11-10 (Depreciation Computations, SYD) The Five Satins Company purchased a piece of equipment at the beginning of 2001. The equipment cost $430,000. It has an estimated service life of 8 years and an expected salvage value of $70,000. The sum-of-the-years'-digits method of depreciation is being used. Someone has already correctly prepared a depreciation schedule for this asset. This schedule shows that $60,000 will be depreciated for a particular calendar year.

Instructions

Show calculations to determine for what particular year the depreciation amount for this asset will be $60,000.

E11-11 (Depreciation—Change in Estimate) Machinery purchased for $60,000 by Joe Montana Co. in 2000 was originally estimated to have a life of 8 years with a salvage value of $4,000 at the end of that time. Depreciation has been entered for 5 years on this basis. In 2005, it is determined that the total estimated life (including 2005) should be 10 years with a salvage value of $4,500 at the end of that time. Assume straight-line depreciation.

Instructions

(a) Prepare the entry to correct the prior years' depreciation, if necessary.
(b) Prepare the entry to record depreciation for 2005.

E11-12 (Depreciation Computation—Addition, Change in Estimate) In 1977, Herman Moore Company completed the construction of a building at a cost of $2,000,000 and first occupied it in January 1978. It was estimated that the building will have a useful life of 40 years and a salvage value of $60,000 at the end of that time.

Early in 1988, an addition to the building was constructed at a cost of $500,000. At that time it was estimated that the remaining life of the building would be, as originally estimated, an additional 30 years, and that the addition would have a life of 30 years, and a salvage value of $20,000.

In 2006, it is determined that the probable life of the building and addition will extend to the end of 2037 or 20 years beyond the original estimate.

Instructions

(a) Using the straight-line method, compute the annual depreciation that would have been charged from 1978 through 1987.
(b) Compute the annual depreciation that would have been charged from 1988 through 2005.
(c) Prepare the entry, if necessary, to adjust the account balances because of the revision of the estimated life in 2006.
(d) Compute the annual depreciation to be charged beginning with 2006.

E11-13 (Depreciation—Replacement, Change in Estimate) Orel Hershiser Company constructed a building at a cost of $2,200,000 and occupied it beginning in January 1985. It was estimated at that time that its life would be 40 years, with no salvage value.

In January 2005, a new roof was installed at a cost of $300,000, and it was estimated then that the building would have a useful life of 25 years from that date. The cost of the old roof was $160,000.

Instructions

(a) What amount of depreciation should have been charged annually from the years 1985 to 2004? (Assume straight-line depreciation.)
(b) What entry should be made in 2005 to record the replacement of the roof?
(c) Prepare the entry in January 2005, to record the revision in the estimated life of the building, if necessary.
(d) What amount of depreciation should be charged for the year 2005?

E11-14 (Error Analysis and Depreciation, SL and SYD) Mike Devereaux Company shows the following entries in its Equipment account for 2005. All amounts are based on historical cost.

Equipment

2005			2005		
Jan. 1	Balance	134,750	June 30	Cost of equipment sold (purchased prior to 2005)	23,000
Aug. 10	Purchases	32,000			
12	Freight on equipment purchased	700			
25	Installation costs	2,700			
Nov. 10	Repairs	500			

Instructions

(a) Prepare any correcting entries necessary.

(b) Assuming that depreciation is to be charged for a full year on the ending balance in the asset account, compute the proper depreciation charge for 2005 under each of the methods listed below. Assume an estimated life of 10 years, with no salvage value. The machinery included in the January 1, 2005, balance was purchased in 2003.

(1) Straight-line.

(2) Sum-of-the-years'-digits.

E11-15 (Depreciation for Fractional Periods) On March 10, 2006, Lost World Company sells equipment that it purchased for $192,000 on August 20, 1999. It was originally estimated that the equipment would have a life of 12 years and a scrap value of $16,800 at the end of that time, and depreciation has been computed on that basis. The company uses the straight-line method of depreciation.

Instructions

(a) Compute the depreciation charge on this equipment for 1999, for 2006, and the total charge for the period from 2000 to 2005, inclusive, under each of the six following assumptions with respect to partial periods.

(1) Depreciation is computed for the exact period of time during which the asset is owned. (Use 365 days for base.)

(2) Depreciation is computed for the full year on the January 1 balance in the asset account.

(3) Depreciation is computed for the full year on the December 31 balance in the asset account.

(4) Depreciation for one-half year is charged on plant assets acquired or disposed of during the year.

(5) Depreciation is computed on additions from the beginning of the month following acquisition and on disposals to the beginning of the month following disposal.

(6) Depreciation is computed for a full period on all assets in use for over one-half year, and no depreciation is charged on assets in use for less than one-half year. (Use 365 days for base.)

(b) Briefly evaluate the methods above, considering them from the point of view of basic accounting theory as well as simplicity of application.

E11-16 (Impairment) Presented below is information related to equipment owned by Suarez Company at December 31, 2004.

Cost	$9,000,000
Accumulated depreciation to date	1,000,000
Expected future net cash flows	7,000,000
Fair value	4,800,000

Assume that Suarez will continue to use this asset in the future. As of December 31, 2004, the equipment has a remaining useful life of 4 years.

Instructions

(a) Prepare the journal entry (if any) to record the impairment of the asset at December 31, 2004.

(b) Prepare the journal entry to record depreciation expense for 2005.

(c) The fair value of the equipment at December 31, 2005, is $5,100,000. Prepare the journal entry (if any) necessary to record this increase in fair value.

E11-17 (Impairment) Assume the same information as E11-16, except that Suarez intends to dispose of the equipment in the coming year. It is expected that the cost of disposal will be $20,000.

Instructions

(a) Prepare the journal entry (if any) to record the impairment of the asset at December 31, 2004.

(b) Prepare the journal entry (if any) to record depreciation expense for 2005.

(c) The asset was not sold by December 31, 2005. The fair value of the equipment on that date is $5,300,000. Prepare the journal entry (if any) necessary to record this increase in fair value. It is expected that the cost of disposal is still $20,000.

E11-18 (Impairment) The management of Luis Andujar Inc. was discussing whether certain equipment should be written off as a charge to current operations because of obsolescence. This equipment has a cost of $900,000 with depreciation to date of $400,000 as of December 31, 2004. On December 31, 2004, management projected its future net cash flows from this equipment to be $300,000 and its fair value to be $230,000. The company intends to use this equipment in the future.

Instructions

(a) Prepare the journal entry (if any) to record the impairment at December 31, 2004.

(b) Where should the gain or loss (if any) on the write-down be reported in the income statement?

(c) At December 31, 2005, the equipment's fair value increased to $260,000. Prepare the journal entry (if any) to record this increase in fair value.
(d) What accounting issues did management face in accounting for this impairment?

E11-19 (Depletion Computations—Timber) Stanislaw Timber Company owns 9,000 acres of timberland purchased in 1993 at a cost of $1,400 per acre. At the time of purchase the land without the timber was valued at $400 per acre. In 1994, Stanislaw built fire lands and roads, with a life of 30 years, at a cost of $84,000. Every year Stanislaw sprays to prevent disease at a cost of $3,000 per year and spends $7,000 to maintain the fire lanes and roads. During 1995, Stanislaw selectively logged and sold 700,000 board feet of timber, of the estimated 3,500,000 board feet. In 1996, Stanislaw planted new seedlings to replace the trees cut at a cost of $100,000.

Instructions

(a) Determine the depreciation expense and the cost of timber sold related to depletion for 1995.
(b) Stanislaw has not logged since 1995. If Stanislaw logged and sold 900,000 board feet of timber in 2006, when the timber cruise (appraiser) estimated 5,000,000 board feet, determine the cost of timber sold related to depletion for 2006.

E11-20 (Depletion Computations—Oil) Diderot Drilling Company has leased property on which oil has been discovered. Wells on this property produced 18,000 barrels of oil during the past year that sold at an average sales price of $15 per barrel. Total oil resources of this property are estimated to be 250,000 barrels.

The lease provided for an outright payment of $500,000 to the lessor before drilling could be commenced and an annual rental of $31,500. A premium of 5% of the sales price of every barrel of oil removed is to be paid annually to the lessor. In addition, the lessee is to clean up all the waste and debris from drilling and to bear the costs of reconditioning the land for farming when the wells are abandoned. It is estimated that this clean-up and reconditioning will cost $30,000.

Instructions

From the provisions of the lease agreement, you are to compute the cost per barrel for the past year, exclusive of operating costs, to Diderot Drilling Company.

E11-21 (Depletion Computations—Timber) Forda Lumber Company owns a 7,000-acre tract of timber purchased in 1997 at a cost of $1,300 per acre. At the time of purchase the land was estimated to have a value of $300 per acre without the timber. Forda Lumber Company has not logged this tract since it was purchased. In 2004, Forda had the timber cruised. The cruise (appraiser) estimated that each acre contained 8,000 board feet of timber. In 2004, Forda built 10 miles of roads at a cost of $7,840 per mile. After the roads were completed, Forda logged and sold 3,500 trees containing 850,000 board feet.

Instructions

(a) Determine the cost of timber sold related to depletion for 2004.
(b) If Forda depreciates the logging roads on the basis of timber cut, determine the depreciation expense for 2004.
(c) If Forda plants five seedlings at a cost of $4 per seedling for each tree cut, how should Forda treat the reforestation?

E11-22 (Depletion Computations—Mining) Alcide Mining Company purchased land on February 1, 2004, at a cost of $1,190,000. It estimated that a total of 60,000 tons of mineral was available for mining. After it has removed all the natural resources, the company will be required to restore the property to its previous state because of strict environmental protection laws. It estimates the cost of this restoration at $90,000. It believes it will be able to sell the property afterwards for $100,000. It incurred developmental costs of $200,000 before it was able to do any mining. In 2004 resources removed totaled 30,000 tons. The company sold 22,000 tons.

Instructions

Compute the following information for 2004.

(a) Per unit material cost.
(b) Total material cost of December 31, 2004, inventory.
(c) Total materials cost in cost of goods sold at December 31, 2004.

E11-23 (Depletion Computations—Minerals) At the beginning of 2004, Aristotle Company acquired a mine for $970,000. Of this amount, $100,000 was ascribed to the land value and the remaining portion to the minerals in the mine. Surveys conducted by geologists have indicated that approximately 12,000,000 units of the ore appear to be in the mine. Aristotle incurred $170,000 of development costs associated with this mine prior to any extraction of minerals and estimates that it will require $40,000 to prepare the land for an alternative use when all of the mineral has been removed. During 2004, 2,500,000 units of ore were extracted and 2,100,000 of these units were sold.

Instructions

Compute the following.

(a) The total amount of depletion of 2004.

(b) The amount that is charged as an expense for 2004 for the cost of the minerals sold during 2004.

E11-24 (Ratio Analysis) The 2001 Annual Report of **Eastman Kodak** contains the following information.

(in millions)	December 31, 2001	December 31, 2000
Total assets	$13,362	$14,212
Total liabilities	10,468	10,784
Net sales	13,234	13,994
Net income	76	1,407

Instructions

Compute the following ratios for Eastman Kodak for 2001.

(a) Asset turnover ratio.

(b) Rate of return on assets.

(c) Profit margin on sales.

(d) How can the asset turnover ratio be used to compute the rate of return on assets?

***E11-25 (Book vs. Tax (MACRS) Depreciation)** Futabatei Enterprises purchased a delivery truck on January 1, 2004, at a cost of $27,000. The truck has a useful life of 7 years with an estimated salvage value of $6,000. The straight-line method is used for book purposes. For tax purposes the truck, having an MACRS class life of 7 years, is classified as 5-year property; the optional MACRS tax rate tables are used to compute depreciation. In addition, assume that for 2004 and 2005 the company has revenues of $200,000 and operating expenses (excluding depreciation) of $130,000.

Instructions

(a) Prepare income statements for 2004 and 2005. (The final amount reported on the income statement should be income before income taxes.)

(b) Compute taxable income for 2004 and 2005.

(c) Determine the total depreciation to be taken over the useful life of the delivery truck for both book and tax purposes.

(d) Explain why depreciation for book and tax purposes will generally be different over the useful life of a depreciable asset.

***E11-26 (Book vs. Tax (MACRS) Depreciation)** Shimei Inc. purchased computer equipment on March 1, 2004, for $31,000. The computer equipment has a useful life of 10 years and a salvage value of $1,000. For tax purposes, the MACRS class life is 5 years.

Instructions

(a) Assuming that the company uses the straight-line method for book and tax purposes, what is the depreciation expense reported in (1) the financial statements for 2004 and (2) the tax return for 2004?

(b) Assuming that the company uses the double-declining balance method for both book and tax purposes, what is the depreciation expense reported in (1) the financial statements for 2004 and (2) the tax return for 2004?

(c) Why is depreciation for tax purposes different from depreciation for book purposes even if the company uses the same depreciation method to compute them both?

PROBLEMS

P11-1 (Depreciation for Partial Period—SL, SYD, and DDB) Onassis Company purchased Machine #201 on May 1, 2004. The following information relating to Machine #201 was gathered at the end of May.

Price	$73,500
Credit terms	2/10, n/30
Freight-in costs	$ 970
Preparation and installation costs	$ 3,800
Labor costs during regular production operations	$10,500

It was expected that the machine could be used for 10 years, after which the salvage value would be zero. Onassis intends to use the machine for only 8 years, however, after which it expects to be able to sell it for $1,200. The invoice for Machine #201 was paid May 5, 2004. Onassis uses the calendar year as the basis for the preparation of financial statements.

Instructions

(a) Compute the depreciation expense for the years indicated using the following methods. (Round to the nearest dollar.)
  (1) Straight-line method for 2004.
  (2) Sum-of-the-years'-digits method for 2005.
  (3) Double-declining balance method for 2004.

(b) Suppose Jackie Ari, the president of Onassis, tells you that because the company is a new organization, she expects it will be several years before production and sales reach optimum levels. She asks you to recommend a depreciation method that will allocate less of the company's depreciation expense to the early years and more to later years of the assets' lives. What method would you recommend?

P11-2 (Depreciation for Partial Periods—SL, Act., SYD, and DDB) The cost of equipment purchased by Boris Becker, Inc., on June 1, 2004 is $67,000. It is estimated that the machine will have a $4,000 salvage value at the end of its service life. Its service life is estimated at 7 years; its total working hours are estimated at 42,000 and its total production is estimated at 525,000 units. During 2004 the machine was operated 6,000 hours and produced 55,000 units. During 2005 the machine was operated 5,500 hours and produced 48,000 units.

Instructions

Compute depreciation expense on the machine for the year ending December 31, 2004, and the year ending December 31, 2005, using the following methods.

(a) Straight-line.
(b) Units-of-output.
(c) Working hours.
(d) Sum-of-the-years'-digits.
(e) Declining balance (twice the straight-line rate).

P11-3 (Depreciation—SYD, Act., SL, and DDB) The following data relate to the Plant Assets account of Arthur Fiedler, Inc. at December 31, 2004.

Plant Assets

	A	B	C	D
Original cost	$35,000	$51,000	$80,000	$80,000
Year purchased	1999	2000	2001	2003
Useful life	10 years	15,000 hours	15 years	10 years
Salvage value	$ 3,100	$ 3,000	$ 5,000	$ 5,000
Depreciation method	Sum-of-the-years'-digits	Activity	Straight-line	Double-declining balance
Accum. Depr. through 2004*	$23,200	$35,200	$15,000	$16,000

*In the year an asset is purchased, Fiedler, Inc. does not record any depreciation expense on the asset. In the year an asset is retired or traded in, Fiedler, Inc. takes a full year's depreciation on the asset.

The following transactions occurred during 2005.

(a) On May 5, Asset A was sold for $13,000 cash. The company's bookkeeper recorded this retirement in the following manner in the cash receipts journal.

Cash	13,000	
Asset A		13,000

(b) On December 31, it was determined that Asset B had been used 2,100 hours during 2005.

(c) On December 31, before computing depreciation expense on Asset C, the management of Fiedler, Inc. decided the useful life remaining from January 1, 2005, was 10 years.

(d) On December 31, it was discovered that a plant asset purchased in 2004 had been expensed completely in that year. This asset cost $22,000 and has a useful life of 10 years and no salvage value. Management has decided to use the double-declining balance method for this asset, which can be referred to as "Asset E."

Instructions

Prepare the necessary correcting entries for the year 2005. Record the appropriate depreciation expense on the above-mentioned assets.

P11-4 (Depreciation and Error Analysis) A depreciation schedule for semitrucks of Oglala Manufacturing Company was requested by your auditor soon after December 31, 2005, showing the additions, retirements, depreciation, and other data affecting the income of the company in the 4-year period 2002 to 2005, inclusive. The following data were ascertained.

Balance of Semitrucks account, Jan. 1, 2002	
Truck No. 1 purchased Jan. 1, 1999, cost	$18,000
Truck No. 2 purchased July 1, 1999, cost	22,000
Truck No. 3 purchased Jan. 1, 2001, cost	30,000
Truck No. 4 purchased July 1, 2001, cost	24,000
Balance, Jan. 1, 2002	$94,000

The Semitrucks—Accumulated Depreciation account previously adjusted to January 1, 2002, and duly entered in the ledger, had a balance on that date of $30,200 (depreciation on the four trucks from the respective dates of purchase, based on a 5-year life, no salvage value). No charges had been made against the account before January 1, 2002.

Transactions between January 1, 2002, and December 31, 2005, and their record in the ledger were as follows.

July 1, 2002	Truck No. 3 was traded for a larger one (No. 5), the agreed purchase price of which was $34,000. Oglala Mfg. Co. paid the automobile dealer $15,000 cash on the transaction. The entry was a debit to Semitrucks and a credit to Cash, $15,000.
Jan. 1, 2003	Truck No. 1 was sold for $3,500 cash; entry debited Cash and credited Semitrucks, $3,500.
July 1, 2004	A new truck (No. 6) was acquired for $36,000 cash and was charged at that amount to the Semitrucks account. (Assume truck No. 2 was not retired.)
July 1, 2004	Truck No. 4 was damaged in a wreck to such an extent that it was sold as junk for $700 cash. Oglala Mfg. Co. received $2,500 from the insurance company. The entry made by the bookkeeper was a debit to Cash, $3,200, and credits to Miscellaneous Income, $700, and Semitrucks, $2,500.

Entries for depreciation had been made at the close of each year as follows: 2002, $20,300; 2003, $21,100; 2004, $24,450; 2005, $27,800.

Instructions

(a) For each of the 4 years compute separately the increase or decrease in net income arising from the company's errors in determining or entering depreciation or in recording transactions affecting trucks, ignoring income tax considerations.

(b) Prepare one compound journal entry as of December 31, 2005, for adjustment of the Semitrucks account to reflect the correct balances as revealed by your schedule, assuming that the books have not been closed for 2005.

P11-5 (Depletion and Depreciation—Mining) Richard Wright Mining Company has purchased a tract of mineral land for $600,000. It is estimated that this tract will yield 120,000 tons of ore with sufficient mineral content to make mining and processing profitable. It is further estimated that 6,000 tons of ore will be mined the first and last year and 12,000 tons every year in between. The land will have a residual value of $30,000.

The company builds necessary structures and sheds on the site at a cost of $36,000. It is estimated that these structures can serve 15 years but, because they must be dismantled if they are to be moved, they have no scrap value. The company does not intend to use the buildings elsewhere. Mining machinery installed at the mine was purchased second-hand at a cost of $48,000. This machinery cost the former owner $100,000 and was 50% depreciated when purchased. Richard Wright Mining estimates that about half of this machinery will still be useful when the present mineral resources have been exhausted but that dismantling and removal costs will just about offset its value at that time. The company does not intend to use the machinery elsewhere. The remaining machinery will last until about one-half the present estimated mineral ore has been removed and will then be worthless. Cost is to be allocated equally between these two classes of machinery.

Instructions

(a) As chief accountant for the company, you are to prepare a schedule showing estimated depletion and depreciation costs for each year of the expected life of the mine.

(b) Also compute the depreciation and depletion for the first year assuming actual production of 7,000 tons. Nothing occurred during the year to cause the company engineers to change their estimates of either the mineral resources or the life of the structures and equipment.

P11-6 (Depletion, Timber, and Extraordinary Loss) Ted Koppel Logging and Lumber Company owns 3,000 acres of timberland on the north side of Mount St. Helens, which was purchased in 1968 at a cost of $550 per acre. In 1980, Koppel began selectively logging this timber tract. In May of 1980, Mount St. Helens erupted, burying the timberland of Koppel under a foot of ash. All of the timber on the Koppel tract was downed. In addition, the logging roads, built at a cost of $150,000, were destroyed, as well as the logging equipment, with a net book value of $300,000.

At the time of the eruption, Koppel had logged 20% of the estimated 500,000 board feet of timber. Prior to the eruption, Koppel estimated the land to have a value of $200 per acre after the timber was harvested. Koppel includes the logging roads in the depletion base.

Koppel estimates it will take 3 years to salvage the downed timber at a cost of $700,000. The timber can be sold for pulp wood at an estimated price of $3 per board foot. The value of the land is unknown, but must be considered nominal due to future uncertainties.

Instructions

(a) Determine the depletion cost per board foot for the timber harvested prior to the eruption of Mount St. Helens.

(b) Prepare the journal entry to record the depletion prior to the eruption.

(c) If this tract represents approximately half of the timber holdings of Koppel, determine the amount of the estimated loss and show how the losses of roads, machinery, and timber and the salvage of the timber should be reported in the financial statements of Koppel for the year ended December 31, 1980.

P11-7 (Natural Resources—Timber) Western Paper Products purchased 10,000 acres of forested timberland in March 2005. The company paid $1,700 per acre for this land, which was above the $800 per acre most farmers were paying for cleared land. During April, May, June, and July 2005, Western cut enough timber to build roads using moveable equipment purchased on April 1, 2005. The cost of the roads was $195,000, and the cost of the equipment was $189,000; this equipment was expected to have a $9,000 salvage value and would be used for the next 15 years. Western selected the straight-line method of depreciation for the moveable equipment. Western began actively harvesting timber in August and by December had harvested and sold 472,500 board feet of timber of the estimated 6,750,000 board feet available for cutting.

In March 2006, Western planted new seedlings in the area harvested during the winter. Cost of planting these seedlings was $120,000. In addition, Western spent $8,000 in road maintenance and $6,000 for pest spraying during calendar-year 2006. The road maintenance and spraying are annual costs. During 2006 Western harvested and sold 774,000 board feet of timber of the estimated 6,450,000 board feet available for cutting.

In March 2007, Western again planted new seedlings at a cost of $150,000, and also spent $15,000 on road maintenance and pest spraying. During 2007, the company harvested and sold 650,000 board feet of timber of the estimated 6,500,000 board feet available for cutting.

Instructions

Compute the amount of depreciation and depletion expense for each of the 3 years. Assume that the roads are usable only for logging and therefore are included in the depletion base.

P11-8 (Comprehensive Fixed Asset Problem) Selig Sporting Goods Inc. has been experiencing growth in the demand for its products over the last several years. The last two Olympic Games greatly increased the popularity of basketball around the world. As a result, a European sports retailing consortium entered into an agreement with Selig's Roundball Division to purchase basketballs and other accessories on an increasing basis over the next 5 years.

To be able to meet the quantity commitments of this agreement, Selig had to obtain additional manufacturing capacity. A real estate firm located an available factory in close proximity to Selig's Roundball manufacturing facility, and Selig agreed to purchase the factory and used machinery from Starks Athletic Equipment Company on October 1, 2002. Renovations were necessary to convert the factory for Selig's manufacturing use.

The terms of the agreement required Selig to pay Starks $50,000 when renovations started on January 1, 2003, with the balance to be paid as renovations were completed. The overall purchase price for the factory and machinery was $400,000. The building renovations were contracted to Malone Construction at $100,000. The payments made, as renovations progressed during 2003, are shown below. The factory was placed in service on January 1, 2004.

	1/1	4/1	10/1	12/31
Starks	$50,000	$100,000	$100,000	$150,000
Malone		30,000	30,000	40,000

On January 1, 2003, Selig secured a $500,000 line-of-credit with a 12% interest rate to finance the purchase cost of the factory and machinery, and the renovation costs. Selig drew down on the line-of-credit to meet the payment schedule shown above; this was Selig's only outstanding loan during 2003.

Rob Stewart, Selig's controller, will capitalize the maximum allowable interest costs for this project. Selig's policy regarding purchases of this nature is to use the appraisal value of the land for book purposes and prorate the balance of the purchase price over the remaining items. The building had originally cost Starks $300,000 and had a net book value of $50,000, while the machinery originally cost $125,000 and had a net book value of $40,000 on the date of sale. The land was recorded on Starks' books at $40,000. An appraisal, conducted by independent appraisers at the time of acquisition, valued the land at $280,000, the building at $105,000, and the machinery at $45,000.

Linda Safford, chief engineer, estimated that the renovated plant would be used for 15 years, with an estimated salvage value of $30,000. Safford estimated that the productive machinery would have a remaining useful life of 5 years and a salvage value of $3,000. Selig's depreciation policy specifies the 200% declining-balance method for machinery and the 150% declining-balance method for the plant. One-half year's depreciation is taken in the year the plant is placed in service and one-half year is allowed when the property is disposed of or retired. Selig uses a 360-day year for calculating interest costs.

Instructions

(a) Determine the amounts to be recorded on the books of Selig Sporting Goods Inc. as of December 31, 2003, for each of the following properties acquired from Starks Athletic Equipment Company.
(1) Land. **(2)** Building. **(3)** Machinery.

(b) Calculate Selig Sporting Goods Inc.'s 2004 depreciation expense, for book purposes, for each of the properties acquired from Starks Athletic Equipment Company.

(c) Discuss the arguments for and against the capitalization of interest costs.

(CMA adapted)

P11-9 (Impairment) Olsson Company uses special strapping equipment in its packaging business. The equipment was purchased in January 2004 for $8,000,000 and had an estimated useful life of 8 years with no salvage value. At December 31, 2005, new technology was introduced that would accelerate the obsolescence of Olsson's equipment. Olsson's controller estimates that expected future net cash flows on the equipment will be $5,300,000 and that the fair value of the equipment is $4,400,000. Olsson intends to continue using the equipment, but it is estimated that the remaining useful life is 4 years. Olsson uses straight-line depreciation.

Instructions

(a) Prepare the journal entry (if any) to record the impairment at December 31, 2005.

(b) Prepare any journal entries for the equipment at December 31, 2006. The fair value of the equipment at December 31, 2006, is estimated to be $4,600,000.

(c) Repeat the requirements for (a) and (b), assuming that Olsson intends to dispose of the equipment and that it has not been disposed of as of December 31, 2006.

P11-10 (Comprehensive Depreciation Computations) Anjelica Huston Corporation, a manufacturer of steel products, began operations on October 1, 2003. The accounting department of Huston has started the fixed-asset and depreciation schedule presented below. You have been asked to assist in completing this schedule. In addition to ascertaining that the data already on the schedule are correct, you have obtained the following information from the company's records and personnel.

1. Depreciation is computed from the first of the month of acquisition to the first of the month of disposition.
2. Land A and Building A were acquired from a predecessor corporation. Huston paid $820,000 for the land and building together. At the time of acquisition, the land had an appraised value of $90,000, and the building had an appraised value of $810,000.
3. Land B was acquired on October 2, 2003, in exchange for 2,500 newly issued shares of Huston's common stock. At the date of acquisition, the stock had a par value of $5 per share and a fair value of $30 per share. During October 2003, Huston paid $16,000 to demolish an existing building on this land so it could construct a new building.
4. Construction of Building B on the newly acquired land began on October 1, 2004. By September 30, 2005, Huston had paid $320,000 of the estimated total construction costs of $450,000. It is estimated that the building will be completed and occupied by July 2006.
5. Certain equipment was donated to the corporation by a local university. An independent appraisal of the equipment when donated placed the fair market value at $30,000 and the salvage value at $3,000.

6. Machinery A's total cost of $164,900 includes installation expense of $600 and normal repairs and maintenance of $14,900. Salvage value is estimated at $6,000. Machinery A was sold on February 1, 2005.
7. On October 1, 2004, Machinery B was acquired with a down payment of $5,740 and the remaining payments to be made in 11 annual installments of $6,000 each beginning October 1, 2004. The prevailing interest rate was 8%. The following data were abstracted from present-value tables (rounded).

Present value of $1.00 at 8%		Present value of an ordinary annuity of $1.00 at 8%	
10 years	.463	10 years	6.710
11 years	.429	11 years	7.139
15 years	.315	15 years	8.559

ANJELICA HUSTON CORPORATION
Fixed Asset and Depreciation Schedule
For Fiscal Years Ended September 30, 2004, and September 30, 2005

Assets	Acquisition Date	Cost	Salvage	Depreciation Method	Estimated Life in Years	Depreciation Expense Year Ended September 30 2004	2005
Land A	October 1, 2003	$ (1)	N/A	N/A	N/A	N/A	N/A
Building A	October 1, 2003	(2)	$40,000	Straight-line	(3)	$17,450	(4)
Land B	October 2, 2003	(5)	N/A	N/A	N/A	N/A	N/A
Building B	Under Construction	$320,000 to date	—	Straight-line	30	—	(6)
Donated Equipment	October 2, 2003	(7)	3,000	150% declining balance	10	(8)	(9)
Machinery A	October 2, 2003	(10)	6,000	Sum-of-the-years'-digits	8	(11)	(12)
Machinery B	October 1, 2004	(13)	—	Straight-line	20	—	(14)

N/A—Not applicable

Instructions

For each numbered item on the foregoing schedule, supply the correct amount. Round each answer to the nearest dollar.

P11-11 (Depreciation for Partial Periods—SL, Act., SYD, and DDB) On January 1, 2002, a machine was purchased for $77,000. The machine has an estimated salvage value of $5,000 and an estimated useful life of 5 years. The machine can operate for 100,000 hours before it needs to be replaced. The company closed its books on December 31 and operates the machine as follows: 2002, 20,000 hrs; 2003, 25,000 hrs; 2004, 15,000 hrs; 2005, 30,000 hrs; 2006, 10,000 hrs.

Instructions

(a) Compute the annual depreciation charges over the machine's life assuming a December 31 year-end for each of the following depreciation methods.
  (1) Straight-line method. **(3)** Sum-of-the-years'-digits method.
  (2) Activity method. **(4)** Double-declining balance method.

(b) Assume a fiscal year-end of September 30. Compute the annual depreciation charges over the asset's life applying each of the following methods.
  (1) Straight-line method.
  (2) Sum-of-the-years'-digits method.
  (3) Double-declining balance method.

***P11-12 (Depreciation—SL, DDB, SYD, Act., and MACRS)** On January 1, 2002, Moshe Dayan Company, a small machine-tool manufacturer, acquired for $1,100,000 a piece of new industrial equipment. The new equipment had a useful life of 5 years, and the salvage value was estimated to be $50,000. Dayan estimates that the new equipment can produce 12,000 machine tools in its first year. It estimates that production will decline by 1,000 units per year over the remaining useful life of the equipment.

The following depreciation methods may be used: (1) straight-line; (2) double-declining balance; (3) sum-of-the-years'-digits; and (4) units-of-output. For tax purposes, the class life is 7 years. Use the MACRS tables for computing depreciation.

Instructions

(a) Which depreciation method would maximize net income for financial statement reporting for the 3-year period ending December 31, 2004? Prepare a schedule showing the amount of accumulated depreciation at December 31, 2004, under the method selected. Ignore present value, income tax, and deferred income tax considerations.

(b) Which depreciation method (MACRS or optional straight-line) would minimize net income for income tax reporting for the 3-year period ending December 31, 2004? Determine the amount of accumulated depreciation at December 31, 2004. Ignore present value considerations.

(AICPA adapted)

CONCEPTUAL CASES

C11-1 (Depreciation Basic Concepts) Prophet Manufacturing Company was organized January 1, 2004. During 2004, it has used in its reports to management the straight-line method of depreciating its plant assets.

On November 8 you are having a conference with Prophet's officers to discuss the depreciation method to be used for income tax and stockholder reporting. Frank Peretti, president of Prophet, has suggested the use of a new method, which he feels is more suitable than the straight-line method for the needs of the company during the period of rapid expansion of production and capacity that he foresees. Following is an example in which the proposed method is applied to a fixed asset with an original cost of $248,000, an estimated useful life of 5 years, and a scrap value of approximately $8,000.

Year	Years of Life Used	Fraction Rate	Depreciation Expense	Accumulated Depreciation at End of Year	Book Value at End of Year
1	1	1/15	$16,000	$ 16,000	$232,000
2	2	2/15	32,000	48,000	200,000
3	3	3/15	48,000	96,000	152,000
4	4	4/15	64,000	160,000	88,000
5	5	5/15	80,000	240,000	8,000

The president favors the new method because he has heard that:

1. It will increase the funds recovered during the years near the end of the assets' useful lives when maintenance and replacement disbursements are high.
2. It will result in increased write-offs in later years and thereby will reduce taxes.

Instructions

(a) What is the purpose of accounting for depreciation?

(b) Is the president's proposal within the scope of generally accepted accounting principles? In making your decision discuss the circumstances, if any, under which use of the method would be reasonable and those, if any, under which it would not be reasonable.

(c) The president wants your advice on the following issues.

(1) Do depreciation charges recover or create funds? Explain.

(2) Assume that the Internal Revenue Service accepts the proposed depreciation method in this case. If the proposed method were used for stockholder and tax reporting purposes, how would it affect the availability of cash flows generated by operations?

C11-2 (Unit, Group, and Composite Depreciation) The certified public accountant is frequently called upon by management for advice regarding methods of computing depreciation. Of comparable importance, although it arises less frequently, is the question of whether the depreciation method should be based on consideration of the assets as units, as a group, or as having a composite life.

Instructions

(a) Briefly describe the depreciation methods based on treating assets as (1) units and (2) a group or as having a composite life.

(b) Present the arguments for and against the use of each of the two methods.

(c) Describe how retirements are recorded under each of the two methods.

(AICPA adapted)

C11-3 (Depreciation—Strike, Units-of-Production, Obsolescence) Presented below are three different and unrelated situations involving depreciation accounting. Answer the question(s) at the end of each situation.

Situation I

Recently, John Brown Company experienced a strike that affected a number of its operating plants. The controller of this company indicated that it was not appropriate to report depreciation expense during this period because the equipment did not depreciate and an improper matching of costs and revenues would result. She based her position on the following points.

1. It is inappropriate to charge the period with costs for which there are no related revenues arising from production.
2. The basic factor of depreciation in this instance is wear and tear, and because equipment was idle, no wear and tear occurred.

Instructions

Comment on the appropriateness of the controller's comments.

Situation II

Andrew Carnegie Company manufactures electrical appliances, most of which are used in homes. Company engineers have designed a new type of blender which, through the use of a few attachments, will perform more functions than any blender currently on the market. Demand for the new blender can be projected with reasonable probability. In order to make the blenders, Carnegie needs a specialized machine that is not available from outside sources. It has been decided to make such a machine in Carnegie's own plant.

Instructions

(a) Discuss the effect of projected demand in units for the new blenders (which may be steady, decreasing, or increasing) on the determination of a depreciation method for the machine.

(b) What other matters should be considered in determining the depreciation method? Ignore income tax considerations.

Situation III

Dorothea Dix Paper Company operates a 300-ton-per-day kraft pulp mill and four sawmills in Wisconsin. The company is in the process of expanding its pulp mill facilities to a capacity of 1,000 tons per day and plans to replace three of its older, less efficient sawmills with an expanded facility. One of the mills to be replaced did not operate for most of 2004 (current year), and there are no plans to reopen it before the new sawmill facility becomes operational.

In reviewing the depreciation rates and in discussing the residual values of the sawmills that were to be replaced, it was noted that if present depreciation rates were not adjusted, substantial amounts of plant costs on these three mills would not be depreciated by the time the new mill came on stream.

Instructions

What is the proper accounting for the four sawmills at the end of 2004?

C11-4 (Depreciation Concepts) As a cost accountant for San Francisco Cannery, you have been approached by Merton Miller, canning room supervisor, about the 2003 costs charged to his department. In particular, he is concerned about the line item "depreciation." Miller is very proud of the excellent condition of his canning room equipment. He has always been vigilant about keeping all equipment serviced and well oiled. He is sure that the huge charge to depreciation is a mistake; it does not at all reflect the cost of minimal wear and tear that the machines have experienced over the last year. He believes that the charge should be considerably lower.

The machines being depreciated are six automatic canning machines. All were put into use on January 1, 2003. Each cost $469,000, having a salvage value of $40,000 and a useful life of 12 years. San Francisco depreciates this and similar assets using double-declining balance depreciation. Miller has also pointed out that if you used straight-line depreciation the charge to his department would not be so great.

Instructions

Write a memo to Merton Miller to clear up his misunderstanding of the term "depreciation." Also, calculate year-1 depreciation on all machines using both methods. Explain the theoretical justification for double-declining balance and why, in the long run, the aggregate charge to depreciation will be the same under both methods.

C11-5 (Depreciation Choice) Billy Williams, Sheffield Corporation's controller, is concerned that net income may be lower this year. He is afraid upper-level management might recommend cost reductions by laying off accounting staff, including him.

Williams knows that depreciation is a major expense for Sheffield. The company currently uses the double-declining balance method for both financial reporting and tax purposes, and he's thinking of a change to the straight-line method. That, of course, would require a cumulative-effect adjustment since it is a change in accounting principle and would be reported separately in the income statement. He doesn't want to highlight the method of increasing income in this manner. He thinks, "Why don't I increase the estimated useful lives and the salvage values? That will decrease depreciation expense and since the changes are accounted for prospectively, they will not be disclosed in the income statement. I may be able to save my job and those of my staff."

Instructions

Answer the following questions.

(a) Who are the stakeholders in this situation?
(b) What are the ethical issues involved?
(c) What should Williams do?

USING YOUR JUDGMENT

FINANCIAL REPORTING PROBLEM

3M Company

The financial statements of 3M are presented in Appendix 5B or can be accessed on the Take Action! CD.

Instructions

Refer to 3M's financial statements and the accompanying notes to answer the following questions.

(a) What descriptions are used by 3M in its balance sheet to classify its property, plant, and equipment?
(b) What method or methods of depreciation does 3M use to depreciate its property, plant, and equipment?
(c) Over what estimated useful lives does 3M depreciate its property, plant, and equipment?
(d) What amounts for depreciation expense did 3M charge to its income statement in 2001, 2000, and 1999?
(e) What were the additions to property, plant, and equipment made by 3M in 2001, 2000, and 1999?

FINANCIAL STATEMENT ANALYSIS CASE

McDonald's Corporation

McDonald's is the largest and best-known global food service retailer, with more than 30,000 restaurants in 121 countries. On any day, McDonald's serves approximately 1 percent of the world's population. Presented on the next page is information related to McDonald's property and equipment.

Instructions

(a) What method of depreciation does McDonald's use?
(b) Does depreciation and amortization expense cause cash flow from operations to increase? Explain.
(c) What does the schedule of cash flow measures indicate?

McDonald's Corporation

Summary of Significant Accounting Policies Section

Property and Equipment. Property and equipment are stated at cost, with depreciation and amortization provided on the straight-line method over the following estimated useful lives: buildings—up to 40 years; leasehold improvements—lesser of useful lives of assets or lease terms including option periods; and equipment—3 to 12 years.

[In the notes to the financial statements:]

Property and Equipment

(in millions)	December 31, 2000	1999
Land	$ 3,932.7	$ 3,838.6
Buildings and improvements on owned land	8,250.0	7,953.6
Buildings and improvements on leased land	7,513.3	7,076.6
Equipment, signs, and seating	3,172.2	2,906.6
Other	700.8	675.4
	23,569.0	22,450.8
Accumulated depreciation and amortization	(6,521.4)	(6,126.3)
Net property and equipment	$17,047.6	$16,324.5

Depreciation and amortization expense was (in millions): 2000—$900.9; 1999—$858.1; 1998—$808.0.

[In the management discussion and analysis section, the following schedule is provided:]

Cash Provided by Operations

(in millions)	2000	1999	1998
Cash provided by operations	$2,751	$3,009	$2,766
Free cash flow	806	1,141	887
Cash provided by operations as a percent of capital expenditures	141%	161%	147%
Cash provided by operations as a percent of average total debt	35	42	41

COMPARATIVE ANALYSIS CASE

The Coca-Cola Company and PepsiCo., Inc.

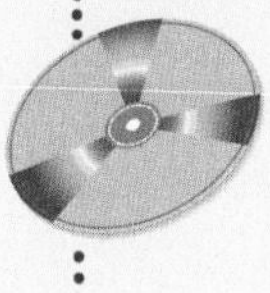

Instructions

Go to the Take Action! CD and use information found there to answer the following questions related to **The Coca-Cola Company** and **PepsiCo, Inc.**

(a) What amount is reported in the balance sheets as property, plant, and equipment (net) of Coca-Cola at December 31, 2001, and of PepsiCo at December 30, 2001? What percentage of total assets is invested in property, plant, and equipment by each company?

(b) What depreciation methods are used by Coca-Cola and PepsiCo for property, plant, and equipment? How much depreciation was reported by Coca-Cola and PepsiCo in 2001, 2000, and 1999?

(c) Compute and compare the following ratios for Coca-Cola and PepsiCo for 2001.

(1) Asset turnover.

(2) Profit margin on sales.

(3) Ratio of return on assets.

(d) What amount was spent in 2001 for capital expenditures by Coca-Cola and PepsiCo? What amount of interest was capitalized in 2001?

RESEARCH CASE

BUSINESS EXTRA

An article by Martin Peers and Robin Sidel, entitled "Days May Be Numbered for Ebitda's Role," appeared in the July 5, 2002, issue of the *Wall Street Journal.* (Subscribers to **Business Extra** can access the article at that site.)

Instructions

Read the article and answer the following questions.

(a) Explain what is meant by Ebitda and why companies are reporting this number.

(b) Why has the WorldCom bankruptcy caused Ebitda to fall into disfavor as a performance metric?

(c) What is wrong with performance metrics such as Ebitda, cash earnings, or other pro-forma income measures?

INTERNATIONAL REPORTING CASE

Companies following international accounting standards are permitted to revalue fixed assets above the assets' historical costs. Such revaluations are allowed under various countries' standards and the standards issued by the International Accounting Standards Board (IASB). **Nestlé SA**, headquartered in Switzerland, follows IASB standards. In a recent year, Nestlé disclosed the following information on revaluations of its tangible fixed assets. The revaluation reserve measures the amount by which tangible fixed assets are recorded above historical cost and is reported in Nestlé's stockholders' equity.

NESTLÉ SA

Tangible fixed assets

The revaluation reserve included in the carrying value of net tangible fixed assets at net replacement value is as follows.

(in millions of Swiss francs)	Land and Buildings	Machinery and Equipment	Tools, Furniture, and Other Equipment	Vehicles	Total
Net replacement value	9,492	10,727	1,571	378	22,168
Net book value	7,474	8,724	1,659	328	18,185
Revaluation reserve	2,018	2,003	(88)	50	3,983

The following additional data were reported by Nestlé. Amounts for Tootsie Roll in the same year are provided for comparison.

	Nestlé (Swiss francs, in millions)	Tootsie Roll ($, in thousands)
Total revenues	69,998	375,594
Average total assets	52,857	413,924
Net income	4,005	60,682

Instructions

(a) Compute the following ratios for Nestlé and Tootsie Roll.

(1) Return on assets.

(2) Profit margin.

(3) Asset turnover.

How do these companies compare on these performance measures?

(b) Nestlé reports a revaluation reserve of 3,983 Swiss francs. Assume that 1,550 of this amount arose from an increase in the net replacement value of land and buildings during the year. Prepare the journal entry to record this increase. (*Hint:* Credit the Revaluation Reserve account.)

(c) Under IASB standards, are Nestlé's assets and equity overstated? If so, why? When comparing Nestlé to U.S. companies, like Tootsie Roll, what adjustments would you need to make in order to have valid comparisons of ratios such as those computed in (a) above?

PROFESSIONAL SIMULATION

Accounting–Property, Plant, and Equipment

Directions | Situation | Explanation | Measurement | Journal Entries | Research | Resources

Directions

In this simulation, you will be asked various questions regarding the accounting for property, plant, and equipment. Prepare responses to all parts.

Situation

Whitley Corporation purchased machinery on January 1, 2003, at a cost of $100,000. The estimated useful life of the machinery is 4 years, with an estimated residual value of $10,000 at the end of that period. The company is considering different depreciation methods that could be used for financial reporting purposes.

Explanation

(a) What is the purpose of depreciation?

(b) Identify the factors that are relevant in determining annual depreciation, and explain whether those factors are determined objectively or whether they are based on judgment.

Measurement

(a) Which depreciation method would result in the highest reported 2003 income? Explain.

(b) Which method would result in the highest total reported earnings over the 4-year period? Explain.

(c) Which method would result in the highest 2003 cash flow? Explain.

Journal Entry

Assume that the company sold the machinery on January 1, 2005, for $84,000 and that the company used the straight-line method. Prepare the journal entry to record the transaction.

www.wiley.com/college/kieso

Remember to check the **Take Action! CD** and the book's **companion Web site** to find additional resources for this chapter.

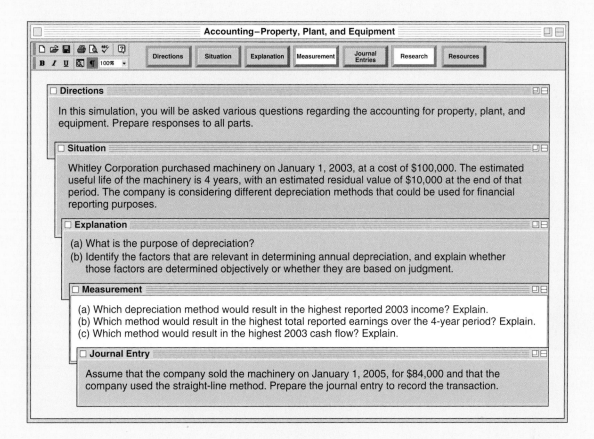

CHAPTER 12

Intangible Assets

Untouchable

As shown in the graph below, tangible assets as a percent of all assets has declined dramatically in the last 45 years.

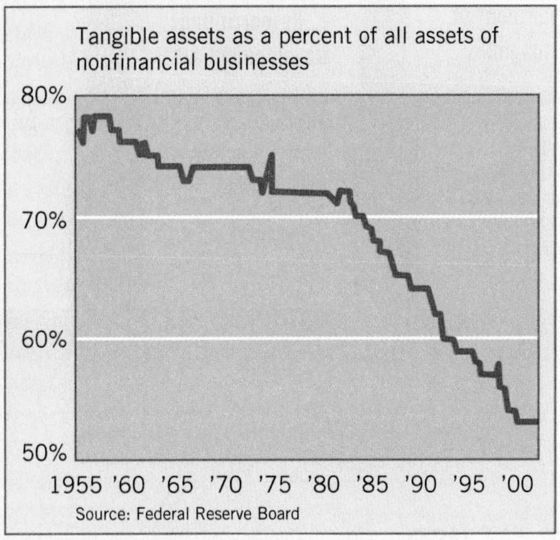

Consequently, value today is increasingly derived from intangible assets—intellectual property, technology, or reputation. For example, many well-known companies make most of their money from intangible assets: **Microsoft Corp.**'s software, **Pfizer Inc.**'s drug patents, and **Walt Disney Co.**'s film and television productions.

Although these formidable franchises are unlikely to erode soon, the experience at **Winstar Communications** illustrates how quickly the value of intangible assets can erode. Just before Winstar filed for bankruptcy in the spring of 2001, it listed $5 billion in assets, a large share comprised of intangible assets related to its customer base. Within just a few short months, its assets fetched just $42 *million*, and Winstar's investors and creditors learned the shocking speed at which the value of such assets can decline. Similarly, the meltdown at **Enron** was accelerated as the market lost confidence in Enron's ability to deliver services in its virtual energy-trading operation.

Perhaps Federal Reserve Chairman Alan Greenspan's remarks are relevant in these turbulent times: ". . . a firm is inherently fragile if its value-added emanates more from conceptual as distinct from physical assets. Trust and reputation can vanish overnight. A factory cannot."[1]

[1]Adapted from Greg Ip, "The Rise and Fall of Intangible Assets Leads to Shorter Company Life Spans," *Wall Street Journal Online* (April 4, 2002).

LEARNING OBJECTIVES

After studying this chapter, you should be able to:

1. **Describe the characteristics of intangible assets.**
2. **Identify the costs included in the initial valuation of intangible assets.**
3. **Explain the procedure for amortizing intangible assets.**
4. **Identify the types of intangible assets.**
5. **Explain the conceptual issues related to goodwill.**
6. **Describe the accounting procedures for recording goodwill.**
7. **Explain the accounting issues related to intangible asset impairments.**
8. **Identify the conceptual issues related to research and development costs.**
9. **Describe the accounting procedures for research and development costs and for other similar costs.**
10. **Indicate the presentation of intangible assets and related items.**

PREVIEW OF CHAPTER 12

As the opening story indicates, the accounting and reporting of intangible assets is taking on increasing importance in this information age, especially for companies like **Microsoft**, **Pfizer**, and **Walt Disney**. The purpose of this chapter is to explain the basic conceptual and reporting issues related to intangible assets. The content and organization of the chapter are as follows.

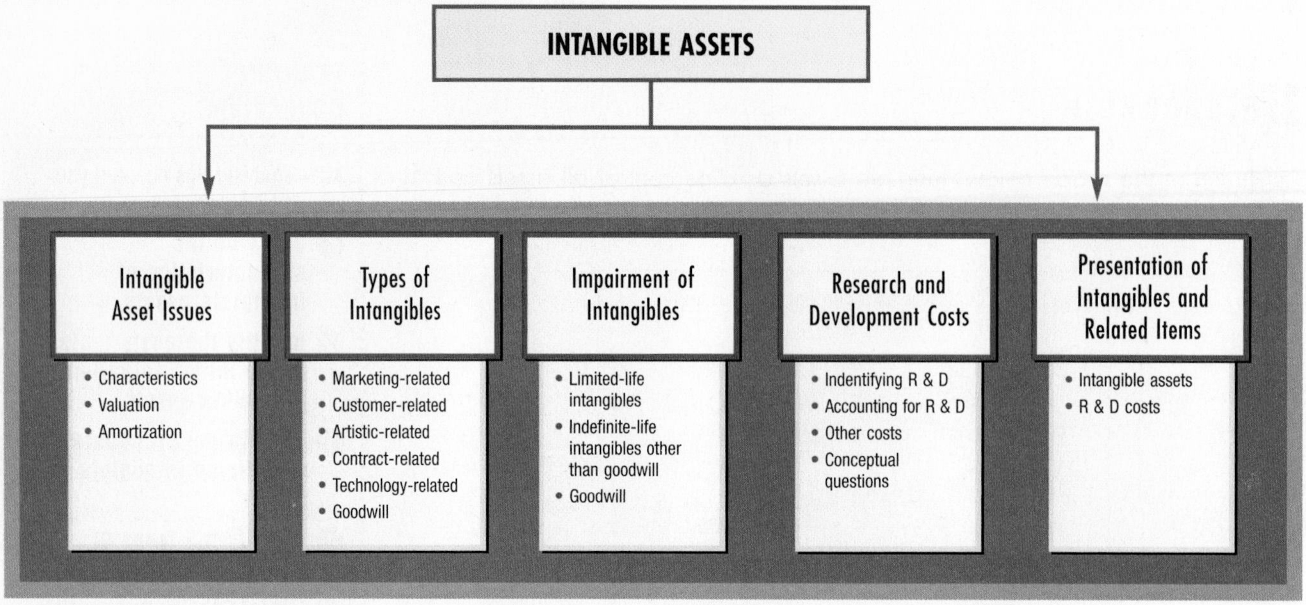

INTANGIBLE ASSET ISSUES

Characteristics

OBJECTIVE 1
Describe the characteristics of intangible assets.

Gap Inc.'s most important asset is not store fixtures—brand image is. The major asset of **Coca-Cola** is not its plant facilities—its secret formula for making Coke is. **America Online**'s most important asset is not its Internet connection equipment—its subscriber base is. As these examples show, we have an economy dominated today by information and service providers, and their major assets are often intangible in nature. Accounting for these intangibles is difficult, and as a result many intangibles are presently not reported on a company's balance sheet. **Intangible assets** have two main characteristics.[2]

1. **They lack physical existence.** Unlike tangible assets such as property, plant, and equipment, intangible assets derive their value from the rights and privileges granted to the company using them.
2. **They are not financial instruments.** Assets such as bank deposits, accounts receivable, and long-term investments in bonds and stocks lack physical substance but are not classified as intangible assets. These assets are **financial instruments**. They derive their value from the right (claim) to receive cash or cash equivalents in the future.

[2]"Goodwill and Other Intangible Assets," *Statement of Financial Accounting Standards No. 142* (Norwalk, Conn.: FASB, 2001).

In most cases, intangible assets provide services over a period of years. As a result, they are normally classified as long-term assets. The most common types of intangibles are patents, copyrights, franchises or licenses, trademarks or trade names, and goodwill.

Valuation

Purchased Intangibles

Intangibles purchased from another party are **recorded at cost**. Cost includes all costs of acquisition and expenditures necessary to make the intangible asset ready for its intended use—for example, purchase price, legal fees, and other incidental expenses.

If intangibles are acquired for stock or in exchange for other assets, **the cost of the intangible is the fair value of the consideration given or the fair value of the intangible received, whichever is more clearly evident**. When several intangibles, or a combination of intangibles and tangibles, are bought in a "basket purchase," the cost should be allocated on the basis of fair values. Essentially the accounting treatment for purchased intangibles closely parallels that followed for purchased tangible assets.

OBJECTIVE 2
Identify the costs included in the initial valuation of intangible assets.

UNDERLYING CONCEPTS

The basic attributes of intangibles, their uncertainty as to future benefits, and their uniqueness have discouraged valuation in excess of cost.

Internally-Created Intangibles

Costs incurred internally to create intangibles are generally expensed as incurred. Thus, even though a company may incur substantial research and development costs to create an intangible, these costs are expensed.

Various reasons are given for this approach. Some argue that the costs incurred internally to create intangibles bear no relationship to their real value; therefore, expensing these costs is appropriate. Others note that with a purchased intangible, a reliable number for the cost of the intangible can be determined; with internally developed intangibles, it is difficult to associate costs with specific intangible assets. And others argue that due to the underlying subjectivity related to intangibles, a conservative approach should be followed—that is, expense as incurred. As a result, the **only internal costs capitalized are direct costs** incurred in obtaining the intangible, such as legal costs.

Amortization of Intangibles

Intangibles have either a **limited (finite) useful life** or an **indefinite useful life**. An intangible asset with a **limited life is amortized**; an intangible asset with an **indefinite life is not amortized**.

OBJECTIVE 3
Explain the procedure for amortizing intangible assets.

Limited-Life Intangibles

As you learned in Chapter 11, the expiration of intangible assets is called **amortization**. **Limited-life intangibles** should be amortized by systematic charges to expense over their useful life. The useful life should reflect the periods over which these assets will contribute to cash flows. Factors considered in determining useful life are:

1. The expected use of the asset by the entity.
2. The expected useful life of another asset or a group of assets to which the useful life of the intangible asset may relate (such as mineral rights to depleting assets).
3. Any legal, regulatory, or contractual provisions that may limit the useful life.
4. Any legal, regulatory, or contractual provisions that enable renewal or extension of the asset's legal or contractual life without substantial cost. (This factor assumes that there is evidence to support renewal or extension and that renewal or extension can be accomplished without material modifications of the existing terms and conditions.)

5. The effects of obsolescence, demand, competition, and other economic factors. (Examples include the stability of the industry, known technological advances, legislative action that results in an uncertain or changing regulatory environment, and expected changes in distribution channels.)
6. The level of maintenance expenditure required to obtain the expected future cash flows from the asset. (For example, a material level of required maintenance in relation to the carrying amount of the asset may suggest a very limited useful life.)[3]

The amount of amortization expense for a limited-life intangible asset should reflect the pattern in which the asset is consumed or used up, if that pattern can be reliably determined. For example, assume that Second Wave, Inc. has purchased a license to provide a limited quantity of a gene product, called Mega. The cost of the license should be amortized following the pattern of production of Mega. If the pattern of production or consumption cannot be determined, the straight-line method of amortization should be used. For homework problems, assume the use of the straight-line method unless stated otherwise.

When intangible assets are amortized, the charges should be shown as expenses, and the credits should be made either to the appropriate asset accounts or to separate accumulated amortization accounts.

The amount of an intangible asset to be amortized should be its cost less residual value. The residual value is assumed to be zero unless at the end of its useful life the intangible asset has value to another entity. For example, if U2D Co. has a commitment from Hardy Co. to purchase its intangible asset at the end of its useful life, U2D Co. should reduce the cost of its intangible asset by the residual value. Similarly, if market values for residual values can be reliably determined, market values should be considered.

What happens if a limited-life intangible asset's useful life is changed? In that case the remaining carrying amount should be amortized over the revised remaining useful life. Limited-life intangibles should be continually evaluated for **impairment**. Similar to property, plant, and equipment, an impairment loss should be recognized if the carrying amount of the intangible is not recoverable and its carrying amount exceeds its fair value.

Indefinite-Life Intangibles

If no legal, regulatory, contractual, competitive, or other factors limit the useful life of an intangible asset, it is considered an **indefinite-life intangible asset. Indefinite** means that there is no foreseeable limit on the period of time over which the intangible asset is expected to provide cash flows. An intangible asset with an indefinite life is not amortized.

To illustrate, assume that Double Clik, Inc. acquired a trademark that is used to distinguish a leading consumer product. The trademark is renewable every 10 years at minimal cost. All evidence indicates that this trademark product will generate cash flows for an indefinite period of time. In this case, the trademark has an indefinite life because it is expected to contribute to cash flows indefinitely.

Indefinite-life intangibles should be tested for impairment at least annually. The **impairment test** compares the fair value of an intangible asset with its carrying amount. This impairment test is different from the one used for a limited-life intangible. That is, there is no recoverability test related to indefinite-life intangibles, only the fair value test. The reason: Indefinite-life intangible assets might never fail the undiscounted cash flows recoverability test because cash flows could extend indefinitely into the future.

In summary, the accounting treatment for intangible assets is shown in Illustration 12-1.

---

[3]Ibid, par. 11.

ILLUSTRATION 12-1
Accounting Treatment for Intangibles

Type of Intangible	Manner Acquired: Purchased	Manner Acquired: Internally Created	Amortization	Impairment Test
Limited-life intangibles	Capitalize	Expense*	Over useful life	Recoverability test and then fair value test
Indefinite-life intangibles	Capitalize	Expense*	Do not amortize	Fair value test

*Except for direct costs, such as legal costs.

TYPES OF INTANGIBLE ASSETS

OBJECTIVE 4
Identify the types of intangible assets.

As indicated, the accounting for intangible assets depends on whether the intangible has a limited or an indefinite life. There are many different types of intangibles, and they are often classified into the following six major categories.[4]

1. Marketing-related intangible assets.
2. Customer-related intangible assets.
3. Artistic-related intangible assets.
4. Contract-related intangible assets.
5. Technology-related intangible assets.
6. Goodwill.

Marketing-Related Intangible Assets

Marketing-related intangible assets are those assets primarily used in the marketing or promotion of products or services. Examples are trademarks or trade names, newspaper mastheads, Internet domain names, and noncompetition agreements.

A very common form of a marketing-related intangible asset is a trademark or trade name. A **trademark** or **trade name** is a word, phrase, or symbol that distinguishes or identifies a particular enterprise or product. Under common law, the right to use a trademark or trade name, whether it is registered or not, rests exclusively with the original user as long as the original user continues to use it. Registration with the U.S. Patent and Trademark Office provides legal protection for an **indefinite number of renewals for periods of 10 years each**. Therefore a business that uses an established trademark or trade name may properly consider it to have an indefinite life. Trade names like Kleenex, Pepsi-Cola, Oldsmobile, Excedrin, Wheaties, and Sunkist create immediate product identification in our minds, thereby enhancing marketability.

If a trademark or trade name is acquired, its capitalizable cost is the purchase price. If a trademark or trade name is developed by the enterprise itself, the capitalizable cost includes attorney fees, registration fees, design costs, consulting fees, successful legal defense costs, and other expenditures directly related to securing it (excluding research and development costs). When the total cost of a trademark or trade name is insignificant, it can be expensed rather than capitalized. In most cases, the life of a trademark or trade name is indefinite, and therefore its cost is not amortized.

The value of a marketing-related intangible can be substantial. Consider Internet domain names as an example. The name **Drugs.com** recently sold for $800,000, and the bidding for the name **Loans.com** approached $500,000.

[4]This classification framework has been adopted from "Business Combinations," *Statement of Financial Accounting Standards No. 141* (Norwalk, Conn.: FASB, 2001).

Company names themselves identify qualities and characteristics that the companies have worked hard and spent much to develop. In a recent year an estimated 1,230 companies took on new names in an attempt to forge new identities. In doing so, they paid over $250 million to corporate-identity consultants. Among these were **Primerica** (formerly American Can), **Navistar** (formerly International Harvester), and **Nissan** (formerly Datsun).[5]

Customer-Related Intangible Assets

Customer-related intangible assets occur as a result of interactions with outside parties. Examples are customer lists, order or production backlogs, and both contractual and noncontractual customer relationships.

To illustrate, assume that We-Market Inc. acquired the customer list of a large newspaper for $6,000,000 on January 1, 2003. The customer list is a database that includes name, contact information, order history, and demographic information for a list of customers. We-Market expects to benefit from the information on the acquired list for 3 years, and it believes that these benefits will be spread evenly over the 3 years. In this case, the customer list is a limited-life intangible that should be amortized on a straight-line basis over the 3-year period.

The entries to record the purchase of the customer list and the amortization of the customer list at the end of each year are as follows.

January 1, 2003		
Customer List	6,000,000	
Cash		6,000,000
(To record purchase of customer list)		
December 31, 2003, 2004, 2005		
Customer List Amortization Expense	2,000,000	
Customer List (or Accumulated Customer List Amortization)		2,000,000
(To record amortization expense)		

In the preceding example it was assumed that the customer list had no residual value. But what if We-Market determines that it can sell the list for $60,000 to another company at the end of 3 years? In that case, this residual value should be subtracted from the cost in order to determine the proper amortization expense for each year. Amortization expense would therefore be $1,980,000, as shown below.

ILLUSTRATION 12-2
Calculation of Amortization Expense with Residual Value

Cost	$6,000,000
Residual value	60,000
Amortization base	$5,940,000
Amortization expense per period: $1,980,000 ($5,940,000 ÷ 3)	

The residual value should be assumed to be zero unless the asset's useful life is less than the economic life and reliable evidence is available concerning the residual value.[6]

[5]To illustrate how various intangibles might arise from a given product, consider what the creators of the highly successful game, Trivial Pursuit, did to protect their creation. First, they copyrighted the 6,000 questions that are at the heart of the game. Then they shielded the Trivial Pursuit name by applying for a registered trademark. As a third mode of protection, the creators obtained a design patent on the playing board's design because it represents a unique graphic creation.

[6]"Goodwill and Other Intangible Assets," *Statement of Financial Accounting Standards No. 142* (Norwalk, Conn.: FASB, 2001), par. B55.

Artistic-Related Intangible Assets

Artistic-related intangible assets involve ownership rights to plays, literary works, musical works, pictures, photographs, and video and audiovisual material. These ownership rights are protected by copyrights.

A **copyright** is a federally granted right that all authors, painters, musicians, sculptors, and other artists have in their creations and expressions. A copyright is granted for the **life of the creator plus 70 years**. It gives the owner, or heirs, the exclusive right to reproduce and sell an artistic or published work. Copyrights are not renewable. The costs of acquiring and defending a copyright may be capitalized, but the research and development costs involved must be expensed as incurred.

Generally, the useful life of the copyright is less than its legal life (life in being plus 70 years). The costs of the copyright should be allocated to the years in which the benefits are expected to be received. The difficulty of determining the number of years over which benefits will be received normally encourages the company to write these costs off over a fairly short period of time.

Copyrights can be valuable. **Really Useful Group** is a company that consists of copyrights on the musicals of Andrew Lloyd Webber—*Cats, Phantom of the Opera, Jesus Christ-Superstar,* and others. It has little in the way of hard assets, yet it has been valued at $300 million. The **Walt Disney Co.** is facing loss of its copyright on Mickey Mouse on January 1, 2004, which may affect sales of billions of dollars of Mickey-related goods and services (including theme parks). Although Disney may be able to use its trademarks on Mickey (which may be renewed indefinitely) to protect itself, many big entertainment companies, Disney included, have been quietly pushing Congress for a copyright extension.

Contract-Related Intangible Assets

Contract-related intangible assets represent the value of rights that arise from contractual arrangements. Examples are franchise and licensing agreements, construction permits, broadcast rights, and service or supply contracts. A very common form of contract-based intangible asset is a franchise.

A **franchise** is a contractual arrangement under which the franchisor grants the franchisee the right to sell certain products or services, to use certain trademarks or trade names, or to perform certain functions, usually within a designated geographical area. For example, when you drive down the street in an automobile purchased from a **Volkswagen** dealer, fill your tank at the corner **Texaco** station, eat lunch at **Subway**, cool off with one of **Baskin-Robbins**' 31 flavors, work at a **Coca-Cola** bottling plant, live in a home purchased through a **Century 21** real estate broker, or vacation at a **Holiday Inn** resort, you are dealing with franchises.

The franchisor, having developed a unique concept or product, protects its concept or product through a patent, copyright, or trademark or trade name. The franchisee acquires the right to exploit the franchisor's idea or product by signing a franchise agreement.

Another type of franchise is the arrangement commonly entered into by a municipality (or other governmental body) and a business enterprise that uses public property. In such cases, a privately owned enterprise is permitted to use public property in performing its services. Examples are the use of public waterways for a ferry service, the use of public land for telephone or electric lines, the use of phone lines for cable TV, the use of city streets for a bus line, or the use of the airwaves for radio or TV broadcasting. Such operating rights, obtained through agreements with governmental units or agencies, are frequently referred to as **licenses** or **permits**.

Franchises and licenses may be for a definite period of time, for an indefinite period of time, or perpetual. The enterprise securing the franchise or license carries an intangible asset account entitled Franchise or License on its books only when there are costs (such as a lump-sum payment in advance or legal fees and other expenditures) that are identified with the acquisition of the operating right. **The cost of a franchise (or license) with a limited life should be amortized as operating expense over the**

life of the franchise. A franchise with an indefinite life, or a perpetual franchise, should be carried at cost and not be amortized.

Annual payments made under a franchise agreement should be entered as operating expenses in the period in which they are incurred. They do not represent an asset to the concern since they do not relate to future rights to use public property.

Technology-Related Intangible Assets

Technology-related intangible assets relate to innovations or technological advances. Examples are patented technology and trade secrets. To illustrate, patents are granted by the U.S. Patent and Trademark Office. A **patent** gives the holder exclusive right to use, manufacture, and sell a product or process **for a period of 20 years** without interference or infringement by others. With this exclusive right, fortunes can be made. For example, companies such as **Merck**, **Polaroid**, and **Xerox** were founded on patents.[7] The two principal kinds of patents are **product patents**, which cover actual physical products, and **process patents**, which govern the process by which products are made.

If a patent is purchased from an inventor (or other owner), the purchase price represents its cost. Other costs incurred in connection with securing a patent, as well as attorneys' fees and other unrecovered costs of a successful legal suit to protect the patent, can be capitalized as part of the patent cost. Research and development costs related to the **development** of the product, process, or idea that is subsequently patented **must be expensed as incurred**, however. See pages 584–586 for a more complete presentation of accounting for research and development costs.

The cost of a patent should be amortized over its legal life or its useful life (the period benefits are received), whichever is **shorter**. If a patent is owned from the date it is granted, and it is expected to be useful during its entire legal life, it should be amortized over 20 years. If it appears that the patent will be useful for a shorter period of time, say, for 5 years, its cost should be amortized to expense over 5 years. Changing demand, new inventions superseding old ones, inadequacy, and other factors often limit the useful life of a patent to less than the legal life. For example, the useful life of patents in the pharmaceutical and drug industry is frequently less than the legal life because of the testing and approval period that follows their issuance. A typical drug patent has 5 to 11 years knocked off its 20-year legal life because 1 to 4 years must be spent on tests on animals, 4 to 6 years on human tests, and 2 to 3 years for the Food and Drug Administration to review the tests—all after the patent is issued but before the product goes on pharmacists' shelves.

WHAT DO THE NUMBERS MEAN?

PATENT BATTLES

From bioengineering to software design to the Internet, battles over patents are heating up as global competition intensifies. For example, **Priceline.com** filed suit against **Microsoft** for launching Hotel Price Matcher, a service that operates pretty much like the name-your-own-price-system pioneered by Priceline. And **Amazon.com** filed a complaint against **Barnesandnoble.com**, its bitter rival in the Web-retailing wars. The suit alleges that Barnesandnoble.com is infringing on Amazon.com's patent for one-click shopping and asks the court to stop Barnesandnoble.com from using its own quick-checkout system, called ExpressLane.

Source: Adapted from "Battle over Patents Threatens to Damp Web's Innovative Spirit," *Wall Street Journal* (November 8, 1999).

---

[7]Consider the opposite result: Sir Alexander Fleming, who discovered penicillin, decided not to use a patent to protect his discovery. He hoped that companies would produce it more quickly to help save sufferers. Companies, however, refused to develop it because they did not have the patent shield and, therefore, were afraid to make the investment.

Legal fees and other costs incurred in successfully defending a patent suit are debited to Patents, an asset account, because such a suit establishes the legal rights of the holder of the patent. Such costs should be amortized along with acquisition cost over the remaining useful life of the patent.

Amortization expense should reflect the pattern in which the patent is used up, if that pattern can be reliably determined. Amortization of patents may be credited directly to the Patent account, or it may be credited to an Accumulated Patent Amortization account. To illustrate, assume that Harcott Co. incurs $180,000 in legal costs on January 1, 2003, to successfully defend a patent. The patent has a useful life of 20 years and is amortized on a straight-line basis. The entries to record the legal fees and the amortization at the end of each year are as follows.

January 1, 2003		
Patents	180,000	
Cash		180,000
(To record legal fees related to patent)		
December 31, 2003		
Patent Amortization Expense	9,000	
Patents (or Accumulated Patent Amortization)		9,000
(To record amortization of patent)		

Amortization on a units-of-production basis would be computed in a manner similar to that described for depreciation on property, plant, and equipment in Chapter 11, page 523.

Although a patent's useful life should not extend beyond its legal life of 20 years, small modifications or additions may lead to a new patent. For example, **Astra Zeneca Plc** has filed additional patents on minor modifications to its heartburn drug, Prilosec. The effect may be to extend the life of the old patent. In that case it is permissible to apply the unamortized costs of the old patent to the new patent if the new patent provides essentially the same benefits.[8] Alternatively, if a patent becomes worthless (impaired) because demand drops for the product, the asset should be written down or written off immediately to expense.

THE VALUE OF A SECRET FORMULA

WHAT DO THE NUMBERS MEAN?

While the nuclear secrets contained within the Los Alamos nuclear lab seem easier to check out than a library book, **Coca-Cola** has managed to keep the recipe for the world's best-selling soft drink under wraps for more than 100 years. How has it done so?

Coca-Cola offers almost no information about its lifeblood. The only written copy of the formula resides in a SunTrust Bank vault in Atlanta. This handwritten sheet isn't available to anyone except by vote of the Coca-Cola board of directors.

Why can't science offer some clues? Coke contains 17 to 18 ingredients. That includes the usual caramel color and corn syrup, as well as a blend of oils known as 7X (rumored to be a mix of orange, lemon, cinnamon, and others). Distilling natural products like these is complicated, since they're made of thousands of compounds. One ingredient you won't find is cocaine. Although the original formula contained trace amounts, today's Coke doesn't. When was it removed? That is a secret too.

Some experts indicate that the power of this formula and related brand image account for almost 95 percent of Coke's $150 billion stock value.

Source: Adapted from Reed Tucker, "How Has Coke's Formula Stayed a Secret?" *Fortune* (July 24, 2000), p. 42.

---

[8]Another example is **Eli Lilly**'s drug Prozac (used to treat depression) which in 1998 accounted for 43 percent of its U.S. sales. The patent on Prozac expired in 2001 and the company was unable to extend its protection with a second-use patent for the use of Prozac to treat appetite disorders. Sales of Prozac were off substantially in 2001 as generic equivalents entered the market.

Goodwill

OBJECTIVE 5
Explain the conceptual issues related to goodwill.

Although companies are permitted to capitalize certain costs to develop specifically identifiable assets such as patents and copyrights, the amounts capitalized are generally not significant. But material amounts of intangible assets are recorded when companies purchase intangible assets, particularly in situations involving the purchase of another business (often referred to as a business combination).

In a business combination, the cost (purchase price) is assigned where possible to the identifiable tangible and intangible net assets, and the remainder is recorded in an intangible asset account called **Goodwill**. Goodwill is often referred to as the most intangible of the intangibles because it can only be identified with the business as a whole. The only way it can be sold is to sell the business.

The problem of determining the proper cost to allocate to intangible assets in a business combination is complex because of the many different types of intangibles that might be considered. Many of these types of intangibles have been discussed earlier. It is extremely difficult not only to identify certain types of intangibles but also to assign a value to them in a business combination. As a result, the approach followed is to record identifiable intangible assets that can be reliably measured. Other intangible assets that are difficult to identify or measure are recorded as goodwill.[9]

Recording Goodwill

OBJECTIVE 6
Describe the accounting procedures for recording goodwill.

Internally Created Goodwill. **Goodwill generated internally should not be capitalized in the accounts.** Measuring the components of goodwill is simply too complex and associating any costs with future benefits too difficult. The future benefits of goodwill may have no relationship to the costs incurred in the development of that goodwill. To add to the mystery, goodwill may even exist in the absence of specific costs to develop it. In addition, because no objective transaction with outside parties has taken place, a great deal of subjectivity—even misrepresentation—might be involved.

UNDERLYING CONCEPTS

Capitalizing goodwill only when it is purchased in an arm's-length transaction and not capitalizing any goodwill generated internally is another example of reliability winning out over relevance.

Purchased Goodwill. Goodwill is recorded only when an entire business is purchased, because goodwill is a "going concern" valuation and cannot be separated from the business as a whole. To record goodwill, the fair market value of the net tangible and identifiable intangible assets are compared with the purchase price of the acquired business. The difference is considered goodwill. This is why goodwill is sometimes referred to as a "plug," or "gap filler," or **"master valuation"** account. **Goodwill is the residual—the excess of cost over fair value of the identifiable net assets acquired.**

To illustrate, Multi-Diversified, Inc. decides that it needs a parts division to supplement its existing tractor distributorship. The president of Multi-Diversified is interested in buying a small concern in Chicago (Tractorling Company) that has an established reputation and is seeking a merger candidate. The balance sheet of Tractorling Company is presented in Illustration 12-3.

ILLUSTRATION 12-3
Tractorling Balance Sheet

TRACTORLING CO.
BALANCE SHEET
AS OF DECEMBER 31, 2003

Assets		Equities	
Cash	$ 25,000	Current liabilities	$ 55,000
Receivables	35,000	Capital stock	100,000
Inventories	42,000	Retained earnings	100,000
Property, plant, and equipment, net	153,000		
Total assets	$255,000	Total equities	$255,000

[9]The new business combination standard provides detailed guidance regarding the recognition of identifiable intangible assets in a business combination. Using this guidance, the expectation is that more identifiable intangible assets will be recognized in the financial statements as a result of business combinations. If this situation occurs, less goodwill will be recognized.

After considerable negotiation, Tractorling Company decides to accept Multi-Diversified's offer of $400,000. What, then, is the value of the goodwill, if any?

The answer is not obvious. The fair market values of Tractorling's identifiable assets are not disclosed in its historical cost-based balance sheet. Suppose, though, that as the negotiations progress, Multi-Diversified conducts an investigation of the underlying assets of Tractorling to determine the fair market value of the assets. Such an investigation may be accomplished either through a purchase audit undertaken by Multi-Diversified's auditors in order to estimate the values of the seller's assets, or by an independent appraisal from some other source. The following valuations are determined.

Expanded Discussion—Valuing Goodwill

ILLUSTRATION 12-4
Fair Market Value of Tractorling's Net Assets

Fair Market Values	
Cash	$ 25,000
Receivables	35,000
Inventories	122,000
Property, plant, and equipment, net	205,000
Patents	18,000
Liabilities	(55,000)
Fair market value of net assets	$350,000

Normally, differences between current fair market value and book value are more common among long-term assets, although significant differences can also develop in the current assets category. Cash obviously poses no problems as to value. And receivables normally are fairly close to current valuation, although at times certain adjustments need to be made because of inadequate bad debt provisions. Liabilities usually are stated at book value, although if interest rates have changed since the liabilities were incurred, a different valuation (such as present value) might be appropriate. Careful analysis must be made to determine that no unrecorded liabilities are present.

The $80,000 difference in Tractorling's inventories ($122,000 − $42,000) could result from a number of factors, the most likely being that the company uses LIFO. Recall that during periods of inflation, LIFO better matches expenses against revenues, but in doing so creates a balance sheet distortion. Ending inventory is comprised of older layers costed at lower valuations.

In many cases, the values of long-term assets such as property, plant, and equipment, and intangibles may have increased substantially over the years. This difference could be due to inaccurate estimates of useful lives, continual expensing of small expenditures (say, less than $300), inaccurate estimates of salvage values, and the discovery of some unrecorded assets (as in Tractorling's case, where Patents are discovered to have a fair value of $18,000). Or, replacement costs may have substantially increased.

Since the fair market value of net assets is now determined to be $350,000, why would Multi-Diversified pay $400,000? Undoubtedly, the seller pointed to an established reputation, good credit rating, top management team, well-trained employees, and so on as factors that make the value of the business greater than $350,000. At the same time, Multi-Diversified placed a premium on the future earning power of these attributes as well as the basic asset structure of the enterprise today. At this point in the negotiations, price can be a function of many factors; the most important is probably sheer skill at the bargaining table.

The difference between the purchase price of $400,000 and the fair market value of $350,000 is labeled goodwill. Goodwill is viewed as one or a group of unidentifiable values (intangible assets) the cost of which "is measured by the difference between the cost of the group of assets or enterprise acquired and the sum of the assigned costs of individual tangible and identifiable intangible assets acquired less liabilities assumed."[10] This procedure for valuation is referred to as a **master valuation approach** because goodwill is assumed to cover all the values that cannot be specifically identified with any identifiable tangible or intangible asset. This approach is shown in Illustration 12-5.

ILLUSTRATION 12-5
Determination of Goodwill—Master Valuation Approach

Assigned to purchase price of $400,000	Cash	$ 25,000
	Receivables	35,000
	Inventories	122,000
	Property, plant, and equipment, net	205,000
	Patents	18,000
	Liabilities	(55,000)
	Fair maket value of net identifiable assets	$350,000
	Purchase price	400,000
	Value assigned to goodwill	$ 50,000

The entry to record this transaction would be as follows.

Cash	25,000	
Receivables	35,000	
Inventory	122,000	
Property, Plant, and Equipment	205,000	
Patents	18,000	
Goodwill	50,000	
Liabilities		55,000
Cash		400,000

Goodwill is often identified on the balançe sheet as the **excess of cost over the fair value** of the net assets acquired.

Goodwill Write-off

Goodwill acquired in a business combination **is considered to have an indefinite life and therefore should not be amortized**. The Board's position is that investors find the amortization charge of little use in evaluating financial performance. In addition, although goodwill may decrease over time, predicting the actual life of goodwill and an appropriate pattern of amortization is extremely difficult.

On the other hand, knowing the amount invested in goodwill is important to the investment community. Therefore, **income statements are not charged unless goodwill has been impaired**. This approach will have a significant impact on the income statements of some companies because goodwill often is the largest intangible asset on a company's balance sheet. Prior to the new FASB standard, companies were required to amortize this intangible. For example, it was estimated that as a result of the new rules, earnings per share in 2001 would increase 21 percent for **International Paper**, 16 percent for **Johnson Controls**, and 30 percent for **Pepsi Bottling Group**.

Some believe that goodwill's value eventually disappears and therefore that goodwill should be charged to expense over the periods affected. Amortizing goodwill, they argue, provides a better matching of expense with revenues. Others note that the accounting treatment for purchased goodwill and goodwill created internally should be consistent. Goodwill created internally is immediately expensed and does not appear as an asset; the same treatment, they argue, should be accorded purchased goodwill. Even though these arguments may have some merit, the FASB decided that nonamor-

[10]The FASB expressed concern about measuring goodwill as a residual, but it noted that there is no real measurement alternative since goodwill is not separable from the enterprise as a whole. "Business Combinations," *Statement of Financial Accounting Standards No. 141* (Norwalk, Conn.: FASB, 2001), par. B145.

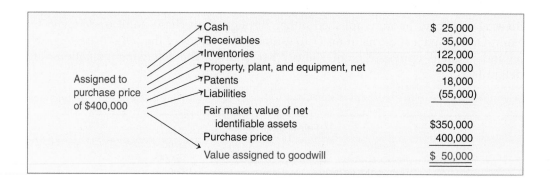

tization of goodwill combined with an adequate impairment test provides the most useful financial information to the investment community.

KITCHEN SINKS AND BATHTUBS

WHAT DO THE NUMBERS MEAN?

Companies will use 2002 to take massive write-offs that will cut earnings by 15 percent to 20 percent, says Goldman Sachs Group Inc. Chief Investment Strategist Abby Joseph Cohen. "Simply stated, many companies are writing off not only the kitchen sink but the bathtub as well," Ms. Cohen wrote. For instance, AOL Time Warner Inc. planned a goodwill write-down in the first quarter that—by itself—would reduce S&P 500 earnings by $2 to $4 on an after-tax basis, Ms. Cohen said.

Ms. Cohen attributed companies' massive write-downs to various factors: the implied or real impacts from the September 11, 2001, terrorist attacks, the official announcement that the country was in a recession, and new rules for the write-down of goodwill. She also says that when all is said and done, 2002 will have seen write-offs that cut into S&P earnings by 35 percent to 40 percent.

Still, Ms. Cohen isn't backing off estimates of 7 percent to 8 percent long-term earnings growth, saying that the hits will be tough to swallow in the quarter during which they are taken, but that they won't be of lasting impact psychologically or operationally. "The quarter in which the write-offs are recorded typically bears the statistical brunt, but may not be reflective of performance in future quarters," according to Ms. Cohen.

Negative Goodwill—Badwill

Negative goodwill arises when the fair value of the assets acquired is higher than the purchase price of the assets. This situation is a result of market imperfection, because the seller would be better off to sell the assets individually than in total. However, situations do occur in which the purchase price is less than the value of the net identifiable assets and therefore a credit develops. Because the Board believes that these situations are generally unrealistic, it decided that any excess should be allocated on a pro-rata basis to certain assets (generally non-financial in nature), to reduce them to a zero basis. Any remaining credit is referred to as **negative goodwill** or, alternatively, as **excess of fair value over the cost acquired**, **badwill**, or **bargain purchase**.

The FASB requires that this remaining excess be recognized as an extraordinary gain. The Board noted that extraordinary gain treatment is appropriate in order to highlight the fact that an excess exists and to reflect the unusual nature and infrequent occurrence of the item. Some disagree with the approach, as it results in a gain at the time of the purchase. However, it appears that the Board took a practical approach, given that this transaction rarely occurs.[11]

IMPAIRMENT OF INTANGIBLE ASSETS

OBJECTIVE 7
Explain the accounting issues related to intangible asset impairments.

In some cases, the carrying amount of a long-lived asset (whether property, plant, and equipment or intangible assets) is not recoverable, and therefore a write-off is needed. This write-off is referred to as an **impairment**.

Impairment of Limited-Life Intangibles

The rules that apply to **impairments of long-lived assets also apply to limited-life intangibles**. As indicated in Chapter 11, long-lived assets to be held and used by a company are to be reviewed for impairment whenever events or changes in circumstances

[11] "Business Combinations," *Statement of Financial Accounting Standards No. 141* (Norwalk, Conn.: FASB, 2001), pars. B187–B192.

indicate that **the carrying amount of the assets may not be recoverable (recoverability test)**. In performing the review for recoverability, the company would estimate the future cash flows expected to result from the use of the asset and its eventual disposition. If the sum of the expected future net cash flows (undiscounted) is less than the carrying amount of the asset, an impairment loss would be measured and recognized. Otherwise, an impairment loss would not be recognized.[12] The impairment loss is the amount by which the carrying amount of the asset exceeds the fair value of the impaired asset (**fair value test**). As with other impairments, the loss is reported as part of income from continuing operations, generally in the "Other expenses and losses" section.

To illustrate, assume that Lerch, Inc. has a patent on how to extract oil from shale rock. Unfortunately, reduced oil prices have made the shale oil technology somewhat unprofitable, and the patent has provided little income to date. As a result, a recoverability test is performed, and it is found that the expected net future cash flows from this patent are $35 million. Lerch's patent has a carrying amount of $60 million. Because the expected future net cash flows of $35 million are less than the carrying amount of $60 million, an impairment loss must be measured. Discounting the expected net future cash flows at the market rate of interest, Lerch determines the fair value of its patent to be $20 million. The impairment loss computation (fair value test) is shown in Illustration 12-6.

ILLUSTRATION 12-6
Computation of Loss on Impairment of Patent

Carrying amount of patent	$60,000,000
Fair value (based on present value computation)	20,000,000
Loss on impairment	$40,000,000

The journal entry to record this loss is:

Loss on Impairment	40,000,000	
Patents		40,000,000

After the impairment is recognized, the reduced carrying amount of the patents is its new cost basis. The patent's new cost should be amortized over its useful life or legal life, whichever is shorter. Even if oil prices increase in subsequent periods, and the value of the patent increases, **restoration of the previously recognized impairment loss is not permitted**.

Impairment of Indefinite-Life Intangibles Other Than Goodwill

Indefinite-life intangibles other than goodwill should be tested for impairment at least annually. The impairment test for an indefinite-life asset other than goodwill is a **fair value test**. This test compares the fair value of the intangible asset with the asset's carrying amount. If the fair value of the intangible asset is less than the carrying amount, impairment is recognized. This one-step test is used because it would be relatively easy for many indefinite-life assets to meet the recoverability test (because cash flows may extend many years into the future). **As a result, the recoverability test is not used.**

To illustrate, assume that Arcon Radio purchased a broadcast license for $2,000,000. The license is renewable every 10 years if the company provides appropriate service and does not violate Federal Communications Commission (FCC) rules and procedures. The license has been renewed with the FCC twice, at a minimal cost. Cash flows were expected to last indefinitely, and therefore Arcon reported the license as an indefinite-life intangible asset. Recently the FCC decided to no longer renew broadcast licenses, but to auction these licenses to the highest bidder. Arcon's existing license has 2 years

[12]"Accounting for the Impairment of Long-Lived Assets," *Statement of Financial Accounting Standards No. 121* (Norwalk, Conn.: FASB, 1994).

remaining, and cash flows are expected for these 2 years. Arcon performs an impairment test and determines that the fair value of the intangible asset is $1,500,000. It therefore reports an impairment loss of $500,000, computed as follows.

ILLUSTRATION 12-7
Computation of Loss on Impairment of Broadcast License

Carrying amount of broadcast license	$2,000,000
Fair value of broadcast license	1,500,000
Loss on impairment	$ 500,000

The license would now be reported at $1,500,000, its fair value. Even if the value of the license increases in the remaining 2 years, restoration of the previously recognized impairment loss is not permitted.

Impairment of Goodwill

The impairment rule for goodwill is a two-step process. First, the fair value of the reporting unit should be compared to its carrying amount including goodwill. If the fair value of the reporting unit is greater than the carrying amount, goodwill is considered not to be impaired, and the company does not have to do anything else.

To illustrate, assume that Kohlbuy Corporation has three divisions in its company. One division, Pritt Products, was purchased 4 years ago for $2 million. Unfortunately, it has experienced operating losses over the last 3 quarters, and management is reviewing the division for purposes of recognizing an impairment. The Pritt Division's net assets including the associated goodwill of $900,000 from purchase are listed in Illustration 12-8.

ILLUSTRATION 12-8
Net Assets of Pritt Division, Including Goodwill

Cash	$ 200,000
Receivables	300,000
Inventory	700,000
Property, plant, and equipment (net)	800,000
Goodwill	900,000
Less: Accounts and notes payable	(500,000)
Net assets	$2,400,000

It is determined that the fair value of Pritt Division is $2,800,000. As a result, no impairment is recognized, because the fair value of the division is greater than the carrying amount of the net assets.

However, if the fair value of Pritt Division is less than the carrying amount of the net assets, then a second step must be performed to determine whether impairment has occurred. In the second step, the fair value of the goodwill must be determined (implied value of goodwill) and compared to its carrying amount. To illustrate, assume that the fair value of Pritt's Division was $1,900,000 instead of $2,800,000. The implied value of the goodwill in this case is computed in Illustration 12-9.[13]

ILLUSTRATION 12-9
Determination of Implied Value of Goodwill

Fair value of Pritt Division	$1,900,000
Net identifiable assets (excluding goodwill) ($2,400,000 − $900,000)	1,500,000
Implied value of goodwill	$ 400,000

[13]Illustration 12-9 assumes that the carrying amount and the fair value of the net identifiable assets (excluding goodwill) are the same. If different, the fair value of the net identifiable assets (excluding goodwill) is used to determine the implied goodwill.

The implied value of the goodwill is then compared to the recorded goodwill to determine whether an impairment has occurred, as shown in Illustration 12-10.

ILLUSTRATION 12-10
Measurement of Goodwill Impairment

Carrying amount of goodwill	$900,000
Implied value of goodwill	400,000
Loss on impairment	$500,000

Illustration 12-11 summarizes the impairment tests for various intangible assets.

ILLUSTRATION 12-11
Summary of Intangible Asset Impairment Tests

Type of Intangible Asset	Impairment Test
Limited life	Recoverability test, then fair value test
Indefinite life other than goodwill	Fair value test
Goodwill	Fair value test on reporting unit, then fair value test on implied goodwill

RESEARCH AND DEVELOPMENT COSTS

OBJECTIVE 8
Identify the conceptual issues related to research and development costs.

Research and development (R & D) costs are not in themselves intangible assets. The accounting for R & D costs is presented here, however, because research and development activities frequently result in the development of something that is patented or copyrighted (such as a new product, process, idea, formula, composition, or literary work).

Many businesses spend considerable sums of money on research and development to create new products or processes, to improve present products, and to discover new knowledge that may be valuable at some future date. The following schedule shows recent outlays for R & D made by selected U.S. companies.

ILLUSTRATION 12-12
R & D Outlays, as a Percentage of Sales and Profits

Company	R & D Dollars	% of Sales	% of Profits
Deere & Co.	$ 444,400,000	3.73%	43.51%
Dell Computer	272,000,000	1.49%	18.63%
General Mills	70,000,000	1.12%	13.10%
Johnson & Johnson	2,269,000,000	9.59%	74.17%
Kellogg	121,900,000	1.80%	24.25%
Merck	1,821,100,000	6.77%	34.70%

INTERNATIONAL INSIGHT

International accounting standards require the capitalization of appropriate development expenditures. This conflicts with U.S. GAAP.

Two difficulties arise in accounting for these research and development (R & D) expenditures: (1) identifying the costs associated with particular activities, projects, or achievements, and (2) determining the magnitude of the future benefits and length of time over which such benefits may be realized. Because of these latter uncertainties, the accounting practice in this area has been simplified by requiring that **all research and development costs be charged to expense when incurred.**[14]

[14]"Accounting for Research and Development Costs," *Statement of Financial Accounting Standards No. 2* (Stamford, Conn.: FASB, 1974), par. 12.

Identifying R & D Activities

To differentiate research and development costs from similar costs, the following definitions are used for **research activities** and **development activities.**[15]

ILLUSTRATION 12-13
R & D Activities

Research Activities	Development Activities

Planned search or critical investigation aimed at discovery of new knowledge.	Translation of research findings or other knowledge into a plan or design for a new product or process or for a significant improvement to an existing product or process whether intended for sale or use.
Examples	**Examples**
Laboratory research aimed at discovery of new knowledge; searching for applications of new research findings.	Conceptual formulation and design of possible product or process alternatives; construction of prototypes and operation of pilot plants.

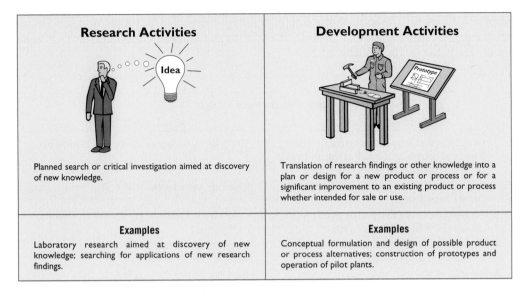

It should be emphasized that R & D activities do not include routine or periodic alterations to existing products, production lines, manufacturing processes, and other ongoing operations even though these alterations may represent improvements. For example, routine ongoing efforts to refine, enrich, or improve the qualities of an existing product are not considered R & D activities.

Accounting for R & D Activities

OBJECTIVE 9
Describe the accounting procedures for research and development costs and for other similar costs.

The costs associated with R & D activities and the accounting treatment accorded them are as follows.

1. *Materials, Equipment, and Facilities.* Expense the entire costs, **unless the items have alternative future uses** (in other R & D projects or otherwise), in which case, carry as inventory and allocate as consumed; or capitalize and depreciate as used.
2. *Personnel.* Salaries, wages, and other related costs of personnel engaged in R & D should be expensed as incurred.
3. *Purchased Intangibles.* Expense the entire cost, **unless the items have alternative future uses** (in other R & D projects or otherwise), in which case, capitalize and amortize.
4. *Contract Services.* The costs of services performed by others in connection with the reporting company's R & D should be expensed as incurred.
5. *Indirect Costs.* A reasonable allocation of indirect costs shall be included in R & D costs, except for general and administrative cost, which must be clearly related in order to be included and expensed.[16]

Consistent with item 1 above, if an enterprise owns a research facility consisting of buildings, laboratories, and equipment that conducts R & D activities and that has

[15]Ibid., par. 8.

[16]Ibid, par. 11.

alternative future uses (in other R & D projects or otherwise), the facility should be accounted for as a capitalized operational asset. The depreciation and other costs related to such research facilities are accounted for as R & D expenses.[17]

To illustrate the identification of R & D activities and the accounting treatment of related costs, assume that Next Century Incorporated develops, produces, and markets laser machines for medical, industrial, and defense uses.[18] The types of expenditures related to its laser machine activities, along with the recommended accounting treatment, are listed in Illustration 12-14.

ILLUSTRATION 12-14
Sample R & D Expenditures and Their Accounting Treatment

Next Century Incorporated

Type of Expenditure	Accounting Treatment
1. Construction of long-range research facility for use in current and future projects (three-story, 400,000-square-foot building).	Capitalize and depreciate as R & D expense.
2. Acquisition of R & D equipment for use on current project only.	Expense immediately as R & D.
3. Acquisition of machinery to be used on current and future R & D projects.	Capitalize and depreciate as R & D expense.
4. Purchase of materials to be used on current and future R & D projects.	Inventory and allocate to R & D projects; expense as consumed.
5. Salaries of research staff designing new laser bone scanner.	Expense immediately as R & D.
6. Research costs incurred under contract with New Horizon, Inc., and billable monthly.	Record as a receivable (reimbursable expenses).
7. Material, labor, and overhead costs of prototype laser scanner.	Expense immediately as R & D.
8. Costs of testing prototype and design modifications.	Expense immediately as R & D.
9. Legal fees to obtain patent on new laser scanner.	Capitalize as patent and amortize to overhead as part of cost of goods manufactured.
10. Executive salaries.	Expense as operating expense (general and administrative).
11. Cost of marketing research to promote new laser scanner.	Expense as operating expense (selling).
12. Engineering costs incurred to advance the laser scanner to full production stage.	Expense immediately as R & D.
13. Costs of successfully defending patent on laser scanner.	Capitalize as patent and amortize to overhead as part of cost of goods manufactured.
14. Commissions to sales staff marketing new laser scanner.	Expense as operating expense (selling).

[17]Costs of research, exploration, and development activities that are unique to companies in the **extractive industries** (e.g., prospecting, acquisition of mineral rights, exploration, drilling, mining, and related mineral development) and those costs discussed which are similar to but not classified as R & D costs may be: (1) expensed as incurred, (2) capitalized and either depreciated or amortized over an appropriate period of time, or (3) accumulated as part of inventoriable costs. Choice of the appropriate accounting treatment for such costs should be guided by the degree of certainty of future benefits and the principle of matching revenues and expenses.

[18]Sometimes enterprises conduct R & D activities for other entities under a **contractual arrangement.** In this case, the contract usually specifies that all direct costs, certain specific indirect costs, plus a profit element, should be reimbursed to the enterprise performing the R & D work. Because reimbursement is expected, such R & D costs should be recorded as a receivable. It is the company for whom the work has been performed that reports these costs as R & D and expenses them as incurred.

For a more complete discussion of how an enterprise should account for its obligation under an arrangement for the funding of its research and development by others, see "Research and Development Arrangements," *Statement of Financial Accounting Standards No. 68* (Stamford, Conn.: FASB, 1982).

Other Costs Similar to R & D Costs

Many costs have characteristics similar to research and development costs. Examples are:

1. Start-up costs for a new operation.
2. Initial operating losses.
3. Advertising costs.
4. Computer software costs.

For the most part, these costs are expensed as incurred, similar to the accounting for R & D costs. A brief explanation of these costs is provided below.

Start-up Costs

Start-up costs are costs incurred for one-time activities to start a new operation. Examples include opening a new plant, introducing a new product or service, or conducting business in a new territory or with a new class of customers. Start-up costs include **organizational costs**. These are costs incurred in the organizing of a new entity, such as legal and state fees of various types.

The accounting for start-up costs is straightforward: **Expense start-up costs as incurred**. The profession recognizes that these costs are incurred with the expectation that future revenues will occur or increased efficiencies will result. However, to determine the amount and timing of future benefits is so difficult that a conservative approach—expensing these costs as incurred—is required.[19]

To illustrate the type of costs that should be expensed as start-up costs, assume that U.S.-based Hilo Beverage Company decides to construct a new plant in Brazil. This represents Hilo's first entry into the Brazilian market. As part of its overall strategy, Hilo plans to introduce the company's major U.S. brands into Brazil, on a locally produced basis. Following are some of the costs that might be involved with these start-up activities.

1. Travel-related costs, costs related to employee salaries, and costs related to feasibility studies, accounting, tax, and government affairs.
2. Training of local employees related to product, maintenance, computer systems, finance, and operations.
3. Recruiting, organizing, and training related to establishing a distribution network.

All of these costs are start-up costs and should be expensed as incurred.

It is not uncommon for start-up activities to occur at the same time as other activities, such as the acquisition or development of assets. For example, property, plant, and equipment or inventory used in Hilo's new plant should not be immediately expensed. These assets should be reported on the balance sheet and charged to operations using appropriate GAAP reporting guidelines.

---

[19]"Reporting on the Costs of Start-Up Activities," *Statement of Position 98-5* (New York: AICPA, 1998).

Initial Operating Losses

Some contend that initial operating losses incurred in the start-up of a business should be capitalized, since they are unavoidable and are a cost of starting a business. For example, assume that Hilo lost money in its first year of operations and wished to capitalize this loss arguing that as the company becomes profitable, it will offset these losses in future periods. What do you think? We believe that this approach is unsound, since losses have no future service potential and therefore cannot be considered an asset.

Our position that operating losses during the early years should not be capitalized is supported by *Statement of Financial Accounting Standards No. 7*, which clarifies the accounting and reporting practices for **development stage enterprises. The FASB concludes that the accounting practices and reporting standards should be no different for an enterprise trying to establish a new business than they are for other enterprises.** The standard says that the same "generally accepted accounting principles that apply to established operating enterprises shall govern the recognition of revenue by a development stage enterprise and shall determine whether a cost incurred by a development stage enterprise is to be charged to expense when incurred or is to be capitalized or deferred."[20]

Advertising Costs

Recently, **PepsiCo** hired pop icon Britney Spears to advertise its products. How should the advertising costs related to Britney Spears be reported? These costs could be expensed in a variety of ways:

1. When she has completed her singing assignment.
2. The first time the advertising takes place.
3. Over the estimated useful life of the advertising.
4. In an appropriate fashion to each of the three periods identified above.
5. Over the period revenues are expected to result.

For the most part advertising costs must be expensed as incurred or the first time the advertising takes place. These two alternatives are permitted because whichever approach is followed, the results are essentially the same. Tangible assets used in advertising, such as billboards or blimps, are recorded as assets because they do have alternative future uses. Again the profession has taken a conservative approach to recording advertising costs because defining and measuring the future benefits are so difficult.[21]

---

[20]"Accounting and Reporting by Development Stage Enterprises," *Statement of Financial Accounting Standards No. 7* (Stamford, Conn.: FASB, 1975), par. 10. A company is considered to be in the developing stages when its efforts are directed toward establishing a new business and either the principal operations have not started or no significant revenue has been earned.

[21]"Reporting on Advertising Costs," *Statement of Position 93-7* (New York: AICPA, 1993). Note that there are some exceptions for immediate expensing of advertising costs when they relate to direct-response advertising, but this subject is beyond the scope of this book.

BRANDED

WHAT DO THE NUMBERS MEAN?

For many companies, developing a strong brand image is as important as developing the products they sell. Now more than ever, companies see the power of a strong brand, which is generally enhanced by significant and effective advertising investments. As indicated in the following chart, the value of such investments is substantial, with **Coca-Cola** leading the list with an estimated brand value of nearly $70 billion.

The World's 10 Most Valuable Brands
(in billions)

1	Coca-Cola	$69.6	6	Nokia	$30.0
2	Microsoft	64.1	7	Disney	29.3
3	IBM	51.2	8	McDonald's	26.4
4	GE	41.3	9	Marlboro	24.2
5	Intel	30.9	10	Mercedes	21.0

Source: 2002 data, from Interbrand Corp. and J. P. Morgan Chase.

Except for the value of a brand that may be included in goodwill, you won't find the estimated values of these brands recorded in these companies' balance sheets. The reason? The subjectivity that goes into estimating the value of a brand. In some cases, brand value is estimated based on opinion polls or based on some multiple of ad spending. In estimating the values in the table, **Interbrand Corp.** develops an estimate of the percentage of the overall future revenues that will be accounted for by the power of the brand and then discounts the net cash flows (after deducting the estimated costs to generate the cash flows), to arrive at a present value. While some believe that information on brand values is relevant, subjectivity in the estimates for revenues, costs, and the risk component of the discount rate introduces valid concerns about the reliability of brand value estimates.

Source: Adapted from Gerry Khermouch, "The Best Global Brands," *Businessweek* (August 5, 2002), pp. 93–95.

Computer Software Costs

A special problem arises in distinguishing R & D costs from selling and administrative activities. The FASB's intent was that the acquisition, development, or improvement of a product or process by an enterprise **for use in its selling or administrative activities** be excluded from the definition of research and development activities. For example, the costs of software incurred by an airline in acquiring, developing, or improving its computerized reservation system, or the costs incurred during the development of a general management information system **are not** research and development costs. Accounting for computer software costs is a specialized and complicated accounting topic that is discussed and illustrated in Appendix 12A (pages 594–597).

UNDERLYING CONCEPTS

The requirement that all R & D costs be expensed as incurred is an example of the conflict between relevance and reliability, with this requirement leaning strongly in support of reliability, as well as conservatism, consistency, and comparability. No attempt is made to match costs and revenues.

Conceptual Questions

The requirement that all R & D costs (as well as other costs mentioned in the previous section) incurred internally be expensed immediately is a conservative, practical solution that ensures consistency in practice and uniformity among companies. But the practice of immediately writing off expenditures made in the expectation of benefiting future periods cannot be justified on the grounds that it is good accounting theory.

Proponents of immediate expensing contend that from an income statement standpoint, long-run application of this standard frequently makes little difference. They contend that because of the ongoing nature of most companies' R & D activities, the amount of R & D cost charged to expense each accounting period would be about the same whether there is immediate expensing or capitalization and subsequent amortization. Critics of this practice argue that the balance sheet should report an intangible asset related to expenditures that have future benefit. To preclude capitalization of all R & D expenditures removes from the balance sheet what may be a company's most valuable asset. This standard represents one of the many trade-offs made among relevance, reliability, and cost-benefit considerations.[22]

INTERNATIONAL INSIGHT

The International Accounting Standards Board issued a standard that is in disagreement with the FASB's standard on accounting for R & D costs. The IASB identified certain circumstances that justify the capitalization and deferral of development costs.

PRESENTATION OF INTANGIBLES AND RELATED ITEMS

OBJECTIVE 10
Indicate the presentation of intangible assets and related items.

Presentation of Intangible Assets

The reporting of intangible assets differs from the reporting of property, plant, and equipment in that contra accounts are not normally shown for intangibles. On the balance sheet, all intangible assets other than goodwill should be reported as a separate item. If goodwill is present, it also should be reported as a separate item. The Board concluded that since goodwill and other intangible assets differ significantly from other types of assets, users of the balance sheet will benefit from this disclosure.

On the income statement, amortization expense and impairment losses for intangible assets other than goodwill should be presented as part of continuing operations. Goodwill impairment losses should also be presented as a separate line item in the continuing operations section, unless the goodwill impairment is associated with a discontinued operation.

The notes to the financial statements should include information about acquired intangible assets, including the aggregate amortization expense for each of the succeeding 5 years. The notes should include information about changes in the carrying amount of goodwill during the period. Illustration 12-15 on page 591 shows the type of disclosure made related to intangible assets in the financial statements and related notes for Harbaugh Company.

Presentation of Research and Development Costs

Acceptable accounting practice requires that disclosure be made in the financial statements (generally in the notes) of the total R & D costs charged to expense each period for which an income statement is presented. **Merck & Co., Inc.**, a global research pharmaceutical company, reported research and development in its recent income statement as shown in Illustration 12-16 on page 592.

---

[22]Recent research suggests that capitalizing research and development costs may be helpful to investors. For example, one study showed that a significant relationship exists between R & D outlays and subsequent benefits in the form of increased productivity, earnings, and shareholder value for R & D–intensive companies. Baruch Lev and Theodore Sougiannis, "The Capitalization, Amortization, and Value-Relevance of R & D," *Journal of Accounting and Economics* (February 1996). Another study found that there was a significant decline in earnings usefulness for companies that were forced to switch from capitalizing to expensing R & D costs and that the decline appears to persist over time. Martha L. Loudder and Bruce K. Behn, "Alternative Income Determination Rules and Earnings Usefulness: The Case of R & D Costs," *Contemporary Accounting Research* (Fall 1995).

ILLUSTRATION 12-15
Intangible Asset Disclosures

HARBAUGH COMPANY

Balance Sheet (partial)
(in thousands)

Intangible Assets (Note C)	$3,840
Goodwill (Note D)	2,575

Income Statement (partial)
(in thousands)

as part of Continuing operations

Amortization expense	$380
Impairment losses (goodwill)	46

Note C: Acquired Intangible Assets

	As of December 31, 2003	
	Gross Carrying Amount	Accumulated Amortization
Amortized intangible assets		
Trademark	$2,000	$(100)
Customer list	500	(310)
Other	60	(10)
Total	$2,560	$(420)
Unamortized intangible assets		
Licenses	$1,300	
Trademark	400	
Total	$1,700	

Aggregate Amortization Expense

For year ended 12/31/03	$380

Estimated Amortization Expense

For year ended 12/31/04	$200
For year ended 12/31/05	90
For year ended 12/31/06	70
For year ended 12/31/07	60
For year ended 12/31/08	50

Note D: Goodwill

The changes in the carrying amount of goodwill for the year ended December 31, 2003, are as follows:

($000s)	Technology Segment	Communications Segment	Total
Balance as of January 1, 2003	$1,413	$904	$2,317
Goodwill acquired during year	189	115	304
Impairment losses	—	(46)	(46)
Balance as of December 31, 2003	$1,602	$973	$2,575

The Communications segment is tested for impairment in the third quarter, after the annual forecasting process. Due to an increase in competition in the Texas and Louisiana cable industry, operating profits and cash flows were lower than expected in the fourth quarter of 2002 and the first and second quarters of 2003. Based on that trend, the earnings forecast for the next 5 years was revised. In September 2003, a goodwill impairment loss of $46 was recognized in the Communications reporting unit. The fair value of that reporting unit was estimated using the expected present value of future cash flows.

ILLUSTRATION 12-16
Income Statement Disclosure of R & D Costs

MERCK

Merck & Co., Inc.
(in millions)

	Years Ended December 31		
	2001	2000	1999
Sales	$47,715.7	$40,363.2	$32,714.0
Costs, expenses, and other			
Materials and production	28,976.5	22,443.5	17,534.2
Marketing and administrative	6,224.4	6,167.7	5,199.9
Research and development	2,456.4	2,343.8	2,068.3
Equity income from affiliates	(685.9)	(764.9)	(762.0)
Other (income) expense, net	341.7	349.0	54.1
	$37,313.1	$30,539.1	$24,094.5

Additional Disclosures of Intangibles and R & D Costs

In addition, Merck provides a discussion about R & D expenditures in its annual report, as shown in Illustration 12-17.

ILLUSTRATION 12-17
Merck's R & D Disclosure

MERCK

Merck & Co., Inc.

Research and development in the pharmaceutical industry is inherently a long-term process. The following data show an unbroken trend of year-to-year increases in research and development spending. For the period 1992 to 2001, the compounded annual growth rate in research and development was 10%. Research and development expenses for 2002 are estimated to approximate $2.9 billion.

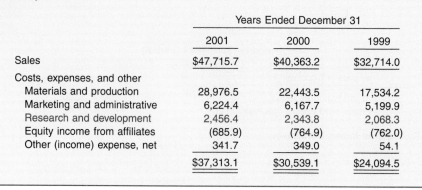

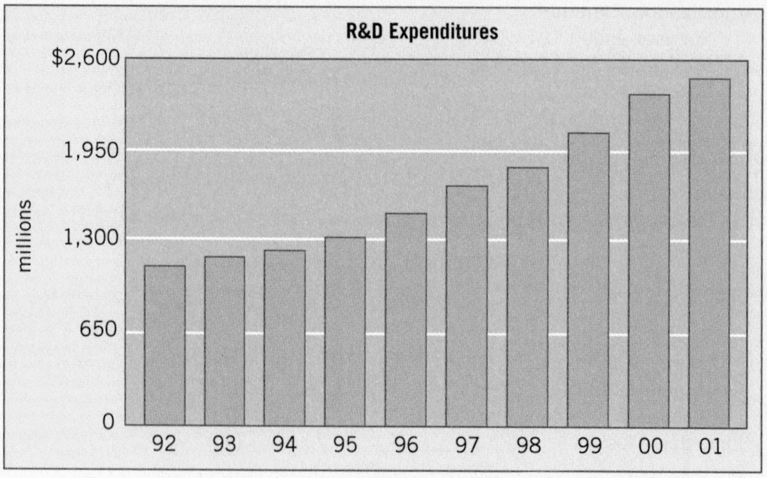

SUMMARY OF LEARNING OBJECTIVES

1 Describe the characteristics of intangible assets. Intangible assets have two main characteristics: (1) They lack physical existence, and (2) they are not financial instruments. In most cases, intangible assets provide services over a period of years. As a result, they are normally classified as long-term assets.

2 Identify the costs included in the initial valuation of intangible assets. Intangibles are recorded at cost. Cost includes all costs of acquisition and expenditures necessary to make the intangible asset ready for its intended use. If intangibles are acquired for stock or in exchange for other assets, the cost of the intangible is the fair value of the consideration given or the fair value of the intangible received, whichever is more clearly evident. When several intangibles, or a combination of intangibles and tangibles, are bought in a "basket purchase," the cost should be allocated on the basis of fair values.

3 Explain the procedure for amortizing intangible assets. Intangibles have either a limited useful life or an indefinite useful life. An intangible asset with a limited life is amortized. An intangible asset with an indefinite life is not amortized. Limited-life intangibles should be amortized by systematic charges to expense over their useful life. The useful life should reflect the period over which these assets will contribute to cash flows. The amount to report for amortization expense should reflect the pattern in which the asset is consumed or used up if that pattern can be reliably determined. Otherwise a straight-line approach should be used.

4 Identify the types of intangible assets. Major types of intangibles are: (1) marketing-related intangibles which are used in the marketing or promotion of products or services; (2) customer-related intangibles which are a result of interactions with outside parties; (3) artistic-related intangibles which involve ownership rights to such items as plays and literary works; (4) contract-related intangibles which represent the value of rights that arise from contractual arrangements; (5) technology-related intangible assets which relate to innovations or technological advances; and (6) goodwill which arises in business combinations.

5 Explain the conceptual issues related to goodwill. Goodwill is unique because unlike receivables, inventories, and patents that can be sold or exchanged individually in the marketplace, goodwill can be identified only with the business as a whole. Goodwill is a "going concern" valuation and is recorded only when an entire business is purchased. Goodwill generated internally should not be capitalized in the accounts, because measuring the components of goodwill is too complex and associating any costs with future benefits too difficult. The future benefits of goodwill may have no relationship to the costs incurred in the development of that goodwill. Goodwill may exist even in the absence of specific costs to develop it.

6 Describe the accounting procedures for recording goodwill. To record goodwill, the fair market value of the net tangible and identifiable intangible assets are compared with the purchase price of the acquired business. The difference is considered goodwill. Goodwill is the residual—the excess of cost over fair value of the identifiable net assets acquired. Goodwill is often identified on the balance sheet as the excess of cost over the fair value of the net assets acquired.

7 Explain the accounting issues related to intangible asset impairments. Impairment occurs when the carrying amount of the intangible asset is not recoverable. Impairments for limited-life intangible assets are based on a recoverability test and a fair value test. Indefinite-life intangibles use only a fair value test. Goodwill impairments use a two-step process: First, test the fair value of the reporting unit, then do the fair value test on implied goodwill.

8 Identify the conceptual issues related to research and development costs. R & D costs are not in themselves intangible assets, but research and development activities frequently result in the development of something that is patented or copyrighted. The difficulties in accounting for R & D expenditures are: (1) identifying the costs associated with particular activities, projects, or achievements, and (2) determining the magnitude of the future benefits and length of time over which such benefits may be realized. Because of these latter uncertainties, the FASB has standardized and simplified accounting practice by requiring that all research and development costs be charged to expense when incurred.

9 Describe the accounting procedures for research and development costs and for other similar costs. The costs associated with R & D activities and the accounting treatment

KEY TERMS

amortization, *571*
badwill, *581*
copyright, *575*
development activities, *585*
fair value test, *582*
franchise, *575*
goodwill, *578*
impairment, *581*
indefinite-life intangibles, *572*
intangible assets, *570*
license (permit), *575*
limited-life intangibles, *571*
master valuation approach, *580*
negative goodwill (badwill), *581*
organizational costs, *587*
patent, *576*
process patent, *576*
product patent, *576*
recoverability test, *582*
research activities, *585*
research and development (R & D) costs, *584*
start-up costs, *587*
trademark, trade name, 573

accorded them are as follows: (1) *Materials, equipment, and facilities:* Expense the entire costs, unless the items have alternative future uses, in which case, carry as inventory and allocate as consumed; or capitalize and depreciate as used. (2) *Personnel:* Salaries, wages, and other related costs of personnel engaged in R & D should be expensed as incurred. (3) *Purchased intangibles:* Expense the entire cost, unless the items have alternative future uses, in which case, capitalize and amortize. (4) *Contract services:* The costs of services performed by others in connection with the reporting company's R & D should be expensed as incurred. (5) *Indirect costs:* A reasonable allocation of indirect costs shall be included in R & D costs, except for general and administrative costs, which must be related to be included and expensed. Many costs have characteristics similar to R & D costs. Examples are start-up costs, initial operating losses, advertising costs, and computer software costs. For the most part, these costs are expensed as incurred, similar to the accounting for R & D costs.

10 **Indicate the presentation of intangible assets and related items.** The reporting of intangibles differs from the reporting of property, plant, and equipment in that contra accounts are not normally shown. On the balance sheet, all intangible assets other than goodwill should be reported as a separate item. If goodwill is present, it too should be reported as a separate item. On the income statement, amortization expense and impairment losses should normally be reported in continuing operations. The notes to the financial statements have additional detailed information. Disclosure must be made in the financial statements for the total R & D costs charged to expense each period for which an income statement is presented.

APPENDIX 12A

Accounting for Computer Software Costs

OBJECTIVE 11
Understand the accounting treatment for computer software costs.

The development of computer software products takes on increasing importance as our economy continues to change from a manufacturing process orientation (tangible outputs) to an information flow society (intangible outputs).[1] This appendix discusses the basic issues involved in accounting for computer software.

DIVERSITY IN PRACTICE

Computer software may be either **purchased** or **created** by a company. It may be purchased or created for **external use** (such as spreadsheet applications like Excel or Lotus 1-2-3) or for **internal use** (e.g., to establish a better internal accounting system).

[1]A major contributing factor was **IBM**'s decision in 1969 to "unbundle" its hardware and software, that is, to state the cost of the hardware and software separately. Prior to the unbundling, most applications software was provided free with the hardware. This unbundling led to the creation of a whole new industry, the software industry, whose members began selling software to hardware users.

Should costs incurred in developing the software be expensed immediately or capitalized and amortized in the future? Prior to 1985, some companies expensed all software costs, and others capitalized such costs. Still others differentiated such costs on the basis of whether the software was purchased or created, or whether it was used for external or internal purposes.

THE PROFESSION'S POSITION

A major question is whether the costs involved in developing software are research and development costs. If they are actually R & D, then the profession requires that they be expensed as incurred. If they are not research and development costs, then a strong case can be made for capitalization. As one financial executive of a software company, who argues for capitalization, noted, "The key distinction between our spending and R & D is recoverability. We know we are developing something we can sell."

In an attempt to resolve this issue (at least for companies that sell computer software), the FASB issued *Statement of Financial Accounting Standards No. 86,* "Accounting for the Costs of Computer Software to Be Sold, Leased, or Otherwise Marketed."[2] The major recommendations of this pronouncement are:

1. Costs incurred in creating a computer software product should be charged to research and development expense when incurred until **technological feasibility** has been established for the product.
2. Technological feasibility is established upon completion of a detailed program design or working model.

In short, the FASB has taken a conservative position in regard to computer software costs. All costs must be expensed until the company has completed planning, designing, coding, and testing activities necessary to establish that the product can be produced to meet its design specifications. Subsequent costs incurred should be capitalized and amortized to current and future periods.

Two additional points should be emphasized. First, **if the software is purchased and it has alternative future uses, then it may be capitalized**. Second, **this standard applies only to the development of software that is to be sold, leased, or otherwise marketed to third parties** (i.e., for external use).

The profession has also indicated how to account for computer software to be used internally. Activities performed during the preliminary project stage of development (conceptual formulation and evaluation of alternatives, for example) are similar to R & D costs and should be expensed immediately. However, once the software is at the application development stage (at the coding or installation into hardware stages, for example), its future economic benefits become probable and so capitalization of costs is required. Costs subsequent to the application development stage related to training and application maintenance should be expensed as incurred.[3]

ACCOUNTING FOR CAPITALIZED SOFTWARE COSTS

If software costs are capitalized, then a proper amortization pattern for these costs must be established. **Companies are required to use the greater of (1) the ratio of current revenues to current and anticipated revenues (percent of revenue approach) or (2) the straight-line method over the remaining useful life of the asset (straight-line**

[2] "Accounting for the Cost of Computer Software to Be Sold, Leased, or Otherwise Marketed," *Statement of Financial Accounting Standards No. 86* (Stamford, Conn.: FASB, 1985). Also see, Robert W. McGee, *Accounting for Software* (Homewood, Ill.: Dow Jones-Irwin, 1985).

[3] "Accounting for the Costs of Computer Software Developed or Obtained for Internal Use," *Statement of Position 98-1* (New York: AICPA, 1998).

approach) as a basis for amortization. These rules can result in the use of the ratio method one year and the straight-line method in another.

To illustrate, assume that AT&T has capitalized software costs of $10 million, and its current (first-year) revenues from sales of this product are $4 million. AT&T anticipates earning $16 million in additional future revenues from this product, which is estimated to have an economic life of 4 years. Using the percent of revenue approach, the current (first) year's amortization would be $2 million ($10,000,000 × $4,000,000/ $20,000,000). Using the straight-line approach, the amortization would be $2.5 million ($10,000,000/4 years). Thus the straight-line approach would be employed because it results in the greater amortization charge.

REPORTING SOFTWARE COSTS

Because much concern exists about the reliability of an asset such as software, the FASB indicated that capitalized software costs should be valued at the **lower of unamortized cost or net realizable value**. If net realizable value is lower, then the capitalized software costs should be written down to this value. Once written down, **they may not be written back up**. In addition to the regular disclosures for R & D costs, the following should be reported in the financial statements.

1. Unamortized software costs.
2. The total amount charged to expense and amounts, if any, written down to net realizable value.

Once again these accounting and reporting requirements apply only to software **developed for external purposes**.

An example of software development cost disclosure, taken from the annual report of Analogic Corporation, is shown below.

ILLUSTRATION 12A-1
Disclosure of Software Development Costs

Analogic Corporation
(in thousands)

	July 31,	
	2001	2000
Total current assets	$268,350	$255,887
Property, plant and equipment, net	68,846	63,524
Investments in and advances to affiliated companies	4,692	4,855
Capitalized software, net	5,488	5,368
Other assets	5,143	3,567
Total assets	$352,519	$333,201

Significant Accounting Policies

Capitalized Software Costs: In accordance with *FAS 86*, the Company capitalizes certain computer software costs, primarily labor and overhead, it develops for use in its own products. Capitalization commences when the Company determines, after a detailed review, that the product is technologically feasible. Capitalized costs are amortized on a straight-line basis over the economic lives of the related products, generally three years. Amortization expense was $1,647, $1,778 and $1,977 in fiscal 2001, 2000, and 1999, respectively. The unamortized balance of capitalized software was $5,488 and $5,368 at July 31, 2001, and 2000, respectively.

SETTING STANDARDS FOR SOFTWARE ACCOUNTING

"It's unreasonable to expense all software costs, and it's unreasonable to capitalize all software costs," said IBM's director of financial reporting. "If you subscribe to those two statements, then it follows that there is somewhere in between where development ends and capitalization begins. Now you have to define that point."[4] The FASB defined that point as "technological feasibility," which is established upon completion of a detailed program design or working model.

The difficulty of applying this criterion to software is that "there is no such thing as a real, specific, baseline design. But you could make it look like you have one as early or as late as you like," says Osman Erlop of **Hambrecht & Quist**.[5] That is, if you wish to capitalize, draw up a detailed program design quickly. If you want to expense lots of development costs, simply hold off writing a detailed program design. And, once capitalized, the costs are amortized over the useful life specified by the developer, which because of either constant redesign or supersession is generally quite short (2 to 4 years).

As another example, some companies "manage by the numbers." That is, they are very careful to identify projects that are worthwhile and capitalize the computer software costs associated with them. They believe that good projects must be capitalized and amortized in the future; otherwise, the concept of properly matching expense and revenues is abused.

Other companies choose not to manage by the numbers and simply expense all these costs. Companies that expense all these costs have no use for a standard that requires capitalization. In their view, it would mean only that a more complex, more expensive cost accounting system would be required, one that would provide little if any benefit.

Financial analysts have reacted almost uniformly against any capitalization. They believe software costs should be expensed because of the rapid obsolescence of software and the potential for abuse that may result from capitalizing costs inappropriately. As Donald Kirk, a former chairman of the FASB, stated, "The Board is now faced with the problem of balancing what it thought was good theory with the costs for some companies of implementing a new accounting system with the concerns of users about the potential for abuse of the standard."[6]

Resolving the software accounting problem again demonstrates the difficulty of establishing reporting standards.

SUMMARY OF LEARNING OBJECTIVE FOR APPENDIX 12A

⑪ **Understand the accounting treatment for computer software costs.** Costs incurred in creating a software product should be charged to R & D expense when incurred until technological feasibility has been established for the product. Subsequent costs should be capitalized and amortized to current and future periods. Software that is purchased for sale or lease to third parties and has alternative future uses may be capitalized and amortized using the greater of the percent of revenue approach or the straight-line approach.

[4]"When Does Life Begin?" *Forbes* (June 16, 1986), pp. 72–74.

[5]Ibid.

[6]Donald J. Kirk, "Growing Temptation & Rising Expectation = Accelerating Regulation," *FASB Viewpoints* (June 12, 1985), p. 7.

Note: All **asterisked** Questions, Brief Exercises, Exercises, Problems, and Conceptual Cases relate to material contained in the appendix to the chapter.

QUESTIONS

1. What are the two main characteristics of intangible assets?

2. If intangibles are acquired for stock, how is the cost of the intangible determined?

3. Intangibles have either a limited useful life or an indefinite useful life. How should these two different types of intangibles be amortized?

4. Why does the accounting profession make a distinction between internally created intangibles and purchased intangibles?

5. In 2003, Sheila Wright Corp. spent $420,000 for "goodwill" visits by sales personnel to key customers. The purpose of these visits was to build a solid, friendly relationship for the future and to gain insight into the problems and needs of the companies served. How should this expenditure be reported?

6. What are factors to be considered in estimating the useful life of an intangible asset?

7. What should be the pattern of amortization for a limited-life intangible?

8. Marcy Co. acquired a trademark that is helpful in distinguishing one of its new products. The trademark is renewable every 10 years at minimal cost. All evidence indicates that this trademark product will generate cash flows for an indefinite period of time. How should this trademark be amortized?

9. Alonzo Mourning Company spent $190,000 developing a new process, $45,000 in legal fees to obtain a patent, and $91,000 to market the process that was patented, all in the year 2003. How should these costs be accounted for in 2003?

10. Yellow 3 purchased a patent for $450,000 which has an estimated useful life of 10 years. Its pattern of use or consumption cannot be reliably determined. Prepare the entry to record the amortization of the patent in its first year of use.

11. Explain the difference between artistic-related intangible assets and contract-related intangible assets.

12. What is goodwill? What is negative goodwill?

13. Under what circumstances is it appropriate to record goodwill in the accounts? How should goodwill, properly recorded on the books, be written off in order to conform with generally accepted accounting principles?

14. In examining financial statements, financial analysts often write off goodwill immediately. Evaluate this procedure.

15. Astaire Inc. is considering the write-off of a limited life intangible because of its lack of profitability. Explain to the management of Astaire how to determine whether a write-off is permitted.

16. Last year Wilde Company recorded an impairment on an intangible asset held for use. Recent appraisals indicate that the asset has increased in value. Should Wilde record this recovery in value?

17. Explain how losses on impaired intangible assets should be reported in income.

18. Logan Company determines that its goodwill is impaired. It finds that its implied goodwill is $380,000 and its recorded goodwill is $400,000. The fair value of its identifiable assets is $1,450,000. What is the amount of goodwill impaired?

19. What is the nature of research and development costs?

20. Research and development activities may include (a) personnel costs, (b) materials and equipment costs, and (c) indirect costs. What is the recommended accounting treatment for these three types of R & D costs?

21. Which of the following activities should be expensed currently as R & D costs?

(a) Testing in search for or evaluation of product or process alternatives.

(b) Engineering follow-through in an early phase of commercial production.

(c) Legal work in connection with patent applications or litigation, and the sale or licensing of patents.

22. Indicate the proper accounting for the following items.

(a) Organization costs.

(b) Advertising costs.

(c) Operating losses.

23. In 2002, Cassie Logan Corporation developed a new product that will be marketed in 2003. In connection with the development of this product, the following costs were incurred in 2002: research and development costs $420,000; materials and supplies consumed $60,000; and compensation paid to research consultants $125,000. It is anticipated that these costs will be recovered in 2005. What is the amount of research and development costs that Cassie Logan should record in 2002 as a charge to expense?

24. Recently, a group of university students decided to incorporate for the purposes of selling a process to recycle the waste product from manufacturing cheese. Some of the initial costs involved were legal fees and office expenses incurred in starting the business, state incorporation fees, and stamp taxes. One student wishes to charge these costs against revenue in the current period. Another wishes to defer these costs and amortize them in the future. Which student is correct?

25. An intangible asset with an estimated useful life of 30 years was acquired on January 1, 1993, for $450,000. On January 1, 2003, a review was made of intangible assets and their expected service lives, and it was determined that this asset had an estimated useful life of 30 more years from the date of the review. What is the amount of amortization for this intangible in 2003?

***26.** An article in the financial press stated, "More than half of software maker **Comserve**'s net worth is in a pile of tapes and ring-bound books. That raises some accountants' eyebrows." What is the profession's position regarding the incurrence of costs for computer software that will be sold?

***27.** Matt Antonio, Inc. has incurred $6 million in developing a computer software product for sale to third parties. Of the $6 million costs incurred, $4 million is capitalized. The product produced from this development work has generated $2 million in 2004 and is anticipated to generate another $8 million in future years. The estimated useful life of the project is 4 years. How much of the capitalized costs should be amortized in 2004?

***28.** In 2004, U-Learn Software developed a software package for assisting calculus instruction in business colleges, at a cost of $2,000,000. Although there are tens of thousands of calculus students in the market, college instructors seem to change their minds frequently on the use of teaching aids. Not one package has yet been ordered or delivered. Prepare an argument to advocate expensing the development cost in the current year. Offer an argument for capitalizing the development cost over its estimated useful life. Which stakeholders are harmed or benefited by either approach?

BRIEF EXERCISES

BE12-1 Doom Troopers Corporation purchases a patent from Judge Dredd Company on January 1, 2004, for $64,000. The patent has a remaining legal life of 16 years. Doom Troopers feels the patent will be useful for 10 years. Prepare Doom Troopers' journal entries to record the purchase of the patent and 2004 amortization.

BE12-2 Use the information provided in BE12-1. Assume that at January 1, 2006, the carrying amount of the patent on Doom Troopers' books is $51,200. In January, Doom Troopers spends $24,000 successfully defending a patent suit. Doom Troopers still feels the patent will be useful until the end of 2013. Prepare the journal entries to record the $24,000 expenditure and 2006 amortization.

BE12-3 Dr. Robotnik's, Inc., spent $60,000 in attorney fees while developing the trade name of its new product, the Mean Bean Machine. Prepare the journal entries to record the $60,000 expenditure and the first year's amortization, using an 8-year life.

BE12-4 Incredible Hulk Corporation commenced operations in early 2004. The corporation incurred $70,000 of costs such as fees to underwriters, legal fees, state fees, and promotional expenditures during its formation. Prepare journal entries to record the $70,000 expenditure and 2004 amortization, if any.

BE12-5 Knuckles Corporation obtained a franchise from Sonic Hedgehog Inc. for a cash payment of $100,000 on April 1, 2004. The franchise grants Knuckles the right to sell certain products and services for a period of 8 years. Prepare Knuckles' April 1 journal entry and December 31 adjusting entry.

BE12-6 On September 1, 2004, Dungeon Corporation acquired Dragon Enterprises for a cash payment of $750,000. At the time of purchase, Dragon's balance sheet showed assets of $620,000, liabilities of $200,000, and owners' equity of $420,000. The fair value of Dragon's assets is estimated to be $800,000. Compute the amount of goodwill acquired by Dungeon.

BE12-7 Nobunaga Corporation owns a patent that has a carrying amount of $330,000. Nobunaga expects future net cash flows from this patent to total $190,000. The fair value of the patent is $110,000. Prepare Nobunaga's journal entry, if necessary, to record the loss on impairment.

BE12-8 Evander Corporation purchased Holyfield Company 3 years ago and at that time recorded goodwill of $400,000. The Holyfield Division's net assets, including the goodwill, have a carrying amount of $800,000. The fair value of the division is estimated to be $1,000,000. Prepare Evander's journal entry, if necessary, to record impairment of the goodwill.

BE12-9 Dorsett Corporation incurred the following costs in 2004.

Cost of laboratory research aimed at discovery of new knowledge	$140,000
Cost of testing in search for product alternatives	100,000
Cost of engineering activity required to advance the design of a product to the manufacturing stage	210,000
	$450,000

Prepare the necessary 2004 journal entry or entries for Dorsett.

BE12-10 Indicate whether the following items are capitalized or expensed in the current year.

(a) Purchase cost of a patent from a competitor.
(b) Research and development costs.
(c) Organizational costs.
(d) Costs incurred internally to create goodwill.

BE12-11 Langer Industries had one patent recorded on its books as of January 1, 2004. This patent had a book value of $240,000 and a remaining useful life of 8 years. During 2004, Langer incurred research and development costs of $96,000 and brought a patent infringement suit against a competitor. On December 1, 2004, Langer received the good news that its patent was valid and that its competitor could not use the process Langer had patented. The company incurred $85,000 to defend this patent. At what amount should patent(s) be reported on the December 31, 2004, balance sheet, assuming monthly amortization of patents?

BE12-12 Wiggens Industries acquired two copyrights during 2004. One copyright related to a textbook that was developed internally at a cost of $9,900. This textbook is estimated to have a useful life of 3 years from September 1, 2004, the date it was published. The second copyright (a history research textbook) was purchased from University Press on December 1, 2004, for $19,200. This textbook has an indefinite useful life. How should these two copyrights be reported on Wiggens' balance sheet as of December 31, 2004?

***BE12-13** Earthworm Jim Corporation has capitalized software costs of $700,000, and sales of this product the first year totaled $420,000. Earthworm Jim anticipates earning $980,000 in additional future revenues from this product, which is estimated to have an economic life of 4 years. Compute the amount of software cost amortization for the first year.

EXERCISES

E12-1 (Classification Issues—Intangibles) Presented below is a list of items that could be included in the intangible assets section of the balance sheet.

1. Investment in a subsidiary company.
2. Timberland.
3. Cost of engineering activity required to advance the design of a product to the manufacturing stage.
4. Lease prepayment (6 months' rent paid in advance).
5. Cost of equipment obtained.
6. Cost of searching for applications of new research findings.
7. Costs incurred in the formation of a corporation.
8. Operating losses incurred in the start-up of a business.
9. Training costs incurred in start-up of new operation.
10. Purchase cost of a franchise.
11. Goodwill generated internally.
12. Cost of testing in search for product alternatives.
13. Goodwill acquired in the purchase of a business.
14. Cost of developing a patent.
15. Cost of purchasing a patent from an inventor.
16. Legal costs incurred in securing a patent.
17. Unrecovered costs of a successful legal suit to protect the patent.
18. Cost of conceptual formulation of possible product alternatives.
19. Cost of purchasing a copyright.
20. Research and development costs.

21. Long-term receivables.
22. Cost of developing a trademark.
23. Cost of purchasing a trademark.

Instructions

(a) Indicate which items on the list above would generally be reported as intangible assets in the balance sheet.

(b) Indicate how, if at all, the items not reportable as intangible assets would be reported in the financial statements.

E12-2 (Classification Issues—Intangibles) Presented below is selected account information related to Martin Burke Inc. as of December 21, 2003. All these accounts have debit balances.

Cable television franchises	Film contract rights
Music copyrights	Customer lists
Research and development costs	Prepaid expenses
Goodwill	Covenants not to compete
Cash	Brand names
Discount on notes payable	Notes receivable
Accounts receivable	Investments in affiliated companies
Property, plant, and equipment	Organization costs
Internet domain name	Land

Instructions

Identify which items should be classified as an intangible asset. For those items not classified as an intangible asset, indicate where they would be reported in the financial statements.

E12-3 (Classification Issues—Intangible Asset) Joni Hyde Inc. has the following amounts included in its general ledger at December 31, 2003.

Organization costs	$24,000
Trademarks	15,000
Discount on bonds payable	35,000
Deposits with advertising agency for ads to promote goodwill of company	10,000
Excess of cost over fair value of net identifiable assets of acquired subsidiary	75,000
Cost of equipment acquired for research and development projects; the equipment has an alternative future use	90,000
Costs of developing a secret formula for a product that is expected to be marketed for at least 20 years	80,000

Instructions

(a) On the basis of the information above, compute the total amount to be reported by Hyde for intangible assets on its balance sheet at December 31, 2003. Equipment has alternative future use.

(b) If an item is not to be included in intangible assets, explain its proper treatment for reporting purposes.

E12-4 (Intangible Amortization) Presented below is selected information for Alatorre Company.

1. Alatorre purchased a patent from Vania Co. for $1,000,000 on January 1, 2002. The patent is being amortized over its remaining legal life of 10 years, expiring on January 1, 2012. During 2004, Alatorre determined that the economic benefits of the patent would not last longer than 6 years from the date of acquisition. What amount should be reported in the balance sheet for the patent, net of accumulated amortization, at December 31, 2004?
2. Alatorre bought a franchise from Alexander Co. on January 1, 2003, for $400,000. The carrying amount of the franchise on Alexander's books on January 1, 2003, was $500,000. The franchise agreement had an estimated useful life of 30 years. Because Alatorre must enter a competitive bidding at the end of 2012, it is unlikely that the franchise will be retained beyond 2012. What amount should be amortized for the year ended December 31, 2004?
3. On January 1, 2000, Alatorre incurred organization costs of $275,000. What amount of organization expense should be reported in 2004?
4. Alatorre purchased the license for distribution of a popular consumer product on January 1, 2004, for $150,000. It is expected that this product will generate cash flows for an indefinite period of time. The license has an initial term of 5 years but by paying a nominal fee, Alatorre can renew the license indefinitely for successive 5-year terms. What amount should be amortized for the year ended December 31, 2004?

Instructions

Answer the questions asked about each of the factual situations.

E12-5 (Correct Intangible Asset Account) As the recently appointed auditor for William J. Bryan Corporation, you have been asked to examine selected accounts before the 6-month financial statements of June 30, 2003, are prepared. The controller for William J. Bryan Corporation mentions that only one account is kept for Intangible Assets. The account is shown below.

Intangible Assets

		Debit	Credit	Balance
Jan. 4	Research and development costs	940,000		940,000
Jan. 5	Legal costs to obtain patent	75,000		1,015,000
Jan. 31	Payment of 7 months' rent on property leased by Bryan	91,000		1,106,000
Feb. 11	Premium on common stock		250,000	856,000
March 31	Unamortized bond discount on bonds due March 31, 2023	84,000		940,000
April 30	Promotional expenses related to start-up of business	207,000		1,147,000
June 30	Operating losses for first 6 months	241,000		1,388,000

Instructions

Prepare the entry or entries necessary to correct this account. Assume that the patent has a useful life of 10 years.

E12-6 (Recording and Amortization of Intangibles) Rolanda Marshall Company, organized in 2003, has set up a single account for all intangible assets. The following summary discloses the debit entries that have been recorded during 2004.

1/2/04	Purchased patent (8-year life)	$ 350,000
4/1/04	Purchased goodwill (indefinite life)	360,000
7/1/04	Purchased franchise with 10-year life; expiration date 7/1/14	450,000
8/1/04	Payment of copyright (5-year life)	156,000
9/1/04	Research and development costs	215,000
		$1,531,000

Instructions

Prepare the necessary entries to clear the Intangible Assets account and to set up separate accounts for distinct types of intangibles. Make the entries as of December 31, 2004, recording any necessary amortization and reflecting all balances accurately as of that date (straight-line amortization).

E12-7 (Accounting for Trade Name) In early January 2003, Gayle Crystal Corporation applied for a trade name, incurring legal costs of $16,000. In January of 2004, Gayle Crystal incurred $7,800 of legal fees in a successful defense of its trade name.

Instructions

(a) Compute 2003 amortization, 12/31/03 book value, 2004 amortization, and 12/31/04 book value if the company amortizes the trade name over 10 years.

(b) Compute the 2004 amortization and the 12/31/04 book value, assuming that at the beginning of 2004, Crystal determines that the trade name will provide no future benefits beyond December 31, 2007.

(c) Ignoring the response for part (b), compute the 2005 amortization and the 12/31/05 book value, assuming that at the beginning of 2005, based on new market research, Crystal determines that the fair value of the trade name is $15,000. Estimated total future cash flows from the trade name is $16,000 on January 3, 2005.

E12-8 (Accounting for Organization Costs) Horace Greeley Corporation was organized in 2002 and began operations at the beginning of 2003. The company is involved in interior design consulting services. The following costs were incurred prior to the start of operations.

Attorney's fees in connection with organization of the company	$15,000
Purchase of drafting and design equipment	10,000
Costs of meetings of incorporators to discuss organizational activities	7,000
State filing fees to incorporate	1,000
	$33,000

Instructions

(a) Compute the total amount of organization costs incurred by Greeley.
(b) Prepare the journal entry to record organization costs for 2003.

E12-9 (Accounting for Patents, Franchises, and R & D) Jimmy Carter Company has provided information on intangible assets as follows.

A patent was purchased from Gerald Ford Company for $2,000,000 on January 1, 2003. Carter estimated the remaining useful life of the patent to be 10 years. The patent was carried in Ford's accounting records at a net book value of $2,000,000 when Ford sold it to Carter.

During 2004, a franchise was purchased from Ronald Reagan Company for $480,000. In addition, 5% of revenue from the franchise must be paid to Reagan. Revenue from the franchise for 2004 was $2,500,000. Carter estimates the useful life of the franchise to be 10 years and takes a full year's amortization in the year of purchase.

Carter incurred research and development costs in 2004 as follows.

Materials and equipment	$142,000
Personnel	189,000
Indirect costs	102,000
	$433,000

Carter estimates that these costs will be recouped by December 31, 2007. The materials and equipment purchased have no alternative uses.

On January 1, 2004, because of recent events in the field, Carter estimates that the remaining life of the patent purchased on January 1, 2003, is only 5 years from January 1, 2004.

Instructions

(a) Prepare a schedule showing the intangibles section of Carter's balance sheet at December 31, 2004. Show supporting computations in good form.
(b) Prepare a schedule showing the income statement effect for the year ended December 31, 2004, as a result of the facts above. Show supporting computations in good form.

(AICPA adapted)

E12-10 (Accounting for Patents) During 2000, George Winston Corporation spent $170,000 in research and development costs. As a result, a new product called the New Age Piano was patented. The patent was obtained on October 1, 2000, and had a legal life of 20 years and a useful life of 10 years. Legal costs of $18,000 related to the patent were incurred as of October 1, 2000.

Instructions

(a) Prepare all journal entries required in 2000 and 2001 as a result of the transactions above.
(b) On June 1, 2002, Winston spent $9,480 to successfully prosecute a patent infringement. As a result, the estimate of useful life was extended to 12 years from June 1, 2002. Prepare all journal entries required in 2002 and 2003.
(c) In 2004, Winston determined that a competitor's product would make the New Age Piano obsolete and the patent worthless by December 31, 2005. Prepare all journal entries required in 2004 and 2005.

E12-11 (Accounting for Patents) Tones Industries has the following patents on its December 31, 2005, balance sheet.

Patent Item	Initial Cost	Date Acquired	Useful Life at Date Acquired
Patent A	$30,600	3/1/02	17 years
Patent B	$15,000	7/1/03	10 years
Patent C	$14,400	9/1/04	4 years

The following events occurred during the year ended December 31, 2006.

1. Research and development costs of $245,700 were incurred during the year.
2. Patent D was purchased on July 1 for $36,480. This patent has a useful life of 9½ years.
3. As a result of reduced demands for certain products protected by Patent B, a possible impairment of Patent B's value may have occurred at December 31, 2006. The controller for Tones estimates the future cash flows from Patent B will be as follows.

Year	Future Cash Flows
2007	$2,000
2008	2,000
2009	2,000

The proper discount rate to be used for these flows is 8%. (Assume that the cash flows occur at the end of the year.)

Instructions

(a) Compute the total carrying amount of Tones' patents on its December 31, 2005, balance sheet.
(b) Compute the total carrying amount of Tones' patents on its December 31, 2006, balance sheet.

E12-12 (Accounting for Goodwill) Fred Moss, owner of Moss Interiors, is negotiating for the purchase of Zweifel Galleries. The balance sheet of Zweifel is given in an abbreviated form below.

ZWEIFEL GALLERIES
BALANCE SHEET
AS OF DECEMBER 31, 2004

Assets		Liabilities and Stockholders' Equity		
Cash	$100,000	Accounts payable		$ 50,000
Land	70,000	Long-term notes payable		300,000
Building (net)	200,000	Total liabilities		350,000
Equipment (net)	175,000	Common stock	$200,000	
Copyright (net)	30,000	Retained earnings	25,000	225,000
Total assets	$575,000	Total liabilities and stockholders' equity		$575,000

Moss and Zweifel agree that:

1. Land is undervalued by $30,000.
2. Equipment is overvalued by $5,000.

Zweifel agrees to sell the gallery to Moss for $350,000.

Instructions

Prepare the entry to record the purchase of Zweifel Galleries on Moss's books.

E12-13 (Accounting for Goodwill) On July 1, 2003, Brigham Corporation purchased Young Company by paying $250,000 cash and issuing a $100,000 note payable to Steve Young. At July 1, 2003, the balance sheet of Young Company was as follows.

Cash	$ 50,000	Accounts payable	$200,000
Receivables	90,000	Stockholders' equity	235,000
Inventory	100,000		$435,000
Land	40,000		
Buildings (net)	75,000		
Equipment (net)	70,000		
Trademarks	10,000		
	$435,000		

The recorded amounts all approximate current values except for land (worth $60,000), inventory (worth $125,000), and trademarks (worth $15,000).

Instructions

(a) Prepare the July 1 entry for Brigham Corporation to record the purchase.
(b) Prepare the December 31 entry for Brigham Corporation to record amortization of intangibles. The trademark has an estimated useful life of 4 years with a residual value of $3,000.

E12-14 (Copyright Impairment) Presented below is information related to copyrights owned by Walter de la Mare Company at December 31, 2004.

Cost	$8,600,000
Carrying amount	4,300,000
Expected future net cash flows	4,000,000
Fair value	3,200,000

Assume that Walter de la Mare Company will continue to use this copyright in the future. As of December 31, 2004, the copyright is estimated to have a remaining useful life of 10 years.

Instructions

(a) Prepare the journal entry (if any) to record the impairment of the asset at December 31, 2004. The company does not use accumulated amortization accounts.
(b) Prepare the journal entry to record amortization expense for 2005 related to the copyrights.
(c) The fair value of the copyright at December 31, 2005, is $3,400,000. Prepare the journal entry (if any) necessary to record the increase in fair value.

E12-15 (Goodwill Impairment) Presented below is net asset information related to the Carlos Division of Santana, Inc.

CARLOS DIVISION
NET ASSETS
AS OF DECEMBER 31, 2004
(IN MILLIONS)

Cash	$ 50
Receivables	200
Property, plant, and equipment (net)	2,600
Goodwill	200
Less: Notes payable	(2,700)
Net assets	$ 350

The purpose of the Carlos division is to develop a nuclear-powered aircraft. If successful, traveling delays associated with refueling could be substantially reduced. Many other benefits would also occur. To date, management has not had much success and is deciding whether a write-down at this time is appropriate. Management estimated its future net cash flows from the project to be $400 million. Management has also received an offer to purchase the division for $335 million. All identifiable assets' and liabilities' book and fair value amounts are the same.

Instructions

(a) Prepare the journal entry (if any) to record the impairment at December 31, 2004.

(b) At December 31, 2005, it is estimated that the division's fair value increased to $345 million. Prepare the journal entry (if any) to record this increase in fair value.

E12-16 (Accounting for R & D Costs) Leontyne Price Company from time to time embarks on a research program when a special project seems to offer possibilities. In 2003 the company expends $325,000 on a research project, but by the end of 2003 it is impossible to determine whether any benefit will be derived from it.

Instructions

(a) What account should be charged for the $325,000, and how should it be shown in the financial statements?

(b) The project is completed in 2004, and a successful patent is obtained. The R & D costs to complete the project are $110,000. The administrative and legal expenses incurred in obtaining patent number 472-1001-84 in 2004 total $16,000. The patent has an expected useful life of 5 years. Record these costs in journal entry form. Also, record patent amortization (full year) in 2004.

(c) In 2005, the company successfully defends the patent in extended litigation at a cost of $47,200, thereby extending the patent life to December 31, 2012. What is the proper way to account for this cost? Also, record patent amortization (full year) in 2005.

(d) Additional engineering and consulting costs incurred in 2005 required to advance the design of a product to the manufacturing stage total $60,000. These costs enhance the design of the product considerably. Discuss the proper accounting treatment for this cost.

E12-17 (Accounting for R & D Costs) Thomas More Company incurred the following costs during 2003 in connection with its research and development activities.

Cost of equipment acquired that will have alternative uses in future research and development projects over the next 5 years (uses straight-line depreciation)	$280,000
Materials consumed in research and development projects	59,000
Consulting fees paid to outsiders for research and development projects	100,000
Personnel costs of persons involved in research and development projects	128,000
Indirect costs reasonably allocable to research and development projects	50,000
Materials purchased for future research and development projects	34,000

Instructions

Compute the amount to be reported as research and development expense by More on its income statement for 2003. Assume equipment is purchased at beginning of year.

***E12-18 (Accounting for Computer Software Costs)** New Jersey Inc. has capitalized computer software costs of $3,600,000 on its new "Trenton" software package. Revenues from 2003 (first year) sales are $2,000,000. Additional future revenues from "Trenton" for the remainder of its economic life, through 2007, are estimated to be $10,000,000.

Instructions

(a) What method or methods of amortization are to be applied in the write-off of capitalized computer software costs?

(b) Compute the amount of amortization for 2003 for "Trenton."

***E12-19 (Accounting for Computer Software Costs)** During 2003, Delaware Enterprises Inc. spent $5,000,000 developing its new "Dover" software package. Of this amount, $2,200,000 was spent before technological feasibility was established for the product, which is to be marketed to third parties. The package was completed at December 31, 2003. Delaware expects a useful life of 8 years for this product with total revenues of $16,000,000. During the first year (2004), Delaware realizes revenues of $3,200,000.

Instructions

(a) Prepare journal entries required in 2003 for the foregoing facts.

(b) Prepare the entry to record amortization at December 31, 2004.

(c) At what amount should the computer software costs be reported in the December 31, 2004, balance sheet? Could the net realizable value of this asset affect your answer?

(d) What disclosures are required in the December 31, 2004, financial statements for the computer software costs?

(e) How would your answers for (a), (b), and (c) be different if the computer software was developed for internal use?

PROBLEMS

P12-1 (Correct Intangible Asset Account) Esplanade Co., organized in 2002, has set up a single account for all intangible assets. The following summary discloses the debit entries that have been recorded during 2002 and 2003.

Intangible Assets

7/1/02	8-year franchise; expiration date 6/30/10	$ 42,000
10/1/02	Advance payment on laboratory space (2-year lease)	28,000
12/31/02	Net loss for 2002 including state incorporation fee, $1,000, and related legal fees of organizing, $5,000 (all fees incurred in 2002)	16,000
1/2/03	Patent purchased (10-year life)	74,000
3/1/03	Cost of developing a secret formula (indefinite life)	75,000
4/1/03	Goodwill purchased (indefinite life)	278,400
6/1/03	Legal fee for successful defense of patent purchased above	12,650
9/1/03	Research and development costs	160,000

Instructions

Prepare the necessary entries to clear the Intangible Assets account and to set up separate accounts for distinct types of intangibles. Make the entries as of December 31, 2003, recording any necessary amortization and reflecting all balances accurately as of that date. (Ignore income tax effects.)

P12-2 (Accounting for Patents) Ankara Laboratories holds a valuable patent (No. 758-6002-1A) on a precipitator that prevents certain types of air pollution. Ankara does not manufacture or sell the products and processes it develops. Instead, it conducts research and develops products and processes which it patents, and then assigns the patents to manufacturers on a royalty basis. Occasionally it sells a patent. The history of Ankara patent number 758-6002-1A is as follows.

Date	Activity	Cost
1993–1994	Research conducted to develop precipitator	$384,000
Jan. 1995	Design and construction of a prototype	87,600
March 1995	Testing of models	42,000
Jan. 1996	Fees paid engineers and lawyers to prepare patent application; patent granted June 30, 1996	62,050
Nov. 1997	Engineering activity necessary to advance the design of the precipitator to the manufacturing stage	81,500

Dec. 1998	Legal fees paid to successfully defend precipitator patent	35,700
April 1999	Research aimed at modifying the design of the patented precipitator	43,000
July 2003	Legal fees paid in unsuccessful patent infringement suit against a competitor	34,000

Ankara assumed a useful life of 17 years when it received the initial precipitator patent. On January 1, 2001, it revised its useful life estimate downward to 5 remaining years. Amortization is computed for a full year if the cost is incurred prior to July 1, and no amortization for the year if the cost is incurred after June 30. The company's year ends December 31.

Instructions

Compute the carrying value of patent No. 758-6002-1A on each of the following dates:

(a) December 31, 1996.
(b) December 31, 2000.
(c) December 31, 2003.

P12-3 (Accounting for Franchise, Patents, and Trade Name) Information concerning Haerhpin Corporation's intangible assets is as follows.

1. On January 1, 2004, Haerhpin signed an agreement to operate as a franchisee of Hsian Copy Service, Inc. for an initial franchise fee of $75,000. Of this amount, $15,000 was paid when the agreement was signed, and the balance is payable in 4 annual payments of $15,000 each, beginning January 1, 2005. The agreement provides that the down payment is not refundable and no future services are required of the franchisor. The present value at January 1, 2004, of the 4 annual payments discounted at 14% (the implicit rate for a loan of this type) is $43,700. The agreement also provides that 5% of the revenue from the franchise must be paid to the franchisor annually. Haerhpin's revenue from the franchise for 2004 was $950,000. Haerhpin estimates the useful life of the franchise to be 10 years. (*Hint:* You may want to refer to Appendix 18A to determine the proper accounting treatment for the franchise fee and payments.)
2. Haerhpin incurred $65,000 of experimental and development costs in its laboratory to develop a patent that was granted on January 2, 2004. Legal fees and other costs associated with registration of the patent totaled $13,600. Haerhpin estimates that the useful life of the patent will be 8 years.
3. A trademark was purchased from Shanghai Company for $32,000 on July 1, 2001. Expenditures for successful litigation in defense of the trademark totaling $8,160 were paid on July 1, 2004. Haerhpin estimates that the useful life of the trademark will be 20 years from the date of acquisition.

Instructions

(a) Prepare a schedule showing the intangible section of Haerhpin's balance sheet at December 31, 2004. Show supporting computations in good form.
(b) Prepare a schedule showing all expenses resulting from the transactions that would appear on Haerhpin's income statement for the year ended December 31, 2004. Show supporting computations in good form.

(AICPA adapted)

P12-4 (Accounting for R & D Costs) During 2001, Florence Nightingale Tool Company purchased a building site for its proposed research and development laboratory at a cost of $60,000. Construction of the building was started in 2001. The building was completed on December 31, 2002, at a cost of $280,000 and was placed in service on January 2, 2003. The estimated useful life of the building for depreciation purposes was 20 years. The straight-line method of depreciation was to be employed, and there was no estimated net salvage value.

Management estimates that about 50% of the projects of the research and development group will result in long-term benefits (i.e., at least 10 years) to the corporation. The remaining projects either benefit the current period or are abandoned before completion. A summary of the number of projects and the direct costs incurred in conjunction with the research and development activities for 2003 appears below.

	Number of Projects	Salaries and Employee Benefits	Other Expenses (excluding Building Depreciation Charges)
Completed projects with long-term benefits	15	$ 90,000	$50,000
Abandoned projects or projects that benefit the current period	10	65,000	15,000
Projects in process—results indeterminate	5	40,000	12,000
Total	30	$195,000	$77,000

Upon recommendation of the research and development group, Florence Nightingale Tool Company acquired a patent for manufacturing rights at a cost of $80,000. The patent was acquired on April 1, 2002, and has an economic life of 10 years.

Instructions

If generally accepted accounting principles were followed, how would the items above relating to research and development activities be reported on the following financial statements?

(a) The company's income statement for 2003.
(b) The company's balance sheet as of December 31, 2003.

Be sure to give account titles and amounts, and briefly justify your presentation.

(CMA adapted)

P12-5 (Goodwill, Impairment) On July 31, 2003, Postera Company paid $3,000,000 to acquire all of the common stock of Mendota Incorporated, which became a division of Postera. Mendota reported the following balance sheet at the time of the acquisition.

Current assets	$ 800,000	Current liabilities	$ 600,000
Noncurrent assets	2,700,000	Long-term liabilities	500,000
Total assets	$3,500,000	Stockholders' equity	2,400,000
		Total liabilities and stockholders' equity	$3,500,000

It was determined at the date of the purchase that the fair value of the identifiable net assets of Mendota was $2,650,000. Over the next 6 months of operations, the newly purchased division experienced operating losses. In addition, it now appears that it will generate substantial losses for the foreseeable future. At December 31, 2003, Mendota reports the following balance sheet information.

Current assets	$ 450,000
Noncurrent assets (including goodwill recognized in purchase)	2,400,000
Current liabilities	(700,000)
Long-term liabilities	(500,000)
Net assets	$1,650,000

It is determined that the fair value of the Mendota Division is $1,850,000. The recorded amount for Mendota's net assets (excluding goodwill) is the same as fair value, except for property, plant, and equipment, which has a fair value $150,000 above the carrying value.

Instructions

(a) Compute the amount of goodwill recognized, if any, on July 31, 2003.
(b) Determine the impairment loss, if any, to be recorded on December 31, 2003.
(c) Assume that fair value of the Mendota Division is $1,500,000 instead of $1,850,000. Determine the impairment loss, if any, to be recorded on December 31, 2003.
(d) Prepare the journal entry to record the impairment loss, if any, and indicate where the loss would be reported in the income statement.

CONCEPTUAL CASES

C12-1 (Accounting for Pollution Expenditure) Phil Mickelson Company operates several plants at which limestone is processed into quicklime and hydrated lime. The Eagle Ridge plant, where most of the equipment was installed many years ago, continually deposits a dusty white substance over the surrounding countryside. Citing the unsanitary condition of the neighboring community of Scales Mound, the pollution of the Galena River, and the high incidence of lung disease among workers at Eagle Ridge, the state's Pollution Control Agency has ordered the installation of air pollution control equipment. Also, the Agency has assessed a substantial penalty, which will be used to clean up Scales Mound.

After considering the costs involved (which could not have been reasonably estimated prior to the Agency's action), Phil Mickelson Company decides to comply with the Agency's orders, the alternative being to cease operations at Eagle Ridge at the end of the current fiscal year. The officers of Mickelson agree that the air pollution control equipment should be capitalized and depreciated over its useful life, but they disagree over the period(s) to which the penalty should be charged.

Instructions

Discuss the conceptual merits and reporting requirements of accounting for the penalty in each of the following ways.

(a) As a charge to the current period.
(b) As a correction of prior periods.
(c) As a capitalizable item to be amortized over future periods.

(AICPA adapted)

C12-2 (Accounting for Pre-Opening Costs) After securing lease commitments from several major stores, Lobo Shopping Center, Inc. was organized and built a shopping center in a growing suburb.

The shopping center would have opened on schedule on January 1, 2003, if it had not been struck by a severe tornado in December. Instead, it opened for business on October 1, 2003. All of the additional construction costs that were incurred as a result of the tornado were covered by insurance.

In July 2002, in anticipation of the scheduled January opening, a permanent staff had been hired to promote the shopping center, obtain tenants for the uncommitted space, and manage the property.

A summary of some of the costs incurred in 2002 and the first nine months of 2003 follows.

	2002	January 1, 2003 through September 30, 2003
Interest on mortgage bonds	$720,000	$540,000
Cost of obtaining tenants	300,000	360,000
Promotional advertising	540,000	557,000

The promotional advertising campaign was designed to familiarize shoppers with the center. Had it been known in time that the center would not open until October 2003, the 2002 expenditure for promotional advertising would not have been made. The advertising had to be repeated in 2003.

All of the tenants who had leased space in the shopping center at the time of the tornado accepted the October occupancy date on condition that the monthly rental charges for the first 9 months of 2003 be canceled.

Instructions

Explain how each of the costs for 2002 and the first 9 months of 2003 should be treated in the accounts of the shopping center corporation. Give the reasons for each treatment.

(AICPA adapted)

C12-3 (Accounting for Patents) On June 30, 2003, your client, Bearcat Company, was granted two patents covering plastic cartons that it had been producing and marketing profitably for the past 3 years. One patent covers the manufacturing process, and the other covers the related products.

Bearcat executives tell you that these patents represent the most significant breakthrough in the industry in the past 30 years. The products have been marketed under the registered trademarks Evertight, Duratainer, and Sealrite. Licenses under the patents have already been granted by your client to other manufacturers in the United States and abroad and are producing substantial royalties.

On July 1, Bearcat commenced patent infringement actions against several companies whose names you recognize as those of substantial and prominent competitors. Bearcat's management is optimistic that these suits will result in a permanent injunction against the manufacture and sale of the infringing products as well as collection of damages for loss of profits caused by the alleged infringement.

The financial vice-president has suggested that the patents be recorded at the discounted value of expected net royalty receipts.

Instructions

(a) What is the meaning of "discounted value of expected net receipts"? Explain.
(b) How would such a value be calculated for net royalty receipts?
(c) What basis of valuation for Bearcat's patents would be generally accepted in accounting? Give supporting reasons for this basis.
(d) Assuming no practical problems of implementation, and ignoring generally accepted accounting principles, what is the preferable basis of valuation for patents? Explain.
(e) What would be the preferable theoretical basis of amortization? Explain.
(f) What recognition, if any, should be made of the infringement litigation in the financial statements for the year ending September 30, 2003? Discuss.

(AICPA adapted)

C12-4 (Accounting for Research and Development Costs) Indiana Jones Co. is in the process of developing a revolutionary new product. A new division of the company was formed to develop, manufacture, and market this new product. As of year-end (December 31, 2003), the new product has not been manufactured for resale. However, a prototype unit was built and is in operation.

Throughout 2003 the new division incurred certain costs. These costs include design and engineering studies, prototype manufacturing costs, administrative expenses (including salaries of administrative personnel), and market research costs. In addition, approximately $900,000 in equipment (with an estimated useful life of 10 years) was purchased for use in developing and manufacturing the new product. Approximately $315,000 of this equipment was built specifically for the design development of the new product. The remaining $585,000 of equipment was used to manufacture the pre-production prototype and will be used to manufacture the new product once it is in commercial production.

Instructions

(a) How are "research" and "development" defined in *Statement of Financial Accounting Standards No. 2*?

(b) Briefly indicate the practical and conceptual reasons for the conclusion reached by the Financial Accounting Standards Board on accounting and reporting practices for research and development costs.

(c) In accordance with *Statement of Financial Accounting Standards No. 2*, how should the various costs of Indiana Jones described above be recorded on the financial statements for the year ended December 31, 2003?

(AICPA adapted)

C12-5 (Accounting for Research and Development Costs) Waveland Corporation's research and development department has an idea for a project it believes will culminate in a new product that would be very profitable for the company. Because the project will be very expensive, the department requests approval from the company's controller, Ron Santo.

Santo recognizes that corporate profits have been down lately and is hesitant to approve a project that will incur significant expenses that cannot be capitalized due to the requirement of *FASB Statement No. 2*. He knows that if they hire an outside firm that does the work and obtains a patent for the process, Waveland Corporation can purchase the patent from the outside firm and record the expenditure as an asset. Santo knows that the company's own R & D department is first-rate, and he is confident they can do the work well.

Instructions

Answer the following questions.

(a) Who are the stakeholders in this situation?

(b) What are the ethical issues involved?

(c) What should Santo do?

USING YOUR JUDGMENT

FINANCIAL REPORTING PROBLEM

3M Company

The financial statements of 3M are presented in Appendix 5B or can be accessed on the Take Action! CD.

Instructions

Refer to 3M's financial statements and the accompanying notes to answer the following questions.

(a) Does 3M report any intangible assets, especially goodwill, in its 2001 financial statements and accompanying notes?

(b) How much research and development (R & D) cost was expensed by 3M in 2001 and 2000? What percentage of sales revenue and net income did 3M spend on R & D in 2001 and 2000?

FINANCIAL STATEMENT ANALYSIS CASE

Merck and Johnson & Johnson

Merck & Co., Inc. and **Johnson & Johnson** are two leading producers of health care products. Each has considerable assets, and each expends considerable funds each year toward the development of new products. The development of a new health care product is often very expensive, and risky. New products frequently must undergo considerable testing before approval for distribution to the public. For example, it took Johnson & Johnson 4 years and $200 million to develop its 1-DAY ACUVUE contact lenses. Below are some basic data compiled from the financial statements of these two companies.

(all dollars in millions)	Johnson & Johnson	Merck
Total assets	$15,668	$21,857
Total revenue	15,734	14,970
Net income	2,006	2,997
Research and development expense	1,278	1,230
Intangible assets	2,403	7,212

Instructions

(a) What kinds of intangible assets might a health care products company have? Does the composition of these intangibles matter to investors—that is, would it be perceived differently if all of Merck's intangibles were goodwill, than if all of its intangibles were patents?

(b) Suppose the president of Merck has come to you for advice. He has noted that by eliminating research and development expenditures the company could have reported $1.3 billion more in net income. He is frustrated because much of the research never results in a product, or the products take years to develop. He says shareholders are eager for higher returns, so he is considering eliminating research and development expenditures for at least a couple of years. What would you advise?

(c) The notes to Merck's financial statements note that Merck has goodwill of $4.1 billion. Where does recorded goodwill come from? Is it necessarily a good thing to have a lot of goodwill on your books?

COMPARATIVE ANALYSIS CASE

The Coca-Cola Company and PepsiCo, Inc.

Instructions

Go to the Take Action! CD and use information found there to answer the following questions related to **The Coca-Cola Company** and **PepsiCo, Inc.**

(a) **(1)** What amounts for intangible assets were reported in their respective balance sheets by Coca-Cola and PepsiCo?

(2) What percentage of total assets is each of these reported amounts?

(3) What was the change in the amount of intangibles from 2000 to 2001 for Coca-Cola and PepsiCo?

(b) **(1)** On what basis and over what periods of time did Coca-Cola and PepsiCo amortize their intangible assets?

(2) What were the amounts of accumulated amortization reported by Coca-Cola and PepsiCo at the end of 2001 and 2000?

(3) What was the composition of the identifiable and unidentifiable intangible assets reported by Coca-Cola and PepsiCo at the end of 2001?

(c) What caused the significant increase in Coca-Cola's intangible assets in 2001?

RESEARCH CASE

The online edition of the March 5, 2002, *Wall Street Journal* includes an article by John Carreyrou entitled "Vivendi May Reveal Write-Down of Up to $13 Billion for Goodwill."

Instructions

Read the story and answer the following questions. (Subscribers to **Business Extra** can access the article at that site.)

(a) Vivendi currently prepares its financial statements using French GAAP. As revealed in the story, how do French and U.S. GAAP differ in the accounting for goodwill impairments? Does the story reveal other areas in which U.S. and French GAAP differ? Explain.

(b) Why are some analysts warning against reading too much negativity into Vivendi's expected goodwill write-down? Do you agree? Explain.

(c) What measure of profitability is used in the media business? Explain how, if at all, this measure of profitability might be affected by Vivendi's changes in accounting, as discussed in the story.

INTERNATIONAL REPORTING CASE

Bayer, Smithkline Beecham, and Merck

MERCK

Presented below are data and accounting policy notes for the goodwill of three international drug companies. **Bayer**, a German company, prepares its statements in accordance with International Accounting Standards (IAS); **Smithkline Beecham** follows United Kingdom (U.K.) rules; and **Merck**, a U.S. company, prepares its financial statements in accordance with U.S. GAAP.

Related Information	Bayer (DM millions)	Smithkline Beecham (£ millions)	Merck ($ millions)
Amortization expense	136	69	0
Net income	3,157	606	5,248
Accumulated goodwill amortization	306	313	0
Stockholders' equity	24,991	1,747	31,853

The following accounting policy notes related to goodwill appeared with the companies' financial statements.

Bayer
Intangible assets that have been acquired are recognized at cost and amortized over their estimated useful lives. Goodwill, including that resulting from capital consolidation, is capitalized in accordance with *IAS 22* (Business Combinations) and normally is amortized over a period of 5 or at most 20 years.

Smithkline Beecham
Goodwill, representing the excess of the purchase consideration over the fair value of the net separable assets acquired, is capitalised and amortised over an appropriate period not exceeding 20 years.

Merck
Goodwill represents the excess of acquisition costs over the fair value of net assets of businesses purchased and is not amortized.

Instructions

(a) Compute the return on equity for each of these companies, and use this analysis to briefly discuss the relative profitability of the three companies.

(b) Assume that each of the companies uses the maximum allowable amortization period for goodwill. Discuss how these companies' goodwill amortization policies affect your ability to compare their amortization expense and income.

(c) Some analysts believe that the only valid way to compare companies that follow different goodwill accounting practices is to treat all goodwill as an asset and record expense only if the goodwill is impaired.* Using the data above, make these adjustments as appropriate, and compare the profitability of the three drug companies, comparing this information to your analysis in (a).

*Trevor Harris, *Apples to Apples: Accounting for Value in World Markets* (New York: Morgan Stanley Dean Witter, February 1998).

PROFESSIONAL SIMULATION

Accounting for Intangibles

Directions | Situation | Journal Entries | Measurement | Financial Statements | Research | Resources

Directions

In this simulation, you will be asked various questions related to intangible assets and similar costs. Prepare responses to all parts.

Situation

Argot Co., organized in 2003, provided you with the following information.

1. Purchased a franchise for $42,000 on July 1, 2003. The rights to the franchise will expire on July 1, 2011.
2. Incurred a net loss of $33,000 in 2003, including a state incorporation fee of $2,000 and related legal fees of organizing, $5,000. (All fees were incurred in 2003.)
3. Purchased a patent on January 2, 2004, for $80,000. It is estimated to have a 10-year life.
4. Costs incurred to develop a secret formula as of March 1, 2004, were $90,000. The secret formula has an indefinite life.
5. On April 1, 2004, Argot Co. purchased a small manufacturing concern for $700,000. Goodwill recorded in the transaction was $180,000.
6. On July 1, 2004, legal fees for successful defense of the patent purchased on January 2, 2004, were $11,400.
7. Research and development costs incurred as of September 1, 2004, were $110,000.

Journal Entries

Prepare the journal entries to record all the entries related to the patent during 2004.

Measurement

At December 31, 2004, an impairment test is performed on the franchise purchased in 2003. It is estimated that the net cash flows to be received from the franchise will be $25,000, and its fair value is $13,000. Compute the amount of impairment, if any, to be recorded on December 31, 2004.

Financial Statements

What is the amount to be reported for intangible assets on the balance sheet at December 31, 2003? At December 31, 2004?

www.wiley.com/college/kieso

Remember to check the **Take Action! CD** and the book's **companion Web site** to find additional resources for this chapter.

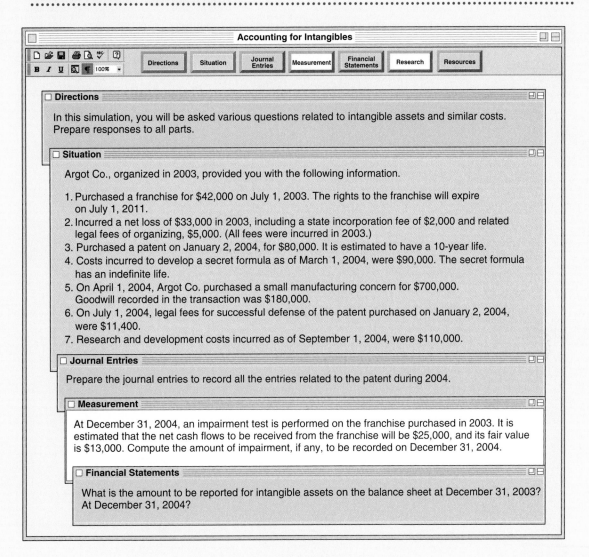

CHAPTER 13

Current Liabilities and Contingencies

Microsoft's Liabilities—Good or Bad?

Users of financial statements generally examine current liabilities to assess a company's liquidity and overall financial flexibility. This is because many current liabilities such as accounts payable, wages payable, and taxes payable must be paid sooner rather than later. Thus, when these liabilities increase substantially, it raises a red flag about a company's financial position.

This is not always the case for all current liabilities. For example, **Microsoft** has a current liability entitled "Unearned Revenue" that has increased substantially year after year. Unearned revenue is a liability that arises from sales of Microsoft products such as *Windows* and *Office*. At the time of a sale, customers pay not only for the current version of the software but also for future improvements to the software. In this case, Microsoft recognizes sales revenue from the current version of the software and records as a liability (unearned revenue) the value of future upgrades to the software that are "owed" to customers.

Market analysts indicate that such an increase in unearned revenue, rather than raising a red flag, often provides a positive signal about sales and profitability. How can information from a liability account provide information about profitability? It works this way: When Microsoft sales are growing, its unearned revenue account increases. Thus, an *increase* in a liability is good news about Microsoft sales.

What happens if the unearned revenue liability declines? After steady increases in recent years, Microsoft's unearned revenue declined from the second to the third quarter of 1999. In response to this decline in unearned revenue, a number of mutual funds sold part of their Microsoft holdings. Many believed that a decline in Microsoft's unearned revenue is bad news for investors. As one analyst noted, when the growth in unearned revenues slows or reverses, as it did for Microsoft, it indicates that sales are slowing. Thus, increases in current liabilities can sometimes be viewed as good signs instead of bad.[1]

LEARNING OBJECTIVES

After studying this chapter, you should be able to:

1. **Describe the nature, type, and valuation of current liabilities.**
2. **Explain the classification issues of short-term debt expected to be refinanced.**
3. **Identify types of employee-related liabilities.**
4. **Identify the criteria used to account for and disclose gain and loss contingencies.**
5. **Explain the accounting for different types of loss contingencies.**
6. **Indicate how current liabilities and contingencies are presented and analyzed.**

[1]Based on David Bank, "Some Fans Cool to Microsoft, Citing Drop in Old Indicator," *Wall Street Journal* (October 28, 1999).

PREVIEW OF CHAPTER 13

As the opening story indicates, careful analysis of current liabilities can provide insights about a company's liquidity and profitability. The purpose of this chapter is to explain the basic principles regarding accounting and reporting for current and contingent liabilities. Chapter 14 addresses issues related to long-term liabilities.

The content and organization of this chapter are as follows.

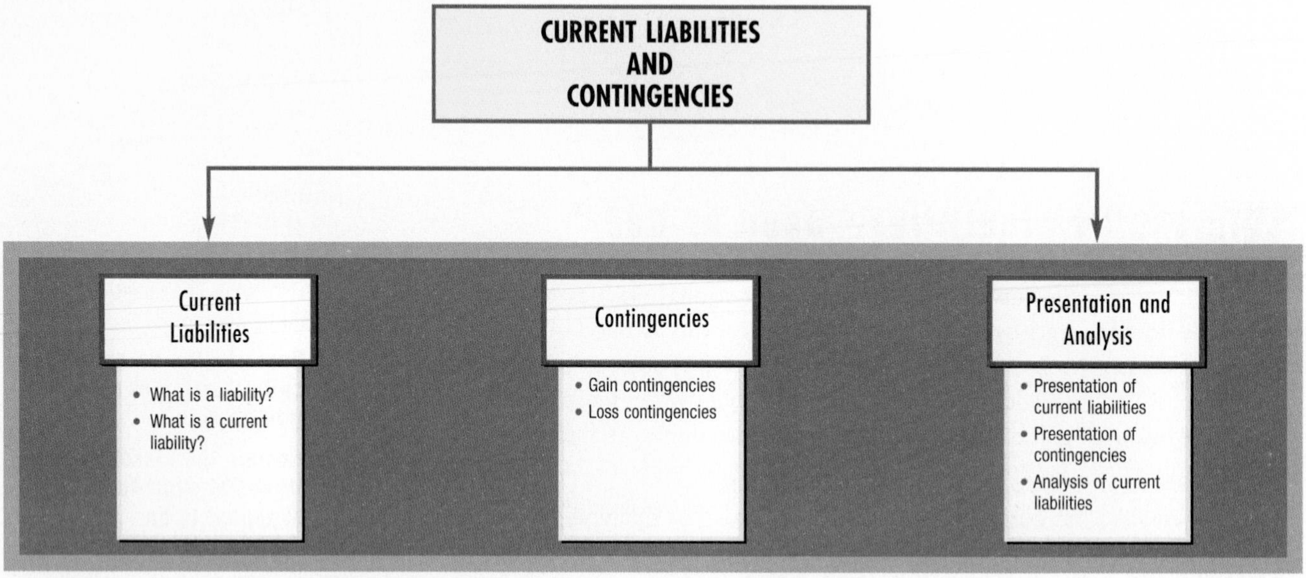

SECTION 1 CURRENT LIABILITIES

WHAT IS A LIABILITY?

The question, "What is a liability?" is not easy to answer. For example, one might ask whether preferred stock is a liability or an ownership claim. The first reaction is to say that preferred stock is in fact an ownership claim and should be reported as part of stockholders' equity. In fact, preferred stock has many elements of debt as well.[2] The issuer (and in some cases the holder) often has the right to call the stock within a specific period of time—making it similar to a repayment of principal. The dividend is in many cases almost guaranteed (cumulative provision)—making it look like interest. And preferred stock is but one of many financial instruments that are difficult to classify.[3]

[2]This illustration is not just a theoretical exercise. In practice, there are a number of preferred stock issues that have all the characteristics of a debt instrument, except that they are called and legally classified preferred stock. In some cases, the IRS has even permitted the dividend payments to be treated as interest expense for tax purposes. This issue is discussed further in Chapter 15.

[3]The FASB has issued a new standard for addressing this issue: "Accounting for Certain Financial Liabilities with Characteristics of Liabilities and Equity," *Statement of Financial Accounting Standards No. 149* (Norwalk, Conn.: FASB, 2003).

To help resolve some of these controversies, the FASB, as part of its conceptual framework project, defined **liabilities** as **"probable future sacrifices of economic benefits arising from present obligations of a particular entity to transfer assets or provide services to other entities in the future as a result of past transactions or events."**[4] In other words, a liability has three essential characteristics:

1. It is a present obligation that entails settlement by probable future transfer or use of cash, goods, or services.
2. It is an unavoidable obligation.
3. The transaction or other event creating the obligation has already occurred.

Because liabilities involve future disbursements of assets or services, one of their most important features is the date on which they are payable. Currently maturing obligations must be satisfied promptly and in the ordinary course of business if operations are to be continued. Liabilities with a more distant due date do not, as a rule, represent a claim on the enterprise's current resources and are therefore in a slightly different category. This feature gives rise to the basic division of liabilities into (1) current liabilities and (2) long-term debt.

UNDERLYING CONCEPTS

To determine the appropriate classification of specific financial instruments, proper definitions of assets, liabilities, and equities are needed. The conceptual framework definitions are often used as the basis for resolving controversial classification issues.

SQUEEZED

WHAT DO THE NUMBERS MEAN?

Investors and creditors closely monitor a company's liquidity. That's because companies with weak liquidity—high levels of current liabilities relative to cash and near-cash assets—lack financial flexibility. As discussed in Chapter 5, a company with a high degree of financial flexibility is better able to survive bad times, to recover from unexpected setbacks, and to take advantage of profitable investment opportunities. A number of companies have experienced the adverse effects of lower liquidity on financial flexibility in the recent economic slowdown.

Companies such as **General Motors**, **El Paso Corp**, and **Tengasco** have increased their reliance on various short-term sources of financing, usually in the form of commercial paper or short-term lines of bank credit. Commercial paper represents short-term loans arranged directly with investors. A line of credit is a bank loan agreement in which the borrower is permitted to draw up to an agreed-upon amount, as needed, on a short-term basis. Relying on these types of short-term liabilities seemed like a good idea for borrowers when the economy was rolling along, especially with the lower interest rates on these obligations relative to long-term debt.

However, in the wake of the World Trade Center disaster in the fall of 2001 and the slowing economy, lenders and short-term investors in commercial paper became reluctant to lend money, thus putting the "squeeze" on short-term borrowers. Many companies experienced a financial flexibility crisis as these short-term obligations came due: They were either unable to refinance, or if they could refinance, it was at much higher rates of interest. In other cases, companies were forced to sell off assets to generate cash for their immediate needs.

Source: Henny Sender, "Firms Feel Consequences of Short-Term Borrowing," *Wall Street Journal Online* (October 12, 2001).

---

[4] "Elements of Financial Statements of Business Enterprises," *Statement of Financial Accounting Concepts No. 6* (Stamford, Conn.: FASB, 1980). The FASB is considering an amendment to the definition of a liability. Under the proposed amendment, some obligations that are settled by issuance of equity shares would be classified as liabilities. "Proposed Amendment to *FASB Statement No. 6* to Revise the Definition of Liabilities," (Norwalk, Conn.: FASB, October 27, 2000).

WHAT IS A CURRENT LIABILITY?

INTERNATIONAL INSIGHT

In France, the balance sheet does not show current liabilities in a separate category. Rather, debts are disclosed separately by maturity in the notes.

Current assets are cash or other assets that can reasonably be expected to be converted into cash or to be sold or consumed in operations within a single operating cycle or within a year if more than one cycle is completed each year. **Current liabilities are "obligations whose liquidation is reasonably expected to require use of existing resources properly classified as current assets, or the creation of other current liabilities."**[5] This definition has gained wide acceptance because it recognizes operating cycles of varying lengths in different industries and takes into consideration the important relationship between current assets and current liabilities.[6]

The **operating cycle** is the period of time elapsing between the acquisition of goods and services involved in the manufacturing process and the final cash realization resulting from sales and subsequent collections. Industries that manufacture products requiring an aging process and certain capital-intensive industries have an operating cycle of considerably more than one year. On the other hand, most retail and service establishments have several operating cycles within a year.

There are many different types of current liabilities. The following ones are covered in this chapter in this order.

OBJECTIVE 1
Describe the nature, type, and valuation of current liabilities.

1. Accounts payable.
2. Notes payable.
3. Current maturities of long-term debt.
4. Short-term obligations expected to be refinanced.
5. Dividends payable.
6. Returnable deposits.
7. Unearned revenues.
8. Sales taxes payable.
9. Income taxes payable.
10. Employee-related liabilities.

Accounts Payable

Accounts payable, or **trade accounts payable**, are balances owed to others for goods, supplies, or services purchased on open account. Accounts payable arise because of the time lag between the receipt of services or acquisition of title to assets and the payment for them. This period of extended credit is usually found in the terms of the sale (e.g., 2/10, n/30 or 1/10, E.O.M.) and is commonly 30 to 60 days.

Most accounting systems are designed to record liabilities for purchases of goods when the goods are received or, practically, when the invoices are received. Frequently there is some delay in recording the goods and the related liability on the books. If title has passed to the purchaser before the goods are received, the transaction should be recorded at the time of title passage. Attention must be paid to transactions occurring near the end of one accounting period and at the beginning of the next. It is essential to ascertain that the record of goods received (the inventory) is in agreement with the liability (accounts payable) and that both are recorded in the proper period.

Measuring the amount of an account payable poses no particular difficulty because the invoice received from the creditor specifies the due date and the exact outlay in money that is necessary to settle the account. The only calculation that may be necessary concerns the amount of cash discount. See Chapter 8 for illustrations of entries related to accounts payable and purchase discounts.

---

[5]Committee on Accounting Procedure, American Institute of Certified Public Accountants, "Accounting Research and Terminology Bulletins," Final Edition (New York: AICPA, 1961), p. 21.

[6]The FASB affirmed this concept of "maturity within one year or the operating cycle whichever is longer" in its definition of short-term obligations in *Statement No. 6*. "Classification of Short-term Obligations Expected to Be Refinanced," *Statement of Financial Accounting Standards No. 6* (Stamford, Conn.: FASB, 1975), par. 2.

Notes Payable

Notes payable are written promises to pay a certain sum of money on a specified future date. They may arise from purchases, financing, or other transactions. In some industries, notes (often referred to as **trade notes payable**) are required as part of the sales/purchases transaction in lieu of the normal extension of open account credit. Notes payable to banks or loan companies generally arise from cash loans. Notes may be classified as short-term or long-term, depending upon the payment due date. Notes may also be interest-bearing or zero-interest-bearing.

Interest-Bearing Note Issued

Assume that Castle National Bank agrees to lend $100,000 on March 1, 2004, to Landscape Co. if Landscape Co. signs a $100,000, 12 percent, 4-month note. The entry to record the cash received by Landscape Co. on March 1 is:

March 1

Cash	100,000	
Notes Payable		100,000
(To record issuance of 12%, 4-month note to Castle National Bank)		

If Landscape Co. prepares financial statements semiannually, an adjusting entry is required to recognize interest expense and interest payable of $4,000 ($100,000 × 12% × 4/12) at June 30. The adjusting entry is:

June 30

Interest Expense	4,000	
Interest Payable		4,000
(To accrue interest for 4 months on Castle National Bank note)		

If Landscape prepared financial statements monthly, the adjusting entry at the end of each month would have been $1,000 ($100,000 × 12% × 1/12).

At maturity (July 1), Landscape Co. must pay the face value of the note ($100,000) plus $4,000 interest ($100,000 × 12% × 4/12).

The entry to record payment of the note and accrued interest is as follows.

July 1

Notes Payable	100,000	
Interest Payable	4,000	
Cash		104,000
(To record payment of Castle National Bank interest-bearing note and accrued interest at maturity)		

Zero-Interest-Bearing Note Issued

A zero-interest-bearing note may be issued instead of an interest-bearing note. A zero-interest-bearing note does not explicitly state an interest rate on the face of the note. Interest is still charged, however, because the borrower is required at maturity to pay back an amount greater than the cash received at the issuance date. In other words, the borrower receives in cash the present value of the note. The present value equals the face value of the note at maturity minus the interest or discount charged by the lender for the term of the note. In essence, the bank takes its fee "up front" rather than on the date the note matures.

To illustrate, we will assume that Landscape Co. issues a $104,000, 4-month, zero-interest-bearing note to Castle National Bank. The present value of the note is $100,000.[7] The entry to record this transaction for Landscape Co. is as follows.

---

[7]The bank discount rate used in this example to find the present value is 11.538 percent.

March 1		
Cash	100,000	
Discount on Notes Payable	4,000	
Notes Payable		104,000
(To record issuance of 4-month, zero-interest-bearing note to Castle National Bank)		

The Notes Payable account is credited for the face value of the note, which is $4,000 more than the actual cash received. The difference between the cash received and the face value of the note is debited to Discount on Notes Payable. **Discount on Notes Payable is a contra account to Notes Payable and therefore is subtracted from Notes Payable on the balance sheet.** The balance sheet presentation on March 1 is as follows.

ILLUSTRATION 13-1
Balance Sheet Presentation of Discount

Current liabilities		
Notes payable	104,000	
Less: Discount on notes payable	4,000	100,000

The amount of the discount, $4,000 in this case, represents the cost of borrowing $100,000 for 4 months. Accordingly, the discount is charged to interest expense over the life of the note. That is, the Discount on Notes Payable balance **represents interest expense chargeable to future periods**. Thus, it would be incorrect to debit Interest Expense for $4,000 at the time the loan is obtained. Additional accounting issues related to notes payable are discussed in Chapter 14.

Current Maturities of Long-Term Debt

The portion of bonds, mortgage notes, and other long-term indebtedness that matures within the next fiscal year—**current maturities of long-term debt**—is reported as a current liability. When only a part of a long-term debt is to be paid within the next 12 months (as in the case of serial bonds that are to be retired through a series of annual installments), **the maturing portion of long-term debt is reported as a current liability.** The balance is reported as a long-term debt.

Long-term debts maturing currently should not be included as current liabilities if they are to be:

1. retired by assets accumulated for this purpose that properly have not been shown as current assets;
2. refinanced, or retired from the proceeds of a new debt issue (see next topic); or
3. converted into capital stock.

In these situations, the use of current assets or the creation of other current liabilities does not occur. Therefore, classification as a current liability is inappropriate. The plan for liquidation of such a debt should be disclosed either parenthetically or by a note to the financial statements.

However, a liability that is **due on demand** (callable by the creditor) or will be due on demand within a year (or operating cycle, if longer) should be classified as a current liability. Liabilities often become callable by the creditor when there is a violation of the debt agreement. For example, most debt agreements specify a given level of equity to debt be maintained, or they specify that working capital be of a minimum amount. If an agreement is violated, classification of the debt as current is required because it is a reasonable expectation that existing working capital will be used to satisfy the debt. Only if it can be shown that it is **probable** that the violation will be cured (satisfied) within the grace period usually given in these agreements can the debt be classified as noncurrent.[8]

[8]"Classification of Obligations That Are Callable by the Creditor," *Statement of Financial Accounting Standards No. 78* (Stamford, Conn.: FASB, 1983).

Short-Term Obligations Expected to Be Refinanced

OBJECTIVE 2
Explain the classification issues of short-term debt expected to be refinanced.

Short-term obligations are those debts that are scheduled to mature within one year after the date of an enterprise's balance sheet or within an enterprise's operating cycle, whichever is longer. Some **short-term obligations** are **expected to be refinanced** on a long-term basis and therefore are not expected to require the use of working capital during the next year (or operating cycle).[9]

At one time, the accounting profession generally supported the exclusion of short-term obligations from current liabilities if they were "expected to be refinanced." Because the profession provided no specific guidelines, however, determining whether a short-term obligation was "expected to be refinanced" was usually based solely on management's **intent** to refinance on a long-term basis. A company may obtain a 5-year bank loan but, because the bank prefers it, handle the actual financing with 90-day notes, which it must keep turning over (renewing). So in this case, what is the loan—a long-term debt or a current liability? Another example of this problem of classification was the **Penn Central Railroad** before it went bankrupt. The railroad was deep into short-term debt and commercial paper but classified it as long-term debt. Why? Because the railroad believed it had commitments from lenders to keep refinancing the short-term debt. When those commitments suddenly disappeared, it was "good-bye Pennsy." As the Greek philosopher Epictetus once said, "Some things in this world are not and yet appear to be."

Refinancing Criteria

As a result of these classification problems, authoritative criteria have been developed for determining the circumstances under which short-term obligations may properly be excluded from current liabilities. A company is required to exclude a short-term obligation from current liabilities only if **both** of the following conditions are met:

1. It must **intend to refinance** the obligation on a long-term basis.
2. It must **demonstrate an ability** to consummate the refinancing.[10]

Intention to refinance on a long-term basis means that the enterprise intends to refinance the short-term obligation so that the use of working capital will not be required during the ensuing fiscal year or operating cycle, if longer. The **ability** to consummate the refinancing may be demonstrated by:

(a) **Actually refinancing** the short-term obligation by issuing a long-term obligation or equity securities after the date of the balance sheet but before it is issued; or

(b) Entering into a **financing agreement** that clearly permits the enterprise to refinance the debt on a long-term basis on terms that are readily determinable.

If an actual refinancing occurs, the portion of the short-term obligation to be excluded from current liabilities may not exceed the proceeds from the new obligation or equity securities that are applied to retire the short-term obligation. For example, **Montavon Winery** with $3,000,000 of short-term debt issued 100,000 shares of common stock subsequent to the balance sheet date but before the balance sheet was issued, intending to use the proceeds to liquidate the short-term debt at its maturity. If the net proceeds from the sale of the 100,000 shares totaled $2,000,000, only that amount of the short-term debt could be excluded from current liabilities.

An additional question relates to whether a short-term obligation should be excluded from current liabilities if it is paid off after the balance sheet date and subsequently replaced by long-term debt before the balance sheet is issued. To illustrate,

[9]*Refinancing a short-term obligation on a long-term basis* means either replacing it with a long-term obligation or with equity securities, or renewing, extending, or replacing it with short-term obligations for an uninterrupted period extending beyond one year (or the operating cycle, if longer) from the date of the enterprise's balance sheet.

[10]"Classification of Short-term Obligations Expected to Be Refinanced," *Statement of Financial Accounting Standards No. 6* (Stamford, Conn.: FASB, 1975), pars. 10 and 11.

Marquardt Company pays off short-term debt of $40,000 on January 17, 2005, and issues long-term debt of $100,000 on February 3, 2005. Marquardt's financial statements dated December 31, 2004, are to be issued March 1, 2005. Because repayment of the short-term obligation **before** funds were obtained through long-term financing required the use of **existing** current assets, the short-term obligations are included in current liabilities at the balance sheet date (see graphical presentation below).

ILLUSTRATION 13-2
Short-Term Debt Paid Off after Balance Sheet Date and Later Replaced by Long-Term Debt

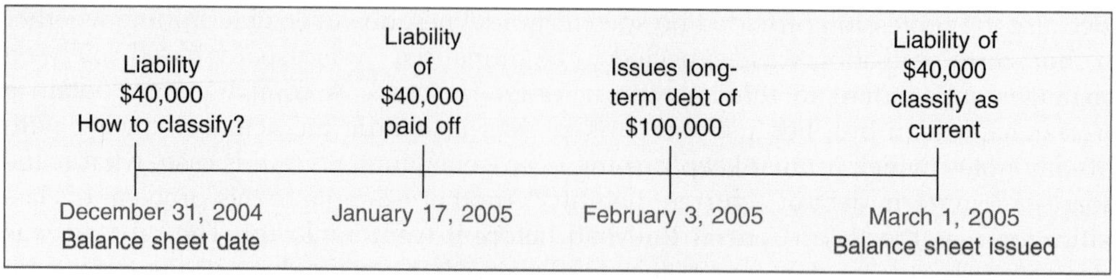

WHAT DO THE NUMBERS MEAN?

WHAT ABOUT THAT SHORT-TERM DEBT?

Investors and creditors are interested in a company's debt-management strategies. Management decisions that are viewed as prudent will be rewarded with lower debt service costs and a higher stock price. The wrong decisions can bring higher debt costs and lower stock prices.

General Electric Capital Corp., a subsidiary of **General Electric**, recently experienced the negative effects of market scrutiny of its debt-management policies when analysts complained that GE had been slow to refinance its mountains of short-term debt. GE had issued these current obligations, with maturities of 270 days or less, when interest rates were low. However, in light of expectations that the Fed would raise interest rates, analysts began to worry about the higher interest costs GE would pay when these loans were refinanced. Some analysts recommended that it was time to reduce dependence on short-term credit. The reasoning was that a shift to more dependable long-term debt, thereby locking in slightly higher rates for the long-term, would be the better way to go.

Thus, scrutiny of GE debt strategies led to analysts' concerns about GE's earnings prospects. Investors took the analysis to heart, and GE experienced a 2-day 6 percent drop in its stock price.

Source: Adapted from Steven Vames, "Credit Quality, Stock Investing Seem to Go Hand in Hand," *Wall Street Journal* (April 1, 2002), p. R4.

Dividends Payable

UNDERLYING CONCEPTS

Preferred dividends in arrears do represent a probable future economic sacrifice, but the expected sacrifice does not result from a past transaction or past event. The sacrifice will result from a future event (declaration by the board of directors). Note disclosure improves the predictive value of the financial statements.

A **cash dividend payable** is an amount owed by a corporation to its stockholders as a result of the board of directors' authorization. At the date of declaration the corporation assumes a liability that places the stockholders in the position of creditors in the amount of dividends declared. Because cash dividends are always paid within one year of declaration (generally within 3 months), they are classified as current liabilities.

Accumulated but undeclared dividends on cumulative preferred stock are not a recognized liability because **preferred dividends in arrears** are not an obligation until formal action is taken by the board of directors authorizing the distribution of earnings. Nevertheless, the amount of cumulative dividends unpaid should be disclosed in a note, or it may be shown parenthetically in the capital stock section of the balance sheet.

Dividends payable in the form of additional shares of stock are not recognized as a liability. Such **stock dividends** (as discussed in Chapter 15) do not require future outlays of assets or services and are revocable by the board of directors at any time prior to issuance. Even so, such undistributed stock dividends are generally reported in the stockholders' equity section because they represent retained earnings in the process of transfer to paid-in capital.

Returnable Deposits

Current liabilities of a company may include **returnable cash deposits** received from customers and employees. Deposits may be received from customers to guarantee performance of a contract or service or as guarantees to cover payment of expected future obligations. For example, telephone companies often require a deposit upon installation of a phone. Deposits may also be received from customers as guarantees for possible damage to property left with the customer. Some companies require their employees to make deposits for the return of keys or other company property. The classification of these items as current or noncurrent liabilities is dependent on the time between the date of the deposit and the termination of the relationship that required the deposit.

Unearned Revenues

A magazine publisher such as **Golf Digest** may receive a customer's check when magazines are ordered, and an airline company, such as **American Airlines**, often sells tickets for future flights. Restaurants may issue meal tickets that can be exchanged or used for future meals. Who hasn't received or given a **McDonald's** gift certificate? And as discussed in the opening story, a company like **Microsoft** issues coupons that allow customers to upgrade to the next version of its software. How do these companies account for **unearned revenues** that are received before goods are delivered or services are rendered?

1. When the advance is received, Cash is debited, and a current liability account identifying the source of the unearned revenue is credited.
2. When the revenue is earned, the unearned revenue account is debited, and an earned revenue account is credited.

To illustrate, assume that Allstate University sells 10,000 season football tickets at $50 each for its five-game home schedule. The entry for the sales of season tickets is:

August 6

Cash	500,000	
Unearned Football Ticket Revenue		500,000
(To record sale of 10,000 season tickets)		

As each game is completed, the following entry is made:

September 7

Unearned Football Ticket Revenue	100,000	
Football Ticket Revenue		100,000
(To record football ticket revenues earned)		

Unearned Football Ticket Revenue is, therefore, unearned revenue and is reported as a current liability in the balance sheet. As revenue is earned, a transfer from unearned revenue to earned revenue occurs. Unearned revenue is material for some companies: In the airline industry, tickets sold for future flights represent almost 50 percent of total current liabilities. At **United Air Lines**, unearned ticket revenue is the largest current liability, recently amounting to over $1.4 billion.

Illustration 13-3 (on page 624) shows specific unearned and earned revenue accounts used in selected types of businesses. The balance sheet should report obligations for any commitments that are redeemable in goods and services. The income statement should report revenues earned during the period.

ILLUSTRATION 13-3
Unearned and Earned Revenue Accounts

Type of Business	Account Title: Unearned Revenue	Account Title: Earned Revenue
Airline	Unearned Passenger Ticket Revenue	Passenger Revenue
Magazine publisher	Unearned Subscription Revenue	Subscription Revenue
Hotel	Unearned Rental Revenue	Rental Revenue
Auto dealer	Unearned Warranty Revenue	Warranty Revenue

Sales Taxes Payable

Sales taxes on transfers of tangible personal property and on certain services must be collected from customers and remitted to the proper governmental authority. A liability is set up to provide for taxes collected from customers but not yet remitted to the tax authority. The Sales Taxes Payable account should reflect the liability for sales taxes due various governments. The entry below is the proper one for a sale of $3,000 when a 4 percent sales tax is in effect.

Cash or Accounts Receivable	3,120	
Sales		3,000
Sales Taxes Payable		120

When the sales tax collections credited to the liability account are not equal to the liability as computed by the governmental formula, an adjustment of the liability account may be made by recognizing a gain or a loss on sales tax collections.

In many companies, however, the sales tax and the amount of the sale are not segregated at the time of sale. Instead, both are credited in total in the Sales account. In that case, to reflect correctly the actual amount of sales and the liability for sales taxes, the Sales account must be debited for the amount of the sales taxes due the government on these sales, and the Sales Taxes Payable account must be credited for the same amount. As an illustration, assume that the Sales account balance of $150,000 includes sales taxes of 4 percent. Because the amount recorded in the Sales account is equal to sales plus 4 percent of sales, or 1.04 times the sales total, sales are $150,000 ÷ 1.04, or $144,230.77. The sales tax liability is $5,769.23 ($144,230.77 × 0.04; or $150,000 − $144,230.77). The following entry would be made to record the amount due the taxing unit.

Sales	5,769.23	
Sales Taxes Payable		5,769.23

WHAT DO THE NUMBERS MEAN?

KILL THE SALES TAX

The use of the sales tax as a source of revenues is coming under increasing scrutiny, especially as more and more purchases are made online. Although under current law one state cannot require businesses in another state to collect sales taxes on Internet purchases, some economists are arguing to eliminate the sales tax altogether. Beyond the difficulty in collecting sales tax on remote purchases, another reason for elimination is that the sales tax does not apply to all sales, which creates a distortion of purchases away from items subject to the sales tax. Furthermore, the sales tax imposes a double tax on businesses. That's because when a business purchases office equipment, it pays sales tax, a cost which is then passed on to consumers in higher prices.

Although there are good reasons to eliminate the sales tax, an important reason for keeping the sales tax is that it is viewed as a hidden tax: Most people know how much income tax they pay each year but are less aware of their sales tax payments. Thus, replacing the revenue from the "hidden" sales tax with more apparent taxes and fees is not likely to be very appealing to many politicians.

Source: Adapted from Hal Varian, "Economic Scene: Forget Net Taxes. Forget Sales Taxes Altogether," *New York Times on the Web* (March 8, 2001).

Income Taxes Payable

Expanded Discussion of Property Taxes Payable

Any federal or state income tax varies in proportion to the amount of annual income. Some consider the amount of income tax on annual income as an estimate because the computation of income (and the tax thereon) is subject to IRS review and approval. The meaning and application of numerous tax rules, especially new ones, are debatable and often dependent on a court's interpretation. Using the best information and advice available, a business must prepare an income tax return and compute the income tax payable resulting from the operations of the current period. The taxes payable on the income of a corporation, as computed per the tax return, should be classified as a current liability.[11]

Unlike the corporation, the proprietorship and the partnership are not taxable entities. Because the individual proprietor and the members of a partnership are subject to personal income taxes on their share of the business's taxable income, income tax liabilities do not appear on the financial statements of proprietorships and partnerships.

Most corporations must make periodic tax payments throughout the year in an authorized bank depository or a Federal Reserve bank. These payments are based upon estimates of the total annual tax liability. As the estimated total tax liability changes, the periodic contributions also change. If in a later year an additional tax is assessed on the income of an earlier year, Income Taxes Payable should be credited. The related debit should be charged to current operations.

Differences between taxable income under the tax laws and accounting income under generally accepted accounting principles sometimes occur. Because of these differences, the amount of income tax payable to the government in any given year may differ substantially from income tax expense, as reported on the financial statements. Chapter 19 is devoted solely to income tax matters and presents an extensive discussion of this complex and controversial problem.

Employee-Related Liabilities

OBJECTIVE 3
Identify types of employee-related liabilities.

Amounts owed to employees for salaries or wages at the end of an accounting period are reported as a current liability. In addition, the following items related to employee compensation are often reported as current liabilities.

1. Payroll deductions.
2. Compensated absences.
3. Bonuses. (Accounting for bonuses is covered in Appendix 13A.)

Payroll Deductions

The most common types of payroll deductions are taxes and miscellaneous items such as insurance premiums, employee savings, and union dues. **To the extent the amounts deducted have not been remitted to the proper authority at the end of the accounting period, they should be recognized as current liabilities.**

Social Security Taxes. Since January 1, 1937, Social Security legislation has provided federal old-age, survivor, and disability insurance (O.A.S.D.I.) benefits for certain individuals and their families through taxes levied on both the employer and the employee. All employers covered are required to collect the employee's share of this tax, by deducting it from the employee's gross pay, and to remit it to the federal government along with the employer's share. Both the employer and the employee are taxed at the same rate, currently 6.2 percent based on the employee's gross pay up to an $84,900 annual limit.

---

[11]Corporate taxes are based on a progressive tax rate structure. Companies with taxable income of $50,000 or less are taxed at a 15 percent rate, while higher levels of income are taxed at rates ranging up to 39 percent.

In 1965 Congress passed the first federal health insurance program for the aged—popularly known as Medicare. It is a two-part program designed to alleviate the high cost of medical care for those over age 65. The Basic Plan, which provides hospital and other institutional services, is financed by a separate Hospital Insurance tax paid by both the employee and the employer at the rate of 1.45 percent on the employee's total compensation. The Voluntary Plan takes care of the major part of doctors' bills and other medical and health services and is financed by monthly payments from all who enroll plus matching funds from the federal government.

The combination of the O.A.S.D.I. tax, often called Federal Insurance Contribution Act (F.I.C.A.) tax, and the federal Hospital Insurance Tax is commonly referred to as the **Social Security tax**. The combined rate for these taxes, 7.65 percent on an employee's wages to $84,900 and 1.45 percent in excess of $84,900, is changed intermittently by acts of Congress. **The amount of unremitted employee and employer Social Security tax on gross wages paid should be reported by the employer as a current liability.**

Unemployment Taxes. Another payroll tax levied by the federal government in cooperation with state governments provides a system of unemployment insurance. All employers who (1) paid wages of $1,500 or more during any calendar quarter in the year or preceding year or (2) employed at least one individual on at least one day in each of 20 weeks during the current or preceding calendar year are subject to the Federal Unemployment Tax Act (F.U.T.A.). This tax is levied only on the employer at a rate of 6.2 percent on the first $7,000 of compensation paid to each employee during the calendar year. The employer is allowed a tax credit not to exceed 5.4 percent for contributions paid to a state plan for unemployment compensation. Thus, if an employer is subject to a state unemployment tax of 5.4 percent or more, only 0.8 percent tax is due the federal government.

State unemployment compensation laws differ from the federal law and differ among various states. Therefore, employers must be familiar with the unemployment tax laws in each state in which they pay wages and salaries. Although the normal state tax may range from 3 percent to 7 percent or higher, all states provide for some form of merit rating under which a reduction in the state contribution rate is allowed. Employers who display by their benefit and contribution experience that they have provided steady employment may be entitled to this reduction—if the size of the state fund is adequate to provide the reduction. In order not to penalize an employer who has earned a reduction in the state contribution rate, the federal law allows a credit of 5.4 percent even though the effective state contribution rate is less than 5.4 percent.

To illustrate, Appliance Repair Co., which has a taxable payroll of $100,000, is subject to a federal rate of 6.2 percent and a state contribution rate of 5.7 percent. Because of stable employment experience, the company's state rate has been reduced to 1 percent. The computation of the federal and state unemployment taxes for Appliance Repair Co. is:

ILLUSTRATION 13-4
Computation of Unemployment Taxes

State unemployment tax payment (1% × $100,000)	$1,000
Federal unemployment tax [(6.2% − 5.4%) × $100,000]	800
Total federal and state unemployment tax	$1,800

The federal unemployment tax is paid quarterly with a tax form filed annually. State contributions generally are required to be paid quarterly. Because both the federal and the state unemployment taxes accrue on earned compensation, the amount of accrued but unpaid employer contributions **should be recorded as an operating expense and as a current liability when financial statements are prepared at year-end**.

Income Tax Withholding. Federal and some state income tax laws require employers to withhold from the pay of each employee the applicable income tax due on those wages. The amount of income tax withheld is computed by the employer according to a government-prescribed formula or withholding tax table. That amount depends on the length of the pay period and each employee's taxable wages, marital status, and claimed dependents. If the income tax withheld plus the employee and the employer Social Security taxes exceeds specified amounts per month, the employer is required to make remittances to the government during the month.

Illustration 13-5 summarizes various payroll deductions and liabilities.

ILLUSTRATION 13-5
Summary of Payroll Liabilities

Item	Who Pays	
Income tax withholding FICA taxes—employee share Union dues	Employee	Employer reports these amounts as liabilities until remitted.
FICA taxes—employer share Federal unemployment State unemployment	Employer	

Payroll Deductions Illustration. Assume a weekly payroll of $10,000 entirely subject to F.I.C.A. and Medicare (7.65%), federal (0.8%) and state (4%) unemployment taxes with income tax withholding of $1,320 and union dues of $88 deducted.

The entry to record the wages and salaries paid and the **employee payroll deductions** would be:

Wages and Salaries Expense	10,000	
Withholding Taxes Payable		1,320
F.I.C.A. Taxes Payable		765
Union Dues Payable to Local No. 257		88
Cash		7,827

The entry to record the **employer payroll taxes** would be:

Payroll Tax Expense	1,245	
F.I.C.A. Taxes Payable		765
Federal Unemployment Tax Payable		80
State Unemployment Tax Payable		400

The employer is required to remit to the government its share of F.I.C.A. tax along with the amount of F.I.C.A. tax deducted from each employee's gross compensation. All unremitted employer F.I.C.A. taxes should be recorded as payroll tax expense and payroll tax payable.[12]

Compensated Absences

Compensated absences are absences from employment—such as vacation, illness, and holidays—for which employees are paid anyway. A liability should be accrued for the cost of compensation for future absences if **all** of the following four conditions are met:[13]

(a) The employer's obligation relating to employees' rights to receive compensation for future absences is attributable to employees' services **already rendered**,

(b) The obligation relates to the rights that **vest or accumulate**,

UNDERLYING CONCEPTS

When these four conditions exist, all elements in the definition of a liability exist. In addition, the matching concept requires that the period receiving the services also should report the related expense.

[12]In a manufacturing enterprise, all of the payroll costs (wages, payroll taxes, and fringe benefits) are allocated to appropriate cost accounts such as Direct Labor, Indirect Labor, Sales Salaries, Administrative Salaries, and the like. This abbreviated and somewhat simplified discussion of payroll costs and deductions is not indicative of the volume of records and clerical work that may be involved in maintaining a sound and accurate payroll system.

[13]"Accounting for Compensated Absences," *Statement of Financial Accounting Standards No. 43* (Stamford, Conn.: FASB, 1980), par. 6.

(c) Payment of the compensation is **probable**, and
(d) The amount can be **reasonably estimated**.[14]

An example of an accrual for compensated absences is shown below in an excerpt from the balance sheet of **Clarcor Inc.** presented in its annual report.

ILLUSTRATION 13-6
Balance Sheet Presentation of Accrual for Compensated Absences

Clarcor Inc.

Current liabilities	
Accounts payable	$ 6,308
Accrued salaries, wages and commissions	2,278
Compensated absences	2,271
Accrued pension liabilities	1,023
Other accrued liabilities	4,572
	$16,452

If an employer meets conditions (a), (b), and (c) but does not accrue a liability because of a failure to meet condition (d), that fact should be disclosed. An example of such a disclosure is the following note from the financial statements of **Gotham Utility Company**.

ILLUSTRATION 13-7
Disclosure of Policy for Compensated Absences

Gotham Utility Company

Employees of the Company are entitled to paid vacation, personal, and sick days off, depending on job status, length of service, and other factors. Due to numerous differing union contracts and other agreements with nonunion employees, it is impractical to estimate the amount of compensation for future absences, and, accordingly, no liability has been reported in the accompanying financial statements. The Company's policy is to recognize the cost of compensated absences when actually paid to employees; compensated absence payments to employees totaled $2,786,000.

Vested rights exist when an employer has an obligation to make payment to an employee even if his or her employment is terminated. Thus, vested rights are not contingent on an employee's future service. **Accumulated rights** are those that can be carried forward to future periods if not used in the period in which earned. For example, assume that you have earned 4 days of vacation pay as of December 31, the end of your employer's fiscal year, and that you will be paid for this vacation time even if you terminate employment. In this situation, your 4 days of vacation pay are considered vested and must be accrued. Now assume that your vacation days are not vested, but that you can carry the 4 days over into later periods. Although the rights are not vested,

[14]These same four conditions are to be applied to accounting for **postemployment benefits**. **Postemployment benefits** are benefits provided by an enterprise to past or inactive employees **after employment but prior to retirement**. Examples include salary continuation, supplemental unemployment benefits, severance pay, job training, and continuation of health and life insurance coverage. *FASB Statement No. 112,* "Employers' Accounting for Postemployment Benefits" requires that the accounting treatment for compensated absences described in *FASB Statement No. 43* be applied to postemployment benefits. "Employers' Accounting for Postemployment Benefits," *Statement of Financial Accounting Standards No. 112* (Norwalk, Conn.: FASB, November 1992), par. 18.

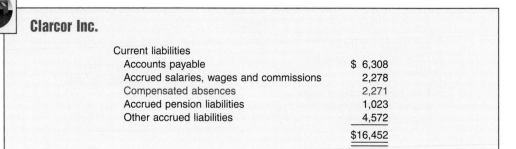

they are accumulated rights for which the employer must provide an accrual, allowing for estimated forfeitures due to turnover.

A modification of the general rules relates to the issue of **sick pay**. If sick pay benefits vest, accrual is required. If sick pay benefits accumulate but do not vest, accrual is permitted but not required. The reason for this distinction is that compensation that is designated as sick pay may be administered in one of two ways. In some companies, employees receive sick pay only if they are absent because of illness. Accrual of a liability is permitted but not required because its payment is contingent upon future employee illness. In other companies, employees are allowed to accumulate unused sick pay and take compensated time off from work even though they are not ill. For this type of sick pay, a liability must be accrued because it will be paid whether or not employees ever become ill.

The expense and related liability for compensated absences should be recognized in the year earned by employees. For example, if new employees receive rights to two weeks' paid vacation at the beginning of their second year of employment, the vacation pay is considered to be earned during the first year of employment.

What rate should be used to accrue the compensated absence cost—the current rate or an estimated future rate? *FASB Statement No. 43* is silent on this subject. Therefore, it is likely that companies will use the current rather than future rate. The future rate is less certain and raises issues concerning the time value of money. To illustrate, assume that Amutron Inc. began operations on January 1, 2003. The company employs ten individuals who are paid $480 per week. Vacation weeks earned by all employees in 2003 were 20 weeks, but none were used during this period. In 2004, the vacation weeks were used when the current rate of pay was $540 per week for each employee. The entry at December 31, 2003, to accrue the accumulated vacation pay is as follows.

Wages Expense	9,600	
Vacation Wages Payable ($480 × 20)		9,600

At December 31, 2003, the company would report on its balance sheet a liability of $9,600. In 2004, the vacation pay related to 2003 would be recorded as follows.

Vacation Wages Payable	9,600	
Wages Expense	1,200	
Cash ($540 × 20)		10,800

In 2004 the vacation weeks were used. Therefore, the liability is extinguished. Note that the difference between the amount of cash paid and the reduction in the liability account is recorded as an adjustment to Wages Expense in the period when paid. This difference arises because the liability account was accrued at the rates of pay in effect during the period when compensated time was earned. The cash paid, however, is based on the rates in effect during the period when compensated time is used. If the future rates of pay had been used to compute the accrual in 2003, then the cash paid in 2004 would have been equal to the liability.[15]

INTERNATIONAL INSIGHT

In Japan, bonuses to members of the Board of Directors and to the Commercial Code auditors are not treated as expenses. They are considered to be a distribution of profits and charged against retained earnings.

Bonus Agreements

For various reasons, many companies give a **bonus** to certain or all officers and employees in addition to their regular salary or wage. Frequently the bonus amount is dependent on the company's yearly profit. For example, **Ford Motor Company** has a plan whereby employees share in the success of the company's operations on the basis of a complicated formula using net income as its primary basis for computation. From the standpoint of the enterprise, **bonus payments to employees** may be considered additional wages and should be included as a deduction in determining the net income for the year.

[15]Some companies have obligations for benefits paid to employees after they retire. The accounting and reporting standards for postretirement benefit payments are complex. These standards relate to two different types of **postretirement benefits**: (1) pensions and (2) postretirement health-care and life insurance benefits. These issues are discussed extensively in Chapter 20.

To illustrate the entries for an employee bonus, assume a company whose income for the year 2004 is $100,000 will pay out bonuses of $10,714.29 in January 2005. (Computations of this and other bonuses are illustrated in Appendix 13A.) An adjusting entry dated December 31, 2004, is made to record the bonus as follows.

Employees' Bonus Expense	10,714.29	
Profit-Sharing Bonus Payable		10,714.29

In January 2005, when the bonus is paid, the journal entry would be:

Profit-Sharing Bonus Payable	10,714.29	
Cash		10,714.29

The expense account should appear in the income statement as an operating expense. **The liability, profit-sharing bonus payable, is usually payable within a short period of time and should be included as a current liability in the balance sheet.**

Similar to bonus arrangements are contractual agreements covering rents or royalty payments conditional on the amount of revenues earned or the quantity of product produced or extracted. Conditional expenses based on revenues or units produced are usually less difficult to compute than bonus arrangements. For example, if a lease calls for a fixed rent payment of $500 per month and 1 percent of all sales over $300,000 per year, the annual rent obligation would amount to $6,000 plus $0.01 of each dollar of revenue over $300,000. Or, a royalty agreement may accrue to the patent owner $1.00 for every ton of product resulting from the patented process, or accrue to the mineral rights owner $0.50 on every barrel of oil extracted. As each additional unit of product is produced or extracted, an additional obligation, usually a current liability, is created.

SECTION 2 *CONTINGENCIES*

A **contingency** is defined in *FASB Statement No. 5* "as an existing condition, situation, or set of circumstances involving uncertainty as to possible gain **(gain contingency)** or loss **(loss contingency)** to an enterprise that will ultimately be resolved when one or more future events occur or fail to occur."[16]

GAIN CONTINGENCIES

OBJECTIVE 4
Identify the criteria used to account for and disclose gain and loss contingencies.

Gain contingencies are claims or rights to receive assets (or have a liability reduced) whose existence is uncertain but which may become valid eventually. The typical gain contingencies are:

1. Possible receipts of monies from gifts, donations, bonuses, and so on.
2. Possible refunds from the government in tax disputes.
3. Pending court cases where the probable outcome is favorable.
4. Tax loss carryforwards (discussed in Chapter 19).

Accountants have adopted a conservative policy in this area. Gain contingencies are not recorded. They are disclosed in the notes only when the probabilities are high that a gain contingency will become a reality. As a result, it is unusual to find infor-

[16] "Accounting for Contingencies," *Statement of Financial Accounting Standards No. 5* (Stamford, Conn.: FASB, 1975), par. 1.

mation about contingent gains in the financial statements and the accompanying notes. An example of a disclosure of a gain contingency is as follows.

ILLUSTRATION 13-8
Disclosure of Gain Contingency

BMC Industries, Inc.

Note 13: Legal Matters. In the first quarter, a U.S. District Court in Miami, Florida, awarded the Company a $5.1 million judgment against **Barth Industries** (Barth) of Cleveland, Ohio and its parent, **Nesco Holdings, Inc.** (Nesco). The judgment relates to an agreement under which Barth and Nesco were to help automate the plastic lens production plant in Fort Lauderdale, Florida. The Company has not recorded any income relating to this judgment because Barth and Nesco have filed an appeal.

LOSS CONTINGENCIES

Loss contingencies are situations involving uncertainty as to possible loss. A liability incurred as a result of a loss contingency is by definition a **contingent liability**. **Contingent liabilities** are obligations that are dependent upon the occurrence or nonoccurrence of one or more future events to confirm either the amount payable, the payee, the date payable, or its existence. That is, one or more of these factors depend upon a contingency.

When a loss contingency exists, the likelihood that the future event or events will confirm the incurrence of a liability can range from probable to remote. The FASB uses the terms **probable**, **reasonably possible**, and **remote** to identify three areas within that range and assigns the following meanings.

> **Probable.** The future event or events are likely to occur.
>
> **Reasonably possible.** The chance of the future event or events occurring is more than remote but less than likely.
>
> **Remote.** The chance of the future event or events occurring is slight.

An estimated loss from a loss contingency should be accrued by a charge to expense and a liability recorded only if **both** of the following conditions are met.[17]

1. Information available prior to the issuance of the financial statements indicates that it is **probable that a liability has been incurred** at the date of the financial statements.
2. The amount of the loss can be **reasonably estimated**.

Neither the exact payee nor the exact date payable need be known to record a liability. **What must be known is whether it is probable that a liability has been incurred.**

The second criterion indicates that an amount for the liability can be reasonably determined. If it cannot, it should not be accrued as a liability. Evidence to determine a reasonable estimate of the liability may be based on the company's own experience, experience of other companies in the industry, engineering or research studies, legal advice, or educated guesses by personnel in the best position to know. The excerpt from the annual report of **Quaker State Oil Refining Corp.** shown in Illustration 13-9 (page 632) is an example of an accrual recorded for a loss contingency.

[17]Those loss contingencies that result in the incurrence of a liability are most relevant to the discussion in this chapter. Loss contingencies that result in the impairment of an asset (e.g., collectibility of receivables or threat of expropriation of assets) are discussed more fully in other sections of this textbook.

ILLUSTRATION 13-9
Disclosure of Accrual for Loss Contingency

Quaker State Oil Refining Corp.

Note 5: Contingencies. During the period from November 13 to December 23, a change in an additive component purchased from one of its suppliers caused certain oil refined and shipped to fail to meet the Company's low-temperature performance requirements. The Company has recalled this product and has arranged for reimbursement to its customers and the ultimate consumers of all costs associated with the product. Estimated cost of the recall program, net of estimated third party reimbursement, in the amount of $3,500,000 has been charged to current operations.

Use of the terms probable, reasonably possible, and remote as guidelines for classifying contingencies involves judgment and subjectivity. The items in Illustration 13-10 are examples of loss contingencies and the general accounting treatment accorded them.

ILLUSTRATION 13-10
Accounting Treatment of Loss Contingencies

Loss Related to	Usually Accrued	Not Accrued	May Be Accrued*
1. Collectibility of receivables	X		
2. Obligations related to product warranties and product defects	X		
3. Premiums offered to customers	X		
4. Risk of loss or damage of enterprise property by fire, explosion, or other hazards		X	
5. General or unspecified business risks		X	
6. Risk of loss from catastrophes assumed by property and casualty insurance companies, including reinsurance companies		X	
7. Threat of expropriation of assets			X
8. Pending or threatened litigation			X
9. Actual or possible claims and assessments**			X
10. Guarantees of indebtedness of others			X
11. Obligations of commercial banks under "standby letters of credit"			X
12. Agreements to repurchase receivables (or the related property) that have been sold			X

*Should be accrued when both criteria—probable and reasonably estimable—are met.
**Estimated amounts of losses incurred prior to the balance sheet date but settled subsequently should be accrued as of the balance sheet date.

INTERNATIONAL INSIGHT

In Germany, company law allows firms to accrue losses for contingencies as long as they are possible and reasonable. Such provisions are one means of smoothing income.

Practicing accountants express concern over the diversity that now exists in the interpretation of "probable," "reasonably possible," and "remote." Current practice relies heavily on the exact language used in responses received from lawyers, but such language is necessarily biased and protective rather than predictive. As a result, accruals and disclosures of contingencies vary considerably in practice. Some of the more common loss contingencies discussed in this chapter are:[18]

1. Litigation, claims, and assessments.
2. Guarantee and warranty costs.
3. Premiums and coupons.
4. Environmental liabilities.
5. Self-insurance risks.

[18] *Accounting Trends and Techniques—2001* reports that of the 600 companies surveyed, loss contingencies of the following nature and number were reported: litigation 468; environmental 249; insurance 58; possible tax assessments 47; governmental investigation 45; and others 47.

Note that general risk contingencies that are inherent in business operations, such as the possibility of war, strike, uninsurable catastrophes, or a business recession, are not reported in the notes to the financial statements.

Litigation, Claims, and Assessments

OBJECTIVE 5
Explain the accounting for different types of loss contingencies.

The following factors, among others, must be considered in determining whether a liability should be recorded with respect to **pending or threatened litigation** and actual or possible **claims** and **assessments**:

1. The **time period** in which the underlying cause of action occurred.
2. The **probability** of an unfavorable outcome.
3. The ability to make a **reasonable estimate** of the amount of loss.

To report a loss and a liability in the financial statements, the cause for litigation must have occurred on or before the date of the financial statements. It does not matter that the company did not become aware of the existence or possibility of the lawsuit or claims until after the date of the financial statements but before they are issued. To evaluate the probability of an unfavorable outcome, consider the following: the nature of the litigation; the progress of the case; the opinion of legal counsel; the experience of your company and others in similar cases; and any management response to the lawsuit.

The outcome of pending litigation, however, can seldom be predicted with any assurance. Even if the evidence available at the balance sheet date does not favor the defendant, it is hardly reasonable to expect the company to publish in its financial statements a dollar estimate of the probable negative outcome. Such specific disclosures could weaken the company's position in the dispute and encourage the plaintiff to intensify its efforts. A typical example of the wording of such a disclosure is the note to the financial statements of **Apple Computer, Inc.** relating to its litigation concerning repetitive stress injuries, as shown in Illustration 13-11.

ILLUSTRATION 13-11
Disclosure of Litigation

Apple Computer, Inc.

"Repetitive Stress Injury" Litigation. The Company is named in numerous lawsuits (fewer than 100) alleging that the plaintiff incurred so-called "repetitive stress injury" to the upper extremities as a result of using keyboards and/or mouse input devices sold by the Company. On October 4, in a trial of one of these cases (*Dorsey v. Apple*) in the United States District Court for the Eastern District of New York, the jury rendered a verdict in favor of the Company, and final judgment in favor of the Company has been entered. The other cases are in various stages of pretrial activity. These suits are similar to those filed against other major suppliers of personal computers. Ultimate resolution of the litigation against the Company may depend on progress in resolving this type of litigation in the industry overall.

With respect to **unfiled suits** and **unasserted claims and assessments**, a company must determine (1) the degree of **probability** that a suit may be filed or a claim or assessment may be asserted and (2) the **probability** of an unfavorable outcome. For example, assume that Nawtee Company is being investigated by the Federal Trade Commission for restraint of trade, and enforcement proceedings have been instituted. Such proceedings are often followed by private claims of triple damages for redress. In this case, Nawtee Company must determine the probability of the claims being asserted **and** the probability of triple damages being awarded. If both are probable, if the loss is reasonably estimable, and if the cause for action is dated on or before the date of the financial statements, then the liability should be accrued.[19]

[19]Contingencies involving an unasserted claim or assessment need not be disclosed when no claimant has come forward unless (1) it is considered probable that a claim will be asserted and (2) there is a reasonable possibility that the outcome will be unfavorable.

Guarantee and Warranty Costs

A **warranty (product guarantee)** is a promise made by a seller to a buyer to make good on a deficiency of quantity, quality, or performance in a product. It is commonly used by manufacturers as a sales promotion technique. Automakers, for instance, "hyped" their sales by extending their new-car warranty to 7 years or 100,000 miles. For a specified period of time following the date of sale to the consumer, the manufacturer may promise to bear all or part of the cost of replacing defective parts, to perform any necessary repairs or servicing without charge, to refund the purchase price, or even to "double your money back."

Warranties and guarantees entail future costs—frequently significant additional costs—which are sometimes called "after costs" or "post-sale costs." Although the future cost is indefinite as to amount, due date, and even customer, a liability is probable in most cases and should be recognized in the accounts if it can be reasonably estimated. The amount of the liability is an estimate of all the costs that will be incurred after sale and delivery and that are incident to the correction of defects or deficiencies required under the warranty provisions. Warranty costs are a classic example of a loss contingency.

There are two basic methods of accounting for warranty costs: (1) the cash basis method and (2) the accrual method.

Cash Basis

Under the **cash basis method**, warranty costs are charged to expense as they are incurred. In other words, **warranty costs are charged to the period in which the seller or manufacturer complies with the warranty**. No liability is recorded for future costs arising from warranties, nor is the period in which the sale is recorded necessarily charged with the costs of making good on outstanding warranties. Use of this method, the only one recognized for income tax purposes, is frequently justified for accounting on the basis of expediency when warranty costs are immaterial or when the warranty period is relatively short. The cash basis method is required when a warranty liability is not accrued in the year of sale either because

1. It is not probable that a liability has been incurred; or
2. The amount of the liability cannot be reasonably estimated.

Accrual Basis

If it is probable that customers will make claims under warranties relating to goods or services that have been sold and a reasonable estimate of the costs involved can be made, the accrual method must be used. Under the **accrual method**, warranty costs are charged to operating expense **in the year of sale**. It is the generally accepted method and should be used whenever the warranty is an integral and inseparable part of the sale and is viewed as a loss contingency. We refer to this approach as the **expense warranty approach**.

Illustration of Expense Warranty Approach. To illustrate the expense warranty method, assume that Denson Machinery Company begins production on a new machine in July 2004 and sells 100 units at $5,000 each by its year-end, December 31, 2004. Each machine is under warranty for one year. The company has estimated, from past experience with a similar machine, that the warranty cost will probably average $200 per unit. Further, as a result of parts replacements and services rendered in compliance with machinery warranties, the company incurs $4,000 in warranty costs in 2004 and $16,000 in 2005.

The journal entry to record the sale of 100 machines at $5,000 each, July through December 2004, would be:

Cash or Accounts Receivable	500,000	
Sales		500,000

The entry to recognize warranty expense, July through December 2004, would be:

Warranty Expense	4,000	
Cash, Inventory, Accrued Payroll		4,000
(Warranty costs incurred)		
Warranty Expense	16,000	
Estimated Liability under Warranties		16,000
(To accrue estimated warranty costs)		

The December 31, 2004, balance sheet would report "Estimated liability under warranties" as a current liability of $16,000. The income statement for 2004 would report "Warranty expense" of $20,000.

The entry to recognize warranty costs incurred in 2005 (on 2004 machinery sales) would be:

Estimated Liability under Warranties	16,000	
Cash, Inventory, or Accrued Payroll		16,000
(Warranty costs incurred)		

If the cash-basis method were applied to the facts in the Denson Machinery Company example, $4,000 would be recorded as warranty expense in 2004 and $16,000 as warranty expense in 2005, with all of the sale price being recorded as revenue in 2004.

In many instances, application of the cash-basis method does not match the warranty costs relating to the products sold during a given period with the revenues derived from such products, and therefore it violates the matching principle. Where ongoing warranty policies exist year after year, the differences between the cash and the expense warranty basis probably would not be so great.

Sales Warranty Approach. A warranty is sometimes **sold separately from the product**. For example, when you purchase a television set or VCR, you will be entitled to the manufacturer's warranty. You also will undoubtedly be offered an extended warranty on the product at an additional cost.[20]

In this case, the seller should recognize separately the sale of the television or VCR with the manufacturer's warranty and the sale of the extended warranty.[21] This approach is referred to as the **sales warranty approach**. **Revenue on the sale of the extended warranty is deferred** and is generally recognized on a straight-line basis over the life of the contract. Revenue is deferred because the seller of the warranty has an obligation to perform services over the life of the contract. Only costs that vary with and are directly related to the sale of the contracts (mainly commissions) should be deferred and amortized. Costs such as employees' salaries, advertising, and general and administrative expenses that would have been incurred even if no contract were sold should be expensed as incurred.

To illustrate, assume you have just purchased a new automobile from Hanlin Auto for $20,000. In addition to the regular warranty on the auto (all repairs will be paid by the manufacturer for the first 36,000 miles or 3 years, whichever comes first), you purchase at a cost of $600 an extended warranty that protects you for an additional 3 years or 36,000 miles. The entry to record the sale of the automobile (with the regular warranty) and the sale of the extended warranty on January 2, 2004, on Hanlin Auto's books is:

Cash	20,600	
Sales		20,000
Unearned Warranty Revenue		600

---

[20]A contract is separately priced **if the customer has the option to purchase** the services provided under the contract for an expressly stated amount separate from the price of the product. An extended warranty or product maintenance contract usually meets these conditions.

[21]"Accounting for Separately Extended Warranty and Product Maintenance Contracts," *FASB Technical Bulletin No. 90–1* (Stamford, Conn.: FASB, 1990).

The entry to recognize revenue at the end of the fourth year (using straight-line amortization) would be as follows.

Unearned Warranty Revenue	200	
Warranty Revenue		200

Because the extended warranty contract does not start until after the regular warranty expires, revenue is not recognized until the fourth year. If the costs of performing services under the extended warranty contract are incurred on other than a straight-line basis (as historical evidence might indicate), revenue should be recognized over the contract period in proportion to the costs expected to be incurred in performing services under the contract.[22]

Premiums and Coupons

Numerous companies offer (either on a limited or continuing basis) premiums to customers in return for boxtops, certificates, coupons, labels, or wrappers. The **premium** may be silverware, dishes, a small appliance, a toy, other goods, or free transportation. Also, **printed coupons** that can be redeemed for a cash discount on items purchased are extremely popular.[23] A more recent marketing innovation is the **cash rebate**, which the buyer can obtain by returning the store receipt, a rebate coupon, and Universal Product Code (UPC label) or "bar code" to the manufacturer.

UNDERLYING CONCEPTS

Warranties and coupons are loss contingencies that satisfy the conditions necessary for a liability. Regarding the income statement, the *matching principle* requires that the related expense be reported in the period in which the sale occurs.

These premiums, coupon offers, and rebates are made to stimulate sales, and their **costs should be charged to expense in the period of the sale** that benefits from the premium plan. At the end of the accounting period many of these premium offers may be outstanding and, when presented in subsequent periods, must be redeemed. The number of outstanding premium offers that will be presented for redemption must be estimated in order to reflect the existing current liability and to match costs with revenues. The cost of premium offers should be charged to Premium Expense. The outstanding obligations should be credited to an account titled Estimated Liability for Premiums.

The following example illustrates the accounting treatment accorded a premium offer. Fluffy Cakemix Company offered its customers a large nonbreakable mixing bowl in exchange for 25 cents and 10 boxtops. The mixing bowl costs Fluffy Cakemix Company 75 cents, and the company estimates that 60 percent of the boxtops will be redeemed. The premium offer began in June 2004 and resulted in the transactions journalized below.

The journal entry to record purchase of 20,000 mixing bowls at 75 cents each would be:

Inventory of Premium Mixing Bowls	15,000	
Cash		15,000

The entry to record sales of 300,000 boxes of cake mix at 80 cents would be:

Cash	240,000	
Sales		240,000

[22]Ibid, par. 3. The FASB recently issued additional disclosure requirements for warranties. A company is required to disclose its accounting policy and the method used to determine its warranty liability, and to present a tabular reconciliation of the changes in the product warranty liability. *FASB Interpretation No. 45,* "Guarantor's Accounting and Disclosure Requirements for Guarantees, Including Indirect Guarantees of Indebtedness of Others" (Norwalk, Conn.: FASB, 2002).

[23]Approximately 4 percent of coupons are redeemed. Redeemed coupons eventually make their way to the corporate headquarters of the stores that accept them. From there they are shipped in 50-pound boxes to Mexico's border towns (Juárez, Tijuana, Nuevo Laredo), where clearinghouses operated by **A. C. Nielsen Company** (of TV rating fame) count them and report back to the manufacturers who, in turn, reimburse the stores.

The entry to record the actual redemption of 60,000 boxtops, the receipt of 25 cents per 10 boxtops, and the delivery of the mixing bowls would be:

Cash [(60,000 ÷ 10) × $0.25]	1,500	
Premium Expense	3,000	
Inventory of Premium Mixing Bowls		4,500

Computation: (60,000 ÷ 10) × $0.75 = $4,500

The end-of-period adjusting entry for estimated liability for outstanding premium offers (boxtops) would be:

Premium Expense	6,000	
Estimated Liability for Premiums		6,000

Computation:

Total boxtops sold in 2004	300,000
Total estimated redemptions (60%)	180,000
Boxtops redeemed in 2004	60,000
Estimated future redemptions	120,000

Cost of estimated claims outstanding
(120,000 ÷ 10) × ($0.75 − $0.25) = $6,000

The December 31, 2004, balance sheet of Fluffy Cakemix Company will report an "Inventory of premium mixing bowls" of $10,500 as a current asset and "Estimated liability for premiums" of $6,000 as a current liability. The 2004 income statement will report a $9,000 "Premium expense" among the selling expenses.

FREQUENT BUYERS

WHAT DO THE NUMBERS MEAN?

Numerous companies offer premiums to customers in the form of a promise of future goods or services as an incentive for purchases today. Premium plans that have widespread adoption are the **frequent-flyer programs** used by all major airlines. On the basis of mileage accumulated, frequent-flyer members are awarded discounted or free airline tickets. Airline customers can earn miles toward free travel by making long-distance phone calls, staying in selected hotels, and charging gasoline and groceries on a credit card. Those free tickets represent an enormous potential liability because people using them may displace paying passengers.

When airlines first started offering frequent-flyer bonuses, they assumed that they could accommodate the free-ticket holders with otherwise-empty seats. That made the additional cost of the program so minimal that airlines didn't accrue it or report the small liability. But, as more and more paying passengers have been crowded off flights by frequent-flyer awardees, the loss of revenues has grown enormously. For example, United Airlines recently reported a liability of $1.4 billion for advance ticket sales, some of which pertains to free frequent-flyer tickets.

Although the accounting for this transaction has been studied by the profession, no authoritative guidelines have been issued.

Environmental Liabilities

Estimates to clean up existing toxic waste sites can run to upward of $752 billion over a 30-year period. In addition, the cost of cleaning up our air and preventing future deterioration of the environment is estimated to cost even more. The average environmental cost per firm in various industries at one time was: high-tech firms $2 million (6.1 percent of revenues); utilities $340 million (6.1 percent of revenues); steel and metals $50 million (2.9 percent of revenues), and oil companies $430 million (1.9 percent of revenues). Given that the average pretax profit of the 500 largest U.S. manufacturing companies recently was 7.7 percent of sales, these figures are staggering!

These costs will only grow when one considers "Superfund" legislation, which provides not only a government-supported fund to clean up pollution, but also a mandate to clean up existing waste sites. Further it provides the Environmental Protection Agency (EPA) with the power to clean up waste sites and charge the clean-up costs to parties the EPA deems responsible for contaminating the site. These potentially responsible parties have an onerous liability. The EPA estimates that it will likely cost an average of $25 million to clean up each polluted site. For the most troublesome sites, the cost could easily reach $100 million or more.

In addition, in many industries the construction and operation of long-lived assets involves obligations associated with the retirement of those assets. For example, when a mining company opens up a strip mine, it may also make a commitment to restore the land on which the mine is located once the mining activity is completed. Similarly, when an oil company erects an offshore drilling platform, it may be legally obligated to dismantle and remove the platform at the end of its useful life.

Accounting Recognition of Asset Retirement Obligations

A company must recognize an **asset retirement obligation (ARO)** when the company has an existing legal obligation associated with the retirement of a long-lived asset and when the amount of the liability can be reasonably estimated. The ARO should be recorded at fair value.[24]

Obligating Events. Examples of existing legal obligations, which would require recognition of a liability include, but are not limited to:

1. decommissioning nuclear facilities,
2. dismantling, restoring, and reclamation of oil and gas properties,
3. certain closure, reclamation, and removal costs of mining facilities, and
4. closure and post-closure costs of landfills.

In order to capture the benefits of these long-lived assets, **the company is generally legally obligated for the costs associated with retirement of the asset, whether the company hires another party to perform the retirement activities or performs the activities with its own workforce and equipment**. AROs give rise to various recognition patterns. For example, the obligation may arise at the outset of the asset's use (e.g., erection of an oil rig), or it may build over time (e.g., a landfill that expands over time).

Measurement. An ARO is initially measured at fair value, which is defined as the amount that the company would be required to pay in an active market to settle the ARO. Although active markets do not exist for many AROs, an estimate of fair value should be based on the best information available. Such information could include market prices of similar liabilities, if available. Alternatively, fair value can be estimated based on present value techniques.

Recognition and Allocation. To record an ARO in the financial statements, the cost associated with the ARO is included in the carrying amount of the related long-lived asset, and a liability is recorded for the same amount. An asset retirement cost is recorded as part of the related asset because these costs are considered a cost of operating the asset and are necessary to prepare the asset for its intended use. Therefore, the specific asset (e.g., mine, drilling platform, nuclear power plant) should be increased because the future economic benefit comes from the use of this productive asset. **The capitalized asset retirement costs should not be recorded in a separate account because there is no future economic benefit that can be associated with these costs alone.**

[24]"Accounting for Asset Retirement Obligations," *Statement of Financial Accounting Standards No. 143* (Norwalk, Conn.: FASB, 2001).

In subsequent periods, the cost of the ARO is allocated to expense over the period of the related asset's useful life. While the straight-line method is acceptable for this allocation, other systematic and rational allocations also are permitted.

Illustration of ARO Accounting Provisions. To illustrate the accounting for AROs, assume that on January 1, 2003, Wildcat Oil Company erected an oil platform in the Gulf of Mexico. Wildcat is legally required to dismantle and remove the platform at the end of its useful life, which is estimated to be 5 years. It is estimated that the total cost of dismantling and removal will be $1,000,000. Based on a 10 percent discount rate, the present value of the asset retirement obligation is $620,920 ($1,000,000 × .62092). Wildcat would make the following journal entry to record this ARO.

January 1, 2003

Drilling Platform	620,920	
Asset Retirement Obligation		620,920

During the life of the asset, the asset retirement cost is allocated to expense. Using the straight-line method, Wildcat would make the following entries to record this expense.

December 31, 2003, 2004, 2005, 2006, 2007

Depreciation Expense ($620,920 ÷ 5)	124,184	
Accumulated Depreciation		124,184

In addition, interest expense must be accrued each period. The entry at December 31, 2003, to record interest expense and the related increase in the asset retirement obligation is as follows.

December 31, 2003

Interest Expense ($620,920 × 10%)	62,092	
Asset Retirement Obligation		62,092

On January 10, 2008, Wildcat contracts with Rig Reclaimers, Inc. to dismantle the platform at a contract price of $995,000. Wildcat would make the following journal entry to record settlement of the ARO.

January 10, 2008

Asset Retirement Obligation	1,000,000	
Gain on Settlement of ARO		5,000
Cash		995,000

More extensive disclosure is needed regarding environmental liabilities. In addition, more of these liabilities should be recorded. The SEC believes that managements should not delay recognition of a liability due to significant uncertainty. The SEC argues that if the liability is within a range and no amount within the range is the best estimate, then management should recognize the minimum amount of the range. That treatment would be in accordance with *FASB Interpretation No. 14*, "Reasonable Estimation of the Amount of a Loss." The SEC also believes that environmental liabilities should be reported in the balance sheet independent of recoveries from third parties. Thus, possible insurance recoveries are not permitted to be netted against liabilities but must be shown separately. Because there is much litigation regarding recovery of insurance proceeds, these "assets" appear to be gain contingencies, and therefore companies will not be reporting these on the balance sheet.[25]

[25] As indicated earlier, the FASB pronouncements on this topic require that, when some amount within the range appears at the time to be a better estimate than any other amount within the range, that amount is accrued. When no amount within the range is a better estimate than any other amount, the dollar amount at the low end of the range is **accrued,** and the dollar amount at the high end of the range is **disclosed**. See *FASB Interpretation No. 14*, "Reasonable Estimation of the Amount of a Loss" (Stamford, Conn.: FASB, 1976), par. 3, and *FASB Statement No. 5*, "Accounting for Contingencies" (Stamford, Conn.: FASB, 1975).

UNDERLYING CONCEPTS

Even if the amount of losses is estimable with a high degree of certainty, the losses are not liabilities because they result from a future event and not from a past event.

Self-Insurance

A company may insure against many contingencies such as fire, flood, storm, and accident by taking out insurance policies and paying premiums to insurance companies. Some contingencies, however, are not insurable, or the insurance rates are prohibitive (e.g., earthquakes and riots). For such contingencies, even though insurance may be available, some businesses adopt a policy of self-insurance.

Despite its name, **self-insurance** is **not insurance, but risk assumption**. Any company that assumes its own risks puts itself in the position of incurring expenses or losses as they occur. There is little theoretical justification for the establishment of a liability based on a hypothetical charge to insurance expense. This is "as if" accounting. The conditions for accrual stated in *FASB Statement No. 5* are not satisfied prior to the occurrence of the event; until that time there is no diminution in the value of the property. And unlike an insurance company, which has contractual obligations to reimburse policyholders for losses, a company can have no such obligation to itself and, hence, no liability either before or after the occurrence of damage.[26]

The following note from the annual report of **Adolph Coors Company** is typical of the self-insurance disclosure.

ILLUSTRATION 13-12
Disclosure of Self-Insurance

Adolph Coors Company

Notes to Financial Statements

Note 4: Commitments and Contingencies. It is generally the policy of the Company to act as a self-insurer for certain insurable risks consisting primarily of physical loss to corporate property, business interruption resulting from such loss, employee health insurance programs, and workers' compensation. Losses and claims are accrued as incurred.

Exposure to **risks of loss resulting from uninsured past injury to others**, however, is an existing condition involving uncertainty about the amount and timing of losses that may develop. In such a case, a contingency exists. A company with a fleet of vehicles would have to accrue uninsured losses resulting from injury to others or damage to the property of others that took place prior to the date of the financial statements (if the experience of the company or other information enables it to make a reasonable estimate of the liability). However, it should not establish a liability for **expected future injury** to others or damage to the property of others, even if the amount of losses is reasonably estimable.

PRESENTATION AND ANALYSIS

OBJECTIVE 6
Indicate how current liabilities and contingencies are presented and analyzed.

Presentation of Current Liabilities

In practice, current liabilities are usually recorded and reported in financial statements at their full maturity value. Because of the short time periods involved, frequently less than one year, the difference between the present value of a current liability and the maturity value is not usually large. The slight overstatement of liabilities that results from carrying current liabilities at maturity value is accepted as immate-

[26]"Accounting for Contingencies," *FASB Statement No. 5*, op. cit., par. 28. A commentary in *Forbes* (June 15, 1974, p. 42) stated its position on this matter quite succinctly: "The simple and unquestionable fact of life is this: Business is cyclical and full of unexpected surprises. Is it the role of accounting to disguise this unpleasant fact and create a fairyland of smoothly rising earnings? Or, should accounting reflect reality, warts and all—floods, expropriations and all manner of rude shocks?"

rial. *APB Opinion No. 21*, "Interest on Receivables and Payables," specifically exempts from present value measurements those payables arising from transactions with suppliers in the normal course of business that do not exceed approximately one year.[27]

The current liabilities accounts are commonly presented as the first classification in the liabilities and stockholders' equity section of the balance sheet. Within the current liabilities section the accounts may be listed in order of maturity, in descending order of amount, or in order of liquidation preference. Illustration 13-13 presents an excerpt of **Best Buy Company**'s published financial statements. This presentation is representative of the reports of large corporations.

ILLUSTRATION 13-13
Balance Sheet Presentation of Current Liabilities

Best Buy Co.
(dollars in thousands)

	March 3, 2001	Feb. 26, 2000
Current assets		
Cash and cash equivalents	$ 746,879	$ 750,723
Receivables	209,031	189,301
Merchandise inventories	1,766,934	1,183,681
Other current assets	205,819	114,755
Total current assets	$2,928,663	$2,238,460
Current liabilities		
Accounts payable	$1,772,722	$1,313,940
Accrued compensation and related expenses	154,159	102,065
Accrued liabilities	545,590	287,888
Accrued income taxes	127,287	65,366
Current portion of long-term debt	114,940	15,790
Total current liabilities	$2,714,698	$1,785,049

Additional Disclosures of Current Liabilities

Detail and supplemental information concerning current liabilities should be sufficient to meet the requirement of full disclosure. Secured liabilities should be identified clearly, and the related assets pledged as collateral indicated. If the due date of any liability can be extended, the details should be disclosed. Current liabilities should not be offset against assets that are to be applied to their liquidation. Current maturities of long-term debt should be classified as current liabilities.

A major exception exists when a currently maturing obligation is to be paid from assets classified as long-term. For example, if payments to retire a bond payable are made from a bond sinking fund classified as a long-term asset, the bonds payable should be reported in the long-term liabilities section. Presentation of this debt in the current liabilities section would distort the working capital position of the enterprise.

If a short-term obligation is excluded from current liabilities because of refinancing, the note to the financial statements should include:

1. A general description of the financing agreement.
2. The terms of any new obligation incurred or to be incurred.
3. The terms of any equity security issued or to be issued.

When refinancing on a long-term basis is expected to be accomplished through the issuance of equity securities, it is not appropriate to include the short-term obligation in stockholders' equity. At the date of the balance sheet, the obligation is a liability and not stockholders' equity. The disclosure requirements are shown in Illustration 13-14 for an actual refinancing situation.

[27]"Interest on Receivables and Payables," *Opinions of the Accounting Principles Board No. 21* (New York: AICPA, 1971), par. 3.

ILLUSTRATION 13-14
Actual Refinancing of Short-Term Debt

	December 31, 2003
Current liabilities	
Accounts payable	$ 3,600,000
Accrued payables	2,500,000
Income taxes payable	1,100,000
Current portion of long-term debt	1,000,000
Total current liabilities	$ 8,200,000
Long-term debt	
Notes payable refinanced in January 2004 (Note 1)	$ 2,000,000
11% bonds due serially through 2014	15,000,000
Total long-term debt	$17,000,000

Note 1: On January 19, 2004, the Company issued 50,000 shares of common stock and received proceeds totaling $2,385,000, of which $2,000,000 was used to liquidate notes payable that matured on February 1, 2004. Accordingly, such notes payable have been classified as long-term debt at December 31, 2003.

Presentation of Contingencies

Additional Disclosures of Contingencies

A loss contingency and a liability is recorded if the loss is both probable and estimable. But, if the loss is **either probable or estimable but not both**, and if there is at least a **reasonable possibility** that a liability may have been incurred, the following disclosure in the notes is required:

1. The nature of the contingency.
2. An estimate of the possible loss or range of loss or a statement that an estimate cannot be made.

Presented in Illustration 13-15 is an extensive litigation disclosure note from the financial statements of **Raymark Corporation**. It shows that although actual losses have been charged to operations and further liability possibly exists, no estimate of this liability is possible.

ILLUSTRATION 13-15
Disclosure of Loss Contingency through Litigation

Raymark Corporation

Note I: Litigation. Raymark is a defendant or co-defendant in a substantial number of lawsuits alleging wrongful injury and/or death from exposure to asbestos fibers in the air. The following table summarizes the activity in these lawsuits:

Claims	
Pending at beginning of year	8,719
Received during year	4,494
Settled or otherwise disposed of	(1,445)
Pending at end of year	11,768
Average indemnification cost	$3,364
Average cost per case, including defense costs	$6,499
Trial activity	
Verdicts for the Company	23
Total trials	36

The following table presents the cost of defending asbestos litigation, together with related insurance and workers' compensation expenses.

Included in operating profit	$ 1,872,000
Nonoperating expense	9,077,000
Total	$10,949,000

The Company is seeking to reasonably determine its liability. However, it is not possible to predict which theory of insurance will apply, the number of lawsuits still to be filed, the cost of settling and defending the existing and unfiled cases, or the ultimate impact of these lawsuits on the Company's consolidated financial statements.

INTERNATIONAL INSIGHT

U.S. GAAP provides more guidance on the content of disclosures about contingencies than do IASB standards.

Certain other contingent liabilities that should be disclosed even though the possibility of loss may be remote are the following.

1. Guarantees of indebtedness of others.
2. Obligations of commercial banks under "stand-by letters of credit."
3. Guarantees to repurchase receivables (or any related property) that have been sold or assigned.

Disclosure should include the nature and amount of the guarantee and, if estimable, the amount that could be recovered from outside parties.[28] **Cities Service Company** disclosed its guarantees of indebtedness of others in the following note.

ILLUSTRATION 13-16
Disclosure of Guarantees of Indebtedness

Cities Service Company

Note 10: Contingent Liabilities. The Company and certain subsidiaries have guaranteed debt obligations of approximately $62 million of companies in which substantial stock investments are held. Also, under long-term agreements with certain pipeline companies in which stock interests are held, the Company and its subsidiaries have agreed to provide minimum revenue for product shipments. The Company has guaranteed mortgage debt ($80 million) incurred by a 50 percent owned tanker affiliate for construction of tankers which are under long-term charter contracts to the Company and others. It is not anticipated that any loss will result from any of the above described agreements.

Analysis of Current Liabilities

The distinction between current liabilities and long-term debt is important because it provides information about the liquidity of the company. Liquidity regarding a liability is the time that is expected to elapse until a liability has to be paid. In other words, a liability soon to be paid is a current liability. A liquid company is better able to withstand a financial downturn. Also, it has a better chance of taking advantage of investment opportunities that develop.

Certain basic ratios such as net cash flow provided by operating activities to current liabilities and the turnover ratios for receivables and inventory are used to assess liquidity. Two other ratios used to examine liquidity are the current ratio and the acid-test ratio.

The **current ratio** is the ratio of total current assets to total current liabilities. The formula is shown below.

ILLUSTRATION 13-17
Formula for Current Ratio

$$\text{Current ratio} = \frac{\text{Current assets}}{\text{Current liabilities}}$$

It is frequently expressed as a coverage of so many times. Sometimes it is called the working capital ratio because working capital is the excess of current assets over current liabilities.

A satisfactory current ratio does not disclose that a portion of the current assets may be tied up in slow-moving inventories. With inventories, especially raw materials and work in process, there is a question of how long it will take to transform them into

[28]As discussed earlier (footnote 22), the FASB recently issued additional disclosure and recognition requirements for guarantees. The interpretation responds to confusion about the application of *SFAS No. 5* to guarantees used in certain transactions. The new rules expand existing disclosure requirements for most guarantees, including loan guarantees such as standby letters of credit. It also will result in companies recognizing more liabilities at fair value for the obligations assumed under a guarantee (*FASB Interpretation No. 45,* op. cit.).

the finished product and what ultimately will be realized in the sale of the merchandise. Elimination of the amount of the inventories, along with the amount of any prepaid expenses from the current assets, might provide better information for the short-term creditors. Many analysts favor an **acid-test** or **quick ratio** that relates total current liabilities to cash, marketable securities, and receivables. The formula for this ratio is shown in Illustration 13-18.

ILLUSTRATION 13-18
Formula for Acid-test Ratio

$$\text{Acid-test ratio} = \frac{\text{Cash} + \text{Marketable securities} + \text{Net receivables}}{\text{Current liabilities}}$$

To illustrate the computation of these two ratios, we use the information for **Best Buy Co.**, reported in Illustration 13-13 on page 641. The computation of the current and acid-test ratios for Best Buy are shown in Illustration 13-19.

ILLUSTRATION 13-19
Computation of Current and Acid-Test Ratios for Best Buy Co.

$$\text{Current ratio} = \frac{\text{Current assets}}{\text{Current liabilities}} = \frac{\$2,929}{\$2,715} = 1.08 \text{ times}$$

$$\text{Acid-test ratio} = \frac{\text{Cash} + \text{Marketable securities} + \text{Net receivables}}{\text{Current liabilities}} = \frac{\$956}{\$2,715} = 0.35 \text{ times}$$

From this information, it appears that Best Buy's current position is adequate. The acid-test ratio is well below 1, and a comparison to another retailer, **Circuit City**, whose acid-test ratio is 0.80, indicates that Best Buy may be carrying more inventory than its industry counterparts.

SUMMARY OF LEARNING OBJECTIVES

KEY TERMS

accumulated rights, *628*
acid-test (quick) ratio, *644*
assessments, *633*
asset retirement obligation, *638*
bonus, *629*
cash dividend payable, *622*
claims, *633*
compensated absences, *627*
contingency, *630*
contingent liabilities, *631*
current liabilities, *618*
current maturities of long-term debt, *620*
current ratio, *643*
expense warranty approach, *634*

1 Describe the nature, type, and valuation of current liabilities. Current liabilities are obligations whose liquidation is reasonably expected to require the use of current assets or the creation of other current liabilities. Theoretically, liabilities should be measured by the present value of the future outlay of cash required to liquidate them. In practice, current liabilities are usually recorded in accounting records and reported in financial statements at their full maturity value. There are several types of liabilities: (1) accounts payable, (2) notes payable, (3) current maturities of long-term debt, (4) dividends payable, (5) returnable deposits, (6) unearned revenues, (7) taxes payable, and (8) employee-related liabilities.

2 Explain the classification issues of short-term debt expected to be refinanced. An enterprise is required to exclude a short-term obligation from current liabilities if both of the following conditions are met: (1) It must intend to refinance the obligation on a long-term basis, *and* (2) it must demonstrate an ability to consummate the refinancing.

3 Identify types of employee-related liabilities. The employee-related liabilities are: (1) payroll deductions, (2) compensated absences, and (3) bonus agreements.

4 Identify the criteria used to account for and disclose gain and loss contingencies. Gain contingencies are not recorded. They are disclosed in the notes only when the probabilities are high that a gain contingency will become a reality. An estimated loss from a loss contingency should be accrued by a charge to expense and a liability recorded only if both of the following conditions are met: (1) Information available prior to the issuance of the financial statements indicates that it is probable that a liability has been incurred at the date of the financial statements, *and* (2) the amount of the loss can be reasonably estimated.

5 Explain the accounting for different types of loss contingencies. The following factors must be considered in determining whether a liability should be recorded with respect to pending or threatened litigation and actual or possible claims and assessments: (1) the time period in which the underlying cause for action occurred; (2) the probability of an unfavorable outcome; and (3) the ability to make a reasonable estimate of the amount of loss.

If it is probable that customers will make claims under warranties relating to goods or services that have been sold and a reasonable estimate of the costs involved can be made, the accrual method must be used. Warranty costs under the accrual basis are charged to operating expense in the year of sale.

Premiums, coupon offers, and rebates are made to stimulate sales, and their costs should be charged to expense in the period of the sale that benefits from the premium plan.

Asset retirement obligations must be recognized when a company has an existing legal obligation related to the retirement of a long-lived asset and the amount can be reasonably estimated.

6 Indicate how current liabilities and contingencies are presented and analyzed. The current liabilities accounts are commonly presented as the first classification in the liabilities and stockholders' equity section of the balance sheet. Within the current liabilities section the accounts may be listed in order of maturity, in descending order of amount, or in order of liquidation preference. Detail and supplemental information concerning current liabilities should be sufficient to meet the requirement of full disclosure. If the loss is either probable or estimable but not both, and if there is at least a reasonable possibility that a liability may have been incurred, disclosure should be made in the notes of the nature of the contingency and an estimate given of the possible loss. Two ratios used to analyze liquidity are the current and acid-test ratios.

gain contingencies, *630*
liabilities, *617*
litigation, claims, and assessments, *633*
loss contingencies, *631*
notes payable (trade notes payable), *619*
operating cycle, *618*
preferred dividends in arrears, *622*
premiums, *636*
probable (contingency), *631*
reasonably possible (contingency), *631*
remote (contingency), *631*
returnable cash deposits, *623*
sales warranty approach, *635*
self-insurance, *640*
short-term obligations expected to be refinanced, *621*
Social Security tax, *626*
trade accounts payable, *618*
trade notes payable, *619*
unearned revenues, *623*
vested rights, *628*
warranty, *634*

APPENDIX 13A

Computation of Employees' Bonuses

OBJECTIVE 7
Compute employee bonuses under differing arrangements.

Because the amount of a bonus is an expense of the business, the problem of computing the amount of bonus based on income becomes more difficult. Say a company has income of $100,000 determined before considering the bonus expense. According to the terms of the bonus agreement, 20 percent of the income is to be set aside for distribution among the employees. If the bonus were not itself an expense to be deducted in determining net income, the amount of the bonus could be computed very simply as 20 percent of the income before bonus of $100,000. However, the bonus itself is an expense that must be deducted in arriving at the amount of income on which the bonus is to be based. Hence, \$100,000 reduced by the bonus is the figure on which the bonus is to be computed. That is, the bonus is equal to 20 percent of \$100,000 less the bonus. Stated algebraically:

$$\begin{aligned} B &= 0.20\ (\$100{,}000 - B) \\ B &= \$20{,}000 - 0.2B \\ 1.2B &= \$20{,}000 \\ B &= \$16{,}666.67 \end{aligned}$$

A similar problem results from the relationship of bonus payments to federal income taxes. Assume income of \$100,000 computed without subtracting either the employees' bonus or taxes on income. The bonus is to be based on income **after deducting income taxes but before deducting the bonus**. The rate of income tax is 40 percent, and the bonus of 20 percent is a deductible expense for tax purposes. The bonus is, therefore, equal to 20 percent of \$100,000 minus the tax, and the tax is equal to 40 percent of \$100,000 minus the bonus. Thus we have two simultaneous equations. By using B as the symbol for the bonus and T for the tax, they may be stated algebraically as follows.

$$\begin{aligned} B &= 0.20\ (\$100{,}000 - T) \\ T &= 0.40\ (\$100{,}000 - B) \end{aligned}$$

These may be solved by substituting the value of T as indicated in the second equation for T in the first equation.

$$\begin{aligned} B &= 0.20\ [\$100{,}000 - 0.40\ (\$100{,}000 - B)] \\ B &= 0.20\ (\$100{,}000 - \$40{,}000 + 0.4B) \\ B &= 0.20\ (\$60{,}000 + 0.4B) \\ B &= \$12{,}000 + 0.08B \\ 0.92B &= \$12{,}000 \\ B &= \$13{,}043.48 \end{aligned}$$

Substituting this value for B into the second equation allows us to solve for T:

$$\begin{aligned} T &= 0.40\ (\$100{,}000 - \$13{,}043.48) \\ T &= 0.40\ (\$86{,}956.52) \\ T &= \$34{,}782.61 \end{aligned}$$

To prove these amounts, both should be worked back into the original equation.

$$\begin{aligned} B &= 0.20\ (\$100{,}000 - T) \\ \$13{,}043.48 &= 0.20\ (\$100{,}000 - \$34{,}782.61) \\ \$13{,}043.48 &= 0.20\ (\$65{,}217.39) \\ \$13{,}043.48 &= \$13{,}043.48 \end{aligned}$$

If the terms of the agreement provide for deducting both the tax and the bonus to arrive at the income figure on which the bonus is computed, the equations would be:

$$\begin{aligned} B &= 0.20\ (\$100{,}000 - B - T) \\ T &= 0.40\ (\$100{,}000 - B) \end{aligned}$$

Substituting the value of T from the second equation into the first equation enables us to solve for B:

$$
\begin{aligned}
B &= 0.20\ [\$100{,}000 - B - 0.40\ (\$100{,}000 - B)] \\
B &= 0.20\ (\$100{,}000 - B - \$40{,}000 + 0.4B) \\
B &= 0.20\ (\$60{,}000 - 0.6B) \\
B &= \$12{,}000 - 0.12B \\
1.12B &= \$12{,}000 \\
B &= \$10{,}714.29
\end{aligned}
$$

The value for B may then be substituted in the second equation above, and that equation solved for T:

$$
\begin{aligned}
T &= 0.40\ (\$100{,}000 - \$10{,}714.29) \\
T &= 0.40\ (\$89{,}285.71) \\
T &= \$35{,}714.28
\end{aligned}
$$

If these values are then substituted in the original bonus equation, they prove themselves as follows.

$$
\begin{aligned}
B &= 0.20\ (\$100{,}000 - B - T) \\
\$10{,}714.29 &= 0.20\ (\$100{,}000 - \$10{,}714.29 - \$35{,}714.28) \\
\$10{,}714.29 &= 0.20\ (\$53{,}571.43) \\
\$10{,}714.29 &= \$10{,}714.29
\end{aligned}
$$

Drawing up a legal document such as a bonus agreement is a task for a lawyer, not an accountant, although accountants are frequently called on to express an opinion on the agreement's feasibility. In this respect, one should always insist that the agreement state specifically whether income taxes and the bonus itself are expenses deductible in determining income for purposes of the bonus computation.

SUMMARY OF LEARNING OBJECTIVE FOR APPENDIX 13A

7 **Compute employee bonuses under differing arrangements.** Because the bonus is based on net income and is deductible in determining net income, the bonus may have to be determined algebraically. Its computation is made more difficult by the bonus being deductible for tax purposes and the taxes being deductible from the income on which the bonus is based.

Note: All **asterisked** Brief Exercises, Exercises, and Problems relate to material contained in the appendix to the chapter.

QUESTIONS

1. Distinguish between a current liability and a long-term debt.

2. Assume that your friend Greg Jonas, who is a music major, asks you to define and discuss the nature of a liability. Assist him by preparing a definition of a liability and by explaining to him what you believe are the elements or factors inherent in the concept of a liability.

3. Why is the liabilities section of the balance sheet of primary significance to bankers?

4. How are current liabilities related by definition to current assets? How are current liabilities related to a company's operating cycle?

5. Jon Bryant, a newly hired loan analyst, is examining the current liabilities of a corporate loan applicant. He ob-

serves that unearned revenues have declined in the current year compared to the prior year. Is this a positive indicator about the client's liquidity? Explain.

6. How is present value related to the concept of a liability?

7. What is the nature of a "discount" on notes payable?

8. How should a debt callable by the creditor be reported in the debtor's financial statements?

9. Under what conditions should a short-term obligation be excluded from current liabilities?

10. What evidence is necessary to demonstrate the ability to consummate the refinancing of short-term debt?

11. Discuss the accounting treatment or disclosure that should be accorded a declared but unpaid cash dividend; an accumulated but undeclared dividend on cumulative preferred stock; a stock dividend distributable.

12. How does deferred or unearned revenue arise? Why can it be classified properly as a current liability? Give several examples of business activities that result in unearned revenues.

13. What are compensated absences?

14. Under what conditions must an employer accrue a liability for the cost of compensated absences?

15. Under what conditions is an employer required to accrue a liability for sick pay? Under what conditions is an employer permitted but not required to accrue a liability for sick pay?

16. Caitlin Carter operates a health food store, and she has been the only employee. Her business is growing, and she is considering hiring some additional staff to help her in the store. Explain to her the various payroll deductions that she will have to account for, including their potential impact on her financial statements, if she hires additional staff.

17. Define (a) a contingency and (b) a contingent liability.

18. Under what conditions should a contingent liability be recorded?

19. Distinguish between a current liability and a contingent liability. Give two examples of each type.

20. How are the terms "probable," "reasonably possible," and "remote" related to contingent liabilities?

21. Contrast the cash basis method and the accrual method of accounting for warranty costs.

22. Kren Company has had a record-breaking year in terms of growth in sales and profitability. However, market research indicates that it will experience operating losses in two of its major businesses next year. The controller has proposed that the company record a provision for these future losses this year, since it can afford to take the charge and still show good results. Advise the controller on the appropriateness of this charge.

23. How does the expense warranty approach differ from the sales warranty approach?

24. Zucker-Abrahams Airlines Inc. awards members of its Flightline program a second ticket at half price, valid for 2 years anywhere on its flight system, when a full-price ticket is purchased. How would you account for the full-fare and half-fare tickets?

25. Northeast Airlines Co. awards members of its Frequent Fliers Club one free round-trip ticket, anywhere on its flight system, for every 50,000 miles flown on its planes. How would you account for the free ticket award?

26. When must a company recognize an asset retirement obligation?

27. Should a liability be recorded for risk of loss due to lack of insurance coverage? Discuss.

28. What factors must be considered in determining whether or not to record a liability for pending litigation? For threatened litigation?

29. Within the current liabilities section, how do you believe the accounts should be listed? Defend your position.

30. How does the acid-test ratio differ from the current ratio? How are they similar?

31. When should liabilities for each of the following items be recorded on the books of an ordinary business corporation?

(a) Acquisition of goods by purchase on credit.

(b) Officers' salaries.

(c) Special bonus to employees.

(d) Dividends.

(e) Purchase commitments.

BRIEF EXERCISES

BE13-1 Congo Corporation uses a periodic inventory system and the gross method of accounting for purchase discounts. On July 1, Congo purchased $40,000 of inventory, terms 2/10, n/30, FOB shipping point. Congo paid freight costs of $1,200. On July 3, Congo returned damaged goods and received credit of $6,000. On July 10, Congo paid for the goods. Prepare all necessary journal entries for Congo.

BE13-2 Desert Storm Company borrowed $50,000 on November 1, 2004, by signing a $50,000, 9%, 3-month note. Prepare Desert Storm's November 1, 2004, entry; the December 31, 2004, annual adjusting entry; and the February 1, 2005, entry.

BE13-3 Kawasaki Corporation borrowed $50,000 on November 1, 2004, by signing a $51,125, 3-month, zero-interest-bearing note. Prepare Kawasaki's November 1, 2004, entry; the December 31, 2004, annual adjusting entry; and the February 1, 2005, entry.

BE13-4 At December 31, 2004, Fifa Corporation owes $500,000 on a note payable due February 15, 2005. (a) If Fifa refinances the obligation by issuing a long-term note on February 14 and using the proceeds to pay off the note due February 15, how much of the $500,000 should be reported as a current liability at December 31, 2004? (b) If Fifa pays off the note on February 15, 2005, and then borrows $1,000,000 on a long-term basis on March 1, how much of the $500,000 should be reported as a current liability at December 31, 2004?

BE13-5 Game Pro Magazine sold 10,000 annual subscriptions on August 1, 2004, for $18 each. Prepare Game Pro's August 1, 2004, journal entry and the December 31, 2004, annual adjusting entry.

BE13-6 Flintstones Corporation made credit sales of $30,000 which are subject to 6% sales tax. The corporation also made cash sales which totaled $19,610 including the 6% sales tax. (a) Prepare the entry to record Flintstones' credit sales. (b) Prepare the entry to record Flintstones' cash sales.

BE13-7 Future Zone Corporation's weekly payroll of $23,000 included FICA taxes withheld of $1,426, federal taxes withheld of $2,990, state taxes withheld of $920, and insurance premiums withheld of $250. Prepare the journal entry to record Future Zone's payroll.

BE13-8 Tale Spin Inc. provides paid vacations to its employees. At December 31, 2004, 30 employees have each earned 2 weeks of vacation time. The employees' average salary is $600 per week. Prepare Tale Spin's December 31, 2004, adjusting entry.

BE13-9 Gargoyle Corporation provides its officers with bonuses based on income. For 2004, the bonuses total $450,000 and are paid on February 15, 2005. Prepare Gargoyle's December 31, 2004, adjusting entry and the February 15, 2005, entry.

BE13-10 Justice League Inc. is involved in a lawsuit at December 31, 2004. (a) Prepare the December 31 entry assuming it is probable that Justice League will be liable for $700,000 as a result of this suit. (b) Prepare the December 31 entry, if any, assuming it is *not* probable that Justice League will be liable for any payment as a result of this suit.

BE13-11 Kohlbeck Company recently was sued by a competitor for patent infringement. Attorneys have determined that it is probable that Kohlbeck will lose the case and that a reasonable estimate of damages to be paid by Kohlbeck is $200,000. In light of this case, Kohlbeck is considering establishing a $100,000 self-insurance allowance. What entry(ies), if any, should Kohlbeck record to recognize this loss contingency?

BE13-12 Darby's Drillers erects and places into service an off-shore oil platform on January 1, 2005, at a cost of $10,000,000. Darby is legally required to dismantle and remove the platform at the end of its useful life in 10 years. The estimated present value of the dismantling and removal costs at January 1, 2005, is $500,000. Prepare the entry to record the asset retirement obligation.

BE13-13 Frantic Factory provides a 2-year warranty with one of its products which was first sold in 2004. In that year, Frantic spent $70,000 servicing warranty claims. At year-end, Frantic estimates that an additional $500,000 will be spent in the future to service warranty claims related to 2004 sales. Prepare Frantic's journal entry to record the $70,000 expenditure, and the December 31 adjusting entry.

BE13-14 Herzog Zwei Corporation sells VCRs. The corporation also offers its customers a 2-year warranty contract. During 2004, Herzog Zwei sold 15,000 warranty contracts at $99 each. The corporation spent $180,000 servicing warranties during 2004, and it estimates that an additional $900,000 will be spent in the future to service the warranties. Prepare Herzog Zwei's journal entries for (a) the sale of contracts, (b) the cost of servicing the warranties, and (c) the recognition of warranty revenue.

BE13-15 Klax Company offers a set of building blocks to customers who send in 3 UPC codes from Klax cereal, along with 50¢. The blocks sets cost Klax $1.10 each to purchase and 60¢ each to mail to customers. During 2004, Klax sold 1,000,000 boxes of cereal. The company expects 30% of the UPC codes to be sent in. During 2004, 120,000 UPC codes were redeemed. Prepare Klax's December 31, 2004, adjusting entry.

***BE13-16** Locke Company provides its president, Cyan Garamonde, with a bonus equal to 10% of income after deducting income tax and bonus. Income *before* deducting income tax and bonus is $265,000, and the tax rate is 40%. Compute the amount of Cyan Garamonde's bonus.

EXERCISES

E13-1 (Balance Sheet Classification of Various Liabilities) How would each of the following items be reported on the balance sheet?

(a) Accrued vacation pay.
(b) Estimated taxes payable.
(c) Service warranties on appliance sales.
(d) Bank overdraft.
(e) Employee payroll deductions unremitted.
(f) Unpaid bonus to officers.
(g) Deposit received from customer to guarantee performance of a contract.
(h) Sales taxes payable.
(i) Gift certificates sold to customers but not yet redeemed.
(j) Premium offers outstanding.
(k) Discount on notes payable.
(l) Personal injury claim pending.
(m) Current maturities of long-term debts to be paid from current assets.
(n) Cash dividends declared but unpaid.
(o) Dividends in arrears on preferred stock.
(p) Loans from officers.

E13-2 (Accounts and Notes Payable) The following are selected 2004 transactions of Sean Astin Corporation.

Sept. 1 Purchased inventory from Encino Company on account for $50,000. Astin records purchases gross and uses a periodic inventory system.
Oct. 1 Issued a $50,000, 12-month, 12% note to Encino in payment of account.
Oct. 1 Borrowed $50,000 from the Shore Bank by signing a 12-month, noninterest-bearing $56,000 note.

Instructions

(a) Prepare journal entries for the selected transactions above.
(b) Prepare adjusting entries at December 31.
(c) Compute the total net liability to be reported on the December 31 balance sheet for:
  (1) the interest-bearing note.
  (2) the non-interest-bearing note.

E13-3 (Refinancing of Short-Term Debt) On December 31, 2004, Hattie McDaniel Company had $1,200,000 of short-term debt in the form of notes payable due February 2, 2005. On January 21, 2005, the company issued 25,000 shares of its common stock for $38 per share, receiving $950,000 proceeds after brokerage fees and other costs of issuance. On February 2, 2005, the proceeds from the stock sale, supplemented by an additional $250,000 cash, are used to liquidate the $1,200,000 debt. The December 31, 2004, balance sheet is issued on February 23, 2005.

Instructions

Show how the $1,200,000 of short-term debt should be presented on the December 31, 2004, balance sheet, including note disclosure.

E13-4 (Refinancing of Short-Term Debt) On December 31, 2004, Chris Atkins Company has $7,000,000 of short-term debt in the form of notes payable to Blue Lagoon State Bank due periodically in 2005. On January 28, 2005, Atkins enters into a refinancing agreement with Blue Lagoon that will permit it to borrow up to 60% of the gross amount of its accounts receivable. Receivables are expected to range between a low of $6,000,000 in May to a high of $8,000,000 in October during the year 2005. The interest cost of the maturing short-term debt is 15%, and the new agreement calls for a fluctuating interest at 1% above the prime rate on notes due in 2009. Atkin's December 31, 2004, balance sheet is issued on February 15, 2005.

Instructions

Prepare a partial balance sheet for Atkins at December 31, 2004, showing how its $7,000,000 of short-term debt should be presented, including footnote disclosure.

E13-5 (Compensated Absences) Zero Mostel Company began operations on January 2, 2003. It employs 9 individuals who work 8-hour days and are paid hourly. Each employee earns 10 paid vacation days and 6 paid sick days annually. Vacation days may be taken after January 15 of the year following the year in which they are earned. Sick days may be taken as soon as they are earned; unused sick days accumulate. Additional information is as follows.

Actual Hourly Wage Rate		Vacation Days Used by Each Employee		Sick Days Used by Each Employee	
2003	2004	2003	2004	2003	2004
$10	$11	0	9	4	5

Zero Mostel Company has chosen to accrue the cost of compensated absences at rates of pay in effect during the period when earned and to accrue sick pay when earned.

Instructions

(a) Prepare journal entries to record transactions related to compensated absences during 2003 and 2004.

(b) Compute the amounts of any liability for compensated absences that should be reported on the balance sheet at December 31, 2003 and 2004.

E13-6 (Compensated Absences) Assume the facts in the preceding exercise, except that Zero Mostel Company has chosen not to accrue paid sick leave until used, and has chosen to accrue vacation time at expected future rates of pay without discounting. The company used the following projected rates to accrue vacation time.

Year in Which Vacation Time Was Earned	Projected Future Pay Rates Used to Accrue Vacation Pay
2003	$10.75
2004	11.60

Instructions

(a) Prepare journal entries to record transactions related to compensated absences during 2003 and 2004.

(b) Compute the amounts of any liability for compensated absences that should be reported on the balance sheet at December 31, 2003, and 2004.

E13-7 (Adjusting Entry for Sales Tax) During the month of June, R. Attenborough Boutique had cash sales of $233,200 and credit sales of $153,700, both of which include the 6% sales tax that must be remitted to the state by July 15.

Instructions

Prepare the adjusting entry that should be recorded to fairly present the June 30 financial statements.

E13-8 (Payroll Tax Entries) The payroll of Rene Auber Company for September 2003 is as follows.

Total payroll was $480,000, of which $110,000 is exempt from Social Security tax because it represented amounts paid in excess of $84,900 to certain employees. The amount paid to employees in excess of $7,000 was $400,000. Income taxes in the amount of $90,000 were withheld, as was $9,000 in union dues. The state unemployment tax is 3.5%, but Auber Company is allowed a credit of 2.3% by the state for its unemployment experience. Also, assume that the current F.I.C.A. tax is 7.65% on an employee's wages to $84,900 and 1.45% in excess of $84,900. No employee for Auber makes more than $125,000. The federal unemployment tax rate is 0.8% after state credit.

Instructions

Prepare the necessary journal entries if the wages and salaries paid and the employer payroll taxes are recorded separately.

E13-9 (Payroll Tax Entries) Green Day Hardware Company's payroll for November 2004 is summarized below.

		Amount Subject to Payroll Taxes		
			Unemployment Tax	
Payroll	Wages Due	F.I.C.A.	Federal	State
Factory	$120,000	$120,000	$40,000	$40,000
Sales	32,000	32,000	4,000	4,000
Administrative	36,000	36,000	—	—
Total	$188,000	$188,000	$44,000	$44,000

At this point in the year some employees have already received wages in excess of those to which payroll taxes apply. Assume that the state unemployment tax is 2.5%. The F.I.C.A. rate is 7.65% on an employee's wages to $84,900 and 1.45% in excess of $84,900. Of the $188,000 wages subject to F.I.C.A. tax, $20,000 of the sales wages is in excess of $84,900. Federal unemployment tax rate is 0.8% after credits. Income tax withheld amounts to $16,000 for factory, $7,000 for sales, and $6,000 for administrative.

Instructions

(a) Prepare a schedule showing the employer's total cost of wages for November by function. (Round all computations to nearest dollar.)

(b) Prepare the journal entries to record the factory, sales, and administrative payrolls including the employer's payroll taxes.

E13-10 (Warranties) Soundgarden Company sold 200 copymaking machines in 2004 for $4,000 apiece, together with a one-year warranty. Maintenance on each machine during the warranty period averages $330.

Instructions

(a) Prepare entries to record the sale of the machines and the related warranty costs, assuming that the accrual method is used. Actual warranty costs incurred in 2004 were $17,000.

(b) On the basis of the data above, prepare the appropriate entries, assuming that the cash basis method is used.

E13-11 (Warranties) Sheryl Crow Equipment Company sold 500 Rollomatics during 2004 at $6,000 each. During 2004, Crow spent $20,000 servicing the 2-year warranties that accompany the Rollomatic. All applicable transactions are on a cash basis.

Instructions

(a) Prepare 2004 entries for Crow using the expense warranty approach. Assume that Crow estimates the total cost of servicing the warranties will be $120,000 for 2 years.

(b) Prepare 2004 entries for Crow assuming that the warranties are not an integral part of the sale. Assume that of the sales total, $150,000 relates to sales of warranty contracts. Crow estimates the total cost of servicing the warranties will be $120,000 for 2 years. Estimate revenues earned on the basis of costs incurred and estimated costs.

E13-12 (Premium Entries) Yanni Company includes 1 coupon in each box of soap powder that it packs, and 10 coupons are redeemable for a premium (a kitchen utensil). In 2004, Yanni Company purchased 8,800 premiums at 80 cents each and sold 110,000 boxes of soap powder at $3.30 per box; 44,000 coupons were presented for redemption in 2004. It is estimated that 60% of the coupons will eventually be presented for redemption.

Instructions

Prepare all the entries that would be made relative to sales of soap powder and to the premium plan in 2004.

E13-13 (Contingencies) Presented below are three independent situations. Answer the question at the end of each situation.

1. During 2004, Salt-n-Pepa Inc. became involved in a tax dispute with the IRS. Salt-n-Pepa's attorneys have indicated that they believe it is probable that Salt-n-Pepa will lose this dispute. They also believe that Salt-n-Pepa will have to pay the IRS between $900,000 and $1,400,000. After the 2004 financial statements were issued, the case was settled with the IRS for $1,200,000. What amount, if any, should be reported as a liability for this contingency as of December 31, 2004?
2. On October 1, 2004, Alan Jackson Chemical was identified as a potentially responsible party by the Environmental Protection Agency. Jackson's management along with its counsel have concluded that it is probable that Jackson will be responsible for damages, and a reasonable estimate of these damages is $5,000,000. Jackson's insurance policy of $9,000,000 has a deductible clause of $500,000. How should Alan Jackson Chemical report this information in its financial statements at December 31, 2004?
3. Melissa Etheridge Inc. had a manufacturing plant in Bosnia, which was destroyed in the civil war. It is not certain who will compensate Etheridge for this destruction, but Etheridge has been assured by governmental officials that it will receive a definite amount for this plant. The amount of the compensation will be less than the fair value of the plant, but more than its book value. How should the contingency be reported in the financial statements of Etheridge Inc.?

E13-14 (Asset Retirement Obligation) Oil Products Company purchases an oil tanker depot on January 1, 2004, at a cost of $600,000. Oil Products expects to operate the depot for 10 years, at which time it is legally required to dismantle the depot and remove the underground storage tanks. It is estimated that it will cost $75,000 to dismantle the depot and remove the tanks at the end of the depot's useful life.

Instructions

(a) Prepare the journal entries to record the depot and the asset retirement obligation for the depot on January 1, 2004. Based on an effective interest rate of 6%, the present value of the asset retirement obligation on January 1, 2004, is $41,879.

(b) Prepare any journal entries required for the depot and the asset retirement obligation at December 31, 2004. Oil Products uses straight-line depreciation; the estimated residual value for the depot is zero.

(c) On December 31, 2013, Oil Products pays a demolition firm to dismantle the depot and remove the tanks at a price of $80,000. Prepare the journal entry for the settlement of the asset retirement obligation.

E13-15 (Premiums) Presented below are three independent situations.

1. Fred McGriff Stamp Company records stamp service revenue and provides for the cost of redemptions in the year stamps are sold to licensees. McGriff's past experience indicates that only 80% of the stamps sold to licensees will be redeemed. McGriff's liability for stamp redemptions was $13,000,000 at December 31, 2003. Additional information for 2004 is as follows.

Stamp service revenue from stamps sold to licensees	$9,500,000
Cost of redemptions (stamps sold prior to 1/1/04)	6,000,000

If all the stamps sold in 2004 were presented for redemption in 2005, the redemption cost would be $5,200,000. What amount should McGriff report as a liability for stamp redemptions at December 31, 2004?

2. In packages of its products, Sam Sosa Inc. includes coupons that may be presented at retail stores to obtain discounts on other Sosa products. Retailers are reimbursed for the face amount of coupons redeemed plus 10% of that amount for handling costs. Sosa honors requests for coupon redemption by retailers up to 3 months after the consumer expiration date. Sosa estimates that 60% of all coupons issued will ultimately be redeemed. Information relating to coupons issued by Sosa during 2004 is as follows.

Consumer expiration date	12/31/04
Total face amount of coupons issued	$800,000
Total payments to retailers as of 12/31/04	330,000

What amount should Sam Sosa report as a liability for unredeemed coupons at December 31, 2004?

3. Bruce Kim Company sold 700,000 boxes of pie mix under a new sales promotional program. Each box contains one coupon, which submitted with $4.00, entitles the customer to a baking pan. Kim pays $6.00 per pan and $0.50 for handling and shipping. Kim estimates that 70% of the coupons will be redeemed, even though only 250,000 coupons had been processed during 2004. What amount should Kim report as a liability for unredeemed coupons at December 31, 2004?

(AICPA adapted)

E13-16 (Financial Statement Impact of Liability Transactions) Presented below is a list of possible transactions.

1. Purchased inventory for $80,000 on account (assume perpetual system is used).
2. Issued an $80,000 note payable in payment on account (see item 1 above).
3. Recorded accrued interest on the note from item 2 above.
4. Borrowed $100,000 from the bank by signing a 6-month, $112,000, noninterest-bearing note.
5. Recognized 4 months' interest expense on the note from item 4 above.
6. Recorded cash sales of $75,260, which includes 6% sales tax.
7. Recorded wage expense of $35,000. The cash paid was $25,000; the difference was due to various amounts withheld.
8. Recorded employer's payroll taxes.
9. Accrued accumulated vacation pay.
10. Recorded an asset retirement obligation.
11. Recorded bonuses due to employees.
12. Recorded a contingent loss on a lawsuit that the company will probably lose.
13. Accrued warranty expense (assume expense warranty approach).
14. Paid warranty costs that were accrued in item 13 above.
15. Recorded sales of product and related warranties (assume sales warranty approach).
16. Paid warranty costs under contracts from item 15 above.
17. Recognized warranty revenue (see item 15 above).
18. Recorded estimated liability for premium claims outstanding.

Instructions

Set up a table using the format shown below and analyze the effect of the 18 transactions on the financial statement categories indicated.

#	Assets	Liabilities	Owners' Equity	Net Income
1				

Use the following code:

I: Increase D: Decrease NE: No net effect

E13-17 (Ratio Computations and Discussion) Sprague Company has been operating for several years, and on December 31, 2004, presented the following balance sheet.

SPRAGUE COMPANY
BALANCE SHEET
DECEMBER 31, 2004

Cash	$ 40,000	Accounts payable	$ 80,000
Receivables	75,000	Mortgage payable	140,000
Inventories	95,000	Common stock ($1 par)	150,000
Plant assets (net)	220,000	Retained earnings	60,000
	$430,000		$430,000

The net income for 2004 was $25,000. Assume that total assets are the same in 2003 and 2004.

Instructions

Compute each of the following ratios. For each of the four indicate the manner in which it is computed and its significance as a tool in the analysis of the financial soundness of the company.

(a) Current ratio.
(b) Acid-test ratio.
(c) Debt to total assets.
(d) Rate of return on assets.

E13-18 (Ratio Computations and Analysis) Hood Company's condensed financial statements provide the following information.

HOOD COMPANY
BALANCE SHEET

	Dec. 31, 2004	Dec. 31, 2003
Cash	$ 52,000	$ 60,000
Accounts receivable (net)	198,000	80,000
Marketable securities (short-term)	80,000	40,000
Inventories	440,000	360,000
Prepaid expenses	3,000	7,000
Total current assets	$ 773,000	$ 547,000
Property, plant, and equipment (net)	857,000	853,000
Total assets	$1,630,000	$1,400,000
Current liabilities	240,000	160,000
Bonds payable	400,000	400,000
Common stockholders' equity	990,000	840,000
Total liabilities and stockholders' equity	$1,630,000	$1,400,000

INCOME STATEMENT
FOR THE YEAR ENDED 2004

Sales	$1,640,000
Cost of goods sold	(800,000)
Gross profit	840,000
Selling and administrative expense	(440,000)
Interest expense	(40,000)
Net income	$ 360,000

Instructions

(a) Determine the following for 2004.
  (1) Current ratio at December 31.
  (2) Acid-test ratio at December 31.
  (3) Accounts receivable turnover.
  (4) Inventory turnover.
  (5) Rate of return on assets.
  (6) Profit margin on sales.

(b) Prepare a brief evaluation of the financial condition of Hood Company and of the adequacy of its profits.

E13-19 (Ratio Computations and Effect of Transactions) Presented below is information related to Carver Inc.

CARVER INC.
BALANCE SHEET
DECEMBER 31, 2004

Cash		$ 45,000	Notes payable (short-term)	$ 50,000
Receivables	$110,000		Accounts payable	32,000
Less: Allowance	15,000	95,000	Accrued liabilities	5,000
Inventories		170,000	Capital stock (par $5)	260,000
Prepaid insurance		8,000	Retained earnings	141,000
Land		20,000		
Equipment (net)		150,000		
		$488,000		$488,000

INCOME STATEMENT
FOR THE YEAR ENDED DECEMBER 31, 2004

Sales		$1,400,000
Cost of goods sold		
Inventory, Jan. 1, 2004	$200,000	
Purchases	790,000	
Cost of goods available for sale	990,000	
Inventory, Dec. 31, 2004	170,000	
Cost of goods sold		820,000
Gross profit on sales		580,000
Operating expenses		170,000
Net income		$ 410,000

Instructions

(a) Compute the following ratios or relationships of Carver Inc. Assume that the ending account balances are representative unless the information provided indicates differently.

(1) Current ratio.
(2) Inventory turnover.
(3) Receivables turnover.
(4) Earnings per share.
(5) Profit margin on sales.
(6) Rate of return on assets on December 31, 2004.

(b) Indicate for each of the following transactions whether the transaction would improve, weaken, or have no effect on the current ratio of Carver Inc. at December 31, 2004.

(1) Write off an uncollectible account receivable, $2,200.
(2) Purchase additional capital stock for cash.
(3) Pay $40,000 on notes payable (short-term).
(4) Collect $23,000 on accounts receivable.
(5) Buy equipment on account.
(6) Give an existing creditor a short-term note in settlement of account.

***E13-20 (Bonus Computation)** Jud Buechler, president of the Supporting Cast Company, has a bonus arrangement with the company under which he receives 15% of the net income (after deducting taxes and bonuses) each year. For the current year, the net income before deducting either the provision for income taxes or the bonus is $299,750. The bonus is deductible for tax purposes, and the effective tax rate may be assumed to be 40%.

Instructions

(a) Compute the amount of Jud Buechler's bonus.
(b) Compute the appropriate provision for federal income taxes for the year.
(c) Prepare the December 31 journal entry to record the bonus (which will not be paid until next year).

***E13-21 (Bonus Computation and Income Statement Preparation)** The incomplete income statement of Scottie Pippen Company follows.

SCOTTIE PIPPEN COMPANY
INCOME STATEMENT
FOR THE YEAR 2004

Revenue		$10,000,000
Cost of goods sold		7,000,000
Gross profit		3,000,000
Administrative and selling expenses	$1,000,000	
Profit-sharing bonus to employees	?	?
Income before income taxes		?
Income taxes		?
Net income		$?

The employee profit-sharing plan requires that 20% of all profits remaining after the deduction of the bonus and income taxes be distributed to the employees by the first day of the fourth month following each year-end. The federal income tax is 45%, and the bonus is tax-deductible.

Instructions
Complete the condensed income statement of Scottie Pippen Company for the year 2004.

*__E13-22 (Bonus Compensation)__ Alan Iverson Company has a profit-sharing agreement with its employees that provides for deposit in a pension trust for the benefit of the employees of 25% of the net income after deducting (1) federal taxes on income, (2) the amount of the annual pension contribution, and (3) a return of 10% on the stockholders' equity as of the end of the year 2004.

Instructions
Compute the amount of the pension contribution under the assumption that the stockholders' equity at the end of 2004 before adding the net income for the year is $700,000; that net income for the year before either the pension contribution or tax is $300,000; and that the pension contribution is deductible for tax purposes. Use 40% as the applicable rate of tax.

PROBLEMS

P13-1 (Current Liability Entries and Adjustments) Described below are certain transactions of James Edwards Corporation.

1. On February 2, the corporation purchased goods from Jack Haley Company for $50,000 subject to cash discount terms of 2/10, n/30. Purchases and accounts payable are recorded by the corporation at net amounts after cash discounts. The invoice was paid on February 26.
2. On April 1, the corporation bought a truck for $40,000 from General Motors Company, paying $4,000 in cash and signing a one-year, 12% note for the balance of the purchase price.
3. On May 1, the corporation borrowed $80,000 from Chicago National Bank by signing a $92,000 non-interest-bearing note due one year from May 1.
4. On August 1, the board of directors declared a $300,000 cash dividend that was payable on September 10 to stockholders of record on August 31.

Instructions
(a) Make all the journal entries necessary to record the transactions above using appropriate dates.
(b) James Edwards Corporation's year-end is December 31. Assuming that no adjusting entries relative to the transactions above have been recorded, prepare any adjusting journal entries concerning interest that are necessary to present fair financial statements at December 31. Assume straight-line amortization of discounts.

P13-2 (Current Liability Entries and Adjustments) Listed below are selected transactions of Kobe Bryant Department Store for the current year ending December 31.

1. On December 5, the store received $500 from the Phil Jackson Players as a deposit to be returned after certain furniture to be used in stage production was returned on January 15.
2. During December, cash sales totaled $834,750, which includes the 5% sales tax that must be remitted to the state by the fifteenth day of the following month.
3. On December 10, the store purchased for cash three delivery trucks for $99,000. The trucks were purchased in a state that applies a 5% sales tax.

4. The store determined it will cost $100,000 to restore the area surrounding one of its store parking lots, when the store is closed in 2 years. Bryant estimates the fair value of the obligation at December 31 is $84,000.

Instructions

Prepare all the journal entries necessary to record the transactions noted above as they occurred and any adjusting journal entries relative to the transactions that would be required to present fair financial statements at December 31. Date each entry. For simplicity, assume that adjusting entries are recorded only once a year on December 31.

P13-3 (Payroll Tax Entries) Star Wars Company pays its office employee payroll weekly. Below is a partial list of employees and their payroll data for August. Because August is their vacation period, vacation pay is also listed.

Employee	Earnings to July 31	Weekly Pay	Vacation Pay to Be Received in August
Mark Hamill	$4,200	$180	—
Carrie Fisher	3,500	150	$300
Harrison Ford	2,700	110	220
Alec Guinness	7,400	250	—
Peter Cushing	8,000	290	580

Assume that the federal income tax withheld is 10% of wages. Union dues withheld are 2% of wages. Vacations are taken the second and third weeks of August by Fisher, Ford, and Cushing. The state unemployment tax rate is 2.5% and the federal is 0.8%, both on a $7,000 maximum. The F.I.C.A. rate is 7.65% on employee and employer on a maximum of $84,900 per employee. In addition, a 1.45% rate is charged both employer and employee for an employee's wage in excess of $84,900.

Instructions

Make the journal entries necessary for each of the four August payrolls. The entries for the payroll and for the company's liability are made separately. Also make the entry to record the monthly payment of accrued payroll liabilities.

P13-4 (Payroll Tax Entries) Below is a payroll sheet for Empire Import Company for the month of September 2004. The company is allowed a 1% unemployment compensation rate by the state; the federal unemployment tax rate is 0.8% and the maximum for both is $7,000. Assume a 10% federal income tax rate for all employees and a 7.65% F.I.C.A. tax on employee and employer on a maximum of $84,900. In addition, 1.45% is charged both employer and employee for an employee's wage in excess of $84,900 per employee.

Name	Earnings to Aug. 31	September Earnings	Income Tax Withholding	F.I.C.A.	State U.C.	Federal U.C.
B.D. Williams	$ 6,800	$ 800				
D. Prowse	6,300	700				
K. Baker	7,600	1,100				
F. Oz	13,600	1,900				
A. Daniels	105,000	15,000				
P. Mayhew	112,000	16,000				

Instructions

(a) Complete the payroll sheet and make the necessary entry to record the payment of the payroll.
(b) Make the entry to record the payroll tax expenses of Empire Import Company.
(c) Make the entry to record the payment of the payroll liabilities created. Assume that the company pays all payroll liabilities at the end of each month.

P13-5 (Warranties, Accrual, and Cash Basis) Jerry Royster Corporation sells portable computers under a 2-year warranty contract that requires the corporation to replace defective parts and to provide the necessary repair labor. During 2004 the corporation sells for cash 300 computers at a unit price of $3,500. On the basis of past experience, the 2-year warranty costs are estimated to be $155 for parts and $185 for labor per unit. (For simplicity, assume that all sales occurred on December 31, 2004.) The warranty is not sold separately from the computer.

Instructions

(a) Record any necessary journal entries in 2004, applying the cash basis method.
(b) Record any necessary journal entries in 2004, applying the expense warranty accrual method.

(c) What liability relative to these transactions would appear on the December 31, 2004, balance sheet and how would it be classified if the cash basis method is applied?
(d) What liability relative to these transactions would appear on the December 31, 2004, balance sheet and how would it be classified if the expense warranty accrual method is applied?

In 2005 the actual warranty costs to Jerry Royster Corporation were $21,400 for parts and $24,900 for labor.

(e) Record any necessary journal entries in 2005, applying the cash basis method.
(f) Record any necessary journal entries in 2005, applying the expense warranty accrual method.

P13-6 (Extended Warranties) Brett Perriman Company sells televisions at an average price of $750 and also offers to each customer a separate 3-year warranty contract for $75 that requires the company to perform periodic services and to replace defective parts. During 2004, the company sold 300 televisions and 270 warranty contracts for cash. It estimates the 3-year warranty costs as $20 for parts and $40 for labor and accounts for warranties separately. Assume sales occurred on December 31, 2004, income is recognized on the warranties, and straight-line recognition of warranty revenues occurs.

Instructions

(a) Record any necessary journal entries in 2004.
(b) What liability relative to these transactions would appear on the December 31, 2004, balance sheet and how would it be classified?

In 2005, Brett Perriman Company incurred actual costs relative to 2004 television warranty sales of $2,000 for parts and $3,000 for labor.

(c) Record any necessary journal entries in 2005 relative to 2004 television warranties.
(d) What amounts relative to the 2004 television warranties would appear on the December 31, 2005, balance sheet and how would they be classified?

P13-7 (Warranties, Accrual, and Cash Basis) Albert Pujols Company sells a machine for $7,400 under a 12-month warranty agreement that requires the company to replace all defective parts and to provide the repair labor at no cost to the customers. With sales being made evenly throughout the year, the company sells 650 machines in 2005 (warranty expense is incurred half in 2005 and half in 2006). As a result of product testing, the company estimates that the warranty cost is $370 per machine ($170 parts and $200 labor).

Instructions

Assuming that actual warranty costs are incurred exactly as estimated, what journal entries would be made relative to the following facts?

(a) Under application of the expense warranty accrual method for:
  (1) Sale of machinery in 2005.
  (2) Warranty costs incurred in 2005.
  (3) Warranty expense charged against 2005 revenues.
  (4) Warranty costs incurred in 2006.
(b) Under application of the cash basis method for:
  (1) Sale of machinery in 2005.
  (2) Warranty costs incurred in 2005.
  (3) Warranty expense charged against 2005 revenues.
  (4) Warranty costs incurred in 2006.
(c) What amount, if any, is disclosed in the balance sheet as a liability for future warranty costs as of December 31, 2005, under each method?
(d) Which method best reflects the income in 2005 and 2006 of Albert Pujols Company? Why?

P13-8 (Premium Entries) To stimulate the sales of its Alladin breakfast cereal, Khamsah Company places 1 coupon in each box. Five coupons are redeemable for a premium consisting of a children's hand puppet. In 2005, the company purchases 40,000 puppets at $1.50 each and sells 440,000 boxes of Alladin at $3.75 a box. From its experience with other similar premium offers, the company estimates that 40% of the coupons issued will be mailed back for redemption. During 2005, 105,000 coupons are presented for redemption.

Instructions

Prepare the journal entries that should be recorded in 2005 relative to the premium plan.

P13-9 (Premium Entries and Financial Statement Presentation) Roberto Hernandez Candy Company offers a CD single as a premium for every five candy bar wrappers presented by customers together with $2.00. The candy bars are sold by the company to distributors for 30 cents each. The purchase price of each CD to the company is $1.80; in addition it costs 30 cents to mail each CD. The results of the premium plan for the years 2004 and 2005 are as follows. (All purchases and sales are for cash.)

	2004	2005
CDs purchased	250,000	330,000
Candy bars sold	2,895,400	2,743,600
Wrappers redeemed	1,200,000	1,500,000
2004 wrappers expected to be redeemed in 2005	290,000	
2005 wrappers expected to be redeemed in 2006		350,000

Instructions

(a) Prepare the journal entries that should be made in 2004 and 2005 to record the transactions related to the premium plan of the Roberto Hernandez Candy Company.

(b) Indicate the account names, amounts, and classifications of the items related to the premium plan that would appear on the balance sheet and the income statement at the end of 2004 and 2005.

P13-10 (Loss Contingencies: Entries and Essay) On November 24, 2004, 26 passengers on Tom Paris Airlines Flight No. 901 were injured upon landing when the plane skidded off the runway. Personal injury suits for damages totaling $5,000,000 were filed on January 11, 2005, against the airline by 18 injured passengers. The airline carries no insurance. Legal counsel has studied each suit and advised Paris that it can reasonably expect to pay 60% of the damages claimed. The financial statements for the year ended December 31, 2004, were issued February 27, 2005.

Instructions

(a) Prepare any disclosures and journal entries required by the airline in preparation of the December 31, 2004, financial statements.

(b) Ignoring the Nov. 24, 2005, accident, what liability due to the risk of loss from lack of insurance coverage should Tom Paris Airlines record or disclose? During the past decade the company has experienced at least one accident per year and incurred average damages of $3,200,000. Discuss fully.

P13-11 (Loss Contingencies: Entries and Essays) Shoyo Corporation, in preparation of its December 31, 2004, financial statements, is attempting to determine the proper accounting treatment for each of the following situations.

1. As a result of uninsured accidents during the year, personal injury suits for $350,000 and $60,000 have been filed against the company. It is the judgment of Shoyo's legal counsel that an unfavorable outcome is unlikely in the $60,000 case but that an unfavorable verdict approximating $225,000 will probably result in the $350,000 case.
2. Shoyo Corporation owns a subsidiary in a foreign country that has a book value of $5,725,000 and an estimated fair value of $8,700,000. The foreign government has communicated to Shoyo its intention to expropriate the assets and business of all foreign investors. On the basis of settlements other firms have received from this same country, Shoyo expects to receive 40% of the fair value of its properties as final settlement.
3. Shoyo's chemical product division consisting of five plants is uninsurable because of the special risk of injury to employees and losses due to fire and explosion. The year 2004 is considered one of the safest (luckiest) in the division's history because no loss due to injury or casualty was suffered. Having suffered an average of three casualties a year during the rest of the past decade (ranging from $60,000 to $700,000), management is certain that next year the company will probably not be so fortunate.

Instructions

(a) Prepare the journal entries that should be recorded as of December 31, 2004, to recognize each of the situations above.

(b) Indicate what should be reported relative to each situation in the financial statements and accompanying notes. Explain why.

P13-12 (Warranties and Premiums) Gloria Estefan's Music Emporium carries a wide variety of musical instruments, sound reproduction equipment, recorded music, and sheet music. Estefan's uses two sales promotion techniques—warranties and premiums—to attract customers.

Musical instruments and sound equipment are sold with a one-year warranty for replacement of parts and labor. The estimated warranty cost, based on past experience, is 2% of sales.

The premium is offered on the recorded and sheet music. Customers receive a coupon for each dollar spent on recorded music or sheet music. Customers may exchange 200 coupons and $20 for a CD player. Estefan's pays $34 for each CD player and estimates that 60% of the coupons given to customers will be redeemed.

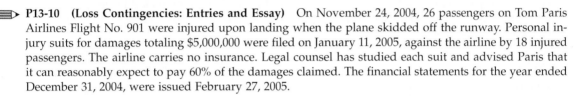

Estefan's total sales for 2004 were $7,200,000—$5,400,000 from musical instruments and sound reproduction equipment and $1,800,000 from recorded music and sheet music. Replacement parts and labor for warranty work totaled $164,000 during 2004. A total of 6,500 CD players used in the premium program were purchased during the year and there were 1,200,000 coupons redeemed in 2004.

The accrual method is used by Estefan's to account for the warranty and premium costs for financial reporting purposes. The balances in the accounts related to warranties and premiums on January 1, 2004, were as shown below.

Inventory of Premium CD Players	$39,950
Estimated Premium Claims Outstanding	44,800
Estimated Liability from Warranties	136,000

Instructions

Gloria Estefan's Music Emporium is preparing its financial statements for the year ended December 31, 2004. Determine the amounts that will be shown on the 2004 financial statements for the following.

(1) Warranty Expense.
(2) Estimated Liability from Warranties.
(3) Premium Expense.
(4) Inventory of Premium CD Players.
(5) Estimated Premium Claims Outstanding.

(CMA adapted)

P13-13 (Liability Errors) You are the independent auditor engaged to audit Christine Agazzi Corporation's December 31, 2004, financial statements. Christine Agazzi manufactures household appliances. During the course of your audit, you discovered the following contingent liabilities.

1. Christine Agazzi began production on a new dishwasher in June 2004 and, by December 31, 2004, sold 100,000 to various retailers for $500 each. Each dishwasher is under a one-year warranty. The company estimates that its warranty expense per dishwasher will amount to $25. At year-end, the company had already paid out $1,000,000 in warranty expenses. Christine Agazzi's income statement shows warranty expenses of $1,000,000 for 2004. Agazzi accounts for warranty costs on the accrual basis.
2. In response to your attorney's letter, Robert Sklodowski, Esq., has informed you that Agazzi has been cited for dumping toxic waste into the Kishwaukee River. Clean-up costs and fines amount to $3,330,000. Although the case is still being contested, Sklodowski is certain that Agazzi will most probably have to pay the fine and clean-up costs. No disclosure of this situation was found in the financial statements.
3. Christine Agazzi is the defendant in a patent infringement lawsuit by Heidi Goldman over Agazzi's use of a hydraulic compressor in several of its products. Sklodowski claims that, if the suit goes against Agazzi, the loss may be as much as $5,000,000; however, Sklodowski believes the loss of this suit to be only reasonably possible. Again, no mention of this suit occurs in the financial statements.

As presented, these contingencies are not reported in accordance with GAAP, which may create problems in issuing a clean audit report. You feel the need to note these problems in the work papers.

Instructions

Heading each page with the name of the company, balance sheet date, and a brief description of the problem, write a brief narrative for each of the above issues in the form of **a memorandum** to be incorporated in the audit work papers. Explain what led to the discovery of each problem, what the problem really is, and what you advised your client to do (along with any appropriate journal entries) in order to bring these contingencies in accordance with GAAP.

***P13-14 (Bonus Computation)** Henryk Inc. has a contract with its president, Nathalie Sarraute, to pay her a bonus during each of the years 2003, 2004, 2005, and 2006. The federal income tax rate is 40% during the 4 years. The profit before deductions for bonus and federal income taxes was $250,000 in 2003, $308,000 in 2004, $350,000 in 2005, and $380,000 in 2006. The president's bonus of 12% is deductible for tax purposes in each year and is to be computed as follows.

(a) In 2003 the bonus is to be based on profit before deductions for bonus and income tax.
(b) In 2004 the bonus is to be based on profit after deduction of bonus but before deduction of income tax.
(c) In 2005 the bonus is to be based on profit before deduction of bonus but after deduction of income tax.
(d) In 2006 the bonus is to be based on profit after deductions for bonus and income tax.

Instructions

Compute the amounts of the bonus and the income tax for each of the 4 years.

P13-15 (Warranty, Bonus, and Coupon Computation) Victor Hugo Company must make computations and adjusting entries for the following independent situations at December 31, 2004.

1. Its line of amplifiers carries a 3-year warranty against defects. On the basis of past experience the estimated warranty costs related to dollar sales are: first year after sale—2% of sales; second year

after sale—3% of sales; and third year after sale—4% of sales. Sales and actual warranty expenditures for the first 3 years of business were:

	Sales	Warranty Expenditures
2002	$ 800,000	$ 6,500
2003	1,100,000	17,200
2004	1,200,000	62,000

Instructions

Compute the amount that Hugo Company should report as a liability in its December 31, 2004, balance sheet. Assume that all sales are made evenly throughout each year with warranty expenses also evenly spaced relative to the rates above.

*2. Hugo Company's profit-sharing plan provides that the company will contribute to a fund an amount equal to one-fourth of its net income each year. Income before deducting the profit-sharing contribution and taxes for 2004 is $1,035,000. The applicable income tax rate is 40%, and the profit-sharing contribution is deductible for tax purposes.

Instructions

Compute the amount to be contributed to the profit-sharing fund for 2004.

3. With some of its products, Hugo Company includes coupons that are redeemable in merchandise. The coupons have no expiration date and, in the company's experience, 40% of them are redeemed. The liability for unredeemed coupons at December 31, 2003, was $9,000. During 2004, coupons worth $25,000 were issued, and merchandise worth $8,000 was distributed in exchange for coupons redeemed.

Instructions

Compute the amount of the liability that should appear on the December 31, 2004, balance sheet.

(AICPA adapted)

CONCEPTUAL CASES

C13-1 (Nature of Liabilities) Presented below is the current liabilities section of Nizami Corporation.

	($000) 2003	2002
Current Liabilities		
Notes payable	$ 68,713	$ 7,700
Accounts payable	179,496	101,379
Compensation to employees	60,312	31,649
Accrued liabilities	158,198	77,621
Income taxes payable	10,486	26,491
Current maturities of long-term debt	16,592	6,649
Total current liabilities	$493,797	$251,489

Instructions

Answer the following questions.

(a) What are the essential characteristics that make an item a liability?
(b) How does one distinguish between a current liability and a long-term liability?
(c) What are accrued liabilities? Give three examples of accrued liabilities that Nizami might have.
(d) What is the theoretically correct way to value liabilities? How are current liabilities usually valued?
(e) Why are notes payable reported first in the current liabilities section?
(f) What might be the items that comprise Nizami's liability for "Compensation to employees"?

C13-2 (Current versus Noncurrent Classification) D'Annunzio Corporation includes the following items in its liabilities at December 31, 2004.

1. Notes payable, $25,000,000, due June 30, 2005.
2. Deposits from customers on equipment ordered by them from D'Annunzio, $6,250,000.
3. Salaries payable, $3,750,000, due January 14, 2005.

Instructions

Indicate in what circumstances, if any, each of the three liabilities above would be excluded from current liabilities.

C13-3 (Refinancing of Short-Term Debt) Levi Eshkol Corporation reports in the current liability section of its balance sheet at December 31, 2004 (its year-end), short-term obligations of $15,000,000, which includes the current portion of 12% long-term debt in the amount of $11,000,000 (matures in March 2005). Management has stated its intention to refinance the 12% debt whereby no portion of it will mature during 2005. The date of issuance of the financial statements is March 25, 2005.

Instructions

(a) Is management's intent enough to support long-term classification of the obligation in this situation?

(b) Assume that Eshkol Corporation issues $13,000,000 of 10-year debentures to the public in January 2005 and that management intends to use the proceeds to liquidate the $11,000,000 debt maturing in March 2005. Furthermore, assume that the debt maturing in March 2005 is paid from these proceeds prior to the issuance of the financial statements. Will this have any impact on the balance sheet classification at December 31, 2004? Explain your answer.

(c) Assume that Eshkol Corporation issues common stock to the public in January and that management intends to entirely liquidate the $11,000,000 debt maturing in March 2005 with the proceeds of this equity securities issue. In light of these events, should the $11,000,000 debt maturing in March 2005 be included in current liabilities at December 31, 2004?

(d) Assume that Eshkol Corporation, on February 15, 2005, entered into a financing agreement with a commercial bank that permits Eshkol Corporation to borrow at any time through 2006 up to $15,000,000 at the bank's prime rate of interest. Borrowings under the financing agreement mature three years after the date of the loan. The agreement is not cancelable except for violation of a provision with which compliance is objectively determinable. No violation of any provision exists at the date of issuance of the financial statements. Assume further that the current portion of long-term debt does not mature until August 2005. In addition, management intends to refinance the $11,000,000 obligation under the terms of the financial agreement with the bank, which is expected to be financially capable of honoring the agreement.

(1) Given these facts, should the $11,000,000 be classified as current on the balance sheet at December 31, 2004?

(2) Is disclosure of the refinancing method required?

C13-4 (Refinancing of Short-Term Debt) Medvedev Inc. issued $10,000,000 of short-term commercial paper during the year 2003 to finance construction of a plant. At December 31, 2003, the corporation's year-end, Medvedev intends to refinance the commercial paper by issuing long-term debt. However, because the corporation temporarily has excess cash, in January 2004 it liquidates $4,000,000 of the commercial paper as the paper matures. In February 2004, Medvedev completes an $18,000,000 long-term debt offering. Later during the month of February, it issues its December 31, 2003, financial statements. The proceeds of the long-term debt offering are to be used to replenish $4,000,000 in working capital, to pay $6,000,000 of commercial paper as it matures in March 2004, and to pay $8,000,000 of construction costs expected to be incurred later that year to complete the plant.

Instructions

(a) How should the $10,000,000 of commercial paper be classified on the December 31, 2003, January 31, 2004, and February 28, 2004, balance sheets? Give support for your answer and also consider the cash element.

(b) What would your answer be if, instead of a refinancing at the date of issuance of the financial statements, a financing agreement existed at that date?

C13-5 (Loss Contingencies) On February 1, 2004, one of the huge storage tanks of Paunee Manufacturing Company exploded. Windows in houses and other buildings within a one-mile radius of the explosion were severely damaged, and a number of people were injured. As of February 15, 2004 (when the December 31, 2003, financial statements were completed and sent to the publisher for printing and public distribution), no suits had been filed or claims asserted against the company as a consequence of the explosion. The company fully anticipates that suits will be filed and claims asserted for injuries and damages. Because the casualty was uninsured and the company considered at fault, Paunee Manufacturing will have to cover the damages from its own resources.

Instructions

Discuss fully the accounting treatment and disclosures that should be accorded the casualty and related contingent losses in the financial statements dated December 31, 2003.

C13-6 (Loss Contingency) Presented below is a note disclosure for Ralph Ellison Corporation.

> **Litigation and Environmental:** The Company has been notified, or is a named or a potentially responsible party in a number of governmental (federal, state and local) and private actions associated

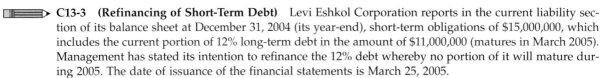

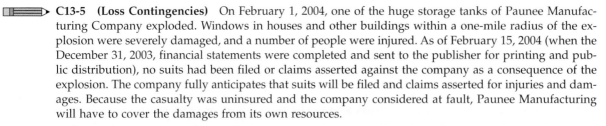

with environmental matters, such as those relating to hazardous wastes, including certain sites which are on the United States EPA National Priorities List ("Superfund"). These actions seek cleanup costs, penalties and/or damages for personal injury or to property or natural resources.

In 2002, the Company recorded a pre-tax charge of $56,229,000, included in the "Other Expense (Income)—Net" caption of the Company's Consolidated Statements of Income, as an additional provision for environmental matters. These expenditures are expected to take place over the next several years and are indicative of the Company's commitment to improve and maintain the environment in which it operates. At December 31, 2002, environmental accruals amounted to $69,931,000, of which $61,535,000 are considered noncurrent and are included in the "Deferred Credits and Other Liabilities" caption of the Company's Consolidated Balance Sheets.

While it is impossible at this time to determine with certainty the ultimate outcome of environmental matters, it is management's opinion, based in part on the advice of independent counsel (after taking into account accruals and insurance coverage applicable to such actions) that when the costs are finally determined they will not have a material adverse effect on the financial position of the Company.

Instructions
Answer the following questions.

(a) What conditions must exist before a loss contingency can be recorded in the accounts?
(b) Suppose that Ralph Ellison Corporation could not reasonably estimate the amount of the loss, although it could establish with a high degree of probability the minimum and maximum loss possible. How should this information be reported in the financial statements?
(c) If the amount of the loss is uncertain, how would the loss contingency be reported in the financial statements?

C13-7 (Warranties and Loss Contingencies) The following two independent situations involve loss contingencies.

Part 1
Clarke Company sells two products, John and Henrick. Each carries a one-year warranty.

1. Product John—Product warranty costs, based on past experience, will normally be 1% of sales.
2. Product Henrick—Product warranty costs cannot be reasonably estimated because this is a new product line. However, the chief engineer believes that product warranty costs are likely to be incurred.

Instructions
How should Clarke report the estimated product warranty costs for each of the two types of merchandise above? Discuss the rationale for your answer. Do not discuss deferred income tax implications, or disclosures that should be made in Clarke's financial statements or notes.

Part 2
Toni Morrison Company is being sued for $4,000,000 for an injury caused to a child as a result of alleged negligence while the child was visiting the Toni Morrison Company plant in March 2004. The suit was filed in July 2004. Toni Morrison's lawyer states that it is probable that Toni Morrison will lose the suit and be found liable for a judgment costing anywhere from $400,000 to $2,000,000. However, the lawyer states that the most probable judgment is $800,000.

Instructions
How should Toni Morrison report the suit in its 2004 financial statements? Discuss the rationale for your answer. Include in your answer disclosures, if any, that should be made in Toni Morrison's financial statements or notes.

(AICPA adapted)

C13-8 (Warranties) The Ray Company, owner of Bleacher Mall, charges Creighton Clothing Store a rental fee of $600 per month plus 5% of yearly profits over $500,000. Harry Creighton, the owner of the store, directs his accountant, Burt Wilson, to increase the estimate of bad debt expense and warranty costs in order to keep profits at $475,000.

Instructions
Answer the following questions.

(a) Should Wilson follow his boss's directive?
(b) Who is harmed if the estimates are increased?
(c) Is Creighton's directive ethical?

USING YOUR JUDGMENT

FINANCIAL REPORTING PROBLEM

3M Company

The financial statements of 3M are presented in Appendix 5B or can be accessed on the Take Action! CD.

Instructions

Refer to these financial statements and the accompanying notes to answer the following questions.

(a) What was 3M's short-term debt and related weighted average interest rate on this debt?

(b) What was 3M's working capital, acid-test ratio, and current ratio? Comment on 3M's liquidity.

(c) What types of commitments and contingencies has 3M reported in its financial statements? What is management's reaction to these contingencies?

FINANCIAL STATEMENT ANALYSIS CASES

Case 1 Northland Cranberries

Despite being a publicly traded company only since 1987, Northland Cranberries of Wisconsin Rapids, Wisconsin, is one of the world's largest cranberry growers. Despite its short life as a publicly traded corporation, it has engaged in an aggressive growth strategy. As a consequence, the company has taken on significant amounts of both short-term and long-term debt. The following information is taken from recent annual reports of the company.

	Current Year	Prior Year
Current assets	$ 6,745,759	$ 5,598,054
Total assets	107,744,751	83,074,339
Current liabilities	10,168,685	4,484,687
Total liabilities	73,118,204	49,948,787
Stockholders' equity	34,626,547	33,125,552
Net sales	21,783,966	18,051,355
Cost of goods sold	13,057,275	8,751,220
Interest expense	3,654,006	2,393,792
Income tax expense	1,051,000	1,917,000
Net income	1,581,707	2,942,954

Instructions

(a) Evaluate the company's liquidity by calculating and analyzing working capital and the current ratio.

(b) The following discussion of the company's liquidity was provided by the company in the Management Discussion and Analysis section of the company's annual report. Comment on whether you agree with management's statements, and what might be done to remedy the situation.

> The lower comparative current ratio in the current year was due to $3 million of short-term borrowing then outstanding which was incurred to fund the Yellow River Marsh acquisitions last year. As a result of the extreme seasonality of its business, the company does not believe that its current ratio or its underlying stated working capital at the current, fiscal year-end is a meaningful indication of the Company's liquidity. As of March 31 of each fiscal year, the Company has historically carried no significant amounts of inventories and by such date all of the Company's accounts receivable from its crop sold for processing under the supply agreements have been paid in cash, with the resulting cash received from such payments used to reduce indebtedness. The Company utilizes its revolving bank credit facility, together with cash generated from operations, to fund its working capital requirements throughout its growing season.

Case 2 Mohican Company

Presented below is the current liabilities section and related note of **Mohican Company**.

	(dollars in thousands) Current Year	Prior Year
Current liabilities		
Current portion of long-term debt	$ 15,000	$ 10,000
Short-term debt	2,668	405
Accounts payable	29,495	42,427
Accrued warranty	16,843	16,741
Accrued marketing programs	17,512	16,585
Other accrued liabilities	35,653	33,290
Accrued and deferred income taxes	16,206	17,348
Total current liabilities	$133,377	$136,796

Notes to Consolidated Financial Statements

1 (in part): Summary of Significant Accounting Policies and Related Data

Accrued Warranty—The company provides an accrual for future warranty costs based upon the relationship of prior years' sales to actual warranty costs.

Instructions

Answer the following questions.

(a) What is the difference between the cash basis and the accrual basis of accounting for warranty costs?

(b) Under what circumstance, if any, would it be appropriate for Mohican Company to recognize deferred revenue on warranty contracts?

(c) If Mohican Company recognized deferred revenue on warranty contracts, how would it recognize this revenue in subsequent periods?

COMPARATIVE ANALYSIS CASE

The Coca-Cola Company and PepsiCo, Inc.

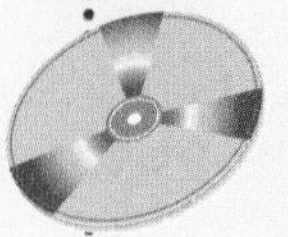

Instructions

Go to the Take Action! CD and use information found there to answer the following questions related to **The Coca-Cola Company** and **PepsiCo, Inc.**

(a) How much working capital do each of these companies have at the end of 2001? Comment on the appropriateness of the working capital they maintain.

(b) Compute both company's (a) current cash debt coverage ratio, (b) cash debt coverage ratio, (c) current ratio, (d) acid-test ratio, (e) receivable turnover ratio and (f) inventory turnover ratio for 2001. Comment on each company's overall liquidity.

(c) In PepsiCo's financial statements, it reports in the long-term debt section "short-term borrowings, reclassified." How can short-term borrowings be classified as long-term debt?

(d) What types of loss or gain contingencies do these two companies have at December 31, 2001?

RESEARCH CASES

Case 1

Instructions

Obtain the most recent edition of *Accounting Trends and Techniques*. Examine the disclosures included under the section regarding gain contingencies, and answer the following questions.

(a) Determine the nature of each of the disclosed gain contingencies. Are there any common themes?

(b) How many of the footnotes include dollar amounts?

(c) What are the smallest and largest amounts disclosed?

Case 2

The January 25, 2002, edition of the *Wall Street Journal* contained an article by Schad Terhune entitled "**Georgia Pacific** Says Asbestos Charge Will Result in Fourth Quarter Net Loss." (Subscribers to **Business Extra** can access the article at that site.)

Instructions

Read the article and answer the following questions.

(a) Under what conditions does GAAP require firms to take charges for "anticipated claims"? Based on the information in the article, does it appear that Georgia-Pacific (GP) meets those conditions? Why or why not?

(b) Prepare the journal entry to record GP's $221 million charge. How would it be reported in the financial statements?

(c) Estimated losses must be based on a "reasonable" estimate. How did GP arrive at its estimate? Do you think this process would result in a reasonable estimate? Why or why not?

INTERNATIONAL REPORTING CASE

An important difference between U.S. and international accounting standards is the accounting for liabilities related to provisions. Due in part to differences in tax laws, accounting standards in some countries and the standards issued by the International Accounting Standards Board (IASB) allow recognition of liabilities for items that would not meet the definition of a liability under U.S. GAAP. The following note disclosure for liabilities related to provisions was provided by **Hoechst A.G.**, a leading German drug company, in its annual report. Hoechst prepares its statements in accordance with IASB standards.

	(in DM millions)	
Other provisions	Current Year	Prior Year
Taxes	2,350	2,349
Restructuring	709	1,109
Damage and product liability claims	795	553
Environmental protection	869	814
Self-insurance loss provisions	631	870
Employee-related commitments	1,123	1,243
Other	2,274	2,538
Total	8,751	9,476
Current portion thereof	(5,013)	(5,679)

Hoechst reported the following additional items in its annual report. Data for **Merck & Co.**, a U.S. drug company, are provided for comparison.

	Hoechst (DM millions)	Merck ($ millions)
Current assets	20,528	10,229
Average current liabilities	5,346	5,819
Liquid assets	391	3,356
Receivables (net)	14,362	3,374
Cash flow from operations	4,628	5,328

Instructions

(a) Compute the following ratios for Hoechst and Merck: current ratio, acid-test ratio, and the current cash debt coverage ratio. Compare the liquidity of these two drug companies based on these ratios.

(b) Identify items in Hoechst's provision disclosure that likely would not be recognized as liabilities under U.S. GAAP. (*Hint:* Refer to Illustration 13-10 in the chapter.)

(c) Discuss how the items identified in (b) would affect the comparative analysis in part (a). What adjustments would you make in your analysis? Assume that 75% of the provisions for restructuring and self-insurance are current liabilities.

PROFESSIONAL SIMULATION

Accounting for Current Liabilities

Directions | Situation | Journal Entries | Explanation | Research | Resources

Directions

In this simulation, you will be asked various questions concerning the accounting for current liabilities. Prepare responses to all parts.

Situation

Alex Rodriguez Inc., a publishing company, is preparing its December 31, 2003, financial statements and must determine the proper accounting treatment for the following situations.

(a) Rodriguez sells subscriptions to several magazines for a 1-year, 2-year, or 3-year period. Cash receipts from subscribers are credited to magazine subscriptions collected in advance, and this account had a balance of $2,300,000 at December 31, 2003. Outstanding subscriptions at December 31, 2003, expire as follows.

During 2004—$600,000
During 2005— 500,000
During 2006— 800,000

(b) On January 2, 2003, Rodriguez discontinued collision, fire, and theft coverage on its delivery vehicles and became self-insured for these risks. Actual losses of $50,000 during 2003 were charged to delivery expense. The 2002 premium for the discontinued coverage amounted to $80,000, and the controller wants to set up a reserve for self-insurance by a debit to delivery expense of $30,000 and a credit to the reserve for self-insurance of $30,000.

(c) A suit for breach of contract seeking damages of $1,000,000 was filed by an author against Rodriguez on July 1, 2003. The company's legal counsel believes that an unfavorable outcome is probable. A reasonable estimate of the court's award to the plaintiff is in the range between $300,000 and $700,000. No amount within this range is a better estimate of potential damages than any other amount.

(d) The following items are listed as liabilities on the balance sheet on December 31, 2003.

Accounts payable	$ 420,000
Notes payable	750,000
Bonds payable	2,250,000

The accounts payable represent obligations to suppliers that were due in January 2004. The notes payable mature on various dates during 2004. The bonds payable mature on July 1, 2004.

Journal Entries

For situations (a), (b), and (c), prepare the journal entry that should be recorded as of December 31, 2003.

Explanation

Prepare a brief memorandum explaining the general rule for classifying a liability as current or non-current. Explain the conditions under which notes payable might be classified as current or non-current.

www.wiley.com/college/kieso

Remember to check the **Take Action! CD** and the book's **companion Web site** to find additional resources for this chapter.

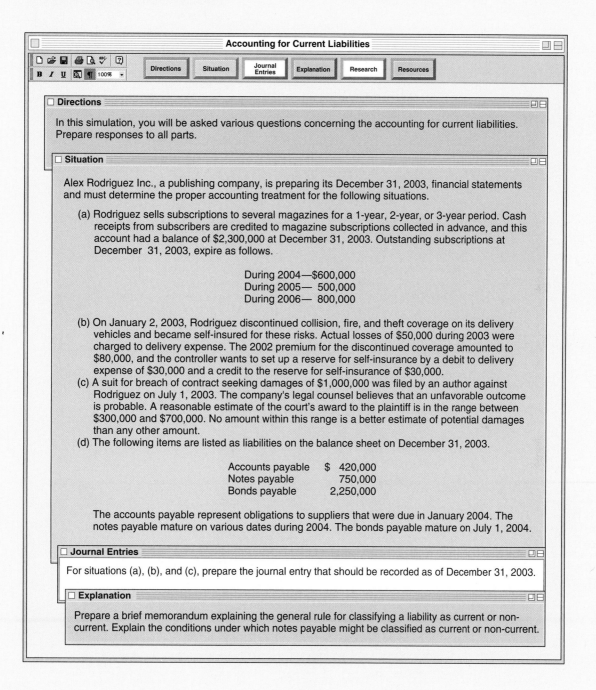

CHAPTER 14

Long-Term Liabilities

Your Debt Is Killing My Stock

Traditionally, investors in the stock and bond markets operate in their own separate worlds. However, in recent volatile markets, even quiet murmurs in the bond market have been amplified into (usually negative) movements in stock prices. At one extreme, these gyrations heralded the demise of a company well before the investors could sniff out the problem.

The swift decline of **Enron** in late 2001 provided the ultimate lesson that a company with no credit is no company at all. As one analyst remarked, "You can no longer have an opinion on a company's stock without having an appreciation for its credit rating." Other energy companies, such as **Calpine**, **NRG Energy**, and **AES Corp.**, also felt the effect of Enron contagion as lenders tightened or closed down the credit supply and raised interest rates on already-high levels of debt. The result? Stock prices took a hit.

Other industries are not immune from the negative stock price effects of credit problems. Industrial conglomerate **Tyco International** felt these effects when questions about its merger accounting turned into concerns over its debt levels and liquidity. Equity investors headed for the exits, driving down the Tyco share price, even as management was reassuring them that the company was not in danger of default. Tyco investors were reluctant to believe the reassurances, given the company's high level of debt taken on to finance its growth through acquisition. This was yet another example of stock prices taking a hit due to concerns about credit quality. Thus, even if your investment tastes are in stocks, keep an eye on the liabilities.[1]

LEARNING OBJECTIVES

After studying this chapter, you should be able to:

1. **Describe the formal procedures associated with issuing long-term debt.**
2. **Identify various types of bond issues.**
3. **Describe the accounting valuation for bonds at date of issuance.**
4. **Apply the methods of bond discount and premium amortization.**
5. **Describe the accounting procedures for the extinguishment of debt.**
6. **Explain the accounting procedures for long-term notes payable.**
7. **Explain the reporting of off-balance-sheet financing arrangements.**
8. **Indicate how long-term debt is presented and analyzed.**

---

[1] Adapted from Steven Vames, "Credit Quality, Stock Investing Go Hand in Hand," *Wall Street Journal* (April 1, 2002), p. R4.

PREVIEW OF CHAPTER 14

As indicated in the opening story, investors are paying considerable attention to the liabilities of companies like **Calpine**, **Tyco**, and **AES**. Companies with high debt levels, and with the related impact on income of higher interest costs, are being severely punished in the stock market. The purpose of this chapter is to explain the accounting issues related to long-term debt.

The content and organization of the chapter are as follows.

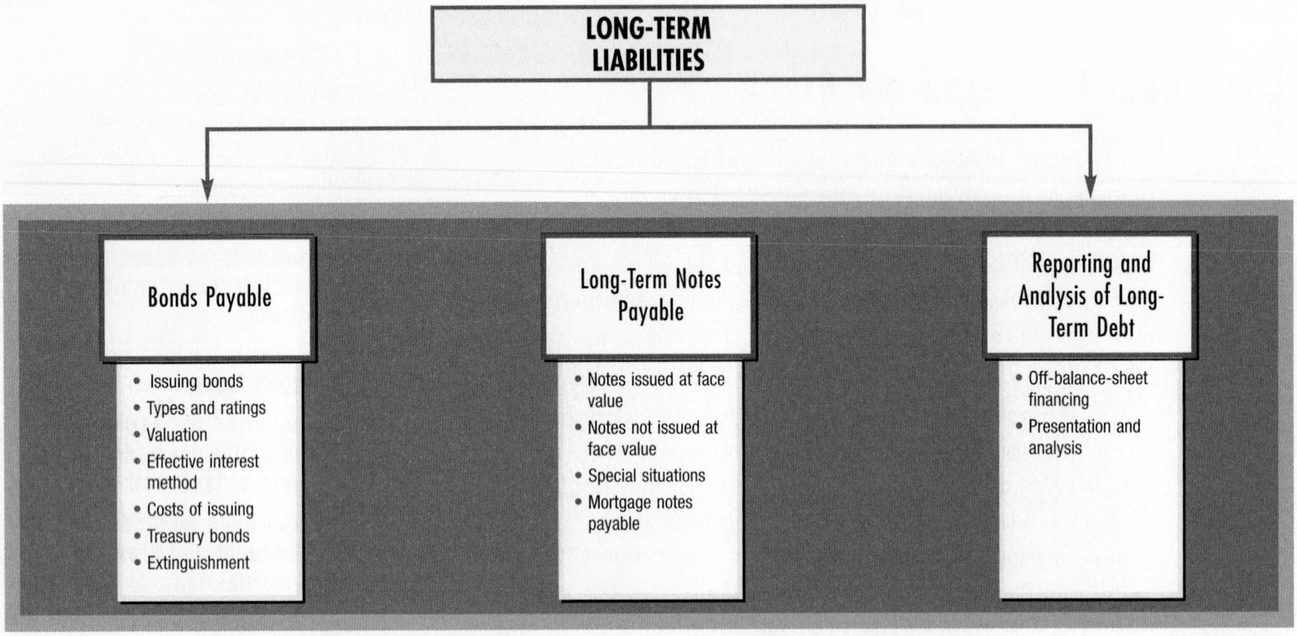

SECTION 1 BONDS PAYABLE

Long-term debt consists of probable future sacrifices of economic benefits arising from present obligations that are not payable within a year or the operating cycle of the business, whichever is longer. Bonds payable, long-term notes payable, mortgages payable, pension liabilities, and lease liabilities are examples of long-term liabilities.

Incurring long-term debt is often accompanied by considerable formality. For example, the bylaws of corporations usually require approval by the board of directors and the stockholders before bonds can be issued or other long-term debt arrangements can be contracted.

OBJECTIVE 1
Describe the formal procedures associated with issuing long-term debt.

Generally, long-term debt has various **covenants** or **restrictions** for the protection of both lenders and borrowers. The covenants and other terms of the agreement between the borrower and the lender are stated in the bond indenture or note agreement. Items often mentioned in the indenture or agreement include the amounts authorized to be issued, interest rate, due date or dates, call provisions, property pledged as security, sinking fund requirements, working capital and dividend restrictions, and limitations concerning the assumption of additional debt. Whenever these stipulations are important for a complete understanding of the financial position and the results of operations, they should be described in the body of the financial statements or the notes thereto.

Although it would seem that these covenants provide adequate protection to the long-term debt holder, many bondholders suffer considerable losses when additional debt is added to the capital structure. Consider what happened to bondholders in the leveraged buyout of **RJR Nabisco**. Solidly rated 9⅜ percent bonds due in 2016 plunged 20 percent in value when management announced the leveraged buyout. Such a loss in value occurs because the additional debt added to the capital structure increases the likelihood of default. Although bondholders have covenants to protect them, they often are written in a manner that can be interpreted in a number of different ways.

ISSUING BONDS

Bonds are the most common type of long-term debt reported on a company's balance sheet. The main purpose of bonds is to borrow for the long term when the amount of capital needed is too large for one lender to supply. By issuing bonds in $100, $1,000, or $10,000 denominations, a large amount of long-term indebtedness can be divided into many small investing units, thus enabling more than one lender to participate in the loan.

A bond arises from a contract known as a **bond indenture** and represents a promise to pay: (1) a sum of money at a designated maturity rate, plus (2) periodic interest at a specified rate on the maturity amount (face value). Individual bonds are evidenced by a paper certificate and typically have a $1,000 face value. Bond interest payments usually are made semiannually, although the interest rate is generally expressed as an annual rate.

An entire bond issue may be sold to an investment banker who acts as a selling agent in the process of marketing the bonds. In such arrangements, investment bankers may underwrite the entire issue by guaranteeing a certain sum to the corporation, thus taking the risk of selling the bonds for whatever price they can get (firm underwriting). Or they may sell the bond issue for a commission to be deducted from the proceeds of the sale (best efforts underwriting).

Alternatively, the issuing company may choose to place privately a bond issue by selling the bonds directly to a large institution, financial or otherwise, without the aid of an underwriter (private placement).

TYPES AND RATINGS OF BONDS

Some of the more common types of bonds found in practice are:

OBJECTIVE 2
Identify various types of bond issues.

TYPES OF BONDS

SECURED AND UNSECURED BONDS. **Secured bonds** are backed by a pledge of some sort of collateral. Mortgage bonds are secured by a claim on real estate. Collateral trust bonds are secured by stocks and bonds of other corporations. Bonds not backed by collateral are **unsecured**. A **debenture bond** is unsecured. A "junk bond" is unsecured and also very risky, and therefore it pays a high interest rate. Junk bonds are often used to finance leveraged buyouts.

TERM, SERIAL, AND CALLABLE BONDS. Bond issues that mature on a single date are called **term bonds**, and issues that mature in installments are called **serial bonds**. Serially maturing bonds are frequently used by school or sanitary districts, municipalities, or other local taxing bodies that receive money through a special levy. **Callable bonds** give the issuer the right to call and retire the bonds prior to maturity.

CONVERTIBLE, COMMODITY-BACKED, AND DEEP DISCOUNT BONDS. If bonds are convertible into other securities of the corporation for a specified time after issuance, they are called **convertible bonds**. Accounting for bond conversions is discussed in Chapter 16. Two new types of bonds have been developed in an attempt to attract capital in a tight money market—commodity-backed bonds and deep discount bonds.

Commodity-backed bonds (also called **asset-linked bonds**) are redeemable in measures of a commodity, such as barrels of oil, tons of coal, or ounces of rare metal. To illustrate, **Sunshine Mining**, a silver mining producer, sold two issues of bonds redeemable with either $1,000 in cash or 50 ounces of silver, whichever is greater at maturity, and that have a stated interest rate of 8½ percent. The accounting problem is one of projecting the maturity value, especially since silver has fluctuated between $4 and $40 an ounce since issuance.

JCPenney Company sold the first publicly marketed long-term debt securities in the United States that do not bear interest. These **deep discount bonds**, also referred to as **zero-interest debenture bonds**, are sold at a discount that provides the buyer's total interest payoff at maturity.

REGISTERED AND BEARER (COUPON) BONDS. Bonds issued in the name of the owner are **registered bonds** and require surrender of the certificate and issuance of a new certificate to complete a sale. A **bearer** or **coupon bond**, however, is not recorded in the name of the owner and may be transferred from one owner to another by mere delivery.

INCOME AND REVENUE BONDS. **Income bonds** pay no interest unless the issuing company is profitable. **Revenue bonds**, so called because the interest on them is paid from specified revenue sources, are most frequently issued by airports, school districts, counties, toll-road authorities, and governmental bodies.

WHAT DO THE NUMBERS MEAN?

HOW'S THE WEATHER?

One of the more interesting recent innovations in the bond market is bonds whose interest payments are tied to changes in the weather. To understand how these *weather bonds* work, let's look at a recent bond issue by **Koch Industries**. Koch provides energy to utilities, distributors, and others around the country. It feels the heat financially when weather is colder than expected and the company has to buy energy in the open market to serve its clients. It also can experience losses if the weather is warmer than usual.

Koch structured a bond offering designed to deal with this problem. With Koch's bonds, if the weather is colder than normal, the interest rate drops ½ percent for each one-quarter degree decline in average temperature. Conversely, the rate goes up by ½ percent if the weather is warmer by one-quarter of a degree. Investors even lose some of their original investment (principal) if weather deviates significantly from the average. However, certain investors like these risky bonds because they add diversification to their portfolios. Mother Nature, rather than economic factors, affects the bond value, thus providing diversification.

Although weather bonds may sound unusual, more and more companies are issuing catastrophe-type bonds. For example, insurance companies are issuing bonds to protect themselves from catastrophes such as earthquakes and storms. Besides financial conditions, it seems that investors must now be concerned with meteorological matters as well.

Source: Adapted from Gregory Zuckerman and Deborah Lohse, "Weather Bonds Hedge Against Mother Nature's Profit Effects," *Wall Street Journal* (October 26, 1999), p. C1.

OBJECTIVE 3
Describe the accounting valuation for bonds at date of issuance.

VALUATION OF BONDS PAYABLE—DISCOUNT AND PREMIUM

The issuance and marketing of bonds to the public does not happen overnight. It usually takes weeks or even months. Underwriters must be arranged, Securities and Exchange Commission approval must be obtained, audits and issuance of a prospectus may be required, and certificates must be printed. Frequently, the terms in a bond indenture are established well in advance of the sale of the bonds. Between the time the terms are set and the bonds are issued, the market conditions and the financial position of the issuing corporation may change significantly. Such changes affect the marketability of the bonds and thus their selling price.

INTERNATIONAL INSIGHT

Valuation of long-term debt varies internationally. In the U.S., discount and premium are booked and amortized over the life of the debt. In some countries (e.g., Sweden, Japan, Belgium), it is permissible to write off the discount and premium immediately.

The selling price of a bond issue is set by such familiar phenomena as supply and demand among buyers and sellers, relative risk, market conditions, and the state of the economy. The investment community values a bond at the present value of its future cash flows, which consist of (1) interest and (2) principal. The rate used to compute the present value of these cash flows is the interest rate that provides an acceptable return on an investment commensurate with the issuer's risk characteristics.

The interest rate written in the terms of the bond indenture (and ordinarily printed on the bond certificate) is known as the **stated**, **coupon**, or **nominal rate**. This rate, which is set by the issuer of the bonds, is expressed as a percentage of the **face value**, also called the **par value**, **principal amount**, or **maturity value**, of the bonds. If the rate employed by the investment community (buyers) differs from the stated rate, the present value of the bonds computed by the buyers will differ from the face value of the bonds. That present value becomes the bond's current purchase price. The difference between the face value and the present value of the bonds is either a discount or premium.[2] If the bonds sell for less than face value, they are sold at a **discount**. If the bonds sell for more than face value, they are sold at a **premium**.

The rate of interest actually earned by the bondholders is called the **effective yield**, or **market rate**. If bonds sell at a discount, the effective yield is higher than the stated rate. Conversely, if bonds sell at a premium, the effective yield is lower than the stated rate. While the bond is outstanding, its price is affected by several variables, most notably the market rate of interest. There is an inverse relationship between the market interest rate and the price of the bond.

To illustrate the computation of the **present value of a bond issue**, assume that ServiceMaster issues $100,000 in bonds, due in 5 years with 9 percent interest payable annually at year-end. At the time of issue, the market rate for such bonds is 11 percent. The following time diagram depicts both the interest and the principal cash flows.

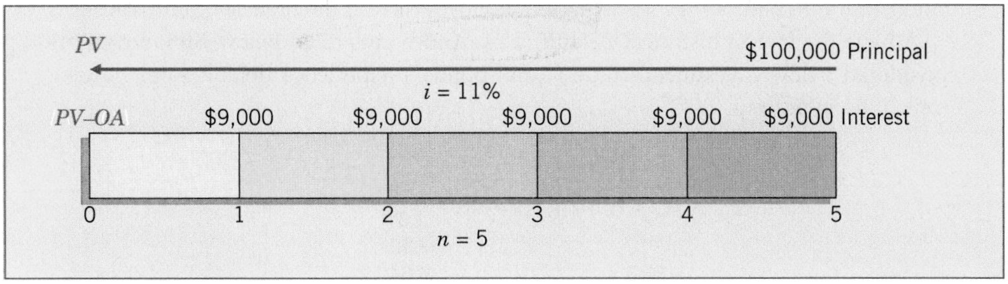

The actual principal and interest cash flows are discounted at an 11 percent rate for 5 periods as shown in Illustration 14-1.

---

[2]Until the 1950s it was common for corporations to issue bonds with low, even-percentage coupons (such as 4 percent) to demonstrate their financial solidity. Frequently, the result was large discounts. More recently, it has become acceptable to set the stated rate of interest on bonds in rather precise fractions (such as 10⅞ percent). Companies usually attempt to align the stated rate as closely as possible with the market or effective rate at the time of issue. While discounts and premiums continue to occur, their absolute magnitude tends to be much smaller; many times it is immaterial. Professor Bill N. Schwartz (Virginia Commonwealth University) studied the 685 new debt offerings in 1985. Of these, none were issued at a premium. Approximately 95 percent were issued either with no discount or at a price above 98. Now, however, zero-interest (deep discount) bonds are more popular, and they cause substantial discounts.

ILLUSTRATION 14-1
Present Value Computation of Bond Selling at a Discount

Present value of the principal:	
$100,000 × .59345 (Table 6-2)	$59,345.00
Present value of the interest payments:	
$9,000 × 3.69590 (Table 6-4)	33,263.10
Present value (selling price) of the bonds	$92,608.10

By paying $92,608.10 at the date of issue, the investors will realize an effective rate or yield of 11 percent over the 5-year term of the bonds. These bonds would sell at a discount of $7,391.90 ($100,000 − $92,608.10). The price at which the bonds sell is typically stated as a percentage of the face or par value of the bonds. For example, the ServiceMaster bonds sold for 92.6 (92.6% of par). If ServiceMaster had received $102,000, we would say the bonds sold for 102 (102% of par).

When bonds sell below face value, it means that investors demand a rate of interest higher than the stated rate. The investors are not satisfied with the stated rate because they can earn a greater rate on alternative investments of equal risk. They cannot change the stated rate, so they refuse to pay face value for the bonds. By changing the amount invested, they alter the effective rate of interest. The investors receive interest at the stated rate computed on the face value, but they are earning at **an effective rate that is higher than the stated rate because they paid less than face value for the bonds.** (An illustration for a bond that sells at a premium is shown later in the chapter, in Illustrations 14-5 and 14-6.)

WHAT DO THE NUMBERS MEAN?

HOW'S MY RATING?

Two major publication companies, **Moody's Investors Service** and **Standard & Poor's Corporation,** issue quality ratings on every public debt issue. The following table summarizes the ratings issued by Standard & Poor's, along with historical default rates on bonds with different ratings. As expected, bonds receiving the highest quality rating of AAA have the lowest historical default rates. And bonds rated below BBB, which are considered below investment grade ("junk bonds") experience default rates ranging from 20 to 50 percent.

Original Rating	Default Rate*
AAA	0.52%
AA	1.31
A	2.32
BBB	6.64
BB	19.52
B	35.76
CCC	54.38

*Percentage of defaults by issuers rated by Standard & Poor's over the past 15 years, based on rating they were initially assigned.
Data: Standard & Poor's Corp.

Because debt ratings reflect credit quality, they are closely monitored by the market when determining the required yield and pricing of bonds at issuance. For example, in late 2001, the spreads in the required yields between corporate investment grade and junk bonds ranged from 6 to 8 percent. For a company such as **WorldCom,** which issued over $11 billion in debt in 2001, every 1 percent of yield it saves by maintaining a higher credit rating translates into over $100 million dollars of reduced interest expense. Thus, it is not surprising that companies also keep a close watch on their credit rating.

Source: A. Borrus, M. McNamee, and H. Timmons, "The Credit Raters: How They Work and How They Might Work Better," *Business Week* (April 8, 2002), pp. 38–40.

Bonds Issued at Par on Interest Date

When bonds are issued on an interest payment date at par (face value), no interest has accrued and no premium or discount exists. The accounting entry is made simply for the cash proceeds and the face value of the bonds. To illustrate, if 10-year term bonds with a par value of $800,000, dated January 1, 2004, and bearing interest at an annual rate of 10 percent payable semiannually on January 1 and July 1, are issued on January 1 at par, the entry on the books of the issuing corporation would be:

Cash	800,000	
Bonds Payable		800,000

The entry to record the first semiannual interest payment of $40,000 ($800,000 × .10 × 1/2) on July 1, 2004, would be as follows.

Bond Interest Expense	40,000	
Cash		40,000

The entry to record accrued interest expense at December 31, 2004 (year-end) would be as follows.

Bond Interest Expense	40,000	
Bond Interest Payable		40,000

Bonds Issued at Discount or Premium on Interest Date

OBJECTIVE 4
Apply the methods of bond discount and premium amortization.

If the $800,000 of bonds illustrated above were issued on January 1, 2004, at 97 (meaning 97% of par), the issuance would be recorded as follows.

Cash ($800,000 × .97)	776,000	
Discount on Bonds Payable	24,000	
Bonds Payable		800,000

Because of its relation to interest, as previously discussed, **the discount is amortized and charged to interest expense over the period of time that the bonds are outstanding.** Under the **straight-line method**,[3] the amount amortized each year is a constant amount. For example, using the bond discount above of $24,000, the amount amortized to interest expense each year for 10 years is $2,400 ($24,000 ÷ 10 years), and if amortization is recorded annually, it is recorded as follows.

Bond Interest Expense	2,400	
Discount on Bonds Payable		2,400

At the end of the first year, 2004, as a result of the amortization entry above, the unamortized balance in Discount on Bonds Payable is $21,600 ($24,000 − $2,400).

If the bonds were dated and sold on October 1, 2004, and if the fiscal year of the corporation ended on December 31, the discount amortized during 2004 would be only 3/12 of 1/10 of $24,000, or $600. Three months of accrued interest must also be recorded on December 31.

Premium on Bonds Payable is accounted for in a manner similar to that for Discount on Bonds Payable. If the 10-year bonds of a par value of $800,000 are dated and sold on January 1, 2004, at 103, the following entry is made to record the issuance.

Cash ($800,000 × 1.03)	824,000	
Premium on Bonds Payable		24,000
Bonds Payable		800,000

---

[3]Although the effective interest method is preferred for amortization of discount or premium, to keep these initial illustrations simple, we have chosen to use the straight-line method (which is acceptable if the results obtained are not materially different from those produced by the effective interest method).

At the end of 2004 and for each year the bonds are outstanding, the entry to amortize the premium on a straight-line basis is:

Premium on Bonds Payable	2,400	
Bond Interest Expense		2,400

Bond interest expense is increased by amortization of a discount and decreased by amortization of a premium. Amortization of a discount or premium under the effective interest method is discussed later.

Some bonds are callable by the issuer after a certain date at a stated price. This call feature gives the issuing corporation the opportunity to reduce its bonded indebtedness or take advantage of lower interest rates. **Whether callable or not, any premium or discount must be amortized over the life to maturity date because early redemption (call of the bond) is not a certainty.**

Bonds Issued between Interest Dates

Bond interest payments are usually made semiannually on dates specified in the bond indenture. When bonds are issued on other than the interest payment dates, **buyers of the bonds will pay the seller the interest accrued from the last interest payment date to the date of issue**. The purchasers of the bonds, in effect, pay the bond issuer in advance for that portion of the full 6-months' interest payment to which they are not entitled, not having held the bonds during that period. **The purchasers will receive the full 6-months' interest payment on the next semiannual interest payment date.**

To illustrate, if 10-year bonds of a par value of $800,000, dated January 1, 2004, and bearing interest at an annual rate of 10 percent payable semiannually on January 1 and July 1, are issued on March 1, 2004, at **par plus accrued interest**, the entry on the books of the issuing corporation is:

Cash	813,333	
Bonds Payable		800,000
Bond Interest Expense ($800,000 × .10 × 2/12)		13,333
(Interest Payable might be credited instead)		

The purchaser advances 2 months' interest, because on July 1, 2004, 4 months after the date of purchase, 6 months' interest will be received from the issuing company. The company makes the following entry on July 1, 2004.

Bond Interest Expense	40,000	
Cash		40,000

The expense account now contains a debit balance of $26,667, which represents the proper amount of interest expense, 4 months at 10 percent on $800,000.

The illustration above was simplified by having the January 1, 2004, bonds issued on March 1, 2004, **at par**. If, however, the 10 percent bonds were issued at 102, the entry on March 1 on the books of the issuing corporation would be:

Cash [($800,000 × 1.02) + ($800,000 × .10 × 2/12)]	829,333	
Bonds Payable		800,000
Premium on Bonds Payable ($800,000 × .02)		16,000
Bond Interest Expense		13,333

The premium would be amortized **from the date of sale**, March 1, 2004, not from the date of the bonds, January 1, 2004.

EFFECTIVE INTEREST METHOD

The profession's preferred procedure for amortization of a discount or premium is the **effective interest method** (also called **present value amortization**). Under the effective interest method:

1. Bond interest expense is computed first by multiplying the **carrying value**[4] of the bonds at the beginning of the period by the effective interest rate.
2. The bond discount or premium amortization is then determined by comparing the bond interest expense with the interest to be paid.

The computation of the amortization is depicted graphically as follows.

ILLUSTRATION 14-2
Bond Discount and Premium Amortization Computation

Bond Interest Expense	−	Bond Interest Paid	=	Amortization Amount
Carrying Value of Bonds at Beginning of Period × Effective Interest Rate	−	Face Amount of Bonds × Stated Interest Rate	=	Amortization Amount

The effective interest method produces a periodic interest expense equal to **a constant percentage of the carrying value of the bonds**. Since the percentage is the effective rate of interest incurred by the borrower at the time of issuance, the effective interest method results in a better matching of expenses with revenues than does the straight-line method.

Both the effective interest and straight-line methods result in the **same total amount of interest expense over the term of the bonds**, and the annual amounts of interest expense are generally quite similar. However, **when the annual amounts are materially different, the effective interest method is required under generally accepted accounting principles**.

Bonds Issued at a Discount

To illustrate amortization of a discount, Evermaster Corporation issued $100,000 of 8 percent term bonds on January 1, 2004, due on January 1, 2009, with interest payable each July 1 and January 1. Because the investors required an effective interest rate of 10 percent, they paid $92,278 for the $100,000 of bonds, creating a $7,722 discount. The $7,722 discount is computed as follows.[5]

ILLUSTRATION 14-3
Computation of Discount on Bonds Payable

Maturity value of bonds payable		$100,000
Present value of $100,000 due in 5 years at 10%, interest payable semiannually (Table 6-2); $FV(PVF_{10,5\%})$; ($100,000 × .61391)	$61,391	
Present value of $4,000 interest payable semiannually for 5 years at 10% annually (Table 6-4); $R(PVF\text{-}OA_{10,5\%})$; ($4,000 × 7.72173)	30,887	
Proceeds from sale of bonds		92,278
Discount on bonds payable		$ 7,722

Illustration 14-4 (on page 678) provides a schedule of bond discount amortization over a 5-year period.

[4]The **book value**, also called the **carrying value**, equals the face amount minus any unamortized discount or plus any unamortized premium.

[5]Because interest is paid semiannually, the interest rate used is 5 percent (10% × 6/12). The number of periods is 10 (5 years × 2).

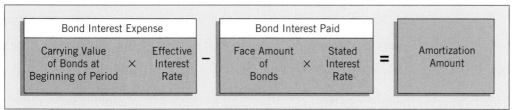

ILLUSTRATION 14-4
Bond Discount Amortization Schedule

Calculator Solution for Present Value of Bonds:

	Inputs	Answer
N	10	
I/YR	5	
PV	?	92,278
PMT	–4,000	
FV	–100,000	

SCHEDULE OF BOND DISCOUNT AMORTIZATION
EFFECTIVE INTEREST METHOD—SEMIANNUAL INTEREST PAYMENTS
5-YEAR, 8% BONDS SOLD TO YIELD 10%

Date	Cash Paid	Interest Expense	Discount Amortized	Carrying Amount of Bonds
1/1/04				$ 92,278
7/1/04	$ 4,000[a]	$ 4,614[b]	$ 614[c]	92,892[d]
1/1/05	4,000	4,645	645	93,537
7/1/05	4,000	4,677	677	94,214
1/1/06	4,000	4,711	711	94,925
7/1/06	4,000	4,746	746	95,671
1/1/07	4,000	4,783	783	96,454
7/1/07	4,000	4,823	823	97,277
1/1/08	4,000	4,864	864	98,141
7/1/08	4,000	4,907	907	99,048
1/1/09	4,000	4,952	952	100,000
	$40,000	$47,722	$7,722	

[a]$4,000 = $100,000 × .08 × 6/12
[b]$4,614 = $92,278 × .10 × 6/12
[c]$614 = $4,614 – $4,000
[d]$92,892 = $92,278 + $614

The entry to record the issuance of Evermaster Corporation's bonds at a discount on January 1, 2004, is:

Cash	92,278	
Discount on Bonds Payable	7,722	
Bonds Payable		100,000

The journal entry to record the first interest payment on July 1, 2004, and amortization of the discount is:

Bond Interest Expense	4,614	
Discount on Bonds Payable		614
Cash		4,000

The journal entry to record the interest expense accrued at December 31, 2004 (year-end) and amortization of the discount is:

Bond Interest Expense	4,645	
Bond Interest Payable		4,000
Discount on Bonds Payable		645

Bonds Issued at a Premium

If the market had been such that the investors were willing to accept an effective interest rate of 6 percent on the bond issue described above, they would have paid $108,530 or a premium of $8,530, computed as follows.

ILLUSTRATION 14-5
Computation of Premium on Bonds Payable

Maturity value of bonds payable		$100,000
Present value of $100,000 due in 5 years at 6%, interest payable semiannually (Table 6-2); $FV(PVF_{10,3\%})$; ($100,000 × .74409)	$74,409	
Present value of $4,000 interest payable semiannually for 5 years at 6% annually (Table 6-4); $R(PVF\text{-}OA_{10,3\%})$; ($4,000 × 8.53020)	34,121	
Proceeds from sale of bonds		108,530
Premium on bonds payable		$ 8,530

Illustration 14-6 (on page 679) provides a schedule of bond premium amortization over a 5-year period.

SCHEDULE OF BOND PREMIUM AMORTIZATION
EFFECTIVE INTEREST METHOD—SEMIANNUAL INTEREST PAYMENTS
5-YEAR, 8% BONDS SOLD TO YIELD 6%

Date	Cash Paid	Interest Expense	Premium Amortized	Carrying Amount of Bonds
1/1/04				$108,530
7/1/04	$ 4,000[a]	$ 3,256[b]	$ 744[c]	107,786[d]
1/1/05	4,000	3,234	766	107,020
7/1/05	4,000	3,211	789	106,231
1/1/06	4,000	3,187	813	105,418
7/1/06	4,000	3,162	838	104,580
1/1/07	4,000	3,137	863	103,717
7/1/07	4,000	3,112	888	102,829
1/1/08	4,000	3,085	915	101,914
7/1/08	4,000	3,057	943	100,971
1/1/09	4,000	3,029	971	100,000
	$40,000	$31,470	$8,530	

[a]$4,000 = $100,000 × .08 × 6/12
[b]$3,256 = $108,530 × .06 × 6/12
[c]$744 = $4,000 − $3,256
[d]$107,786 = $108,530 − $744

ILLUSTRATION 14-6
Bond Premium Amortization Schedule

Calculator Solution for Present Value of Bonds:

	Inputs	Answer
N	10	
I/YR	3	
PV	?	108,530
PMT	−4,000	
FV	−100,000	

The entry to record the issuance of Evermaster bonds at a premium on January 1, 2004, is:

Cash	108,530	
Premium on Bonds Payable		8,530
Bonds Payable		100,000

The journal entry to record the first interest payment on July 1, 2004, and amortization of the premium is:

Bond Interest Expense	3,256	
Premium on Bonds Payable	744	
Cash		4,000

The discount or premium should be amortized as an adjustment to interest expense over the life of the bond in such a way as to result in a **constant rate of interest** when applied to the carrying amount of debt outstanding at the beginning of any given period.[6] Although the effective interest method is recommended, the straight-line method is permitted if the results obtained are not materially different from those produced by the effective interest method.

Accruing Interest

In our previous examples, the interest payment dates and the date the financial statements were issued were the same. For example, when Evermaster sold bonds at a premium (page 677), the two interest payment dates coincided with the financial reporting dates. However, what happens if Evermaster wishes to report financial statements at the end of February 2004? In this case, the premium is prorated by the appropriate number of months to arrive at the proper interest expense as follows.

Interest accrual ($4,000 × 2/6)	$1,333.33
Premium amortized ($744 × 2/6)	(248.00)
Interest expense (Jan.–Feb.)	$1,085.33

ILLUSTRATION 14-7
Computation of Interest Expense

[6]"Interest on Receivables and Payables," *Opinions of the Accounting Principles Board No. 21* (New York: AICPA, 1971), par. 16.

The journal entry to record this accrual is as follows.

Bond Interest Expense	1,085.33	
Premium on Bonds Payable	248.00	
Bond Interest Payable		1,333.33

If the company prepares financial statements 6 months later, the same procedure is followed. That is, the premium amortized would be as follows.

ILLUSTRATION 14-8
Computation of Premium Amortization

Premium amortized (March–June) ($744 × 4/6)	$496.00
Premium amortized (July–August) ($766 × 2/6)	255.33
Premium amortized (March–August 2004)	$751.33

The computation is much simpler if the straight-line method is employed. For example, in the Evermaster situation, the total premium is $8,530, which is allocated evenly over the 5-year period. Thus, premium amortization per month is $142.17 ($8,530 ÷ 60 months).

Classification of Discount and Premium

Discount on bonds payable is **not an asset** because it does not provide any future economic benefit. The enterprise has the use of the borrowed funds, but must pay interest for that use. A bond discount means that the company borrowed less than the face or maturity value of the bond and therefore is faced with an actual (effective) interest rate higher than the stated (nominal) rate. Conceptually, discount on bonds payable is a liability valuation account. That is, it is a reduction of the face or maturity amount of the related liability.[7] This account is referred to as a **contra account**.

Premium on bonds payable has no existence apart from the related debt. The lower interest cost results because the proceeds of borrowing exceed the face or maturity amount of the debt. Conceptually, premium on bonds payable is a liability valuation account. That is, it is an addition to the face or maturity amount of the related liability.[8] This account is referred to as an **adjunct account**. As a result, the profession requires that **bond discount and bond premium be reported as a direct deduction from or addition to the face amount of the bond**.

COSTS OF ISSUING BONDS

The issuance of bonds involves engraving and printing costs, legal and accounting fees, commissions, promotion costs, and other similar charges. According to *APB Opinion No. 21*, these items should be debited to a **deferred charge account** (asset) for Unamortized Bond Issue Costs and amortized over the life of the debt, in a manner similar to that used for discount on bonds.[9]

The FASB, however, in *Concepts Statement No. 6* takes the position that debt issue cost can be treated as either an expense or a reduction of the related debt liability. Debt issue cost is not considered an asset because it provides no future economic benefit. The cost of issuing bonds, in effect, reduces the proceeds of the bonds issued and in-

[7]"Elements of Financial Statements of Business Enterprises," *Statement of Financial Accounting Concepts No. 6* (Stamford, Conn.: FASB, 1985), par. 236.

[8]Ibid., par. 238.

[9]"Interest on Receivables and Payables," op. cit., par. 15.

creases the effective interest rate. Thus it may be accounted for the same as the unamortized discount.

There is an obvious difference between GAAP and *Concepts Statement No. 3*'s view of debt issue costs. Until a standard is issued to supersede *Opinion No. 21*, however, **acceptable GAAP for debt issue costs is to treat them as a deferred charge and amortize them over the life of the debt.**

To illustrate the accounting for costs of issuing bonds, assume that Microchip Corporation sold $20,000,000 of 10-year debenture bonds for $20,795,000 on January 1, 2005 (also the date of the bonds). Costs of issuing the bonds were $245,000. The entries at January 1, 2005, and December 31, 2005, for issuance of the bonds and amortization of the bond issue costs would be as follows.

January 1, 2005		
Cash	20,550,000	
Unamortized Bond Issue Costs	245,000	
Premium on Bonds Payable		795,000
Bonds Payable		20,000,000
(To record issuance of bonds)		
December 31, 2005		
Bond Issue Expense	24,500	
Unamortized Bond Issue Costs		24,500
(To amortize one year of bond issue costs—straight-line method)		

Although the bond issue costs should be amortized using the effective interest method, the straight-line method is generally used in practice because it is easier and the results are not materially different.

TREASURY BONDS

Bonds payable that have been reacquired by the issuing corporation or its agent or trustee and have not been canceled are known as **treasury bonds**. They should be shown on the balance sheet at par value—as a deduction from the bonds payable issued, to arrive at a net figure representing bonds payable outstanding. When they are sold or canceled, the Treasury Bonds account should be credited.

EXTINGUISHMENT OF DEBT

OBJECTIVE 5
Describe the accounting procedures for the extinguishment of debt.

How is the payment of debt—often referred to as **extinguishment of debt**—recorded? If the bonds (or any other form of debt security) are held to maturity, the answer is straightforward: No gain or loss is computed. Any premium or discount and any issue costs will be fully amortized at the date the bonds mature. As a result, the carrying amount will be equal to the maturity (face) value of the bond. Because the maturity or face value is also equal to the bond's market value at that time, no gain or loss exists.

In some cases, debt is extinguished before its maturity date.[10] The amount paid on extinguishment or redemption before maturity, including any call premium and ex-

[10]Some companies have attempted to extinguish debt through an in-substance defeasance. **In-substance defeasance** is an arrangement whereby a company provides for the future repayment of one or more of its long-term debt issues by placing purchased securities in an irrevocable trust, the principal and interest of which are pledged to pay off the principal and interest of its own debt securities as they mature. The company, however, is not legally released from its primary obligation for the debt that is still outstanding. In some cases, debt holders are not even aware of the transaction and continue to look to the company for repayment. This practice is not considered an extinguishment of debt, and therefore no gain or loss is recorded.

pense of reacquisition, is called the **reacquisition price**. On any specified date, the **net carrying amount** of the bonds is the amount payable at maturity, adjusted for unamortized premium or discount and cost of issuance. Any excess of the net carrying amount over the reacquisition price is a **gain from extinguishment**. In contrast, the excess of the reacquisition price over the net carrying amount is a **loss from extinguishment**. At the time of reacquisition, **the unamortized premium or discount, and any costs of issue applicable to the bonds, must be amortized up to the reacquisition date**.

To illustrate, assume that on January 1, 1994, General Bell Corp. issued bonds with a par value of $800,000 at 97, due in 20 years. Bond issue costs totaling $16,000 were incurred. Eight years after the issue date, the entire issue is called at 101 and canceled.[11] The loss on redemption (extinguishment) is computed as follows. (Straight-line amortization is used for simplicity.)

ILLUSTRATION 14-9
Computation of Loss on Redemption of Bonds

Reacquisition price ($800,000 × 1.01)		$808,000
Net carrying amount of bonds redeemed:		
Face value	$800,000	
Unamortized discount ($24,000* × 12/20)	(14,400)	
Unamortized issue costs ($16,000 × 12/20)		
(both amortized using straight-line basis)	(9,600)	776,000
Loss on redemption		$ 32,000

*[$800,000 × (1 − .97)]

The entry to record the reacquisition and cancellation of the bonds is:

Bonds Payable	800,000	
Loss on Redemption of Bonds	32,000	
Discount on Bonds Payable		14,400
Unamortized Bond Issue Costs		9,600
Cash		808,000

It is often advantageous for the issuing corporation to acquire the entire outstanding bond issue and replace it with a new bond issue bearing a lower rate of interest. The replacement of an existing issuance with a new one is called **refunding**. Whether the early redemption or other extinguishment of outstanding bonds is a non-refunding or a refunding situation, the difference (gain or loss) between the reacquisition price and the net carrying amount of the redeemed bonds should be recognized currently in income of the period of redemption.[12]

[11]The issuer of callable bonds is generally required to exercise the call on an interest date. Therefore, the amortization of any discount or premium will be up to date and there will be no accrued interest. However, early extinguishments through purchases of bonds in the open market are more likely to be on other than an interest date. If the purchase is not made on an interest date, the discount or premium must be amortized and the interest payable must be accrued from the last interest date to the date of purchase.

[12]Until recently, gains and losses on extinguishment of debt were reported as extraordinary items. In response to concerns that such gains or losses are neither unusual nor infrequent, the FASB eliminated extraordinary item treatment for extinguishment of debt. "Recission of *FASB Statements No. 4, 44,* and *64* and Technical Corrections," *Statement of Financial Accounting Standards No. 145* (Norwalk, Conn.: FASB, 2002).

MORE DEBT, PLEASE

WHAT DO THE NUMBERS MEAN?

As shown in the following charts, growth of U.S. corporate and consumer debt is outpacing the growth in assets. This increase in debt levels is sparking some concern for stock prices, with corporate debt exceeding \$4.9 trillion and consumer debt exceeding \$7.5 trillion in 2001. Both are more than twice their 1989 levels.

Growth Rates for Corporate and Consumer Debt and Assets

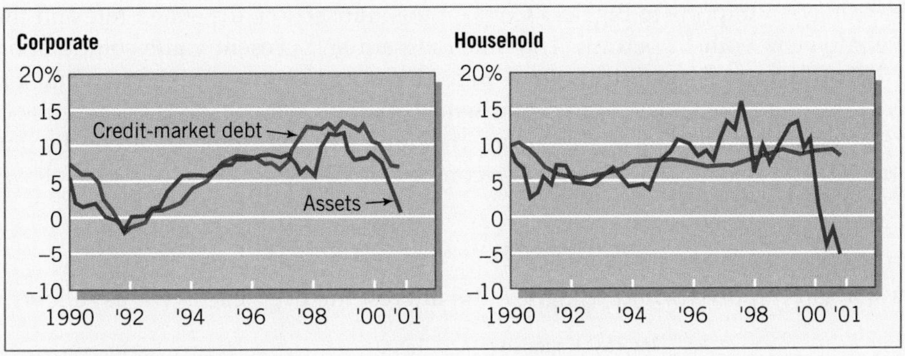

Increasing debt levels can be good indicators of the vibrancy of the economy, especially when the borrowed money is used to expand productive capacity or communications networks to better serve growing customer demand. Unfortunately, a substantial amount of the money borrowed by corporations in the recent debt run-up was used in share buybacks, some of which were used to compensate management via stock option plans.

Source: Adapted from Gregory Zuckerman, "Climb of Corporate Debt Trips Analysts' Alarm," *Wall Street Journal* (December 31, 2001), p. C1.

LONG-TERM NOTES PAYABLE — SECTION 2

OBJECTIVE 6
Explain the accounting procedures for long-term notes payable.

The difference between current notes payable and **long-term notes payable** is the maturity date. As discussed in Chapter 13, short-term notes payable are expected to be paid within a year or the operating cycle—whichever is longer. Long-term notes are similar in substance to bonds in that both have fixed maturity dates and carry either a stated or implicit interest rate. However, notes do not trade as readily as bonds in the organized public securities markets. Noncorporate and small corporate enterprises issue notes as their long-term instruments. In contrast, larger corporations issue both long-term notes and bonds.

Accounting for notes and bonds is quite similar. **Like a bond, a note is valued at the present value of its future interest and principal cash flows, with any discount or premium being similarly amortized over the life of the note.**[13] The computation

[13]According to *APB Opinion No. 21*, all payables that represent commitments to pay money at a determinable future date are subject to present value measurement techniques, except for the following specifically excluded types:

1. Normal accounts payable due within one year.
2. Security deposits, retainages, advances, or progress payments.
3. Transactions between parent and subsidiary.
4. Convertible debt securities.
5. Obligations payable at some indeterminable future date.

of the present value of an **interest-bearing note**, the recording of its issuance, and the amortization of any discount or premium and accrual of interest are as shown for bonds on pages 673–680 of this chapter.

As you might expect, accounting for long-term notes payable parallels accounting for long-term notes receivable as was presented in Chapter 7.

NOTES ISSUED AT FACE VALUE

In Chapter 7, we discussed the recognition of a $10,000, 3-year note issued at face value by Scandinavian Imports to Bigelow Corp. In this transaction, the stated rate and the effective rate were both 10 percent. The time diagram and present value computation on page 327 of Chapter 7 (see Illustration 7-8) for Bigelow Corp. would be the same for the issuer of the note, Scandinavian Imports, in recognizing a note payable. Because the present value of the note and its face value are the same, $10,000, no premium or discount is recognized. The issuance of the note is recorded by Scandinavian Imports as follows.

Cash	10,000	
Notes Payable		10,000

Scandinavian Imports would recognize the interest incurred each year as follows.

Interest Expense	1,000	
Cash		1,000

NOTES NOT ISSUED AT FACE VALUE

Zero-Interest-Bearing Notes

Calculator Solution for Effective Interest on Note:

	Inputs	Answer
N	8	
I/YR	?	15
PV	-327	
PMT	0	
FV	1,000	

If a zero-interest-bearing (non-interest-bearing) note[14] is issued solely for cash, its present value is measured by the cash received by the issuer of the note. The implicit interest rate is the **rate that equates the cash received with the amounts received in the future**. The difference between the face amount and the present value (cash received) is recorded as **a discount and amortized to interest expense over the life of the note**.

An example of such a transaction is Beneficial Corporation's offering of $150 million of zero-coupon notes (deep discount bonds) having an 8-year life. With a face value of $1,000 each, these notes sold for $327—a deep discount of $673 each. The present value of each note is the cash proceeds of $327. The interest rate can be calculated by determining the interest rate that equates the amount currently paid by the investor with those amounts to be received in the future. Thus, Beneficial amortized the discount over the 8-year life of the notes using an effective interest rate of 15 percent.[15]

To illustrate the entries and the amortization schedule, assume that your company is the one that issued the 3-year, $10,000, zero-interest-bearing note to Jeremiah Company as illustrated on page 328 of Chapter 7 (notes receivable). The implicit rate that equated the total cash to be paid ($10,000 at maturity) to the present value of the future cash flows ($7,721.80 cash proceeds at date of issuance) was 9 percent (The present value of $1 for 3 periods at 9 percent is $0.77218.) The time diagram depicting the one cash flow is shown at the top of page 684.

[14]Although the term "note" is used throughout this discussion, the basic principles and methodology are equally applicable to other long-term debt instruments.

[15] $\$327 = \$1{,}000\ (PVF_{8,i})$

$$PVF_{8,i} = \frac{\$327}{\$1{,}000} = .327$$

$.327 = 15\%$ (in Table 6-2 locate .32690).

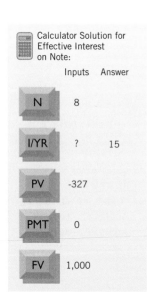

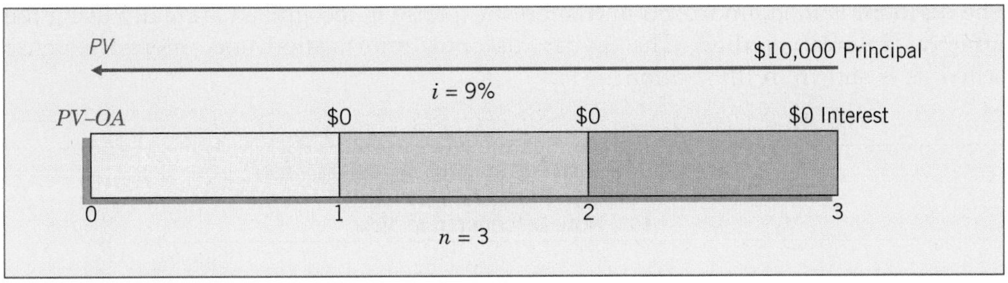

Your entry to record issuance of the note is as follows.

Cash	7,721.80	
Discount on Notes Payable	2,278.20	
Notes Payable		10,000.00

The discount is amortized and interest expense is recognized annually using the **effective interest method**. The 3-year discount amortization and interest expense schedule is shown in Illustration 14-10. (This schedule is similar to the note receivable schedule of Jeremiah Company in Illustration 7-9.)

ILLUSTRATION 14-10
Schedule of Note Discount Amortization

SCHEDULE OF NOTE DISCOUNT AMORTIZATION
EFFECTIVE INTEREST METHOD
0% NOTE DISCOUNTED AT 9%

	Cash Paid	Interest Expense	Discount Amortized	Carrying Amount of Note
Date of issue				$ 7,721.80
End of year 1	$-0-	$ 694.96[a]	$ 694.96[b]	8,416.76[c]
End of year 2	-0-	757.51	757.51	9,174.27
End of year 3	-0-	825.73[d]	825.73	10,000.00
	$-0-	$2,278.20	$2,278.20	

[a]$7,721.80 × .09 = $694.96
[b]$694.96 − 0 = $694.96
[c]$7,721.80 + $694.96 = $8,416.76
[d]5¢ adjustment to compensate for rounding

Interest expense at the end of the first year using the effective interest method is recorded as follows.

Interest Expense ($7,721.80 × 9%)	694.96	
Discount on Notes Payable		694.96

The total amount of the discount, $2,278.20 in this case, represents the expense to be incurred on the note over the 3 years.

Interest-Bearing Notes

The zero-interest-bearing note above is an example of the extreme difference between the stated rate and the effective rate. In many cases, the difference between these rates is not so great. Take, for example, the illustration from Chapter 7 where Marie Co. issued a $10,000, 3-year note bearing interest at 10 percent to Morgan Corp. for cash. The market rate of interest for a note of similar risk is 12 percent. The time diagram depicting the cash flows and the computation of the present value of this note are shown on page 329 (Illustration 7-10). In this case, because the effective rate of interest (12%) is greater than the stated rate (10%), the present value of the note is less than the face value. That is, the note is exchanged at a **discount**. The issuance of the note is recorded by Marie Co. as follows.

Cash	9,520	
Discount on Notes Payable	480	
Notes Payable		10,000

The discount is then amortized and interest expense is recognized annually using the **effective interest method**. The 3-year discount amortization and interest expense schedule is shown in Illustration 14-11.

ILLUSTRATION 14-11
Schedule of Note Discount Amortization

SCHEDULE OF NOTE DISCOUNT AMORTIZATION
EFFECTIVE INTEREST METHOD
10% NOTE DISCOUNTED AT 12%

	Cash Paid	Interest Expense	Discount Amortized	Carrying Amount of Note
Date of issue				$ 9,520
End of year 1	$1,000[a]	$1,142[b]	$142[c]	9,662[d]
End of year 2	1,000	1,159	159	9,821
End of year 3	1,000	1,179	179	10,000
	$3,000	$3,480	$480	

[a]$10,000 × 10% = $1,000
[b]$9,520 × 12% = $1,142
[c]$1,142 − $1,000 = $142
[d]$9,520 + $142 = $9,662

Payment of the annual interest and amortization of the discount for the first year are recorded by Marie Co. as follows (amounts per amortization schedule).

Interest Expense	1,142	
Discount on Bonds Payable		142
Cash		1,000

When the present value exceeds the face value, the note is exchanged at a premium. The premium on a note payable is recorded as a credit and amortized using the effective interest method over the life of the note as annual reductions in the amount of interest expense recognized.

SPECIAL NOTES PAYABLE SITUATIONS

Notes Issued for Property, Goods, and Services

Sometimes, when a note is issued, property, goods, or services may be received. When the debt instrument is exchanged for property, goods, or services in a bargained transaction entered into at arm's length, the stated interest rate is presumed to be fair unless:

1. No interest rate is stated, or
2. The stated interest rate is unreasonable, or
3. The stated face amount of the debt instrument is materially different from the current cash sales price for the same or similar items or from the current market value of the debt instrument.

In these circumstances the present value of the debt instrument is measured by the fair value of the property, goods, or services or by an amount that reasonably approximates the market value of the note.[16] **The interest element other than that evidenced by any stated rate of interest is the difference between the face amount of the note and the fair value of the property.**

For example, assume that Scenic Development Company sold land having a cash sale price of $200,000 to Health Spa, Inc. in exchange for Health Spa's 5-year, $293,860 zero-interest-bearing note. The $200,000 cash sale price represents the present value of the $293,860 note discounted at 8 percent for 5 years. If the transaction is recorded by both parties on the sale date at the face amount of the note, $293,860, Health Spa's Land

[16]"Interest on Receivables and Payables," op. cit., par. 12.

account and Scenic's sales would be overstated by $93,860, because the $93,860 represents the interest for 5 years at an effective rate of 8 percent. Interest revenue to Scenic and interest expense to Health Spa for the 5-year period correspondingly would be understated by $93,860.

Because the difference between the cash sale price of $200,000 and the $293,860 face amount of the note represents interest at an effective rate of 8 percent, the transaction is recorded at the exchange date as follows.

ILLUSTRATION 14-12
Entries for Noncash Note Transactions

Health Spa, Inc. Books			Scenic Development Company Books		
Land	200,000		Notes Receivable	293,860	
Discount on Notes Payable	93,860		Discount on Notes Rec.		93,860
Notes Payable		293,860	Sales		200,000

During the 5-year life of the note, Health Spa amortizes annually a portion of the discount of $93,860 as a charge to interest expense. Scenic Development records interest revenue totaling $93,860 over the 5-year period by also amortizing the discount. The effective interest method is required, although other approaches to amortization may be used if the results obtained are not materially different from those that result from the effective interest method.

Choice of Interest Rate

In note transactions, the effective or real interest rate is either evident or determinable by other factors involved in the exchange, such as the fair market value of what is given or received. But, if the fair value of the property, goods, services, or other rights is not determinable, and if the note has no ready market, the problem of determining the present value of the note is more difficult. To estimate the present value of a note under such circumstances, an applicable interest rate that may differ from the stated interest rate must be approximated. This process of interest-rate approximation is called **imputation**, and the resulting interest rate is called an **imputed interest rate**.

The choice of a rate is affected by the prevailing rates for similar instruments of issuers with similar credit ratings. It is also affected specifically by restrictive covenants, collateral, payment schedule, the existing prime interest rate, etc. Determination of the imputed interest rate is made when the note is issued; any subsequent changes in prevailing interest rates are ignored.

To illustrate, assume that on December 31, 2004, Wunderlich Company issued a promissory note to Brown Interiors Company for architectural services. The note has a face value of $550,000, a due date of December 31, 2009, and bears a stated interest rate of 2 percent, payable at the end of each year. The fair value of the architectural services is not readily determinable, nor is the note readily marketable. On the basis of the credit rating of Wunderlich Company, the absence of collateral, the prime interest rate at that date, and the prevailing interest on Wunderlich's other outstanding debt, an 8 percent interest rate is imputed as appropriate in this circumstance. The time diagram depicting both cash flows is shown as follows.

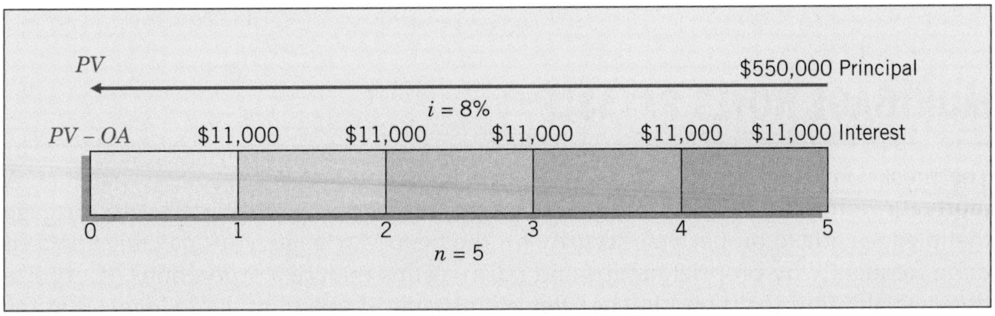

The present value of the note and the imputed fair value of the architectural services are determined as follows.

ILLUSTRATION 14-13
Computation of Imputed Fair Value and Note Discount

Face value of the note		$550,000
Present value of $550,000 due in 5 years at 8% interest payable annually (Table 6-2); $FV(PVF_{5,8\%})$; ($550,000 × .68058)	$374,319	
Present value of $11,000 interest payable annually for 5 years at 8%; $R(PVF\text{-}OA_{5,8\%})$; ($11,000 × 3.99271)	43,920	
Present value of the note		418,239
Discount on notes payable		$131,761

The issuance of the note in payment for the architectural services is recorded as follows.

December 31, 2004		
Building (or Construction in Process)	418,239	
Discount on Notes Payable	131,761	
Notes Payable		550,000

The 5-year amortization schedule appears below.

ILLUSTRATION 14-14
Schedule of Discount Amortization Using Imputed Interest Rate

SCHEDULE OF NOTE DISCOUNT AMORTIZATION
EFFECTIVE INTEREST METHOD
2% NOTE DISCOUNTED AT 8% (IMPUTED)

Date	Cash Paid (2%)	Interest Expense (8%)	Discount Amortized	Carrying Amount of Note
12/31/04				$418,239
12/31/05	$11,000[a]	$ 33,459[b]	$ 22,459[c]	440,698[d]
12/31/06	11,000	35,256	24,256	464,954
12/31/07	11,000	37,196	26,196	491,150
12/31/08	11,000	39,292	28,292	519,442
12/31/09	11,000	41,558[e]	30,558	550,000
	$55,000	$186,761	$131,761	

[a]$550,000 × 2% = $11,000
[b]$418,239 × 8% = $33,459
[c]$33,459 − $11,000 = $22,459
[d]$418,239 + $22,459 = $440,698
[e]$3 adjustment to compensate for rounding.

Calculator Solution for the Fair Value of Services:

	Inputs	Answer
N	5	
I/YR	8	
PV	?	418,239
PMT	11,000	
FV	550,000	

Payment of the first year's interest and amortization of the discount is recorded as follows.

December 31, 2005		
Interest Expense	33,459	
Discount on Notes Payable		22,459
Cash		11,000

MORTGAGE NOTES PAYABLE

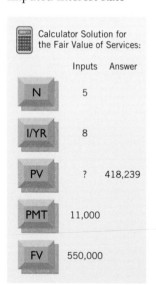

The most common form of long-term notes payable is a mortgage note payable. A **mortgage note payable** is a promissory note secured by a document called a mortgage that pledges title to property as security for the loan. Mortgage notes payable are used more frequently by proprietorships and partnerships than by corporations. (Corporations usually find that bond issues offer advantages in obtaining large loans.) On the balance sheet, the liability should be reported using a title such as "Mortgage Notes Payable" or "Notes Payable—Secured," with a brief disclosure of the property pledged in notes to the financial statements.

The borrower usually receives cash in the face amount of the mortgage note. In that case, the face amount of the note is the true liability and no discount or premium is involved. When "points" are assessed by the lender, however, the total amount paid by the borrower exceeds the face amount of the note.[17] Points raise the effective interest rate above the rate specified in the note. A point is 1 percent of the face of the note. For example, assume that a 20-year mortgage note in the amount of $100,000 with a stated interest rate of 10.75 percent is given by you to Local Savings and Loan Association as part of the financing of your new house. If Local Savings demands 4 points to close the financing, you will receive 4 percent less than $100,000—or $96,000—but you will be obligated to repay the entire $100,000 at the rate of $1,015 per month. Because you received only $96,000, and must repay $100,000, your effective interest rate is increased to approximately 11.3 percent on the money you actually borrowed.

Mortgages may be payable in full at maturity or in installments over the life of the loan. If payable at maturity, the mortgage payable is shown as a long-term liability on the balance sheet until such time as the approaching maturity date warrants showing it as a current liability. If it is payable in installments, the current installments due are shown as current liabilities, with the remainder shown as a long-term liability.

The traditional **fixed-rate mortgage** has been partially supplanted with alternative mortgage arrangements. Most lenders offer **variable-rate mortgages** (also called floating-rate or adjustable rate mortgages) featuring interest rates tied to changes in the fluctuating market rate. Generally the variable-rate lenders adjust the interest rate at either 1- or 3-year intervals, pegging the adjustments to changes in the prime rate or the U.S. Treasury bond rate.

REPORTING AND ANALYSIS OF LONG-TERM DEBT — SECTION 3

Reporting of long-term debt is one of the most controversial areas in financial reporting. Because long-term debt has a significant impact on the cash flows of the company, reporting requirements must be substantive and informative. One problem is that the definition of a liability established in *Concepts Statement No. 6* and the recognition criteria established in *Concepts Statement No. 5* are sufficiently imprecise that arguments can still be made that certain obligations need not be reported as debt.

OFF-BALANCE-SHEET FINANCING

OBJECTIVE 7
Explain the reporting of off-balance-sheet financing arrangements.

What do **Krispy Kreme, Cisco, Enron,** and **Adelphia Communications** have in common? They all have been accused of using off-balance-sheet financing to minimize the reporting of debt on their balance sheets. **Off-balance-sheet financing** is an attempt to borrow monies in such a way that the obligations are not recorded. It has become an issue of extreme importance because many allege that Enron, in one of the largest corporate failures on record, hid a considerable amount of its debt off the balance sheet. As a result, any company that uses off-balance-sheet financing today is taking the risk that investors (given their concerns about what happened at Enron) will dump their stock, and share price will suffer. Nevertheless, a considerable amount of off-balance-sheet financing will continue to exist. As one writer noted, "The basic drives of humans are few: to get enough food, to find shelter, and to keep debt off the balance sheet."

[17]Points, in mortgage financing, are analogous to the original issue discount of bonds.

Different Forms

Off-balance-sheet financing can take many different forms. Here are a few examples:

1. **Non-Consolidated Subsidiary:** Under present GAAP, a parent company does not have to consolidate a subsidiary company that is less than 50 percent owned. In such cases, the parent therefore does not report the assets and liabilities of the subsidiary. All the parent reports on its balance sheet is the investment in the subsidiary. As a result, users of the financial statements may not understand that the subsidiary has considerable debt for which the parent may ultimately be liable if the subsidiary runs into financial difficulty.
2. **Special Purpose Entity (SPE):** A **special purpose entity** is an entity created by a company to perform a special project. To illustrate, assume that Clarke Company has decided to build a new factory. In determining whether to build the new factory, an important variable in the decision is that management does not want to report on its balance sheet the borrowing used to fund the construction. It therefore creates an SPE whose sole purpose is to build the plant (referred to as a **project financing arrangement**). The SPE finances and builds the plant, and then Clarke Company guarantees that all the products produced by the plant will be purchased, either by Clarke Company or some outside party. (Some refer to this as a **take-or-pay contract**). As a result, Clarke Company does not report the asset or liability on its books. It should be emphasized that the accounting rules in this area are complex, but a company can achieve this objective with relative ease.
3. **Operating Leases:** Another way that companies keep debt off the balance sheet is by leasing. Instead of owning the assets, companies lease them. Again, by meeting certain conditions, the company has to report only rent expense each period and to provide note disclosure of the transaction. It should be noted that SPEs often use leases to accomplish off-balance-sheet treatment. Accounting for lease transactions is discussed extensively in Chapter 21.

Rationale

Why do companies engage in off-balance-sheet financing? A major reason is that many believe that **removing debt enhances the quality of the balance sheet** and permits credit to be obtained more readily and at less cost.

Second, loan covenants often impose a limitation on the amount of debt a company may have. As a result, off-balance-sheet financing is used, because **these types of commitments might not be considered in computing the debt limitation.**

Third, it is argued by some that the asset side of the balance sheet is severely understated. For example, companies that use LIFO costing for inventories and depreciate assets on an accelerated basis will often have carrying amounts for inventories and property, plant, and equipment that are much lower than their current values. As an offset to these lower values, some managements believe that part of the debt does not have to be reported. In other words, **if assets were reported at current values**, less pressure would undoubtedly exist for off-balance-sheet financing arrangements.

Whether the arguments above have merit is debatable. The general idea "out of sight, out of mind" may not be true in accounting. Many users of financial statements indicate that they factor these off-balance-sheet financing arrangements into their computations when assessing debt to equity relationships. Similarly, many loan covenants also attempt to take these complex arrangements into account. Nevertheless, many companies still believe that benefits will accrue if certain obligations are not reported on the balance sheet.

The FASB's response to off-balance-sheet financing arrangements has been increased disclosure (note) requirements. In addition, the SEC, in response to the Sarbanes-Oxley Act of 2002, now requires companies in their Management Discussion and

Analysis section to provide information on (1) all contractual obligations in a tabular format and (2) contingent liabilities and commitments in either a textual or tabular format.[18] The authors believe that financial reporting would be enhanced if more obligations were recorded on the balance sheet instead of merely described in the notes to the financial statements. Given the problems with companies such as **Enron, Dynergy, Williams Companies, Adelphia Communications**, and **Calpine**, our expectation is that less off-balance-sheet financing will occur in the future.

PRESENTATION AND ANALYSIS OF LONG-TERM DEBT

Presentation of Long-Term Debt

OBJECTIVE 8
Indicate how long-term debt is presented and analyzed.

Companies that have large amounts and numerous issues of long-term debt frequently report only one amount in the balance sheet and support this with comments and schedules in the accompanying notes. Long-term debt that **matures within one year** should be reported as a current liability, unless retirement is to be accomplished with other than current assets. If the debt is to be refinanced, converted into stock, or is to be retired from a bond retirement fund, it should continue to be reported as non-current and accompanied with a note explaining the method to be used in its liquidation.[19]

Note disclosures generally indicate the nature of the liabilities, maturity dates, interest rates, call provisions, conversion privileges, restrictions imposed by the creditors, and assets designated or pledged as security. Any assets pledged as security for the debt should be shown in the assets section of the balance sheet. The fair value of the long-term debt should also be disclosed if it is practical to estimate fair value. Finally, disclosure is required of future payments for sinking fund requirements and maturity amounts of long-term debt during each of the next 5 years.[20] The purpose of these disclosures is to aid financial statement users in evaluating the amounts and timing of future cash flows. An example of the type of information provided is shown on page 692 for **Best Buy Co.**

Note that if the company has any unconditional long-term obligations (such as project financing arrangements) that are not reported in the balance sheet, extensive note disclosure must be provided.[21]

Analysis of Long-Term Debt

Long-term creditors and stockholders are interested in a company's long-run solvency, particularly its ability to pay interest as it comes due and to repay the face value of the debt at maturity. Debt to total assets and times interest earned are two ratios that provide information about debt-paying ability and long-run solvency.

The **debt to total assets ratio** measures the percentage of the total assets provided by creditors. It is computed as shown in Illustration 14-15 by dividing total debt (both current and long-term liabilities) by total assets.

[18]It is unlikely that accounting regulators will be able to stop all types of off-balance-sheet transactions. Financial information is the Holy Grail of Wall Street. Developing new financial instruments and arrangements to sell and market to customers is not only profitable, but also adds to the prestige of the investment firms that create them. Thus, new financial products will continue to appear that will test the ability of regulators to develop appropriate accounting standards for them.

[19]"Balance Sheet Classification of Short-Term Obligations Expected to Be Refinanced," *FASB Statement of Financial Accounting Standards No. 6* (Stamford, Conn.: FASB, 1975), par. 15. See also "Disclosure of Information about Capital Structure," *FASB Statement of Financial Accounting Standards No. 129* (Norwalk, Conn.: FASB, 1997), par. 4.

[20]"Disclosure of Long-Term Obligations," *Statement of Financial Accounting Standards No. 47* (Stamford, Conn.: FASB, 1981), par. 10.

[21]Ibid., par. 7.

ILLUSTRATION 14-15
Computation of Debt to Total Assets Ratio

$$\text{Debt to total assets} = \frac{\text{Total debt}}{\text{Total assets}}$$

The higher the percentage of debt to total assets, the greater the risk that the company may be unable to meet its maturing obligations.

ILLUSTRATION 14-16
Long-Term Debt Disclosure

Best Buy Co.
(dollars in thousands)

	March 3, 2001	Feb. 26, 2000
Total current assets	$2,928,663	$2,238,460
Current liabilities		
Accounts payable	$1,772,722	$1,313,940
Accrued compensation and related expenses	154,159	102,065
Accrued liabilities	545,590	287,888
Accrued income taxes	127,287	65,366
Current portion of long-term debt	114,940	15,790
Total current liabilities	2,714,698	1,785,049
Long-term liabilities	121,952	99,448
Long-term debt (Note 3.)	181,009	14,860

Note 3. Debt (in part)

	March 3, 2001	Feb. 26, 2000
Senior subordinated notes, face amount $109,500, unsecured, due 2003, interest rate 9.0%, effective rate 8.9%	$ 110,471	$ —
Senior subordinated notes, face amount $150,000, unsecured, due 2008, interest rate 9.9%, effective rate 8.5%	160,574	—
Mortgage and other debt, interest rates ranging from 5.3% to 9.4%	24,904	30,650
Total debt	295,949	30,650
Less current portion	(114,940)	(15,790)
Long-term debt	$ 181,009	$ 14,860

The mortgage and other debt are secured by certain property and equipment with a net book value of $43,500 and $35,600 at March 3, 2001, and February 26, 2000, respectively.
During fiscal 2001, 2000, and 1999, interest paid totaled $7,000, $5,300, and $23,800, respectively.
During fiscal 2001, 2000, and 1999, interest expense totaled $6,900, $5,100, and $19,400, respectively, and is included in net interest income. The fair value of long-term debt approximates the carrying value.
The future maturities of long-term debt consist of the following:

Fiscal Year	
2002	$114,940
2003	2,036
2004	895
2005	745
2006	810
Thereafter	176,523
	$295,949

The **times interest earned ratio** indicates the company's ability to meet interest payments as they come due. It is computed by dividing income before interest expense and income taxes by interest expense, as shown in Illustration 14-17.

$$\text{Times interest earned} = \frac{\text{Income before income taxes and interest expense}}{\text{Interest expense}}$$

ILLUSTRATION 14-17
Computation of Times Interest Earned Ratio

To illustrate these ratios, we will use data from **Best Buy**'s 2001 Annual Report, which disclosed total liabilities of $3,018 million, total assets of $4,840 million, interest expense of $6.9 million, income taxes of $246 million, and net income of $396 million. Best Buy's debt to total assets and times interest earned ratios are computed as follows.

$$\text{Debt to total assets} = \frac{\$3{,}018}{\$4{,}840} = 62.4\%$$

$$\text{Times interest earned} = \frac{(\$396 + \$6.9 + \$246)}{\$6.9} = 94 \text{ times}$$

ILLUSTRATION 14-18
Computation of Long-Term Debt Ratios for Best Buy

Even though Best Buy has a relatively high debt to total assets percentage of 62.4, its interest coverage of 94 times indicates it can easily meet its interest payments as they come due.

SUMMARY OF LEARNING OBJECTIVES

1 Describe the formal procedures associated with issuing long-term debt. Incurring long-term debt is often a formal procedure. The bylaws of corporations usually require approval by the board of directors and the stockholders before bonds can be issued or other long-term debt arrangements can be contracted. Generally, long-term debt has various covenants or restrictions. The covenants and other terms of the agreement between the borrower and the lender are stated in the bond indenture or note agreement.

2 Identify various types of bond issues. Types of bond issues are: (1) *Secured and unsecured bonds.* (2) *Term, serial, and callable bonds.* (3) *Convertible, commodity-backed, and deep discount bonds.* (4) *Registered and bearer (coupon) bonds.* (5) *Income and revenue bonds.* The variety in the types of bonds is a result of attempts to attract capital from different investors and risk takers and to satisfy the cash flow needs of the issuers.

3 Describe the accounting valuation for bonds at date of issuance. The investment community values a bond at the present value of its future cash flows, which consist of interest and principal. The rate used to compute the present value of these cash flows is the interest rate that provides an acceptable return on an investment commensurate with the issuer's risk characteristics. The interest rate written in the terms of the bond indenture and ordinarily appearing on the bond certificate is the stated, coupon, or nominal rate. This rate, which is set by the issuer of the bonds, is expressed as a percentage of the face value, also called the par value, principal amount, or maturity value, of the bonds. If the rate employed by the buyers differs from the stated rate, the present value of the bonds computed by the buyers will differ from the face value of the bonds. The difference between the face value and the present value of the bonds is either a discount or premium.

4 Apply the methods of bond discount and premium amortization. The discount (premium) is amortized and charged (credited) to interest expense over the period of time that the bonds are outstanding. Bond interest expense is increased by amortization of a discount and decreased by amortization of a premium. The profession's preferred procedure for amortization of a discount or premium is the effective interest method. Under the effective interest method, (1) bond interest expense is computed by multiplying the carrying value of the bonds at the beginning of the period by the effective

KEY TERMS

bearer (coupon) bonds, *672*
bond discount, *673*
bond indenture, *671*
bond premium, *673*
callable bonds, *671*
carrying value, *677*
commodity-backed bonds, *672*
convertible bonds, *671*
debenture bonds, *671*
debt to total assets ratio, *691*
deep discount (zero-interest) debenture bonds, *672*
effective interest method, *676*
effective yield, or market rate, *673*
extinguishment of debt, *681*
face, par, principal or maturity value, *673*
imputed interest rate, *687*
income bonds, *672*
long-term debt, *670*
long-term notes payable, *683*
mortgage notes payable, *688*

interest rate, and (2) the bond discount or premium amortization is then determined by comparing the bond interest expense with the interest to be paid.

5 Describe the accounting procedures for the extinguishment of debt. At the time of reacquisition, the unamortized premium or discount and any costs of issue applicable to the debt must be amortized up to the reacquisition date. The amount paid on extinguishment or redemption before maturity, including any call premium and expense of reacquisition, is the reacquisition price. On any specified date, the net carrying amount of the debt is the amount payable at maturity, adjusted for unamortized premium or discount and cost of issuance. Any excess of the net carrying amount over the reacquisition price is a gain from extinguishment. The excess of the reacquisition price over the net carrying amount is a loss from extinguishment. Gains and losses on extinguishments are recognized currently in income.

6 Explain the accounting procedures for long-term notes payable. Accounting procedures for notes and bonds are quite similar. Like a bond, a note is valued at the present value of its future interest and principal cash flows, with any discount or premium being similarly amortized over the life of the note. Whenever the face amount of the note does not reasonably represent the present value of the consideration given or received in the exchange, the entire arrangement must be evaluated to properly record the exchange and the subsequent interest.

7 Explain the reporting of off-balance-sheet financing arrangements. Off-balance-sheet financing is an attempt to borrow funds in such a way that the obligations are not recorded. Examples of off-balance-sheet arrangements are (1) non-consolidated subsidiaries, (2) special purpose entities, and (3) operating leases.

8 Indicate how long-term debt is presented and analyzed. Companies that have large amounts and numerous issues of long-term debt frequently report only one amount in the balance sheet and support this with comments and schedules in the accompanying notes. Any assets pledged as security for the debt should be shown in the assets section of the balance sheet. Long-term debt that matures within one year should be reported as a current liability, unless retirement is to be accomplished with other than current assets. If the debt is to be refinanced, converted into stock, or is to be retired from a bond retirement fund, it should continue to be reported as non-current and accompanied with a note explaining the method to be used in its liquidation. Disclosure is required of future payments for sinking fund requirements and maturity amounts of long-term debt during each of the next 5 years. Debt to total assets and times interest earned are two ratios that provide information about debt-paying ability and long-run solvency.

APPENDIX 14A

Accounting for Troubled Debt

During periods of depressed economic conditions or other financial hardship, some debtors have difficulty meeting their financial obligations. For example, owing to rising interest rates and corporate mismanagement, the savings and loan industry experienced a decade of financial crises. The banking industry also faced credit concerns: During the late 1980s bad energy loans and the rescheduling of loans between "less developed countries," such as Argentina, Brazil, and Mexico, and major U.S. banks created considerable uncertainty about the soundness of our banking system. Electric utilities with large nuclear plant construction programs suffered from the financial strains of illiquidity. More recently, companies such as **Xerox**, **Kmart**, and **Polaroid** had to restructure their debts or in some other way be bailed out of negative cash flow situations when the economy, technology, competition, or a combination thereof, turned against them.

ACCOUNTING ISSUES

The major accounting issues related to troubled debt situations involve recognition and measurement. In other words, when should a loss be recognized and at what amount?

To illustrate the major issue related to recognition, assume that Metro Bank has a \$10,000,000, 5-year, 10 percent loan to Brazil, with interest receivable annually. At the end of the third year, Metro Bank has determined that it probably will be able to collect only \$7,000,000 of this loan at maturity. Should it wait until the loan becomes uncollectible, or should it record a loss immediately? The general recognition principle is this: **Losses should be recorded immediately if it is probable that the loss will occur.**

Assuming that Metro Bank decides to record a loss, at what amount should the loss be recorded? Three alternatives are:

1. ***Aggregate Cash Flows.*** Some argue that a loss should not be recorded unless the aggregate cash flows from the loan are less than its carrying amount. In the Metro Bank example, the aggregate cash flows expected are \$7,000,000 of principal and \$2,000,000 of interest (\$10,000,000 × 10% × 2), for a total of \$9,000,000. Thus, a loss of only \$1,000,000 (\$10,000,000 − \$9,000,000) would be reported.

   Advocates of this position argue that Metro Bank will recover \$9,000,000 of the \$10,000,000, and therefore its loss is only \$1,000,000. Others disagree, noting that this approach ignores present values. That is, the present value of the future cash flows is much less than \$9,000,000, and therefore the loss is much greater than \$1,000,000.

2. ***Present Value—Historical Effective Rate.*** Those who argue for the use of present value, however, disagree about the interest rate to use to discount the expected future cash flows. The two rates discussed are the **historical (original) effective rate** and the **market rate** at the time the loan is recognized as troubled.

   Those who favor the historical effective rate believe that losses should reflect only a deterioration in credit quality. When the historical effective loan rate is used, the value of the investment will change only if some of the legally contracted cash flows are reduced. A loss in this case is recognized because the expected future cash flows have changed. Interest rate changes caused by current economic events that affect the fair value of the loan are ignored.

3. ***Present Value—Market Rate.*** Others believe that expected future cash flows of a troubled loan should be discounted at market interest rates, which reflect current economic events and conditions that are commensurate with the risks involved. The historical effective interest rate reflects the risk characteristics of the loan at the time it was originated or acquired, but not at the time it is troubled. In short, proponents of the market rate believe that a fair value measure should be used.

OBJECTIVE 9
Distinguish among and account for: (1) a loss on loan impairment, (2) a troubled debt restructuring that results in the settlement of a debt, and (3) a troubled debt restructuring that results in a continuation of debt with modification of terms.

This appendix addresses issues concerning the accounting by debtors and creditors for troubled debt. Two different types of situations result with troubled debt:

1. Impairments.
2. Restructurings:
   - **a.** Settlements.
   - **b.** Modification of terms.

In a troubled debt situation, the creditor usually first recognizes a loss on impairment. Subsequently either the terms of the loan are modified, or the loan is settled on terms unfavorable to the creditor. In unusual cases, the creditor forces the debtor into bankruptcy in order to ensure the highest possible collection on the loan. Illustration 14A-1 shows this continuum.

ILLUSTRATION 14A-1
Usual Progression in Troubled Debt Situations

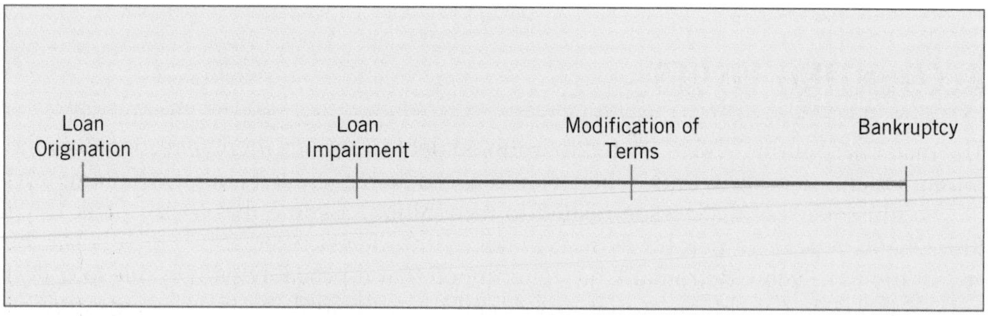

IMPAIRMENTS

A loan[1] is considered **impaired** when, based on current information and events, it is **probable**[2] that the creditor will be unable to collect all amounts due (both principal and interest) according to the contractual terms of the loan. Creditors should apply their normal review procedures in making the judgment as to the probability of collection.[3] If a loan is considered impaired, the loss due to the **impairment** should be measured as the difference between the investment in the loan (generally the principal plus accrued interest) and the expected future cash flows discounted at the loan's historical effective interest rate.[4] In estimating future cash flows the creditor should employ all reasonable and supportable assumptions and projections.[5]

Illustration of Loss on Impairment

On December 31, 2003, Prospect Inc. issued a $500,000, 5-year, zero-interest-bearing note to Community Bank. The note was issued to yield 10 percent annual interest. As a result, Prospect received and Community Bank paid $310,460 ($500,000 × .62092) on December 31, 2003.[6] A time diagram at the top of the next page illustrates the factors involved.

[1]*FASB Statement No. 114*, "Accounting by Creditors for Impairment of a Loan" (Norwalk, Conn.: FASB, May 1993), defines a loan as "a contractual right to receive money on demand or on fixed and determinable dates that is recognized as an asset in the creditor's statement of financial position." For example, accounts receivable with terms exceeding one year are considered loans.

[2]Recall the definitions of probable, reasonably possible, and remote with respect to contingencies, as defined in *FASB Statement No. 5*.

[3]Normal review procedures include examination of "watch lists," review of regulatory reports of examination, and examination of management reports of total loan amounts by borrower.

[4]The creditor may also, for the sake of expediency, use the market price of the loan (if such a price is available) or the fair value of collateral if it is a collateralized loan. *FASB Statement No. 114*, par. 13.

[5]*FASB Statement No. 114*, par. 15.

[6]Present value of $500,000 due in 5 years at 10%, annual compounding (Table 6-2) equals $500,000 × .62092.

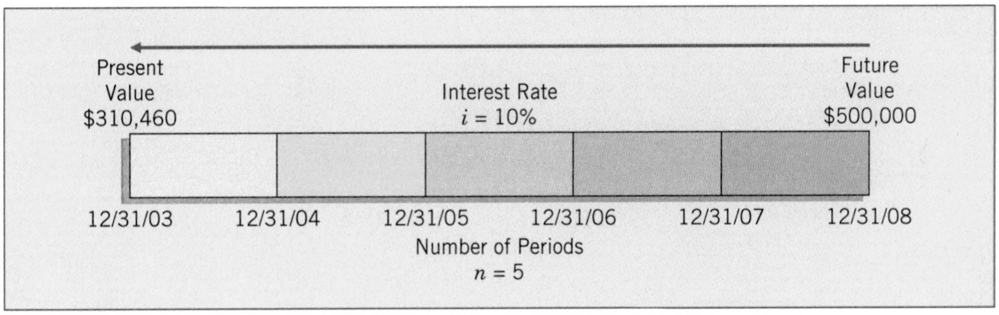

The entries to record this transaction on the books of Community Bank (creditor) and Prospect Inc. (debtor) are as follows.

ILLUSTRATION 14A-2
Creditor and Debtor Entries to Record Note

December 31, 2003					
Community Bank (Creditor)			**Prospect Inc. (Debtor)**		
Notes Receivable	500,000		Cash	310,460	
Discount on Notes Receivable		189,540	Discount on Notes Payable	189,540	
Cash		310,460	Notes Payable		500,000

Assuming that Community Bank and Prospect Inc. use the effective interest method to amortize discounts, Illustration 14A-3 shows the amortization of the discount and the increase in the carrying amount of the note over the life of the note.

ILLUSTRATION 14A-3
Schedule of Interest and Discount Amortization (Before Impairment)

COMMUNITY BANK

Date	Cash Received (0%)	Interest Revenue (10%)	Discount Amortized	Carrying Amount of Note
12/31/03				$310,460
12/31/04	$0	$ 31,046[a]	$ 31,046	341,506[b]
12/31/05	0	34,151	34,151	375,657
12/31/06	0	37,566	37,566	413,223
12/31/07	0	41,322	41,322	454,545
12/31/08	0	45,455	45,455	500,000
Total	$0	$189,540	$189,540	

[a]$31,046 = $310,460 × .10
[b]$341,506 = $310,460 + $31,046

Unfortunately, during 2005 Prospect's business deteriorated due to increased competition and a faltering regional economy. After reviewing all available evidence at December 31, 2005, Community Bank determined that it was probable that Prospect would pay back only $300,000 of the principal at maturity. As a result, Community Bank decided that the loan was impaired and that a loss should be recorded immediately.

To determine the loss, the first step is to compute the present value of the expected cash flows discounted at the historical effective rate of interest. This amount is $225,396. The time diagram on the next page highlights the factors involved in this computation.

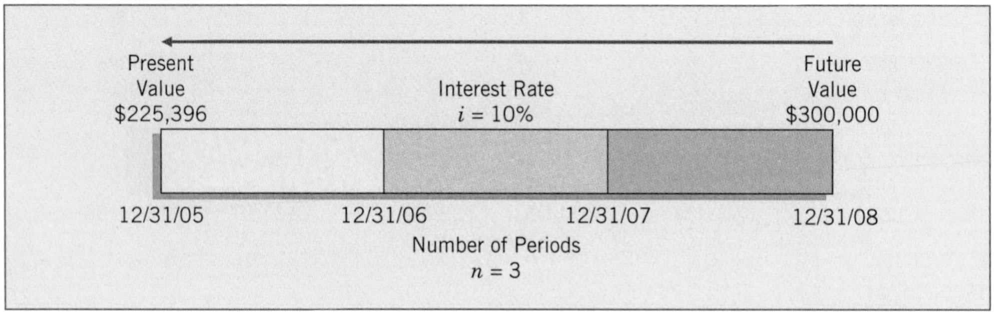

The loss due to impairment is equal to the difference between the present value of the expected future cash flows and the recorded carrying amount of the investment in the loan. The calculation of the loss is shown in Illustration 14A-4.

ILLUSTRATION 14A-4
Computation of Loss Due to Impairment

Carrying amount of investment (12/31/05)—Illustration 14A-3	$375,657
Less: Present value of $300,000 due in 3 years at 10% interest compounded annually (Table 6-2); $FV(PVF_{3,10\%})$; ($300,000 × .75132)	225,396
Loss due to impairment	$150,261

The loss due to the impairment is $150,261, not $200,000 ($500,000 − $300,000). The reason is that the loss is measured at a present value amount, not an undiscounted amount, at the time the loss is recorded.

The entry to record the loss is as follows.

ILLUSTRATION 14A-5
Creditor and Debtor Entries to Record Loss on Note

December 31, 2005

Community Bank (Creditor)			Prospect Inc. (Debtor)
Bad Debt Expense	150,261		No entry
Allowance for Doubtful Accounts		150,261	

Community Bank (creditor) debits Bad Debt Expense for the expected loss. At the same time, it reduces the overall value of its loan receivable by crediting Allowance for Doubtful Accounts.[7] On the other hand, Prospect Inc. (debtor) makes no entry because it still legally owes $500,000.[8]

---

[7]In the event that the loan is written off, the loss is charged against the allowance. In subsequent periods, if the estimated expected cash flows are revised based on new information, the allowance account and bad debt account are adjusted (either increased or decreased depending whether conditions improved or worsened) in the same fashion as the original impairment. The terms "loss" and "bad debt expense" are used interchangeably throughout this discussion. Losses related to receivables transactions should be charged to Bad Debt Expense or the related Allowance for Doubtful Accounts because these are the accounts used to recognize changes in values affecting receivables.

[8]Many alternatives are permitted to recognize income in subsequent periods. See *FASB Statement No. 118*, "Accounting by Creditors for Impairment of a Loan—Income Recognition and Disclosures" (Norwalk, Conn.: FASB, October 1994) for appropriate methods.

TROUBLED DEBT RESTRUCTURINGS

A **troubled debt restructuring** occurs when a creditor "for economic or legal reasons related to the debtor's financial difficulties grants a concession to the debtor that it would not otherwise consider."[9] Thus a **troubled debt restructuring** does not apply to modifications of a debt obligation that reflect general economic conditions that dictate a reduction in interest rates. Nor does it apply to the refunding of an old debt with new debt having an effective interest rate approximately equal to that of similar debt issued by nontroubled debtors.

A troubled debt restructuring involves one of two basic types of transactions:

1. Settlement of debt at less than its carrying amount.
2. Continuation of debt with a modification of terms.

Settlement of Debt

A transfer of noncash assets (real estate, receivables, or other assets) or the issuance of the debtor's stock can be used to settle a debt obligation in a troubled debt restructuring. In these situations, **the noncash assets or equity interest given should be accounted for at their fair market value**. The debtor is required to determine the excess of the carrying amount of the payable over the fair value of the assets or equity transferred (gain). Likewise, the creditor is required to determine the excess of the receivable over the fair value of those same assets or equity interests transferred (loss). The debtor recognizes a gain equal to the amount of the excess, and the creditor normally would charge the excess (loss) against Allowance for Doubtful Accounts. In addition, the debtor recognizes a gain or loss on disposition of assets to the extent that the fair value of those assets differs from their carrying amount (book value).

Transfer of Assets

Assume that American City Bank has loaned $20,000,000 to Union Mortgage Company. Union Mortgage in turn has invested these monies in residential apartment buildings, but because of low occupancy rates it cannot meet its loan obligations. American City Bank agrees to accept from Union Mortgage real estate with a fair market value of $16,000,000 in full settlement of the $20,000,000 loan obligation. The real estate has a recorded value of $21,000,000 on the books of Union Mortgage Company. The entry to record this transaction on the books of American City Bank (creditor) is as follows.

Real Estate	16,000,000	
Allowance for Doubtful Accounts	4,000,000	
Note Receivable from Union Mortgage Company		20,000,000

The real estate is recorded at fair market value, and a charge is made to the Allowance for Doubtful Accounts to reflect the bad debt write-off.

The entry to record this transaction on the books of Union Mortgage Company (debtor) is as follows.

Note Payable to American City Bank	20,000,000	
Loss on Disposition of Real Estate	5,000,000	
Real Estate		21,000,000
Gain on Restructuring of Debt		4,000,000

Union Mortgage Company has a loss on the disposition of real estate in the amount of $5,000,000 (the difference between the $21,000,000 book value and the $16,000,000 fair market value), which should be shown as an ordinary loss on the income statement. In addition, it has a gain on restructuring of debt of $4,000,000 (the difference

[9]"Accounting by Debtors and Creditors for Troubled Debt Restructurings," *FASB Statement No. 15* (Norwalk, Conn.: FASB, June, 1977), par. 1.

between the $20,000,000 carrying amount of the note payable and the $16,000,000 fair market value of the real estate).

Granting of Equity Interest

Assume that American City Bank had agreed to accept from Union Mortgage Company 320,000 shares of Union's common stock ($10 par) that has a fair market value of $16,000,000 in full settlement of the $20,000,000 loan obligation. The entry to record this transaction on the books of American City Bank (creditor) is as follows.

Investment	16,000,000	
Allowance for Doubtful Accounts	4,000,000	
Note Receivable from Union Mortgage Company		20,000,000

The stock received by American City Bank is recorded as an investment at the fair market value at the date of restructure.

The entry to record this transaction on the books of Union Mortgage Company (debtor) is as follows.

Note Payable to American City Bank	20,000,000	
Common Stock		3,200,000
Additional Paid-in Capital		12,800,000
Gain on Restructuring of Debt		4,000,000

The stock issued by Union Mortgage Company is recorded in the normal manner with the difference between the par value and the fair value of the stock recorded as additional paid-in capital.

Modification of Terms

In some cases, a debtor will have serious short-run cash flow problems that lead it to request one or a combination of the following modifications:

1. Reduction of the stated interest rate.
2. Extension of the maturity date of the face amount of the debt.
3. Reduction of the face amount of the debt.
4. Reduction or deferral of any accrued interest.

Under *FASB Statement No. 114*, the creditor's loss is based upon cash flows discounted at the historical effective rate of the loan. The FASB concluded that, "because loans are recorded originally at discounted amounts, the ongoing assessment for impairment should be made in a similar manner."[10] The debtor's gain is calculated based upon **undiscounted amounts**, as required by the previous standard. As a consequence, **the gain recorded by the debtor will not equal the loss recorded by the creditor under many circumstances.**[11]

Two illustrations demonstrate the accounting for a troubled debt restructuring by debtors and creditors:

1. The debtor does not record a gain.
2. The debtor records a gain.

In both instances the creditor has a loss.

[10] *FASB Statement No. 114*, par. 42.

[11] In response to concerns expressed about this nonsymmetric treatment, the FASB stated that *Statement No. 114* does not address debtor accounting because the FASB was concerned that expansion of the scope of the statement would delay its issuance.

Illustration 1—No Gain for Debtor

This illustration demonstrates a restructuring in which no gain is recorded by the debtor.[12] On December 31, 2003, Morgan National Bank enters into a debt restructuring agreement with Resorts Development Company, which is experiencing financial difficulties. The bank restructures a $10,500,000 loan receivable issued at par (interest paid to date) by:

1. Reducing the principal obligation from $10,500,000 to $9,000,000;
2. Extending the maturity date from December 31, 2003, to December 31, 2007; and
3. Reducing the interest rate from 12% to 8%.

Debtor Calculations. The total future cash flow after restructuring of $11,880,000 ($9,000,000 of principal plus $2,880,000 of interest payments[13]) exceeds the total pre-restructuring carrying amount of the debt of $10,500,000. Consequently, **no gain is recorded, and no adjustment is made by the debtor** to the carrying amount of the payable. As a result, no entry is made by Resorts Development Co. (debtor) at the date of restructuring.

A new effective interest rate must be computed by the debtor in order to record interest expense in future periods. The new effective interest rate equates the present value of the future cash flows specified by the new terms with the pre-restructuring carrying amount of the debt. In this case, the new rate is computed by relating the pre-restructure carrying amount ($10,500,000) to the total future cash flow ($11,880,000). The rate necessary to discount the total future cash flow ($11,880,000) to a present value equal to the remaining balance ($10,500,000) is 3.46613 percent.[14]

On the basis of the effective rate of 3.46613 percent, the schedule shown in Illustration 14A-6 is prepared.

RESORTS DEVELOPMENT CO. (DEBTOR)

Date	Cash Paid (8%)	Interest Expense (3.46613%)	Reduction of Carrying Amount	Carrying Amount of Note
12/31/03				$10,500,000
12/31/04	$ 720,000[a]	$ 363,944[b]	$ 356,056[c]	10,143,944
12/31/05	720,000	351,602	368,398	9,775,546
12/31/06	720,000	338,833	381,167	9,394,379
12/31/07	720,000	325,621	394,379	9,000,000
	$2,880,000	$1,380,000	$1,500,000	

[a]$720,000 = $9,000,000 × .08
[b]$363,944 = $10,500,000 × 3.46613%
[c]$356,056 = $720,000 − $363,944

ILLUSTRATION 14A-6
Schedule Showing Reduction of Carrying Amount of Note

Calculator Solution for Interest Rate

	Inputs	Answer
N	4	
I/YR	?	3.466
PV	10,500,000	
PMT	720,000	
FV	9,000,000	

[12]Note that the examples given for restructuring assume no previous entries were made by the creditor for impairment. In actuality it is likely that, in accordance with *Statement No. 114*, the creditor would have already made an entry when the loan initially became impaired, and restructuring would simply require an adjustment of the initial estimated bad debt by the creditor. Recall, however, that the debtor makes no entry upon impairment.

[13]Total interest payments are: $9,000,000 × .08 × 4 years = $2,880,000.

[14]An accurate interest rate i can be found by using the formulas given at the tops of Tables 6-2 and 6-4 to set up the following equation.

$$\$10{,}500{,}000 = \underbrace{\frac{1}{(1+i)^4}}_{\text{(from Table 6-2)}} \times \$9{,}000{,}000 + \underbrace{\frac{1 - \frac{1}{(1+i)^4}}{i}}_{\text{(from Table 6-4)}} \times \$720{,}000$$

Solving algebraically for i, we find that i = 3.46613%.

Thus, on December 31, 2004 (date of first interest payment after restructure), the debtor makes the following entry.

December 31, 2004		
Notes Payable	356,056	
Interest Expense	363,944	
Cash		720,000

A similar entry (except for different amounts for debits to Notes Payable and Interest Expense) is made each year until maturity. At maturity, the following entry is made.

December 31, 2007		
Notes Payable	9,000,000	
Cash		9,000,000

Creditor Calculations. Morgan National Bank (creditor) is required to calculate its loss based upon the expected future cash flows discounted at the historical effective rate of the loan. This loss is calculated as follows.

ILLUSTRATION 14A-7
Computation of Loss to Creditor on Restructuring

Pre-restructure carrying amount		$10,500,000
Present value of restructured cash flows:		
Present value of $9,000,000 due in 4 years at 12%, interest payable annually (Table 6-2); $FV(PVF_{4,12\%})$; ($9,000,000 × .63552)	$5,719,680	
Present value of $720,000 interest payable annually for 4 years at 12% (Table 6-4); $R(PVF\text{-}OA_{4,12\%})$; ($720,000 × 3.03735)	2,186,892	
Present value of restructured cash flows		7,906,572
Loss on restructuring		$ 2,593,428

As a result, Morgan National Bank records a bad debt expense as follows (assuming no allowance balance has been established from recognition of an impairment).

Bad Debt Expense	2,593,428	
Allowance for Doubtful Accounts		2,593,428

In subsequent periods, interest revenue is reported based on the historical effective rate. Illustration 14A-8 provides the following interest and amortization information.

ILLUSTRATION 14A-8
Schedule of Interest and Amortization after Debt Restructuring

MORGAN NATIONAL BANK (CREDITOR)

Date	Cash Received (8%)	Interest Revenue (12%)	Increase of Carrying Amount	Carrying Amount of Note
12/31/03				$7,906,572
12/31/04	$ 720,000[a]	$ 948,789[b]	$ 228,789[c]	8,135,361
12/31/05	720,000	976,243	256,243	8,391,604
12/31/06	720,000	1,006,992	286,992	8,678,596
12/31/07	720,000	1,041,404[d]	321,404[d]	9,000,000
Total	$2,880,000	$3,973,428	$1,093,428	

[a]$720,000 = $9,000,000 × .08
[b]$948,789 = $7,906,572 × .12
[c]$228,789 = $948,789 − $720,000
[d]$28 adjustment to compensate for rounding.

On December 31, 2004, Morgan National Bank would make the following entry.

December 31, 2004		
Cash	720,000	
Allowance for Doubtful Accounts	228,789	
Interest Revenue		948,789

A similar entry (except for different amounts debited to Allowance for Doubtful Accounts and credited to Interest Revenue) is made each year until maturity. At maturity, the following entry is made.

December 31, 2007		
Cash	9,000,000	
Allowance for Doubtful Accounts	1,500,000	
Notes Receivable		10,500,000

Illustration 2—Gain for Debtor

If the pre-restructure carrying amount exceeds the total future cash flows as a result of a modification of the terms, the debtor records a gain. To illustrate, assume the facts in the previous example except that Morgan National Bank reduced the principal to $7,000,000 (and extended the maturity date to December 31, 2007, and reduced the interest from 12 percent to 8 percent). The total future cash flow is now $9,240,000 ($7,000,000 of principal plus $2,240,000 of interest[15]), which is $1,260,000 less than the pre-restructure carrying amount of $10,500,000. Under these circumstances, Resorts Development Company (debtor) would reduce the carrying amount of its payable $1,260,000 and record a gain of $1,260,000. On the other hand, Morgan National Bank (creditor) would debit its Bad Debt Expense for $4,350,444. This computation is shown in Illustration 14A-9.

ILLUSTRATION 14A-9
Computation of Loss to Creditor on Restructuring

Pre-restructure carrying amount		$10,500,000
Present value of restructured cash flows:		
Present value of $7,000,000 due in 4 years at 12%, interest payable annually (Table 6-2); $FV(PVF_{4,12\%})$; ($7,000,000 × .63552)	$4,448,640	
Present value of $560,000 interest payable annually for 4 years at 12% (Table 6-4); $R(PVF\text{-}OA_{4,12\%})$; ($560,000 × 3.03735)	1,700,916	6,149,556
Creditor's loss on restructuring		$ 4,350,444

Entries to record the gain and loss on the debtor's and creditor's books at the date of restructure, December 31, 2003, are shown in Illustration 14A-10.

ILLUSTRATION 14A-10
Debtor and Creditor Entries to Record Gain and Loss on Note

December 31, 2003 (date of restructure)

Resorts Development Co. (Debtor)			Morgan National Bank (Creditor)		
Notes Payable	1,260,000		Bad Debt Expense	4,350,444	
Gain on Restructuring of Debt		1,260,000	Allowance for Doubtful Accounts		4,350,444

[15]Total interest payments are: $7,000,000 × .08 × 4 years = $2,240,000.

For Resorts Development (debtor), because the new carrying value of the note ($10,500,000 − $1,260,000 = $9,240,000) equals the sum of the undiscounted cash flows ($9,240,000), the imputed interest rate is 0 percent. Consequently, all of the future cash flows reduce the principal balance, and no interest expense is recognized. For Morgan National the interest revenue would be reported in the same fashion as the previous example—that is, using the historical effective interest rate applied toward the newly discounted value of the note. Interest computations are shown in Illustration 14A-11.

ILLUSTRATION 14A-11
Schedule of Interest and Amortization after Debt Restructuring

MORGAN NATIONAL BANK (CREDITOR)

Date	Cash Received (8%)	Interest Revenue (12%)	Increase in Carrying Amount	Carrying Amount of Note
12/31/03				$6,149,556
12/31/04	$ 560,000[a]	$ 737,947[b]	$177,947[c]	6,327,503
12/31/05	560,000	759,300	199,300	6,526,803
12/31/06	560,000	783,216	223,216	6,750,019
12/31/07	560,000	809,981[d]	249,981[d]	7,000,000
Total	$2,240,000	$3,090,444	$850,444	

[a]$560,000 = $7,000,000 × .08
[b]$737,947 = $6,149,556 × .12
[c]$177,947 = $737,947 − $560,000
[d]$21 adjustment to compensate for rounding.

ILLUSTRATION 14A-12
Debtor and Creditor Entries to Record Periodic Interest and Final Principal Payments

The following journal entries illustrate the accounting by debtor and creditor for periodic interest payments and final principal payment.

Resorts Development Co. (Debtor)			Morgan National Bank (Creditor)		
December 31, 2004 (date of first interest payment following restructure)					
Notes Payable	560,000		Cash	560,000	
Cash		560,000	Allowance for Doubtful Accounts	177,947	
			Interest Revenue		737,947
December 31, 2005, 2006, and 2007 (dates of 2nd, 3rd, and last interest payments)					
(Debit and credit same accounts as 12/31/04 using applicable amounts from appropriate amortization schedules.)					
December 31, 2007 (date of principal payment)					
Notes Payable	7,000,000		Cash	7,000,000	
Cash		7,000,000	Allowance for Doubtful Accounts	3,500,000	
			Notes Receivable		10,500,000

SUMMARY OF LEARNING OBJECTIVE FOR APPENDIX 14A

KEY TERMS

impairment, *696*
troubled debt restructuring, *699*

9 Distinguish among and account for: (1) a loss on loan impairment, (2) a troubled debt restructuring that results in the settlement of a debt, and (3) a troubled debt restructuring that results in a continuation of debt with modification of terms. An impairment loan loss is based on the difference between the present value of the future cash flows and the carrying amount of the note. There are two types of settlement of debt restructurings: (1) transfer of noncash assets, and (2) granting of equity interest. For accounting purposes there are also two types of restructurings with continuation of debt with modified terms: (1) the carrying amount of debt is less than the future cash flows, and (2) the carrying amount of debt is greater than the total future cash flows.

Note: All **asterisked** Questions, Brief Exercises, Exercises, and Problems relate to material contained in the appendix to the chapter.

QUESTIONS

1. (a) From what sources might a corporation obtain funds through long-term debt? (b) What is a bond indenture? What does it contain? (c) What is a mortgage?

2. Differentiate between term bonds, mortgage bonds, collateral trust bonds, debenture bonds, income bonds, callable bonds, registered bonds, bearer or coupon bonds, convertible bonds, commodity-backed bonds, and deep discount bonds.

3. Distinguish between the following interest rates for bonds payable:

(a) yield rate
(b) nominal rate
(c) stated rate
(d) market rate
(e) effective rate

4. Distinguish between the following values relative to bonds payable:

(a) maturity value
(b) face value
(c) market value
(d) par value

5. Under what conditions of bond issuance does a discount on bonds payable arise? Under what conditions of bond issuance does a premium on bonds payable arise?

6. How should discount on bonds payable be reported on the financial statements? Premium on bonds payable?

7. What are the two methods of amortizing discount and premium on bonds payable? Explain each.

8. Zeno Company sells its bonds at a premium and applies the effective interest method in amortizing the premium. Will the annual interest expense increase or decrease over the life of the bonds? Explain.

9. How should the costs of issuing bonds be accounted for and classified in the financial statements?

10. Where should treasury bonds be shown on the balance sheet? Should treasury bonds be carried at par or at reacquisition cost?

11. What is the "call" feature of a bond issue? How does the call feature affect the amortization of bond premium or discount?

12. Why would a company wish to reduce its bond indebtedness before its bonds reach maturity? Indicate how this can be done and the correct accounting treatment for such a transaction.

13. How are gains and losses from extinguishment of a debt classified in the income statement? What disclosures are required of such transactions?

14. What is done to record properly a transaction involving the issuance of a non-interest-bearing long-term note in exchange for property?

15. How is the present value of a non-interest-bearing note computed?

16. When is the stated interest rate of a debt instrument presumed to be fair?

17. What are the considerations in imputing an appropriate interest rate?

18. Differentiate between a fixed-rate mortgage and a variable-rate mortgage.

19. What disclosures are required relative to long-term debt and sinking fund requirements?

20. What is off-balance-sheet financing? Why might a company be interested in using off-balance-sheet financing?

21. What are some forms of off-balance-sheet financing?

22. What are take-or-pay contracts and through-put contracts?

***23.** What are three measurement bases that might be used to value troubled debt? What are the advantages of each method?

***24.** What are the general rules for measuring and recognizing gain or loss by both the debtor and the creditor in an impairment?

***25.** What are the general rules for measuring gain or loss by both creditor and debtor in a troubled debt restructuring involving a settlement?

***26.** (a) In a troubled debt situation, why might the creditor grant concessions to the debtor?

(b) What type of concessions might a creditor grant the debtor in a troubled debt situation?

(c) What is meant by "impairment" of a loan? Under what circumstances should a creditor or debtor recognize an impaired loan?

***27.** What are the general rules for measuring and recognizing gain or loss by both the debtor and the creditor in a troubled debt restructuring involving a modification of terms?

***28.** What is meant by "accounting symmetry" between the entries recorded by the debtor and creditor in a troubled debt restructuring involving a modification of terms? In what ways is the accounting for troubled debt restructurings and impairments non-symmetrical?

***29.** Under what circumstances would a transaction be recorded as a troubled debt restructuring by only one of the two parties to the transaction?

BRIEF EXERCISES

BE14-1 Ghostbusters Corporation issues $300,000 of 9% bonds, due in 10 years, with interest payable semiannually. At the time of issue, the market rate for such bonds is 10%. Compute the issue price of the bonds.

BE14-2 The Goofy Company issued $200,000 of 10% bonds on January 1, 2005. The bonds are due January 1, 2010, with interest payable each July 1 and January 1. The bonds are issued at face value. Prepare Goofy's journal entries for (a) the January issuance, (b) the July 1 interest payment, and (c) the December 31 adjusting entry.

BE14-3 Assume the bonds in BE14-2 were issued at 98. Prepare the journal entries for (a) January 1, (b) July 1, and (c) December 31. Assume The Goofy Company records straight-line amortization annually on December 31.

BE14-4 Assume the bonds in BE14-2 were issued at 103. Prepare the journal entries for (a) January 1, (b) July 1, and (c) December 31. Assume The Goofy Company records straight-line amortization annually on December 31.

BE14-5 Toy Story Corporation issued $500,000 of 12% bonds on May 1, 2005. The bonds were dated January 1, 2005, and mature January 1, 2010, with interest payable July 1 and January 1. The bonds were issued at face value plus accrued interest. Prepare Toy Story's journal entries for (a) the May 1 issuance, (b) the July 1 interest payment, and (c) the December 31 adjusting entry.

BE14-6 On January 1, 2005, Qix Corporation issued $400,000 of 7% bonds, due in 10 years. The bonds were issued for $372,816, and pay interest each July 1 and January 1. Qix uses the effective interest method. Prepare the company's journal entries for (a) the January 1 issuance, (b) the July 1 interest payment, and (c) the December 31 adjusting entry. Assume an effective interest rate of 8%.

BE14-7 Assume the bonds in BE14-6 were issued for $429,757 and the effective interest rate is 6%. Prepare the company's journal entries for (a) the January 1 issuance, (b) the July 1 interest payment, and (c) the December 31 adjusting entry.

BE14-8 Izzy Corporation issued $400,000 of 7% bonds on November 1, 2005, for $429,757. The bonds were dated November 1, 2005, and mature in 10 years, with interest payable each May 1 and November 1. Izzy uses the effective interest method with an effective rate of 6%. Prepare Izzy's December 31, 2005, adjusting entry.

BE14-9 At December 31, 2005, Treasure Land Corporation has the following account balances:

Bonds payable, due January 1, 2013	$2,000,000
Discount on bonds payable	98,000
Bond interest payable	80,000

Show how the above accounts should be presented on the December 31, 2005, balance sheet, including the proper classifications.

BE14-10 James Bond 007 Corporation issued 10-year bonds on January 1, 2005. Costs associated with the bond issuance were $180,000. Bond uses the straight-line method to amortize bond issue costs. Prepare the December 31, 2005, entry to record 2002 bond issue cost amortization.

BE14-11 On January 1, 2005, Uncharted Waters Corporation retired $600,000 of bonds at 99. At the time of retirement, the unamortized premium was $15,000 and unamortized bond issue costs were $5,250. Prepare the corporation's journal entry to record the reacquisition of the bonds.

BE14-12 Jennifer Capriati, Inc. issued a $100,000, 4-year, 11% note at face value to Forest Hills Bank on January 1, 2005, and received $100,000 cash. The note requires annual interest payments each December 31. Prepare Capriati's journal entries to record (a) the issuance of the note and (b) the December 31 interest payment.

BE14-13 Joe Montana Corporation issued a 4-year, $50,000, zero-interest-bearing note to John Madden Company on January 1, 2005, and received cash of $31,776. The implicit interest rate is 12%. Prepare Montana's journal entries for (a) the January 1 issuance and (b) the December 31 recognition of interest.

BE14-14 Larry Byrd Corporation issued a 4-year, $50,000, 5% note to Magic Johnson Company on January 1, 2005, and received a computer that normally sells for $39,369. The note requires annual interest payments each December 31. The market rate of interest for a note of similar risk is 12%. Prepare Larry Byrd's journal entries for (a) the January 1 issuance and (b) the December 31 interest.

BE14-15 King Corporation issued a 4-year, $50,000, zero-interest-bearing note to Salmon Company on January 1, 2005, and received cash of $50,000. In addition, King agreed to sell merchandise to Salmon at an amount less than regular selling price over the 4-year period. The market rate of interest for similar notes is 12%. Prepare King Corporation's January 1 journal entry.

***BE14-16** Assume that Toni Braxton Company has recently fallen into financial difficulties. By reviewing all available evidence on December 31, 2003, one creditor of Toni Braxton, the National American Bank, determined that Toni Braxton would pay back only 65% of the principal at maturity. As a result, the bank decided that the loan was impaired. If the loss is estimated to be $225,000, what entries should both Toni Braxton and National American Bank make to record this loss?

EXERCISES

E14-1 (Classification of Liabilities) Presented below are various account balances of K.D. Lang Inc.

(a) Unamortized premium on bonds payable, of which $3,000 will be amortized during the next year.
(b) Bank loans payable of a winery, due March 10, 2008. (The product requires aging for 5 years before sale.)
(c) Serial bonds payable, $1,000,000, of which $200,000 are due each July 31.
(d) Amounts withheld from employees' wages for income taxes.
(e) Notes payable due January 15, 2007.
(f) Credit balances in customers' accounts arising from returns and allowances after collection in full of account.
(g) Bonds payable of $2,000,000 maturing June 30, 2006.
(h) Overdraft of $1,000 in a bank account. (No other balances are carried at this bank.)
(i) Deposits made by customers who have ordered goods.

Instructions
Indicate whether each of the items above should be classified on December 31, 2005, as a current liability, a long-term liability, or under some other classification. Consider each one independently from all others; that is, do not assume that all of them relate to one particular business. If the classification of some of the items is doubtful, explain why in each case.

E14-2 (Classification) The following items are found in the financial statements.

(a) Discount on bonds payable
(b) Interest expense (credit balance)
(c) Unamortized bond issue costs
(d) Gain on repurchase of debt
(e) Mortgage payable (payable in equal amounts over next 3 years)
(f) Debenture bonds payable (maturing in 5 years)
(g) Notes payable (due in 4 years)
(h) Premium on bonds payable
(i) Treasury bonds
(j) Income bonds payable (due in 3 years)

Instructions
Indicate how each of these items should be classified in the financial statements.

E14-3 (Entries for Bond Transactions) Presented below are two independent situations.

1. On January 1, 2004, Paul Simon Company issued $200,000 of 9%, 10-year bonds at par. Interest is payable quarterly on April 1, July 1, October 1, and January 1.
2. On June 1, 2004, Graceland Company issued $100,000 of 12%, 10-year bonds dated January 1 at par plus accrued interest. Interest is payable semiannually on July 1 and January 1.

Instructions
For each of these two independent situations, prepare journal entries to record the following.

(a) The issuance of the bonds.
(b) The payment of interest on July 1.
(c) The accrual of interest on December 31.

E14-4 (Entries for Bond Transactions—Straight-Line) Celine Dion Company issued $600,000 of 10%, 20-year bonds on January 1, 2005, at 102. Interest is payable semiannually on July 1 and January 1. Dion Company uses the straight-line method of amortization for bond premium or discount.

Instructions

Prepare the journal entries to record the following.

(a) The issuance of the bonds.
(b) The payment of interest and the related amortization on July 1, 2005.
(c) The accrual of interest and the related amortization on December 31, 2005.

E14-5 (Entries for Bond Transactions—Effective Interest) Assume the same information as in E14-4, except that Celine Dion Company uses the effective interest method of amortization for bond premium or discount. Assume an effective yield of 9.75%.

Instructions

Prepare the journal entries to record the following. (Round to the nearest dollar.)

(a) The issuance of the bonds.
(b) The payment of interest and related amortization on July 1, 2005.
(c) The accrual of interest and the related amortization on December 31, 2005.

E14-6 (Amortization Schedules—Straight-line) Dan Majerle Company sells 10% bonds having a maturity value of $2,000,000 for $1,855,816. The bonds are dated January 1, 2004, and mature January 1, 2009. Interest is payable annually on January 1.

Instructions

Set up a schedule of interest expense and discount amortization under the straight-line method.

E14-7 (Amortization Schedule—Effective Interest) Assume the same information as E14-6.

Instructions

Set up a schedule of interest expense and discount amortization under the effective interest method. (*Hint:* The effective interest rate must be computed.)

E14-8 (Determine Proper Amounts in Account Balances) Presented below are three independent situations.

(a) CeCe Winans Corporation incurred the following costs in connection with the issuance of bonds: (1) printing and engraving costs, $12,000; (2) legal fees, $49,000, and (3) commissions paid to underwriter, $60,000. What amount should be reported as Unamortized Bond Issue Costs, and where should this amount be reported on the balance sheet?
(b) George Gershwin Co. sold $2,000,000 of 10%, 10-year bonds at 104 on January 1, 2004. The bonds were dated January 1, 2004, and pay interest on July 1 and January 1. If Gershwin uses the straight-line method to amortize bond premium or discount, determine the amount of interest expense to be reported on July 1, 2004, and December 31, 2004.
(c) Ron Kenoly Inc. issued $600,000 of 9%, 10-year bonds on June 30, 2004, for $562,500. This price provided a yield of 10% on the bonds. Interest is payable semiannually on December 31 and June 30. If Kenoly uses the effective interest method, determine the amount of interest expense to record if financial statements are issued on October 31, 2004.

E14-9 (Entries and Questions for Bond Transactions) On June 30, 2005, Mischa Auer Company issued $4,000,000 face value of 13%, 20-year bonds at $4,300,920, a yield of 12%. Auer uses the effective interest method to amortize bond premium or discount. The bonds pay semiannual interest on June 30 and December 31.

Instructions

(a) Prepare the journal entries to record the following transactions.
  (1) The issuance of the bonds on June 30, 2005.
  (2) The payment of interest and the amortization of the premium on December 31, 2005.
  (3) The payment of interest and the amortization of the premium on June 30, 2006.
  (4) The payment of interest and the amortization of the premium on December 31, 2006.
(b) Show the proper balance sheet presentation for the liability for bonds payable on the December 31, 2006, balance sheet.
(c) Provide the answers to the following questions.
  (1) What amount of interest expense is reported for 2006?
  (2) Will the bond interest expense reported in 2006 be the same as, greater than, or less than the amount that would be reported if the straight-line method of amortization were used?
  (3) Determine the total cost of borrowing over the life of the bond.
  (4) Will the total bond interest expense for the life of the bond be greater than, the same as, or less than the total interest expense if the straight-line method of amortization were used?

E14-10 (Entries for Bond Transactions) On January 1, 2004, Aumont Company sold 12% bonds having a maturity value of $500,000 for $537,907.37, which provides the bondholders with a 10% yield. The bonds are dated January 1, 2004, and mature January 1, 2009, with interest payable December 31 of each year. Aumont Company allocates interest and unamortized discount or premium on the effective interest basis.

Instructions

(a) Prepare the journal entry at the date of the bond issuance.
(b) Prepare a schedule of interest expense and bond amortization for 2004–2006.
(c) Prepare the journal entry to record the interest payment and the amortization for 2004.
(d) Prepare the journal entry to record the interest payment and the amortization for 2006.

E14-11 (Information Related to Various Bond Issues) Karen Austin Inc. has issued three types of debt on January 1, 2004, the start of the company's fiscal year.

(a) $10 million, 10-year, 15% unsecured bonds, interest payable quarterly. Bonds were priced to yield 12%.
(b) $25 million par of 10-year, zero-coupon bonds at a price to yield 12% per year.
(c) $20 million, 10-year, 10% mortgage bonds, interest payable annually to yield 12%.

Instructions

Prepare a schedule that identifies the following items for each bond: (1) maturity value, (2) number of interest periods over life of bond, (3) stated rate per each interest period, (4) effective interest rate per each interest period, (5) payment amount per period, and (6) present value of bonds at date of issue.

E14-12 (Entry for Retirement of Bond; Bond Issue Costs) On January 2, 1999, Banno Corporation issued $1,500,000 of 10% bonds at 97 due December 31, 2008. Legal and other costs of $24,000 were incurred in connection with the issue. Interest on the bonds is payable annually each December 31. The $24,000 issue costs are being deferred and amortized on a straight-line basis over the 10-year term of the bonds. The discount on the bonds is also being amortized on a straight-line basis over the 10 years. (Straight-line is not materially different in effect from the preferable "interest method".)

The bonds are callable at 101 (i.e., at 101% of face amount), and on January 2, 2004, Banno called $900,000 face amount of the bonds and retired them.

Instructions

Ignoring income taxes, compute the amount of loss, if any, to be recognized by Banno as a result of retiring the $900,000 of bonds in 2004 and prepare the journal entry to record the retirement.

(AICPA adapted)

E14-13 (Entries for Retirement and Issuance of Bonds) Larry Hagman, Inc. had outstanding $6,000,000 of 11% bonds (interest payable July 31 and January 31) due in 10 years. On July 1, it issued $9,000,000 of 10%, 15-year bonds (interest payable July 1 and January 1) at 98. A portion of the proceeds was used to call the 11% bonds at 102 on August 1. Unamortized bond discount and issue cost applicable to the 11% bonds were $120,000 and $30,000, respectively.

Instructions

Prepare the journal entries necessary to record issue of the new bonds and the refunding of the bonds.

E14-14 (Entries for Retirement and Issuance of Bonds) On June 30, 1996, Gene Autry Company issued 12% bonds with a par value of $800,000 due in 20 years. They were issued at 98 and were callable at 104 at any date after June 30, 2004. Because of lower interest rates and a significant change in the company's credit rating, it was decided to call the entire issue on June 30, 2005, and to issue new bonds. New 10% bonds were sold in the amount of $1,000,000 at 102; they mature in 20 years. Autry Company uses straight-line amortization. Interest payment dates are December 31 and June 30.

Instructions

(a) Prepare journal entries to record the retirement of the old issue and the sale of the new issue on June 30, 2005.
(b) Prepare the entry required on December 31, 2005, to record the payment of the first 6 months' interest and the amortization of premium on the bonds.

E14-15 (Entries for Retirement and Issuance of Bonds) Linda Day George Company had bonds outstanding with a maturity value of $300,000. On April 30, 2005, when these bonds had an unamortized discount of $10,000, they were called in at 104. To pay for these bonds, George had issued other bonds a month earlier bearing a lower interest rate. The newly issued bonds had a life of 10 years. The new bonds were issued at 103 (face value $300,000). Issue costs related to the new bonds were $3,000.

Instructions

Ignoring interest, compute the gain or loss and record this refunding transaction.

(AICPA adapted)

E14-16 (Entries for Non-Interest-Bearing Debt) On January 1, 2005, Ellen Greene Company makes the two following acquisitions.

1. Purchases land having a fair market value of $200,000 by issuing a 5-year, non-interest-bearing promissory note in the face amount of $337,012.
2. Purchases equipment by issuing a 6%, 8-year promissory note having a maturity value of $250,000 (interest payable annually).

The company has to pay 11% interest for funds from its bank.

Instructions

(a) Record the two journal entries that should be recorded by Ellen Greene Company for the two purchases on January 1, 2005.

(b) Record the interest at the end of the first year on both notes using the effective interest method.

E14-17 (Imputation of Interest) Presented below are two independent situations:

(a) On January 1, 2005, Robin Wright Inc. purchased land that had an assessed value of $350,000 at the time of purchase. A $550,000, non-interest-bearing note due January 1, 2008, was given in exchange. There was no established exchange price for the land, nor a ready market value for the note. The interest rate charged on a note of this type is 12%. Determine at what amount the land should be recorded at January 1, 2005, and the interest expense to be reported in 2005 related to this transaction.

(b) On January 1, 2005, Sally Field Furniture Co. borrowed $5,000,000 (face value) from Gary Sinise Co., a major customer, through a non-interest-bearing note due in 4 years. Because the note was non-interest-bearing, Sally Field Furniture agreed to sell furniture to this customer at lower than market price. A 10% rate of interest is normally charged on this type of loan. Prepare the journal entry to record this transaction and determine the amount of interest expense to report for 2005.

E14-18 (Imputation of Interest with Right) On January 1, 2003, Margaret Avery Co. borrowed and received $400,000 from a major customer evidenced by a non-interest-bearing note due in 3 years. As consideration for the non-interest-bearing feature, Avery agrees to supply the customer's inventory needs for the loan period at lower than the market price. The appropriate rate at which to impute interest is 12%.

Instructions

(a) Prepare the journal entry to record the initial transaction on January 1, 2003. (Round all computations to the nearest dollar.)

(b) Prepare the journal entry to record any adjusting entries needed at December 31, 2003. Assume that the sales of Avery's product to this customer occur evenly over the 3-year period.

E14-19 (Long-Term Debt Disclosure) At December 31, 2003, Helen Reddy Company has outstanding three long-term debt issues. The first is a $2,000,000 note payable which matures June 30, 2006. The second is a $6,000,000 bond issue which matures September 30, 2007. The third is a $17,500,000 sinking fund debenture with annual sinking fund payments of $3,500,000 in each of the years 2005 through 2009.

Instructions

Prepare the note disclosure required by *FASB Statement No. 47,* "Disclosure of Long-term Obligations," for the long-term debt at December 31, 2003.

***E14-20 (Settlement of Debt)** Larisa Nieland Company owes $200,000 plus $18,000 of accrued interest to First State Bank. The debt is a 10-year, 10% note. During 2004, Larisa Nieland's business deteriorated due to a faltering regional economy. On December 31, 2004, First State Bank agrees to accept an old machine and cancel the entire debt. The machine has a cost of $390,000, accumulated depreciation of $221,000, and a fair market value of $190,000.

Instructions

(a) Prepare journal entries for Larisa Nieland Company and First State Bank to record this debt settlement.

(b) How should Larisa Nieland report the gain or loss on the disposition of machine and on restructuring of debt in its 2004 income statement?

(c) Assume that, instead of transferring the machine, Larisa Nieland decides to grant 15,000 shares of its common stock ($10 par) which has a fair market value of $190,000 in full settlement of the loan obligation. If First State Bank treats Larisa Nieland's stock as a trading investment, prepare the entries to record the transaction for both parties.

***E14-21 (Term Modification without Gain—Debtor's Entries)** On December 31, 2004, the Firstar Bank enters into a debt restructuring agreement with Nicole Bradtke Company, which is now experiencing financial trouble. The bank agrees to restructure a 12%, issued at par, $2,000,000 note receivable by the following modifications:

1. Reducing the principal obligation from $2,000,000 to $1,600,000.
2. Extending the maturity date from December 31, 2004, to December 31, 2007.
3. Reducing the interest rate from 12% to 10%.

Bradtke pays interest at the end of each year. On January 1, 2008, Bradtke Company pays $1,600,000 in cash to Firstar Bank.

Instructions

(a) Based on *FASB Statement No. 114*, will the gain recorded by Bradtke be equal to the loss recorded by Firstar Bank under the debt restructuring?
(b) Can Bradtke Company record a gain under the term modification mentioned above? Explain.
(c) Assuming that the interest rate Bradtke should use to compute interest expense in future periods is 1.4276%, prepare the interest payment schedule of the note for Bradtke Company after the debt restructuring.
(d) Prepare the interest payment entry for Bradtke Company on December 31, 2006.
(e) What entry should Bradtke make on January 1, 2008?

***E14-22 (Term Modification without Gain—Creditor's Entries)** Using the same information as in E14-21 above, answer the following questions related to Firstar Bank (creditor).

Instructions

(a) What interest rate should Firstar Bank use to calculate the loss on the debt restructuring?
(b) Compute the loss that Firstar Bank will suffer from the debt restructuring. Prepare the journal entry to record the loss.
(c) Prepare the interest receipt schedule for Firstar Bank after the debt restructuring.
(d) Prepare the interest receipt entry for Firstar Bank on December 31, 2006.
(e) What entry should Firstar Bank make on January 1, 2008?

***E14-23 (Term Modification with Gain—Debtor's Entries)** Use the same information as in E14-21 above except that Firstar Bank reduced the principal to $1,300,000 rather than $1,600,000. On January 1, 2008, Bradtke pays $1,300,000 in cash to Firstar Bank for the principal.

Instructions

(a) Can Bradtke Company record a gain under this term modification? If yes, compute the gain for Bradtke Company.
(b) Prepare the journal entries to record the gain on Bradtke's books.
(c) What interest rate should Bradtke use to compute its interest expense in future periods? Will your answer be the same as in E14-21 above? Why or why not?
(d) Prepare the interest payment schedule of the note for Bradtke Company after the debt restructuring.
(e) Prepare the interest payment entries for Bradtke Company on December 31, of 2005, 2006, and 2007.
(f) What entry should Bradtke make on January 1, 2008?

***E14-24 (Term Modification with Gain—Creditor's Entries)** Using the same information as in E14-21 and E14-23 above, answer the following questions related to Firstar Bank (creditor).

Instructions

(a) Compute the loss Firstar Bank will suffer under this new term modification. Prepare the journal entry to record the loss on Firstar's books.
(b) Prepare the interest receipt schedule for Firstar Bank after the debt restructuring.
(c) Prepare the interest receipt entry for Firstar Bank on December 31, 2005, 2006, and 2007.
(d) What entry should Firstar Bank make on January 1, 2008?

***E14-25 (Debtor/Creditor Entries for Settlement of Troubled Debt)** Petra Langrova Co. owes $199,800 to Mary Joe Fernandez Inc. The debt is a 10-year, 11% note. Because Petra Langrova Co. is in financial trouble, Mary Joe Fernandez Inc. agrees to accept some property and cancel the entire debt. The property has a book value of $80,000 and a fair market value of $120,000.

Instructions

(a) Prepare the journal entry on Langrova's books for debt restructure.
(b) Prepare the journal entry on Fernandez's books for debt restructure.

***E14-26 (Debtor/Creditor Entries for Modification of Troubled Debt)** Steffi Graf Corp. owes $225,000 to First Trust. The debt is a 10-year, 12% note due December 31, 2004. Because Graf Corp. is in financial trouble, First Trust agrees to extend the maturity date to December 31, 2006, reduce the principal to $200,000, and reduce the interest rate to 5%, payable annually on December 31.

Instructions

(a) Prepare the journal entries on Graf's books on December 31, 2004, 2005, 2006.
(b) Prepare the journal entries on First Trust's books on December 31, 2004, 2005, 2006.

***E14-27 (Impairments)** On December 31, 2003, Iva Majoli Company borrowed $62,092 from Paris Bank, signing a 5-year, $100,000 non-interest-bearing note. The note was issued to yield 10% interest. Unfortunately, during 2005, Majoli began to experience financial difficulty. As a result, at December 31, 2005, Paris Bank determined that it was probable that it would receive back only $75,000 at maturity. The market rate of interest on loans of this nature is now 11%.

Instructions

(a) Prepare the entry to record the issuance of the loan by Paris Bank on December 31, 2003.
(b) Prepare the entry (if any) to record the impairment of the loan on December 31, 2005, by Paris Bank.
(c) Prepare the entry (if any) to record the impairment of the loan on December 31, 2005, by Majoli Company.

***E14-28 (Impairments)** On December 31, 2002, Conchita Martinez Company signed a $1,000,000 note to Sauk City Bank. The market interest rate at that time was 12%. The stated interest rate on the note was 10%, payable annually. The note matures in 5 years. Unfortunately, because of lower sales, Conchita Martinez's financial situation worsened. On December 31, 2004, Sauk City Bank determined that it was probable that the company would pay back only $600,000 of the principal at maturity. However, it was considered likely that interest would continue to be paid, based on the $1,000,000 loan.

Instructions

(a) Determine the amount of cash Conchita Martinez received from the loan on December 31, 2002.
(b) Prepare a note amortization schedule for Sauk City Bank up to December 31, 2004.
(c) Determine the loss on impairment that Sauk City Bank should recognize on December 31, 2004.

PROBLEMS

P14-1 (Analysis of Amortization Schedule and Interest Entries) The following amortization and interest schedule reflects the issuance of 10-year bonds by Terrel Brandon Corporation on January 1, 1997, and the subsequent interest payments and charges. The company's year-end is December 31, and financial statements are prepared once yearly.

Amortization Schedule

Year	Cash	Interest	Amount Unamortized	Book Value
1/1/97			$5,651	$ 94,349
1997	$11,000	$11,322	5,329	94,671
1998	11,000	11,361	4,968	95,032
1999	11,000	11,404	4,564	95,436
2000	11,000	11,452	4,112	95,888
2001	11,000	11,507	3,605	96,395
2002	11,000	11,567	3,038	96,962
2003	11,000	11,635	2,403	97,597
2004	11,000	11,712	1,691	98,309
2005	11,000	11,797	894	99,106
2006	11,000	11,894		100,000

Instructions

(a) Indicate whether the bonds were issued at a premium or a discount and how you can determine this fact from the schedule.
(b) Indicate whether the amortization schedule is based on the straight-line method or the effective interest method and how you can determine which method is used.
(c) Determine the stated interest rate and the effective interest rate.

(d) On the basis of the schedule above, prepare the journal entry to record the issuance of the bonds on January 1, 1997.
(e) On the basis of the schedule above, prepare the journal entry or entries to reflect the bond transactions and accruals for 1997. (Interest is paid January 1.)
(f) On the basis of the schedule above, prepare the journal entry or entries to reflect the bond transactions and accruals for 2004. Brandon Corporation does not use reversing entries.

P14-2 (Issuance and Retirement of Bonds) Sam Sluggers Co. is building a new hockey arena at a cost of $2,000,000. It received a downpayment of $500,000 from local businesses to support the project, and now needs to borrow $1,500,000 to complete the project. It therefore decides to issue $1,500,000 of 10.5%, 10-year bonds. These bonds were issued on January 1, 2002, and pay interest annually on each January 1. The bonds yield 10%. Sluggers paid $50,000 in bond issue costs related to the bond sale.

Instructions

(a) Prepare the journal entry to record the issuance of the bonds and the related bond issue costs incurred on January 1, 2002.
(b) Prepare a bond amortization schedule up to and including January 1, 2006, using the effective interest method.
(c) Assume that on July 1, 2005, Sam Sluggers Co. retires half of the bonds at a cost of $800,000 plus accrued interest. Prepare the journal entry to record this retirement.

P14-3 (Negative Amortization) Slippery Sales Inc. developed a new sales gimmick to help sell its inventory of new automobiles. Because many new car buyers need financing, Slippery offered a low downpayment and low car payments for the first year after purchase. It believes that this promotion will bring in some new buyers.

On January 1, 2004, a customer purchased a new $25,000 automobile, making a downpayment of $1,000. The customer signed a note indicating that the annual rate of interest would be 8% and that quarterly payments would be made over 3 years. For the first year, Slippery required a $300 quarterly payment to be made on April 1, July 1, October 1, and January 1, 2005. After this one-year period, the customer was required to make regular quarterly payments that would pay off the loan as of January 1, 2007.

Instructions

(a) Prepare a note amortization schedule for the first year.
(b) Indicate the amount the customer owes on the contract at the end of the first year.
(c) Compute the amount of the new quarterly payments.
(d) Prepare a note amortization schedule for these new payments for the next 2 years.
(e) What do you think of the new sales promotion used by Slippery?

P14-4 (Issuance and Retirement of Bonds; Income Statement Presentation) Chris Mills Company issued its 9%, 25-year mortgage bonds in the principal amount of $5,000,000 on January 2, 1990, at a discount of $250,000, which it proceeded to amortize by charges to expense over the life of the issue on a straight-line basis. The indenture securing the issue provided that the bonds could be called for redemption in total but not in part at any time before maturity at 104% of the principal amount, but it did not provide for any sinking fund.

On December 18, 2004, the company issued its 11%, 20-year debenture bonds in the principal amount of $6,000,000 at 102, and the proceeds were used to redeem the 9%, 25-year mortgage bonds on January 2, 2005. The indenture securing the new issue did not provide for any sinking fund or for retirement before maturity.

Instructions

(a) Prepare journal entries to record the issuance of the 11% bonds and the retirement of the 9% bonds.
(b) Indicate the income statement treatment of the gain or loss from retirement and the note disclosure required.

P14-5 (Comprehensive Bond Problem) In each of the following independent cases the company closes its books on December 31.

1. Danny Ferry Co. sells $250,000 of 10% bonds on March 1, 2004. The bonds pay interest on September 1 and March 1. The due date of the bonds is September 1, 2007. The bonds yield 12%. Give entries through December 31, 2005.
2. Brad Dougherty Co. sells $600,000 of 12% bonds on June 1, 2004. The bonds pay interest on December 1 and June 1. The due date of the bonds is June 1, 2008. The bonds yield 10%. On October 1, 2005, Dougherty buys back $120,000 worth of bonds for $126,000 (includes accrued interest). Give entries through December 1, 2006.

Instructions

(Round to the nearest dollar.)

For the two cases prepare all of the relevant journal entries from the time of sale until the date indicated. Use the effective interest method for discount and premium amortization (construct amortization tables where applicable). Amortize premium or discount on interest dates and at year-end. (Assume that no reversing entries were made.)

P14-6 (Issuance of Bonds between Interest Dates, Straight-line, Retirement) Presented below are selected transactions on the books of Michael Cage Powerglide Corporation.

May 1, 2004	Bonds payable with a par value of $700,000, which are dated January 1, 2004, are sold at 106 plus accrued interest. They are coupon bonds, bear interest at 12% (payable annually at January 1), and mature January 1, 2014. (Use interest expense account for accrued interest.)
Dec. 31	Adjusting entries are made to record the accrued interest on the bonds, and the amortization of the proper amount of premium. (Use straight-line amortization.)
Jan. 1, 2005	Interest on the bonds is paid.
April 1	Bonds of par value of $420,000 are purchased at 102 plus accrued interest, and retired. (Bond premium is to be amortized only at the end of each year.)
Dec. 31	Adjusting entries are made to record the accrued interest on the bonds, and the proper amount of premium amortized.

Instructions

Prepare journal entries for the transactions above.

P14-7 (Entries for Life Cycle of Bonds) On April 1, 2004, Jerry Fontenot Company sold 12,000 of its 11%, 15-year, $1,000 face value bonds at 97. Interest payment dates are April 1 and October 1, and the company uses the straight-line method of bond discount amortization. On March 1, 2005, Fontenot took advantage of favorable prices of its stock to extinguish 3,000 of the bonds by issuing 100,000 shares of its $10 par value common stock. At this time, the accrued interest was paid in cash. The company's stock was selling for $31 per share on March 1, 2005.

Instructions

Prepare the journal entries needed on the books of Fontenot Company to record the following.

(a) April 1, 2004: issuance of the bonds.
(b) October 1, 2004: payment of semiannual interest.
(c) December 31, 2004: accrual of interest expense.
(d) March 1, 2005: extinguishment of 3,000 bonds. (No reversing entries made.)

P14-8 (Entries for Non-Interest-Bearing Debt) On December 31, 2004, Jose Luis Company acquired a computer from Cuevas Corporation by issuing a $400,000 non-interest-bearing note, payable in full on December 31, 2008. Jose Luis Company's credit rating permits it to borrow funds from its several lines of credit at 10%. The computer is expected to have a 5-year life and a $50,000 salvage value.

Instructions

(a) Prepare the journal entry for the purchase on December 31, 2004.
(b) Prepare any necessary adjusting entries relative to depreciation (use straight-line) and amortization (use effective interest method) on December 31, 2005.
(c) Prepare any necessary adjusting entries relative to depreciation and amortization on December 31, 2006.

P14-9 (Entries for Non-Interest-Bearing Debt; Payable in Installments) Sun Yat-sen Cosmetics Co. purchased machinery on December 31, 2003, paying $40,000 down and agreeing to pay the balance in four equal installments of $30,000 payable each December 31. An assumed interest of 12% is implicit in the purchase price.

Instructions

Prepare the journal entries that would be recorded for the purchase and for the payments and interest on the following dates.

(a) December 31, 2003.
(b) December 31, 2004.
(c) December 31, 2005.
(d) December 31, 2006.
(e) December 31, 2007.

P14-10 (Comprehensive Problem; Issuance, Classification, Reporting) Presented below are four independent situations.

(a) On March 1, 2005, Heide Co. issued at 103 plus accrued interest $3,000,000, 9% bonds. The bonds are dated January 1, 2005, and pay interest semiannually on July 1 and January 1. In addition, Heide Co. incurred $27,000 of bond issuance costs. Compute the net amount of cash received by Heide Co. as a result of the issuance of these bonds.

(b) On January 1, 2004, Reymont Co. issued 9% bonds with a face value of $500,000 for $469,280 to yield 10%. The bonds are dated January 1, 2004, and pay interest annually. What amount is reported for interest expense in 2004 related to these bonds, assuming that Reymont used the effective interest method for amortizing bond premium and discount?

(c) Czeslaw Building Co. has a number of long-term bonds outstanding at December 31, 2005. These long-term bonds have the following sinking fund requirements and maturities for the next 6 years.

	Sinking Fund	Maturities
2006	$300,000	$100,000
2007	100,000	250,000
2008	100,000	100,000
2009	200,000	—
2010	200,000	150,000
2011	200,000	100,000

Indicate how this information should be reported in the financial statements at December 31, 2005.

(d) In the long-term debt structure of Marie Curie Inc., the following three bonds were reported: mortgage bonds payable $10,000,000; collateral trust bonds $5,000,000; bonds maturing in installments, secured by plant equipment $4,000,000. Determine the total amount, if any, of debenture bonds outstanding.

P14-11 (Effective Interest Method) Mathilda B. Reichenbacher, an intermediate accounting student, is having difficulty amortizing bond premiums and discounts using the effective interest method. Furthermore, she cannot understand why GAAP requires that this method be used instead of the straight-line method. She has come to you with the following problem, looking for help.

On June 30, 2003, Joan Elbert Company issued $3,000,000 face value of 13%, 20-year bonds at $3,225,690, a yield of 12%. Elbert Company uses the effective interest method to amortize bond premiums or discounts. The bonds pay semiannual interest on June 30 and December 31. Compute the amortization schedule for four periods.

Instructions

Using the data above for illustrative purposes, write a short memo (1–1.5 pages double-spaced) to Mathilda, explaining what the effective interest method is, why it is preferable, and how it is computed. (Do not forget to include an amortization schedule, referring to it whenever necessary.)

***P14-12 (Loan Impairment Entries)** On January 1, 2004, Bostan Company issued a $1,200,000, 5-year, zero-interest-bearing note to National Organization Bank. The note was issued to yield 8% annual interest. Unfortunately, during 2005, Bostan fell into financial trouble due to increased competition. After reviewing all available evidence on December 31, 2005, National Organization Bank decided that the loan was impaired. Bostan will probably pay back only $800,000 of the principal at maturity.

Instructions

(a) Prepare journal entries for both Bostan Company and National Organization Bank to record the issuance of the note on January 1, 2004. (Round to the nearest $10.)

(b) Assuming that both Bostan Company and National Organization Bank use the effective interest method to amortize the discount, prepare the amortization schedule for the note.

(c) Under what circumstances can National Organization Bank consider Bostan's note to be "impaired"?

(d) Compute the loss National Organization Bank will suffer from Bostan's financial distress on December 31, 2005. What journal entries should be made to record this loss?

***P14-13 (Debtor/Creditor Entries for Continuation of Troubled Debt)** Jeremy Hillary is the sole shareholder of Hillary Inc., which is currently under protection of the U.S. bankruptcy court. As a "debtor in possession," he has negotiated the following revised loan agreement with Valley Bank. Hillary Inc.'s $400,000, 12%, 10-year note was refinanced with a $400,000, 5%, 10-year note.

Instructions

(a) What is the accounting nature of this transaction?

(b) Prepare the journal entry to record this refinancing:

(1) On the books of Hillary Inc.
(2) On the books of Valley Bank.

(c) Discuss whether generally accepted accounting principles provide the proper information useful to managers and investors in this situation.

***P14-14 (Restructure of Note under Different Circumstances)** Sandro Corporation is having financial difficulty and therefore has asked Botticelli National Bank to restructure its $3 million note outstanding. The present note has 3 years remaining and pays a current rate of interest of 10%. The present market rate for a loan of this nature is 12%. The note was issued at its face value.

Instructions

Presented below are four independent situations. Prepare the journal entry that Sandro and Botticelli National Bank would make for each of these restructurings.

(a) Botticelli National Bank agrees to take an equity interest in Sandro by accepting common stock valued at $2,200,000 in exchange for relinquishing its claim on this note. The common stock has a par value of $1,000,000.

(b) Botticelli National Bank agrees to accept land in exchange for relinquishing its claim on this note. The land has a book value of $1,950,000 and a fair value of $2,400,000.

(c) Botticelli National Bank agrees to modify the terms of the note, indicating that Sandro does not have to pay any interest on the note over the 3-year period.

(d) Botticelli National Bank agrees to reduce the principal balance due to $2,500,000 and require interest only in the second and third year at a rate of 10%.

***P14-15 (Debtor/Creditor Entries for Continuation of Troubled Debt with New Effective Interest)** Mildred Corp. owes D. Taylor Corp. a 10-year, 10% note in the amount of $110,000 plus $11,000 of accrued interest. The note is due today, December 31, 2004. Because Mildred Corp. is in financial trouble, D. Taylor Corp. agrees to forgive the accrued interest, $10,000 of the principal, and to extend the maturity date to December 31, 2007. Interest at 10% of revised principal will continue to be due on 12/31 each year.

Assume the following present value factors for 3 periods.

	2¼%	2⅜%	2½%	2⅝%	2¾%	3%
Single sum	.93543	.93201	.92859	.92521	.92184	.91514
Ordinary annuity of 1	2.86989	2.86295	2.85602	2.84913	2.84226	2.82861

Instructions

(a) Compute the new effective interest rate for Mildred Corp. following restructure. (*Hint:* Find the interest rate that establishes approximately $121,000 as the present value of the total future cash flows.)

(b) Prepare a schedule of debt reduction and interest expense for the years 2004 through 2007.

(c) Compute the gain or loss for D. Taylor Corp. and prepare a schedule of receivable reduction and interest revenue for the years 2004 through 2007.

(d) Prepare all the necessary journal entries on the books of Mildred Corp. for the years 2004, 2005, and 2006.

(e) Prepare all the necessary journal entries on the books of D. Taylor Corp. for the years 2004, 2005, and 2006.

CONCEPTUAL CASES

C14-1 (Bond Theory: Balance Sheet Presentations, Interest Rate, Premium) On January 1, 2005, Branagh Company issued for $1,075,230 its 20-year, 13% bonds that have a maturity value of $1,000,000 and pay interest semiannually on January 1 and July 1. Bond issue costs were not material in amount. Below are three presentations of the long-term liability section of the balance sheet that might be used for these bonds at the issue date.

1. Bonds payable (maturing January 1, 2025)	$1,000,000
Unamortized premium on bonds payable	75,230
Total bond liability	$1,075,230
2. Bonds payable—principal (face value $1,000,000 maturing January 1, 2025)	$ 97,220[a]
Bonds payable—interest (semiannual payment $65,000)	978,010[b]
Total bond liability	$1,075,230

3. Bonds payable—principal (maturing January 1, 2025)	$1,000,000
Bonds payable—interest ($65,000 per period for 40 periods)	2,600,000
Total bond liability	$3,600,000

[a]The present value of $1,000,000 due at the end of 40 (6-month) periods at the yield rate of 6% per period.
[b]The present value of $65,000 per period for 40 (6-month) periods at the yield rate of 6% per period.

Instructions

(a) Discuss the conceptual merit(s) of each of the date-of-issue balance sheet presentations shown above for these bonds.

(b) Explain why investors would pay $1,075,230 for bonds that have a maturity value of only $1,000,000.

(c) Assuming that a discount rate is needed to compute the carrying value of the obligations arising from a bond issue at any date during the life of the bonds, discuss the conceptual merit(s) of using for this purpose:
  (1) The coupon or nominal rate.
  (2) The effective or yield rate at date of issue.

(d) If the obligations arising from these bonds are to be carried at their present value computed by means of the current market rate of interest, how would the bond valuation at dates subsequent to the date of issue be affected by an increase or a decrease in the market rate of interest?

(AICPA adapted)

C14-2 (Various Long-Term Liability Conceptual Issues) Emma Thompson Company has completed a number of transactions during 2004. In January the company purchased under contract a machine at a total price of $1,200,000, payable over 5 years with installments of $240,000 per year. The seller has considered the transaction as an installment sale with the title transferring to Thompson at the time of the final payment.

On March 1, 2004, Thompson issued $10 million of general revenue bonds priced at 99 with a coupon of 10% payable July 1 and January 1 of each of the next 10 years. The July 1 interest was paid and on December 30 the company transferred $1,000,000 to the trustee, Hollywood Trust Company, for payment of the January 1, 2005, interest.

Due to the depressed market for the company's stock, Thompson purchased $500,000 par value of their 6% convertible bonds for a price of $455,000. It expects to resell the bonds when the price of its stock has recovered.

As the accountant for Emma Thompson Company, you have prepared the balance sheet as of December 31, 2004, and have presented it to the president of the company. You are asked the following questions about it.

1. Why has depreciation been charged on equipment being purchased under contract? Title has not passed to the company as yet and, therefore, they are not our assets. Why should the company not show on the left side of the balance sheet only the amount paid to date instead of showing the full contract price on the left side and the unpaid portion on the right side? After all, the seller considers the transaction an installment sale.
2. What is bond discount? As a debit balance, why is it not classified among the assets?
3. Bond interest is shown as a current liability. Did we not pay our trustee, Hollywood Trust Company, the full amount of interest due this period?
4. Treasury bonds are shown as a deduction from bonds payable issued. Why should they not be shown as an asset, since they can be sold again? Are they the same as bonds of other companies that we hold as investments?

Instructions

Outline your answers to these questions by writing a brief paragraph that will justify your treatment.

C14-3 (Bond Theory: Price, Presentation, and Retirement) On March 1, 2005, Chuck Norris Company sold its 5-year, $1,000 face value, 9% bonds dated March 1, 2005, at an effective annual interest rate (yield) of 11%. Interest is payable semiannually, and the first interest payment date is September 1, 2005. Norris uses the effective interest method of amortization. Bond issue costs were incurred in preparing and selling the bond issue. The bonds can be called by Norris at 101 at any time on or after March 1, 2006.

Instructions

(a) (1) How would the selling price of the bond be determined?
  (2) Specify how all items related to the bonds would be presented in a balance sheet prepared immediately after the bond issue was sold.

(b) What items related to the bond issue would be included in Norris' 2005 income statement, and how would each be determined?

(c) Would the amount of bond discount amortization using the effective interest method of amortization be lower in the second or third year of the life of the bond issue? Why?
(d) Assuming that the bonds were called in and retired on March 1, 2006, how should Norris report the retirement of the bonds on the 2006 income statement?

(AICPA adapted)

C14-4 (Bond Theory: Amortization and Gain or Loss Recognition)
Part I. The appropriate method of amortizing a premium or discount on issuance of bonds is the effective interest method.

Instructions

(a) What is the effective interest method of amortization and how is it different from and similar to the straight-line method of amortization?
(b) How is amortization computed using the effective interest method, and why and how do amounts obtained using the effective interest method differ from amounts computed under the straight-line method?

Part II. Gains or losses from the early extinguishment of debt that is refunded can theoretically be accounted for in three ways:

1. Amortized over remaining life of old debt.
2. Amortized over the life of the new debt issue.
3. Recognized in the period of extinguishment.

Instructions

(a) Develop supporting arguments for each of the three theoretical methods of accounting for gains and losses from the early extinguishment of debt.
(b) Which of the methods above is generally accepted and how should the appropriate amount of gain or loss be shown in a company's financial statements?

(AICPA adapted)

C14-5 (Off-Balance-Sheet Financing) Brad Pitt Corporation is interested in building its own soda can manufacturing plant adjacent to its existing plant in Partyville, Kansas. The objective would be to ensure a steady supply of cans at a stable price and to minimize transportation costs. However, the company has been experiencing some financial problems and has been reluctant to borrow any additional cash to fund the project. The company is not concerned with the cash flow problems of making payments, but rather with the impact of adding additional long-term debt to their balance sheet.

The president of Pitt, Aidan Quinn, approached the president of the Aluminum Can Company (ACC), their major supplier, to see if some agreement could be reached. ACC was anxious to work out an arrangement, since it seemed inevitable that Pitt would begin their own can production. The Aluminum Can Company could not afford to lose the account.

After some discussion a two part plan was worked out. First ACC was to construct the plant on Pitt's land adjacent to the existing plant. Second, Pitt would sign a 20-year purchase agreement. Under the purchase agreement, Pitt would express its intention to buy all of its cans from ACC, paying a unit price which at normal capacity would cover labor and material, an operating management fee, and the debt service requirements on the plant. The expected unit price, if transportation costs are taken into consideration, is lower than current market. If Pitt did not take enough production in any one year and if the excess cans could not be sold at a high enough price on the open market, Pitt agrees to make up any cash shortfall so that ACC could make the payments on its debt. The bank will be willing to make a 20-year loan for the plant, taking the plant and the purchase agreement as collateral. At the end of 20 years the plant is to become the property of Pitt.

Instructions

(a) What are project financing arrangements using special purpose entities?
(b) What are take-or-pay contracts?
(c) Should Pitt record the plant as an asset together with the related obligation?
(d) If not, should Pitt record an asset relating to the future commitment?
(e) What is meant by off-balance-sheet financing?

C14-6 (Bond Issue) Roland Carlson is the president, founder, and majority owner of Thebeau Medical Corporation, an emerging medical technology products company. Thebeau is in dire need of additional capital to keep operating and to bring several promising products to final development, testing, and production. Roland, as owner of 51% of the outstanding stock, manages the company's operations. He places heavy emphasis on research and development and long-term growth. The other principal stockholder is Jana Kingston who, as a nonemployee investor, owns 40% of the stock. Jana would like to deemphasize the R & D functions and emphasize the marketing function to maximize short-run sales and profits from existing products. She believes this strategy would raise the market price of Thebeau's stock.

All of Roland's personal capital and borrowing power is tied up in his 51% stock ownership. He knows that any offering of additional shares of stock will dilute his controlling interest because he won't be able to participate in such an issuance. But, Jana has money and would likely buy enough shares to gain control of Thebeau. She then would dictate the company's future direction, even if it meant replacing Roland as president and CEO.

The company already has considerable debt. Raising additional debt will be costly, will adversely affect Thebeau's credit rating, and will increase the company's reported losses due to the growth in interest expense. Jana and the other minority stockholders express opposition to the assumption of additional debt, fearing the company will be pushed to the brink of bankruptcy. Wanting to maintain his control and to preserve the direction of "his" company, Roland is doing everything to avoid a stock issuance and is contemplating a large issuance of bonds, even if it means the bonds are issued with a high effective-interest rate.

Instructions

(a) Who are the stakeholders in this situation?
(b) What are the ethical issues in this case?
(c) What would you do if you were Roland?

USING YOUR JUDGMENT

FINANCIAL REPORTING PROBLEM

3M Company

The financial statements of 3M are presented in Appendix 5B or can be accessed on the Take Action! CD.

Instructions

Refer to 3M's financial statements and the accompanying notes to answer the following questions.

(a) What cash outflow obligations related to the repayment of long-term debt does 3M have over the next 5 years?

(b) 3M indicates that it believes that it has the ability to meet business requirements in the foreseeable future. Prepare an assessment of its solvency and financial flexibility using ratio analysis.

FINANCIAL STATEMENT ANALYSIS CASES

Case 1 Commonwealth Edison Co.

The following article appeared in the *Wall Street Journal.*

> **Bond Markets**
> *Giant Commonwealth Edison Issue Hits Resale Market With $70 Million Left Over*
> NEW YORK—**Commonwealth Edison Co.**'s slow-selling new $9\frac{1}{4}\%$ bonds were tossed onto the resale market at a reduced price with about $70 million still available from the $200 million offered Thursday, dealers said.
>
> The Chicago utility's bonds, rated double-A by Moody's and double-A-minus by Standard & Poor's, originally had been priced at 99.803, to yield 9.3% in 5 years. They were marked down yesterday the equivalent of about $5.50 for each $1,000 face amount, to about 99.25, where their yield jumped to 9.45%.

Instructions

(a) How will the development above affect the accounting for Commonwealth Edison's bond issue?

(b) Provide several possible explanations for the markdown and the slow sale of Commonwealth Edison's bonds.

PEPSICO

Case 2 PepsiCo, Inc.

PepsiCo, Inc. based in Purchase, New York, is a leading company in the beverage industry. Assume that the following events occurred relating to PepsiCo's long-term debt in a recent year.

1. The company decided on February 1 to refinance $500 million in short-term 7.4% debt to make it long-term 6%.
2. $780 million of long-term zero-coupon bonds with an effective interest rate of 10.1% matured July 1 and were paid.
3. On October 1, the company issued $200 million in Australian dollar 6.3% bonds at 102 and $95 million in Italian lira 11.4% bonds at 99.
4. The company holds $100 million in perpetual foreign interest payment bonds that were issued in 1989, and presently have a rate of interest of 5.3%. These bonds are called perpetual because they have no stated due date. Instead, at the end of every 10-year period after the bond's issuance, the bondholders and PepsiCo have the option of redeeming the bonds. If either party desires to redeem the bonds, the bonds must be redeemed. If the bonds are not redeemed, a new interest rate is set, based on the then-prevailing interest rate for 10-year bonds. The company does not intend to cause redemption of the bonds, but will reclassify this debt to current next year, since the bondholders could decide to redeem the bonds.

Instructions

(a) Consider event 1. What are some of the reasons the company may have decided to refinance this short-term debt, besides lowering the interest rate?

(b) What do you think are the benefits to the investor in purchasing zero-coupon bonds, such as those described in event 2? What journal entry would be required to record the payment of these bonds? If financial statements are prepared each December 31, in which year would the bonds have been included in short-term liabilities?

(c) Make the journal entry to record the bond issue described in event 3. Note that the bonds were issued on the same day, yet one was issued at a premium and the other at a discount. What are some of the reasons that this may have happened?

(d) What are the benefits to PepsiCo in having perpetual bonds as described in event 4? Suppose that in the current year the bonds are not redeemed and the interest rate is adjusted to 6% from 7.5%. Make all necessary journal entries to record the renewal of the bonds and the change in rate.

COMPARATIVE ANALYSIS CASE

The Coca-Cola Company and PepsiCo, Inc.

Instructions

Go to the Take Action! CD and use information found there to answer the following questions related to **The Coca-Cola Company** and **Pepsi Co, Inc.**

(a) Compute the debt to total assets ratio and the times interest earned ratio for these two companies. Comment on the quality of these two ratios for both Coca-Cola and PepsiCo.

(b) What is the difference between the fair value and the historical cost (carrying amount) of each company's debt at year-end 2001? Why might a difference exist in these two amounts?

(c) Both companies have debt issued in foreign countries. Speculate as to why these companies may use foreign debt to finance their operations. What risks are involved in this strategy, and how might they adjust for this risk?

RESEARCH CASES

Case 1

Instructions

Use an appropriate source (such as those identified in Chapter 2 Research Case 1) to identify a firm that recently had its bond rating changed. Answer the following questions.

(a) Which rating agency(ies) changed the rating?

(b) What was the bond rating before and after the change?

(c) What reasons did the rating agency give in support of its action? What accounting data was used as support?

(d) Are additional changes possible?

Case 2

BUSINESS EXTRA

The February 2, 2002, edition of the *Wall Street Journal* includes an article by Mark Maremount entitled "Tyco May Alter Plan to Buy Back $11 Billion in Bonds with Tenders." (Subscribers to **Business Extra** can access the article at that site.)

Instructions

Read the article and answer the following questions.

(a) Tyco had announced earlier that it intended to "tender" for $11 billion of its bonds. Now it says it may repurchase the bonds in the open market. What's the difference between a "tender" and an open-market purchase?

(b) How would the transaction (tender or repurchase) be reported in the income statement? That is, what amount would be reported, and where would it appear?

(c) Under U.S. GAAP, should Tyco write down its bonds to their current market value? What accounting principle would justify this treatment?

PROFESSIONAL SIMULATION

Long-Term Liabilities

Directions | Situation | Journal Entries | Financial Statements | Research | Resources

Directions

In this simulation, you will be asked various questions concerning the accounting for long-term liabilities. Prepare responses to all parts.

Situation

Honoré de Balzac Inc. has been producing quality children's apparel for more than 25 years. The company's fiscal year runs from April 1 to March 31. The following information relates to the obligations of Balzac as of March 31, 2003.

Bonds Payable

Balzac issued $5,000,000 of 11% bonds on April 1, 2002. Market interest rates on that date for bonds of similar risk were 10%. Bonds mature on April 1, 2012; interest is paid annually on April 1.

Notes Payable

Balzac has signed several long-term notes with financial institutions and insurance companies. The maturities of these notes are given in the schedule below. The total unpaid interest for all of these notes amounts to $210,000 on March 31, 2003.

Due Date	Amount Due
April 1, 2003	$ 200,000
July 1, 2003	300,000
October 1, 2003	150,000
January 1, 2004	150,000
April 1, 2004–March 31, 2005	600,000
April 1, 2005–March 31, 2006	500,000
	$1,900,000

Asset Retirement Obligation

Balzac purchased a warehouse in 1998 for $300,000. In February 2003, due to the passage of a new wetlands restoration law, Balzac will be required to restore the wetlands surrounding the warehouse site when the warehouse is abandoned in 2007. Balzac has estimated that the present value of the cost to restore the site is $35,000.

Journal Entry

Prepare the journal entry for the issuance of the bonds and on the first interest payment date.

Resources

Use a computer spreadsheet to prepare an amortization schedule for the bonds.

Financial Statements

Prepare the long-term liabilities section of the balance sheet and appropriate notes to the financial statements for Balzac Inc. as of March 31, 2003.

www.wiley.com/college/kieso

Remember to check the **Take Action! CD**
and the book's **companion Web site**
to find additional resources for this chapter.

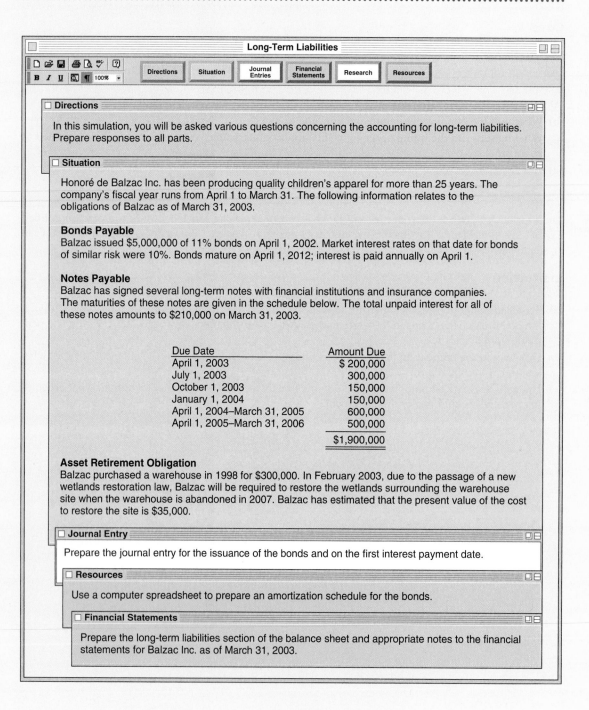

Logo Credits

The following companies have granted permission for their logos to be included in this text.

3M Company

Alterra Healthcare Corporation

Anchor BanCorp Wisconsin Inc.

Avon Rubber p.l.c. The Avon logo is a registered trademark supplied by kind permission of Avon Rubber p.l.c.

Brown Shoe Company, Inc.

The Coca-Cola Company

The Walt Disney Company

Gateway, Inc.

The Gillette Company

Johnson & Johnson

Kellogg Company. KELLOGG'S™ is a trademark of Kellogg Company. All rights reserved. Used with permission.

Mack Trucks, Inc.

Mattel, Inc. Mattel logo courtesy of Mattel, Inc.

Merck & Co. Inc.

Occidental Petroleum Corporation

PepsiCo, Inc. © 2002 PepsiCo, Inc. All rights reserved. Used with permission.

Quaker Oats Company. The Quaker name and Quaker Oats logo are registered trademarks of the Quaker Oats Company.

Southwest Airlines

Tompkins PLC

Tootsie Roll Industries, Inc.

Union Planters Corporation

Uniroyal Technology Corporation

Westinghouse Electric Corporation

Index

OFFICIAL ACCOUNTING PRONOUNCEMENTS

The following list of official accounting pronouncements constitutes the major part of *generally accepted accounting principles* (GAAP) and represents the authoritative source documents for much of the discussion contained in this book.

Accounting Research Bulletins (ARB's), Committee on Accounting Procedures, AICPA (1953–1959)

Date Issued		No.	Title
June	1953	No. 43	Restatement and Revision of Accounting Research Bulletins Nos. 1–42, and Accounting Terminology Bulletin No. 1 (originally issued 1939–1953)
Oct.	1954	No. 44	Declining-Balance Depreciation; Revised July, 1958 (amended)
Oct.	1955	No. 45	Long-term Construction-type Contracts (unchanged)
Feb.	1956	No. 46	Discontinuance of Dating Earned Surplus (unchanged)
Sept.	1956	No. 47	Accounting for Costs of Pension Plans (superseded)
Jan.	1957	No. 48	Business Combinations (superseded)
April	1958	No. 49	Earnings Per Share (superseded)
Oct.	1958	No. 50	Contingencies (superseded)
Aug.	1959	No. 51	Consolidated Financial Statements (amended and partially superseded)

Accounting Terminology Bulletins, Committee on Terminology, AICPA

Aug.	1953	No. 1	Review and Résumé (of the eight original terminology bulletins) (amended)
Mar.	1955	No. 2	Proceeds, Revenue, Income, Profit, and Earnings (amended)
Aug.	1956	No. 3	Book Value (unchanged)
July	1957	No. 4	Cost, Expense, and Loss (amended)

Accounting Principles Board (APB) Opinions, AICPA (1962–1973)

Nov.	1962	No. 1	New Depreciation Guidelines and Rules (amended)
Dec.	1962	No. 2	Accounting for the "Investment Credit" (amended)
Oct.	1963	No. 3	The Statement of Source and Application of Funds (superseded)
Mar.	1964	No. 4	Accounting for the "Investment Credit" (Amending No. 2)
Sept.	1964	No. 5	Reporting of Leases in Financial Statements of Lessee (superseded)
Oct.	1965	No. 6	Status of Accounting Research Bulletins (partially superseded)
May	1966	No. 7	Accounting for Leases in Financial Statements of Lessors (superseded)
Nov.	1966	No. 8	Accounting for the Cost of Pension Plans (superseded)
Dec.	1966	No. 9	Reporting the Results of Operations (amended and partially superseded)
Dec.	1966	No. 10	Omnibus Opinion—1966 (amended and partially superseded)
Dec.	1967	No. 11	Accounting for Income Taxes (superseded)
Dec.	1967	No. 12	Omnibus Opinion—1967 (partially superseded)
Mar.	1969	No. 13	Amending Paragraph 6 of APB Opinion No. 9, Application to Commercial Banks (unchanged)
Mar.	1969	No. 14	Accounting for Convertible Debt and Debt Issued with Stock Purchase Warrants (unchanged)
May	1969	No. 15	Earnings per Share (superseded)
Aug.	1970	No. 16	Business Combinations (superseded)
Aug.	1970	No. 17	Intangible Assets (superseded)
Mar.	1971	No. 18	The Equity Method of Accounting for Investments in Common Stock (amended)
Mar.	1971	No. 19	Reporting Changes in Financial Position (amended)
July	1971	No. 20	Accounting Changes (amended)
Aug.	1971	No. 21	Interest on Receivables and Payables (amended)
April	1972	No. 22	Disclosure of Accounting Policies (amended)
April	1972	No. 23	Accounting for Income Taxes—Special Areas (superseded)
April	1972	No. 24	Accounting for Income Taxes—Equity Method Investments (unchanged)
Oct.	1972	No. 25	Accounting for Stock Issued to Employees (unchanged)
Oct.	1972	No. 26	Early Extinguishment of Debt (amended)
Nov.	1972	No. 27	Accounting for Lease Transactions by Manufacturer or Dealer Lessors (superseded)
May	1973	No. 28	Interim Financial Reporting (amended and partially superseded)
May	1973	No. 29	Accounting for Nonmonetary Transactions (amended)
June	1973	No. 30	Reporting the Results of Operations (amended)
June	1973	No. 31	Disclosure of Lease Commitments by Lessees (superseded)

Financial Accounting Standards Board (FASB), Statements of Financial Accounting Standards (1973–2002)

Dec.	1973	No. 1	Disclosure of Foreign Currency Translation Information (superseded)
Oct.	1974	No. 2	Accounting for Research and Development Costs (amended)
Dec.	1974	No. 3	Reporting Accounting Changes in Interim Financial Statements
Mar.	1975	No. 4	Reporting Gains and Losses from Extinguishment of Debt (superseded)
Mar.	1975	No. 5	Accounting for Contingencies (amended)
May	1975	No. 6	Classification of Short-term Obligations Expected to be Refinanced
June	1975	No. 7	Accounting and Reporting by Development Stage Enterprises
Oct.	1975	No. 8	Accounting for the Translation of Foreign Currency Transactions and Foreign Financial Statements (superseded)

Date Issued		No.	Title
Oct.	1975	No. 9	Accounting for Income Taxes—Oil and Gas Producing Companies (superseded)
Oct.	1975	No. 10	Extension of "Grandfather" Provisions for Business Combinations (superseded)
Dec.	1975	No. 11	Accounting for Contingencies—Transition Method
Dec.	1975	No. 12	Accounting for Certain Marketable Securities (superseded)
Nov.	1976	No. 13	Accounting for Leases (amended, interpreted, and partially superseded)
Dec.	1976	No. 14	Financial Reporting for Segments of a Business Enterprise (amended)
June	1977	No. 15	Accounting by Debtors and Creditors for Troubled Debt Restructurings (amended)
June	1977	No. 16	Prior Period Adjustments (amended)
Nov.	1977	No. 17	Accounting for Leases—Initial Direct Costs
Nov.	1977	No. 18	Financial Reporting for Segments of a Business Enterprise—Interim Financial Statements
Dec.	1977	No. 19	Financial Accounting and Reporting by Oil and Gas Producing Companies (amended)
Dec.	1977	No. 20	Accounting for Forward Exchange Contracts (superseded)
April	1978	No. 21	Suspension of the Reporting of Earnings per Share and Segment Information by Nonpublic Enterprises (amended)
June	1978	No. 22	Changes in the Provisions of Lease Agreements Resulting from Refundings of Tax-Exempt Debt (amended)
Aug.	1978	No. 23	Inception of the Lease
Dec.	1978	No. 24	Reporting Segment Information in Financial Statements That Are Presented in Another Enterprise's Financial Report
Feb.	1979	No. 25	Suspension of Certain Accounting Requirements for Oil and Gas Producing Companies
April	1979	No. 26	Profit Recognition on Sales-Type Leases of Real Estate
May	1979	No. 27	Classification of Renewals or Extensions of Existing Sales-Type or Direct Financing Leases
May	1979	No. 28	Accounting for Sales with Leasebacks
June	1979	No. 29	Determining Contingent Rentals
Aug.	1979	No. 30	Disclosure of Information about Major Customers
Sept.	1979	No. 31	Accounting for Tax Benefits Related to U.K. Tax Legislation Concerning Stock Relief
Sept.	1979	No. 32	Specialized Accounting and Reporting Principles and Practices in AICPA Statements of Position and Guides on Accounting and Auditing Matters (amended and partially superseded)
Sept.	1979	No. 33	Financial Reporting and Changing Prices (amended and partially superseded)
Oct.	1979	No. 34	Capitalization of Interest Cost (amended)
Mar.	1980	No. 35	Accounting and Reporting by Defined Benefit Pension Plans (amended)
May	1980	No. 36	Disclosure of Pension Information (superseded)
July	1980	No. 37	Balance Sheet Classification of Deferred Income Taxes (amended)
Sept.	1980	No. 38	Accounting for Preacquisition Contingencies of Purchased Enterprises (superseded)
Oct.	1980	No. 39	Financial Reporting and Changing Prices: Specialized Assets—Mining and Oil and Gas
Nov.	1980	No. 40	Financial Reporting and Changing Prices: Specialized Assets—Timberlands and Growing Timber
Nov.	1980	No. 41	Financial Reporting and Changing Prices: Specialized Assets—Income-Producing Real Estate
Nov.	1980	No. 42	Determining Materiality for Capitalization of Interest Cost
Nov.	1980	No. 43	Accounting for Compensated Absences (amended)
Dec.	1980	No. 44	Accounting for Intangible Assets of Motor Carriers (superseded)
Mar.	1981	No. 45	Accounting for Franchise Fee Revenue (amended)
Mar.	1981	No. 46	Financial Reporting and Changing Prices: Motion Picture Films
Mar.	1981	No. 47	Disclosure of Long-Term Obligations (amended)
June	1981	No. 48	Revenue Recognition When Right of Return Exists
June	1981	No. 49	Accounting for Product Financing Arrangements
Nov.	1981	No. 50	Financial Reporting in the Record and Music Industry
Nov.	1981	No. 51	Financial Reporting by Cable Television Companies (amended)
Dec.	1981	No. 52	Foreign Currency Translation (amended)
Dec.	1981	No. 53	Financial Reporting by Producers and Distributors of Motion Picture Films (superseded)
Jan.	1982	No. 54	Financial Reporting and Changing Prices: Investment Companies (superseded)
Feb.	1982	No. 55	Determining Whether a Convertible Security is a Common Stock Equivalent (superseded)
Feb.	1982	No. 56	Designation of AICPA Guide and SOP 81-1 on Contractor Accounting and SOP 81-2 on Hospital-Related Organizations as Preferable for Applying APB Opinion 20 (superseded)
Mar.	1982	No. 57	Related Party Disclosures
April	1982	No. 58	Capitalization of Interest Cost in Financial Statements that Include Investments Accounted for by the Equity Method
April	1982	No. 59	Deferral of the Effective Date of Certain Accounting Requirements for Revision Plans of State and Local Governmental Units
June	1982	No. 60	Accounting and Reporting by Insurance Enterprises (amended)
June	1982	No. 61	Accounting for Title Plant (amended)
June	1982	No. 62	Capitalization of Interest Cost in Situations Involving Certain Tax-Exempt Borrowings and Certain Gifts and Grants
June	1982	No. 63	Financial Reporting by Broadcasters (amended)

Date Issued		No.	Title
Sept.	1982	No. 64	Extinguishment of Debt Made to Satisfy Sinking-Fund Requirements (superseded)
Sept.	1982	No. 65	Accounting for Certain Mortgage Bank Activities (amended)
Oct.	1982	No. 66	Accounting for Sales of Real Estate (amended)
Oct.	1982	No. 67	Accounting for Costs and Initial Rental Operations of Real Estate Projects (amended)
Oct.	1982	No. 68	Research and Development Arrangements (amended)
Nov.	1982	No. 69	Disclosures about Oil and Gas Producing Activities
Dec.	1982	No. 70	Financial Reporting and Changing Prices: Foreign Currency Translation
Dec.	1982	No. 71	Accounting for the Effects of Certain Types of Regulation (amended)
Feb.	1983	No. 72	Accounting for Certain Acquisitions of Banking or Thrift Institutions (amended)
Aug.	1983	No. 73	Reporting a Change in Accounting for Railroad Track Structures
Aug.	1983	No. 74	Accounting for Special Termination Benefits Paid to Employees
Nov.	1983	No. 75	Deferral of the Effective Date of Certain Accounting Requirements for Pension Plans of State and Local Governmental Units (superseded)
Nov.	1983	No. 76	Extinguishment of Debt (superseded)
Dec.	1983	No. 77	Reporting by Transferors for Transfers of Receivables with Recourse (superseded)
Dec.	1983	No. 78	Classifications of Obligations that Are Callable by the Creditor
Feb.	1984	No. 79	Elimination of Certain Disclosures for Business Combinations by Nonpublic Enterprises (superseded)
Aug.	1984	No. 80	Accounting for Futures Contracts (superseded)
Nov.	1984	No. 81	Disclosure of Postretirement Health Care and Life Insurance Benefits
Nov.	1984	No. 82	Financial Reporting and Changing Prices: Elimination of Certain Disclosures
Mar.	1985	No. 83	Designation of AICPA Guides and Statement of Position on Accounting by Brokers and Dealers in Securities, by Employee Benefit Plans, and by Banks as Preferable for Purposes of Applying APB Opinion 20
Mar.	1985	No. 84	Induced Conversions of Convertible Debt
Mar.	1985	No. 85	Yield Test for Determining Whether a Convertible Security Is a Common Stock Equivalent (superseded)
Aug.	1985	No. 86	Accounting for the Costs of Computer Software to be Sold, Leased, or Otherwise Marketed
Dec.	1985	No. 87	Employers' Accounting for Pensions (amended)
Dec.	1985	No. 88	Employers' Accounting for Settlements and Curtailments of Defined Benefit Pension Plans and for Termination Benefits (amended)
Dec.	1986	No. 89	Financial Reporting and Changing Prices (amended)
Dec.	1986	No. 90	Regulated Enterprises—Accounting for Abandonments and Disallowances of Plant Costs
Dec.	1986	No. 91	Accounting for Nonrefundable Fees and Costs Associated with Originating or Acquiring Loans and Initial Direct Costs of Leases
Aug.	1987	No. 92	Regulated Enterprises—Accounting for Phase-in Plans
Aug.	1987	No. 93	Recognition of Depreciation by Not-for-Profit Organizations
Oct.	1987	No. 94	Consolidation of All Majority-Owned Subsidiaries
Nov.	1987	No. 95	Statement of Cash Flows (amended)
Dec.	1987	No. 96	Accounting for Income Taxes (superseded)
Dec.	1987	No. 97	Accounting and Reporting by Insurance Enterprises for Certain Long-Duration Contracts and for Realized Gains and Losses from the Sale of Investments
June	1988	No. 98	Accounting for Leases; Sale-Leaseback Transactions Involving Real Estate; Sales-Type Leases of Real Estate; Definition of the Lease Term; Initial Direct Costs of Direct Financing Leases
Sept.	1988	No. 99	Deferral of the Effective Date of Recognition of Depreciation by Not-for-Profit Organizations
Dec.	1988	No. 100	Accounting for Income Taxes—Deferral of the Effective Date of FASB Statement No. 96
Dec.	1988	No. 101	Regulated Enterprises—Accounting for the Discontinuation of Application of FASB Statement No. 71 (amended)
Feb.	1989	No. 102	Statement of Cash Flows—Exemption of Certain Enterprises and Classification of Cash Flows from Certain Securities Acquired for Resale (amended)
Dec.	1989	No. 103	Accounting for Income Taxes—Deferral of the Effective Date of FASB Statement No. 96
Dec.	1989	No. 104	Statement of Cash Flows—Net Reporting of Certain Cash Receipts and Cash Payments and Classification of Cash Flows from Hedging Transactions
Mar.	1990	No. 105	Disclosure of Information About Financial Instruments with Off-Balance-Sheet Risk and Financial Instruments with Concentrations of Credit Risk (superseded)
Dec.	1990	No. 106	Employers' Accounting for Postretirement Benefits Other Than Pensions (amended)
Dec.	1991	No. 107	Disclosures about Fair Value of Financial Instruments (amended)
Dec.	1991	No. 108	Accounting for Income Taxes—Deferral of the Effective Date of FASB Statement No. 96
Feb.	1992	No. 109	Accounting for Income Taxes (amended)
Aug.	1992	No. 110	Reporting by Defined Benefit Pension Plans of Investment Contracts
Nov.	1992	No. 111	Rescission of FASB Statement No. 32 and Technical Corrections
Nov.	1992	No. 112	Employers' Accounting for Postemployment Benefits
Dec.	1992	No. 113	Accounting and Reporting for Reinsurance of Short-Duration and Long-Duration Contracts
May	1993	No. 114	Accounting by Creditors for Impairment of a Loan (amended)
May	1993	No. 115	Accounting for Certain Investments in Debt and Equity Securities (amended)

Date Issued		No.	Title
June	1993	No. 116	Accounting for Contributions Received and Contributions Made
June	1993	No. 117	Financial Statements of Not-for-Profit Organizations (amended)
Oct.	1994	No. 118	Accounting by Creditors for Impairments of a Loan—Income Recognition and Disclosures
Oct.	1994	No. 119	Disclosure about Derivative Financial Instruments and Fair Value of Financial Instruments (superseded)
Jan.	1995	No. 120	Accounting and Reporting by Mutual Life Insurance Enterprises
Mar.	1995	No. 121	Accounting for the Impairment of Long-Lived Assets (superseded)
May	1995	No. 122	Accounting for Mortgage Servicing Rights (superseded)
Oct.	1995	No. 123	Accounting for Stock-Based Compensation (amended)
Nov.	1995	No. 124	Accounting for Certain Investments Held by Not-for-Profit Organizations
June	1996	No. 125	Accounting for Transfers and Servicing of Financial Assets and Extinguishment of Liabilities (amended)
Dec.	1996	No. 126	Exemption from Certain Required Disclosures about Financial Instruments for Certain Nonpublic Entities
Dec.	1996	No. 127	Deferral of the Effective Date of Certain Provisions of FASB Statement No. 125
Feb.	1997	No. 128	Earnings per Share (amended)
Feb.	1997	No. 129	Disclosure of Information about Capital Structure
June	1997	No. 130	Reporting Comprehensive Income
June	1997	No. 131	Reporting Disaggregated Information about a Business Enterprise
Feb.	1998	No. 132	Employers' Disclosures about Pensions and Other Postretirement Benefits an amendment of FASB Statements No. 87, 88, and 106
June	1998	No. 133	Accounting for Derivative Instruments and Hedging Activities (amended)
Oct.	1998	No. 134	Accounting for Mortgage-Backed Securities Retained after the Securitization of Mortgage Loans Held for Sale by a Mortgage Banking Enterprise (an amendment of FASB Statement No. 65)
Feb.	1999	No. 135	Rescission of FASB Statement No. 75 and Technical Corrections (amended)
June	1999	No. 136	Transfers of Assets to a Not-for-Profit Organization or Charitable Trust That Raises or Holds Contributions for Others (amended)
June	1999	No. 137	Accounting for Derivative Instruments and Hedging Activities—Deferral of the Effective Date for FASB Statement No. 133 (an amendment of Statement No. 133)
June	2000	No. 138	Accounting for Certain Derivative Instruments and Certain Hedging Activities (an amendment of FASB Statement No. 133)
June	2000	No. 139	Rescission of FASB Statement No. 53 and amendments to FASB Statements No. 63, 89, and 121
Sept.	2000	No. 140	Accounting for Transfers and Servicing of Financial Assets and Extinguishments of Liabilities (a replacement of FASB Statement 125)
June	2001	No. 141	Business Combinations (amended)
June	2001	No. 142	Goodwill and Other Intangible Assets (amended)
June	2001	No. 143	Accounting for Asset Retirement Obligations (amended)
Aug.	2001	No. 144	Accounting for the Impairment or Disposal of Long-Lived Assets (amended)
April	2002	No. 145	Rescission of FASB Statements No. 4, 44, and 64, Amendment of FASB Statement No. 13, and Technical Corrections
June	2002	No. 146	Accounting for Costs Associated with Exit or Disposal Activities
Oct.	2002	No. 147	Acquisitions of Certain Financial Institutions, an Amendment of FASB Statements No. 72 and 144 and FASB Interpretation No. 9
Dec.	2002	No. 148	Accounting for Stock-Based Compensation—Transition and Disclosure
Feb.	2003	No. 149	Accounting for Certain Financial Instruments with Characteristics of Liabilities and Equity

Financial Accounting Standards Board (FASB), Interpretations (1974–2002)

June	1974	No. 1	Accounting Changes Related to the Cost of Inventory (APB Opinion No. 20)
June	1974	No. 2	Imputing Interest on Debt Arrangements Made Under the Federal Bankruptcy Act (APB Opinion No. 21) (superseded)
Dec.	1974	No. 3	Accounting for the Cost of Pension Plans Subject to the Employee Retirement Income Security Act of 1974 (APB Opinion No. 8)
Feb.	1975	No. 4	Applicability of FASB Statement No. 2 to Purchase Business Combinations (amended)
Feb.	1975	No. 5	Applicability of FASB St. No. 2 to Development Stage Enterprises (superseded)
Feb.	1975	No. 6	Applicability of FASB Statement No. 2 to Computer Software
Oct.	1975	No. 7	Applying FASB Statement No. 7 in Statements of Established Enterprises
Jan.	1976	No. 8	Classification of a Short-Term Obligation Repaid Prior to Being Replaced by a Long-Term Security (FASB Std. No. 6)
Feb.	1976	No. 9	Applying APB Opinion No. 16 and 17 when a Savings and Loan or Similar Institution is Acquired in a Purchase Business Combination (APB Op. No. 16 & 17) (amended)
Sept.	1976	No. 10	Application of FASB Statement No. 12 to Personal Financial Statements (FASB Std. No. 12)
Sept.	1976	No. 11	Changes in Market Value after the Balance Sheet Date (FASB Std. No. 12)
Sept.	1976	No. 12	Accounting for Previously Established Allowance Accounts (FASB Std. No. 12)
Sept.	1976	No. 13	Consolidation of a Parent and Its Subsidiaries Having Different Balance Sheet Dates (FASB Std. No. 12)
Sept.	1976	No. 14	Reasonable Estimation of the Amount of a Loss (FASB Std. No. 5)

Date Issued		No.	Title
Sept.	1976	No. 15	Translation of Unamortized Policy Acquisition Costs by Stock Life Insurance Company (FASB Std. No. 8) (amended and partially superseded)
Feb.	1977	No. 16	Clarification of Definitions and Accounting for Marketable Equity Securities That Become Nonmarketable (FASB Std. No. 12)
Feb.	1977	No. 17	Applying the Lower of Cost or Market Rule in Translated Financial Statements (FASB Std. No. 8) (superseded)
Mar.	1977	No. 18	Accounting for Income Taxes in Interim Periods (APB Op. No. 28) (amended)
Oct.	1977	No. 19	Lessee Guarantee of the Residual Value of Leased Property (FASB Std. No. 13)
Nov.	1977	No. 20	Reporting Accounting Changes under AICPA Statements of Position (APB Op. No. 20)
April	1978	No. 21	Accounting for Leases in a Business Combination (FASB Std. No. 13) (amended)
April	1978	No. 22	Applicability of Indefinite Reversal Criteria to Timing Differences (APB Op. No. 11 and 23)
Aug.	1978	No. 23	Leases of Certain Property Owned by a Governmental Unit or Authority (FASB Std. No. 13)
Sept.	1978	No. 24	Leases Involving Only Part of a Building (FASB Std. No. 13)
Sept.	1978	No. 25	Accounting for an Unused Investment Tax Credit (APB Op. No. 2, 4, 11, and 16)
Sept.	1978	No. 26	Accounting for Purchase of a Leased Asset by the Lessee During the Term of the Lease (FASB Std. No. 13)
Nov.	1978	No. 27	Accounting for a Loss on a Sublease (FASB Std. No. 13 and APB Op. No. 30) (amended)
Dec.	1978	No. 28	Accounting for Stock Appreciation Rights and Other Variable Stock Option or Award Plans (APB Op. No. 15 and 25) (amended)
Feb.	1979	No. 29	Reporting Tax Benefits Realized on Disposition of Investments in Certain Subsidiaries and Other Investees (APB Op. No. 23 and 24)
Sept.	1979	No. 30	Accounting for Involuntary Conversions of Nonmonetary Assets to Monetary Assets (APB Op. No. 29)
Feb.	1980	No. 31	Treatment of Stock Compensation Plans in EPS Computations (APB Op. No. 15 and Interp. 28) (superseded)
Mar.	1980	No. 32	Application of Percentage Limitations in Recognizing Investment Tax Credit (APB Op. No. 2, 4, and 11)
Aug.	1980	No. 33	Applying FASB Statement No. 34 to Oil and Gas Producing Operations (FASB Std. No. 34)
Mar.	1981	No. 34	Disclosure of Indirect Guarantees of Indebtedness of Others (FASB Std. No. 5)
May	1981	No. 35	Criteria for Applying the Equity Method of Accounting for Investments in Common Stock (APB Op. No. 18)
Oct.	1981	No. 36	Accounting for Exploratory Wells in Progress at the End of a Period
July	1983	No. 37	Accounting for Translation Adjustments upon Sale of Part of an Investment in a Foreign Entity (Interprets FASB Statement No. 52)
Aug.	1984	No. 38	Determining the Measurement Date for Stock Option, Purchase, and Award Plans Involving Junior Stock (Interprets APB Opinion No. 25)
Mar.	1992	No. 39	Offsetting of Amounts Related to Certain Contracts (Interprets APB Opinion No. 10 and FASB Statement No. 105) (amended)
Apr.	1993	No. 40	Applicability of Generally Accepted Accounting Principles to Mutual Life Insurance and Other Enterprises (Interprets FASB Statements No. 12, 60, 97, and 113)
Dec.	1994	No. 41	Offsetting of Amounts Related to Certain Repurchase and Reverse Repurchase Agreements
Sept.	1996	No. 42	Accounting for Transfers of Assets in Which a Not-for-Profit Organization is Granted Variance Power
June	1999	No. 43	Real Estate Sales (Interprets FASB Statement No. 66) (amended)
		No. 44	Accounting for Certain Transactions involving Stock Compensation (an interpretation of APB Opinion No. 25) (amended)
Nov.	2002	No. 45	Guarantor's Accounting and Disclosure Requirements for Guarantees, Including Indirect Guarantees of Indebtedness of Others
Jan.	2003	No. 46	Consolidation of Variable Interest Entities (an interpretation of ARB No. 51)

Financial Accounting Standards Board (FASB), Technical Bulletins (1979–2002)

Dec.	1979	No. 79-1	Purpose and Scope of FASB Technical Bulletins and Procedures for Issuance
Dec.	1979	No. 79-2	Computer Software Costs
Dec.	1979	No. 79-3	Subjective Acceleration Clauses in Long-Term Debt Agreements
Dec.	1979	No. 79-4	Segment Reporting of Puerto Rican Operations
Dec.	1979	No. 79-5	Meaning of the Term 'Customer' as it Applies to Health Care Facilities under FASB Statement No. 14
Dec.	1979	No. 79-6	Valuation Allowances Following Debt Restructuring
Dec.	1979	No. 79-7	Recoveries of a Previous Writedown under a Troubled Debt Restructuring Involving a Modification of Terms
Dec.	1979	No. 79-8	Applicability of FASB Statements 21 and 33 to Certain Brokers and Dealers in Securities
Dec.	1979	No. 79-9	Accounting in Interim Periods for Changes in Income Tax Rates
Dec.	1979	No. 79-10	Fiscal Funding Clauses in Lease Agreements
Dec.	1979	No. 79-11	Effect of a Penalty on the Term of a Lease
Dec.	1979	No. 79-12	Interest Rate Used in Calculating the Present Value of Minimum Lease Payments
Dec.	1979	No. 79-13	Applicability of FASB Statement No. 13 to Current Value Financial Statements
Dec.	1979	No. 79-14	Upward Adjustment of Guaranteed Residual Values
Dec.	1979	No. 79-15	Accounting for Loss on a Sublease Not Involving the Disposal of a Segment
Dec.	1979	No. 79-16	Effect on a Change in Income Tax Rate on the Accounting for Leveraged Leases

Date Issued		No.	Title
Dec.	1979	No. 79-17	Reporting Cumulative Effect Adjustment from Retroactive Application of FASB No. 13
Dec.	1979	No. 79-18	Transition Requirements of Certain FASB Amendments and Interpretations of FASB Statement No. 13
Dec.	1979	No. 79-19	Investor's Accounting for Unrealized Losses on Marketable Securities Owned by an Equity Method Investee
Dec.	1980	No. 80-1	Early Extinguishment of Debt through Exchange for Common or Preferred Stock (amended)
Dec.	1980	No. 80-2	Classification of Debt Restructuring by Debtors and Creditors
Feb.	1981	No. 81-1	Disclosure of Interest Rate Futures Contracts and Forward and Standby Contracts
Feb.	1981	No. 81-2	Accounting for Unused Investment Tax Credits Acquired in a Business Combination Accounted for by the Purchase Method
Feb.	1981	No. 81-3	Multiemployer Pension Plan Amendments Act of 1980
Feb.	1981	No. 81-4	Classification as Monetary or Nonmonetary Items
Feb.	1981	No. 81-5	Offsetting Interest Cost to be Capitalized with Interest Income
Nov.	1981	No. 81-6	Applicability of Statement 15 to Debtors in Bankruptcy Situations
Jan.	1982	No. 82-1	Disclosure of the Sale or Purchase of Tax Benefits through Tax Leases (amended)
Mar.	1982	No. 82-2	Accounting for the Conversion of Stock Options into Incentive Stock Options as a Result of the Economic Recovery Tax Act of 1981
July	1983	No. 83-1	Accounting for the Reduction in the Tax Basis of an Asset Caused by the Investment Tax Credit (ITC)
Mar.	1984	No. 84-1	Accounting for Stock Issued to Acquire the Results of a Research and Development Arrangement (amended)
June	1984	No. 79-1	Purpose and Scope of FASB Technical Bulletins and Procedures for Issuance (Revised)
Sept.	1984	No. 84-2	Accounting for the Effects of the Tax Reform Act of 1984 on Deferred Income Taxes Relating to Domestic International Sales Corporations
Sept.	1984	No. 84-3	Accounting for the Effects of the Tax Reform Act of 1984 on Deferred Income Taxes of Stock Life Insurance Enterprises
Oct.	1984	No. 84-4	In-Substance Defeasance of Debt
Mar.	1985	No. 85-1	Accounting for the Receipt of Federal Home Loan Mortgage Corporation Participating Preferred Stock
Mar.	1985	No. 85-2	Accounting for Collateralized Mortgage Obligations (CMOs) (superseded)
Nov.	1985	No. 85-3	Accounting for Operating Leases with Scheduled Rent Increases
Nov.	1985	No. 85-4	Accounting for Purchases of Life Insurance (superseded)
Dec.	1985	No. 85-5	Issues Relating to Accounting for Business Combinations (amended)
Dec.	1985	No. 85-6	Accounting for a Purchase of Treasury Shares
Oct.	1986	No. 86-1	Accounting for Certain Effects of the Tax Reform Act of 1986
Dec.	1986	No. 86-2	Accounting for an Interest in the Residual Value of a Leased Asset (amended)
April	1987	No. 87-1	Accounting for a Change in Method of Accounting for Certain Postretirement Benefits
Dec.	1987	No. 87-2	Computation of a Loss on an Abandonment
Dec.	1987	No. 87-3	Accounting for Mortgage Servicing Fees and Rights (amended)
Dec.	1988	No. 88-1	Issues Relating to Accounting for Leases
Dec.	1988	No. 88-2	Definition of a Right of Setoff
Dec.	1990	No. 90-1	Accounting for Separately Priced Extended Warranty and Product Maintenance Contracts
Apr.	1994	No. 94-1	Application of Statement 115 to Debt Securities Restructured in a Troubled Debt Restructuring
Dec.	1997	No. 97-1	Accounting under Statement 123 for Certain Employee Stock Purchase Plans with a Look-Back Option
July	2001	No. 01-1	Effective Date for Certain Financial Institutions of Certain Provisions of Statement No. 140 Related to the Isolation of Transferred Financial Assets

Financial Accounting Standards Board (FASB), Statements of Financial Accounting Concepts (1978–2002)

Nov.	1978	No. 1	Objectives of Financial Reporting by Business Enterprises
May	1980	No. 2	Qualitative Characteristics of Accounting Information
Dec.	1980	No. 3	Elements of Financial Statements of Business Enterprises
Dec.	1980	No. 4	Objectives of Financial Reporting by Nonbusiness Organizations
Dec.	1984	No. 5	Recognition and Measurement in Financial Statements of Business Enterprises
Dec.	1985	No. 6	Elements of Financial Statements
Feb.	2000	No. 7	Using Cash Flow Information and Present Value in Accounting Measurements

NATIONAL ACCOUNTING BOARDS AND ORGANIZATIONS

American Accounting Association (AAA)
5717 Bessie Drive
Sarasota, FL 34233
(941) 921-7747
www.aaa-edu.org

American Institute of Certified Public Accountants (AICPA)
1211 Avenue of the Americas
New York, NY 10036
(212) 596-6200
www.aicpa.org

Association of Government Accountants (AGA)
2208 Mount Vernon Ave.
Alexandria, VA 22301
(703) 684-6931
www.agacgfm.org

Financial Accounting Standards Board (FASB)
401 Merritt 7
P.O. Box 5116
Norwalk, CT 06856
(203) 847-0700
www.fasb.org

Financial Executives Institute (FEI)
10 Madison Ave.
P.O. Box 1938
Morristown, NJ 07962-1938
(973) 898-4600
www.fei.org

Governmental Accounting Standards Board (GASB)
401 Merritt 7
P.O. Box 5116
Norwalk, CT 06856
(203) 847-0700
www.fasb.org

International Accounting Standards Board (IASB)
30 Cannon Street
London EC4M 6XH, United Kingdom
Telephone: +44 (0)20 7246 6410
e-mail: iasb@iasb.org.uk

Institute of Certified Management Accountants
10 Paragon Drive
Montvale, NJ 07645-1718
(201) 573-9000
www.imanet.org

Institute of Internal Auditors (IIA)
249 Maitland Avenue, P.O. Box 1119
Altamonte Springs, FL 32701
(407) 830-7600
www.theiia.org

Institute of Management Accountants (IMA)
10 Paragon Drive
Montvale, NJ 07645-1718
(201) 573-9000
www.imanet.org

Securities and Exchange Commission (SEC)
450 Fifth Street NW
Washington, DC 20549
(202) 942-7040
www.sec.gov